Red Hat® Linux® 7.2 Bible

Unlimited Edition™

Red Hat® Linux® 7.2 Bible

Unlimited Edition™

Christopher Negus

Hungry Minds™

Best-Selling Books • Digital Downloads • e-Books • Answer Networks • e-Newsletters • Branded Web Sites • e-Learning

New York, NY✦ Cleveland, OH ✦ Indianapolis, IN

Red Hat® Linux® 7.2 Bible, Unlimited Edition™

Published by
Hungry Minds, Inc.
909 Third Avenue
New York, NY 10022
www.hungryminds.com

Library of Congress Control Number: 2001094147

ISBN: 0-7645-3630-3

Printed in the United States of America

10 9 8 7 6 5 4 3

1B/SZ/QT/QS/IN

Distributed in the United States by Hungry Minds, Inc.

Distributed by CDG Books Canada Inc. for Canada; by Transworld Publishers Limited in the United Kingdom; by IDG Norge Books for Norway; by IDG Sweden Books for Sweden; by IDG Books Australia Publishing Corporation Pty. Ltd. for Australia and New Zealand; by TransQuest Publishers Pte Ltd. for Singapore, Malaysia, Thailand, Indonesia, and Hong Kong; by Gotop Information Inc. for Taiwan; by ICG Muse, Inc. for Japan; by Intersoft for South Africa; by Eyrolles for France; by International Thomson Publishing for Germany, Austria, and Switzerland; by Distribuidora Cuspide for Argentina; by LR International for Brazil; by Galileo Libros for Chile; by Ediciones ZETA S.C.R. Ltda. for Peru; by WS Computer Publishing Corporation, Inc., for the Philippines; by Contemporanea de Ediciones for Venezuela; by Express Computer Distributors for the Caribbean and West Indies; by Micronesia Media Distributor, Inc. for Micronesia; by Chips Computadoras S.A. de C.V. for Mexico; by Editorial Norma de Panama S.A. for Panama; by American Bookshops for Finland.

For general information on Hungry Minds' products and services please contact our Customer Care department within the U.S. at 800-762-2974, outside the U.S. at 317-572-3993 or fax 317-572-4002.

For sales inquiries and reseller information, including discounts, premium and bulk quantity sales, and foreign-language translations, please contact our Customer Care department at 800-434-3422, fax 317-572-4002 or write to Hungry Minds, Inc., Attn: Customer Care Department, 10475 Crosspoint Boulevard, Indianapolis, IN 46256.

For information on licensing foreign or domestic rights, please contact our Sub-Rights Customer Care department at 212-884-5000.

For information on using Hungry Minds' products and services in the classroom or for ordering examination copies, please contact our Educational Sales department at 800-434-2086 or fax 317-572-4005.

For press review copies, author interviews, or other publicity information, please contact our Public Relations department at 650-653-7000 or fax 650-653-7500.

For authorization to photocopy items for corporate, personal, or educational use, please contact Copyright Clearance Center, 222 Rosewood Drive, Danvers, MA 01923, or fax 978-750-4470.

Hungry Minds™ is a trademark of Hungry Minds, Inc.

Credits

Acquisitions Editor
Debra Williams Cauley

Project Editor
Marcia Brochin

Technical Editor
Jason Luster

Development/Copy Editor
Andrea Boucher

Permissions Editor
Laura Moss

Editorial Manager
Ami Sullivan

Senior Vice President, Technical Publishing
Richard Swadley

Vice President and Publisher
Mary Bednarek

Project Coordinator
Regina Snyder

Graphics and Production Specialists
Sean Decker
Jackie Nicholas
Laurie Petrone
Jill Piscitelli
Brian Torwelle
Jeremey Unger
Erin Zeltner

Quality Control Technicians
Laura Albert
Valery Bourke
Andy Hollandbeck

Media Development Specialist
Gregory Stephens

Media Development Coordinator
Marisa Pearman

Illustrator
Kate Shaw

Proofreading and Indexing
TECHBOOKS Production Services

About the Author

Chris Negus has been working with UNIX systems, the Internet, and (more recently) Linux systems for more than two decades. During that time, Chris worked at AT&T Bell Laboratories, UNIX System Laboratories, and Novell, helping to develop the UNIX operating system. Features from many of the UNIX projects Chris worked on at AT&T have found their way into Red Hat and other Linux systems.

During the past few years, Chris has written several books on UNIX and the Internet, including *Caldera OpenLinux Bible, Internet Explorer 4 Bible,* and *Netscape Plug-ins For Dummies* for Hungry Minds (formerly IDG Books Worldwide). He also co-wrote several books for Que Corporation, including *The Complete Idiot's Guide to Networking* (second and third editions) and *Using UNIX* (second edition). Chris's other writings include articles for *Internet World, NetWare Connection,* and *Visual Developer* magazines.

At home, Chris enjoys spending time with his wife, Sheree, and his boys, Caleb and Seth. His hobbies include soccer, singing, and exercising with Sheree.

I dedicate this book to my wife, Sheree. This book would never have happened without her love and support.

Preface

Many Linux books resemble someone's throwing a bunch of high-performance car parts on the floor and saying, "Go ahead and build a Porsche." Although it's true that the parts you need for power computing are in Linux, you still need to know how to put them together. *Red Hat® Linux® 7.2 Bible, Unlimited Edition™* takes you through those steps.

Who Are You?

To use this book, you don't have to be a programmer. You could be someone who just wants to use Red Hat Linux (to run programs, access the Internet, and so on). Or you may want to know how to administer a Linux system in a workgroup or on a network.

I assume that you are somewhat computer literate but have had little or no experience with Linux (or UNIX). You might be migrating from Microsoft operating systems to Red Hat Linux because of its networking and multiuser features. You might be looking to start a career as a computer technician or network administrator and find that spending a few dollars for an entire operating system and book is more economical than taking those technical classes offered on late-night television. Or you might just think a "free" operating system is cool.

In any case, after you peruse this book you should have a good idea of how to run applications, set up a small network, connect to the Internet, and configure a variety of server types (Web servers, print servers, file servers, and so on). This book represents a great first couple of steps toward your becoming someone who can set up a home network or a small office network and maintain a group of computers.

This Book's Learn-Through-Tasks Approach

The best way to learn a computer system is to get your hands on it. To help you learn Red Hat Linux, this book takes a task-oriented approach. Where possible, I step you through the process of working with a feature, such as setting up a network or configuring your desktop.

When you are done with a task, you should have a good, basic setup of the feature that it covers. After that, I often provide pointers to further information on tweaking and tuning the feature.

Instead of assuming that you already know what cryptic topics such as troff, NFS, and TCP/IP are, I ease you into those features with headings such as "Publishing with Linux," "Setting up a File Server," and "Connecting to the Internet." Heck, if you already knew what all those things were and how to get them working, you wouldn't need me, would you?

When many tools can be used to achieve the same results, I usually present one or two examples. In other words, I don't describe six different Web browsers, twelve different text editors, and three different news servers. I tell you how to get one or two similar tools really working and then note the others that are available.

What You Need

To follow along with this book, you need to install the software that comes with the accompanying CDs. To do that, you need a PC with the following general configuration:

- ✦ An Intel 80386, 80486, Pentium, or compatible CPU.

- ✦ At least 32MB of RAM, although 64MB or more is recommended. To run the GNOME or KDE desktop, Red Hat recommends at least 64MB.

- ✦ At least 350MB of hard disk space (you have to deselect some packages during installation to get down to the 350MB limit and you don't get a graphical interface). You need 1.5GB of hard disk space for a typical workstation installation or at least 1GB of space for a server installation. To install everything, you need about 3GB of space.

- ✦ A CD-ROM drive. This is recommended for installation, although you can install over a network or from a local hard disk instead. For those types of installs, you need at least a 3.5-inch floppy disk drive and either an extra hard disk partition or another computer (that can be reached over the network) that has images of the Red Hat Linux CDs on it.

Not every piece of PC hardware works with Red Hat Linux. You can find a list of computer hardware that will work with Red Hat at http://www.redhat.com/hardware. You will probably want to use other types of hardware (also on that list) with your Red Hat Linux system, including video cards, mice, sound cards, modems, printers, scanners, joysticks, PCMCIA devices, and tape drives.

 Cross-Reference   I describe hardware requirements in more detail during descriptions of Red Hat Linux installation in Chapter 2.

Conventions Used in This Book

Throughout the book, special typefaces indicate code or commands. I also use icons to set apart certain pieces of information. Commands and code are shown in monospace type, such as the following:

```
This is how code looks.
```

On the occasion that an example includes both input and output, monospace is still used, but input is presented in bold type to distinguish the two. Here is an example:

```
$ ftp ftp.handsonhistory.com
Name (home:jake): jake
Password: ******
```

Icons appear in the left margin. The following icons are used to call your attention to points that are particularly important.

A Note icon provides extra information to which you need to pay special attention.

A Tip icon shows a special way of performing a particular task.

A Caution icon alerts you that you need to take special care when executing a procedure, or damage to your computer hardware or software could result.

A Cross-Reference icon is used to refer to further information on a subject that you can find outside the current chapter.

How This Book Is Organized

The book is organized into four parts.

Part I: Getting Started in Red Hat Linux

Part I consists of Chapters 1 and 2, which contain brief descriptions of the Linux technology and tell you what you need in order to get the operating system installed. Chapter 1 serves as an introduction to the Linux OS and to Red Hat Linux in particular. Chapter 2 discusses what you need to install Red Hat Linux and then how to make the decisions you are faced with during installation. It includes procedures for installing from CD-ROM, hard disk, or network connection (NFS, FTP, or HTTP servers).

Part II: Using Red Hat Linux

Part II consists of Chapters 3 through 9, which include information for the average user who needs to use Linux to run applications and access the Internet. Chapter 3 describes ways of exploring and understanding Red Hat Linux, primarily from the Linux shell command interpreter. You learn how to use the bash shell, the vi text editor, and the commands for moving around the Linux file system. In Chapter 4, you learn about the GNOME desktop environment, the KDE desktop environment, and the X Window System. These GUIs provide graphical means of using Red Hat Linux.

Chapter 5 contains information on obtaining, installing, and running Linux applications. It also helps you run applications from other operating systems in Linux. Chapter 6 describes both old-time (free) publishing tools and new, graphical word processors that are available with Red Hat Linux. Old tools include the troff and TeX text processing tools, whereas newer, commercially available publishing software includes StarOffice, and WordPerfect.

Graphical and character-based games that run in Red Hat Linux are described in Chapter 7. This chapter also describes game console emulators and commercial games, such as "Civilization: Call to Power" and "Myth II," some of which have demo versions available. Chapter 8 describes how to use audio and video players, as well as how to configure sound cards and CD burners and set up your Internet browser to play multimedia. Chapter 9 describes tools for browsing the Web (such as Netscape's browser) and related tools (such as e-mail clients and newsreaders).

Part III: Administering Red Hat Linux

Part III consists of Chapters 10 through 14, which cover general setup and system maintenance tasks, including how to set up user accounts, automate system tasks, and back up your data. Chapter 10, in which you learn what you need to know about basic system administration, describes the root login, administrative commands, configuration files, and log files. Chapter 11 describes how to set up and provide support for multiple users on your Red Hat Linux system.

You learn to create shell scripts and to use the cron facility to automate a variety of tasks on your Red Hat Linux system in Chapter 12. Techniques for backing up your system and restoring files from backup are described in Chapter 13. Chapter 14 describes issues related to securing your computing assets in Red Hat Linux.

Part IV: Red Hat Linux Network and Server Setup

Part IV consists of Chapters 15 through 23, which describe step-by-step procedures for setting up a variety of server types. Simple configurations for what might otherwise be complex tasks are contained in each chapter. Learn to arrange, address, and connect your Linux computers to a local area network (LAN) in Chapter 15. Chapter 16 describes techniques for connecting your Linux computer and LAN to the Internet, using features such as Point-to-Point Protocol (PPP), IP forwarding, IP masquerading, and proxy servers.

Chapter 17 describes how to set up different types of print server interfaces, including Samba (to share with Windows systems), NetWare, and native Linux printing. Chapter 18 describes file servers, such as Network File System (NFS) servers, Samba file servers, and NetWare file servers. Chapter 19 describes how to configure an e-mail server.

Chapter 20 describes how to configure and secure an FTP server, as well as how to access the server using FTP client programs. Chapter 21 teaches you how to set up Red Hat Linux as a Web server, focusing on the popular Apache server software. Chapter 22 describes how to set up an INN news server, including determining how to set up news feeds, choosing news storage methods, and enabling access to your INN server. Chapter 23 describes how to set up NIS services to distribute information to client workstations on the network. Chapter 24 describes how to configure and start up MySQL database server, as well as how to add MySQL databases and tables.

Appendixes

This book also has three appendixes. Appendix A describes the contents of the companion CD-ROMs, and Appendix B lists the hundreds of RPMs (software packages) that come with the Red Hat Linux distribution. Appendix C contains an overview of setting up and running network services.

New in this Edition

Improvements to Red Hat Linux 7.2 that are described in this book include a new boot loader (GRUB), a new default file system type (ext3), and continued improvements to a variety of hardware drivers to work with the Linux 2.4 kernel added in Red Hat Linux 7.1. Many new software packages were added in this release as well. See Chapter 1 for details of significant new packages and Appendix B for a complete package list.

General improvements to the book have been made in the areas of network security, monitoring, and server operations. The following major enhancements have been made:

✦ The Ethereal window was added to this release, to allow administrators to monitor activity on their Ethernet LANs. Ethereal is described in Chapter 15.

✦ Descriptions of PortSentry and LogCheck have been added to Chapter 14. PortSentry is used to monitor ports and deny access to those who might be trying to break in through those ports. LogCheck is a tool for helping you sort through error messages gathered by your system.

✦ Chapter 24 was added to describe how to configure and start up a MySQL database server. It also shows examples of how to add MySQL databases and tables.

✦ The Internet News Server (INN) descriptions in Chapter 22 were significantly enhanced.

Special Unlimited Edition

One of the best features about this book is that it doesn't end at the last page. As the owner of this book, you have access to the Unlimited Edition Web site (http://www.unltded.com).

For up to a year after the book is published (or until a new edition becomes available), new material is posted to the Web site to cover new or expanded topics in Red Hat Linux. You will also have access to every chapter of the book from this site.

About the Companion CD-ROMs

The CD-ROMs that come with this book provide the software that you need to have a working Red Hat Linux system. With this software, you can set up a Red Hat Linux workstation or server as described throughout this book. See Appendix A for a description of the contents of the Red Hat Linux CD-ROMs.

Reach Out

The publisher and I would like your feedback. After you have had a chance to use this book, send any feedback to my2cents@hungryminds.com. Please include the book's ISBN and/or title in the subject line so that your comments reach the right people.

Of course, if you have any questions or comments about *Red Hat Linux 7.2 Bible*, feel free to contact me by e-mail at this address: chris.negus@iname.com

Acknowledgments

Anyone writing a book on Linux should first and foremost thank the Linux development community. To everyone who created a piece of code, contributed a binary, wrote a HOW-TO, or just helped answer a question in a Linux newsgroup, thank you for helping create this phenomenon known as Linux.

Thanks to everyone at Red Hat for putting together a great Linux distribution. Special thanks to the members of the Red Hat Linux 7.2 beta team for answering my questions and providing insight into the product during beta testing. Thanks to Debra Williams Cauley, Marcia Brochin, Terri Varveris and the others at Hungry Minds for your support through the entire writing and editing process. Thanks to freelance editor Andrea Boucher and technical editor Jason Luster for their excellent work. Thanks to Margot Maley Hutchison and the others at Waterside Productions for bringing me this project. Thanks to Forrest Cavalier for helping with questions regarding Internet News servers.

On the writing side, I'd especially like to thank Thad Phetteplace for his updates of security information, as well as his help for bringing this book in on schedule. Thanks to Deanne Clark for her speedy turnaround, sifting through all the packages in the Red Hat Linux distribution and updating Appendix B. I'd also like to thank Thad and Andy Wagliardo for their contributions of several chapters to the first edition of this book.

Thanks to my family for helping me through this project. Sheree managed to keep our family going as we settled into our home in the Pacific Northwest. Seth has grown up enough to take over one of my computers, so he can play balloon-popping games next to me while I work. Caleb contributed his "System Down" image to the multimedia chapter.

Special Acknowledgment

In recognition of the World Trade Center attack, I'd like to send my condolences to the families of those who died and my admiration for those who have participated in the massive clean-up effort. For myself, I plan to support those organizations that are themselves struggling to survive in the aftermath of the disaster.

If you are using this book to create a Web server, consider adding a link on your Web site to a site where visitors can donate to a relief effort (for the Red Cross, send a request to `linkagreement@usa.redcross.org`). Maybe you could send a donation to an organization fighting to create open source software. Let's thank God for our blessings and work to preserve them.

Contents at a Glance

Contents

Part IV: Red Hat Linux Network and Server Setup   591

Chapter 15: Setting Up a Local Area Network 593

Chapter 16: Connecting to the Internet 623

Getting Started in Red Hat Linux

An Overview of Red Hat Linux

Linux was a phenomenon waiting to happen. The computer industry suffered from a rift. In the 1980s and 1990s, people had to choose between inexpensive, market-driven PC operating systems from Microsoft and expensive, technology-driven operating systems such as UNIX. Free software was being created all over the world, but lacked a common platform to rally around. Linux has become that common platform.

Red Hat Linux is the most popular commercial distribution of Linux. Red Hat and other commercial distributions, such as Caldera's OpenLinux, have taken the Linux concept a step further. With Red Hat Linux, users no longer have to download, compile, and check Linux source code to make sure that all the right pieces are put together for Linux to work. Basically, Red Hat has made it possible for Linux to be used by people other than computer geeks.

Red Hat Linux has also made Linux a more viable alternative for corporate users. Many companies have felt insecure about relying on a free operating system to handle their critical data. With Red Hat Linux, they can rely on Red Hat Software, Inc. (www.redhat.com) to provide tested versions of that software and technical support if there are problems.

Introducing Red Hat Linux

Red Hat Linux 7.2 is the best representation of a Linux community that is coming of age. With version 7.2, Red Hat Linux has become a solid, polished platform for both desktop and server computing.

More than 1,200 individual software packages (compared to just over 600 in Red Hat Linux 6.2) are included in this latest release. These packages contain features that would cost you hundreds or thousands of dollars to duplicate if you bought them as separate commercial products. These features let you:

✦ Connect your computers to a LAN or the Internet.

✦ Create documents and publish your work on paper or on the Web.

✦ Work with multimedia content to manipulate images, play MPEG music files, view video, and even burn your own CDs.

✦ Play games individually or over a network.

✦ Communicate over the Internet using a variety of Web tools for browsing, chatting, transferring files, participating in newsgroups, and sending and receiving e-mail.

✦ Configure a computer to act as a network server, such as a print server, Web server, file server, mail server, news server, and a database server.

This is just a partial list of what you can do with Red Hat Linux. Using this book as your guide, you will find that there are many more features built into Red Hat Linux as well.

Support for new video cards, printers, storage devices, and applications are being added every day. Linux programmers around the world are no longer the only ones creating hardware drivers. Every day more hardware vendors are creating their own drivers, so they can sell products to the growing Linux market. New applications are being created to cover everything from personal productivity tools to programs that access massive corporate databases.

Remember that old x486 computer in your closet? Don't throw it away! Just because a new release of Red Hat Linux is out doesn't mean that you need all new hardware for it to run. Support for many old computer components get carried from one release to the next. There are old PCs running Red Hat Linux today as routers (to route data between your LAN and the Internet), firewalls (to protect your network from outside intrusion), and file servers (to store shared files on your LAN) — with maybe an Ethernet card or an extra hard disk added.

Past versions of Linux showed the promise of what Linux could be. Red Hat Linux 7.2 could be the realization of that promise. This brings us to the more basic question: What is Linux?

What Is Linux?

Linux is a free operating system that was created by Linus Torvalds when he was a student at the University of Helsinki in 1991. Torvalds started Linux by writing a *kernel*—the heart of the operating system—partly from scratch and partly by using publicly available software. (For the definition of an operating system and a kernel, see the sidebar "What Is an Operating System?" later in this chapter.) Torvalds then released the system to his friends and to a community of "hackers" on the Internet and asked them to work with it and enhance it. It took off.

Cross-Reference See Chapter 14 for a discussion about the difference between hackers (people who just like to play with computers) and crackers (people who break into computer systems and cause damage).

What Is an Operating System?

An operating system is made up of software instructions that lie between the computer hardware (disks, memory, ports, and so on) and the application programs (word processors, Web browsers, spreadsheets, and so on). At the center is the kernel, which provides the most basic computing functions (managing system memory, sharing the processor, opening and closing devices, and so on). Besides the kernel, an operating system provides other basic services needed to operate the computer, including:

✦ **File systems**—The file system provides the structure in which information is stored on the computer. Information is stored in files, primarily on hard disks inside the computer. Files are organized within a hierarchy of directories. The Linux file system holds the data files that you save, the programs you run, and the configuration files that set up the system.

✦ **Device drivers**—These provide the interfaces to each of the hardware devices connected to your computer. A device driver enables a program to write to a device without needing to know details about how each piece of hardware is implemented. The program opens a device, sends and receives data, and closes a device.

✦ **User interfaces**—An operating system needs to provide a way for users to run programs and access the file system. Linux has both graphical and text-based user interfaces. Gnome and KDE provide graphical user interfaces, whereas shell command interpreters (such as bash) run programs by typing commands and options.

✦ **System services**—An operating system provides system services, many of which can be started automatically when the computer boots. In Linux, system services can include processes that mount file systems, start your network, and run scheduled tasks.

Without an operating system, an application program would have to know the details of each piece of hardware, instead of just being able to say, "open that device and write a file there."

Bonus content at www.unltded.com

Today, there are hundreds of software developers around the world contributing software to the Linux effort. Because the source code for the software is freely available, anyone can work on it, change it, or enhance it. On top of the Linux kernel effort, the creators of Linux also drew on a great deal of system software and applications that are now bundled with Linux from the GNU software effort (GNU stands for "GNU is Not UNIX"), which is directed by the Free Software Foundation (FSF). There is a vast amount of software that can be used with Linux, all of which includes features that can compete with or surpass those of any other operating system in the world.

If you have heard Linux described as a free version of UNIX, there is good reason for it. Although much of the code for Linux started from scratch, the blueprint for what the code would do was created to follow POSIX standards. POSIX (Portable Operating System Interface for UNIX) is a computer industry operating system standard that every major version of UNIX complied with. In other words, if your operating system was POSIX-compliant, it was UNIX. See the next section describing Linux's roots in the UNIX operating system.

Linux's Roots in UNIX

Linux grew within a culture of free exchange of ideas and software. Like UNIX—the operating system on which Linux is based—the focus was on keeping communications open among software developers. Getting the code to work was the goal, without much concern about who owned the code, and the Internet was the primary communications medium. What, then, were the conditions that made the world ripe for a computer system such as Linux?

In the 1980s and 1990s, while Microsoft flooded the world with personal computers running DOS and Windows operating systems, power users demanded more from an operating system. They ached for systems that could run on networks, support many users at once (multiuser), and run many programs at once (multitasking). DOS (Disk Operating System) and Windows didn't cut it.

If there was an early operating system that might have risen to meet this challenge, it had to be UNIX, which came out of AT&T Bell Laboratories in 1969. Compare the cultures in which UNIX and Windows arose. Microsoft bought rights to the Disk Operating System (DOS), then set out to make it (or its successors) the only operating system choice on personal computers. Microsoft's goal was to dominate the market for personal computers running personal productivity applications.

UNIX, on the other hand, grew out of a culture where technology was king and marketing people were, well, hard to find. Bell Laboratories in Murray Hill, New Jersey, was a think tank where ideas came first and profits were somebody else's problem. A quote from Dennis Ritchie, co-creator of UNIX and designer of the C programming language, in a 1980 lecture on the evolution of UNIX, sums up the spirit that started UNIX. He was commenting on both his hopes and those of his colleagues for the UNIX project after a similar project called Multics had just failed:

What we wanted to preserve was not just a good environment in which to do programming, but a system around which a fellowship could form. We knew from experience that the essence of communal computing as supplied by remote-access, time-shared machines, is not just to type programs into a terminal instead of a keypunch, but to encourage close communication.

In that spirit, the first source code of UNIX was distributed free to universities. Like Linux, the availability of UNIX source code made it possible for a diverse population of software developers to make their own enhancements to UNIX and share them with others.

By the early 1980s, UNIX development moved from the organization in Murray Hill to a more commercially oriented development laboratory in Summit, New Jersey (a few miles down the road). During that time, UNIX began to find commercial success as the computing system of choice for applications such as AT&T's telephone switching equipment, for supercomputer applications such as modeling weather patterns, and for controlling NASA space projects.

Major computer hardware vendors licensed the UNIX source code to run on their computers. To try to create an environment of fairness and community to its OEMs (original equipment manufacturers), AT&T began standardizing what these different ports of UNIX had to be able to do to still be called UNIX. To that end, compliance with POSIX standards and the AT&T UNIX System V Interface Definition (SVID) were specifications UNIX Vendors could use to create compliant UNIX systems. Those same documents also served as road maps for the creation of Linux.

Common Linux Features

No matter what version of Linux you use, the piece of code common to all is the Linux kernel. Although the kernel can be modified to include support for the features you want, every Linux kernel can offer the following features:

✦ **Multiuser** — Not only can you have many user accounts available on a Linux system, you can also have multiple users logged in and working on the system at the same time. Users can have their own environments arranged the way they want: their own home directory for storing files and their own desktop interface (with icons, menus, and applications arranged to suit them).

✦ **Multitasking** — In Linux, it is possible to have many programs running at the same time, which means that not only can you have many programs going at once, but that Linux, itself, can have programs running in the background. Many of these system processes make it possible for Linux to work as a server, with these background processes listening to the network for requests to log in to your system, view a Web page, print a document, or copy a file. These background processes are referred to as *daemons*.

✦ **Graphical User Interface (X Window System)** — The powerful framework for working with graphical applications in Linux is referred to as the X Window System (or simply X). X handles the functions of opening X-based GUI applications and displaying them on an X server process (the process that manages your screen, mouse, and keyboard).

On top of X, you use an X-based desktop environment to provide a desktop metaphor and window manager to provide the specific look-and-feel of your GUI (icons, window frames, menus, and colors). There are several desktop environments and dozens of desktop managers to choose from. (Red Hat provides several desktop managers, but focuses on Gnome and KDE desktop environments.)

✦ **Hardware support** — You can configure support for almost every type of hardware that can be connected to a computer. There is support for floppy disk drives, CD-ROMs, removable disks (such as Zip drives), sound cards, tape devices, video cards, and most anything else you can think of.

Note   Not every hardware manufacturer provides Linux drivers with their peripheral devices and adapter cards. Although most popular hardware will be supported eventually in Linux, it can sometimes take a while for a member of the Linux community to write a driver.

✦ **Networking connectivity** — To connect your Linux system to a network, Linux offers support for a variety of Local Area Network (LAN) boards, modems, and serial devices. In addition to LAN protocols, such as Ethernet and Token Ring protocols, all the most popular upper-level networking protocols can be built-in. The most popular of these protocols is TCP/IP (used to connect to the Internet). Other protocols, such as IPX (for Novell networks) and X.25 (a packet-switching network type that is popular in Europe), are also available.

✦ **Network servers** — Providing networking services to the client computers on the LAN or to the entire Internet is what Linux does best. A variety of software packages are available that enable you to use Linux as a print server, file server, FTP server, mail server, Web server, news server, or workgroup (bootp or NIS) server.

✦ **Application support** — Because of compatibility with POSIX and several different application programming interfaces (APIs), a wide range of freeware and shareware software is available for Linux. Most GNU software from the Free Software Foundation will run in Linux.

Note   Because of the popularity of the Red Hat Package Management (RPM) format for packaging software, many software packages are available on the Internet in RPM format. If the RPM version matches your processor type, you can install the package without building and compiling the package. See Chapter 5 for information on working with RPM packages.

Primary Advantages of Linux

When compared to different commercially available operating systems, Linux's best assets are its price and its reliability. Most people know that its initial price is free (or at least under $100 when it comes in a box or with a book). However, when people talk about Linux's affordability, they are usually thinking of its total cost, which includes the capability of using inexpensive hardware and compatible free add-on applications. Although commercial operating systems tend to encourage upgrading to later hardware, Linux doesn't.

In terms of reliability, the general consensus is that Linux is comparable to many commercial UNIX systems but more reliable than most desktop-oriented operating systems. This is especially true if you rely on your computer system to stay up because it is a Web server or a file server.

Another advantage of using Linux is that help is always available on the Internet. There is probably someone out there in a Linux newsgroup who is willing to help you get around your problem. Because the source code is available, if you need something fixed you can even patch the code yourself! On the other hand, I've seen commercial operating system vendors sit on reported problems for months without fixing them. Remember that the culture of Linux is one that thrives on people helping other people.

Note   If you have general questions about Red Hat Linux, try the `linux.redhat.misc` newsgroup. For specific questions about networking or hardware, try `comp.os.linux.networking` and `comp.os.linux.hardware`, respectively.

What Is Red Hat Linux?

Having directories of software packages floating extraneously around the Internet was not a bad way for hackers to share software. However, for Linux to be acceptable to a less technical population of computer users, it needed to be simple to install and use. Likewise, businesses that were thinking about committing their mission-critical applications to a computer system would want to know that this system had been carefully tested.

To those ends, several companies and organizations began gathering and packaging Linux software together into usable forms called *distributions*. The main goal of a Linux distribution is to make the hundreds of unrelated software packages that make up Linux work together as a cohesive whole. The most popular distribution is Red Hat Linux.

Red Hat Linux is a commercial product produced by Red Hat Software, Inc. You can walk into a store and buy a boxed set of CDs and manuals. Or you can get Red Hat Linux free by downloading it over the Internet or by installing it from CDs that come with books such as this one. The boxed set provides technical support on installation and an extra CD that contains limited and demo versions of commercially available Linux application packages (such as word processors and database applications). Check the Red Hat Web site (www.redhat.com) for details on what is included with Red Hat products.

Why Choose Red Hat Linux?

To distinguish themselves from other versions of Linux, each distribution adds some extra features. Because most of the power features are already built-in, most enhancements for a particular distribution exist to make it easier to install, configure, and use Linux. Also, because there are different software packages available to do the same jobs (such as window managers or a particular server type), a distribution can distinguish itself by which packages it chooses to include and feature.

Red Hat Linux has set itself apart from other Linux distributions in these ways:

✦ **Software packaging** — Red Hat Software, Inc. created the Red Hat Package Management (RPM) method of packaging Linux. RPMs allow less technically savvy users to easily install Linux software. With RPM tools, you can install from CD, hard disk, over your LAN, or over the Internet. It's easy to track which packages are installed or to look at the contents of a package. Because RPM is available to the Linux community, it has become one of the de facto standards for packaging Linux software.

Chapter 5 describes how to install RPM packages.

✦ **Easy installation** — The Red Hat Linux installation process provides easy steps for installing Linux. During installation, Red Hat also helps you take the first few steps toward configuring Linux. You can choose which packages to install and how to partition your hard disk. You can even get your desktop GUI ready to go by configuring your video card, user accounts, and even your network.

Chapter 2 covers Red Hat Linux installation.

✦ **UNIX System V–style run-level scripts** — To have your system services (daemon processes) start up and shut down in an organized way, Red Hat Linux uses the UNIX System V mechanism for starting and stopping services. Shell scripts (that are easy to read and change) are contained in subdirectories of /etc. When the run level changes, such as when the system boots up or you change to single-user mode, messages tell you whether each service started correctly or failed to execute properly (a very nice feature!). Chapter 12 describes how to use run-level scripts.

✦ **Desktop environments (Gnome and KDE)** — To make it easier to use Linux, Red Hat Linux is ready to use the Gnome or KDE desktop environments. Gnome is installed by default and offers some nice features that include drag-and-drop protocols and windows that operate like window shades. KDE is another popular desktop manager that includes several tools, such as the KDE Control Center for configuring the desktop and the KOrganizer for managing appointments.

✦ **Administration tools** — There are some helpful configuration tools for setting up some of the trickier tasks in Linux. Several different GUI tools provide a graphical, form-driven interface for configuring networking, users, file systems, and initialization services. Instead of creating obtuse command lines or having to create tricky configuration files, these graphical tools can set up those files automatically.

Note

There are advantages and disadvantages of using a GUI-based program to manipulate text-based configuration files. GUI-based configuration tools can lead you through a setup procedure and error-check the information you enter. However, some features can't be accessed through the GUI, and if something goes wrong, it can be trickier to debug. Also, by adding proprietary interfaces to standard features, different Linux versions start to diverge.

✦ **Testing** — The exact configuration that you get on a Red Hat Linux distribution has been thoroughly tested by experts around the world. On the other hand, when you download Linux over the Internet, you can't guarantee that what you get will match the system that is on the CD.

New Features in Red Hat Linux 7.2

While the inclusion of the Linux 2.4 kernel was the major enhancement for version 7.1, Red Hat Linux 7.2 includes new features that span different areas of the operating system. In case you are upgrading from a Red Hat Linux 7.0 or earlier system, I have included descriptions of the Linux 2.4 kernel (which you may be seeing for the first time). Features that appear in Red Hat Linux for the first time in version 7.2 include a new boot manager (GRUB), a new journaling file system (ext3), and a handful of new application packages.

Improvements to Linux 2.4 kernel

With Red Hat Linux 7.2, Red Hat continues to tune and improve the Linux 2.4 kernel that was added to the distribution in version 7.1. Though many new features and fixes have been added to the Linux 2.4 kernel, the most prominent features are aimed at enterprise computing. The term enterprise computing implies that the computing systems serve a lot of people and are expected to be able to handle high volumes of data reliably.

Here is a list of many of the new features:

✦ **Enhanced Symetric Multiprocessing** — With the Linux development community getting support from major computer hardware vendors such as IBM, Dell Computer, Hewlett-Packard, Silicon Graphics, and Intel, the Linux 2.4 kernel has been enhanced to handle more powerful, multiprocessor computers. The Linux 2.2 kernel could manage up to eight processors. However, it is limited by being able to handle only 1,024 simultaneous threads.

The Linux 2.4 kernel is intended to handle multiple processors more efficiently and effectively than the 2.2 kernel. The 2.4 kernel is designed to be able to scale up at runtime to handle many more threads if necessary.

✦ **Greater capacity** — Besides being able to manage many processors, the Linux 2.4 kernel is made to support more RAM (up to 4GB), more IDE controllers (up to 10), and more network interface cards (up to 16 Ethernet NICs).

✦ **Networking enhancements** — Key networking components have been redesigned to be able to handle the greater system loads in enterprise computing environments. In particular, security features such as firewalls (using the iptables feature) have been built into the kernel. Support for new networking hardware, such as high-speed ATM network adapters, has also been added to the kernel.

✦ **Improved Universal Serial Bus (USB) support** — Though some USB support is included with Red Hat Linux 7, more USB devices are supported in the Linux 2.4 kernel. In Red Hat Linux 7, USB devices are limited to USB mouse support and USB keyboard support. The new kernel supports new USB video camera drivers, printer drivers, and Abstract Control Module drivers.

✦ **New file system interface** — Besides including, and presumably improving, previously supported file-system types such as DOS and Windows file systems (FAT, NTFS, VFAT, and FAT32), several new file-system types have been added. These include the DVD disk file system (UDF), the UNIX NFS file system, and the IRIX XFS (EFS) file system.

In general, the Linux 2.4 kernel enhancements are aimed at helping Red Hat Linux, as well as other Linux distributions, run faster, more efficiently, and more reliably in large-scale computing environments. The new kernel should also help limit the number of Linux kernel variants by including the features in Linux 2.4 that allow the same kernel to work on everything from single-user workstations to enterprise servers that can support thousands of simultaneous transactions.

GRUB boot manager

The GRand Unified Bootloader (GRUB) replaces the LInux LOader (LILO) as the default boot manager for Red Hat Linux 7.2. When your computer starts up, the first thing it does is run the boot manager. The boot manager lets you select which operating system to boot (if you have more than one on your computer), and then hands control of the rest of the boot process to the operating system you chose.

GRUB can boot both multiboot and non-multiboot operating systems. Multiboot operating systems let you pass arguments to the operating system when you boot. Non-multiboot systems simply allow you to use a feature called chain-loading, which allows it to simply load another boot loader to start the operating system. Here are examples of operating systems that GRUB can selectively boot from the same computer:

✦ **Multiboot Operating Systems**—Red Hat Linux, FreeBSD, NetBSD, OpenBSD, and OpenLinux.

✦ **Non-Multiboot Operating Systems**—DOS, OS/2, Windows 95, Windows 98, Windows NT, Windows ME, and Windows 2000.

For multiboot systems, GRUB allows you to pass options to the kernel at boot time. For example, you can identify a hardware device to use a particular driver or override auto-detection of a device. You can also use a configuration file to name and identify the locations of boot images on your computer.

Journaling file system (ext3)

The default file system for Red Hat Linux has changed from ext2 to ext3 for this release. The ext3 file system is what is referred to as a *journaling file system*. Journaling file systems are designed to recover quickly from system crashes. Quick recovery makes ext3 an important asset for computers that need to be up all the time.

The ext3 file system is really just an ext2 file system with the ability to recover faster after the system goes down. File systems can grow larger and larger with ext3, without accepting a penalty of long file system checks after a crash.

Additional software packages

Red Hat Linux can't go from 600 to over 1,200 software packages in a few years' time without having lots of new features spread across the operating system. The following bullet list should give you an idea of some of the new software packages for Red Hat Linux 7.2:

✦ **alien**—Contains programs for converting software packages to different formats.

✦ **cdlabelgen**—Contains tools for printing CD labels.

✦ **cdrdao**—Contains software for duplicating CDs.

✦ **curl**—Contains utility for copying files over the Internet.

✦ **docbook**—Contains tools for creating documents in docbook format.

✦ **ethereal**—Contains utilities for analyzing network traffic.

✦ **GConf** — Contains tools for managing Gnome configuration information.

✦ **gnucash** — Contains tools for managing personal finances.

✦ **grip** — Contains tools for playing and copying music CDs.

✦ **hotplug** — Contains utilities for configuring USB devices.

✦ **iptraf** — Contains tools for monitoring IP traffic.

✦ **w3m** — Contains the w3m utility for browsing the Web in text mode.

✦ **webalizer** — Contains webalizer for analyzing Web server log files.

✦ **xawtv** — Contains the xawtv command that allows you to watch TV on your computer screen.

There are other new packages in Red Hat Linux 7.2 as well. For a more complete list, see Appendix B, "Red Hat Linux RPMs."

The Culture of Free Software

I would be remiss to not say something about the culture of free software development from which Linux has thrived and will continue to thrive. The copyright for Red Hat Linux is covered under the GNU public license. That license, which most free software falls under, provides the following:

✦ **Author rights** — The original author retains the rights to his or her software.

✦ **Free distribution** — People can use the GNU software in their own software, changing and redistributing it as they please. They do, however, have to include the source code with their distribution (or make it easily available).

✦ **Copyright maintained** — Even if you were to repackage and resell the software, the original GNU agreement must be maintained with the software. This means that all future recipients of the software must have the opportunity to change the source code, just as you did.

It is important to remember that there is no warranty on GNU software. If something goes wrong, the original developer of the software has no obligation to fix the problem. However, the Linux culture has provided resources for that event. Experts on the Internet can help you iron out your problems, or you can access one of the many Linux newsgroups to read how others have dealt with their problems and to post your own questions about how to fix yours. Chances are that someone will know what to do — maybe even going so far as to provide the software or configuration file you need.

Note The GNU project uses the term *free software* to describe the software that is covered by the GNU license. On occasion, you may see the term *open source software* being used to describe software. Though source code availability is part of the GNU license, the GNU project claims that software defined as open source is not the same as free software because it can encompass semi-free programs and even some proprietary programs. See `www.opensource.org` for a description of open source software.

Summary

Linux is a free computer operating system that was created by Linus Torvalds in 1991 and that has grown from contributions from software developers all over the world. Red Hat Linux is a distribution of Linux that packages together the software needed to run Linux and makes it easier to install and run.

Features in Red Hat Linux include a simplified installation procedure, Red Hat Package Management (RPM) tools for managing the software, and easy-to-use Gnome and KDE desktop environments. You can get Red Hat Linux from the Internet, from distributions that come with books such as this one, or from a commercially available boxed set of Red Hat Linux software.

✦　　✦　　✦

Installing Red Hat Linux

A simplified installation procedure is one of the best reasons for using a Linux distribution such as Red Hat Linux. In many cases, for a computer dedicated to using Linux, you can just pop in the Red Hat Linux CDs (that come with this book), choose from several preset configurations, and be up and running Linux in less than an hour.

If you want to share your computer with both Linux and Microsoft Windows, Red Hat offers several ways to go about doing that. If your computer doesn't have a CD drive, Network and Hard Disk installs are available. To preconfigure Red Hat Linux to install on multiple, similar computers, you can use the Kickstart installation.

Quick Installation

It can be a little intimidating to see a thick chapter on installation. But the truth is, if you have a little bit of experience with computers and a computer with common hardware, you can probably install Red Hat Linux pretty easily. The procedure in this section will get you going quickly if you have:

✦ The Red Hat Linux Installation CDs that come with this book.

✦ A PC with a built-in, bootable CD-ROM drive, at least 32MB of RAM, at least 350MB of free hard disk space for a minimal custom install, at least 1.5GB of free space for a workstation install, and at least 1GB for a server install.

For this quick procedure, you must either be dedicating your entire hard disk to Linux, have a preconfigured Linux partition, or have free space on your hard disk outside any existing Windows partition.

Caution If you are not dedicating your whole hard disk to Red Hat Linux and you don't understand partitioning, skip to the "Detailed Installation Instructions" section in this chapter. That section describes choices for having both Linux and Windows on the same computer.

Here's how you get started:

1. Insert the first Red Hat Linux installation CD into your computer's CD-ROM drive.

2. Reboot your computer.

3. When you see the Welcome screen, press Enter to begin the installation.

During installation, you are asked questions about your computer hardware and the network connections. After you have completed each answer, click Next. The following list describes the information you will need to enter. (If you need help, all of these topics are explained later in this chapter.)

✦ **Language** — Choose your language.

✦ **Keyboard** — Choose your keyboard type.

✦ **Mouse** — Identify the type of mouse you are using.

✦ **Install type** — Choose a configuration, such as Workstation (adds Linux and leaves Windows partitions), Server (adds Linux server packages and *erases* entire disk), Laptop (ensures that special laptop packages, such as PCMCIA and power management support, are included), or Custom (adds selected Linux packages and lets you choose partitioning). If you have an earlier version of Red Hat Linux installed, you can choose Upgrade to upgrade your system (hopefully) without losing data files.

✦ **Partitions** — Either have Red Hat choose your partitions or customize your own (with Disk Druid or fdisk). You must have at least one Linux partition, which must be assigned to root (/), and a swap partition. You may be asked to format that partition. (Because repartitioning can result in lost data, I recommend that you refer to descriptions on repartitioning your hard disk later in this chapter.)

✦ **GRUB** — Add the GRUB boot manager to control the boot process. (GRUB is described later in this chapter.)

✦ **Network configuration** — Set up your LAN connection. Information includes your computer's IP address, netmask, network number, broadcast address, host name, default gateway, and DNS servers. You can also indicate whether to activate your network when Linux boots.

✦ **Firewall** — Choose a default firewall configuration. Select High if you plan to connect to the Internet but don't plan to use Linux as a server. Choose Custom if you want to make particular services available to the network.

Select No Firewall only if you are connected to a trusted network, with no connection to a public network. You can also customize the firewall to allow selected interfaces or services.

✦ **Language support** — Choose to install support for additional languages.

✦ **Time zone** — Identify the time zone in which you are located.

✦ **User accounts** — Add the root user account password and add at least one regular user.

✦ **Authentication** — Choose whether to use encrypted or shadow passwords. You can instead choose to use a network-based authentication scheme, including the following: NIS, LDAP, or Kerberos. (These methods require special configuration.)

✦ **Packages** — For custom installations, choose groups of software packages to install. (You can also choose individual packages, if you like.)

✦ **Video** — Identify your video card.

✦ **Installing packages** — Up to this point, you can quit the installation process without having written anything to hard disk. After you select Next, the packages you selected are installed.

✦ **Boot disk** — Create a boot disk (optional).

✦ **Monitor** — Identify your monitor by selecting the vendor and model.

✦ **Custom X Configuration** — Indicate the color depth and screen. You can also choose your GUI environment (GNOME or KDE, if both are available) and whether you will see a graphical or text-based login prompt.

During installation, you can choose to install software based on the type of system you want (workstation, laptop, or server) or to select package groups individually (custom). I installed all packages, which I recommend doing only if you are trying out Linux in a nonproduction environment and have the disk space.

Caution　If your computer is connected to the Internet, you should be more selective about which server packages you install because they can pose potential security risks. A misconfigured server can be like an open window to your computer.

After answering the questions, the actual installation of packages takes between 20 and 40 minutes, depending on the number of packages and the speed of the computer hardware. The time will vary depending on your hardware. During this time, you may be asked to insert the other Red Hat installation CD.

When installation is done, remove the Red Hat Linux CD and click Exit to reboot your computer. When you see the boot screen, use up and down arrows to select a partition. Linux should boot by default. After Linux boots, it presents you with a login prompt. If you need more information than this procedure provides, go to the detailed installation instructions just ahead.

Detailed Installation Instructions

This section provides more detail on installation. Besides expanding on the installation procedure, this section also provides information on different installation types and on choosing computer hardware.

Tip

If anything goes wrong during installation and you get stuck, go to the "Troubleshooting Your Installation" section later in this chapter. It will give you suggestions about how to solve common installation problems.

Caution

If you are installing a dual-boot system that includes a Windows operating system, try to install the Windows system first and the Red Hat Linux system later. Some Windows systems blow away the Master Boot Record (MBR), making the Red Hat Linux partition inaccessible.

If, when installing Windows or Red Hat Linux, you find that the other operating system is no longer available on your boot screen, don't panic and don't immediately reinstall. You can usually recover from the problem by booting with the Red Hat Linux emergency boot disk, and then using either the `grub-install` or `lilo` commands to reinsert the proper MBR. If you are uncomfortable working in emergency mode, seek out an expert to help you.

Choosing an installation method

Red Hat Linux offers very flexible ways of installing the operating system. Of course, I recommend installing Red Hat Linux from the CDs that come with this book. However, if you don't have the Red Hat CDs or if you don't have a working CD-ROM drive, you can install Red Hat Linux from any of several different types of media. There are also several special types of installation. The installation types noted here are described fully in the "Special Installation Procedures" section.

First you should determine if you are doing a new install or an upgrade. If you are upgrading an existing Red Hat Linux system to the latest version, the installation process will try to leave your data files and configuration file intact as much as possible. This type of installation takes longer than a new install. A new install will simply erase all data on the Linux partitions (or whole hard disk) that you choose.

You can install Red Hat Linux from any of the locations described here. Each of the installation procedures from locations other than a CD requires a Red Hat Linux installation boot disk. (Creating an installation boot disk is described later.)

✦ **HTTP server**—Lets you install from a Web page address.

✦ **FTP server**—Lets you install from any FTP site.

✦ **NFS server**—Allows you to install from any shared directory on another computer on your network using the Network File System (NFS) facility.

✦ **Hard disk** — If you can place a copy of the Red Hat Linux distribution on your hard disk, you can install it from there. (Presumably, the distribution is on a hard disk partition to which you are *not* installing.)

The following specialty installation type also may be of interest to you:

✦ **Kickstart installation** — Lets you create a set of answers to the questions Red Hat Linux asks you during installation. This can be a timesaving method if you are installing Red Hat Linux on many computers with similar configurations.

The Red Hat Installation Guide is available on the Red Hat Documentation CD. If you don't have Red Hat Linux installed yet, you can open this CD on any Windows computer you have available. The guide is in HTML format, so you can view it from your browser. Open the `index-en.html` file in the `RH-DOCS` directory to start from the table of contents for Installation and other guides. Another document you may find useful before installing is the Red Hat Linux Reference Guide (also listed on the `index-en.html` page).

Choosing computer hardware

This may not really be a choice. You may just have an old PC lying around that you want to try Red Hat Linux on. Or you may have a killer workstation with some extra disk space and want to try out Red Hat Linux on a separate partition. To install the PC version of Red Hat Linux successfully (that is, the version on the accompanying CD), there are a few things that the computer must have:

✦ **x86 processor** — Your computer needs an Intel-compatible CPU. Unlike with some commercial operating systems, you don't need the latest Pentium processor to run Red Hat Linux (although it wouldn't hurt). Red Hat Linux can run on older processors. I've even seen the Intel 80386 on compatibility lists, although I haven't tried installing Red Hat Linux on a computer with that CPU.

✦ **Floppy disk drive or CD-ROM** — You need to be able to boot up the installation process from either floppy disk or CD-ROM. If you don't have a CD-ROM drive, you need a LAN connection to install Red Hat Linux from a server on the network or figure out a way to copy the contents of the CD to a hard disk.

✦ **Hard disk** — You need a hard disk, or a partition from a hard disk, that contains at least 350MB of hard-disk space for the most minimal custom install. (The actual amount of space you need varies depending on the installation type and packages you select. Workstation installs require 1.5GB, while an "Everything" install requires nearly 3GB.)

✦ **RAM** — You should have at least 32MB of RAM to install Red Hat Linux. If you are running in graphical mode, you will probably want at least 64MB.

✦ **Keyboard and monitor**—Although this seems obvious, the truth is that you only need a keyboard and monitor during installation. You can operate Red Hat Linux quite well over a LAN using either a shell interface from a network login or an X terminal.

There are versions of Red Hat Linux that run on Alpha and Sparc workstations, instead of just on PCs. The CD that comes with this book and the installation procedures presented here, however, are specific to PCs. Most of the other software described in this book, however, will work the same in any of those hardware environments.

Note The list of hardware supported by Red Hat Linux is available on the Internet at `www.redhat.com/hardware`.

If your computer's CD-ROM device is connected to a PCMCIA port (such as those that come on laptop computers), you will need to install PCMCIA support during installation. PCMCIA support is available only on Intel-based computers. See the sidebar on installing Red Hat Linux on a laptop for further information.

Beginning the installation

If you feel you have chosen the right type of installation for your needs, you can begin the installation procedure. Throughout most of the procedure, you can click Back to make changes to earlier screens. However, once you are warned that packages are about to be written to hard disk, there's no turning back. Most items that you configure can be changed after Red Hat Linux is up and running.

Installing Red Hat Linux on a Laptop

If your laptop computer has a built-in CD-ROM drive, you can install from that drive without any special considerations. However, if your laptop doesn't have a built-in CD-ROM drive, you probably need to install from a device that is connected to a PCMCIA slot on your laptop.

PCMCIA slots let you connect a variety of devices to your laptop using credit-card-sized cards (sometimes called PC Cards). Linux supports hundreds of PCMCIA devices. You may use your laptop's PCMCIA slot to install Red Hat Linux from several different types of PCM-CIA devices, including:

✦ A CD-ROM drive

✦ A LAN adapter

If you would like to know which PCMCIA devices are supported in Linux, see the `SUPPORTED.CARDS` file (located in the `/usr/share/doc/kernel-pcmcia-cs*` directory). In any of these cases, you need the PCMCIA support disk to use the device as an installation medium. The section on creating install disks describes how to create these installation floppy disks.

Caution   It is quite possible that your entire hard disk is devoted to a Windows 95, 98, 2000, ME, NT, or XP operating system and you may want to keep much of that information after Red Hat Linux is installed. Workstation and Custom install classes let you retain existing partitions, but they don't let you take space from existing DOS partitions without destroying them. See the section on reclaiming free disk space called "Using the FIPS utility" for information on how to assign your extra disk space to a different partition before you start this installation process.

Choosing Different Install Modes

Though most computers will allow you to install Red Hat Linux in the default mode (graphical), there are times when your video card may not support that mode. Also, though the install process will detect most computer hardware, there may be times when your hard disk, Ethernet card, or other critical hardware cannot be detected and require special information at boot time.

Here is a list of different installation modes you can use to start the Red Hat Linux install process. You would typically only try these modes if the default mode failed (that is, if the screen was garbled or hardware wasn't detected).

✦ **text**: Type **text** to run installation in a text-based mode. Do this if installation doesn't seem to recognize your graphics card. The installation screens aren't as pretty, but they work just as well.

✦ **lowres**: Type **lowres** to run installation in 640×480 screen resolution for graphics cards that can't support the higher resolution.

✦ **nofb**: Type **nofb** to turn off frame buffer.

✦ **expert**: Type **expert** if you believe that the installation process is not properly auto-probing your hardware. This mode bypasses probing so you can choose your mouse, video memory, and other values that may otherwise be chosen for you.

✦ **linux rescue**: The `linux rescue` mode is not really an installation mode. This mode boots from CD, mounts your hard disk, and lets you access useful utilities to correct problems preventing your Linux system from operating properly.

✦ **linux dd**: Type **linux dd** if you have a driver disk you want to use to install.

You can add other options to the linux boot command to identify particular hardware that is not being detected properly. For example, to specify the number of cylinders, heads, and sectors for your hard disk (if you believe the boot process is not detecting these values properly), you could pass the information to the kernel as follows:

```
linux hd=720,32,64
```

In this example, the kernel is told that the hard disk has 720 cylinders, 32 heads, and 64 sectors. You can find this information in documentation that comes with your hard disk (or stamped on the hard disk itself on a sticker near the serial number).

1. **Insert the CD-ROM in the CD-ROM drive.**

   If you are doing an install from a local hard disk or network, you can insert an installation boot disk instead. Refer to the section on creating install disks for information on making the disk (or disks) that you need.

2. **Start your computer.**

   If you see the "Red Hat Linux Welcome" screen, continue to the next step.

Tip   If you don't see the Welcome screen, your CD-ROM drive may not be bootable. Creating a bootable floppy may be the best way to proceed. However, you also may have the choice of making your CD-ROM drive be bootable. Here's how: Restart the computer. Immediately, you should see a message telling you how to go into setup, such as by pressing the F1, F2 or Del key. Enter setup and look for an option such as "Boot Options" or "Boot from." If the value is "A: First, Then C:" change it to "CD-ROM First, Then C:" or something similar. Save the changes and try to install again.

   If installation succeeds, you may want to restore the boot settings. If your CD drive still won't boot, you may need to create an installation boot disk from the `boot.img` (for most computers), `bootnet.img` (for network installs), or `pcmcia.img` (for laptops) files on your CD. Create that boot disk from descriptions provided later in this chapter. Then insert the floppy, reboot, and continue this procedure.

3. **Start the boot procedure.**

   At the boot prompt, press Enter to start the boot procedure in graphical mode. If for some reason your computer will not let you install in graphical mode (16-bit color, 800×600 resolution, framebuffer), refer to the "Choosing Different Install Modes" sidebar. You are asked to choose a language.

4. **Choose a language.**

   When prompted, indicate the language that you would like to use during the installation procedure by moving the arrow keys and selecting Next. (Later, you will be able to add additional languages.) You are asked to choose a keyboard.

5. **Choose a keyboard and then click Next.**

   Select the correct keyboard model (Generic 101-key PC by default), layout (U.S. English by default), and whether or not you want to enable dead keys (on by default). Dead keys allow you to enter characters with special markings (such as circumflexes and umlauts).

6. **Add a mouse.**

   When prompted, indicate the kind of mouse and click Next.

   If possible, choose an exact match to the model of mouse you have. Otherwise, you can choose a generic serial mouse (if it connects to a COM port) or a generic PS/2 mouse (if it connects to a PS/2 port). Support exists also for two-button and three-button USB mice. For a serial mouse, you need to identify which COM port the mouse is connected to. If you are using a two-button mouse, you can click Emulate 3 Buttons. This allows you to use the Shift key with a mouse button to emulate the center button from a three-button mouse.

7. Continue installation.

From the Welcome to Red Hat Linux screen, click Next to continue. You will see the Install Options screen.

8. Choose install type.

Select either Install for a new install (along with the type of install) or Upgrade to upgrade the software for an existing version of Red Hat.

To upgrade, you must have at least a Linux 2.0 kernel installed. With an upgrade, all of your configuration files are saved as `filename`.rpmsave (for example, the hosts file is saved as `hosts.rpmsave`). The locations of those files, as well as other upgrade information, is written to `/tmp/upgrade.log`. The upgrade installs the new kernel, any changed software packages, and any packages that the installed packages depend on being there. Your data files and configuration information should remain intact.

See the section on partitioning to learn to use Disk Druid or fdisk to partition your disk. See Appendix B for descriptions of Red Hat packages.

For a new install, you must choose one of the following types (also referred to as classes) of installation:

- **Workstation** — It automatically selects the partitioning and installs packages that are appropriate for a Linux workstation. Either GNOME or KDE is the desktop environment and the X Window System provides the underlying GUI framework. GNOME is the default window manager for Red Hat Linux. You can select to install one or both of them later in the installation process.

Any Linux partitions or free space on your hard disk(s) will be assigned to the new installation with the Workstation and Laptop types of installation. Any Windows partitions (VFAT file system types) will not be touched by this install. After installation, you will be able to boot Linux or Windows. If there is no free space outside of your Windows partition, you must run the FIPS program (described later) before proceeding, or you will lose your Window installation.

- **Server** — A Server installs the software packages that you would typically need for a Linux server (for example, Web server, file server, and so on). This type of install does not install the X Window System by default (so you need to either add X when you select packages or you'd better know how to use the shell). This type of install also erases all hard disks and assigns all disks to Linux by default.

Caution   This is a big one. In case you didn't catch the previous paragraph, Server installs erase the whole hard disk by default! If you have an existing Windows partition that you want to keep, change the Automatic Partitioning option that appears next to either only remove the Linux Partitions or to only use existing free space.

- **Laptop** — A Laptop install is similar to a Workstation install. The primary differences between the two are that the Laptop install includes PCMCIA support, IRDA (infrared) utilities, and wireless tools.

- **Custom System** — You are given the choice of configuring your own partitions and selecting your own software packages.

Note   If you are at all computer literate, I recommend choosing Custom System install. It will give you a better feel for what is going on with your installation.

At this point, the procedure will continue through a Custom System installation. If you are doing a Workstation installation, you can indicate that you want to do automatic partitioning, then skip to the Configure Networking step. If you select Server installation, you can indicate that you want to erase the entire disk, then skip to the Configure Networking step. For Custom System installs, continue on.

9. **Choose your partitioning strategy.**

   You have three choices related to how your disk is partitioned for Red Hat Linux installation:

   - **Have the installer automatically partition for you** — With this selection, all Linux partitions on all hard disks are erased and used for the installation. The installation process automatically handles the partitioning.

   - **Manually Partition with Disk Druid** — With this selection, the Disk Druid utility is run to let you partition your hard disk. This interface is more intuitive than fdisk's.

   - **Manually Partition with fdisk [experts only]** — With this selection, the fdisk utility is run to let you partition your hard disk. This interface is more appropriate for seasoned Linux/UNIX users.

   Click Next to continue.

10. **Choose partitioning.**

    If you selected to have the installer automatically partition for you, you can choose from the following options:

Note   If you selected to use Disk Druid or fdisk for partitioning, refer to the section on partitioning your hard disk later in this chapter for details on using those tools.

- **Remove all Linux partitions on this system** — Windows and other non-Linux partitions remain intact with this selection.

- **Remove all partitions on this system** — This erases the entire hard disk.

- **Keep all partitions and use existing free space** — This only works if you have enough free space on your hard disk that is not currently assigned to any partition.

If you have multiple hard disks, you can select which of those disks should be used for your Red Hat Linux installation. Leave the Review check box on to see how Linux is choosing to partition your hard disk.

After reviewing the Partitions screen, you can change any of the partitions you choose, providing you have at least one root (/) partition that can hold the entire installation and one swap partition. The swap partition is usually twice the size of the amount of RAM on your computer (for example, for 128MB RAM you could use 256MB of swap).

Click the Next button to continue.

11. **Choose a boot loader.** Select whether you want to use the GRUB or LILO boot loader. Or you can choose to not install a boot loader (for example, if you want to use a boot loader that is already installed on your computer or if you want to boot Linux from floppy disk). You can also choose where to store the boot loader. Your choices are:

- **Master Boot Record (MBR)** — This is the preferred place for GRUB or LILO. It causes either GRUB or LILO to control the boot process for all operating systems installed on the hard disk.

- **First Sector of Boot Partition** — If another boot loader is being used on your computer, you can have GRUB or LILO installed on your Linux partition (first sector). This lets you have the other boot loader refer to your GRUB or LILO boot loader to boot Red Hat Linux.

Note

If you select the GRUB boot loader, which is the default, you have the option of adding a GRUB password. The password protects your system from having potentially dangerous kernel options sent to the kernel by someone without that password. GRUB and LILO boot loaders are described later in this chapter.

You can choose to add Kernel Parameters (which may be needed if your computer can't detect certain hardware). For example, if you have an IDE writeable CD drive, you would want it to operate in SCSI emulation mode by setting the drive to use the ide-scsi module.

You can select to use linear mode (which is required if you use LILO to boot from a disk with more than 1024 cylinders and you want to have the Linux boot partition exist above that partition). The bottom of the screen indicates the bootable partitions on your computer. Select the default boot partition by clicking the partition and selecting "Default boot image." You can also change the label on any partition by clicking it and then changing the value in the Boot label box.

Note

For further information on configuring GRUB or LILO, refer to the section on those two boot loaders later in this chapter.

12. Configure networking.

At this point, you are asked to configure your networking. This applies only to configuring a local area network. If you will use only dial-up networking, skip this section by clicking Next. If your computer is not yet connected to a LAN, you should skip this section.

Network address information is assigned to your computer in two basic ways: statically (you type it in) or dynamically (a DHCP server provides that information from the network at boot time). A system administrator will give you information about a DHCP server, or the administrator may give you a static IP address that is permanently assigned to your computer, as well as other information that is needed to complete your network configuration. Besides this information, you should also indicate whether you want the network to start at boot time (you probably do if you have a LAN).

Refer to Chapter 15 for descriptions of IP addresses, netmasks, and other information that you need to set up your LAN and to Chapter 16 for information related to domain names.

If you have selected to enter your networking information statically, you may need to deselect the Configure Using DHCP option and add the following information:

- **IP Address** — This is the four-part, dot-separated number that represents your computer to the network. How IP addresses are formed and how you choose them is more than can be said in a few sentences (see Chapter 15 for a more complete description). An example of a private IP address is 10.0.0.12.

- **Netmask** — The netmask is used to determine what part of an IP address represents the network and what part represents a particular host computer. An example of a netmask for a Class A network is 255.0.0.0. (Red Hat installation does a good job of guessing your netmask.)

- **Network** — This number represents the network number. For example, if you have an IP number of 10.0.0.12 on a Class A network (255.0.0.0), the network number is 10 (although it would be represented here as 10.0.0.0).

- **Broadcast** — This is the IP number that is reserved for broadcast data on the network. For a Class A network with a network number 10, the broadcast number could be 10.255.255.255.

- **Hostname** — This is the name identifying your computer within your domain. For example, if your computer were named "baskets" in the handsonhistory.com domain, your full hostname may be baskets.handsonhistory.com.

- **Gateway** — This is the IP number of the computer that acts as a gateway to networks outside your LAN. This typically represents a host computer or router that routes packets between your LAN and the Internet.

- **Primary DNS** — This is the IP address of the host that translates computer names you request into IP addresses. It is referred to as a Domain Name Service (DNS) server. You may also have Secondary and Ternary name servers in case the first one can't be reached. (Most ISPs will give you two DNS server addresses.)

Cross-Reference

To configure your LAN after installation, see Chapter 15.

13. **Choose a firewall configuration.**

The use of a firewall has significant impact on the security of your computer. If you are connected to the Internet or to another public network, a firewall can limit the ways an intruder may break into your Linux system. Here are your choices for configuring a firewall during installation:

- **High** — Select this security level if you are connecting your Linux system to the Internet for Web browsing but don't plan to offer your system as a server to the Internet. Only explicitly defined connections are accepted. To allow Web browsing and basic network setup, DNS replies and DHCP (to serve addresses) are allowed.

- **Medium** — Select this security level if you want to block access to ports used to offer most basic TCP/IP services (standard, reserved ports lower than 1023). This selection denies access to ports used for NFS servers, remote X clients, and the X font server.

- **No firewall** — Select this security level if you are not connected to a public network and do not want to deny requests for services from any computer on your local network. Of course, you can still restrict access to services by starting up only the services you want to offer and by using configuration files to restrict access to individual services.

If you know you want to allow access to particular services, you can click Customize and allow incoming requests for the following: DHCP, SSH, Telnet, WWW, Mail, and/or FTP services. You can also add a comma-separated list of port numbers to the Other Ports box to open access to those ports. (The /etc/services file lists which services are associated with which port numbers.)

If you have a LAN that consists of trusted computers, you can click the box representing your interface to that LAN (probably eth0). Clicking the box allows access to any services you care to share with the computers on your LAN.

Tip   Adding firewall rules here results in rules being added to the /etc/sysconfig/ ipchains file. The rules are run from the /etc/init.d/ipchains start-up script when you boot your computer. I recommend that you edit the rules file to change your firewall rules. This makes sure that your rules are configured automatically each time the system starts.

Cross-Reference   For more information on configuring firewalls, see Chapter 14.

14. Choose language support.

Your installation language should be selected automatically on this screen. You can select to install support for additional languages by clicking the check boxes next to the languages you want.

15. Choose a time zone.

Select the time zone from the list of time zones shown. Either click a spot on the map or choose from the scrolling list. To see a more specific view of your location, click World and choose your continent. From the UTC Offset tab, you can choose a time zone according to the number of hours away from Greenwich Mean Time (GMT), known as the UTC offset.

16. Configure user accounts.

You need to choose a password for your root user at this point and add one or more regular user accounts. The root password provides complete control of your Red Hat Linux system. Without it, and before you add other users, you will have no access to your own system. Enter the Root Password, and then type it again in the Confirm box to confirm it. (Remember the root user's password and keep it confidential!)

Tip   Use the passwd command to change your password later. See Chapter 14 for suggestions on how to choose a good password. See Chapter 11 for information on setting up user accounts.

Add an account name for a regular user on your computer. Type the password, confirm it, type a full name for the user, and click Add to add the account. Click Next to continue.

17. Enable authentication.

In most situations, you will enable shadow passwords and MD5 passwords (as selected by default). The shadow password file prevents access to encrypted passwords.

Note   MD5 is an algorithm used to encrypt passwords in Linux and other UNIX systems. It replaces an algorithm called crypt, which was used with early UNIX systems. When you enable MD5 passwords, your users can have longer passwords that are harder to break than those encrypted with crypt.

If you are on a network that supports one of several different forms of network-wide authentication, you may choose one of the following features:

- **Enable NIS.** Select this button and type the NIS Domain name and NIS server location if your network is configured to use the Network Information System (NIS). Instead of selecting an NIS Server, you can click the button to broadcast to find the server on your network.

For more information on NIS, see Chapter 23.

- **Enable LDAP.** If your organization gathers information about users, you can click this button to search for authentication information in an LDAP server. You can enter the LDAP Server name and optionally an LDAP distinguished name to look up the user information your system needs.

- **Enable Kerberos 5.** Click this button to enable network authentication services available through Kerberos. After enabling Kerberos, you can enter information about a Kerberos Realm (a group of Kerberos servers and clients), KDC (a computer that issues Kerberos tickets), and Admin server (a server running the Kerberos kadmind daemon).

- **SMB.** Click on this tab to configure your computer to use Samba for file and print sharing with Windows systems. If you Enable SMB Authentication, you can enter the name of the SMB server for your LAN and indicate the Workgroup you want your computer to belong to.

18. **Select Packages.**

You are presented with groups of packages at this point. Which packages are selected by default depends on the type of installation you chose earlier. In general, either more workstation-oriented or server-oriented packages are selected. Select the ones you want and click Next.

If you have enough disk space and you want to try out lots of different areas of Linux, I recommend you do a Custom install and select "Everything" at the bottom of the Package Group list. As you try out procedures in this book, you won't have to keep installing packages if everything is already installed. Again, I don't recommend this on production computers because many server software packages open security holes. Installing everything can also consume about 3GB of space.

Because each group represents several packages, you can click the "Select individual packages" button to select more specifically the packages you want.

Appendix B describes the software packages that come with Red Hat Linux.

A listing of all of the software packages in each Package Group is contained in the file RedHat/base/comps on the Red Hat installation CD-ROM.

19. Configure video hardware.

Your video card should have been detected automatically and should be high-lighted. If not, choose the correct video driver from the list, and select the amount of video RAM contained on the board. You can also choose to skip X configuration. (If you do, you can configure X after Linux is installed and running by using the Xconfigurator command.)

Tip   If you have problems getting your video card and monitor to work properly, refer to the XFree86 Web site (www.xfree86.org). Select a link to a driver status document to view problems with specific video cards. See the troubleshooting section later in this chapter.

20. Begin installing?

A screen tells you that you are about to begin writing to hard disk. You can still back out now, and the disk will not have changed. Click Next to proceed. (To quit without changes, eject the CD and restart the computer.) Now the file systems are created and the packages are installed.

You are prompted to insert additional installation CDs as they are needed.

21. Create boot disk.

If you chose to create a boot disk earlier, you are prompted here to insert a blank floppy and click Next to create the boot floppy. (You can still skip it, if you like, by clicking Skip Boot Disk Creation.)

22. Select Monitor Configuration.

Scroll down the list to find your monitor's manufacturer; then click the plus sign to choose the model. When you select the model, the correct horizontal and vertical sync rates are added or you can type your own values. If your model is not found, consult the monitor's manual. Click Next to continue.

23. Choose Custom X Configuration (Color and Resolution).

Based on what your hardware can support, you will see possible combinations of the number of colors and screen resolutions. The number of bits per pixel represents the total number of colors that can be displayed. You can choose 8 bits and possibly 16 bits and 32 bits. (Some applications require at least 16-bit color.) Standard screen resolution begins with 640×480. Higher resolutions allow you to fit more windows on your screen, but everything is smaller and performance can be degraded. Click the Test This Configuration button to try out the selected resolution/color combination. Click Next to continue.

If you installed both GNOME and KDE, you can choose which to use by default (you can switch between them once your system is running). You can also choose whether or not you want a graphical login screen (run level 5) or a text-based login screen (run level 3). Click Next to continue.

24. Finish installing.

When you see the "Congratulations" screen, eject the CD and click Exit.

Your computer will restart. If you installed GRUB or LILO, you will see a graphical boot screen that displays the bootable partitions. Press the Up Arrow and Down Arrow keys to choose the partition you want to boot, and press Enter. If Linux is the default partition, you can wait a few moments and it will boot automatically.

Depending on whether you set your computer to use graphical login or not, you will either see the Red Hat graphical login screen or a simple command-line login prompt. Go to Chapter 3 for a description on how to login to Red Hat Linux and begin learning how to use Linux.

If after installation you decide to add or remove hardware from your computer, there is a tool that will allow you to reconfigure your hardware when the system boots up. See the sidebar describing kudzu for detecting and configuring new and changed hardware.

Special Installation Procedures

If you don't want to, or can't, use the procedure to install Red Hat Linux from CD, the procedures in this section give you alternatives. The first procedure tells how to install Red Hat Linux from alternative media (using FTP, HTTP, NFS, or hard disk installs). The next procedure describes how to do kickstart installations.

Reconfiguring Hardware at Boot Time with kudzu

Sometimes as Red Hat Linux is booting up, you may want to make changes to the system configuration. You may have added a new piece of hardware (or removed one). You may want to turn off a particular system service because it is hanging during the boot. With kudzu, you can change hardware and service configurations as your computer is booting.

To enter kudzu while Red Hat Linux is booting, look for a message on the screen that says "Press 'I' to enter interactive startup." Press I and you will be prompted to enter interactive startup. The kudzu Hardware Discovery Utility will check for hardware that has been removed or added and allow you to add or remove configuration for the hardware or do nothing.

When all the new or changed hardware has been reconfigured, you are prompted to start service reconfiguration. Type Y and you will be stepped through each service that is configured to start at boot time. This is an excellent way to temporarily turn off a service that is hanging your system or that is no longer needed.

Installing from other media

Your CD-ROM drive may not be working, you may not have a CD-ROM drive, or maybe you just want to install a new version of Red Hat Linux that is available from another computer on the network. In any of these cases, Red Hat will let you install Linux from a Web server (HTTP), an FTP server, a shared NFS directory, or local hard disk.

Note   To use HTTP, FTP, or NFS installations, your computer must be connected to a LAN that can reach the computer containing the Red Hat Linux distribution. You cannot use a direct dial-up connection. For a local hard disk install, the distribution must have been copied to a local disk that is not being used for installation. See the section "Setting up an install server" for details on copying the distribution and making it available.

Beginning installation

To begin any of these types of installation, you need to boot the installation process from a floppy disk. Refer to the section on creating boot disks later in this chapter. With the appropriate boot disk in hand (`bootnet.img` for a network install and `boot.img` for a hard disk install), start the installation for these types of installs as follows:

1. **Insert the floppy boot disk.**

2. **Reboot the computer.** You should see the "Welcome to Red Hat" boot screen.

3. **Press Enter.** You are prompted to select a language.

4. **Select the language.** You are prompted to choose a keyboard type.

5. **Select your keyboard type.** You are prompted to select an installation method.

6. **Choose install method.** Select any of the following installation methods: NFS Image, FTP, HTTP, or Hard disk.

7. **Configure TCP/IP.** For any of the network install types (NFS, FTP, and HTTP), you are prompted to configure TCP/IP. (See the section on configuring networking earlier in this chapter for descriptions of information you need to add to these fields.)

8. **Identify location of Red Hat.** You need to identify the NFS server name, FTP site name, or Web site name that contains the Red Hat directory that holds the distribution. Or, if you are installing from hard disk, you must identify the partition containing the distribution and the directory that actually contains the Red Hat directory.

9. **Continue with installation.** If the distribution is found in the location you indicated, continue the installation as described in the previous section.

The next section describes how to set up your own server for installing Red Hat Linux.

Setting up an install server

If you have a LAN connection from your computer to a computer that has a CD-ROM drive and about 1.3GB of disk space and offers NFS, FTP, or Web services, you can install Red Hat Linux from that server. Likewise, you can install from a spare disk partition by using a hard disk install. The following procedures let you set up a Linux install server:

Because there are two CDs in the Red Hat Linux distribution, you can't just identify the location of the mounted CD as you could with previous Red Hat Linux distributions. You must install the contents of both CDs in the same directory structure on the server's hard disk. For example, you could do the following:

```
# mkdir /tmp/rh
# mount /mnt/cdrom              With first CD inserted
# cp -r /mnt/cdrom/* /tmp/rh/
# umount /mnt/cdrom ; eject /mnt/cdrom
# mount /mnt/cdrom              With second CD inserted
# cp -r /mnt/cdrom/* /tmp/rh/
```

Just type "y" when it asks to overwrite some files. The distribution directory must contain at least the RPMS and base directories, which must include all necessary software packages. In this example, all files were copied. What you do next depends on the type of install server you are using.

NFS server

Add an entry to the /etc/exports file to share the distribution directory you created. This entry would make the directory available in read-only form to any computer:

```
/tmp/rh   (ro)
```

Next, restart NFS by typing the following as root user:

```
/etc/init.d/nfs restart
```

If your computer were named pine, the computer installing the distribution from your shared directory would identify it as pine:/tmp/rh.

Web server

If your computer is configured as a Web server, you need to simply make the distribution directory available. For example, after creating the distribution directory as described above, type the following:

```
# ln -s /tmp/rh /var/www/html/rh
```

If your computer were named pine.handsonhistory.com, you would identify the install server as http://pine.handsonhistory.com/rh.

FTP server

If your computer is configured as an FTP server, you need to make the distribution directory available in much the same way you did with the Web server. For example, after creating the distribution directory as described above, type the following:

```
# ln -s /tmp/rh /var/ftp/pub/rh
```

If your computer were named pine.handsonhistory.com, you would identify the install server as ftp://pine.handsonhistory.com/pub/rh.

Hard disk install

For a hard disk install, you need to copy the ISO images of each CD (for example, type cp /dev/cdrom /tmp/rh/cd1.iso). If the ISO images existed in the /tmp/rh directory of the first partition of your IDE hard disk, you could identify the device as /dev/hda1 and the directory holding the images as /tmp/rh.

Tip   Because I had a dual-boot system (Linux and Windows ME) with a lot of space on my Windows partition, I copied iso images of each Red Hat Linux distribution CD to a top level directory called rh. The install procedure had no trouble accessing the Windows (VFAT) partition and installation went smoothly.

Kickstart installation

If you are installing Red Hat Linux on multiple computers, you can save yourself some trouble by preconfiguring the answers to questions asked during installation. The method of automating the installation process is referred to as a kickstart installation.

Caution   Based on the information you provide in your ks.cfg file, kickstart will silently go through and install Red Hat Linux without intervention. If this file is not correct, you could easily remove your master boot record and erase everything on your hard disk. Check the ks.cfg file carefully and test it on a noncritical computer before trying it on a computer holding critical data.

The general steps of performing a kickstart installation are as follows:

1. **Create a kickstart file.** The kickstart file, named ks.cfg, contains the responses to questions that are fed to the installation process.

2. **Install kickstart file.** You have to place the ks.cfg on a floppy disk, on a local hard disk, or in an accessible location on the network.

3. **Start kickstart installation.** When you boot the installation procedure, you need to identify the location of the ks.cfg file.

Tip

If you already have a Red Hat Linux installation completed, you can use the settings given for that installation to create a ks.cfg file that you can use for the next computer. Type the following from a terminal window on that computer.

```
# mkkickstart > /tmp/ks.cfg
```

Be sure to open the ks.cfg file you just created, in any text editor, and change it as you desire. The output is not perfect, so you will need to correct it. In particular, you need to create good partitioning information. It is useful, however, for gathering a list of packages. You can then copy the ks.cfg file to a floppy disk to use for your next kickstart installation.

Creating the kickstart file

The best way to begin creating your kickstart file is from a working ks.cfg file. You can do this either by copying one that comes with your Red Hat installation or by creating one using the mkkickstart command described in the previous section. From the Red Hat Documentation CD, copy the sample.ks file to a temporary directory so you can work on it. Here is an example:

```
# cp /mnt/cdrom/RH-DOCS/sample.ks /tmp/ks.cfg
```

Use any text editor to edit the ks.cfg file. Remember that required items should be in order and that any time you omit an item, the user will be prompted for an answer. Entries from the sample ks.cfg file are described in the text that follows. Use some of these entries as they are and modify others to suit your needs. Commented lines begin with a pound sign (#).

The required lang command sets the language (and to be more specific, the country as well) in which Red Hat is installed. The set value is U.S. English (en_US).

```
### Installation Language
lang en_US
```

The optional network command lets you configure your Red Hat system's interface to your network. The example tells your computer to get its IP address and related network information from a DHCP server (--bootproto dhcp). If you want to assign a particular IP address, comment out the dhcp line and uncomment the --bootproto static line. Then change the IP address (--ip), netmask (--netmask), IP address of the gateway (--gateway), and IP address of the DNS name server (--nameserver) to suit your system.

Note

Although the network --bootproto static values appear to be on two lines, when you remove the pound signs all values must be on the same line.

```
### Network Configuration
network --bootproto dhcp
```

```
#network --bootproto static --ip 192.168.0.1 --netmask 255.255.254.0 --
gateway 192.168.0.1 --nameserver 192.168.0.254
```

The next value identifies where Red Hat software is located: cdrom, nfs, url, or harddrive. The cdrom value requires no options. To install from harddrive, you must identify the partition and directory containing the distribution. For an NFS server, you must identify the server and directory. For a url installation, you must provide the URL for an FTP or HTTP location that contains the installation software. (The nfs example must be changed for your situation.)

```
### Source File Location
cdrom
#url --url http://<server>/<dir>
#harddrive --partition /dev/sda2 --dir /home/dist/6.2/i386
#nfs --server porkchop.redhat.com --dir /mnt/test/qa0301/i386
```

The optional device command example allows you to pass parameters to identify your Ethernet card, or other device, so it can be recognized by the install process. In this example, you can set the IO and IRQ for a card that cannot be auto-probed by removing the comment character and setting the options appropriate to your card.

```
### Ethernet Device Configuration
#device ethernet wd --opts "io=0x280, irq=3"
```

The required keyboard command identifies a United States (us) keyboard by default. More than 70 other keyboard types are supported.

```
### Keyboard Configuration
keyboard us
```

Partitioning is required for a new install, optional for an upgrade. The code that follows is from the sample ks.cfg file. The zerombr yes value clears the Master Boot Record (to leave the MBR alone, set this to no). The clearpart --linux value removes existing linux partitions (or use --all to clear all partitions). The part /boot, swap, and / lines sets the sizes of those partitions (--size) to 35MB, 128MB, and 1000MB, respectively. The root partition (/) can grow to a --maxsize of 1400MB (if that much space is available).

```
### Partitioning Information
zerombr yes
clearpart --linux
part /boot --size 35
part swap --size 128
part / --size 1000 --grow --maxsize 1400
```

There are also optional RAID partition examples shown in this file. In the examples, raid.0 and raid.1 are each set to 80MB. Their locations are set to the first and second SCSI disks (sda and sdb, respectively).

The `install` option runs a new installation. You can use the `upgrade` keyword instead to upgrade an existing system. (For an upgrade, only a language, an install method, an install device, a keyboard, and a boot loader configuration are required.)

```
install
```

Two options are commented out for you to consider. The `text` option causes the installation process to be done in text mode instead of the default graphical mode. The `interactive` option causes kickstart to stop at each installation screen (by default, kickstart just continues so that the install can be unattended).

```
### Perform kickstart installation in text mode
#text

### Stop at each screen during the kickstart
### installation
#interactive
```

The required `mouse` value identifies the mouse type. The example shows a generic three-button PS/2 type mouse (`generic3ps/2`). You could replace it with a two-button serial mouse (`generic`), a two-button PS/2 mouse (`genericps/2`), or a Microsoft Intellimouse (`msintellips/2`). For a serial mouse, identify the device (for example, `--device ttyS0` for the COM1 port). To configure other types of mice, you must run `mouseconfig`. To see other mouse types, run the `mouseconfig --help` command.

```
### Mouse Configuration
#mouse generic --device ttyS0
mouse generic3ps/2
```

The `firewall` command lets you set the default firewall used by your Red Hat Linux system. The default value is `high` (high security). Or you can set firewall to `medium` (medium security) or `disabled` (no firewall). (These values are described in the installation procedure earlier in this chapter.) As you see in the commented example, you can optionally indicate that there are no restrictions from host computers on a particular interface (`--trust eth0`). You can also allow an individual service (`--ssh`) or a particular port:protocol pair (`--port 1234:upd`).

```
### Firewall Configuration
### options are high, medium, and disabled
# firewall --high --trust eth0 --ssh --port 1234:udp
firewall --high
```

The `timezone` command sets the timezone for your Linux system. The default, shown here, is United States, New York (`America/New_York`). If you don't set a time zone, `US/Eastern` is used. Run the `timeconfig` command to see other valid time zones.

```
### Time Zone Configuration
timezone --utc America/New_York
```

The optional xconfig command can be used to configure your monitor and video card. If the skipx command is used instead (which it is by default), no X configuration is done. (After the system is installed, run Xconfigurator to set up your X configuration.) Along with the xconfig command, you can identify the type of X server to use based on your video card (--server) and monitor (--monitor). A handful of other options let you set the color depth in bits (--depth 16), the screen resolution (--resolution 800x600), the default desktop to GNOME or KDE (--defaultdesktop=GNOME), whether the login screen is graphical (--startonboot), a name identifying the card (--card "Matrox Millennium"), and the amount of RAM on your video card (--videoram 1024).

```
### X Configuration
skipx
#xconfig --server "SVGA" --monitor "viewsonic g773" --depth 16
--resolution 800x600 --defaultdesktop=GNOME --startonboot --
card "Matrox Millennium" --videoram 1024
```

The rootpw command sets the password to whatever word follows (in this example, paSSword). Understand that it is a security risk to leave this password hanging around, so you should change this password (with the passwd command) after Linux is installed. You also have the option of adding an encrypted password instead (--iscrypted g.UJ.RQeOV3Bg).

```
### Root Password Designation
rootpw paSSword
#rootpw --iscrypted g.UJ.RQeOV3Bg
```

If you want the system to reboot after installation is completed, uncomment the optional reboot command. Otherwise, installation waits for you to explicitly indicate that the system should reboot.

```
#reboot
```

The required auth command sets the type of authentication used to protect your user passwords. The --useshadow option enables the /etc/shadow file to store your passwords. The --enablemd5 option enables up to 256 character passwords. (You would typically use both.)

```
### Authorization Configuration
auth --useshadow --enablemd5
```

The bootloader command sets the location of the boot loader. By default, the GRUB boot loader is used. For example, --location mbr adds GRUB to the master boot record. Use --location none to not add GRUB. You can also add kernel options to be read at boot time using the append option (--append hdd=ide-scsi) or an optional password for GRUB (--password=XYZ).

```
### Boot Loader Configuration
bootloader --location mbr
#bootloader --location=mbr --append hdd=ide-scsi --password=GRUBpassword
```

To indicate which packages to install, begin a section with the `%packages` command. A few examples follow. Designate whole installation groups, individual groups, or individual packages. After the `%packages`, start an entry with an @ sign for a group of packages, and add each individual package by placing its name on a line by itself. The example does a Server install, adds all X packages, and adds the ElectricFence package.

Tip You can find a listing of package groups and individual packages on the Red Hat installation CD. Find the `comps` file in the `RedHat/base` directory. However, if you have a working Red Hat Linux system with packages that you like already installed, you can use the `mkkickstart` command, described in the previous section, to come up with packages and other kickstart settings.

```
### Package Designation
%packages
# Use one of these whole installation groups:
@ Server
# @ KDE Workstation
# @ Gnome Workstation
# Add an individual group, such as X Window System:
@ X Window System
# Add an individual package, such as ElectricFence:
ElectricFence
```

Note The `%packages` command is not supported for an upgrade.

The `%post` command starts the postinstallation section. Any shell commands you want to run after installation is completed can be added after the `%post` command.

```
### Commands To Be Run Post-Installation
%post
echo "Kickstart installation" > /tmp/message
```

If you want to find out more about using Kickstart commands, see the Red Hat Linux Reference Guide. The guide is available on the Red Hat Docs CD. It includes an appendix that describes the kickstart commands in detail. If the Red Hat Docs CD is not available, look for both the Reference Guide and the Kickstart sample file (`sample.ks`) in the doc/ directory of any Red Hat mirror site (see `www.redhat.com/mirrors.html` for a list of sites).

Installing the kickstart file

Once the `ks.cfg` file is created, you need to put it somewhere accessible to the computer doing the installation. Typically, you will place the file on a floppy disk. However, you can also put the file on a computer that is reachable on the network or on a hard disk.

To copy the file to a floppy disk, create a DOS floppy and copy the file as follows:

```
# mcopy ks.cfg a:
```

When you do the Red Hat installation, you must have this floppy disk with you.

Being able to place the `ks.cfg` file on a computer on the network requires a bit more configuration. The network must have a DHCP or a BOOTP server configured that is set up to provide network information to the new install computer. The NFS server containing the `ks.cfg` file must export the file so that it is accessible to the computer installing Linux. To use a `ks.cfg` file from the local hard disk, you can place the file on any partition that is a Windows (VFAT) or Linux (ext3) partition.

Booting a kickstart installation

If the kickstart file (`ks.cfg`) has been created and installed in an accessible location, you can start the kickstart installation. Here is an example of how you can do a kickstart installation using the Red Hat Linux CD and a floppy containing a `ks.cfg` file:

1. Insert the Red Hat Linux CD and restart the computer.

2. When you see the boot prompt, insert the floppy containing the `ks.cfg` file and type the following (quickly, before the installation boots on its own):

   ```
   boot: linux ks=floppy
   ```

   You should see messages about formatting the file system and reading the package list. The packages should install without any intervention, and you should see a post install message. Finally, you should see the "Complete" message.

3. Remove the floppy; then press the Spacebar to restart your computer (the CD should eject automatically).

Special Installation Topics

Some things that you run into during installation merit whole discussions by themselves. Rather than bog down the procedures with details that not everyone needs, I have added these topics to this section. Descriptions expand on things such as reclaiming disk space, partitioning, and other topics, such as reconfiguring your kernel.

Partitioning your disks

The hard disk (or disks) on your computer provides the permanent storage area for your data files, applications programs, and the operating system (such as Red Hat Linux). Partitioning is the act of dividing a disk into logical areas that can be worked with separately. There are several reasons you may want to do partitioning:

✦ **Multiple operating systems**—If you install Red Hat Linux on a PC that already has a Windows operating system, you may want to keep both operating systems on the computer. To run efficiently, they must exist on completely separate partitions. When your computer boots, you can choose which system to run.

✦ **Multiple partitions within an operating system**—To protect from having your entire operating system run out of disk space, people often assign separate partitions to different areas of the Red Hat Linux file system. For example, if /home and /var were assigned to separate partitions, then a gluttonous user who fills up the /home partition wouldn't prevent logging daemons from continuing to write to log files in the /var/log directory.

Multiple partitions also make it easier to do certain kinds of backups (such as an image backup). For example, an image backup of /home would be much faster (and probably more useful) than an image backup of the root file system (/).

✦ **Different file system types**—Different kinds of file systems that have different structures. File systems of different types must be on their own partitions. In Red Hat Linux, you need at least one file system type for / (typically ext3) and one for your swap area. File systems on CD-ROM use the iso9660 file system type.

When you create partitions for Red Hat Linux, you will usually assign the file system type as Linux native (using the ext3 type). Reasons to use other types include needing a file system that allows particularly long filenames or many inodes (each file consumes an inode). For example, if you set up a news server, it can use many inodes to store news articles. Another reason for using a different file system type is to copy an image backup tape from another operating system to your local disk (such as one from an OS/2 or Minix operating system).

If you have only used Windows operating systems before, you probably had your whole hard disk assigned to C: and never thought about partitions. With Red Hat Linux, you can do a Server class of install (and have Linux erase the whole disk, take it over, and partition it) or a Workstation class (and have Linux keep separate partitions for Windows 9x/2000 and Linux). With the latest version of Red Hat Linux, you also have the opportunity to view and change the default partitioning for the different installation types.

During installation, Red Hat lets you partition your hard disk using either the Disk Druid or the fdisk utility. The following sections describe those and other related tools. See the section "Tips for creating partitions" for some ideas for creating disk partitions.

Partitioning with Disk Druid during installation

During a custom installation, you are given the opportunity to change how your hard disk is partitioned. Red Hat recommends using the Disk Druid. Figure 2-1 is an example of the Disk Druid screen from the Red Hat Linux Installation Guide.

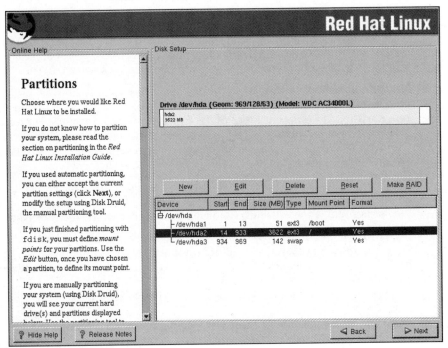

Figure 2-1: Change disk partitions during installation using Disk Druid.

The Disk Druid screen is divided into two sections. The top shows general information about each hard disk and primary partition. The bottom shows details of each partition.

For each of the hard disk partitions, you can see:

✦ **Device** — The device name is the name representing the hard disk partition in the /dev directory. Each disk partition device begins with two letters: hd for IDE disks, sd for SCSI disks, ed for ESDI disks, or xd for XT disks. After that is a single letter representing the number of the disk (disk 1 is a, disk 2 is b, disk 3 is c, and so on). The partition number for that disk (1, 2, 3, and so on) follows that.

✦ **Start/End** — Represents the partition's starting and ending cylinders on the hard disk.

✦ **Size (MB)** — The amount of disk space actually allocated for the partition. If you selected to let the partition grow to fill the existing space, this number may be much larger than the requested amount.

✦ **Type** — The type of file system that is installed on the disk partition. In most cases, the file system will be Linux (ext3), Win 95 FAT16 (fat), Win VFAT (vfat), or Linux swap. Table 2-1 lists the types of file systems that are available to assign to a disk partition. The number associated with each type of file system is what you would actually type if you were to assign that file system to a partition.

Not all these types are supported in Red Hat Linux. Of those that are, some are not built into the kernel by default (such as NTFS). Even fewer are available to be created in Disk Druid. Type `cat /proc/filesystems` to see which file systems are built into the kernel. Others are available as loadable modules, while others may require you to reconfigure the kernel. Most needs should be served by ext3 (Linux), vfat (DOS/Windows), swap (Linux swap) and iso9660 (CD-ROM).

✦ **Mount Point** — The directory where the partition is connected into the Linux file system (if it is). You must assign the root partition (/) to a native Linux partition before you can proceed.

✦ **Format** — Indicates whether (Yes) or not (No) the installation process should format the hard disk partition.

Table 2-1
File System Types and Numbers for Disk Partition

Number	File System Type	Number	File System Type	Number	File System Type
01	FAT12	42	SFS	87	NTFS volume set
02	XENIX root	4D	QNX4.x	93	Amoeba
03	XENIX usr	4E	QNX4.x 2nd part	94	Amoeba BBT
04	FAT16 <32M	4F	QNX4.x 3rd part	A0	IBM Thinkpad hiberna
05	Extended	50	OnTrack DM	A5	BSD/386
06	FAT16	51	OnTrack DM6 Aux1	A6	OpenBSD
07	HPFS/NTFS	52	CP/M	A7	NeXTSTEP
08	AIX	53	OnTrack DM6 Aux3	B7	BSDI fs

Continued

Table 2-1 *(continued)*

Number	File System Type	Number	File System Type	Number	File System Type
09	AIX bootable	54	OnTrackDM6	B8	BSDI swap
0A	OS/2 Boot Manager	55	EZ-Drive	C1	DRDOS/sec (FAT-12)
0B	Win95 FAT32	56	Golden Bow	C4	DRDOS/sec (FAT-16 <
0C	Win95 FAT32 (LBA)	5C	Priam Edisk	C6	DRDOS/sec (FAT-16)
0E	Win95 FAT16 (LBA)	61	SpeedStor	C7	Syrinx
0F	Win95 Ext'd (LBA)	63	GNU HURD or SysV	DB	CP/M/CTOS /...
10	OPUS	64	Novell Netware 286	E1	DOS access
11	Hidden FAT12	65	Novell Netware 386	E3	DOS R/O
12	Compaq diagnostics	70	DiskSecure Multi-Boo	E4	SpeedStor
14	Hidden FAT16 <32M	75	PC/IX	EB	BeOS fs
16	Hidden FAT16	80	Old Minix	F1	SpeedStor
17	Hidden HPFS/ NTFS	81	Minix/ old Linux	F4	SpeedStor
18	AST Windows swapfile	82	Linux swap	F2	DOS secondary
24	NEC DOS	83	Linux (ext3)	FE	LANstep
3C	PartitionMagic recov	84	OS/2 hidden C: drive	FF	BBT
40	Venix 80286	85	Linux extended		
41	PPC PReP Boot	86	NTFS volume set		

In the Disk Setup section, you can see each of the hard disks that are connected to your computer. The drive name is shown first. The Geometry section (Geom) shows the numbers of cylinders, heads, and sectors, respectively, on the disk. The total amount of disk space, the amount used, and the amount free are shown in megabytes.

Reasons for partitioning

There are different opinions about how to divide up a hard disk. Here are some issues:

✦ **Do you want to install another operating system?** If you want Windows on your computer along with Linux, you will need at least one Windows (Win95 FAT16 or VFAT type), one Linux (Linux ext3), and one Linux swap partition.

✦ **Is it a multiuser system?** If you are using the system yourself, you probably don't need many partitions. One reason for partitioning an operating system is to keep the entire system from running out of disk space at once. That also serves to put boundaries on what an individual can use up in his or her home directory.

✦ **Do you have multiple hard disks?** You need at least one partition per hard disk. If your system has two hard disks, you may assign one to / and one to /home.

Deleting, adding, and editing partitions

Before you can add a partition, there needs to be some free space available on your hard disk. If all space on your hard disk is currently assigned to one partition (as it often is in DOS or Windows), you must delete or resize that partition before you can claim space on another partition. The section on reclaiming disk space discusses how to add a partition without losing information in your existing single-partition system.

Caution Make sure that any data that you want to keep are backed up before you delete the partition. When you delete a partition, all its data are gone.

The Disk Druid is less flexible, but more intuitive, than the `fdisk` utility. Disk Druid lets you delete, partition, and edit partitions. Select OK to assign the changes.

Tip If you create multiple partitions, make sure that there is enough room in the right places to complete the installation. For example, most of the Linux software is installed in the /usr directory (and subdirectories), whereas most user data are eventually added to the /home directory.

To delete a partition in Disk Druid, do the following:

1. Select a partition from the list of Current Disk Partitions on the main Disk Druid window (click it or use the arrow keys).

2. To immediately delete the partition (no confirmation!), click Delete.

3. If you made a mistake, click Reset to return to the partitioning as it was when you started Disk Druid.

To add a partition in Disk Druid, follow these steps from the main Disk Druid window:

1. Select New. A window appears, enabling you to create a new partition.

2. Type the name of the Mount Point (the directory where this partition will connect to the Linux file system). You need at least a root (/) partition.

3. Select the type of file system to be used on the partition. You can select from Linux native (ext2 or ext3), software RAID, Linux swap (swap), or Windows FAT (vfat)

Tip   To create a different file system type than those shown, leave the space you want to use free for now. You can click on the Back button and select fdisk instead of Disk Druid. Or, you could wait until after installation is done and use `fdisk` or `cfdisk` to create a partition of the type you want.

4. Type the number of megabytes to be used for the partition (in the Size field). If you want this partition to grow to fill the rest of the hard disk, you can put any number in this field (1 will do fine).

5. If you have more than one hard disk, select the disk on which you want to put the partition from the Allowable Drives box.

6. Type the size of the partition (in megabytes) into the Size (MB) box.

7. Select one of the following Additional Size Options:

   • **Fixed size** — Click here to use only the number of megabytes you entered into the Size box when you create the partition.

   • **Fill all space up to (MB)** — If you want to use all remaining space up to a certain number of megabytes, click here and fill in the number. (You may want to do this if you are creating a VFAT partition up to the 2048MB limit that Disk Druid can create).

   • **Fill to maximum allowable size** — If you want this partition to grow to fill the rest of the disk, click here.

8. Optionally select Force to Be a Primary Partition if you want to be sure to be able to boot the partition or Check for Bad Blocks if you want to have the partition checked for errors.

9. Select OK if everything is correct. (The changes don't take effect until several steps later when you are asked to begin installing the packages.)

To edit a partition in Disk Druid from the main Disk Druid window, follow these steps:

1. Click the partition you want to edit.

2. Click the Edit button. A window appears, ready to let you edit the partition definition.

3. Change any of the attributes (as described in the add partition procedure). For a new install, you may need to add the mount point (/) for your primary Linux partition.

4. Select OK. (The changes don't take effect until several steps later, when you are asked to begin installing the packages.)

Note   If you want to create a RAID device, you need to first create at least two RAID partitions. Then click the Make RAID button to make the two partitions into a RAID device. For more information on RAID, refer to the Red Hat Linux Customization guide on the DOC CD that comes with this book.

Partitioning with fdisk

During installation, Red Hat recommends using the Disk Druid to change partitioning but gives you the option of using fdisk instead. fdisk and related tools do the same job as Disk Druid, but they can be run after installation. Tools include the fdisk, sfdisk, and cfdisk commands.

Caution   Remember that any partition commands can easily erase your disk or make it inaccessible. Back up critical data before using any tool to change partitions! Then be very careful about the changes you do make. Keeping an emergency boot disk handy is a good idea, too.

The fdisk command is one that is available on many different operating systems (although it looks and behaves differently on each). In Linux, fdisk is a menu-based command. If you use fdisk, type **m** to see the options. The sfdisk command is command-line oriented. Type the full command line to list or change partitions.

The best choice for ease of use is the cfdisk command because it is screen oriented, enabling you to see your partitions and options. Move the arrow keys to select the partition that you are interested in. The options that are available for the selected partition are displayed on the bottom of the screen.

Here is what you can do with cfdisk:

✦ **Delete a partition** — Position the cursor over the partition you want to delete and press D. The disk space that is released is made available in the Free Space listing so that you can reclaim it for another partition. (The deletion won't take effect until you write the change. Until then, it's not too late to back out.)

✦ **Create a partition** — If free space is shown, position the cursor over that entry and press N. Choose whether to create a primary or logical partition. Choose how many megabytes you want assigned to the partition (the whole extra amount is assumed). Next, press T to choose the type of file system. For a Linux file system, use the number 83; use 82 for a Linux swap partition.

✦ **Print the partition table** — Position the cursor over a partition listing and press P. Next, select Table and, either press Enter to display the table on the screen, or type a filename and press Enter to save the file to your hard disk. You can see the sector where each partition starts and stops, as well as the disk space used.

If you don't like a change you make to your partitions, press Q to exit without saving. To write your changes to the partition table, press W. You are warned about how dangerous it is to change partitions and asked to confirm the change.

Tips for creating partitions

Changing your disk partitions to handle multiple operating systems can be very tricky. Part of the reason is that each different operating system has its own ideas about how partitioning information should be handled, as well as different tools for doing it. Here are some tips to help you get it right.

✦ You can have up to 63 partitions on an IDE hard disk. A SCSI hard disk can have up to 15 partitions. You won't need nearly that many partitions.

✦ The fdisk man page recommends that you use partitioning tools that come with an operating system to create partitions for that operating system. For example, the DOS fdisk knows how to create partitions that DOS will like, and the Red Hat Linux cfdisk will happily make your Linux partitions.

✦ If you are creating a dual boot system, particularly for Windows ME and Windows XP, try to install the Windows operating system first. Otherwise, the Windows installation may make the Linux partitions inaccessible.

If you are using Red Hat Linux as a desktop system, you probably don't need a lot of different partitions within your Red Hat Linux system. There are, however, some very good reasons for having multiple partitions for Red Hat Linux systems that are shared by a lot of users or are public Web servers or file servers. Multiple partitions within Red Hat Linux offer the following advantages:

✦ **Protection from attacks** — Denial-of-service attacks sometimes take action that tries to fill up your hard disk. If public areas, such as /var, are on separate partitions, a successful attack can fill up a partition without shutting down the whole computer.

✦ **Protection from corrupted file systems** — If you have only one file system (/), corruption of that file system can cause the whole Red Hat Linux system to be damaged. Corruption of a smaller partition can be easier to correct and can often allow the computer to stay in service while the corruption is fixed.

Here are some directories that you may want to consider making into separate file system partitions.

✦ /boot —Sometimes the BIOS in older PCs can access only the first 1024 cylinders of your hard disk. To make sure that the information in your /boot directory is accessible to the BIOS, create a separate disk partition (of only a few MB) for /boot and make sure that it exists below cylinder 1024. Then, the rest of your Linux system can exist outside of that 1024-cylinder boundary if you like. Even with several boot images, there is no need for /boot to be larger than 64MB. For newer hard disks, you can sometimes avoid this problem by selecting "linear mode" during installation. Then the boot partition can be anywhere on the disk.

✦ /usr —This directory structure contains most of the applications and utilities available to Red Hat Linux users. Having /usr on a separate partition lets you mount that file system as read-only after the operating system has been installed. This prevents attackers from replacing or removing important system applications with their own versions that may cause security problems. A separate /usr partition is also useful if you have diskless workstations on your local network. Using NFS, you can share /usr over the network with those workstations.

✦ /var —Your FTP (/var/ftp) and Web server (/var/www) directories are stored under /var. Having a separate /var partition can prevent an attack on those facilities from corrupting or filling up your entire hard disk.

✦ /home —Because your user account directories are located in this directory, having a separate /home account can prevent an indiscriminate user from filling up the entire hard disk.

✦ /tmp —Protecting /tmp from the rest of the hard disk by placing it on a separate partition can ensure that applications that need to write to temporary files in /tmp are able to complete their processing, even if the rest of the disk fills up.

Though people who use Red Hat Linux casually rarely see a need for lots of partitions, those who maintain and occasionally have to recover large systems are thankful when the system they need to fix has several partitions. Multiple partitions can localize deliberate damage (such as denial-of-service attacks), problems from errant users, and accidental file system corruption.

Reclaiming disk space from existing partitions

Like many people, your PC probably came with a Windows operating system already installed on the entire disk. Installing Red Hat, while keeping Windows on your hard disk, presents a problem. Red Hat Linux and Windows operating systems are typically put on separate disk partitions, and right now there is only one partition (and it isn't for Red Hat Linux).

If you are in this predicament, but you have a lot of unused space in your Windows partition (at least 1GB or more), follow this procedure to reclaim the disk space:

If you value the information on your Windows partition, you need to understand what you are doing before you run the procedure that follows. Three mini-HOWTOs cover issues related to Red Hat Linux and Windows 9x/2000 coexisting on a computer. These are the Linux+DOS+Win95+OS2, Linux+Win95, and Linux+NT-Loader mini-HOWTOs. Check for them in your HOWTOS/mini directory on the Red Hat documentation CD.

Backing up and repartitioning

One way to divide a disk that is currently totally used for DOS (DOS, Windows 9x/2000, and so on) is not very complicated, but it can take some time. The method is to do a full system backup of your data, erase the whole disk, repartition the disk, restore your Windows 9x/2000 operating system to the hard disk (on a smaller partition), and add Red Hat Linux to the hard disk (using new partitions). Whew!

The problem with the backup/repartition approach is that it can be a pain. If your backup device is a 1.44MB floppy disk and your hard disk holds a gigabyte or more, a full backup is not a pleasant prospect. Alternatively, there is a DOS utility called FIPS.

Using the FIPS utility

The FIPS utility came about to solve the problem of a would-be Linux user with a monolithic DOS hard disk. With FIPS, you can change the size of your DOS partition without erasing it. Though this process is risky, and nobody recommends it without major "buyer beware" warnings, many use it safely and save a lot of time and effort.

FIPS works by changing the values in the partition table and boot sector. Space is gained by changing the partition table that is used to create a new primary DOS partition. After that, the new DOS partition can be converted to a Linux partition.

Warnings that come with FIPS documentation have mostly to do with older, non-standard hard disks. I recommend reading the warnings that come with this documentation. You can find them on the Red Hat Linux installation CD in the `dosutils/fipsdocs` directory. Especially read `fips.doc`.

Split your DOS (Windows) disk into separate DOS and Linux partitions as follows:

1. Check your DOS partition.

In a DOS window, run `chkdsk` to check for disk errors. The output shows how your disk space is used, as well as errors found and corrected. Next, run scan-disk in Windows 9x/2000. Scandisk will deal with lost file fragments, invalid filenames, and cross-linked files. It can also scan for disk surface errors. The point is to correct any hard disk errors encountered.

2. Create a bootable FIPS floppy.

You need to create a bootable floppy disk. Insert a blank, 3.5-inch floppy disk in drive A. Then, from DOS (or a DOS window), type the following to create a boot floppy:

```
format a:/s
```

After creating the boot floppy, copy the following files from the first Red Hat Linux installation CD (CD-1) to this bootable floppy: `restorrb.exe`, `fips.exe`, and `errors.txt`. (These files are located in the `dosutils/fips20` directory.) To make sure that the bootable floppy is working properly, insert the floppy disk into a PC that has a DOS (Windows 9*x*/2000) partition and reboot the computer. Now make sure that you can access the partition by typing `dir C:\` at the prompt.

3. Defragment your hard disk.

Reboot your PC so that Windows 9*x*/2000 starts up. To defragment your disk, so that all of your used space is put in order on the disk, open My Computer, right-click your hard disk icon (C:), select Properties, click Tools, and select Defragment Now.

Defragmenting your disk can be a fairly long process. The result of defragmentation is that all the data on your disk are contiguous, creating a lot of contiguous free space at the end of the partition. There are cases where you will have to do the following special tasks to make this true:

- If the Windows swapfile is not moved during defragmentation, you must remove it. Then, after you defragment your disk again and run FIPS, you will need to restore the swapfile. To remove the swap file, open the Control Panel, open the System icon, and then click the Performance tab and select Virtual Memory. To disable the swap file, click Disable Virtual Memory.

- If your DOS partition has hidden files that are on the space you are trying to free up, you need to find them. In some cases, you won't be able to delete them. In other cases, such as swap files created by a program, you can safely delete those files. This is a bit tricky because some files should not be deleted, such as DOS system files. You can use the `attrib -s -h` command from the root directory to deal with hidden files.

4. Reboot (FIPS boot disk).

Before you reboot to the FIPS disk, you want to make sure that nothing is written to the hard disk when DOS/Windows shuts down. Look for programs in `config.sys` and `autoexec.bat` that write to disk. When you are satisfied, insert the boot floppy and reboot.

5. Run FIPS.

With your computer now booted in DOS (with C: drive accessible), run the FIPS program by typing:

```
# fips
```

You can quit FIPS at any time by pressing Ctrl+C. If you have more than one hard disk, FIPS will ask which one you want to use. FIPS then displays the partition table and asks you the number of the partition you want to split:

- Type the number of the partition you want to split. FIPS checks the partition for free space and asks if you want to make a copy of your root and boot sector before you go on (this is recommended).

- Type Y to backup your root and boot sector. FIPS asks if you have your FIPS bootable floppy in the drive.

- Make sure the floppy is in the drive and type Y. FIPS copies a file called rootboot.000 to your A: drive. Then FIPS determines how much free space is available on the partition. If FIPS can't find at least one cylinder free, it probably means that you need to remove a mirror or image file (after you do that, you will have to defragment the drive again before you can rerun FIPS). If all goes well, you will see output that looks similar to the following:

```
Old partition          Cylinder          New Partition
   2753.3 MB              351               35393.2 MB
```

Note If the New Partition doesn't show enough disk space, you may need to go back and remove some files until there is enough free space.

- Use Right Arrow and Left Arrow keys to choose what cylinder the new partition should start on. As you press those keys, you can see the sizes of the old and new partitions change. When the partitions are the sizes you want, press Enter.

- When the new partition table appears, you can accept it or re-edit the table.

- Press C to continue if everything is okay. You are asked if you are ready to write the new partition table to disk.

- Press Y to proceed. When FIPS is done, it will say Bye! and exit.

6. Reboot (FIPS boot disk) and test.

Reboot from the DOS/FIPS disk again. Then run the fips command again, but this time in test mode as follows:

```
# fips -t
```

If the partition table looks okay, exit FIPS by pressing Ctrl+C. You can also use a program such as chkdsk to be sure the old partition is still working.

Caution If the partitions are not correct, you can restore your original partitioning by running the restorrb command from the FIPS floppy disk.

7. Restart your computer.

At this point, you can restart your computer as you would normally (remove the FIPS boot disk). Try using the Windows 9*x*/2000 system to make sure that everything is working okay.

With partitioning done, you can install Red Hat Linux using the reclaimed space. (Don't assign the free disk space to anything yet. Just go ahead and install Red Hat Linux and assign the Linux partitions you need during installation.)

If you have a problem with FIPS, its creator asks that you make a transcript of the FIPS session (using the `-d` option) and send it to `schaefer@rbg.informatik.` `th-darmstadt.de`. The transcript will appear in the `fipsinfo.dbg` file.

Creating install floppy disks

There are several cases in which you need to have one or more floppy disks to install Red Hat Linux. In general, you need an install disk any time the computer you are installing on doesn't have a built-in CD-ROM. This includes network installs and PCMCIA device installs, such as external CD-ROM drives or network adapters on laptops.

Each disk that you may need is available on the Red Hat Linux CD as an image file. If you need to create a disk, copy the image file from the CD to a blank, formatted 1.44MB 3.5-inch floppy disk (using a program that can copy raw data).

The image files are available from the images directory on the Red Hat CD (if the CD were mounted in Red Hat Linux, images may be in the `/mnt/cdrom/images` directory). Here is a list of the boot images and what each is used for:

✦ **Boot** (`boot.img`) — Use this boot image to create a boot disk for installing Red Hat Linux from a CD or from a copy of Red Hat on the local disk.

✦ **Network Boot** (`bootnet.img`) — Create a boot disk from this image for installing Red Hat Linux over a network (NFS, HTTP, or FTP).

✦ **PCMCIA support** (`pcmcia.img`) — Use this image if you need to use a PCMCIA adapter to install Red Hat Linux (such as a LAN card on your laptop).

Create the install/boot disks in DOS or Linux. The `rawrite` command for copying the images from DOS to floppy is on the Red Hat CD. In Linux, use the `dd` command. There are also other image files you can use to create disks to support different types of hardware. These image files include the following:

✦ **Block Devices** (`drvblock.img`) — Use this image to support special types of hard disks and other block devices.

✦ **Network Devices** (`drvnet.img`) — Use this image to support different types of network interface cards and other network devices.

✦ **CD-ROM Devices** (`oldcdrom.img`) — Use this image to support certain old CD-ROM devices.

✦ **PCMCIA Devices** (`pcmciadd.img`) — Use this image if you need support for a PCMCIA adapter to install Red Hat Linux that isn't supported by the `pcmcia.img` boot image.

Creating a floppy disk in Linux

Using the `dd` command, you can copy data from one device to another in Linux (or other UNIX system). To copy a disk image from the installation CD to a disk, you need:

✦ A blank 3.5-inch floppy disk (formatted).

✦ Write permission to the disk drive (probably drive A, which in Red Hat Linux is `/dev/fd0`). The root user should have write permission, but root would have to open write permission to allow another user to write to floppy disk.

✦ An available copy of the disk image to be copied. (The best way to get access to this in Red Hat Linux is by inserting the CD and typing `mount /dev/cdrom`, then typing `cd /mnt/cdrom/images`.)

To copy the `boot.img` file from the images directory on the CD, type the following:

```
# dd if=boot.img of=/dev/fd0 bs=1440k
```

Replace `boot.img` with the name of any other image file you want to copy.

Creating a disk in DOS

The Red Hat CD has both image files and DOS utilities needed to create the installation disks while you are in DOS or Windows. From a DOS prompt, do the following:

1. Insert the Red Hat CD into the drive and change to the CD's drive letter (probably D: or E:).

2. Insert a blank, formatted 3.5-inch floppy disk into drive A.

3. Change to the `dosutils` directory (`cd \dosutils`).

4. Run the `rawrite` command as follows:

```
C:\> rawrite
Enter disk image source file name: D:\images\boot.img
Enter target diskette drive: a:
Please insert a formatted diskette into drive A: and
        press -Enter- :
```

5. Press Enter. The image is written to the disk. Remove the disk and mark it.

Using GRUB or LILO boot loaders

For Red Hat Linux 7.2, the default boot loader changed from LILO to GRUB. The boot loader lets you choose when and how to boot any of the bootable operating systems installed on your computer's hard disks. The following sections describe both the GRUB and LILO boot loaders.

Booting your computer with GRUB

With multiple operating systems installed and several partitions set up, how does your computer know which operating system to start? To select and manage which partition is booted and how it is booted, you need a boot loader. The boot loader that is installed by default with Red Hat Linux is called the GRand Unified Boot loader (GRUB).

GRUB is a GNU software package (`www.gnu.org/software/grub`) that replaced the LILO boot loader by default in Red Hat Linux 7.2. GRUB offers the following features:

✦ Support for multiple executable formats.

✦ Support for Multiboot operating systems (such as Red Hat Linux, FreeBSD, NetBSD, OpenBSD, and other Linux systems).

✦ Support for non-Multiboot operating systems (such as Windows 95, Windows 98, Windows NT, Windows ME, Windows XP and OS/2) via a chain-loading function. Chain-loading is the act of loading another boot loader (presumably one that is specific to the proprietary operating system) from GRUB to start the selected operating system.

✦ Support for multiple filesystem types.

✦ Support for automatic decompression of boot images.

✦ Support for downloading boot images from a network.

For more information on how GRUB works, type `man grub` or `info grub`. The `info` command contains more details about GRUB.

Booting with GRUB

When you install Red Hat Linux, information needed to boot your computer (with one or more operating systems) is automatically set up and ready to go. Simply restart your computer. When you see the GRUB boot screen (it says Red Hat Linux at the top and lists bootable partitions in the left column), do one of the following:

✦ **Default:** If you do nothing, the default operating system will boot automatically after a few seconds.

✦ **Select an operating system:** Use the up and down arrow keys to select any of the operating systems shown on the screen. Then press Enter to boot that operating system.

✦ **Edit the boot process:** If you want to change any of the options used during the boot process, use the arrow keys to select the operating system you want and type the letter e to select it. Follow the procedure described next to change your boot options temporarily.

If you want to change your boot options so that they take effect every time you boot your computer, see the section on permanently changing boot options. Changing those options involves editing the /boot/grub/grub.conf file.

Temporarily changing boot options

From the GRUB boot screen, you can select to change or add boot options for the current boot session. First, select the operating system you want (using the arrow keys) and type e (as described earlier). You will see a text screen that looks like the following:

```
GRUB version 0.90 (639K lower / 129792K upper memory)

root (hd0,1)
kernel /boot/vmlinuz-2.4.7-10 ro root=/dev/hda3 hdc=ide-scsi
initrd /boot/initrd-2.4.7-10.img

Use the ↑ and ↓ keys to select which entry is highlighted.
Press 'b' to boot, 'e' to edit the selected command in the
boot sequence, 'c' for a command-line, 'o' to open a new line
after ('O' for before) the selected line, 'd' to remove the
selected line, or escape to go back to the main menu.
```

There are three lines in the example of the GRUB editing screen that identify the boot process for the operating system you chose. The first line (beginning with root) shows that the entry for the GRUB boot loader is on the second partition of the first hard disk (hd0,1). GRUB represents the hard disk as hd, regardless of whether it is a SCSI, IDE, or other type of disk. You just count the drive number and partition number, starting from zero.

The second line of the example (beginning with kernel) identifies the boot image (/boot/vmlinuz-2.4.7-10) and several options. The options identify the partition as initially being loaded ro (read-only) and the location of the root file system on the third partition of the first SCSI disk (root=/dev/sda3). The third line (beginning with initrd) identifies the location of the initial RAM disk contents, which contains the minimum files and directories needed during the boot process.

If you are going to change any of the lines related to the boot process, you would probably change only the second line to add or remove boot options. Here is how you go about doing that:

1. Position the cursor on the kernel line and type e.

2. Either add or remove options after the name of the boot image. You can use a minimal set of bash shell command line editing features to edit the line. You can even use command completion (type part of a file name and press Tab to complete it). Here are a few options you may want to add or delete:

   - **Boot to a shell:** If you forgot your root password or if your boot process hangs, you can boot directly to a shell by adding init=/bin/sh to the boot line. (The file system is mounted read-only, so you can copy files out. You need to remount the file system with read/write permission to be able to change files.)

   - **Select a run level:** If you want to boot to a particular run level, you can add the word *linux,* followed by the number of the run level you want. For example, to have Red Hat Linux boot to run level 3 (multiuser plus networking mode), add linux 3 to the end of the boot line. You can also boot to single-user mode (1), multi-user mode (2), or X GUI mode (5).

3. Press Enter to return to the editing screen.

4. Type b to boot the computer with the new options. The next time you boot your computer, the new options will not be saved. To add options so they are saved permanently, see the next section.

Permanently changing boot options

You can change the options that take effect each time you boot your computer by changing the GRUB configuration file. In Red Hat Linux, GRUB configuration centers around the /boot/grub/grub.conf file.

The /boot/grub/grub.conf file is created when you install Red Hat Linux. Here is an example of a grub.conf file.

```
# grub.conf generated by anaconda
#
# Note that you do not have to rerun grub after making
# changes to this file.
# NOTICE: You have a /boot partition.  This means that
# all kernel and initrd paths are relative to /boot/, eg.
#        root (hd0,1)
#        kernel /vmlinuz-version ro root=/dev/hda3
#        initrd /initrd-version.img
#boot=/dev/hda
default=0
timeout=10
```

```
splashimage=(hd0,1)/grub/splash.xpm.gz
title Red Hat Linux (2.4.7-10)
     root (hd0,1)
     kernel /vmlinuz-2.4.7-10 ro root=/dev/hda3 hdc=ide-scsi
     initrd /initrd-2.4.7-10.img
title Windows ME
     rootnoverify (hd0,0)
     chainloader +1
```

The `default=0` line indicates that the first partition in this list (in this case Red Hat Linux) will be the one that is booted by default. The line `timeout=5` causes GRUB to pause for five seconds before booting the default partition. The `splashimage` line looks in the second partition on the first disk (`hd0,1`) for the boot partition (`/dev/hda2` in this case). GRUB loads `splash.xpm.gz` as the image on the splash screen (`/boot/grub/splash.xpm.gz`). In the default, the splash screen consists of a blue background and a Red Hat logo that appears as the background of the boot screen.

Note   GRUB indicates disk partitions using the following notation: (hd0,0). The first number represents the disk, and the second is the partition on that disk. So, (hd0,1) is the second partition (1) on the first disk (0).

The two bootable partitions in this example are `Red Hat Linux` and `Windows ME`. The title lines for each of those partitions are followed by the name that appears on the boot screen to represent each partition.

For the Red Hat Linux system, the `root` line indicates the location of the boot partition as the second partition on the first disk. So, to find the bootable `kernel` (`vmlinuz-2.4.7-10`) and the `initrd` initial RAM disk boot image that is loaded (`initrd-2.4.7-10.img`), GRUB looks in the root of `hd0,1` (which is represented by `/dev/hda2` and is eventually mounted as `/boot`). Other options on the `kernel` line set the partition as read-only initially (`ro`), set the root file system to `/dev/hda3` (the fourth partition on the first disk), and add an option to make an IDE CD-ROM drive operate in SCSI emulation.

For the Windows ME partition, the `rootnoverify` line indicates that GRUB should not try to mount the partition. In this case, Windows ME is on the first partition of the first hard disk (`hd0,0`) or `/dev/hda1`. Instead of mounting the partition and passing options to the new operating system, the `chainloader +1` indicates to hand control the booting of the operating system to another boot loader. The +1 indicates that the first sector of the partition is used as the boot loader.

Note   Microsoft operating systems require that you use the `chainloader` to boot them from GRUB.

If you make any changes to the `/boot/grub/grub.conf` file, you *do not* need to load those changes. Those changes are automatically picked up by GRUB when you reboot your computer. If you are accustomed to using the LILO boot loader, this may confuse you at first, as LILO requires you to rerun the `lilo` command for the changes to take effect.

Adding a new GRUB boot image

You may have different boot images for kernels that include different features. Here is the procedure for modifying the `grub.conf` file:

1. Copy the new image from the directory in which it was created (such as `/usr/src/linux-2.4/arch/i386/boot`) to the `/boot` directory. Name the file something that reflects its contents, such as `bz-2.4.7-10`. For example:

   ```
   # cp /usr/src/linux-2.4/arch/i386/boot/bzImage /boot/bz-
   2.4.7-10
   ```

2. Add several lines to the `/boot/grub/grub.conf` file so that the image can be started at boot time if it is selected. For example:

   ```
   title Red Hat Linux (IPV6 build)
       root (hd0,1)
       kernel /bz-2.4.7-10 ro root=/dev/hda3 hdc=ide-scsi
       initrd /initrd-2.4.7-10.img
   ```

3. Reboot your computer.

4. When the GRUB boot screen appears, move your cursor to the title representing the new kernel and press Enter.

The advantage to this approach, as opposed to copying the new boot image over the old one, is that if the kernel fails to boot, you can always go back and restart the old kernel. When you feel confident that the new kernel is working properly, you can use it to replace the old kernel or perhaps just make the new kernel the default boot definition.

Booting your computer with LILO

LILO stands for LInux LOader. It is the program that can stand outside the operating systems installed on the computer so you can choose which system to boot. It also lets you give special options that modify how the operating system is booted.

Note LILO has been replaced by GRUB as the default boot loader for Red Hat Linux. Unless you have explicitly changed your system to use LILO, you should be reading the GRUB section for boot loader information.

If LILO is being used on your computer, it is installed in either the master boot record or the first sector of the root partition. The master boot record is read directly by the computer's BIOS. In general, if LILO is the only loader on your computer, install it in the master boot record. If there is another boot loader already in the master boot record, put LILO in the root partition.

Using LILO

When your computer boots with the Red Hat Linux version of LILO installed in the master boot record, a graphical Red Hat screen appears, displaying the bootable partitions on the computer. Use the Up Arrow and Down Arrow keys on your keyboard to select the one you want and press Enter. Otherwise, the default partition that you set at installation will boot after a few seconds.

If you want to add any special options when you boot, press Ctrl+X. You will see a text-based boot prompt that appears as follows:

```
boot:
```

LILO pauses for a few seconds and then automatically boots the first image from the default bootable partition. To see the bootable partitions again, quickly press Tab. You may see something similar to the following:

```
LILO boot:
linux linux-up dos
boot:
```

This example shows that three bootable partitions are on your computer, called `linux`, `linux-up`, and `dos`. The first two refer to two different boot images that can boot the Linux partition. The third refers to a bootable DOS partition (presumably containing a Windows operating system). The first bootable partition is loaded if you don't type anything after a few seconds. Or you could type the name of the other partition to have that boot instead.

Here are explanations of what the different boot images are for:

✦ **linux**—This is for a bootable image that can be used for computers with multiple processors (SMP).

✦ **linux-up**—This is for a bootable image for a standard installation.

If you have multiple boot images, press Shift, and LILO will ask you which image you want to boot. Available boot images and other options are defined in the `/etc/lilo.conf` file.

Setting up the /etc/lilo.conf file

The `/etc/lilo.conf` file is where LILO gets the information it needs to find and start bootable partitions and images. By adding options to the `/etc/lilo.conf` file, you can change the behavior of the boot process. The following is an example of some of the contents of the `/etc/lilo.conf` file:

```
prompt
timeout=50
default=linux
boot=/dev/hda
map=/boot/map
install=/boot/boot.b
message=/boot/message
linear
```

```
image=/boot/vmlinuz-2.4.7-10
        label=linux
        initrd=/boot/initrd-2.4.7-10.img
        read-only
        root=/dev/hda6
        append="hdc=ide-scsi"
other=/dev/hda1
        label=dos
```

With prompt on, the boot prompt appears when the system is booted without requiring that any keys are pressed. The timeout value, in this case 50 tenths of a second (5 seconds), defines how long to wait for keyboard input before booting the default boot image. The boot line indicates that the bootable partition is on the hard disk represented by /dev/hda (the first IDE hard disk).

The map line indicates the location of the map file (/boot/map, by default). The map file contains the name and locations of bootable kernel images. The install line indicates that the /boot/boot.b file is used as the new boot sector. The message line tells LILO to display the contents of the /boot/message file when booting (that contains the graphical Red Hat boot screen that appears). The linear line causes linear sector addresses to be generated (instead of sector/head/cylinder addresses).

In the sample file, there are two bootable partitions. The first (image=/boot/ vmlinuz-2.4.7-10) shows an image labeled linux. The root file system (/) for that image is on partition /dev/hda6. Read-only indicates that the file system is first mounted read-only, though it is probably mounted as read/write after a file system check. The inidrd line indicates the location of the initial RAM disk image used to start the system.

The second bootable partition, which is indicated by the word *other* in this example, is on the /dev/hda1 partition. Because it is a Windows ME system, it is labeled a DOS file system. The table line indicates the device that contains the partition.

Other bootable images are listed in this file, and you can add another boot image yourself (like one you create from reconfiguring your kernel as discussed in the next section) by installing the new image and changing lilo.conf.

After you change lilo.conf, you then must run the lilo command for the changes to take effect. You may have different boot images for kernels that include different features. Here is the procedure for modifying the lilo.conf file:

1. Copy the new image from the directory in which it was created (such as /usr/src/linux/arch/i386/boot) to the /boot directory. Name the file something that reflects its contents, such as zImage-2.4.7-10.

2. Add several lines to the /etc/lilo.conf file so that the image can be started at boot time if it is selected. For example:

```
image=/boot/zImage-2.4.7-10
label=new
```

3. Type the `lilo -t` command (as root user) to test that the changes were okay.

4. Type the `lilo` command (with no options) for the changes to be installed.

To boot from this new image, either select new from the graphical boot screen or type `new` and Enter at the LILO boot prompt. If five seconds is too quick, increase the timeout value (such as 100 for 10 seconds).

Options that you can use in the `/etc/lilo.conf` file are divided into global options, per-image options, and kernel options. There is a lot of documentation available for LILO. For more details on any of the options described here or for other options, you can see the `lilo.conf` manual page (type `man lilo.conf`) or any of the documents in `/usr/share/doc/lilo*/doc`.

A few examples follow of global options that you can add to `/etc/lilo.conf`. Global options apply to LILO as a whole, instead of just to a particular boot image.

You can use the `default=label` option, where label is replaced by an image's label name, to indicate that a particular image be used as the default boot image. If that option is excluded, the first image listed in the `/etc/lilo.conf` file is used as the default. For example, to start the image labeled new by default, add the following line to `lilo.conf`:

    default=new

Change the delay from 5 seconds to something greater if you want LILO to wait longer before starting the default image. This gives you more time to boot a different image. To change the value from 5 seconds (50) to 15 seconds (150), add the following line:

    delay=150

You can change the message that appears before the LILO prompt by adding that message to a file and changing the message line. For example, you could create a `/boot/boot.message` file and add the following words to that file: `Choose linux, new, or dos`. To have that message appear before the boot prompt, add the following line to `/etc/lilo.conf`:

    message=/boot/boot.message

All per-image options begin with either an `image=` line (indicating a Linux kernel) or `other=` (indicating some other kind of operating system, such as Windows XP). The per-image options apply to particular boot images rather than to all images (as global options do). Along with the image or other line is a `label=` line, which gives a name to that image. The name is what you would select at boot time to boot that image. Here are some of the options that you can add to each of those image definitions:

✦ `lock` — This enables automatic recording of `boot` command lines as the defaults for different boot options.

✦ `alias=`*name* — You can replace *name* with any name. That name becomes an alias for the image name defined in the label option.

✦ `password=`*password* — You can password-protect the image by adding a password option line and replacing *password* your own password. The password would have to be entered to boot the image.

✦ `restricted` — This option is used with the password option. It indicates that a password should be used only if command-line options are given when trying to boot the image.

For Linux kernel images, there are specific options that you can use. These options let you deal with hardware issues that can't be auto-detected, or provide information such as how the root file system is mounted. Here are some of kernel image–specific options:

✦ `append` — Add a string of letters and numbers to this option that need to be passed to the kernel. In particular, these can be parameters that need to be passed to better define the hard disk when some aspect of that disk can't be autodetected.

✦ `ramdisk` — Add the size of the RAM disk that you want to use so as to override the size of the RAM disk built into the kernel.

✦ `read-only` — Indicates to mount the root file system read-only. It is typically remounted read-write after the disk is checked.

✦ `read-write` — Indicates to mount the root file system read/write.

Changing your boot loader

If you don't want to use the GRUB boot loader, or if you tried out LILO and want to switch back to GRUB, it's not hard to change to a different boot loader. To switch your boot loader from GRUB to LILO, do the following:

1. Configure the `/etc/lilo.conf` file as described in the "Booting your computer with LILO" section.

2. As root user from a Terminal window, type the following:

   `# lilo`

   The new Master Boot Record is written, including the entries in `/etc/lilo.conf`.

3. Reboot your computer. You should see the LILO boot screen.

To change your boot loader from LILO to GRUB, do the following:

1. Configure the `/boot/grub/grub.conf` file as described in the "Booting your computer with GRUB" section.

2. You need to know the device on which you want to install GRUB. For example, to install GRUB on the master boot record of the first disk, type the following as root user from a Terminal window:

   `# grub-install /dev/hda`

   The new Master Boot Record is written to boot with the GRUB boot loader.

3. Reboot your computer. You should see the GRUB boot screen.

Reconfiguring the kernel

When you install Red Hat Linux, the kernel (which represents the core of the operating system) is automatically configured for you and ready to run. Many assumptions are built into this kernel, including the types of drivers that you will need to run your hardware and the services that the kernel provides. There are times when you may want to change these assumptions. To do that, you can reconfigure your kernel.

Note   Not all changes to the features in your kernel require that you rebuild it. Many drivers are available to an installed Red Hat Linux system in the form of *loadable modules.* Loadable modules can be used to add features to a running kernel. For example, the PCMCIA feature uses loadable modules. You can use the `insmod` and `modprobe` commands to load modules that you need.

Reconfiguring your kernel is a tedious job. It consists of answering a lot of questions (some of which you will have no idea how to answer). In most cases, the kernel configuration process has defaults set up. So, if you run into a question you can't answer, press Enter to use the default. Kernel configuration also takes time. The Kernel-HOWTO suggests that the process can take from 20 to 90 minutes, depending on hardware.

To simplify the process of reconfiguring your kernel, the `xconfig` option to make for rebuilding the kernel offers a graphical interface. Using `make xconfig`, you can focus on the drivers you want to add and remove, instead of having to page through all the drivers.

Deciding to reconfigure the kernel

There are times when you need to reconfigure the kernel for it to work the way you need it to. A lot of the features that are turned off by default are off either because they relate to experimental features or because they are needed to supports bugs (or limited features) in some older computer hardware. Here are a few examples:

✦ **Processor type and features** — If you are using any 386 CPU or a 486 CPU with no math coprocessor, you must turn off the math emulation value in the kernel. Also, you can have your kernel more specifically tuned to your processor by choosing 386, 486/Cx486, 586/K5/5x86/6x86, Pentium/K6/TSC, or PPro/6x86MX (depending on the CPU in your computer).

✦ **Networking options** — Network should be on by default. It should be on even if you are not connected to a network because the X Window system (your graphical desktop) relies on it. Otherwise, you will want to reconfigure networking options if Linux is operating as a router and you want to optimize it as such (by default, it is optimized to act as a host). Certain experimental options (X.25, SPX, and others) are also turned off by default.

✦ **Block devices** — For some older disk drives, you may need to use an old disk-only driver on the primary interface. With that selected, you won't be able to have an IDE/ATAPI CD-ROM attached to the primary IDE interface. However, turning on the disk-only driver may be necessary for some older disk drives.

✦ **QoS and/or fair queuing** — If your network devices include some real-time devices that require a minimum quality of service (QoS), you can change some of these QoS values to favor certain interfaces when there is a lot of demand for service. Turning on QoS lets you try any of a handful of different algorithms.

As you read this and other documents that describe how to use Red Hat Linux, the documents may describe features that require changing the kernel for those features to work. By using tools such as the X kernel configuration tool, you can determine which features are turned on and off by default, and build a kernel to suit your needs.

Note

If you need to support a hardware device that is only added temporarily or occasionally to your computer, you should try to configure it as a loadable module. In that way, you can load and unload the module as needed, without making the kernel bear any performance penalty when the device is not needed.

Installing kernel source code

To reconfigure the kernel, you need the Linux source code. You can install that source code from the second Red Hat Linux installation CD that comes with this book (CD-2). If the source code is already installed on your Linux system, it should be in the `/usr/src/linux*` directory (for example, `/usr/src/linux-2.4`).

The kernel source code is contained in the kernel-source package in RedHat/RPMS directory on the second installation CD. When I checked the disk space, the source code consumed about 114MB of disk space in `/usr/src/linux-2.4` (which is a link to a directory that has a name reflecting the kernel release, such as `linux-2.4.7-10`). To install the kernel source code from the RPMS directory, type:

```
# rpm -i kernel-source*
```

Starting to reconfigure the kernel

The steps for reconfiguring your kernel include configuring the options, checking for dependencies, cleaning up the files, and compiling the new kernel. Each of these steps is fairly straightforward and described in the text that follows:

Protect your system

During Red Hat Linux installation, you should have created an emergency boot disk. This floppy disk allows you to boot your Linux system in case the new kernel doesn't boot or in case your `grub.conf` file doesn't work (so that the boot loader fails). If you did not create one, or if you can't find it, insert a blank floppy disk in the first floppy drive and type the following:

```
# mkbootdisk --device /dev/fd0 2.4.7-10
```

Replace the number `2.4.7-10` with the version number of your kernel. Press Enter to continue, as prompted.

Setting up the configuration

To begin reconfiguring the kernel, you should be in a bash shell. (If you are not sure, type `bash` at the command line.) Then go to the `/usr/src/linux*` directory and type:

```
# make mrproper
```

This prepares you to create the new kernel configuration. It thoroughly cleans up the kernel configuration directories.

Making the configuration

To choose the kernel options that you want, you must run `make` with the `config`, `menuconfig`, or `xconfig` options. By far, the easiest option is `xconfig`, though it requires that you run an X desktop (such as GNOME or KDE). Here is an example:

```
# make xconfig
```

If you are not running X, you can use `config` or `menuconfig`. Using `make config` presents you with a pure text-based, question-and-answer way of rebuilding your kernel. Typing `make menuconfig` from `/usr/src/linux*` provides a menu-driven interface (which runs in a character terminal).

Besides being a bit nicer to look at, the `menuconfig` and `xconfig` kernel configuration tools enable you to select only those areas of the kernel that you want to change. With `make config`, you have to step through each category. With the `xconfig` tool, you see all selections available in a category, though if a category is turned off, selections within that category are grayed out. Also, if you make a mistake, just select the category again.

Checking for dependencies

When you are done configuring the kernel, save the changes. After you have made the kernel configuration changes that you want, you have to go back to the `/usr/src/linux*` directory and type the following:

```
# make dep
```

The `make dep` command checks that dependencies of the packages are met. Next you need to prepare the source tree.

Preparing the source tree

To prepare the source tree for the new kernel build, run the `make clean` command as follows:

```
# make clean
```

Compiling the new kernel

You have several choices for compiling the new kernel. You can create the new kernel boot image so that it is stored on your hard disk or have a copy placed on floppy disk. The latter is good for testing the new kernel. You can boot the image from floppy before you install it. So, if the new kernel doesn't work, you can simply not install it.

To compile the kernel and save it to a floppy disk (as well as to the hard disk), place a floppy disk in the disk drive and run: `make zdisk`. The other option results in saving the new image only to hard disk. To do that, type `make zImage` to compile the kernel. If the image created by `make zImage` is too large, type the following to create a more compressed image:

```
# make bzImage
```

This process takes a while, so be patient. In any case, the image is placed in the `arch/i386/boot` directory. The resulting file is a compressed boot image.

Making modules

Modules that are not compiled into the kernel can be compiled as loadable modules using the `modules` option. Once the modules are compiled, you can install them in `/lib/modules/kernel` (where kernel is replaced by the number representing the current kernel) with the `modules_install` option. Here is what you need to type:

```
# make modules
# make modules_install
```

To add a module when your system is running, you could use the `modprobe` or `insmod` commands.

Creating an initrd image

If your computer does not have a SCSI adapter, skip this step. However, if your computer does have a SCSI adapter and needs to load the SCSI module at boot time, you need to create an initrd image. First, check that your /etc/modules.conf file contains a line for your SCSI adapter. For example:

```
alias scsi_hostadapter aic7xxx
```

Next, use the mkinitrd command to build the new image. The mkinitrd command takes two options. The first option indicates the name of the new image. The second indicates the kernel from which the modules are taken (such as /lib/modules/2.4.7-10). For example:

```
# mkinitrd /boot/newinitrd-image 2.4.7-10
```

When you create an entry for this new kernel in /etc/lilo.conf, make sure you add the new initrd image to that entry. For example:

```
initrd=/boot/newinitrd-image
```

Installing the new kernel

To install the new kernel files in their proper places, type the following:

```
# make install
```

The most common way to install the new kernel is to set it up to boot by LILO. You can do that either by replacing the old boot image with the new one (which is a bit risky until you know that the new one is working) or by adding the new one as an alternative bootable image. Ways of setting up boot images in the GRUB or LILO boot loader are described in the GRUB and LILO sections, respectively, earlier in this chapter.

Troubleshooting Your Installation

After you have finished installing Red Hat Linux, you can check how the installation went by checking your log files. There are three places to look once the system comes up:

✦ /tmp/upgrade.log—When upgrading packages, output from each installed package is sent to this file. You can see what packages were installed and if any of them failed.

✦ /var/log/dmesg—This file contains the messages that are sent to the console terminal as the system boots up, including messages relating to the kernel being started and hardware being recognized. If a piece of hardware isn't working, you can check here to make sure that the kernel found the hardware and configured it properly.

✦ `/var/log/boot.log` — This file contains information about each service that is started up at boot time. You can see if each service started successfully. If a service fails to start properly, there may be clues in this file that will help you learn what went wrong.

If something was set wrong (such as your mouse) or just isn't working quite right (such as your video display), you can always go back after Red Hat Linux is running and correct the problem. Here is a list of utilities you can use to reconfigure different features that were set during installation:

✦ **Changing or adding a mouse:** `mouseconfig`

✦ **Adding or deleting software packages:** `gnorpm` or `rpm`

✦ **Partitioning:** `fdisk` or `cfdisk`

✦ **Boot loader:** `/boot/grub/grub.conf` (for GRUB); `lilo` and `/etc/lilo.conf` (for LILO)

✦ **Networking (Ethernet & TCP/IP):** `neat`

✦ **Time zone:** `timeconfig`

✦ **User accounts:** `useradd` or `linuxconf`

✦ **X Window System:** `Xconfigurator`

Here are a few other random tips that can help you during installation:

✦ If installation fails because the installation procedure is unable to detect your video card, try restarting installation in text mode. After Red Hat Linux is installed and running, use the `Xconfigurator` command to configure your video card and monitor.

✦ If your mouse is not detected during installation, you can use arrow keys and the Tab key to make selections.

✦ Probably the best resource for troubleshooting your installation problems is the Red Hat Support site (`www.redhat.com/apps/support`). Links from that page can take you to documentation, updates and errata, and information about support programs. If you are having problems with a particular piece of hardware, try searching the Solutions Database, using the name of the hardware in the search box. If you are having problems with particular hardware, chances are someone else did too.

Summary

Installing Linux is not nearly the adventure it once was. Precompiled binary software and preselected packaging and partitions can make most Red Hat Linux installations a simple proposition. This type of installation has made entering the Linux arena more possible for computer users who are not programmers.

Besides providing some step-by-step installation procedures, this chapter discussed some of the trickier aspects of Red Hat Linux installation. In particular, ways of partitioning your hard disk, creating installation boot disks, and changing the boot procedure were described. The chapter also discussed how to reconfigure and install a new kernel.

✦   ✦   ✦

Using Red Hat Linux

Getting to Know Red Hat Linux

This chapter presents a view of Red Hat Linux from the shell. The shell is a command-line interpreter that lets you access some of the most critical Red Hat Linux tools. The shell is powerful, complex, and almost completely unintuitive.

Although, at first, it isn't obvious how to use the shell, with the right help you can quickly learn many of the most important shell features. This chapter is your guide to logging in and working with the Linux system commands, processes, and file system from the shell. After describing the simple process of logging in to Red Hat Linux, this chapter describes the shell environment and helps you tailor it to your needs. It also describes how to use and move around the file system.

Logging in to Red Hat Linux

Because Red Hat Linux was created as a multiuser computer system, even if you are the only person using the computer, you start by logging in. Logging in identifies you as a particular user. With that identity, Red Hat Linux can start up your configuration and give you appropriate permissions to files and programs.

After the computer has been turned on and the operating system has started, you see either a graphical login screen (default) or a text-based login prompt. The text-based prompt should look similar to this:

```
Red Hat Linux release 7.2
Kernel 2.4.7-2 on an i686

localhost login:
```

The graphical login is typically your entry into the X Window System graphical user interface (GUI). Figure 3-1 is an example of the login window you see if you are using the Gnome desktop environment.

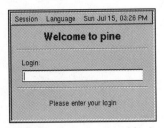

Figure 3-1: A graphical login can access the Red Hat Linux GUI.

Notice the several menu buttons on the login screen. You can ignore them and simply log in. Or you can use these buttons as follows:

✦ **Session** — Usually when you log in, your graphical desktop starts up (either Gnome or KDE desktops). Click Session to choose a different desktop (if available) or to select Failsafe. If you can't remember which desktop to use, you can choose Last (to use the desktop you used most recently) or Default (to use the desktop set as your default). You use Failsafe if you want only a shell interface (the shell is described later in this chapter).

The failsafe session is used primarily to correct problems when, for some reason, your desktop session won't start properly. For example, graphics settings may be wrong, resulting in a garbled screen. The failsafe session simply opens a shell window so you can type commands to correct the problem before you log in again. When you are done with a failsafe session, type **exit** to be allowed to log in again.

✦ **Language** — Click Language to select a language other than the last language you used (indicated by the Last button on this menu). (You need additional software packages to use different languages.)

✦ **System** — If instead of logging in, you want to shut down or restart the computer, click System, and select either Reboot or Halt.

For a normal login, at the login prompt type your user name and, when prompted, your password. Every Linux system has a *root* user and at least one non-root user (with a name of your choosing) assigned when Linux is installed. The root user has the capability to run programs, use files, and change the computer setup in any way. Because the root user has special powers, and can therefore do special damage, you usually log in as a regular user (which only has access to that user's own files and those that are open to everyone).

As someone just using the Linux system, you probably have your own unique user name and password. Often that name is associated with your real name (such as johnb, susanp, or dave4). If you are still not sure why you need a user login, see the sidebar "Why Do I Need a User Login?" for more information.

 See Chapter 10 for a description of the root user and Chapter 11 for information on how to set up and use other user accounts. Refer to Chapter 14 for suggestions on how to choose a good password.

The login session

As you log in, Red Hat Linux starts up a user environment that is unique to your user account. Various attributes are set that remain active during your login session until they are changed. Some of the features that make up your user environment are:

✦ **A home directory** — The home directory identifies a location on the computer's hard disk where you can save and protect the files that you need. You can organize your files any way you like and assign permissions to those files to prevent or allow access to them by others.

Why Do I Need a User Login?

If you are accustomed to using a PC, and you are the only one using your Linux computer, you may wonder why you need a user account and password. Unlike Windows, Linux (as its predecessor UNIX) was designed from the ground up to be a multiuser system. Here are several good reasons why you should use separate user accounts:

✦ Even as the only person using a Linux system, you will want a user name besides the root user for running applications and working with files to prevent you from changing critical system files by mistake during your everyday computer use.

✦ If several people are using a Linux system, separate user accounts let you protect your files from being accessed or changed by others.

✦ Networking is probably the best reason for using a Linux system. If you are on a network, a unique user name is useful in many ways. Your user name can be associated with resources on other computers: file systems, application programs, and mailboxes to name a few. Often a root user is not allowed to share resources on remote Linux systems.

✦ Over time, you will probably change personal configuration information associated with your account. For example, you may add aliases, create your own utility programs, or set properties for the applications you use. By gathering this information in one place, it's easy to move your account or add a new account to another computer in the future.

The root user's home directory in Linux is usually /root. Other users typically have home directories in the /home directory. For example, if your user name were johnq, your home directory would probably be /home/johnq.

✦ **A shell configuration** — There are several shells available for use with Linux, with each having slightly different features. The *bash* shell (which stands for Bourne Again SHell) is most commonly used with Linux. (In this chapter, bash is used to show how to work with the shell.)

Within your home directory are several configuration files that set up properties for your shell login session. These files may identify the path (where programs are located that you can use), contain environment variables and aliases (described later), and define functions that make your work more efficient.

Note Configuration files usually begin with a dot (.), so they do not appear by default when you list the contents of the directory (type `ls -a` to see dot files). Examples of these files and descriptions of how to configure them are discussed later in this chapter.

✦ **A graphical configuration** — If you are set up to use Linux through a GUI, there are many ways you can configure how that GUI behaves. Most GUIs used with Linux are based on the X Window System (often referred to simply as X). While X provides a framework for a GUI that lets you run applications, it enables you to choose from many different *desktop environments*. For Red Hat Linux, the Gnome and KDE desktop environments are available to provide a cohesive interface to the applications, menus, and windows of your GUI. Different *window managers* can be used as well, to provide a specific look and feel of the GUI. (Window managers can define the colors, fonts, mouse behavior, window controls, menus, and other surface features of your desktop.)

Besides choosing a desktop environment, you can set up your own desktop properties. These properties can change such things as colors, locations of icons, application menus, and other attributes to make your GUI efficient and, if you like, attractive to the eye.

When the login process is complete, either a shell or a GUI is started automatically. This chapter goes into detail about how to use the shell.

Cross-Reference Chapter 4 describes how to use the Gnome and KDE desktop environments, as well as the X Window System itself.

The shell interface

If your Red Hat Linux system has no GUI (or one that isn't working at the moment), you must enter commands from the shell. If you are using a shell interface, the first thing you see is the shell prompt. The default prompt for a user is simply a dollar sign:

$

The default prompt for the root user is a pound sign (also called a hash sign):

```
#
```

For most Red Hat Linux systems, the $ or # prompts are preceded by your user name, system name, and current directory name. So, for example, a login prompt for the user named `jake` on a computer named `pine` with `/tmp` as the current directory would appear as follows:

```
[jake@pine tmp]$
```

You can change the prompt to display any characters you like. You could use as your prompt the current directory, the date, the local computer name, or any string of characters that pleases you. (Configuring your prompt is described in the "Setting your prompt" section later in this chapter.)

Although there are a tremendous number of features available with the shell, it's easy to begin by just typing a few commands. Try some of the commands shown in the remainder of this section to become familiar with your current shell environment.

> **Tip**   If, instead of a shell prompt, you see a GUI when you log in, you can still try out the shell commands shown in the next section. To access a shell from the GUI, you can open a Terminal window by clicking a Terminal icon on the desktop panel. As an alternative, you can select Terminal from the main menu on your desktop. Click the window that appears, and you are ready to begin typing commands.

In the examples that follow, the $ or # symbols indicate a prompt. The prompt is followed by the command that you type and then by Enter or Return (depending on your keyboard). The lines that follow show the output that results from the command.

Checking your login session

When you log in to a Linux system, Linux views you as having a particular identity. That identity includes your user name, group name, user ID, and group ID. Linux also keeps track of your login session: it knows when you logged in, how long you have been idle, and where you logged in from.

To find out information about your identity, use the `id` command as follows:

```
$ id
  uid=101(chris) gid=105(sales) groups=105(sales),4(adm),7(lp)
```

This shows that the user name is `chris`, which is represented by the numeric user ID (uid) 101. Here, the primary group for chris is called `sales`, which has a group ID (gid) of 105. Chris also belongs to other groups called adm (uid 4) and lp (uid 7). These names and numbers represent the permissions that chris has to access computer resources. (Permissions are described later in this chapter in the section on working with files.)

You can see information about your current login session by using the who command. In the following example, the -i option tells the who command to print the login time, -m says to print information about the current user, and -H asks that a header be printed:

```
$ who -imH
                      USER   LINE   LOGIN-TIME    IDLE  FROM
host1.twostory.com!chris   tty1    Jun 18 20:57
```

The output from this who command shows that the user name is chris on a computer named host1, which is in a domain named twostory.com. Here, chris is logged in on tty1 (which is the monitor connected to the computer), and his login session began at 20:57 on June 18. The IDLE time shows how long the shell has been open without any command being typed (the dot indicates that it is currently active). FROM would show the name of the remote computer the user had logged in from, if that user had logged in from another computer on the network.

Checking directories and permissions

Associated with each shell is a location in the Linux file system known as the *current* or *working directory*. As previously mentioned, each user has a directory that is identified as the user's home directory. When you first log in to Linux, you begin with your home directory as the current directory.

When you request to open or save a file, your shell uses the current directory as the point of reference. Simply give a filename when you save a file and it will be placed in the current directory. Alternatively, you can identify a file by its relation to the current directory (relative path). Or you can ignore the current directory and identify a file by the full directory hierarchy that locates it (absolute path). The structure and use of the file system is described in detail later in this chapter.

To find out what your current directory is, type the pwd command:

```
$ pwd
/usr/bin
```

In this example, the current/working directory is /usr/bin. To find out the name of your home directory, type the **echo** command, followed by the $HOME variable:

```
$ echo $HOME
/home/chris
```

In the above example, the home directory is /home/chris. To get back to your home directory, you can simply type the change directory (cd) command. Although cd changes the current directory to any directory that you choose, simply typing cd takes you to your home directory:

```
$ cd
```

At this point, list the contents of your home directory, using the ls command. Either you can type the full path to your home directory to list its contents, or you can use the ls command without a directory name to list the contents of the current directory. Using the -a option to ls enables you to view the hidden files (dot files) as well as other files. With the -l option, you can see a long, detailed list of information on each file. (You can put multiple single-letter options together after a single dash, for example, -la.)

```
$ ls -la /home/chris
total 158
drwxrwxrwx      2   chris   sales      1024  Jan 12 13:55 .
drwxr-xr-x      3   root    root       1024  Jan 10 01:49 ..
-rw-r--r--      1   chris   sales      1155  Jan 10 01:50 .Xdefaults
-rw-------      1   chris   sales      2204  Jan 18 21:30 .bash_history
-rw-r--r--      1   chris   sales        24  Jan 10 01:50 .bash_logout
-rw-r--r--      1   chris   sales       230  Jan 10 01:50 .bash_profile
-rw-r--r--      1   chris   sales       124  Jan 10 01:50 .bashrc
-rw-rw-r--      1   chris   sales    149872  Jan 11 22:49 letter
```

Displaying a long list (-l option) of the contents of your home directory shows you more about file sizes and directories. Directories such as the current directory (.) and the directory above the current directory (..) are noted as directories by the letter "d" at the beginning of each entry. In this case, dot (.) represents /home/chris and two dots (..), which is also referred to as the parent directory, represents /home. The /home directory is owned by root. All other files are owned by the user chris (who belongs to the sales group).

The filenames shown on the right are mostly dot (.) files that are used to store GUI properties (.Xdefaults) or shell properties (.bash files). The only non-dot file shown in this example is the one named letter. At the beginning of each line are the permissions set for each file. (Permissions and configuring shell property files are described later in this chapter.) Other information in the listing includes the size of each file in bytes (column 4) and the date and time each file was most recently modified (column 5).

Checking system activity

In addition to being a multi-user operating system, Linux is also a multitasking system. *Multitasking* means that many programs can be running at the same time. An instance of a running program is referred to as a process. Linux provides tools for listing running processes, monitoring system usage, and stopping (or killing) processes when necessary.

The most common utility for checking running processes is the ps command. With ps, you can see which programs are running, the resources they are using, and who is running them. The following is an example of the ps command:

```
$ ps au
USER    PID %CPU %MEM  VSZ   RSS   TTY    STAT START  TIME COMMAND
root   2146 0.0  0.8  1908  1100   ttyp0  S    14:50  0:00 login -- jake
jake   2147 0.0  0.7  1836  1020   ttyp0  S    14:50  0:00 -bash
jake   2310 0.0  0.7  2592   912   ttyp0  R    18:22  0:00 ps au
```

In this example, the -a option asks to show processes of all users that are associated with your current terminal, and the -u option asks that user names (as opposed to numeric user IDs) be shown, as well as the time the process started. The concept of terminal comes from the old days, when people worked exclusively from character terminals, so a terminal typically represented a single person. Now you can have many "terminals" on one screen by opening multiple Terminal windows.

On this shell session, there isn't much happening. The first process shows that the user named jake logged in to the login process (which is controlled by the root user). The next process shows that jake is using a bash shell and has just run the ps au command. The terminal device ttyp0 is being used for the login session. The STAT column represents the state of the process, with R indicating a currently running process and S representing a sleeping process.

The USER column shows the name of the user who started the process. Each process is represented by a unique ID number referred to as a process ID (PID). (You can use the PID if you ever need to kill a runaway process.) The %CPU and %MEM columns show the percentage of the processor and random access memory, respectively, that the process is consuming. VSZ (virtual set size) shows size of the image process (in kilobytes), and RSS (resident set size) shows the size of the program in memory. START shows the time the process began running, and TIME shows the cumulative system time used.

Many processes running on a computer are not associated with a terminal. A normal Red Hat Linux system has many processes running in the background. Background system processes perform such tasks as logging system activity or listening for data coming in from the network. They are often started when Red Hat Linux boots up and runs continuously until it shuts down. To see and thereby monitor all the processes running on your Red Hat Linux system, type:

```
$ ps aux | less
```

I added the pipe (|)and the less command to ps aux to allow you to page through the many processes that will appear on your screen. A pipe lets you direct the output of one command to be the input of the next command.

Exiting the shell

To exit the shell when you are done, either type exit or press Ctrl+D. If you are exiting from your login shell (the shell that started when you first logged in), type logout to exit the shell.

I just showed a few commands designed to familiarize you quickly with your Linux system. There are hundreds of other commands that you can try that are contained in directories such as /bin and /usr/bin. There are also administrative commands in /sbin or /usr/sbin directories. Many of these commands are described in the remainder of this chapter.

Understanding the Red Hat Linux Shell

Before icons and windows took over computer screens, you typed commands to run most computers. On UNIX systems, from which Red Hat Linux was derived, the program used to interpret and manage commands was referred to as the shell.

The shell provides a way to run programs, work with the file system, compile computer code, and manage the computer. Although the shell is less intuitive than common GUIs, most Linux experts consider the shell to be much more powerful than GUIs. Because shells have been around for so long, many advanced features have been built into them. Many old-school Linux administrators and programmers primarily use a GUI in their work as a means of opening lots of shells.

The Red Hat Linux shell illustrated in this chapter is called the bash shell, which stands for Bourne Again SHell. The name is derived from the fact that bash is compatible with the first UNIX shell: the Bourne shell (represented by the sh command). Other popular shells include the C Shell (csh), which is popular among BSD UNIX users, and the Korn Shell (ksh), which is popular among UNIX System V users. Linux also has a tcsh shell (a C shell look-alike) and an ash shell (another Bourne shell look-alike).

Although most Red Hat Linux users have a preference for one shell or another, when you know how to use one shell, you can quickly learn any of the others by occasionally referring to the shell's man page (for example, type man bash). In Red Hat Linux, the bash shell is roughly compatible with the sh shell.

Caution   When you run the sh shell in Linux, a link to the bash shell is actually invoked, instead of the sh shell. To have bash behave like an sh shell when the sh shell is run, bash uses the /etc/profile and ~/.profile files to configure the shell. Likewise, when csh is run, the tcsh shell is invoked instead.

Using the Shell in Red Hat Linux

When you type a command in a shell, you can also include other characters that change or add to how the command works. In addition to the command itself, these are some of the other items that you can type on a shell command line:

✦ **Options**—Most commands have one or more options you can add to change their behavior. Options typically consist of a single letter, preceded by a dash. You can also usually combine several options after a single dash. For example, the command ls -la lists the contents of the current directory. The -l asks for a detailed (long) list of information, and the -a asks that files beginning with a dot (.) also be listed. When a single option consists of a word or abbreviation, it is usually preceded by a double dash (--). For example, to use the help option on many commands, you would enter --help on the command line.

✦ **Arguments**—Many commands also accept arguments after any options are entered. An argument is an extra piece of information, such as a filename, that can be used by the command. For example, cat /etc/passwd prints out the contents of the /etc/passwd file. In this case, /etc/passwd is the argument.

✦ **Environment variables**—The shell itself stores information that may be useful to the user's shell session in what are called *environment variables.* Examples of environment variables include $SHELL (which identifies the shell you are using), $PS1 (which defines your shell prompt), and $MAIL (which identifies the location of your mailbox).

Tip

You can check your environment variables at any time. Type declare to list the current environment variables. Or you can type echo $*VALUE*, where *VALUE* is replaced by the name of a particular environment variable you want to list.

✦ **Metacharacters**—These are characters that have special meaning to the shell. Metacharacters can be used to direct the output of a command to a file (>), pipe the output to another command (|), or run a command in the background (&), to name a few. Metacharacters are discussed later in this chapter.

To save you some typing, there are shell features that store commands you want to reuse, recall previous commands, and edit commands. You can create aliases that allow you to type a short command to run a longer one. The shell stores previously entered commands in a history list, which you can display and from which you can recall commands. This is discussed further in the remainder of this section.

Unless you specifically change to another shell, the bash shell is the one you use with Red Hat Linux. The bash shell contains most of the powerful features available in other shells. Although the description in this chapter steps you through many bash shell features, you can learn more about the bash shell by typing **man bash**. For other ways to learn about using the shell, refer to the sidebar "Getting Help with Using the Shell."

Locating commands

If you know where a command is located in your Linux file system, one way to run it is to type the full path to that command. For example, you get the date command from the bin directory by typing:

```
$ /bin/date
```

Getting Help with Using the Shell

When you first start using the shell, it can be intimidating. All you see is a prompt. How do you know which commands are available, which options they use, or how to use more advanced features? Fortunately, lots of help is available. Here are some places you can look to supplement what you learn in this chapter:

✦ **Check the PATH** — Type `echo $PATH`. The result is a listing of the directories containing commands that are immediately accessible to you. Listing the contents of those directories displays most of the standard Linux commands.

✦ **Use the** `help` **command** — Some commands are built into the shell, so they do not appear in a directory. The `help` command lists those commands and shows you the options available with each of them. (Because the list is long, type `help | more` to page through the list.) For help with a particular built-in command, type `help` *command*, replacing *command* with the name that interests you.

✦ **Use the** `man` **command** — If you know a command name and want to find out more about it, type `man` *command*. Replace *command* with the command name in which you are interested. A description of the command and its options appears on the screen.

Of course, this can be inconvenient, especially if the command resides in a directory with a long name. The better way is to have commands stored in well-known directories, and then add those directories to your shell's PATH environment variable. The path consists of a list of directories that are checked sequentially for the commands you enter. To see your current path, type the following:

```
$ echo $PATH
/bin:/usr/bin:/usr/local/bin:/usr/bin/X11:/usr/X11R6/bin:/home/chris/bin
```

The results show the default path for a regular Linux user. Directories in the path list are separated by colons. Most user commands that come with Linux are stored in the `/bin`, `/usr/bin`, or `/usr/local/bin` directories. Graphical commands (that are used with GUIs) are contained in `/usr/bin/X11` and `/usr/X11R6/bin` directories. The last directory shown is the bin directory in the user's home directory.

Tip

If you want to add your own commands or shell scripts, place them in the bin directory in your home directory (such as `/home/chris/bin` for the user named chris). This directory is automatically added to your path. So as long as you add the command to your bin with execute permission (described in the "Understanding file permissions" section), you can immediately begin using the command by simply typing the command name at your shell prompt.

If you are the root user, directories containing administrative commands are in your path. These directories include /sbin and /usr/sbin.

The path directory order is important. Directories are checked from left to right. So, in this example, if there was a command called foo located in both the /bin and /usr/bin directories, the one in /bin would be executed. To have the other foo command run, you would have to either type the full path to the command or change your PATH variable. (See the section on configuration files later in this chapter for information on changing your PATH or adding directories to it.)

Not all the commands that you run are located in directories in your PATH. Some commands are built into the shell. Other commands can be overridden by creating aliases that define any commands and options that you want the command to run. There are also ways of defining a function that consists of a stored series of commands. Here is the order in which the shell checks for the commands you type:

1. **Aliases**—Names set by the alias command that represent a particular command and a set of options.

2. **Shell reserved word**—Words that are reserved by the shell for special use. Most of these are words that you would use in programming-type functions, such as do, while, case, and else.

3. **Function**—A set of commands that are executed together within the current shell.

4. **Built-in command**—A command that is built into the shell.

5. **File system command**—This is a command that is stored in and executed from the computer's file system. (These are the commands that are indicated by the value of the PATH variable.)

Note   To see a list of bash built-in commands (and options), type the help command. For more information on a particular built-in, use the info command, followed by the name of the built-in command.

To find out where a particular command is taken from, you can use the type command. For example, to find out where the bash shell command is located, type the following:

```
$ type bash
bash is /bin/bash
```

Try these few words with the type command to see other locations of commands: which, case, and mc. If a command resides in several locations, you can add the -a option to have all the known locations of the command printed.

Tip   Sometimes you run a command and receive an error message that the command was not found or that permission to run the command was denied. In the first case, check that you spelled the command correctly and that it is located in your PATH. In the second case, the command may be in the PATH, but may not be executable. The section on working with files describes how to add execute permissions to a command.

Rerunning commands

It's annoying, after typing a long or complex command line, to learn that you mistyped something. Fortunately, some shell features let you recall previous command lines, edit those lines, or complete a partially typed command line.

The shell *history* is a list of the commands that you have entered before. Using the history command, you can view your previous commands. Then, using various shell features, you can recall individual command lines from that list and change them however you please.

The rest of this section describes how to do command-line editing, how to complete parts of command lines, and how to recall and work with the history list.

Command-line editing

If you type something wrong on a command line, the bash shell ensures that you don't have to delete the entire line and start over. Likewise, you can recall a previous command line and change the elements to make a new command.

By default, the bash shell uses command-line editing that is based on the emacs text editor. So, if you are familiar with emacs, you probably already know most of the keystrokes described here.

Tip   If you prefer the vi command for editing shell command lines, you can easily make that happen. Add the line:

```
set -o vi
```

to the .bashrc file in your home directory. The next time you open a shell, you can use vi commands (as described in the tutorial later in this chapter) to edit your command lines.

To do the editing, you can use a combination of control keys, meta keys, and arrow keys. For example, Ctrl+f means to hold the control key and type f. Alt+f means to hold the Alt key and type f. (Instead of the Alt key, your keyboard may use a Meta key or the Esc key instead. On a Windows keyboard, use the Windows key.)

To try out a bit of command-line editing, type the following command:

```
$ ls /usr/bin | sort -f | more
```

This command lists the contents of the /usr/bin directory, sorts the contents in alphabetical order (regardless of upper- and lowercase), and pipes the output to more (so you can page through the results). Now, suppose you want to change /usr/bin to /bin. These are steps you can use to change the command:

1. Press Ctrl+a. This moves the cursor to the beginning of the command line.

2. Press Ctrl+f (or the right arrow (→) key). Repeat this command a few times to position the cursor under the first slash (/).

3. Press Ctrl+d. Type this command four times to delete /usr.

4. Press Enter. This executes the command line.

As you edit a command line, at any point you can type regular characters to add those characters to the command line. The characters appear at the location of your cursor. You can use right (→) and left (←) arrows to move the cursor from one end to the other on the command line. You can also press the up (↑) and down (↓) arrow keys to step through previous commands in the history list to select a command line for editing. (See the following discussion on command recall for details on how to recall commands from the history list.)

There are many keystrokes you can use to edit your command lines. Table 3-1 lists the keystrokes that you can use to move around the command line.

Table 3-1
Keystrokes for Navigating Command Lines

Keystroke	Full Name	Meaning
Ctrl+f	Character forward.	Go forward one character.
Ctrl+b	Character backward.	Go backward one character.
Alt+f	Word forward.	Go forward one word.
Alt+b	Word backward.	Go backward one word.
Ctrl+a	Beginning of line.	Go to the beginning of the current line.
Ctrl+e	End of line.	Go to the end of the line.
Ctrl+l	Clear screen.	Clear screen and leave line at the top of the screen.

Table 3-2 lists the keystrokes for editing command lines.

Table 3-2 Keystrokes for Editing Command Lines		
Keystroke	**Full Name**	**Meaning**
Ctrl+d	Delete current.	Delete the current character.
Backspace or Rubout	Delete previous.	Delete the previous character.
Ctrl+t	Transpose character.	Switch positions of current and previous characters.
Alt+t	Transpose words.	Switch positions of current and previous characters.
Alt+u	Uppercase word.	Change the current word to uppercase.
Alt+l	Lowercase word.	Change the current word to lowercase.
Alt+c	Capitalize word.	Change the current word to an initial capital.
Ctrl+v	Insert special character.	Add a special character. For example, to add a Tab character, press Ctrl+v+Tab.

Table 3-3 lists the keystrokes for cutting and pasting text on a command line.

Table 3-3 Keystrokes for Cutting and Pasting Text in Command Lines		
Keystroke	**Full Name**	**Meaning**
Ctrl+k	Cut end of line.	Cut text to the end of the line.
Ctrl+u	Cut beginning of line.	Cut text to the beginning of the line.
Ctrl+w	Cut previous word.	Cut the word located behind the cursor.
Alt+d	Cut next word.	Cut the word following the cursor.
Ctrl+y	Paste recent text.	Paste most recently cut text.
Alt+y	Paste earlier text.	Rotate back to previously cut text and paste it.
Ctrl+c	Delete whole line.	Delete the entire line.

Command line completion

To save you a few keystrokes, the bash shell offers several different ways of completing partially typed values. To attempt to complete a value, type the first few characters, and then press Tab. Here are some of the values you can type partially:

✦ **Environment variable**—If the text begins with a dollar sign ($), the shell completes the text with an environment variable from the current shell.

✦ **User name**—If the text begins with a tilde (~), the shell completes the text with a user name.

✦ **Command, alias, or function**—If the text begins with regular characters, the shell tries to complete the text with a command, alias, or function name.

✦ **Hostname**—If the text begins with an at (@) sign, the shell completes the text with a hostname taken from the /etc/hosts file.

Tip

To add host names from an additional file, you can set the HOSTFILE variable to the name of that file. The file must be in the same format as /etc/hosts.

Here are a few examples of command completion. (When you see <Tab>, it means to press the Tab key on your keyboard.) Type the following:

```
$ echo $OS<Tab>
$ cd ~ro<Tab>
$ fing<Tab>
$ mailx root@loc<Tab>
```

The first example causes $OS to be expanded to the $OSTYPE variable. In the next example, ~ro is expanded to the root user's home directory (~root/). Next, fing is expanded to the finger command. Finally, the address of root@loc is expanded to the computer named localhost (the local computer).

Of course, there will be times when there are several possible completions for the string of characters you have entered. In that case, you can check the possible ways text can be expanded by pressing Esc+? at the point where you want to do completion. Here is an example of the result you would get if you checked for possible completions on $P.

```
$ echo $P<Esc+?>
$PATH $PPID $PS1 $PS2 $PS4 $PWD
$ echo $P
```

In this case, there are six possible environment variables that begin with $P. After the possibilities are displayed, the original command line is returned, ready for you to complete it as you choose.

If the text you are trying to complete is not preceded by a $, ~, or @, you can still try to complete the text with a variable, user name, or hostname. Press the following to complete your text:

✦ Alt+~ — Complete the text before this point as a user name.

✦ Alt+$ — Complete the text before this point as a variable.

✦ Alt+@ — Complete the text before this point as a host name.

✦ Alt+! — Complete the text before this point as a command name (alias, reserved word, shell function, built-in, and filenames are checked in that order). In other words, complete this key sequence with a command that you previously ran.

✦ C+x+/ — List possible user name text completions.

✦ C+x+$ — List possible environment variable completions.

✦ C+x+@ — List possible hostname completions.

✦ C+x+! — List possible command name completions.

Command line recall

After you type a command line, that entire command line is saved in your shell's history list. The list is stored in a history file, from which any command can be recalled to run again. After it is recalled, you can modify the command line, as described earlier.

To view the contents of your history list, use the `history` command. You can either type the command without options or follow it with a number to list that number of the most recent commands. Here's an example:

```
$ history 8
 382 date
 383 ls /usr/bin | sort -a | more
 384 man sort
 385 cd /usr/local/bin
 386 man more
 387 useradd -m /home/chris -u 101 chris
 388 passwd chris
 389 history 8
```

A number precedes each command line in the list. There are several ways to run a command immediately from this list, including:

✦ **Run Command Number** (`!n`) — Replace the *n* with the number of the command line, and the command line indicated is run.

✦ **Run Previous Command** (`!!`) — Runs the previous command line.

✦ **Run Command Containing String** (`!?string?`) — Runs the most recent command that contains a particular *string* of characters.

Instead of just running a `history` command line immediately, you can recall a particular line and edit it. You can use these keys to do that:

✦ **Step** (Arrow Keys) — Press the up (↑) and down (↓) arrow keys to step through each command line in your history list to arrive at the one you want.

✦ **Reverse Incremental Search** (Ctrl+r) — After you press these keys, you are asked to enter a search string to do a reverse search. As you type the string, a matching command line appears that you can run or edit.

✦ **Forward Incremental Search** (Ctrl+s) — After you press these keys, you are asked to enter a search string to do a forward search. As you type the string, a matching command line appears that you can run or edit.

✦ **Reverse Search** (Alt+p) — After you press these keys, you are asked to enter a string to do a reverse search. Type a string and press Enter to see the most recent command line that includes that string.

✦ **Forward Search** (Alt+n) — After you press these keys, you are asked to enter a string to do a forward search. Type a string, and press Enter to see the most recent command line that includes that string.

✦ **Beginning of History List** (Alt+<) — Brings you to the first entry of the history list.

✦ **Beginning of History List** (Alt+>) — Brings you to the last entry of the history list.

Another way to work with your history list is to use the `fc` command. Type `fc` followed by a history line number, and that command line is opened in a text editor. Make the changes that you want. When you exit the editor, the command runs. You could also give a range of line numbers (for example, fc 100 105). All the commands open in your text editor, and then run one after the other when you exit the editor.

The history list is stored in the `.bash_history` file in your home directory. Up to 1000 history commands are stored for you by default.

Connecting and expanding commands

A truly powerful feature of the shell is the capability to redirect the input and output of commands to and from other commands and files. To allow commands to be strung together, the shell uses metacharacters. As noted earlier, a metacharacter is a typed character that has special meaning to the shell for connecting commands or requesting expansion.

Piping commands

The pipe (|) metacharacter connects the output from one command to the input of another command. This lets you have one command work on some data, then have the next command deal with the results. Here is an example of a command line that includes pipes:

```
$ cat /etc/password | sort | more
```

This command prints the contents of the /etc/password file and pipes the output to the sort command. The sort command takes the user names that begin each line of the /etc/password file, sorts them alphabetically, and pipes the output to the more command. The more command displays the output one page at a time, so that you can go through the output a line or a page at a time.

Pipes are an excellent illustration of how UNIX, the predecessor of Linux, was created as an operating system made up of building blocks. A standard practice in UNIX was to connect utilities in different ways to get different jobs done. For example, before the days of integrated, graphical word processors, users would create plain-text files that included macros to indicate formatting. Then, to see how the document really appeared, they would use a command such as the following:

```
$ nroff -man grep.1 | lpr
```

In this example, the nroff command is used to format the file grep.1 (which is the grep manual page) using the manual macro (-man). The output is piped to the lpr command to print the output. Because the file being printed is in plain text, you could have substituted any number of options to work with the text before printing it. You could sort the contents, change or delete some of the content, or bring in text from other documents. The key is that, instead of all those features being in one program, you get results from piping and redirecting input and output between multiple commands.

Sequential commands

Sometimes you may want a sequence of commands to run with one command to complete before the next command begins. You can use a semicolon (;) metacharacter to run commands in a sequence. To run a sequence of commands, type them all on the same command line and separate them with semicolons (;). For example:

```
$ date ; troff -me verylargedocument | lpr ; date
```

In this example, I was formatting a huge document and wanted to know how long it would take. The first command (date) showed the date and time before the formatting started. The troff command formatted the document and then piped the output to the printer. When the formatting was done, the date and time was printed again (so I know how long the troff command took to complete).

Background commands

Some commands can take a while to complete. Sometimes you may not want to tie up your shell waiting for a command to finish. In those cases, you can have the commands run in the background by using the ampersand (&).

Text formatting commands (such as nroff and troff, which were described earlier) are examples of commands that you may want to run in the background if you are formatting a large document. You also may want to create your own shell scripts that run in the background to check continuously for certain events to occur, such as the hard disk filling up or particular users logging in.

Here is an example of a command being run in the background:

```
$ troff -me verylargedocument &
```

There are other ways of managing background and foreground processes. These different methods are described in detail in the "Managing background and foreground processes" section.

Expanding commands

With command substitution, you can have the output of a command interpreted by the shell instead of by the command itself. In this way, you can have the standard output of a command become an argument for another command. The two forms of command substitution are $(command) or 'command'.

The command in this case can include options, metacharacters, and arguments. Here is an example of using command substitution:

```
$ vi $(find / -print | grep xyzzy)
```

In this command line, the command substitution is done before the vi command is run. First, the find command starts at the root directory (/) and prints out all files and directories in the entire file system. This output is piped to the grep command, which filters out all files except for those that include the string xyzzy. Finally, the vi command opens all filenames for editing (one at a time) that include xyzzy.

This particular example may be useful if you knew that you wanted to edit a file for which you knew the name but not the location. As long as the string was fairly uncommon, you could find and open every instance of a particular filename existing in the file system.

Expanding arithmetic expressions

There may be times when you want to pass arithmetic results to a command. There are two forms you can use to expand an arithmetic expression and pass it to the shell: $[expression] or $((expression)). Here is an example:

```
$ echo "I am $[2002 - 1957] years old."
I am 45 years old.
```

In this example, the shell interprets the arithmetic expression first (2002 - 1957), and then passes that information to the echo command. The echo command displays the text, with the results of the arithmetic (45) inserted.

Expanding variables

Environment variables that store information within the shell can be expanded using the dollar sign ($) metacharacter. When you expand an environment variable on a command line, the value of the variable is printed instead of the variable name itself, as follows:

```
$ ls -l $BASH_ENV
-rw-r—r-- 1 chris   sales  124  Jan 10 01:50 /home/chris/.bashrc
```

In this example, you wanted to see the location of your bash environment file, and then check its size and when it was last changed. The BASH_ENV environment variable contains the name of your bash environment file. Using $BASH_ENV as an argument to ls -l causes a long listing of that file to be printed. (The $BASH_ENV variable isn't automatically set for the root user, though it should be for all others.) For more information on shell environment variables, see the following section.

Using shell environment variables

Every active shell stores pieces of information that it needs to use in what are called environment variables. An environment variable can store things such as locations of configuration files, mailboxes, and path directories. They can also store values for your shell prompts, the size of your history list, and type of operating system.

To see the environment variables currently assigned to your shell, type the declare command. (It will probably fill more than one screen, so type declare | more.) You can refer to the value of any of those variables by preceding it with a dollar sign ($) and placing it anywhere on a command line. For example:

```
$ echo $USER
chris
```

This command prints the value of the USER variable, which happens to be the user name (chris). You can substitute any other value for USER to print its value instead.

Common shell environment variables

When you start a shell (by logging in or opening a Terminal window), there is a bunch of environment variables already set. The following are some of the variables that are either set when you use a bash shell in Linux or that can be set by you to use with different features.

✦ BASH—Contains the full path name of the bash command. This is usually /bin/bash.

✦ BASH_VERSION—A number that represents the current version of the bash command.

✦ ENV—This value identifies the location of a file that contains commands used to initialize the shell. For the bash shell, this file is probably $HOME/.bashrc. See the section about creating configuration files for information on working with the .bashrc file.

✦ EUID—This is the effective user ID number of the current user. It is assigned when the shell starts.

✦ FCEDIT—If set, this indicates the text editor used by the fc command to edit history commands. If this variable isn't set, the vi command is used.

✦ HISTFILE—The location of your history file. It is typically located at $HOME/.bash_history.

✦ HISTFILESIZE—The number of history entries that can be stored. After this number is reached, the oldest commands are discarded. The default value is 1000.

✦ HISTCMD—This returns the number of the current command in the history list.

✦ HOME—This is your home directory. It is your current working directory each time you log in or type the cd command with any options.

✦ HOSTTYPE—A value that describes the computer architecture on which the Linux system is running. For Intel-compatible PCs, the value is i386.

✦ MAIL—This is the location of your mailbox file. The file is typically your user name in the /var/spool/mail directory.

✦ OLDPWD—The directory that was the working directory before you changed to the current working directory.

✦ OSTYPE—A name identifying the current operating system. In our case, this will say Linux. (Bash can run on other operating systems as well.)

✦ PATH—The colon-separated list of directories used to find commands that you type. This value is initially set by the operating system, although most people modify it. The default value for regular users is: /usr/local/bin:/bin:/usr/bin:/usr/X11R6/bin:$HOME/bin. For the root user, the value also includes /sbin, /usr/sbin, and /usr/local/sbin.

✦ PPID—The process ID of the command that started the current shell (for example, its parent process).

✦ PROMPT_COMMAND—Can be set to a command name that is run each time before your shell prompt is displayed. Setting PROMPT_COMMAND=date prints the current date and time before the prompt line appears.

✦ PS1 — Sets the value of your shell prompt. There are many items that you can read into your prompt (date, time, user name, hostname, and so on). Sometimes a command requires additional prompts, which you can set with the variables PS2, PS3, and so on. (Setting your prompt is described later in this chapter.)

✦ PWD — This is the directory that is assigned as your current directory. This value changes each time you change directories using the cd command.

✦ RANDOM — Accessing this variable causes a random number to be generated. The number is between 0 and 99999.

✦ SECONDS — The number of seconds since the time the shell was started.

✦ SHLVL — The number of shell levels associated with the current shell session. When you log in to the shell, the SHLVL is 1. Each time you start a new bash command (by, for example, using su to become a new user, or by simply typing bash), this number is incremented.

✦ TMOUT — Can be set to a number representing the number of seconds the shell can be idle without receiving input. After the number of seconds is reached, the shell exits. This is a security feature that can help make it less likely for unattended shells to be accessed by unauthorized people. (This must be set in the login shell for it to actually cause the shell to log out the user.)

✦ UID — The user ID number assigned to your user name. The user ID number is permanently stored in the /etc/password file.

Set your own environment variables

Environment variables can provide a handy way of storing bits of information that you use often from the shell. You are free to create any variables that you want (although I would avoid those that are already in use) so that you can read in the values of those variables as you use the shell. (See the bash man page for a listing of shell environment variable names that are already in use.)

To set an environment variable temporarily, you can simply type a variable name and assign it to a value. Here is an example:

```
$ AB=/usr/dog/contagious/ringbearer/grind ; export AB
```

This example causes a long directory path to be assigned to the AB variable. The export AB command says to export the value to the shell so that it can be propagated to other shells you may open. With AB set, you can go to the directory by typing the following:

```
$ cd $AB
```

Tip
You may have noticed that environment variables shown here are in all caps. Though case does matter with these variables, setting them as uppercase is a convention, not a necessity. You could just as easily set a variable to xyz as to XYZ (they are not the same, but either will work).

The problem with setting environment variables in this way is that as soon as you exit the shell in which you set the variable, the setting is lost. To set variables more permanently, you should add variable settings to your bash configuration files, which is described later in the section on adding environment variables.

If you want to have other text right up against the output from an environment variable, you can surround the variable in braces. This protects the variable name from being misunderstood. For example, if you wanted to add a command name to the AB variable shown earlier, you could do the following:

```
$ echo ${AB}/adventure
/usr/dog/contagious/ringbearer/grind/adventure
```

Remember that you need to export the variable for it to be picked up by other commands. You need to add the export line to a shell configuration file for it to take effect the next time you login. The export command is fairly flexible. Instead of running the export command after you set the variable, you could do it all in one step, as follows:

```
$ export XYZ=/home/xyz/bin
```

You can override the value of any environment variable at any time. This can be temporary by typing the new value in the shell. Or you can add the changed variable command line to your $HOME/.bashrc file. One useful variable to update is the PATH variable. Here is an example:

```
$ export PATH=$PATH:/home/xyz/bin
```

In this example, I temporarily added the /home/xyz/bin directory to the PATH. This is useful if, during a shell session, you find yourself wanting to run a bunch of commands from a directory that is not normally in your PATH. This temporary addition saves you from typing the full or relative path each time you want to run a command.

If you decide that you no longer want a variable to be set, you can use the unset command to erase its value. For example, you could type unset XYZ, which would cause XYZ to have no value set. (Remember to remove the export from the $HOME/.bashrc file—if you added it there— or it will return the next time you open a new shell.)

Managing background and foreground processes

If you are using Linux over a network or from a *dumb* terminal (a monitor that allows only text input with no GUI support), your shell may be all that you have. You may be used to a windowing environment where you have a lot of programs active at the same time so that you can switch among them as needed. This shell thing can seem pretty limited.

Though the bash shell doesn't offer you a GUI for running many programs, it does offer a way to move active programs between the background and foreground. In this way, you can have a lot of stuff running, while selectively being able to choose the one you want to deal with at the moment.

There are several ways to place an active program in the background. One mentioned earlier is to add an ampersand (&) to the end of a command line. Another way is to use the at command to run one or more commands in a way in which they are not connected to the shell.

To stop a running command and put it in the background, press Ctrl+z. After the command is stopped, you can either bring it to the foreground to run (the fg command) or start it running in the background (the bg command).

Starting background processes

If you have programs that you want to run while you continue to work in the shell, you can place the programs in the background. To place a program in the background at the time you run the program, type an ampersand (&) at the end of the command line. For example:

```
$ find /usr -print > /tmp/allusrfiles &
```

This command finds all files on your Red Hat Linux system (starting from the /usr directory), prints those file names, and puts those names in the file /tmp/allusrfiles. The ampersand (&) runs that command line in the background. To check which commands you have running in the background, use the jobs command, as follows:

```
$ jobs
[1]  Stopped (tty output)  vi /tmp/myfile
[2]  Running           find /usr -print > /tmp/allusrfiles &
[3]  Running           nroff -man /usr/man2/* >/tmp/man2 &
[4]- Running           nroff -man /usr/man3/* >/tmp/man3 &
[5]+ Stopped           nroff -man /usr/man4/* >/tmp/man4
```

The first job shows a text-editing command (vi) that was placed in the background and stopped by pressing Ctrl+z while I was editing. Job two shows the find command I just ran. Jobs three and four show nroff commands currently running in the background. Job five had been running in the shell (foreground) until I decided too many processes were running and pressed Ctrl+z to stop job five until a few processes had completed.

The plus sign (+) next to number 5 shows that this is the job that was most recently placed in the background. The minus sign (-) next to number 4 shows that it was placed in the background just before the most recent background job. Because job 1 requires terminal input, it cannot run in the background. As a result, it appears as Stopped until it is brought to the foreground again.

Tip   To see the process ID for the background job, add an -l option to the jobs command. If you type **ps**, you can use the process ID to figure out which command is associated with a particular background command.

Using foreground and background commands

Continuing with the example shown, you can bring any of the commands on the jobs list into the foreground. For example, if you are ready to edit myfile again, you can type:

```
$ fg %1
```

As a result, the vi command opens again, with all the text as it was when you stopped the vi job.

Caution   Before you put a text processor, word processor, or similar program in the background, make sure you save your file. It's easy to forget you have a program in the background and you will lose your data if you log out or the computer reboots later on.

To refer to a background job (to cancel it or bring it to the foreground), you can use a percent sign (%) followed by the job number. You can also use the following to refer to a background job:

✦ % — A percent sign alone refers to the most recent command put into the background (indicated by the plus sign). This action brings the command to the foreground.

✦ %string — Refers to a job where the command begins with a particular string of characters. The string must be unambiguous. (In other words, typing %vi when there are two vi commands in the background, results in an error message.)

✦ %?string — Refers to a job where the command line contains a string at any point. The string must be unambiguous or the match will fail.

✦ %-- — Refers to the previous job stopped before the one most recently stopped.

If a command is stopped, you can start it running again in the background using the bg command. For example, take job number 5 from the jobs list in the previous example:

```
[5]+ Stopped            nroff -man man4/* >/tmp/man4
```

Type the following:

```
$ bg %5
```

After that, the job runs in the background. Its jobs entry appears as follows:

```
[5]  Running              nroff -man man4/* >/tmp/man4 &
```

Tip

After a background command is done, an Exit message will be displayed the next time you press Enter (before a new shell prompt is displayed). If you want to have the exit message appear the moment the command completes, you must set the `notify` variable. To do this, type `export notify=yes`.

Configuring your shell

You can tune your shell to help you work more efficiently. Your prompt can provide pertinent information each time you press Enter. You can set aliases to save your keystrokes and permanently set environment variables to suit your needs. To make each change occur when you start a shell, you can add this information to your shell configuration files.

Several configuration files support how your shell behaves. Some of these files are executed for every user and every shell. Others are specific to the particular user that creates the configuration file. Here are the files that are of interest to anyone using the bash shell in Linux:

✦ `/etc/profile` — This file sets up user environment information for every user. It is executed when you first log in and the shell starts. This file provides default values for your path, your prompt, the maximum file size that you can create, and the default permissions for the files that you create. It also sets environment variables for such things as the location of your mailbox and the size of your history files.

✦ `/etc/bashrc` — This file is executed for every user that runs the bash shell. It is read each time a bash shell is opened. It sets the default prompt and may add one or more aliases. Values in this file can be overridden by information in each user's `~/.bashrc` file.

✦ `~/.bash_profile` — This file is used by each user to enter information that is specific to their own use of the shell. It is executed only once, when the user logs in. By default it sets a few environment variables and executes the user's `.bashrc` file.

✦ `~/.bashrc` — This file contains the bash information that is specific to your bash shells. It is read when you log in and also each time you open a new bash shell. This is the best location to add environment variables and aliases so that your shell picks them up.

✦ `~/.bash_logout` — This file executes each time you log out (exit the last bash shell). By default, it simply clears your screen.

To change the /etc/profile or /etc/bashrc files, you must be the root user. Any user can change the information in the $HOME/.bash_profile, $HOME/.bashrc, and $HOME/.bash_logout files in their own home directories.

The following sections provide ideas about things to add to your shell configuration files. In most cases, you add these values to the .bashrc file in your home directory. However, if you are an administrator for a system, you may want to set some of these values as defaults for all of your Linux system's users.

Setting your prompt

Your prompt consists of a set of characters that appear each time the shell is ready to accept a command. Exactly what that prompt contains is determined by the value in the PS1 environment variable. If your shell requires additional input, it uses the values of PS2, PS3, and PS4.

When your Red Hat Linux system is installed, your prompt is set to include the following information: your user name, your hostname, and the base name of your current working directory. That information is surrounded by brackets and followed by a dollar sign (for regular users) or a pound sign (for the root user). Here is an example of that prompt:

```
[chris@myhost bin]$
```

If you were to change directories, the bin name would change to the name of the new current working directory. Likewise, if you were to log in as a different user or to a different host, that information would change.

You can use several special characters (indicated by adding a backslash to a variety of letters) to include different information in your prompt. These can include your terminal number, the date, and the time, as well as other pieces of information. Here are some examples:

✦ \! —Shows the current command history number. This includes all previous commands stored for your user name.

✦ \# —Shows the command number of the current command. This includes only the commands for the active shell.

✦ \$ —Shows the standard user prompt ($) or root prompt (#), depending on which user you are.

✦ \W —Shows only the current working directory base name. For example, if the current working directory was /var/spool/mail, this value would simply appear as mail.

✦ \[—Precedes a sequence of nonprinting characters. This could be used to add a terminal control sequence into the prompt for such things as changing colors, adding blink effects, or making characters bold. (Your terminal determines the exact sequences available.)

✦ \] — Follows a sequence of nonprinting characters.

✦ \\ — Shows a backslash.

✦ \d — Displays the day, month, and number of the date. For example: Sat Jan 23.

✦ \h — Shows the hostname of the computer running the shell.

✦ \n — Causes a newline to occur.

✦ \nnn — Shows the character that relates to the octal number replacing nnn.

✦ \s — Displays the current shell name. For example, for this bash shell the value would be bash.

✦ \t — Prints the current time in hours, minutes, and seconds. For example, 10:14:39.

✦ \u — Prints your current user name.

✦ \w — Displays the full path to the current working directory.

Tip

If you are setting your prompt temporarily by typing at the shell, you should put the value of PS1 in quotes. For example, you could type export PS1="[\t \w]\$ " to see a prompt that looks like this: [20:26:32 /var/spool]$.

To make a change to your prompt permanent, add the value of PS1 to your .bashrc file in your home directory (assuming that you are using the bash shell). There is probably already a PS1 value in that file that you can modify.

Adding environment variables

You may consider adding a few environment variables to your .bashrc file. These can help make working with the shell more efficient and effective:

✦ TMOUT — This sets how long the shell can be inactive before bash automatically exits. The value is the number of seconds for which the shell has not received input. This can be a nice security feature, in case you leave your desk while you are still logged in to Linux. So as not to be annoyed by logging you off while you are still working, you may want to set the value to something like TMOUT=1800 (to allow 30 minutes of idle time).

✦ PATH — As described earlier, the PATH variable sets the directories that are searched for the commands that you type. If you often use directories of commands that are not in your PATH, you can permanently add them. To do this, add a new PATH variable to your .bashrc file. For example, to add a new directory called /getstuff/bin to your path, add the following line:

```
PATH=$PATH:/getstuff/bin ; export PATH
```

This example first reads all the current path directories into the new PATH ($PATH), adds the /getstuff/bin directory, and then exports the new PATH.

Caution

Some people add the current directory to their PATH by adding a directory identified simply as a dot (.), as follows:

```
PATH=.:$PATH ; export PATH
```

This lets you always run commands in your current directory (which people may be used to if they have used DOS). However, the security risk with this procedure is that you could be in a directory that contains a command that you don't intend to run from that directory. For example, a hacker could put an ls command in a directory that, instead of listing the content of your directory, does something devious.

✦ WHATEVER—You can create your own environment variables to provide short-cuts in your work. Choose any name that is not being used and assign a useful value to it. For example, if you do a lot of work with files in the /work/time/files/info/memos directory, you could set the following variable:

```
M=/work/time/files/info/memos ; export M
```

You could make that your current directory by typing cd $M. You could run a program from that directory called hotdog by typing $M/hotdog. You could edit a file from there called bun by typing vi $M/bun.

Adding aliases

Setting aliases can save you even more typing than setting environment variables. With aliases, you can have a string of characters execute an entire command line. You can add and list aliases with the alias command. Here are some examples:

```
alias p='pwd ; ls -CF'
alias rm='rm -i'
```

In the first example, the letter p is assigned to run the command pwd, and then to run ls -CF to print the current working directory and list its contents in column form. The second runs the rm command with the -i option each time you simply type rm. (This is an alias that is often set automatically for the root user, so that instead of just removing files, you are prompted for each individual file removal. This prevents you from removing all the files in a directory by mistakenly typing something such as rm *.)

While you are in the shell, you can check which aliases are set by typing the alias command. If you want to remove an alias, you can type unalias. (Remember that if the alias is set in a configuration file, it will be set again when you open another shell.)

Working with the Red Hat Linux File System

The Red Hat Linux file system is the structure in which all the information on your computer is stored. Files are organized within a hierarchy of directories. Each directory can contain files, as well as other directories.

If you were to map out the files and directories in Red Hat Linux, it would look like an upside down tree. At the top is the root directory, which is represented by a single slash (/). Below that is a set of common directories in the Linux system, such as /bin, /dev, /home, /lib, and /tmp, to name a few. Each of those directories, as well as directories added to the root, can contain subdirectories.

Figure 3-2 illustrates how the Linux file system is organized as a hierarchy. To illustrate how directories are connected, Figure 3-2 shows a /home directory that contains subdirectories for three users: chris, mary, and tom. Within the chris directory are three subdirectories: briefs, memos, and personal. To refer to a file called inventory in the chris memos directory, you could type the full path of /home/chris/memos/inventory. If your current directory were /home/chris/memos, you could refer to the file as simply inventory.

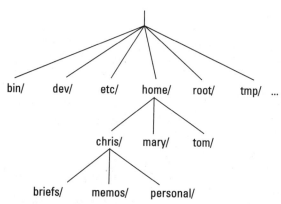

Figure 3-2: The Red Hat Linux file system is organized as a hierarchy of directories.

Some of the Red Hat Linux directories that may be of interest to you include the following:

✦ /bin—Contains common Linux user commands, such as ls, sort, date, and chmod.

✦ /dev—Contains files representing access points to devices on your systems. These include terminal devices (tty*), floppy disks (fd*), hard disks (hd*), RAM (ram*), and CD-ROM (cd*). (Users normally access these devices directly through the device files.)

✦ `/etc` — Contains administrative configuration files.

✦ `/home` — Contains directories assigned to each user with a login account.

✦ `/mnt` — Provides a location for mounting devices, such as remote file systems and removable media (with directory names of cdrom, floppy, and so on).

✦ `/root` — Represents the root user's home directory.

✦ `/sbin` — Contains administrative commands and daemon processes.

✦ `/tmp` — Contains temporary files used by applications.

✦ `/usr` — Contains user documentation, games, graphical files (X11), libraries (lib), and a variety of other user and administrative commands and files.

The file systems in the DOS or MS Windows operating systems differ from Linux's file structure. See the sidebar on the Linux file system versus MS file systems.

Creating files and directories

As a Red Hat Linux user, most of the files you save and work with will probably be in your home directory. Here are some of the commands you use in the file creation process:

Red Hat Linux File System versus MS File Systems

Although similar in many ways, the Linux file system has some striking differences from the file systems used in MS-DOS and Windows operating systems. Here are a few:

✦ In MS-DOS and Windows file systems, drive letters represent different storage devices (for example, A: is a floppy drive and C: is a hard disk). In Linux, all storage devices are fit into the file system hierarchy. So, the fact that all of `/usr` may be on a separate hard disk or that `/mnt/rem1` is a file system from another computer is invisible to the user.

✦ Slashes, rather than backslashes, are used to separate directory names in Linux. So, `C:\home\chris` in an MS system is `/home/chris` in a Linux system.

✦ Filenames almost always have suffixes in DOS (such as .txt for text files or .doc for word-processing files). Though at times you can use that convention in Linux, three-character suffixes have no required meaning in Linux. They can be useful for identifying a file type.

✦ Every file and directory in a Linux system has permissions and ownership associated with it. Security varies among Microsoft systems. Because DOS and MS Windows began as single-user systems, file ownership was not built into those systems when they were designed. Later releases added features such as file and folder attributes to address this problem.

✦ cd —Change to another current working directory

✦ pwd —Print the name of the current working directory

✦ mkdir —Create a directory

✦ chmod —Change the permission on a file or directory

✦ ls —List the contents of a directory

The following procedure steps you through creating directories within your home directory, moving among your directories, and setting appropriate file permissions:

1. First, go to your home directory. To do this, simply type cd.

   (For other ways of referring to your home directory, see the sidebar on identifying directories.)

2. To make sure that you got to your home directory, type pwd. When I do this, I get the following response (yours will reflect your home directory):

   ```
   $ pwd
   /home/chris
   ```

3. Create a new directory called test in your home directory, as follows:

   ```
   $ mkdir test
   ```

4. Check the permissions of the directory by typing:

   ```
   $ ls -ld test
   drwxr-xr-x  2 chris  sales  1024  Jan 24 12:17 test
   ```

   Notice that this listing says that test is a directory (d), the owner is chris, the group is sales, and the file was most recently modified on Jan 24 at 12:17 p.m. Suppose that you want to prevent everyone else who uses this computer from using or viewing the files in this directory. The permissions for the directory are rwxr-xr-x. I explain what these permissions mean later in this section.

5. For now, type the following:

   ```
   $ chmod 700 test
   ```

   This changes the permissions of the directory to give you complete access and everyone else no access at all. (The new permissions should read like rwx------.)

6. Next, make the test directory your current directory as follows:

   ```
   $ cd test
   ```

Identifying Directories

When you need to identify your home directory on a shell command line, you can use the following:

✦ $HOME—This environment variable stores your home directory name.

✦ ~—The tilde (~) represents your home directory on the command line.

You can also use the tilde to identify someone else's home directory. For example, ~chris would be expanded to the chris home directory (probably /home/chris).

Other special ways of identifying directories in the shell include the following:

✦ .—A single dot (.) refers to the current directory.

✦ ..—Two dots (..) refers to a directory directly above the current directory.

✦ $OLDPWD—This environment variable refers to the previous working directory before you changed to the current one.

Using metacharacters and operators

To make more efficient use of your shell, the bash shell lets you use certain special characters, referred to as metacharacters and operators. Metacharacters can help you match one or more files without typing each file out completely. Operators let you direct information from one command or file to another command or file.

Using file-matching metacharacters

To save you some keystrokes and to be able to refer easily to a group of files, the bash shell lets you use metacharacters. Anytime you need to refer to a file or directory, such as to list it, open it, or remove it, you can use metacharacters to match the files you want. Here are some useful metacharacters for matching filenames:

✦ *—This matches any number of characters.

✦ ?—This matches any one character.

✦ [...]—This matches any one of the characters between the brackets, which can include a dash-separated range of letters or numbers.

To try out some of these file-matching metacharacters, go to an empty directory (such as the test directory described in the previous section) and create some files. Here's an example of how to create some empty files:

```
$ touch apple banana grape grapefruit watermelon
```

The next few commands show you how to use shell metacharacters to match file names so they can be used as arguments to the ls command. Using metacharacters shown below, you can match the file names you just created with the touch command. Type the following commands and see if you get the same responses:

```
$ ls a*
apple
$ ls g*
grape
grapefruit
$ ls g*t
grapefruit
$ ls *e*
apple grape grapefruit watermelon
$ ls *n*
banana watermelon
```

The first example matches any file that begins with an a (apple). The next example matches any files that begin with g (grape, grapefruit). Next, files beginning with g and ending in t are matched (grapefruit). Next, any file that contains an e in the name is matched (apple, grape, grapefruit, watermelon). Finally, any file that contains an n is matched (banana, watermelon).

Here are a few examples of pattern matching with the question mark (?):

```
$ ls ????e
apple grape
$ ls g???e*
grape grapefruit
```

The first example matches any five-character file that ends in e (apple, grape). The second example matches any file that begins with g and has e as its fifth character (grape, grapefruit).

Here are a few examples of using braces to do pattern matching:

```
$ ls [abw]*
apple banana watermelon
$ ls [agw]*[ne]
apple grape watermelon
```

In the first example, any file beginning with a, b, or w is matched. In the second, any file that begins with a, g, or w and also ends with either n or e is matched.

Using file-redirection metacharacters

Commands receive data from standard input and send it to standard output. Using pipes (described earlier), you can direct standard output from one command to the standard input of another. With files, you can use less than (<) and greater than (>) signs to direct data to and from files. Here are the file redirection characters:

✦ <—Direct the contents of a file to the command.

✦ >—Direct the output of a command to a file, deleting the existing file.

✦ >>—Direct the output of a command to a command, adding the output to the end of the existing file.

Here are some examples of command lines where information is directed to and from files:

```
$ mail root < ~/.bashrc
$ nroff -man /usr/share/man/man1/chmod.1* > /tmp/chmod
$ echo "I finished the project on $(date)" > ~/projects
```

In the first example, the contents of the .bashrc file in the home directory are sent in a mail message to the computer's root user. The second command line formats the chmod man page (using the nroff command) and sends the output to the file /tmp/chmod (erasing the previous /tmp/chmod file, if it existed). The final command results in the following text being added to the user's project file:

```
I finished the project on Sun Nov 25 13:46:49 PST 2001
```

Understanding file permissions

After you've worked with Linux for a while, you are almost sure to get a *Permission Denied* message. Permissions associated with files and directories in Linux were designed to keep users from accessing other users' private files and to protect important system files.

The nine bits assigned to each file for permissions define the access that you and others have to your file. Permission bits appear as *rwxrwxrwx*. The first three bits apply to the owner's permission, the next three apply to the owner's group, and the last three apply to all others. The *r* stands for *read*, the *w* stands for *write*, and the *x* stands for *execute permissions*. If a dash appears instead of the letter, it means that permission is turned off for that associated read, write, or execute.

You can see the permission for any file or directory by typing the ls -ld command. The named file or directory appears as those shown in the example below:

```
$ ls -ld ch3 test
-rw-rw-r--  1 chris  sales   4983  Jan 18 22:13  ch3
drwxr-xr-x  2 chris  sales   1024  Jan 24 13:47  test
```

The first line shows a file (ch3) that has read and write on for the owner and the group. All other users have read permission, which means they can view the file but cannot change its contents or remove it. The second line shows a directory (indicated by the letter d before the permission bits). The owner has read, write, and execute permission, while the group and other users have only read and execute permissions. As a result, only the owner can add, change, or delete files in that directory. Any other user, however, can only read the contents, change to that directory, and list the contents of the directory.

If you own a file, you can change the permission on it as you please. You can do this with the chmod command. For each of the three sets of permission on a file (read, write, and execute), the r is assigned to the number 4, w to 2, and x to 1. So to make permissions wide open for yourself as owner, you would set the first number to 7 (4 plus 2 plus 1). The same would be true for group and other permission. Any combination of permissions can result from 0 (no permission) through 7 (full permission).

Here are some examples of how to change permission on a file and what the resulting permission would be:

```
chmod 777 files  →  rwxrwxrwx
chmod 755 files  →  rwxr-xr-x
chmod 644 files  →  rw--r--r--
chmod 000 files  →  ---------
```

When you try to create a file, by default it is given the permission: rw-r–r–. A directory is given the permission rwxr-xr-x. These default values are determined by the value of umask. Type umask to see what your umask value is. For example:

```
$ umask
022
```

Subtract the number you see in each of the three sets from seven and you will see the value of each of the fields. The umask of 022 results in permission for a directory of 755 (rwxr-xr-x). That same umask results in a file permission of 644 (rw-r–r–). (Execute permissions are off by default for regular files.)

Tip

Here's a great tip for changing the permission for lots of files at once. Using the -R options of chmod, you could change the permission for all of the files and directories within a directory structure at once. For example, if you wanted to open permissions completely to all files and directories in the /tmp/test directory, you could type the following:

```
$ chmod -R 777 /tmp/test
```

This command line runs chmod recursively (-R) for the /tmp/test directory, as well as any files or directories that exist below that point in the file system (for example, /tmp/test/hat, /tmp/test/hat/baseballcaps, and so on). All would be set to 777 (full read/write/execute permissions).

Caution

The -R option of chmod works best if you are opening permissions completely or adding execute permission (as well as the appropriate read/write permission). The reason is that if you turn off execute permission recursively, you close off your ability to change to any directory in that structure. For example, chmod -R 644 /tmp/test turns off execute permission for the /tmp/test directory, then fails to change any files or directories below that point.

Moving, copying, and deleting files

Commands for moving, copying, and deleting files are fairly straightforward. To change the location of a file, use the mv command. To copy a file from one location to another, use the cp command. To remove a file, use the rm command. Here are some examples:

```
$ mv abc def
$ mv abc ~
$ cp abc def
$ cp abc ~
$ rm abc
$ rm *
```

Of the two move (mv) commands, the first moves the file abc to the file def in the same directory (essentially renaming it), whereas the second moves the file abc to your home directory (~). The first copy command (cp) copies abc to the file def, whereas the second copies abc to you home directory (~). The first remove command (rm) deletes the abc file, whereas the second removes all the files in the current directory.

Note   For the root user, the mv, cp, and rm commands are aliased to each be run with the -i option. This causes a prompt to appear asking you to confirm each move, copy, and removal, one file at a time. This is done to prevent the root user from messing up a large group of files by mistake.

Using the vi Text Editor

It's almost impossible to use Red Hat Linux for any period of time and not need to use a text editor. If you are using a GUI, you can run xedit, which has a fairly intuitive interface for editing text. Most Red Hat Linux shell users will use either the vi or emacs commands to edit plain-text files. The advantage of using vi or emacs, instead of a graphical editor, is that you can use it from a Terminal window, a character terminal, or a character-based connection over a network (using telnet or ssh, for example). No GUI is required.

This section provides a brief tutorial of the vi text editor. Any time in this book that I suggest you manually edit a configuration file, you can use vi to do that editing (from any shell prompt). The vi editor is difficult to learn at first. But when you know it, you will be able to edit and move files around quickly and efficiently. Your fingers never have to leave the keyboard to pick up a mouse or hit a function key.

Starting with vi

Most often, you start vi to open a particular file. For example, to open a file called /tmp/test, type the following command:

```
$ vi /tmp/test
```

If this is a new file, you should see something similar to the following:

```
~
~
~
~
~
"/tmp/test" [New File]
```

The box at the top represents where your cursor is. The bottom line keeps you informed about what is going on with your editing (here you just opened a new file). In between, there are tildes (~) as filler because there is no text in the file yet. Now here's the intimidating part: there are no hints, menus, or icons to tell you what to do. On top of that, you can't just start typing. If you do, the computer is likely to beep at you.

The first things you need to know are the different operating modes. The vi editor operates in either command mode or input mode. When you start vi, you are in command mode. Before you can add or change text in the file, you have to type a command to tell vi what you want to do. A command consists of one or two letters and an optional number. To get into input mode, you need to type an input command. To start out, type either of the following input commands:

✦ a —Add. After you type a, you can input text that starts to the right of the cursor.

✦ i —Insert. After you type i, you can input text that starts to the left of the cursor.

Type a few words and press Enter. Repeat that a few times until you have a few lines of text. When you are done typing, press Esc. You are now back in command mode. Remember the Esc key! It always places you back into command mode. Now that you have a file with some text in it, try moving around within that text with the following keys or letters:

✦ **Arrow keys** —Use the arrow keys to move up, down, left, or right in the file one character at a time. To move left and right you can also use Backspace and the spacebar, respectively. If you prefer to keep your fingers on the keyboard, use h (left), l (right), j (down), or k (up) to move the cursor.

✦ **w** —Moves the cursor to the beginning of the next word.

✦ **b** —Moves the cursor to the beginning of the previous word.

✦ **0** (zero) —Moves the cursor to the beginning of the current line.

✦ **$** —Moves the cursor to the end of the current line.

✦ **H** —Moves the cursor to the upper-left corner of the screen (first line on the screen).

✦ **M**—Moves the cursor to the first character of the middle line on the screen.

✦ **L**—Moves the cursor to the lower-left corner of the screen (last line on the screen).

Now that you know how to input text and move around in text, the only other editing you need to know is how to delete text. Here are a few vi commands for deleting text:

✦ **x**—Deletes the character under the cursor.

✦ **X**—Deletes the character directly before the cursor.

✦ **dw**—Deletes from the current character to the end of the current word.

✦ **d$**—Deletes from the current character to the end of the current line.

✦ **d0**—Deletes from the previous character to the beginning of the current line.

If you feel pretty good about creating text and moving around the file, you may want to wrap things up. Several keystrokes for saving and quitting the file follow:

✦ **ZZ**—Save the current changes to the file and exit from vi.

✦ **:w**—Save the current file but continue editing.

✦ **:wq**—Same as ZZ.

✦ **:q**—Quit the current file. This works only if you don't have any unsaved changes.

✦ **:q!**—Quit the current file and DON'T save the changes you just made to the file.

Tip   If you've really trashed the file by mistake, the :q! command is the best way to exit and abandon your changes. The file reverts to the most recently changed version. So, if you just did a :w, you are stuck with the changes up to that point. If you just want to undo a few bad edits, press u to back out of changes.

You have learned a handful of vi editing commands. I describe many, many more commands in the following sections. However, before I do, here are a few tips to smooth out your first trials with vi:

✦ **Esc**—Remember that Esc gets you back to command mode. (I've watched people press every key on the keyboard trying to get out of a file.) Esc followed by ZZ gets you out of command mode, saves the file, and exits.

✦ **u**—Press u to undo the previous change you made. Continue to press u to undo the change before that, and the one before that.

✦ **Ctrl-r**—If you decide you didn't want to undo the previous command, use Ctrl-r for Redo. Essentially, this command undoes your undo.

✦ **Caps Lock** — Beware of hitting the Caps Lock by mistake. Everything you type in vi has a different meaning when the letters are capitalized. You don't get a warning that you are typing capitals — things just start acting weird.

✦ **:! *command*** — You can run a command while you are in vi using :! followed by a command name. For example, type :!date to see the current date and time, type :!pwd to see what your current directory is, or type :!jobs to see if you have any jobs running in the background. When the command completes, press Enter and you are back to editing the file. You could even do that with a shell (:!bash) to run a few commands from the shell, then type exit to return to vi. (I recommend doing a save before escaping to the shell, just in case you forget to go back to vi.)

✦ **– INSERT –** — When you are in insert mode, the word INSERT appears at the bottom of the screen. Other messages also appear at the line at the bottom of the screen.

✦ **Ctrl+g** — If you forget what you are editing, pressing these keys prints the name of the file that you are editing and the current line that you are on. It also prints the total number of lines in the file, the percentage of how far you are through the file, and the column number the cursor is on. This just helps you get your bearings.

Moving around the file

Besides the few movement commands described earlier, there are other ways of moving around a vi file. To try these out, you may want to open a large file that you can't do much damage to. (How about copying /var/log/messages to /tmp?) Here are some possibilities:

✦ **Ctrl+f** — Page ahead, one page at a time.

✦ **Ctrl+b** — Page back, one page at a time.

✦ **Ctrl+d** — Page ahead 1/2 page at a time.

✦ **Ctrl+u** — Page back 1/2 page at a time.

✦ **G** — Go to the last line of the file.

✦ **1G** — Go to the first line of the file. (Instead of 1, you could use any number to go to that line number in the file.)

Searching for text

To search for the next occurrence of text in the file, use either the slash (/) or the question mark (?) character. Within the search, you can also use metacharacters. Here are some examples:

✦ /hello—Searches forward for the word hello.

✦ ?goodbye—Searches backwards for the word goodbye.

✦ /The*foot—Searches forward for a line that has the word The in it and also, after that at some point, the word foot.

✦ ?[pP]rint—Searches backward for either the word print or Print. Remember that case does matter in Linux, so using brackets is one way to search for words that could have different capitalization:

The vi editor was originally based on the ex editor. That editor did not let you work in full-screen mode. However, it did enable you to run commands that let you find and change text on one or more lines at a time. When you type a colon and the cursor goes to the bottom of the screen, you are essentially in ex mode. Here is an example of some of those ex commands for searching for and changing text. (I chose the words Local and Remote to search for, but you can use any appropriate words.)

✦ :g/Local—Searches for the word Local and prints every occurrence of that line from the file. (If there is more than a screen full, the output is piped to the more command.)

✦ :s/Local/Remote—Substitutes the word Remote for the word Local on the current line.

✦ :g/Local/s//Remote—Substitutes the first occurrence of the word Local on every line of the file with the word Remote.

✦ :g/Local/s//Remote/g—Substitutes every occurrence of the word Local with the word Remote in the entire file.

✦ :g/Local/s//Remote/gp—Substitutes every occurrence of the word Local with the word Remote in the entire file, then prints each line so that you can see the changes (piping it through more if output fills more than one page).

Using numbers with commands

You can precede most vi commands with numbers to have the command repeated that number of times. This is a handy way to deal with several lines, words, or characters at a time. Here are some examples:

✦ 3dw—Deletes the next three words.

✦ 5cl—Changes the next five letters (that is, removes the letters and goes into input mode).

✦ 12j—Moves down 12 lines.

Putting a number in front of most commands just repeats those commands. At this point, you should be fairly proficient at using the vi command.

Summary

Working from a shell command-line interpreter within Red Hat Linux may not be as simple as using a GUI, but it offers many powerful and flexible features. This chapter describes how to log in to Red Hat Linux and work with shell commands. Features for running commands include recalling commands from a history list, completing commands, and joining commands in various ways.

This chapter describes how shell environment variables can be used to store and recall important pieces of information. It also teaches you to modify shell configuration files to tailor the shell to suit your needs. Finally, the chapter describes how to use the Red Hat Linux file system to create files and directories, understand permissions, and work with files (moving, copying, and removing them).

✦　　✦　　✦

Working with the Desktop

Add a graphical user interface (*GUI*) to an otherwise unintuitive operating system, and it immediately becomes something anyone can use. Icons can represent programs and files. Clicking a mouse button can start applications. In keeping with other UNIX-like systems, Linux uses the *X Window System* (also referred to as X11 or just X) as the framework for its graphical desktop. On top of this framework, Red Hat Linux lets you choose either (or both) of two powerful desktop environments: GNOME and KDE.

This chapter describes how to get your X environment working, start up the desktop, and use the GNOME and KDE desktop environments. It also describes a variety of X features you can use to manipulate the desktop.

Configuring Your Desktop

If you installed Red Hat Linux as a desktop system and everything went smoothly, you should have configured your video card and chosen a desktop environment (GNOME or KDE). If so, you can skip ahead to the *Starting the X Desktop* section. If you were unable to configure your desktop or if you need to change it (for example, you may have added a video card or changed your monitor), this section is here for your reference.

If Red Hat Linux has been successfully installed (along with the desired desktop environment) but the GUI wasn't configured properly, you will only see a simple text-based login prompt when you start Red Hat Linux. This login prompt may look something like this:

```
Red Hat Linux release 7.2
Kernel 2.4 on an i686
YourComputer login:
```

Log in as the root user. Because there is no graphical desktop interface set up yet, you need to do some work from the shell command line. First, try the Xconfigurator command.

Running Xconfigurator

The Xconfigurator command can be used to set up the links and configuration files needed to run your graphical X desktop environment. It checks that the correct X server is installed and configures the /etc/X11/XF86Config file. The following is an example of an Xconfigurator session:

1. Type **Xconfigurator** from the shell prompt (as the root user). A welcome screen appears.

2. Highlight the Ok button (using tab and arrow keys) and press Enter. Xconfigurator probes for your video card. If it finds one, it displays the name of the card, the X server, and the Xfree4 driver.

3. Highlight Ok and press Enter to continue. A list of monitors appears.

4. Select the type of monitor you are using. You can use Page Up and Page Down to search through the list. Type a letter to go directly to a monitor name that begins with that letter. Highlight the correct monitor, highlight Ok, and press Enter. The next window asks you to identify your video memory.

> **Note**   If your monitor is not on the list, select Custom. To install a custom monitor, you need to determine the vertical refresh rate and the horizontal sync rate to properly configure your monitor. Check the manual that comes with your monitor for that information.

5. Select how much memory is on your video card, highlight OK, and press Enter. The next window asks you to identify your clock configuration.

6. Select No Clockchip Setting (unless you know that your card requires a special clockchip setting). Highlight Ok and press Enter. The next window displays video modes that are available to your video card.

7. Select the number of colors and video resolutions for each number of colors. A higher number of colors (8-bit, 16-bit, or 24-bit) allow better quality graphics, but can slow performance. Higher resolutions (800×600, 1024×768, or 1152×864) allow more space for windows, but everything is smaller. You can select several resolutions for each set of colors. Position the cursor over a selection and press the space bar to select it. Highlight Ok and press Enter to continue. The window warns you that it is about to test X.

8. Highlight Ok and press Enter. If X is working properly, you should see a pop-up window that asks if you can see it. If you don't see this window, it will timeout after a few seconds and return to your Xconfigurator. You'll need to try configuring the card again. If you do see the pop-up window, click the Yes button. You are asked if you want to start X at boot-time.

9. Click Yes (to have X start when you boot your computer) or No (to start from a text-based prompt and start X later manually). A pop-up window alerts you that the new configuration has been saved.

10. Click OK and you are done.

You should now be able to start your X environment. The next section describes the XF86Config file.

Note   If your GUI is still not working, go to `www.xfree86.org` and click the Driver Status Document link for your version of XFree86 (probably version 4.1). Find the manufacturer of your video card (or at least of the chip set in your video card) and select that link to find out if your card is supported or if a workaround is needed.

Understanding the XF86Config file

The XF86Config file (located in the `/etc/X11` directory) contains definitions used by the X server to use your video card, keyboard, mouse, and monitor. In general, novice users should not edit this file directly, but rather, use Xconfigurator to change its contents. For some video cards, however, there is a need for some manual configuration to get the card working properly.

The following is a description of the basic information contained in the XF86Config file:

✦ **Files section** — Sets the locations of the RGB (color) and fonts databases.

✦ **Server flags section** — Allows you to disable abort and mode switching key sequences (usually you will leave this section alone).

✦ **Keyboard section** — Sets keyboard settings, including the layout of the keyboard and how certain key sequences are mapped to the keyboard.

✦ **Pointer section** — Selects the pointer you are using (typically a mouse linked to `/dev/mouse`). Also sets speed and button emulation, when appropriate.

✦ **Monitor section** — Sets the type of monitor, along with its horizontal sync rate, vertical refresh rate, and settings needed to operate at different resolutions.

✦ **Screen section** — Binds together the graphics board and monitor information to be referenced later by the ServerLayout section.

✦ **Graphics device section** — Identifies your video card and, optionally, video RAM and clock information for the chipset.

✦ **ServerLayout section** — Sets server definitions for different X servers (if necessary).

For further information on the XF86Config file, see the XF86Config man pages (type **man XF86Config**).

Getting more information

If you tried configuring X and you still have a server that crashes or has a garbled display, your video card may either be unsupported or may require special configuration. Here are several locations you can check for further information:

✦ **XFree86.org** (www.xfree86.org) — The latest information about the X servers that come with Red Hat Linux is available from the XFree86.org Web site. XFree86 is the freeware version of X used with all major Linux distributions.

✦ **Red Hat Support** (www.redhat.com/support) — Search the Red Hat support database for the model of your card. There may already be reports of problems (and hopefully fixes) related to your card.

✦ **X documentation** — README files that are specific to different types of video cards are delivered with XFree86. Look in the XFree86 doc directory (/usr/X11R6/lib/X11/doc) for a README file specific to the type of video card (or more specifically, the video chip set) you are using.

Starting the X Desktop

There are several different ways you can start your desktop in Red Hat Linux. If Red Hat Linux starts up and you see a graphical login screen, you can just log in and your desktop environment should appear. If Red Hat Linux starts up to a simple text-based login prompt, you can have the desktop environment start after you log in (either manually or automatically). Each of these methods is described in this section.

Cross-Reference Procedures in this chapter assume that you have already configured your monitor and video driver. If this is not the case, see either Chapter 2 (to configure at installation time) or the *Configuring Your Desktop* section earlier in this chapter.

The X Window System GUI (or X GUI) can be started in several different ways, including:

✦ **At boot-time** — After your video card and monitor are properly configured, you may want to have the X GUI start automatically when Red Hat Linux is booted. You can do this by setting your system initialization state to 5. After you log in, you will see the GNOME or KDE desktop environments.

✦ **From the shell (or starting it yourself)** — If you have logged in to a shell interface, you can start the GUI at any time using the startx command. When you quit from the GUI, you will be back at your shell prompt.

✦ **At login time** — To start with a text-based login screen, but have the X GUI started after you log in, you can add the startx command to one of your personal startup files (such as $HOME/.bash_profile).

Each of these methods results in the startup of the X GUI and either the GNOME or KDE desktop environment. Along with the GNOME desktop environment, the sawfish window manager (or possibly some other window manager) starts up in order to provide the look-and-feel of the desktop.

Tip If your X screen ever gets garbled to the point where you don't know how to exit, or if you want to go to a command-line interface, you can do either by using control keys. From the X GUI, press Ctrl+Alt+F2. You will see a text login. After you log in, you can look for the X process (ps ax | less) and kill it (kill *pid*, where *pid* is the X process). Or you can return to the GUI by pressing Ctrl+Alt+F7. These extra screens, referred to as *virtual terminals*, can be accessed using any function keys from Ctrl+Alt+F2 to Ctrl+Alt+F7.

Starting the GUI at boot time

After Red Hat Linux boots up, a Red Hat logo and a GNOME (default) or KDE login window appears. You are ready to start using Red Hat Linux from an X Window GUI (probably GNOME and sawfish). Figure 4-1 shows an example of the login window that is used with GNOME:

Figure 4-1: Log in to start your desktop environment.

Type your login and password, as prompted, and your personal desktop is displayed.

It is possible to change several important options when you log in using the graphical login screen. In fact, you can even select a desktop environment other than the default. Here are menu options you can select:

✦ **Session** — From this menu item, you can select the desktop interface that is used with your login session. Besides GNOME, you can possibly choose Default, Failsafe, WindowMaker, or KDE as your interface (depending on which interfaces you have installed).

✦ **Language** — You can choose from more than a dozen languages to use during your desktop session (all languages are not completely supported).

✦ **System** — Instead of logging in, you can choose Reboot or Halt from the System selection to restart or halt Red Hat Linux.

The graphical login screen is started by the xdm command (which stands for X Display Manager). The xdm process manages both logging in and starting the GUI for your console monitor, as well as graphical logins from other computers and X terminals.

Normally, you start xdm by setting the system's default run state to 5. You can determine your system's default run state by checking the /etc/inittab file for an entry that looks similar to the following:

```
id:5:initdefault:
```

If the initdefault state is 3, the system boots to a text-based login prompt. At the bottom of that file, you will see that the xdm command is run in system state 5. (Instead of xdm, a GNOME version of xdm called prefdm or gem may run. Either command results in the same functions as xdm.)

Cross-Reference See Chapter 12 for information on Linux run states and startup processes.

When xdm starts up, it reads a series of configuration files that set up both the login screen and the desktop environment that appears. The identity of many configuration files is contained in the xdm-config file (usually in the /etc/X11/xdm directory). Here are some of the files identified in xdm-config that may interest you:

✦ **Error Log** (/var/log/xdm-error.log) — Contains error messages output from xdm. You can check this log if you have problems starting X.

✦ **Servers** (/etc/X11/xdm/Xservers) — Identifies the X server used for your display. If your computer has extra displays or X terminals that access it, you can add X server entries here.

✦ **Login Setup** (/etc/X11/xdm/Xsetup_0) — Identifies the client processes that are run on the console display login screen. These processes include the xsetroot command (to set the background color) and the xsri command (to display the Red Hat logo).

✦ **Session Setup** (/etc/X11/xdm/Xsession) — Defines how to start up your window manager session.

Note Settings that you put into any of the above files, such as the Xsession file, are likely to be overridden by settings that are specific to your desktop environment (GNOME or KDE). For example, I changed the background color of my desktop in the Xsession file to red (xsetroot -solid 'red'). When X started, the screen background flashed red; then GNOME took over and changed the background to blue.

Starting the GUI yourself

If you log in to a nongraphical interface, you can start yo
the startx command. The startx command is a shell sc...
figuration files, and starts the xinit command (which starts th
the startx command, simply type the following:

```
$ startx
```

Tip If startx fails with a message "Server is already active," it may be that a lock file
was not removed the last time X ran. Assuming you are using display 0 (which is
the default), type rm /tmp/.X0-lock.

If you don't create your own configuration files, startx will read several preset
configuration files instead. Just as with xdm, by default you will see the GNOME
desktop environment and the sawfish window manager, and possibly some clients
(such as the File Manager and a Help Browser).

To override the default behavior of startx, you need to create a $HOME/.xinitrc
file. Like the .xsession file described earlier, the .xinitrc file can start up some
client processes and run the window manager you choose. Here is an example of
the contents of a $HOME/.xinitrc file:

```
xeyes &
xterm &
xpmroot /usr/share/pixmaps/redhat/shadowman-64.xpm &
exec twm
```

In this example, the .xinitrc file tells startx to run the xeyes and xterm clients.
Then the xpmroot entry sets the background of the root window to lots of little
Red Hat icons. Finally, the file starts up the twm window manager. Because your
.xinitrc file overrides the system xinitrc file, you may want to add the following
lines to your .xinitrc file to read in systemwide and personal X resources
(.Xresources) and modifications to keyboard mappings (.Xmodmap):

```
xrdb -merge /usr/X11R6/lib/X11/xinit/.Xresources
xmodmap /usr/X11R6/lib/X11/xinit/.Xmodmap
xrdb -merge $HOME/.Xresources
xmodmap $HOME/.Xmodmap
```

By default, the .Xresources and .Xmodmap files don't exist in your home directory.
Information on how to create and use these files is contained later in this chapter.

When you exit your window manager, the X server is halted. You are then returned
to your login shell.

Starting the GUI at login time

If you want to be able to use the X GUI when other users on your system choose not to, set up your user account to start the GUI when you log in. You do this by adding a `startx` command to one of your personal startup files. One place you can add the `startx` command is to your `$HOME/.bash_profile` file (assuming you are using the bash shell as your login shell).

```
exec startx
```

The default window manager will start immediately after you log in. Then, when you exit the window manager later, you are logged out and returned to the login prompt.

Using the GNOME Desktop Environment

GNOME (pronounced guh-nome) provides the desktop environment that you get by default when you install Red Hat Linux. This desktop environment provides the software that is between your X Window System framework and the look-and-feel provided by the window manager. GNOME offers a stable and reliable desktop environment, with a few cool features built in.

GNOME is not a window manager, so it must be used with a window manager to provide such things as window borders and window controls. Currently, sawfish is the default window manager with GNOME. You can, however, use other window managers with GNOME, including:

+ Enlightenment
+ Window Maker
+ Twm

You can change to any of these window managers using the GNOME Window Manager window, which you can start from the GNOME menu by choosing Programs ⇨ Settings ⇨ Desktop ⇨ Window Manager. (How to configure GNOME is described later in this section.)

This section describes the GNOME desktop environment and ways of using it. If your Red Hat Linux system is configured to use a GUI by default, you simply need to log in from the graphical login screen. Otherwise, type **startx** from a shell prompt after you log in. In either case, you should see the GNOME desktop environment similar to that shown in Figure 4-2.

The GNOME desktop that appears the first time it is started by a new user account includes the GNOME panel, desktop area, desktop icons, and file manager. Descriptions of those elements follow.

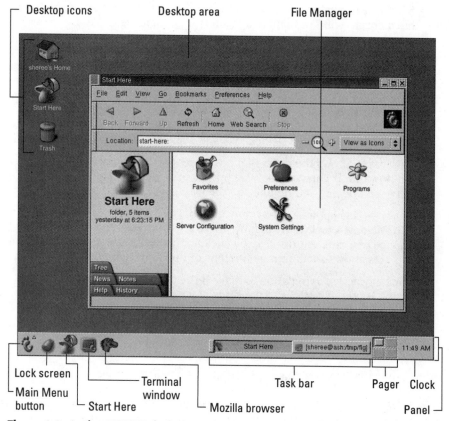

Figure 4-2: In the GNOME desktop environment, you can manage applications from the panel.

The panel contains most of the controls you need to use the desktop. When it first starts, the panel contains buttons for starting applications, a list of active applications, several applets, and a few controls. This is what you should see:

✦ **Main menu button** (footprint icon) — Click this button to see a list of menu items from which you can select. These menu items include selections for starting applications (such as the Run program window, Lock screen, and Log out selections) and submenus of selections.

The Programs menu (under the main menu) includes the following submenus: Applications, Utilities, Games, Graphics, Internet, Multimedia, Settings, and System. There is also a Help System selection from this menu.

✦ **Lock screen** (lock icon) — Lets you lock the screen so it can be reopened using your password only.

✦ **Start Here** (mushroom icon) — Opens a Start Here window, which is actually a file manager window displaying icons for configuring GNOME.

✦ **Terminal window** (terminal icon) — Opens a Terminal window, which provides access to a Red Hat Linux shell.

✦ **Mozilla browser** (red monster head logo) — Opens the Mozilla browser window. This software is for browsing the World Wide Web or for running related programs to use e-mail, to compose Web pages, or to view newsgroups. (Mozilla has recently replaced Netscape Navigator as the default browser for Red Hat Linux, though Netscape is still available from the GNOME menu.)

✦ **Taskbar** — Shows the tasks that are currently running on the desktop. The window that is currently active appears pressed in. Click a task to toggle between opening and minimizing the window.

✦ **Pager** — This applet shows a tiny view of the multiple desktop areas of your GNOME environment. By default, there are four desktops available. You can change to a different desktop by clicking the area in the pager. Each minidesktop area shows small representations of the active windows within that desk.

Click any active application to make it the current application. A sticky application is one that sticks to the same place on the screen, regardless of which desktop you move to. People stick things such as clocks or e-mail notification windows.

✦ **Clock** — This applet shows the current date and time.

Other useful GNOME controls are located in the following places:

✦ **Desktop Area** — This is the screen area on which you can use the windows, icons, and menus that make up the GNOME desktop. Right-click the desktop area to see a menu of options.

✦ **File Manager** — This window contains a graphical means of moving up and down your Red Hat Linux file system, opening files, and running applications. It supports expected features for creating, opening, copying, deleting, and moving files and folders. However, it also has some special features, such as drag-and-drop, launching applications based on MIME type, and file finding. The File Manager is called Nautilus. Nautilus is now the default file manager for Red Hat Linux 7.2.

✦ **Desktop icons** — Icons on the desktop each represent a directory, application, or file that you can work with. You can double-click a desktop icon to open it, drag-and-drop it to move it to another location, or right-click it to see a menu of options related to the icon. The icons added to your Red Hat Linux GNOME desktop include one that opens a File Manager to your home directory, one that opens the Start Here window, and a Trash icon for deleting files.

The GNOME desktop is quite intuitive. However, you may want to read some of the following descriptions of GNOME if you are a novice user or if you want to learn some of the less obvious features of the GNOME desktop.

Using the GNOME panel

The GNOME panel is intended to be the place from which you manage your desktop. From this panel you can start applications (from buttons or menus), see what programs are active, and monitor how your system is running. There are also many ways to change the panel, such as by adding applications or monitors, or changing the placement or behavior of the panel.

Click the GNOME menu, then select the Panel menu. From this menu, you can perform a variety of functions, including:

✦ **Add to panel** — You can add an applet, menu, launcher, drawer, button (logout, lock, or run), a swallowed application, or a status dock.

✦ **Create panel** — You can create additional panels for your desktops in different styles.

✦ **Remove this panel** — You can delete the current panel.

Procedures for each of these functions are described in the following sections. For information on changing properties of the panel itself, see the section on changing GNOME preferences.

Adding an applet

There are several small GNOME applications, called applets, that you can run directly on the GNOME panel. These applets can show information you may want to see on an ongoing basis or may just provide some amusement. To see what applets are available and to add applets that you want to your panel, perform the following steps:

1. Click the GNOME menu button on the panel (the paw print icon), then select Panel ⇨ Add to panel ⇨ Applet.

2. Select an applet from one of the following categories:

   • **Amusements** — Includes a puzzle game (Fifteen), eyes that follow your mouse around, and a few other amusements.

   • **Monitors** — Includes useful tools for monitoring CPU/Memory usage, CPU load, disk usage, load average, memory load, network load, and swap load.

   • **Multimedia** — Includes applets for playing CDs or MP3 audio files or using an audio mixer.

   • **Network** — Includes applets for checking for AOL instant messaging (GAIM), checking incoming mail, displaying stock prices or headlines, showing modem incoming and outgoing traffic, dialing a PPP connection, or opening a Web site (HTML page).

- **Utility** — Includes applets for monitoring battery levels, mounting floppy drives, managing print queues, and performing other useful tasks.
- **Clock** — Runs a clock applets.

3. Select the applet to add from the category you selected. The applet appears on the panel, ready for you to use.

After an applet is installed, right-click it to see what options are available. If you don't like its location, right-click it, click Move applet, slide the mouse until the applet is where you want it, then click again to set its location.

If you no longer want an applet to appear on the panel, right-click it, and then click Remove from panel. The icon representing the applet will disappear. If you find that you have run out of room on your panel, you can add a new panel to another part of the screen, as described in the next section.

Adding another panel

You can have several panels on your GNOME desktop. You can either add edge panels (that run along the entire bottom, top, or side of the screen) or a corner panel (that only expands as needed to show the applets it contains). To add a panel, do the following:

1. Click the GNOME menu button on the panel (the paw print icon), then select Panel ➪ Create panel.

2. Select from the following menu items:

- **Menu panel** — Places a menu bar across the top of the screen.
- **Edge panel** — Creates a panel along the edge of the screen (top, sides, or bottom).
- **Aligned panel** — Adds a panel that stretches out only as far as is required to display the applets it contains.
- **Sliding panel** — Creates a panel that stretches out only as far as required to display the applets it contains. When you hide/unhide the panel, it closes in the middle of the display instead of just at the edges.
- **Floating panel** — Adds a panel that begins from the middle of the edge of a display (instead of from a corner).

After you've added a panel, you can add applets or application launchers to it as you did to the default panel. You can change an edge panel to a corner panel (or vice versa), by right-clicking the edge panel, and then selecting Panel ➪ Properties ➪ Type ➪ and selecting the type of panel that you want. To remove a panel, right-click it and select Panel ➪ Remove this panel.

Adding an application launcher

Icons on your panel that show the terminal and the Mozilla logo are used to launch Terminal and Netscape Communicator applications, respectively. You can add your own icons to launch applications from the panel.

Icons that are available to use to represent your application are contained in the /usr/share/pixmaps directory. These icons are either in png or xpm formats. If there isn't an icon in that directory that you want to use, create your own and assign it to the application. To add a new application launcher to the panel, do the following:

1. Right-click the panel.

2. Select Panel ➪ Add to panel ➪ Launcher. The Create launcher applet window appears.

3. Provide the following information for the application that you want to add:

   - **Name** — A name to identify the application.

   - **Comment** — A comment describing the application. This information appears when you later move your mouse over the launcher.

   - **Command** — The command line that is run when the application is launched. You should use the full path name, plus any required options.

   - **Type** — Select either Application (if you are launching an application), URL (to open a Web address in a browser) or Directory (if you are opening a directory in a File Manager window).

   - **Run in Terminal** — If it is a character-based or ncurses application. (Applications written using the curses library run in a Terminal window but offer screen-oriented mouse and keyboard controls.)

4. Click the Icon box (it may say No Icon). Select one of the icons shown and click OK. Alternatively, you can browse the Red Hat Linux file system to choose an icon. (Icons should be in png or xpm graphics formats.)

5. Click OK.

The application should now appear in the panel. Click it to start the application.

Adding a drawer

By adding a drawer to your GNOME panel, you can add several applets and launchers and have them take up only one slot on your panel. You can use the drawer to show the applets and launchers as though they were being pulled out of a drawer icon on the panel.

To add a drawer to your panel, right-click the panel and then select Panel ➪ Add to panel ➪ Drawer. The drawer should appear on the panel. The drawer behaves just like a panel. Right-click the drawer area, and add applets or launchers to it as you would to a panel. Click the drawer icon to retract the drawer.

Changing panel properties

There are both global and specific panel properties that you may want to consider changing. To change global panel preferences, open the GNOME menu and choose Panel ➪ Global Preferences. The Panel window appears.

Five tabs are used to change the behavior of your GNOME panels. The Animation tab enables you to change animation speeds that affect how windows and icons are moved and minimized. The Buttons tab lets you set tiles used for the backgrounds of Launcher, Drawer, Menu, and Special buttons. The Panel Objects tab is used to set how applets change positions on the panel when you move them. The Menu tab sets the positions of different global menu items on the GNOME menu. The Miscellaneous tab enables you to assign properties that are used with tool tips and various other miscellaneous options.

To open the Panel properties window that applies to a specific panel, open the GNOME menu on that panel. Then choose Panel ➪ Properties ➪ All Properties. The Panel properties window that appears enables you to change the following values:

✦ **Type**—You can see whether the panel is an Edge, Aligned, Sliding, or Floating panel.

✦ **Hiding policy**—You can select whether or not a panel is explicitly hidden (by clicking the hide/unhide buttons) or automatically hidden (appearing only when the mouse pointer is in the area).

✦ **Hide buttons**—You can choose whether or not the Hide/Unhide buttons (with pixmap arrows on them) appear on the edges of the panel.

✦ **Size and position**—You can select the size of your panel, from Ultra Tiny (12 pixels) to Ridiculous (128 pixels).

✦ **Background**—You can assign a color to the background of the panel, assign a pixmap image, or just leave the standard background (sort of gray). Click the Background tab, and then select the pixmap (from the /usr/share/pixmaps or other directory) or color to assign to the panel.

Tip   I usually turn on the AutoHide feature and turn off the Hide buttons. Using AutoHide gives you more space to work with on your desktop. When you move your mouse to the edge where the panel is, it pops up—obviating any need for the Hide buttons.

Using the Nautilus file manager

At one time, file managers did little more than let you run applications, create data files, and open folders. These days, as the information a user needs expands beyond the local system, file managers are expected to also display Web pages, access FTP sites, and play multimedia content. The Nautilus file manager, which is the default GNOME file manager, is an example of just such a file manager.

When you open the Nautilus file manager window (from the GNOME main menu or by launching a directory), you will see a sidebar in the left column and the files and directories contained in the current directory in the right column. Figure 4-3 is an example of the File manager window displaying the home directory of a user named jake (/home/jake).

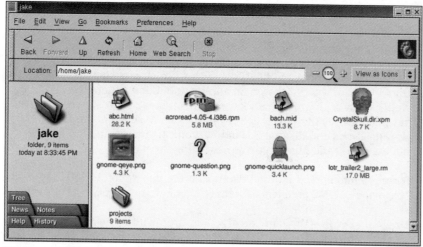

Figure 4-3: Move around the file system, open directories, launch applications, and browse the Web from Nautilus.

Icons on the toolbar of the Nautilus window let you move forward and back among the directories and Web sites you visit. To move up the directory structure, click the Up arrow. To refresh the view of the folder or Web page, click the Refresh button. The Home button takes you to your home page and the Web search button lets you search the Web.

Many data files are represented by icons that indicate the type of data they contain. The contents or file extension of each file can determine which application is used to work with the file. Or, you can right-click an icon to open the file it represents with a particular application or viewer.

Some of the more interesting features of Nautilus are described below:

✦ **Sidebar**—The left column of the screen consists of a sidebar. From the sidebar, you can click on tabs that represent different types of information you can select. The Tree tab shows a tree view of the directory structure, so you can easily traverse your directories. The News tab lets you select from a variety of news sites and has headlines displayed from those sites.

The Notes tab lets you add notes that become associated with the current Directory or Web page. The Help tab opens links to the GNOME Help system. The History tab displays a history of directories and Web sites you have visited, allowing you to click those items to return to the sites they represent.

✦ **Web browsing**—By typing a Web address (URL) in the Location box on the Nautilus window or by clicking on a link, Nautilus acts as a Web browser by displaying the requested content. Select Web search to have your favorite search engine displayed to search for Web sites (www.google.com is used by default).

✦ **MIME types and file types**—To handle different types of content that may be encountered in the Nautilus window, you can set applications to respond based on MIME type and file type. With a directory being displayed, click a file for which you want to assign an application. Click either Open With an Application or Open With a Viewer. If no application or viewer has been assigned for the file type, click OK to be able to select an application. From the File Types and Programs window, you can add an application based on the file extension and MIME type representing the file.

For more information in MIME types, see the description of MIME types in the "Changing GNOME preferences" section later in this chapter.

✦ **Drag-and-Drop**—You can use drag-and-drop within the Nautilus window, between the Nautilus and the desktop, or between multiple Nautilus windows. As other GNOME-compliant applications become available, they are expected to also support the GNOME drag-and-drop feature.

If you need more information on the Nautilus file manager, visit the Eazel Web site at http://nautilus.eazel.com. Eventually, support for Nautilus will move to the GNOME Web site (www.gnome.org/nautilus).

Changing GNOME preferences

There are many ways to change the behavior, look, and feel of your GNOME desktop. Some of these relate directly to GNOME, whereas others must be changed for the window manager (in this case, sawfish). Most GNOME preferences can be modified in the Control Center window. You can open that window from a Terminal window as follows:

```
# gnomecc &
```

The Control Center window contains categories for changing preferences related to the Desktop, Document Handlers (editors, MIME types, and URLs), the current window manager, and other features. The following sections describe the preferences that you can change.

Changing the desktop

From the Control Center window, you can change the Background, Launch Feedback, Panel, Screensaver, Theme Selector, or Window Manager for your GNOME desktop. After you open the Control Center window, select one of those categories. Here are the preferences that you can change from each:

✦ **Background** — From the Background preferences, you can choose a single solid color, a two-color gradient (shading from top to bottom or left to right), or a pixmap image to use as wallpaper. If you choose a single solid color, click the color box under Primary Color, choose a color from the palette, and select OK. To have the color fade into another color, click Vertical or Horizontal Gradient, and then select the second color. Choosing Vertical has the colors transform from top to bottom, while Horizontal causes the colors to change from left to right.

To use wallpaper for your background, click Browse. You can choose from a variety of images in the /usr/share/nautilus directory. Then, choose to have the image tiled, centered, scaled (in proportion), or scaled (using any proportion to fill the screen).

✦ **Launch Feedback** — From the Launch Feedback preferences, you can indicate the kind of behavior the GNOME exhibits while an application is being launched. While an application is being launched from the desktop, you can enable feedback in a tasklist, have an hourglass appear for the mouse cursor, have a splash screen displayed while the application launches, or have an animated star displayed.

✦ **Panel** — From the Panel section, you can change global behavior of the panels on your desktop. These selections are described earlier in the Using the GNOME Panel section.

✦ **Screensaver** — You can choose dozens of screensavers from the Screen Saver preferences window. Select Random Screensaver to have your screen saver chosen randomly, or select one that you like from the list. Next, choose how long your screen must be idle before the screen saver starts (default is 20 minutes). You can also choose to require a password or to enable power management to shut down your monitor after a set number of minutes.

✦ **Theme Selector** — You can choose to have an entire theme of elements be used on your desktop. A desktop theme affects not only the background, but also the way that many buttons and menu selections appear. There are about a dozen themes available with the Red Hat Linux distribution. See the sidebar "Finding Desktop Themes" for information on how to get additional desktop themes.

Finding Desktop Themes

New desktop themes for GNOME/Sawfish are available from the `sawfish.themes.org` Web site. To select and download a Sawfish desktop theme, do the following:

1. Make sure that the Sawfish themes directory is available for downloading the themes. You can use either of the following two directories: `/usr/share/sawfish/themes` or `$HOME/.sawfish/themes`.

   Use the first directory if you want any user on your Red Hat Linux system to be able to use the theme. Use the second directory if you want the theme available only for your own use.

2. Go to the following Web site: `http://sawfish.themes.org`.

   (To search for themes other than the ones listed on the main Sawfish themes page, go to the Sawfish themes search page. Click the Themes link from the main page or go directly to `sawfish.themes.org/themes.phtml`.)

3. Click any theme that looks interesting from those available at `sawfish.themes.org`. You can select from a list of themes that were most downloaded today and those that have been downloaded most over time. You can also choose themes that have recently been added.

4. On the page that appears describing the theme, select the Download link. You will be prompted again to download the theme.

5. Click Download. You are asked to select a location to which to download the file.

6. Type the path to either of the Sawfish themes directories noted in Step 1. The theme file is downloaded to that directory. (You can close the browser for the moment.)

7. Go to the Sawfish themes directory and unzip the file. For example, to unzip a theme called `Whatever.tar.gz`, you would type the following from a Terminal window: `cd /usr/share/sawfish/themes` and then `tar xvfz Whatever.tar.gz`.

At this point, the desktop theme is ready to be used.

✦ **Window Manager** — The list of available window managers appears when you select Window Manager from the Control Center. Currently, sawfish is the default window manager with GNOME. If you want to try other window managers, however, here are a few that are compatible with GNOME:

- Enlightenment
- Twm
- Window Maker

To change window manager properties for Sawfish, click Sawfish and select Run Configuration Tool for Sawfish. You can change dozens of window manager features from the window that appears.

Selecting a default editor

If GNOME needs to open a file in a text editor, by default it will use the emacs editor. If you want to change that, you can do so using the GNOME Default selection under Document Handlers from the Control Center. To make the change, click the down arrow under GNOME editor. Then select from among more than a dozen different text editors.

Note Although several of the text editors available are mentioned in this book, the vi editor is the only one that is described in a full tutorial. A graphical editor, such as gEdit, may be easier for you if you are not used to nongraphical text editors.

Configuring MIME types

By assigning MIME types and file extensions to particular types of data files, you can assign how those types of data are handled when the file is opened from GNOME (such as in the File Manager window). This can be a very powerful feature. It enables you to identify which application is started to handle a file that you open.

Click the File Types and Programs selection from the Control Center. You will see a list of MIME Types and file extensions. You can change which application is used to open a particular file type by clicking the MIME type/extension that represents it and selecting Edit. For example, the PostScript file type (eps and ps extensions) is handled by the GhostView application (gv).

To add your own MIME type and file extension, click Add and fill in the MIME type and extension. You can also add regular expressions (strings of text and optional wildcards) to identify the files you want to match. After you have added that information, click OK. Then, with the entry still selected, click Edit to add actions that are taken for the MIME type/file extension.

Exiting GNOME

When you are done with your work, you can either log out from your current session or shut down your computer completely. To exit from GNOME, do the following:

1. Open the GNOME main menu.

2. Select Log out from the Main menu. A pop-up window should appear, asking if you want to Logout, Halt, or Reboot.

Tip At this point, you can also select to save your session by clicking Save current setup. This is a great way to have the applications that you use all the time restart the next time you log in. Make sure you save your data before you exit, however. Most applications do not yet support the data-saving feature.

3. Select Logout from the pop-up menu. This will log you out and return you to either the graphical login screen or to your shell login prompt. If, instead, you select Halt, the system is shut down; if you select Reboot, the system is restarted.

Note   You will need the root password if you want to either halt or reboot your Red Hat Linux system.

4. Select Yes to finish exiting from GNOME.

If you are unable to get to the Log out button (if, for example, your Pager was deleted by mistake), there are two other exit methods. Try one of these two ways, depending on how you started the desktop:

✦ If you started the desktop by typing `startx` from your login shell, press Ctrl+Alt+F1 to return to your login shell. Then type `Ctrl+c` to kill the desktop.

✦ If you started the desktop from a graphical login screen, first open a Terminal window (right-click the desktop and then select New ➪ Terminal). In the Terminal window, type `ps x | more` to see a list of running processes. Look for a command name gnome-session and determine its number under the PID column. Then type `kill PID`, where `PID` is replaced by the PID number.

Although these are not the most graceful ways to exit the desktop, they work. You should be able to log in again and restart the desktop.

Using the KDE Desktop Environment

The KDE desktop was developed to provide an interface to Linux and other UNIX systems that could compete with MacOS or Microsoft Windows operating systems for ease of use. Integrated within KDE are tools for managing files, windows, multiple desktops, and applications. If you can work a mouse, you can learn to navigate the KDE desktop.

The lack of an integrated, standardized desktop environment in the past has held back Linux and other UNIX systems from acceptance on the desktop. While individual applications could run well, you rarely could drag-and-drop files or other items between applications. Likewise, you couldn't open a file and expect it to launch the correct application to deal with it. KDE provides a platform for developers who want to create applications that can easily share information and detect how to deal with different types of data.

The following section describes how to get started with KDE. This includes using the KDE Setup wizard, maneuvering around the desktop, managing files, windows, virtual desktops, and adding application launchers.

Starting with KDE

You can select the KDE desktop from the login screen (provided that both GNOME and KDE are installed). Choose Session ➪ KDE. Then, type your login name and password, as prompted. The KDE desktop should appear, as shown in Figure 4-4.

Note

If you are currently using GNOME and want to switch to KDE as your desktop environment, type `switchdesk` from your GNOME desktop. The switchdesk window that appears will let you change to KDE as the default desktop environment. If by chance the GUI is still GNOME when you log in again, try restarting X as root user by typing the following command line: `init 3 ; init 5`

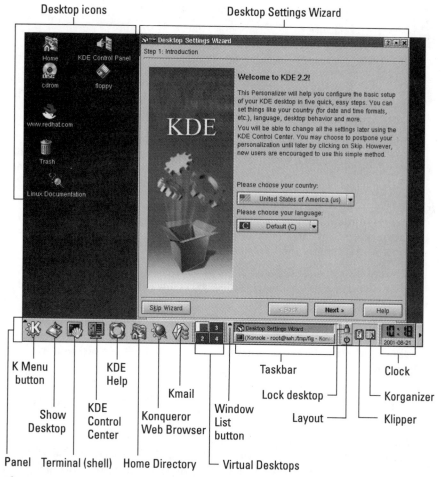

Figure 4-4: Manage files and applications graphically with the KDE desktop.

KDE desktop described

When you start the KDE desktop for the first time, you will probably see the Desktop Settings Wizard window, some icons on the desktop, and the panel (bottom). Here are some quick descriptions of what you can expect to find on the desktop:

✦ **Desktop Settings Wizard** — This window appears when you first log in to KDE. It allows you to configure your desktop to your liking. I recommend you step through this window to configure your desktop initially. The window lets you:

- Choose your country and language.

- Set the system behavior to be in the style of KDE, other UNIX systems, Microsoft Windows, or Apple MacOS. Select each one to see how features would be set before choosing which one to use.

- Turn on more or fewer special effects. More effects may look nicer, but be harmful to system performance. If you have a slow processor, you probably want fewer special effects.

- Choose a theme to use for your desktop. The theme effects the look of your screen, panel, and icons, as well as the location of some controls.

- Change the content that is added to the KDE panel.

✦ **Desktop icons** — The desktop starts with several icons on it to provide quick access to selected features. By default, you will probably have icons that give you access to your Home directory, CD-ROM, and floppy disk drive. There will also be icons representing the KDE Control Panel, the Red Hat Web site, the Trash can, and Linux Documentation.

✦ **Panel** — Provides some quick tools for launching applications and managing the desktop. You can adapt the panel to your needs by resizing it, adding tools, and changing the look and feel.

✦ **K Menu button** — This panel button has the letter *K* on it. Click this button to see a menu of applications, utilities, and configuration tools that are available to run on your KDE desktop.

✦ **Show Desktop** — This button toggles on and off the elements on your desktop, so you can see the full desktop background. This makes it easier to see your menus and icons, so you can easily start a new application when your desktop is cluttered.

✦ **Terminal (shell)** — This button resembles a computer terminal with a shell in front of it. Click this button to open a Terminal window. The Terminal window provides a way for you to enter commands at a shell prompt.

✦ **KDE Control Center** — This button looks like a computer screen, with half of the screen covered by a remote control box. Click it to open the KDE Control Center window. This window is your primary tool for configuring your KDE desktop. (This interface is described in detail a little later.)

✦ **KDE Help** — This button is an image of a lifesaver. Click it to open the KDE Help window. From this window, you can browse lists of KDE applications, Linux man page listings, or info command contents. You can also do a keyword search to find keywords in the different online documents that are available.

✦ **Home Directory** — This panel button looks like a house in front of a file folder. Click this button to open your home folder in a file manager window.

✦ **Konqueror Web Browser** — This panel button looks like a globe with pointy things on it. Click it to open the Konqueror Web Browser. Konqueror can be used to traverse your computer's file system as well as the Web.

✦ **Kmail** — This panel button is the image of an E with a letter resting on it. Click it to open the Kmail window for sending, receiving, and managing your e-mail.

✦ **Virtual Desktops** — There are four virtual desktops available to you, by default. These are labeled 1, 2, 3, and 4. You begin your KDE session on virtual desktop 1. You can change to any of the four desktops by clicking it.

✦ **Window List button** — This is a slender button with an up-arrow on it. Click it to see a list of virtual desktops and open windows on your desktop. Click an entry to go right to the virtual desktop or window you select.

✦ **Taskbar** — Shows the tasks that are currently running on the desktop. The window that is currently active appears pressed in. Click a task to toggle between opening and minimizing the window.

✦ **Lock Desktop** — This button looks like a small lock. Click it to lock your desktop from access. You need to enter your user password to access the desktop again.

✦ **Logout** — Click this button to end your KDE session. A window asks if you want to save the current state of your desktop to return to the next time you log in to KDE.

✦ **Klipper** — This button looks like a clipboard. Click it to see a list of contents on your desktop's clipboard.

✦ **Korganizer** — This button contains an image of a calendar. Click it to open the Korganizer window. Korganizer is an online calendar and to-do list.

✦ **Clock** — The current time and date are shown in the far right side of the panel. Click it to see a calendar of the current month. Click arrow keys on the calendar to step forward and back to other months.

Getting around the desktop

Navigating the desktop is done with your mouse and keyboard. You can use a two-button or three-button mouse. Using the keyboard to navigate requires using different Alt and Ctrl key sequences.

Using the mouse

The responses from the desktop to your mouse depend on which button you press and where the mouse pointer is located. Table 4-1 shows the results of clicking each mouse button with the mouse pointer placed in different locations:

<table>
<tr><th colspan="3">Table 4-1
Mouse Actions</th></tr>
<tr><th>*Pointer Position*</th><th>*Mouse Button*</th><th>*Results*</th></tr>
<tr><td>Window title bar or frame (current window active)</td><td>Left</td><td>Raise current window.</td></tr>
<tr><td>Window title bar or frame (current window active)</td><td>Middle</td><td>Lower current window.</td></tr>
<tr><td>Window title bar or frame (current window active)</td><td>Right</td><td>Open operations menu.</td></tr>
<tr><td>Window title bar or frame (current window not active)</td><td>Left</td><td>Activate current window and raise it to the top.</td></tr>
<tr><td>Window title bar or frame (current window not active)</td><td>Middle</td><td>Activate current window and lower it.</td></tr>
<tr><td>Window title bar or frame (current window not active)</td><td>Right</td><td>Activate current window without changing position.</td></tr>
<tr><td>Inner window (current window not active)</td><td>Left</td><td>Activate current window, raise it to the top, and pass the click to the window.</td></tr>
<tr><td>Inner window (current window not active)</td><td>Middle</td><td>Activate current window and pass the click to the window.</td></tr>
<tr><td>Inner window (current window not active)</td><td>Right</td><td>Activate current window and pass the click to the window.</td></tr>
<tr><td>Any part of a window</td><td>Left (plus hold Alt key)</td><td>Move the window to a new location.</td></tr>
<tr><td>Any part of a window</td><td>Middle (plus hold Alt key)</td><td>Toggle between raising and lowering the window.</td></tr>
<tr><td>Any part of a window</td><td>Right (plus hold Alt key)</td><td>Resize the window.</td></tr>
<tr><td>On the desktop area</td><td>Left (hold and drag)</td><td>Select a group of icons.</td></tr>
<tr><td>On the desktop area</td><td>Right</td><td>Open system pop-up menu.</td></tr>
</table>

The mouse actions in the table are all single-click actions. Use single-click with the left mouse button to open an icon on the desktop. On a window title bar, double-clicking results in a window-shade action, where the window scrolls up and down into the title bar.

Using keystrokes

If you don't happen to have a mouse or you just like to keep your hands on the keyboard, there are several keystroke sequences you can use to navigate the desktop. Here are some examples:

✦ **Step through desktops** (Ctrl+Tab) — To go from one virtual desktop to the next, hold down the Ctrl key and press the Tab key until you see the desktop that you want to make current. Then release the Ctrl key to select that desktop.

✦ **Step through windows** (Alt+Tab) — To step through each of the windows that are running on the current desktop, hold down the Alt key and press the Tab key until you see the one you want. Then release the Alt key to select it.

✦ **Open Run Command box** (Alt+F2) — To open a box on the desktop that lets you type in a command and run it, hold the Alt key and press F2. Next, type the command in the box and press Enter to run it. You can also type a URL into this box to view a Web page.

✦ **Close the current window** (Alt+F4) — To close the current window, press Alt+F4.

✦ **Close another window** (Ctrl+Alt+Esc) — To close an open window on the desktop, press Ctrl+Alt+Esc. When a skull and cross bones appears as the pointer, move the pointer over the window you want to close and click the left mouse button. (This is a good technique for killing a window that has no borders or menu.)

✦ **Switch virtual desktops** (Ctrl+F1, F2, F3 or F4 key) — To step through virtual desktops, press and hold the Ctrl key and press F1, F2, F3, or F4 to go directly to desktop one, two, three or four, respectively. You could do this for up to eight desktops, if you have that many configured.

✦ **Open window operation menu** (Alt+F3) — To open the operations menu for the active window, press Alt+F3. When the menu appears, move the arrow keys to select an action (Move, Size, Minimize, Maximize, etc.), then press Enter to select it.

Managing files with the Konqueror File Manager

The Konqueror File Manager helps elevate the KDE environment from just another X window manager to an integrated desktop that can compete with GUIs from Apple Computing or Microsoft. The features in Konqueror rival those that are offered by those user-friendly desktop systems. Figure 4-5 shows an example of the Konqueror File Manager window.

Figure 4-5: Konqueror provides a network-ready tool for managing files.

Some of Konqueror's greatest strengths over earlier file managers are the following:

✦ **Network desktop** — If your computer is connected to the Internet or a LAN, features built into Konqueror let you create links to files (using FTP) and Web pages (using HTTP) on the network and open them within the Konqueror window. Those links can appear as file icons in a Konqueror window or on the desktop. When a link is opened (single-click), the contents of the FTP site or Web page appears right in the Konqueror window.

✦ **Web browser interface** — The Konqueror interface works like Netscape Navigator, Mozilla, Internet Explorer, or another Web browser in the way you select files, directories, and Web content. A single-click opens a file, link to a network resource, or application program. You can also open content by typing Web-style addresses in a Location box.

Tip

Web pages that contain Java content will not run by default in Konqueror. To turn on Java support, choose Settings ➪ Configure Konqueror. From the Settings window, click Konqueror Browser and select the Java tab. To enable Java, click the Enable Java Globally box and click Apply.

✦ **File types and MIME types** — If you want a particular type of file to always be launched by a particular application, you can configure that file yourself. KDE already has dozens of MIME types defined that can automatically detect particular file and data types and start the right application. There are MIME types defined for audio, image, text, video, and a variety of other content types.

Of course, you can also perform many standard file manager functions with Konqueror. For manipulating files, you can use features like Select, Move, Cut,

Paste, and Delete. You can search directories for files, create new items (files, folders, and links, to name a few), view histories of the files and Web sites you have opened, and create bookmarks.

Working with files

Because most of the ways of working with files in Konqueror are quite intuitive (by intention), I'll just give a quick rundown of how to do basic file manipulation:

✦ **Open a file** — Single-click the left mouse button on a file. The file will open in the default application set for the file type. For example, a plain-text file will open in the Text Editor (kedit). You can also open a directory (to make it the current directory), application (to start the application), or link (to open the target of a link) in this way.

✦ **Choose an application** — Single-click the right mouse button. When you right-click a data file, select the Open With menu. The menu that appears shows which applications are set up to open the file.

✦ **Delete a file** — Single-click the right mouse button ⇨ Delete. You are asked if you really want to delete the file. Click Yes to permanently delete it.

✦ **Copy a file** — Single-click the right mouse button ⇨ Copy. This copies the file to your clipboard. After that, you can paste it to another folder. (See the "Move a file" bullet for a drag-and-drop method of copying.)

✦ **Paste a file** — Single-click the right mouse button (on an open area of a folder) ⇨ Paste. A copy of the file you copied previously is pasted in the current folder.

✦ **Move a file** — With the original folder and target folder both open on the desktop, press and hold the right mouse button on the file you want to move, drag the file to an open area of the new folder, and release the mouse button. From the menu that appears, click Move. (You could also copy or create a link to the file using this menu.)

✦ **Link a file** — Drag-and-drop a file from one folder to another (as described in "Move a file"). When the menu appears, click Link Here. (A linked file lets you access a file from a new location without having to make a copy of the original file. When you open the link, a pointer to the original file causes it to open.)

There are also several features for viewing information about the files and folders in your Konqueror windows:

✦ **View quick file information** — Position the mouse pointer over the file. When a mouse pointer is over a file in a Konqueror window, information appears in the window footer. This includes the file name, file size, and file type.

✦ **View hidden files** — Select View ⇨ Show Hidden Files. This allows you to see files that begin with a dot (.). Dot files tend to be used for configuration and don't generally need to be viewed in your daily work.

✦ **View file system tree** — Select View ➪ View Mode ➪ Tree View. This presents a tree view of your folder, displaying folders above the current folder in the file system. You can click a folder in the tree view to jump directly to that folder. There are also Multicolumn, Detailed List and Text views available.

✦ **Change icon view** — Select View ➪ Icon Size, and then choose Large, Medium, or Small to select the size of the icons that are displayed on the window. You can also choose Default Size, to return to the default icon size.

To act on a group of files at the same time, there are a couple of actions you can take. Choose Edit ➪ Select. A pop-up window lets you match all (*) or any group of documents indicated by typing letters, numbers, and wildcard characters. Or, to select a group of files, left-click in an open area of the folder and drag the pointer across the files you want to select. All files within the box will be highlighted. When files are highlighted, you can move, copy, or delete the files as described earlier.

Searching for files

If you are looking for a particular file or folder, you can use the Konqueror Find feature. To open a Find window to search for a file, choose Tools ➪ Find File. (You could also start the kfind window by typing kfind from a Terminal window.) Figure 4-6 shows the kfind window.

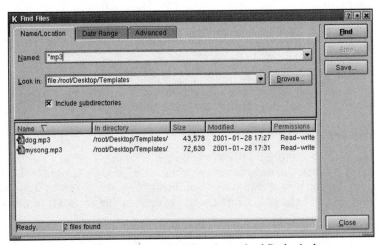

Figure 4-6: Search for files and folders from the kfind window.

Simply type the name of the file you want to search for (in the Named box) and the folder, including all subfolders, you want to search in (in the Look in box). Then click the Find button. Use metacharacters, if you like, with your search. For example, search for *.rpm to find all files that end in .rpm or z*.doc to find all files that begin with z and end with .doc. You can also select to have the search be case-sensitive or click the Help button to get more information on searching.

To further limit your search, you can click the Date Range tab, then enter a date range (between), a number of months before today (during the previous x months), or the number of days before today (during the previous x days). Select the Advanced tab to choose to limit the search to files of a particular type (of Type), files that include text that you enter (Containing Text), or that are of a certain size (Size is) in kilobytes.

Creating new files and folders

You can create a variety of file types when using the Konqueror window. Choose Edit ➪ Create New, and select one of the following types:

✦ **Illustration Document** — Opens a box that lets you create a document in kontour format (an illustration). Type the document name you want to create and click OK. The document should have a .kil suffix if you want it to automatically open in kontour.

✦ **Presentation Document** — Opens a box that lets you create a document in kpresenter format (a presentation). Type the document name you want to create and click OK. The document should have a .kpr or .kpt suffix if you want it to automatically open in kpresenter.

✦ **Spreadsheet Document** — Opens a box that lets you create a document in kspread format (a spreadsheet). Type the document name you want to create and click OK. The document should have a .ksp suffix if you want it to automatically open in kspread.

✦ **Text Document** — Opens a box that lets you create a document in KWord format (a word processing document). Type the document name you want to create and click OK. The document should have a .kwd or .kwt suffix if you want it to automatically open in kword.

✦ **Directory** — Opens a box that lets you type in a new directory name. Type the name, click OK, and an icon representing the new directory appears.

✦ **HTML File** — Opens a box that lets you type in an address of an HTML file.

✦ **Text File** — Opens a box that lets you create a text file. Type a file name for the text file and click OK.

✦ **CDROM Device** — Opens a box that lets you type a new CDROM device name. Click the Device tab and type the name of the device (/dev/cdrom), the mount point (such as /mnt/cdrom), and the file system type (you can use iso9660 for the standard CDROM files system, ext2 for Linux or msdos for DOS). When the icon appears, you can open it to mount the CDROM and display its contents.

✦ **Floppy Device** — Opens a box that lets you type a new floppy name. Click the Device tab and type the name of the device (/dev/fd0), the mount point (such as /mnt/floppy), and the file system type (you can use auto, to autodetect the contents, ext2 for Linux, or msdos for DOS). When the icon appears, you can open it to mount the floppy and display its contents.

✦ **Hard Disc Device** — Opens a box that lets you type a new hard disk or hard disk partition name. Click the Device tab and type the name of the device (/dev/hda1), the mount point (such as /mnt/win), and the file system type (you can use auto to autodetect the contents, ext2 or ext3 for Linux, or vfat for a Windows file system). When the icon appears, you can open it to mount the file system and display its contents.

✦ **Link to Application** — Opens a window that lets you type the name of an application. Click the Permissions tab to set file permissions (Exec must be on to run the file as an application). Click the Execute tab and type the name of the program to execute (Execute on click) and a title to appear in the title bar of the application (Window Title). If it is a text-based command, select the Run in terminal box. Click the box to Run as a different user, and add the user name. Click the Application tab to assign this application to handle files of particular MIME types. Click OK.

✦ **Link to Location (URL)** — Selecting either of these two menu items opens a box that lets you type a name that represents a Web address. Type the name of the address and click OK. Right-click the icon that appears, and click Properties. Click URL and type the name of the URL (Web address) for the site.

Creating MIME types and applications are described later in this chapter.

Using other browser features

Because Konqueror performs like a Web browser as well as a file manager, it includes several other browser features. For example, you can keep a bookmark list of Web sites you have visited, using the bookmarks feature. Any bookmarks that you add to your bookmarks list show up in the pull-down menu that appears when you click Bookmarks. Select from that list to return to a site. There are several ways to add and change your bookmarks list:

✦ **Add Bookmark** — To add the address of the page that is currently being displayed to your bookmark list, choose Bookmarks ➪ Add Bookmark. The next time you click Bookmarks, you will see the bookmark you just added on the Bookmarks menu.

✦ **Edit Bookmarks** — Because your bookmarks are stored as URL link files to the sites you choose, they are all stored in a folder. Selecting Bookmarks ➪ Edit Bookmarks opens the folder containing your bookmarks. From that folder, you can rearrange your bookmarks and change their properties using the same controls as you would with any other file.

✦ **New Folder** — You can add a new folder of bookmarks to your Konqueror bookmarks list. To create a bookmarks folder, choose Bookmarks ➪ New Folder. Then type a name for the new bookmarks folder and click OK. The new bookmark folder appears on your bookmarks menu. You can add the current location to that folder by clicking on the folder name and selecting Add Bookmark.

Configuring Konqueror options

You can change many of the visual attributes of the Konqueror window. You can select which menubars and toolbars appear. You can have any of the following bars appear on the Konqueror window: Menubar, Toolbar, Extra Toolbar, Location Toolbar, Bookmark Toolbar. Select Settings and then click the menu item for the bar you want to appear (or not appear). The bar appears when the checkmark is shown next to it.

You can modify a variety of options for Konqueror by choosing Settings ⇨ Configure Konqueror. The Konqueror Settings window appears, offering the following options:

✦ **File Manager** — This feature is described later in this chapter.

✦ **File Associations** — This feature is described later in this chapter.

✦ **Konqueror Browser** — Click the Konqueror Browser button to open a window to configure your Web browser features of Konqueror. There are tabs on this window for configuring your Web browsing, including HTTP (to set how links and images are handled), Appearance (to change font sizes and types), and Java/JavaScript (to enable Java and JavaScript, which are disabled by default).

✦ **Enhanced Browsing** — Click the Enhanced Browsing buttons to see a list of keyword shortcuts you can use to go to different Internet sites. For example, follow the word "ask" with a search string to search the Ask Jeeves (www.ask.com) Web site.

✦ **Cookies** — Click the Cookies button to select whether or not cookies are enabled in Konqueror. By default, you are asked to confirm that it is okay each time a Web site tries to create or modify a cookie. You can change that to either accept or reject all cookies. You can also set policies for acceptance or rejection of cookies based on host and domain names.

✦ **Proxies and Cache** — Click the Proxies and Cache button if you are accessing the Internet through a proxy server. You need to enter the address and port number of the computer that is providing HTTP and/or FTP proxy services. You can also add a caching setting, to indicate how much space on your hard disk can be used to store the sites you have visited (Average Cache Size).

✦ **Stylesheets** — Click the Stylesheets button to select whether to use the default stylesheet, a user-defined stylesheet, or a custom stylesheet. The stylesheet sets the font family, font sizes and colors that are applied to Web pages. (This won't change particular font requests made by the Web page.) If you select a custom stylesheet, click the Customize tab to customize your own fonts and colors.

✦ **Crypto** — Click the Crypto button to display a list of secure certificates that can be accepted by the Konqueror browser. By default, Secure Socket Layer (SSL) version 2 and 3 certificates are accepted, as is TLS support (if supported by the server). You can also select to be notified when you are entering or leaving a secure Web site.

✦ **User Agent**—Click the User Agent button to set the user agent that is used for browsing. By default, the Mozilla Web browser is used as the Konqueror Web browser for all servers. You can define different Web browsers to be used by Konqueror for displaying Web content from different servers.

✦ **Netscape Plugins**—Click the Netscape Plugins button to see a list of plugins that are available for use by Mozilla. Mozilla can also scan your computer to find plugins that are installed for other browsers in other locations.

Managing windows

If you have a lot of windows open at the same time, tricks for organizing and managing the windows on your desktop are very helpful. KDE helps you out by maintaining window lists you can work with and shortcuts for keeping the windows in order.

Using the taskbar

When you open a window, a button representing the window appears in the taskbar at the bottom of the screen. Here is how you can manage windows from the taskbar:

✦ **Toggle windows**—You can left-click any running task in the taskbar to toggle between opening the window and minimizing it.

✦ **Move windows**—You can move a window from the current desktop to any other virtual desktop. Right-click any task in the taskbar, select To Desktop, then select any desktop number. The window moves to that desktop.

Only the windows that are running in the current virtual desktop appear in the taskbar. Click any virtual desktop icon on the taskbar to see the windows in that virtual desktop.

Uncluttering the desktop

If your windows are scattered willy-nilly all over the desktop, here are a couple of ways you can make your desktop's appearance a little neater:

✦ **Unclutter windows**—Right-click the desktop, and then click Unclutter Windows on the menu. All windows that are currently displayed on the desktop are lined up along the left side of the screen, starting from the top down.

✦ **Cascade windows**—Right-click the desktop, and then click Cascade windows on the menu. The windows are aligned as they are with the Uncluttered selection, except that the windows are each indented.

✦ **Rolling up windows**—Double-click the title bar of a window to roll it up like a window shade. Double-click the title bar again to roll the window down again. This is a great way to clear a window away for a time, without fully minimizing it.

Moving windows

The easiest way to move a window from one location to another is to place the pointer on the windows title bar, move the mouse so the window goes to a new location, and release the mouse button to drop the window. Another way to do it is to click the window menu button (top left corner of the title bar), click Move, move the mouse to relocate the window, and then click again to place it.

If somehow the window gets stuck in a location where the title bar is off the screen, there is a way you can move it back to where you want it. Hold down the Alt key and press the left mouse button in the inner window. Then move the window where you want it and release.

Resizing windows

To resize a window, place the pointer over a corner or side of the window border, then move it until it is the size you want. Grabbing a corner lets you resize vertically and horizontally at the same time. Grabbing the side lets you resize in only one direction.

You can also resize a window from the window menu button. Click the window menu button (top left corner of the title bar) and select Size. Move the mouse until the window is resized and click to leave it there.

Using virtual desktops

To give you more space to run applications than will fit comfortably on your physical screen, KDE gives you access to several virtual desktops at the same time. Using the 1, 2, 3, and 4 buttons on the Panel, you can easily move between the different desktops. Just click the one you want.

If you want to move an application from one desktop to another, you can do so from the Window menu. Click the Window menu button for the window you want to move, click To Desktop, then select Desktop 1, 2, 3, or 4. The window will disappear from the current desktop and move to the one you selected.

Using sticky windows

When you are using multiple virtual desktops (the 1, 2, 3, or 4 on the Panel), there are times when you want the same window to appear on every one of them. For example, you may want a clock to appear in the upper corner of all desktops or a stock ticker to run along the bottom of all desktops.

To stick the window, click the pushpin icon so it appears to be pressed in. To unstick a window, use the same control. Click the pushpin again.

Any application that you always want available is a candidate for sticking. Some good examples are xclock (to always view a clock), xconsole (to see system messages), xeyes (so eyes can watch your every move), and xbiff (to have an indicator show you when mail arrives).

Configuring the desktop

If you want to change the look, feel, or behavior of your KDE desktop, the best place to start is the KDE Control Center. The KDE Control Center window lets you configure dozens of attributes associated with colors, fonts, backgrounds, and screensavers used by KDE. You can also change attributes relating how you work with windows and files.

To open the KDE Control Center from the desktop, either click the KDE Control Center icon on the Panel or click the K button ⇨ Control Center. The KDE Control Center window appears, as shown in Figure 4-7.

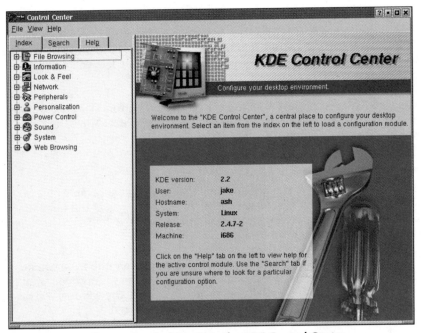

Figure 4-7: Configure your desktop from the KDE Control Center.

Click the plus (+) sign next to topics you want to configure. Then select the particular item you want to configure. The following sections describe some of the features you can configure from the KDE Control Center.

Changing the display

There are several ways you can change the look and feel of your desktop display. Under the Look & Feel topic (click the +), you can change Background, Colors, Desktop, Fonts, Icons, Key Bindings, Launch Feedback, Panel, Screensaver, Style, Taskbar, Theme Manager, and Window Behavior, and Window Decoration.

Here are a few of the desktop features you may want to change:

✦ **Change the background** — Under the Look & Feel heading in the KDE Control Center, select Background. You can remove the "X" next to Common Backgrounds to choose to have a common background for all four of your virtual desktops or assign backgrounds to individual desktops.

First select the Mode: Flat (single color); Pattern (two colors and click Setup to select a pattern); Background Program (click Setup to choose a program to run on the background); Horizontal Gradient (two colors that fade from left to right); Vertical Gradient (two colors that fade from top to bottom); Pyramid Gradient (two colors that fade from outside in); Pipecross Gradient (two colors that fade from the outside to a cross in the middle); and Elliptic Gradient (two colors that fade from outside to an ellipse in the middle).

If you prefer to use a wallpaper on the background, click the Wallpaper tab and select a desktop. Choose a Mode (to indicate the position of the wallpaper) and click the Wallpaper box to scroll down to choose the wallpaper. If you have a JPEG image you would like to use instead, click the Browse button to select the image you want from your file system. Click the Multiple box if you want to assign several wallpapers that change at set intervals.

Click Apply to apply your selections.

✦ **Change the screensaver** — Under the Look & Feel heading, select Screensaver. From the window that appears, select from about 25 different screen savers. Click Setup to modify the behavior of the screen saver. Under settings, select how many minutes of inactivity before the screensaver turns on. You can also click Require password to require that a password be entered before you can access your display after the screensaver has come on.

Tip If you are working in a place where you want your desktop to be secure, be sure to turn on the Require Password feature. This prevents others from gaining access to your computer when you forget to lock it or shut it off. If you have any virtual terminals open, switch to them and type `vlock` to lock each of them as well. (You need to install the vlock package if the `vlock` command isn't available.)

✦ **Change fonts** — You can assign different fonts to places that fonts appear on the desktop. Under the Look & Feel heading, select Fonts. Select one of the categories of fonts (General, Fixed width, Desktop icon, File manager, Toolbar, Menu, and Window title fonts). Then click the Choose box to select a font from the Select Font box that you want to assign to that category. If the font is available, you will see an example of the text in the Sample text box.

Tip If you want to use 100 dpi fonts, you need to add an entry for 100 dpi fonts to the `/etc/XF86Config` file. After you make that change, you need to restart the X server for it to take effect.

Other attributes you can change for the selected fonts are size (in points) and character set (to select an ISO standard character set). Select Apply to apply the changes.

✦ **Change the colors** — Under the Look & Feel heading in the KDE Control Center, select Colors. The window that appears lets you change the color of selected items on the desktop. Select a whole color scheme from the Color Scheme box. Or select an item from the Widget color box to change a particular item. Items you can change include text, backgrounds, links, buttons, and title bars.

Changing panel attributes

For most people, the panel is the place where they select which desktop is active and which applications are run. You can change some of the behavior of the panel from the KDE Control Center. (Select Panel under the Look & Feel heading.) Here are the features you can change from each of the tabs:

✦ **Position** — Change the location of the panel by clicking on Top, Left, Bottom, or Right in the Panel Location box. The Panel Style selection lets you change the size of the panel from Medium to Tiny, Small, or Large.

✦ **Hiding** — There are selections that allow you to autohide the panel and hide buttons. Under the Hide Buttons heading, choose whether or not hide buttons are put on each outside edge (left/top or right/bottom) of the Panel. Sliders let you select the delay and speed at which panels and buttons are hidden.

✦ **Look & Feel** — You can enable icon zooming (so icons bulge out as the mouse passes over them), have tooltips appear, and enable background tiles. You can select a background image for the panel. You can also assign different tile colors for different types of applications you add to the Panel.

✦ **Menus** — Choose options associated with menus. You can clear the menu cache after a set number of seconds or select to show hidden files on browser menus. For the K Menu, you can select to merge different menu locations, show the recent documents submenu, and show the quick browser submenu. By defining a Quick Start section, you can have the most recently or most frequently used items accessible from that menu.

✦ **Applets** — Select the security level associated with the applets on your panel. You can indicate that only trusted applets can be used, then choose which applets to add to your Trusted list.

Adding application launchers and MIME types

You want to be able to quickly access the applications that you use most often. One of the best ways to make that possible is to add icons to the panel or the desktop that can launch the applications you need with a single click. Procedures for adding applications to the panel and desktop are described in the following sections.

Adding applications to the panel

You can add any KDE application to the KDE panel quite easily. From the K menu button on the panel, do the following:

1. Right-click an open space on the panel.
2. Choose Panel Menu ⇨ Add ⇨ Button.
3. Select one of the categories of applications.
4. Click any application from the category you selected (or select Add this menu to add the whole menu of applications).

An icon representing the application should immediately appear on the panel. At this point, you can change any properties associated with the application by right-clicking on the application icon in the panel and then selecting Preferences. Here are the properties you can change:

✦ **General** — Lets you change the file name associated with the icon. (This is not recommended, since the file name is not exposed from the panel.) You can also click the icon on this tab to select a different icon to represent it.

✦ **Permissions** — Lets you change read, write, and execute permissions associated with the application. Because this is a special KDE link file (.kdelnk or .desktop), it only needs to be readable by all and not executable.

✦ **Execute** — Lets you change the complete command line that is run when the command is executed, as well as the icon representing the application. Click Run in terminal if the application is a text-based, and not a GUI-based, application.

✦ **Application** — Lets you add a Comment to the application. This comment is displayed as a tooltip when the pointer is positioned over the icon. The Name you enter is what appears in the title bar for the application. If you want the application to be launched if a particular type of data (MIME Type) is encountered, you can click a MIME Type in the right text box, then click the left arrow button to move the MIME Type to the left box.

If you decide later that you no longer want this application to be available on the panel, right-click it and click Remove. To move it to a different location on the panel, right-click it, click Move, move it to where you want it on the panel, and click again.

Adding applications to the desktop

To add an application to the desktop, you can use the desktop menu. Here's how:

1. Right-click an open area of the desktop.
2. Select Create New ⇨ Link to Application from the menu.
3. In the Properties window that appears, replace the Program name. (This name will appear under the icon on the desktop.)

4. Add Permissions, Execute, and Application information for the application as described in the previous section about adding applications to the panel. In this case, much of the information will have to be entered manually. You will at least want to enter the command to execute, along with any options, on the Execute tab. You will probably also want to enter the Comment and Name on the Application tab. Click OK to save the application icon to the desktop.

If you decide later that you no longer want this application to be available on the desktop, right-click it and click Delete or Move to Trash.

Configuring MIME types

By assigning MIME types and file extensions to particular types of data files, you can assign how those types of data are handled when the file is opened from KDE (such as in the Konqueror File Manager window). This can be a very powerful feature. It enables you to identify which application is started to handle a file that you open.

MIME, which stands for Multipurpose Internet Mail Extension, was originally created as a way of adding different kinds of data to a mail message. For example, the data could be an image, a sound clip, or a video. Because this data may not have a file extension associated with it (.doc, .gif, and so on), the MIME type associated with the file could indicate to the mail reader or other application what to do with the data.

When you add a MIME type to the Konqueror window, it tells it how to deal with particular kinds of data when a file is encountered in a folder (based on file extension) or some data is encountered when you open a Web page (based on MIME type). The following example shows a MIME type entry that was created to cause a particular application to be launched based on a file extension:

1. From the K menu, click the Control Center.

2. From the KDE Control Center, choose File Browsing ⇨ File Associations. A File Associations screen appears in the KDE Control Center.

3. Click Add to create a new MIME Type. A Create new file type window appears.

4. Select a group that the MIME type you are adding applies to by clicking the arrows next to the Group box. Then enter a Type name for the new MIME type and click OK.

5. Add the following information to the General tab that appears for the new MIME type:

   • **Filename Patterns** — Click Add and enter the file name extension for files that should be handled by this MIME type.

   • **Icon** — Click the icon on this tab to see the Select Icon window. From there, you can select the icon you want to represent the MIME type and click OK.

- **Description** — Type a description of the MIME type.

- **Application Preference Order** — Click Add, then select an application that will handle the MIME type that you just added and click OK. You can add several applications, in order, that could be used to handle the data type. The first application launches when you select a matching file type; other applications will appear on the menu when you right-click a matching file type and select Open With.

   6. Click Apply. The new MIME time is now saved.

At this point, any file created with the file extension that was just added will be launched by the application you indicated when the file is opened from the desktop or File Manager window. Right-click a file of that type to choose to launch the file by a different application from the Open With list (if more than one application is listed for the file type).

Changing X Settings

No matter what window manager you use, there are X resources that you can change that apply to your desktop in general, as well as specific X clients you run. Most X clients use standard options to set background and foreground colors, window titles, placement on the screen, and other resources. This section describes how to set X resources that apply to the general desktop, as well as to X client programs.

The most common ways to set X resources are by:

   ✦ **X Client Command-Line Options** — Most X clients support standard command-line options (as well as some options specific to each client) that set resources. For example, the option `-geometry` can be used to set the default size and position of most X clients.

   ✦ **X Resource Files** — System and user resource files can be loaded by the `xrdb` command at desktop startup time. When you start the X GUI, it loads resources from either the system-wide Xresources file or from your personal .Xresources file (if either exists). Default resources for many X clients are stored in files in the `/usr/lib/X11/app-defaults` directory. You can override any X client resources files in app-defaults by creating files of the same names in your home directory.

There are also commands that you can run to change attributes related to general desktop features (`xsetroot` command) or your keyboard mappings (`xmodmap` command). The following sections describe how to change X resources using both X client command-line options and X resource files.

X client command-line options

When you run X client commands, or put them in a configuration file to start automatically, you can add options that affect how the client looks and behaves. These options are part of the X toolkit, so they are available regardless of what window manager you are using. Table 4-2 describes options that can be used with many different X client commands.

<table>
<tr><td colspan="2" align="center">Table 4-2
Command Options for Setting X Clients</td></tr>
<tr><td>*Option*</td><td>*Description*</td></tr>
<tr><td>-bg color or -background color</td><td>Set the background color of the window by replacing color with the color you choose. See the Colors section for a list of valid colors.</td></tr>
<tr><td>-fg color or -foreground color</td><td>Set the window's foreground color by replacing color with the color you choose. This color is used for text or graphics in the window.</td></tr>
<tr><td>-rv or -reverse</td><td>Reverse the window's background and foreground colors.</td></tr>
<tr><td>+rv</td><td>Restore the window's original background and foreground colors.</td></tr>
<tr><td>-bd color or -bordercolor color</td><td>Set the color of the window border by replacing color with the color you choose. See the Colors section for a list of valid colors.</td></tr>
<tr><td>-bw pixels or -borderwidth pixels</td><td>Set the window border width in terms of number of pixels.</td></tr>
<tr><td>-display display</td><td>Set the client program to appear on a particular display. The display can be set as the display on the local system (:0.0) or to a display on a remote computer (host:0.0). See Chapter 5 for a more in-depth description of how to direct the output of an X client to a remote display.</td></tr>
<tr><td>-fn fontname or -font fontname</td><td>Set the font used in the display text to fontname. See the Fonts section to find valid font names.</td></tr>
</table>

Option	Description
`-geometry WidthxHeight+Xoff+Yoff`	Set the size and placement of the window on the screen. `Width` and `Height` are numbers indicating either pixels or characters. `Xoff` and `Yoff` set the offset of where on the screen the window begins. A plus sign (+) offsets the window from the left or top of the screen. A minus (-) sign offsets the window from the right or bottom of the screen. (See examples that follow.)
`-iconic`	Start the application minimized (reduced to an icon). This is a nice option for running several clients at startup time so they are immediately ready for use, but not cluttering up your screen.
`-name "app name"`	Assign a name to the client (`app name`) that can be used to identify the application's resources. This is useful when the client has been renamed or aliased, but you still want it to use its resources. The `app name` you assign appears on the icon representing the window when it is minimized and, possibly, in the window's title bar. The name can be overridden in those locations using the option `-title`.
`-title "Window Name"`	Set the title used in the window's title bar and, possibly, the icon representing the window when it is minimized.
`-xnllanguage lang[_terr][.codeset]`	Set the language, territory, and codeset used to resolve filenames (such as resource files).
`-xrm "resource:value"`	Set a `resource` to a particular `value`. This is useful for setting any X resource for the client that can't be changed with a specific option. (Separate the `resource` and `value` with a colon and surround them with quotes to avoid special characters from being interpreted by the shell.)

In most cases, you can use several of these X options on the same command line. The following are some examples of X command options that are used with some common X clients:

Note   You can type these commands in a Terminal window in your GUI. The results should appear on your desktop. If the clients don't appear, refer to Chapter 5 for information on running X applications.

Example one

The `xeyes` command opens a small window that contains a pair of eyes. Those eyes follow your mouse movements around the screen. Here is an example of the `xeyes` command with several options:

```
$ xeyes -fg red -center yellow &
```

This runs the `xeyes` command with the pupils (`-fg`) set to red and the whites of the eyes (`-center`) set to yellow. The `-center` option is specific to `xeyes`. The ampersand (&) runs the command in the background.

Example two

The `xlogo` command simply displays an X (representing the X Window System) on your display. Here is an example of the `xlogo` command with several options:

```
$ xlogo -geometry 300x300-0-0 -bg green -fg red &
```

This places an X logo in the lower right-hand corner of the screen (`-0-0`) at a size of 300 x 300 pixels. The background behind the X is green (`-bg`), whereas the X itself is red (`-fg`). If the location had been set to `+0+0`, the X would have been placed in the upper left-hand corner. The ampersand (&) runs the command in the background.

Note   For an xterm window, `-geometry` is interpreted in characters. So, a geometry of 80 × 15 would result in the text area of the xterm window being 80 characters wide and 15 lines long.

Example three

The `xterm` command starts a Terminal window on your desktop. Here is an example of an `xterm` command with several options:

```
$ xterm -title "Login to Comp1" -e ssh comp1
```

This command opens an xterm window and attempts to log in to a remote computer called `comp1` (`-e ssh comp1`). The words *Login to Comp1* will appear in the xterm window's title bar. To try this on your own computer, substitute `comp1` with the name of a computer on your network.

This example represents a great way to start an application and identify the activity of that application in the title bar of the xterm window. (This is a particularly good technique when an `xterm` command is used to log in to another computer. The title reminds you that you are not working on your own computer within that window, because you're logged in somewhere else.)

Example four

X resources can also be set on a command line. The following is an example of an `-xrm` option being used to set resources for an xterm window.

```
$ xterm -xrm "XTerm*cursorColor:Blue"
```

This command opens an xterm window with the color of the cursor set to blue. You can set any xterm resource using the `-xrm` option. Try a few others, such as `-xrm XTerm*background:Red` or `-xrm XTerm*foreground:Yellow`. You can have more than one resource set at a time, but each must be preceded with `-xrm`.

Caution

Be careful not to set background, foreground, and other adjacent items to the same color. If your text, cursor, or other items seem to have disappeared, they may just be set to the same color.

X resource files

When you specify a resource for an X client, that resource follows a fairly simple form. It consists of class name, attribute, and a value. The class name is just the name of the application with the first letter capitalized. Some class names that begin with the letter x, however, capitalize the second letter as well (for example, the classname for the xterm application is XTerm). The attribute identifies the element within that application. The value is what that element is set to.

Here is an example of an X resource:

```
XTerm*background: Red
```

The object of this attribute is the `xterm` command. The attribute is the `background`. The value sets the background to red. X resources that are specific to a particular client are organized in a hierarchy, in what is called a widget class. To find this hierarchy for an X client, check its man page and look for the WIDGETS heading. (Not all man pages have this heading.)

Tip

To see the widget tree for an X client that is running, use the `editres` command. From `editres`, choose Commands ➪ Get Tree, and then click the window of the client for which you want to see resources. To see an extensive list of resources, try clicking the editres window itself.

Because the hierarchy of resources can allow long names, you can use an asterisk in a resource name for what is called a *loose binding*. This means that any number of characters can be matched by the asterisk (the way an asterisk is used as a wildcard in the shell). So, in the example just shown, any resource that ends with the attribute *background* for the *XTerm* class will be *Red*.

If you want to be more specific in how you match a resource name, use a period (.) to create a *tight binding* in a resource name. A tight binding enables you to be more specific about the resource you want. For example, if you want all backgrounds in the xterm window to be Black and foregrounds to be White, but you want the scrollbar background to be Red and the foreground to be Yellow, use the following resources:

```
XTerm*background: Black
XTerm*foreground: White
XTerm*scrollbar.background: Red
XTerm*scrollbar.foreground: Yellow
```

Most X applications accept these attributes: *background*, *foreground*, *borderwidth*, and *bordercolor*. Many also accept *title* (to change the name in the title bar), *geometry* (to set the window size and location), and *font* (to change the font used in the window).

Remember that you can add resources in several ways: .Xdefaults, .Xresources, application-specific resource files in your home directory (such as XTerm), or using the -xrm "*resource*" option on an X client's command line. Here are a few X resource examples you can try to get a feel for:

```
xfontsel*MenuButton.background: Red
XClock*geometry: +0-0
XTerm*font: 9x15bold
```

In these examples, the first line shows buttons on the xfontsel window in red. The second line places the xclock utility in the lower-left corner of the screen. The third line sets the fonts used in an xterm window to be the 9x15bold font.

X colors

When you define X resources, there are several ways to refer to colors. One way that is easy to understand is to use common names: red, blue, black, etc. However, to be more specific, you can also use hexadecimal notation or specific numeric red, green, and blue values to refer to more subtle colors.

The table of colors that are supported by X are contained in /usr/lib/X11/ rgb.txt file. Each entry in this file consists of three numbers and a name. The three numbers represent the intensity of red, green, and blue, respectively. A zero (0) represents no trace of the color, whereas 255 represents full intensity. Here are some examples of colors in this file:

```
250 235 215          AntiqueWhite
230 230 250          lavender
255 228 225          misty rose
255 255 255          white
  0   0   0          black
 47  79  79          DarkSlateGray
190 190 190          gray
  0   0 128          navy
  0   0 255          blue
135 206 235          sky blue
175 238 238          PaleTurquoise
  0 255 255          cyan
  0 255   0          green
255 255   0          yellow
165  42  42          brown
255 165   0          orange
255   0   0          red
255   0 255          magenta
160  32 240          purple
```

You can use any of these names as arguments to color resource options. (Remember to put multiword colors in quotes.) Another way to refer to a color is with hexadecimal notation. In this form, there are six integers, each representing a number from 0 to 16. The first two integers refer to red, the next two refer to blue, and the final two refer to green. So, in the first two integers, ff is 255 (all red) and 00 is zero (no red). The same is true for setting the amounts of blue and green used. Here are some common colors in hexadecimal notation.

```
black      #000000
blue       #0000ff
cyan       #00ffff
green      #00ff00
magenta    #ff00ff
red        #ff0000
white      #ffffff
yellow     #ffff00
```

Depending on where you enter colors in hexadecimal notation, you may need to put the numbers in quotes. For example, to set the background color to green for an xterm window, you would type `xterm -bg "#00ff00"` at the command line.

X fonts

To see the fonts that are available to X on your computer, use the `xlsfonts` command. The `xlsfonts` command just dumps a listing of fonts to your screen. So, to view the contents you should either pipe the output to the `more` command or direct the output to a file. Here are two ways to run the command:

```
$ xlsfonts | more
$ xlsfonts > /tmp/allfonts
```

Here are some fonts you can try. Use the command `xterm -fn "font"` to try some of these fonts:

```
12x24romankana
-adobe-utopia-bold*
lucidasanstypewriter-bold-18
```

The X server maintains a list of font locations in what is called the *font path*. When you display a list of fonts or choose particular fonts to assign as resources, the font path is checked to determine whether the font exists. Font path is similar to the shell PATH, which searches for commands by checking a list of directories, using the order in which they appear in the PATH. Likewise, X checks for a font using the order set by font path. To see the current font path, type `xset -q| grep -i font`.

Changing X display resources

Resources associated with your X server display affect the behavior of the mouse and keyboard, and can modify such things as the sounds and background of your desktop. There are several commands that are used to change and view the resources that are set for your display:

✦ `xset` — Sets and displays a variety of resources associated with your X display. It can control sounds from the desktop, set the font path, change mouse parameters, change the screen saver, and set background color of the desktop.

✦ `xmodmap` — Modifies how the keys on your keyboard and pointer buttons are mapped. It can also display existing key map and pointer map tables.

✦ `xsetroot` — Sets parameters associated with your root window. You can change the cursor for the mouse pointer or set the background window to a color or bitmap image.

✦ `xv` — Although `xv` can be used to capture and display images in a variety of formats, it can also be used to show an image as a background for your display. (The `xv` command does not come with the Red Hat Linux distribution, though it is available from Red Hat FTP sites as shareware.)

Typically, you would try different values with these commands to find settings that look and behave the way you want. Then you could add these commands, with options, to your `.xinitrc` or `.xsession` files so that they are in effect each time you start the desktop.

There are several attributes of your mouse, cursor, and keyboard mappings that you can change. You can speed your mouse motion. You can change what each mouse button does. You can assign a different cursor to the mouse pointer. You can modify annoying sounds. You can set the background of your display. You can set the idle time of your screen saver.

Mouse speed

To change the speed your mouse cursor travels in proportion to how far you move the mouse, change the acceleration value with the xset command. To set the m option to xset, enter a number to represent acceleration. You can also add a number, following the first one that represents a threshold. The movement of the cursor is the first number (acceleration) times the movement of the mouse (the distance the mouse is moved), after it passes the set threshold of pixels. (The reason for waiting for the threshold to be reached is so that you can move the cursor in a refined way for short distances.) Here is an example:

```
$ xset m 5 10
```

This example sets the mouse to move five times as fast as it would normally move for the amount that you move the mouse. Acceleration begins after the mouse moves 10 pixels. If you try this option, you will see that the mouse cursor starts out moving slowly for a short distance, then begins moving quickly.

Mouse buttons

If you are left-handed, you can use the xmodmap command to change the arrangement of the mouse buttons. To have the mouse button you most often use to select items under your index finger, reverse the order of the three mouse buttons. First, use the following command to check the current arrangement of your mouse buttons:

```
$ xmodmap -pp
There are 5 pointer buttons defined.

    Physical        Button
    Button          Code
      1               1
      2               2
      3               3
      4               4
      5               5
```

This output shows that the five mouse buttons are assigned in order. The code for the first button is assigned to button one and so on. To change the order (for a left-handed person), type the following:

```
$ xmodmap -e "pointer = 3 2 1 4 5"
```

Tip   If your mouse isn't working, there may be a problem in your mouse configuration. Try running mouseconfig. Mouse information in your /etc/X11/XF86Config file may be wrong. If you are careful, you can manually edit mouse information in that file.

Mouse cursor

By default, the cursor representing the location of the mouse pointer when it is over the root window is an X. If you like, you can change the cursor to a different representation with the xsetroot command. The full list of cursors is available in the X Windows include file (/usr/X11R6/include/X11/cursorfont.h). Here is an example of how you can change the mouse cursor to a different icon:

```
$ xsetroot -cursor_name draped_box
```

This example changes the X cursor to a box with a small mosaic pattern in it. You can also change the cursor to any of the following values:

```
hand1
hand2
iron_cross
left_ptr
plus
top_left_arrow
watch
```

Sounds

You can modify the annoying sounds your computer makes using the xset command. You can turn off the beep your computer makes when you make a mistake by typing the following:

```
$ xset b off
```

You can turn the beep back on as follows:

```
$ xset b on
```

You can change how loud your computer beeps by using a numeric value after the b option. The number represents a percentage of the maximum loudness (from 1 to 100). For example, the following sets the bell to 90 percent of its maximum loudness:

```
$ xset b 90
```

Backgrounds

Note   Because GNOME and KDE take over control of the background of your desktop, you may not be able to see the effects of these commands unless you turn on GNOME or KDE background settings.

With the xsetroot command, you can set the background of your desktop to a solid color or to a repeated bitmap pattern. Here's how to set the background to a solid color:

```
$ xsetroot -solid Black
```

This sets the background to solid black. You can also set the background to any valid color (using names or hexadecimal notation). The following example shows how to set the background to a bitmap image:

```
$ xsetroot -bitmap /usr/X11R6/include/X11/bitmaps/terminal -fg Red -bg Black
```

This command fills the background with tiny bitmap terminals. The foreground of each image is red and the background is black. You can try this command using other images from the bitmap directory and using other foreground and background colors.

You can set your background to a grid using the -mod option of the xsetroot command. The two integers that follow represent the x and y coordinates of the grid. Each integer can be a number between 1 and 16 (to change how close together the grid lines are). Here is an example:

```
$ xsetroot -mod 5 16
```

If you want to use an image type other than a bitmap for your background, you can use the xv command. (Though xv doesn't come with Red Hat Linux, it can be obtained from a Red Hat FTP site.) The xv command can display a variety of image types: GIF, JPEG, TIFF, PBM, PGM, PPM, X11 bitmap, PCX, XPM, and a variety of others. (If you have an image in a different format, you may be able to use the convert command to change it to a format you can display.) Here is an example of the syntax of the xv command for displaying an image as your desktop background:

```
$ xv -quit -root -max /usr/share/pixmaps/backgrounds/space/apollo17_earth.jpg
```

As noted earlier, any of these attributes that you want set each time you start your desktop can be added to your .xinitrc or .xsession files.

Tip   You can find some nice background images in the Propaganda directories (/usr/share/pixmaps/backgrounds/Propaganda/*). There are also many places to find nice background images on the Web, including Digital Blasphemy (www.digitalblasphemy.com) and Background Pics for Linux (http://heimat.de/ruebe/linux/bgs.html).

Screen saver

There is an option that you can add when you run the X server to have a screen saver come on after a set number of minutes of idle time. Using the xset command, you can change that timeout value. (As with the background examples just shown, your desktop environment may take over control of the screensaver function.)

There are different ways to initially set the screen saver timeout value when you start X.

```
$ X -s 15
$ xinit -- -s 15 serverargs="-s 15"
```

In the first example, you simply run the X command with the -s 15 option to have the screen saver come on after 15 minutes of inactivity. If you run xinit, two dashes on the command line indicate that the next arguments are to be passed to the X server (in this case, -s 15 is passed). The last example isn't a command at all. It is a line in the startx command. As the root user, edit the startx command and add -s 15 to the serverargs line between the quotes. This causes the -s 15 argument to be passed to the server.

To change the screen saver timeout value after X has started, use the xset command as follows:

```
$ xset s 15
```

You can also add the xset command line to an initialization file (such as .xinitrc), to have it set the timeout value each time the desktop starts up. If you simply want the screen saver off, type xset s off. To turn it on, type xset s on. To have the screen be blanked when it times out, type xset s blank.

Tip   You now know how to set your screen saver for the desktop. But what if you want to turn off the screen saver when you are in text mode? Just type setterm -blank 0. The screen saver will never come on.

X Application resources

Most X applications support some, or all, of the standard X options (geometry, foreground, background, etc.), as well as some options that are specific to the application. Many of them start with a set of default options defined. You can override these default options in several different ways.

There are separate resource files for each X application (that chooses to create one) in the /usr/lib/X11/app-defaults directory. Each file is named after the X client it represents, with the exception that the first one or two characters are capitalized. Although it is not recommended, you could edit these files and change the resources. In that way everyone who starts X on your system will start with the same set of resources set for their applications.

The preferred way to change resources for your X clients is to copy the resource file you want to change to your home directory. Then make changes and additions to it. When you start the X client that is associated with that file, the resources are incorporated into the client. Even if there is no default resource file for an X client, you can create one. For example, I created a $HOME/XEyes file and added the following lines to it:

```
XEyes*title: My Eyes
XEyes*foreground: Red
XEyes*background: Yellow
```

When I ran the xeyes command, the title "My Eyes" appeared on the task bar for the application. The eyeballs were colored yellow and the pupils were red.

Instead of using individual files, you can add X resources associated with any client into your .Xresources or .Xdefaults file. When you make a change to those files, you can immediately merge those changes into the current desktop as follows:

```
$ xrdb -merge $HOME/.Xresources
```

Summary

The X Window System provides the basis for most graphical user interfaces available for Red Hat and other Linux systems today. Although X provides the framework for running and sharing applications, the GNOME and KDE desktop environments, along with a window manager, provide the look-and-feel of your desktop.

Using various configuration files and commands, you can change nearly every aspect of your graphical environment. Backgrounds can be assigned a single color or can be filled with single or tiled graphic images. Menus can be changed or enhanced. Multiple virtual workspaces can be used and managed.

There are also many settings associated with X itself that you can use directly to change the behavior of your desktop.

✦ ✦ ✦

Accessing and Running Applications

To get your work done on a computer, you use application programs. They let you create documents, crunch data, and communicate with others. As an engine for running applications, Red Hat Linux is becoming more viable every day. Not too long ago, there were only a handful of user-friendly applications available. Now there are hundreds — and they're getting more powerful and friendlier all the time.

This chapter describes how to get applications for Red Hat Linux and run them. Because Red Hat Linux is still, at its heart, a programmer's and network administrator's operating system, this chapter teaches you how to download applications from the Internet and to uncompress and install them. For running native Linux applications, this chapter focuses on graphical-based applications (run on an X desktop, including applications distributed over the network).

Besides programs that were specifically created for (or ported to) Linux, it is possible to run applications that were intended for other operating systems. This chapter describes emulators that are available to use with Red Hat Linux for running applications created for Windows, DOS, and Macintosh operating systems.

Using Red Hat Linux as an Application Platform

Although operating systems are nice, people use desktop computers to run application programs. A strong case can be made for using Red Hat Linux as a server, but as a desktop system, Red Hat Linux is still a long way from challenging Microsoft's operating system dominance for several reasons:

✦ Although you can get word processing programs, spreadsheet programs, graphics programs, and almost any other type of application that you want for Linux, many of the most popular applications in each category don't run well in Linux or don't run at all. For example, the latest Microsoft Office product will not run in Linux. If your company uses Microsoft Word for word processing or Microsoft Excel for spreadsheets, you could try converting files from those applications to run in StarOffice in Red Hat Linux. However, those files won't always convert cleanly.

✦ There are many more commercial, battle-tested applications for Microsoft Windows operating systems than there are for Linux. Because the user market is so huge for Windows systems, many software companies develop their products solely for that market.

✦ Linux applications, as a rule, are more difficult to configure and use than are many commercial Windows applications.

That's the bad news. The good news is that Linux is gaining ground. You can now use Linux on your desktop to do almost everything you would want to do on a desktop computer with Windows (it's often just a bit tougher getting there). In the near term, making a case for replacing all desktop computers with Red Hat Linux is difficult, but I believe there are many good reasons to think that, in the long term, Linux will be the superior operating system for running applications. Here are some of those reasons:

✦ Many people believe that, in time, networked applications will drive the future of computing. Unlike the first Windows systems, which had their roots in the single-user, one-task-at-a-time DOS system, Red Hat Linux is based on UNIX systems. UNIX was designed from the ground up to deal with many users and many tasks in a networked environment. Although it could still use a coat of paint, Red Hat Linux offers a strong foundation for networked applications.

✦ A huge development community is working on open source to meet the needs of the Linux community. In the past couple of years, some strong commercial offerings have been added.

✦ In the spirit of Linux and the GNU (which stands for "GNU is Not UNIX"), most application programs are free or inexpensive. This means that you can try out most applications for little or no money. Getting started running Linux applications can be done at a small cost. For example, StarOffice is free to download (and only $39.95 for the boxed set), whereas if you just want Word, you need to pay hundreds of dollars for the entire Microsoft Office package.

The bottom line is that it will take some effort for most people to discard their Windows operating systems completely. However, if you are committed to making Red Hat Linux your sole application platform, there are several ways to ease that transition. Emulation programs let you run many programs that were created for other operating systems. Conversion programs can help you convert graphics and word processing from other formats to those supported by Linux applications.

See Chapter 6 for information on importing and exporting word processing and graphics files.

If you are running Linux on a PC, chances are that you already paid for a Windows 95, 98, ME, XP, NT, or 2000 operating system. You can either run the different operating systems on different PCs or have Windows and Linux on separate partitions of your hard disk. The latter requires that you reboot each time you want to switch operating systems.

The following sections describe how to find and work with application programs that are created specifically for Linux.

Obtaining Red Hat Linux Applications

Unfortunately, you won't be able to walk into the average computer store and find a lot of Linux application programs. By far, the best way to get Linux applications is to download them from the Internet. They can also be ordered on CD-ROM from several Linux Web sites.

Finding applications on the Internet

Here are a few places to look for Linux applications on the Internet:

✦ **Freshmeat** (`www.freshmeat.net`) — This site maintains a massive index of Linux software. Type the name of a software package into the find box and you can find where it is available on the Web. This is one of the best sites to check first for Linux software.

✦ **SourceForge** (`www.sourceforge.net`) — This site hosts thousands of open source software projects. You can download software and documentation from those projects from the SourceForge site.

✦ **Linux Applications Web site** (`www.linuxapps.com/`) — If you don't already know which applications you are looking for, this is a great place to start. The site offers more than 30 categories of applications. Instead of just presenting a list of package names, Linux Applications has descriptions of each application along with links to the applications' home pages.

✦ **Red Hat Application Index** (`www.redhat.com/apps/marketplace/`) — You can find commercial applications for Red Hat Linux at this site. Contact information and pricing, along with descriptions of each application, are provided.

✦ **Linux Mall** (`www.linuxmall.com`) — This site offers a large selection of Linux software. It describes each software package and provides a listing of the top 40 Linux products sold at the Linux Mall.

✦ **Linux Applications and Utilities page** (www.xnet.com/~blatura/linapps. shtml)—This site has links to a variety of freeware, shareware, and commercial Linux applications (either in binary or source code).

When you purchase a commercial application, you usually get the application on CD. Installation is often simplified, and hard copy documentation is provided. Of course, when you download software, you get immediate gratification—when you purchase it, you have to wait for the package to arrive in the mail.

Sometimes software packages will be available in both libc5 and libc6 formats. This refers to the version of C programming language libraries that are used by the application. If you have a choice, choose the libc6 packages. The libc6 packages are compatible with Red Hat Linux 7 (or any Linux kernel version 2.2 and higher). In fact, all major Linux distributions now use libc6.

If you already have some idea of the software you want, you can go right to any of the many FTP sites that hold Linux software on the Internet. Here are a few ways to get to Linux FTP sites:

✦ **Red Hat FTP Mirrors** (www.redhat.com/mirrors.html)—Go to this page for a listing of FTP sites that contain Red Hat software that you can download. Most of these sites also have a variety of freeware and shareware applications that are usable with Linux.

Because Red Hat recently discontinued its PowerTools CD, you may need to hunt around a bit more for popular applications that were once on that CD. The following Web site is intended to eventually become a gathering place for software packages that are intended for Red Hat Linux, but didn't make the main distribution: http://rhcontrib.bero.org. You can also try the RpmFind site (www.rpmfind.net).

✦ **Sunsite FTP Site** (ftp://metalab.unc.edu/pub/Linux/apps)—There are many FTP sites from which you can download Linux software. The link shown here takes you to a directory of "large useful packages and applications for Linux." The University of North Carolina-Chapel Hill MetaLab maintains this FTP site.

✦ **Free Software Foundation** (ftp://ftp.gnu.org/pub/gnu)—The Free Software Foundation (the organization that maintains the GNU) also has a lot of software at its FTP site, as well as electronic copies of printed manuals.

The FTP sites are good if you already have some idea of what you are looking for. You can start by reading the README and INDEX files for a particular software product to get your bearings. When you find the software you want, simply click the link to begin downloading the software to your computer.

A great way to find software packages that are part of the Red Hat Linux distribution or the former Red Hat Linux PowerTools is the rpmfind command. Using rpmfind, you can locate Linux software packages in RPM format and download them. The rpmfind command is described later in this chapter.

Downloading Linux software

You can download Linux software from the Internet using a Web browser (such as Netscape Navigator) or an FTP program (such as the `ftp` command). The browser often enables you to view the contents of an FTP site through a Web interface (look for an `index.html` file in an FTP directory). The FTP command has more options, but is less intuitive. There are also GUI-based FTP applications, such as `gFTP`, to make FTP services easier to use. (The `gFTP` command is described in Chapter 20.)

Note The following procedures assume that you have a connection to the Internet.

Downloading with Netscape

To download a Linux software package from the Internet using Netscape Navigator, follow this procedure:

1. From the desktop, start Netscape Navigator.
2. Type the name of an FTP site that has Linux software in the location box and press Enter. For example, try `ftp://sunsite.unc.edu/pub/Linux/apps`.
3. To move around the FTP site, click Up to Higher Level Directory to move up, or click on a directory to move down.
4. When you find a package that you want to install, position the cursor over it, click the right mouse button, and then select Save Link As.
5. In the Save As box, into the Selection box, type the location (such as `/tmp/abcpkg/abc.rpm`) on your local system where you would like to save the package.

Tip When you download software, you should place it in an empty directory with an appropriate name. Not only does this help you remember where you put the software, but it also keeps the unarchived files separate from other files. I also recommend that you not change the name of the package, so as not to lose information about the package's contents.

6. Press OK.

As the package is downloaded to your computer, a dialog box displays the progress. When the download is complete, the application is ready to be uncompressed and installed.

Downloading with FTP

If you want to use a text-based method of downloading files (instead of Netscape), you can use the `ftp` command. Here's an example of an FTP procedure:

1. From a shell or a Terminal window, type `ftp` *location*, where *location* is an FTP site. For example:

   ```
   ftp metalab.unc.edu
   ```

   If the FTP site is available, it will prompt you for a user name.

2. Type anonymous for the Name and press Enter.

   The site prompts you for a password.

3. Type your e-mail address for the password and press Enter.

4. When your login is accepted, you can use these commands to find the software package or document that you are looking for:

   - ls -CF—To list the contents of the current directory.

   - cd *dir*—To change the current directory to the subdirectory *dir*. If you prefer, you can use two dots (cd ..) to go up a directory level. For example, try cd /pub/Linux/apps/doctools.

5. Type binary (to make sure the file is downloaded as a binary file).

6. To download a file from the current working directory, type get *file* where *file* is the application name. For example, to download the whichman application while /pub/Linux/apps/doctools is the current directory, type:

   get whichman-2.0.tar.gz

7. When the download is complete, type exit.

Tip

Before you start the ftp command, make sure that your current directory is the one in which you want to download the file. Alternatively, you could change to the directory you want by using the lcd command within ftp. For example, to change to /tmp/abcapp, **type** lcd /tmp/abcapp.

Using rpmfind for Downloading

If you are looking for software packages you know are in RPM format, rpmfind is probably the best tool for finding and downloading them. Besides finding the packages you request, rpmfind checks your Linux system so it can find packages that best match your current configuration.

To use rpmfind, type rpmfind along with the software package you want. If you are connected to the Internet, rpmfind finds the package and asks if you want to download it. Here is an example of how you may use the rpmfind command to find the xv software packages:

```
# cd /tmp
# rpmfind xv
Installing xv will require 943 KBytes
Non-qualified hostname: maple(none)
ftp://ftp.redhat.com/pub/redhat/redhat-7.1/powertools/i386/RedHat/RPMS/
    xv-3.10a-23.i386.rpm
Do you want to download these files to /tmp? [Y/n/a/i] ? : Y
```

After you type Y, the software package is downloaded to your current directory (in this case, /tmp). You can then use the rpm -i /tmp/xv* command to install the package. (Replace the /tmp/xv* with the name of the package you are installing.)

Note I particularly recommend using the `rpmfind` command to get software packages that were part of the Red Hat Linux PowerTools that was discontinued for Red Hat Linux 7.2. Those packages are not included with this book, though several previous PowerTools packages (such as xv) are referenced in this book.

Understanding package names and formats

You just downloaded a massive file from the Internet that contains lots of names, numbers, dots, gzs, and tars. What does all that stuff mean? Well, when you break it down, it's really not that complicated.

Most of the names of archive files containing Linux applications follow the GNU-style package-naming conventions. The following example illustrates the package-naming format:

```
mycoolapp-4.2.3.i386.rpm
mycoolapp-4.2.3.tar.gz
mycoolapp-4.2.3.src.tar.gz
mycoolapp-4.2.3.bin.SPARC.tar.gz
mycoolapp-4.2.3.bin.ELF.static.tar.gz
```

These examples represent several different packages of the same software application. The name of this package is `mycoolapp`. Following the package name is a set of numbers that represent the version of the package. In this case, it is version 4.2.3 (the major version number is 4, followed by minor version number and patch level 2.3). After the version number is a dot, followed by some optional parts, which are followed by indications of how the file is archived and compressed.

The first line shows a package that is in Red Hat Package Manager (`.rpm`) format. The `.i386` before the `.rpm` indicates that the package contains binaries that are built to run Intel i386 architecture computers (in other words, PCs). See the sidebar "RPM versus Building from Source" for the pros and cons of using prebuilt RPM binary packages as opposed to compiling the program yourself.

In the next two lines, each file contains the source code for the package. The files that make up the package were archived using the `tar` command (`.tar`) and compressed using the `gzip` command (`.gz`). You use these two commands to expand and uncompress the packages when you are ready to install the applications.

Between the version number and the `.tar.gz` suffixes there can be optional tags, separated by dots, which provide specific information about the contents of the package. In particular, if the package is a binary version, this information provides details about where the binaries will run. In the third line, the optional `.src` tag is added because the developer wanted to differentiate between the source and binary versions of this package. In the fourth line, the `.bin.SPARC` indicates that it is a binary package, ready to run on a SPARC workstation. The final line indicates that it is a binary package, consisting of ELF format executables that are statically linked.

RPM versus Building from Source

Binaries created in RPM format are easily installed, managed, and uninstalled using Red Hat tools. This is the recommended installation method for Red Hat Linux novices. Sometimes, however, building an application from source code may be preferable. Here are some arguments on both sides:

✦ **RPM** — Installing applications from an RPM archive is easy. After the application is installed, there are both shell commands and GUIs for managing, verifying, updating, and removing the RPM application. You don't need to know anything about Makefiles or compilers. When you install an RPM package, RPM tools even check to make sure that other packages that the package depends on are installed.

Because Red Hat has released RPM under the GNU, other Linux distributions have begun using it to distribute their software. Thus, most Linux applications are, or will be, available in RPM format.

✦ **Source Code** — It sometimes takes a while for a source code package to be made into RPM binaries. You may find yourself with software that is several versions old by using RPM, when you could simply download the latest source code and run a few `tar` and `make` commands. Also, by modifying the source code, you may be able to tailor the application to better suit your needs.

Here is a breakdown of the parts of a package name:

✦ *name* — This is generally an all-lowercase string of characters that identifies the application.

✦ dash (-)

✦ version — This is shown as major to minor version number from left to right.

✦ dot (.)

✦ `src` or `bin` — This is optional, with `src` usually implied if no indication is given.

✦ dot (.)

✦ type of binary — This is optional and can include several different tags to describe the content of the binary archive. For example, i386 indicates binaries intended for Intel architectures (386, 486, Pentium, and so on) and SPARC indicates binaries for a Sparc CPU.

✦ dot (.)

✦ archive type — Often `tar` is used (`.tar`)

✦ compression type — Often `gzip` is used (`.gzip`)

Using different archive and document formats

Many of the software packages that are not associated with a specific distribution (such as Red Hat, Debian, or Open Linux) use the `tar/gzip` method for archiving and compressing files. However, you may notice files with different suffixes at Linux FTP sites. Sometimes these files represent documents that can be in various formats. Also, several of the distributions have their own software packaging format, which are indicated by a different suffix.

Note Because we are using Red Hat Linux, most of the software applications we install are in Red Hat Package Management format (`.rpm`). Unless you want to build the software yourself — in which case you'll need the source code — RPM is the format to look for. When it is available, an RPM package from a Red Hat FTP site will provide your best chance for getting a software package that will run without modification on a Red Hat Linux system. RPM packages also let you use RPM tools to query packages, add packages, and remove the packages.

Table 5-1 describes the different file formats that you will encounter as you look for software at a Linux FTP site. Table 5-2 lists some of the common document formats that are used in distributing information in Linux.

<table>
<tr><td colspan="3">Table 5-1
Linux Archive File Formats</td></tr>
<tr><td>*Format*</td><td>*Suffix*</td><td>*Description*</td></tr>
<tr><td>Gzip file</td><td>`.gz` or `.z`</td><td>File was compressed using the GNU `gzip` utility. It can be uncompressed using the `gzip` or `gunzip` utilities (they are both the same).</td></tr>
<tr><td>Tar file</td><td>`.tar`</td><td>File was archived using the `tar` command. Tar is used to gather multiple files into a single archive file. You can expand the archive into separate files using tar with different options.</td></tr>
<tr><td>Bzip2</td><td>`.bz2`</td><td>File was compressed with the `bzip2` program.</td></tr>
<tr><td>Tar/compressed</td><td>`.taz` or `.tz`</td><td>File was archived with `tar` and compressed with the UNIX `compress` command. (The `compress` command is not part of the GNU because it is patented.)</td></tr>
</table>

Continued

Table 5-1 *(continued)*

Format	Suffix	Description
Linux Software Map	`.lsm`	File contains text that describes the content of an archive.
Debian Binary Package	`.deb`	File is a binary package used with the Debian Linux distribution. (See descriptions of how to convert Debian to Red Hat formats later in this chapter.)
Red Hat Package Management	`.rpm`	File is a binary package used with the Red Hat distribution. The format is also available to other Linux distributions.

Table 5-2
Linux Document Formats

Format	Suffix	Description
Hypertext Markup Language	`.html` or `.htm`	File is in hypertext format for reading by a Web browser program (such as Netscape Communicator).
PostScript	`.ps`	File is in PostScript format for outputting on a PostScript printer.
SGML	`.sgml`	File is in SGML, a standard document format. SGML is often used to produce documents that can later be output to a variety of formats.
DVI	`.dvi`	File is in DVI, the output format of the LaTeX text-processing tools. Convert these files to PostScript or Hewlett-Packard's PCL using the `dvips` and `dvilj` commands.
Plain text		Files without a suffix are usually plain text files (in ASCII format).

If you are not sure what format a file is in, use the `file` command as follows:

```
file archive-file
```

This command tells you if it is a GNU `tar` file, RPM, `gzip`, or other file format. (This is a good technique if a file was renamed and lost its suffix.)

Converting software packages with the alien command

If there is a package available in a non-RPM format that you want to use on your Red Hat Linux system, you may be able to use the `alien` command to convert the package to RPM format. The `alien` command lets you convert packages from Debien (.deb), Stampede (.slp), Slackware (.slp), or Red Hat package management (.rpm) to any of those other formats.

The advantage of converting a package from another format to RPM is that you can then manage that package using various RPM tools. As an example, I downloaded the bsdgames package from the Debian FTP site (`ftp://ftp.us.debian.org`). I then converted the package, which was in .deb format, to RPM format as follows:

```
# alien --to-rpm bsdgames_2.9-3.deb
```

In this case, an RPM file was created from the Debian package. The new file was called bsdgames-2.9-4.i386.rpm. After it was created, I could install it as I would any RPM file:

```
# rpm -i bsdgames-2.9-4.i386.rpm
```

After that, I could query the bsdgames package as I would any RPM package. For example, I could type `rpm -ql bsdgames` to list the contents of the package. Later, to delete the package, I can use the `rpm -e bsdgames` command.

With the `alien` command, you can also make Debian packages (`--to-deb` option), Slackware packages (`--to-tgz`), or Stampede packages (`--to-slp`). To create Debian packages, you need extra software packages that include gcc, make, debgmake, dpg-dev, and dpkg packages.

Caution   Though alien provides a quick way to convert software package to different formats, it should not be used to convert critical operating system packages. For example, you shouldn't expect system initialization packages to be reliably converted so they can be used in Red Hat Linux.

Installing Red Hat Linux Applications

Most of the Linux applications that you want to install are available in RPM format. There is probably a binary version of the application that specifically suits your platform. If no RPMs are available for the applications, you can probably find a source code version (often stored as a `tar/gzip` archive) that you can use to build the software yourself.

This section describes how to install and manage applications using tools created for RPM archive files. Later in this section, you will learn how to build and install applications that come as source code packages.

Installing and managing RPM files

When you get an application that is packaged in RPM format, you typically get a single file. The command used to work with RPM package files is *rpm*. To manage RPM packages, the rpm command has options that let you list all the packages that are installed, upgrade existing packages to newer versions, and query packages for information (such as the files or documentation included with the package). There is also a verify option that lets you check that all files that make up the package are present and unchanged.

The rpm command has these modes of operation:

- ✦ install (-i)
- ✦ upgrade (-U)
- ✦ query (-q)
- ✦ verify (-V)
- ✦ signature check (--checksig)
- ✦ uninstall (-e)
- ✦ build (-b)
- ✦ rebuild database (--rebuilddb)
- ✦ fix permissions (--setperms)
- ✦ set owners/groups (--setugids)
- ✦ show RC (--showrc)

With these options, you can install RPM packages and verify that their contents are properly installed, correcting any problems that occur.

The following sections describe how to use rpm to install and work with your RPM applications.

Caution   You must be logged in as the root user to add or remove packages. You may, however, list installed packages, query packages for information, or verify a package's contents without being logged in as the root user.

Installing with rpm

To install an RPM archive file with the rpm command, use the following syntax:

```
rpm -i [options] package
```

Package is the name of the RPM archive file. This package may be in the current directory, on a mounted CD (for example, /mnt/cdrom/RedHat/RPMS/whatever.rpm), or on an accessible FTP site (for example, ftp://sunsite.unc.edu/pub/Linux/apps/sound/cdrom/X/xcd-2.0-1.i386.rpm).

Note When you indicate a package from an FTP site, the file is downloaded before it is installed.

Along with the -i option, you can use these options to get feedback during the installation:

✦ -vv — Prints debugging information during installation. This is a good way to see everything that happens during the install process. (This output can be long, so you may want to pipe it to more.)

✦ -h — Prints 50 hash marks (#) as the package is unpacked. The intent is just to see the progress of the unpacking process (so you can tell if the program is still working or stalled).

✦ -percent — Prints the percentage of the total package that has been installed throughout the install process.

Before installing a package, rpm checks to make sure that it is not overwriting newer files or installing a package that has dependencies on other packages that are not installed. The following install options can be used to override conditions that may otherwise cause the installation to fail:

✦ --force — Forces the contents of the current package to be installed, even if the current package is older than the one already installed, contains files placed there by other packages, or is already installed. (This is the same as using the oldpackage, replacefiles, and replacepkgs options.)

✦ --oldpackage — Forces the package to be installed, even if the current package is older than the one already installed.

✦ --replacefiles — Forces files in this package to be installed, even if the files were placed there by other packages.

✦ --replacepkgs — Forces packages in this archive to be installed, even if they are already installed on the system.

✦ --nodeps — Skips package dependency checks and installs the package, even if packages it depends on are not installed.

✦ --ignorearch — Forces package to be installed, even if the binaries in the package don't match the architecture of your host computer.

✦ --ignoreos — Forces package to be installed, even if the binaries in the package don't match the architecture of your operating system.

The following is a simple rpm command line used to install an RPM archive.

```
rpm -i audiofile-devel-0.1.6-1.i386.rpm
```

I personally like to see some feedback when I install something (by default, rpm is suspiciously quiet when it succeeds). Here is what the command looked like when I added the -vv option to get more verbose feedback, along with some of the output:

```
# rpm -ivv audiofile-devel-0.2.1-2.i386.rpm
D: counting packages to install
D: found 1 packages
D: looking for packages to download
D: retrieved 0 packages
D: finding source and binary packages
D: New Header signature
       .
       .
D: opening database in //var/lib/rpm/
D: installing binary packages
Installing audiofile-devel-0.2.1-2.i386.rpm
       .
       .
D: package: audiofile-devel-0.2.1-2 files test = 0
D: running preinstall script (if any)
D: running postinstall script (if any)
```

From this output, you can see that rpm finds one package in this archive, verifies the signature, opens the RPM database, installs the packages, and runs any pre- or postinstall scripts. Another way of getting verification that the install is actually working is to add the -h option, as in the following example:

```
# rpm -ivh audiofile-devel-0.2.1-2.i386.rpm
audiofile-devel ###############################################
```

With the -h option, rpm chugs out 50 number signs (#) until the package is done installing. As you can see, when everything goes well, installing with rpm is quite simple. Some problems can occur, however. Here are a couple of them:

✦ Package dependencies errors—If the package you are installing requires an additional package for it to work properly, you will see an error noting the missing package. You should get and install that package before trying your package again. (You can override the failure with install options described above, but I don't recommend that because your package may not work without the dependent package.)

✦ Nonroot user errors—If rpm -i is run by someone who is not the root user, the command will fail. The output will indicate that the /var/lib/rpm database could not be opened. Log in as root user and try again.

Upgrading packages with rpm

The upgrade option (-U) with rpm behaves pretty much like the install option. The difference is that it uninstalls the old package before installing the new version of the package. The format is:

```
rpm -U [options] package
```

Tip You can use the -U option regardless of whether you are doing a new install or an upgrade. With -U, the package will install in either case. So `rpm -U` will always work, while `rpm -i` will fail if the package is already installed.

One issue when upgrading is installing an older version of a package. For example, if you install a new version of some software and it doesn't work as well, you will want to go back to the old version. To do this, you can use the `--oldpackage` option as follows:

```
rpm -U --oldpackage AnotherLevel-0.7.4-1.noarch.rpm
```

If a later package of this name already exists, it is removed and the older version is installed.

Removing packages with rpm

If you no longer want to use a package (or you just want to recover some disk space), use the -e option to remove a package. In its simplest form, you use `rpm` with the -e option as follows:

```
rpm -e package
```

If there are no dependencies on this package, it is silently removed. Before you remove a package, however, you may want to do a quick check for dependencies. The -q option is used for a variety of query options. (Checking for dependencies isn't necessary because `rpm` checks for dependencies before it removes a package. You may want to do this for your own information, however.) To check for dependencies, do the following:

```
rpm -q --whatrequires package
```

If you decide to remove the package, I recommend using the -vv option with `rpm -e`. This lets you see the actual files that are being removed. I also suggest that you either direct the output to a file or pipe it to `more` because the output will probably run off the screen. Here's an example:

```
rpm -evv xpilot | more
```

This example removes the `xpilot` package and shows you the files that are being removed one page at a time. (Press the Spacebar to page through the output.)

Other options that you can run with `rpm -e` can be used to override conditions that would prevent the package from being removed or to prevent some processing (such as not running preuninstall and postuninstall scripts). Three of those options are as follows:

✦ --nodeps — Uninstall the package without checking for dependencies.

✦ --noscripts — Uninstall the package without running any preuninstall or postuninstall scripts.

✦ --notriggers — Uninstall the package without executing scripts that are triggered by removing the package.

If you feel nervous about boldly removing a package, you can always run the uninstall in test mode (--test) before you do the real uninstall. Test mode shows you everything that would happen in the uninstall without actually uninstalling. (Add the --vv option to see the details.) Here's an example:

```
# rpm -evv --test xpilot | more
D: counting packages to uninstall
D: opening database in //var/lib/rpm/
D: found 1 packages to uninstall
D: uninstalling record number 4545368
D: will remove files test = 1
D: /usr/share/doc/xpilot-4.3.2-1/doc/man/xpilots.man.msub -
removing
D: /usr/share/doc/xpilot-4.3.2-1/doc/man/xpilots.man - removing
   .
   .
   .
D: /etc/X11/wmconfig/xpilot - removing
D: removing database entry
```

If the results look fine, you can run the command again, without the --test option, to have the package removed.

Querying packages with rpm

Using the query options (-q) of rpm, you can get information about RPM packages. This can be simply listing the packages that are installed or printing detailed information about a package. Here is the basic format of an rpm query command (at least one option is required):

```
rpm -q [options]
```

The following are some useful options you can use with an rpm query:

✦ -qa — Lists all installed packages.

✦ -qf *file* — Lists the package that owns *file*. (The file must include the full path name or rpm assumes the current directory.)

✦ -qi *package* — Lists lots of information about a package.

✦ -qR *package* — Lists components (such as libraries and commands) that *package* depends on.

✦ -ql *package* — Lists all the files contained in *package*.

✦ -qd *package*—Lists all documentation files that come in *package*.

✦ -qc *package*—Lists all configuration files that come in *package*.

To list all the packages installed on your computer, use the -a query option. Because this is a long list, you should either pipe the output to more or, possibly, use grep to find the package you want. The following command line displays a list of all installed RPM packages, and then shows only those names that include the string of characters xfree. (The -i option to grep says to ignore case.)

```
rpm -qa |grep -i xfree
```

If you are interested in details about a particular package, you can use the rpm -i query option. In the following example, information about the dosfstools package (for working with DOS filesystems in Linux) is displayed:

```
# rpm -qi dosfstools
Name        : dosfstools          Relocations: (not relocatable)
Version     : 2.7                      Vendor: Red Hat, Inc.
Release     : 1                    Build Date: Fri 06 Jul 2001 08:29:15 AM PDT
Install date: Sun 29 Jul 2001 01:12:47 PM PDT  Build Host: devel.redhat.com
Group       : Applications/System  Source RPM: dosfstools-2.7-1.src.rpm
Size        : 194162                  License: GPL
Packager    : Red Hat, Inc. <bugzilla.redhat.com/bugzilla>
Summary     : Utilities for making and checking MS-DOS FAT filesystems in Linux.
Description : The dosfstools package includes the mkdosfs and dosfsck utilities,
which respectively make and check MS-DOS FAT filesystems on hard
drives or on floppies.
```

To find out more about a package's contents, you can use the -l (list) option with your query. The following example shows the complete path names of files contained in the xpilot package:

```
# rpm -ql xpilot | more
/etc/X11/wmconfig/xpilot
/etc/X11/wmconfig/xpilots
/usr/X11R6/bin/xp-replay
/usr/X11R6/bin/xpilot
    .
    .
    .
```

Would you like to know how to use the components in a package? Using the -d option with query will display the documentation (man pages, README files, HOWTOs, etc.) that is included with the package. If you are having trouble getting your X Window System running properly, you can use the following command line to find documents that may help:

```
# rpm -qd XFree86 | more
/usr/X11R6/man/man1/editres.1x.gz
/usr/X11R6/man/man1/iceauth.1x.gz
```

```
/usr/X11R6/man/man1/lbxproxy.1x.gz
/usr/X11R6/man/man1/libxrx.1x.gz
/usr/X11R6/man/man1/lndir.1x.gz
/usr/X11R6/man/man1/makedepend.1x.gz
/usr/X11R6/man/man1/makepsres.1x.gz
/usr/X11R6/man/man1/makestrs.1x.gz
/usr/X11R6/man/man1/mkcfm.1x.gz
        .
        .
        .
```

Many packages have configuration files associated with them. To see what configuration files are associated with a particular package, use the -c option with a query. For example, this is what you would type to see configuration files that are used with the ppp package:

```
# rpm -qc ppp
/etc/pam.d/ppp
/etc/ppp/chap-secrets
/etc/ppp/options
/etc/ppp/pap-secrets
```

If you ever want to know which package a particular command or configuration file came from, you can use the -qf option. In the following example, the -qf option displays the fact that the chgrp command comes from the fileutils package:

```
# rpm -qf /bin/chgrp
fileutils-4.1-4
```

Verifying packages with rpm

If something in a software package isn't working properly, or if you suspect that your system has been tampered with, the verify (-V) option of rpm can help you verify the contents of your software packages. Information about each installed package is stored on your computer in the RPM database. By using the verify option, you can check if any changes were made to the components in the package.

Various file size and permissions tests are done during a verify operation. If everything is fine, there is no output. Any components that have been changed from when they were installed, however, will be printed along with information indicating how they were changed. Here's an example:

```
# rpm -V ppp
S.5....T c /etc/ppp/chap-secrets
S.5....T c /etc/ppp/options
S.5....T c /etc/ppp/pap-secrets
```

This output shows that the ppp package (used to dial-up a TCP/IP network such as the Internet) has had three files changed since it was installed. The notation at the beginning shows that the file size (S), the MD5 sum (5), and the modification time

(T) have all changed. The letter c shows that these are all configuration files. By reviewing these files and seeing that the changes were only those that I made to get PPP working, I can verify that the package is okay.

The indicators that you may see when you verify the contents of a configuration file are:

- ✦ 5 — MD5 Sum — An md5 checksum indicates a change to the file contents.
- ✦ S — File size — The number of characters in the file has changed.
- ✦ L — Symlink — The file has become a symbolic link to another file.
- ✦ T — Mtime — The modification time of the file has changed.
- ✦ D — Device — The file has become a device special file.
- ✦ U — User — The user name that owns the file has changed.
- ✦ G — Group — The group assigned to the file has changed.
- ✦ M — Mode — If the ownership or permission of the file changed.

Tip

There is a utility available for browsing the contents of RPM files in a Windows system. By using the `rpmbrowser.exe` utility, you can list and extract files from an RPM distribution. This utility is available from `winsite.com` (search for `rpmbrowser` from `www.winsite.com/ws_search.html`).

Building and installing from source code

If no binary version of the package that you want is available, or if you just want to tailor a package to your needs, you can always install the package from source code. The source code CD that comes with Red Hat Linux contains the source code equivalent (SRPMS) of the binary packages you installed. You can modify the source code and rebuild it to suit your needs.

Note

Though the Red Hat Linux source code CD is not included with this book, you can obtain a copy of the CD from Hungry Minds. Refer to the Linux source code mail-in coupon available on the third CD with this book.

Software packages that are not available in SRPMS format are typically available in `tar/gzip` format. Although the exact instructions for installing an application from a source code archive vary, many packages that are in the `.gz` and `.tar` formats follow the same basic procedure.

Tip

Before you install from source code, you will need to install a variety of software development packages. If you have the disk space, I recommend that you install all software development packages that are recommended during Red Hat installation. (It's annoying to have an install fail because of a missing component. You can end up wasting a lot of time figuring out what is missing.)

The following is a minimal list of C-programming software development tools:

✦ `glibc` — Contains important shared libraries, the C library, and standard math library.

✦ `glibc-devel` — Contains standard header files needed to create executables.

✦ `binutils` — Contains utilities needed to compile programs (such as the assembler and linker).

✦ `kernel-source` — Contains the Linux kernel source code and is needed to build most C programs.

✦ `libc` — Contains libraries needed for programs that were based on `libc` 5, so older applications can run on `glibc` (`libc` 6) systems.

Installing software in SRPMS format

To install a source package from the Red Hat Linux source CD, use the following procedure:

1. Insert the Red Hat Linux source CD into the CD-ROM drive. It should mount automatically. (If it doesn't, type `mount /mnt/cdrom` in a Terminal window.)

2. Change to the source directory on the CD. For example:

   `cd /mnt/cdrom/SRPMS`

3. Choose the package you want to install (type `ls` to see the packages) and install it using the following command:

   `rpm -iv packagename*.src.rpm`

   (Replace *packagename* with the name of the package you are installing.) The source is installed in the Red Hat Linux source tree (`/usr/src/redhat`). Spec files are copied to `/usr/src/redhat/SPECS`.

4. Change to the SPECS directory as follows:

   `cd /usr/src/redhat/SPECS`

5. Unpack the source code as follows:

   `rpm -bp packagename*.spec`

   The source code for the package is installed into the `/usr/src/redhat/BUILD/package` directory.

6. You can now make changes to the files in the package's BUILD directory. Read the README, Makefile, and other documentation files for details on how to build the individual package.

Installing software in gzip/tar format

Here are some generic instructions that you can use to install many Linux software packages that are in `gzip/tar` format:

1. Get the source code package from the Internet or from a CD distribution and copy it into an empty directory (preferably using a name that identifies the package).

2. Assuming the file is compressed using `gzip`, uncompress the file using the following command:

   ```
   gzip -d package.tar.gz
   ```

   The result is that the package is uncompressed and the `.gz` is removed from the package name (for example, `package.tar`).

3. From the resulting `tar` archive, run the `tar` command as follows:

   ```
   tar xvf package.tar
   ```

   This command extracts the files from the archive and copies them to a subdirectory of the current directory.

4. Change directories to the new subdirectory created in Step 3, as follows:

   ```
   cd newdir
   ```

5. Look for a file called `INSTALL` or `README`. One of these files should give you instructions on how to proceed with the installation. In general, the `make` command is used to install the package. Here are a few things to look for in the current directory:

   - If there is a `Make.in` file, try running:

     ```
     ./configure -prefix=/usr
     make all
     ```

   - If there is an `Imake` file, try running:

     ```
     xmkmf -a
     make all
     ```

   - If there is a `Make` file, try running:

     ```
     make all
     ```

After the program is built and installed, you may need to do additional configuration. You should consult the `man` pages and/or the HOWTOs that come with the software for information on how to proceed.

 Tip Even if you are not a programmer, reading the source code used to make a program can often give you insight into how that program works.

To try out this procedure, I downloaded the `whichman` package, which includes utilities that let you find manual pages by entering keywords. The file I downloaded, `whichman-1.5.tar.gz`, was placed in a directory that I created called `/usr/sw/which`. I then ran the `gzip` and `tar` commands, using `whichman-1.5.tar.gz` and `whichman-1.5.tar` as options, respectively.

I changed to the new directory, `cd /usr/sw/which/whichman-1.5`. I then listed its contents. The README file contained information about the contents of the package and how to install it. As the README file suggested, I typed `make`, and then `make install`. The commands `whichman`, `ftwhich`, and `ftff` were installed in `/usr/bin`. (At this point, you can check the `man` page for each component to see what it does.)

The last thing I found in the README file was that a bit of configuration needed to be done. I added a `MANPATH` variable to my `$HOME/.bashrc` to identify the location of `man` pages on my computer to be searched by the `whichman` utility. The line I added looked like this:

```
export MANPATH=/usr/man:/usr/X11R6/man:/usr/doc/samba-2.0.2/docs
```

In case you are wondering, `whichman`, `ftwhich`, and `ftff` are commands that you can use to search for `man` pages. They can be used to find several locations of a `man` page, `man` pages that are close to the name you enter, or `man` pages that are located beneath a point in the directory structure, respectively.

Running X Window Applications

Setting up and configuring the X Window System to your liking is the hard part. By comparison, using X to run applications is relatively easy. If you have used Microsoft Windows operating systems, you already know the most basic ways of running an application from a graphical desktop. X, however, provides a much more flexible environment for running native Linux applications.

See Chapter 4 for information on setting up an X desktop.

Starting applications from a menu

To run applications on your own desktop, most X window managers provide a menu, similar to the Microsoft Start menu, to display and select X applications. Applications are usually organized in categories. Open the menu, select the category, and then select the application to run. Figure 5-1 is an example of the GNOME Main Menu.

Figure 5-1: Start X applications from the GNOME Main Menu.

Starting applications from a Run Program window

Not all installed applications appear on the menus provided with your window manager. For running other applications, some window managers provide a window, similar to the GNOME Run Program window, that lets you type in the name of the program you want to run.

To access the Run Program window:

1. Open the GNOME Main Menu

2. Click Run.

   The Run Program window displays a list of programs you can select from.

3. Click the program you want and then click Run.

   If the application you want isn't on the list, you can click Advanced. Then you can either type the command you want to run (along with any options) and click Run, or you can click Browse to browse through your directories to select a program to run. If you are running a program that needs to run in a Terminal window, such as the vi command, click the Run in Terminal button before running the command. Figure 5-2 is an example of the Run Program window.

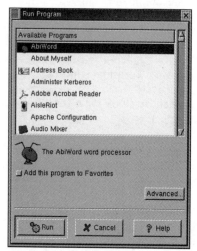

Figure 5-2: Select a program to run from the list in the Run Program window.

Starting applications from a Terminal window

I prefer to run an X application, at least for the first time, from a Terminal window. There are several reasons why I prefer a Terminal window to selecting an application from a menu or Run Program window:

✦ If there is a problem with the application, you get to see error messages. Applications usually just fail silently if an application that is started from a menu or Run Program window fails.

✦ Applications selected from menus are run with set options. If you want to change those options, you have to change the configuration file that set up the menu and make the changes there.

✦ If you want to try out a few different options with an application, a Terminal window is an easy way to start it, stop it, and change its options.

When you have found an application and figured out the options that you like, you can add it to a menu or a panel (if your window manager supports those features). In that way, you can run a program exactly as you want, instead of the way it is given to you on a menu.

Tip   To add an application so that it appears in your GNOME desktop Panel, open the GNOME menu and choose Panel ⇨ Add to Panel ⇨ Launcher. Fill in the fields needed to identify the application. In the Command field, type in the command name and the options that you like. Click the Icon box to select an icon to represent the command. Click OK when you are done, and the application appears on the launcher.

Here is a procedure to run X applications from a Terminal window.

1. Open a Terminal window from your desktop (look for a Terminal icon on your Panel or a Terminal selection on a menu.)

2. Type

   ```
   $ echo $DISPLAY
   ```

   The result should be something similar to the following:

   ```
   :0
   ```

   This indicates that the Terminal window will, by default, direct any X application you run from this window to display 0 on your system. (If you don't see a value when you type that command, type `export DISPLAY=:0` to set the display value.)

3. Type the following command:

   ```
   $ xmms &
   ```

   The `xmms` program should appear on your desktop, ready to work with. You should note the following:

- The `xmms` command runs in the background of the Terminal window (&). This means that you can continue to use the Terminal window while `xmms` is running. Because it is a child process of the Terminal window, `xmms` will close if you close the Terminal window.

- I encountered no errors running `xmms` on this occasion. With other applications at times, however, text appeared in the Terminal window after the command was run. The text may tell me that the command can't find certain information or perhaps that certain fonts or colors cannot be displayed. That information would be lost if I had run the command from a menu.

4. If you want to know what options are available, type:

   ```
   $ xmms --help
   ```

5. Try it with a few options. For example, if you want to begin by playing a file, you could type:

   ```
   $ xmms file.wav
   ```

 Refer to Chapter 4 for information on X resources and options that are available to most X commands.

6. When you are ready to close the window, you can either do so from the `xmms` window (right-click on the `xmms` window and select Exit) or you can kill the process in the Terminal window. Type `jobs` to see the job number of the process. If it was job number 2, for example, you would type `kill %2` to kill the `xmms` program.

You should try running a few other X commands. Many X commands are stored in `/usr/X11R6/bin`. A few of these commands are described in the following sections.

Using X Window utilities

A common set of X utilities comes with most versions of the X Window System. The Terminal window (`xterm` command) is a useful X Window utility because it enables you to run other commands and utilities. To get a feel for using X utilities, try several, such as a simple text editor (`xedit`), a calculator (`xcalc`), and some clock programs (`xclock`, `rclock`, `wmclock`, and `xdaliclock`).

Using a Terminal window

The UNIX system, on which Red Hat Linux is based, began as a completely text-based system. There were no colors or graphics. There was no mouse. Everything had to be done by typing letters, numbers, and special keys (for example, function keys, Ctrl, Alt, and so on) from a keyboard. The shell command interpreter (usually just referred to as the *shell*) interpreted the keystrokes.

Cross-Reference   See Chapter 3 for a description of the shell command interpreter.

If you are accessing Red Hat Linux from the X Window System, the Terminal window provides your text-based interface to Linux. As you use Red Hat Linux, you will find that there are many times when you want to use a Terminal window. Moving up and down the file system can be quicker in a Terminal window than in a file manager. Some useful utilities don't have graphical equivalents. And, as I stated earlier, there are even reasons for starting X applications from a Terminal window.

Every window manager provides a menu selection for one or more ways of opening a Terminal window. As an alternative, there are several different commands available with Red Hat Linux that can be used to start a Terminal window, like the following:

✦ xterm—This is the most common command used to open a Terminal window. Most other Terminal windows are based on this command.

✦ rxvt—A reduced-size Terminal window, which is designed to run more efficiently.

✦ gnome-terminal—A Terminal window available with the GNOME window manager.

If you are using the GNOME window manager, which is the default, there are several features that make it easier for you to customize the GNOME Terminal window (gnome-terminal command). This window has a menu bar that offers File, Settings, and Help buttons. Figure 5-3 shows a GNOME Terminal window.

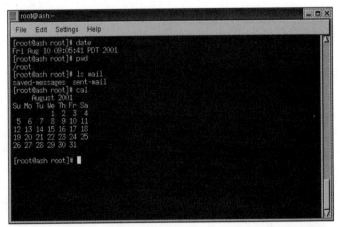

Figure 5-3: An added menu bar helps customize the GNOME Terminal window.

With the GNOME Terminal window, you can change the Terminal window attributes by selecting Settings ⇨ Preferences instead of messing around with command-line options or X resources. From the window that appears, you can change the following Terminal window preferences:

✦ Font

✦ Bold text

✦ Blinking cursor

✦ Menu bar (hidden or not)

✦ Terminal bell (silent or not)

✦ Erase key (DEL or backspace)

✦ Background image

✦ Color (foreground and background)

✦ Scrolling (scrollbar position and number of scrollback lines)

If you get really stuck, you can click Help to view the GNOME Terminal User's Guide.

Using a Text Editor

One of the most intimidating tasks in Linux is learning to use a text editor. The most popular editors are vi and emacs. People who use one of these editors typically claim that their editor is the most powerful and easy to use. The truth is that both take some time to learn.

See Chapter 3 for a description of how to use the vi editor.

One editor that takes almost no time to learn, however, is the xedit text editor. If you are using X, this editor is a good way to go. To edit a text file with xedit, simply type the following:

```
xedit file
```

Replace *file* with the name of the file that you want to edit. Editing is quite intuitive. Click the mouse pointer where you want the text to begin, then just type. You can move around using the arrow keys. Scroll up and down a page using the PgUp and PgDn keys. When you are done, click Save, and then Quit to close the file.

If you are a bit more adventurous, there are a few keystrokes you can use to work with xedit, which are listed in Table 5-3.

Table 5-3
Keystrokes for Editing with xedit

Keystrokes	Description
Alt+b	Go back one word
Ctrl+b	Go back one character
Alt+v	Go to previous page
Alt+<	Go to file beginning
Ctrl+p	Go to previous line
Ctrl+a	Go to line beginning
Ctrl+z	Scroll down one line
Alt+f	Go forward one word
Ctrl+f	Go forward one character
Alt+z	Scroll up one line
Ctrl+v	Go to next page
Alt+>	Go to file end
Ctrl+e	Go to line ending
Ctrl+d	Delete next character
Alt+d	Delete next word
Alt+H	Delete previous word
Alt+k	Delete to end of paragraph
Ctrl+k	Delete to the end of line
Ctrl+h	Delete previous character
Alt+h	Delete previous word

Using a calculator

The X Calculator window (xcalc) provides the functions of a scientific calculator. The calculator can operate in modes that emulate two different types of calculators: the Texas Instruments TI-30 and the Hewlett-Packard HP-10C. To start up a scientific calculator, type:

```
$ xcalc &
```

This starts the calculator in TI-30 mode. To start the calculator in HP-10C mode, type the following:

```
$ xcalc -rpn &
```

Figure 5-4 shows the calculator in two different modes. The TI-30 is on the right and the HP-10C is on the left.

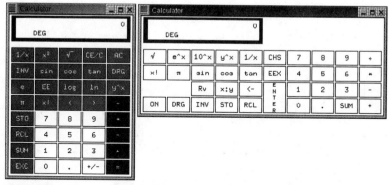

Figure 5-4: The `xcalc` calculator operates in TI-30 (right) and HP-10C (left) modes.

Along with the calculator buttons, you can use keyboard accelerators to operate the calculator. Table 5-4 lists some of the keyboard controls that you can use with the calculator.

Table 5-4 Keyboard Accelerators for xcalc Calculator	
Keystrokes	*Description*
Numbers	Type any number to have it appear in the display
Spacebar	Clear the calculator
Del or Backspace	Delete previous number
q or Ctrl+c	Quit
+	Add
-	Subtract
*	Multiply
/	Divide
=	Equals
c	Cosine
d	Degree

Continued

Keystrokes	Description
i	Inverse
s	Sine
t	Tangent
p	Pi
!	Factorial
(	Left parenthesis
)	Right parenthesis

Table 5-4 *(continued)*

Using a clock

There are several X clock programs that come with the Red Hat Linux distribution. A lot of people like to have one on their desktop and some of the clocks have nice features. Figure 5-5 shows four different X clocks (from left to right): xclock, rclock, wmclock, and xdaliclock (bottom).

Figure 5-5: Red Hat Linux provides a choice of clock programs, including xclock, rclock, wmclock, and xdaliclock.

Note   You may not have every clock available that is shown here. The following is a list of clocks, with the package for each clock listed next to it: xclock (XFree86-tools package), rclock (rxvt package), wmclock (WindowMaker package), and xdaliclock (xdaliclock package).

Some of the things you can do with the different clock programs are as follows:

✦ xclock — You can set xclock to display a clock face and hands (-analog option) or numbers (-digital option). Set -chime to have the clock ring twice on the hour and once on the half-hour. Set xclock to update the time every few seconds (-update *seconds*). Set the update to less than 30 seconds and a second hand is added to the display.

✦ rclock — Besides displaying the time and date, rclock can tell you when incoming mail arrives; it can start applications at specific times, and alert you to appointments. Place a .rclock file in your home directory and add the following types of entries to it:

```
09:00 mtwrf * Hello.\nRead your mail?;rxvt -e mail
11:45 mtwrf * Put your mail out before noon!
```

The first line has the message "Hello. Read your mail?" appear in a dialog box every morning (Monday through Friday) at 9:00 a.m. If you click Start in that box, the mail program starts in a Terminal window. The second line simply displays a dialog box with the message "Put your mail out before noon!" every weekday morning at 11:45 a.m. (Consult the rclock man page for more ways to use the .rclock file.)

✦ wmclock — The wmclock program comes with the WindowMaker window manager package. This clock doesn't seem to do much, but it is more pleasing to the eye than the others and comes in a compact size. (This clock may not be installed by default.)

✦ xdaliclock — The numbers on the digital readout of the xdaliclock program melt into each other. It's cool to watch. There are a few options that let you set the clock to a 12-hour clock (-12) or 24-hour clock (-24). You can also set it to update every second (-seconds option). To have the clock continuously change colors, use the -cycle option. (This clock may not be installed by default.)

Running remote X applications

X lets you start an application from anywhere on the network and have it show up on your X display. Suddenly, instead of being limited by the size of your hard disk and the power of your CPU and RAM, you can draw on resources from any computer that gives you access to those resources.

Think about the possibilities. You can work with applications launched from any other computer that can run an X application — from a small PC to a supercomputer. Given the proper permission, you can work with files, printers, backup devices, removable drives, other users, and any other resources on the remote computer as though you were working on that computer.

With this power, however, comes responsibility. You need to protect the access to your display, especially in networks where the other machines and users are not known or trusted. For example, you wouldn't want to allow anyone to display a login screen on your display, encouraging you to inadvertently give some cracker your login and password.

To run remote X applications, you basically only need to know how to identify remote X displays and how to use whatever security measures are put in place to protect your network resources. Those issues are described in the following sections.

Identifying remote X displays

If there is an X application installed on another computer on your network and you want to use it from your desktop, follow these steps:

✦ Open permissions to your X server so that the remote application can access your display.

✦ Identify your X server display to the application when it starts up.

When you run an X client on your local system, your local display is usually identified as :0. The :0 represents the first display on the local system. To identify that display to a remote system, however, you need to add your computer's hostname. For example, if your computer were named *whatever*, your display name would be:

```
whatever:0
```

Tip

In most cases, the hostname is the TCP/IP name. For the computers on your local network, the name may be in your /etc/hosts file, or it may be determined using the Domain Name System (DNS) service. You could also use a full domain name, such as hatbox.handsonhistory.com. X does support other types of transport, such as DECnet. A DECnet address has two colons separating the hostname and display number (for example, whatever::0).

You will probably use the display name in this form at least 99 percent of the time you run a remote X application. In certain cases, however, the information may be different. If your computer had multiple X displays (keyboard, mouse, and monitor), you may have numbers other than :0 (:1, :2, and so on). It is also possible for one keyboard and mouse to be controlling more than one monitor, in which case you could add a screen number to the address, like this:

```
whatever:0.1
```

This address identifies the second screen (.1) on the first display (:0). The first screen is identified as .0 (which is the default because most displays only have one screen). Unless you have multiple physical screens, however, you can skip the screen identifier.

There are two ways to identify your display name to a remote X application:

✦ `DISPLAY` shell variable—The `DISPLAY` shell variable can be set to the system name and number identifying your display. After this is done, the output from any X application run from that shell will appear on the display indicated. For example, to set the `DISPLAY` variable to the first display on `whatever`, type one of the following:

```
export DISPLAY=whatever:0
setenv DISPLAY whatever:0
```

The first example is how you would set it on a `bash` or `ksh` shell. The second example works for a `csh` shell.

✦ `-display` option—Another method for identifying a remote display is to add the `-display` option to the command line when you run the X application. This overrides the `DISPLAY` variable. For example, to open an `xterm` window on a remote system so that it appears on the first display on `whatever`, type the following:

```
xterm -display whatever:0
```

With this information, you should be able to run an X application from any computer that you can access from your local computer. The following sections describe how you may use this information to start a remote X application.

Launching a remote X application

Suppose you want to run an application from a computer named `remote1` on your local area network (in your same domain). Your local computer is `local1`, and the remote computer is `remote1`. The following steps show how to run an X application from `remote1` from your X display on `local1`.

Caution

This procedure assumes that no special security procedures are implemented. It is the default situation and is designed for sharing applications among trusted computers (usually single-user workstations) on a local network. This method is inherently insecure and requires that you trust all users on computers to which you allow access.

1. Open a Terminal window on the local computer.

2. Allow access for the remote computer (`remote1`) to the local X display by typing the following from the Terminal window:

```
$ xhost +remote1
remote1 being added to access control list
```

3. Log in to the remote computer (`remote1`) using the following command:

```
$ rlogin -l user remote1
Password:
```

Replace *user* with the name of the user login that you have on the remote computer. (If you have the same user name on both computers, which is sometimes the case, you can skip the -l *user* option. The rlogin command assumes your current login name.) You will be prompted for a password.

Note   By default, the rlogin service is not enabled in Red Hat Linux. The server (in this example, remote1) must consider the security consequences of enabling remote login services.

4. Type the password for the remote user login. (You are now logged in as the remote user in the Terminal window.)

5. Set the DISPLAY variable on the remote computer to your local computer. For example, if your computer were named pine, the command would appear as:

```
export DISPLAY=pine:0
```

(If you are using a csh shell on the remote system, you may need to type setenv DISPLAY pine:0.)

6. At this point, any X application you run from the remote system from this shell will appear on the local display. For example, to run a remote Terminal window so that it appears locally, type:

```
$ xterm -title "Terminal from Remote1"
```

The Terminal window appears on the local display with the word *Remote1* in the title bar.

Tip   As a rule, I use the -title option when I run remote X applications. In the title, I try to indicate the remote computer name. That way, I am reminded that the application is not running locally.

You need to remember some things about the remote application that is now appearing on your display:

✦ If you only use the login to run remote applications, you can add the line exporting the DISPLAY variable to a user configuration file on the remote system (such as .bashrc, if you use the bash shell). After that, any application that you run will be directed to your local display.

✦ Even though the application looks as though it is running locally, all the work is being done on the remote system. For example, if you ran a word processing program remotely, it would use the remote CPU and when you save a file, it is saved to the remote file system.

Caution   Don't forget when a remote shell or file editor is open on your desktop. Sometimes people forget that a window is remote and will edit some important configuration file on the remote system by mistake (such as the /etc/fstab file). You could damage the remote system with this type of mistake.

Securing X remote applications

There are several different methods available to prevent just any X application from appearing on your display. Each method offers a different level of security, as well as different amounts of setup. The major security methods that are supported include:

✦ **Host Access**—This method, described earlier as a default method, lets you decide which host computers can have access to your computer's X display. Use the `xhost` command to indicate those computers that are allowed access (`xhost +`*hostname*) and those that are not (`xhost -`*hostname*). If you allow a host access, any user from that computer is allowed access. This security method works best with small networks and single-user computers owned by people you trust.

✦ **Magic Cookie**—This method, referred to as the MIT-MAGIC-COOKIE-1 method, lets you grant an individual user remote access to your display. The remote client must present a valid cookie before it can access your display.

The steps go something like this: You generate a magic cookie (using the `mcookie` command); you refer to the cookie when you start your X server (usually from a copy of the cookie in your `$HOME/.Xauthority` file); you distribute this cookie to remote computers that want to show X clients on your display; and the remote client refers to this cookie when it starts.

There are other X security methods that are also based on storing one or more randomly generated keys in the `.Xauthority` file. XDM-AUTHORIZATION-1 uses a two-part key—a DES encryption key (56-bit) and some random data (64-bit)—to enable access. When a system supports secure RPC, the SUN-DES-1 method can be used to enable access by setting up public and private key pairs that can be validated on a per user basis. Finally, the MIT-KERBEROS-5 method enables both the X client and X server to validate each other (using a Kerberos trusted third party).

For more information about Kerberos, visit the Kerberos home page at `web.mit.edu/kerberos/www/index.html`. For general information on Linux security, you could refer to the *Linux Security Toolkit* by David A. Bandel, published by Hungry Minds, Inc.

To create secure connections, where information is encrypted for transfer, use the `ssh` secure shell. You can use `ssh` instead of `rlogin` to do remote logins as described in a previous example. The `ssh` utility has recently become available with Red Hat Linux because the United States Government has changed export restrictions that relate to encryption technology. For more information about `ssh`, visit the Secure Shell Community site (`www.ssh.org`).

Using Emulators to Run Applications from Other Operating Systems

Linux is ready to run applications that were created specifically for Linux, the X Window System, and many UNIX systems. Many other applications that were originally created for other operating systems have also been ported to Linux. There are still, however, thousands of applications created for other operating systems for which there are no Linux versions.

Linux can run some applications that are intended for other operating systems using *emulator* programs. An emulator, as the name implies, tries to act like something it is not. In the case of an operating system, an emulator tries to present an environment that looks to the application like the intended operating system. In the next sections, I discuss emulators that enable you to run applications that are intended for the following operating systems:

✦ DOS

✦ Windows 3.1

✦ Windows 95

✦ Windows 98

✦ Windows NT

✦ Macintosh

Note There is currently no product that offers a way to run Windows 2000 applications specifically in Linux. However, any application that is Win32 compatible should, in theory, be able to run using software such as WINE (described later). Whether or not a Windows application will run in an emulator in Linux must really be checked on a case-by-case basis.

Emulation programs for running DOS programs are available for Red Hat Linux. You need to install the dosemu and/or xdosemu packages (which are available from Red Hat Linux FTP sites, though not part of the basic Red Hat Linux distribution). DOS emulation commands from these packages include: dos, xtermdos, dosdebug, xdos, and dosexec. Other operating system emulation programs can be added to your system, including:

✦ WINE, which lets you run Windows 3.1, Windows 95, Windows 98, and Windows NT binaries. (Windows NT programs are not well supported.)

✦ Bochs, which is a PC emulation software package that emulates the x86 CPU to run DOS, Windows 95, Minix 2.0, and other operating systems.

✦ ARDI Executor, which enables you to run applications that are intended for the Macintosh operating system.

In general, the older and less complex a program is, the better chance it has to run in an emulator. Character-based applications generally run better than graphics-based applications. Also, programs tend to run slower in emulation, due sometimes to additional debugging code put into the emulators.

Running DOS applications

Because Linux was originally developed on PCs, a variety of tools were developed to help developers and users bridge the gap between Linux and DOS systems. A set of Linux utilities called *Mtools* lets you work with DOS files and directories from within Linux. A DOS emulator called `dosemu` lets you run DOS applications from within a DOS environment that is actually running within Linux (much the way a DOS window runs within a Windows operating system).

Using mtools

`Mtools` are mostly DOS commands that have the letter *m* in front of them and that run in Linux (though there are a few exceptions that are named differently). Using these commands, you can easily work with DOS files and file systems. Table 5-5 lists `mtools` that are available with Linux (if you have the `mtools` package installed):

Table 5-5
Mtools Available with Linux

Command	Function
mattrib	The DOS attrib command, which is used to change an MS-DOS file attribute flag.
mbadblocks	The DOS badblocks command, which is used to test a floppy disk and mark any bad blocks contained on the floppy in its FAT.
mcd	The DOS cd command, which is used to change the working directory to another DOS directory. (The default directory is A:\) that is used by other mtools.
mcheck	The DOS check command, which is used to verify a file.
mcopy	The DOS copy command, which is used to copy files from one location to another.
mdel	The DOS del command, which is used to delete files.
mdeltree	The DOS deltree command, which is used to delete an MS-DOS directory along with the files and subdirectories it contains.
mdir	The DOS dir command, which is used to list the contents of a directory.

Continued

Table 5-5 *(continued)*

Command	Function
mdu	The Linux du command, which is used to show the amount of disk space used by a DOS directory.
mformat	The DOS format command, which is used to format a DOS floppy disk.
minfo	This command is used to print information about a DOS device, such as a floppy disk.
mkmanifest	This command is used to create a shell script that restores Linux filenames that were truncated by DOS commands.
mlabel	The DOS label command, which is used to make a DOS volume label.
mmd	The DOS md command, which is used to create a DOS directory.
mmount	This command is used to mount a DOS disk in Linux.
mmove	The DOS move command, which is used to move a file to another directory and/or rename it.
mrd	The DOS rd command, which is used to remove a DOS directory.
mread	The DOS copy command, which is used to copy a DOS file from one location to another.
mren	The DOS ren command, which is used to rename a DOS file.
mshowfat	This command is used to show the FAT entry for a file in a DOS file system.
mtoolstest	This command is used to test the mtools configuration files.
mtype	The DOS type command, which is used to display the contents of a DOS text file.
mzip	This command is used to perform operations with Zip disks, including eject, write protect, and query.

I usually use the mtools to copy files between my Linux system and a Windows system that is not on my network. I most often use mcopy, which lets me copy files using drive letters instead of device names. In other words, to copy the file vi.exe from floppy drive A: to the current directory in Linux, I would type:

```
# mcopy a:\vi.exe
```

Caution

By default, the floppy disk drive can be read from or written to only by the root user. To make the floppy drive accessible to everyone (assuming it is floppy drive A:), type the following as root user: **chmod 666 /dev/fd0**.

Using dosemu and xdosemu

The DOS emulator packages `dosemu` and `xdosemu` no longer come with the Red Hat Linux distribution. These packages were previously part of the Red Hat PowerTools. Now you can obtain these packages from a Red Hat Linux FTP site or by using the `rpmfind` command.

With the utilities that come with the `dosemu` and `xdosemu` packages, you can run DOS applications, as well as use your computer as if it were running DOS. This includes accessing hardware, working with DOS configuration files, and using the DOS file system.

The following commands can be used to start `dosemu` within Linux:

✦ `dos` — Starts the DOS emulator in any shell.

✦ `xdos` — Starts the DOS emulator in its own X window.

✦ `xtermdos` — Starts the DOS emulator in an xterm window.

✦ `dosdebug` — Starts a debug program to view information and error messages about a running DOS program.

Basic information about your DOS environment is set in the `/etc/dosemu.conf` file. The following list contains information about how the DOS environment is set up and how to change it:

✦ **CPU** — The CPU is set to emulate an 80386 (Intel 386-compatible). You can change the `$_cpu` value to 80486 or 80586 (for Pentium).

✦ **Keyboard** — The keyboard is set to `auto`, which tries to set the keyboard based on the current Linux console settings. You can specifically change the keyboard type by setting the `$_layout` value to a variety of other country/language combinations listed in the `dosemu.conf` file (such as `us` for United States/English, `de` for German, or `it` for Italian).

✦ **X Settings** — There are several X settings (beginning with `$_X`) that enable you to change such things as the title in the DOS window, the font used, and the blink rate for the cursor.

✦ **Floppy Disks** — Floppy disk A (`/dev/fd0`) is set to a 3.5-inch floppy (`threeinch`) and floppy disk B (`/dev/fd1`) is not assigned. Either disk can be assigned to be 3.5-inch (`threeinch`), 5.25-inch (`fiveinch`), `atapi`, or `empty`.

✦ **Hard Disk Images** — The file system that appears when you start DOS is actually a disk image file stored in `/var/lib/dosemu`. By default, `dosemu` uses `hdimage.first` (which is linked to `hdimage.freedos`). You can change that to another DOS image or to a DOS file system (such as `/dev/hda1`, if that partition were a DOS partition).

✦ **Serial Ports** — No serial ports are assigned by default. You can assign any of the serial ports (`$_com1` to `$_com4`) to a device such as a modem (`/dev/modem`), a mouse (`/dev/mouse`), or a terminal line (`/dev/tty0`).

Dosemu is set up for the root user. It is not very secure to allow multiple users to have access to DOS because DOS does not have the same security protections for files and devices that Linux does. If you want other users on your Linux system to use DOS, however, edit the /etc/dosemu.users file so that it includes the following lines:

```
root c_all
all c_all
```

For more information on dosemu, visit the dosemu home page at www.dosemu.org.

Running Windows and Macintosh applications

Although Red Hat Linux doesn't provide software with the base operating system that lets you run software that is intended for Microsoft Windows or Macintosh operating systems, there are several emulation packages that you can add to Red Hat Linux for those purposes. WINE and Bochs are used to run Windows 95 applications. ARDI Executor can run many Macintosh programs.

WINE

The WINE project (www.winehq.com) seems to be the project for running applications intended for Microsoft Windows that has the most weight behind it. WINE is not really an emulator, because it doesn't emulate the entire Windows operating system. Instead, by implementing Win32 application programming interfaces (APIs) and Windows 3.x interfaces, the WINE project is more of a "Windows compatibility layer."

Besides developing software, the WINE project maintains a database of applications that run under WINE. More than 1000 applications are listed, although many of them are only partially operational. The point is, however, that the list of applications is growing, and special attention is being paid to getting important Windows 3.1, 95, and 98 applications running.

Tip　Although not an open source product, VMware is another good way to run Windows applications along with a Linux system on the same running computer. With VMware you can simultaneously run Windows 98, Windows NT, Windows 2000 and Linux operating systems on the same PC. You can get more information about VMware from www.vmware.com.

Bochs

Bochs is a PC-emulation software package that can run DOS, Minix 2.0, and Windows 95 applications. You can download Bochs from the TUCOWS site (www.tucows.com). The Bochs developers claim that the following Windows operating system applications will run in Bochs:

✦ Access 97

✦ CorelDRAW 7

✦ Excel 97

✦ Lotus 1-2-3 97

✦ Word 97

✦ PowerPoint 97

✦ Quattro Pro 7

✦ WordPerfect 7

Though previously available for a small fee, in March 2000 Bochs was purchased by MandrakeSoft (`www.linux-mandrake.com`), which committed Bochs to Open Source. The Bochs code is being included in the Plex86 project (`www.plex86.org`). The Plex86 project claims to be able to run Windows 95, FreeDOS, and Linux on the same computer in virtualization mode. Plex86 could someday be an open-source alternative to VMware for running multiple operating systems simultaneously.

ARDI Executor

Besides enabling you to run many popular Macintosh applications on the PC, the ARDI Executor (`www.ardi.com`) from ARDI, Incorporated lets you work with Mac-formatted floppies and a variety of Mac drives. There is a charge for this software (currently $75 for a single Linux version, although only $35 for students. Lower prices are available if you buy in quantity).

ARDI also maintains a listing of compatible Mac software. There are literally hundreds of Mac applications listed. Each application is color coded (green, yellow, orange, red, or black) to indicate how well the software runs under ARDI. Green and yellow are fully usable and largely usable, respectively. Orange is mostly unusable. Red means the application won't run at all, and black means it won't run because it requires features that aren't implemented in ARDI. At a glance, about two-thirds of the applications listed were either green or yellow.

Summary

Between applications written directly for Linux and other UNIX systems, those that have been ported to Linux, and those that can run in emulation, there are hundreds of applications available that can be used with Red Hat Linux. There are dozens of locations on the Internet for downloading Linux applications, and many more that can be purchased on CD.

To simplify the process of installing and managing your Linux applications, Red Hat developed the Red Hat Package Manager (RPM). Using tools developed for RPM, such as the `rpm` command, you can easily install, remove, and do a variety of queries on Linux packages that are in RPM format.

Of the types of applications that can run in Linux, those created for the X Window System provide the greatest level of compatibility and flexibility when used in Linux. However, using emulation software, it is possible to run applications intended for DOS, Windows 95/98, and Macintosh operating systems.

✦   ✦   ✦

Publishing with Red Hat Linux

To survive as a desktop system, an operating system must be able to perform at least one task well: produce documents. It's no accident that, after Windows, Word (now bundled into Microsoft Office) is the foundation of Microsoft's success on the desktop. Many people bought their first desktop computer specifically to write and format documents.

Right out of the box, Red Hat Linux includes tools for producing documents. The free document and graphics tools that come with Red Hat Linux are mostly built on older, text-based tools. Many technical people use these tools (such as Groff and LaTeX) quite happily. For those who want a friendlier word processor, however, some new open source graphical word processing tools are becoming available, as well as several commercial word processing applications that provide graphical, X-based interfaces.

In this chapter, I look at the pros and cons of using Red Hat Linux as a publishing platform. I include descriptions of text-based and GUI-based document preparation software that either comes with Red Hat Linux or is available as an add-on (usually at very reasonable costs). I also describe tools for printing and displaying documents, software for working with graphic images in a variety of formats, and software for using a scanner.

Choosing Red Hat Linux as Your Publishing Platform

The allure of a free publishing platform is probably as enticing to you as a free operating system. Imagine not having to drop several hundred dollars each time Microsoft comes out with a new version of Microsoft Office. So, should you take the plunge?

The answer is a resounding . . . maybe. Thousands of people have used Linux and other UNIX systems as their sole means of producing documents. In particular, computer software developers, college students, scientists, and other technical people have been quite satisfied creating text and publishing it using the same tools that are available with Linux today.

Before you jump into the Red Hat Linux publishing swimming pool, however, you may want to make sure there is some water in it. Red Hat Linux is definitely not the publishing platform for everyone — at least not yet.

Before you purge your old documents and erase your Windows partitions, I recommend that you read the following sections. They contain some of my observations about the pros and cons of publishing in Red Hat Linux, as well as information I gathered from others who chose to use Linux for either some or all of their document publishing needs.

Note   You should understand the difference between text processing and word processing before you go any further. With word processors (such as Star Office), you mark up text and see the basic layout of the document as you write. With old-school text processors (such as Groff and TeX), the author can ignore the appearance of the document while writing. Plain text macros, inserted into the document, are used to process documents for printing after the writing is done.

Checklist of your document requirements

I have prepared a list of questions that will help you understand what you are getting into by publishing with Red Hat Linux. These questions will help you understand what Red Hat Linux documentation tools can and cannot currently do, as well as help you evaluate your own document needs.

1. Do you want to see the layout as you create the document?

Most of the document publishing tools that come free with Red Hat Linux have you work with plain text files. Even graphical editors, such as the LyX LaTeX editor, won't show you an exact screen representation of the printed document.

Within each text file, you indicate formatting by adding *macros*. The macros are interpreted when you either display the document (using programs such as Ghostview or Acrobat) or print the document. In other words, you can't see what the document will look like as you write it.

If you prefer a WYSIWYG (What-You-See-Is-What-You-Get) document system, I recommend commercial graphical word processors for Linux, such as Anyware Office, WordPerfect, or Star Office. In addition to enabling you to see the layout, these software applications tend to have simplified ways of integrating text with graphics, tables, and other document elements. They also support conversion programs from many popular document formats. See the section on attributes of Linux publishing to understand the characteristics of each type of document processing system.

2. Are you working with a set of documents that need to be converted?

If you or your organization is currently using a word processing system to create documents, it is not a trivial task to move those documents to Red Hat Linux. In particular, if your documents are complex (including multiple columns, forms, or other items), or if there are many documents to convert, the conversion process can hurt your workflow.

Here is a list of document elements that don't always convert cleanly:

✦ Multiple columns

✦ Forms

✦ Breaks (page breaks, section breaks, and column breaks)

✦ Tables

✦ Styles (you might lose the markup during conversion)

Tip Before committing to converting all the documents in your organization to a Linux platform, test converting a few first. Make sure that the documents you test contain many of the most complex elements used by your co-workers. In particular, look for the elements shown in the previous list.

Red Hat Linux comes with a set of tools for converting documents and images from a variety of formats to other formats. Likewise, most WYSIWYG word processors enable you to import and export different document and image formats. In general, the older the document format, the better it will convert. That is because later word processing formats contain more complex features that are harder to cleanly convert. See the section on converting documents for information about Red Hat Linux tools for converting different document formats.

3. Do you need to exchange documents with other groups?

Some organizations are set up to accept documents that use a particular document format. If you need to hand your work to such an organization, you may have your hands tied when it comes to changing how you do your work. Even if you can import a document from another format, you may not be able to convert the document back cleanly. And though your co-workers may accept a one-time conversion, converting each time you send and receive a document can become tedious.

4. Does your organization need to keep running while you change over?

Most businesses can't afford to stop working while their documents are converted. The changeover to Red Hat Linux from a Windows 9*x*/2000 operating system can bring all work to a halt if upgrades don't go smoothly. If you have the resources, a transition period where some Red Hat Linux systems are brought up in parallel, instead of replacing all existing systems, enables work to go on if something goes wrong.

You can read about one person's experience replacing a small office's Windows 95/98 systems with Linux and Star Office in "Star Office Wars." The document is located at: `http://users.smileys.net/~leonb/StarOffice-wars.html`.

5. Are you comfortable fiddling to make things work?

To get the formatting right when you are using Groff or LaTeX, you usually have to reformat a few times. That either entails using a tool such as Ghostview (which can be slow) or running back and forth to the printer. You may also want to set up shell scripts to run your formatting and printing commands. All this requires some fiddling. If you, or the people who need to work with the document system you set up, are not comfortable with fiddling, you may want to stick with a commercial word processor. Running tools such as LaTeX (the editor) and Ghostview (the viewer) side by side can get you closer to the WYSIWYG experience.

6. Do you need special features, such as color separations?

Most of the advanced publishing features are not yet available in Red Hat Linux. Some professional publishing operations have noted, for example, that there are no Linux tools for doing color separations or some of the other advanced photographic image manipulations.

Attributes of Linux publishing

Some attributes of the traditional Linux publishing tools make them particularly well suited for certain types of document publishing. As noted earlier, Groff and LaTeX (which is based on TeX) come with Red Hat Linux and are very popular among technical people. There are several reasons why technical people take well to the traditional UNIX/Linux document tools:

✦ You can easily manipulate files that are in plain text. Using tools like `perl`, `sed`, and `grep`, you can scan and change one document or hundreds of documents with a single command or script.

✦ Scientific and mathematical notation is supported. With `geqn`, you can create complex equations that can be output with Groff. LaTeX and TeX are particularly suited for technical notation. Some mathematical publications require LaTeX.

✦ Editing can be faster because traditional Linux documents are created with a text editor. You can usually get better performance out of a text editor than a word processor. Some people who learn the `vi` or `emacs` text editor don't miss a mouse at all. Plus there are X-based text processors today that incorporate many word processing features (such as spell checking and menus for editing functions).

Documents with straightforward page layouts work well with Linux documentation tools. For example, a technical book with a few flow charts and images can be easily produced and maintained using Red Hat Linux documentation tools. Letters and memos are also easy to do with these tools. And, of course, Red Hat Linux man pages (which provide separate write-ups for every command, file, and device in Linux) and other Linux documentation are created with these tools.

Additionally, Linux likes PostScript. Though many people think of PostScript as a printer output language, it is really more of a programming language (that is, you could write PostScript code directly, if you had the courage). Some document-processing software only includes print drivers for PostScript (although you can get around that problem using conversion programs). Also, many documents on the Web are distributed in PostScript (.ps) format.

The drawback to the traditional Linux document tools is that they are not intuitive. Though there are some easier front-ends to LaTeX (see the description of LyX later on), if you are creating documents in a text editor, you will need to learn what macros to type into your documents to format them. This is not as easy as just clicking a style or selecting fonts from a pop-up window. You also need to know which formatting and print commands to use and how to use them.

Note

For many years, the UNIX system documentation distributed by AT&T was created in troff/nroff formats, which predate Groff. The documents used separate macro packages, man pages, and guide material. Using a source code control system (SCCS), thousands of pages of documentation could be ported to different UNIX systems. Today, Red Hat Linux still includes the same tools to work with man pages.

Creating Documents in Groff or LaTeX

You can create documents for either of Linux's Groff (troff/nroff) or LaTeX (TeX) styles of publishing using any text editor. Red Hat Linux comes with several of these text editors, or you can download lots of others from the Internet. See the "Choosing a Text Editor" sidebar for information on different text editors.

The process for creating documents in Groff and LaTeX is generally the same. Use the following steps:

1. Create a document with any text editor. The document will contain text and markup (macros) to indicate how the document is to be formatted.

2. Format the document using a formatting command that matches the style of the document that you created (for example, with groff or latex). During this step, you may need to indicate the type of output device the document is intended for. If the document contains special content, such as equations (eqn command), tables (tbl command), or line drawings (pic command), you may also need to indicate how the file is to be preprocessed.

3. Send the document to an output device. The output device may be a printer or program that displays the page on your screen.

Choosing a Text Editor

Hardcore UNIX/Linux users tend to edit files with either the vi or emacs text editor. These text editors have been around a long time and are hard to learn, but efficient to use. (Your fingers never have to leave the keyboard). The emacs editor has some native GUI support, though it will run fine in a Terminal window. There are also GUI versions of vi and emacs that add menu and mouse features to those editors. These are GVim (gvim command) and Xemacs (xemacs command) editors, respectively.

Some of the other, simpler text editors that can run on your graphical desktop are:

✦ **gedit** (gedit **command**) — This text editor, which comes with Red Hat Linux, is the lightweight text editor for the Gnome interface. A menu bar lets you create, open, or save files. It also has simple edit functions (cut, copy, paste, select all, and find). Settings let you set indentations and word wrap.

A plug-ins feature lets you select various special functions, such as a spell checker and a diff feature (to compare the contents of the document with another document). You can start gedit from the Start menu by selecting Programs ⇨ Applications ⇨ gedit. For more information about gedit, go to http://gedit.pn.og.

✦ **Advanced Editor** (kwrite **command**) — This text editor includes a menu bar to quickly create, open, or save files. It also has simple edit functions (cut, copy, paste, undo, and help). Other edit features let you set indentations, find/replace text, and select all text. This comes with the KDE desktop, so you can access it by selecting KDE menus ⇨ Editors ⇨ Advanced Editor.

✦ **Text Editor** (kedit **command**) — This is another fairly simple text editor. Its features include the ability to open files from your file system or from a Web address (URL). It also includes a convenient toolbar and a spell checker. It comes with the KDE desktop, so you can access it by selecting KDE menus ⇨ Editors ⇨ Text Editor.

If you are used to a word processor with a GUI, you may find either of these publishing tools difficult to work with. In general, Groff is useful if you need to work with or create your own man pages for Red Hat Linux. LaTeX may be useful if you need to produce mathematical documents, perhaps for publication in a technical journal.

Text processing with Groff

The nroff and troff text formatting commands were the first interfaces available for producing typeset quality documents with the UNIX system. They aren't editors; rather, they are commands that you send your text through, with the result being formatted pages:

✦ nroff — Produces formatted plain text and includes the ability to do pagination, indents, and text justification, as well as other features.

✦ `troff` — Produces typeset text, including everything `nroff` can do, plus the capability to produce different kinds of fonts and spacing. The `troff` command also supports kerning.

The `groff` command is the front-end for producing `nroff/troff` documentation. Because `nroff` and `troff` were so popular with UNIX, they were used to produce the documentation for most UNIX systems. That tradition continues to a small extent with Linux in that Linux man pages are formatted and output in Groff. Therefore, most of the examples here help you create and print man pages with Groff.

People rarely use primitive `nroff/troff` markup to create documents. Instead, there are several common macro packages that simplify creating `nroff/troff` formatted documents. The most popular macro packages are:

✦ `man` — The `man` macros are used to create Linux man pages. You can format a man page using the `-man` option to the `groff` command. (The `man` macros are discussed further in the section on creating a man page with `groff`.)

✦ `mm` — The `mm` macros (memorandum macros) were created to produce memos, letters, and technical white papers. This macro package includes macros for creating a table of contents, lists of figures, references, and other features that are helpful for producing technical documents. These macros were developed and used by AT&T and UNIX System V versions of UNIX. You can format an `mm` document using the `-mm` option to the `groff`, `nroff`, or `troff` commands.

✦ `me` — The `me` macros were also used for producing memos and technical papers. This macro package was popular with Berkeley UNIX systems. This macro package is still in use in some places today. You can format an `me` document using the `-me` option to the `groff` command.

Groff macro packages are stored in `/usr/share/groff/tmac`. You can look in these files to see what macro definitions look like. The `man` macros are contained in the tmac.an file, `mm` macros are in tmac.m, and `me` macros are in tmac.e. The naming convention for each macro package is tmac.*xxx*, where the *xxx* is replaced by one or more letters representing the macro package. In each case, you can understand the name of the macro package by adding an `m` to the beginning of the file suffix.

Tip Instead of indicating `-man` or `-mm` on a command line to specify a macro package, you can use `-mandoc`. This causes Groff to choose the appropriate macro package for the file.

When you run the `groff` formatting command, you can indicate on the command line which macro packages you are using. You can also indicate that the document should be run through any of the following commands that preprocess text from special formats for equations, pictures, or tables:

✦ eqn — This preprocessor formats macros that produce equations in `groff`.

✦ `pic` — This preprocessor formats macros used to create simple pictures in `groff` (mostly line drawings).

✦ `tbl` — This preprocessor formats macros that produce tables within `groff`.

The formatted Groff document is output for a particular type of device. The device the document is intended for can be a printer, a display program, or (in the case of plain ASCII text) your shell window. Here are the output forms supported by Groff:

✦ **ps** — Produces PostScript output that can be printed on a PostScript printer or displayed on a PostScript previewer.

✦ **lj4** — Produces output for an HP LaserJet4-compatible printer or other PCL5-compatible printer.

✦ **ascii** — Produces plain text output that can be viewed from a Terminal window. (This is how you produce nroff output with the `groff` command.)

✦ **dvi** — Produces output in TeX dvi format, which can be output on a variety of devices using commands described later.

✦ **X75** — Produces output for an X11 75 dots/inch previewer.

✦ **X100** — Produces output for an X11 100 dots/inch previewer.

✦ **latin1** — Produces typewriter-like output using the ISO Latin-1 character set.

Formatting and printing documents with Groff

The best way to try out Groff is to try formatting and printing an existing Groff document. Start by using any man pages on your Red Hat Linux system (such as those in `/usr/share/man/*`). (Those man pages are compressed, so you may want to copy them to a temporary directory and unzip them to try out Groff.)

The following command lines copy the chown man page to the `/tmp` directory and unzips it. After that, the `groff` command is used to format the chown man page in plain text so you can page through it on your screen.

```
$ cp /usr/share/man/man1/chown.1.gz /tmp
$ gunzip /tmp/chown.1.gz
$ groff -Tascii -man /tmp/chown.1 | less
```

In the previous example, the chown man page (`chown.1.gz`) is copied to the `/tmp` directory. Then the man page is unzipped (using the `gunzip` command). Finally, the chown man page (`chown.1`) is output in plain text (`-Tascii`) using the man macros (`-man`). The output is piped to the `less` command, so you can page through it on your screen. Instead of piping the output to `less` (`| less`), you could direct the output to a file (`> /tmp/chown.txt`).

To format a man page for typesetting, you could specify PostScript or HP LaserJet output. In this case, you don't want to format the document to your screen. You should either direct the output to a file or to a printer. Here are a couple of examples:

```
$ groff -Tps -man /tmp/chown.1 > /tmp/chown.ps
$ groff -Tlj4 -man -l /tmp/chown.1
```

The first example creates PostScript output (-Tps) and directs it to a file called /tmp/chown.ps. That file can be read by a PostScript previewer (such as ghostscript) or sent to a printer (lpr /tmp/chown.ps). The second example creates HP LaserJet output (-Tlj4) and directs it to the default printer (-l option). If your default printer is a PostScript printer, use -Tps instead.

Creating a man page with Groff

Before HOW-TOs and info files, man pages were the foundation for information about UNIX (and UNIX-like) systems. Each command, file format, device, or other component either had its own man page or was grouped on a man page with similar components. To create your own man page requires that you learn only a few macros (in particular, man macros). Figure 6-1 is an example of the source file for a fictitious man page for a command called *waycool*.

Tip Most man pages are stored in subdirectories of /usr/share/man. Before you create a man page, refer to similar man pages to see the markup and the headings they include. In man1 are commands; man2 contains system calls; man3 has library functions; man4 has special device files (/dev/*, /*); man5 has file formats; man6 has games; man7 has miscellaneous components, and man8 has administrative commands.

```
.\"
.\" waycool.1 - the *roff document processor source for the waycool command
.\"
.TH waycool 1 "June 15, 1999" GNU "Linux Programmer's Manual"
.SH NAME
waycool - My cool command
.SH SYNTAX
\fBwaycool\fR [ \fB-abcv\fR ] [ \fI file ...\fR ]
.SH VERSION
This man page documents GNU waycool version X.XX.
.SH DESCRIPTION
\fBwaycool\fR is a way cool command.
.SP
This version of \fBwaycool\fR is better than the last one.
.SH OPTIONS
.IP -a
Run all options with it.
.IP -b
Run some options.
.IP -c
Run one or two options.
.IP -v
Print the version number with the command.
.SH COMMENTS
If you don't like the command, don't tell me. It will just hurt my feelings.
.SH ENVIRONMENT VARIABLES
These  environment variables are used  by \fBwaycool\fR:
.IP "DISPLAY"
This sets the X Display variable.
.IP "WAYCOOL"
This contains the location of the waycool database.
.SH FILES
/usr/local/waycool - Directory containing waycool stuff.
.SH AUTHOR
Chris Craft (chris@handsonhistory.com)
.SH ACKNOWLEDGEMENTS
I'd like to thank all my friends.
```

Figure 6-1: Simple markup is required to create man pages.

Most man pages begin with commented lines (. \") that contain descriptive information about the component. Often, information about the GNU license is commented out at the beginning. The first command is the title command (which uses the .TH macro), which includes the title of the man page, section number, source of the component (such as the distribution or kernel name), and the title of the manual. Section headings begin with the .SH macro. Every command should have at least a NAME, SYNTAX, and DESCRIPTION section heading. Your man page may have different types of information, such as environment variables, bugs, or files.

A few other kinds of macros are also used in the man page. The .IP macros format indented paragraphs for things such as options. The man page also contains some lower-level font requests; for example, \fB says to change the current font to bold, \fI changes the font to italic, and \fR changes it back to regular font. (This markup is better than asking for a particular font type because it just changes to bold, italic, or regular for the current font.) Figure 6-2 shows what the waycool man page looks like after it is formatted with the man macros and sent to your printer by the following command:

```
$ groff -man -Tps -1 waycool.1
```

Macro	Description	Macro	Description
.B	Bold.	.BI	Bold, then italics (alternating).
.BR	Bold, then roman (alternating).	.DT	Set default tabs.
.B	Begin a hanging indent.	.I	Italics.
.IB	Italics, then bold (alternating).	.IP	Begin a hanging tag. Used to describe options. Use .TP with long tags.

Figure 6-2: Man page formatting adds headers and lays out the page of text.

Table 6-1 lists the macros that you can use on your man pages. These macros are defined in the tmac.an macro file (usually located in /usr/share/groff/tmac). They are also described on the man(7) manual page (type man 7 man to view that page).

Table 6-1 Man Macros			
Macro	*Description*	*Macro*	*Description*
.B	Bold	.BI	Bold, then italics (alternating)
.BR	Bold, then roman (alternating)	.DT	Set default tabs
.HP	Begin a hanging indent	.I	Italics

Macro	Description	Macro	Description
.IB	Italics, then bold (alternating)	.IP	Begin a hanging tag. Used to describe options. Use .TP with long tags.
.IR	Italics, then roman (alternating)	.LP	Begin paragraph (same as .PP)
.PD	Set distance between paragraphs	.PP	Begin paragraph (same as .LP)
.RB	Roman, then bold (alternating)	.RE	End relative indent (used after .RS)
.RI	Roman, then italics (alternating)	.RS	Begin relative indent (use .RE to end indent)
.SB	Small text, then bold (alternating)	.SM	Small text. Sometimes used to show words in all caps.
.SH	Section head	.SS	Subheading within a .SH heading.
.TH	Title heading. Used once at the beginning of the man page.	.TP	Begin a hanging tag. Similar to .IP, but .TP begins text on next line, rather than same line as tag.

Creating a letter, memo, or white paper with Groff

Memorandum macros (which are used with the -mm option of Groff) were once popular among UNIX users for producing technical documents, letters, and memos. Although more modern word processors with a variety of WYSIWYG templates have made mm outdated, in a pinch mm can still be a quick way to create a typeset-style document in a text environment.

To format and print a document with mm macros, use the following command line (assuming your default printer is a PostScript printer):

```
$ groff -mm -Tps -l letter.mm
```

The following is a simple example of how to use mm macros to produce a letter:

```
.WA "Christopher T. Craft"
999 Anyway Way
Anytown, UT 84111 USA
.WE
.IA
John W. Doe
111 Notown Blvd.
Notown, UT 84111
.IE
.LO RN "Our telephone conversation"
.LO SA "Dear Mr. Doe:"
```

```
.LT
In reference to our telephone conversation on the 4th, I am
calling to confirm our upcoming appointment on the 18th. I look
forward to discussing the merger. I believe we have a win-win
situation here.
.FC "Yours Truly,"
.SG
```

In this example, the .WA, .IA, .IE, .LO, .LT, .FC, and .SG macros are used. The .WA macro begins the writer's address and the .WE ends the address. The .IA begins the recipient's name and address and .IE ends the recipient's address. The .LO RN adds an `In reference to:` line to the letter that is followed by the text `Our telephone conversation`. The .LO SA is used to add a salutation line. The .LT indicates that the document is in letter format.

Following the text of the letter, .FC indicates the formal closing to use. Finally, the .SG adds the writer's name as a signature line. The output of the letter, if you use the `groff` command line mentioned in the paragraph preceding the code example, is shown in Figure 6-3.

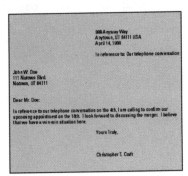

Figure 6-3: Create a simple letter using mm macros.

The mm macros were often used to produce technical memos. The following is an example of a sign-off sheet that might go at the front of a larger technical memo.

```
.TL
Merger Technical Specifications
.AF "ABC Corporation"
.AU "Christopher Craft"
.AT "President"
.AS
This memo details the specifications for the planned merger.
.AE
.MT "Merger Description and Marching Orders"
As a result of our talks with XYZ corporation, we plan to go
forward with the merger. This document contains the following:
```

```
.BL
.LI
Schedule and time tables.
.LI
Financial statements.
.LI
Asset allocations.
.LE
.SP
Please add corrections and sign the approval line.
.FC
.SG
.AV "John W. Doe, XYZ Corporation President"
.AV "Sylvia Q. Public, XYZ Corporation CFO"
.NS
Everyone in the corporation.
.NE
```

In this example, the subject of the memorandum follows the .TL macro. The .AF, .AU, and .AT macros identify the company name, author, and author title, respectively. The .AS and .AE macros surround the abstract. The .MT indicates that this is a memorandum-type document. Within the text of the memo, there is a bulleted list, started by .BL, with each item noted by a .LI and ended by a .LE.

Next is .SP, which adds a line of space. To end the memo, the .FC indicates a formal closing of the memo (`Yours Very Truly,`), and .SG adds the author's name as the signature line. The .AV macros each indicate which people need to approve the document. Finally, the .NS and .NE macros surround the `copy to:` list. Figure 6-4 shows the output of this memo.

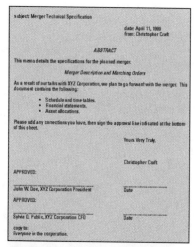

Figure 6-4: Add headings and approval lines automatically to memos.

Note   For a complete listing of mm macros, see the `groff_mm` man page. More than 100 mm macros exist. Also, dozens of defined strings let you set and recall information (such as figure names, tables, table of contents information, and text) that is automatically printed with different headings.

Adding equations, tables, and pictures

There are several sets of Groff macros that let you add special content to Groff documents. These macros require special preprocessors. You can add mathematical equations with EQN macros. Using the TBL macros, you can format tables in Groff. With the PIC macros, you can create simple line drawings.

To interpret these macros, you can run separate commands (eqn, tbl, and pic commands) on the file before you run the groff command. As an alternative, you can add options to the groff command line to have the file preprocessed automatically by any of the commands (-e for eqn, -t for tbl, and -p for pic).

Here are some examples of EQN, TBL, and PIC markup that can be included in a Groff document. The first example shows an equation that can be processed by eqn for a Groff document:

```
.EQ
a ~ mark = ~ 30
.EN
.EQ
a sup 2 ~ + ~ b sup 2~lineup = ~ 1000
.EN
.EQ
x sup 3 ~ + ~ y sup 3 ~ + ~ z sup 3~lineup = ~ 1400
.EN
```

If this appeared in a memo called memoeqn.mm, the memo would be preprocessed by eqn and then sent to the printer using the following command:

```
$ groff -Tps -l -mm -e memoeqn.mm
```

All data between the .EQ and .EN macros are interpreted as equations. The resulting output from the equation would appear as shown in Figure 6-5.

$$a = 30$$
$$a^2 + b^2 = 1000$$
$$x^3 + y^3 + z^3 = 1400$$

Figure 6-5: Produce equations in documents with the use of the eqn command's .EQ and .EN macros.

To create a table in a Groff document, use the .TS and .TE macros of the tbl preprocessor. The following is an example of the markup used to produce a simple table.

```
.TS
center, box, tab(:);
c s s
c | c | c
l | l | l.
Mergers and Acquisitions Team
=
Employee:Title:Location
_
Jones, James:Marketing Manager:New York Office
Smith, Charles:Sales Manager:Los Angeles Office
Taylor, Sarah:R&D Manager:New York Office
Walters, Mark:Information Systems Manager:Salt Lake City Office
Zur, Mike:Distribution Manager:Portland Office
.TE
```

After the .TS macro starts the table, the next line indicates that the table should be
centered on the page (center) and surrounded by a line box and that a colon will
be used to separate the data into cells (tab(:)). The next line shows that the
heading should be centered in the box (c) and should span across the next two
cells (s s). The line after that indicates that the heading of each cell should be
centered (c | c | c) and that the data cells that follow should be left justified
(l | l | l).

Caution   There must be a period at the end of the table definition line. In this case, it is after
the l | l | l. line. If the period is not there, tbl will try to interpret the text as
part of the table definition. In this case, tbl will fail and stop processing the table,
so the table will not print.

The rest of the information in the table is the data. Note that the tab separators are
colon characters (:). When the table is done, you end it with a .TE macro.

If the table were in a memo called memotbl.mm, tbl could preprocess the memo
and then send it to the printer using the following command:

```
$ groff -Tps -l -mm -t memotbl.mm
```

Data between .TS and .TE macros are interpreted as tables. Figure 6-6 shows an
example of this table in the previous example's output.

Employee	Title	Location
Jones, James Smith, Charles Taylor, Sarah Walters, Mark Zur, Mike	Marketing Manager Sales Manager R&D Manager Information Systems Manager Distribution Manager	Jones, James Smith, Charles Taylor, Sarah Walters, Mark Zur, Mike

Figure 6-6: Set how text is justified and put in columns with the use of the tbl command's .TS and .TE macros.

The PIC macros (.PS and .PE) enable you to create simple diagrams and flow charts to use in Groff. PIC is really only qualified to create simple boxes, circles, ellipses, lines, arcs, splines, and some text. The following is an example of some PIC code that could be included in a Groff document:

```
.PS
box invis "Start" "Here"; arrow
box "Step 1"; arrow
circle "Step 2"; arrow
ellipse "Step 3"; arrow
box "Step 4"; arrow
box invis "End"
.PE
```

After the .PS, the first line indicates an invisible box (`invis`) that contains the words Start Here, followed by an arrow. That arrow connects to the next box containing the words Step 1. The next elements (connected by arrows) are a circle (Step 2), an ellipse (Step 3), another box (Step 4), and another invisible box (End). The .PE indicates the end of the pic drawing.

If these lines appeared in a document called memopic.mm, you could preprocess the PIC code and print the file using the following command:

```
$ groff -Tps -l -mm -p memopic.mm
```

Figure 6-7 shows an example of this drawing:

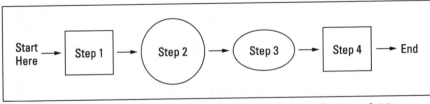

Figure 6-7: Create simple flow diagrams with the pic command's .PS and .PE macros.

For information on the `eqn`, `tbl`, or `pic` command or formatting markup, see their respective man pages.

Text processing with TeX/LaTeX

TeX is a collection of document formatting commands used primarily to produce scientific and mathematical typeset documents. The most common way to use TeX is by calling a macro package. The most popular macro package for Tex is LaTeX, which takes a higher-level approach to formatting TeX documents. TeX and LaTeX tools are contained in the tetex-latex package.

Note

The tetex-* packages described in this section are not installed by default in a Red Hat Linux workstation install. The required packages are contained on CD-2 that comes with this book.

TeX interprets the LaTeX macros from the latex format file (`latex.fmt`). By default, the `latex.fmt` and `plain.fmt` format files are the only ones that are automatically built when the TeX package is installed. Besides LaTeX, there are other macro format files that you can use with TeX, including:

✦ **amstex** — The American Mathematical Society uses this as their official typesetting system. Many mathematical publications use this macro set.

✦ **amslatex** — Adds amstex features to LaTeX.

✦ **eplain** — Includes macros for indexing, table of contents, and symbolic cross-referencing.

✦ **lamstex** — Can be used with amstex to provide many features that are compatible with LaTeX.

✦ **texinfo** — Macros used by the Free Software Foundation to produce software manuals. Text output from these macros can be used with the Red Hat Linux `info` command.

You can create a TeX/LaTeX file using any text editor. After the text and macros (formatting instructions) are created, you can run the `tex` command (or one of several other related utilities) to format the file. The input file is in the form *filename*`.tex`. The output is generally three different files:

✦ *filename*`.dvi` — This is the device independent output file that can be translated for use by several different types of output devices (such as PostScript).

✦ *filename*`.log` — This is a log file that contains diagnostic messages.

✦ *filename*`.aux` — This is an auxiliary file used by LaTeX.

The .dvi file that is produced can be formatted to output the document to the particular device you are using. For example, you could use the `dvips` command to output the resulting .dvi file to your PostScript printer (`dvips` *filename*`.dvi`). Or you could use the `xdvi` command to preview the dvi file in an X window.

Creating and formatting a LaTeX document

Because LaTeX is the most common way of using TeX, this section describes how to create and format a LaTeX document. A LaTeX macro (often referred to as a command) appears in a document in one of the two following forms:

✦ *string*{*option*}[*required*] — First there is a backslash (\\), which is followed by a string of characters. (Replace *string* with the name of the command.) Optional arguments are contained in braces ({ }), and required arguments are in brackets ([ ]).

✦ *?*{*option*}[*required*] — First there is a backslash (\\), which is followed by a single character that is not a letter. (Replace *?* with the command character.) Optional arguments are contained in braces ({ }), and required arguments are in brackets ([ ]).

Each command defines some action to be taken. The action can control page layout, the font used, spacing, paragraph layout, or a variety of other actions on the document. The minimum amount of formatting that a LaTeX document can contain is the following:

```
\documentclass{name}

\begin{document}

  TEXT GOES HERE!

\end{document}
```

You should replace *{name}* with the name of the class of document you are creating. Valid document classes include article, book, letter, report, and slides. The text for the file, along with your formatting commands, goes between the begin and end document commands.

The best way to get started with LaTeX is to use the LyX editor. LyX provides a GUI for creating LaTeX documents. It also contains a variety of templates you can use instead of just creating a document from scratch. Figure 6-8 shows an example of the LyX editor.

Note   The LyX editor doesn't come with the Red Hat Linux distribution on the CD-ROMs that accompany this book. You can find an RPM package for LyX from the LyX FTP site at `ftp://ftp.lyx.org/pub/lyx/bin`. Besides needing to have several tetex packages installed, to install LyX you will also need the xforms package (which is available from the Lyx.org FTP site).

If you want to edit LaTeX in a regular text editor, you need to be familiar with the LaTeX commands. For a complete listing of the LaTeX commands, type **$ info latex** and then go to the section "Commands within a LaTeX document."

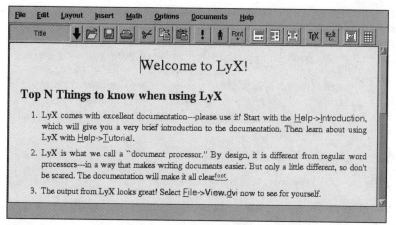

Figure 6-8: Create LaTeX documents graphically with the LyX editor.

Using the LyX LaTeX Editor

You can start the LyX LaTeX editor with the `lyx` command (probably located in `/usr/bin/lyx`). LyX comes with a lot of supporting documentation. Click Help to select a Tutorial, User's Guide, Reference Manual, or other information.

To start your first document, I recommend that you select one of the templates provided with LyX. Templates are located in `/usr/share/lyx/templates`. To open a template, click File ➪ New from template, and select Templates. There are templates available for a letter, technical paper, and a Linux document, to name a few.

Besides offering standard editing functions, such as cut, copy and paste, you can perform a variety of markup functions from the Layout menu. You can change character fonts, paragraph alignment and spacing, and document features (such as columns, drivers, and page styles). From the Insert menu, you can import Encapsulated PostScript pictures, tables, and different file types (including ASCII and LyX files).

As for mathematical functions, the Math menu enables you to insert fractions, square root, exponent, sum, and integral functions into your document. When you are done, you can:

- ✦ Print the file to a PostScript printer or output a PostScript (`.ps`) file. (Click File ➪ Print, select the printing method, and then click OK.)

- ✦ Output the file to dvi format. (Click File ➪ View.dvi.) Your document will appear in the xdvi window, which displays how the document will appear when it is printed.

- ✦ Export the file to LaTeX, DVI, PostScript, or ASCII Text. (Click File ➪ Export and choose from the list of file formats.)

LyX calls itself a WYSIWYM editor—What You Say Is What You Mean. As a result, what you see on the screen as you edit is not exactly what the printed document will look like. For example, no extra white space will appear between lines by pressing Enter multiple times. Likewise, pagination is done during the printing/formatting stage.

Because LyX supports style files, it enables you to create documents that meet several different standards. For example, LyX supports typesetting for the American Mathematics Society (AMS) journals using the articles textclass. Other textclasses supported include:

- **article**—One-sided paper with no chapters.
- **report**—Two-sided report, tending to be longer than an article.
- **book**—Same as report, with additional front and back matter.
- **slides**—For producing transparencies.
- **letter**—Includes special environments for addresses, signatures, and other letter elements.

Printing LaTeX files

Whether you create your own LaTeX file, export one from the LyX LaTeX editor, or download one from the Internet, several utilities are available to format, print, or display the output. Here are some of your choices:

- To format a LaTeX file (`filename.tex`), run the following command:

  ```
  $ latex filename.tex
  ```

- To print a .dvi file (`filename.dvi`), send it to your default PostScript printer, and type the following:

  ```
  $ dvips filename.dvi
  ```

- To display a .dvi file in an X window, type the following:

  ```
  $ xdvi filename.dvi
  ```

- To print a .dvi file to a PCL printer, such as an HP LaserJet, type the following:

  ```
  $ dvicopy filename.dvi
  $ dvilj filename.dvi
  ```

  The `dvilj` command doesn't support virtual fonts directly. The `dvicopy` command converts the fonts so that the PCL printer can handle them.

Converting documents

Documents can come to you in many different formats. Search just some of the Linux FTP sites on the Internet and you will find files in PostScript, DVI, man, PDF, HTML, and TeX. There is also a variety of graphics formats.

The capability to convert files from one format to another can be especially important if you are switching your documentation platforms from one word processing application to another. Red Hat Linux comes with lots of utilities for converting documents and graphics from one format to another. To convert document files that come from popular word processors, such as Microsoft Word, see the descriptions of commercial Linux word processors later in this chapter.

The following is a list of document and graphics conversion utilities:

✦ **dos2unix** — Converts a DOS text file to a UNIX (Linux) text file.

✦ **fax2ps** — Converts TIFF facsimile image files to a compressed PostScript format. The PostScript output is optimized to send to a printer on a low-speed line. This format is less efficient for images with a lot of black or continuous tones. (In those cases, tiff2ps might be more effective.)

✦ **fax2tiff** — Converts fax data (Group 3 or Group 4) to a TIFF format. The output is either low-resolution or medium-resolution TIFF format.

✦ **g32pbm** — Converts a Group 3 fax file (either digifax or raw) to a portable bitmap.

✦ **gif2tiff** — Converts a GIF (87) file to a TIFF format.

✦ **man2html** — Converts a man page to an HTML format.

✦ **pal2rgb** — Converts a TIFF image (palette color) to a full-color RGB image.

✦ **pbm2g3** — Converts a portable bitmap image to a fax file (Group 3).

✦ **pdf2dsc** — Converts a Portable Document Format (PDF) file to a PostScript document dsc file. The PostScript file conforms to Adobe Document Structuring Conventions (DSC). The output enables PostScript readers (such as Ghostview) to read the PDF file a page at a time.

✦ **pdf2ps** — Converts a Portable Document Format (PDF) file to a PostScript file (level 2).

✦ **pfb2pfa** — Converts a Type 1 PostScript font (in a binary MS-DOS representation) to an ASCII-readable format.

✦ **pk2bm** — Converts a TeX pkfont font file to a bitmap (ASCII file). This bitmap can be used to create X11 applications.

✦ **ppm2tiff** — Converts a PPM image file to a TIFF format.

✦ **ps2ascii** — Converts PostScript or PDF files to ASCII text. (The `pstotext` command can handle font encoding and kerning better than ps2ascii. However, pstotext works only with PostScript files.)

✦ **ps2epsi** — Converts a PostScript file to Encapsulated PostScript (EPSI). Some word processing and graphic programs can read EPSI. Output is often low quality.

✦ **ps2pdf** — Converts PostScript file to Portable Document Format (PDF).

✦ **ps2pk**—Converts a Type 1 PostScript font to a TeX pkfont.

✦ **pstotext**—Converts a PostScript file to ASCII text. `pstotext` is similar to ps2ascii, but it handles font encoding and kerning better than ps2ascii. Also, pstotext doesn't convert PDF files.

✦ **ras2tiff**—Converts a Sun raster file to a TIFF format.

✦ **texi2html**—Converts a Texinfo file to HTML.

✦ **tiff2bw**—Converts an RGB or Palette color TIFF image to a grayscale TIFF image.

✦ **tiff2ps**—Converts a TIFF image to PostScript.

✦ **unix2dos**—Converts a UNIX (Linux) text file to a DOS text file.

Creating DocBook Documents

Documentation projects often need to produce documents that are output in a variety of formats. For example, the same text that describes how to use a software program may need to be output as a printed manual, an HTML page, and a PostScript file. The standards that have been embraced most recently by the Linux community for creating what are referred to as *structured documents* are SGML, XML, and DocBook.

Understanding SGML and XML

Standard Generalized Markup Language (SGML) was created to provide a standard way of marking text so that it could be output later in a variety of formats. Because SGML markup is done with text tags, you can create SGML documents using any plain text editor (such as `vi`, `emacs` or `gedit` commands). Each document consists of the text of your document and tags that identify each type of information in the text.

Unlike markup languages such as groff and HTML, SGML markup is not intended to enforce a particular look when you are creating the document. So, for example, instead of marking a piece of text as being bold or italic, you would identify it as an address, paragraph, or a name. Later, a style sheet would be applied to the document to take the tagged text and assign a look and presentation.

Because SGML consists of many tags, to simplify producing documents based on SGML other projects have cropped up to better focus the ways in which SGML is used. In particular, the Extensible Markup Language (XML) was created to offer a manageable subset of SGML that would be specifically tailored to work well with Web-based publishing.

So far in describing SGML and XML, I have only referred to the frameworks that are used to produce structured documents. Specific documentation projects need to create and, to some extent, enforce specific markup definitions for the type of documents they need to produce. These definitions are referred to as Data Type Definitions (DTDs). For producing writing that document Linux and other open source projects, DocBook has become the DTD of choice.

Understanding DocBook

DocBook is a DTD that particularly well-suited for producing computer software documents in a variety of formats. It was originally created by the OASIS Consortium (www.oasis-open.org) and is now supported by many different commercial and open source tools.

DocBook's focus is on marking content, instead of indicating a particular look (that is, font type, size, position, and so on.). It includes mark-up that lets you automate the process of creating indices, lists of figures, and tables of contents, to name a few. Tools, that are included with Red Hat Linux, let you output DocBook documents into HTML, PDF, DVI, PostScript, RTF and other formats.

DocBook is important to the Linux community because many open source projects are using DocBook to produce their documentation. For example, the following is a list of organizations, and related Web sites, that use DocBook to create the documents that describe their software:

✦ Linux Documentation Project (www.linuxdoc.org/LDP/LDP-Author-Guide)

✦ Gnome Documentation Project (http://developer.gnome.org/projects/gdp)

✦ KDE Documentation Project (www.kde.org/documentation)

✦ Open Source Writers Group (www.oswg.org)

✦ FreeBSD Documentation Project (www.freebsd.org/docproj)

If you wanted to contribute to any of the above documentation projects, refer to the Web sites for each organization. In all cases, they publish writers' guides or style guides that describe the DocBook tags that they support for their writing efforts.

Creating DocBook Documents

You can create the documents in any text editor, using tags that are similar in appearance to HTML tags (with beginning and end tags appearing between less-than and greater-than signs). There are also word processing programs that allow you to create DocBook markup.

The following procedure contains an example of a simple DocBook document that is produced with a plain text editor and output into HTML using tools that come with Red Hat Linux.

1. Create a directory in your home directory to work in and go to that directory. For example, you could type the following from a Terminal window:

```
$ mkdir $HOME/doctest
$ cd $HOME/doctest
```

2. Open a new document to hold your DocBook document using your favorite text editor. For example, you could type:

```
$ nedit cardoc.sgml
```

3. Enter the tags and text that you want to appear in your document. Most DocBook documents are either <book> type (for large, multi-chapter documents) or <article> type (for single chapter documents). You could type in the following text to try out a DocBook document:

```
<xml version="1.0">
<article>
  <title>Choosing a new car</title>
  <artheader>
    <abstract>
      In this article, you will learn how to price,
      negotiate for, and purchase an automobile.
    </abstract>
  </artheader>
  <section>
    <title>Getting Started</title>
    <para>
      The first thing you will learn is how to figure out
      what you can afford.
    </para>
  </section>
  <section>
    <title>The Next Step</title>
    <para>
    After you know what you can afford, you can begin your
    search.

    </para>

  </section>

</article>
```

There are a few things you should notice about this simple document. The entire document is wrapped in article tags (<article></article>). The title of the article appears in title tags (<title></title>). The section tags (<section></section>) indicate separate sections of text that have a title and paragraph each. These separate sections can later be treated separately in the table of contents and appear on separate pages (as seen later).

4. Save the file and exit from the text editor.

5. Next, you can try translating the document you just created into several different formats. For example, to create HTML output you could type the following:

```
$ db2html cardoc.sgml
```

The result is a new directory called `cardoc`. When I ran that command, the result was the following in the cardoc directory: a stylesheet-images directory, a `t2.html` file, and an `x12.html` file.

6. To view the HTML file just created, I typed the following:

```
$ netscape $HOME/doctest/cardoc/t2.html
```

Figure 6-9 shows an example of the output created from the `db2html` command. The screen on the left shows the first page. The second page is shown on the right. During the conversion to HTML, the `db2html` command adds Next and Previous buttons to each page. It also gathers the title of each section into a Table of Contents on the first page. The title also appears in the title bar of the browser window.

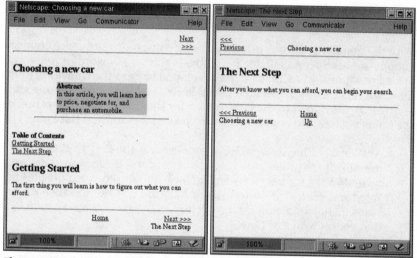

Figure 6-9: The DocBook file is output in HTML with the db2html command.

From this point, you can continue to add content and different types of tags. If you are writing documents for a particular project (such as the Linux projects mentioned earlier), you should get information on the particular tags and other style issues they require.

Converting DocBook documents

The previous example shows how to create a simple DocBook document and convert it to HTML output. Because DocBook tags are based on content rather than a specific markup, a DocBook document can be output to different formats. The following is a list of utilities that come with Red Hat Linux for converting DocBook files:

✦ **docbook2dvi** — Converts a DocBook file to Device Independent file format.

✦ **docbook2html** — Converts a DocBook file to Hypertext Markup Language (HTML) format.

✦ **docbook2man** — Converts a DocBook file to man page format.

✦ **docbook2pdf** — Converts a DocBook file to Portable Document Format (PDF).

✦ **docbook2ps** — Converts a DocBook file to PostScript format.

✦ **docbook2rtf** — Converts a DocBook file to Rich Text Format (RTF).

✦ **docbook2texi** — Converts a DocBook file to man page format.

✦ **docbook2txt** — Converts a DocBook file to TeXinfo format.

Using Free and Commercial Word Processors

With the number of Linux systems growing daily, more and more commercial applications are becoming available for Linux. In the area of word processing, several strong products have already been developed to ease the transition to Red Hat Linux for less technical-oriented users. In Red Hat 7, a free word processor (ABIWord) was added to the distribution for the first time. This section describes the following free and commercial word processors for Red Hat Linux:

✦ **AbiWord** — The AbiWord word processor is the first application produced by the AbiSource project (www.abisource.com). Besides working with files in its own AbiWord format (.abw and .zabw), AbiWord can import files in Microsoft Word and several other formats. If AbiWord was not installed during Red Hat Linux installation, you can install it from the second installation CD (CD-2) that comes with this book.

✦ **Anyware Office** — The Anyware Office suite (formerly Applixware) contains all the basics for desktop publishing and a whole bunch of extras. Anyware Words provides word processing and publishing features. Anyware Graphics is a drawing, charting, and graphics-editing application. Anyware Spreadsheets provides custom spreadsheets, numerical analysis, goal seeking, charts, graphs, and projection tables. In addition, Anyware Office includes features for creating presentations, managing e-mail, authoring HTML, accessing databases, and building custom decision support applications.

✦ **Star Office** — The Star Office office productivity suite contains applications for word processing, spreadsheets, presentation graphics, e-mail, news, charting, and graphics. It was created to run on Linux systems but runs in other environments as well. It can import and export a variety of Microsoft file formats. Star Office is owned by Sun Microsystems, which offers it free for those who want to download it. A deluxe version of Star Office is available for purchase.

✦ **WordPerfect** — At one time, WordPerfect was the most popular word-processing software for the PC. Although it was unseated by Word (and passed from WordPerfect Corporation to Novell, Incorporated to Corel Corporation), it continues to be a very powerful word processor. WordPerfect version 8 has been ported to Linux.

AbiWord comes with Red Hat 7.1. Star Office is an Open Source product, so you can download a free copy from the Internet. WordPerfect offers a 90-day trial period for its software. A demo of the Anyware Office suite is now available from Vistasource.com and can be launched from your Web browser. Purchase prices are all very reasonable — only a small fraction of what you would pay for the Microsoft Office suite (and Microsoft Office doesn't have a Linux version).

If you are committed to using Red Hat Linux as your computing platform but still want to use some of your older Windows applications, there are some workarounds:

✦ Set up separate Red Hat Linux and Windows 9x/2000 partitions on your computer (the most inefficient way), and reboot to a different partition (if you need to run Microsoft Word or some other application occasionally).

✦ Use Windows 9x/2000 or DOS emulators to run your older applications from those operating systems.

Cross-Reference

For information about obtaining Windows 3.1 or 95 emulators, such as WABI and WINE, refer to Chapter 5. VMWare (`www.vmware.com`), which is also referenced in Chapter 5, is a commercial product that lets you run Windows and Linux software on the same desktop.

Using Anyware Office

The Anyware Office Suite for Linux from VistaSource (`www.vistasource.com`) contains a full set of publishing and office-productivity applications that run under Linux. Publishing applications that come with the suite include:

✦ **Anyware Words** — This WYSIWYG word processor contains a full set of document-publishing features for editing text and formatting pages. You can also import files from many other word processors, including Word (including Microsoft Office 97).

✦ **Anyware Graphics** — You can create and edit graphical images in Anyware Graphics format (.ag) or import files in a variety of other graphics formats.

✦ **Anyware Spreadsheets** — You can create customized, graphical spreadsheets with this application. Using the spreadsheet data, you can create charts, graphs, and projection tables.

These publishing applications integrate with each other so that, for example, you can import spreadsheets into a Words document or a graphic into a Spreadsheets file. The publishing applications also integrate with other office productivity applications that come with Anyware. Office productivity applications in the suite include:

- ✦ **Anyware Presents** — Software to create presentations. You can create presentations that can be viewed as an onscreen slideshow, printed on paper or transparencies (color or monochrome), or output as 35mm slides.

- ✦ **Anyware Mail** — Send, receive, and manage e-mail messages with this application. Common e-mail features, such as maintaining recipient lists and adding attachments, are supported.

- ✦ **Anyware HTML Author** — Create your own Web pages with this HTML editor. Like Anyware Words, the HTML author is WYSIWYG so you can see what your Web page will look like as you edit.

- ✦ **Anyware Data** — Query SQL databases with this application. The interface enables you to query the databases without writing SQL statements.

- ✦ **Anyware Builder** — Create custom, user-friendly applications with Anyware Builder.

Applications in the Anyware Office suite are colorful and intuitive. Menus and icons make it easy to find and select functions. If you are used to Word or WordPerfect, you will find it very easy to begin using Anyware Office. Check theVistasource.com Web site for the price of Anyware Office. At the time of this publication, Anyware Office was offered at $49.99 to customers in North America (down from its $99 previous price). This is an excellent price, considering all the software you get and how well it is integrated. Also, you can try out an older demo of Anyware Office before you decide to buy. See the description of the demo later in this section.

Anyware Office runs not only on Linux, but also on Windows 9*x*/2000 and Windows NT. So, if your organization uses several different computing platforms, as do most organizations, the work you create can be used across all those platforms without modification.

Anyware Office import/export filters

If you are coming from another desktop publishing environment, you will find that Anyware Office enables you to open or import documents from many of the most popular formats. Import filters for graphics, document, and spreadsheet formats also exist. Here are the filters for these formats supported by Anyware Office.

Caution Don't expect every format to translate perfectly into Anyware Office. Also, after you import a file, you may not be able to export it back exactly as it was. If you have to return a file to its original form, you may have to use Rich Text Format (RTF) as an intermediate format before returning to the original form. As a precaution, be sure to keep a copy of your original file before you convert it to another format.

Words import filters

Anyware Words enables you to import documents from a variety of formats, including the following: ASCII (with line breaks or paragraph breaks); DCA Revisable Form Text (.rft); Framemaker's Maker Interchange Format (versions 4.0 and 5.5, .mif); HTML (.html); Interleaf ASCII format (versions 4.0, 5.x, and 6.x); Word (DOS); Word for Windows 2.0; Word (versions 6.0, 7.0/95, and 97); Word 5.1 (Macintosh); OfficeWriter (SPC version 6.0); Rich Text Format (.rtf); and WordPerfect (versions 4.2, 5.0, 5.1, 6.0, and 7.0).

Graphics import filters

Anyware Graphics lets you import graphics from these formats: Anyware Bitmap (.im); Computer Graphics Meta File (.cgm); Document Interchange Format (.dxf); Encapsulated PostScript Interchange (.epsi); FAX (Group 3 and Group 4 CALS, .fax); GEM Image Format (.img); GIF (.gif); HPGL (.hpgl); Amiga IFF ILBM (.iff); JPEG (.jpg); MacPaint (.mpnt); Windows Bitmap (.bmp); Portable Bitmap (.pbm); Portable Graymap (.pgm); Portable Pixmap (.ppm); PC Paintbrush PCX (.pcx); MacDraw (PICT and PICT2, .pict); PowerPoint (versions 3.0, 4.0, and 7.0); raw bitmap; SGI raster file; Sun Raster (.rs); TruVision Targa file (.tga); TIFF (.tif); MS Windows Metafile (.wmf); WordPerfect Graphics (.wpg); X Window Bitmap (.xbm); X Window Pixmap (.xpm); and X Window Dump (.xwd).

Spreadsheets import filters

Anyware Spreadsheets enables you to import these spreadsheet formats: Lotus (.wks, .wk1, .wk3, and .wk4); Microsoft Excel (versions 3.0, 4.0, 5.0, 7.0, and 97, .xls); Symbolic Link file (.slk); Data Interchange Format (.sdi, .dif, and .xdf); ASCII (any format); and Comma Separated Values (.csv).

The Anyware Office demo

A demo version of Anyware Office is available from VistaSource. The demo can be launched from your Web browser and run over the Internet.

To run the demo from Red Hat Linux, you need to start Netscape Navigator (version 4 or greater is required) and have it Java-enabled (which it is by default). From the VistaSource Web site (www.vistasource.com), you need to set up a demo user account. Then visit the following site to log in and begin the demo:

```
http://www.anywareoffice.com
```

The demo opens an Anyware Office icon bar. Move the mouse over the icon bar to see tool tips identifying each application. From left to right, the icon bar lets you open the following applications: Words, Spreadsheets, Presents, Graphics, Data, Inbox, Sendmail, Data, and Directory Displayer. The last two buttons let you select Tools and Preferences. Figure 6-10 shows an example of the Anyware Office icon bar, Anyware Words, and Anyware Sendmail.

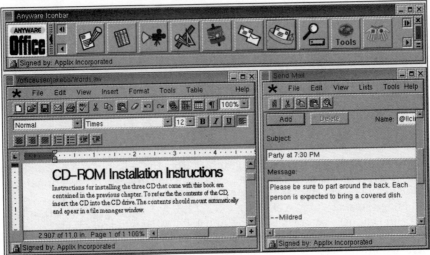

Figure 6-10: Select Anyware Office applications, such as Words, from the Anyware Office iconbar.

Though the demo runs on your computer, you cannot save any file locally. Any files you save are stored on a remote server. So you can use all the features of Anyware Office, but you can't really do any work with it unless you purchase the product.

Tips for running Anyware Office

Here are a few tips for running applications in the Anyware Office suite:

✦ The star button on the menu bar of any Anyware Office application lets you open any other Anyware Office application.

✦ When you open Anyware Presents, select the Content of Presentation menu box. From that menu you can select from several types of presentations to begin with, including General Purpose, Reporting Bad News, Progress Report, Instructional/Training, Promotion of Products, and Recommendation.

✦ To keep track of your changes in a Word document, click Tools ⇨ Change Bars ⇨ Add Change Bars.

✦ You can add an index and cross-references with Words. Click a word or phrase, and then select Tools ⇨ Book Building ⇨ Index Entry to add an index entry. Click a word, and then select Tools ⇨ Cross Reference ⇨ Cross Reference Source to create a cross-reference.

✦ If you want to discard all the changes you made to a document since it was last saved, click File ⇨ Revert.

✦ You can open a window to send the document you are working on by e-mail with one click. Click the mail icon on the Words menu bar and an Anyware Mail window appears. The current document is added to the message as an attachment. You can add an e-mail address, type a message, and send it to the recipients.

✦ When you use Anywhere Data, you can choose the database server you want to access by clicking Query ➪ Choose Server. From the dialog box that appears, you can enter the name and address information for an Informix, Ingres, ODBC, Oracle, or Sybase server. (Anyware Data is disabled in the demo.)

Using Star Office

The Star Office suite from Sun Microsystems Inc. (www.sun.com/staroffice) is another product that runs on several different operating systems. Like Anyware Office, Star Office contains many features that make it compatible with Microsoft Office applications. In particular, it includes the capability to import Microsoft Word and Excel files. There is also strong support for producing HTML files.

Star Office for Linux includes these applications:

✦ **StarWriter** — This is the Star Office word processing application. It can import documents from a variety of formats, with special emphasis on working with Microsoft Word documents.

✦ **StarCalc** — This is the spreadsheet program that comes with Star Office. You can import spreadsheets from Microsoft Excel and other popular programs.

✦ **StarImpress** — You can create presentations with the StarImpress application.

✦ **StarDraw** — This is a vector-oriented drawing program. It includes the capability to create 3D objects and to use texturing.

✦ **StarBase** — You can manage your data with StarBase. It can access a variety of database interfaces.

✦ **StarSchedule** — Use this application to manage your schedule, track events, and store your contacts. You can even interface StarSchedule to a PalmPilot.

There are also other applications in Star Office that create business graphics (StarChart), edit images (StarImage), edit mathematical formulas (StarMath), and manage e-mail (StarMail). You can manage all these applications from the StarDesktop. The StarDesktop features an explorer tree for navigation and a task bar (so you can easily switch between tasks).

You can download a free version of Star Office for Linux from the Star Office Web site at www.sun.com/staroffice. Just look for the downloads links on that page. If you want to purchase the Star Office Deluxe for Linux, the cost, at time of this writing, was $39.99. The Deluxe version includes an installation CD and printed manuals. More clip art and fonts are also included.

Sun Microsystems has recently launched the OpenOffice project (www.openoffice.org). Visit that site for download links and other information related to Star Office.

Using Corel WordPerfect

At one time, WordPerfect was the world's most popular word-processing program. Although MS Word overtook WordPerfect a few years ago, WordPerfect is still very popular and is loaded with features. Corel Corporation (www.corel.com) now owns WordPerfect and continues its development. Fortunately for Red Hat Linux users, WordPerfect is available for Linux.

Instead of having a lot of different applications for drawing and graphics editing, those features are built into the WordPerfect application. Other tools in WordPerfect include a spell checker, a thesaurus, and a grammar checker.

The latest version of WordPerfect that runs on Linux is WordPerfect 2000 for Linux, available in both standard and deluxe editions. The deluxe edition contains more clip art, a few additional applications, and more support features.

WordPerfect can import many different word-processing and image file formats, including: AmiPro (1.2, 1.2a, 1.2b, 2.0, 3.0); Applix Words 4.0; ASCII (Delimited Text, Text, Text/LineFeed-SRt); CGM; Encapsulated PostScript; Framemaker Maker Interchange Format (versions 3, 4, and 5); HPGL; HTML; Interleaf (3.1cx, 3.1ps, 4.0cx, 4.0ps, 5.0); Island Write (3.0, 4.0); ISO Latin Text; Kermit (7-bit transfer); Lotus 1-2-3 (2.3, 2.4, 3.0, 3.1); Microsoft Word (4.0, 5.0, 5.5); Word for Windows (2.0, 2.0a, 2.0b, 2.0c, 6.0/7.0); Word 97; Navy DIF Standard; RTF; WordPerfect for Macintosh (2.0, 2.1, 3.0); WordPerfect (4.2, 5.0, 5.1/5.2, 6.x/7/8); WordPerfect 7.0 OLE Doc File; and AutoCAD DXF (ASCII).

The following are the image file formats that WordPerfect can import: CompuServe GIF; Enhanced Windows Metafile; Framemaker Vector; IBM Graphics Data Format; GEM Metafile; CALS format; Mac PICT2; Lotus PIC; IBM PIF; NAPLPS Standard ANSI Profile; Targa; Windows Metafile; X Window bitmap; JPEG; CorelDraw; Harvard Chart (3.0); Micrografx Product; PCX; Sun RasterFile; TIFF Graphic; Windows Bitmap; WordPerfect Graphic (1.0, 2.0); and X Window Dump (xwd).

AbiWord

The AbiWord word processor is a very nice, free word processor from the AbiSource project (www.abisource.com). If you are creating documents from scratch, AbiWord includes many of the basic functions you need to create good-quality documents.

Basic word processing features include the ability to select several font types, font sizes, bold, italics, underscore, overline, strikethrough, superscript, and subscript. You can do left, center, and right adjustment. You can cut, copy, and paste text, and undo and redo editing changes. File operations let you create new documents, open an existing document, or save the current document.

With AbiWord, you can select what type of document the file contains. You can select to read the file in the following formats:

✦ AbiWord (.abw)

✦ GZipped AbiWord (.zabw)

✦ Rich Text Format (.rtf)

✦ Microsoft Word (.doc)

✦ UTF8 (.utf8)

✦ Text (.txt)

AbiWord doesn't yet import all of these file types cleanly. For example, styles are not supported. When I imported a Microsoft Word file, all text came in as Normal, though some attempt was made to interpret a few different font types. If you want to work with a Word document in AbiWord, open it as AbiWord, correct any font problems, and save the document in AbiWord format. There's no clean way to go back to Word at that point.

AbiWord is a great first try as a usable word processor. Listed but nonimplemented features imply good things to come (styles, bullets, borders and shading, etc.). It's not competitive with comparable commercial products, but its developers continue to improve it. Remember — they said the same thing about Linux a few years ago.

Printing Documents with Red Hat Linux

Printers are configured in Red Hat Linux using the LPRng service. As a nonroot user, you don't have a lot of control over how the printers are configured. You can, however, check which printers are available, choose which printer to print to, check the status of print queues (documents waiting to print), and remove any of your own queued print jobs.

 Cross-Reference For information on configuring local and remote printers for Red Hat Linux, see Chapter 17.

Printing to the default printer

When your system administrator configured printers for your computer, one of those printers was defined as the default printer. If you are not sure which printer is your default printer, look for the word Default next to one of the printers in the /etc/printcap file.

Commercial word processors, such as Anyware Office, let you choose a printer from those available. WordPerfect also lets you choose a default printer. Some of the less sophisticated Linux utilities that run from the command line, however, use only the default printer. For example, `dvips` (to print a PostScript file) and `groff -l` (to print a troff/nroff file) automatically send the output to the default printer.

As a regular user, you can override the default printer using the `PRINTER` environment variable. For example, if the default printer on your computer is `lp0` and you want to print on a regular basis to `lp1`, you could change your default printer by setting the `PRINTER` variable as follows:

    $ export PRINTER=lp1

To have this take effect all the time, you could add this line to one of your shell configuration files (such as `$HOME/.bashrc`, if you use the bash shell).

Printing from the shell

In Red Hat Linux, `lpr` is the shell command used to print files. While some text formatting commands can automatically print their output when they are done, if you have a file that is already formatted, use `lpr` to print it.

For example, if you have a PostScript output file (file.ps) and you want to print it to your PostScript printer, use the following command line:

    $ lpr file.ps

If you want to specify a particular printer (other than the default printer), add the `-Pprinter` option. For example:

    $ lpr -Plp0 file.ps

If you want to print more than one copy of a document, use the `-#num` option, where `num` is replaced by the number of copies you want. For example, to print five copies of a file, use the following command:

    $ lpr -#5 file.ps

The `lpr` command can also accept standard output for printing. For example, you could print the output of a `groff` command by piping that output to `lpr` as follows:

    $ groff -Tps -man /tmp/chown.1 | lpr -Plp0

Some of the commands that bypass the `lpr` command for printing are described in the sections, "Text Processing with Groff" and "Text Processing with TeX/LaTeX," earlier in this chapter.

Tip   The `enscript` command is another useful tool for printing plain text files. It converts the files to PostScript and sends them to a printer or to a specified file.

Checking the print queues

To check the status of print jobs that have been queued, you can use the lpq command. By itself, lpq prints a listing of jobs that are in the queue for the default printer. For example:

```
$ lpq
Rank  Owner   Job   Files            Total Size
1st   root     0    (standard input)  625 bytes
2nd   root     1    memo1.ps         12273 bytes
3rd   chuck    5    bikes.ps         10880 bytes
```

The output from lpq shows the files waiting to be printed. Rank lists the order in which they are in the queue. Owner is the user who queued the job. Job shows the job number. The Files column shows the name of the file or standard output (if the file was piped to lpr). Total Size shows how large each file is in bytes.

You can add options to lpq to print different kinds of information. By adding -Pprinter, you can see the queue for any available printer. You can also add the job number (to see the status of a particular print job) or a user name (to see all queued jobs for a user).

Removing print jobs

If you have ever sent a large print job to the printer by mistake, you understand the value of being able to remove a print job from the queue. Likewise, if a printer is going to be down for a while and everyone has already printed their jobs to another printer, it's sometimes nice to be able to clear all the print jobs when the printer comes back online.

You can remove print jobs in Red Hat Linux using the lprm command. For example, to remove all jobs for the user named chuck (assuming you are either chuck or the root user), type the following:

```
$ lprm chuck
```

The root user can remove all print jobs from the queue. To do this you add a dash (-) to the lprm command line as follows:

```
$ lprm -
```

You can also remove queued print jobs for a particular printer (-Pprinter) or for a particular job number by just adding the job number to the lprm command line.

Checking printer status

Sometimes nothing comes out of a printer and you have no idea why. The lpc command is a printer status command you can run that might give you a clue as to what is going on with your printer. The lpc command is intended for administrators, so it may not be in your default PATH. To start the lpc command, type the following:

```
# /usr/sbin/lpc
lpc> status
lp:
  queuing is enabled
  printing is enabled
  4 entries in spool area
  waiting for queue to be enabled on maple
lp0:
  queuing is enabled
  printing is enabled
  no entries
  no daemon present
lpc>
```

When the command returns the lpc> prompt, type the word status. This example shows the status of two printers: lp and lp0. The lp printer has four jobs waiting to be printed. Though the queuing and printing are enabled, they haven't printed because the print queue is not enabled. (It is a remote printer on a computer called maple that may be down or disabled.) The lp0 printer seems to be working fine. No print jobs are waiting.

Displaying Documents with Ghostscript and Acrobat

Red Hat Linux publishing can be very paper-intensive if you send a groff or LaTeX document to the printer each time you want to make a change to the document's content or formatting. To save paper and time spent running around, you can use some print preview programs to display a document on screen as it will appear on the printed page. The following sections describe the ghostscript command for displaying PostScript files and the Adobe Acrobat reader for displaying Portable Document Format (PDF) files.

Using the ghostscript and gv commands

To display PostScript or PDF documents in Red Hat Linux, you can use the ghostscript command. The ghostscript command is a fairly crude interface, intended to let you step through documents and interpret them one line at a time. (If the ghostscript command is not installed on your system, you can get it by installing the ghostscript package from CD-1 that comes with this book.)

You can display any .ps or .pdf file you happen to have on your computer. For example, if the vnc-doc package is installed, you could type the following to display a PDF file (otherwise, you could find your own PDF file to try it):

```
$ ghostscript /usr/share/doc/vnc-doc-*/rfbprotoheader.pdf
>>showpage, press <return> to continue<<
```

At the GS> prompt, press Enter (or Return) to go through the file one page at a time. When the file is done, you can type the name of another PostScript file and page through that file. When you are done, type quit.

The gv command (ghostview) is another, more friendly way of viewing PostScript files. (If the gv command is not installed on your system, you can get it by installing the gv package from CD-2 that comes with this book.)

To use gv to open a file called rbash.ps, you would type the following:

```
$ gv /usr/share/doc/bash-doc-*/bashref.ps
```

When the ghostview window opens, you can see the document. Left-click your mouse on the page and move it up and down to scroll the document. Use Page Up and Page Down keys to page through the document.

Using Adobe Acrobat Reader

The Portable Document Format (PDF) provides a way of storing documents as they would appear in print. With Adobe Acrobat Reader, you can view PDF files in a very friendly way. Adobe Acrobat makes it easy to move around a PDF file. A PDF file may include hyperlinks, a table of contents, graphics, and a variety of type fonts.

You can also download a free copy of Acrobat Reader from the Adobe site: www.adobe.com/support/downloads. The Acrobat Reader is free so as to encourage people to buy the Acrobat 4 program for creating PDF documents. With Acrobat 4, you can convert nearly any kind of document to PDF, create PDF files from scanned images, add electronic notes and highlights to PDF documents, and apply digital signatures (for security reasons).

After you have installed the Adobe Acrobat Reader, type the following command to start the program:

```
$ acroread
```

Click File ➪ Open, and then select the name of a PDF file you have to display. Figure 6-11 shows an example of a PDF file viewed in Adobe Acrobat Reader.

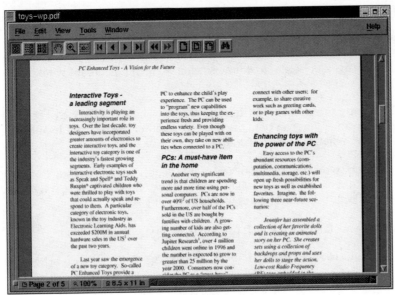

Figure 6-11: Display PDF files in the Adobe Acrobat Reader.

Acrobat Reader has a lot of nice features. For example, you can display a list of bookmarks alongside the document and click on a bookmark to take you to a particular page. You can also display thumbnails of the pages to quickly scroll through and select a page.

Using the menu bar or buttons, you can page through the PDF document, zoom in and out, go to the beginning or end of the document, and display different views of the document (as well as display bookmarks and page thumbnails). To print a copy of the file, click File ⇨ Print.

Working with Graphics

Tools for creating and manipulating graphics are becoming both more plentiful and more powerful in Red Hat Linux. Leading the list is the GNU Image Manipulation Program (GIMP). GIMP lets you compose and author images as well as retouch photographs. Other tools that come with Red Hat Linux for creating graphics include xv (a program for taking screen captures) and xpaint (for working with bitmap images).

Cross-Reference See Chapter 8 for descriptions of other multi-media applications, such as the gphoto window for working with images from digital cameras.

Manipulating photos and images

The GIMP program is a free software program that comes with Red Hat Linux for manipulating photographs and graphical images. To create images with GIMP, you can either import a drawing, photograph, or 3D-image, or you can create one from scratch. You can start GIMP from the system menu by clicking on Graphics ➪ The GIMP or by typing gimp& from a Terminal window.

Note   If GIMP is not on your system or is not installed properly, you can install it from CD-1 that comes with this book. Alternatively, you can obtain the latest copy of GIMP from www.gimp.org.

In many ways, GIMP is similar to Adobe Photoshop. Some people feel that GIMP's scripting features are comparable to, or even better than, Actions in Adobe Photoshop. One capability that GIMP lacks, however, is support for CMYK separations.

Taking screen captures

If you want to show examples of the work you do on Red Hat Linux, you can use the xv utility to capture screen images. This utility is particularly handy for those of us who write computer books. (Most of the images in this book were captured using the xv utility.) Because xv is shareware, to use it commercially you should send a $25 fee to the creator of xv (click the About XV button to find out about the license and where to send the fee).

The xv utility is no longer part of the Red Hat Linux distribution. You can obtain a copy of the xv package, however, from Red Hat Linux FTP sites (such as ftp://ftp. redhat.com/pub/contrib/libc6/i386/). To open the xv window, type:

```
xv&
```

When you first start xv, the xv image display window (where your screen captures will appear) is displayed. Click on that window to see the xv controls window (which contains buttons for grabbing and saving screens). Figure 6-12 shows the xv controls. Notice that the version of xv that comes with Red Hat Linux (shown in the figure) is unregistered. I strongly recommend you register a copy if you use it for your work.

To grab an image with xv, click Grab. A dialog box lets you select Grab (to grab a window with the left mouse button) or AutoGrab (to grab a window that the cursor is positioned over after a set number of seconds). For Grab, you can either just click on the window you want or use the middle mouse button (on a 3-button mouse) to drag open a rectangular area to grab. Before you can use AutoGrab, you must type in a Delay (in seconds) that xv should wait before AutoGrab grabs the window indicated by your cursor.

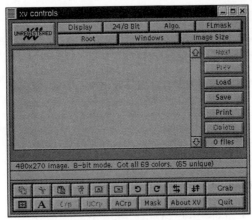

Figure 6-12: Capture screen images and save to a variety of formats using xv.

After you have grabbed an image, you can do some manipulation with it. Select a rectangular area on the image window. Then, from the control window, click Scissors (to cut the area), Crop (to cut outside the area), or either of the arrow buttons (to flip the selected area up/down or right/left). Click the rotation arrows to rotate the image in one direction or the other.

To save the image, click Save. Select the format to choose from 15 different image output types. Select Full Color, B/W Dithered, or Greyscale. Choose the directory and filename for the image. Then click OK. If you want to review any of the images on your computer, click Load and select the file that you want.

Note   If you just want to do quick screen shots, screenshooter is a free utility that comes with the Gnome desktop that lets you do just that. Add it to your Gnome panel (Gnome menu ➪ Panel ➪ Add to panel ➪ Applet ➪ Utility ➪ Screenshooter). Then click the left side of the screenshooter icon to select a window or swipe an area to capture. Click the right side of the screenshooter icon to grab the whole desktop. The captured images are saved as JPEG files in your home directory.

Creating bitmap images

Create bitmap images from scratch, or import a variety of image formats with the xpaint program. The xpaint program can read and write GIF, JPEG, BMP, XBM, XPM, and PPM image formats. Figure 6-13 shows an example of the xpaint toolbox and canvas.

Start xpaint from either the System menu (click on Programs ➪ Graphics ➪ Paint) or from a Terminal window (/usr/X11R6/bin/xpaint&). Start with either a blank canvas (File ➪ New Canvas) or by opening an image in one of the supported formats (File ➪ Open, browse for a file, and then select OK).

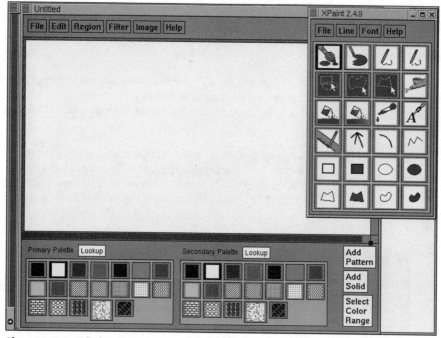

Figure 6-13: Edit bitmap images with xpaint.

The painting tools enable you to draw arcs, boxes, polygons, and other shapes; change the brush being used; create a series of connected lines; make dots on the canvas; erase a section of the image; choose from various fills; reshape objects; and add text. Using the Filter menu, you can have selected image processing done on an area of the image, such as inverting the colors, adding noise (random dots), and spreading the image by a set number of pixels. Using the Region menu, you can do common flips and rotations on objects in the image.

Using Scanners Driven by SANE

Software for using a scanner with Linux is being driven by an effort called Scanner Access Now Easy (SANE). This effort hopes to standardize how device drivers for equipment such as scanners, digital still cameras, and digital video cameras are created, as well as help simplify the interfaces for applications that use those devices.

SANE is now included with the Red Hat Linux distribution. The sane-backends and sane-frontends packages are on the first Red Hat Linux installation CD (CD-1) that comes with this book. You can get the latest SANE driver packages from www. mostang.com/sane.

Someone wanting to use Linux as a publishing platform is generally interested in two issues about scanners: which scanners are supported and which applications are available to use the scanners. In general, more SCSI scanners are supported than parallel scanners.

Because of the ongoing development effort, new scanners are being supported all the time. You can find a current list of supported scanners at www.mostang.com/sane/sane-backends.html. As for applications, these are currently available with Red Hat Linux:

✦ **xsane** — This is an X-based graphical front end for SANE scanners; xsane can work as a GIMP plug-in or as a separate application. It supports 8-bit output in JPG, TIFF, PNG, PostScript, and PNM formats. There is experimental 16-bit support for PNM (ASCII), PNG, and raw formats. Figure 6-14 shows the xsane window.

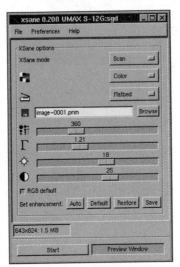

Figure 6-14: Use xsane to access scanners in Red Hat Linux.

✦ **xscanimage** — Another X-based window used to preview and scan images from a Linux scanner or digital camera. Starting xscanimage from the command line lets you save images in PBM (black-and-white), PGM (grayscale), or PPM (color). When used as a GIMP plug-in, GIMP processes the images.

✦ **scanimage** — This is a command-line interface for obtaining scanned images. It supports the same formats as xscanimage. The command acquires the scanned image, and then directs the data to standard output (so you can send it to a file or pipe it to another program).

✦ **xcam** — This graphical interface lets you grab continuous images from a video camera interface on your system.

Because of the architecture of SANE scanner drivers, it is possible to separate scanner drivers from scanner applications. This makes it possible to share scanners and video cameras across a network.

Summary

In recent times, modern GUI-based publishing tools have augmented the text-based publishing tools that have always been available with Red Hat Linux (and other UNIX systems). Publishing tools that come with Red Hat Linux include Groff (which implements traditional troff/nroff text processing) and LaTeX (a TeX macro interface that is particularly suited for scientific and mathematical publishing). In recent years, DocBook, an SGML-based data type definition, has become the standard for producing documentation of Linux and other software projects.

Along with Red Hat Linux's growing popularity, more commercial publishing applications have appeared that work with Red Hat Linux. Anyware Office and Star Office are two application suites that provide powerful publishing features in Linux. The popular WordPerfect word processor has also been ported to Linux. Although you do have to pay for Anyware Office and WordPerfect, their prices are reasonable (especially when measured against comparable MS Windows applications). Red Hat Linux does include one free word processor: AbiWord. Though AbiWord isn't up to the level of the best commercial word processors, it does have good, basic features and potential for the future.

To create and manage graphics, Red Hat Linux comes with applications like GIMP, xv, and xpaint. Each of these applications enables you to input and output graphics files from a variety of formats. There is also an interface to scanners called Scanner Access Now Easy (SANE). With SANE, a variety of applications can access scanner devices, and the devices can be shared across a network.

✦   ✦   ✦

Playing Games with Red Hat Linux

The advancement of computer games has mirrored the improvements in computers themselves. In the 1970s, the first games for UNIX systems were visually simple and could run on slow, character-based terminal connections. Today, games that combine graphics, animation, and sound have helped drive improvements in computer technology in general.

Availability of gaming software useable with Red Hat Linux is similar to that of Linux publishing software. A lot of the old software is still around (and is free), while newer software is available in demo form but will cost some money to get a full version. Some experts predict that gaming will be the software category that brings Linux into homes. Although the number of popular game applications is limited at the moment, like everything else in Linux, more are becoming available each day.

This chapter addresses the current state of gaming in Linux, including the basics on getting your gaming environment going, and hardware and networking considerations for multiuser gaming. It describes the free games (mostly character-based and fairly simple X Window games) that come with Red Hat Linux or that can be easily downloaded. For running games that were created for other platforms, this chapter describes some game emulators.

This chapter also discusses some graphical games, such as Quake III, that have demo versions available for Linux, as well as the full commercial game being packaged for Linux, such as Civilization: Call to Power.

Basic Linux Gaming Information

There isn't much you need to know to run most of the text-based or X Window-based game applications that come with Red Hat Linux. Most of the gaming issues that may trip you up pertain to those commercial games that need special hardware and software to run 3D graphics and animation. Outside of that, however, there are a few bits of game information that may be useful.

✦ Games are often placed in /usr/games or /usr/X11R6/bin, though many KDE games are simply piled in /usr/bin. If a game that you play a lot is in /usr/games or some other directory that is not in your PATH by default, you may want to add them to your PATH. That way, you don't have to type the whole directory structure with the command. The games may also be installed in /usr/local/games or some other directory (such as a subdirectory of /opt).

✦ Man pages for older Linux games are in section 6 (in the /usr/share/man/man6 directory).

Tip   After I install a game package, I type rpm -ql *package*, where package is the name of the game package. This shows me where the executables and documentation are, if any.

Where to get information on Linux gaming

To find news on the latest games available for Linux, as well as links to download sites, go to some of the several Web sites available. Here are a few to get you started:

✦ **The Linux Game Tome** (http://happypenguin.org) — This site contains news on Linux gaming and lots of links to other gaming sites. In particular, there are links to news from other gaming sites. Links to recently updated or reviewed games are also included.

✦ **Linuxgames.com** (http://linuxgames.com) — This site can help you get the latest information on the games you are interested in. There are links to HOW-TOs and Frequently Asked Questions (FAQs), as well as forums for discussing Linux games (so far, most of the action is in the Games Development forum). There are also links to Web sites that have information on a particular game you are interested in.

✦ **id Software** (www.idsoftware.com/archives) — Go to the id Software site for information and download links for Linux demo versions of the Quake and Doom games.

✦ **Loki Entertainment Software** (www.lokigames.com) — Loki ports best-selling games to Linux. Their products include Civilization: Call to Power, Myth II: Soulblighter, SimCity 3000, Railroad Tycoon II, and the Linux version of Quake III Arena. Check the Web site for other games in development.

✦ **Tux Games** (www.tuxgames.com)—If you are ready to purchase a game, the Tux Games Web site is a dedicated to the sale of Linux games. Besides offering Linux gaming news and products, the site lists its top-selling games and includes notices of games that are soon to be released.

If the idea of developing your own games interests you, try the Linux Game Development Center (http://lgdc.sunsite.dk).

Graphical gaming interfaces

Most new games that require a graphical interface to run under Red Hat Linux offer a version that runs under the X Window System. Other graphical interfaces, however, are available. In some cases, you need to install special software packages for these interfaces to work. Graphical interfaces include the X Window System, SVGALIB, and GGI interfaces.

X Window System

The X Window System (X) is the graphical interface used with every Red Hat Linux desktop by default. Most new games offer X versions since everyone has X. Because X doesn't provide a dedicated graphical screen for the game, performance can be degraded. There is more overhead in X that is devoted to running the desktop and managing X applications than is needed, if you just need a GUI to play a game.

Tip   It is the X window manager that typically consumes most of your processing power. If you want to run a game in X, you might consider using the twm window manager, which consumes a very small amount of system resources.

Linux Super VGA Library

The Super VGA Library (SVGALIB) interface can run games in a more dedicated way than X. An SVGALIB game fills the whole screen. Because SVGALIB can run your game without having to manage a desktop and other applications (as X does), SVGALIB can run some games faster than X. When you run an SVGALIB application, it takes over the screen and control of the mouse.

Note   The svgalib software package is not part of the basic Red Hat Linux operating system. However, it is included on the Red Hat Linux FTP site or from a Red Hat mirror site.

At the moment, the development effort behind SVGALIB seems to be lagging. Also, the GGI effort (discussed next) could eventually make SVGALIB obsolete. So far, it has not. To use games intended for SVGALIB, you need to have the svgalib package installed.

Tip   If your mouse isn't working in SVGALIB, you may need to configure it for SVGALIB. To do this, edit the /etc/vga/libvga.config file. This file contains details about configuring your mouse, keyboard, monitor, and video chips so that they work properly with SVGALIB.

OpenGL Support

Many advanced games in Linux rely on the OpenGL (www.opengl.org) graphics environment for high-performance graphics rendering. To see a list of games (as well as other applications) that rely on OpenGL, you can refer to the Applications and Tools for Linux list that is maintained at the OpenGL Web site (www.opengl.org/users/apps_hardware/applications/linux_apps.html).

Chances are that if you don't have a recent model computer, the video card you have may not support the OpenGL features that are required by some of today's more demanding Linux games. You might want to consider replacing the card with a newer card. For example, here is a list of video cards and the Linux games from Loki Software that they can be used to play:

✦ **3Dfx cards** — Voodoo, Voodoo Rush, Voodoo 2, Voodoo Banshee, Voodoo 3, Voodoo 4, and Voodoo 5

✦ **ATI cards** — Rage Pro, Rage Pro/Mobility, Rage 128, Rage 128 PRO, and Radeon

✦ **Matrox cards** — G200, G400, and G450

✦ **nVidia cards** — TNT, TNT2, TNT Ultra, and GeForce

For more details on how to configure specific cards to work with Loki Software games, refer to the company's FAQs page (http://faqs.lokigames.com). In particular, refer to the OpenGL on XFree86 FAQs for information on setting up and troubleshooting particular video cards.

To do hardware acceleration in XFree86, DRI (Direct Rendering Infrastructure) GLX drivers are used. An exception is that DRI drivers are not included for nVidia cards because nVidia provides closed-source binary drivers for their cards. Because DRI drivers are actually compatible with the chipsets used on supported boards, boards that used the same chipsets may also be supported. For more specific information about which chipsets are supported in DRI, refer to the DRI support Web page (http://dri.sourceforge.net/status.phtml).

Tip   To use hardware DRI acceleration on Voodoo 3 cards, you must have your display set to use 16bpp resolution. On Voodoo 5 cards, only 16bpp and 24bpp resolutions are supported.

X Window Games

The X Window System created a great opportunity for games in Red Hat Linux and other UNIX systems to move from character-based to graphical-based games. (Character-based games are discussed later in the chapter.) So, instead of having little character symbols representing robots and arrows, they could actually show pictures of little robots and arrows.

There are a lot of diverting games that come with Red Hat Linux and run in X. Unless otherwise noted, all of the X games described in this section are free. Also, each of the major desktop environments that come with Red Hat Linux (described in Chapter 4) has a set of games associated with it.

Gnome games

The Gnome games consist of some old text-based UNIX games, some card games, and a bunch of games that look suspiciously like games you would find on Windows systems. If you are afraid of losing your favorite applications (such as Solitaire, Freecell, and Minesweeper) when you leave Windows 9x/2000, have no fear. You can find many of them under Gnome games.

Table 7-1 lists the games available by selecting Programs ➪ Games from the Main Gnome menu.

Table 7-1
Gnome Games

Game	Description	Game	Description
AisleRiot (solitaire)	Lets you select from among 28 different solitaire card games.	Chess	Gnuchess game in X. (Runs the `xboard` and `gnuchess` commands.)
Chromium-Setup	Set options such as skill level, screen size, and sound for Chromium.	Chromium	Deliver supplies to troops in battle in this action game.
FreeCell	A popular solitaire card game.	Freeciv (Engels tileset)	In this strategy game, you try to lead your civilization to extinguish all others. (Uses Engels tileset to represent cities, oceans, and other terrain.)
Freeciv (Trident tileset)	In this strategy game, you try to lead your civilization to extinguish all others. (Uses Trident tileset to represent cities, oceans, and other terrain.)	Freeciv Server (new game)	Server program needed to play Freeciv.

Continued

Table 7-1 *(continued)*

Game	Description	Game	Description
Gataxx	Board game where you flip over circles to consume enemy pieces.	Glines	Match five colored balls in a row to score points.
Gnibbles	Steer a worm around the screen while avoiding walls.	GnobotsII	Later version of Gnobots, which includes movable junk heaps.
Gnome Mines	Minesweeper clone. Click on safe spaces and avoid the bombs.	Gnome-Stones	Move around a cave, collect diamonds, and avoid rocks.
Gnotravex	Tetravex clone. Move blocks so that numbers on each side align.	Gnotski	Move pieces around to allow one piece to escape.
GTali	Yahtzee clone. Roll dice to fill in categories.	Iagno	Flip black and white chips to maneuver past the opponent.
Maelstrom	Navigate a space ship through an asteroid field.	Mahjongg	Classic oriental tile game.
Same Gnome	Eliminate clusters of balls for high score.	Tux Race	Steer a penguin as he races down a hill on his belly.
xbill	Prevent Bill from stealing operating systems. Whack Bill and return the OSs.	xbl	Drop 3-D blocks and fit them together in this Tetris-like game.
Xsnow	Add a snowy backdrop to your desktop.		

KDE games

If you install KDE, there are a bunch of games that come with the desktop. These games also show up on the Gnome menu. To see the KDE Games from the Gnome menu, select KDE menus ➪ Games, and then choose the game you want from the following categories: Arcade, Card, Board, Tactic/Strategy. The games available in KDE are listed in Table 7-2.

Cross-Reference   See Chapter 4 for a description of the KDE desktop.

Table 7-2
Games for the KDE Desktop

Game	Description	Game	Description
Abalone	Board game whose object is to push opponents' pieces off the board.	Asteroids	Destroy asteroids in the classic asteroids arcade game.
Atomic Entertainment	Move pieces to create different chemical compounds.	BlackBox	Find hidden balls by shooting rays.
Foul Eggs	Squish eggs in this Tetris-like game.	Jezzball	Trap bouncing balls to progress to higher levels.
KBackgammon	Online version of backgammon.	KBattleship	Sink the opponent's battleship in this online version of the board game.
KJumping Cube	Click squares to increase numbers and take over adjacent squares.	Klines	Move marbles to form 5-in-a-row and score points.
Kwin4	Drop colored pieces to get 4-in-a-row.	Konquest	Expand your interstellar empire in this multiplayer game.
Lieutenant Skat	Play the card game Skat.	Mahjongg	Classic oriental tile game.
Minesweeper	Minesweeper clone. Click safe spaces and avoid the bombs.	Patience	Choose from nine different solitaire card games.
Poker	Video poker clone. Play five-card draw, choosing which cards to hold and which to throw.	Reversi	Flip game pieces to outmaneuver the opponent.
SameGame	Erase game pieces to score points.	Shisen-Sho	Tile game similar to Mahjongg.
Sirtet	Tetris clone. Try to fill in lines of blocks as they drop down.	Smiletris	Tetris with smiley faces.

Continued

Bonus content at www.unltded.com

Table 7-2 *(continued)*

Game	Description	Game	Description
Snake Race	Race your snake around a maze.	Sokoban	The Japanese warehouse keeper game.
SpaceDuel	Fire at another space ship as you spin around a planet.	Tron	Snake-style race game.

The games on the KDE menu range from diverting to quite challenging. If you are used to playing games in Windows, Minesweeper and Patience will seem like old favorites. Asteroids and Poker are good for the mindless game category. For a mental challenge (it's harder than it looks), try Sokoban. For a challenging multiuser game on the GNOME menu, try Freeciv. (The commercial version of Freeciv, Civilization: Call to Power, is described later in this chapter.) For chess enthusiasts, there is xboard.

If the games that run in X that come with KDE aren't enough for you, lots of X games are available for download from the Web. For example, the Freshmeat site lists more than 200 games in its application index that you can be downloaded to run in X (go to `http://www.freshmeat.com/appindex/x11/games.html`).

The following sections describe a couple of the more interesting Red Hat Linux games that run in X. First is the xboard game and some related chess programs. Next is a description of Freeciv.

Chess games

Chess was one of the first games played on computer systems. While the game hasn't changed over the years, the way it's played on computers has. The set of chess programs that come with Red Hat Linux lets you play against the computer (in text or graphical modes), has the computer play against itself, or replays stored chess games. You can even play chess against other users on the Internet using Internet Chess Servers (ICS).

The `xboard` program is an X-based chess game that provides a graphical interface for gnuchess. GNU Chess (represented by the gnuchess package) describes itself as a communal chess program. It has had many contributors, and it seeks to advance a "more open and friendly environment of sharing" among the chess community.

With `xboard`, you can move graphical pieces with your mouse. To play against the computer, click Programs ⇨ Games ⇨ Chess from the GNOME menu, then start by just moving a piece with your mouse. While in the `xboard` window, select Mode ⇨ Two Machines to have the computer play itself. Select File ⇨ Load Game to load a game in Portable Game Notation (PGN). Figure 7-1 shows the xboard window with a game in progress.

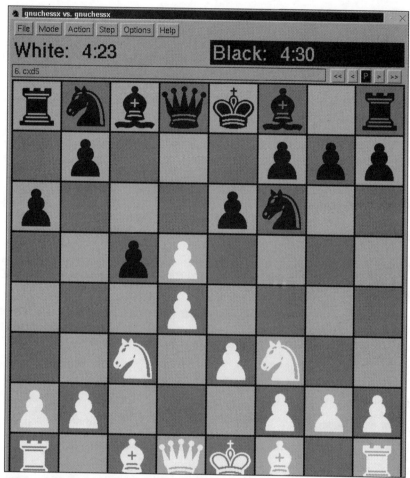

Figure 7-1: In the xboard window, you can set xgame to either play against the computer or to replay saved games.

You can use xboard to play online against others, by connecting an xboard session to an Internet Chess Server (ICS). To start xboard as an interface to an ICS, type the following command line:

```
xboard -ics -icshost name
```

In this example, *name* is the name of the ICS host. In ICS mode, you can just watch games, play against other users, or replay games that have finished. The ICS host acts as a gathering place for enthusiasts who want to play chess against others on the Internet, watch games, participate in tournaments, or just meet chess people. Here are Web pages you can use to get to a few ICS host computers:

✦ **Internet Chess Club: ICC** (www.chessclub.com)

✦ **Chess.net** (www.chess.net)

✦ **Free Internet Chess Server** (www.freechess.org)

As an alternative to xboard, you can sometimes use Web-based applications to play chess on the Internet. For example, if you were to visit the Chess.net Web site (www.chess.net), you could click the Play link to start. You could then choose the chess software to use. (Chess.net for Java works in Red Hat Linux with Netscape.) After the software downloads, you can sign up for a Chess.net account. After that, the window that appears lets you choose someone to play against or to watch a game in progress.

Chess-related commands that come with Red Hat Linux in the gnuchess package provide different ways of playing chess or manipulating chess output. Here are some examples:

✦ game—A command that takes the output of gnuchess (a chess.lst file) and outputs a PostScript file, board by board. The move and current score are printed with each board.

✦ gnuchess—A simple, curses-based chess game that runs on character terminals or in an xterm window. (The curses interface in UNIX is used for creating and using menus and screen controls in character terminals.)

✦ gnuchessn—A command that is similar to gnuchess, but produces a fancier version (using features such as reverse video).

✦ gnuchessr—A completely ASCII-based version of chess.

✦ gnuchessx—Another ASCII-based chess game that is compatible with xboard.

✦ gnuan—A command that is used to analyze a chess game.

✦ zic2xpm—A command that translates ZIICS chess pieces into xboard pieces. (ZIICS was a popular interface for creating chess pieces that could be displayed in DOS.)

Freeciv

With Freeciv, you create a civilization that challenges competing civilizations for world dominance. The version of Freeciv that comes with Red Hat Linux contains both client software (to play the game) and server software (to connect players together). You can connect to your server and try the game yourself or (with a network connection) play against up to 14 others on the Internet.

You can start Freeciv from the Gnome menu by clicking on Games ➪ FreeCiv (either the Engels or Trident tile set). If for some reason Freeciv doesn't start, try starting it from a Terminal window by typing:

```
civ &
```

Figure 7-2 shows the two windows that appear when you start Freeciv. The Connect to Freeciv Server window contains your user name, host name, and port number. The Freeciv window is where you play the game.

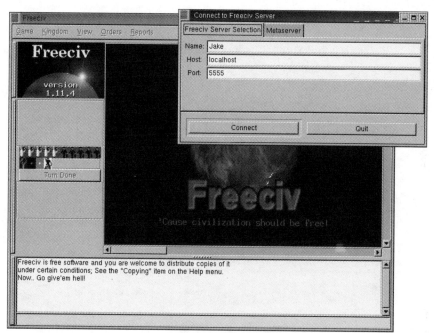

Figure 7-2: Play Freeciv to build civilizations and to compete against others.

Note If Freeciv won't start, one reason may be because you are logged in as root. You must be logged in as a regular user to run the `civ` command. (The root user is prevented from running Freeciv for security reasons.)

Starting Freeciv

You can go ahead and play a few games by yourself, if you like, to get to know the game before you play against others on the network. The following procedure describes how to start your first practice Freeciv game.

1. Start Freeciv (K ➪ Games ➪ FreeCiv, or type **civ&**).

   The Freeciv windows appear, as shown in Figure 7-2.

2. From a Terminal window, start the Freeciv server by typing:

   ```
   $ civserver
   You can learn a lot about Freeciv at http://www.freeciv.org
   1: Now accepting new client connections.

   Get a list of available commands with 'help'.
   >
   ```

3. Click Connect from the Connect to Freeciv Server window.

4. From the server prompt, type the following:

```
> start
Starting game.
1: Loading rulesets
>
```

A "What Nation Will You Be?" window appears on the client screen, as shown in Figure 7-3.

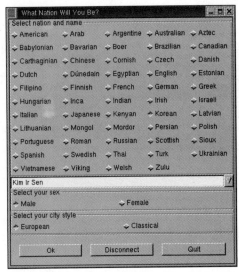

Figure 7-3: Choose a nation to begin Freeciv.

5. After you start Freeciv from the server prompt, choose a nation, the name of a leader, your sex, and the style of the city, and then click OK. At this point, you are ready to return to the Freeciv window.

Beginning with Freeciv

Check out the Freeciv window. Here are things you should know when you are starting. (You can find more help at the Freeciv site: `www.freeciv.org`.)

✦ Click the Help button for topical information on many different subjects that will be useful to you as you play.

✦ The world (by default) is 80×50 squares, with 11×8 squares visible at a time.

✦ The active square contains an icon of the active unit (flashing alternatively with the square's terrain).

✦ Some squares contain special resources. Press and hold the middle mouse button for information on what special resources a square contains. Try this a few times to get a feel for the land around you. This action also identifies any units on the terrain, as well as statistics for the unit.

✦ To see the world outside of your 11 × 8 viewing area, click the scroll bars outside of the map. At first the world outside will be black. As units are added, areas closer to those units will be visible. (Press the letter c to return to the active part of your map.)

✦ An overview map is in the upper-left corner of the Freeciv window. As the world becomes more civilized, this provides a good way to get an overview of what is going on. Right-click a spot on the overview map to have your viewport centered there.

✦ The menu bar contains buttons you can use to play the game. The Game menu lets you change settings and options, view player data, view messages, and clear your log. The Kingdom menu lets you change tax rates, find cities, and start revolutions. The View menu lets you place a grid on the map or center the view. The Orders menu is where you choose the items you build and the actions you take. The Reports menu lets you display reports related to cities, military, trade, and science, as well as other special reports.

✦ A summary of the economy of your civilization appears under the overview map. Information includes number of people, current year, money in the treasury, and percent of money distributed to tax, luxury, and science.

✦ Ten icons below the overview information represent how money is divided between luxuries (an entertainer), research (a researcher), and taxes (a tax collector). Essentially, these icons represent how much of your resources are placed into improving each of those attributes of your community.

✦ When you have made all your moves for a turn, click Turn Done. Next to that, a lightbulb indicates the progress of your research (increasing at each turn). A sun icon starts clear, but becomes brighter from pollution to warn of possible global warming. A government symbol indicates that you begin with a despotic government. The last icon tells you how much time is left in a turn.

The Unit box shows information about your current unit. You begin with two Settlers units and one Explorer unit.

Building your civilization

Begin to build your civilization. Here are some things to try, as recommended by the Freeciv manual:

✦ To change the distribution of money, choose Kingdom ➪ Tax Rates. Move the slider bars to redistribute the percentage of assets assigned to luxury, research, and taxes. Try increasing research and reducing taxes to start off.

✦ Change the current unit to be a settler as follows: click the stack of units on the map and click one of the Settlers from the menu that appears.

✦ Begin building a city by clicking on Orders ➪ Build City. When prompted, type a name for the city and click OK. The window that appears shows information about the city. It starts with one happy citizen, represented by a single icon (more citizens will appear as the game progresses).

✦ The Food, Prod, and Trade lines reflect the raw productivity statistics for the city. The first number shows how much is being produced, the second (in parens) shows the surplus above what is needed to support the units. The Gold, Luxury, and Science lines indicate the city's trade output. Granary numbers show how much food is stored and the size of the food store. The pollution level begins at zero.

✦ The Units at this point are not yet supported by a city (so nothing appears under Supported Units). When Units require support, they will be assigned to cities, and they will draw on city resources. Units present appear under that heading.

✦ The map area shown consists of 21 squares that make up the city. The number 1 indicates the size of the city. The number 211 reflects the production of food, manufacturing production, and trade, respectively. The number 210 shows where the city's citizen is working and the results of the work.

✦ The Phalanx line shows that the city can build a Phalanx and that it will take 20 production points to produce. Click Change to view other units the city could produce, select one you want to build, and click Change. Below that is a list of your current buildings (of which you have only a Palace to start out).

✦ Close the city window by clicking on Close.

Exploring your world

To begin exploring, move the Settler.

1. Using the numeric keypad, press the 9 key three times to begin exploring. You can move the explorer up to three times per turn. You begin to see more of the world.

2. When the next unit (the Settler) begins blinking, move it one square in another direction. Click Turn Done. Information for the city will be updated.

3. Click the City to see the city window. Notice that information about the city has been updated. In particular, you should see food storage increase. Close the city window.

4. Continue exploring and build a road. With the explorer flashing, use the numeric keypad to move it another three sections. When the settler begins blinking, press **r** to build a road. A small R appears on the square to remind you that the Settler is busy building a road. Click Turn Done.

Using more controls and actions

Now that you have some understanding of the controls and actions, the game can begin taking a lot of different directions. Here are a few things that may happen next and some things you can do:

✦ After you take a turn, the computer gets a chance to play as well. As it plays, its actions are reported to you. You can make decisions on what to do about those actions. Choose Game ➪ Message Options. The Message options window appears, containing a listing of different kinds of messages that can come from the server and how they will be presented to you.

✦ As you explore, you will run into other explorers and eventually other civilizations. Continue exploring by selecting different directions on your numeric keypad.

✦ Continue to move the Settler one square at a time, once it has finished creating the road. (The Settler will blink again when it is available.) Click Turn Done.

✦ At this point, you should see a message that your city has finished building Warriors. When buildings and units are complete, you should usually check out what has happened. Click the message associated with the city, then click Popup City. The city window appears, showing you that it has additional population. The food storage may appear empty, but the new citizens are working to increase the food and trade. You may see an additional warrior unit.

✦ A science advisory may also appear at this point to let you choose your city's research goals. Click Change and select Writing as your new research goal. You can then select a different long-term goal as well. Click Close when you are done.

✦ If your new Warrior is now blinking, click s to assign sentry mode to the Warrior.

You should be familiar with some of the actions of Freeciv at this point. To learn some basic strategies going forward, choose Help ➪ Help Playing. It will provide you with some general strategy steps for playing the game.

X games you can download

There is no shortage of games you can download from the Web. The following are a few action and strategy games you can download and start playing. You can find links to these packages at either www.freshmeat.com or by using the rpmfind command. The examples shown here include LinCity, Xgalaga, and XSoldier.

LinCity

LinCity simulates building and maintaining a city, or a suburban or rural area. You add residences, monuments, communes, tracks, markets, potteries, ore mines, and other sites to create a thriving community. Connect areas together with tracks, roads, or railways. Remember that the game simulates a living community, so watch that resources aren't consumed too rapidly and that pollution doesn't grow too quickly. Try to recycle and make sure you don't spend all of your resources and go broke.

Get LinCity from the Red Hat FTP site. Or, you can get it from the LinCity home page (www.floot.demon.co.uk/lincity.html) and look for a download link. Download and install the package as directed. To start LinCity, type the following command (it's probably located in /usr/local/bin):

```
$ xlincity
```

The first time you run LinCity, it asks if it can create a directory in which to save your games. Yes is a good answer to that. Then, when the LinCity window opens, the game helps you get started by letting you load a built-in scene or begin with a random village.

Here are some tips for playing LinCity:

✦ Right-click a button to see a description of an item before you add it to your community.

✦ Use the Tips button to create a place to put your trash. If you accumulate too much trash, you may need to burn it (which causes pollution). When the trash area fills up, it gets covered in grass.

✦ Build monuments to improve unemployment temporarily, add inspiration to a community, and increase the community's technological capability.

✦ While a mill can produce goods, be careful because the people who run the mill also consume a lot of food.

✦ Either import or have farms for producing food. If you run out of food, people will either die or move away.

Figure 7-4 shows an example of a LinCity community in action.

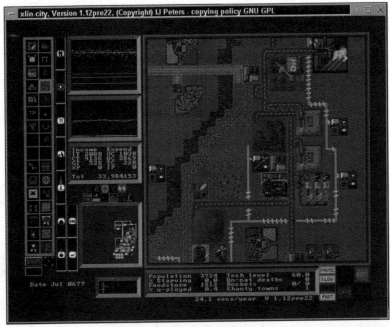

Figure 7-4: Create a thriving community with LinCity.

Xgalaga

Xgalaga is your basic Space Invaders-type game. You fire back at alien spaceships as they attack you. Select either keyboard (arrows to move and Spacebar to shoot) or mouse controls (move with mouse, shoot with right-click). Then just move and shoot. There's not much else to it, but it's fun if your brain needs to rest for a while. To start Xgalaga, type the following:

```
$ xgalaga
```

You need to install the xgalaga software package. You can find the xgalaga package using the rpmfind command. It puts the executable in the /usr/X11R6/bin directory. Figure 7-5 shows the Xgalaga window. Your level and score appear at the top.

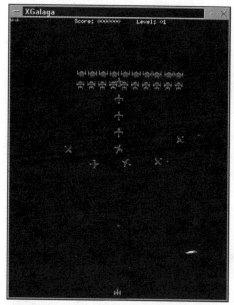

Figure 7-5: Destroy enemy spaceships in Xgalaga.

Maelstrom

In Maelstrom, you maneuver your spaceship to dodge asteroids, then use your shield and plasma cannons to destroy them. Besides asteroids, you need to look out for stars that go nova, Shenobi autonominous mines, vortexes, and Shenobi fleet ships.

Start Maelstrom from the Gnome menu (Programs ⇨ Games ⇨ Maelstrom). Then click the P button to start the game, or click the C button to change the keyboard controls for the game. Here are the keyboard controls assigned by default:

Action	Key
Fire	Tab
Thrust	Up Arrow
Shield	Spacebar
Turn clockwise	Right arrow
Turn counterclockwise	Left Arrow
Pause	Pause
Abort game	Esc

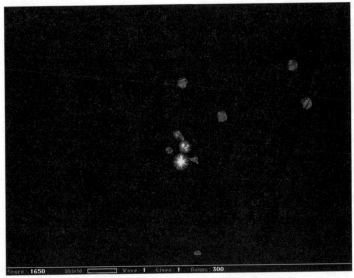

Figure 7-6: Avoid and destroy asteroids in Maelstrom.

Character-Based Games

There aren't many character-based games delivered with the basic Red Hat Linux installation. If you are interested in trying some of the legacy UNIX games, some of which were created many years ago, you can install the bsd-games package (which is available from Red Hat FTP sites).

The games that come in the bsd-games package include simple card games, shooting games, and adventure games. As previously noted, games are stored in the /usr/games directory by default, so you may want to add that directory to your PATH.

Some of the games have score files, which should be created as writable by everyone (if multiple people use your system). Or you can make those games that write to score files into setgid games, and then make the file permissions 664. The owner and group of each game command is root by default. Only one game (Hunt) allows multiple players and has a daemon program (in /usr/sbin) for coordinating game play.

Cross-Reference See Chapter 3 for information on adding a directory to your PATH and setting file permissions.

If you want to control who runs these games and when the games are run, you can use the dm command (Dungeon Master) for controlling access to games. You can add controlled games into a hidden directory (/usr/games/dm), then create a configuration file (/etc/dm.conf) to determine when each controlled game can be run.

Table 7-3 lists all of the games available in the bsd-games package. For a simple game, try Fish (/usr/games/fish). If you are adventurous, try Adventure (/usr/games/adventure). Here are a few hints that will help you with Adventure:

✦ Move around the caves in Adventure by asking for an adjacent room or by naming a direction (N, S, E, SW, NE, etc.).

✦ As you explore the caves, draw a map as you go—it helps you return to places later.

✦ Take valuable things and bring them back to the building.

✦ Typing xyzzy and plugh sometimes transports you to a remote location.

Table 7-3
Games in the bsd-games Package

Game	Description	Game	Description
adventure	Explore the Colossal caves and find treasures.	arithmetic	Answer simple, timed arithmetic questions.
atc	Air traffic controller game. Direct jets and propeller planes through flight area and airports.	backgammon	Backgammon board game.
Banner	Print large-letter banners on your printer.	battlestar	A tropical adventure game.
canfield	The canfield solitaire game.	cribbage	The cribbage board game.
dm	Dungeon master to regulate game playing.	factor	Factor numbers.

Continued

Table 7-3 (continued)

Game	Description	Game	Description
fish	The go fish card game.	gomoku	Two-player game to get five in a row.
hunt	Multiplayer maze game with the object of killing the other players.	mille	The Mille Bornes game.
monop	The Monopoly game for multiple players.	number	Converts arabic numbers to words.
phantasia	Role playing fantasy game for fighting monsters.	pig	Reformat input as pig latin.
pom	Displays the current phase of the moon.	primes	Generate prime numbers.
quiz	Answer questions on selected topics.	rain	Displays animated raindrops.
random	Generate random numbers.	robots	Fight evil robots.
sail	Multiuser fighting ships game.	snake	Avoid getting eaten by a snake.
tetris-bsd	Tetris game.	trek	Trekkie space game.
wargames	No thermonuclear warfare. Not dangerous.	worm	A growing worm game.
worms	Animated worms.	wump	Shoot at the wumpus in an underground cave.

The xmame Gaming Emulator

Creators of gaming emulators set out to take games that were designed for home gaming consoles or arcades and have those games run on a computer. As a result, games that were created for gaming machines that are now outdated or broken can be resurrected on your home computer.

A compilation of gaming emulators has been put together into one project called Multiple Arcade Machine Emulator (MAME). Nicola Salmoria started the MAME project in January 1997. There are now more than 100 contributors. An X Window

System version of MAME called xmame runs in Red Hat Linux. There are also several other versions that run in different video modes, allowing the use of 3Dfx, SVGALIB, and other video technologies.

No games are delivered with the xmame package. Games that can be used with the xmame package are listed in a file that comes with xmame. That file lists more than 600 games that are supported by xmame. (Up to 2000 games have been listed as compatible with MAME on other computing platforms — in particular, old Windows 3.1/95 platforms.)

You can download the xmame package from any Red Hat FTP site. If you prefer to install from source code, you can download the most recent version from the XMAME home page at `http://x.mame.net`. Although it can be a bit trickier getting xmame installed and working, the real trick is getting legal software (ROMs) and getting them to run properly. (I discuss that a bit later.)

Supported xmame hardware

To control your gaming, xmame supports several different types of gaming hardware, including:

✦ **Joysticks** — Xmame supports i386-style joystick driver, the Fm Town Pad, the X11 input extension joystick, and the newer i386 linux 1.x.x joystick driver, if those drivers are compiled into Linux.

✦ **Mouse** — Common device for moving the pointer on the screen.

✦ **Trackball** — A ball device, used instead of a mouse particularly on laptop computers, for controlling how the pointer moves on the screen.

✦ **Game pad** — A pad device (accessible through the `/dev/pad00` device).

For sound, the audio device is defined as `/dev/dsp`. If you want to change any of the game controlling devices or sound device, you can edit the `xmamerc` file in your `$HOME/xmame` directory. You can set the system-wide configuration information in `/usr/lib/games/xmame/xmamerc`.

To use a gaming device for a particular game, indicate that on the `xmame` command line. To use a joystick, add `-joy`; to use a mouse, add `-mouse`; to use a trackball, add `-trak`; and to use a game pad, add `-pad`. (The game pad requires the Linux FM-TOWNS game pad driver.) For example, to add a mouse for a particular game, type:

```
$ xmame -mouse game
```

Getting and installing xmame games

The xmame package doesn't come with any games. Because the games that run on xmame and other emulators are copyright protected and intended for other machines, it is illegal for you to obtain copies of these games without already owning the original arcade machine.

The games that can be used by xmame are copied and distributed in what are called ROM images. Each game is usually stored in a single zip file that is uncompressed to a half-dozen or more files that are used by xmame. ROM images are created by special hardware that can copy software from game cartridges and other media. Because most of these games are covered by copyright protection, ROMs can only be used in particular ways so as not to be illegal.

Sites that have ROMS to download come with some very strong warnings. Likewise, MAME itself gives strong warnings about how to use ROMs and asks that if you repackage MAME that you not include ROMs with it. When you visit a ROM download site, you will see the rules under which you can download and use the ROMs. You will be asked to agree with those rules before you proceed. Warnings typically include the following:

✦ You must own the game cartridge of the game you are downloading. You are legally entitled to a backup copy of any software you purchase, according to some of these sites.

✦ You must not sell ROMs for profit.

Caution   I recommend that you do not use any game ROMs that are copyright protected. If you decide to obtain ROMs, you are responsible for researching the legal aspects of your actions.

Some sites say that you are allowed to copy a game ROM for a 24-hour period, after which you must either purchase the game machine or delete the game. However, those sites also warn that many of the ROMs cannot be used legally in North and Central America. Again, buyer (or in this case, downloader) beware.

Finding gaming ROM Sites

The best place to begin looking for ROMs that run in xmame is at the MAME ROMs site (http://surf.to/mameroms). That site has links to sites that have the latest MAME ROMs.

Check the gameslist.txt file that came with the xmame package you installed. It lists the games that are known to work with xmame and describes any known problems. Checking this file can prevent you from wasting time downloading ROMs that are known not to work with your gaming emulator.

Installing game ROMs

When you look at the gamelist.txt file, notice that there is a directory name associated with each game. Typically, that is the name that identifies the game. You use that name to create the ROM directory and to ask for the game on the xmame command line. The following procedure describes how to install a fictitious ROM called hoohah.zip so that it can be used by xmame:

1. Create the directory for the game:

   ```
   $ mkdir /usr/lib/games/xmame/hooha
   ```

2. Copy the zip file to the ROM directory:

   ```
   $ cp wherever/hooha.zip /usr/lib/games/xmame/roms/hooha/
   ```

3. Change to the ROM directory and unzip the file:

   ```
   $ unzip -L hooha
   ```

4. Try the xmame command to see if the ROMs work. For example:

   ```
   $ xmame hooha
   ```

   Again, if this command doesn't work, check that:

   - The xmame command is in your PATH (or type the full PATH).
   - The game's ROM directory is in the base ROM directory. (Set the ROM directory with the rompath value in the /usr/lib/games/xmame/xmamerc file or in your $HOME/xmame/xmamerc file.)
   - The directory name and the game name are the same.
   - The case for the ROM files is correct. When the command fails, it will list the proper case for each ROM (probably lowercase and numbers).

Note In Linux, case matters. In Step 3, use the -L option to unzip files so that they are in all lowercase. If the xmame command fails later, it will tell you the ROM files it needs. Make sure the files are there and in the proper case.

Known problems are listed in the readme.unix file (for general problems) and gamelist.txt file (for specific game problems) in the /usr/doc/xmame* directory. If you get stuck, try the MAME newsgroup: alt.games.mame. The group is quite active and participants in the group are very helpful.

Commercial Linux Games

Commercial software vendors believe that Linux will become a viable gaming platform. Popular commercial games like Quake, Myth II, and Civilization: Call to Power all have shrink-wrapped versions that you can purchase for Linux. To support those games, video card manufacturers such as Nvidia, ATI, and Matrox offer 3D graphic accelerator drivers that work in Linux. There still aren't a ton of commercial games that run in Linux, but some of the best are making their way to Linux.

To get an idea of the state of the art in Linux gaming, you need to try out some of these commercial games. Demo versions of games like Civilization: Call to Power and Myth II provide a good way to learn the games and help you decide if you want to purchase full versions. These demos often include the ability to play against other people on the Internet.

The following section describes some of the most popular commercial games that are available for Linux. More popular titles are being added all the time.

To find the latest Linux gaming news, try the Linux Gaming Tome (`http://happypenguin.org`) and the Linux Games site (`www.linuxgames.com`). You should also check out the Web site for Loki Entertainment Software (`www.lokigames.com`), which has ported many popular games from other gaming platforms to Linux.

If you try to download any of the demos described in the next sections, make sure you have plenty of disk space available. It is common for one of these demos to require several hundred megabytes of disk space to run. If you like a game, I strongly encourage you to purchase it, to help grow the market for high-quality Linux games.

Loki Software Games Demos

Loki Software's catalog of action and strategy games for Linux has grown significantly in the past few years. To encourage people to get to know their games, Loki offers a demo program that lets you choose from among more than a dozen of its games to download and try.

The Loki Demo Launcher for downloading demos is available from the Demo Launcher page (`www.lokigames.com/products/demos.php3`). From that page, there are links to FTP sites from which you can download the Demo Launcher. Save the file to a directory (such as `/tmp/loki`) and do the following:

1. Change to the directory where you downloaded the demo. For example:

```
# cd /tmp/loki
```

You may not need to be root user to install these games. However, the default paths where the Demo Launcher tries to write by default are only accessible to the root user.

2. As root user, run the following command (the program may have a different name if it has been updated):

```
# sh loki_demos-full-1.0e.x86.run
```

If you have not used the Demo Launcher before, a screen appears asking you to identify the paths used to place the Install Tool.

3. If the default locations shown are okay with you, click Begin Install.

Assuming that there was no problem writing to the install directories, you should see an Install Complete message.

4. Click Exit. Next you should see the Uninstall Tool window.

5. If the paths for holding the Uninstall Tool are okay, click Begin Install.

The Install Complete message appears.

6. Click Exit.

A window appears that allows you to set the locations for installing the Demo Pack.

7. If the paths are okay, click Begin Install.

Next you should see a box that shows the different demo games that are available. Figure 7-7 shows an example of the window for selecting the demos you want to download:

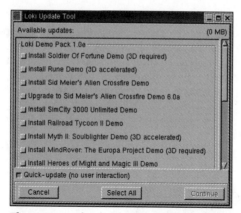

Figure 7-7: Check which Loki game demos you want to download.

8. As you move the cursor over each game, the disk space is displayed for that game. Click the games you want to install, then click Continue. A window appears, displaying the progress of each download.

9. You may need to click an Update button to complete the update and Finish to finish it.

The demo should now be ready to start.

10. Either click Play or type **loki_demos** from a Terminal window to start the program.

Select to start the game and you're ready to go.

The following sections describe some of the games that are available.

Civilization: Call to Power

You can build online civilizations with Civilization: Call to Power (CCP). Like earlier versions and public spin-offs (such as the Freeciv described earlier in this chapter), Civilization: Call to Power for Linux lets you explore the world, build cities, and manage your empire. This latest version offers multiplayer network competition and extensions that let you extend cities into outer space and under the sea.

CCP is produced by Activision (www.activision.com), although the Linux version was created by Loki Entertainment Software (www.lokigames.com). CCP is one of the best selling games of all time, so it is considered quite a plus for Linux users that a boxed version of the product is being produced for Linux.

If you like the Freeciv game that comes with Red Hat Linux, you will love CCP. Engaging game play is improved with enhanced graphics, sound, and animation. English, French, German, Italian, and Spanish versions are available. Each, at the time of publication, was priced at $49.95. If you are not quite ready to make the commitment, a demo version is available using the Demo Launcher described earlier.

The game won't run on just any computer. The Red Hat Linux software that comes with this book will satisfy your operating system requirements. Your computer must have at least a Pentium 133 MHz processor, 32MB RAM, 80MB of swap space, 16-bit color, and X Window System running. To play over the network, you need network connection hardware (a network card or dialup Internet connection). To use sound, you will need an Open Sound System (OSS) compatible sound card.

The CCP demo comes with an excellent tutorial to start you out. If you have never played a civilization game before, the tutorial is a great way to start. Figure 7-8 shows an example of a scene from the Civilization: Call to Power for Linux demo.

Figure 7-8: Civilization: Call to Power features excellent graphics and network play.

Myth II: Soulblighter

If you like knights and dwarves and storming castles, Myth II: Soulblighter for Linux might be for you. In Myth II, you are given a mission and some troops with various skills. From there, you need strategy and the desire to shed lots of virtual blood to meet your goal.

Myth II was created by Bungie Software (www.bungie.com) and ported to Linux by Loki Entertainment Software (www.lokigames.com). This version of the popular Myth game includes improved graphics and new scenarios.

A demo version is available that runs well in Red Hat Linux. You can get it via the Demo Launcher described earlier. As usual, you will need a fairly powerful computer (at least a Pentium 133 MHz, 32MB RAM, 80MB swap space, and 100MB of free disk space). You need network hardware for multiuser network play (network card or dialup) and a sound card if you want audio. A screen shot of Myth II is shown in Figure 7-9.

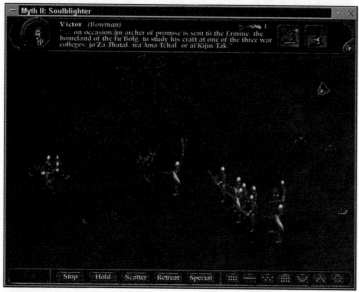

Figure 7-9: Use warriors, archers, and dwarves to battle in Myth II.

Quake III Arena

The latest version of the Quake series of games, Quake III Arena, is available in a Linux version. Quake was the big follow-up game by id Software to their Doom line. Like Doom, Quake is a first-person (you) game in which you travel through corridors, armed and looking for trouble. As with Doom, the main point is to shoot a lot of monsters. The monsters, however, are much more varied and have different strengths and weaknesses. There are also complex missions that need to be carried out.

If you want to try out Quake III Arena, you can get a demo version of Quake III Arena from the Quake III Arena site: `www.quake3arena.com`. Figure 7-10 shows the Quake III Arena demo setup.

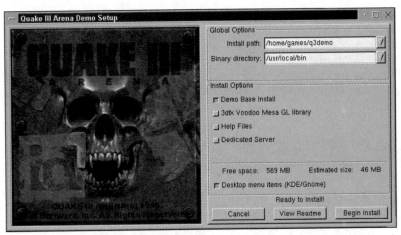

Figure 7-10: Try out Quake III Arena from quake3arena.com.

Summary

While Red Hat Linux has not yet become a dominant gaming platform, there are still plenty of games running on Red Hat Linux that you can spend your time on. Old UNIX games that have made their way to Linux include a variety of text-based and X Window-based games. There are card games, strategy games, and some action games.

For games that were intended for certain gaming consoles and arcade machines, the xmame emulator provides an environment within the Linux system in which those games could be played. Hundreds of game ROMs are available on the Internet, although copyright laws restrict what you can legally download and use.

On the commercial front, Civilization: Call to Power for Linux, Myth II, and Quake III Arena are available to use on your Red Hat Linux system. Most of these games offer excellent graphics and animation, but they require certain video cards and drivers to work effectively.

✦   ✦   ✦

Multimedia in Red Hat Linux

Where UNIX systems, like Red Hat Linux, were once represented by mere words on a screen, advancements in graphical video cards and interfaces (such as the X Window System) have made working with powerful computing systems more friendly. By adding a sound card and some software to your Red Hat Linux system, you can now experience music, sound effects, animation, and video where there were once just words.

In this chapter, you learn to add sound, video, and other multimedia support to your Red Hat Linux system. The chapter describes how to configure a sound card to work with Red Hat Linux. Then it tells you how to get and use software to play music CDs and a variety of sound formats from your Red Hat Linux system.

Video clips that are readily available on the Internet, that come in formats such as AVI, MPEG, and QuickTime, can be viewed using several different players in Red Hat Linux. Also, to view the huge amount of RealMedia content available on the Web, Real Networks offers a version of its RealPlayer software that runs in Linux. This chapter describes how to get that player and how to find content to use with it.

Because CD-ROM is the medium of choice for recorded music, this chapter describes how to set up and use CD burners to create your own music CDs. Once your CD burner is set up to record music, the same CD burner can be used to create CDs to back up your data or to create software CDs.

Listening to Audio

If you want sound on your computer to be more than the speaker on your PC going "bing" occasionally, you need to add a sound card to your computer. Games are a reason to add a sound card, if the games rely on sound effects or talking back to you. Moreover, sound cards also allow you to play music and communicate with others on the Internet using telephony software.

To give you an idea of the features that a sound card can provide, the following lists features that are included in the popular Sound Blaster 16 sound card:

✦ **Sound recording and playback** — The card can convert analog sound into 8-bit or 16-bit digital numbers. To convert the sound, the board samples the sound in waves from 5 kHz to 44.1 kHz, or 5000 to 44,100 times per second. (Of course, the higher the sampling, the better the sound and larger the output.)

✦ **Full-duplex support** — This allows for recording and playback to occur at the same time. This is particularly useful for bidirectional Internet communication.

✦ **Input/output ports** — Several different ports on the board enable you to connect other input/output devices. These ports include:

- **Line-In** — Connects an external CD player, cassette deck, synthesizer, or other device for recording or playback.

- **Microphone** — Connects a microphone for audio recording.

- **Line-Out (Speaker Out)** — Connects non-powered speakers, headphones, or a stereo amplifier.

- **Joystick/MIDI** — Connects a joystick or MIDI device.

- **Internal CD Audio** — This internal port connects the sound card to your computer's internal CD-ROM board (this port isn't exposed when the board is installed).

Tip

In general, the most popular hardware has the best chance of working in Red Hat Linux. I use the Sound Blaster 16 card because it is fairly inexpensive and I know it has been thoroughly tested in Linux. Linux drivers are not always immediately available for the latest sound cards or other hardware.

In Red Hat Linux, sound drivers that are provided have come from a variety of sources, including a project that no longer exists called the Open Sound System/Free (OSS/Free) project. If your sound card isn't supported in Red Hat Linux, try the OSS/Linux package to see if that package supports your sound card (go to `www.opensound.com/oss.html`). If it works, you can purchase the sound package.

Caution

Before you install a separate sound driver distribution, check to see if your current Red Hat distribution already has the most recent sound driver. When possible, use the driver that's distributed with the kernel. If you have tried the procedures in this book and you still don't have a working sound card, read the Readme.OSS file that comes with Red Hat Linux (probably in `/usr/src/linux*/Documentation/sound`).

The devices that the audio programs use to access audio hardware in Red Hat Linux include:

✦ `/dev/audio`, `/dev/audio1` — Devices that are compatible with Sun workstation audio implementations (audio files with the .au extension).

✦ /dev/cdrom—Device representing your first CD-ROM drive. (Additional CD-ROM drives are located at /dev/cdrom1, /dev/cdrom2, etc.)

✦ /dev/dsp, /dev/dsp1—Digital sampling devices, to which many audio applications direct sound.

✦ /dev/mixer, /dev/mixer1—Sound-mixing devices.

✦ /dev/sequencer—Device that provides low-level interface to MIDI, FM, and GUS.

✦ /dev/midi00—Device that provides raw access to midi ports.

✦ /dev/sndstat—Device that displays the status of sound drivers.

Nodes in the /dev directory, such as /dev/audio, aren't just regular files. They represent access points to the physical devices (hard disks, COM ports, etc.) that are connected to your system, or to pseudo-devices (such as Terminal windows). For example, to find out the device of your current Terminal window, type **tty**. Then send some data to that device. For example, if your device name is /dev/pts/0, type:

```
echo "Hello There" > /dev/pts/0
```

The words "Hello There" appear in that Terminal window. You can try sending messages among several Terminal windows. If other users who are logged on to the computer have their terminal permissions open, you can send messages to them in this way, too. (I knew people who would direct the output of a dictionary file to an unsuspecting user's terminal. Though it wasn't destructive, it was quite annoying if you were trying to get work done.)

For information that is specific to your sound card in Red Hat Linux, look for the appropriate file in the /usr/src/linux*/Documentation/sound directory. The README files also have general information about the sound drivers. For general information about sound in Linux, see the Sound-HOWTO (for tips about sound cards and general sound issues) and the Sound-Playing-HOWTO (for tips on software for playing different types of audio files).

You can find Linux HOWTOs on the DOC CD (CD-3) that comes with this book. Refer to the HOWTOS top level directory of the CD.

Configuring your sound card

Before you can use sound on your Red Hat Linux system, you need to install your sound card and connect the speakers. Red Hat Linux should detect this card when you install Red Hat Linux or when you reboot and install the proper driver. Drivers for many common sound cards are available when you first install Red Hat Linux. Earlier releases of Red Hat Linux did not have sound card devices built into the kernel, but the current release of Red Hat Linux automatically builds sound support into the kernel.

Probably the easiest way to check if your sound card is working is to insert a music CD into the drive and (if one doesn't start automatically) start one of the CD players described in the next section. As an alternative, you can check if the basic sound module is installed. For example, you could type:

```
$ cat /proc/modules | grep soundcore
soundcore          4112   4 [es1371]
```

This example shows that the soundcore module has been loaded and that the sound card driver is the Ensoniq ES1371 driver.

Note   If you have a sound file, you can send it directly to a sound device (for example, `cat file.wav > /dev/audio`) to test your sound card. You can use a sound file from `/usr/share/sndconfig` to test your sound card in Red Hat Linux. To find a sound file on your Windows 95/98 system, use the `Find` window (Start ⇨ Find ⇨ Files or Folders) and do an advanced search for Sound Clip.

If you hear a sound clip, then your sound card is working. If your speakers are plugged in and the volume is up, but you don't hear any sounds, continue with the next procedure to configure your sound card.

1. Run `/usr/sbin/sndconfig` (this starts the Sound Card Configuration Utility).

2. A sndconfig window is displayed, asking ask if you want to probe for Plug-and-Play cards. Press Enter to select OK.

   If the utility finds a sound card that it recognizes, it displays the name of that card and asks if you want to configure it. The sndconfig window just described is shown in Figure 8-1.

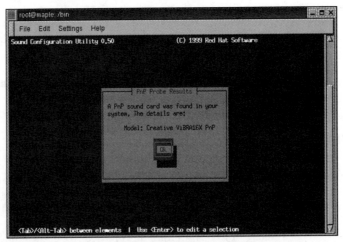

Figure 8-1: The sndconfig utility finds and configures your sound card.

3. In this example, sndconfig detects a Creative Sound Blaster 16 card (Creative ViBRA16X PnP). Press Enter to select OK.

4. A message warns you that you are replacing the old `/etc/conf.modules` file. Press Enter to select OK.

5. A message tells you that a sound sample will play to check if the card is configured properly. Press Enter to select OK.

6. You are asked if you heard the sound.

7. If you hear the sound, select Yes and skip to step 12. Otherwise select No to continue.

8. You are asked to manually configure your sound card. Press Enter to select OK.

9. A list of sound cards is displayed. Select your card and press Enter to select OK.

10. Select OK to try the sound card again.

11. You are asked again if you were able to hear the sample. If you hear the sound, select Yes to continue. Otherwise select No to try a different card.

12. You are warned that a new `/etc/modules.conf` file is being created (and the old one is being backed up). Press Enter to select OK.

At this point, you can try to run an audio file again. Type **cat *file*.au > /dev/audio**. If all went well, you should hear the audio file this time. At this point, you should be able to use any of the CD music players or applications that use sound to play sound through your sound card.

Tip When I configured my sound card, the default sound level was a bit low for my taste. I inserted a music CD to have something to listen to. Then I ran the `aumix` command to adjust the volume levels. Volume (Vol) should be highlighted when `aumix` opens. You can use the right and left arrows to adjust volume levels. Use the up and down arrows to choose particular sound devices: speaker, line, mic, CD, and so on. With a device highlighted, use the tab key to be able to adjust balance for the device. Type **s** to save the changes and **q** when you are done.

Audio file conversion

If you have a sound file in one format, but you want it to be in another format, Linux offers some conversion tools you can use to convert the file. The Sox utility can translate to and from any of the audio formats listed in Table 8-1.

Tip It may be that not all audio types are compiled into your version of Sox. Type **sox -h** to see the supported audio types. This also shows the options and effects that Sox supports.

Table 8-1
Sound Formats Supported by Sox Utility

File Extension or Pseudonym	Description	File Extension or Pseudonym	Description
.8svx	8SVX Amiga musical instrument description format.	.aiff	Apple IIc/IIgs and SGI AIFF files. May require a separate archiver to work with these files.
.au	Sun Microsystems AU audio files. This is a popular format.	.cdr	CD-R files used to master compact disks.
.cvs	Continuously variable slope delta modulation, which is used for voice mail and other speech compression.	.dat	Text data files, which contain a text representation of sound data.
.gsm	Lossy Speech Compression (GSM 06.10), used to shrink audio data in voice mail and similar applications.	.hcom	Macintosh HCOM files.
.maud	Amiga format used to produce sound that is 8-bit linear, 16-bit linear, A-law, and u-law in mono or stereo.	.ossdsp	Pseudo file, used to open the OSS /dev/dsp file and configure it to use the data type passed to Sox. Used to either play or record.
.sf	IRCAM sound files, used by CSound package and MixView sample editor.	.smp	SampleVision files from Turtle Beach, used to communicate with different MIDI samplers.
.sunau	Pseudo file, used to open a /dev/audio file and set it to use the data type being passed to Sox.	.txw	Yamaha TX-16W from a Yamaha sampling keyboard.
.vms	Used to compress speech audio for voice mail and similar applications.	.voc	Sound Blaster VOC file.

File Extension or Pseudonym	Description	File Extension or Pseudonym	Description
`.wav`	Microsoft WAV RIFF files. This is the native MS Windows sound format.	`.wve`	8-bit, a-law, 8 kHz sound files used with Psion Palmtop computers.
`.raw`	Raw files (contain no header information, so sample rate, size, and style must be given).	`.ub, .sb, .uw, .sw, .ul`	Raw files with certain characteristics. ub is unsigned byte; sb is signed byte; uw is unsigned word; sw is signed word; and ul is ulaw.

If you are not sure about the format of an audio file, you can add the .auto extension to the filename. This triggers Sox to guess what kind of audio format is contained in the file. The .auto extension can only be used for the input file. If Sox can figure out the content of the input file, it translates the contents to the sound type for the output file you request.

In its most basic form, you can convert one file format (such as a .wav file) to another format (such as an .au file) as follows:

```
sox file1.wav file1.au
```

Note   I had good luck getting .wav files to play with my sound card by converting them to .au and directing them to `/dev/audio` (that is, `cat   file1.au > /dev/audio`). If the file is a `.voc` file, I direct it to `/dev/dsp` (that is, `cat file1.voc > /dev/dsp`).

To see what Sox is doing, use the `-V` option. For example,

```
$ sox -V file1.wav file1.voc

sox: Reading Wave file: Microsoft PCM format, 1 channel, 11025 samp/sec
sox:        11025 byte/sec, 1 block align, 8 bits/samp, 676354 data bytes
sox: Input file: using sample rate 11025
        size bytes, style unsigned, 1 channel
sox: Input file: comment "file1.wav"

sox: Output file: using sample rate 11025
        size bytes, style unsigned, 1 channel
sox: Output file: comment "file1.wav"
```

You can apply sound effects during the Sox conversion process. The following example shows how to change the sample rate (using the `-r` option) from 10,000 kHz to 5000 kHz:

```
$ sox -r 10000 file1.wav -r 5000 file1.voc
```

To reduce the noise, you can send the file through a low-pass filter. Here's an example:

```
$ sox file1.voc file2.voc lowp 2200
```

For more information on Sox and to get the latest download, go to the SoX — Sound eXchange — home page (`sourceforge.net/projects/sox/`).

CD audio players

The same CD-ROM drive that you use to install software can be used to play music CDs. A couple of basic CD players that you get with Red Hat are `gtcd` (an X-based CD player) and `cdp` (a text-based CD player).

Tip   Before you try any of the CD players, unmount the CD in your drive (if one is mounted) by typing **umount /mnt/cdrom**. Then you can eject the old CD and place an audio CD in the drive.

One feature to look for in a CD player to use with Red Hat Linux is CD Database (CDDB) support. With CDDB, the player can detect which CD is loaded and download Title, Artist, and Track name information from the database. After you store that information for your favorite CDs, you will always be able to see what CD is in your player and what each track is.

Note   If you try some of these CD players and your CD-ROM drive is not working, see the sidebar "Troubleshooting Your CD-ROM" for further information.

Automatically playing CDs

You insert a music CD into your computer, and suddenly it begins to play. If you are using the Gnome desktop, you can thank magicdev. The magicdev process monitors your CD-ROM drives and starts a CD player automatically.

The fact that inserting a CD starts a player automatically is nice to some people and annoying to others. If you just want the CD to play, this behavior is a good thing. However, if you want to choose your own CD player or not play the CD until you choose, you may find auto-playing a bother. If you insert a data CD, magicdev exhibits different behavior. Here is what magicdev does by default:

Troubleshooting Your CD-ROM

If you are unable to play CDs on your CD-ROM drive, there are a few things you can check to correct the problem:

✦ Check that your sound card is installed and working properly (see "Configuring your sound card" earlier in this chapter).

✦ There could be a problem with the physical connection between your sound card and your CD-ROM drive. Check that the wire between your CD-ROM and sound card is connected.

✦ Check that the CD-ROM was detected when you booted Linux. If your CD-ROM drive is an IDE drive, type **dmesg | grep ^hd**.

You should see messages about your CD-ROM that look like hdc: CD-ROM CDU701, ATAPI CDROM drive or hdc: ATAPI 14X CD-ROM drive, 128kB Cache.

If there is no indication of a CD-ROM drive, check that the power supply and cables to the CD-ROM are connected. To make sure that the hardware is working, you can also boot to DOS and try to access the CD.

✦ If it turns out that the CD-ROM hardware is working in DOS but still doesn't show up in Linux, you may need to rebuild your kernel. At this point, you may want to get some help about your specific CD-ROM drive by asking about it in some Linux newsgroup.

✦ Try mounting a software CD-ROM. If you are running the Gnome or KDE desktop, a window should appear indicating that the CD has mounted automatically. If a window doesn't appear, go to a Terminal window and type **mount /mnt/cdrom**. Then change to the /mnt/cdrom directory and list the contents (type **cd /mnt/cdrom; ls**). This tells you if the CD-ROM is accessible.

✦ If you get the CD-ROM working, but it fails when you try to play music as a nonroot user with the message — CDROM device: Permission denied — the problem may be that /dev/cdrom (which is typically a link to the actual hardware device) is not readable by anyone but root. Type **ls -l /dev/cdrom** to see what the device is linked to. Then, assuming the device name it is linked to is /dev/hdc, as the root user type **chmod 644 /dev/hdc** to enable all users to read your CD-ROM and the root user to write to it. One warning: if others are using your computer, they will be able to read any CD you place in this drive.

✦ **Music CD** — When the music CD is inserted, magicdev starts the gtcd player to play the first track of the CD.

✦ **Data CD** — When a data CD is inserted, the CD is mounted on your file system, and you are asked if you want to run any auto-run program that may be on the CD. The mount point for the first CD-ROM drive (/dev/cdrom) is /mnt/cdrom. If you have two drives, the second (/dev/cdrom1) is mounted on /mnt/cdrom1 (and so on).

You can change the behavior of magicdev from the Gnome Control Panel. Here's how:

1. Open the Gnome Control Center from the Gnome menu by choosing Programs ➪ Settings ➪ Gnome Control Center.

2. Under the Peripherals heading, click CD Properties.

   CD properties information for data and music CDs appears.

3. For Data CDs, select from the following options:

   - **Automatically mount CD when inserted** — If this is selected, when a data CD is inserted it is automatically mounted in a subdirectory of /mnt. This option is on by default.

   - **Automatically start auto-run program on newly mounted CD** — If this is selected, after a data CD is mounted, the user is asked to choose whether to run an auto-run program from the CD. This option is on by default.

   - **Open file manager window for newly mounted CD** — If this is selected, after a data CD is mounted, a file manager window opens to display the contents of the top-level directory of the CD. For the first CD drive, the directory is /mnt/cdrom. This option is on by default.

4. For Audio CDs, you can select Run Command When CD Is Inserted to have the CD start playing automatically after it's inserted. The command shown in the box labeled Command is used to play the CD. By default, the option is on, and the gtcd command is used, though you can change the CD player to any player you prefer.

5. Click OK.

Playing CDs with gtcd

The gtcd CD player is the one that pops up automatically when you insert a CD as you use the Gnome desktop. This player has controls that look similar to what you would see on a physical CD player. If you are using the Gnome desktop, from the System Menu select Multimedia ➪ CD Player; from a Terminal window, type:

```
$ gtcd &
```

Adding track information

The interface for adding information about the CD and its tracks is very nice. Click the Open Track Editor button. If you have an active connection to the Internet, gtcd automatically tries to grab track information for your CD. So, you may already see the CD title and track name for each song when you open the editor.

If information about the CD doesn't appear, you can add Artist and Title information about the CD yourself. Then you can select each track to type in the track name. To add the name of the artist and the CD name, click in the Artist/Title box and type in that information. Figure 8-2 shows the CD Player and the Track Editor.

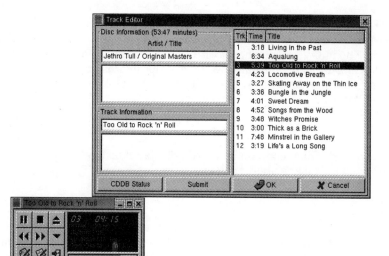

Figure 8-2: Play CDs and store artist, title, and track information with gtcd.

Using the CD database

By default, the player contacts the freedb.freedb.org server to get CD artist and track information from the CD Database. However, you can add the address of a different CDDB server if you choose.

To get information about the CD you are playing from the CD Database, do the following from your gtcd window:

1. Click the Open Track Editor button.

2. From the Track Editor window that appears, click the CDDB Status button.

3. From the CDDB Status window that appears, click the Get CDDB Now button. The CDDB Status window opens a connection to the CD Database on the Internet and tries to download artist, title, and track information for the current CD.

If the procedure is successful, information about the CD should appear in the Track Editor window. You will see the name of the artist, the title of the CD, and the title of each track.

Note   You need a connection to the Internet from your Red Hat Linux system to take advantage of Internet CD databases.

Playing CDs with cdp

If you are working from a dumb terminal or just don't have your X desktop running, you can run the cdp utility (which comes with Red Hat Linux) to play CDs. I don't suggest running this from an X Terminal window; it doesn't display properly. First, insert the music CD you want to play. Then, to start cdp, go to a virtual terminal (Ctrl+Alt+F3) and type:

```
$ cdp
```

You should see a blue screen containing the cdp display. If instead of starting on the first track you want to start on another track (for example, track 5), type:

```
$ cdp play 5
```

When cdp starts, you can see all the tracks, how long each track plays, and total play time. To control the play of the CD, use the following controls (turn on Num Lock to use these numbers from the numeric keypad):

✦ 9 — Play

✦ 8 — Pause/Resume

✦ 7 — Stop

✦ 6 — Next Track

✦ 5 — Replay Current Track

✦ 4 — Previous Track

✦ 3 — Forward 15 Seconds

✦ 2 — Quit (Stop Music and Exit)

✦ 1 — Back 15 Seconds

✦ 0 — Exit (Continue Music and Exit)

✦ . — Help (Press the period key)

The cdp display also lets you enter the names of the Artist, CD, and each song. Because this information is saved, you can see it each time you play the CD. Type these commands while the cdp display is showing to edit information about the CD currently playing:

✦ a — Edit the Artist Name

✦ c — Edit the CD Name

✦ Enter — Edit the title of the current song

Caution   If you try to edit a song name and cdp crashes, type **eject** to stop the CD from playing. Editing the song name seems to work better if you pause the song first.

The arrow keys are also pretty handy for controlling CDs in cdp. The up arrow is for pause/play, and the left arrow is to go back a track. The right arrow is to go forward a track, and the down arrow is to eject.

MP3 audio players

One of the most popular, and controversial, audio formats is the MPEG layer 3 audio format (MP3). This format produces relatively small music files that can produce excellent sound quality for recorded music. MP3 is becoming the format of choice for high-quality music distribution on the Web.

An MPEG file is usually identifiable by the .mp3 suffix. For music, 1MB of MPEG sound plays about one minute of music. Files that play only spoken words can hold many more minutes of content per megabyte.

There are literally thousands of MPEG music files available on the Web. Because of the lawsuits from the music industry to stop copyright infringement, many sites that once promoted the free exchange of music files (such as MP3.com and Napster.com) are moving toward subscription/fee-based businesses. If you are okay with the fees, these services are a great way to get the songs you like in the time it takes to do a download.

For playing MP3 content in Red Hat Linux, I describe, in the following sections, the mpg321 command (text-based), the xmms player, and the freeamp player (X Window–based). In general, mpg321 is the more reliable way to play an MP3 (or other MPEG format) audio file, while the xmms player has a great interface.

Note   The RealPlayer, described later in this chapter, is also capable of playing MP3 audio files. Its primary function, however, is to play RealMedia files (.ram) and streaming video and audio.

Playing MP3 with mpg321

The mpg321 player is a free version of the not-free mpg123 player. Besides playing MPEG layer 3 files (MP3), the mpg321 utility also plays MPEG layer 1 and layer 2 files. This utility runs at the command line, by entering the command and the name of the file (or files) you want to play. Here is an example:

```
$ mpg321 music_file.mp3
```

There are several options available with mpg321. You can test your mp3 file, without producing any output, using the -t option. There are also several options that allow you to decode or mix only selected channels. If you use the verbose option (-v), you can see the frame numbers being played and the elapsed time (and time remaining). The Verbose output looks similar to this:

```
$ mpg321 -v music_file.mp3
Frame# 2456 [ 3456 }, Time: 01:40.34 [01:23.52],
```

Output from mpg321 is usually directed to your sound card (usually /dev/audio or /dev/dsp). You can also direct output directly to the speaker (-o s), headphones (-o h), or the line-out connector (-o l). To play the output faster, use the -d # option, where # is replaced by the number of times faster. For example, -d 2 plays the output twice as fast. To play the output half as fast, use -h 2.

Playing MP3 with XMMS Audio Player

The XMMS Audio Player (which stands for X Multimedia System) provides a graphical interface for playing your MP3 audio files, as well as audio files in a variety of other formats. It has some nice extras too, which include an equalizer and a playlist editor. If the player looks familiar to you, that's because it is styled after the Windows winamp program.

You can start the XMMS Audio Player from the Gnome desktop menu by choosing Programs ➪ Multimedia ➪ XMMS. Or you can run the xmms command from a Terminal window. Figure 8-3 consists of the XMMS Audio Player with the associated equalizer below and the Playlist Editor to the right.

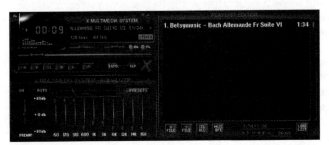

Figure 8-3: Play MP3 and other audio files from the XMMS playlist.

As noted earlier, you can play other formats of audio files as well as MP3. Supported audio file formats include the following:

✦ MP2 and MP3 streams

✦ WAV

✦ AU

✦ CD Audio

✦ CIN Movies

The XMMS Audio Player can be used in the following way:

1. Obtain music files to play. One way is to download files from the Web (for instance, from MP3.com) and store them in an accessible directory.

2. Choose Programs ⇨ Multimedia ⇨ XMMS from the Gnome desktop menu to open the XMMS player. (Or type **xmms** from a Terminal window.)

3. Click the Play button (the arrow pointing to the right) on the console. A Load Files window appears.

4. Select the .mp3 or other music file you want to play and click OK. (Change directories as required to locate the file.) The music file starts playing.

5. With a file selected and playing, here are a few actions you can take:

   - **Control play** — Buttons for controlling play are what you may expect to see on a physical CD player. From left to right, the buttons let you go to a previous track, play, pause, stop, go to the next track, or eject. The eject button opens a window, allowing you to load the next file.

   - **Adjust sound** — Use the left slider bar to adjust the volume. Use the right slider bar to change the right-to-left balance.

   - **Display time** — Click in the elapsed time area to toggle between elapsed time and time remaining.

   - **View file information** — Click the button in the upper-left corner of the screen to see the XMMS menu. Then select View File Info. You can usually find out a lot of information about the file: title, artist, album, comments, and genre. For an MP3 file, you can see specific information about the file itself, such as the format, bit rate, sample rate, frames, file size, and more. You can change or add to the tag information and click Save to keep it.

6. When you are done playing music, click the Stop button to stop the current song. Then click the X in the upper-right corner of the display to close the window.

Special features of the XMMS Audio Player let you adjust high and low frequencies using a graphic equalizer and gather and play songs using a Playlist Editor. Click the button marked EQ next to the balance bar on the player to open the Equalizer. Click the button marked PL next to that to open the Playlist Editor.

Using the Equalizer

The Equalizer lets you use slider bars to set different levels to different frequencies played. Bars on the left adjust lower frequencies, and those on the right adjust higher frequencies. Select the EQ button to open the Equalizer. Here are some tasks you can perform with the Equalizer:

   ✦ If you like the settings you have for a particular song, you can save them as a Preset. Set each frequency as you like it and click the Preset button. Then choose Save ⇨ Preset. Type a name for the preset and click OK.

   ✦ To reload a preset you created earlier, click the Preset button and select Load ⇨ Preset. Select the preset you want and click OK. The settings change to those of the preset you just loaded.

The small window in the center/top of the Equalizer shows the sound wave formed by your settings. You can adjust the Preamp bar on the left to boost different levels in the set range.

Using the Playlist Editor

The Playlist Editor lets you put together a list of audio files that you want to play. You can add and delete files from this list, save them to a file, and use them again later. Click the PL button in the XMMS window to open the Playlist Editor.

The Playlist Editor allows you to:

✦ **Add files to the playlist** — Click the "+ File" button. The Load Files window appears. Select the directory containing your audio files (it's useful to keep them all in one place) from the left column. Then either select a file from the right column and click Add selected files or click Add all files in the directory. Click OK. The selected file or files appear in the playlist.

✦ **Select files to play** — To select from the files in the playlist, use the previous track and next track buttons in the main XMMS window. The selected file is highlighted. Click the Play button to play that file. Alternatively, you can double-click on any file in the playlist to start it playing.

✦ **Delete files from the playlist** — To remove a file from the playlist, select the file you want to remove (next/previous track buttons) and click the "- File" button. The file is removed.

✦ **Sort files on the playlist** — To sort the playlist in different ways, click and hold the Misc Opt button and move the mouse to select Sort List. Then you can select Sort List to sort the list by Title, Filename, or Path and Filename. You can also randomize or reverse the list.

✦ **Save the playlist** — To save the current playlist, hold the mouse button down on the Load List button and then select Save List. Type the name you want to assign to the playlist and click OK.

✦ **Load the playlist** — To reload a saved playlist, click the Load List button. Select a previously saved playlist from the file list and click OK.

There is also a tiny set of buttons on the bottom of the Playlist Editor screen. These are the same buttons as those on the main screen used for selecting different tracks or playing, pausing, stopping, or ejecting the current track.

Playing MP3 with freeamp

The freeamp MP3 player has some clever controls. You can click in the display area to cycle through the current time, remaining time, and total time associated with the music. Press and hold the left mouse button on dials on either side of the display, then move them to adjust the volume (left dial) or to seek a particular place in the song (right dial).

Freeamp is not part of the Red Hat Linux distribution. The freeamp player is available from the FreeAmp Home Page (`www.freeamp.org`), or you can type `rpmfind freeamp` to find it from a Red Hat mirror site. To start freeamp to run on your X display, type the following:

```
$ freeamp &
```

Figure 8-4 shows the freeamp display window.

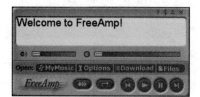

Figure 8-4: Use dials to adjust volume and to seek songs in freeamp.

Preferences for freeamp are stored in the `$HOME/.freeamp/preferences` file. Subdirectories to the .freeamp directory store information about your stored music, fonts, and themes used with the freeamp player.

You can also run freeamp in text mode. To do this, add the `-ui TextUI` option to the `freeamp` command line. However, you don't have to add the `-ui` options. If the DISPLAY variable is set, the X interface of freeamp is started; if DISPLAY is not set, freeamp starts in text mode.

The My Music Collection feature of freeamp lets you create and manage your own library of music. You can include MPEG-1 and MPEG-2 audio files. You can also save individual playlists. When you open a stored playlist, freeamp finds the files you listed and plays them back in the order you specified.

To play a SHOUTcast/http stream or an RTP/multicast stream, specify a URL on the `freeamp` command line. For example, the first command line that follows represents a SHOUTcast stream and the second line represents a multicast stream:

```
$ freeamp http://123.48.23.4:8000
$ freeamp rtp://132.43.21.4:4420
```

You can change the look and the arrangement of buttons on your freeamp window by changing the theme. Click the options button, click the Themes tab (from the Preferences window), select a theme from the Theme Selection area, and click OK. The new theme is immediately applied to freeamp.

MIDI audio players

MIDI stands for Musical Instrument Digital Interface. MIDI files are created from synthesizers and other electronic music devices. MIDI files tend to be smaller than other kinds of audio files because, instead of storing the complete sounds, they contain the notes played. The MIDI player reproduces the notes to sound like a huge variety of MIDI instruments.

There are lots of sites on the Internet for downloading MIDI files. Try the Ifni MIDI Music site (www.ifni.com), which contains songs by the Beatles, Led Zeppelin, Nirvana, and others that are organized by album. Most of the MIDI music is pretty simple, but you can have some fun playing with it.

Red Hat Linux comes with several different MIDI players, including playmidi (from the playmidi package) and xplaymidi (from the playmidi-X11 package). The playmidi command is a text-based MIDI player. The xplaymidi command provides an X interface to the playmidi command.

For any of the commands, you simply type the command followed by the name of the MIDI file you want to play. The few options include choices to mask a particular channel number (-c#, where # is replaced by the channel to mask) or to ignore any percussion tracks (-d). If you use xplaymidi, however, the interface enables you to selectively turn tracks off and on. Figure 8-5 shows the xplaymidi window (playing Bach's Brandenburg Concerto No. 3).

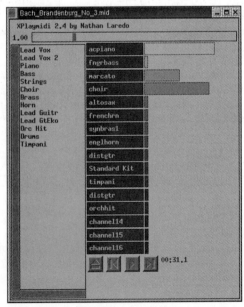

Figure 8-5: The xplaymidi window shows each MIDI track as it plays.

The instrument name is shown for each track (on the left), while bars (to the right) show the sound level for each track as it plays. Click the button representing each track to turn the track off or on. To hear what just a few tracks are doing, click the buttons on the tracks that you don't want to hear; you will then only hear the tracks you want.

Playing Video

If you want to show video clips or play streaming video from the Internet, your choices of software to do that are somewhat limited in Linux. You can play a variety of video formats, such as Quicktime and AVI, with the Xanim Viewer for X. There is a Linux version of the RealPlayer for playing a large volume of RealMedia content.

Because you may be viewing video clips or streaming video from the Internet, you may want to incorporate some of this video technology in your Internet browser. Netscape includes the capability to play video (and other data types) in the Netscape Navigator Internet browser by adding what are called plug-ins or helper apps. The Plugger plug-in for Linux lets you incorporate several different video and audio technologies in Netscape.

Xanim viewer

The Xanim program is a viewer that runs on your X desktop. It can play animation, video, and audio files. Until Red Hat Linux 7.1, the xanim package was part of the Red Hat Linux Powertools CD. Though there is no longer a Powertools CD, you can download the xanim package from any Red Hat FTP site.

The types of media formats Xanim supports are:

✦ **Animations** — Supports FLI, FLC, IFF (with support for various compression, color cycling, and display modes), GIF87a (single and multiple image support) and GIF89a (with animation extensions), DL animations, Amiga PFX, Amiga MovieSetter, and Utah Raster Toolkit.

✦ **AVI Animations** — Supports several video codecs (*coders/dec*oders), including: IBM Ultimotion, JPEG, Motion JPEG, Intergraph JPEG, Microsoft Video 1, Radius Cinepak, Intel Indeo 3.1, Intel Indeo 3.2, Intel Raw YUV, Creative CYUV, Uncompressed RGB, run length encoded, and editable MPEG.

✦ **Quicktime Animations** — Supports several video codecs, including: Uncompressed raw video, Apple Graphics, Apple Animation, Apple Video, Radius Cinepak, Intel Indeo 3.1, Intel Indeo 3.2, Intel Raw YUV, Component Video, Photo JPEG, Kodak Photo CD, and Microsoft Video 1.

✦ **SGI Movie Format Files**—Supports several video codecs, including: Uncompressed RGB, MVC1, MVC2, and JPEG.

✦ **MPEG Animations**—Supports only Type I MPEG frames (ignoring Type GB and Type P frames).

There are separate readme files that you need to read to add Radius Cinepak, Intel Indeo, and Creative Technology CYUV support. You can find those readme files in the directory `/usr/share/doc/xanim*`. Besides video and animations, Xanim can play several different audio formats as well. The following is a list of audio formats that Xanim supports:

✦ **Quicktime Audio**—Supports these codecs: Unsigned PCM, signed PCM, uLAW, IMA4, GSM 6.10.

✦ **SGI Movie Format Audio**—Supports these codecs: Unsigned PCM and signed PCM.

✦ **WAV Audio**—Supports these WAV audio codecs: PCM, uLAW, MSADPCM, Intel DVI, and GSM. Any animation that doesn't already have audio can add a WAV audio and be played with Xanim.

✦ **AU Audio**—Any animation that doesn't already have audio can add an AU audio and be played with Xanim.

Tip To play an audio file along with a video clip, type **xanim *vidfile audfile*,** where *vidfile* is the name of a video clip or animation and *audfile* is the name of a WAV or AU audio file. The two files begin playing together.

To start Xanim, type the following command from a Terminal window on your desktop:

```
xanim file
```

where *file* is the name of a video, animation, or audio file in a supported format. Figure 8-6 shows the Xanim viewer. The image on the right is an AVI file being played. On the left are the controls.

Figure 8-6: Use controls to play and control video content with Xanim.

The controls are fairly straightforward. Controls along the top row (in the order they appear) let you go back one frame at a time, play backward, pause, play forward, and go forward one frame at a time, respectively. Plus and minus keys let you speed up and slow down play, respectively. The plus and minus speakers let you increase or decrease the sound volume.

You can also control Xanim play from the mouse or the keyboard. Move forward or backward a frame at a time using the right and left mouse buttons, respectively. Press the middle mouse button to start and stop the animation. From the keyboard, press the Spacebar to start and stop the animation. To quit Xanim, press Q.

Here are a few cool things to do with Xanim:

✦ Try starting Xanim with the +root option. This causes the video or animation to be tiled on to the root X screen as it plays.

✦ Add the +Sr option to the end of the xadmin command line. This enables you to resize the animation window on the fly. (A larger window can slow down playback.)

✦ Add the +T2 option to the end of the command line to show the frame numbers along with the filename of the animation as it plays.

RealPlayer

A tremendous amount of content is available on the Internet in the RealMedia and RealAudio formats. You can see and hear video clips of popular musicians and comics. You can view live events, such as conferences, news stories, and concerts. You can also listen to your favorite radio stations when you are out of town.

To play RealMedia and RealAudio content you need, as you may have guessed, the RealPlayer. Real Networks (www.real.com) is a leader in streaming media on the Internet. More than 50 million unique users have registered with Real Networks and their Web site, downloading more than 175,000 files per day. And that's not even the good news. The good news is that a RealPlayer is available to run in Red Hat Linux.

To get a free download of RealPlayer, go to the RealPlayer download page (www.real.com/products/player). When you get there, click a link to the free player (RealPlayer 8 Basic), then select the OS as UNIX or Linux. You are asked to fill out a form to get a free download. You need to select the type of system you are using and the CPU. Choose the Linux version that supports libc6 for i386 (or if there is an RPM available, choose that). The RealPlayer for Linux is also available via the Linux area of download.com.

The instructions for configuring RealPlayer are delivered in HTML format, so you can read it in Netscape or some other Web browser. If any patches or workarounds are required, you can find them in the Real Networks Knowledge Base. To get there, click Support (from most Real Networks pages), then click Knowledge Base. When there, query for the word Linux to find any problem reports and fixes.

When you install the RealPlayer, you are asked if you want to configure it to be used as a Netscape plug-in (which I strongly recommend you do). After that, when you open any Real content, the RealPlayer automatically opens to handle the content. As an alternative, you can start the RealPlayer from a Terminal window on your desktop by typing the following:

```
realplay &
```

Figure 8-7 shows the RealPlayer window.

Figure 8-7: Play music videos, sports, and news from the Web with RealPlayer.

After you have RealPlayer, you can visit some sites to get content to play on your RealPlayer. I suggest starting at the RealGuide site (realguide.real.com). This is a guide to audio and video on the Internet that plays on RealPlayers. The guide has links to radio shows and events that are live at the moment. There are also special news reports and links to music, show business, sports, science/technical, society, money, and shopping sites that use this technology.

Using a Digital Camera with gPhoto

With the gPhoto window, you can download images from digital cameras. gPhoto works by attaching one of the supported digital cameras to a serial port on your computer. You can view an index of thumbnails of the digital images from the camera, view full-size digital images, and download the ones you select from the camera to your Linux system.

Check the gPhoto Web site (www.gphoto.org) for information on supported cameras as well as other topics related to gPhoto. Here is a list of digital cameras that are currently supported.

- ✦ **Agfa ePhoto** — Supported models: 307, 708, 708C, 1280, and 1680.
- ✦ **Apple QuickTake** — Supported models: 150 and 200.

✦ **Cannon PowerShot** — Supported models: A5, A5 Zoom, A50, A70, S10, and S20.

✦ **Casio QV** — Supported models: 10, 10A, 11, 30, 70, 100, 200, 700, and 5000SX.

✦ **Chinon** — Supported model: ES-1000.

✦ **Epson PhotoPC** — Supported models: 500, 550, 600, 700, and 800.

✦ **Fuji** — Supported models: DS-7, DX-5, DX-10, MX-500, MX-600, MX-700, MX-1200, and MX 2700.

✦ **Hewlett-Packard PhotoSmart** — Supported models: C20, C30, and C2000.

✦ **Kodak DC** — Supported models: 20, 25, 200+, 210, 210+ Zoom, 215 Zoom, 220 +, 240, and 280.

✦ **Konica** — Supported models: QM100, QM100V, Q-EZ, Q-M100, Q-M100V, and Q-M200.

✦ **Leica** — Supported model: Digilux Zoom.

✦ **Minolta** — Supported model: Dimage V.

✦ **Mustek** — Supported model: MDC 800 v2.

✦ **Nicon CoolPix** — Supported models: 100, 300, 600, 700, 800, 900, 900S, 950, and 950S.

✦ **Olympus** — Supported models: D-100Z, D-200L, D-220L, D-300L, D-320L, D-330R, D-340L, D-340R, D-400L Zoom, D-450Z, D-500L, D-600L, D-620L, C-400L, C-410L, C-800L, C-820L, C-830L, C-840L, C-900 Zoom, C-900L Zoom, C-1000L, C-1400L, and C-2000Z.

✦ **Panasonic** — Supported models: Coolshot KXI-600A and Cardshot NV-DCF5E.

✦ **Philips** — Supported models: ESP60 and ESP 80.

✦ **Polaroid** — Supported model: PDC 640.

✦ **Ricoh RDC** — Supported models: 300, 300Z, 4200, 4300, and 5000.

✦ **Samsung** — Supported models: Kenox SSC-350N and Digimax 800K.

✦ **Sanyo VPC** — Supported models: G210, G200, G250, and X350.

✦ **Sony** — Supported models: DSC-F1, DSC-F55, DSC-F505, Memory Stick Adapter, and MSAC-SR1 and DCR-PC100.

✦ **Toshiba** — Supported model: PDR-M1.

To start gPhoto from the Gnome desktop menu, choose Programs ⇨ Applications ⇨ gPhoto. A pop-up window asks you to identify the type of camera you are using and the port that it is connected to. At this point you should have your camera attached to a serial port (such as COM1 or COM2) on your computer. After identifying your camera and port, click Save. The main gPhoto window appears, as shown in Figure 8-8.

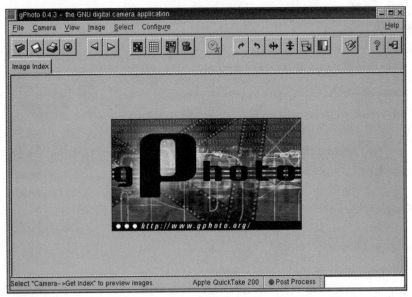

Figure 8-8: Download images from digital cameras from the gPhoto window.

To view images from your digital camera, choose Camera ⇨ Download Index. Then either select Thumbnails (to display thumbnail views of each image) or No Thumbnails to simply see a gray box representing each image. Thumbnails take much longer to appear than the gray boxes. So if you want to just select one image at a time to view, you can click No Thumbnails.

After images are selected, choose Camera ⇨ Download Selected ⇨ Thumbnails. Then select either Images or Thumbnails. After that, you can select either Open in window (to view the selected images) or Save to disk (to save the selected images).

After images are displayed, you can rotate the images, flip them vertically or horizontally, resize them, or modify colors. You can also save, print, or delete selected images.

MultiMedia Netscape Plug-ins and Helper Apps

Because much of your stock of video clips, audio clips, and other multimedia content will probably come from the Internet, it makes sense to be able to play that content in your Internet browser. Software added to Netscape Navigator to play different content takes the form of plug-ins and helper apps.

In simple terms, a Netscape plug-in is software that plays a particular type of data (a video, sound clip, or other form of content) within the Netscape display area. A helper app is software that is launched as a separate application by Netscape to handle a particular type of data (usually by opening a separate window).

Compared to the number of plug-ins available for the Windows platforms, very few plug-ins can be used with your Red Hat Linux system. Those plug-ins that apply to multimedia content are described in the text that follows. Any application that can play multimedia content in Red Hat Linux, however, can be added to Netscape as a helper application. See Chapter 9 for a description of how to add helper applications to Netscape.

Here are two plug-ins for Netscape that come with Red Hat Linux and allow you to play some types of multimedia content that you may not otherwise be able to play in Linux.

✦ **Shockwave Flash Player** — This plug-in plays multimedia FutureSplash content created by Flash 3 authoring software from Macromedia (www. macromedia.com). It also plays Shockwave Flash multimedia content. Flash content can contain animation, vector graphics, sound, and interactive interfaces.

✦ **Plugger** — This is a streaming multimedia plug-in for Netscape on UNIX platforms. On the back end of Plugger are applications such as Xanim, MpegTV, and several other applications that actually process the data. (In other words, these other applications need to be installed so that Plugger can use them to provide the features you select.)

Another plug-in you should consider installing is the Adobe Acrobat Reader plug-in. You can get it by installing the acroread. (You can use the rpmfind acroread command to locate a copy of the acroread package from the Internet.)

Installing a plug-in often means simply copying the plug-in file to the directory where Netscape will find it. On my system the location is the /usr/lib/netscape/ plugins directory. The best way to find this location, as well as a list of other plug-ins that are already installed, is to open Netscape and then choose Help ⇨ About Plug-ins. Figure 8-9 shows what this listing looks like after I installed the Adobe Acrobat Reader plug-in.

The listing of plug-ins shows the name of the plug-in, the MIME type of the content it can play, and the filename extensions on the files it can play.

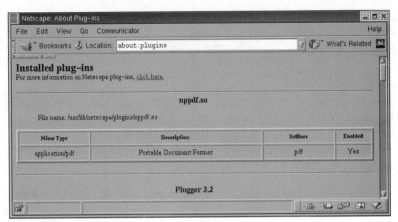

Figure 8-9: Find what plug-ins are installed in Netscape using
Help ➪ About Plug-ins.

Recording Music CDs

Writable CD-ROM drives are fast becoming a standard device on computers. Where
once you had to settle for a floppy disk (1.44MB) or a Zip disk (100MB) to store
personal data, a CD-ROM burner lets you store more than 600MB of data in a format
that can be exchanged with most computers. On top of that, you can create CD
music disks!

Both graphical and command-line tools exist for creating CDs in Red Hat Linux. The
`cdrecord` command lets you create audio and data CDs from the command line.
The `xcdroast` provides a graphical interface. Both tools let you write to CD-
Recordable (CD-R) and CD-Rewritable (CD-RW) drives. The `cdrecord` command
and xcdroast window are described in the next section of this chapter.

Only SCSI CD-ROM drives can be used to create CDs in Linux with the current tools.
If you have an IDE writable CD-ROM, however, don't despair. With a bit of extra
configuration, you can set up your drive for SCSI emulation. After that, Linux CD
writing tools write to it as though it were a SCSI drive.

Configuring an IDE CD-ROM for recording

If you are using a SCSI drive, you are probably ready to begin recording; CD recording tools in Linux should recognize and be able to use your drive automatically. If
you are using an IDE-based drive, however, you may have some work to do.

In most cases, your IDE writable CD drive should be recognized and properly configured when you install Red Hat Linux. The following boot option should automatically appear as an option to your bootloader:

```
hdc=ide-scsi
```

This shows that IDE disk device "c"(hdc) is set up to do SCSI emulation. If this is working properly, you should be able to type the following to see if the CD drive appears on the list of accessible SCSI devices.

```
$ cdrecord --scanbus
```

If your IDE writable CD drive is not working, check that the following basic steps are done: 1) have SCSI emulation built into the kernel; 2) remove the IDE-CD module; and 3) add the IDE-SCSI module. By default, SCSI emulation should be built into your kernel, so unless you remove it, there's nothing you have to do there. Here's how you accomplish the other two steps:

1. To remove the ide-cd module, as root user add the following line to the /etc/modules.conf file (using any text editor).

   ```
   options ide-cd ignore=hdc
   ```

   In this example, the writable CD-ROM device is located at /dev/hdc. Replace hdc with the location of your CD device. If you are not sure, type **dmesg | grep ^hd** to see a list of IDE disks on your computer.

2. Restart your computer.

3. To add the ide-scsi module, type the following command:

   ```
   # modprobe -a ide-scsi
   ```

4. To make sure Linux can recognize your CD writer, type the following command:

   ```
   # cdrecord -scanbus
   Cdrecord 1.10 (i686-pc-linux-gnu) Copyright (C) 1995-2001
       J!!rg Schilling
   Linux sg driver version: 3.1.19
   Using libscg version 'schily-0.5'
   scsibus0:
       0,0,0    0) 'IDE-CD' 'R/RW 4x4x24 ''1.04' Removable CD-ROM
       0,1,0    1) 'SONY ''CD-ROM CDU701 ''1.0f' Removable CD-ROM
       0,2,0    2) *
       0,3,0    3) *
       0,4,0    4) *
       0,5,0    5) *
       0,6,0    6) *
       0,7,0    7) *
   ```

   Here you can see that cdrecord has detected two CD drives on SCSI bus 0. A writable CD drive is at 0,0,0 and a read-only CD is located at 0,1,0. You need to remember these numbers later when you use cdrecord to create a CD. Until your CD burners show up on this list, cdrecord cannot write to them.

5. After you have added your CD writer as a SCSI device, it may no longer be available to the CD players described in this chapter. By default, those players play the /dev/cdrom device, which in this case points to an IDE drive. To fix that, type the following as root user:

```
# cd /dev
# rm cdrom
# ln -s scd0 cdrom
```

If you have two CD drives, repeat this step, replacing cdrom with cdrom1, and scd0 with scd1.

Creating an Audio CD with cdrecord

You can use the cdrecord command to create either data or music CDs. You can create a data CD, by setting up a separate file system and copying the whole image of that file system to CD. Creating an audio CD consists of selecting the audio tracks you want to copy and copying them all at once to the CD.

This section focuses on using cdrecord to create audio CDs. The cdrecord command can use audio files in .au, .wav, or .cdr format, automatically translating them when necessary. If you have audio files in other formats, you can convert them to one of the supported formats by using the sox command (described previously in this chapter).

Cross-Reference   See Chapter 13 for a description of how to use cdrecord to create data CDs.

One way to create an audio CD is to copy the music tracks you want to a directory; then copy them to the writable CD. To extract the tracks, you can use the cdda2wav command. Then you write them to CD by using the cdrecord command. Here is an example:

1. Create a directory to hold the audio files, and change to that directory. Make sure the directory can hold up to 660MB of data (or less if you are burning fewer songs). For example:

```
# mkdir /tmp/cd
# cd /tmp/cd
```

2. Type the cdrecord --scanbus command (as shown earlier) to determine the SCSI device number of your CD-ROM drive.

3. Insert the music CD into your CD-ROM drive. (If a CD player opens on the desktop, close it.)

4. Extract the music tracks you want by using the `cdda2wav` command. For example:

```
# cdda2wav -D0,0,0 -B -owav
```

This example reads all of the music tracks from the CD-ROM drive located at SCSI device number 0,0,0. The `-B` option says to output each track to a separate file. The `-owav` option tells the `cdda2wav` command to output the files to WAV audio format.

Instead of extracting all songs, you can choose a single track or a range of tracks to extract. For example, to extract tracks 3 through 5, add the `-t3+5` option. To extract just track 9, add `-t9+9`. To extract track 7 through the end of the CD, add `-t7`.

5. Insert a blank CD into your writable CD drive.

6. Use the `cdrecord` command to write the music tracks to the CD. For example:

```
# cdrecord -v dev=0,0,0 -audio *.wav
```

The options to `cdrecord` tell the command to create an audio CD (`-audio`) on the writable CD device located on 0,0,0. The `cdrecord` command writes all files from the current directory that end in `.wav`. The `-v` option causes verbose output.

If you want to change the order of the tracks, you can type their names in the order you want them written (instead of using `*.wav`). If your CD writer supports higher speeds, you can use the speed option to double (`speed=2`) or to quadruple (`speed=4`) the writing speed.

Once you have created the music CD, indicate the contents of the CD on the front of the CD. The CD should now be ready to play on any standard music CD player.

Ripping CDs with grip

The grip window provides a more graphical method of copying music from CDs to your hard disk. You can then play the songs directly from your hard disk or burn them back on to a blank CD.

You can open Grip from the Gnome menu by choosing Programs ⇨ Multimedia ⇨ grip or by typing grip from a Terminal window. Figure 8-10 shows an example of the Grip window.

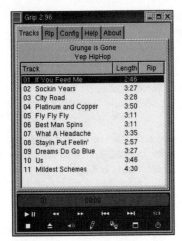

Figure 8-10: Rip and play songs from the grip window.

To rip audio tracks from a CD with grip, do the following:

1. With the grip window open, insert a music CD into your CD drive. If you have an active connection to the Internet and the CD is known to the CD database, then title, artist, and track information appear for the CD.

2. Right click on each track that you want to rip (that is, copy to your hard disk).

   A check mark appears under the Rip column for the song.

3. Click the Rip tab at the top of the page.

   The Rip tab appears.

4. Click one of the following:

   - Rip+Encode — This rips the selected songs in MP3 format. You need an MP3 player to play the songs after they have been ripped in this format.

   - Rip only — This rips the selected songs in WAV format. You can use a standard CD player to play these songs.

   Songs are copied to the hard disk in the format you selected. By default, the files are copied into a subdirectory of $HOME/ogg (that is, the ogg directory in your home directory, such as /home/jake/ogg). The subdirectory is named for the artist and CD. For example, if the user jake were ripping the called High Life by the artist Mumbo, the directory containing the ripped songs would be /home/jake/ogg/mumbo/high_life. Each song file would be named for the song (for example, fly_fly_fly.wav).

At this point you can play any of the files using a player that can play WAV or MP3 files, such as xmms. Or you can copy the files back to the CD using CD record. Because the file names are the song names, they don't appear in the same order as they appear on the CD. So if you want to copy them back to a writable CD in the same order where they originally appeared, you may have to type each file name individually on the cdrecord command line. Here is an example:

```
# cdrecord -v dev=0,0,0 -audio fly_fly_fly.wav big_news.wav
about_time.wav
```

The grip window can also be used to play CDs. Use the buttons on the bottom of the display to play/pause, skip ahead/back, stop and eject the CD. The Toggle track display button lets you shrink the size of the display so it doesn't take up much space on the desktop. Click Toggle disc editor to see and change title, artist, and track information.

Creating CD labels with cdlabelgen

The cdlabelgen command can be used to create tray cards and front cards to fit in CD jewel cases. You gather information about the CD and cdlabelgen produces a PostScript output file that you can send to the printer. The cdlabelgen package also comes with graphics (in /usr/share/cdlabelgen) that you can incorporate into your labels.

Here is an example of a cdlabelgen command line that you can use to generate a CD label file in PostScript format. (Type it all on one line or use backslashes, as shown here, to put it on multiple lines.)

```
cdlabelgen -c "Grunge is Gone" -s "Yep HipHop" \
-i "If You Feed Me%Sockin Years%City Road%Platinum and Copper%Fly Fly Fly% \
Best Man Spins%What A Headache%Stayin Put Feelin%Dreams Do Go Blue%Us% \
Mildest Schemes" -o yep.ps
```

In this example, the title of the CD is indicated by -c "Grunge is Gone" and the artist by the -s "Yep HipHop" option. The tracks are entered after the -i option, with each line separated by a % sign. The output file is sent to the file yep.ps with the -o option. To view and print the results, you can use the gv command as follows:

```
$ gv yep.ps
```

The results of this example are shown in Figure 8-11.

Figure 8-11: Generate CD jewel case labels with cdlabelgen and print them with gv.

You will probably want to edit the command and re-run gv a few times to get the CD label correct. When you are ready to print the label (assuming you have a printer configured for your computer), click Print All to print the label.

Multimedia Technologies in Waiting

Some multimedia technologies are on the horizon for Linux. Here are two technologies that have varied levels of support in Linux: DVD and Virtual Reality.

DVD movies

DVD (which stands for Digital Video Disk or Digital Versatile Disk, depending on whom you ask) is the latest medium for selling movies to consumers. Some believe that DVDs will eventually make VHS video a thing of the past. DVD technology is being built into standalone players as well as computers. Currently, all official DVD players that are built into computers run only under MS Windows operating systems.

Several efforts are underway to make DVDs usable in Linux. Linux drivers have been developed for a PCI DVD decoder board by a German company called Convergence Integrated Media (www.convergence.de). The company is developing a PCI DVD board to use the drivers.

If you can't wait that long, check out the latest happenings of the Linux Video and DVD project (or LiViD). There is a collection of video and DVD Linux projects that are accessible from the LiViD site (www.linuxvideo.org).

Caution The entertainment industry has filed several lawsuits, attempting to protect the decryption scheme used in DVD movies. Because the legality of using the DeCSS software described by OpenDVD.org to decrypt DVD movies is still in question, I recommend that you study the legal issues before using the software. One site you can visit is the DeCSS Central Web page (www.lemuria.org/DeCSS).

Virtual reality

Some people believed that virtual reality would one day be the interface of choice on the Internet. Imagine being able to wander through virtual malls to do your shopping or a virtual town to make vacation plans. So far, virtual reality mania has not overrun the Internet. As for Linux support, the VRwave plug-in seems to be the only software available for viewing virtual reality content (VRML format). And that software hasn't been updated for quite some time. If you are interested, go to www.iicm.edu/vrwave for more information and links to download the plug-in.

Summary

Getting your Red Hat Linux system set up for sound and video can take some doing, but once it's done you can play most audio and video content that is available today. This chapter took you through the steps of setting up and troubleshooting your sound card. When that was done, you learned how to find software to play music through that card.

Video players, such as Xanim, were described for playing video clips in Red Hat Linux. The chapter also covered how to get the RealPlayer from Real Networks so you can draw from the large pool of RealMedia content available on the Web. To download images from a digital camera, the gPhoto window was described.

If your computer has a CD burner, use descriptions in this chapter to create your own music CDs and CD labels. The chapter described a few plug-ins that you can add to your Netscape browser to play some types of multimedia content as you browse the Web. Finally, it described the current state of DVD and VRML content in Linux.

✦   ✦   ✦

Tools for Using the Internet and the Web

♦ ♦ ♦ ♦

In This Chapter

Understanding Internet tools

Browsing the Web

Communicating via e-mail

Participating in newsgroups

Using remote login, copy, and execution commands

♦ ♦ ♦ ♦

Because Linux and other UNIX systems were such an integral part of the creation and growth of the Internet and the World Wide Web, there are many tools available for using the Internet. Although most of the most powerful Internet tools for Linux were once text-based, user-friendly Internet applications have been added in recent years to give you the power to access a wide range of Internet content from your desktop.

This chapter describes some of the most important tools available with Red Hat Linux for working with the Internet. These descriptions include Web browsers, e-mail readers, newsreaders, instant messaging clients, and remote commands for login, copy, and remote execution.

Overview of Internet Tools

The most important client Internet program these days is the Web browser. Red Hat Linux features the Mozilla and Netscape Communicator software packages, each of which includes a Web browser as well as several other Web client software for reading mail, participating in newsgroups, and creating Web pages (to name a few). Other Web browsers are available for Red Hat Linux as well, such as the Lynx browsers.

Running a close second to Web browsers is the e-mail reader (referred to in network standards terms as a Mail User Agent or MUA.) Both Mozilla and Netscape Communicator have integrated an e-mail program into their packages. If you are looking for a friendly e-mail program, mail programs that come with those two browsers are good choices. Mail programs that have been around in Linux and other UNIX systems since the time when most mail was plain text, include elm and mail.

You can choose from thousands of newsgroups to participate in discussions on the Internet. Red Hat Linux has a variety of newsreaders available. Again, Mozilla and Netscape Communicator include applications for participating in newsgroups. Also, the Pan and xrn newsreaders are available for the desktop.

Besides browsing, e-mail, and news, there are many ways of communicating with other computers and users on the Internet. A set of commands, sometimes referred to as "r" commands, lets you log in to other computers (`rlogin`), execute remote programs (`rsh`), and copy files to and from remote computers (`rcp`). These, and a few other utilities described later, are usually most effective when used on your LAN or private network (particularly with other Linux/UNIX systems). That's because they sometimes require that certain network services be made available that are usually restricted between computers that don't know each other.

Browsing the Web

More and more businesses today need to provide World Wide Web access to their employees. In the few years since the Web was created, it has become a necessary tool for keeping in touch with customers, suppliers, and business partners. For the home user, the Internet provides access to shopping, educational information, news, and many other resources.

Although the Internet has been around since the 1960s, the Web is a relatively new technology (it was created in 1985). The Web places an additional framework over Internet addresses that were once limited to hostnames and domain names. Before the Web, finding resources on the Internet was difficult. However, the Web now provides several features that make it much easier to access these resources:

✦ **Uniform Resource Locators (URLs)** — URLs identify the location of resources on the Web. Besides identifying the domain and host on which a resource resides, they can also identify the type of content and the specific location of the content.

✦ **Hypertext Markup Language (HTML) Web pages** — When people talk about a Web page, they are generally referring to information that is presented in HTML format. HTML changed the Internet from a purely plain text-based resource to one that could present graphics and font changes. An HTML page can also contain hypertext links. Links are the threads that join together the Web, enabling someone viewing a Web page to be immediately transported to another Web page (or other content) by simply selecting a linked text string or image in the page.

The primary tool for displaying HTML Web pages is the Web browser. Mozilla and Netscape Communicator are the most popular Web browsers for Red Hat Linux. Both can display HTML (Web pages) as well as a variety of other types of Web content. This section contains general information about the Web and some specific hints for using Netscape Communicator or Mozilla to browse the Web from your Red Hat Linux system.

Uniform Resource Locators

To visit a site on the Internet, you either type a URL into the Location box on your browser or click on a link (either on a Web page or from a menu or button on the browser). Although URLs are commonplace these days — you can find them on everything from business cards to cereal boxes — you may not know how URLs are constructed. The form of the URL is generally as follows:

```
protocol://host-domain/path
```

The protocol identifies the kind of content that you are requesting. By far, the most common protocol you come across is Hypertext Transfer Protocol (HTTP). HTTP is the protocol used to request Web pages. In addition to HTTP, however, there are other protocols that might appear at the beginning of a Web address. Instead of showing you a Web page, these other types of protocols may display different kinds of information in your browser, or open a completely different application for working with the content.

Table 9-1 lists some of the protocols that can appear in a Web URL.

Table 9-1	
Protocols in Web URLs	
Protocol Name	*Description*
http	Hypertext Transfer Protocol. Used to identify HTML Web pages and related content.
file	Identifies a file on a specific host. Most often used to display a file from your local computer.
ftp	File Transfer Protocol. Identifies a location where there are file archives from which you might want to download files.
gopher	Gopher Protocol. Provides databases of mostly text-based documents that are distributed across the Internet. (Web pages and search engines have made gopher nearly obsolete.)

Continued

Table 9-1 *(continued)*

Protocol Name	Description
mailto	Electronic Mail Address. Identifies an e-mail address, such as `mailto://webmaster@handsonhistory.com`. Typing this type of address into Netscape results in a new mail message window opening, ready to create a message to the address named.
news	USENET newsgroup. Identifies a newsgroup, such as `news://news.myisp.com/comp.os.linux.networking`. If you type this address into Netscape, a Messenger window appears, with the newsgroup displayed from the news server you identified.
nntp	USENET news using nntp protocol. Identifies a USENET newsgroup, using nntp protocol.
telnet	Login to a remote computer and begin an interactive session. An example of a telnet address is `telnet://localhost.handsonhistory.com`. Type a telnet address into Netscape and a Telnet window will open and attempt to log you in to the named computer. (You couldcan replace `localhost` with any computer name or IP address that will allows you to login to it.)
wais	Wide Area Information Server protocol. A WAIS address might look like the following: `wais://handsonhistory.com/waisdb`. A WAIS address provides access to a WAIS database. (Like gopher, WAIS databases are nearly obsolete.)

The first part of a URL is the protocol. If you have used Netscape Communicator or another Web browser before, you will notice that you don't always have to type in the protocol. Netscape is pretty good at guessing what kind of content you are looking for (mostly it guesses HTTP). If the address you type in starts with www, it assumes HTTP; if it starts with ftp, it assumes FTP protocol.

The second part of a URL takes you to the computer that is hosting the Web content. By convention, Web servers begin with www (or sometimes home). However, as long as you type the correct protocol (usually http), you will be directed to the right service within the host computer. The next piece of this name is just the host.domain style of Internet address that has always been used with the Internet (such as redhat.com, handsonhistory.com, or whitehouse.gov). Finally, an optional port number can be tacked on to the host.domain name. For example, to specifically request the port used for HTTP services (port 80) from the host/domain called handsonhistory.com, you can type: `http://handsonhistory.com:80`.

Tip You can see the standard ports and services used by your Red Hat Linux computer. Most are contained in the /etc/services file on your Red Hat Linux system. A port number is a lot like a telephone extension in a big company. A main telephone number (like the host.domain name) gets you to a company switchboard. The telephone extension (like the port number) connects you to the right person (like the service associated with a port).

The third and final part of a URL identifies the specific location of the content on the host computer. Sections within a Web page can be identified by following the Web page location with a pound sign (#) and an identifier. For example, the craft section of the dsched.htm page at handsonhistory.com would be identified by the following URL: http://handsonhistory.com/dsched.htm#craft. Notice that the file name extension (such as .htm or .html) can further identify the type of content (in this case, as an HTML page).

Web pages

If you look at the HTML source code that produces Web pages, you see that it consists of a combination of information and markup tags, all of which are in plain-text format. The idea was to have Web pages be very portable and flexible. You can create a Web page with vi, emacs, Notepad, or any text editor on any computing platform. Or simplified front-end programs can be used to provide WYSIWYG (What You See Is What You Get) interfaces that let you see what you are creating as you go.

HTML tags are set apart by right and left angle brackets. Tags come in pairs, with a beginning tag, followed by information, and then an ending tag. The beginning tag contains the tag name, whereas an ending tag contains a forward slash (/) and the tag name. A minimal HTML page includes the following code:

```
<HTML>
<HEAD>
<TITLE>Greetings from Washington</TITLE>
</HEAD>
<BODY>
Here we are in beautiful Gig Harbor.
</BODY>
</HTML>
```

You can see that the document begins and ends with HTML tags (<HTML> and </HTML>). The beginning part of the Web page is contained within the HEAD tags. The body of the page is contained within the BODY tags. The title of the page (which appears in the browser's title bar) is set apart by TITLE tags.

Between the beginning and ending BODY tags, you can add all kinds of stuff. You can have different types of bulleted or numbered lists. You can have headings, images, and text. More complex pages can include forms, dynamic HTML (which changes the content as you move or select items), or special data. Figure 9-1 is an example of a Web page as it appears in Netscape Communicator.

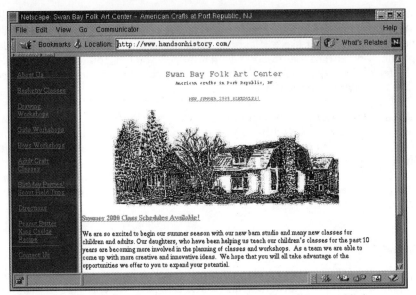

Figure 9-1: Many Web pages contain text, images, headings, and links.

Some of the HTML code that was used to create the Web page shown in Figure 9-1 follows. The title of the Web page appears between two TITLE tags.

```
<TITLE>Swan Bay Folk Art Center - American Crafts
in Port Republic, NJ</TITLE>
```

The following code is used to create a link that opens a new mail message window:

```
A HREF="mailto:webmaster@handsonhistory.com">Contact Us</A>;
```

The text Contact Us is a link to the e-mail address that you would contact for more information. When someone clicks on that link, a new message window appears, allowing that person to send e-mail to that address.

```
<FONT FACE="Copperplate Gothic Bold"><A HREF=" draw.htm">
     Drawing Workshops</A></FONT>
```

A special font face was used for the words Drawing Workshops and if someone were to click on that word, the draw.htm page would appear.

Netscape Communicator package

A few years ago, Netscape Navigator was overwhelmingly the most popular Web browser. Although Microsoft Internet Explorer (IE) has overtaken it on Microsoft operating systems, Netscape, and its open source cousin Mozilla, are still the most popular browsers on Linux and other UNIX systems. A lot of that has to do with the fact that there is no version of IE running on Red Hat or other Linux systems. (Don't hold your breath waiting for it, either.)

Netscape Communicator is a repackaging of Netscape Navigator, with additional software for other Web-related features besides browsing. While the Netscape Communicator package for Red Hat Linux doesn't have everything in it that you might expect (see the sidebar "What's Missing in Netscape for Red Hat Linux?"), it is still an excellent browser to use with Red Hat Linux.

You can start Netscape Navigator from a menu or from a Terminal window on your desktop. If you are using the Gnome desktop (which is the default), you can choose Programs ➪ Internet ➪ Netscape Communicator. Otherwise, you can start Netscape from a Terminal window by typing:

```
netscape&
```

Figure 9-2 shows an example of the Netscape Navigator window displaying the Red Hat home page (`www.redhat.com`).

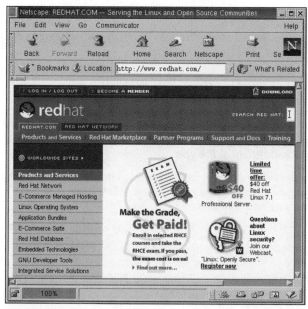

Figure 9-2: The Red Hat Linux opening page appears when you first open Netscape Navigator to browse the World Wide Web.

What's Missing in Netscape for Red Hat Linux?

Unfortunately, the Red Hat Linux version of Netscape Navigator doesn't contain some of the features that are available in the Windows versions of Netscape. Here is a partial list:

✦ Some major features, including Conference, Calendar, IBM-Host On Demand, Netcaster, and AOL Instant Messenger Service, are not supported.

✦ Very few plug-ins are supported, and only a few of those that are available are supplied. (Plug-ins are described later.)

Although you can read HTML files from your local computer, Netscape Navigator is most often used with a connection to the Internet. To use most of the preset bookmarks and even to get Netscape help files, you need to access sites on the Web.

The following sections describe how to use Netscape controls, select other Netscape Communicator features, use plug-ins and helper apps, and set preferences.

Using Netscape controls

There is a good set of controls in Netscape for opening, saving, searching, and otherwise working with Web pages in Netscape. Here is a list of control features and how you go about using them:

✦ **Open a New Navigator Window:** Choose File ➪ New ➪ Navigator Window.

✦ **Open a New Mail Message:** Choose File ➪ New ➪ New Message.

✦ **Open a Local or Internet Web Page:** Choose File ➪ Open Page. Then either type a URL for a Web page, type a local filename, or browse your computer (click Choose File) to find the local file you want.

✦ **Save the Current Web Page:** Choose File ➪ Save As, and then select a location in your file system to save the whole page. Choose File ➪ Save Frame As to save only the currently selected frame.

✦ **Send Web Content:** You can send an e-mail containing either the current Web page (File ➪ Send Page) or the URL of the current Web page (File ➪ Send Link) to selected recipients.

✦ **Print the Current Page:** Choose File ➪ Print to print the current Web page. The Print dialog box lets you select to print to a particular printer or to save the printed output to a PostScript file. You can also select to print the page in landscape or portrait modes, choose the order in which pages are printed, select gray scale or color, and select the paper size.

✦ **Close the Navigator Window:** Choose File ➪ Close. Or you can click on the X in the upper-right corner of the window frame. (This action closes only the current Navigator window. If you have several Navigator windows open, choose File ➪ Exit to close them all.)

✦ **Copy Text:** To copy text from the page, click and drag the mouse pointer over the text you want to copy. Choose Edit ➪ Copy to copy the text. You can also choose Edit ➪ Select All to select all the text.

✦ **Paste Text:** To paste text that you have previously copied, click on the location you want to paste the text and choose Edit ➪ Copy. Paste can be useful if you happen to be filling out a form or need to cut and paste a URL into the location box.

✦ **Find Text:** To find text in the Web page, choose Edit ➪ Find in Page, fill in the text you want to search for, then click Find. To find the same text again, choose Edit ➪ Find Again.

✦ **Search the Internet:** You can search the Internet for a keyword phrase in many different ways. Choose Edit ➪ Search Internet to open a page from the Netscape Web site that lets you search the Internet. Or type a question mark (**?**) followed by one or more keywords in the Location box and press Enter. Besides the two Netscape search tools, there are entire Web sites devoted to doing keyword searches of the Internet. Here are a few to try: `yahoo.com`, `altavista.com`, `hotbot.lycos.com`, `excite.com`, `lycos.com`, and `goto.com`.

✦ **Display Tool Bars:** You can choose which toolbars are and are not displayed on your Navigator window. Choose View, and then click the buttons next to Navigation Toolbar, Location Toolbar, or Personal Toolbar to have those toolbars displayed or not displayed.

✦ **Reload the Web Page:** If a page is taking too long to load or if you want to update the information on the current page, either click Reload or choose View ➪ Reload.

✦ **Stop Loading a Web Page:** If you want to stop a Web page that is in the process of loading, choose View ➪ Stop Loading.

✦ **View the Page's Source Code:** To view the underlying HTML code for the Web page, choose View ➪ Page Source.

✦ **View Information about a Page:** You can view information about the location of a Web page, the location of each of its components, the dates the page was modified, and other information by choosing View ➪ Page Info. Figure 9-3 shows the Page Info window for a Web page.

✦ **Returning to Web Sites:** You can step backward and forward among the pages you have visited or select from the list of recently visited pages. Click and hold on Back to select from a list of sites that you visited. After you have stepped back, click and hold Forward to go forward to a page that you visited. These options, plus a list of sites that you visited during this session can be accessed under the Go menu as well.

✦ **Getting Help:** Click Help to get a list of help resources available with Netscape. Most of these are accessible from the Web. To determine the version of your Netscape Communicator and its components, choose Help ➪ About Communicator.

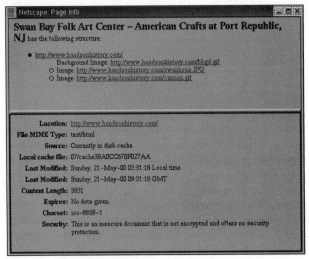

Figure 9-3: Display information about a Web page by selecting Page Info.

Selecting other Netscape Communicator features

Other client programs and features are included with Netscape Communicator, besides the Netscape Navigator browser. Here is a list of those clients and features:

✦ **Messenger:** Choose Communicator ➪ Messenger to open a Messenger window for viewing mail and newsgroups. The Messenger window is described in the E-mail and Newsgroup sections of this chapter.

✦ **Compose:** Choose Communicator ➪ Compose to display the Composer window for creating your own Web pages.

✦ **Radio:** Select the Radio to play music from the Internet. Netscape Radio lets you choose from among 15 different channels. You can display information about the recording artists and purchase music you like online.

✦ **Bookmarks:** Netscape starts you off with a number of bookmarked pages. Click Bookmarks to select from the lists of bookmarks. Click Add to add the current page to the bookmarks. Click Edit to open a Bookmark Edit window to organize your bookmarks.

Tip

The Personal Toolbar should have bookmarks that you use often. To delete the bookmarks that Netscape provides, choose Bookmarks ➪ Edit Bookmarks and select the bookmarks under the Personal Toolbar heading, and then choose Edit ➪ Delete. Now you can add your own. The bookmarks you add to the Personal Toolbar are only one click away.

✦ **Address Book:** Netscape includes an address book that you can use to keep track of people's e-mail addresses and other personal information. It is integrated with the mail and newsgroup features, so you can easily send messages to people you contact regularly. Choose Communicator ⇨ Address Book to open the Address Book.

✦ **Security:** If you are dealing with sensitive material, you can take advantage of several security features that are built into Netscape. Click the Security icon on the toolbar. Figure 9-4 shows the Security Info page that appears.

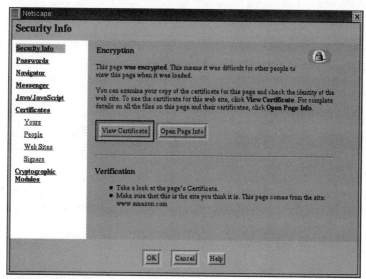

Figure 9-4: Check the security of Web content from the Security Info window.

✦ The first page of the Security Info window (shown here) describes whether the current page is encrypted. You can configure certificates as a means of verifying the identity of other people and sites, as well as to verify yourself to them. Select Password to enter a password that you will be prompted for if your certificate is needed.

✦ Under Navigator, choose whether you should receive warnings if you enter or leave an encrypted Web site. Choose whether your mail should be encrypted and signed. Under Cryptographic Modules, you can add modules to provide your encryption technology (by default, Netscape's Internal PKCS #11 module is used).

Using plug-ins and helper apps

Although the main type of content provided by Web pages is HTML, many other content types can be displayed, played, or presented by a Web browser. Most additional data encountered by Netscape is handled in one of two ways: plug-ins or helper apps.

Plug-ins are self-contained programs that allow data to play within the Netscape window. A helper app can be any program that is available on your Red Hat Linux system. It is up to you to identify the plug-in or helper app to be launched by your Netscape browser when a certain type of data is encountered.

Adding helper apps

To see what types of data your Netscape browser can handle with helper apps and plug-ins, do the following:

1. Choose Edit ➪ Preferences.

   The Netscape Preferences window appears.

2. Click the arrow next to the Navigator category.

3. Select Applications.

   Descriptions of the plug-ins and helper applications that are configured for Netscape on your computer appear, along with information on how the plug-ins are handled.

If you have never added any plug-ins or helper apps to this instance of Netscape, you probably noticed that there are very few plug-ins. Most of the entries represent helper apps that are launched when certain types of data are encountered. Netscape determines what kind of data it has encountered (and subsequently, what helper app or plug-in to launch) based on one of the following criteria:

✦ **Suffixes:** If the browser is reading a file that has a particular suffix attached to the filename (such as exe for an application or gz for a compressed zip file), it can use that suffix to determine the file's contents. When a file's suffix matches a suffix configured for a particular helper app or plug-in, the helper app or plug-in is used to play or display the data.

✦ **MIME type:** Because data may come to the browser in a stream or have no suffix, Netscape can use the MIME type attached to the data to determine which plug-in or helper app to use. (MIME stands for Multipurpose Internet Mail Extensions.)

With the Netscape Preferences window open to the Applications page, as described in the previous procedure, you can add your own helper app to automatically handle a particular type of data in your browser. Here's how:

1. Click New.

   A dialog box appears that enables you to add information about the helper app and the data that it can handle.

2. Type in a description of the data, the MIME type (if any), and the file suffixes (if any) on files that contain that type of data.

Note   When you add the suffix, don't put the dot in with it.

3. Select one of the following, depending on the type of helper app you want to add:

- **Navigator** — Click here if you want Netscape Navigator to handle this type of data. Besides HTML, Navigator can also handle various image types (such as GIF, JPEG, and BMP files).

- **Plug-in** — Click here if you want a plug-in that is already installed to handle the data type. Click the down arrow next to the plug-in field to select from the list of available plug-ins.

- **Application** — Click here to choose an application to handle the data type. If the application needs a Terminal window to run, type `xterm -e`, followed by the command line you need to enter. This executes the command in an xterm window, reading in data as needed.

- **Save to Disk** — Click here to be prompted to download the data when you encounter it in your Netscape browser.

- **Unknown: Prompt User** — Click here to be prompted about what to do with data of this type when it is encountered.

Tip   Notice in the window that there are a lot of data types set as Unknown: Prompt User. Many of these entries represent common data types that you might encounter. If you know an application that can handle one of these data types, click it, select Edit, click Application, type in the application to handle the data, and click OK.

4. Click OK when you are done.

Adding plug-ins

There are not that many plug-ins available for use in the version of Netscape Communicator that comes with Red Hat Linux. To see a list of plug-ins that are associated with your Netscape Navigator browser, choose Help ⇨ About Plug-ins. A window similar to the one shown in Figure 9-5 should appear.

It's quite likely that you have only the default plug-in and the Plugger plug-in configured to use with Netscape. There are very few plug-ins available for Netscape in Red Hat Linux. There are probably 20 plug-ins that run in Windows 9x/2000 for every one that runs in Red Hat Linux. Most plug-ins are authored by companies that sell products to create Web content, then give away the plug-ins so anyone can play that content. So, there are probably not a lot of good economic reasons for creating Linux plug-ins (yet).

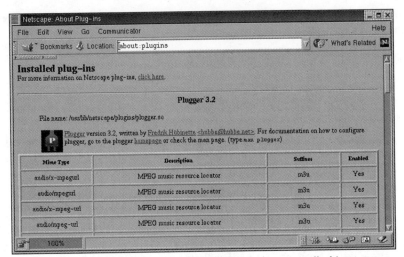

Figure 9-5: About Plug-ins shows which plug-ins are installed in Netscape.

That notwithstanding, there are some plug-ins available for Netscape that do work with your Red Hat Linux system. These are the ones that I could uncover:

✦ **Adobe Acrobat Plug-in** (www.adobe.com) — Displays PDF (Portable Document Format) files from Adobe Systems. (You can search the Adobe site for "Acrobat Linux" to find the current download page.)

✦ **Cult3D Plug-in** (www.cult3d.com) — Displays high-quality, interactive real-time 3D images on the Web. This plug-in is from Cycore Computers. (Click Download to find the plug-in.)

✦ **DjVu Plug-in** (www.djvu.att.com/software/plugin.html) — Displays images in DjVu image compression technology. This plug-in is from AT&T.

✦ **Gig Plug-in** (www.genlogic.com) — Plays data-driven interactive graphic in your Netscape window. This plug-in is from Generic Logic.

✦ **Plugger** (http://fredrik.hubbe.net/plugger.html) — A multimedia plug-in that handles QuickTime, MPEG, MP2, AVI, SGI-movie, Tiff, DL, IFF-anim, MIDI, Soundtracker, AU, WAV, and Commodore 64 audio files by relying on external programs to play the data. This is one of the few plug-ins that is probably already installed on your computer.

✦ **Real Audio** (www.real.com) — Plays Real Audio and Video content. This plug-in is from Real Networks.

✦ **Macromedia Flash Player** (www.macromedia.com/shockwave/download/) — Displays multimedia vector graphics and animation. This plug-in is from Macromedia, Inc.

✦ **Xswallow** (www.csn.ul.ie/~caolan/docs/Xswallow.html) — Allows X window programs to be used as an inline viewer.

✦ **Mpeg TV Plug-in** (www.mpegtv.com) — Play full-screen MPEG video and VCD with this plug-in.

More plug-ins may be added in the future for use with Red Hat Linux. One site you can check is the Netscape Browser Plug-ins site (www.netscape.com/plugins). At that site, most of the plug-ins are for Windows systems, but Linux versions are noted.

When you download a plug-in, follow the instructions that come with the plug-in for installing it. If the plug-in comes in an RPM file, install it as you would any other software package in Red Hat Linux (rpm -i *package* command). Otherwise, you probably just have to copy the plug-in file (a .so file) to either the system plug-in directory (probably /usr/lib/netscape/plugins) or your personal plug-ins directory (probably $HOME/.netscape/plugins). When you restart Netscape, the plug-ins will automatically be picked up from those locations.

When a plug-in is installed, it is automatically assigned to handle data for certain data types. Using the procedure described for adding helper apps, you can add additional data types to be handled by the plug-in.

Setting Netscape preferences

You can change a lot about how Netscape Navigator appears and behaves. Most of those changes can be done from the Preferences window, which can be opened by choosing Edit ⇨ Preferences.

In each category (Navigator, Roaming User, Appearance, Advanced, Composer, and Mail & Newsgroups), there are several pages of preferences that you can change. (Mail & Newsgroups preferences are described later in this chapter.) Click the arrow next to each category to see preference pages that are available with each one.

As you set your personal preferences, changes are made to files in your $HOME/.netscape directory. Don't edit the files there directly! Because they are updated from Netscape menus and windows, any changes you make will be overwritten the next time you change something from the Netscape window.

Setting a home page

Your home page is the Web page that appears in your Netscape Navigator window when you click Home. By default in Red Hat Linux, when Netscape Navigator first starts it displays a "Welcome to Red Hat Linux" page.

Most people choose to set a home page (using a page that includes their favorite news headlines, search engine, or weather report) that they can return to often. To set up your own home page from the Preferences window, click the Navigator category. Click to select the Browser starts with Home Page button. Then type the URL of the location you want to be used for your start page into the Location box and click OK.

Using roaming access

If you use the Internet on someone else's computer, you can utilize the Roaming User feature to have Netscape start and load preferences that are specific to you over the network. Before you can use this feature, your personal information must be configured in a LDAP Directory Server. LDAP stands for Lightweight Directory Access Protocol. (A network administrator can help you set this up.)

To enable roaming access, click the Roaming User category in the Preferences window. Select Enable Roaming Access for this Profile (to turn on the feature), then type in the user name associated with your Roaming Access account. Next, click the down arrow next to Roaming User and select Server Information. On this page, you can select the LDAP Directory server and type the address of the server and your User DN (i.e., your user name). Next, click the Item Selection page and select the user profile items to download.

Changing Netscape's appearance

To alter the appearance of Netscape, change the toolbars that are displayed, as well as the fonts and the colors that are used. The toolbars can appear as Pictures and Text, Pictures Only, or Text Only. To change how toolbars appear, select the Appearance category in the Preferences window, then select one of the types of appearances shown.

Instead of selecting specific fonts, Web pages often just include markup for headings, paragraphs, and characteristics (italic, bold, etc.) that result in the default fonts of the browser being used. You can change the default fonts used in your Netscape window from the Fonts Preferences page. (To get to the Fonts Preferences page, click the down arrow next to the Appearance menu item, then select Fonts.) The default variable width is Times (Adobe) and the default fixed width is Courier (Adobe). You can also change the point size of each font (default is 12 points).

If a Web page does indicate that specific fonts be used, Netscape uses those fonts instead of the defaults. If you want to use your default fonts instead, you can click Use My Default Fonts on the Preferences page. You can also choose to disable Dynamic Fonts by selecting that option. (Dynamic fonts tend to load more slowly because they must be rendered, as opposed to just being displayed.)

The default colors used in Netscape cause the text to be black and the background white. A link that you haven't visited yet is light blue, while one that you have visited is dark blue. Also, links are underlined by default. You can change any of those colors from the Colors Preferences page (click the Appearance down arrow and then select Colors). Click on the color you want to change, then select the new color from the Color Picker window (from swatches or by moving Red, Green, and Blue (RGB) bars to make the color you want).

Changing Netscape's behavior

Several preferences are available to control how Netscape reacts in certain situations (such as encountering some types of data or getting requests to accept cookies). If you have a very slow Internet connection or if you have some concerns about security, you can change some of these settings on the Advanced Preferences page. To do this, select the Advanced category in the Preferences window, and then click the advanced down arrow to get to the Advanced Preferences page. The following are some of the security settings that can be changed:

✦ **Automatically load images and other data types** — Normally this is selected and images that are placed on a Web page will appear. If you have a slow Internet connection, and don't want to wait for images to download, click this item to deselect it. If you want images to be loaded for the current page being displayed, click the Images button that appears on your Navigation Toolbar.

✦ **Enable Java/JavaScript** — With Java and JavaScript, a Web author can add content that is more like a program (forms, calculations, and other features) than like a document (headings, images, and text). Although Java is quite secure (these programs can't just grab your /etc/passwd file), it can access more areas of your computer than the average Web page can. Also, Java tends be a bit slow sometimes. You can disable Java and/or JavaScript from appearing in your Netscape window by deselecting either of those two buttons.

Caution

You will be missing significant amounts of content from some Web pages if you disable Java and JavaScript. Keep in mind, however, that JavaScript can cause significant security risks. Before entering passwords or personal information, be sure that the JavaScript content is coming from a trusted source.

✦ **Enable JavaScript for Mail and News** — JavaScript can also be included in mail and newsgroup messages. You can turn off that feature by deselecting this button.

✦ **Enable Style Sheets** — Style sheets can create a sort of template for Web designers so a whole set of pages can have the same look and feel without having to re-create large amounts of HTML for each page. I suppose there may be some small performance hit interpreting pages that include style sheets (actually, by excluding the images and font changes they include you might be able to speed up the page's download). For the most part, however, I think you should leave this one on.

✦ **Send e-mail address as anonymous FTP password** — When you visit an FTP site (that is, the URL begins with ftp://), that site typically enables a user login named anonymous. By convention, behind the scenes your browser will send the word *anonymous* when you connect to an FTP site. When the FTP site asks for a password, it requests that you enter your e-mail address. By default, this feature is off with Netscape; however, it is probably the courteous thing to do to turn it on.

✦ **Cookies**—*Cookies* are small pieces of information that a Web page can place on your computer in a set area. That information is typically stuff about you, such as profile information about the news items that interest you, your favorite sports teams, or the name of your city (so the page can show you local events and weather).

The advantage of allowing cookies (which is on by default) is that you can tailor the information you get from a Web page, and then the next time you return to it, you can get the same information again (without having to enter it again). The disadvantages of cookies are that the owners of the Web page might misuse that information—or other Web pages might get access to the information (and misuse it).

Most people keep Accept All Cookies on. You can disable cookies, however, by selecting Do Not Accept or Send Cookies. Alternatively, you could limit the effects of cookies by selecting Only Accept Cookies Originating from the Same Server as Page Being Viewed or by selecting Warn Me Before Accepting a Cookie. (The latter option can become quite overwhelming for a page that uses lots of cookies.)

If you do turn off cookies, some e-commerce sites will not work. For example, some Web shopping sites require that cookies be enabled or you will not be able to order from the Web site. Also, many sites use cookies to gather information about users, then sell that information to other vendors.

An interesting exercise is to turn on the "Warn Me Before Accepting a Cookie" feature for a while. With this on, you can get a feel for what sites are saving cookies on your computer and how often they do it. You might want to leave the feature on if you feel uncomfortable about the sites that are keeping track of you. In this way, you can individually reject cookies.

Controlling disk space use by Netscape

If you are like most people who browse the Web, you probably find yourself returning to some of the same pages over and over (even within the same session). Netscape helps to make browsing more efficient by storing recently visited Web pages on the local computer. That way, when you press Forward and Back, you usually don't have to wait again for a page you just visited to download.

The temporary storage area for Web pages is referred to as cache. Web content that has been visited very recently is stored in the memory cache (RAM), while typically larger amounts and less recent content is stored in disk cache (hard disk). You can change the amount of cache space available or clear the current cache areas on the Cache Preferences Page (click the arrow next to Advanced, then click Cache).

If you have lots of disk space available, you may want to increase the amount of Disk Cache (5000K by default) and Memory Cache (3000K by default) available to Netscape. If your system ever runs out of disk space, you can click Clear Disk Cache. You can also empty the Memory Cache by clicking Clear Memory Cache. (Of course, these are only temporary measures. Caches will fill up again as you continue to use Netscape.)

The first time you access a document in Netscape for a particular session, a Web page held in Cache is compared to the actual Web page on the Internet (to see if it has changed). After that, Netscape will continue to use the page stored in Cache throughout the current session. You can change that behavior to have the page checked for changes each time you access it (click Every time) or to always continue to use the locally stored copy of the page (click Never).

Tip   Regardless of how you set the compare document to cache selection, if the content of a Web page needs to be updated, you can simply click Reload.

Using the Mozilla browser

When the Netscape Communicator source code was released to the world as open-source code, Mozilla.org was formed to coordinate the development of the new browser from that code. The result is the Mozilla browser now available with Red Hat Linux, as well as with many other computing platforms.

Because Mozilla comes from the same code that is at the core of Netscape, you may notice that it has many of the same features. At the center of Mozilla, of course, is the Navigator Web browser. Mozilla also includes the following features:

✦ **Mail** — A full-featured program for sending, receiving, and managing e-mail.

✦ **IRC Chat** — An Internet Relay Chat (IRC) window, called ChatZilla, for participating in online, typed conversations.

✦ **Composer** — A Web page (HTML) composer application.

✦ **Address Book** — An application for managing names, addresses, and telephone numbers.

✦ **History List** — A feature for recalling and searching for previously visited Web sites.

You can click directly on the Mozilla icon on the GNOME desktop panel to start Mozilla. Or, you can open Mozilla from the Gnome menu by selecting Programs ➪ Internet ➪ Mozilla. Figure 9-6 shows an example of the Mozilla browser as it displays the Mozilla home page (www.mozilla.org).

Though the development paths of Netscape and Mozilla are diverging, there are still many features that work the same way between the two browsers. For that reason, if there are particular features you want to be able to do with Mozilla, refer to the previous section describing Netscape and try action that is recommended.

A few nice extras are in Mozilla that you won't find in the Netscape Navigator that comes with Red Hat Linux. For example, in Mozilla you can change the theme so that the buttons and other controls have a different look and feel (choose View ➪ Apply Theme; then either select an existing theme, or click Get New Themes to find new ones). Also, Mozilla's Web search interface is very friendly and flexible.

Figure 9-6: Mozilla is the open-source Web browser created from Netscape source code.

Using text-based Web browsers

If you become a Linux administrator or power user, over time you will inevitably find yourself working on a computer from a remote login or where there is no desktop GUI available. At some point while you are in that state, you will probably want to check an HTML file or a Web page. To solve the problem, Red Hat Linux includes several text-based Web browsers.

With text-based Web browsers, any HTML file available from the Web, your local file system, or a computer where you're remotely logged in can be accessed from your shell. There's no need to fire up your GUI or read pages of HTML markup if you just want to take a peek at the contents of a Web page. Though, obviously, you can't display graphics from the shell, text-based browsers do let you call up Web pages, move around with those pages, and follow links to other pages.

Which text-based browser you use is a matter of which you are more comfortable with. Browsers that are available include:

> ✦ links — With links, you can open a file or a URL, and then traverse links from the pages you open. Use search forward (/string) and back (?string) features to find text strings in pages. Use up and down arrows to go forward and back among links. Then press Enter to go to the current link. Use right and left arrows to go forward and back among pages you have visited. Press Esc to see a menu bar of features to select from.

✦ lynx — The lynx browser has a good set of help files that come with it (press the ? key). Step through pages using the space bar. Though can display pages containing frames, it cannot display them in the intended positioning. Use arrow keys to display the selected link (right arrow), go back to the previous document (left arrow), select the previous link (up arrow), and select the next link (down arrow).

✦ w3m — The w3m text-based Web browser can display HTML pages containing text, links, frames, and tables. There are both English and Japanese help files available (press H with w3m running). You can also use w3m to page through an HTML document (for example, cat index.html | w3m). Use Page Up and Page Down to page through a document. Press Enter on a link to go to that link. Search forward and back for text using / and ? keys, respectively.

The w3m command seems the most sophisticated of the browsers mentioned here. It features a nice default font selection, seems to handle frames neatly, and its use of colors also makes it easy to use.

You can start any of these text-based Web browsers by giving it a file name, or if you have an active connection to the network, a Web address. For example, to read the links documentation (which is in HTML format) with a w3m browser, you can type the following from a Terminal window or other shell interface:

```
$ w3m /usr/share/doc/links*/manual*/index.html
```

An all-text version of the Links User Reference Manual is displayed. You can also have started links without giving it a file name (in which case, you will have to open one later from the menu). Or you can give it a URL to a Web page, such as the following:

```
$ w3m www.handsonhistory.com
```

After a page is open, you can begin viewing the page and moving around to links to the page. Start by using the arrow keys to move around and select links. Use Page Up and Page Down keys to page through text.

Communicating with E-mail

If you are using Mozilla or Netscape Navigator to browse the Web, it's a short step to using those same programs to handle your e-mail as well. If you are used to a graphical mail program, Netscape Messenger mail and Mozilla Mail are fairly intuitive and have all the common features for sending, receiving, and managing messages.

If you don't mind text-based interfaces, or if you are a UNIX person who likes to sort, grep, troff, col, and cat your e-mail, there are still plenty of UNIX-like mail tools around. The mail command itself provides an easy interface for plain-text messages sent to other users on your UNIX system or on your LAN. There are also text-based mail applications, such as the mutt command, that let you handle mail attachments.

After covering some e-mail basics, this section will lead you through the steps that allow you to use e-mail with Mozilla Mail. If you are interested in text-based, command-driven mail tools, some of which have been around UNIX systems for many years, descriptions of many of those commands are also in this section.

E-mail basics

E-mail is one of the oldest uses of computer networks — predating the Web by more than 20 years. In fact, e-mail was one of the first applications used to transport information on the Internet, when the Internet consisted of only a few computers.

Today, there are millions of users around the world that have e-mail addresses. Although there are several different styles of e-mail addressing, by far the most popular e-mail address format is the domain style address (used with the Internet and other TCP/IP networks). The e-mail address consists of the user name and the domain name, separated by an at (@) sign. Here is an example:

```
webmaster@handsonhistory.com
```

As someone using e-mail, you need a program (such as Netscape Messenger) that enables you to get your e-mail, manage your e-mail messages, and send messages. Although mail messages were originally only plain text, and still are in most cases today, there are some newer features that let you enhance the kinds of content that you can send and receive. Here are two ways to enhance your mail messages:

✦ **Attachments** — You can attach files of information to your mail messages. These attachments can contain data that you couldn't ordinarily keep in a mail message, such as a binary program, a word processing file, or an image. The recipient of the mail attachment can either save the file to a local hard disk or open it in a program designed to read the attachment.

✦ **HTML** — The same stuff that can be used to create Web pages can be included in mail messages that you create with certain mail clients (including Netscape Messenger). This enables you to change fonts and colors, add backgrounds, insert images, or add most other valid HTML features.

Caution   To people who use text-based mail clients, HTML content can't be interpreted (it shows up as a bunch of markers that overwhelm the text). In general, don't use HTML in messages that are being distributed to a large group of people (such as in a newsgroup).

Depending on the mail program you are using (which is also referred to as a Mail User Agent or MUA), e-mail management features let you direct incoming e-mail into different folders and sort your messages by date, mail sender, or other attributes. E-mail-sending features enable you to reply to messages, forward messages, and draw names from personal address books or directory servers.

Before you get started, you may need to do some setup (unless you are lucky enough to have a system administrator do it for you). Most of the setup you need to do is based on the location and type of e-mail server that you are using. If you are getting your e-mail from an ISP, the ISP probably provides the mail server address, server type, user account information, and passwords that you need to get your mail.

If you are using the local sendmail program (so that your computer is acting as your mail server), the setup you need to do may be much simpler. For example, you may be able to just type the mail command from the shell to see the e-mail for your user account.

Cross-Reference   For information on setting up a mail server, see Chapter 19.

Mozilla Mail client

The Mozilla Mail client program provides a simple interface for using e-mail in Red Hat Linux. You can access the Mozilla Mail window from your Mozilla browser window by choosing Tasks ➪ Mail. Figure 9-7 shows an example of the Mozilla Mail window that is ready to use mail and news.

Note   If you are using Mozilla instead of Netscape, you can choose Communicator ➪ Messenger to open the Netscape Messenger mail program. Because both mail programs came from the same source code, many of the procedures described for using Mozilla Mail will work for Netscape Messenger as well. Setup and preferences, however, are rather different between the two.

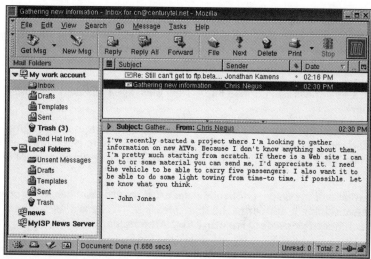

Figure 9-7: Manage your e-mail from the Mozilla Mail window.

Note If an administrator has already set up your e-mail account to work with Mozilla Mail, you can go ahead and start following the descriptions for using it. Otherwise, skip to the "Connecting to the mail server" section to see how to set up Mozilla Mail to send and receive e-mail.

Managing incoming mail

You typically get your incoming e-mail messages by downloading them from a mail server. There are various ways to store and manage those messages. The following is a quick rundown of how to use Mozilla Mail for managing incoming mail:

✦ Your e-mail messages are typically stored on a mail server that is contacted over the network. To download your mail messages from the mail server, click File ➪ Get New Messages (or click Get Msg on the toolbar).

✦ Mail messages are stored in folders under the Mail Folders heading in the left column. There should be a separate heading for each mail account you have. For each mail account, incoming messages are stored (by default) in your Inbox folder. You can create additional folders to better keep track of your mail. Other folders contain messages that have been queued but not yet sent (Unsent Messages), drafts of mail messages that you have set aside for a time (Drafts), templates for creating messages (Templates), messages you have sent (Sent), and messages that you have discarded (Trash).

✦ Messages are sorted by date for the folder you select, in the upper-right corner of the display. You can click on the heading over the messages to sort by subject, sender, or priority instead.

✦ When you select a message, it appears in the lower-right corner of the display.

Composing and sending mail

To compose e-mail messages, you can either start from scratch or respond to an existing e-mail message. The following are some quick descriptions of how to create outgoing mail:

✦ To create a new message, choose File ➪ New Message (or select New Msg from the toolbar).

✦ To reply to a mail message, click on the message on the right side of your screen, and then choose Message ➪ Reply (to reply only to the author of the message) or Message ➪ Reply to All (to reply to everyone listed as copied on the message).

✦ To forward a mail message, choose Message ➪ Forward. You can also forward a message and have it appear in the text (Message ➪ Forward As ➪ Inline) or as an attachment (Message ➪ Forward As ➪ Attachment).

In each case of outgoing mail, a mail Compose window appears, as shown in Figure 9-8, in which you compose your e-mail message.

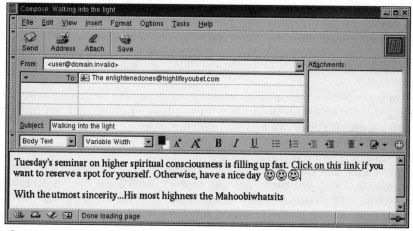

Figure 9-8: Compose messages in HTML or plain-text formats in the Compose window.

As you compose your message in the Compose window, you can:

✦ Add e-mail addresses from your personal address book (or from one of several different directory servers) by choosing Options ➪ Select Addresses. A list of your stored addresses appears for you to choose from. Click Collected Addresses to see a list of addresses that have been collected from e-mail messages you have received.

✦ Add attachments to the message (such as a word processing file, image, or executable program) by choosing File ➪ Attach File. After that, you can select a file from your file system to attach. (You can also choose File ➪ Attach Web Page to choose the URL of a Web page that you want to attach.)

✦ Add certificates or view security information about your mail message by clicking the Security button. In the window that appears, you can add certificates (used to verify your identify) or view general security information about the message.

You can have your messages be in plain text or rich text (HTML) formats. From the Compose window, choose Options ➪ Format and select one of the following:

✦ **Auto-Detect** — Use the default type of message.

✦ **Plain Text Only** — Only text and no HTML markup.

✦ **Rich Text (HTML) Only** — The whole text in HTML.

✦ **Plain and Rich (HTML) Text** — A mixture of plain text and HTML.

If you are using HTML markup, you can choose View ⇨ Show/Hide ⇨ Formatting Toolbar. This displays a toolbar that lets you add markup to your message. You can select different paragraph styles, font types, and point sizes of text, or add bold, italic, or underline. You can also insert links, anchors, images, lines, and tables. There is even a selection for adding emoticons (such smile, frown, and wink faces).

When you are finished composing the message, click Send to send the message. If you prefer, you can queue the message to be sent later by choosing File ⇨ Send Later. (Send Later is useful if you have a dial-up connection to the network and you are not currently online.)

Tip   If you decide that you want to quit and finish the e-mail message later, you can choose File ⇨ Save As ⇨ Draft. Then click on the X in the upper right corner to close the window. When you are ready to resume work on the message, click the Draft folder in the Mozilla Mail window and double-click the message.

Connecting to the mail server

You need to identify information about yourself and your mail server before you can download or send your mail messages. If you are getting your mail from an ISP or from your place of business, you should get some information when you get your user account. There is, however, other information that you need to add about yourself:

✦ **E-mail address** — The *name@domain* address that is assigned to you.

✦ **Name** — The name that appears on the messages you send (for example, John Smith).

✦ **Incoming Mail Server** — The name or IP address of the mail server from which you get your messages. You also need to know what type of server it is (POP or IMAP). POP servers require a POP login and password. POP stands for Post Office Protocol. IMAP stands for Internet Message Protocol.

✦ **Outgoing Mail Server** — If there is a different outgoing mail server, you will need the name or IP address of that server. Likewise, you will probably need login and password information to send mail on that server. You can choose to use Secure Socket Layer (SSL) to protect your outgoing messages (if it is supported by the server).

There are preferences associated with how your e-mail is downloaded and sent that you can set as well. You can decide how often you want to download messages (you can set this to be done automatically at certain intervals). Here is a procedure for adding information about your mail server to your Mozilla Mail interface:

1. From the Mozilla Mail window, choose File ⇨ New ⇨ Account.

   The Account Wizard window appears.

2. Click ISP or Email Provider and select Next.

   An identity window appears.

3. Type your name into the Your Name box and e-mail address into the Email Address box; then click Next.

The name should be as you would want it to appear to people receiving your email messages. The address should be "@" separated address (for example, `cn@handsonhistory.com`).

4. Select whether it is a POP or IMAP server and type in the name of the incoming mail server (that is, where you get your mail) and click Next to continue. By convention, the server name often has the word mail in it, such as `mail.example.net.`

5. Type your user name into the User Name box and then click Next.

This name should be given to you by your ISP. It is often the same as the first part of your email address (the part before the @ sign). However, it may be different.

6. Type any name that you want to associate with this account into the Account Name box and click Next.

All the information you just entered is then displayed.

7. If the information is correct, click Finish.

The new mail account appears in the Mozilla Mail main window under the left-hand Mail Folders column.

8. Click on the new account name in the Mail Folders column.

Options appear to the right of that column.

9. Click View Settings for This Account.

The Account Settings window appears. From there you can set lots of options by selecting each of the following headings under the account: Account Settings, Server Settings, Copies and Folders, Addressing, and Disk Space. Here's what you might want change under each of those headings:

- Account Settings — You can add a Reply-to address if you want recipients of your mail message to respond to you at a different address. You can also identify your Organization and attach a signature file (for signing off at the end of your messages).

- Server Settings — The server settings let you set how and when your e-mail messages are downloaded. If you don't want messages downloaded each time you open the Mail window and checked every 10 minutes (the default), change these settings.

- Copies and Folders — Copies of the messages you send are automatically placed in your Sent folder. Drafts (messages you started and want to get back to later) and Templates (used to add form to a message) are stored in their respective folders. You can change those setting, or add recipients of blind carbon copies of every message you sent, under this heading.

- Addressing — You can indicate that a particular LDAP server be used to look-up mail addresses.

- Disk Space — By default, there is no maximum size of e-mail message that someone can send you. Under this heading, you can click the Do Not Download... box to limit the size of messages you receive to 50k. Or you can change the maximum size to any number you are comfortable with.

10. Click OK before leaving the page associated with an Account Setting to save the changes you make. Mozilla Mail should now be ready to send mail to and receive mail from your mail servers. To actually download messages, choose File ➪ Get New Messages (or select Get Msg on the toolbar). You have to enter your incoming mail user password at least the first time you ask for mail. If you set the option to save that password, you won't have to enter it again.

Text-based mail programs

There are many text-based mail programs for reading, sending, and working with your mail. Many of these programs have been around for a long time, so they are full of features and have been well debugged. As a group, however, they are not very intuitive. The following sections describe some text-based commands.

Tip

Most of these programs use the value of your $MAIL environment variable as your local mailbox. Usually, that location is /var/spool/mail/*user*, where *user* is your user name. To set your $MAIL so that it points to your Netscape mailbox (so you can use either Netscape Messenger or a text-based mail program), add the following line to one of your startup files:

```
export MAIL=$HOME/nsmail/Inbox
```

If you usually use Netscape for mail, you can set this variable temporarily to try out some of these mail programs. You can do the same thing with your Mozilla Mail Inbox, though it's a bit trickier to locate. The location of that Inbox is something like the following: $HOME/.mozilla/default/*/Mail/*servername*. (Your actual mailbox name varies depending on your mail server name.)

Mail readers and managers

Mail readers described below are text-based and use the entire screen. Although some features are different, menu bars show available options right on the screen.

Mutt mail reader

Note

To use the mutt mail reader you must have the mutt software package installed.

The mutt command is a text-based, full-screen mail user agent for reading and sending e-mail. The interface is quick and efficient. Type mutt to start the mail program. Move arrow keys up and down to select from your listed messages. Press Enter to see a mail message and type i to return to the Main menu.

The menu bar indicates how to mark messages for deletion or undelete them, save messages to a directory, or reply to a message. Type m to compose a new message and it opens your default editor (for me, vi) to create the message. If you want to read your mail without having your fingers leave your keyboard, mutt is a nice choice. (It even handles attachments!)

Pine mail reader

Note   To use the pine mail reader you must have the pine software package installed.

The pine mail reader is another full-screen mail reader, but it offers many more features than does mutt. With pine, you can manage multiple mail folders. You can also manage newsgroup messages, as well as mail messages. As text-based applications go, pine is quite easy to use. It was developed by a group at the University of Washington for use by students on campus, but has become widely used in UNIX and Linux environments.

Start this mail program by typing pine. The following menu is displayed, from which you can make a selection by typing the associated letter or using up and down arrows and pressing Enter:

```
?   HELP              Get help using Pine
C   COMPOSE MESSAGE   Compose and send a message
I   MESSAGE INDEX     View messages in current folder
L   FOLDER LIST       Select a folder to view
A   ADDRESS BOOK      Update address book
S   SETUP             Configure Pine Options
Q   QUIT              Leave the Pine program
```

To read your e-mail, select either I or L. Commands are listed along the bottom of the screen and change to suit the content you are viewing. Left (←) and right (→) arrow keys let you step backward and forward among the pine screens.

Elm mail reader

This is yet another text-based and form-based mail reader. When you first start elm, it sets up several mail directories and files in your home directory. Then it opens a very basic interface to your incoming mailbox (as set by the $MAIL variable).

On the Mailbox screen, elm identifies your mailbox and shows the headings for the first page of mail messages. Move up and down among the messages with arrow keys (or with j and k keys, as in the vi editor). Press Enter to open the current mail message and press i to return to the index. Other commands are shown at the bottom of the screen.

Mail reader

The `mail` command was the first mail reader for UNIX. It is text-based, but not screen-oriented. Type `mail` and you will see the messages in your mailbox. Because mail is not screen-oriented, you just get a prompt after message headings are displayed—you are expected to know what to do next. Type ? to see which commands are available.

While in mail, type h to see your mail headings again. Simply type a message number to see the message. Type d# (replacing # with a message number) to delete a message. To create a new message, type m. To respond to a message, type r# (replacing # with the number to respond to).

Printmail reader

Though printmail isn't strictly a mail reader, it can be used as a part of managing your mail messages. The `printmail` command formats the mail in any file you give it (either your default mailbox or a saved mail message file) and formats the mail in a nicer form for printing. A command such as `printmail | lpr` will format the contents of your mailbox and output it to the formatted messages to the printer (printmail assumes plain-text files).

Incoming mail checkers

There are a couple of commands that aren't e-mail readers or composers. However, these programs let you quickly check whether you have any messages in your mailbox. The following are two such programs:

✦ **messages**—Does a quick count of the messages in your mailbox.

✦ **newmail**—Monitors mailboxes at intervals you choose (every so many seconds) and sends a message to your Terminal window when new mail arrives.

Commands for handling attachments

The following commands are used for handling data so that it can be included in a mail message as an attachment. Attachments in UNIX systems were originally handled by uuencode format. Now most mail attachments are handled using MIME format with various encoding.

Note   Because newer graphical mail programs, such as Mozilla Mail and Netscape Messenger, can handle attachments automatically, it is inefficient to go through the trouble of using most of these commands.

✦ uuencode—Used to convert a binary file into a form that allows it to be transmitted in a mail message. The uuencode command reads a file and writes it to another encoded file. The user can then insert that file into a mail message and send it to the recipient. Here is an example of the uuencode command:

```
cat file1 | uuencode myfile > myfile.uu
```

In this example, the contents of the file called file1 are encoded and the output is sent to the `myfile.uu` command. When the file is later decoded (see uudecode), the new file is called myfile.

✦ `uudecode` — When a user receives a mail message that includes a uuencoded file, the user saves that part of the message to a new file and runs `uudecode` on it. This returns the file to its original form. Here is an example of decoding a message that was created using the example shown in `uuencode` above.

```
cat myfile.uu |uudecode
```

In this example, the result is a decoded file called myfile.

✦ `metasend` — Provides a simple interface for sending binary data or other nontext file as an e-mail message. Type `metasend` as follows:

```
metasend
```

The program prompts you for address information and the location of the file to send.

✦ `mailto` — Like `metasend`, this command is used to send e-mail that includes MIME content. Along with the mailing address, you need to indicate the type of content being sent (i.e., the MIME type) and the type of encoding that you want to use. Supported encoding includes 7-bit ASCII, base64 (recommended), quoted-printable encoding, or uuencode formats. Here is an example of a simple `mailto` command:

```
mailto jim bill -s "Hi Jim and Bill" -c frank
```

In this example, e-mail is sent to the users named `jim` and `bill`. The subject of the message is `"Hi Jim and Bill"` and a carbon copy of the message is sent to `frank`. At this point, you type in the content of the message. When you are done, type a dot (.) on a line by itself to send the message.

A couple of other commands that you might want to look at are the `mimecode` command (to convert data to or from MIME format), `metamail` (to display nontext content of a mail message in MIME format), and `splitmail` (to divide a large mail message into smaller MIME messages).

Participating in Newsgroups

Usenet news is another feature that has been around almost as long as the Internet. Using a newsreader, and even many regular mail readers, you can select from literally thousands of topics and participate in discussions on those topics. To participate, you simply read the messages people have posted to the group, respond to those that you have something to say about, and send your own messages to start a discussion yourself.

To get started, you basically need a newsreader and access to a news server computer. As with e-mail, Mozilla uses Mozilla Mail and Netscape Navigator uses the Messenger mail program to let you participate in newsgroups. Traditional UNIX-style newsreaders include `trn` and `tin`, which are full-screen, text-based newsreaders.

Tip   If you have never used a newsgroup before, check out the `news.announce.newusers` newsgroup. It's there to answer questions from new users.

Netscape Messenger for newsgroups

Before you can begin using news groups you need to identify the news server you are using, identify yourself, and choose the newsgroups you want to access.

Connecting to the news server

To begin using newsgroups, you need to open the Netscape Preferences window and add the news server's name and port number as follows:

1. From the Messenger window, choose Edit ⇨ Preferences to bring up the Netscape Preferences window.

2. In the Netscape Preferences window, click the down-arrow next to Mail & Newsgroups, then select Newsgroups Servers.

3. On the Newsgroup and Server page that appears, click Add.

   A pop-up window appears.

4. Type the name of your news server and, if necessary, the port number for news on that server.

   (The default news port is 119. You can obtain the name of the news server from your ISP or your system administrator at work. By convention, the name often has "news" or "nw" at the beginning.)

5. You can select to use encrypted (Secure Socket Layer) connections or to always use a name and password with the connection to your news server. (Both are probably unnecessary.)

6. Click OK to accept the news server entry.

7. Other selections on the Newsgroups Servers page let you select a server and set it as the default or prompt you if there are more than a certain number of newsgroup messages downloaded to you (500 by default). Finally, you can choose which directory to use to hold your newsgroup messages.

8. Click OK.

   If your news server was properly identified and your connection to that server is working, you can open the Netscape Messenger window to begin participation in newsgroups. Connection to the news server occurs when you select news in the Messenger window. You need to have a Netscape Messenger mail account configured if you want to be able to post messages to the newsgroups.

Using newsgroups

To participate in newsgroups, you need to choose the ones that interest you from a list of available newsgroups. You can then subscribe to your favorite newsgroups so that they are available every time you use Netscape Messenger.

Subscribing to newsgroups

The following procedure describes how to subscribe to a newsgroup in Netscape Messenger.

1. Open Netscape Messenger (Communicator ➪ Messenger from the Netscape browser window).

2. Right-click on the news server name in the left column.

3. In the menu that appears, click Subscribe to Newsgroups.

   A newsgroup subscription window appears, as shown in Figure 9-9.

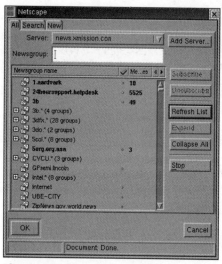

Figure 9-9: Choose from thousands of newsgroups in the newsgroup subscription window in Netscape Messenger.

What appears (after a few minutes or more) in the subscription list are top-level newsgroup names. Newsgroups are organized in a hierarchy, similar to Internet domain names — levels are separated by dots (although newsgroup names start at the left and go down to the right).

4. Click the plus sign next to a category to see which groups in that category interest you.

5. When you see a newsgroup that interests you, click it and select Subscribe.

6. Click OK.

   The subscribed newsgroup appears in your Messenger window under the name of the news server.

7. Click the newsgroup in Messenger.

   Recent messages from that newsgroup are downloaded to your Messenger window.

Reading newsgroup messages

Reading newsgroup messages is similar to reading mail messages. You simply click on a message that interests you or move to it using the up and down arrow keys. The message will appear in the message pane in the lower-right corner of the Messenger window.

The concept of threads should be mentioned here: When someone posts a message to a newsgroup, usually one or more people respond to it. Because it is useful to read messages and responses together, these messages are grouped together in *threads*. A plus (+) next to a message indicates that there are responses to that message. Click the plus to see the available threads. Threads make it easy to see a group of messages on a topic that interests you or to skip over a topic that doesn't.

The Pan newsreader

Note   You can get a recent version of the Pan news reader from the PAN site: `http://pan.rebelbase.com`. An rpm package is probably available.

The Pan news reader is a graphical application for reading, managing, and interacting with newsgroups. It is particularly adept at displaying attached pictures and downloading binaries. The interface is very intuitive and easy to use.

Pan is designed for the Gnome desktop. If you are running another desktop environment, however, you can still use Pan as long as you have the gnome-libs software package installed. After that, Pan works fine on KDE, Window Maker, AfterStep, or a variety of other desktop environments.

To open the Pan news reader from the Gnome desktop menu, choose Programs ➪ Internet ➪ Pan. The first time you start Pan, the Pan wizard runs to allow you to configure the news reader. Have your e-mail address and your news server's ready. When the wizard is done, you can download the list of newsgroups available from your news server.

The trn newsreader

Note The trn newsreader was recently removed from the Red Hat Linux distribution. You can download a copy of trn from the following Web site: `http://sourceforge.net/projects/trn`.

The `trn` command is a full-screen, text-based newsreader. It was based on the original read news program called `rn`. The `trn` command added thread support to `rn` and thus named itself `trn`.

The `trn` command finds the news server from listings in `/usr/lib/trn/server`. You could also set the `NNTPSERVER` variable to identify your server. Running `trn` lets you select the groups to subscribe to. All newsgroups are stored in your `$HOME/.newsrc` file.

The interface to `trn` is managed using arrow keys, letters, and numbers to select the newsgroups and messages that you want to read and respond to. Because it is a plain-text application, `trn` doesn't handle HTML messages well (you can see the markup and the text in the messages).

The tin newsreader

Note The tin newsreader was recently removed from the Red Hat Linux distribution. You can download a copy of tin from the following Web site: `http://www.tin.org`.

The `tin` command is another text-based newsreader. With `tin`, you can read news from a local news directory (`/var/spool/news`) or from a remote Network News Transport Protocol (NNTP) server. The `tin` display operates at several different levels. First, the group selection level, then the group level, followed by the thread level, and then the article. You go through the levels to reach articles that interest you.

As with `trn`, a list of newsgroups is stored in the `$HOME/.newsrc` file. The news server is specified in the `$HOME/.tin/newsrctable` file. Or you can specify the server on the command line using the `-g server` option.

Participating in AOL Instant Messaging with Gaim

Gaim is an AOL Instant Messaging client program that runs in Linux. Because it is based on AOL's Open IM architecture (`http://aim.aol.com/openim`), it has the same messaging features you get from AOL's own messaging application.

To start Gaim from a Gnome desktop menu, choose Programs ➪ Internet ➪ Gaim. Figure 9-10 contains an example of the Gaim window:

Figure 9-10: Access your AOL Instant Messaging using GAIM.

From the main Gaim window, you have the following options:

- ✦ **Cancel**—Exit from Gaim.

- ✦ **Accounts**—Add screen names, passwords, and options associated with your AOL Instant Messaging accounts.

- ✦ **Signon**—Sign on to AOL Instant Messaging by using your selected screen name.

- ✦ **Register**—Open the Web site that lets you register for an AOL Instant Messaging account.

- ✦ **Options**—Set options associated with your AOL Instant Messaging and Chat windows.

- ✦ **Plug-ins**—Load plug-ins that can perform special functions, such as spell checking and auto-reconnection.

Besides AOL IM protocols, Gaim supports other messaging protocols, including instant messaging protocols from Yahoo!, the Microsoft Network, ICQ, and IRC.

Using Remote Login, Copy, and Execution

This section describes some features for allowing users to transparently use resources across a network. They are the `telnet`, `ssh`, `ftp`, `rlogin`, `rcp`, and `rsh` commands.

Because using these commands can represent significant security risks, Red Hat Linux is not configured to allow any of these commands to connect to it by default. For information on how to turn on these services on a Red Hat Linux server, refer to Chapter 14 (Computer Security Issues) and Appendix C (Running Network Services).

There is a nice set of commands available with Red Hat Linux for moving information between computers on a network—particularly between trusted computers. Two of the commands described in this section that are generally available are remote login and file transfer programs: `telnet` and `ftp`, respectively.

Other commands described in this section are more specific to Red Hat Linux and other UNIX systems, but provide simplified ways of copying files, logging in, and executing commands among trusted systems: `rcp`, `rlogin`, and `rsh`, respectively. Also, a more secure tool for remote login called `ssh` has recently been added to the Red Hat Linux distribution. The `ssh` command can be used for remote execution as well.

Using telnet for remote login

Telnet is a service provided by many different types of computer systems to enable remote users to log in to their machines over TCP/IP networks. The `telnet` command is the client program that you use to do the remote login. The most common way to use telnet is with a hostname. The following is a typical telnet session:

```
$ telnet maple
Trying 10.0.0.11 ...
Connected to maple (10.0.0.11).
Escape character is '^]'.
Red Hat Linux release 7.2
Kernel 2.4.6-3.1 on an i686
login: mike
Password:
Last login: Mon Dec 18 13:15:57 from pine
[mike@maple mike]$
```

This example shows what happens when the `telnet` command is used to log in from a computer named pine to a computer named maple by typing `telnet maple`. My computer tries to connect to the telnet port on maple (IP address 10.0.0.11). Because maple is also a Red Hat Linux computer, once the connection is established, I see the standard `login: prompt`. I type the user name (mike) and the password when prompted. When the login and password are accepted, I see the shell prompt for the user named mike.

The telnet service is available by default on Red Hat Linux systems. So, if you can reach the Linux system from your LAN or Internet connection, you can try to log in using telnet. (Of course, you need the user name and password to get past the login prompts.) Other remote computer systems may not have the telnet service on by default. If you try to telnet to your Windows 95 system, you will probably get a Connection Refused message.

Here are a few useful options you can use with telnet:

✦ `-a` — Automatic login. With this option, your computer attempts to log in to the remote computer using your local user name. In other words, if you are logged into your computer as `mike` and you use telnet to log in to a remote computer, the remote computer assumes that you want to log in as `mike`. So it simply prompts you for `mike`'s password.

✦ `-l user` — User name. This option is similar to the `-a` option, except that instead of using your current user name, you can ask to log in using any user name you choose.

✦ `-r` — Rlogin-style interface. This option lets you use tilde (~) options. For example, to disconnect while in rlogin mode, type ~. (tilde+dot), or to suspend the telnet session, type ~^z (tilde+Ctrl+z). Only use ~. if your remote shell is hung (exit is a better way to quit normally). If you use ~^z to temporarily suspend your telnet session, you are returned to your local system shell. To get back to the suspended session, type `fg` to put telnet back in the foreground. See the description of rlogin later in this chapter for more features you can use in rlogin mode.

Another way to use telnet is in command mode. Instead of using a hostname, simply type the word `telnet`. You will see a telnet prompt as follows:

```
$ telnet
telnet>
```

At this point, there are several commands available to you. You are not yet connected to a remote host. To open a login session to a remote computer from the telnet prompt (for example, to a computer named `maple`), type:

```
telnet> open maple
```

After you do connect to a remote computer, you can return to the telnet session at any time by typing `Ctrl+]`. Here are other options you can use during your telnet session:

✦ `?` — Print help information.

✦ `!` — Escape to the shell.

✦ `close` — If you have an open connection, type `close` to close it.

✦ `display` — Shows the operating parameters that are in effect.

✦ `logout` — Logs you off any remote connection in this session and closes the connection.

✦ `mode` — Tries to enter line mode or character mode. (Type `mode ?` to see other options that go with the mode option.)

◆ quit — Close telnet and exit.

◆ z — Suspend the current telnet session.

If you suspend a telnet session or escape to the shell, you can return to your telnet session by typing fg.

Copying files with FTP

Like telnet, FTP is a protocol that is available on many different operating systems. Archives of files on the Internet are stored on what are called FTP servers. To connect to those servers from Red Hat Linux, you can either type the URL of that server into a Web browser or you can use the ftp command or graphical ftp windows such as gFTP.

Using the ftp command

The ftp command is available on Red Hat Linux, as well as every other Linux and UNIX system, for copying files to and from FTP servers. Like telnet, FTP has a command mode or you (more typically) can use it to connect directly to a remote computer. For example:

```
$ ftp maple
Connected to maple.
220 maple FTP server (Version wu-2.6.1-18) ready.
530 Please login with USER and PASS.
Name (maple:mike): jake
331 Password required for jake.
Password: *********
230 User jake logged in.
Remote system type is UNIX.
Using binary mode to transfer files.
ftp>
```

In this example, ftp connects to a computer called maple (ftp maple). When I was prompted for a name, it assumed that I was going to use my current login name on maple (maple:mike). I could have pressed Enter to use the name mike, but instead I logged in as jake and typed the password when prompted. The password was accepted and, after some information was printed, I was given an ftp> prompt.

Unlike telnet, instead of being in a regular UNIX shell after I logged in with FTP, I was placed in FTP command mode. Command mode with FTP includes a whole lot of commands for moving around the remote file system and for copying files (which is its main job).

FTP directory commands

To get your bearings and move around the remote file system, you could use some of the following commands from the ftp> prompt. The commands are used to work with both the remote and local directories associated with the FTP connection.

✦ `pwd`—Shows the name of the current directory on the remote system.

✦ `ls`—Lists the contents of the current remote directory using the UNIX `ls` command. You can use any valid `ls` options with this command.

✦ `dir`—Same as `ls`.

✦ `cd`—Use the `cd` command to move to the directory named.

✦ `cdup`—Moves up one directory in the file system.

✦ `lcd`—Lists the name of the current local directory.

If you want to make changes to any of the remote files or directories, use the following commands:

✦ `mkdir`—Creates a directory on the remote system.

✦ `rename`—Renames a file or directory on the remote system.

✦ `rmdir`—Removes a remote directory.

✦ `delete`—Removes a remote file.

✦ `mdelete`—Removes multiple remote files.

FTP file copying commands

Before you copy files between the remote and local systems, consider the type of transfer you want to do. The two types of transfer modes are:

✦ binary—For transferring binary files (such as data files and executable commands). This is also referred to as an image transfer.

✦ ascii—For transferring plain-text files.

The Linux `ftp` command seems to set the default to binary when you start FTP. Binary seems to work well for either binary or text files. However, binary transfers may not work transferring ascii files from non-UNIX systems. If you transfer an executable file in ascii mode, the file may not work (that is, run as a command) when you try to run it on your local system.

Most file copying is done with the `get` and `put` commands. Likewise, you can use the `mget` and `mput` commands to transfer multiple files at once. Here are descriptions of those commands:

✦ `get` *file*—Copies a file from the current directory on the remote file system and copies it to the current directory on the local file system. You can use a full path along with the filename. You can also specify the path to the local file where the remote file will be placed. Here are some examples:

```
get route
get /tmp/options /home/mike/op
get /tmp/sting
```

The first example takes the file `route` from the current remote directory and copies it to the current local directory. The second example copies the remote file `/tmp/options` and copies it to the local file `/home/mike/op`. The third example copies the file `/tmp/sting` from the remote system to the file `/tmp/sting` on the local system (not to the current local directory).

✦ `put` *`file`*—Copies a file from the current local directory to the current remote directory. The usage of this command is essentially the same as the `get` command, except that files are copied from the local to the remote system.

> **Note** Anonymous FTP sites (described later) usually let you copy files *from* them, but not *to* them. If they do allow you to put files on their server, it will usually be in a restricted area.

✦ `mget` *`file . . .`*—This command lets you get multiple files at once. You can specify multiple files either individually or by using metacharacters (such as the asterisk). FTP prompts you for each file to make sure you want to copy it.

✦ `mput` *`file . . .`*—This command lets you put multiple files on the remote computer. Like `mget`, `mput` prompts you before transferring each file.

FTP Exiting Commands

While a connection is open to a remote computer, you can use several commands to either temporarily or permanently exit from that connection. Here are some useful commands:

✦ `!`—This temporarily exits you to the local shell. After you have done what you need to do, type `exit` to return to your FTP session. You can also use this command to run other local commands. For example, you can type `!pwd` to see what the current directory is on the local system, `!uname -a` to remind yourself of your local system name, or `!ls -l` to see the contents of your current directory. The last example is useful if you want to make sure a file copy succeeded.

✦ `close`—Closes the current connection.

✦ `bye`—Closes the connection and exits the `ftp` command.

When you exit FTP, you see information about how many files you transferred and how much data was sent during those transfers.

Using the gFTP window

If you prefer a more graphical interface for accessing FTP servers, you can use the gFTP window. You can open a gFTP window by typing `gftp` or by choosing Programs ➪ Internet ➪ gFTP from the main menu on the GNOME desktop. An example of the gFTP window is shown in Figure 9-11.

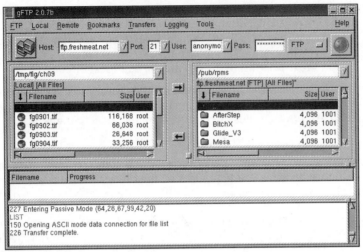

Figure 9-11: View local and remote files simultaneously from the gFTP window.

Unlike the `ftp` command, the gFTP window lets you simultaneously see the contents of the current remote and local directories. To transfer a file from one side to the other, simply double-click it or drag-and-drop it to the other pane. (Normally, you will just be copying files from FTP sites, unless a site provides you with permission to write to it.)

Follow this procedure to connect to an FTP site:

1. Type the name of the FTP server to which you want to connect (for example, `ftp.freshmeat.net`) into the Host box.

2. Type the port number on the ftp server (you can leave this blank to use the default port number 21).

3. Type the user name that will be used to log in to the FTP server. Type `anonymous` if you don't have a specific user name and the server is accessible to the public.

4. Type the password for the user name you entered. The convention with FTP servers is to use your e-mail address as the password.

5. Click the icon displaying two little monitors to connect to the FTP site.

   If you entered the information correctly, the bottom pane on the window should show that the transfer was complete and the right pane should show the contents of the current directory of the FTP site. Here are some actions you can take once you are connected:

   • **Move around.** Double-click a directory to move into that directory or the two dots (. .) to move up a directory level. You can do this on both the remote and local directories.

- **Drag-and-drop files.** You can drag-and-drop files from the FTP site on to the left pane (representing your current local directory).

- **Save this site.** If you want to return to this site later, choose Bookmarks ⇨ Add Bookmark. A pop-up window lets you name this site for the bookmarks list. After you do, you can select that entry from the list at a later date to connect to that site. The gFTP window will have stored not only the hostname, but also the port, user name, and password. So you are just one click away from connecting.

A nice feature of gFTP is that it stores log information. Choose Logging ⇨ View Log. A window appears showing you the conversations that have taken place between your computer and each FTP site. You can look at these messages to figure out what is wrong if you are unable to connect to a site or to remember where you have been and what you have done on an FTP site.

Using ssh for remote login/remote execution

Although the `telnet` and `rlogin` login commands and `rsh` remote execution command have been around much longer, the `ssh` command is quickly becoming the preferred tool for remote logins and executions. The reason is that `ssh` provides encrypted communication so that it can be used securely over insecure, public networks between hosts that are not known to each other.

In the following example, `ssh` is being used to log in to a computer named maple. Because no user is specified, `ssh` tries to log in as the current user (which is the root user in this case).

```
# ssh maple
mike@pine's password:
```

If you wanted to log in as a different user, you could use the `-l` option. For example, to log in to the computer named maple as the user named jake, you could type the following:

```
# ssh -l jake maple
jake@pine's password:
```

The `ssh` command can also be used to execute a command on the remote computer. For example, if you wanted to monitor the messages file on a remote computer for a minute, you could type the following command:

```
# ssh maple "tail -f /var/log/messages"
password:
```

After you typed the password in the above case, the last several lines of the `/var/log/messages` file on the remote computer would be displayed. As messages were received, they would continue to be displayed until you decided to exit (type Ctrl+D).

Note   You can find out more about the ssh command from the SSH Web site (www. ssh.com).

Using the "r" commands: rlogin, rcp, and rsh

The rlogin, rcp, and rsh commands all use the same underlying security mechanism to enable remote login, remote file copy, and remote execution, respectively, among computers. If you use these commands, you will find that they are a quick and convenient way of exchanging information among a group of trusted computers.

Caution   The default security mechanism used by the "r" commands is not very secure. Don't use these commands if your computers protect national secrets.

I recommend using these commands — and the security arrangement I'm about to describe — between computers within an organization in which the other computers are trusted and there are no connections to the outside world. They provide a great way for people who work on multiple computers to easily exchange data and execute commands among those computers.

One of the main problems with the "r" commands is that the underlying security mechanism simply believes that you are who you say you are. For example, suppose permission is open to allow joe from the computer named maple to run any program as though he were the local user named joe. Any computer with access to your network could claim to be that computer and user to gain access to your computer. Even the basic password mechanism is bypassed.

Setting up rhosts security

Let's say you have a private network at your place of business and you want your employees to be able to draw on resources from many of those computers. You give each user a login account to several different computers (using the same login name on each). For a user to be able to freely exchange information among the computers, you or the user can simply change a configuration file to enable the user to run the rlogin, rcp, and rsh commands freely between the computers.

Caution   The reason the security measures described here are not terribly secure is that they rely on the computer on the networks to supply user names. There is no guarantee that the names supplied are real user names. For that reason, you should use this method only among trusted machines.

An individual user can create a .rhosts file in the user's home directory. That file can contain a list of host computers on which the user has accounts of the same name. For example, a user named mike on the machine named pine also has a user login (of the same name) on computers named maple, spruce, and fig. He adds the following entries to a .rhosts file that looks like the following in the home directory on each computer:

```
maple
spruce
fig
pine
```

After the files are added, `mike` can use the `rlogin`, `rsh`, and `rcp` commands between the four computers without having to type a password. For each command, `mike` will have permission to copy files, access files and directories, and execute programs with the permission available on the computer being accessed.

Instead of using the `.rhosts` files, a system administrator can add similar contents to the `/etc/hosts.equiv` file. A `/etc/hosts.equiv` file that had those four computer names in it would enable any users with the same user name on those computers to exchange information between them without entering a password. Besides hostnames, the `/etc/hosts.equiv` file can limit the user names that can use "r" commands without passwords. Here's an example of a `/etc/hosts.equiv` file:

```
maple mike sally bill sheree
spruce mike sally
fig
pine
```

In this example, users with the same names on `fig` and `pine` can exchange information freely. However, only `mike`, `sally`, `bill`, and `sheree` can freely exchange information on `maple`, whereas `mike` and `sally` can exchange information on `spruce`. If users aren't included in the `hosts.equiv` file, they can still create their own `.rhosts` file. You can also add a plus (+) to an entry to indicate that access permission should be added for that entry.

Note   Although the .rhosts feature is on by default, a host computer can turn it off by running rlogin's server daemon (`rlogind`) with the `-l` option (to prevent the use of an individual's .rhosts file) or the `-L` option (which prevents `/etc/hosts.equiv` from being read).

Here are some commands that you could run between trusted hosts that were set up as described above:

```
$ rlogin maple
$ rcp file1 spruce:/home/mike
$ rsh fig df
```

The user named `mike` from the computer name `pine` runs the commands shown. With the first command, `mike` is logged in immediately as `mike` to the computer named `maple` (no password is necessary). Next, the `rcp` command copies the file1 file to the `/home/mike` directory on `spruce`. In the last example, the remote execution command (`rsh`) runs the `df` command and the output (a disk space listing from `fig`) appears on his local screen.

Note Other security measures can be used instead of the .rhosts method. One of the most popular methods is called Kerberos. With Kerberos, each user sets up a .klogin file that lists Kerberos principal names. A user trying to gain access to a remote user account is authenticated to a principal named in the user's .klogin file before access is allowed.

Using rlogin for remote logins

The `rlogin` command is not as widely available as telnet for logging in to remote computers. However, it does offer some features that make it easier to use among Red Hat Linux and other UNIX systems. In particular, `rlogin` can be set up to do no-password logins (described in the previous section) and it has some tilde (~) escape features that you can use to escape from the login session.

Some people expect `rlogin` to be replaced by telnet as more features (such as tilde escapes) are added to telnet. To use `rlogin`, simply type:

```
$ rlogin hostname
```

In the above code, *hostname* is replaced by the computer that you want to login to. You can use any hostname that is in your `/etc/hosts` file or that can be obtained through DNS. Once you have started `rlogin`, you can use any of the following key sequences:

✦ `~.` — Exit. This causes the rlogin program to exit (ungracefully). I use this option if the remote shell is hung or if I get stuck at the login prompt (from a forgotten password or logged into the wrong system).

✦ `~Ctrl+Shift+z` — Suspend. (Press Ctrl and Shift while pressing z.) This puts the current rlogin session in the background, returning you to a local shell command line. To return to the suspended session, type `fg`.

Using rcp for remote copies

The `rcp` command is handy for copying one file or a whole directory structure of files from one computer to another. It is quicker than `ftp` because you don't have to start a session and log in before you copy a file. However, because `rcp` doesn't prompt for a password, it requires that you configure rhosts authentication (discussed above) for it to work.

To copy a file from one computer to another, use the following command:

```
$ rcp fileX maple:/home/mike
```

That command would copy the file (`fileX`) to `/home/mike` on the computer named `maple`. You could also take a file from another computer by typing the following:

```
. $ rcp maple:/home/mike/fileZ .
```

That command would copy the file (fileZ) from /home/mike on maple and place it in the current directory (.).

If rhosts authentication is set up among several hosts on your network, you can have both the source and destination of the file on different computers. For example:

```
$ rcp maple:/home/mike/fileY pine:/tmp
```

You can use shell metacharacters (*, ?, etc.) in a path name. However, you must surround them in quotes (or escape them with backslashes) if you want them to refer to a remote location so the local shell doesn't interpret them. Here is an example:

```
$ rcp maple:/tmp/p\* /tmp
```

The previous command would copy all files in the /tmp directory on the computer named maple that begin with the letter p (p*) to the /tmp directory on the local system.

Perhaps the most useful option for the rcp command is the -r option. The -r option enables you to copy all the files in a directory structure from one computer to another. This can provide a quick and easy way of backing up a large area of data in one command. Here is an example:

```
$ rcp -r /a maple:/backup/pine
```

The previous example is one that I use. I store all my software and data files in the directory /a. If I want to do a quick backup or if I want to reinstall Red Hat Linux, I can copy all of my data and software to maple, reinstall the local system, then rcp the files back again. This command creates a directory on maple in a directory called /backup/pine/a. That directory can contain hundreds of files and subdirectories.

Using rsh for remote execution

While previous commands, such as rcp and ftp, can help you share files among computers on your network, rsh lets you share the processors. With rsh, it is simple to ask that a command be run on any computer for which you have rhosts access. Likewise, you can have the command's output printed on your screen, directed to a local file, or directed to a remote file.

Here are four examples of the rsh command:

```
$ rsh spruce who
$ rsh maple "tail -f /var/log/messages"
$ rsh pine "man rlogin" >> /tmp/rlman
$ rsh fir "uname -a" ">>" /tmp/name
```

In the first example, the who command is run on the remote computer named spruce and the output appears on the local screen. The second example runs the tail -f command to display messages as they arrive in the /var/log/messages file on maple. (This is a good way to remotely monitor log files in one quick command line.) The next command runs the man command to output the rlogin man page and outputs the results to the /tmp/rlman file on the local system. In the final example, the uname -a command runs on fir, but by quoting the arrows, the output is sent to the /tmp/name file on the remote computer, rather than the local one.

Summary

Most use of the World Wide Web centers on the Web browser. Over your existing Internet connection, the browser lets you indicate Web pages and other content that you want to access using addresses referred to as URLs (Uniform Resource Locators). Mozilla and Netscape are the most popular browsers with Red Hat and other Linux systems, and are accessible from a button on your desktop.

E-mail is probably the Internet application that is used most. The e-mail program that comes with Mozilla, called Mozilla Mail, integrates well with the Mozilla browser and provides most everything needed for reading, sending, and managing your mail. There are several traditional UNIX mail programs available with Red Hat Linux as well, including elm, pine, and mail.

To read newsgroups, you can use Netscape Messenger. Text-based newsreaders are also available.

To pass data around freely between trusted hosts, you can use a set of commands sometimes referred to as "r" commands. The rlogin command lets you log in to other computers over the network. With the rcp command, you can copy one file, many files, or a whole directory structure of files among computers on the network. The rsh command lets you run programs on different computers on a network and direct the output to the local computer or to a remote computer. Commands such as telnet (for remote login) and ftp (for remote file copying) are also available with Red Hat Linux.

✦   ✦   ✦

Administering Red Hat Linux

Understanding System Administration

Red Hat Linux, like other UNIX systems, was intended for use by more than one person at a time. Multiuser features allow many people to have accounts in Red Hat Linux, with their data kept secure from others. Multitasking allows many people to use the computer at the same time. Sophisticated networking protocols and applications make it possible for a Red Hat Linux computer to extend its capabilities to network users and computers around the world. The person assigned to manage all of this stuff is referred to as the *system administrator.*

Even if you are the only person using a Red Hat Linux system, system administration is still set up to be separate from other computer use. To do most tasks, you need to be logged in as the root user (also referred to as the super user). Other users cannot change, or in some cases, even see some of the configuration information for a Red Hat Linux system. In particular, security features such as passwords are protected from general view.

General principles of Red Hat Linux system administration are described in this chapter. In particular, this chapter covers some of the basic tools you need to administer your Red Hat Linux system. It also helps teach you how to work with file systems and monitor the setup and performance of your Linux system.

Using the root Login

The root user has complete control of the operation of your Red Hat Linux system. That user can open any file or run any program. The root user also installs applications and adds accounts for other people who use the system.

When you first install Red Hat Linux, you should have added a password for the root user. You need to remember and protect this password. You will need it to log in as root or to obtain root permission while you are logged in as some other user.

The home directory for the root user is /root. That and other information associated with the root user account is located in the /etc/passwd file. Here is what the root entry looks like in the /etc/passwd file:

```
root:x:0:0:root:/root:/bin/bash
```

This shows that for the user named root, the user ID is set to 0 (root user), the group ID is set to 0 (root group), the home directory is /root, and the shell for that user is /bin/bash. You can change the home directory or the shell used, if you like, by simply editing the values in this file.

See the section on setting up users in Chapter 11 for further information about the /etc/passwd file.

Among the defaults that are set for the root user are aliases for certain dangerous commands. Aliases for the rm, cp, and mv commands allow those commands to be run with the -i option. This prevents massive numbers of files being removed, copied, or moved by mistake. The -i option causes each deletion, copy, or move to prompt you before the actual change is made.

Becoming Super User (The su Command)

Though the normal way to become the super user is to log in as root, sometimes that is not convenient. For example, you may be logged into a regular user account and just want to make a quick administrative change to your system without having to log out and log back in. Or, you may need to log in over the network to make a change to a Linux system but find that the system doesn't allow root users in from over the network (a common practice).

The answer is that you can use the su command. From any Terminal window or shell, you can simply type:

```
$ su
Password: ******
#
```

When you are prompted, type in the root user's password. The prompt for the regular user ($) will be changed to the super user prompt (#). At this point, you have full permission to run any command and use any file on the system. However, one thing that the su command doesn't do when used this way is read in the root user's environment. As a result, you may type a command that you know is available and get the message "command not found." To fix this problem, you can use the su command with the dash (-) option instead, as follows:

```
$ su -
Password: ******
#
```

You still need to type the password, but after you do that, everything that normally happens at login for the root user will happen after the su command is completed. Your current directory will be root's home directory (probably /root), and things like the root user's PATH variable will be used. With the other way of running root, you would not have changed directories or the environment of the current login session.

Tip When you become super user during someone else's session, a common mistake is to leave files or directories behind in the user's directories that are owned by root. If you do this, be sure to use the chown or chmod command to make the files and directories you modify open to the user that you want to own them. Otherwise, you will probably get a phone call in a short time, asking you to come back and fix it.

You can also use the su command to become another user than root. For example, to have the permissions of a user named chum, you could type the following:

```
$ su - chum
```

Even if you were root user before you typed this command, you would only have the permission to open files and run programs that are available to chum. As root user, however, after you type the su command to become another user, you don't need a password to continue.

When you are finished using your super user permissions, you can return to the previous shell by exiting the current shell. Do this by pressing Ctrl+D or by typing exit. If you are the administrator for a computer that is accessible to multiple users, don't leave a root shell open on someone else's terminal (unless you want to let that person do anything they like to the computer)!

One useful thing to do with su is to become super user on an X desktop where another user is currently logged in, then run administrative GUI programs from that desktop. If you want to find out how to do that (it can be a bit tricky), see the sidebar "Becoming Super User in X."

Becoming Super User in X

There may be times when an X GUI is running on Red Hat Linux as a nonroot user and you want to run a graphical administration program (such as `netcfg` or `linuxconf`). Here is a procedure you can follow to do just that:

First, open a Terminal window on the X desktop.

Then, open permission to the X window display to everyone on the local computer (this is just a temporary measure) by typing:

```
$ xhost +localhost
```

Type the following and enter the root password when prompted, to become super user:

```
$ su -
Password: ******
#
```

Next, type the following to see the current display value:

```
# echo $DISPLAY
```

If the value is something like `:0`, that means that any X command you run from that shell will appear on the console terminal for the computer. If you are at the console and that's what you see, then you can skip the next step. If you see no value (which is quite possible) or the wrong value, you need to set the `DISPLAY` variable.

Type the following (assuming you are using a `bash` or `sh` shell):

```
# export DISPLAY=:0
```

At this point, you can run any administrative X command (such as `netcfg` or `linuxconf`) and have it appear on your X desktop. If you are running an administrative command from a remote computer and you want it to appear on your local desktop, you can set the `DISPLAY` to `host:0`, where *host* is replaced by the name of your computer.

When you are done, be sure to exit the application you are running. Then restore the security of your X desktop by typing the following:

```
$ xhost -localhost
```

Learning about Administrative Commands, Configuration Files, and Log Files

Whether you administer Red Hat Linux from the shell or from a GUI, underlying your activities are many administrative commands, configuration files, and log files. Understanding where these commands and files are located and how they are used will help you effectively maintain your Red Hat Linux system. Although most administrative features are intended for the root user, other administrative users (described later in this section) have limited administrative capabilities.

Administrative commands

Many commands are only intended for root. When you log in as root, your $PATH variable is set to include some directories that contain commands for the root user. These include the following directories:

✦ /sbin—This contains commands for modifying your disk partitions (such as fdisk), changing boot procedures (grub), and changing system states (init).

✦ /usr/sbin—This contains commands for managing user accounts (such as adduser) and configuring your mouse (mouseconfig) or keyboard (kbdconfig). Many commands that are run as daemon processes are also contained in this directory. (Look for commands that end in "d" such as lpd, pppd, and crond.)

Some administrative commands are contained in regular user directories (such as /bin and /usr/bin). This is especially true of commands that have some options that are available to everyone and others that are root-only options. An example is the /bin/mount command, which anyone can use to list mounted file systems, but which only root can use to mount file systems.

To find commands that are intended primarily for the system administrator, check out the section 8 manual pages (usually in /usr/share/man/man8). They contain descriptions and options for most Red Hat Linux administrative commands.

Some third-party applications will add administrative commands to directories that are not in your PATH. For example, an application may put commands in /usr/local/bin or /usr/local/sbin. In those cases, you may want to add those directories to your PATH.

Administrative configuration files

Configuration files are another mainstay of Linux administration. Almost everything you set up for your particular computer—user accounts, network addresses, or GUI preferences—is stored in plain-text files. This has some advantages and some disadvantages.

The advantage of plain-text files is that it is easy to read and change them. Any text editor will do. On the downside, however, is that as you edit configuration files, no error checking is going on. You have to run the program that reads these files (such as a network daemon or the X desktop) to find out if you set up the files correctly. A comma or a quote in the wrong place can sometimes cause a whole interface to fail.

Throughout this book, I describe the configuration files you need to set up the different features that make up Red Hat Linux. In terms of a general perspective on configuration files, however, there are several locations in the Red Hat Linux file system where configuration files are stored. Here are some of the major locations:

✦ $HOME — All users store information in their home directories that directs how their login accounts behave. Most configuration files begin with a dot (.), so they don't appear as a user's directory when you use a standard `ls` command (you need to type **ls -a** to see them). There are dot files that define how each user's shell behaves, the look and feel of the desktop, and what options are used with your text editor. There are even files (such as `.rhosts`) that configure network permissions for each user.

✦ /etc — This contains many of the most basic Linux system configuration files. Here are some /etc configuration files that are of interest:

   • `aliases` — Can contain distribution lists used by the Linux mail service.

   • `bashrc` — Sets system-wide defaults for bash shell users. (By default, it sets the shell prompt to include the current user name, hostname, and current directory, as well as a few other values.)

   • `crontab` — Sets cron environment and times for running automated tasks.

   • `csh.cshrc` (or `cshrc`) — Sets system-wide defaults for csh (C shell) users.

   • `exports` — Contains a list of local directories that are available to be shared by remote computers using the Network File System (NFS).

   • `fdprm` — Sets parameters for common floppy disk formats.

   • `fstab` — Identifies the devices for common storage media (hard disk, floppy, CD-ROM, etc.) and locations where they are mounted in the Linux system. This is used by the `mount` command to choose which file systems to mount.

   • `gettydefs` — Contains line definitions used by terminal devices (including modems, dumb terminals, and remote logins over terminal devices).

   • `group` — Identifies group names and group IDs (GIDs) that are defined on the systems. Group permissions in Red Hat Linux are defined by the second of three sets of rwx (read, write, execute) bits associated with each file and directory.

   • `host.conf` — Sets the locations in which domain names (e.g., redhat.com) are searched for on TCP/IP networks (such as the Internet). By default, the local hosts file is searched, then any nameserver entries in `resolv.conf`.

- `hosts` — Contains IP addresses and hostnames that you can reach from your computer. (Usually this file is used just to store names of computers on your LAN or larger private network.)

- `hosts.allow` — Lists host computers that are allowed to use TCP/IP services from the local computer.

- `hosts.deny` — Lists host computers that are *not* allowed to use TCP/IP services from the local computer.

- `xinetd.conf` — Contains simple configuration information used by the `xinetd` daemon process. This file mostly points to the `/etc/xinetd.d` directory for information about individual services (described later).

- `info-dir` — Contains the top heading for information that is available from the `info` command.

- `inittab` — Contains information that defines what programs start and stop when Red Hat Linux boots, shuts down, or goes into different states in between.

- `issue` — Contains the lines that are displayed when a terminal is ready to let you log in to Red Hat Linux from a local terminal, or the console in text mode.

- `issue.net` — Contains login lines that are displayed to users that try to log in to the Linux system from a computer on the network using the telnet service.

- `lilo.conf` — Sets various parameters used by the Linux boot loader (lilo) to boot your Linux system. In particular, it lists information about the bootable partitions on your computer. (If you are using grub, which has replaced lilo as the default boot manager, the lilo.conf file is not used.)

- `mail.rc` — Sets system-wide parameters associated with using mail.

- `man.config` — Used by the `man` command to determine the default path to the location of `man` pages.

- `modules.conf` — Contains aliases and options related to loadable kernel modules used by your computer.

- `mtab` — Contains a list of file systems that are currently mounted.

- `passwd` — Stores account information for all valid users for the system. Also includes other information, such as the home directory and default shell.

- `printcap` — Contains definitions for the printers configured for your computer.

- `profile` — Sets system-wide environment and start-up programs for all users. This file is read when the user logs in.

- `protocols`—Sets protocol numbers and names for a variety of Internet services.

- `redhat-release`—Contains a string identifying the current Red Hat release number.

- `resolv.conf`—Identifies the locations of DNS name server computers that are used by TCP/IP to translate Internet host.domain names into IP addresses.

- `rpc`—Defines remote procedure call names and numbers.

- `rpmfind`—Contains configuration information used by the `rpmfind` command to search for RPM software packages on the Internet.

- `services`—Defines TCP/IP services and their port assignments.

- `shadow`—Contains encrypted passwords for users that are defined in the `passwd` file. (This is viewed as a more secure way to store passwords than the original encrypted password in the `passwd` file. The `passwd` file needs to be publicly readable, whereas the `shadow` file can be unreadable by all but the root user.)

- `shells`—Lists the shell command line interpreters (`bash`, `sh`, `csh`, etc.) that are available on the system, as well as their locations.

- `sudoers`—Sets commands that can be run by users, who may not otherwise have permission to run the command, using the `sudo` command. In particular, this file is used to provide selected users with root permission.

- `syslog.conf`—Defines what logging messages are gathered by the syslogd daemon and what files they are stored in. (Typically, log messages are stored in files contained in the `/var/log` directory.)

- `termcap`—Lists definitions for character terminals, so that character-based applications know what features are supported by a given terminal. Graphical terminals and applications have made this file obsolete to most people. (Termcap was the BSD UNIX way of storing terminal information; UNIX System V used definitions in `/usr/share/terminfo` files.)

✦ `/etc/X11`—Contains subdirectories that each contain system-wide configuration files used by X and different X window managers available with Red Hat Linux. The `XF86Config` file (which makes your computer and monitor usable with X) and configuration directories containing files used with `xdm` and `xinit` to start X are contained here.

Directories relating to window managers contain files that include the default values that a user will get if that user starts one of these window managers on your system. Window managers that may have system-wide configuration files in these directories include: WindowMaker, fvwm2, GNOME (`gdm`), and Twm (`twm`).

Note Some of the files and directories in /etc/X11 are linked to locations in the /usr/X11R6 directory structure.

✦ **/etc/cron*** — Directories in this set contain files that define how the crond utility runs applications on a daily (cron.daily), hourly (cron.hourly), monthly (cron.monthly), or weekly (cron.weekly) schedule.

✦ **/etc/default** — Contains files that set default values for various utilities. For example, the file for the useradd command defines the default group number, home directory, password expiration date, shell, and skeleton directory (/etc/skel) that are used when creating a new user account.

✦ **/etc/httpd** — Contains a variety of files used to configure the behavior of your Apache Web server (specifically, the httpd daemon process).

✦ **/etc/init.d** — Contains the permanent copies of run-level scripts. These scripts are linked to files in the /etc/rc?.d directories to have each service associated with a script started or stopped for the particular run level. The ? is replaced by the run level number (0 through 6).

✦ **/etc/pcmcia** — Contains configuration files that allow you to have a variety of PCMCIA cards configured for your computer. (PCMCIA slots are those openings on your laptop that allow you to have credit-card-sized cards attached to your computer. You can attach such devices as modems and external CD-ROMs.)

✦ **/etc/ppp** — Contains several configuration files used to set up Point-to-Point protocol (so that you can have your computer dial out to the Internet).

✦ **/etc/rc?.d** — There is a separate rc?.d directory for each valid system state: rc0.d (shutdown state), rc1.d (single-user state), rc2.d (multiuser state), rc3.d (multiuser plus networking state), rc4.d (user-defined state), rc5.d (multiuser, networking, plus GUI login state), and rc6.d (reboot state).

✦ **/etc/security** — Contains files that set a variety of default security conditions for your computer.

✦ **/etc/skel** — Any files contained in this directory are automatically copied to a user's home directory when that user is added to the system. By default, most of these files are dot (.) files, such as .kde (a directory for setting KDE desktop defaults) and .bashrc (for setting default values used with the bash shell).

✦ **/etc/sysconfig** — Contains important system configuration files that are created and maintained by several Red Hat applications (including netcfg and linuxconf).

✦ **/etc/uucp** — Contains configuration files used with Taylor UUCP (a nonstandard version of the uucp facility that is used to create modem, direct line, and other serial connections with other computers).

✦ /etc/xinetd.d—Contains a set of files, each of which defines a network service that the xinetd daemon listens for on a particular port. When the xinetd daemon process receives a request for a service, it uses the information in these files to determine which daemon processes to start to handle the request.

Administrative log files

One of the things that Linux does well is keep track of itself. This is a good thing, when you consider how much can go wrong with a complex operating system. Sometimes you are trying to get a new facility to work and it fails without giving you the foggiest reason why. Other times you want to monitor your system to see if people are trying to access your computer illegally. In any of those cases, you can use log files to help track down the problem.

The main utilities for logging error and debugging messages for Linux are the syslogd and klogd daemons. General system logging is done by syslogd. Logging that is specific to kernel activity is done by klogd. Logging is done according to information in the /etc/syslog.conf file. Messages are typically directed to log files that are usually in the /var/log directory. Here are some common log files from that directory and the messages they contain:

✦ boot.log—Contains messages related to system services starting and stopping when Linux boots up and shuts down, respectively.

✦ cron—Contains messages output by the cron command (which is used to run tasks at set times). Here you can see when tasks start and any error conditions that may have occurred.

✦ dmesg—Contains boot-up messages that can be useful in debugging hardware failures. (You can run the dmesg command to see these messages.)

✦ maillog—Activities of the sendmail daemon (which forwards e-mail to other computers) are logged in this file.

✦ messages—Messages associated with many daemon processes are directed to the messages file.

✦ secure—Contains messages that may indicate security breeches. Connections from remote hosts are logged, as are attempts to log in to your system.

✦ xferlog—Shows which files have been transferred to and from your FTP server.

Besides these files, messages are also directed to several directories located in the /var/log directory. These directories include:

✦ httpd—Messages from the Apache Web server are logged to files in this directory.

✦ news—Messages related to the Internet News service (INN).

✦ samba—Messages from the Samba service, for sharing files and printers with Windows systems.

✦ uucp—Messages from the UNIX-to-UNIX copy (uucp) facility are stored here.

Using other administrative logins

You don't hear much about other administrative logins (besides root) being used with Red Hat Linux. It was a fairly common practice in UNIX systems to have several different administrative logins that allowed administrative tasks to be split among several users. For example, a person sitting near a printer could have lp permissions to move print jobs to another printer if they knew a printer wasn't working. These logins are available with Linux, however, so you may want to look into using them.

Tip

Because most Red Hat Linux administrative features are expected to be administered by the root user, e-mail for other administrative accounts is routed to the root user. If you want other administrative users to receive their own e-mail, delete the aliases for those users from the /etc/aliases file.

Here are the administrative logins that are configured automatically for Linux systems. By tradition, these logins are assigned UID numbers under 100. These logins have no passwords by default, so you can't use any administrative login separately until you assign it a password. To make an administrative login useful, you may need to change permissions of some executables, spool files, and log files so that they are owned by the administrative login:

✦ **lp**—This user can control some printing features. Having a separate lp administrator allows someone other than the super user to do such things as move or remove lp logs and print spool files. The home directory for lp is /var/spool/lpd.

✦ **mail**—This user can work with administrative e-mail features. The mail group has group permissions to use mail files in /var/spool/mail (which is also the mail user's home directory).

✦ **uucp**—This user owns various uucp commands (once used as the primary method for dial-up serial communications). It is the owner of log files in /var/log/uucp, spool files in /var/spool, administrative commands (such as uuchk, uucico, uuconv, and uuxqt) in /usr/sbin, and user commands (uucp, cu, uuname, uustat, and uux) in /usr/bin. The home directory for uucp is /var/spool/uucp.

✦ **bin**—This user owns many commands in /bin in traditional UNIX systems. This is not the case in Red Hat Linux, because root tends to own most executable files. The home directory of bin is /bin.

✦ **news**—This user could be used to do administration of Internet news services, depending on how you set permission for /var/spool/news and other news-related resources. The home directory for news is /var/spool/news.

Getting to Know Your System

Knowing how your Red Hat Linux system is set up will help you with your task of administering that system. This is especially true if you did not set up the system yourself. This section covers a few commands you can run to understand how a Linux system is configured.

Hostname and Linux version

The uname command can print some basic information about your Linux system. This information can include:

✦ Operating system name (i.e., Linux)

✦ System's host name

✦ Linux release number

✦ Current date and time

✦ Processor type

The following is an example of the uname -a command (the -a prints all the information at once):

```
$ uname -a
Linux mycomputer 2.4.6-3.1 #1 Sat Oct 27 19:09:11 EDT 2001 i686
unknown
```

The system's hostname is used to identify your computer (in particular, it is used by remote systems to contact you over a network). The Linux release number (2.4.6-3.1) identifies the release of the Linux kernel that you have installed. Check this number to make sure you have the latest kernel.

You can change your computer name using the hostname command as follows:

```
# hostname yourcomputer
```

The hostname is read automatically by different programs that need to indicate what computer is being used. For example, your shell command line prompt probably automatically displays the hostname. You can also print other information that relates to how your computer is named from the perspective of the network. For example, `dnsdomainname` lists your domain name (used for the Internet). If your computer uses NIS services, you can print your NIS domain name with the `domainname` command.

Disk partitions and sizes

Before Red Hat Linux can be installed, areas of the hard disk are divided up to hold Linux data, swap space, and any other operating systems you may want on your computer. These divisions are called *partitions*. You can view and change your disk partitions, using the `fdisk` command (described later in this chapter).

If you have multiple partitions, you need to watch the percentage of space used on each mounted partition. If, for example, space runs out on a separate `/var` file system, programs that need to spool data (such as mail and printing utilities), write to log files in `/var/log`, or use temporary file space in `/var/tmp` may fail. Even if plenty of space is available in the root partition or another partition, if the assigned partition runs out of space, it won't draw from other partitions.

More information on monitoring and managing file systems is included later in this chapter.

Users

User login accounts are listed in the `/etc/passwd` file. You can list the contents of this file to see what users have accounts on your Linux system as follows:

```
# less /etc/passwd
```

Administrative logins (up to UID 100 in the third colon-separated field) should make up most of the first few entries in this file. Regular user accounts (with UIDs above 100) are usually added in after the administrative accounts.

As an administrator of a multiuser Red Hat Linux system, you need to make sure that user accounts are kept up to date. To keep your Red Hat Linux system secure, you need to remove users when they leave your organization (or at least deactivate their passwords if their home directories still contain information that your organization needs).

Chapter 11 contains information on how to set up and manage users in Linux.

The kernel

The heart of the Linux system is called the *kernel*. The kernel provides the interface between you (and the programs you run) and the hardware (hard disks, RAM, network cards, etc.). Using the /proc file system, you can find out a lot of information about your kernel, by simply displaying the contents of /proc files.

For each process currently running in Linux, there is a directory in /proc consisting of the process number for the running process. (Type ps aux | more to see the running processes and their associated PID numbers.) The /proc directory contains other files that are connected to certain features (such as networking, SCSI devices, and other components).

To display the contents of /proc files, you can use the cat command. For example, change to the /proc directory (cd /proc), then type the following command:

```
# cat version
```

The output of this command contains the Linux version number and other information (such as the compiler version and the system install date). There are other files under the /proc directory structure that you can also list to find out interesting information about your running Linux system. Here are a few files that you can "cat" to get information:

- ✦ cpuinfo — Tells you the type of CPU in your computer, the speed (CPU MHz), the CPU family, and other information related to your computer's processor.

- ✦ devices — Displays the character and block devices currently being used on your computer, along with their major device numbers.

- ✦ ioports — Shows the I/O port addresses for the devices on your computer.

- ✦ meminfo — Contains information about memory usage and swap space usage. You can see the total amounts of memory and the how much is currently being used.

- ✦ modules — Shows a list of modules that are currently installed in the system.

- ✦ mounts — Displays the file systems that are currently mounted in the system.

- ✦ partitions — Contains the names of your hard disk partitions, the number of blocks in each partition, and each partition's major and minor device number.

- ✦ pci — Lists the PCI devices installed in your computer. You can see the bus device numbers, names, and other information. For cards that are installed (such Ethernet or modem cards), you can see their IRQs, addresses, and other information.

✦ swaps —Shows the swap partitions that are currently mounted on your system, along with their sizes and the amount of space being used.

✦ net/dev —Displays the contents of the net/dev file to see your active network interfaces.

✦ sys/* —Looks at the contents of these directories for information related to debugging (debug), devices (dev), file systems (fs), the kernel (kernel), networks (net), and processes (proc). The net directory contains some of the most useful information. Go to /proc/sys/net/ipv4 and list the contents of these files to see when certain features are turned on or off. For example, ip_forward will tell you if IP forwarding is turned on for your computer (0 for off or 1 for on).

Graphical Administrative Interfaces

To try to simplify Linux administration, several graphical administrative utilities are now available. These interfaces attempt to organize the information you need to get a whole job done in one place. The interface handles putting the information you enter into the correct configuration files and setting up the correct commands to run.

Graphical interfaces are a step in the right direction toward making Linux useable by the general population. The problem is, however, that these don't yet allow you to do everything you need to do, so you will often find yourself having to edit a configuration file by hand after you have entered the information into that file using a graphical application. You will find that you need to do this less for simple tasks (such as adding a user account) than you will for more complex tasks (such as configuring servers).

Another downside of graphical administrative interfaces in Linux is that they tend to cause versions of Linux to diverge. For example, the configuration files created when you set up a dial-out Internet connection using PPP with the Network configurator in Red Hat Linux are different from the files you would create setting up PPP on a different version of Linux. This can make it a bit difficult to get information on your particular situation.

The following sections describe the major graphical interfaces used to do administration for Red Hat Linux.

Using linuxconf

The most complete graphical utility for working with Red Hat Linux is linuxconf. It contains features for configuring networking (client and server tasks), creating user accounts, and working with the file system.

Note   Red Hat is phasing out support for linuxconf. In fact, unless you do an "everything" install of Red Hat Linux, it's likely that linuxconf isn't even installed on your system. If linuxconf is not found, you can install it from the second Red Hat Linux installation CD (CD-2). As Red Hat creates GUI interfaces to replace linuxconf features (particularly in the area of network configuration), you should consider using those tools instead of linuxconf.

As a GUI, linuxconf isn't fancy. Don't expect to see lots of icons or to be able to drag and drop items on the display. It does, however, offer some advantages over just editing configuration files directly:

✦ Configuration and control tools for many different features are all contained in one place. Just click an activity in the left column and a form for configuring the item appears in the right column. You don't have to search blindly in /etc for the right files to edit.

✦ Some error checking is done. In many cases, linuxconf will prevent you from entering invalid values in the fields.

✦ Options are offered. If, for example, you are adding a network interface, you can click a pull-down menu to select from the interfaces that Linux knows about (such as PPP or Ethernet).

Administrative activities are divided into three major categories in linuxconf: Config, Control, and Status. Config activities let you set up your network interfaces (for both client and server features), work with user accounts, configure file systems, and manage how Linux boots. Control activities let you work with features that have already been configured, including starting and stopping services, mounting/unmounting file systems, and controlling the files and systems used by linuxconf. Status activities let you view system logs.

Starting linuxconf

You can start linuxconf from the System menu (Programs ➪ System ➪ LinuxConf) or from a Terminal window (linuxconf &). Figure 10-1 shows the LinuxConf window.

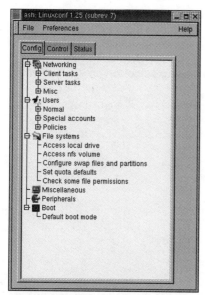

Figure 10-1: linuxconf centralizes Linux administration in one graphical window.

Tip

linuxconf can also be operated from Netscape or another Web browser. To allow that, you must simply allow the local or remote computer to access the service. To use the service from a remote computer, the remote computer requests port number 98 from your computer. For example, if the linuxconf server is named comp1, you can start linuxconf by typing the Web address: http://comp1:98/ from the remote host. Before you can use the service, you need to enter the root password.

You need to activate the linuxconf service to allow a user from a remote computer to use linuxconf. From the linuxconf Config tab, select Networking, Misc, and Linuxconf network access. Then click Enable network access and type the names of the hosts and/or networks you want to allow to access the service. Next, you need to edit the /etc/xinetd.d/linuxconf-web file and change disable = yes to disable = no. Then type /etc/init.d/xinetd restart to make the linuxconf Web service available.

To choose a task to perform in linuxconf, click the task in the left column. A form representing the task appears on the right. Select the options you want and fill in the necessary information. Accept the changes by clicking Accept or OK. Click Cancel when you are done. You can also use the following function keys and control keys with `linuxconf`:

✦ **Ctrl+X** — If the current field contains a pop-up selection list (indicated by a down arrow), this key opens the list.

✦ **F3** — Escapes from any dialog.

✦ **Ctrl+A** — Goes to the beginning of the line.

✦ **Ctrl+B** — Goes up one page.

✦ **Ctrl+D** — Deletes the current character.

✦ **Ctrl+E** — Goes to the end of the line.

✦ **Ctrl+F** — Goes down one page.

✦ **Ctrl+K** — Deletes text to the end of the line.

Linuxconf configuration tasks

Under the configuration section in `linuxconf` are tasks for setting up your network, creating user accounts, working with file systems, initializing system services, and choosing boot modes. Networking tasks are divided into those that apply to your computer as a client and those that apply to it as a server.

Linuxconf networking tasks

Client networking tasks let you view and configure information associated with your computer's host name, the network interfaces that are attached to your computer, and the routes you can use to get to other hosts and networks. Click the plus sign (+) next to Client tasks and select Host name and IP network devices. From the window that appears, here are some of the items you can change:

✦ **Hostname** — Your hostname is how other computers on the network identify yours. It can contain the full hostname.domainname form.

✦ **Adaptor** — The network interfaces (i.e., Ethernet cards, PPP dial-up connections, etc.) that give you access to the network can be viewed by clicking the Adaptor tabs on this form. The information you would need to enter in this form is described in detail in Chapter 15, "Setting Up a Local Area Network."

Your system resolves Internet host names into IP addresses by identifying DNS servers that can do name to address resolution. Click the Name Server Specification (DNS) task to add your default domain and one or more name servers. You can also indicate which domains to search for addresses.

Under Routing and Gateways, you can define how your networking requests are routed across gateway machines (those that are connected to your subnetwork and another subnetwork) to reach beyond your local network. You can also specify routes to other local area networks.

Another network service you can configure includes configuring an IPX interface. IPX is a networking interface protocol popular with NetWare servers.

If you make any changes to your network configuration, you can activate those changes by clicking the Act/Changes button. You can either preview what needs to be done to activate the changes or click Activate the changes for the changes to be implemented and the network to be restarted.

Under Server tasks, you can share your file systems with other computers on the network (using NFS) and set up IP aliases for virtual hosts.

Other linuxconf configuration tasks

Besides networking tasks, you can select from several other basic system tasks in `linuxconf`. Under User Accounts, you can add normal user accounts, special user accounts, and policies regarding user accounts. Under File systems, you can add definitions of mountable local drives or NFS file systems (from remote systems) that can later be added to or removed from your system (using mount and unmount tasks described in the Control section). Finally, you can add parameters that have an impact on how your Linux system boots.

Linuxconf control tasks

The Control section of `linuxconf` lets you work with Linux features that change the ongoing operation of your Red Hat Linux system. Here are some of the tasks you can do from this section:

✦ **Activate configuration** — For changes that you make to take effect, some services have to be stopped and restarted. This task checks what needs to be restarted, based on the changes you have made, then restarts those services when you say you are ready.

✦ **Shutdown/Reboot** — Use this task to either shut down and halt your computer or reboot it.

✦ **Control service activity** — You can enable or disable a variety of network services by selecting this task.

✦ **Mount/Unmount file systems** — Any local or NFS file systems you configured to be mountable (in the Configuration section) can be mounted or unmounted using these tasks.

✦ **Configure superuser scheduled tasks** — You can add commands that are run at a set schedule (using the cron facility) as the root user by adding entries under this task.

✦ **Archive configurations**—With this task, you can archive the configuration files you have set up so that you can recall these saved configuration files later. This can be used to get you back to a sane state if your configuration files get wrecked.

✦ **Switch system profile**—You can recall a past archive of configuration files (and save the current configuration files) using this task.

✦ **Linuxconf management**—Select tasks from this section to change the way configuration files, commands, file permissions, modules, system profiles, and `linuxconf` add-ons are configured and used in `linuxconf`.

✦ **Date & time**—Change the date, time, and time zone from this task.

When you have made changes to any configurations that require programs to be restarted, you can click Act/Changes. Then click the Activate the Changes button that appears. If errors are reported, click Yes to view those messages. Then you can view the log that was created from the changes.

Linuxconf subsection commands

Instead of using `linuxconf`, you can use commands to go directly to particular configuration sections. Here those commands:

✦ **Filesystem configurator** (`fsconf`)—Configures the file systems that your computer can access. This can include local drives and NFS volumes (mounted from remote computers). It also allows you to configure swap files and partitions, set quota defaults, and check the permissions of certain files. Figure 10-2 shows the Filesystem configurator window.

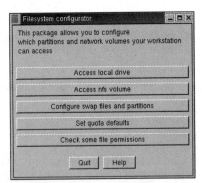

Figure 10-2: Mount local and remote file systems using Filesystem configurator.

✦ **Network configurator** (netconf)—Configures your TCP/IP network. It lets you add everything you need to create connections to modems and Ethernet LANs. You can set up the Domain Name System (DNS), routing and gateways, and serial communications (PPP, SLIP, or PLIP). Figure 10-3 shows the Network configurator window.

While the Network configurator (netconf) window works well in most cases, I recommend that you refer to Chapter 15 before you configure your networking interfaces. That chapter contains more in-depth descriptions on setting up a network and recommends using some different tools for configuration.

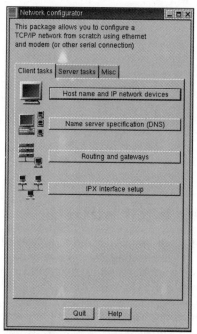

Figure 10-3: Set up TCP/IP network connections with the Network configurator.

✦ **User Account configurator** (userconf)—Manage your computer's user accounts. It lets you add regular user and group definitions, then assign passwords to users. You can also add special user accounts, such as those that let you automatically log in and start a PPP, SLIP, UUCP, or POP connection. Figure 10-4 shows the User Account configurator window.

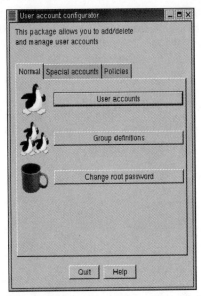

Figure 10-4: Add regular and special user accounts in the User Account configurator.

Reconfiguring Hardware with kudzu

When you add or remove hardware from your computer and reboot Red Hat Linux, a window appears during the reboot process advising that hardware has either been added or removed and asking if you want to reconfigure it. The program that detects and reconfigures your hardware is called kudzu.

The kudzu program is a hardware autodetection and configuration tool that runs automatically at boot time. If you like, you can also start kudzu while Red Hat Linux is running. In either case, here is what kudzu does:

1. It checks the hardware connected to your computer.

2. It compares the hardware it finds to the database of hardware information stored in the /etc/sysconfig/hwconf file.

3. It prompts you to change your system configuration, based on new or removed hardware that was detected.

The following is a list of hardware that kudzu can detect (according to the kudzu README file), followed by a description of what kudzu does to configure the device. Other devices may be detected as well (such as USB devices).

✦ **Network devices** — Adds an Ethernet interface alias (eth0, eth1, etc.) if necessary and either migrates the old device configuration or creates a new one.

✦ **SCSI** — Adds an alias for `scsi_hostadapter`.

✦ **Video card** — Runs the `Xconfigurator` command to configure the video card.

✦ **Sound card** — Runs the `sndconfig` command to configure and test the sound card.

✦ **Mouse** — Links the new mouse device to `/dev/mouse` and runs the `mouseconfig` command to configure and test the mouse.

✦ **Modem** — Links the new modem device to `/dev/modem`.

✦ **CD-ROM** — Links the CD-ROM device to `/dev/cdrom`.

✦ **Scanner** — Links the new scanner device to `/dev/scanner`.

✦ **Keyboard** — Runs the `kbdconfig` command to reconfigure the keyboard. Also, if you are using a serial console, it makes sure `/etc/inittab` and `/etc/securetty` are configured to be used by a serial console.

The following is a list of actions kudzu takes when a device is removed:

✦ **Network** — Removes the alias for the Ethernet interface (eth0, eth1, etc.).

✦ **SCSI** — Removes the alias for the SCSI host adapter (scsi_hostadapter).

✦ **Mouse** — Removes the link to `/dev/mouse`.

✦ **Modem** — Removes the link to `/dev/modem`.

✦ **CD-ROM** — Removes the link to `/dev/cdrom`.

✦ **Scanner** — Removes the link to `/dev/scanner`.

The only known problems with kudzu have to do with probing serial devices and video cards on a running Red Hat Linux system. If serial devices or older video cards are in use while kudzu is probing them, activity on those devices can be disturbed.

Configuring Modules

In a perfect world, by the time you have installed and booted Red Hat Linux, all of your hardware should be detected and available for access. While Red Hat Linux is rapidly moving closer to that world, there are times when you need to take special steps to get your computer hardware working.

Red Hat Linux comes with tools for configuring the drivers that stand between the programs you run (such as CD players and Web browsers) and the hardware they use (CD-ROM drives and network cards). The intention is to have the drivers your system needs most often built into the kernel; these are called *resident drivers*. Other drivers that are added dynamically as needed are referred to as *loadable modules*.

Cross-Reference

Chapter 2 contain descriptions of how to rebuild your kernel, including how to place drivers into your system as either resident kernel drivers or to have them available as loadable modules. This section describes how to display, add, and remove loadable modules in Linux.

Note

Besides providing hardware interfaces, modules can also provide interfaces for file systems, network services, binary formats, and other operating system features.

Finding available modules

If you have installed the Linux kernel source code (kernel-source package), source code files for available drivers are stored in subdirectories of the /usr/src/linux-2.4/drivers directory. There are several ways of finding information about these drivers:

+ **make xconfig**—With /usr/src/linux-2.4 as your current directory, type **make xconfig** from a Terminal window on the desktop. Select the category of module you are interested in and click Help next to the driver that interests you. The help information that appears tells you the module name and a description of the driver.

+ **Documentation**—The /usr/src/linux-2.4/Documentation directory contains lots of plain-text files describing different aspects of the kernel and related drivers. Of particular interest is the modules.txt file (which describes how to work with modules) and the Configure.help file (which contains all the help files hardware drivers).

+ **kernel-doc**—The kernel-doc software package (available on CD-2 of the Red Hat Linux distribution) contains a large set of documents describing the kernel and drivers. These documents are stored in the /usr/share/doc/kernel-doc* directory.

After modules have been built, they are installed in the /lib/modules/2.4* directory. The name of the directory is based on the current release number of the kernel. Modules that are in that directory can then be loaded and unloaded as they are needed.

Note

In previous releases, Red Hat Linux stored modules in the /lib/modules directory, rather than the /lib/moduels/2.4* directory. This structure allows you to store modules on your system that relate to different kernel versions you may be running.

Listing loaded modules

To see which modules are currently loaded into the running kernel on your computer, you can use the lsmod command. Here is an example:

```
# lsmod
Module                  Size  Used by
sr_mod                 15120  0  (autoclean)
es1371                 26784  0  (autoclean)
ac97_codec              8704  0  (autoclean) [es1371]
gameport                1920  0  (autoclean) [es1371]
soundcore               4112  4  (autoclean) [es1371]
binfmt_misc             6272  1
nuscsitcp              17200  0  (unused)
autofs                 10816  1  (autoclean)
tulip                  46400  1
ipchains               36960  0  (unused)
ide-scsi                8192  0
scsi_mod               93568  3  [sr_mod nuscsitcp ide-scsi]
hid                    18160  0  (unused)
input                   3456  0  [hid]
usb-uhci               21440  0  (unused)
usbcore                50432  1  [hid usb-uhci]
ext3                   50656  2
jbd                    39376  2  [ext3]
```

This output shows a variety of modules that have been loaded on a Linux system. The modules loaded on this system include several to support the Ensoniq 1371 sound card that is installed (es1371, ac97_codec, gameport, and soundcore). There are also modules to support the IDE CD-ROM drive that runs in SCSI emulation on this system (scsi_mod, sr_mod, nuscsitcp, and ide-scsi).

To find information about any of the loaded modules, you can use the modinfo command. For example, you could type the following:

```
# modinfo -d es1371
"ES1371 AudioPCI97 Driver"
```

Not all modules have descriptions available. In this case, however, the es1371 module is described as an ES1371 AudioPCI87 Driver. You can also use the -a option to see the author of the module or -n to see the object file representing the module. The author information often has the e-mail address of the driver's creator, so you can contact the author if you have problems or questions about it.

Loading modules

You can load any module that has been compiled and installed (to the /lib/ modules directory) into your running kernel using the insmod command. The most common reasons for loading a module are that you want to use a feature temporarily (such as loading a module to support a special file system on a floppy you want to access) or to identify module that will be used by a particular piece of hardware that could not be autodetected.

Here is an example of the `insmod` command being used to load the parport module. The parport module is used to provide the core functions for sharing a parallel port with multiple devices.

```
# insmod parport
Using /lib/modules/2.4.6-3.1/kernel/drivers/parport/parport.o
```

After parport is loaded you could load the parport_pc module to define the PC-style ports that are available through the interface. The parport_pc module lets you optionally define the addresses and IRQ numbers associated with each device sharing the parallel port. Here is an example:

```
# insmod parport_pc io=0x3bc irq=auto
```

In the previous example, a device is identified as having an address of 0x3bc. The IRQ for the device is auto-detected.

The `insmod` command loads modules temporarily. At the next system reboot, the modules you enter disappear. To permanently add the module to your system, add the `insmod` command line to one of the start-up scripts that are run a boot time.

Removing modules

You can remove a module from a running kernel using the `rmmod` command. For example, to remove the module parport_pc from the current kernel, type the following:

```
# rmmod parport_pc
```

If the module is not currently busy, the parport_pc module is removed from the running kernel.

Working with File Systems

File systems in Red Hat Linux are organized in a hierarchy, beginning from root (/) and continuing downward in a structure of directories and subdirectories. As an administrator of a Red Hat Linux system, it is your duty to make sure that all the disk drives that represent your file system are available to the users of the computer. It is also your job to make sure that there is enough disk space in the right places in the file system for users to store the information they need.

File systems are organized differently in Linux than they are in MS Windows operating systems. Instead of drive letters (e.g., A:, B:, C:) for each local disk, network file system, CD-ROM, or other type of storage medium, everything fits neatly into the directory structure. It is up to an administrator to create a mount point in the file system and then connect the disk to that point in the file system.

 Cross-Reference Information on how the Linux file system is organized is provided in Chapter 3.

The organization of your file system begins when you install Linux. Part of the installation process is to divide your hard disk (or disks) into partitions. Those partitions can then be assigned to:

✦ A part of the Linux file system,

✦ Swap space for Linux, or

✦ Other file system types (perhaps containing other bootable operating systems.)

For our purposes, I want to focus on partitions that are used for the Linux file system. To see what partitions are currently set up on your hard disk, you can use the `fdisk` command as follows:

```
# fdisk -l
```

Figure 10-5 shows how the `fdisk` command displays partition information in a Terminal window.

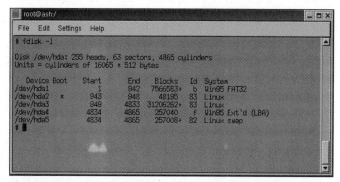

Figure 10-5: View disk partitions with the fdisk command.

This output shows the disk partitioning for a computer running both Red Hat Linux and Microsoft Windows. You can see that the Linux partition on /dev/hda3 has most of the space available for data. There is a Windows partition (/dev/hda1) and a Linux swap partition (/dev/hda5). There is also a small /boot partition (49MB) on /dev/hda2. In this case, the root partition for Linux has 31.881GB of disk space and resides on /dev/hda3.

Next, to see what partitions are actually being used for your Linux system, you can use the mount command (with no options). The mount command can show you which of the available disk partitions are actually mounted and where they are mounted.

```
# mount
/dev/hda3 on / type ext3 (rw)
none on /proc type proc (rw)
/dev/hda2 on /boot type ext3 (rw)
none on /dev/pts type devpts (rw,gid=5,mode=0620)
```

Notice that /proc and /dev/pts are shown as file systems because they represent different file system types (proc and devpts, respectively). The word "none," however, indicates that they are not associated with a separate partition.

The only mounted partitions in this case are /dev/hda2 and /dev/hda3, which provide space for the /boot directory (which contains data for booting Linux) and rest of the Linux file system beginning from the root (/), respectively. If you were to have multiple partitions mounted on your file system, they would be shown here as well. After the word "type," you can see the type of file system contained on the device. (See the description of different file system types later in this chapter.) Particularly on larger Linux systems, you may have multiple partitions for several reasons:

✦ **Multiple hard disks**—You may have several hard disks available to your users. In that case you would have to mount each disk (and possibly several partitions from each disk) in different locations in your file system.

✦ **Protecting different parts of the file system**—If you have many users on a system, and the users become suddenly very piggy and consume all of the file system space, the entire system can fail. For example, there may be no place for temporary files to be copied (so the programs writing to temporary files may fail), and incoming mail may fail to be written to mail boxes. With multiple mounted partitions, if one partition runs out, the others can continue to work fine.

✦ **Backups**—There are some fast ways of backing up data from your computer that involve copying the entire image of a disk or partition. If you want to restore that partition later, you can simply copy it back (bit-by-bit) to a hard disk. With smaller partitions, this approach can be done fairly efficiently.

✦ **Protecting from disk failure**—If one disk (or part of one disk) fails, by having multiple partitions mounted on your file system, you may be able to continue working and just fix the one disk that fails.

When a disk partition is mounted on the file system, all directories and subdirectories below that mount point are then stored on that partition. So, for example, if you were to mount one partition on / and one on /usr, everything below the /usr mount point would be stored on the second partition while everything else would be stored on the first partition. If you then mounted another partition on /usr/local, everything below that mount point would be on the third partition, while everything else below /usr would be on the second partition.

Tip Here's something to look out for, particularly if you are mounting file systems from other computers. What if a remote file system is unmounted from your computer, then you go to save a file in that mount point directory? What happens is that you will write the file to that directory and it will be stored on your local hard disk. When the remote file system is remounted, however, the file you saved will seem to disappear. To get the file back, you will have to unmount the remote file system (causing the file to reappear), move the file to another location, remount the file system, and copy the file back there.

Mount points that are often mentioned as being candidates for separate partitions include: /, /home, /usr, and /var. The root file system (/) is the catchall for directories that aren't in other mount points. The /home file systems is where all the user accounts are typically stored. Applications and documentation are stored in /usr. Below the /var mount point is where log files, temporary files, server files (Web, FTP, and so on), and lock files are stored (i.e., items that need disk space for your computer's applications to keep running).

Cross-Reference See Chapter 2 for further information on partitioning techniques.

The fact that multiple partitions are mounted on your file system is basically invisible to people using your Red Hat Linux system. The only times they will care will be if a partition runs out of space or if they need to save or use information from a particular device (such as a floppy disk or file system on another computer). Of course, any user can check this by simply typing the mount command.

For a personal Red Hat Linux system, I don't see much need for different partitions. Many people just mount their entire file system on root (/). Then, they just have to make sure that the entire file system doesn't run out of room.

Mounting file systems

Most of your hard disks are mounted automatically for you. When you installed Red Hat Linux, you were asked to create partitions and indicate the mount points for those partitions. When you boot Red Hat Linux, all Linux partitions should be mounted. For that reason, this section focuses mostly on how to mount other types of devices so that they become part of your Red Hat Linux file system.

Besides being able to mount other types of devices, you can also use `mount` to mount other kinds of file systems on your Linux file systems. This means that you can store files from other operating systems or use file systems that are appropriate for certain kinds of activities (such as writing large block sizes). The most common use of this feature for the average Linux user, however, is to allow that user to obtain and work with files from floppy disks or CD-ROMs.

Supported file systems

To see file system types that are currently in use on your system, type **cat /proc/filesystems**. The following file system types are supported in Linux.

- ✦ **ext3**—The ext file systems are the most common file systems used with Linux. The ext3 file system is new for Red Hat Linux 7.2 and is used as the default file system type. The root file system (/) must be ext3, ext2, or minux. The ext3 file system is also referred to as the Third Extended file system. The ext3 file system includes journaling features that improves a file system's ability to recover from crashes, as compared to ext2 file systems.

- ✦ **ext2**—The default file system type for previous versions of Red Hat Linux. Features are the same as ext3, except that ext2 doesn't include journaling features.

- ✦ **ext**—This is the first version of ext3. It is not used very often anymore.

- ✦ **iso9660**—This file system evolved from the High Sierra file system (which was the original standard used on CD-ROM). By adding extensions to that standard (called Rock Ridge extensions), the file system can support long filenames and UNIX-style information (such as file permissions, ownership, and links).

- ✦ **minix**—This is the Minix file system type, used originally with the Minix version of UNIX. This file system type only supports filenames up to 30 characters.

- ✦ **msdos**—This is an MS-DOS file system. You can use this type to mount floppy disks that come from Microsoft operating systems.

- ✦ **umsdos**—This is an MS-DOS file system with extensions to allow features that are similar to UNIX (including long filenames).

- ✦ **proc**—This is not a real file system, but rather a file system interface to the Linux kernel. You probably won't do anything special to set up a proc file system. However, the /proc mount point should be a proc file system. Many utilities rely on /proc to gain access to Linux kernel information.

- ✦ **swap**—This is used for swap partitions. Swap areas are used to temporarily hold data when RAM is currently used up. Data is swapped to the swap area, then returned to RAM when it is needed again.

- ✦ **nfs**—This is the Network File System (NFS) type of file system. File systems that are mounted from another computer on your network use this type of file system.

Information on using NFS to export and share file systems over a network is contained in Chapter 18, "Setting Up a File Server."

✦ **hpfs** — This file system is used to do read-only mounts of an OS/2 HPFS file system.

✦ **ncpfs** — This relates to Novell NetWare file systems. NetWare file systems can be mounted over a network.

For information on using NetWare file systems over a network, see the section on setting up a file server in Chapter 18.

✦ **ntfs** — This is the Windows NT file system. It is supported as a read-only file system (so that you can mount and copy files from it). Read-write support is available, but not built into the kernel by default and is considered unreliable (some say, dangerous).

✦ **affs** — This file system is used with Amiga computers.

✦ **ufs** — This file system is popular on Sun Microsystems operating systems (i.e., Solaris and SunOS).

✦ **xenix** — This was added to be compatible with Xenix file systems (one of the first PC versions of UNIX). The system is obsolete and will probably be removed at some time.

✦ **xiafs** — This file system supports long filenames and larger inodes than file systems such as minux.

✦ **coherent** — This is the file system type used with Coherent or System V files. Like the xenix file system type, it will be removed some time in the future.

Using the fstab file to define mountable file systems

The hard disks on your local computer and the remote file systems you use every day are probably set up to automatically mount when you boot Linux. The definitions for which of these file systems are mounted are contained in the /etc/fstab file. Here's an example of an /etc/fstab file:

```
LABEL=/          /             ext3      defaults                      1 1
LABEL=/boot      /boot         ext3      defaults                      1 2
none             /dev/pts      devpts    gid=5,mode=620                0 0
/dev/fd0         /mnt/floppy   auto      noauto,owner                  0 0
none             /proc         proc      defaults                      0 0
/dev/hda5        swap          swap      defaults                      0 0
/dev/cdrom       /mnt/cdrom    iso9660   noauto,owner,kudzu,ro         0 0
/dev/hda1        /mnt/win      vfat      noauto                        0 0
```

All file systems that are listed in this file are mounted at boot time, except for those that are set to noauto in the fourth field. In this example, the root (/) and boot

(/boot) hard disk partitions are mounted at boot time, along with the /proc and /dev/pts file systems (which are not associated with particular devices). The floppy disk (/dev/fd0) and CD-ROM drives (/dev/cdrom) are not mounted at boot time. Definitions are put in the fstab file for floppy and CD-ROM drives so that they can be mounted in the future (as described later). I also added one additional line for /dev/hda1, which allows me to mount the Windows (vfat) partition on my computer so I don't have to always boot Windows to get at the files on my Windows partition.

Here is what is in each of the fields of the fstab file:

✦ **Field 1** — The name of the device representing the file system. The word "none" is often placed in this field for file systems (such as /proc and /dev/pts) that are not associated with special devices. Notice that this field can now include the LABEL option. Using LABEL, you can indicate a universally unique identifier (UUID) or volume label instead of a device name. The advantage to this approach is that, since the partition is identified by volume name, you can move a volume to a different device name and not have to change the fstab file.

✦ **Field 2** — The mount point in the file system. The file system contains all data from the mount point down the directory tree structure, unless another file system is mounted at some point beneath it.

✦ **Field 3** — The file system type. Valid file system types are described in the *Supported File Systems* section earlier in this chapter.

✦ **Field 4** — Options to the mount command. In the preceding example, the noauto option prevents the indicated file system from being mounted at boot time. Also, ro says to mount the file system read-only (which is reasonable for a CD-ROM player). Commas must separate options. See the mount command manual page (under the -o option) for information on other supported options.

Tip   Normally only the root user is allowed to mount a file system using the mount command. However, to allow any user to mount a file system (such as a file system on a floppy disk), you could add the user option to Field 4 of /etc/fstab.

✦ **Field 5** — The number in this field indicates whether or not the indicated file system needs to be dumped. A number 1 assumes that the file system needs to be dumped. A number 2 assumes that the file system doesn't need to be dumped.

✦ **Field 6** — The number in this field indicates whether or not the indicated file system needs to be checked with fsck. A number 1 assumes that the file system needs to be checked. A number 2 assumes that the file system doesn't need to be checked.

If you want to add an additional local disk or an additional partition, you can create an entry for the disk or partition in the /etc/fstab file. To get instructions on how to add entries for an NFS file system, see Chapter 18, "Setting Up a File Server."

Using the mount command to mount file systems

Your Red Hat Linux system automatically runs `mount -a` (mount all file systems) each time you boot. For that reason, you would typically only use the `mount` command for special situations. In particular, the average user and administrator uses the `mount` command in two ways:

✦ To display the disks, partitions, and remote file systems that are currently mounted.

✦ To temporarily mount a file system.

Any user can type the `mount` command (with no options) to see what file systems are currently mounted on the local Linux system. The following is an example of the `mount` command. It shows a single hard disk partition (`/dev/hda1`) containing the root (`/`) file system, and proc and devpts file system types mounted on `/proc` and `/dev`, respectively. The last entry shows a floppy disk, formatted with a standard Linux file system (ext3) mounted on the `/mnt/floppy` directory.

```
$ mount
/dev/hda3 on / type ext3 (rw)
none on /proc type proc (rw)
/dev/hda2 on /boot type ext3 (rw)
none on /dev/pts type devpts (rw,gid=5,mode=0620)
/dev/fd0 on /mnt/floppy type ext3 (rw)
```

The most common devices to mount by hand are your floppy disk and your CD-ROM. However, depending on the type of desktop you are using, CD-ROMs and floppy disks may be mounted for you automatically when you insert them. (In some cases, the autorun program may also run automatically. For example, autorun may start a CD music player or software package installer to handle the data on the medium.)

If you want to mount a file system manually, however, the `/etc/fstab` file helps make it simple to mount a floppy disk or a CD-ROM. In some cases, you can use the `mount` command with a single option to indicate what you want to mount, and information is taken from the `/etc/fstab` file to fill in the other options. Entries probably already in your `/etc/fstab` file let you do these quick mounts in the following two cases:

✦ **CD-ROM** — If you are mounting a CD-ROM that is in the standard ISO 9960 format (as most software CD-ROMs are), you can mount that CD-ROM by placing it in your CD-ROM drive and typing the following:

`# mount /mnt/cdrom`

By default, your CD-ROM is mounted on the `/mnt/cdrom` directory. (The file system type, device name, and other options are filled in automatically.) To see the contents, type `cd /mnt/cdrom`, then type `ls`. Files from the CD-ROM's root directory will be displayed.

✦ **Floppy Disk** — If you are mounting a floppy disk that is in the standard Linux file system format (ext3), you can mount that floppy disk by inserting it in your floppy drive and typing the following:

```
# mount /mnt/floppy
```

The file system type (ext3), device (/dev/fd0), and mount options are filled in automatically from the /etc/fstab file. You should be able to change to the floppy disk directory (cd /mnt/floppy) and list the contents of the floppy's top directory (ls).

Note
In both of the two previous cases, you could give the device name (/dev/cdrom or /dev/fd0, respectively) instead of the mount point directory to get the same results.

Of course, it is possible that you may get floppy disks you want to use that are in all formats. Someone may give you a floppy containing files from a Microsoft operating system (in MS-DOS format). Or you may get a file from another UNIX system. In those cases, you can fill in your own options, instead of relying on options from the /etc/fstab file. In some cases, Linux autodetects that the floppy disk contains an MS-DOS (or Windows vfat) file system and mount it properly without additional arguments. However, if it doesn't, here is an example of how to mount a floppy containing MS-DOS files:

```
# mount -t msdos /dev/fd0 /mnt/floppy
```

This shows the basic format of the mount command you would use to mount a floppy disk. You could change the msdos to any other supported file system type (described earlier in this chapter) to mount a floppy of that type. Instead of using floppy drive A: (/dev/fd0), you could use drive B: (/dev/fd1) or any other accessible drive. Instead of mounting on /mnt/floppy, you could create any other directory and mount the floppy there.

Here are some other useful options you could add along with the mount command:

✦ -t auto — If you aren't sure exactly what type of file system is contained on the floppy disk (or other medium you are mounting), use the -t auto option to indicate the file system type. The mount command will query the disk to try to guess what type of data it contains.

✦ -r — If you don't want to make changes to the mounted file system (or can't because it is a read-only medium), use this option when you mount it. This will mount it read-only.

✦ -w — This mounts the file system with read/write permission.

Some options to mount are available only for a specific file system type. See the mount manual page for those and other useful options.

Using the umount command to unmount a file system

When you are done using a temporary file system, or you want to unmount a permanent file system temporarily, you can use the umount command. This command detaches the file system from its mount point in your Red Hat Linux file system. To use umount, you can give it either a directory name or a device name. For example:

```
# umount /mnt/floppy
```

This unmounts the device (probably /dev/fd0) from the mount point /mnt/floppy. You could also have done this using the form:

```
# umount /dev/fd0
```

Note If you get a message that the "device is busy," the umount request has failed. The reason is that either a process has a file open on the device or that a you have a shell open with a directory on the device as a current directory. Stop the processes or change to a directory outside of the device you are trying to un-mount for the umount request to succeed.

Using the mkfs command to create a file system

It is possible to create a file system, for any supported file system type, on a disk or partition that you choose. This is done with the mkfs command. While this is most useful for creating file systems on hard disk partitions, you can create file systems on floppy disks as well.

Note Though supposedly you should be able to create a file system of several different supported file system types, my installation of Linux allowed me to create only ext3 and minix file systems.

Here is an example of mkfs for creating a file system:

```
# mkfs -t ext2 /dev/fd0
mke2fs 1.22, 22-Jun-2001 for EXT2 FS 0.5b, 95/08/09
Filesystem label=
OS type: Linux
Block size=1024 (log=0)
Fragment size=1024 (log=0)
184 inodes, 1440 blocks
72 blocks (5.00%) reserved for the super user
First data block=1
1 block group
8192 blocks per group, 8192 fragments per group
184 inodes per group

Writing inode tables: done
```

```
Writing superblocks and filesystem accounting information: done

The filesystem will be checked every 25 mounts or 180 days,
whichever comes first. Use tune2fs -c or -i to override.
```

You can see the statistics that are output with the formatting done by the mkfs command. The number of inodes and block created are output. Likewise, the number of blocks per group and fragments per group are also output. You could now mount this file system (mount /mnt/floppy), change to it as your current directory (cd /mnt/floppy), and create files on it as you please.

Adding a hard disk

Adding a new hard disk to your computer so that it can be used by Linux requires a combination of steps described in previous sections. The general steps are as follows:

1. Install the hard disk hardware.

2. Identify the partitions on the new hard disk.

3. Create the file systems on the new hard disk.

4. Mount the file systems.

The easiest way to add a hard disk to Linux is to have the whole hard disk devoted to a single Linux partition. You can have multiple partitions, however, and assign them each to different types of file systems and different mount points, if you like. The procedure below describes how to add a hard disk containing a single Linux partition. Along the way, however, it also notes which steps you need to repeat to have multiple file systems with multiple mount points.

Note

This procedure assumes that Red Hat Linux is already installed and working on the computer. If this is not the case, follow the instructions for adding a hard disk on your current operating system. Later, when you install Red Hat Linux, you can identify this disk when you are asked to partition your hard disk(s).

1. Install the hard disk into your computer. Follow the manufacturer's instructions for physically installing and connecting the new hard disk. If, presumably, this is a second hard disk, you may need to change jumpers on the hard disk unit itself to have it operate as a slave hard disk. You may also need to change the BIOS settings.

2. Boot your computer to Red Hat Linux.

3. Determine the device name for the hard disk. As root user from a shell, type the following:

```
# dmesg | less
```

From the output, look for an indication that the new hard disk was found. For example, if it is a second IDE hard disk, you should see "hdb:" in the output. For a second SCI drive, you should see "sdb:" instead. Be sure you identify the right disk or you will erase all the data from disks you probably want to keep!

4. Use the `fdisk` command to format the new disk. For example, if you are formatting the second IDE disk (hdb), you could type the following:

   `# fdisk /dev/hdb1`

5. If the disk had existing partitions on it, you can change or delete those partitions now. Or, you can simply reformat the whole disk to blow everything away. Use "p" to view all partitions and "d" to delete a partition.

6. To create a new partition, type the following:

   `n`

   You are asked to choose an extended or primary partition.

7. To choose a primary partition, type the following:

   `p`

   You are asked the partition number.

8. If you are creating the first partition (or if there will only be one partition), type the number one:

   `1`

   You are asked to enter the first cylinder number (with one being the default).

9. To begin at the second cylinder, type the number two as follows:

   `2`

   You are asked to enter the last cylinder.

10. If you are using the hard disk, use the last cylinder number shown. Otherwise, either choose the ending cylinder number or indicate how many MB the partition should contain.

11. If you are creating multiple partitions on this hard disk, repeat the previous five steps to create each partition.

12. Type `w` to write the changes to the hard disk. At this point, you should be back at the shell.

13. To make a file system on the new disk partition, use the `mkfs` command. By default, this command creates an ext2 file system, which is useable by Linux. To create an ext2 file system on the first partition of the second hard disk, type the following:

    `# mkfs /dev/hdb1`

If you created multiple partitions, repeat this step for each partition (such as `/dev/hdb2`, `/dev/hdb3`, and so on).

Tip

This example creates an ext2 file system, which is the default. You can use other commands, or options to this command, to create other file system types. For example, use the `mkfs.vfat` command to create a VFAT file system, `mkfs.bfs` for BFS, `mkfs.minix` for Minix, `mkfs.msdos` for DOS, or `mkfs.reiserfs` for Reiser file system type. The `tune2fs` command, described later in this section, can be used to change the ext2 file system to an ext3 file system.

14. Once the file system is created, you can have the partition permanently mounted by editing the `/etc/fstab` and adding the new partition. Here is an example of a line you might add to that file:

```
/dev/hdb1          /abc          ext2          defaults          1 1
```

In this example, the partition (`/dev/hdb1`) is mounted on the `/abc` directory as an ext2 file system. The default keyword causes the partition to be mounted at boot time. The numbers "1 1" cause the disk to be checked for errors. Add one line like the one shown above for each partition you created.

15. Create the mount point. For example, to mount the partition on `/abc` (as shown in the previous step), type the following:

```
# mkdir /abc
```

Create your other mount points if you created multiple partitions. The next time you boot Red Hat Linux, the partition will be automatically mounted on the `/abc` directory, as will any other partitions you added.

Once you have created the file systems on your partitions, a nice tool for adjusting those file systems is the `tune2fs` command. Using `tune2fs`, you can change volume labels, how often the file system is checked, and error behavior. You can also use `tune2fs` to change an ext2 file system to an ext3 file system so that the file system can use journaling. Here is an example:

```
# tune2fs -j /dev/hdb1
tune2fs 1.23, 15-Aug-2001 for EXT2 FS 0.5b, 95/08/09
Creating journal inode: done
This filesystem will be automatically checked every 33 mounts
or
180 days, whichever comes first. Use tune2fs -c or -i to
override.
```

By adding the `-J` option to `tune2fs`, you can change either the journal size or attach the file system to an external journal block device. After you have used `tune2fs` to change your file system type, you probably need to correct your `/etc/fstab` file to include changing the file system type from ext2 to ext3.

Checking System Space

Running out of disk space on your computer is not a happy situation. Using tools that come with Red Hat Linux, you can keep track of how much disk space has been used on your computer, and you can keep an eye on users who consume a lot of disk space.

Displaying system space with df

You can display the space available in your file systems using the df command. To see the space available on all of the mounted file systems on your Linux computer, type df with no options:

```
$ df
Filesystem   1k-blocks      Used   Available  Use%  Mounted on
/dev/hda3    30645460    2958356    26130408   11%  /
/dev/hda2       46668       8340       35919   19%  /boot
/dev/fd0         1412         13        1327    1%  /mnt/floppy
```

The output here shows the space available on the hard disk partition mounted on the root partition (/dev/hda1), /boot partition (/dev/hda2), and the floppy disk mounted on the /mnt/floppy directory (/dev/fd0). Disk space is shown in 1K blocks. To produce output in a more human-readable form, use the -h option as follows:

```
$ df -h
Filesystem          Size  Used  Avail  Use% Mounted on
/dev/hda3           29G   2.9G   24G   11% /
/dev/hda2           46M   8.2M   25M   19% /boot
/dev/fd0            1.4M   13k  1.2M    1% /mnt/floppy
```

With the df -h option, output appears in a friendlier megabyte or gigabyte listing. Other options with df let you:

- ✦ Print only file systems of a particular type (-t *type*)
- ✦ Exclude file systems of a particular type (-x *type*)
- ✦ Include file systems that have no space, such as /proc and /dev/pts (-a)
- ✦ List only available and used inodes (-i)
- ✦ Display disk space in certain block sizes (--block-size=*#*)

Checking disk usage with du

To find out how much space is being consumed by a particular directory (and its subdirectories), you can use the du command. With no options, du lists all directories below the current directory, along with the space consumed by each directory. At the end, du produces total disk space used within that directory structure.

The du command is a good way to check how much space is being used by a particular user (du /home/user1) or in a particular file system partition (du /var). By default, disk space is displayed in 1K block sizes. To make the output more friendly (in kilobytes, megabytes, and gigabytes), use the -h option as follows:

```
$ du -h /home/jake
114k    /home/jake/httpd/stuff
234k    /home/jake/httpd
137k    /home/jake/uucp/data
701k    /home/jake/uucp
1.0M    /home/jake
```

The output shows the disk space used in each directory under the home directory of the user name jake (/home/jake). Disk space consumed is shown in kilobytes (k) and megabytes (M). The total space consumed by /home/jake is shown on the last line.

Finding disk consumption with find

The find command is a great way to find file consumption of your hard disk using a variety of criteria. You can get a good idea of where disk space can be recovered by finding files that are over a certain size or were created by a particular person.

Note   You need to be root user to run this command effectively.

In the following example, the find command searches the root file system (/) for any files owned by the user named jake (-user jake) and prints the filenames. The output of the find command is then listed with a long listing in size order (ls -ldS). Finally that output is sent to the file /tmp/jake. When you read the file /tmp/jake, you will find all of the files that are owned by the user jake, listed in size order. Here is the command line:

```
# find / -user jake -print -xdev | xargs ls -ldS > /tmp/jake
```

Tip   The -xdev option prevents file systems other than the selected file system from being searched. This is a good way to cut out a lot of junk that may be output from the /proc file system. It could also keep large remotely mounted file systems from being searched.

The next example is similar to the previous one, except that instead of looking for a user's files, this command line looks for files that are larger than 100 kilobytes (`-size 100k`). Here is the command line:

```
# find / -size 100k -print -xdev | xargs ls -ldS > /tmp/size
```

You can often save yourself a lot of disk space by just removing some of the largest files that are no longer needed. Open the `/tmp/size` file in this example and large files are sorted by size.

Monitoring System Performance

If your Linux system is being used as a multiuser computer, sharing the processing power of that computer can be a major issue. Likewise, any time you can stop a runaway process or reduce the overhead of an unnecessary program running, your Linux server can do a better job serving files, Web pages, or e-mail to the people that rely on it.

Utilities are included with Linux that can help you monitor the performance of your Linux system. The kinds of features you want to monitor in Linux include CPU usage, memory usage (RAM and swap space), and overall load on the system. The following sections describe tools for monitoring Linux.

Checking system load average with xload

One way of keeping an eye on general system performance is to open an xload window on your desktop and put it off in the corner somewhere. The xload window graphically represents the performance of your system. It periodically checks the load on the system and then charts demand on the system over time.

By default, xload updates the display every 10 seconds. Scale lines on the window help you monitor when xload has exceeded certain limits. The label in the xload window shows the system name. By running xload windows from various host computers and displaying them on your screen, you can monitor a whole set of computers at once.

Figure 10-6 shows the xload window.

Figure 10-6: Xload graphically represents performance of a Linux system.

Monitoring CPU usage with top and gtop

Start the `top` utility in a terminal window, and it displays the top CPU consuming processes on your computer. Every five seconds, `top` will determine which processes are consuming the most CPU time and display them in descending order on your screen.

By adding the `-S` option to `top`, you can have the display show you the cumulative CPU time that the process, as well as any child processes that may already have exited, has spent. If you want to change how often the screen is updated, you can add the `-d` *secs* option, where *secs* is replaced by the number of seconds between updates.

Tip
If you prefer a more graphical version of top, try the Gnome System Monitor. You can start this monitor by typing the `gtop` command from a Terminal window. Because gtop is an X application, you need to have your desktop running to use it (while `top` can run in any shell). The cool thing about `gtop` is that you can click on columns in the `gtop` display to sort data by application size, memory usage, CPU usage, or a variety of other variables. You may need to install Gnome libraries to use gtop from a different desktop environment (such as KDE).

Figure 10-7 shows an example of the gtop.

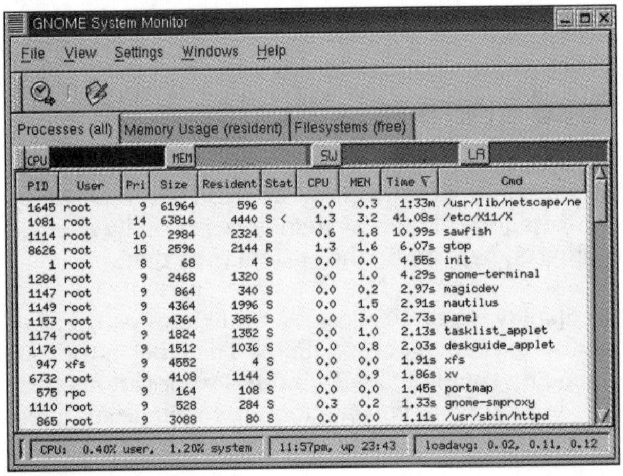

Figure 10-7: Note the graphical components in this example of gtop.

You can see from the Gnome System Monitor display that much of the processing power of this system is being consumed by graphical components. This includes the X Window system itself, Netscape Navigator, sawfish (the window manager), and gtop itself.

Checking virtual memory and CPU usage with vmstat

Nothing can slow down system performance more than running out of virtual memory. Waiting for CPU time can also keep processes from running efficiently. The vmstat command displays a variety of statistics that can tell you how efficiently your Linux system is running.

Figure 10-8 shows an example of a vmstat command output. In this example, vmstat is run with a five-second delay between updates and with a count of five updates before exiting.

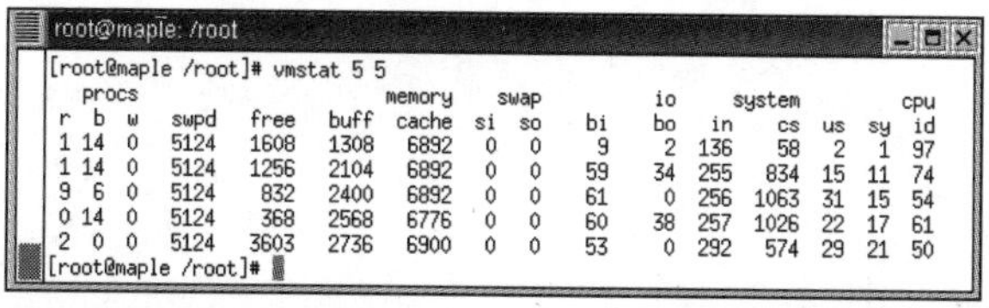

```
root@maple: /root                                                    _ □ X
[root@maple /root]# vmstat 5 5
   procs                    memory   swap       io       system        cpu
 r  b  w   swpd   free   buff  cache  si  so   bi   bo   in    cs   us  sy  id
 1 14  0   5124   1608   1308  6892   0   0    9    2   136    58    2   1  97
 1 14  0   5124   1256   2104  6892   0   0   59   34   255   834   15  11  74
 9  6  0   5124    832   2400  6892   0   0   61    0   256  1063   31  15  54
 0 14  0   5124    368   2568  6776   0   0   60   38   257  1026   22  17  61
 2  0  0   5124   3603   2736  6900   0   0   53    0   292   574   29  21  50
[root@maple /root]#
```

Figure 10-8: Display the processes consuming the most CPU time with top.

The following is some of the information that can be interpreted from this output:

✦ Where there are not a lot of processes running on this CPU, under the procs runtime column (r), you can see that in each case there were processes waiting for runtime (in the third update, nine processes were waiting to run). Up to 14 processes (b) were waiting in an uninterruptible sleep.

✦ Under the memory free column, you can see that the amount of idle memory was down in the third and fourth update, then recovered for the fifth update.

✦ Despite the demands on the CPU time, no memory was swapped to or from the hard disk (swap si and so).

✦ While there were processes waiting for CPU time, the processor itself was idle half the time or more in each instance (cpu id was between 50 and 97 percent). Demand from user processes (us) was greater than demand from system processes (sy).

Summary

Even though you may be using Red Hat Linux as a single-user system, many of the tasks you must do to keep your computer running are defined as administrator tasks. A special user account called the root user is needed to do many of the things necessary to keep Linux working as you would like it to.

If you are administering a Linux system that is used by lots of people, the task of administration becomes even larger. You need to be able to add and support users, maintain the file systems, and make sure that system performance serves your users well.

To help the administrator, Linux comes with a variety of command-line utilities and graphical windows for configuring and maintaining your system. The `linuxconf` program contains dozens of configuration and control tasks for everything from network configuration to user setup to run level management tools. The kudzu program can be used to probe and reconfigure Red Hat Linux when you add or remove hardware. Commands such as `mkfs` and `mount` let you create and mount file systems, respectively. Tools like `top`, `gtop`, and `vmstat` let you monitor system performance.

✦   ✦   ✦

Setting Up and Supporting Users

One of the more fundamental tasks of administering a Red Hat Linux server is setting up and supporting user accounts. Computers, after all, are tools to be used by people. Apocalyptic science fiction plots aside, without users, computers have no purpose.

When you install Red Hat Linux, you are required to create at least two user accounts: one for the root user (administrator) and one for any name you choose (regular user). Several other administrative user accounts are set up automatically that you will probably never use.

Cross-Reference For a description of the root user account and how to use it, see Chapter 10.

This chapter discusses the basics of setting up a user account and offers tips on easing the burdens of supporting a large number of Red Hat Linux users.

Creating User Accounts

Every person who uses your Red Hat Linux system should have a separate user account. Having a user account provides each person with an area in which to securely store files, as well as a means of tailoring his or her user interface (GUI, path, environment variables, and so on) to suit the way that he or she uses the computer.

You can add user accounts to your Red Hat Linux system in several different ways. This chapter describes how to use the useradd command to add user accounts to Red Hat Linux.

Note The linuxconf facility, which is a general-purpose administration tool that can also be used for adding users, is no longer being installed by default in a Red Hat Linux workstation install. It is also likely to be dropped altogether from the Red Hat Linux distribution at some future release. However, if you prefer a more menu-driven approach to adding users, you can currently install the linuxconf package from CD-2 of the Red Hat Linux distribution that comes with this book.

The most straightforward method for creating a new user from the shell is with the useradd command. After opening a Terminal window with root permission, you simply invoke the useradd command at the command prompt, passing the details of the new account as parameters. The only required parameter is the login name of the user, but you will probably want to include some additional information. Each item of account information is preceded by a single letter option code with a dash in front of it. Table 11-1 lists the options that are available with the useradd command.

Table 11-1
useradd Command Options

Option	Description
-c comment	Provide a description of the new user account. Usually just the person's full name. Replace comment with the name of the user account.
-d home_dir	Set the home directory to use for the account. The default is to name it the same as the login name and to place it in /home. Replace home_dir with the directory name to use.
-D	Rather than create a new account, save the supplied information as the new default settings for any new accounts that are created.
-e expire_date	Assign the expiration date for the account in MM/DD/YYYY format. Replace expire_date with the expiration date to use.
-f inactivity	Set the number of days after a password expires until the account is permanently disabled. Setting this to 0 disables the account immediately after the password has expired. Setting it to -1 disables the option, which is the default behavior. Replace inactivity with the number to use.
-g group	Set the primary group (as listed in the /etc/group file) that the new user will be in. Replace group with the group name to use.

Option	Description
-G grouplist	Add the new user to the supplied comma-separated list of groups.
-k skel_dir	Set the skeleton directory containing initial configuration files and login scripts that should be copied to a new user's home directory. This parameter can only be used in conjunction with the -m option. Replace skel_dir with the directory name to use.
-m	Automatically create the user's home directory and copy the files in the skeleton directory (/etc/skel) to it.
-M	Do not create the new user's home directory, even if the default behavior is set to create it.
-n	Turn off the default behavior of creating a new group that matches the name and user ID of the new user.
-r	Allows you to create a new account with a user ID in the range reserved for system accounts.
-s shell	Specify the command shell to use for this account. Replace shell with the command shell.
-u user_id	Specify the user ID number for the account. The default behavior is to automatically assign the next available number. Replace user_id with the ID number.

As an example, let's create an account for a new user named Mary Smith with a login name of mary. First, log in as root, then type the following command:

```
# useradd -c "Mary Smith" mary
```

Next, set Mary's initial password using the passwd command. It prompts you to type the password twice.

```
# passwd mary
New UNIX password: *******
Retype new UNIX password: *******
```

Cross-
Reference   Refer to Chapter 14 for tips on picking good passwords.

In creating the account for Mary, the useradd command performs several actions:

✦ Reads the /etc/login.defs file to learn the default values it should use when creating accounts.

✦ Parses the command line parameters to find out which default values should be overridden.

✦ Creates a new user entry in the `/etc/passwd` and `/etc/shadow` files based on the default values and command-line parameters.

✦ Creates any new group entries in the `/etc/group` file.

✦ Creates a home directory based on the user's name and located within the `/home` parent directory.

✦ Copies any files located within the `/etc/skel` directory to the new home directory. This usually includes login and application startup scripts.

The preceding example uses a bare minimum of the available `useradd` options. Most of the account settings are assigned using default values. Here is an example that uses a few more options:

```
# useradd -m -g users -G wheel,sales -s /bin/tcsh -c "Mary Smith" mary
```

In this case, the `useradd` command is told to create a home directory for `mary` (`-m`), make `users` the primary group she belongs to (`-g`), add her to the groups `wheel` and `sales`, and assign `tcsh` as her primary command shell (`-s`). This results in a line similar to the following being added to the `/etc/passwd` file:

```
mary:x:500:100:Mary Smith:/home/mary:/bin/tcsh
```

In the `/etc/passwd` file, each line represents a single user account record. Each field is separated from the next by a colon (`:`) character. The field's position determines what it is. As you can see, the login name is first. The password field contains an `x` because we are using a shadow password file to store encrypted password data. The user ID selected by the `useradd` command was 500. The primary group ID is 100, which corresponds to the `users` group in the `/etc/group` file. The comment field was correctly set to Mary Smith, the home directory was automatically assigned as `/home/mary`, and the command shell was assigned as `/bin/tcsh`, exactly as specified with the `useradd` options.

The `/etc/group` file holds information about the different groups on your Red Hat Linux system and the users that belong to them. Groups are useful for allowing multiple people to share access to the same files while denying access to others. If you peek at the `/etc/group` file, you should find something similar to this:

```
bin::1:root,bin,daemon
daemon::2:root,bin,daemon
sys::3:root,bin,adm
adm::4:root,adm,daemon
tty::5:
disk::6:root
lp::7:daemon,lp
mem::8:
```

```
kmem::9:
wheel::10:root,joe,mary
mail::12:mail
news::13:news
uucp::14:uucp
man::15:
games::20:
gopher::30:
dip::40:
ftp::50:
nobody::99:
users::100:
sales::500:bob,jane,joe,mary
```

Each line in the group file contains the name of a group, the group ID number associated with it, and a list of users in that group. Note that `mary` was added to the `wheel` and `sales` groups. Though Mary's primary group is `users`, her name doesn't need to be added there. The `useradd` command did that for you when you included the `-G` flag.

It is actually rather significant that `mary` was added to the `wheel` group. By doing this, we are granting her the ability to use the `su` command to become root (assuming she knows the root password). If a user who is not in the `wheel` group attempts to `su` to root, he or she will receive an error message.

Cross-Reference See Chapter 10 for a description of the `su` command.

In this example, we used the `-g` option to assign `mary` to the `users` group. If you leave off the `-g` parameter, the default behavior is for `useradd` to create a new group with the same name and ID number as the user, which is assigned as the new user's primary group. For example, look at the following `useradd` command:

```
# useradd -m -G wheel,sales -s /bin/tcsh -c "Mary Smith" mary
```

It would result in a `/etc/passwd` line like this:

```
mary:x:500:500:Mary Smith:/home/mary:/bin/tcsh
```

It would also result in a new group line like this:

```
mary:x:500:
```

Note that the user ID and group ID fields now have the same number. If you set up all of your users this way, you will have a unique group for every user on the system, which allows for increased flexibility in the sharing of files among your users.

Setting User Defaults

The useradd command determines the default values for new accounts by reading the /etc/login.defs file. You can modify those defaults by either editing that file manually with a standard text editor or by running the useradd command with the -D option. If you choose to edit the file manually, here is what you will face:

```
# *REQUIRED*
# Directory where mailboxes reside, _or_ name of file,
relative
# to the home directory. If you _do_ define both, MAIL_DIR
# takes precedence.
# QMAIL_DIR is for Qmail
#
#QMAIL_DIR Maildir
MAIL_DIR      /var/spool/mail
#MAIL_FILE .mail

# Password aging controls:
#
# PASS_MAX_DAYS Maximum number of days a password may be used.
# PASS_MIN_DAYS Minimum number of days allowed between
password
# changes.
# PASS_MIN_LEN Minimum acceptable password length.
# PASS_WARN_AGE Number of days warning given before a password
# expires.
#
PASS_MAX_DAYS     99999
PASS_MIN_DAYS      0
PASS_MIN_LEN       5
PASS_WARN_AGE     7

#
# Min/max values for automatic uid selection in useradd
#
UID_MIN                  500
UID_MAX                60000

#
# Min/max values for automatic gid selection in groupadd
#
GID_MIN                  500
GID_MAX                60000
```

```
#
# If defined, this command is run when removing a user.
# It should remove any at/cron/print jobs etc. owned by
# the user to be removed (passed as the first argument).
#
#USERDEL_CMD /usr/sbin/userdel_local


#
# If useradd should create home directories for users by
# default. On RH systems, we do. This option is ORed with on
# the -m flag useradd command line.
#
CREATE_HOME yes
```

Blank lines and comments beginning with a pound sign (#) are ignored by the useradd command. All other lines contain keyword/value pairs. For example, the very first noncomment line is the keyword MAIL_DIR followed by some white space and the value /var/spool/mail. This tells useradd that the initial user e-mail mailbox should be created in that directory. Following that are keyword/value pairs, which enable you to customize the valid range of automatically assigned user ID numbers or group ID numbers. A comment section that explains that keyword's purpose precedes each keyword. Altering a default value is as simple as editing the value associated with that keyword and then saving the login.defs file.

If you want to view the defaults, type the useradd command with the -D option as follows:

```
# useradd -D
GROUP=100
HOME=/home
INACTIVE=-1
EXPIRE=
SHELL=/bin/bash
SKEL=/etc/skel
```

You can also use the -D option to change defaults. When run with this flag, useradd refrains from actually creating a new user account; instead, it saves any additionally supplied options as the new default values in /etc/login.defs. Not all useradd options can be used in conjunction with the -D option. You may use only the five options listed in Table 11-2.

Table 11-2
useradd Options for Changing User Defaults

Options	Description
`-b default_home`	Set the default directory in which user home directories will be created. Replace `default_home` with the directory name to use. Usually this is `/home`.
`-e default_expire_date`	Set the default expiration date on which the user account is disabled. The `default_expire_date` value should be replaced with a date in the form MM/DD/YYYY—for example, 10/15/2001.
`-f default_inactive`	Set the number of days after a password has expired before the account is disabled. Replace `default_inactive` with a number representing the number of days.
`-g default_group`	Set the default group that new users will be placed in. Normally `useradd` creates a new group with the same name and ID number as the user. Replace `default_group` with the group name to use.
`-s default_shell`	Set the default shell for new users. Normally this is /bin/sh. Replace default_shell with the full path to the shell that you want as the default for new users.

To set any of the defaults, give the `-D` option first; then add any of the defaults you want to set. For example, to set the default home directory location to `/home/everyone` and the default shell to `/bin/tcsh`, type the following:

```
# useradd -D -b /home/everyone -s /bin/tcsh
```

Besides setting up user defaults, an administrator can create default files that are copied to each user's home directory for use. These files can include login scripts and shell configuration files (such as `.bashrc`). The following sections describe some of these files.

Supplying initial login scripts

Many Red Hat Linux applications, including the command shell itself, read a configuration file at startup. It is traditional that these configuration files are stored in the users' home directories. In this way, each user can customize the behavior of the command shell and other applications without affecting that behavior for other users. In this way, global defaults can be assigned from `/etc/profile`, then those settings can be enhanced or overridden by a user's personal files.

The bash command shell, for example, looks for a file called .bashrc in the current user's home directory whenever it starts up. Similarly, the tcsh command shell looks for a file called .tcshrc in the user's home directory. You may see a repeating theme here. Startup scripts and configuration files for various applications usually begin with a dot (.) character and end in the letters rc. You can supply initial default versions of these and other configuration files by placing them in the /etc/skel directory. When you run the useradd command, these scripts and configuration files are copied to the new user's home directory.

Supplying an initial .bashrc file

By supplying your users with an initial .bashrc file, you provide them a starting point from which they can further customize their shell environment. Moreover, you can be sure that the file is created with the appropriate access permissions so as not to compromise system security. This script is, after all, run each time the user starts a new bash shell. So, security is a concern. It is also a good place to supply useful command aliases and additions to the command search path. Let us look at an example:

```
# .bashrc
# User specific aliases and functions
alias rm='rm -i'
alias cp='cp -i'
alias mv='mv -i'

if [ -f /etc/bashrc ]; then
        . /etc/bashrc
fi

PATH=$PATH:/usr/bin:/usr/local/bin
export PATH
```

This sample .bashrc file creates aliases for the rm, cp, and mv commands that result in the -i option always being used (unless overridden with the -f option). This protects against the accidental deletion of files. Next, the file executes the /etc/bashrc (if it exists) to read any further global bash values. This file also sets the search path.

Supplying an initial .tcshrc file

This following example .tcshrc file does basically the same thing as the preceding .bashrc example. However, this file (which is for the root user) has the additional task of setting the appearance of the command prompt:

```
# .tcshrc

# User specific aliases and functions
```

```
alias rm 'rm -i'
alias cp 'cp -i'
alias mv 'mv -i'

setenv PATH "$PATH:/usr/bin:/usr/local/bin"

set prompt='[%n@%m %c]# '
```

Instead of using the export command to set environment variables, the tcsh shell uses the setenv command. In the example, setenv is used to set the PATH variable. The shell prompt is set to include your user name (%n), your computer name (%m), and the name of the current directory (%c). So, if you were to use the tcsh shell as the root user on a computer named maple with /tmp as your current directory, your prompt would appear as follows:

```
[root@maple /tmp]#
```

The .tcshrc file can also be named .cshrc. The tcsh shell is really an extended version of the csh shell (in fact, you can invoke it by the csh name). When a tcsh shell is started, it first looks for a .tcshrc file in the current user's home directory. If it can't find a file by that name, it looks for the other name, .cshrc. Thus, either name is appropriate.

Configuring systemwide shell options

Allowing individually customizable shell startup files for each user is a very flexible and useful practice. But sometimes you need more centralized control than that. You may have an environment variable or other shell setting that you want set for every user, without exception. If you add that setting to each individual shell, the user has the ability to edit that file and remove it. Furthermore, if that setting must be changed in the future, you must change it in every single user's shell startup file.

Fortunately, there is a better way. There are default startup files that apply to all users of the computer that each command shell reads before reading the user-specific files. In the case of the bash command shell, it reads the /etc/bashrc file before doing anything else.

Similarly, the tcsh shell reads the /etc/csh.cshrc file before processing the .cshrc or .tcshrc file found in the user's home directory. The /etc/csh.cshrc file that ships with Red Hat Linux is as follows:

```
# /etc/cshrc
#
# csh configuration for all shell invocations.

# by default, we want this to get set.
```

```
# Even for non-interactive, non-login shells.
 [ `id -gn` = `id -un` -a `id -u` -gt 99 ]
if $status then
  umask 022
else
  umask 002
endif

if ($?prompt) then
  if ($?tcsh) then
    set prompt='[%n@%m %c]$ '
  else
    set prompt=\[`id -nu`@`hostname -s`\]\$\
  endif
endif

if ( -d /etc/profile.d ) then
  set nonomatch
      foreach i ( /etc/profile.d/*.csh )
       if ( -r $i ) then
                    source $i
       endif
      end
  unset i nonomatch
endif
```

The /etc/cshrc and /etc/bashrc files set a variety of shell environment options. If you wish to modify or add to the shell environment supplied to every single user on the system, the /etc/bashrc or /etc/cshrc files are the place to do it.

Creating Portable Desktops

Linux is an operating system that was born on the Internet, so it is not surprising that it has such strong networking capabilities. This makes Linux an excellent server, but it also allows Linux to be an excellent desktop workstation, especially in a highly networked environment. Red Hat Linux lets you easily set up your users with a portable desktop that follows them from computer to computer. With other leading desktop operating systems, it is not nearly as easy.

Normally, a Red Hat Linux user's home directory is located within the /home directory. I suggest an alternative. Within the home directory, create a directory named after the system's hostname. Within that directory, create the users' home directories. Thus, on a Linux system named dexter, the user mary would have a home directory of /home/dexter/mary instead of /home/mary. There is a very good reason for doing this.

If you are logged into the Linux system `ratbert` and wish to access your home directory on `dexter` as if it were stored locally, the best approach is to use Network File System (NFS) to mount `dexter`'s `/home` directory on the `/home` on `ratbert`. This results in having the same contents of your home directory available to you no matter which machine you log in to.

Cross-Reference You can read more about NFS in Chapter 18.

To mount `dexter`'s `/home` directory as described, you would add a line similar to the following in `ratbert`'s `/etc/fstab` file:

```
dexter:/home /home nfs defaults 0 0
```

You would also add an entry similar to the following in `dexter`'s `/etc/exports` directory:

```
/home ratbert
```

Now, when `ratbert` boots up, it automatically mounts `dexter`'s home partition over the network. This enables us to treat the remote files and directories on `dexter`'s `/home` as if they are locally stored on `ratbert`. Unfortunately, this has the side effect of "covering up" `ratbert`'s actual `/home` directory.

This is where the extra directory level based on the system name comes to the rescue. With all of `dexter`'s home directories located in `/home/dexter` and all of `ratbert`'s home directories located in `/home/ratbert`, we can remove the danger of one system covering up the home directories of another. In fact, let us take this example one step further: Imagine a scenario in which the systems `dexter`, `ratbert`, and `daffy` all have portable desktops that are shared with the other systems. The `/etc/fstab` and `/etc/exports` files for each system should have the following lines added to them.

The `/etc/exports` and `/etc/fstab` files for `dexter` are as follows:

/etc/exports file
```
/home/dexter ratbert,daffy
```
/etc/fstab file
```
Ratbert:/home/ratbert /home/ratbert nfs defaults 0 0
Daffy:/home/daffy     /home/daffy   nfs defaults 0 0
```

The `/etc/exports` and `/etc/fstab` files for `ratbert` are:

/etc/exports
```
/home/ratbert dexter,daffy
```

/etc/fstab

```
dexter:/home/dexter  /home/dexter  nfs  defaults  0 0
daffy:/home/daffy    /home/daffy   nfs  defaults  0 0
```

The /etc/exports and /etc/fstab files for daffy are:

/etc/exports

```
/home/dexter ratbert,dexter
```

/etc/fstab

```
Ratbert:/home/ratbert  /home/ratbert  nfs  defaults  0 0
Dexter:/home/dexter    /home/dexter   nfs  defaults  0 0
```

As you can see, each system uses NFS to mount the home directories from the other two systems. A user can travel from server to server and see exactly the same desktop on each system.

Providing Support to Users

Creating new user accounts is just one small administrative task among many. No single chapter can adequately discuss all the tasks that are involved in the ongoing support of users. But I share with you a few hints and procedures to ease that burden.

Creating a technical support mailbox

E-mail is a wonderful communication tool, especially for the overworked system administrator. In my experience, people put more thought and effort into their e-mail messages than into the voice messages that they leave. A text message can be edited for clarity before being sent, and important details can be cut and pasted from other sources. This makes e-mail an excellent method for Red Hat Linux users to communicate with their system administrator.

In an office with only a few users, you can probably get away with using your personal mailbox to send and receive support e-mails. In a larger office, however, you should create a separate mailbox reserved only for technical support issues. This has several advantages over the use of your personal mailbox:

✦ Support messages will not be confused with personal or other non-support-related messages.

✦ Multiple people can check the mailbox and share administrative responsibility without needing to read each other's personal e-mail.

✦ Support e-mail is easily redirected to another person's mailbox when you go on vacation. Your personal e-mail continues to go to your personal mailbox.

One easy solution is to simply create a support e-mail alias that redirects messages to an actual mailbox or list of mailboxes. For example, suppose you wish to create a support alias that redistributes e-mail to the user accounts for support staff members Joe, Mary, and Bob. You would log in as root, edit the /etc/alias file, and add lines similar to the following:

```
# Technical support mailing list
support: joe, mary, bob
```

After saving the file, you need to run the newaliases command to recompile the /etc/aliases file into a database format. Now your users can send e-mail to the support e-mail address, and the message is automatically routed to everyone on the list. When a member of the list responds to that message, he or she should use the "Reply To All" option so that the other support staff members also see the message. Otherwise, multiple people may attempt to solve the same problem, resulting in wasteful duplication of effort.

You may also choose to create an actual support user account. The technical support staff would log in to this account to check messages and send replies. In this manner, all replies are stamped with the support login name and not the personal e-mail address of a staff member.

Resetting a user's password

A common (if not the most common) problem that your users will encounter is the inability to log in. The most common causes for this are:

✦ They have the Caps Lock key on.

✦ They have forgotten the password.

✦ The password has expired.

If the Caps Lock key is not on, then you probably need to reset the individual's password. Looking up the password and telling it to the user is not an option. Red Hat Linux stores passwords in an encrypted format. Instead, use the passwd command to assign a new password to the user's account. Tell the user what that new password is (preferably in person), but then set the password to expire soon so that he or she must choose one (hopefully, a new one that is more easily remembered).

See Chapter 14 for advice on how to select good passwords.

If you must reset a user's password, do so with the passwd command. While logged in as root, type passwd followed by the login name you are resetting. You are prompted to enter the password twice.

```
# passwd mary
```

After resetting the password, set it to expire so that the user is forced to change it the next time she logs in. You can use the `chage` command to set an expiration period for the password and to trick the system into thinking that the password is long overdue to be changed.

```
# chage -M 30 -d 0 mary
```

The `-M 30` option tells the system to expire Mary's password every 30 days. The `-d 0` option tricks the system into thinking that her password has not been changed since January 1, 1970.

 Cross-Reference   You can read more about password security and the `chage` command in Chapter 14.

Modifying accounts

Occasionally, a user needs more done to an account than just a resetting of the password. A person may become married and need the full name in the comment field changed. You may need to change the groups that user is in, or the drive that a home directory resides on. The `usermod` command is the tool for these tasks.

The `usermod` command is similar to the `useradd` command and even shares some of the same options. However, instead of adding new accounts, it enables you to change various details of existing accounts. When invoking the `usermod` command, you must provide account details to change followed by the login name of the account. Table 11-3 lists the available options for the `usermod` command.

Table 11-3
usermod Options for Changing Existing Accounts

Options	Description
`-c comment`	Change the description field of the account. You can also use the `chfn` command for this. Replace *comment* with a name or other description of the user account, placing multiple words in quotes.
`-d home_dir`	Change the home directory of the account to the specified new location. If the `-m` option is included, copy the contents of the home directory as well. Replace *home_dir* with the full path to the new directory.
`-e expire_date`	Assign a new expiration date for the account, replacing *expire_date* with a date in MM/DD/YYYY format.

Continued

Table 11-3 (continued)

Options	Description
-f *inactivity*	Set the number of days after a password expires until the account is permanently disabled. Setting inactivity to 0 disables the account immediately after the password has expired. Setting it to -1 disables the option, which is the default behavior.
-g *group*	Change the primary group (as listed in the /etc/group file) that the user is in. Replace *group* with the name of the new group.
-G *grouplist*	Set the list of groups that user belongs to. Replace *grouplist* with a list of groups.
-l *login_name*	Change the login name of the account to the name supplied after the -l option. Replace *login_name* with the new name. This automatically change the name of the home directory; use the -d and -m options for that.
-m	This option is used only in conjunction with the -d option. It causes the contents of the user's home directory to be copied to the new directory.
-o	This option is used only in conjunction with the -u option. It removes the restriction that user IDs must be unique.
-s *shell*	Specify a new command shell to use with this account. Replace *shell* with the full path to the new shell.
-u *user_id*	Change the user ID number for the account. Replace user_id with the new user ID number. Unless the -o option is used, the ID number must not be in use by another account.

Assume that a new employee named Jenny Barnes will be taking over Mary's job. We want to convert the mary account to a new name (-l jenny), new comment (-c "Jenny Barnes"), and home directory (-d /home/jenny). We could do that with the following command:

```
# usermod -l jenny -c "Jenny Barnes" -m -d /home/jenny mary
```

Furthermore, if after converting the account we learn that Jenny prefers the tcsh shell, we could make that change with the -s option (-s /bin/tcsh):

```
# usermod -s /bin/tcsh jenny
```

Alternatively, we could use the chsh command to change the shell. The following is an example:

```
# chsh -s /bin/tcsh jenny
```

The chsh command is handy because it enables a user to change his or her own shell setting. Simply leave the user name parameter off when invoking the command, and chsh assumes the currently logged-in user as the account to change.

Deleting User Accounts

Occasionally, it is necessary to remove a user account from your Red Hat Linux system. This can be done with the userdel command. The userdel command takes a single argument, which is the login name of the account to delete. If you supply the optional -r option, it also deletes the user's home directory and all the files in it. To delete the user account with login name mary, you would type this:

```
# userdel mary
```

To wipe out her home directory along with her account, type this:

```
# userdel -r mary
```

Files owned by the deleted user but not located in the user's home directory will not be deleted. The system administrator must search for and delete those files manually. The find command comes in very handy for this type of thing. I won't describe all the capabilities of the find command (that would take a very fat chapter of its own). I do, however, provide a few simple examples of how to use find to locate files belonging to a particular user, even when those files are scattered throughout a file system. You can even use the find command to delete or change the ownership of files, as they are located. Table 11-4 has a few examples of the find command in action.

Table 11-4 Using find to Locate and Change User Files	
Find Command	**Description**
find / -user mary -print	Search the entire file hierarchy (start at /) for all files and directories owned by mary and print the filenames to the screen.
find /home -user mary -exec rm {} \;	Search for all files and subdirectories under /home that are owned by user mary. Run the rm command to delete each of those files.

Continued

Table 11-4 *(continued)*

Find Command	Description
`find / -user mary -exec chown jenny {} \;`	Search for all files and subdirectories under /home that are owned by user `mary` and run the `chown` command to change each file so that it is owned by `jenny` instead.
`find / -uid 500 -exec chown jenny {} \;`	This command is basically the same as the previous example, but it uses the user ID number instead of the user name to identify the matching files. This is useful if you have deleted a user before converting her files.

There are a few common things about each invocation of the `find` command. The first parameter is always the directory to start the recursive search in. After that come the file attributes to match. We can use the `-print` option to just list the matching files, or the `-exec` parameter to run a command against each matching file or directory. The {} characters designate where the matching filename should be filled in when `find` runs the `-exec` option. The \; at the end simply tells Linux where the command ends. These are only a few of `find`'s capabilities. I encourage you to read the online man page to learn more about `find`. (Type man `find` to view the page.)

Checking Disk Quotas

Limited disk space can be another source of user support calls. A stock Red Hat Linux system lacks true disk quotas, so it is possible for a single user to use up an entire disk, causing problems for the rest of the users. The duty then falls on the system administrator to recover enough disk space for everyone to keep working. The long-term solution is to install a larger hard drive, but in the short term, the solution is usually to contact individual users and convince them to remove unneeded files.

You can discover the most voracious consumers of disk space using the `du` command. Invoke `du` with the `-s` option and give it a list of directories; it reports the total amount of disk space used by all the files in each directory. You can thus use the `du` command to list the total disk space used by each subdirectory within the /home directory. Try the following:

```
# du -s /home/*
```

This should result in a list of all of your users' home directories preceded by the number of kilobytes that each directory structure uses, generally similar to this:

```
60      /home/bob
1       /home/jane
1960    /home/joe
7       /home/mary
9984    /home/thad
```

Of course, manually checking the disk usage of every user on a regular basis is a real pain in the neck. Fortunately, Red Hat Linux lets you automate this sort of thing. The following is a script that uses du to check the home directory of every user on your system. You could put this script in an accessible location, such as /usr/local/bin/quota.csh. (Shell scripts are described in Chapter 12.)

```csh
#!/bin/csh
#
# quota.csh: This script scans the home directories of all
#            nonsystem accounts and e-mails a warning message
#            to any user that is consuming an excessive
#            amount of disk space.

# set the maximum space per home directory to 5000 kilobytes.
set maxusage=5000

#
# Loop through every login name, but skip the first 17 accounts
#
foreach user ( `awk -F: '{ print $1 }' /etc/passwd | tail +17` )
    # Get the users home directory
    set dir=`grep "^"$user":" /etc/passwd | awk -F: '{ print $6 }'`

    # Find out home much disk space the home dir is using
    set usage=`du -s $dir | awk '{ print $1 }'`

    # Check if the space used exceeds the max allowed
    if ( $usage > $maxusage ) then
        #
        # Send a warning message to the user
        #
        set subject="Warning! You are using $usage KB of disk space"
        mail -s "$subject" $user < /usr/local/etc/quota.txt

        # print the violators to the screen
        echo User $user is using $usage KB of disk space
    endif
end
```

The maximum amount of disk space allowed for each user is defined in the variable `maxusage`. It is set to 5000KB in this example; feel free to change that to whatever makes sense for your situation. Simply modify the set `maxuser= line` located toward the top of the file. When run, the script mails the file `/usr/local/etc/quota.txt` to the users exceeding the quota. The `quota.txt` file may contain a message similar to the following:

```
You have exceeded the maximum allowed disk quota of 5000
kilobytes. Please remove any unnecessary files from your
home directory.
```

You can log in as root and run the script manually, or add the script to the root `cron` jobs so that it automatically runs on a regular basis. (The `cron` facility is described in detail in Chapter 12.) To do that, run the `crontab -e` command as root and add the following line to the `crontab` file.

```
0 3 * * * /usr/local/bin/quota.csh
```

The `quota.csh` script will now automatically run once a day at 3:00 a.m. This method of enforcing quotas actually has some advantages over implementations built into the operating system. Built-in quotas stop a user from creating new files when his or her quota is exceeded. To that user, it is effectively the same as if the disk has become full. This inevitably results in a support call to the system administrator. The `quota.csh` script, however, does not suffer from this problem. Users can temporarily exceed the quota if they need to; they are simply be nagged with automated e-mail messages until they reduce their file usage to acceptable levels again. In this respect, you can think of it as a "kinder and gentler" quota system.

Caution

When typing in the `quota.csh` script, pay close attention to the type of quote characters being used. The script uses two different types of single quote character, and the type used is significant; they are not interchangeable.

The backward slanting quote character (usually located just below Esc on your keyboard) is used in several places. It is the outermost set of quotes on the "`foreach user`" line, the "`set dir`" line, and the "`set usage`" line, causing the text it surrounds to be interpreted as a command. The other type of single quote (located on the double quote key) causes the text to be interpreted literally but does not cause it to run as a command.

Sending Mail to All Users

Occasionally, you need to send messages to all users on your system. Warning users of planned downtime for hardware upgrades is a good example. Sending e-mail to each user individually is extremely time consuming and wasteful; this is precisely the kind of task that e-mail aliases and mailing lists were invented for. Keeping a mailing list of all the users on your system can be problematic, however. If you are not diligent about keeping the mailing list current, it becomes increasingly inaccurate as you add and delete users. Also, if your system has many users, the mere size of the alias list can become unwieldy.

The following script, called `mailfile`, provides a simple method of working around these problems. It grabs the login names directly from the /etc/passwd file and sends e-mail to all the users.

```csh
#!/bin/csh
#
# mailfile: This script mails the specified file to all users
#           of the system.  It skips the first 17 accounts so
#           we do not send the email to system accounts like
#           'root'.
#
# USAGE: mailfile "Subject goes here" filename.txt

#
# Check for a subject
#
if ( `echo $1 | awk '{ print $1 }'` == "" ) then
    echo You did not supply a subject for the message.
    echo Be sure to enclose it in quotes.
    exit 1
else
    # Get the subject of the message
    set subject=$1
endif

#
# Check for a filename
#
if ( $2 == "" ) then
    echo You did not supply a file name.
    exit 2
else
    # Get the name of the file to send
    set filename=$2
endif

#
# Check that the file exists
#
if ( -f $filename ) then
    echo Sending file $filename
else
    echo File does not exist.
    exit 3
endif

#
```

```
# Loop through every login name, but skip the first 17 accounts
#
foreach user ( `awk -F: '{ print $1 }' /etc/passwd | tail +17`
)
    # Mail the file
    echo Mailing to $user
    mail -s "$subject" $user < $filename

    # sleep for a few seconds so we don't overload the mailer
    # On fast systems or systems with few accounts, you can
    # probably take this delay out.
    sleep 2
end
```

The script accepts two parameters. The first is the subject of the e-mail message, which is enclosed in quotes. The second is the name of the file containing the text message to send. Thus, to send an e-mail message to all users warning them about an upcoming server hardware upgrade, I may do something similar to the following.

```
mailfile "System upgrade at 5:00pm" upgrade.txt
```

The file upgrade.txt contains the text of the message to be sent to each user. The really useful thing about this approach is that I can save this text file and easily modify and resend it the next time I upgrade the system.

Tip   If your users log in to your system using text-based logins instead of graphical logins, you can add messages to the /etc/motd file to have them reach your users. Any text in that file will be displayed on each user's screen after the user logs in and before the first shell prompt appears.

Summary

It is not uncommon for a Red Hat Linux system to be used as a single-task server with no actual users. It sits quietly in a server room, serving Web pages or handling domain name service, never crashing, and rarely needing attention. This is not always the case, however. You may have to support users on your Red Hat Linux server, and that can be the most challenging part of your system-administration duties.

Red Hat Linux provides a variety of tools that help you with your administrative chores. The useradd, usermod, and userdel commands enable easy command-line manipulation of user account data. Furthermore, creating a support mailbox and building shell scripts to automate repetitive tasks lightens your load even more. Red Hat Linux builds on top of the rich history of UNIX and provides an ideal platform to support the diverse needs of your users.

✦   ✦   ✦

Automating System Tasks

◆ ◆ ◆ ◆

In This Chapter

Understanding shell scripts

System initialization

System start-up and shutdown

Scheduling system tasks

◆ ◆ ◆ ◆

You'd never get any work done if you had to type every command that needs to be run on your Red Hat Linux system when it starts up. Likewise, you could work more efficiently if you grouped together sets of commands that you run all the time. Shell scripts can handle these tasks.

A *shell script* is a group of commands, functions, variables, or just about anything else you can use from a shell. These items are typed into a plain-text file. Then that file can be run as a command. Red Hat Linux uses system initialization shell scripts during system start-up to run commands needed to get things going. You can create your own shell scripts to automate the tasks you need to do regularly.

This chapter provides a rudimentary overview of the inner workings of shell scripts and how they can be used. You learn how shell scripts are responsible for the messages that scroll by on the system console during booting and how simple scripts can be harnessed to a scheduling facility (such as cron or at) to simplify administrative tasks.

You also learn to fine-tune your machine to start at the most appropriate run level and to only run the daemons that you need. With that understanding, you'll be able to personalize your environment and cut down on the amount of time you spend repetitively typing the same commands.

Understanding Shell Scripts

A shell script is a plain-text file containing a sequence of commands. It can be a simple one-line command that you'd prefer not to type repetitively; a complex program containing several loops, conditional statements, mathematical operations, and control structures; or anything in between.

Shell scripts are equivalent to batch files in DOS/Windows but offer greater flexibility and control through advanced looping constructs, logical operators, functions, and a larger base of commands to use. Shell scripts have much the same syntax as programming languages and are capable of handling many of the same tasks.

Nearly a dozen different shells are available in Red Hat Linux, some of which function virtually identically in an interactive environment. From a programming standpoint, there are basically two varieties, those based on the Bourne shell (sh), and those derived from the C shell (csh). All code and examples in this chapter are based on the bash (Bourne-again shell) environment, which implements a superset of the original Bourne shell. In fact, /bin/sh is a symbolic link to /bin/bash.

The syntax (that is, the way commands and options are constructed) of the C shell is similar to that of the C programming language. It has interactive capabilities that are not included in most Bourne shells. Each shell also uses different configuration files and different methods of setting shell environment variables.

Executing shell scripts

Shell scripts are files of text commands, functions, environment variables, and/or comments that you can run as commands. In theory, a shell script is a way of grouping a sequence of commands instead of typing them at a shell prompt. In reality, shell scripts can be as complex as any executable program.

An advantage of shell scripts is that they can be opened in any text editor to see what it does. A disadvantage is that shell scripts often execute more slowly than compiled programs. There are two ways to execute a shell script:

+ The filename is used as an argument to the shell (e.g., bash script_file). In this method, the file does not need to be executable; it just contains a list of shell commands. The shell specified on the command line is used to interpret the commands in the script file. This is most common for quick, simple tasks.

+ The shell script is executed by specifying the name of the file on the command line. This requires that the first line of the shell script contain the name of the shell interpreter that is to be used (e.g., #!/bin/bash as the first line of the file) and that the execute bit is set. This method is most common for complex scripts that may be used frequently. The first line of a shell script is the only line where the pound sign (#) isn't interpreted as a comment.

Cross-Reference   See Chapter 3 for information on chmod and read/write/execute file permissions.

The examples in this chapter are of the second variety. When scripts are executed in either manner, options to the program may be specified on the command line. Anything following the name of the script is referred to as a *command-line argument*.

These are referenced within the script as the variables $1, $2, $3, . . . $n. The name of the script itself is held within the variable $0. Note that these are positional parameters, meaning that they refer to a position of information on the command line.

While it is recommended that you choose meaningful variable names, there's still no substitute for active commenting throughout the design of the shell script. The pound sign (#) prefaces comments and can take up an entire line or exist on the same line as script code.

When you are writing more complex shell scripts, it is best to implement them in stages, making sure the logic is sound at each step before continuing. One way to make sure things are working as expected during testing is to place an echo statement at the beginning of lines within the body of a loop. That way, rather than executing the code, you can see what will be executed without making any permanent changes. Another way to accomplish the same goal is to place dummy echo statements at various places throughout the code. If these lines get printed, you know the correct logic branch is being taken. With the bash shell, you could also use set +x near the beginning of the script to display each command that is executed.

Besides commands, shell scripts can contain such components as user-defined variables, program constructs (such as loops and conditionals), and arithmetic instructions. These topics are described in the following sections.

Creating user-defined variables in shell scripts

Often within a shell script, you want to reuse certain items of information. During the course of processing the shell script, the name or number representing this information may change. To store information used by a shell script in a way that it can be easily reused, you can set variables. Variable names within shell scripts are case-sensitive and can be defined in the following manner:

```
NAME=value
```

The first part of a variable is the variable name, and the second part is the value set for that name. For example, you can define a variable containing the city in which you live as follows:

```
City="Springfield"
```

Technically, quoting is only necessary to preserve spacing within values, but it may aid in readability. Double quotes (") are considered weak quotes, while single quotes (') are considered strong quotes. Any special characters contained in a string surrounded by single quotes (for example, 'string') are disabled. With double quotes, however, all special characters are disabled except dollar sign ($), single quote ('), and backslash (\).

Variables can contain the output of a command. The advantage of having a variable set to the output of a command is that you can take advantage of information that changes in certain conditions. In the following example, the MACHINE variable is set to the output of the uname -n command. This always sets MACHINE to the name of your current computer, as follows:

```
MACHINE=`uname -n`
```

The command contained within the back quotes is executed in a subshell, and the output is stored in the variable name. In this case, the uname -n command outputs the computer's hostname (such as baskets.handsonhistory.com) and assigns that value to the MACHINE variable.

Note   A subshell provides a way to execute a command, or series of commands, outside of the current shell. The subshell is similar to the current shell in that it remembers locations of commands and values of environment variables from the parent shell. However, changes to the subshell's environment are not automatically passed back to the parent shell.

Variables can also take on the values of other variables. This is a way of taking advantage of changing information as the shell script runs. For example, a shell script could determine an account balance ($CurrentBalance) and then store that value in the BALANCE variable, enabling the value to be saved as follows:

```
BALANCE=$CurrentBalance
```

Note   When being assigned, only the variable name is necessary. When being referenced, the variable name must be prefaced by a dollar sign ($).

Performing arithmetic evaluation in shell scripts

While variables in shell scripts can contain numbers, all values are treated as alphanumeric strings unless otherwise instructed by the built-in typeset command. Integer arithmetic can be performed using the built-in let command or through the external expr command. For example, given that the variable BIGNUM contains the value 1024, the following two commands would both store the value 64 in the RESULT variable:

```
let Result=$BIGNUM/16
Result=`expr $BIGNUM / 16`
```

Note   While most elements of shell scripts are relatively free form (where white space, such as spaces or tabs, is insignificant), both of the previous commands are particular about spacing. The let command insists on no spaces between each operand and the mathematical operator, whereas the syntax of the expr command requires white space between each operand and its operator.

Valid mathematical operations available in bash's built-in `let` command are listed in Table 12-1 in order of decreasing precedence. Multiple operators in the same row indicate equal precedence. Table 12-2 similarly lists the valid mathematical operators for the `expr` command.

Table 12-1
Mathematical Operations in let

Operator	Description
+ -	unary plus and minus
! ~	logical and bitwise negation
* / %	multiplication, division, and modulus (remainder)
+ -	addition and subtraction
<< >>	left and right bitwise shift
< <= >= >	less than; less than or equal to; greater than or equal to; and greater than comparisons
== !=	equality and inequality
&	bitwise AND
^	bitwise XOR (exclusive OR)
|	bitwise OR
&&	logical AND
||	logical OR
= *= /= %= += -= <<= >>= &= ^= |=	assignment

Table 12-2
Mathematical Operations in expr

Operator	Description
* / %	multiplication, division, and modulus (remainder)
+ -	addition and subtraction
< <= >= > != = ==	Comparison: less than; less than or equal to; greater than or equal to; greater than; not equal to; and two representations of equal to

Continued

Operator	Description
&	logical AND
|	logical OR
-eq	equal to
-ne	not equal to
-lt	less than
-le	less than or equal to
-gt	greater than
-ge	greater than or equal to
|	logical OR

Table 12-2 *(continued)*

Using programming constructs in shell scripts

One of the features that make shell scripts so powerful is their implementation of looping constructs similar to those found in compiled programming languages. You can use several different types of loops, depending on your needs.

The for . . . do loop

One of the most commonly used loops is the `for . . . do` loop. It iterates through a list of values, executing the body of the loop for each element in the list. The syntax and examples are presented here:

```
for VAR in LIST
do
    { body }
done
```

In the preceding example, the `for` loop assigns the values in `LIST` to `VAR` one at a time. Then for each value, the body in braces between `do` and `done` are executed. `VAR` can be specified by any valid variable name. `LIST` can be composed of any values that can be defined (numbers, letters, path names, dates, etc.) because each item in the list is treated as a string value in the body of the loop. Any commands can appear in the body. The beginnings of some possible loops are shown here:

```
for SECTION in 1 2 3 4 5 6 7 8
for DIRS in /home /etc /usr /var
for DISK in /dev/hda /dev/hdb /dev/sda
for PARTITION in a b d e
```

Each element in the loop is separated from the next by white space. For that reason, you should be careful if you are directing output of a command to use as your LIST. As soon as the for loop sees a space or a tab, it runs the loop on it. For example, if you direct the output of the ls command to the loop, the loop evaluates each filename separately. However, if you use the output of ls -l, the loop also evaluates every other piece of information in the list (such as file owner, permission bits, and so on) — something that you probably don't want to do.

The if . . . then test statements

Another common way of testing variables is within an if statement. The possible variations of if . . . then selection constructs are shown here:

```
if [ expression ]
then
   { body }
fi

if [ expression ]
then
    { body }
else
    { body }
fi

if [ expression ]
then
    { body }
elif [ expression ]
then
    { body }
else
    { body }
fi
```

In these types of statements, each of the expressions is tested. Based on the results of that test, one of the actions that follow is taken.

Table 12-3 lists the possible test expressions that can exist between the brackets in an if statement. The left bracket itself begins the "test" part of the statement. In fact, each of the preceding if statements can be rewritten without brackets as in:

```
if test expression
```

When the expression is evaluated, the result is either a 0 (indicating "true") or a 1 (indicating "false").

Table 12-3
Operators for Test Expressions

Operator	What Is Being Tested?
-b *file*	Is the file block special (e.g., a block device)? Used to identify disk and tape devices.
-c *file*	Is the file character special (e.g., a character device)? Used to identify serial lines and terminal devices.
-d *file*	Is the file a directory?
-e *file*	Does the file exist?
-f *file*	Does the file exist, and is it a regular file (e.g., not a directory, socket, pipe, link, or device file)?
-g *file*	Does the file have the set-group-id bit set?
-G *file*	Does the file exist and is its group ownership the same as the current user's primary group?
-k *file*	Does the file have the sticky bit set?
-L *file*	Is the file a symbolic link?
-n *string*	Is the length of the string greater than 0 bytes?
-O *file*	Does the file exist and does the current user own it?
-p *file*	Is the file a named pipe?
-r *file*	Does the file exist, and is it readable?
-s *file*	Does the file exist, and is it larger than 0 bytes?
-S file	Does the file exist, and is it a socket?
-t fd	Is the file descriptor open?
-u file	Does the file have the set-user-id bit set?
-w file	Does the file exist, and is it writable?
-x file	Does the file exist, and is it executable?
-z string	Is the length of the string 0 bytes?
expr1 -a expr2	Are both the first expression and the second expression true?
expr1 -o expr2	Is either of the two expressions true?
file1 -nt file2	Is the first file newer than the second file (using the modification timestamp)?
file1 -ot file2	Is the first file older than the second file (using the modification timestamp)?
file1 -ef file2	Are the two files associated by a link (a hard link or a symbolic link)?

Operator	What Is Being Tested?
`var1 -eq var2`	Is the first variable equal to the second variable?
`var1 -ge var2`	Is the first variable greater than or equal to the second variable?
`var1 -gt var2`	Is the first variable greater than the second variable?
`var1 -le var2`	Is the first variable less than or equal to the second variable?
`var1 -lt var2`	Is the first variable less than the second variable?
`var1 -ne var2`	Is the first variable not equal to the second variable?

Here are some examples that demonstrate the uses of the `if` statement and a test expression:

```
if [ -x /sbin/ifconfig ]
if [ $4 -eq "nl" ]
if [ $# -gt 2 ]
if [ -z $HOSTNAME ]
```

In the previous example, the first statement checks if the `/sbin/ifconfig` program is executable. The second example checks if the string value `nl` is equal to the value stored in `$4` (the fourth command-line argument). The next line checks if the number of command-line arguments (represented by the `$#` variable) is greater than two. The last example determines if the variable `$HOSTNAME` is empty.

The case command for nested if statements

Another frequently used construct is the `case` command. Similar to a `switch` statement in programming languages, this can take the place of several nested `if` statements. A general form of the `case` statement is as follows:

```
case "VAR" in
   Result1)   { body }
         ;;
   Result2)   { body }
         ;;
   *)       { body }
         ;;
esac
```

An example of the `case` command follows. This fragment of code sets the `TYPE` and `RCFILE` variables based on the user's default shell as reported in the seventh (colon-separated) field of the `/etc/passwd` file:

```
Shell=`grep "^$USER:" /etc/passwd | awk -F: '{ print $7 }'`
case "$Shell" in
    /bin/sh)    TYPE=Bourne
            RCFILE=".profile"
            ;;
    /bin/csh)    TYPE=C
            RCFILE=".cshrc"
            ;;
    /bin/bash)    TYPE=Bourne
            RCFILE=".bashrc"
            ;;
    /bin/tcsh)    TYPE=C
            RCFILE=".tcshrc"
            ;;
    *)        TYPE=other
            RCFILE="unknown"
            ;;
    esac
```

The asterisk (*) is used as a catchall. If none of the other entries are matched on the way down the list, the asterisk is matched and the value is set to unknown.

The while . . . do and until . . . do loops

Two other possible looping constructs are the while . . . do loop and the until . . . do loop. The structure of each is presented here:

```
while condition        until condition
do                     do
    { body }              { body }
done                   done
```

In a while loop, the condition is usually a test statement, but it can also be used to read input until an End-of-File (<EOF>) is encountered. If a test condition is used, the body of the loop is executed until the condition evaluates to false (a return code of 1). A sample is included here:

```
while read COL1 COL2 COL3 COL4
do
    echo -n " |  X    $COL2    |    $COL3    " > /home/ben/DB
    echo "|    $COL4    |    $COL1    X  |" > /home/ben/DB
done
```

This loop reads values (in groups of four) from the keyboard, rearranges the column order, and outputs them to a file in a particular format.

The until loop executes the code in the body until the test evaluates to true (a return code of 0). At that point, the loop exits.

```
COUNT=1
until [ $Count -eq 34 ]
do
    DIR=/home/grd/proj/$Count
    if [ ! -d $DIR ]
    then
        mkdir $DIR
        cp /home/grd/proj/template $DIR/file_def
    fi
    let Count+=1
done
```

The preceding loop creates a directory, if the directory doesn't already exist, and copies a template file to it. This repeats until the value of the COUNT variable is equal to 34 (requiring 33 iterations).

Trying some simple shell scripts

Sometimes the simplest of scripts can be the most useful. If you type the same sequence of commands repetitively, it makes sense to store those commands (once!) in a file. Here are some examples of simple, but useful, shell scripts.

A simple backup script

If you've been collecting data for a research project for the past two years, you'll want to keep backup copies of your work in case something should happen to the original files. Rather than type out the full command each time you'd like to make a backup, simply store the commands in a shell script:

```
#!/bin/bash
#
mt /dev/rft0 rew
cd /home/rp008a/data
tar cvf /dev/rft0
mt /dev/rft0 rewoffl
exit 0
```

This script runs the mt command with the rew option to rewind the tape in the tape drive, attached to the floppy controller (/dev/rft0). Next, the cd command changes the current directory to /home/rp008a/data. The tar command creates the archive (c) from files in the current directory, verbosely (v) describes what it is doing, and outputs the archive file to the tape device (f /dev/rft0). Then the mt command rewinds and ejects the tape (rewoffl) from the tape device (/dev/rft0). For further automation, see the section on the cron facility later in this chapter.

Cross-Reference It is just as important to back up the operating system. See Chapter 13 for details on backing up and restoring files.

Scripts to check disk space

Another common administrative issue is disk space, a resource that always seems to be in short supply. If you find yourself regularly checking the size of users' home directories, the following script may be handy:

```
#!/bin/bash
#
cd /home ; du -s * | sort -rn
```

Cross-Reference Use the -h option with du to make the output of du friendlier.

This script looks at all directories in /home and reports on their size in kilobytes. The output is sorted numerically, with the largest directory at the top of the list. If you have users with home directories other than the /home directory, the following (slightly more complex) script is more useful:

```
#!/bin/bash
#
TMPfile=/tmp/sh$$tmp
for I in `awk -F: '{ if ($3 >= 500) print $6 }' /etc/passwd`
do
    du -s $I > $TMPfile
done
sort -rn $TMPfile
rm $TMPfile
exit 0
```

In this script, awk chooses particular bits of information from the /etc/passwd file. Using the colon as a field separator (the -F: option), awk checks whether the third field on each line (the user ID, or UID) is greater than or equal to 500 (by default, the starting point for regular user accounts). If so, that user's home directory (the sixth field) is returned. The for loop cycles through the list returned by awk, and performs a disk usage check on each directory. The results are stored in a unique temporary file (the $$ variable represents the process ID of the running program). The temporary file is numerically sorted and then removed. The results from either of the preceding programs may look like:

```
936890      /home/jsmith
489349      /home/oracle
20439       /home/wilhelm
748         /home/acorad
8           /home/gandalf
8           /home/johnson
8           /home/cseitz
8           /home/buchanan
```

Cross-
Reference The awk command is used to scan a file for particular patterns, based on rules that you provide. It can then output that information in a form that you choose.

A script for checking scripts

Occasionally, when testing scripts, it's helpful to take a look at what the script has accomplished so far. When called from another shell script, the following script suspends the running program and lets you (via another Terminal window or virtual terminal) look for expected temporary files or altered conditions. This can indicate whether a program is performing as expected, or if it needs a little more work.

```
#!/bin/bash
#
Count=1
while :
do
    echo -n "$Count   Continue? (y/n): "
    read ANS
    case "$ANS" in
    y|Y)   break
       ;;
    esac
    let Count+=1
done
exit 0
```

The colon (:) on the fourth line does absolutely nothing. It functions only as a placeholder, and allows the while loop to repeat until a y or Y is entered (causing the break to exit the loop). The Count variable keeps track of the number of times the loop has run. The -n option to echo suppresses printing the new line and positions the cursor just beyond the Continue? (y/n): prompt to wait for input.

A script to kill processes

Another example that may be used frequently is the following script to kill processes nicely. This script gives the processes every opportunity to clean up any temporary files, notify the parent process that it is exiting, and terminate quietly.

```
#!/bin/bash
#
for I in `echo $*`
do
    for J in 15 2 1 9
    do
        kill -$J $I && sleep 1
    done
done
exit 0
```

This script cycles through a list of process IDs specified on the command line. To ensure that the process has been terminated, several signals are sent to the process in increasing levels of severity. The first signal attempted is 15 (signal number 15 is SIGTERM), which requests the termination of the process. The next signal is 2 (signal 2 is SIGINT), representing an attempted interrupt from the keyboard (i.e., a Ctrl+C sequence or similar action). Signal 1, SIGHUP, is then tried, which attempts to kill the process by indicating that the controlling terminal has "hung up," terminology left over from when serial consoles were more prevalent.

Finally, signal 9, SIGKILL, is sent to the process. This last resort signal doesn't allow the process to perform any activities on exiting—it just tries to "kill with impunity." A one-second delay, induced only if previous attempts to kill the process have failed, gives the process some time to trap each signal and exit properly.

For a complete list of signals, refer to the signal 7 manual page (type man 7 signal). More advanced scripts are examined throughout the course of this chapter.

System Initialization

In the boot process, the transfer from the kernel phase (the loading of the kernel, probing for devices, and loading drivers) to init is indicated by the following lines:

```
INIT: version 2.78 booting
                        Welcome to Red Hat Linux
```

The init program, part of the SysVinit RPM package, is now in control. Known as "the father of all processes," the output from ps always lists init as PID (process identifier) 1. Its actions are directed by the /etc/inittab file, which is reproduced next.

The inittab file

The following text shows the contents of the /etc/inittab file as it is delivered with Red Hat Linux:

```
#
# inittab       This file describes how the INIT process should set up
#               the system in a certain run level.
#
# Author:       Miquel van Smoorenburg, <miquels@drinkel.nl.mugnet.org>
#               Modified for RHS Linux by Marc Ewing and Donnie Barnes
#

# Default runlevel. The runlevels used by RHS are:
#   0 - halt (Do NOT set initdefault to this)
#   1 - Single user mode
```

```
#   2 - Multiuser, without NFS (The same as 3, if you do not have networking)
#   3 - Full multiuser mode
#   4 - unused
#   5 - X11
#   6 - reboot (Do NOT set initdefault to this)
#
id:3:initdefault:

# System initialization.
si::sysinit:/etc/rc.d/rc.sysinit

l0:0:wait:/etc/rc.d/rc 0
l1:1:wait:/etc/rc.d/rc 1
l2:2:wait:/etc/rc.d/rc 2
l3:3:wait:/etc/rc.d/rc 3
l4:4:wait:/etc/rc.d/rc 4
l5:5:wait:/etc/rc.d/rc 5
l6:6:wait:/etc/rc.d/rc 6


# Things to run in every runlevel.
ud::once:/sbin/update

# Trap CTRL-ALT-DELETE
ca::ctrlaltdel:/sbin/shutdown -t3 -r now

# When our UPS tells us power has failed, assume we have a few minutes
# of power left. Schedule a shutdown for 2 minutes from now.
# This does, of course, assume you have powerd installed and your
# UPS connected and working correctly.
pf::powerfail:/sbin/shutdown -f -h +2 "Power Failure; System Shutting Down"

# If power was restored before the shutdown kicked in, cancel it.
pr:12345:powerokwait:/sbin/shutdown -c "Power Restored; Shutdown Cancelled"


# Run gettys in standard runlevels
1:2345:respawn:/sbin/mingetty tty1
2:2345:respawn:/sbin/mingetty tty2
3:2345:respawn:/sbin/mingetty tty3
4:2345:respawn:/sbin/mingetty tty4
5:2345:respawn:/sbin/mingetty tty5
6:2345:respawn:/sbin/mingetty tty6

# Run xdm in runlevel 5
# xdm is now a separate service
x:5:respawn:/etc/X11/prefdm -nodaemon
```

Format of the inittab file

The plain-text `inittab` file consists of several colon-separated fields in the format:

```
id:runlevels:action:command
```

The id field is a unique identifier, one to four alphanumeric characters in length that represents a particular action to take during system start-up. The run levels field contains a list of run levels in which the command will be run. Common run levels are 0, 1, 2, 3, 4, 5, and 6 (s and S represent single-user mode, which is equivalent to 1). Run levels 7, 8, and 9 are not standard; they can also be used as the special run levels associated with the on demand action (a, b, and c, which are equivalent to A, B, and C). The next field represents the type of action to be taken by init (valid actions and the results of those actions are listed in Table 12-4), and the last field is the actual command that is to be executed.

Table 12-4
Valid init Actions

Action	How the Command Is Run
once	The command is executed once when entering the specified run level.
wait	The same as once, but init waits for the command to finish before continuing with other inittab entries.
respawn	The process is monitored, and a new instance is started if the original process terminates.
powerfail	The command is executed on receiving a SIGPWR signal from software associated with an UPS unit.
powerwait	The same as powerfail, but init waits for the command to finish.
powerwaitok	The command is executed on receiving a SIGPWR signal if the /etc/powerstatus file contains the word OK. This is generally accomplished by the UPS software, and indicates that a normal power level has been restored.
ondemand	The command is executed when init is manually instructed to enter one of the special run levels a, b, or c (equivalent to A, B, and C, respectively). No change in run level actually takes place. The program is restarted if the original process terminates.
sysinit	The command is executed during the system boot phase; the runlevelsfield is ignored.
boot	The command is executed during the system boot phase, after all sysinit entries have been processed; the runlevels field is ignored.
bootwait	The same as boot, but init waits for the command to finish before continuing with other inittab entries; the runlevels field is also ignored.
initdefault	The run level to enter after completing the boot and sysinit actions.

Action	How the Command Is Run
off	Nothing happens (perhaps useful for testing and debugging).
ctrlaltdel	Traps the Ctrl+Alt+Del key sequence, and is typically used to gracefully shut down the system.
kbrequest	Used to trap special key sequences, as interpreted by the keyboard handler.

Breakdown of the inittab file

Because the inittab file is a configuration file and not a sequential shell script, the order of lines is not significant. Lines beginning with a # character are considered comments and are not processed.

The first noncommented line in the preceding sample inittab file sets the default run level to 3. A default of 3 means that, following the completion of all commands associated with the sysinit, boot, and bootwait actions, run level 3 will be entered (booting to a text-based login). The other common initdefault level is run level 5 (booting to a GUI). Table 12-5 describes each of the run levels and helps you choose the run level that is best suited as the default in your environment.

Table 12-5
Possible Run Levels

Run Level	What Happens in This Run Level
0	All processes are terminated and the machine comes to an orderly halt. As the inittab comments point out, this is not a good choice for initdefault, because as soon as the kernel, modules, and drivers are loaded, the machine will halt.
1, s, S	This represents single-user mode, which is most frequently used for system maintenance and in situations where it may be preferable to have few processes running and no services activated. In single-user mode, the network is nonexistent, the X server is not running, and it is possible that some file systems are not mounted.
2	Multiuser mode. Multiple user logins are allowed, all configured file systems are mounted, and all processes except X, the at daemon, the xinetd daemon, and NIS/NFS are started. If your machine doesn't have (or perhaps doesn't need) a permanent network connection, this is a good choice for initdefault.

Continued

	Table 12-5 *(continued)*
Run Level	**What Happens in This Run Level**
3, 4	Multiuser mode with network services. Run level 3 is the typical value for `initdefault` on a Red Hat Linux server, but run level 4 (generally left to be user-defined) is almost identical in a default Red Hat 7.0 Linux configuration.
5	Multiuser mode with network services and X. This run level starts the X server and presents a graphical login window, visually resembling any of the more expensive UNIX-based workstations. This is a common `initdefault` value for a Red Hat Linux workstation.
6	All processes are terminated and the machine is gracefully rebooted. Again, the comments in the `inittab` file mention that this is not a good choice for `initdefault`, perhaps even worse than run level 0. The effect is a possibly infinite cycle of booting, followed by rebooting.
7, 8, 9	Generally unused and undefined, these run levels have the potential to meet any needs not covered by the default options.
a, b, c, A, B, C	Used in conjunction with the `ondemand` action. These don't really specify a run level but can launch a program or daemon "on demand" if so instructed.

Note   If there is no `initdefault` specified in the `inittab` file, the boot sequence will be interrupted and you will be prompted to specify a default run level into which the machine will boot.

The next line in the `inittab` file instructs `init` to execute the `/etc/rc.d/rc.sysinit` script before entering the default run level. This script performs many initialization routines such as choosing a keymap file, checking and mounting the root and proc file systems, setting the clock and hostname, configuring swap space, cleaning up temporary files, and loading system modules.

The seven following lines control the commands executed within each major run level. In each, the `/etc/rc.d/rc` script is called, using the desired run level as an argument. It, in turn, descends into the appropriate directory tree (for example, the `/etc/rc3.d` directory is entered for run level 3).

The next line specifies that no matter what run level the machine is in, the update daemon should be running. The update daemon is a program that flushes kernel buffers from memory to disk (generally every 30 seconds) to ensure that, in the event of an unintended shutdown, a minimum amount of data is lost.

The `ctrlaltdel` tells `init` to perform exactly what PC users would expect if the Ctrl, Alt, and Delete keys were pressed simultaneously. The system reboots itself in an orderly fashion (a switch to run level 6) after a three-second delay.

The next two lines (with their comments) deal with graceful shutdowns if you have an uninterruptible power supply (UPS) and software installed. The first line initiates a halt (a switch to run level 0) two minutes after receiving a signal from the UPS indicating a power failure. The second line cancels the shutdown in the event that power is restored.

The six `getty` lines start up virtual consoles to allow logins. These processes are always running in any of the multiuser run levels. When someone connected to a virtual console logs out, that `getty` process dies, and the `respawn` action instructs `init` to start a new `getty` process.

The last line indicates that as long as the system is in run level 5, the "preferred display manager" (xdm, gnome, KDE, etc.) will be running. This presents a graphical login prompt rather than the usual text-based login, and eliminates the need to run startx.

System Start-up and Shutdown

During system start-up, a series of scripts are run to start the services that you need. These include scripts to start network interfaces, mount directories, and monitor your system. Most of these scripts are run from subdirectories of `/etc/rc.d`. The program that starts most of these services up when you boot and stops them when you shut down is the `/etc/rc.d/rc` script. The following sections describe run-level scripts and what you can do with them.

Starting run-level scripts

As previously mentioned, the `/etc/rc.d/rc` script is a script that is integral to the concept of run levels. Any change of run level causes the script to be executed, with the new run level as an argument. This simple yet powerful script is shown and discussed here:

```
#!/bin/bash
#
# rc            This file is responsible for starting/stopping
#               services when the runlevel changes. It is also
#               responsible for the very first setup of basic
#               things, such as setting the hostname.
#
# Original Author:
#               Miquel van Smoorenburg, <miquels@drinkel.nl.mugnet.org>
#

# Now find out what the current and what the previous runlevel are.
argv1="$1"
```

```
set `/sbin/runlevel`
runlevel=$2
previous=$1
export runlevel previous

# Source function library.
. /etc/init.d/functions

# See if we want to be in user confirmation mode
if [ "$previous" = "N" ]; then
if grep -i confirm /proc/cmdline >/dev/null || [ -f /var/run/confirm ] ; then
    rm -f /var/run/confirm
    CONFIRM=yes
  else
    CONFIRM=
     echo "Entering non-interactive startup"
   fi
fi

export CONFIRM

# Get first argument. Set new runlevel to this argument.
[ "$1" != "" ] && runlevel="$argv1"

# Tell linuxconf what runlevel we are in
[ -d /var/run ] && echo "/etcrc$runlevel.d" > /var/run/runlevel.dir

# Is there an rc directory for this new runlevel?
if [ -d /etc/rc$runlevel.d ]; then
   # First, run the KILL scripts.
   for i in /etc/rc$runlevel.d/K*; do
      # Check if the script is there.
      [ ! -f $i ] && continue

      # Don't run [KS]??foo.{rpmsave,rpmorig} scripts
      [ "${i%.rpmsave}" != "${i}" ] && continue
      [ "${i%.rpmorig}" != "${i}" ] && continue
      [ "${i%.rpmnew}" != "${i}" ] && continue

      # Check if the subsystem is already up.
      subsys=${i#/etc/rc$runlevel.d/K??}
      [ ! -f /var/lock/subsys/$subsys ] && \
         [ ! -f /var/lock/subsys/${subsys}.init ] && continue

      # Bring the subsystem down.
      if egrep -q "(killproc |action )" $i ; then
         $i stop
      else
         action "Stopping $subsys" $i stop
      fi
   done
```

```
# Now run the START scripts.
for i in /etc/rc$runlevel.d/S*; do
   # Check if the script is there.
   [ ! -f $i ] && continue

   # Don't run [KS]??foo.{rpmsave,rpmorig} scripts
   [ "${i%.rpmsave}" != "${i}" ] && continue
   [ "${i%.rpmorig}" != "${i}" ] && continue
   [ "${i%.rpmnew}" != "${i}" ] && continue

   # Check if the subsystem is already up.
   subsys=${i#/etc/rc$runlevel.d/S??}
   [ -f /var/lock/subsys/$subsys ] || \
      [ -f /var/lock/subsys/${subsys}.init ] && continue

   # If we're in confirmation mode, get user confirmation
   [ -n "$CONFIRM" ]  &&
     {
       confirm $subsys
       case $? in
         0)
            :
         ;;
         2)
           CONFIRM=
         ;;
         *)
           continue
         ;;
       esac
     }


   # Bring the subsystem up.
   if egrep -q "(daemon |action )" $i ; then
         if [ "$subsys" = "halt" -o "$subsys" = "reboot" ]; then
                 unset LANG
                 unset LC_ALL
                 unset TEXTDOMAIN
                 unset TEXTDOMAINDIR
                 exec $i start
         else
             $i start
         fi
   else
         if [ "$subsys"= "halt" -o "$subsys" = "reboot" -o
             "$subsys" = "single" -o "$subsys" = "local" ]; then
             if [ "$subsys" = "halt" -o "$subsys" = "reboot" ]; then
                         unset LANG
                         unset LC_ALL
                         unset TEXTDOMAIN
```

```
                               unset TEXTDOMAINDIR
                               exec $i start
                    fi
                    $i start
          else
              action "Starting $subsys" $i start
          fi
      fi
    done
fi
```

As with the `inittab` file, lines beginning with a # character are considered comments. Well, almost: The first line indicates that a unique instance of `/bin/bash` will be run for the execution of the script. The first noncommented lines deal with past, present, and future run levels. The variable `argv1` takes on the value of the first (and only) command-line argument ($1). This represents the desired run level. The `set` command places the output of the `runlevel` command (explained later in this section) into $1 and $2, which are then distributed to the `previous` (the previous run level) and `runlevel` (the current run level) variables.

The next line reads `/etc/init.d/functions`, which contains several segments of shell script code (such as the `action`, `killproc`, and `confirm` subroutines) used to provide a consistent interface for each process started from the `rc` script.

If the confirm option is passed to the boot loader at boot time, no daemons or server processes will start without first being confirmed by a user at the system console. This next block of code checks if processes will need to be confirmed and sets the `CONFIRM` variable appropriately.

In the next line, if the first part evaluates to a `true` (0) value (the value of $1 does not equal a null string), the second part following the && is run. The run-level variable is set to the desired run level as stored in the variable `argv1`.

In the same manner on the next line, if the directory `/var/run` exists, the `/var/run/runlevel.dir` is created or overwritten. This file will contain the name of the directory that contains the commands about to be run (i.e., `/etc/rc3.d`).

The next block begins by checking if that directory exists, terminating if it does not. At this point, the program begins the loop where all scripts in the run-level directory that begin with the letter K (representing those programs that should be stopped in the new run level) are run. Various checks are performed, skipping over such things as broken symbolic links (where the actual file to which the link points no longer exists) and files left around as conflicts when new RPM packages are installed over existing files that had been modified.

In the line beginning with `subsys=`, conditional parameter expansion is performed within the curly braces ({ }), removing the regular expression following the # from the variable specified before it. For example, if the value of the variable $i was /etc/rc3.d/K60lpd, the resultant value stored in the variable subsys would be lpd. The rc script will not attempt to kill a daemon if its lock files in the /var/lock/subsys directory do not exist, indicating that the daemon is not running.

The next block of code checks whether the script that is about to run contains a reference to the killproc or action procedures as defined in the /etc/init.d/functions file. If such a reference exists, the script is called with stop as a command-line argument. Otherwise, the action procedure is called directly. Using this mechanism ensures that the output on the console is consistent for all daemons that are stopped.

At the end of that loop, all daemons that should not be running in the new run level will have been terminated. The next loop similarly cycles through the files in the same directory that begin with the letter S, representing all daemons or server processes that should be running in the new run level.

This loop performs the same checks to ignore broken links and files lingering from previous RPM package installations. Also, the rc script will not attempt to start a daemon if its lock files in the /var/lock/subsys directory exist, indicating that the daemon is already running.

The next block of code implements the aforementioned daemon startup confirmation process, prompting the user to type y, Y, or the Enter key to start the daemon; n or N to refrain from starting the daemon; or c or C to proceed with a normal, non-confirmed startup sequence.

Again, the script that is about to run is checked for a reference to the daemon or action procedures from the /etc/init.d/functions file. If such a reference exists (or if the script about to run is halt or reboot, the scripts that alter the run level), some variables are unset (LANG, LC_ALL, TEXTDOMAIN, and TEXTDOMAINDIR) and the script will be called with start as a command-line argument. This mechanism ensures that the output on the console is consistent for all daemons that are started.

When that loop completes, all daemons that should be running at that run level will have been started. The rc script then terminates.

Using run level 3 as an example of a common run level to start up your system (as set by the initdefault described earlier), the rc script traverses the /etc/rc3.d directory. It first looks for any program (most likely a shell script) with a name beginning with K. It runs each of these in turn, giving it an argument of stop, with the intention of killing the named processes. It then executes all programs that begin with S, using an argument of start, to run the named processes.

Note The other common start-up run level for a Linux workstation is run level 5. The main difference between 3 and 5 is that the GUI starts at level 5 while you are just in command mode at level 3. (To start the GUI while you are in run level 3, type startx.)

Understanding run-level scripts

A software package that has a service that needs to start at boot time (or when the system changes to any run level) can add a script to the /etc/init.d directory. That script can then be linked to an appropriate run-level directory and either be started or stopped (to start or stop the service).

Table 12-6 lists many of the typical run-level scripts that are found in /etc/init.d, and explains their function. Depending on the Red Hat Linux software packages you installed on your system, you may have dozens more run-level scripts than you see here. (Later, I describe how these files are linked into particular run-level directories.)

Table 12-6	
Run-Level Scripts Contained in /etc/init.d	
Run-Level Scripts	**What Does It Do?**
apmd	Controls the Advanced Power Management daemon, which monitors battery status, and which can safely suspend or shut down all or part of a machine that supports it.
atd	Starts or stops the at daemon to receive, queue, and run jobs submitted via the at or batch commands. (The anacron run-level script runs at and batch jobs that were not run because the computer was down.)
autofs	Starts and stops the automount daemon, for automatically mounting file systems (so, for example, a CD can be automatically mounted when it is inserted).
crond	Starts or stops the cron daemon to periodically run routine commands.
dhcpd	Starts or stops the dhcpd daemon, which automatically assigns IP addresses to computers on a LAN.
gpm	Controls the gpm daemon, which allows the mouse to interact with console- and text-based applications.
halt	Terminates all processes, writes out accounting records, removes swap space, unmounts all file systems, and either shuts down or reboots the machine (depending upon how the command was called).

Run-Level Scripts	*What Does It Do?*
httpd	Starts the httpd daemon, which allows your computer to act as an HTTP server (i.e., to serve Web pages).
iptables	Starts the iptables firewall daemon, which manages any iptables-style firewall rules set up for your computer.
keytable	Loads the predefined keyboard map.
killall	Shuts down any subsystems that may still be running prior to a shutdown or reboot.
kudzu	Detects and configures new hardware at boot time.
linuxconf	Loads any customized linuxconf policies or modules, as well as a few default modules (for use with the linuxconf system configuration tool).
lpd	Controls the lpd line printer daemon that handles spooling printing requests.
netfs	Mounts or unmounts network (NFS, SMB, and NCP) file systems.
network	Starts or stops all configured network interfaces and initializes the TCP/IP and IPX protocols.
nfs	Starts or stops the NFS-related daemons (rpc.nfsd, rpc.mountd, rpc.statd, and rcp.rquotad) and exports shared file systems.
pcmcia	Loads or unloads modules, drivers, and programs (including the cardmgr daemon) to support PCMCIA cards (Ethernet adapters, modems, memory cards, etc.) in laptop computers.
portmap	Starts or stops the portmap daemon, which manages programs and protocols that utilize the Remote Procedure Call (RPC) mechanism.
random	Loads or saves the current state of the machine's random number generator's random seed to ensure more random randomness.
reconfig	Runs the anaconda reconfiguration screens during certain start-up situations (such as a reconfig request from the LILO boot prompt).
routed	Starts or stops the routed daemon, which controls dynamic-routing table updates via the Router Information Protocol (RIP).
rstatd	Starts or stops the rpc.rstatd daemon, which enables others on the network to probe the machine for performance statistics.
rusersd	Starts or stops the rpc.rusersd daemon, which enables others on the network to locate users on the machine.

Continued

Table 12-6 *(continued)*

Run-Level Scripts	What Does It Do?
rwhod	Starts or stops the rwhod daemon, which enables others on the network to obtain a list of all currently logged-in users.
sendmail	Controls the sendmail daemon, which handles incoming and outgoing SMTP (Simple Mail Transport Protocol) mail messages.
single	Terminates all running processes and enters run level 1 (single-user mode).
smb	Starts or stops the smbd and nmbd daemons for allowing access to Samba file and print services.
snmpd	Starts or stops the snmpd (Simple Network Management Protocol) daemon, which enables others to view machine-configuration information.
squid	Starts or stops the squid services, which enables proxy service to clients on your network.
syslog	Starts or stops the klogd and syslogd daemons that handle logging events from the kernel and other processes, respectively.
xfs	Starts or stops xfs, the X Window font server daemon.
xinetd	Sets the machine's hostname, establishes network routes, and controls xinetd, the network services daemon which listens for incoming TCP/IP connections to the machine.
ypbind	Binds to an NIS (Network Information Service) master server (if NIS is configured), and starts or stops the ypbind process, which communicates with the master server.

Each script representing a service that you want to start or stop is linked to a file in each of the run-level directories. For each run level, a script beginning with K stops the service, whereas a script beginning with S starts the service.

The two digits following the K or S in the filename provide a mechanism to select the priority in which the programs are run. For example, S30syslog is run before S40crond. However, while humans can readily see that 85 is less than 110, the file S110my_daemon is run before S85gpm. This is because the "ASCII collating sequence orders the files," which simply means that one positional character is compared to another. Therefore, a script beginning with the characters S110 is executed between S10network and S15netfs in run level 3.

All of the programs within the /etc/rc*X*.d directories (where *X* is replaced by a run-level number) are symbolic links, usually to a file in /etc/init.d. The /etc/rc*X*.d directories include the following:

- ✦ /etc/rc0.d: Run level 0 directory
- ✦ /etc/rc1.d: Run level 1 directory
- ✦ /etc/rc2.d: Run level 2 directory
- ✦ /etc/rc3.d: Run level 3 directory
- ✦ /etc/rc4.d: Run level 4 directory
- ✦ /etc/rc5.d: Run level 5 directory
- ✦ /etc/rc6.d: Run level 6 directory

In this manner, /etc/rc0.d/K60atd, /etc/rc1.d/K60atd, /etc/rc2.d/K60atd, /etc/rc3.d/S40atd, /etc/rc4.d/S40atd, /etc/rc5.d/S40atd, and /etc/rc6.d/K60atd are all symbolic links to /etc/init.d/atd. Using this simple, consistent mechanism, you can customize which programs are started at boot time.

Understanding what startup scripts do

Despite all the complicated rcXs, Ss, and Ks, the form of each start-up script is really quite simple. Because they are in plain text, you can just open one with a text editor to take a look at what it does. For the most part, a run-level script can be run with a start option, a stop option, and possibly a restart option. For example, the following lines are part of the contents of the smb script that defines what happens when the script is run with different options to start or stop the Samba file and print service:

```
#!/bin/sh
#
# chkconfig: - 91 35
# description: Starts and stops the Samba smbd and nmbd daemons \
#              used to provide SMB network services.
#

     .
     .
     .
start() {
        KIND="SMB"
        echo -n $"Starting $KIND services: "
        daemon smbd $SMBDOPTIONS
        RETVAL=$?
        echo
```

```
        KIND="NMB"
        echo -n $"Starting $KIND services: "
        daemon nmbd $NMBDOPTIONS
        RETVAL2=$?
        echo
        [ $RETVAL -eq 0 -a $RETVAL2 -eq 0 ] && touch /var/lock/subsys/smb || \
            RETVAL=1
        return $RETVAL
}

stop() {
        KIND="SMB"
        echo -n $"Shutting down $KIND services: "
        killproc smbd
        RETVAL=$?
        echo
        KIND="NMB"
        echo -n $"Shutting down $KIND services: "
        killproc nmbd
        RETVAL2=$?
        [ $RETVAL -eq 0 -a $RETVAL2 -eq 0 ] && rm -f /var/lock/subsys/smb
        echo ""
        return $RETVAL
}

restart() {
        stop
        start
}

case "$1" in
  start)
        start
        ;;
  stop)
        stop
        ;;
  restart)
        restart
        ;;

  *)
        echo $"Usage: $0 {start|stop|restart|status|condrestart}"
        exit 1
esac

exit $?
```

To illustrate what this script essentially does, I skipped some of the beginning of the script (where it checked if the network was up and running and set some values). Here are the actions `smb` takes when it is run with `start` or `stop`:

- `start`—This part of the script starts the `smbd` and `nmbd` servers when the script is run with the start option.

- `stop`—When run with the `stop` option, the `/etc/init.d/smb` script stops the `smbd` and `nmbd` servers.

The restart option runs the script with a `stop` option followed by a `start` option. If you wanted to start the `smb` service yourself, you could type the following command (as root user):

```
# /etc/init.d/smb start
Starting SMB services:                    [ OK ]
Starting NMB services:                    [ OK ]
```

To stop the service, you could type the following command:

```
# /etc/init.d/smb stop
Shutting down SMB services:               [ OK ]
Shutting down NMB services:               [ OK ]
```

The `smb` run-level script is different from other run-level scripts in that it supports several other options than `start` and `stop`. For example, this script has options (not shown in the example) that allow you to reload the `smb.conf` configuration file (`reload`) and check the status of the service (`rhstatus`).

Changing run-level script behavior

Modifying the start-up behavior of any such script merely involves opening the file in a text editor. For example, the `atd` daemon queues jobs submitted from the `at` and `batch` commands. Jobs submitted via `batch` are executed only if the system load is below a particular value, which can be set with a command-line option to the `atd` command. The default value of 0.8 is based on the assumption that a single-processor machine with less than 80 percent CPU utilization could handle the additional load of the batch job. However, if you were to add another CPU to your machine, the default threshold value would be too low and the batch jobs would not be sufficiently restricted.

You can change the system load threshold value from 0.8 to 1.6 to accommodate the increased processing capacity. To do this, simply modify the following line (in the `start` section) of the `/etc/init.d/atd` script:

```
daemon /usr/sbin/atd
```

Replace it with this line, using the `-l` argument to specify the new minimum system load value:

```
daemon /usr/sbin/atd -l 1.6
```

After saving the file and exiting the editor, you can reboot the machine or just run any of the following three commands to begin using the new batch threshold value:

```
/etc/init.d/atd reload
/etc/init.d/atd restart
/etc/init.d/atd stop ; /etc/rc.d/init.d/atd start
```

Note   Always make a copy of a run-level script before you change it. Also, keep track of changes you make to run-level scripts before you upgrade the packages they come from. You need to make those changes again after the upgrade.

Reorganizing or removing run-level scripts

There are several ways to deal with removing programs from the system startup directories, adding them to particular run levels, or changing when they are executed. The first method is to manually delete the symbolic links (to remove it) or renumber it (to change its order of execution). If you wanted to keep the sendmail daemon from starting in run level 2 (active only in run levels 3, 4, and 5), you could delete the `/etc/rc2.d/S80sendmail` link. However, it may be more convenient to rename the link to something that does not begin with S (e.g., `/etc/rc2.d/_S80sendmail`), just in case you want to reenable it later. To change the order in which it is run, simply rename the file and change the number 80 to a higher or lower number.

Caution   You should never remove the actual file (in this case, `/etc/init.d/sendmail`). Because no scripts are run directly from the `/etc/init.d` directory automatically, it does no harm to keep them there. The scripts in `/etc/init.d` are only accessed as links from the `/etc/rcX.d` directories. By keeping scripts in the `init.d` directory, you can always add them later by re-linking them to the appropriate run level directory.

Another way to reorganize or remove run-level scripts is to use the Service Configuration window. Log in as root user and type the following from a Terminal window:

```
# serviceconf &
```

Figure 12-1 shows an example of the Service Configuration window:

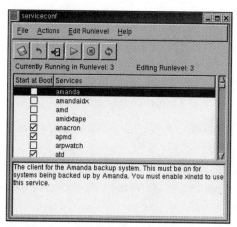

Figure 12-1: Reorganize, add, and remove run-level scripts from the Service Configuration window.

The Service Configuration window lets you reconfigure services for run levels 3, 4, and 5. The run levels that you are currently running and currently editing are displayed near the top of the screen. Services that are available for the run level appear in the middle of the frame, with check marks next to the ones configured to start at that level. Here is what you can do from this window:

✦ **Add** — Click the box next to each service you want to start automatically at that run level so that a check mark appears in the box.

✦ **Remove** — Click the run-level script that you want to remove for a particular run level to remove the check mark.

✦ **Save Changes** — Click Save Changes on the window to save any changes you have made to the run-level scripts.

✦ **Start, Stop, or Restart** — Click a service on the list. Select Action; then select either Start Service, Stop Service, or Restart Service. The selected service immediately starts, stops, or restarts.

Some administrators prefer text-based commands for managing run-level scripts and for managing other system services that start automatically. The chkconfig command can be used to list whether services that run-level scripts start, as well as services the xinetd daemon starts, are on or off. To see a list of all system services, with indications that they are on or off, type the following:

```
# chkconfig --list | less
```

You can then page through the list to see those services. If you want to view the status of an individual service, you can add the service at the end of the list option. For example, to see whether the nfs service starts in each run level, type the following:

```
# chkconfig --list nfs
nfs      0:off  1:off  2:off  3:on  4:on  5:on  6:off
```

This example shows that the nfs service is set to be on for run levels 3, 4, and 5, but that it is set to off for run levels 0, 1, 2, and 6.

Another tool that can be run from the shell to change which services start and do not start at various levels is the ntsysv command. Type the following as root user from the shell:

```
# ntsysv &
```

A screen appears with a list of available services. Use the up and down arrow keys to locate the service you want. With the cursor on a service, press the spacebar to toggle the service on or off. Press the Tab key to highlight the OK button, and press the spacebar to save the change and to exit. The ntsysv tool is somewhat clever; it checks your default run level (the initdefault set in the /etc/inittab file) and turns on the service so that it starts at that run level.

Adding run-level scripts

Adding the appropriate files for new run-level scripts is very similar, for both methods. After installing the binaries for the fictitious my_daemon program, it needs to be configured to start up in run levels 3, 4, and 5, and terminated in any other run level. To do this, just place a shell script called my_daemon (or some other reasonably intuitive name) in /etc/init.d. This script should minimally support the start and stop command-line options. For the manual method, just create the following symbolic links:

```
cd /etc/rc0.d ; ln -s ../init.d/my_daemon K28my_daemon
cd /etc/rc1.d ; ln -s ../init.d/my_daemon K28my_daemon
cd /etc/rc2.d ; ln -s ../init.d/my_daemon K28my_daemon
cd /etc/rc3.d ; ln -s ../init.d/my_daemon S82my_daemon
cd /etc/rc4.d ; ln -s ../init.d/my_daemon S82my_daemon
cd /etc/rc5.d ; ln -s ../init.d/my_daemon S82my_daemon
cd /etc/rc6.d ; ln -s ../init.d/my_daemon K28my_daemon
```

Alternatively, to use chkconfig, ensure that the following lines are included in the /etc/init.d/my_daemon script:

```
# chkconfig: 345 82 28
```

```
# description: Does something pretty cool - you really \
#    have to see it to believe it!
# processname: my_daemon
```

With those lines in place, simply run the following command:

```
# chkconfig --add my_daemon
```

The appropriate links are created automatically. This can be verified with the following command:

```
# chkconfig --list my_daemon
```

The resulting output should look like:

```
my_daemon 0:off 1:off 2:off 3:on 4:on 5:on 6:off
```

Managing xinetd services

There are a bunch of services, particularly Internet services, that are not handled by separate run-level scripts. Instead, a single run-level script called xinetd (formerly inetd) is run to handle incoming requests for a variety of network services. For that reason, xinetd is sometimes referred to as the super-server. The xinetd run-level script (along with the xinetd daemon that it runs) offers the following advantages:

✦ **Less daemon processes.** Instead of one (or more) daemon processes running on your computer to monitor incoming requests for each service, the xinetd daemon can listen for requests for many different services. As a result, when you type ps -ax to see what processes are running, dozens of fewer daemon processes will be running than there would be if each service had its own daemon.

✦ **Access control and logging.** By using xinetd to oversee the management of services, consistent methods of access control (such as PAM) and consistent logging methods (such as the /var/log/messages file) can be used across all of the services.

When a request comes into your computer for a service that xinetd is monitoring, xinetd uses the /etc/xinetd.conf file to read configuration files contained in the /etc/xinetd.d directory. Then, based on the contents of the xinetd.d file for the requested service, a server program is launched to handle the service request.

Each server process is one of two types: single-thread or multithread. A single-thread server will handle only the current request, whereas a multithread server will handle all incoming requests for the service as long as there is still a client holding the process open. Then the multithread server will close and xinetd will begin monitoring that service again.

The following are a few examples of services that are monitored by xinetd. The daemon process that is started up to handle each service is also listed.

Note   Some of the following services are actually launched by the tcpd daemon. The tcpd daemon acts as an extra level of security, logging each incoming request and performing other security checks.

✦ **comsat** (`/usr/sbin/in.comsat`)—Used to alert the biff client program that new mail has arrived.

✦ **eklogin** (`/usr/kerberos/sbin/klogind`)—Kerberos-related login daemon.

✦ **finger** (`/usr/sbin/in.fingerd`)—Handles incoming finger requests for information from remote users about local users.

✦ **gssftp** (`/usr/kerberos/sbin/ftpd`)—Kerberos-related daemon for handling file transfer requests (FTP).

✦ **imap** (`/usr/sbin/imapd`)— Daemon for handling requests from remote mail clients to get their mail from this IMAP server.

✦ **linuxconf** (`/sbin/linuxconf`)—Accepts requests from Web browsers from other computers to run `linuxconf`.

✦ **ntalk** (`/usr/sbin/in.ntalkd`)—Daemon for handling requests to set up chats between a remote user and a local one (using the `talk` command).

✦ **rlogin** (`/usr/sbin/in.rlogind`)—Daemon for responding to remote login requests (from a remote `rlogin` command).

✦ **rsh** (`/usr/sbin/in.rshd`)—Handles requests from a remote client to run a command on the local computer.

✦ **wu-ftpd** (`/usr/sbin/in.ftpd`)—Accepts FTP requests to the wu-ftpd server.

Other services that can be launched by requests that come in to xinetd include services for POP mail, remote telnet requests, Samba configuration requests, and amanda network backups.

Manipulating run levels

Aside from the run level chosen at boot time (usually 3 or 5) and the shutdown or reboot levels (0 and 6, respectively), you can change the run level at any time while you're logged in (as root user). The `telinit` command (really just a symbolic link to `init`) enables you to specify a desired run level, causing the termination of all system processes that shouldn't exist in that run level, and starting all processes that should be running.

Note The `telinit` command is also used to instruct `init` to reload its configuration file, `/etc/inittab`. This is accomplished with either the `telinit q` or the `telinit Q` commands.

For example, if you encountered a problem with your hard disk on startup, you may be placed in single-user mode (run level 1) to perform system maintenance. After the machine is stable, you can just execute the command as follows:

```
# telinit 5
```

The `init` command handles terminating and starting all processes necessary to present you with a graphical login window.

Determining the current run level

You can determine the machine's current run level with the aptly named `runlevel` command. Using the previous example of booting into single-user mode and then manually changing the run level, the output of the `runlevel` command would be:

```
# runlevel
S 5
```

This means that the previous run level was S (for single-user mode) and the current run level is 5. If the machine had booted properly, the previous run level would be listed as N to indicate that there really wasn't a previous run level.

Changing to a shutdown run level

Shutting down the machine is simply a change in run level. With that in mind, other ways to change the run level include the `reboot`, `halt`, `poweroff`, and `shutdown` commands. The `reboot` command, which is a symbolic link to the `halt` command, executes a `shutdown -r now`, terminating all processes and rebooting the machine. The `halt` command executes `shutdown -h now`, terminating all processes and leaving the machine in an idle state (but still powered on). Similarly, the `poweroff` command, which is also a link to the `halt` command, executes a change to run level 0, but if the machine's BIOS supports Advanced Power Management (APM), it will switch off the power to the machine.

Note A time must be given to the `shutdown` command, either specified as +m (representing the number of minutes to delay before initiating the shutdown) or as hh:mm (an absolute time value, where hh is the hour and mm is the minute that you would like the shutdown to begin). Alternatively, now is commonly used to initiate the shutdown immediately.

Scheduling System Tasks

Frequently the need arises to run a process unattended or during off-hours. The at facility is designed to run such jobs at specific times. Submitted jobs are spooled in the directory /var/spool/at, awaiting execution by the at daemon atd. The jobs are executed using the current environment and directory that was active when the job was submitted. Any output or error messages that haven't been redirected elsewhere are e-mailed to the user that submitted the job.

The following sections describe how to use the at, batch, and cron facilities to schedule tasks to run at specific times. These descriptions also include ways of viewing which tasks are scheduled and deleting scheduled tasks that you don't want to run anymore.

Using at.allow and at.deny

There are two access control files designed to limit which users can use the at facility. The file /etc/at.allow contains a list of users that are granted access, and the file /etc/at.deny contains a similar list of those who may not submit at jobs. If neither file exists, only the superuser is granted access to at. If a blank /etc/at.deny file exists (as in the default configuration), all users are allowed to utilize the at facility.

Specifying when jobs are run

There are many different ways to specify the time at which an at job should run (most of which closely resemble a spoken command). A few examples are presented in Table 12-7. These are not complete commands — they only provide a sample of how to specify the time that a job should run.

Table 12-7 Samples for Specifying Times in an at Job	
Command Line	**When the Command Is Run**
at now	The job is run immediately.
at now + 2 minutes	The job will start 2 minutes from the current time.
at now + 1 hour	The job will start one hour from the current time.
at now + 5 days	The job will start five days from the current time.
at now + 4 weeks	The job will start four weeks from the current time.
at now next minute	The job will start in exactly 60 seconds.
at now next hour	The job will start in exactly 60 minutes.

Command Line	When the Command Is Run
`at now next day`	The job will start at the same time tomorrow.
`at now next month`	The job will start on the same day and at the same time next month.
`at now next year`	The job will start on the same date and at the same time next year.
`at now next fri`	The job will start at the same time next Friday.
`at teatime` `at 16:00 today`	The job will run at 4 p.m. They keywords noon and midnight can also be used.
`at 16:00 tomorrow`	The job will run at 4 p.m. tomorrow.

`at 2:45pm`
 	
`at 14:45`
	The job will run at 2:45 p.m. on the current day.

`at 5:00 Jun 14 2001` `at 5:00 6/14/01`	The job will begin at 5 a.m. on June 14, 2001.

Submitting scheduled jobs

The `at` facility offers a lot of flexibility in how you can submit scheduled jobs. There are three ways to submit a job to the `at` facility:

✦ Piped in from standard input. For example, the following command will attempt to build the Perl5.005_56 distribution from source in the early morning hours while the machine is likely to be less busy:

```
echo "cd /tmp/perl5.005_56 ; make ; ls -al" | at 2am tomorrow
```

An ancillary benefit to this procedure is that a full log of the compilation process will be e-mailed to the user that submitted the job.

✦ Read as standard input. If no command is specified, `at` will prompt you to enter commands at the special `at>` prompt, as shown in the following example. You must indicate the end of the commands by pressing Ctrl+D, which signals an End of Transmission (<EOT>) to at.

```
$ at 23:40
at> cd /tmp/perl5.005_56
at> make
at> ls -al
at> <Ctrl-d>
```

✦ Read from a file. When the -f command-line option is followed by a valid file-name, the contents of that file are used as the commands to be executed, as in the following example:

```
$ at -f /root/bin/runme now + 5 hours
```

This runs the commands stored in /root/bin/runme in five hours. The file can either be a simple list of commands or a shell script to be run in its own subshell (that is, the file begins with #!/bin/bash or the name of another shell).

Viewing scheduled jobs

You can use the atq command (effectively the same as at -l) to view a list of your pending jobs in the at queue, showing each job's sequence number, the date and time the job is scheduled to run, and the queue in which the job is being run.

The two most common queue names are "a," which represents the at queue, and "b," which represents the batch queue. All other letters (upper- and lowercase) can be used to specify queues with even lower priority levels. If the atq command lists the queue name as =, this indicates that the job is currently running. The following is an example of output from the atq command:

```
# atq
2      2001-06-02 00:51 a
3      2001-06-02 00:52 a
4      2001-06-05 23:52 a
```

Here you can see that there are three at jobs pending (job numbers 2, 3, and 4, all indicated as "a"). After the job number, the output shows the date and hour that each job is scheduled to run.

Deleting scheduled jobs

If you decide that you'd like to cancel a particular job, you can use the atrm command (equivalent to at -d) with the job number (or more than one) as reported by the atq command. For example, using the following output from atq:

```
# atq
18       2001-06-01 03:00 a
19       2001-06-29 05:27 a
20       2001-06-30 05:27 a
21       2001-06-14 00:01 a
22       2001-06-01 03:00 a
```

you can remove the jobs scheduled to run at 5:27 a.m. on June 29 and June 30 from the queue with the command `atrm 19 20`.

Using the batch command

If system resources are at a premium on your machine, or if the job you submit can run at a priority lower than normal, the `batch` command (equivalent to `at -q b`) may be useful. It is controlled by the same atd daemon, and it allows job submissions in the same format as `at` submissions (although the time specification is optional).

However, to prevent your job from usurping already scarce processing time, the job will run only if the system load average is below a particular value. The default value is 0.8, but specifying a command-line option to `atd` can modify this. This was used as an example in the earlier section describing start-up and shutdown. Here is an example of the `batch` command:

```
$ batch
at> du -h /home > /tmp/duhome
at> <Ctrl-d>
```

In this example, after I type the `batch` command, the `at` facility is invoked to enable me to enter the command(s) I want run. Typing the `du -h /home > /tmp/duhome` command line has the disk usages for everything in the /home directory structure output to the /tmp/duhome file. On the next line, Ctrl+D is pressed to end the batch job. As soon as the load average is low enough, the command is run.

Using the cron facility

Another way to run commands unattended is via the `cron` facility. Part of the vixie-cron RPM package, `cron` addresses the need to run commands periodically or routinely (at least, more often than you'd care to manually enter them) and allows considerable flexibility in automating the execution of the command. As with the `at` facility, any output or error messages that haven't been redirected elsewhere are e-mailed to the user that submitted the job.

Also like the `at` facility, `cron` includes two access control files designed to limit which users can use it. The file /etc/cron.allow contains a list of users that are granted access, and the file /etc/cron.deny contains a similar list of those who may not submit `cron` jobs. If neither file exists, all users are granted access to `cron`.

There are four places where a job can be submitted for execution by the cron daemon crond:

✦ The /var/spool/cron/*username* file. This method, where each individual user (indicated by *username*) controls his or her own separate file, is the method used on UNIX System V systems.

✦ The /etc/crontab file. This is referred to as the system crontab file, and was the original crontab file from BSD UNIX and its derivatives. Only root has permission to modify this file.

✦ The /etc/cron.d directory. Each file placed in this directory has the same format as the /etc/crontab file. Only root has permission to create or modify the files in this directory.

✦ The /etc/cron.hourly, /etc/cron.daily, /etc/cron.weekly, and /etc/cron.monthly directories. Each file in these directories is a shell script that runs at the times specified in the /etc/crontab file (by default at one minute after the hour, at 4:02 a.m. every day, Sunday at 4:22 a.m., and 4:42 a.m. on the first day of the month, respectively). Only root has permission to create or modify the files in these directories.

The standard format of an entry in the /var/spool/cron/*username* file consists of five fields specifying when the command should run: minute, hour, day of the month, month, and day of the week. The sixth field is the actual command to be run.

The files in the /etc/cron.d directory and the /etc/crontab file use the same first five fields to determine when the command should run. However, the sixth field represents the name of the user submitting the job (because it cannot be inferred by the name of the file as in a /var/spool/cron/*username* directory), and the seventh field is the command to be run. Table 12-8 lists the valid values for each field common to both types of files.

Table 12-8
Valid /etc/crontab Field Values

Field Number	Field	Acceptable Values
1	minute	Any integer between 0 and 59
2	hour	Any integer between 0 and 23
3	day of the month	Any integer between 0 and 31
4	month	Any integer between 0 and 12, or an abbreviation for the name of the month (Jan, Feb, Mar, Apr, May, Jun, Jul, Aug, Sep, Oct, Nov, Dec)
5	day of the week	Any integer between 0 and 7 (where both 0 and 7 can represent Sunday), or abbreviation for the day (Sun, Mon, Tue, Wed, Thu, Fri, Sat)

An asterisk (*) in any field indicates all possible values for that field. For example, an asterisk in the second column is equivalent to 0,1,2 . . . 22,23, and an asterisk in the fourth column means Jan,Feb,Mar . . . Nov,Dec. In addition, lists of values, ranges of values, and increments can be used. For example, to specify the days Monday, Wednesday, and Friday, the fifth field could be represented as the list Mon,Wed,Fri. To represent the normal working hours in a day, the range 9–5 could be specified in the second field. Another option is to use an increment, as in specifying 0–31/3 in the third field to represent every third day of the month, or */5 in the first field to denote every five minutes.

Lines beginning with a # character in any of the crontab-format files are comments, which can be very helpful in explaining what task each command is designed to perform. It is also possible to specify environment variables (in Bourne shell syntax, e.g., NAME="*value*") within the crontab file. Any variable can be specified to fine-tune the environment in which the job will run, but one that may be particularly useful is MAILTO. The following line will send the results of the cron job to a user other than the one that submitted the job:

```
MAILTO=otheruser
```

If the following line appears in a crontab file, all output and error messages that haven't already been redirected will be discarded:

```
MAILTO=
```

Modifying scheduled tasks with crontab

The files in /var/spool/cron should not be edited directly. They should only be accessed via the crontab command. To list the current contents of your own personal crontab file, type the following command:

```
$ crontab -l
```

All crontab entries can be removed with the following command:

```
$ crontab -r
```

Even if your personal crontab file doesn't exist, you can use the following command to begin editing it:

```
$ crontab -e
```

The file automatically opens in the text editor that is defined in your EDITOR or VISUAL environment variables, with vi as the default. When you're done, simply exit the editor. Provided there were no syntax errors, your crontab file will be installed. For example, if your username is jsmith, you have just created the file /var/spool/cron/jsmith. If you add a line (with a descriptive comment, of course) to remove any old core files from your source code directories, that file may look similar to this:

```
# DO NOT EDIT THIS FILE - edit the master and reinstall.
# (/tmp/crontab.618 installed on Sat March 17 13:58:38 2001)
# (Cron version -- $Id: crontab.c,v 2.13 1994/01/17 03:20:37 vixie Exp $)
#  Early every Sunday and Wednesday morning (1:05am), silently remove
#  old core files from directories where code is being developed:
5 1 * * Sun,Wed find /home/jsmith/src -name core -exec rm {} \; > /dev/null 2>&1
```

The root user can access any user's individual `crontab` file by using the `-u username` option to the `crontab` command.

Understanding cron files

There are separate `cron` directories set up to contain `cron` jobs that run hourly, daily, weekly, and monthly. These `cron` jobs are all set up to run from the `/etc/crontab` file. The default `/etc/crontab` file looks like this:

```
SHELL=/bin/bash
PATH=/sbin:/bin:/usr/sbin:/usr/bin
MAILTO=root
HOME=/

# run-parts
01 * * * * root run-parts /etc/cron.hourly
02 4 * * * root run-parts /etc/cron.daily
22 4 * * 0 root run-parts /etc/cron.weekly
42 4 1 * * root run-parts /etc/cron.monthly
```

The first four lines initialize the run-time environment for all subsequent jobs (the subshell in which jobs will run, the executable program search path, the recipient of output and error messages, and that user's home directory).

The next four lines execute (as the user root) the `run-parts` program that controls programs that you may wish to run periodically. `run-parts` is a shell script that takes a directory as a command-line argument. It then sequentially runs every program within that directory (shell scripts are most common, but binary executables and links are also evaluated). The default configuration executes programs in `/etc/cron.hourly` at one minute after every hour of every day; `/etc/cron.daily` at 4:02 a.m. every day; `/etc/cron.weekly` at 4:22 a.m. on Sundays; and `/etc/cron.monthly` at 4:42 a.m. on the first day of each month.

The following files are installed in `cron` directories by default:

✦ `/etc/cron.daily/logrotate.cron`—Automates rotating, compressing, and manipulating system logfiles.

✦ `/etc/cron.daily/makewhatis.cron`—Updates the whatis database (contains descriptions of man pages), which is used by the `man -k`, `apropos`, and `whatis` commands to find man pages related to a particular word.

✦ /etc/cron.daily/slocate.cron—Updates the /var/lib/slocate/slocate.db database, which contains a searchable list of files on the machine (excluding temporary directories and network-mounted file systems).

✦ /etc/cron.daily/tetex.cron—Removes TeX font files from /var/lib/texmf that haven't been accessed in 90 days.

✦ /etc/cron.daily/tmpwatch—Removes files from /tmp, /var/tmp, and /var/catman that haven't been accessed in 10 days.

The makewhatis.cron script installed in /etc/cron.weekly is similar to the one in /etc/cron.daily, but it completely rebuilds the whatis database, rather than just updating the existing database.

In the /etc/cron.d directory, each individual file has the same format as the /etc/crontab file. The only file installed is /etc/cron.d/kmod, which executes the rmmod command every 10 minutes to remove from memory any unused kernel modules:

```
# rmmod -a is a two-hand sweep module cleaner
*/10 * * * *    root    /sbin/rmmod -as
```

Splitting up cron jobs in separate files in such a manner can be useful if different environment variables are necessary for each individual task.

Summary

Shell scripts are an integral part of the Red Hat Linux system for configuring, booting, administering, and customizing Red Hat Linux. They are used to eliminate typing repetitive commands. They are frequently executed from the scheduling facilities within Red Hat Linux, allowing much flexibility in determining when and how often a process should run. And they control the start-up of most daemons and server processes at boot time.

The init daemon and its configuration file, /etc/inittab, also factor heavily in the initial start-up of your Red Hat Linux system. They implement the concept of run levels that is carried out by the shell scripts in /etc/rc.d/init.d, and they provide a means by which the machine can be shut down or rebooted in an orderly manner.

To have shell scripts configured to run on an ongoing basis, you can use the cron facility. Cron jobs can be added by editing cron files directly or by running commands such as at and batch to enter the commands to be run.

✦   ✦   ✦

Backing Up and Restoring Files

I f you've ever suffered a hard drive crash, you know just how aggravating it can be. Irreplaceable data can be lost. Countless hours may be spent reinstalling your operating system and applications. It is not a fun experience. It need happen only once for you to learn the importance of making regular backups of your critical data.

Today, larger and faster backup media can help simplify the process of backing up your data. Red Hat Linux supports many different types of media — such as writable CD-ROM and magnetic tape — for creating backups. Using tools such as `cron`, you can configure backups to run unattended at scheduled times.

This chapter describes how to create a backup strategy and how to select media for backing up data on your Red Hat Linux system. It tells how to do automated backups and backups over a network. It also describes how to restore individual files, or entire file systems, using tools such as the `restore` command.

Selecting a Backup Strategy

There are several approaches to backing up your data. You need to ask yourself a few questions to decide which approach is best for you. Some things that you should consider are:

- ✦ In the event of a crash, how much downtime can I tolerate?
- ✦ Will I ever need to recover older versions of my files, or is just the most recent revision sufficient?
- ✦ Do I need to back up files for just one computer or for many computers on a network?

Your answers to these questions will help you decide how often to do full backups and how often to do incremental backups. If the data is particularly critical, you may even decide that you need to have your data duplicated constantly, using a technique called disk mirroring. The following sections describe different backup methods.

Full backup

A full backup is one that stores every file on a particular disk or partition. If that disk should ever crash, you can rebuild your system by restoring the entire backup to a new disk. Whatever backup strategy you decide on, some sort of full backup should be part of it. You may perform full backups every night or perhaps only once every week; it depends on how often you add or modify files on your system, as well as the capacity of your backup equipment.

Incremental backup

An incremental backup is one that contains only those files that have been added or modified since the last time a more complete backup was made. You may choose to do incremental backups to conserve your backup media. Incremental backups also take less time to complete. This can be important when systems are in high use during the work week and running a full backup would degrade system performance. Full backups can be reserved for the weekend when the system is not in use.

Disk mirroring

Full and incremental backups can take time to restore, and sometimes you just can't afford that downtime. By duplicating your operating system and data on an additional hard drive, you can greatly increase the speed with which you can recover from a server crash.

With disk mirroring, it is usually common for the system to continuously update the duplicate drive with the most current information. In fact, with a type of mirroring called RAID 1, the duplicate drive is written to at the same time as the original, and if the main drive fails, the duplicate can immediately take over. This is called *fault-tolerant* behavior, which is a must if you are running a mission-critical server of some kind.

Network backup

All of the preceding backup strategies can be performed over a network. This is good because you can share a single backup device with many computers on a network. This is much cheaper and more convenient than installing a tape drive or other backup device in every system on your network. If you have many computers, however, your backup device will require a lot of capacity. In such a case, you may consider a mechanical tape loader or writable CD jukebox.

It is even possible to do a form of disk mirroring over the network. For example, a Web server may store a duplicate copy of its data on another server. If the first server crashes, a simple TCP/IP hostname change can redirect the Web traffic to the second server. When the original server is rebuilt, it can recover all of its data from the backup server and be back in business.

Selecting a Backup Medium

Armed with a backup strategy in mind, it is time to select a backup medium. Several types of backup hardware and media are available for use with Red Hat Linux. Each type has its advantages and disadvantages.

The type of medium to choose depends largely on the amount of data you need to archive, how long you will store backups, how often you expect to recover data from your backups, and how much you can afford to spend. Table 13-1 compares the most common backup media.

	Table 13-1	
	Comparison of Common Backup Media	
Backup Medium	**Advantage**	**Disadvantage**
Magnetic tape	High capacity, low cost for archiving massive amounts of data.	Sequential access medium, so recovery of individual files can be slow.
Writable CDs	Random access medium, so recovery of individual files is easier. Backups can be restored from any CD-ROM.	Limited storage space (approximately 650MB per CD).
Additional hard drive	Allows faster and more frequent backups. Fast recovery from crashes. No media to load. Data can be located and recovered more many revisions of your files. quickly. You can configure the second disk to be a virtual clone of the first disk, so that you can boot off of the second disk if the first disk crashes.	Data cannot be stored offsite, thus there is risk of data loss if the entire server is destroyed. This method is not well suited to keeping historical archives of the The hard drive will eventually fill up.

The following sections describe how to use magnetic tape and writable CDs as backup media. How to use additional hard drives as backup media is described later in this chapter.

Magnetic tape

Magnetic tape is the most common medium used for backing up large amounts of computer data. Tapes provide a low-cost, convenient way to archive your files. Today's high-capacity tape drives can back up many gigabytes of data on an amazingly small tape, allowing vast amounts of information to be safely stored.

The primary disadvantage of magnetic tape is that it is a sequential access medium. This means that tapes are read or written from beginning to end, and searching for a particular file can be a time-consuming process. For this reason, tape is a good choice for backing up and restoring entire file systems, but not the ideal choice if you need to recover individual files on a regular basis.

Red Hat Linux can use a wide variety of tape drives. Most SCSI tape drives will work with the generic Linux kernel. Even many IDE tape drives are supported via a "SCSI emulation" mode. Some drives, however, require installation of additional software.

Using Ftape tools for magnetic tape

If your tape drive is attached to an IDE floppy controller cable, you will need to use the ftape driver to access it. Fortunately, version 3.04 of the ftape loadable module is bundled with the Linux 2.4 kernel. When your Linux system boots, it should autodetect the tape drive and load the ftape driver. To verify that your system loaded the tape driver, type the following command:

```
dmesg | grep ftape
```

This searches the most recent kernel messages for lines containing the word *ftape*. If the ftape module was loaded, you should see something like this:

```
ftape v3.04d 25/11/97
[000] ftape-init.c (ftape_init) - installing QIC-117 floppy tape hardware
drive... .
[001] ftape-init.c (ftape_init) - ftape_init @ 0xd08b0060.
[002] ftape-buffer.c (add_one_buffer) - buffer nr #1 @ c1503914, dma area @
c02c0000.
[003] ftape-buffer.c (add_one_buffer) - buffer nr #2 @ c1503c44, dma area @
c0298000.
[004] ftape-buffer.c (add_one_buffer) - buffer nr #3 @ c50abaac, dma area @
c0328000.
[005] ftape-calibr.c (time_inb) - inb() duration: 1109 nsec.
[006] ftape-calibr.c (ftape_calibrate) - TC for `ftape_udelay()' = 310 nsec (at
20479 counts).
[007] ftape-calibr.c (ftape_calibrate) - TC for `fdc_wait()' = 2208 nsec (at
2559 counts).
```

If the module was not loaded, then you should check if your kernel is compiled with support for the ftape module and your particular tape drive. Refer to the section on reconfiguring the kernel located in Chapter 2. When running the `make config` or `make menuconfig` command, choose Character Devices ⇨ Ftape, the floppy tape device driver. You can then verify that the ftape module is enabled and that your specific hardware is supported. Continue with compiling and installing the kernel in the normal way.

In most cases, an ftape device can be accessed just like a SCSI device. The primary difference is that an ftape device file contains the letters *qft* (for QIK Floppy Tape) where a SCSI tape contains *st*. For example, the device file for the first SCSI tape on your system will probably be /dev/st0; the device file for the first floppy tape will likely be `/dev/qft0`.

All of the standard tape and archiving related programs should work fine with both types of hardware. Nevertheless, there are a few extra programs that you may find useful when working with a floppy tape drive. These programs can be found in the ftape-tools package located at `ftp://metalab.unc.edu/pub/Linux/kernel/tapes/`. Download the file named `ftape-tools-1.09.tar.gz`. If a version higher than 1.09 is available, download that instead. Extract the ftape package using the `tar` command.

```
$ tar -xzvf ftape-tools-1.09.tar.gz
```

This extracts the package into an `ftape-tools-1.09` directory. Use the `dcd` command to go to that directory and to run the `./configure` script to prepare the package's makefiles. Next, compile the package by typing the `make` command:

```
$ ./configure
$ make
```

Finally, assume root privilege using the `su` command and type **make install** to install the ftape-tools programs and online man pages to the appropriate directories:

```
# make install
```

Testing the magnetic tape drive

You should now be ready to test your tape drive. Insert a blank tape into the tape drive and type the following command:

```
$ mt -f /dev/qft0 rewind
```

You should hear the tape spin as the system rewinds the tape. This will be a very short process if the tape is already rewound. The `mt` command provided with ftape-tools is used to scan, rewind, and eject magnetic tapes in a floppy controller tape drive. It is very similar in operation to the st command, which is used to perform the same functions on SCSI tapes.

Formatting magnetic tapes

The ftape-tools package also includes a tool for formatting tapes as well. Most tapes now come preformatted. In the event that you have an older floppy controller tape drive that uses unformatted tapes, use the ftformat command to format them:

```
$ /usr/local/bin/ftformat -f /dev/qft0
```

Usually, the -f parameter with the device name is the only parameter that you need to supply. Nevertheless, you are encouraged to read the online man page for ftformat to learn more about its options and capabilities.

Writable CD-ROM drives

Another backup medium that is gaining popularity is the writable CD-ROM drive. Writable CD-ROM drives have several advantages over tape, the primary one being that CDs are a random access medium. This means that the CD drive can quickly locate a particular file on the CD without sequentially scanning through the entire disc. This is useful when you need to keep a revision history of frequently changing data files (such as source code for a software project or drafts of legal documents).

Another advantage is the extremely long life span of CDs. If you wish to archive your backups for a very long time, a writable CD drive is a good choice. If your backups are intended for short-term storage, you should probably consider a rewritable CD drive. A rewritable CD (unlike plain writable CDs) can be reformatted and used to store new backups.

The biggest drawback is that a CD can store at most about 650MB of data. In contrast, many tape drives can store multiple gigabytes of data.

Getting cdrecord for writable CDs

To write CDs with Red Hat Linux you need to install the cdrecord package. This package contains components such as the cdrecord, devdump, isodump, isoinfo, isovfy, and readcd command. The cdrecord package is included with the Red Hat Linux distribution.

Note The cdrecord package requires that you use a SCSI CD drive. If you have an IDE/ATAPI CD drive, which is a very popular device, you maymay need to configure that drive to do SCSI emulation. See Chapter 8 for a description of how to configure an IDE/ATAPI CD drive for SCSI emulation.

Writing to CDs

Because the data written to a CD becomes permanent once it is written, you need to format the CD and copy files to it all in one step. If you formatted it first, you would end up with an empty file system on a CD that can no longer be written to.

The first step is to create an image of the CD file system as a file on your computer. You do this with the mkisofs command. As an example, imagine that we want to back up the home directory for user mary. We would invoke the mkisofs command and pass it the name of the file system image file to create, followed by the directory to base it on:

```
$ mkisofs -o /var/tmp/mary.cd /home/mary
```

This creates an ISO9660 file system image in a file named mary.cd located in the /var/tmp directory. If your /var partition does not have enough room for the image, choose a different location.

Tip

By default, mkisofs preserves the ownership and access rights of files and directories when it creates the file system image. This is appropriate when you are making a backup, but not when you are creating a software distribution CD. In such a case, add the -r option as the first parameter to mkisofs. It will then store all files as publicly readable.

Before we can write this image file to a CD, we must first discover the SCSI bus number, device ID number, and Logical Unit Number (LUN) of the CD drive. Unless you have an actual SCSI bus in your computer, the emulated SCSI bus is probably numbered zero. You can confirm this using the dmesg command combined with grep:

```
# dmesg | grep ^scsi
```

This scans recent kernel messages and prints out any that begin with scsi. For example, if you have an IDE/ATAPT CD drive emulating a SCSI device, you should see output similar to this:

```
scsi0 : SCSI host adapter emulation for IDE ATAPI devices
scsi : 1 host.
scsi : detected 1 SCSI cdrom total.
```

Sure enough, the emulated SCSI bus is identified as scsi0. Next, you need to find out which SCSI device ID the CD drive is using. Invoke the cdrecord command with the single parameter -scanbus:

```
# cdrecord -scanbus
```

You should see a response similar to the following:

```
Cdrecord 1.10 (i686-pc-linux-gnu) Copyright (C) 1995-2001 J!!rg Schilling
Linux sg driver version: 3.1.19
Using libscg version 'schily-0.5'
scsibus0:
        0) 'Memorex ' 'CRW-1622 ' 'D4.0' Removable CD-ROM
        1) *
        2) *
        3) *
        4) *
        5) *
        6) *
        7) *
```

This tells us that the CD drive is using SCSI ID zero. The Logical Unit Number in this case should always be zero, so we now have all three numbers. We supply them to cdrecord as part of the dev parameter. The SCSI bus number is listed first; it is followed by the ID number, and then by the LUN. The entire command should look similar to this:

```
# cdrecord -v speed=2 dev=0,0,0 -data /var/tmp/mary.cd
```

Several additional parameters are included in the command. The -v parameter tells cdrecord to supply verbose output to the screen. The speed parameter tells cdrecord what speed to record at (in this case X2). The -data parameter tells cdrecord that the next parameter is the name of the file system image to write to the CD. As it works, cdrecord should display status messages that look similar to the following:

```
Cdrecord 1.10 (i686-pc-linux-gnu) Copyright (C) 1995-2001 J!!rg
Schilling
TOC Type: 1 = CD-ROM
scsidev: '0,0,0'
scsibus: 0 target: 0 lun: 0
Linux sg driver version: 3.1.19
Using libscg version 'schily-0.5'
atapi: 1
Device type      : Removable CD-ROM
Version          : 0
Response Format: 1
Vendor_info      : 'Memorex '
Identifikation : 'CRW-1622            '
Revision         : 'D4.0'
Device seems to be: Generic mmc CD-RW.
Using generic SCSI-3/mmc CD-R driver (mmc_cdr).
Driver flags     : SWABAUDIO
Drive buf size : 786432 = 768 KB
FIFO size        : 4194304 = 4096 KB
Track 01: data    90 MB
```

```
Total size:     103 MB (10:18.05) = 46354 sectors
Lout start:     104 MB (10:20/04) = 46354 sectors
Current Secsize: 2048
ATIP start of lead in:  -11580 (97:27/45)
  ATIP start of lead out: 333226 (74:05/01)
Disk type:    Short strategy type (Phthalocyanine or similar)
Manuf. index: 9
Manufacturer: Kodak Japan Limited
Blocks total: 333226 Blocks current: 333226 Blocks remaining:
286872
RBlocks total: 343358 RBlocks current: 343358 RBlocks
remaining: 297004
Starting to write CD/DVD at speed 2 in write mode for single
session.
Last chance to quit, starting real write in 0 seconds.
Operation starts.
Waiting for reader process to fill input buffer ... input
buffer ready.
Performing OPC...
Starting new track at sector: 0
Track 01:  90 of  90 MB written (fifo 100%).
Track 01: Total bytes read/written: 94928896/94928896 (46352
sectors).
Writing  time:  319.345s
Fixating...
Fixating time:  133.394s
cdrecord: fifo had 1496 puts and 1496 gets.
cdrecord: fifo was 0 times empty and 1424 times full, min fill
was 95%.
```

After cdrecord finishes writing the CD and your shell prompt returns, delete the file system image file /var/tmp/mary.cd.

Cross-Reference You can learn more about installing and troubleshooting writable CD drives from the CD-Writing-HOWTO (available from the Red Hat Linux documentation CD). You can also get a copy of the HOWTO by visiting the Web site www.linuxdocs.org.

Backing Up to a Hard Drive

Removable media such as tapes or CDs are not the only choice for backing up your data. You may find it useful to install a second hard drive in your system and use that drive for backups. This has several advantages over other backup media:

✦ Data can be backed up quickly and throughout the day; thus, backed up data will be more current in the event of a crash.

✦ No media to load. Data can be located and recovered more quickly.

✦ You can configure the second disk to be a virtual clone of the first one. If the first disk crashes, you can simply boot off of the second disk rather than installing new hardware. With disk mirroring software, this process can even be automated.

There are, however, a few disadvantages to backing up to a hard drive:

✦ This method is not well suited to keeping historical archives of the many revisions of your files because the hard drive will eventually fill up.

✦ The backups cannot be stored offsite, which means that if the entire server is destroyed, your data is lost.

Because of these disadvantages, you should probably not use a hard drive as your only backup medium. Instead, combine it with some sort of removable media backup such as a tape drive. Hard-drive mirroring can provide you a *snapshot* backup that will get you up and running again quickly, while the removable backups can provide longer-term storage of data and protection from more catastrophic failures. Hard-drive mirroring is discussed in the next section.

The simplest form of second-hard-drive backup is to simply copy important files to the other drive using the cp or tar command. The most sophisticated method is to provide fault-tolerant disk mirroring using RAID software. The latter choice requires special kernel drivers that are still somewhat experimental in Red Hat Linux and require a bit of work to configure. If you don't need the high level of protection from data loss that RAID disk mirroring provides, but you still like the idea of having a complete duplicate of your data on-hand and ready for use, there is an alternative.

Getting and installing mirrordir to clone directories

The mirrordir package is a way of doing hard-drive mirroring. Mirrordir is a powerful tool that enables you to make and maintain an exact copy of a hierarchy of directories. You can find its official Web site at http://mirrordir.sourceforge. net. It can be downloaded by selecting the Download RPM button from that site.

After downloading the file, install it in the same way you install any rpm. For example, if you have downloaded the rpm file to /tmp, you can type:

```
# rpm -i /tmp/mirrordir*rpm
```

Cloning a directory with mirrordir

Now that you have mirrordir installed, you can use it to clone a directory. Suppose you have a second hard drive with a partition large enough to hold a copy of your /home partition. Your first step is to create a directory to mount the partition on, and then mount it. Log in as root and type the following:

```
# mkdir -p /mirror/home
# mount /dev/hdb5 /mirror/home
```

In this example, we are mounting the fifth partition of the second hard drive, hence the device name /dev/hdb5. The b refers to the second disk, and the 5 refers to the partition number. You may use a different drive or partition. If so, adjust the device name accordingly. Assuming the mount command successfully mounted the drive, you are ready to copy your /home partition. Enter the following command:

```
# mirrordir /home /mirror/home
```

This command causes the contents of the /home directory to be exactly duplicated in the /mirror/home directory.

Caution

It is very important that you get the order of these parameters correct. If you reverse them, the entire contents of your /home directory will be deleted! You will, in essence, be copying an empty directory back to your /home directory.

You now have a backup of your entire /home partition. You can run mirrordir again in the future, and it will again make the /mirror/home directory an exact duplicate of /home. It will copy to /mirror/home only those files that have been added or modified since the previous run of mirrordir. Also, it will delete any files from /mirror/home that are no longer on /home. Thus, the mirror is kept current without copying the entire /home partition each time. If the disk with the /home partition should ever crash, you can replace the disk and then copy the file system back by issuing the mirrordir command with the parameters reversed:

```
# mirrordir /mirror/home /home
```

Furthermore, you can be up and running even faster by simply turning the mirrored partition into the actual home partition. Just edit the /etc/fstab file and change the device name for /home so that it matches the mirrored directory. Now unmount and remount the /home partition (or reboot the computer), and the mirrored directory will be mounted to /home. Your users will never be the wiser. You may even consider mirroring every partition on your main disk. Then, even a complete disk crash can be recovered from quickly. Simply turn the secondary disk into the primary disk, and you are up and running again.

Automating mirroring

To automate the mirroring process, I suggest creating a small script that mounts the mirror partition, runs the mirrordir command, and then unmounts the partition. Leaving the partition unmounted when not in use reduces the chance of data being accidentally deleted from it. Create a script named mirror.sh and place it in the /usr/local/sbin directory. Something similar to the following should do the trick:

```
#!/bin/sh
#
#  mirror.sh:  Mirror the /home partition to a second hard
drive
```

```
#
/bin/mount /dev/hdb5 /mirror/home
mirrordir /home /mirror/home
/bin/umount /mirror/home
```

Now tell `cron` to periodically run this script. Invoke the `cron` command with the `-e` option. This brings up an editor containing root's `cron` jobs. Add a line similar to the following at the end of the list.

```
0 * * * * /usr/local/sbin/mirror.sh
```

Save and exit the editor. This cron entry causes the `mirror.sh` script to run once an hour. If you decide to mirror other partitions, you can do it quite easily by creating appropriate mount points in `/mirror` and then adding matching sections to the `mirror.sh` script.

Backing Up Files with dump

The `dump` command is the most commonly used tool for performing backups on UNIX systems. This command traces its history back to the early days of UNIX and thus is a standard part of nearly every version of UNIX. Likewise, the dump package is included in the Red Hat Linux distribution. If it was not installed by default when you first set up your Linux system, you can install it from the dump RPM file located on the second Red Hat Linux installation CD.

The dump package actually consists of several commands. You can read their online man pages for more information about them, but Table 13-2 has a short description of the programs.

Table 13-2
Programs in the dump Package

Command	Description
dump	Used to create backup archives of entire disk partitions or individual directories.
restore	Can be used to restore an entire archive or individual files from an archive to the hard drive.
rmt	A program used by the `dump` and `restore` commands to copy files across the network. You should never need to use this command directly.

Creating a backup with dump

When making a file system backup using the dump command, you must supply parameters specifying the dump level, the backup media, and the file system to back up. You can also supply optional parameters to specify the size of the backup media, the method for requesting the next tape, and the recording of file system dump times and status.

The first parameter to dump is always a list of single-letter option codes. This is followed by a space-separated list of any arguments needed by those options. The arguments appear in the same order as the options that require them. The final parameter is always the file system or directory being backed up.

```
dump <options> <arguments> <filesystem>
```

Table 13-3 lists the various one-letter option codes for the dump command.

<table>
<tr><td colspan="2" align="center">Table 13-3
Options to dump</td></tr>
<tr><td>**Dump Options**</td><td>**Description**</td></tr>
<tr><td>0-9</td><td>The dump level. Selecting a dump level of 0 backs up all files (a full dump). A higher number backs up only those files modified since the last dump of an equal or lower number (in essence, an incremental dump). The default dump level is 9.</td></tr>
<tr><td>B</td><td>The number of dump records per volume. Basically, the amount of data you can fit on a tape. This option takes a numeric argument.</td></tr>
<tr><td>b</td><td>The number of kilobytes per dump record. Useful in combination with the B option. This option takes a numeric argument.</td></tr>
<tr><td>h</td><td>Files can be marked with a nodump attribute. This option specifies the dump level at or above which the nodump attribute is honored. This option takes a numeric argument of 1-9.</td></tr>
<tr><td>f</td><td>The name of the file or device to write the dump to. This can even be a file or device on a remote machine. This option takes a single alphanumeric argument.</td></tr>
<tr><td>d</td><td>Sets the tape density. The default is 1600 bits per inch. This option takes a numeric argument.</td></tr>
<tr><td>n</td><td>When a dump needs attention (such as to change a tape), dump will send a message to all of the users in the operator group. This option takes no arguments.</td></tr>
</table>

Continued

	Table 13-3 *(continued)*	
Options	**Description**	
s	Specifies the length in feet of the dump tape. This calculation is dependent on tape density (option d) and the dump record (options B and b). This takes a numeric argument.	
u	Record this backup in the /etc/dumpdates file. It is a good idea to use this option, especially if you create incremental backups.	
T	Specify a date and time on which to base incremental backups. Any files modified or added after that time will be backed up. This option causes dump to ignore the /etc/dumpdates file. It takes a single argument, a date in the format specified by the ctime man page.	
W	This option causes dump to list the file systems that need to be backed up. It does this by looking at the /etc/dumpdates file and the /etc/fstab file.	
w	This works like the W option but lists the individual files that should be backed up.	

Thus, a typical dump command may look similar to the following:

```
# dump 0uBf 500000 /dev/qft0 /dev/hda6
```

This command results in dump performing a level zero (full) backup of the /dev/hda7 file system, storing the backup on the tape drive /dev/qft0, and recording the results in /etc/dumpdates. The B option is used to increase the expected tape block count to 500000; otherwise, dump would prompt for a new tape far earlier than required. The dump command prints status messages to the screen, letting you know how far along the backup has progressed and estimating how much time it will take to complete. The output looks similar to this:

```
DUMP: Date of this level 0 dump: Thu Aug 16 23:33:37 2001
DUMP: Dumping /dev/hda6 (/home) to /dev/qft0
DUMP: Exclude ext3 journal inode 8
DUMP: Label: /home
DUMP: mapping (Pass I) [regular files]
DUMP: mapping (Pass II) [directories]
DUMP: estimated 93303 tape blocks on 0.19 tape(s).
DUMP: Volume 1 started with block 1 at: Thu Aug 16 23:33:47
DUMP: dumping (Pass III) [directories]
DUMP: dumping (Pass IV) [regular files]
DUMP: Closing /dev/qft0
DUMP: Volume 1 completed at: Thu Aug 16 23:35:35 2001
DUMP: Volume 1 94360 tape blocks (92.15MB)
DUMP: Volume 1 took 0:01:48
DUMP: Volume 1 transfer rate: 873 kB/s
```

```
DUMP: 94360 tape blocks (92.15MB) on 1 volume(s)
DUMP: finished in 108 seconds, throughput 873 kBytes/sec
DUMP: Date of this level 0 dump: Thu Aug 16 23:33:37 2001
DUMP: Date this dump completed:  Thu Aug 16 23:35:35 2001
DUMP: Average transfer rate: 873 kB/s
DUMP: DUMP IS DONE
```

Understanding dump levels

The dump command has the capacity to back up all files on a file system, or it can selectively back up only those files that have changed recently. The dump level parameter is used to specify this behavior. A dump level of 0 results in a full backup of all files on the file system. Specifying a higher number (1-9) backs up only those files that have been changed or added since the most recent dump of the same or lower dump level. I recommend you use dump levels to implement a full and incremental backup schedule similar to that shown in Table 13-4.

Table 13-4
Recommended dump Schedule

Day of Week	Dump Level
Sunday	Level 0 (full dump). Eject the tape when done.
Monday	Level 9 (incremental dump).
Tuesday	Level 8 (incremental dump).
Wednesday	Level 7 (incremental dump).
Thursday	Level 6 (incremental dump).
Friday	Level 5 (incremental dump).
Saturday	Level 4 (incremental dump).

Note that after the full backup on Sunday, a level 9 incremental dump is done the next day, and a successively lower dump level is done each day after that. This results in all the files that have changed since Sunday being backed up on every single incremental backup. Each incremental backup is thus larger than the previous; the backup contains all of the files from the previous incremental backup plus any files that have changed since then. This may seem wasteful of storage space on the backup tape, but it will save a lot of time and effort should there be a need to restore the file system.

For example, let us imagine that your hard drive crashed on Friday. After replacing the hard drive, you can restore the entire file system in two steps: restore the full backup from the prior Sunday and then the most recent incremental backup from

Thursday. We can do this because Thursday's backup contains all of the files from Monday, Tuesday, and Wednesday's tape as well as the files that changed after that. If the dump levels had progressed in positive order (level 1 for Monday, level 2 for Tuesday, and so on), *all* of the incremental backups would have to be restored in order to restore the file system to its most current state.

Automating Backups with cron

You can automate most of your backups with shell scripts and the cron daemon. Use the su command to become root, and then cd to the /usr/local/bin directory. Use any text editor to create a shell script called backups.sh that looks similar to the following:

```
#!/bin/sh
#
# backups.sh - A simple backup script, by Thad Phetteplace
#
# This script takes one parameter, the dump level.
# If the dump level is not provided, it is
# automatically set to zero. For level zero (full)
# dumps, rewind and eject the tape when done.
#

if [ $1 ]; then
        level=$1
else
        #
        # No dump level was provided, so set it
        # to zero
        #
        level="0"
fi

/sbin/dump $level'uf' /dev/nrft0 /
/sbin/dump $level'uf' /dev/nrft0 /home
/sbin/dump $level'uf' /dev/nrft0 /var
/sbin/dump $level'uf' /dev/nrft0 /usr              .


#
# If we are doing a full dump, rewind and eject
# the tape when done.
#
if [ $level = "0" ]; then
        #
        # Note: We should replace this with the /bin/st command
        # instead if we ever switch to a SCSI tape drive.
        #
        /bin/mt -f /dev/nrft0 rewind
        /bin/mt -f /dev/nrft0 offline
fi
```

You may choose to change the partitions being backed up to match your situation, but this script should otherwise work quite well for you. After saving and exiting the editor, change the permissions on the file so that it is executable only by root:

```
chmod 700 backups.sh
```

You can now back up your entire system by running the `backups.sh` script when logged in as root. The script accepts the dump level as its only parameter. If you leave the parameter off, it will automatically assume a level zero dump. Thus, the following two commands are equivalent:

```
backups.sh
backups.sh 0
```

You may need to customize this script for your situation. For example, I am using the tape device `/dev/nrft0`. You may be using a different tape device. Whatever device you use, you should probably use the version of its device name that begins with a the letter *n*. That tells the system that after it finishes copying data to the tape, it should *not* rewind the tape. As an example, I used `/dev/nrft0` instead of `/dev/rst0` in the preceding script. If I had used `/dev/rst0`, each successive incremental backup would have overwritten the previous one.

Other things that you may change in this script include the partitions being backed up and the dump level at which the tape is ejected. It is not uncommon to eject the tape after the last incremental backup just before performing a full backup.

The most useful thing about this script is that you can easily configure your system to run it automatically. Simply add a few lines to the root `crontab` file, and the cron daemon will invoke the script on the days and times specified. While logged in as root, enter the `crontab` command with the `-e` option:

```
# crontab -e
```

This brings up the root `crontab` file in an editor. Add the following lines at the end of the file:

```
0 22 * * 0 /usr/local/bin/backup.sh 0
0 22 * * 1 /usr/local/bin/backup.sh 9
0 22 * * 2 /usr/local/bin/backup.sh 8
0 22 * * 3 /usr/local/bin/backup.sh 7
0 22 * * 4 /usr/local/bin/backup.sh 6
0 22 * * 4 /usr/local/bin/backup.sh 5
0 22 * * 5 /usr/local/bin/backup.sh 4
```

Save and exit the file. The cron daemon will now run the backup script at 10:00 p.m. (22:00 in military time) every day of the week. This example implements the dump schedule outlined earlier. A full dump is performed on Sunday, and the tape is ejected when it is done. A new tape should be loaded on Monday, and then incremental backups will be written to that same tape for the rest of the week. The next full dump will be written to the end of that tape, unless someone is around on Sunday to eject and replace the tape before 10:00 p.m.

Restoring Backed Up Files

The `restore` command is used to retrieve files from a backup tape or other media. You can use `restore` to recover an entire file system or to interactively select individual files. It recovers files from the specified media and copies them into the current directory (the one you ran the `recover` command in), re-creating subdirectories as needed. Much as with the `dump` command, the first parameter passed to the `restore` command is a list of single character option codes, as shown in Table 13-5.

Table 13-5
Restore Command Options

Restore Options	Description
r	Restore the entire dump archive.
C	Compare the contents of the dump file with the files on the disk. This is used to check the success of a restore.
R	Start the restore from a particular tape of a multitape backup. This is useful for restarting an interrupted restore.
x	Extract only specific files or directories from the archive. This option takes one argument, a list of files or directories to extract.
t	List the contents of the dump archive. If a file or directory is given as an argument, list only the occurrence of that file, directory, or anything within the directory.
I	Restore files in interactive mode.
b	Specify the block size of the dump in kilobytes. This option takes a numeric argument.
D	Specify the name of the file system to be compared when using the C option. The file system name is passed as an argument.
f	Specify the name of the dump archive to restore from. This option takes an alphanumeric argument.
h	If this option is specified, `restore` re-creates directories marked for extraction but will not extract their contents.
m	Files are extracted by inode number instead of name. This is generally not very useful.

Restore Options	Description
N	Instead of extracting files, print their names.
s	Specify the dump file to start with on a multiple file tape. This takes a numeric argument.
T	This tells `restore` where to write any temporary files. This is useful if you have booted from a floppy (which has no space for temporary files).
v	Run in verbose mode. This causes `restore` to print information about each file as it restores it.
y	The restore command will always continue when it encounters a bad block, rather than asking you if you want to continue.

Restoring an entire file system

Let us return to our earlier example of the Friday disk crash. You installed a shiny new hard drive and your backup tapes are in hand. It is time to restore the files. For the purpose of this example, I am assuming that the crashed drive contained only the /home partition and that the Red Hat Linux operating system is still intact. If the crashed drive had contained the Red Hat Linux operating system, you would first have to reinstall Red Hat Linux before restoring the backup.

Before any files can be recovered to your new hard drive, an empty file system must be created on it. You will use the `mkfs` command to do this. The `mkfs` command can accept a variety of parameters, but usually you only need to supply the name of the device to create the file system on. Thus, to prepare the new hard drive type:

    # mkfs /dev/hda6

Alternatively, because our /home drive is listed in the /etc/fstab file, we can simply specify the mount point /home *mountpoint* and `mkfs` will figure out the correct device. Thus, the preceding command could be replaced with this:

    # mkfs /home

Caution   You should, of course, exercise extreme caution when using the `mkfs` command. If you specify the wrong device name, you could unintentionally wipe out all data on an existing file system.

After creating a file system on your new disk, mount the partition to a temporary mount point.

    # mount /dev/hda6 /mnt

This connects the new file system to the /mnt directory. Now change into the directory (cd /mnt) and use the restore command to recover the entire file system off of your backup tape. Of course, it is assumed that you have loaded the correct tape into the tape drive.

```
# cd /mnt
# restore rf /dev/nrft0
```

When the restore is finished, you can unmount the partition and remount it to the appropriate mount point. If you have restored the file system to a different physical partition than it was originally on, be sure to modify the /etc/fstab file appropriately so that the correct partition is mounted next time the system is rebooted.

Recovering individual files

The restore command can also be used to recover individual files and directories. By using restore in interactive mode, you can type a series of restore commands to selectively restore files. To run restore in interactive mode, use the i parameter instead of r:

```
# restore if /dev/nrst0
```

The restore command will then read the file index from the backup tape and present you with a restore prompt. At this prompt, you can type the commands that enable you to select which directories and files to recover. You can navigate the directory structure of the backup index much the same way that you navigate an actual file system using a shell prompt. The interactive restore command even has its own version of the familiar cd and ls commands, as shown in Table 13-6.

	Table 13-6 **Interactive restore Commands**
Command	**Description**
Add	Add a file or directory to the list of files to be extracted. If a directory is marked for extraction, all of the directories and files within it will also be extracted.
Cd	Change the current directory being viewed within the dump archive. Works similar to the cd command used at a shell prompt.
Delete	Delete a file or directory from the list of files to be extracted. Deleting a directory from the list results in all of the files and directories within it also being deleted.

Command	Description
Extract	Extract all of the marked files and directories from the archive and write them back to the file system.
help	List the available commands.
ls	List the contents of the current directory. If a directory name is provided as an argument, list the contents of that directory. Files or directories marked for extraction have a * character in front of them.
pwd	Print the full path name of the current directory of the dump archive.
quit	Exit the interactive restore program.
setmodes	Do not restore the files; instead, set the modes of already existing files on the target disk to match the modes recorded in the dump file. This is useful for recovering from a restore that was prematurely aborted.
verbose	Toggles verbose output versus quite output during the restore process. Verbose output mode will echo information to the screen for every file that is restored.

As an example, let us pretend that the user `joe` has accidentally deleted his Mail subdirectory from his home directory. Joe happens to be your boss, so it is urgent that you recover his files. Here is how you may go about it.

Load the appropriate tape into the tape drive and log in as root. Use the `cd` command to go to the top of the `/home` partition, and then run the `restore` program in interactive mode:

```
# cd /home
# restore if /dev/nrft0
```

Verify that you have the backup tape for the `/home` partition by entering the `ls` command. You should see something like the following list of directories, representing users that have home directories in `/home`:

```
restore > ls
.:
bob/        jane/       joe/            lost+found/ mary/
thad/
```

Yes, this is the home partition. Now change the current directory to Joe's home directory using the `cd` command. Type **ls** again to view the contents of his home directory.

```
restore > cd joe
restore > ls
./joe:
```

```
.netscape/        Desktop/        report.html
.tcshrc           Mail/           letter.txt
.xinitrc          News/           www/
```

Now mark the Mail directory for extraction using the add command:

```
restore > add Mail
```

If we use the ls command again, we see that the Mail directory is preceded with an asterisk (*) character, which means it has been marked for extraction.

```
restore > ls
./joe:
.netscape/        Desktop/        report.html
.tcshrc           *Mail/          letter.txt
.xinitrc          News/           www/
```

Now use the extract command to begin the extraction process. Restore will prompt you for the number of the tape to start with. This is a single tape backup, so just enter the number 1. When it prompts you to "set owner/mode for '.'?," answer yes by typing **y** and pressing Enter. Restore will then set restore the file permissions (if necessary) of the directory it is restoring to. This isn't critical when extracting individual files like this, but you should always answer yes to this prompt when doing a full restore. Anyway, your screen should now contain the following:

```
restore > extract
You have not read any tapes yet.
Unless you know which volume your file(s) are on you
should start with the last volume and work toward
the first.
Specify next volume #: 1
set owner/mode for '.'? [yn] y
restore >
```

At this point, the files have been recovered and you can exit the restore program by issuing the quit command. That's all there is to it. You now know the basics of using the dump and restore commands.

Backing Up Over the Network

Using dump as described earlier works great when you have a tape drive physically connected to the system that you are backing up. But installing backup hardware in every single device on your network is hardly cost effective. Fortunately, dump has the capability to send data over the network to be written to a device on another server.

To direct the output of dump to a server on the network, you need to modify the backup device argument supplied with the -f option. Include the hostname followed by a colon (:) character before the name of the backup device. The dump command will then look for that device on the remote system. For example, to make a backup of the /dev/hda7 partition but write it to a tape drive connected to the computer named ratbert, type the following:

```
# dump 0uBf 500000 ratbert:/dev/nrf0 /dev/hda7
```

Similarly, the restore command can also access devices connected to remote systems. Thus to restore the dump you just made, you would type:

```
# restore rf ratbert:/dev/nrft0
```

The dump and restore commands use the same authentication for remote access as the remote shell service, meaning that you must have appropriate entries in the .rhosts or hosts.equiv files on the remote system for this to work. Because dump usually runs with root privilege, this can be a security risk.

Cross-Reference Refer to Chapter 14 for an explanation of remote shell services and the risks involved using dump and restore over a network.

Another issue with remote dumps is the complications inherent in coordinating backups among many computers. The next section discusses a solution to that problem.

Performing Network Backups with Multiple Computers

Backing up a single workstation is not a terribly complex job, but backing up an entire network of computers can be. When multiple computers all want to back up their data to the same network-accessible tape drive, coordinating the access so that each computer gets a turn can be difficult.

Simply setting different backup times with each system's cron daemon is not sufficient to manage network backups. If a single backup runs long, all the backups scheduled after it could begin to collide. Fortunately, there is a tool that can help.

The software package Amanda, the Advanced Maryland Automatic Network Disk Archiver, is designed specifically for coordinating the network backup of many machines. With Amanda, you can turn your Red Hat Linux system into a backup server that will archive files for other Linux systems, UNIX, and even Windows 9x/2000 and Windows NT systems.

Getting and installing the Amanda package

As of Red Hat Linux 7, Amanda is included as one of the standard packages in the Red Hat Linux distribution. Actually, it is split into three distinct packages: the base Amanda package, the client package, and the server package. The base package must be installed before you can install either the client package or the server package. Furthermore, the Amanda server cannot be installed unless the gnuplot utility has been installed on your system. Thus, to install Amanda, you should obtain the following four RPM files either from your Red Hat CD media or from a Red Hat Linux FTP site.

```
gnuplot
amanda
amanda-client
amanda-server
```

Log in as root, and use the rpm command to install these packages. On the system that will be your Amanda server on which your backups will be stored, you would install gnuplot, amanda, and amanda-server packages.

On each Linux system that will be an Amanda client, you should log in as root and install amanda and amanda-client packages.

Configuring Amanda for network backups

The Amanda package includes a variety of commands. The online man page for Amanda describes the commands as shown in Table 13-7.

Table 13-7
Backup Commands Used with Amanda

Command	Description
amdump	Take care of automatic Amanda backups. It is normally executed by cron on a computer called the tape server host and requests backups of file systems located on backup clients. amdump backs up all disks in the disklist file to tape or, if there is a problem, to a special holding disk. After all backups are done, amdump sends mail reporting failures and successes.
amflush	Flush backups from the holding disk to tape. amflush is used after amdump has reported it could not write backups to tape for some reason. When this happens, backups stay in the holding disk. After the tape problem is corrected, run amflush to write backups from the holding disk to the tape.
amcleanup	Clean up after an interrupted amdump. This command is only needed if amdump was unable to complete for some reason, usually because the tape server host crashed while amdump was running.

Command	Description
amrecover	Provide an interactive interface to browse the Amanda index files and select which tapes to recover files from. `amrecover` can also run `amrestore` and the system restore program (for example, tar) in some cases.
amrestore	Read an Amanda tape, searching for requested backups. `amrestore` is suitable for everything from interactive restores of single files to a full restore of all partitions on a failed disk.
amlabel	Write an Amanda format label onto a tape. All Amanda tapes must be labeled with `amlabel`. `amdump` and `amflush` will not write to an unlabeled tape.
amcheck	Verify the correct tape is in the tape drive and that all file systems on all backup client systems are ready to be backed up. Can optionally be run by cron before `amdump`, so someone will get mail warning that backups will fail unless corrective action is taken.
amadmin	Take care of administrative tasks, such as finding out which tapes are needed to restore a file system, forcing hosts to do full backups of selected disks, and looking at schedule balance information.
amtape	Take care of tape changer control operations, such as loading particular tapes, ejecting tapes, and scanning the tape rack.
amverify	Check Amanda backup tapes for errors (GNU tar format backups only).
amrmtape	Delete a tape from the tape list and from the Amanda database.
amstatus	Give the status of a running amdump.

The `amdump` command is the one that you will use the most, but before you can get started, you need to configure a few things on both the backup server (the system with the tape drive) and the backup clients (the systems being backed up).

Creating Amanda directories

You need to create some directories to hold the Amanda configuration files and to provide a location to write Amanda log files. The configuration files go in an `/etc/amanda` directory, and the log files go in `/usr/adm/amanda`. In both cases, you create subdirectories within those directories, one subdirectory for each backup schedule that you intend to run, as shown here:

```
# mkdir -p /usr/adm/amanda/normal
# mkdir -p /etc/amanda/normal
```

For the purpose of this example, I have created only a normal backup configuration that backs up the data drives on several machines. You may also decide to create an upgrade backup configuration that backs up the operating system partitions. You could then run that backup before you perform any operating system upgrades.

You also need to specify a holding disk that Amanda can use to temporarily spool backups before it writes them to disk. This directory should be on a disk with a lot of free space. I have a large /home partition on my server, so I created an Amanda directory there to use as a holding disk as follows:

```
# mkdir /home/amanda
```

Creating the amanda.conf file

Next you must create two configuration files for Amanda and store them in the /etc/amanda/normal directory. The amanda.conf file sets a variety of general configuration values, and the disklist file defines which machines and partitions to back up. The amanda.conf file can be rather complicated, but, fortunately, most of its values can be left at their default values. Here is a simplified amanda.conf file with some comments embedded in it to help explain things:

```
#
# amanda.conf - sample Amanda configuration file. This started
#               life as the actual config file in use at
#               CS.UMD.EDU.

org "GLACI"         # your organization name for reports
mailto "root"       # space separated list of operators at
                    # your site
dumpuser "root"     # the user to run dumps under

# Specify tape device and/or tape changer. If you don't have a tape
# changer, and you don't want to use more than one tape per run of
# amdump, just comment out the definition of tpchanger.

runtapes 1          # number of tapes to be used in a single
        # run of amdump
tapedev "/dev/nrft0"    # the no-rewind tape device to be used
rawtapedev "/dev/rft0"  # the raw device to be used (ftape only)

tapetype HP-DAT     # what kind of tape it is
        # (see tapetypes below)
labelstr "^DailySet1[0-9][0-9]*$"   # label constraint all
        # tapes must match

# Specify holding disks. These are used as a temporary
# staging area for dumps before they are written to tape and
# are recommended for most sites.
```

```
holdingdisk hd1 {
    comment "main holding disk"
    directory "/home/amanda"   # where the holding disk is
    use 290 Mb      # how much space can we use on it
    chunksize -1        # size of chunk
    }

# Note that, although the keyword below is infofile, it is
# only so for historic reasons, since now it is supposed to
# be a directory (unless you have selected some database
# format other than the `text' default)

infofile "/usr/adm/amanda/normal/curinfo"   # database DIRECTORY
logdir   "/usr/sdm/amanda/normal"      # log directory
indexdir "/usr/adm/amanda/normal/index"   # index directory

# tapetypes

# Define the type of tape you use here, and use it in "tapetype"
# above. Some typical types of tapes are included here. The
# tapetype tells amanda how many MB will fit on the tape, how
# big the filemarks are, and how fast the tape device is.

define tapetype HP-DAT {
    comment "DAT tape drives"
    # data provided by Rob Browning <rlb@cs.utexas.edu>
    length 1930 mbytes
    filemark 111 kbytes
    speed 468 kbytes
}

# dumptypes
#
# These are referred to by the disklist file.

define dumptype global {
    comment "Global definitions"
    # This is quite useful for setting global parameters, so you
    # don't have to type them everywhere.
}

define dumptype always-full {
    global
    comment "Full dump of this filesystem always"
    compress none
    priority high
    dumpcycle 0
}
```

This example amanda.conf was trimmed down from a larger example located in /etc/amanda/DailySet1. Rather than type a configuration file from scratch, I recommend you start with the example amanda.conf and modify it as needed. The example amanda.conf file provides additional information on the available configuration options. Also, the online man page for Amanda should be helpful (type man amanda to read it). You can find more instructions in the /usr/share/doc/amanda-server* directory. Generally, you have to do the following:

✦ Modify the org name for reports.

✦ Change the device names specified for tapedev and rawtapedev so that they match your tape device.

✦ Select a tape type entry that is appropriate for your tape drive.

✦ Change the name of the directory specified in the holding disk section to match the directory you created earlier.

Creating a disklist file

You also must create a disklist file in the /etc/amanda/normal directory. This simply contains a list of the systems and disk partitions to back up. The qualifier always-full is included on each entry to tell Amanda what type of backup to perform. It means to use full, rather than incremental, backups.

```
# sample Amanda2 disklist file
#
# File format is:
#
#        hostname diskdev dumptype [spindle [interface]]
#
# where the dumptypes are defined by you in amanda.conf.

dexter hda5 always-full
dexter hda6 always-full
dexter hda7 always-full
dexter hda8 always-full

daffy hda5 always-full
daffy hda6 always-full
daffy hda7 always-full
daffy hdb1 always-full
daffy hdb2 always-full
```

This example file backs up two systems, dexter and daffy. The order of the systems and the partitions is selected so that the most important data is backed up first. This way, if a tape drive becomes full, you have still managed to back up the most important data.

Adding Amanda network services

Amanda is designed to perform backups over a network. The following `amanda` services are defined in the `/etc/services` file:

```
amanda          10080/udp
amandaidx       10082/tcp
amidxtape       10083/tcp
```

To offer these services to the network in Red Hat Linux, you need to configure the xinetd daemon to listen for those services. You do this by enabling the services in the `amandaidx` and `amidxtape` files in the `/etc/xinetd.d` directory. In each of those files, you need to change the disable line to `no`, as follows:

```
disable         = no
```

This enables Amanda to accept requests from the client system and to start the backup process without any user intervention. You need to tell the xinetd daemon to reload the `/etc/xinetd.d` files before this change takes place. You can do this by typing the following as root user:

```
# /etc/init.d/xinetd restart
```

You next need to create an `.amandahosts` file in the `/root` directory. This file should contain the fully qualified host and domain name of any backup servers that will connect to this client. For example, to create an `.amandahosts` file on the system `dexter.glaci.com` that will enable the backup server `ratbert.glaci.com` to connect, do the following:

```
# echo ratbert.glaci.com > /root/.amandahosts
# chmod 600 /root/.amandahosts
```

I used `chmod` to change the access permissions of the file. This assures that only root can read or modify this account.

Performing an Amanda backup

Now that everything is configured, you are ready to perform an Amanda backup. While logged in as root, type the following command:

```
# /usr/sbin/amdump normal
```

This runs the `amdump` command and tells it to read the configuration files it finds in the `/etc/amanda/normal` directory. It then works its way down the list of systems and partitions in the `disklist` file, backing up each partition in the order it occurs. The results of the `amdump` are written to the `/usr/adm/amanda/normal` directory.

Read the files you find there to check on the results of the backup. (See the previous section on how to create a `disklist` file to understand the process that `amdump` goes through.)

You can, of course, automate this process with `cron`. To create an `amdump` schedule similar to the regular dump schedule discussed in an earlier section, do the following. While logged in as root, enter the `crontab` command with the `-e` option:

```
# crontab -e
```

This brings up the root `crontab` file in an editor. Add the following lines to the end of the file:

```
0 22 * * 0 /usr/sbin/amdump normal
0 22 * * 1 /usr/sbin/amdump incremental
0 22 * * 2 /usr/sbin/amdump incremental
0 22 * * 3 /usr/sbin/amdump incremental
0 22 * * 4 /usr/sbin/amdump incremental
0 22 * * 5 /usr/sbin/amdump incremental
0 22 * * 6 /usr/sbin/amdump incremental
```

Save and exit the file. The cron daemon will now run `amdump` at 10:00 p.m. (22:00 in military time) every day of the week. This example assumes that a second incremental configuration has been created. You can do this by creating a subdirectory named `incremental` under `/etc/amanda` and populating it with appropriately modified `amanda.conf` and `disklist` files. You also need to create a subdirectory named `incremental` under `/usr/adm/amanda` so that `amanda` has somewhere to write the logfiles for this configuration.

It may be a bit of work to get it all in place, but once you do, Amanda can make your network backups much easier to manage. It is perhaps overkill for a small office, but in a large enterprise network situation, it enables Red Hat Linux to act as a powerful backup server.

Using the pax Archiving Tool

Over the years, a variety of UNIX operating systems have arisen, resulting in a variety of similar but incompatible file archiving formats. Even tools that go by the same name may use slightly different storage formats on different systems. This can lead to big problems when trying to archive and retrieve data in a multiplatform environment. Fortunately, there is a solution.

The `pax` program is a POSIX standard utility that can read and write a wide variety of archive formats. An RPM package for `pax` is included with Red Hat Linux. If it is not already installed, copy the `pax-1.5-4.i386.rpm` file from your distribution media, or download it from a Red Hat Linux FTP site, and then use the `rpm` command to install it.

```
# rpm -i pax-1.5-4.i386.rpm
```

Remember that you need to be logged in as root when installing software with the `rpm` command.

Pax takes a variety of command-line options. The last parameter is usually the file or directory to archive. You may use wildcard characters such as "*" or "?" to specify multiple files or directories. The options you will use most often include the `-r` and `-w` parameters for specifying when you are reading or writing an archive. These are usually used in conjunction with the `-f` parameter, which is used to specify the name of the archive file.

By using `pax` parameters in different combinations, it is possible to extract an archive, create an archive, list the contents of an archive, or even copy an entire directory hierarchy from one location to another. Table 13-8 shows a few examples of the `pax` command in action.

<table>
<tr><td colspan="2" align="center">**Table 13-8**
Examples of pax Use</td></tr>
<tr><td>*Pax Command*</td><td>*Description*</td></tr>
<tr><td>`pax -f myfiles`</td><td>List the contents of the archive named `myfiles`.</td></tr>
<tr><td>`pax -r -f myfiles`</td><td>Extract the contents of the archive named `myfiles`.</td></tr>
<tr><td>`pax -w -f myfiles /etc`</td><td>Create an archive named `myfiles` containing everything within the `/etc` directory.</td></tr>
<tr><td>`pax -w -f myfiles *.txt`</td><td>Archive all of the files in the current directory that have a `.txt` file extension.</td></tr>
<tr><td>`pax -r -w /olddir /newdir`</td><td>Copy the entire contents of the directory `/oldir` into a new directory called `/newdir`.</td></tr>
<tr><td>`pax -w -B 1440000 -f /dev/fd0 *`</td><td>Archive the contents of the current directory onto multiple floppy disks.</td></tr>
<tr><td>`pax -w -x cpio -f myfiles *`</td><td>Archive the contents of the current directory into an archive file named `myfiles` using the `cpio` format.</td></tr>
<tr><td>`pax -r -U mary -f backups`</td><td>Extract all of the files owned by user `mary` from the archive named `backups`.</td></tr>
</table>

Note that by leaving off both the -r and -w options, you cause pax to simply list the contents of the archive. If you specify both the -r and -w options, then you should leave off the -f option and supply source and destination directories instead. This will cause the source directory to be completely cloned in the specified destination directory.

You can use additional parameters to further modify pax's behavior. For example, you may use the -x option in conjunction with the -w option to specify the specific archive type to create, or you may use the -B option to specify the number of bytes to write to each volume of a multi-volume archive.

Table 13-9 briefly describes the many optional parameters to the pax command. You are encouraged to read the online pax man page to see an in-depth discussion of these parameters.

Table 13-9
Options to pax

Pax Options	Description
-r	Read files from an archive.
-w	Write files to an archive.
-a	Append files to a previously created archive.
-b blocksize	Specify the data block size of the archive. This must be a multiple of 512.
-c	Match all files except those that match the specified pattern.
-d	Match filename wildcards against file or directory names only, not the complete path.
-f archive	Specify the name of the archive.
-i	Interactively rename files when archiving.
-k	Do not overwrite existing files.
-l	Link files with hard links when in copy mode (-r -w).
-n	Match only the first file that matches the supplied pattern.
-o options	Extra options specific to the archiving format used.
-p string	Specify the file characteristics to retain when archiving or copying. Read the pax man page for more information on this option.
-s replstr	Modify the archived filenames using the supplied regular expression.
-t	Preserve the access times of archived files.
-u	Do not overwrite files with older versions.
-v	Provide verbose output when running.

Pax Options	Description
-x *format*	Specify format of the archive. Valid formats include cpio, bcpio, sv4cpio, sv4crc, tar, and ustar. The default is to use ustar when creating an archive. Pax will automatically determine the correct file type when reading an archive.
-B *bytes*	Specify the number of bytes per archive volume. Use this option to create multivolume archives on removable media.
-D	Do not overwrite existing files with files that have an older inode modification time.
-E *limit*	Limit the number of times pax will retry on encountering a read or write error.
-G *group*	Select files based on a group name or GID. To select by GID, place a # sign in front of the group number.
-H	Follow only command-line symbolic links while performing a physical file system traversal.
-L	Follow all symbolic links when traversing a directory hierarchy.
-P	Do not follow symbolic links. This is the default.
-T *time*	Select files based on their modification time. Read the pax man page for complete discussion of this parameters syntax.
-U *user*	Select files based on the owners user name, or by UID with a # sign in front of it.
-X	Do not traverse into directories that reside on a different device.
-Y	This option is the same as the -D option, except that the inode change time is checked using the pathname created after all the filename modifications have completed.
-Z	This option is the same as the -u option, except that the modification time is checked using the pathname created after all the filename modifications have completed.

As you can see, pax is a very flexible and powerful archiving tool. It can be particularly helpful in migrating data from older legacy systems to your new Linux system. When you are faced with the task of recovering archived data from an antiquated or even nonfunctioning UNIX system, the multiple file format support of pax can be a literal lifesaver.

Summary

It may take some work to put a proper backup schedule in place, but the effort is well worth it. Hopefully, you will never experience a major hard drive crash, but if you ever do, the effort of making backups will repay itself many times over. Think of it as an insurance policy. You hope to never use it, but you're glad you have it when disaster strikes.

A variety of low-cost backup hardware is available to use with your Red Hat Linux system. The traditional tape drive is an excellent choice for backing up large amounts of data. If long-term archiving of data is needed, a writable CD drive is a good choice. If minimizing downtime is your main concern, mirroring data to a second hard drive is another smart choice. Whatever backup strategy you choose to use with your Red Hat Linux system, be sure to choose one, and stick with it. You have invested a lot of time creating your data. Invest a little more to keep it safe.

✦   ✦   ✦

Computer Security Issues

With the growth of the Internet, computer and network security has become more important than ever. Increasingly, we hear of malicious individuals breaking into corporate and government computer systems around the world. The media calls these people *hackers*. That description is not entirely accurate. Within the subculture of computer hobbyists and software enthusiasts, the term *hacker* usually refers to a particular kind of programmer. A cracker, on the other hand, is someone who breaks into computers, often to do something malicious.

This chapter describes ways of protecting your Red Hat Linux system from crackers and other behavior that could do damage to your computer. Subjects discussed include password protection, network filtering, and security audits.

Hacker versus Cracker

In short, a hacker is someone who programs creatively and usually for the pure enjoyment of it (most programmers who work on Linux are hackers in this sense). The correct term for someone who breaks into computer systems is a cracker. (Refer to the sidebar that describes hackers in this chapter.)

There are many types of crackers, ranging from professional computer criminals to the hobbyist types that break into computers for the thrill. The growth of the cracker problem has kept pace with the growth of the Internet. A new, younger generation of cracker is emerging. These teenage pseudocrackers do not have all the knowledge and skill of their true cracker counterparts, but they have access to a growing number of cracker tools that automate the breaking of a system's security.

What Is a Hacker?

The Jargon File (www.tuxedo.org/~esr/jargon/) defines a hacker as the following:

hacker n.

[originally, someone who makes furniture with an axe]

1. A person who enjoys exploring the details of programmable systems and how to stretch their capabilities, as opposed to most users, who prefer to learn only the minimum necessary.

2. One who programs enthusiastically (even obsessively) or who enjoys programming rather than just theorizing about programming.

3. A person capable of appreciating hack value.

4. A person who is good at programming quickly.

5. An expert at a particular program, or one who frequently does work using it or on it; as in a *Unix hacker*. (Definitions 1 through 5 are correlated, and people who fit them congregate.)

6. An expert or enthusiast of any kind. One may be an astronomy hacker, for example.

7. One who enjoys the intellectual challenge of creatively overcoming or circumventing limitations.

8. [deprecated] A malicious meddler who tries to discover sensitive information by poking around. Hence *password hacker, network hacker*. The correct term for this sense is *cracker*.

By using programs and scripts created by the truly talented crackers, youngsters can often break into systems without really knowing the details of how it is done. Because they are usually rather young and mostly dependent on tools provided by others, they are sometimes referred to as "scriptkiddies." Make no mistake, if your system is not properly secured, scriptkiddies can do just as much damage as any other cracker.

Whatever you call them, crackers pose a serious risk to anyone connecting a computer to the Internet. Their reasons for breaking into systems are varied; some hope to steal financial information, others wish to gain bragging rights among their peers. Often, a system is broken into solely for use as a jumping-off point to launch further attacks on other systems. In some cases, the damage may be as little as an altered Web page, the Internet equivalent of graffiti. In other cases, the cracker may wipe out your entire hard drive to cover his or her tracks. Fortunately, there are ways to protect yourself. This chapter will show you some of them.

Password Protection

Passwords are the most fundamental security tool of any modern operating system and, consequently, the most commonly attacked security feature. It is natural to want to choose a password that is easy to remember, but very often this means choosing a password that is also easy to guess. Crackers know that on any system with more than a few users, at least one person is likely to have an easily guessed password.

By using the "brute force" method of attempting to log in to every account on the system and trying the most common passwords on each of these accounts, a persistent cracker has a good shot of finding a way in. Remember that a cracker will automate this attack, so thousands of login attempts are not out of the question. Obviously, choosing good passwords is the first and most important step to having a secure system.

Here are some things to avoid when choosing a password:

✦ Do not use any variation of your login name or your full name. Even if you use varied case, append or prepend numbers or punctuation, or type it backwards, this will still be an easily guessed password.

✦ Do not use a dictionary word, even if you add numbers or punctuation to it.

✦ Do not use proper names of any kind.

✦ Do not use any contiguous line of letters or numbers on the keyboard (such as "qwerty" or "asdfg").

Choosing good passwords

A good way to choose a strong password is to take the first letter from each word of an easily remembered sentence. The password can be made even better by adding numbers, punctuation, and varied case. The sentence you choose should have meaning only to you, and should not be publicly available (choosing a sentence on your personal Web page is a bad idea). Table 14-1 lists examples of strong passwords and the tricks used to remember them.

Table 14-1 Ideas for Good Passwords	
Password	*How to Remember It*
Mrci7yo!	My rusty car is 7 years old!
2emBp1ib	2 elephants make BAD pets, 1 is better
ItMc?Gib	Is that MY coat? Give it back

As you can see, I even placed emphasis on particular words and used that to remember capitalization of certain letters. The passwords look like gibberish, but are actually rather easy to remember. You set your password using the `passwd` command. Type the `passwd` command within a command shell, and it will enable you to change your password. First, it will prompt you to enter your old password. To protect against someone "shoulder surfing" and learning your password, the password will not be displayed as you type.

Assuming you type your old password correctly, the `passwd` command will prompt you for the new password. It will ask you to enter the new password a second time to make sure there are no typos (which are hard to detect when you can't see what you are typing). When running as root, it is possible to change a user's password by supplying that user's login name as a parameter to the `passwd` command. Typing this:

```
passwd joe
```

results in the `passwd` command prompting you for joe's new password. It does not prompt you for his old password in this case. This allows root to reset a user's password when that user has forgotten it (an event that happens all too often).

Changing passwords periodically

Even really good passwords can be broken if a cracker has enough time to work at it. That is why periodically changing your password is an extremely good idea. This way, by the time a cracker does arrive at the correct password, it will already be changed to something different. It is even possible to set an expiration date on Linux passwords. You can use the `chage` command to change the expiration date of passwords on your Red Hat Linux system. For example, to set the password expiration so that user Mary is prompted to change her password every 30 days, you would log in as root and type the following command:

```
# chage -M 30 mary
```

The `-M` parameter tells the `chage` command that you are setting the maximum number of days to keep the password. The number of days follows the `-M` switch, and the user name is always the last parameter. When 30 days have passed and Mary's password expires, she will be greeted with the following message the next time she logs in:

```
Your password has expired; please change it!
Changing password for mary
```

The system will then prompt her once for her old password and then twice for her new password. She will not be able to log in until she successfully sets a new password.

Table 14-2 lists the valid options for the chage command. The options are case sensitive.

	Table 14-2 **Options for the chage Command**
Option	**Description**
-m	The minimum number of days before a user may change his or her password. If set to zero, he or she may change it at any time.
-M	The maximum number of days a password should stay valid.
-d	Set the date that the password was last changed.
-I	Set the number of allowed days of inactivity for the account. If the account is unused for that long, it is deactivated.
-E	Set the date on which the user account will expire and automatically be deactivated.
-W	Set the number of days before the password expires that the user will be warned to change it.
-l	List the number of days until the password expires.

To set Mary's account so it warns her five days before she must select a new password, use the -W option.

```
# chage -W 5 mary
```

On the appropriate day, Mary will be greeted with the following warning message when she logs in.

```
Warning: your password will expire in 5 days
```

The system will greet her with a similar message each day (showing the appropriate number of days) until the password actually expires.

You can combine parameters to set several properties at a time. For example, the following example configures Mary's account so that her password expires every 30 days (-M 30) and she is warned 5 days before she has to change it (-W 5). Also, her account will completely expire on January 1, 2002 (-E 01/01/2002).

```
# chage -M 30 -W 5 -E 01/01/2002 mary
```

To examine what values her account properties are set to, type this:

```
# chage -l mary
```

and you should see something similar to this:

```
Minimum:            0
Maximum:           30
Warning:            5
Inactive:          -1
Last Change:              May 05, 2001
Password Expires:         Jun 04, 2001
Password Inactive:        Never
Account Expires:          Jan 01, 2002
```

Setting expiration times on passwords and accounts is an important part of your security strategy. By setting a default password rotation and an expiration date for every account you create, you minimize the risk that crackers will exploit a forgotten account with an unchanging password.

Using a shadow password file

In early versions of UNIX, all user account and password information was stored in a file that all users could read (although only root could write to it). This was generally not a problem because the password information was encrypted. The password was encrypted using a *trapdoor algorithm*, meaning the nonencoded password could be encoded into a scrambled string of characters, but that scrambled string could not be translated back to the nonencoded password.

How does the system check your password in this case? Simple. When you log in, the system encodes the password you entered, compares the resulting scrambled string with the scrambled string that is stored in the password file, and grants you access only if the two match. Have you ever asked a system administrator what the password on your account is only to hear, "I don't know" in response? If so, this is why: The administrator really doesn't have the password, only the encrypted version. The nonencoded password exists only in that brief moment when you type it in.

Breaking encrypted passwords

There is a problem with people being able to see encrypted passwords, however. Although it may be difficult (or even impossible) to reverse the encryption of a trapdoor algorithm, it is very easy to encode a large number of password guesses and compare them to the encoded passwords in the password file. This is, in orders of magnitude, more efficient than trying actual login attempts for each user name and password. If a cracker can get a copy of your password file, the cracker has a much better chance of breaking into your system.

Fortunately, Linux and all modern UNIX systems support a shadow password file. It may sound ominous, but it really is a good thing. The shadow file is a special version of the password file that only root can read. It contains the encrypted password information, so that the passwords may be left out of the world readable password file. Linux supports both the older, single password file method as well as the newer shadow password file. You should always use the shadow password file; it provides an important extra layer of defense against cracker attacks. In fact, the only time it is permissible to forego the shadow file is when your system is not plugged into a network, not plugged into a power outlet, and you've buried it under several feet of concrete.

Checking for the shadow password file

The password file is named passwd and can be found in the /etc directory. The shadow password file is named shadow and is also located in /etc. If your /etc/shadow file is missing, then it is likely that your Linux system is storing the password information in the /etc/passwd file instead. You can verify this by printing the file to the screen using the more command.

```
# more /etc/passwd
```

Something similar to the following should be displayed:

```
root:DkkS6Uke799fQ:0:0:root:/root:/bin/bash
bin:*:1:1:bin:/bin:
daemon:*:2:2:daemon:/sbin:
adm:*:3:4:adm:/var/adm:
lp:*:4:7:lp:/var/spool/lpd:
sync:*:5:0:sync:/sbin:/bin/sync
shutdown:*:6:0:shutdown:/sbin:/sbin/shutdown
halt:*:7:0:halt:/sbin:/sbin/halt
mail:*:8:12:mail:/var/spool/mail:
news:*:9:13:news:/var/spool/news:
uucp:*:10:14:uucp:/var/spool/uucp:
operator:*:11:0:operator:/root:
games:*:12:100:games:/usr/games:
gopher:*:13:30:gopher:/usr/lib/gopher-data:
ftp:*:14:50:FTP User:/u/ftp:
nobody:*:99:99:Nobody:/:
postgres:!:100:101:PostreSQL Server:/var/lib/pgsql:/bin/bash
mary:KpRUp2ozmY5TA:500:100:Mary Smith:/home/mary:/bin/sh
joe:OsXrzvKnQaksI:501:100:Joe Johnson:/home/joe:/bin/sh
jane:ptNoiueYEjwX.:502:100:Jane Anderson:/home/jane:/bin/sh
bob:Ju2vY7AOX6Kzw:503:100:Bob Renolds:/home/bob:/bin/sh
```

Each line in this listing corresponds to a single user account on the Linux system. Each line is made up of seven fields separated by colon (:) characters. From left to right the fields are the login name, the encrypted password, the user ID, the group ID, the description, the home directory, and the default shell. Looking at the first line, you see that it is for the root account and has an encrypted password of DkkS6Uke799fQ. We can also see that root has a user ID of zero, a group ID of zero, and a home directory of /root, and that root's default shell is /bin/sh.

All of these values are quite normal for a root account, but seeing that encrypted password should set off alarm bells in your head. It confirms that your system is not using the shadow password file. At this point, you should immediately convert your password file so that it uses /etc/shadow to store the password information. You do this by using the pwconv command. Simply log in as root (or use the su command to become root) and enter the pwconv command at a prompt. It will print no messages, but when your shell prompt returns, you should have a /etc/shadow file and your /etc/passwd file should now look like this:

```
root:x:0:0:root:/root:/bin/bash
bin:x:1:1:bin:/bin:
daemon:x:2:2:daemon:/sbin:
adm:x:3:4:adm:/var/adm:
lp:x:4:7:lp:/var/spool/lpd:
sync:x:5:0:sync:/sbin:/bin/sync
shutdown:x:6:0:shutdown:/sbin:/sbin/shutdown
halt:x:7:0:halt:/sbin:/sbin/halt
mail:x:8:12:mail:/var/spool/mail:
news:x:9:13:news:/var/spool/news:
uucp:x:10:14:uucp:/var/spool/uucp:
operator:x:11:0:operator:/root:
games:x:12:100:games:/usr/games:
gopher:x:13:30:gopher:/usr/lib/gopher-data:
ftp:x:14:50:FTP User:/u/ftp:
nobody:x:99:99:Nobody:/:
postgres:x:100:101:PostreSQL Server:/var/lib/pgsql:/bin/bash
mary:x:500:100:Mary Smith:/home/mary:/bin/sh
joe:x:501:100:Joe Johnson:/home/joe:/bin/sh
jane:x:502:100:Jane Anderson:/home/jane:/bin/sh
bob:x:503:100:Bob Renolds:/home/bob:/bin/sh
```

All the encrypted password data is now replaced with an x character. The password data has been moved to /etc/shadow.

There is also a screen-oriented command called authconfig that you can use to manage shadow passwords and other system authentication information. This tool also has features that let you work with MD5 passwords, LDAP authentication, or Kerberos 5 authentication as well. Type authconfig and step through the screens to use it.

To work with passwords for groups, you can use the grpconv command to convert passwords in /etc/groups to shadowed group passwords in /etc/gshadow. If you change passwd or group passwords and something breaks (you are unable to log in to the accounts), you can use the pwunconv and grpunconv commands, respectively, to reverse the password conversion.

So, now you are using the shadow password file, picking good passwords, and changing them regularly. You have made a great start toward securing your system. You may also have noticed by now that security is not just a one-time job. It is an ongoing process, as much about policies as programs. Keep reading to learn more.

Protection from Break-ins

Crackers have a wide variety of tools and techniques to assist them in breaking into your computer. Fortunately, there are many tools and techniques for combating them. This section discusses the most common break-in methods and the tools available to protect your system. Though the examples shown are specific to Red Hat Linux systems, the tools and techniques are generally applicable to any other Linux or UNIX-like operating system.

Testing your passwords with Crack

In a previous section, I described the importance of choosing good passwords. If you are the only person who uses your Red Hat Linux box, it is obviously not a big problem to verify the robustness of the passwords used on it. You, after all, are the person who assigned all those passwords.

On a multiuser system, however, the task of ensuring good passwords is more complex. If you have many people with accounts on your Red Hat Linux server, the likelihood that some users will pick weak passwords is almost certain. How can you be certain that your users are not using passwords that are easily cracked? The best approach is to use tools that are similar to the ones that crackers use and try to "break" the passwords on your system. Probably the best tool for this is the aptly named Crack utility.

Obtaining the Crack package

For general information about the Crack software, read the Frequently Asked Questions Web page at `www.users.dircon.co.uk/~crypto/download/c50-faq.html`. Crack can be downloaded via FTP from the `/pub/tools/unix/pwdutils/crack/` directory at `ftp.cerias.purdue.edu`. At the time of this writing, 5.0 is the current version of Crack. In this case, the file `crack5.0.tar.gz` is the one to download. If you find a higher version number when you look in the directory, download that newer version instead.

Alternatively, you can download the file `Crack_5.0a.tar.gz` from the directory `/pub/tools/password/Crack/` on the server `ftp.cert.dfn.de`.

After you have downloaded the file, extract it using the `tar` command. From the same directory that contains the downloaded file, type the following command

```
# tar -xzvf crack5.0.tar.gz
```

to uncompress and extract the Crack package. It will create a directory called c50a in the current directory. That directory will contain the `Crack` program as well as the other files and directories that the Crack package requires.

To use the Crack 5.0a package, follow these steps:

1. Using a Web browser, go to the page `www.users.dircon.co.uk/~crypto/` `download/c50-linux-util-makefile.txt` and save the page to the file `c50a/src/util/Makefile` in the directory to which you extracted the Crack package. Your browser should prompt you to replace the existing Makefile.

2. Click Yes to overwrite the older Makefile with the newer version that fixes the compile problem.

3. Next, compile the Crack package. Change your current directory to the c50a directory (using the `cd` command) and then type the following:

```
# ./Crack  -makeonly
```

to convert the source code for the Crack package into executable code.

4. Next, you need to prepare the dictionary files that Crack will use when trying to guess passwords. Do that with the following command:

```
# ./Crack  -makedict
```

Running the Crack command

Crack is now ready to run. Before you can run it, however, you must make your password file available in a format that Crack can read. The easiest way to do this is to run the `shadmrg.sv` script provided with Crack. You must be running as root to run the script, so use the `su` command to assume root privilege. The `shadmrg.sv` script is in the scripts directory within the primary Crack directory. It prints the merged password data to the screen, so you will need to redirect the output to a file when you invoke the command:

```
# ./scripts/shadmrg.sv > mypasswd
```

You should now be back at a command prompt. The new mypasswd file should be in the current directory. Unfortunately, it is still owned by root, and unless you plan to run Crack as root, you will need to change this. Type the following commands, replacing `myname` with your actual login name:

```
# chown myname mypasswd
# chmod 600 mypasswd
```

The `chown` command modifies the file so that it is owned by you rather than by root. (Replace *myname* with your user name.) The `chmod` command changes the file permissions so that only you can read it. THIS IS EXTREMELY IMPORTANT! You must change the permissions on this file so it is readable only by you; otherwise, you are opening a security hole on your system. If the file is readable by other users on the system, they can copy the file and then run Crack against it themselves.

Finally, exit the root shell using the `exit` command, and then run Crack against the merged password file using the following command:

```
# ./Crack mypasswd
```

This will start up the password cracking process, put it into the background, and return you to a command prompt. This does not mean that Crack is already done. Cracking a password file can take hours or even days depending on the size of the file. Crack will work on the file in the background and automatically exit when finished. You can pause, stop, or check the progress of Crack at any time. Table 14-3 lists the command lines that you are likely to find useful.

Table 14-3	
Different Options for the Crack Utility	
Command Line	**Description**
`./Crack mypasswd`	Crack the password file.
`./Crack -mail mypasswd`	Crack the password file and e-mail a warning to each user with a weak password.
`./Crack -nice 10 mypasswd`	Run Crack with a lower priority so it will take longer but not bog down the system.
`./Crack -kill mypasswd`	Terminate the current Crack run.
`./Crack -recover mypasswd`	Resume an abnormally terminated Crack run.
`./Reporter`	Show the progress or final results of a Crack run.

Showing the progress of a Crack run

After you have started a Crack session, the most useful command is the Reporter script. This will show you the progress or the final results of a Crack run, listing any passwords that it succeeded in cracking. An example of output from the Reporter script is shown below:

```
---- passwords cracked as of Wed May 16 21:43:07 CDT 2001 ----

Guessed jane [nosredna]  Jane Anderson [passwd.tmp /bin/sh]
Guessed joe [scuba]  Joe Johnson [passwd.tmp /bin/sh]

---- errors and warnings ----
StoreDataHook: invalid ciphertext: postgres !
StoreDataHook: wg='postgres PostreSQL Server' un='postgres' cm='PostreSQL Server
[/etc/passwd /bin/bash]' ct='!' sk='!'
ignoring locked entry: adm:*:3:4:adm:/var/adm:
```

```
ignoring locked entry: bin:*:1:1:bin:/bin:
ignoring locked entry: daemon:*:2:2:daemon:/sbin:
ignoring locked entry: ftp:*:14:50:FTP User:/u/ftp:
ignoring locked entry: games:*:12:100:games:/usr/games:
ignoring locked entry: gopher:*:13:30:gopher:/usr/lib/gopher-data:
ignoring locked entry: halt:*:7:0:halt:/sbin:/sbin/halt
ignoring locked entry: lp:*:4:7:lp:/var/spool/lpd:
ignoring locked entry: mail:*:8:12:mail:/var/spool/mail:
ignoring locked entry: news:*:9:13:news:/var/spool/news:
ignoring locked entry: nobody:*:99:99:Nobody:/:
ignoring locked entry: operator:*:11:0:operator:/root:
ignoring locked entry: shutdown:*:6:0:shutdown:/sbin:/sbin/shutdown
ignoring locked entry: sync:*:5:0:sync:/sbin:/bin/sync
ignoring locked entry: uucp:*:10:14:uucp:/var/spool/uucp:

---- done ----
```

In the above example, the users joe and Jane both had their passwords cracked. The user named joe used the dictionary word "scuba" and Jane used her last name backwards. You can use this report to identify accounts with weak passwords and warn those users that they must change their passwords.

Crack even has a nifty feature that automates the sending of warning messages to users with bad passwords. If you invoked the Crack script with the `-mail` parameter, such as:

```
# ./Crack -mail passwd
```

Crack will then send an e-mail message to each user when that person's password is cracked. Before you do this, however, you should probably edit the nastygram script. It is located in the scripts subdirectory of the Crack distribution, and you can edit it with the command:

```
# vi ./scripts/nastygram
```

Your editor should then contain the following:

```
#!/bin/sh
###
# This program was written by and is copyright Alec Muffett 1991,
# 1992, 1993, 1994, 1995, and 1996, and is provided as part of the
# Crack v5.0 Password Cracking package.
#
# The copyright holder disclaims all responsibility or liability with
# respect to its usage or its effect upon hardware or computer
# systems, and maintains copyright as set out in the "LICENCE"
# document which accompanies distributions of Crack v5.0 and upwards.
###

for username in $*
```

```
        do
                mail $username <<EndOfLetter
                                                `date`
Dear $username,

The login password you use for the account "$username" has been found
to be insecure by the "Crack" password guessing program. You must
change your password as soon as possible.

Passwords which are not easily compromised by programs such as "Crack"
are based upon non-dictionary words, hence any word which may appear
in a dictionary, EVEN IF IT IS SUPPOSEDLY AN OBSCURE WORD is
unsuitable.

Similarly, any password which is derived from your name, department or
other personal information is unsuitable because it can be easily
guessed.

It is important that password security be maintained at a high level
for the sake of ALL the people who use these computers. We thank you
for your co-operation in this matter.

        Yours,

                [insert the name of your system administrator]

ps:     This is a recorded announcement.
        Please bear this in mind in all correspondence.

EndOfLetter
done
```

If you specify the `-email` option, Crack will run this script whenever a user's password is cracked. The majority of the script is taken up with the text of the letter that will be sent to each user. You will probably want to customize this text so it is appropriate for your situation. In particular, replace the "`insert the name of your system administrator`" line with the appropriate person's name, e-mail, and phone number.

You can also combine multiple parameters when invoking Crack. Thus, if you want to run Crack at a lower (nice) priority so as not to bog down the system, and you also want to e-mail nastygrams to users with bad passwords, invoke Crack like this:

```
# ./Crack -nice 10 -email mypasswd
```

Be sure to read the online documentation for more information about Crack's many features. The documentation is available in both text and HTML format in the same directory as the Crack script (the c50a directory). Look for the files manual.txt and manual.html.

Protecting Your Computer by Filtering Network Access

Password vulnerability is only one potential weakness that a cracker may exploit to gain access to your system. Red Hat Linux and its UNIX kin provide a wide variety of network services, and with them a variety of avenues for cracker attacks. It is important that you know these services and how to limit access to them.

So what do I mean by a network service? Basically, I am referring to any task that the computer performs that requires it to send and receive information over the network using some predefined set of rules. Routing e-mail is a network service. So is serving Web pages. Your Linux box has the potential to provide thousands of services. Many of them are listed in the /etc/services file. Let's look at a snippet of that file:

```
# /etc/services:
# $Id: services,v 1.13 2000/12/01 03:20:17 nalin Exp $
#
# Network services, Internet style
#
# Note that it is presently the policy of IANA to assign a single well-known
# port number for both TCP and UDP; hence, most entries here have two entries
# even if the protocol doesn't support UDP operations.
# Updated from RFC 1700, ``Assigned Numbers'' (October 1994).  Not all ports
# are included, only the more common ones.
#
# Each line describes one service, and is of the form:
#
# service-name  port/protocol  [aliases ...]   [# comment]

tcpmux        1/tcp                           # TCP port service multiplexer
tcpmux        1/udp                           # TCP port service multiplexer
rje           5/tcp                           # Remote Job Entry
rje           5/udp                           # Remote Job Entry
echo          7/tcp
echo          7/udp
discard       9/tcp           sink null
discard       9/udp           sink null
systat        11/tcp          users
systat        11/udp          users
daytime       13/tcp
daytime       13/udp
qotd          17/tcp          quote
qotd          17/udp          quote
msp           18/tcp                          # message send protocol
msp           18/udp                          # message send protocol
chargen       19/tcp          ttytst source
chargen       19/udp          ttytst source
ftp-data      20/tcp
ftp-data      20/udp
```

```
ftp            21/tcp
ftp            21/udp
ssh            22/tcp                          # SSH Remote Login Protocol
ssh            22/udp                          # SSH Remote Login Protocol
telnet         23/tcp
telnet         23/udp
# 24 - private mail system
smtp           25/tcp           mail
```

The first 14 lines of the file are just comments (identified as such by the # character at the beginning of each line). After the comments, however, you will notice three columns of information. The leftmost column contains the name of each service. The middle column defines the port number and protocol type used for that service. The rightmost field can contain an optional alias or list of aliases for the service.

As an example, let us examine the last entry in the above file snippet. It describes the SMTP (Simple Mail Transfer Protocol) service, which is the service used for delivering e-mail over the Internet. The middle column contains the text 25/tcp, which tells us that the SMTP protocol uses port 25 and uses the Transmission Control Protocol (TCP) as its protocol type.

So, what exactly is a port number? It is a unique number that has been set aside for a particular network service. It allows network connections to be properly routed to the software that handles that service. For example, when an e-mail message is delivered from some other computer to your Linux box, the remote system must first establish a network connection with your system. Your computer receives the connection request, examines it, sees it labeled for port 25, and thus knows that the connection should be handed to the program that handles e-mail (which happens to be sendmail).

Note A program that stays quietly in the background handling service requests (such as sendmail) is called a daemon. Usually, daemons are started automatically when your system boots up, and they keep running until your system is shut down. Daemons may also be started on an as-needed basis by xinetd, a special daemon that listens on a large number of port numbers, then launches the requested process.

I mentioned that SMTP uses the TCP protocol. Some services use UDP, the User Datagram Protocol. All you really need to know about TCP and UDP (for the purpose of this security discussion anyway) is that they provide different ways of packaging the information sent over a network connection. A TCP connection provides error detection and retransmission of lost data. UDP doesn't check to ensure that the data arrived complete and intact; it is meant as a fast way to send non-critical information.

It is important that you understand the concept of services and port numbers because you use this information to selectively filter which services can be accessed on your Linux system and who can access those services.

Securing remote shells and logins

UNIX has a long history of providing many flexible ways to share information and tasks among networked computers. Red Hat Linux follows in that tradition by including all the traditional UNIX services for remote login, invocation of commands, and transfer of data. Although these services can be very useful, they can also create security risks on your system when not used properly.

One of these useful but risky features is the remote shell service, which traditionally runs on TCP port 514 and is serviced by the `in.rshd` daemon invoked by xinetd. The remote shell service enables you to invoke a command on a remote system without supplying a password for that system. You do this with the remote shell command `rsh`. For example, if you are logged in to a computer named ren and wish to check the contents of your home directory on a computer named stimpy, you would type the following:

```
# rsh stimpy ls
```

This invokes the `ls` command on stimpy just as if you logged in, typed in the command, and logged back out. It does this without prompting you for a password because ren is "trusted" by stimpy.

How do you tell one system that it should trust another? One way is by listing the trusted hosts in the `/etc/hosts.equiv` file on the trusting system. By listing a system in the `hosts.equiv` file, you are telling your computer that any user on that remote system should be allowed to run commands on your system without logging in and without supplying a password. They only need a user name on the remote system that matches a user name on your local system. Your computer will assume that this user is the same person and will allow the remote user to run commands with the matching local user's privileges. Placing a plus (+) sign in the `hosts.equiv` file tells your system to trust all systems. This action naturally has horrendous security ramifications, and you should NEVER do it.

Even if you do not have a `hosts.equiv` file, individual users can enable remote shell access to their accounts by creating a `.rhosts` file in their home directory. The `.rhosts` file is basically the same as the `hosts.equiv` file, but it affects only that user's account instead of all users on the system. Other commands that use the `hosts.equiv` and `.rhosts` file for establishing trust include the `rlogin` (remote login) command and the `rcp` (remote copy) command.

 Cross-Reference   Refer to Chapter 9 to learn more about remote shell and other network services.

Using these remote services poses some risks. Your system becomes only as secure as the most vulnerable of the systems you "trust." If one of the computers listed in your `hosts.equiv` is cracked, the crackers will easily be able to jump from that system to yours.

Unless you absolutely have to use remote shell or remote copy services, I recommend that you disable them completely.

Disabling network services

The remote shell service is just one of many services that is handled by the xinetd process. Xinetd is a daemon that listens on a great number of network port numbers. When a connection is made to a particular port number, xinetd automatically starts the appropriate program for that service and hands the connection to it. The configuration file /etc/xinetd.conf is used to tell xinetd what ports to listen on and what programs to start. To disable remote shell services, edit the xinetd.conf file and look for a section similar to the following:

```
service shell
{
        socket_type             = stream
        wait                    = no
        user                    = root
        instances               = UNLIMITED
        flags                   = IDONLY
        log_on_success += USERID
        server                  = /usr/sbin/in.rshd
}
```

Note that the first line of this example identifies the service as "shell." This exactly matches the service name listed in the /etc/services file. To disable shell services, you could simply delete this section from the xinetd.conf file. Better yet, you could add the line "disabled = yes" somewhere between the lines with the curly brackets "{" and "}". Thus, the above example with shell services disabled would look like this:

```
service shell
{
        socket_type             = stream
        wait                    = no
        user                    = root
        instances               = UNLIMITED
        flags                   = IDONLY
        log_on_success += USERID
        server                  = /usr/sbin/in.rshd
        disabled                = yes
}
```

Similarly, you should disable the rlogin service by making sure that disabled=yes is set in the /etc/xinetd.d/rlogin file.

Tip   It is possible to leave the remote login service active but disable the use of the /etc/host.equiv and .rhosts files, requiring rlogin to always prompt for a password. Rather than deleting the section or adding a "disabled" line, locate the line "server = /usr/sbin/in.rshd" and add a space followed by an -L at the end of it.

You now need to send a signal to the xinetd process to tell it to reload its configuration file. The quickest way to do that is to restart the xinetd service. As the root user, type the following from a shell:

```
# /etc/init.d/xinetd restart
Stopping xinetd:          [ OK ]
Starting xinetd:          [ OK ]
```

That's it—you have disabled the remote shell and remote login services. If someone attempts to use those services, he or she will receive a Connection Refused error message.

Using TCP wrappers

Completely disabling an unused service is fine, but what about the services that you really need? How can you selectively grant and deny access to these services? In previous versions of Red Hat Linux, the TCP wrapper daemon (tcpd) was used to facilitate this sort of selective access. In the current version of Red Hat Linux, TCP wrapper support has been integrated into xinetd. Xinetd will look at the files /etc/hosts.allow and /etc/hosts.deny to determine when a particular connection should be granted or refused. It scans through the hosts.allow and hosts.deny files and stops as soon as it finds an entry that matches the IP address of the connecting machine. The following checks are made each time a connection attempt occurs:

✦ If the address is listed in the hosts.allow file, the connection is allowed and hosts.deny is not checked.

✦ Otherwise, if the address is in hosts.deny, the connection is denied.

✦ Finally, if the address is in neither file, the connection is allowed.

It is not necessary (or even possible) to list every single address that may connect to your computer. The hosts.allow and hosts.deny files enable you to specify entire subnets and groups of addresses. You can even use the keyword ALL to specify all possible addresses. You can also restrict specific entries in these files so they only apply to specific network services. Let's look at an example of a typical pair of hosts.allow and hosts.deny files.

```
#
# hosts.allow    This file describes the names of the hosts are
```

```
#                   allowed to use the local INET services, as decided
#                   by the '/usr/sbin/tcpd' server.
#

imapd, ipop3d: 199.170.177.
in.telnetd: 199.170.177., .glaci.com
ftpd: ALL

#
# hosts.deny    This file describes the names of the hosts which are
#               *not* allowed to use the local INET services, as
#               decided by the '/usr/sbin/tcpd' server.
#

ALL: ALL
```

The above example is a rather restrictive configuration. It allows connections to the imap, ipop3d, and telnet services from certain hosts but then denies all other connections. Let's examine the files in detail.

As usual, lines beginning with a # character are comments and are ignored by tcpd when parsing the file. Each noncomment line consists of a comma-separated list of daemons followed by a colon (:) character and then a comma-separated list of client addresses to check. In this context, a client is any computer that attempts to access a network service on your system.

A client entry can be a numeric IP address (such as 199.170.177.25) or a hostname (such as dexter.glaci.com) but is more often a wildcard variation that specifies an entire range of addresses. A client entry can take four different forms. The online manual page for the hosts.allow file describes them as follows:

✦ A string that begins with a dot (.) character. A hostname is matched if the last components of its name match the specified pattern. For example, the pattern .tue.nl matches the host name wzv.win.tue.nl.

✦ A string that ends with a dot (.) character. A host address is matched if its first numeric fields match the given string. For example, the pattern 131.155. matches the address of (almost) every host on the Eindhoven University network (131.155.x.x).

✦ A string that begins with an at (@) sign is treated as an NIS (formerly YP) netgroup name. A hostname is matched if it is a host member of the specified netgroup. Netgroup matches are not supported for daemon process names or for client user names.

✦ An expression of the form *n.n.n.n/m.m.m.m* is interpreted as a *net/mask* pair. A host address is matched if *net* is equal to the bitwise AND of the address and the mask. For example, the net/mask pattern 131.155.72.0/255.255.254.0 matches every address in the range 131.155.72.0 through 131.155.73.255.

The example host.allow contains the first two types of client specification. The entry 199.170.177. will match any IP address that begins with that string, such as 199.170.177.25. The client entry .glaci.com will match host names such as dexter.glaci.com or scooby.glaci.com.

Let's examine what happens when a host named daffy.glaci.com (with IP address 199.170.179.18) connects to your Red Hat Linux box using the telnet protocol:

1. Xinetd receives the connection request.

2. Xinetd begins comparing the address and name of daffy.glaci.com to the rules listed in /etc/hosts.allow. It starts at the top of the file and works its way down the file until finding a match. Both the daemon (the program handling the network service on your Red Hat Linux box) and the connecting client's IP address or name must match the information in the hosts.allow file. In this case, the second rule that is encountered matches the request:

   ```
   in.telnetd: 199.170.177., .glaci.com
   ```

3. Daffy is not in the 199.170.177 subnet, but it is in the glaci.com domain. Xinetd stops searching the file as soon as it finds this match.

How about if daffy connects to your box using the imap protocol? In this case, it matches none of the rules in hosts.allow; the only line that refers to the imapd daemon does not refer to the 199.170.179 subnet or to the glaci.com domain. Xinetd continues on to the hosts.deny file. The entry ALL: ALL matches with anything, so tcpd promptly denies the connection.

The ALL wildcard was also used in the hosts.allow file. In this case, we are telling xinetd to permit absolutely any host to connect to the FTP service on the Linux box. This is appropriate for running an anonymous FTP server that anyone on the Internet can access. If you are not running an anonymous FTP site, you probably should not use the ALL flag.

A good rule of thumb is to make your hosts.allow and hosts.deny files as restrictive as possible and then explicitly enable only those services that you really need. Also, grant access only to those systems that really need access. Using the ALL flag to grant universal access to a particular service may be easier than typing in a long list of subnets or domains, but better a few minutes spent on proper security measures than many hours recovering from a break-in.

Tip   You can further restrict access to services by using various options within the /etc/xinetd.conf file itself, even to the point of limiting access to certain services to specific times of the day. Read the online manual page for xinetd (by typing man xinetd at a command prompt) to learn more about these options.

Protecting Your Network with Firewalls

What is a firewall? In the non-computer world, a firewall is a physical barrier that keeps a fire from spreading. Computer firewalls serve a similar purpose, but the "fires" that they attempt to block are attacks from crackers on the Internet. In this context, a firewall is a physical piece of computer hardware that sits between your network and the Internet, regulating and controlling the flow of information.

Using filtering or proxy firewalls

The two primary types of firewalls are the filtering firewall and the proxy firewall. Often both types are employed to protect a network. A single piece of hardware may even serve both roles.

Filtering firewalls

A filtering firewall does just what the name implies; it filters the traffic flowing between your network and the Internet, blocking certain things that may put your network at risk. It can limit access to and from the Internet to only specific computers on your network. It can also limit the type of communication, selectively permitting or denying various Internet services.

Usually the router that connects your network to the Internet acts as your filtering firewall. Linux has the capability to connect directly to the Internet and even act as an Internet router, allowing other computers on your network to communicate with the Internet through your Linux server. Unsurprisingly, network-filtering capabilities have been added to Linux, allowing it to function as a filtering firewall.

Proxy firewalls

A proxy firewall does not let any direct network traffic through. Instead, it acts as the intermediary between the Internet and the computers on your internal network. The firewall handles various network services itself rather than passing them straight through. In this sense, it is a "proxy" for the systems making the request.

For example, suppose you request an Internet Web page while logged in to a computer on your network. Instead of connecting directly to the Internet Web server providing the page (the usual approach), your computer connects to a proxy server on your own network. This server recognizes the proxied Web request and passes it to the appropriate Internet Web server in the normal way. The remote Web server sees it as a normal Web request coming from the firewall server (not your system) and delivers the appropriate page. The firewall server then sends that page back to your computer.

In this way, the firewall "hides" from the Internet server the fact that your computer even exists. Furthermore, a proxy firewall will commonly handle all incoming connections from the Internet (such as Web traffic, FTP downloads, and e-mail deliveries). Again, this is to minimize the visibility of your internal network to the outside world.

Configuring Red Hat Linux as a filtering firewall

A Red Hat Linux server can make a great firewall. A variety of tools are available to help you configure your Linux box to fulfill that role. For Linux to act as a filtering firewall, it is only necessary to use the ipchains or iptables features. The iptables feature is the newer of the two and is intended to replace ipchains for configuring Linux firewalls. However, because Red Hat Linux sets up a firewall for you during installation by using ipchains, this chapter describes how to continue firewall setup with ipchains.

Note   You can read about the differences between ipchains and iptables in the iptables HOWTO at the following Web site: `http://netfilter.kernelnotes.org/ unreliable-guides/packet-filtering-HOWTO/packet-filtering- HOWTO.linuxdoc-7.html`.

Checking your ipchains firewall setup

Ipchains works by examining packets as they are sent and received on a network interface and deciding which packets should be delivered and which should be stopped. It does this by examining a list (also called a chain) of rules. It stops at the first rule that matches the packet and examines that rule's target.

If you have configured a firewall during Red Hat Linux installation, some rules have already been set up for you. These rules are probably quite restrictive. After your system is up and running after installation, the first task you should do is check the current status of your firewall. Do that by typing the following as root user:

```
# ipchains -L
Chain input (policy ACCEPT):
target  prot opt     source         destination ports
ACCEPT  all  ------  anywhere       anywhere    n/a
ACCEPT  udp  ------  a.myisp.net    anywhere    domain - any
ACCEPT  udp  ------  b.myisp.net    anywhere    domain - any
DENY    tcp  -y----  anywhere       anywhere    any - any
DENY    udp  ------  anywhere       anywhere    any - any
Chain forward (policy ACCEPT):
Chain output (policy ACCEPT):
```

Preceding is the output I get when I choose the default firewall settings during Red Hat Linux installation (High security). Notice that only input is restricted. In other words, restrictions are on which services outside users can request. The first

ACCEPT line results from a rule that allows all requests made from users on the local system (that is, it allows the loopback driver, as indicated by n/a under ports). With that enabled, you can request any service from your local system without the packet being denied.

The next two ACCEPT lines allow the computers I indicate as my DNS servers (from /etc/resolv.conf) to request DNS services (domain) from my computer. The last two rules (DENY) result in all tcp and udp requests to be denied that don't match previous rules.

This default firewall configuration is set up in the /etc/sysconfig/ipchains file. When the ipchains service starts during system boot time (/etc/init.d/ipchains), the service reads the rules from /etc/sysconfig/ipchains. Here is what the rules from that file look like to create the preceding configuration:

```
:input ACCEPT
:forward ACCEPT
:output ACCEPT
-A input -s 0/0 -d 0/0 -i lo -j ACCEPT
-A input -s 192.160.0.253 53 -d 0/0 -p udp -j ACCEPT
-A input -s 192.160.0.254 53 -d 0/0 -p udp -j ACCEPT
-A input -s 0/0 -d 0/0 -p tcp -y -j DENY
-A input -s 0/0 -d 0/0 -p udp -j DENY
```

Because ipchains rules are cleared and reloaded from this file each time you start your system, I recommend the /etc/sysconfig/ipchains file as a good place to set up your firewall rules. With computer-cracker attacks on the rise, the current approach to security the experts recommend is to be secure by default. This means you should start by restricting most services and should then add only those services you want enabled. Put in the rules that allow services first, and then have all other services denied in the last two lines.

Understanding ipchains firewall rules

An ipchains target can be a simple command like ACCEPT or DENY, or it can be the name of another rule chain to begin examining. There are three default rule chains that the kernel will always examine. They are the input, output, and forward chains. You can create additional user-defined chains and call them from these original three, but for simple firewall configurations, the standard three should be sufficient.

Tip   Because ipchains stops examining a rule chain after finding the first match, you should pay special attention to the order of your rules. Rules with very specific conditions should generally go before those with similar but broader conditions. If you accept all TCP connections but then follow that with a rule to deny telnet access, telnet (being a TCP service) will still be allowed. Reverse the order of the rules (deny telnet, then accept TCP) and you will have the desired effect.

The general syntax is to invoke `ipchains` with a parameter specifying the action to take, followed by the rule chain to take it on. This may be followed by a rule description and a rule target. Table 14-4 shows action parameters you can use with ipchains.

Table 14-4 Ipchains Action Parameters	
Action Parameter	**Description**
`-A, --append`	Append a new rule to the end of the specified list.
`-D, --delete`	Delete a rule from the specified list. You can specify the rule by its numeric place in the list or by the rule parameters that match it.
`-R, --replace`	Replace a rule with a new one.
`-I, --insert`	Insert a new rule into a specific position in the list.
`-L, --list`	List all the rules in a chain. If the chain name is left off, list all rules in all chains.
`-F, --flush`	Flush all the rules out of a chain.
`-Z, --zero`	Zero out the packet counters for all chains.
`-N, --new-chain`	Create a new chain with the specified name.
`-X, --delete-chain`	Delete the chain with the specified name.
`-P, --policy`	Set the policy for the chain to the specified target. The policy of a chain describes what action to take if no rule matches the packet. The default policy for all chains is ACCEPT.
`-M, --masquerading`	Allows viewing of masqueraded connections. IP Masquerading is discussed in Chapter 16.
`-S, --set`	Set the timeouts for TCP, TCPFIN, and UDP packets.
`-C, --check`	Check a supplied packet against the given chain. This is useful mainly for debugging.
`-h`	Print a Help message describing parameters to ipchains.

As you can see in Table 14-4, the ipchains action parameters can be expressed in two forms, either as a dash followed by a single capital letter, or two dashes followed by a descriptive word. Both will work, so use whichever you prefer. In the example in this chapter, I will use the abbreviated version.

Usually, we follow the action parameter with the rule chain to apply it to. Rules added to the input chain will be examined only when filtering network packets being received by the Linux box. Similarly, the output chain is examined only for packets being transmitted from the Linux box. The forward chain is examined only for network packets that are received by the Linux system but will be delivered to some other network system. Packet forwarding only occurs when your system is configured as a router.

After specifying a chain to act on, you may specify some optional parameters to define a rule. Table 14-5 lists the available optional parameters.

Table 14-5
Ipchains Optional Parameters

Parameter	Description
`-p, --protocol[!] protocol`	Specify the protocol that the rule should match against. This should be TCP, UDP, or ICMP.
`-s, --source [!] address`	Specify the source address to match against. This can be an individual address, or you can specify an entire subnet by following the address with a / and the number of 1 bits in the left side of the subnet mask. Thus, the address 199.170.177.0/24 would have a subnet mask of 255.255.255.0.
`--source-port [!]port`	The source TCP or UDP port number as specified in /etc/services. You can also specify a range of ports by listing the first and last port number separated by a ':' colon character.
`-d, --destination [!] address`	Specify the destination address to match against. This can be an individual address, or you can specify an entire subnet by following the address with a / and the number of 1 bits in the left side of the subnet mask. Thus, the address 199.170.177.0/24 would have a subnet mask of 255.255.255.0.
`--destination-port [!] port`	The destination TCP or UDP port number as specified in /etc/services. You can also specify a range of ports by listing the first and last port number separated by a ':' colon character.
`--icmp-type [!] typename`	Set the type of ICMP packet to use.
`-j, --jump target`	The name of the target (action) to execute when the rule matches. This could be the name of another ipchain or one of several predefined targets.

Continued

Table 14-5 (continued)

Parameter	Description
`-i. --interface [!] name`	The name of the network interface that this rule applies to. If this option is not supplied, the rule will apply to all interfaces.
`[!] -f, --fragment`	The rule will apply only to fragmented packets, excluding the first packet. In other words, it applies to all packet fragments after the first one.
`-b, --bidirectional`	The rule should apply to both incoming and outgoing packets.
`-v, --verbose`	Print debug messages when processing this ipchains command.
`-n, --numeric`	Use IP addresses instead of hostnames when printing output to the screen.
`-1, --log`	Turn on kernel logging of matching packets. This will slow things down and fill up your hard drive. It is intended mainly for debugging.
`-o, --output [maxsize]`	Divert packets to a user space process. Another debugging feature.
`-m, --mark markvalue`	Mark the packet with a 32-bit signature. This is probably only useful to you if you are a kernel hacker.
`-t, --TOS andmask xormask`	Examine the TOS field of the packet using the supplied bit masks. Read the ipchains man page for a complete discussion of this option.
`-x, --exact`	Display exact values of packet counters rather than numbers rounded to the kilobyte.
`[!] -y, --syn`	Examine the SYN bit in the TCP packet being looked at. Useful for blocking TCP connection from being initiated in one direction but not the other.
`--line-numbers`	Show line numbers when listing rules. This is useful if you plan to delete or modify rules by position number.
`--no-warnings`	Disable all warning messages.

After specifying a rule for a particular type of packet, you must specify the target for it using the `-j` or `--jump` option. This tells ipchains what to do with that packet when it finds a rule that matches it. The target could be the name of another rule chain to traverse, but more often it is one of the predefined actions described in Table 14-6.

Table 14-6
Ipchains Targets

Target	Description
ACCEPT	Accept the packet and deliver it in the normal way.
DENY	Drop the packet completely.
REJECT	Drop the packet and then send an ICMP packet with an explanation to the sending host. This is primarily useful for debugging.
MASQ	Use IP Masquerading for this packet type. Refer to Chapter 16 for an explanation of masquerading.
REDIRECT	Redirect the packet to a new location.
RETURN	Return from this chain to the chain that called it. Continue examining rules in the calling chain where you left off.

I've shown you the various components of an `ipchains` command. It is time to put them together into some practical examples. It is possible to create some very sophisticated and complicated rule lists with `ipchains`, but I will keep my examples rather simple. Keeping things simple is generally a good policy, since large, complicated rule chains can impact system performance. More time spent examining rules means less time delivering packets and serving up information. The higher the traffic level on your Linux box, the greater the performance impact of those complicated rule chains.

Changing ipchains firewall rules

Now let us try adding a rule. As an example, let us imagine we want to block ICMP packets to disallow "pinging" of our Linux box. You may do that to avoid various Denial of Service attacks that could be launched against your system. Block ICMP with a command like the following:

```
# ipchains -A input -p icmp -j DENY
```

This specifies that we are adding a rule to the input chain. It will match any ICMP packet and will drop it rather than allowing it through. Now if you are using the `ping` command against your Linux box, you should receive no response. Type the `ipchains -L` command again, and you will see something like this:

```
    Chain input  (policy ACCEPT):
    target    prot opt     source         destination ports
    DENY      icmp ------   anywhere       anywhere    any  -> any
    Chain forward (policy ACCEPT):
    Chain output  (policy ACCEPT):
```

You can see your new rule listed. This rule will block all ICMP packets entering your system, regardless of which computer sent those packets. If your Linux system is acting as a router, it will also block ICMP packets that are being forwarded from the Internet to your network, or vice versa. People on the Internet will be unable to ping anything on your network. Likewise, you will be unable to ping anything on the Internet. Perhaps that is not what you want. Let us assume then that you wish to block pinging of systems on your network by people on the Internet, but allow pinging of the router and allow the router to ping hosts on the Internet. First, we should flush the contents of the input chains using the -F parameter; then we can add our new rule.

```
# ipchains -F input
# ipchains -A forward -p icmp -j DENY
```

Now we can ping the Linux system and the Linux system can ping other boxes, but ping requests will not be passed through the Linux system. If you wish, use the ipchains -L command to verify that the rule has now been added to the forward chain rather than the input chain.

You may also wish to block the telnet protocol when coming from the Internet. For this example, let us assume that our Linux router is connected to the Internet via a dialup connection called ppp0 and is connected to our internal LAN via an Ethernet connection called eth0. In that case, you could block telnet with a command like the following:

```
# ipchains -A input -i ppp0 -p tcp --dport 23 -j DENY
```

This rule basically says that any TCP packet with a destination port of 23 (the telnet port as specified in /etc/services) that is arriving on the ppp0 interface should be dropped. This does not prevent you from telneting to your Linux box from your internal network, but it does block telnet access from the Internet.

I'm going to finish up with one more useful example. Imagine you want to allow any type of outbound TCP connection to the Internet, but want to block any inbound TCP connection. Every TCP connection sends packets in both directions, so at first glance it would seem impossible. Block all inbound TCP packets, and the reply packets to your outbound connections will also be blocked. The trick is to block only the initial TCP packet that is used to start an inbound connection. We can do this because all TCP connection requests start with a packet that has something called the SYN bit set. We can use the --syn option to tell ipchains to look for that bit. Try the following command:

```
# ipchains -A input -i ppp0 -p tcp --syn -j DENY
```

There are many useful ways to filter traffic using ipchains. I encourage you to read the ipchains man page (type man ipchains) and the ipchains HOWTO document to learn more about it. You can find the HOWTO document under the /usr/share/doc directory on your Linux system or at the Web site at www.linuxdoc.org/HOWTO/IPCHAINS-HOWTO.html.

Saving ipchains firewall rules

After you have created the ipchains rules you want, it is important to save them to a file; otherwise, they will be lost when you reboot the server. Fortunately, a pair of useful scripts (`ipchains-save` and `ipchains-restore`) is provided for exactly this purpose. Essentially, `ipchains-save` will echo the current ipchains rule list to the screen. The `ipchains-restore` script reads in the specially formatted rule list and makes it active. After customizing the ipchains configuration, save it to a file by running `ipchains-save` and directing the output to a file like this:

```
# /sbin/ipchains-save > /tmp/ipchains.rules
```

Next, you can add the rules you have created to the `/etc/sysconfig/ipchains` file. As root user, open the file in any text editor. Then read in the ipchains.rules file you have created in the preceding example.

Using firewall-config

If you really do not enjoy building your ipchains rules from the command line, you can use the new graphical application, firewall-config. You must be running within the X environment and logged in as root. Click the GNOME menu button ➪ Programs ➪ System ➪ firewall-config, or run the firewall-config application from a command shell; you should see the window shown in Figure 14-1.

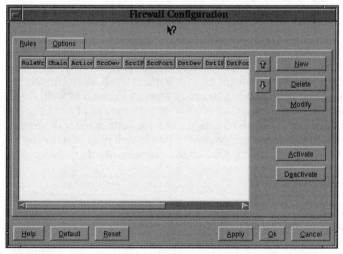

Figure 14-1 The main firewall-config window will display the list of all ipchain rules.

You can then add, modify, and delete rules simply by clicking the buttons on the right side of the form. Add a new rule, and the form shown in Figure 14-2 appears.

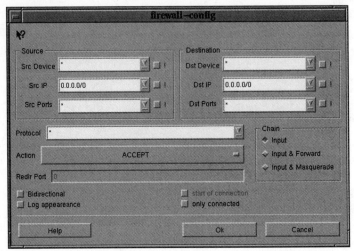

Figure 14-2: Clicking New on the main firewall-config window brings up a window for composing a new ipchain rule.

> **Tip**   The `firewall-config` application overwrites the contents of the `/etc/sysconfig/ipchains` file. Therefore, any rules entered manually into that file are lost. You should make a copy of the `/etc/sysconfig/ipchains` file before using `firewall-config`.

Configuring Red Hat Linux as a proxy firewall

We have seen that Red Hat Linux can act as a filtering firewall. With the addition of the socks5 package, Linux can be made to act as a proxy firewall as well. An RPM version of socks5 is available from `ftp://ftp.redhat.com/pub/contrib/libc6/i386`. Type `rpmfind socks5` to locate the socks5 package if the Red Hat FTP site is busy. Download the socks5 package; then install it as you do any RPM package. With the socks5 package installed in the current directory, type:

```
# rpm -i socks5*
```

The program that actually understands the socks protocol and handles the proxy service is the socks5 daemon. Before you use it, however, you must create a socks5.conf file in the /etc directory. Socks5 looks at the `/etc/socks5.conf` file to learn what protocols and services it will proxy, and which computers will be enabled to use the proxy service.

Creating the socks5.conf file

The `socks5.conf` file is divided into six sections. Each section controls a specific aspect of how the socks5 daemon handles a particular connection. When a client computer connects to proxy server, socks5 sequentially searches through each line of each section and determines what action to take based on the rules it encounters.

It stops when it finds a rule line that matches the connection being processed, so the order of rules is important. I briefly discuss each section, taking the most time to discuss the Access Control section, as that is the section that you are likely to use the most.

First, let's examine some of the syntax that is common to all sections. Each line within any section is made up of a keyword followed by several user-definable parameters. The keyword determines what section that line belongs in and what its function is. The parameters tell socks5 such useful things as the source and destination addresses to permit or deny proxy services, what protocols or service ports to permit or deny, and what type of authentication to use.

Host address notation

A host address can be a complete hostname or IP address, such as ratbert.glaci.com or 199.170.177.18. It can also be a partial hostname or address, such as .glaci.com or the 199.170.177. IP address. Note that the partial hostname begins with a dot (.) character. This allows socks5 to recognize it as a partial hostname and use it to match any host in the glaci.com domain. Likewise, the partial IP address ends with a dot (.) character, allowing socks5 to recognize it as a partial address. It will match any IP address in the 199.170.177.0 subnet.

You may recognize this as the same notation used in the `hosts.allow` and `hosts.deny` files that are used by the tcpd daemon. Socks5 does one thing differently, however. Instead of using the keyword `ALL` as a wildcard to match all hosts, it uses the dash (-) character.

Service port notation

A port can be specified using the service name as listed in the `/etc/services` file (such as http or telnet), or the corresponding integer number can be used (such as 80 or 23). For both the source-host and source-port entries, a dash (-) character can be used to match any host or port.

The ban host section

The ban host section is used to deny proxy services to specific hosts and protocols. A ban host line always starts with the keyword `ban` followed by the source-host parameters and a source-port parameter.

```
ban    source-host    source-port
```

The source-host designates the hostname or IP address that the connection is coming from. The source port designates the service port number that the connecting system is requesting. Table 14-7 lists examples of valid `ban` host lines.

Table 14-7
Valid ban Host Lines

Valid ban Host Lines	Description
ban ratbert.glaci.com http	The host ratbert is not allowed to access the Web server on this system.
ban .glaci.com 1880	No host in the glaci.com domain is allowed access to port 1880 on this system.
ban 199.170.177.22 ptelnet	The host 199.170.177.22 is not allowed to access the proxy telnet service in this system.
ban 199.170.176. -	No hosts on the 199.170.176.x subnet can access any proxy service on this system.
ban - -	No host anywhere is allowed to access any proxy service on this system.

The authentication section

An authentication line tells socks5 how it should authenticate connections from a particular host for a particular service. The line always begins with the auth keyword followed by the source-host, source-port, and the type of authentication to use.

```
auth   source-host   source-port   auth-methods
```

Valid auth methods include username/password, kerberos, any, or none. A single letter (u, k, -, or n) is used to indicate each authentication type.

- ✦ u — Username/Password
- ✦ k — Kerberos 5
- ✦ - — Any authentication method
- ✦ n — No authentication

The auth-method parameter can be a single authentication type or a comma-separated list of types. If you specify multiple types, socks5 will check them in reverse order so that the last one in the list is the preferred type.

Omitting the authentication section results in any authentication method being allowed for all permitted connections. This is appropriate if you are primarily using socks for outgoing proxy services (from your network to the Internet) and thus are permitting or denying connections based on the address and port. This is the most common way of configuring a proxy server.

The interfaces section

The interfaces section is only used if your Linux system is dual-homed, which means that it has more than one network interface. This is usually the case if your Linux system is also acting as a filtering firewall (not just a proxy) or as a router. The interface section enables you to specify different rules for how connections are handled on different interfaces.

The variables and flags section

The variables and flags section is used to adjust the level of logging and debug messages that socks5 generates. Entries in this section always begin with the `set` keyword followed by the variable being set and the value it is being set to, as shown here:

```
set variable value
```

Generally, the default settings are sufficient. Read the Environment section of the socks5 online manual page (using the `man socks5` command) to learn more about setting variables and flags.

The proxies section

Use the proxy section to tell socks how and when it should relay a connection to another proxy server. This is not a common occurrence in normal Internet usage, but you may have situations on your intranet where this would be useful.

The access control section

This is probably the most used section of the socks5.conf file. The access control section is used to permit or deny proxy connections based on the host address or port number of either the source or destination machine. An access control line always starts with either the keyword `permit` or the keyword `deny`. Six required parameters and an optional seventh parameter follow the keyword.

```
permit auth cmd src-host dest-host src-port dest-port [user-list]
deny   auth cmd src-host dest-host src-port dest-port [user-list]
```

When a client computer connects to the proxy server, socks5 scans through the list of access control lines until it finds one that matches the incoming connection. If even a single parameter on a line does not match the connection, that line is not considered a match and socks5 continues to the next line. If no matching lines are found, socks5 denies the connection. If a match is found, socks5 looks at the keyword for that line and permits or denies the connection as appropriate.

The `auth` parameter is used to describe the authentication methods allowed for the connection. Refer to the authentication section discussion for details on the different authentication schemes.

The `cmd` parameter is used to tell socks5 what sort of actions can be performed on a particular connection. The allowed values are:

- ✦ c — Connect
- ✦ b — Bind
- ✦ u — UDP
- ✦ p — Ping
- ✦ t — Traceroute
- ✦ - — All Commands

The `src-host` parameter matches the hostname or IP address of the connecting machine, while the `dest-host` parameter matches the hostname or address of the machine it is trying to connect to. Similarly, the `src-port` matches the service port number that the client machine is connecting to, and the `dest-port` matches the port number that the proxy server is redirecting the connection to.

The `user-list` is an optional parameter that can limit the connection to only the specified users. It is a comma-separated list of user names with no spaces.

As you can see, many of the capabilities of the other sections are also available in the access section. It is not uncommon to have a `socks5.conf` file that contains only permit and deny access lines. Here is an example of a `socks5.conf` file. Each permit or deny line is preceded by a comment that explains its function.

```
# Sample socks5.conf file
# Allow hosts in the 199.170.177.x subnet to access
# the web (http protocol) through proxy port 1880
permit - - 199.170.177. - 1880 http

# Allow any host within the glaci.com domain to
# connect to the proxy telnet service. Require
# user/password authentication to access it.
permit u c .glaci.com - ptelnet telnet

# Deny all other connections
deny - - - - - -
```

You can find additional `socks5.conf` examples in the examples directory within the main socks directory. The man page for `socks5.conf` also has additional useful information.

Starting socks5 services

By installing the socks5 RPM, your Red Hat Linux system is automatically set up to start the socks5 service. When your system boots, the `/etc/init.d/socks5` script is run from the appropriate run-level directory (for system states 3, 4, and 5). If you want to start the service immediately, type the following as root user:

```
# /etc/init.d/socks5 start
```

This results in socks5 daemons running on your computer to handle incoming requests for proxy service.

Protection against NFS Vulnerabilities

The Network File Service (NFS) provides a convenient way to share files over a local area network. However, as with any service that transfers information over the network, there are security risks. Fortunately, these risks can be minimized with a few simple precautions.

Cross-Reference   If you are not familiar with NFS, refer to Chapter 18.

The file /etc/exports is the configuration file that tells your Red Hat Linux system which file systems and directories to make available over the network. A proper understanding of this file will help you avoid common mistakes that may let uninvited individuals access your private information.

Here is a very simple example of an /etc/exports file:

```
/usr/local
/home
/var
```

This basic exports file is really nothing more than a list of the file systems being exported via NFS. There is also no security at all in this example. Each of the listed file systems may be connected to by anyone on the Internet who cares to attempt it. A better example looks similar to this:

```
/usr/local ratbert.glaci.com(ro),dexter.glaci.com(ro)
/home ratbert.glaci.com,dexter.glaci.com
/var ratbert.glaci.com,dexter.glaci.com
```

In the above example, access is restricted to two machines, ratbert and dexter. Furthermore, we have exported the /usr/local directory read only using the (ro) flag. It is a good idea to grant no more access to your exported file systems than you feel comfortable with. Also, if at all possible, never export a / or /etc directory on critical systems. Doing so makes it easier for crackers to access or alter system configuration files.

Running Security Audits with Tiger

By now you have observed that attending to the security of your Red Hat Linux box can be a time-consuming process. Fortunately, there are some tools that help automate the more routine tasks performed in crack-proofing your system. Tiger is one such tool. It performs security audits, automatically scanning your computer for bad configuration files, altered programs, and other potential security problems. It looks for weaknesses in all the following:

✦ cron entries

✦ mail aliases

✦ NFS exports

✦ inetd entries

✦ PATH variables

✦ rhosts and .netrc files

✦ Specific file and directory access permissions

Tiger also performs file system scans to locate unusual files and checks path names that are embedded in any files reported by most of the other checks.

When Tiger is run, it records in a file all the weaknesses it finds. You can then review that file and correct any of the security problems, and then rerun Tiger to verify that everything has been fixed correctly. It is even possible to configure Tiger to run periodically and to e-mail its results to you. This is generally a good idea. Even the most secure system can drift back toward being unsecured as new software packages are installed and new users are added.

Tiger is part of the TAMU security tools collection created by the Texas A&M University. You can read about TAMU security toolkit at the Web page `http://net.net.tamu.edu/network/public.html`. You can download the Tiger package from `www.net.tamu.edu/ftp/security/TAMU/`. Download the file `tiger-2.2.4p1.tgz` (or if a higher version number is available, download that). Extract the file using the `tar` command:

```
# tar -xzvf tiger-2.2.4p1.tgz
```

This will create a `tiger-2.2.4` directory and extract the Tiger files to it. Use the `cd` command to change to the `tiger-2.2.4` directory. Now, install the Tiger package in the appropriate system directories by typing the `make install` command.

```
# cd tiger-2.2.4p1
# make install
```

This creates a directory called /usr/local/tiger and copies various scripts and configuration files into it. Next, you will need to make the temporary directories that Tiger will use as a scratchpad while auditing your system. Use the mkdir command to create a few subdirectories in the /var/spool directory:

```
# mkdir /var/spool/tiger
# mkdir /var/spool/tiger/work
# mkdir /var/spool/tiger/logs
```

Next, you should customize the tigerrc file located in the /usr/local/tiger directory. Use the cd command to change to that directory and load the tigerrc file in an editor such as vi:

```
# cd /usr/local/tiger
# vi tigerrc
```

You should then see a file that looks similar to the following:

```
#
# 'rc' file for tiger. This file is preprocessed, and thus
# can *only* contain variable assignments and comments.
#
#-------------------------------------------------------------
#
# Select checks to perform. Specify 'N' (uppercase) for checks
# you don't want performed.
#
Tiger_Check_PASSWD=Y              # Fast
Tiger_Check_GROUP=Y               # Fast
Tiger_Check_ACCOUNTS=Y            # Time varies on # of users
Tiger_Check_RHOSTS=Y              # Time varies on # of users
Tiger_Check_NETRC=Y               # Time varies on # of users
Tiger_Check_ALIASES=Y             # Fast
Tiger_Check_CRON=Y                # Fast
Tiger_Check_ANONFTP=Y             # Fast
Tiger_Check_EXPORTS=Y             # Fast
Tiger_Check_INETD=Y               # Could be faster, not bad though
Tiger_Check_KNOWN=Y               # Fast
Tiger_Check_PERMS=Y               # Could be faster, not bad though
Tiger_Check_SIGNATURES=Y          # Several minutes
```

As usual, comments start with #. All other lines start with a Tiger_Check parameter that is set to yes or no (indicated by an uppercase Y or N, respectively). After each parameter is a comment describing approximately how long it takes to run that check. To turn off a particular test, simply change the Y to N. Save and exit the file when you are done making changes.

To run the tiger audit script, type ./tiger at the command prompt:

```
# ./tiger
```

The script will print out status messages as it runs. The final line it prints will tell you the name of the file where security problems have been reported.

```
Security report is in
`/var/spool/logs/security.report.ratbert.glaci.com.010123-17:39
'.
```

As noted, this file can be found in the /var/spool/tiger/logs directory. Use the cd command to change to that directory and then use the more command or an editor to view its contents. Here is a part of a typical Tiger security report:

```
# Performing NFS exports check...
--FAIL-- [nfs006f] Directory /home exported R/W to everyone.
--FAIL-- [nfs006f] Directory /var exported R/W to everyone.
# Performing check of system file permissions...
--WARN-- [perm006w] /root/.bashrc should not have group read.
--WARN-- [perm006w] /root/.bashrc should not have world read.
--WARN-- [perm006w] /root/.cshrc should not have group read.
--WARN-- [perm006w] /root/.cshrc should not have world read.
--FAIL-- [perm007f] /etc/aliases should not have group read.
--FAIL-- [perm007f] /etc/aliases should not have world read.
```

The security report is divided into sections with each section labeled with a comment. In the above example, the NFS exports section has two problems. The /home and /var partitions are exported without restrictions. The system file permissions section reports several problems. Some are labeled with –WARN– in front of them. These are not as critical as the ones with –FAIL– in front of them. Nevertheless, in both cases you should use the chown or chgrp command to alter the permissions.

Detecting Intrusions from Log Files

Preparing your system for a cracker attack is only part of the battle. You must also recognize a cracker attack when it is occurring. Understanding the various log files in which Red Hat Linux records important events is critical to this goal. The log files for your Red Hat Linux system can be found in the /var/log directory. You can cd to that directory and use the ls command to list its contents. Table 14-8 lists some of the log files.

Table 14-8
Log Files in the /var/log Directory

Filename	Description
boot.log	Contains messages indicating which systems services have started up and shut down successfully and which (if any) have failed to start or stop.
cron	Contains status messages from the crond, a daemon that periodically runs scheduled jobs, such as backups and log file rotation.

Filename	Description
dmesg	A recording of messages printed by the kernel when the system boots.
lastlog	The latest login date and time for each user on the system.
log.smb	Messages from the Samba SMB file service daemon.
maillog	Contains information about addresses to which and from which e-mail was sent. Useful for detecting spamming.
messages	A general-purpose log file to which many programs record messages.
news	Directory containing logs of messages from the Usenet News server, if you are running one.
secure	Records the date, time, and duration of login attempts and sessions.
sendmail	Error messages recorded by the sendmail daemon.
uucp	Status messages from the Unix to Unix Copy Protocol daemon.
wtmp	Information about who is currently logged into the system and what he or she is doing. (This is not a text file, so you must use tools such as the who command to see the information.)
xferlog	Information about files transferred using the FTP service.

The role of syslogd

Most of the files in the /var/log directory are maintained by the syslogd process. The syslogd daemon is the System Logging Daemon. It accepts log messages from a variety of other programs and writes them to the appropriate log files. This is better than having every program write directly to its own log file because it allows you to centrally manage how log files are handled. It is possible to configure syslogd to record varying levels of detail in the log files. It can be told to ignore all but the most critical message, or it can record every tiny detail.

The syslogd daemon can even accept messages from other computers on your network. This is particularly handy because it enables you to centralize the management and reviewing of the log files from many systems on your network. There is also a major security benefit to this practice. If a system on your network is broken into, the cracker cannot delete or modify the log files because those files are stored on a separate computer.

It is not uncommon to run a dedicated loghost, a computer that serves no other purpose than to record log messages from other computers on the network. Because this system runs no other services, it is unlikely that it will be broken into. This makes it nearly impossible for a cracker to erase his or her tracks.

Redirecting logs to a loghost with syslogd

To redirect your computer's log files to another computer's syslogd, you must make some changes to your local syslogd's configuration file. The file that you need to work with is /etc/syslog.conf. Become root using the su command and then load the /etc/syslog.conf file in a text editor (such as vi). You should see something similar to this:

```
# Log all kernel messages to the console.
# Logging much else clutters up the screen.
#kern.*                                    /dev/console

# Log anything (except mail) of level info or higher.
# Don't log private authentication messages!
*.info;mail.none;news.none;authpriv.none;cron.none  /var/log/messages

# The authpriv file has restricted access.
authpriv.*                                 /var/log/secure

# Log all the mail messages in one place.
mail.*                                     /var/log/maillog

# Log cron stuff
cron.*                                         /var/log/cron

# Everybody gets emergency messages, plus log them on another
# machine.
*.emerg                                        *

# Save mail and news errors of level err and higher in a
# special file.
uucp,news.crit                             /var/log/spooler

# Save boot messages also to boot.log
local7.*                                       /var/log/boot.log


#
# INN
#
news.=crit                                 /var/log/news/news.crit
news.=err                                  /var/log/news/news.err
news.notice                                /var/log/news/news.notice
```

The lines beginning with a # character are comments. Other lines contain two columns of information, separated by colons (spaces won't work). The left field is a semicolon-separated list of message types and message priorities. The right field is the log file to which those messages should be written. To send the messages to another computer (the loghost) instead of a file, simply replace the log file name with the @ character followed by the name of the loghost. For example, to redirect the output normally sent to the `messages`, `secure`, and `maillog` log files, make these changes to the above file:

```
# Log anything (except mail) of level info or higher.
# Don't log private authentication messages!
*.info;mail.none;news.none;authpriv.none;cron.none   @loghost

# The authpriv file has restricted access.
authpriv.*                              @loghost

# Log all the mail messages in one place.
mail.*                                  @loghost
```

The messages will now be sent to the `syslogd` running on the computer named loghost. The name loghost was not an arbitrary choice. It is customary to create such a hostname and make it an alias to the actual system acting as the loghost. That way, if you ever need to switch the loghost duties to a different machine, you only need to change the loghost alias; you do not need to reedit the `syslog.conf` file on every computer.

Understanding the messages logfile

Because of the many programs and services that record information to the messages logfile, it is important that you understand the format of this file. Examining this file will often give you a good early warning of problems developing on your system. Each line in the file is a single message recorded by some program or service. Here is a snippet of an actual messages log file.

```
May 20 18:26:17 ratbert PAM_pwdb[3043]: (su) session opened for user root by
(uid=0)
May 20 18:27:15 ratbert PAM_pwdb[3049]: (login) session opened for user mary by
(uid=0)
May 20 18:27:15 ratbert login[3049]: LOGIN ON ttyp1 BY mary FROM dexter
May 20 18:27:15 ratbert PAM_pwdb[3049]: (login) session closed for user mary
May 20 23:27:46 ratbert ftpd[3060]: ANONYMOUS FTP LOGIN FROM dexter.glaci.com
[199.170.177.25], thad@glaci.com
May 20 23:28:01 ratbert ftpd[3060]: FTP session closed
```

This is really very simple when you know what to look for. Each message is divided into five main parts. From left to right they are:

- ✦ The date and time that the message was logged

- ✦ The name of the computer that the message came from

- ✦ The program or service name that the message pertains to

- ✦ The process number (enclosed in square brackets) of the program sending the message

- ✦ The actual text message itself

Let's examine the last line in the above file snippet. First, we see that it was logged on May 20 at 23:28:01 (11:28 p.m. expressed in nonmilitary time). Also, it came from the system named ratbert and was sent by the FTP daemon (`ftpd`) on that system. The process number of that ftpd is 3060. The message it sent was "FTP session closed." If you look at the line just above, you see another message, also from `ftpd` process 3060 on ratbert. This one shows the FTP session in question being opened. Other messages in the file record password authentication, login attempts, and `su` sessions. As you can see, the messages file gives you a pretty good snapshot of the activity that is taking place on your system. Another file that you should examine is the secure log file. It has the same format as the `messages` file, but contains only login attempt and failure information for a variety of services.

By occasionally reviewing the messages file and the secure file, it is possible to catch a cracking attempt before it is successful. If you see an excessive number of connection attempts for a particular service, especially if they are coming from systems on the Internet, you may be under attack.

Using Tripwire to Detect Tampered Files

What can you do to minimize the damage if, despite all of your best efforts, a cracker actually does break into your system? A savvy cracker will delete or modify your system logs, making it nearly impossible to know for certain what he or she has been up to. Important system programs may have been replaced with Trojan horses. Backdoors may have been hidden in your security. Examining and repairing the damage by hand can be a painstaking process.

Simply restoring from backups is not enough because you cannot be certain when the cracker first broke in. Backdoors and Trojan horses may have been on your system for some time and thus already on your backups. It becomes tempting simply to reinstall the entire operating system from scratch.

Do not despair. The security tool Tripwire can save you from this worst-case nightmare. Tripwire is a file-integrity checking system that was originally developed by Dr. Eugene Spafford and Gene Kim at Purdue University. It is now maintained and supported by the commercial organization Tripwire Security Systems, Inc. Much like a physical tripwire, the Tripwire software package can warn you when your security has been breached.

Specifically, Tripwire can warn you when important system programs or configuration files have been modified, allowing you to repair or replace just the altered files without having to resort to a complete reinstall of the system. It does this by keeping a database of cryptographic checksums for every important file on your system. A cryptographic checksum is a unique number created by sending every byte of a file through a special mathematical algorithm. Change even a single byte in the file, and you change the checksum number that the file generates. Thus, by comparing a file's current checksum against older checksums stored in a database, it is possible to tell if the file has been changed.

Configuring Tripwire

Tripwire was added to the Red Hat Linux distribution for the first time in version 7.1. After it is installed, you need to configure it. You can start by running the `twinstall.sh` script as the root user, by typing the following:

```
# /etc/tripwire/twinstall.sh
        .
        .
        .
        .

Creating key files...

(When selecting a passphrase, keep in mind that good passphrases typically
have upper and lower case letters, digits and punctuation marks, and are
at least 8 characters in length.)

Enter the site keyfile passphrase: ********
Verify the site keyfile passphrase: ********
Enter the local keyfile passphrase: ********
Verify the local keyfile passphrase: ********
```

As prompted, you need to select local and site passphrases. *Passphrases* are special passwords used to digitally sign various files that Tripwire creates and uses. A digital signature is used to verify the origin and integrity of a file. It is a protection against crackers tampering with the Tripwire package. The install script will first prompt you to enter the site passphrase. The passphrase will not display as you type it, so you will be asked to enter it a second time to verify that you typed it correctly the first time. You should take the same care in selecting this passphrase as you do in selecting your login password. Basically, avoid dictionary words, proper names, and other easily guessed passwords. (The script recommends using at least eight characters, with a combination of cases, numbers, and punctuation marks.)

The Tripwire configuration file is created next. You are prompted for your site passphrase. It is used to digitally sign the file.

```
Signing configuration file...
Please enter your site passphrase:
```

Next, the policy file is created. Again, you will be asked for your site passphrase, so it may be used to digitally sign the policy file.

```
Signing policy file...
Please enter your site passphrase:
```

The Tripwire software is now installed on your system and ready to run. A text version of the Tripwire policy file is copied to the `/etc/tripwire/tw.pol` file. The main `tripwire` command has four modes that it runs in.

Initializing the Tripwire database

The first of the four modes that Tripwire can run in is database initialization mode. This mode creates a new checksum database for files on your system. While logged in as root, type the following command:

```
# tripwire --init
```

You are prompted for your site passphrase, after which the checksum database will be built. The database is written to the file /var/lib/tripwire/*host*.twd, where *host* is replaced by your computer's host name.

Tripwire selects which files and directories to checksum by examining its policy file. Tripwire ships with a policy file that is appropriate for most newly installed Red Hat Linux systems, but it is possible that it will try to look for a few files that your system does not contain. If this happens, you will see error messages similar to this:

```
### Warning: File system error.
### Filename: /usr/bin/dos
### No such file or directory
### Continuing...
```

These error messages do not affect the creation of the checksum database, but they can make it difficult to recognize real error messages. To get rid of them, you must modify the policy file.

Rebuilding the policy file

A Tripwire policy file is used to describe the behavior that is expected of the system and data files. Tripwire uses the policy file information to create a snapshot of the file system. Later, this snapshot (referred to as the baseline) is compared against the running system, to see if your system has been modified by someone trying to break in.

To modify the policy file for Tripwire, you must first edit the text configuration file /etc/tripwire/twpol.txt. Open the file in an editor and comment out the lines that mention those missing files that resulted in error message. For example, if you wish to get rid of the error message for the missing /usr/bin/dos file, look for the following line in the policy text file:

```
/usr/bin/dos                    -> $(SEC_SUID)   ;
```

Comment out the line by placing a # character at the beginning of it. It should now look like this:

```
#   /usr/bin/dos                    -> $(SEC_SUID)   ;
```

You now must process the policy text file and create the encrypted and digitally signed policy file that Tripwire actually uses when creating or checking the checksum database. Type the `tripwire` command, passing it the `--update-policy` parameter and the name of the policy text file:

```
# tripwire --update-policy /etc/tripwire/twpol.txt
```

You will be prompted for your site and local passphrases. After that, a new policy will be built. You can then rebuild the checksum database with the `tripwire --init` command. The "No such file" error messages should not appear this time.

Checking file integrity

After the checksum database is built, you should periodically run Tripwire in integrity-checking mode. Integrity-checking mode will recompute the checksum for each file and check it against the checksum stored in the database, printing a warning message for any files that have changed. Use the `--check` parameter to do this:

```
# tripwire --check
```

Normally, no error messages will be reported. If, however, a file has been modified, you may receive a message that indicates that a cracker has gotten into your system and modified some of the operating system files, such as the `telnetd` program. The `telnetd` program may have been replaced with a version containing a backdoor through your security. It is critical that you replace any altered programs with the original versions from your Linux install CD or from a valid Linux distribution FTP site. Also, temporarily remove your system from the Internet while you perform a thorough audit of your security logs, closing any revealed security holes.

It is possible for Tripwire to report file changes that are not the result of a break-in. This most often happens when you have upgraded your operating system or installed software patches. Your best strategy is to run a Tripwire check just before installing any upgrades or patches. Assuming that there are no errors, proceed with the upgrade or patch, and then use the `tripwire` command to update the checksum database. It is not necessary to completely rebuild the database; you may run Tripwire in update mode to rebuild only the checksums of those files that changed.

Updating the database

To run Tripwire in update mode, invoke it with the `--update` parameter.

```
# tripwire --update
```

This will recalculate the checksums for any files that have changed since the last update and save those changes to the database. This is much less time-consuming than totally rebuilding the checksum database with the `tripwire --init` command.

Tip   You can greatly improve the security of Tripwire by running it from a read-only media such as a CD-ROM, or at least from a media that is only mounted when Tripwire is run. Also, storing the checksum database on a removable media that is mounted only when needed is another way of improving Tripwire security.

I store my Tripwire executable and database on a CD-R writable CD-ROM drive. You will, of course, need to specify the different file paths when running the `tripwire` command. The `-d` parameter can be used to change the location of the checksum database. On my Linux system ratbert, I run the `tripwire` command by loading my Tripwire CD and typing:

```
# /mnt/cdrom/tss/bin/tripwire --check -d /mnt/cdrom/tss/db/ratbert.db
```

If I upgrade my operating system, I must generate a new database and burn that to a new CD, but that is a small price to pay to be certain that my Tripwire database has not been compromised.

Protection from Denial-of-Service Attacks

Break-ins are not the only security risk your system may face. Your computer could suffer from a denial-of-service attack. This is an attack that attempts to crash your computer or at least degrade its performance to an unusable level. There are a variety of denial-of-service exploits. Most focus on overloading some system resource, such as your available disk space or your Internet connection. The most common attacks and their defenses are discussed in the following sections.

Mailbombing

Mailbombing is the practice of sending so much e-mail to a particular user or system that the computer's hard drive becomes full. There are several ways to protect yourself from mailbombing. You can install an e-mail-filtering tool such as procmail or configure your sendmail daemon.

Cross-Reference   See Chapter 19 for a more complete description of sendmail.

Blocking mail with Procmail

The Procmail e-mail-filtering tool is installed by default with RedHat Linux and is tightly integrated with the sendmail e-mail daemon and thus can be used to selectively block or filter out specific types of e-mail. You can learn more about Procmail at the Procmail Web site `www.procmail.org/`.

To enable Procmail for your user account, create a `.procmailrc` file in your home directory. The file should be mode 0600 (readable by you but nobody else). Type in the following, replacing *evilmailer* with the actual e-mail address that is mailbombing you.

```
# Delete mail from evilmailer
:0
* ^From.*evilmailer
/dev/null
```

The online manual page for Procmail explains its capabilities in greater detail. Type `man procmail` at a command prompt to view it. The procmailrc and procmailex man pages will tell you more about the `.procmailrc` file and give numerous examples of how to selectively process different types of mail. You should also examine the Web page "Timo's procmail tips and recipes" located at `www.uwasa.fi/~ts/info/proctips.html`.

Blocking mail with sendmail

The Procmail e-mail tool works quite well when only one user is being mailbombed. If, however, the mailbombing affects many users, you should probably configure your sendmail daemon to block all e-mail from the mailbomber. You do this by adding the mailbomber's e-mail address or system name to the access file located in the `/etc/mail` directory.

Each line of the access file contains an e-mail address, hostname, domain, or IP address followed by a tab and then a keyword specifying what action to take when that entity sends you a message. Valid keywords are OK, RELAY, REJECT, DISCARD, and ERROR. Using the REJECT keyword will cause a sender's e-mail to be bounced back with an error message. The keyword DISCARD will cause the message to be silently dropped without sending an error back. You can even return a custom error message by using the ERROR keyword.

Thus, an example `/etc/mail/deny file` may look similar to this:

```
# Check the /usr/share/doc/sendmail-8.11.4/README.cf file
# for a description of the format of this file. (search for
# access_db in that file) The
# /usr/share/doc/sendmail-8.11.4/README.cf is part of the
# sendmail-doc package.
#
# by default we allow relaying from localhost...
localhost.localdomain            RELAY
localhost                        RELAY
127.0.0.1                        RELAY
#
# Senders we want to Block
#
evilmailer@yahoo.com    REJECT
stimpy.glaci.com        REJECT
cyberpromo.com          DISCARD
199.170.176.99          ERROR:"550 Die Spammer Scum!"
199.170.177             ERROR:"550 Email Refused"
```

As with most Linux configuration files, lines that begin with a # pound sign are comments. Our list of blocked spammers is at the end of this example file. Note that the address to block can be a complete e-mail address, a full hostname, a domain only, an IP address, or a subnet.

To block a particular e-mail address or host from mailbombing you, log in to your system as root, edit the /etc/mail/access file, and add a line to DISCARD mail from the offending sender. After saving the file and exiting the editor, you must convert the access text file to the database format used by the sendmail daemon by using the makemap command. To convert the deny file into a hash indexed database called access.db, type the following at a command prompt:

```
# makemap hash access.db < access
```

Sendmail should now discard e-mail from the addresses you added.

Spam relaying

Another way in which your e-mail services can be abused is by having your system used as a Spam Relay. *Spam* refers to the unsolicited junk e-mail that has become a common occurrence on the Internet. Spammers usually deliver their annoying messages from a normal dial-up Internet account. They need some kind of high capacity e-mail server to accept and buffer the payload of messages. They deliver the spam to the server all in one huge batch, and then log off and let the server do the work of delivering the messages to the many victims.

Naturally, no self-respecting Internet Service Provider will cooperate with this action, so spammers resort to hijacking servers at another ISP to do the dirty work. Having your mailserver hijacked to act as a spam relay can have a devastating effect on your system's performance. Fortunately, mail relaying is deactivated by default on new Red Hat Linux installations. This is one security issue that you will not have to attend to. You can allow specific hosts or domains to relay mail through your system by adding those senders to your /etc/mail/access file with keyword RELAY. Refer to the chapter 'Setting Up a Mail Server' as well as the sendmail documentation for more information.

Smurfing

Smurfing refers to a particular type of denial-of-service attack aimed at flooding your Internet connection. It can be a difficult attack to defend against because it is not easy to trace the attack back to the attacker. Here is how smurfing works.

The attack makes use of the ICMP protocol, a service intended for checking the speed and availability of network connections. Using the ping command, you can send a network packet from your computer to another computer on the Internet. The remote computer will recognize the packet as an ICMP request and echo back a reply packet to your computer. Your computer can then print a message revealing that the remote system is up and telling you how long it took to reply to the ping.

A smurfing attack uses a malformed ICMP request to bury your computer in network traffic. The attacker does this by bouncing a ping request off an unwitting third party in such a way that the reply is duplicated dozens or even hundreds of times. An organization with a fast Internet connection and a large number of computers is used as the relay. The destination address of the ping is set to an entire subnet instead of a single host. The return address is forged to be your machine's address instead of the actual sender. When the ICMP packet arrives at the unwitting relay's network, every host on that subnet replies to the ping! Furthermore, they reply to your computer instead of the actual sender. If the relay's network has hundreds of computers, your Internet connection can be quickly flooded.

The best fix is to contact the organization being used as a relay and inform them of the abuse. Usually they only need to reconfigure their Internet router to stop any future attacks. If the organization is uncooperative, you can minimize the effect of the attack by blocking the ICMP protocol on your router. This will at least keep the traffic off your internal network. If you can convince your ISP to block ICMP packets aimed at your network, it will help even more.

Using Encryption Techniques

The previous sections told you how to lock the doors to your Red Hat Linux system to deny access to crackers. The best dead bolt lock, however, is useless if you are mugged in your own driveway and have your keys stolen. Likewise, the best computer security can be for naught if you are sending passwords and other critical data unprotected across your network or the Internet.

A savvy cracker can use a tool called a protocol analyzer or a network sniffer to peek at the data flowing across a network and pick out passwords, credit card data, and other juicy bits of information. The cracker does this by breaking into a poorly protected system on the same network and running software, or by gaining physical access to the same network and plugging in his or her own equipment.

You can combat this sort of theft by using encryption. The two main types of encryption in use today are Symmetric Cryptography and Public-Key Cryptography.

Symmetric Cryptography

Symmetric Cryptography, also called Private Key Cryptography, uses a single key to both encrypt and decrypt the message. The disadvantage of this method is that it must have a secure method of distributing the key. This method is fine when you are sending messages among computers on your own network. It is relatively easy for you to install the encryption key on each of your computers. The task becomes prohibitively complex, however, when the computers are scattered around the Internet.

Public-Key Cryptography

Public-Key Cryptography does not suffer from the key distribution problem, and that is why it is the preferred encryption method for secure Internet communication. This method uses two keys, one to encrypt the message and another to decrypt the message. The key used to encrypt the message is called the Public Key because it is made available for all to see. The key used to decrypt the message is the Private Key and is kept hidden. The entire process works like this:

Let's imagine that you want to send me a secure message using public-key encryption. Here is what we need:

1. I must have a public and private key pair. Depending on the circumstances, I may generate the keys myself (using special software) or obtain the keys from a Key Authority.

2. You wish to send me a message, so you first look up my Public Key (or more accurately, the software you are using looks it up).

3. You encrypt the message with the public key. At this point, the message can only be decrypted with the private key (the public key cannot be used to decrypt the message).

4. I receive the message and use my private key to decrypt it.

Exporting encryption technology

Before describing how to use the various encryption tools, I need to warn you about an unusual policy of the U.S. government.

For many years, the U.S. government treated encryption technology like munitions. As a result, anyone wishing to export encryption technology had to get an export license from the Commerce Department. This applied not only to encryption software developed within the United States, but also to software obtained from other countries and then re-exported to another country (or even to the same country you got it from). Thus, if you installed encryption technology on your Linux system and then transported it out of the country, you were violating federal law! Furthermore, if you e-mailed encryption software to a friend in another country or let him or her download it from your server, you violated the law.

In January 2000, U.S. export laws relating to encryption software were relaxed considerably. However, in many cases, the U.S. Commerce Department's Bureau of Export Administration still requires a review of encryption products before they can be exported. U.S. companies are also still prohibited from exporting encryption technology to countries classified as supporting terrorism.

Using the Secure Shell package

The Secure Shell package (SSH) is a package that provides shell services similar to the rsh, rcp, and rlogin commands, but encrypts the network traffic. It uses Private Key Cryptography, so it is ideal for use with Internet connected computers. The Red Hat Linux distribution contains the following client and server software packages for SSH: openssh, openssh-client, and openssh-server packages.

Starting the SSH service

If you have installed the openssh-server software package, the SSH server is automatically configured to start. The SSH daemon is started from the /etc/init.d/sshd start-up script. To make sure the service is set up to start automatically, type the following (as root user):

```
# chkconfig --list sshd
sshd        0:off   1:off   2:off   3:on    4:on    5:on    6:off
```

This shows that the sshd service is set to run in system states 3, 4, and 5 (normal bootup states) and set to be off in all other states. You can turn on the SSH service, if it is off, for your default run state, by typing the following as root user:

```
# chkconfig --level 345 sshd on
```

This line turns on the SSH service when you enter run levels 3, 4, or 5. To start the service immediately, type the following:

```
# /etc/init.d/sshd start
```

Using the ssh and scp commands

Two commands you most likely want to use with the SSH service are ssh and scp. Remote users use the ssh command to login to your system securely. The scp command allows remote users to copy files to and from your system.

Like the normal remote shell services, secure shell looks in the /etc/hosts.equiv file and in a user's .rhost file to determine whether it should allow a host to connect. It also looks in the ssh-specific files /etc/shosts.equiv and .shosts. Using the shosts.equiv and the .shosts files is preferable because it avoids granting access to the regular, nonencrypted remote shell services. The /etc/shosts.equiv and .shosts files are functionally equivalent to the traditional hosts.equiv and .rhosts, so the same instructions and rules apply.

Now you are ready to test the SSH service. From another computer on which SSH has been installed (or even from the same computer if another is not available), type the ssh command followed by a space and the name of the system you are connecting to. For example, to connect to the system ratbert.glaci.com, type:

```
# ssh ratbert.glaci.com
```

If this is the first time you have ever logged in to that system using ssh, it will ask you to confirm that you really want to connect. Type `yes` and press Enter when it asks this:

```
Host key not found from the list of known hosts.
Are you sure you want to continue connecting (yes/no)?
```

It should then prompt you for a user name and password in the normal way. The connection will then function like a normal telnet connection. The only difference is that the information is encrypted as it travels over the network. You should now also be able to use the `ssh` command to run remote commands.

The syntax for the `scp` command is similar to that of the `rcp` command for copying files to and from Linux systems. Here is an example of using the `scp` command to copy a file called `memo` from the home directory of the user named jake to the `/tmp` directory on a computer called maple:

```
$ scp /home/jake/memo maple:/tmp
passwd: ********
memo            100%|***************|   153    0:00
```

Enter the password for your user name (if a password is requested). If the password is accepted, the remote system indicates that the file has been copied successfully.

Monitoring Log Files with Logcheck

Red Hat Linux has the ability to monitor and log nearly every activity that can occur on your computer. On a busy system, massive amounts of informational and error messages are produced and placed in log files. For the administrator, the hard part of monitoring log files isn't detecting or logging security problems; the hard part is remembering to check the log files and sift out those messages that pose a threat from all the other stuff that gets logged. This section describes how to monitor log files with the Logcheck package.

The Logcheck package is a handy tool that you can use to easily manage your system log files. Because you're more likely to glance through an e-mail than you are to remember to check log files, Logcheck puts information in front of you that may otherwise go unnoticed.

Logcheck checks standard log files that are produced by the standard Linux `syslog` facility, attempts to filter out messages that don't represent any security threat, and then categorizes messages that could represent a threat and e-mails those messages to the system administrator. By default, Logcheck will check messages in the `messages`, `secure`, and `mail` log files in the `/var/log` directory. By changing the Logcheck configuration files, you can change which log files are checked, how messages are filtered, and how often log summary e-mail messages are sent. You may also want to change which features the syslog facility monitors and the level of syslog monitoring, if you are interested in debugging a particular system feature.

Logcheck and Portsentry (described later) are produced by Psionic Software, Inc., (`www.psionic.com`) as part of its Abacus Project. The Abacus Project aims to produce free host-based Internet security software that can detect and respond to intrusions from the network.

A package called HostSentry (`www.psionic.com/abacus/hostsentry`) is also available from Psionic Software, Inc. HostSentry monitors login sessions to try and detect behavior that may indicate that a user is breaking into your system. Though this software is currently in alpha form (that is, not yet ready for prime time), you may want to try it out on non-production systems and look for a stable version when it becomes available.

Downloading and installing Logcheck

You can find the `logcheck` package in the contrib directory of any Red Hat Linux FTP mirror site. If you have a connection to the Internet, you can use the following command to find an available logcheck package:

```
# rpmfind logcheck
```

After Logcheck is downloaded, to install the package simply run the following command from the directory you downloaded it to:

```
# rpm -i logcheck*
```

The installed Logcheck package consists of several configuration files (in the `/etc/logcheck` directory), the `cron` file that runs the `logcheck` command (in `/etc/cron.hourly/logcheck`), and the `logcheck` and `logtail` commands (in `/usr/sbin`). There are also several README files of interest in the `/usr/doc/logcheck*` directory.

Because there are several different versions of Logcheck floating around on the Web, the locations of commands and instructions for using Logcheck may be different than what I describe here. For example, your Logcheck package may include a `logcheck.sh` script in `/usr/bin` for running logcheck. The Logcheck package used in this section, which reflects its version, is Logcheck-1.1.1-1.i386.rpm.

Setting up Logcheck

You don't have to do anything to get Logcheck working. After Logcheck is installed, it runs every hour, on the hour. The results are then e-mailed to the root user on the local host computer. There are several things you can do, however, to tailor Logcheck to suit your particular needs. See the "Configuring Logcheck to suit your needs" section, later in this chapter, for more information.

Running Logcheck

When you install the Logcheck package, a script named `logcheck` is placed in the `/etc/cron.hourly` directory. Files in the `/etc/cron.hourly` directory are run hourly. In this case, the `/etc/cron.hourly/logcheck` script simply runs the `/usr/sbin/logcheck` script.

Because the `logcheck` script runs hourly, this means that you (or the administrator) will receive 24 e-mail messages each day, each containing the filtered log messages. If you want fewer e-mail messages, you can move the script to the `/etc/cron.daily` file (so you only get one message a day). Or you can create your own cron script to have the `logcheck` launched on any schedule you choose.

Note   The `/usr/sbin/logcheck` script uses the `/usr/sbin/logtail` command to gather only those log messages that you haven't already seen. The `logtail` command does this by creating a `.offset` file for each log file that Logcheck monitors. The next time Logcheck is run, only log messages that have arrived since the previous run are checked.

Using Logcheck

After Logcheck has been set up and run, to begin using Logcheck you start by simply reading the e-mail that Logcheck sends you. By default, the `root` user on your Red Hat Linux system will receive an e-mail message from Logcheck each hour. Log messages that are matched, and not excluded, are sorted under one of the following three headings in each e-mail message:

✦ **Active System Attack Alerts:** Represents messages that may represent an attack on your system.

✦ **Security Violations:** Includes failures and violations that may indicate a problem, but not necessarily an attack on your system.

✦ **Unusual System Events:** Includes all log messages that are neither matched nor excluded.

The following is an example of a Logcheck e-mail message.

```
Return-Path: <root@localhost.localdomain>
Received: (from root@localhost)
Subject: maple 04/06/01:19.01 ACTIVE SYSTEM ATTACK!
Status: R

Active System Attack Alerts
=-=-=-=-=-=-=-=-=-=-=-=-=
Apr  6 18:02:28 maple portsentry[1102]: attackalert: Possible stealth scan from
unknown host to TCP port: 111 (accept failed)
Apr  6 18:33:26 maple sendmail[1863]: f371XJw01863: "wiz" command from
duck.handsonhistory.com [10.0.0.28] (127.0.0.1)
Apr  6 18:33:29 maple sendmail[1863]: f371XJw01863: "debug" command from
duck.handsonhistory.com [10.0.0.28] (127.0.0.1)

Security Violations
=-=-=-=-=-=-=-=-=-=
Apr  6 18:02:28 maple portsentry[1102]: attackalert: Possible stealth scan from
unknown host to TCP port: 111 (accept failed)
Apr  6 18:39:14 maple  -- root[1121]: ROOT LOGIN ON tty1

Unusual System Events
=-=-=-=-=-=-=-=-=-=-=
Apr  6 18:01:35 maple last message repeated 291877 times
Apr  6 18:14:10 maple last message repeated 297510 times
Apr  6 18:20:58 maple kernel: SB 4.16 detected OK (220)
Apr  6 18:20:58 maple kernel: SB16: Bad or missing 16 bit DMA channel
Apr  6 18:20:58 maple kernel: sb: 1 Soundblaster PnP card(s) found.
Apr  6 18:38:37 maple syslog: syslogd startup succeeded
Apr  6 18:38:37 maple kernel: klogd 1.4-0, log source = /proc/kmsg started.
Apr  6 18:38:37 maple kernel: Inspecting /boot/System.map-2.4.2-0.1.49
```

In the above e-mail, under the Active System Attack Alerts heading, you can see that a scan of port 111 (portmapper service) was detected by the PortSentry service. The next two messages indicate that a user from the host duck. handsonhistory.com tried to scan sendmail to see if debug and wiz services could be accessed. Under the Security Violations heading, the possible stealth scan appeared again. A normal login by the root user was also detected (although it represented no particular threat in this case).

Under the Unusual System Events heading, as noted earlier, are included all messages not matched (specifically added to another category) or excluded (specifically ignored) by any of the filter files. A lot of normal system activity messages appear here. Over time, you may want to explicitly include or exclude message that you see all the time or that catch your eye as being a potential problem you need to watch. For example, the lines above that say last message repeated 291877 times indicate a potential denial-of-service attack. You may want to add the keywords "message repeated" to your logcheck.hacking list. Likewise, the words "Soundblaster PnP card(s) found" could be added to the logcheck.ignore file, because that message reflects normal processing.

Tip   In general, you want to react to attacks that you detect by preventing an attacker from gaining access to your system. If an attacker does get in, you want to get that attacker out of your system and clean up the damage as best you can. An excellent tool for detecting, logging, and denying access to your system by attackers is the PortSentry package discussed later in this chapter.

Configuring Logcheck to suit your needs

After Logcheck is installed, it will run without requiring any configuration. However, to better suit your needs, there are several configuration files you can modify. The following section describes those files.

Editing the logcheck script

The /usr/sbin/logcheck script scans your log files and sorts the log messages that are e-mailed. You can change much of the behavior of the logcheck script by changing the values of the variables within the script. To change the behavior of the logcheck script, follow these steps:

1. Make a copy of the /usr/sbin/logcheck file. For example:

   # cp /usr/sbin/logcheck /usr/sbin/logcheck.old

2. Open the script in any text editor while logged in as the root user and make any changes to the script. The following bullet list describes values that you may want to change in this script.

   - **SYSADMIN:** This variable defines the root user as the one to receive the e-mail messages resulting from running Logcheck. You can change root to anyone you want to receive the Logcheck messages. This can be either local users or users on other computers (that is, *user@hostname*).

     SYSADMIN=root

   - **TMPDIR:** Sets where Logcheck writes its temporary files during processing. The directory is created when Logcheck starts and is removed before Logcheck finishes. You can change the location by modifying the following entry:

     TMPDIR=/tmp/logcheck$$-$RANDOM

   - **GREP:** The logcheck script relies on a grep command that supports the -i, -v, and -f options to search the log files. By default, the egrep command is used for this purpose. You could change the value to grep or another command by modifying the following variable:

     GREP=egrep

   - **MAIL:** E-mail is sent by Logcheck using the mail command. To have Logcheck use a command other than the mail command to send e-mail messages to the administrator, change the following mail variable:

     MAIL=mail

- **Filter files:** There are four filter files defined by Logcheck. The files each contain keywords that are either used to find messages or exclude messages that contain those keywords. The following variables are set to indicate the location of the four Logcheck filter files.

```
HACKING_FILE=/etc/logcheck/logcheck.hacking
VIOLATIONS_FILE=/etc/logcheck/logcheck.violations
VIOLATIONS_IGNORE_FILE=/etc/logcheck/logcheck.violations.ignore

IGNORE_FILE=/etc/logcheck/logcheck.ignore
```

  For more information on filter files, see the "Changing Logcheck filter files" section, later in this chapter.

- **Log files:** The last entries in the /usr/sbin/logcheck script that you may want to change designate which log files are monitored by the logcheck script. By default, the logcheck script runs the logtail command to check the messages, secure, and maillog files (in /var/log). The following lines define which log files that are checked and determine the locations where the output of logtail is temporarily written.

```
$LOGTAIL /var/log/messages > $TMPDIR/check.$$
$LOGTAIL /var/log/secure >> $TMPDIR/check.$$
$LOGTAIL /var/log/maillog >> $TMPDIR/check.$$
```

Tip   If you like, you can have more log files checked by adding more lines like the ones above. Just make sure that the first line includes a single arrow (to overwrite a previous check file) and that all subsequent lines contain double arrows (to append to the current check file).

Changing Logcheck filter files

The /etc/logcheck directory contains four filter files that define which messages are matched and e-mailed to the administrator. The contents of these files are simply keywords. Log files are searched (or *grepped*) for these keywords and sorted or discarded based on the results of the search.

Some keyword filter files are intended to uncover words or phrases that would appear in a log message in the event of a system break-in or misuse. Other keyword files are intended to find messages that pose no security threat (so that the messages can be excluded from the e-mailed log messages). Messages that match neither the included or excluded keywords are appended to the Unusual System Events heading of the e-mail summary output.

You can use the filter files as they are. However, over time, you may want to modify these files for several reasons. If you are receiving repetitive, non-threatening messages in the Logcheck e-mails, you can add keywords that can filter out those messages. Also, you can add keywords later as you learn about new types of security breaches that you may want to look for.

Besides including alphanumeric characters, keywords can also include wildcard characters. For example, you could use an asterisk (*) to match any string of characters, a question mark (?) to match any single character, or a dollar sign ($) to match a keyword that appears at the end of a line.

Caution   Use wildcards carefully. A mistaken wildcard character can result in too many or too few messages being included or excluded.

The four Logcheck filter files in the `/etc/logcheck` directory are

✦ `logcheck.hacking`: Contains keywords that appear in log messages that represent known hacking attacks.

✦ `logcheck.ignore`: Contains keywords that represent messages that should always be ignored.

✦ `logcheck.violations`: Contains keywords that represent negative activities that may or may not represent real intrusions on your system.

✦ `logcheck.violations.ignore`: Contains keywords that represent messages that should be ignored from those that are found as part of the violations check.

Each of these files is described in the following sections.

Note   It is important to note that messages that are neither explicitly matched (from `logcheck.hacking` and `logcheck.violations`) nor explicitly excluded (from `logcheck.ignore` and `logcheck.violations.ignore`) are included in the e-mail sent by Logcheck to the administrator. Those messages are displayed under the following catchall heading:

```
Unusual System Events
=-=-=-=-=-=-=-=-=-=-=-=
```

logcheck.hacking

Keywords from the `/etc/logcheck/logcheck.hacking` file are meant to uncover log messages representing attacks on your system. Log messages that are matched by keywords in this file are output in e-mail messages to your system administrator under the logcheck.hacking heading.

Messages that appear under this heading are the first messages to appear in the e-mail message. You can add other keywords to this file as you learn about messages that represent different types of attacks on your system.

Following are some examples of keywords that appear in the `logcheck.hacking` file:

```
"wiz"
"WIZ"
"debug"
"DEBUG"
```

```
ATTACK
nested
VRFY bbs
VRFY decode
VRFY uudecode
rlogind.*: Connection from .* on illegal port
rshd.*: Connection from .* on illegal port
sendmail.*: user .* attempted to run daemon
uucico.*: refused connect from .*
tftpd.*: refused connect from .*
login.*: .*LOGIN FAILURE.* FROM .*root
login.*: .*LOGIN FAILURE.* FROM .*guest
```

Most of the messages in this file are used to match log messages that result from someone probing your system with the Internet Security Scanner (ISS). ISS is a tool that can scan a set of IP addresses for potential security weaknesses. Though most of the security holes ISS checks for have been plugged over time, these log messages alert you to the fact that someone is checking the security of your system.

The debug and wiz keywords shown in the above file will catch attempts by ISS to access wiz and debug services from the sendmail service. Likewise, VRFY is a command that ISS sends to requests of the sendmail service to ask for different user names. Other keyword phrases shown in the previous example match failed attempts to connect using different Linux network services (such as rlogind, rshd, sendmail, uucico, and so on).

logcheck.ignore

Keywords in the /etc/logcheck/logcheck.ignore file are used to find log messages that should be excluded (that is, ignored) by Logcheck and will therefore not appear in e-mail summaries. The keywords in this file reduce the amount of log messages that are e-mailed to the administrator, making it easier to find the real problems. The following are some examples of keywords from the logcheck.ignore file.

```
cron.*CMD
cron.*RELOAD
cron.*STARTUP
ftp-gw.*: exit host
ftp-gw.*: permit host
ftpd.*ANONYMOUS FTP LOGIN
http-gw.*: exit host
http-gw.*: permit host
identd.*Successful lookup
identd.*from:
named.*Response from
```

Most of the entries in this file are used to match messages that represent the normal operation of various system services. The keywords shown in the previous example represent normal processing of cron, ftp, http, identd, and named features.

Note Notice that all of the keyword phrases shown in the preceding example include an asterisk (*) wildcard. If you add your own keywords to this file, using asterisks and other wildcards can help you be specific about the log messages you exclude.

logcheck.violations

There are certain words that imply negative behavior occurring on your computer. Though these words may not be associated with any particular attack, Logcheck notes messages containing these words and displays them under the following heading and e-mails them to the system administrator:

```
Security Violations
=-=-=-=-=-=-=-=-=-=
```

The following is an example of some of the keywords that appear in the `logcheck.violations` file:

```
ATTACK
BAD
DEBUG
FAILURE
ILLEGAL
REFUSED
denied
failed
unapproved
attackalert
```

Adding your own keywords to the file can help you flag log messages that may be of particular concern for your computer. For example, you can add keywords that represent failures or improper use of services that are not standard Linux features but can be accessed from the network.

logcheck.violations.ignore

Use the `logcheck.violations.ignore` file to exclude messages that were matched from the `logcheck.violations` file, but are known to not represent security problems. By default, only the following entry is contained in this file:

```
stat=Deferred
```

The previous keyword causes Logcheck to ignore log messages from `sendmail` that represent e-mail messages that haven't been sent because the receiving server was temporarily unavailable. As you use Logcheck on your system, you will likely to repeatedly encounter certain log messages that represent no security threat. Add keywords here (as specifically as possible) to exclude those messages from appearing continuously in your e-mail messages from Logcheck.

Modifying syslog

The `syslog` service gathers the log messages of system activity that are used by Logcheck. Red Hat Linux, as well as most other Linux and UNIX systems, comes with `syslog` installed and operational by default. You can modify the `/etc/syslog.conf` file to tailor the behavior of `syslog` to best suit the way you use your system.

The `syslog` service is part of the `sysklogd` software package. To make sure that `sysklogd` is installed, type the following at a shell prompt:

```
# rpm -q sysklogd
```

The `syslogd` service is started automatically from the `/etc/init.d/syslog` start-up script. After that script has been run on your system, two daemon processes should be active on your system: `syslogd` and `klogd`. To see if they are running, type the following:

```
# ps -ax | grep log
```

The `/etc/syslog.conf` file contains information that defines which activities are logged, and from which system. Logcheck monitors three of the log files created by `syslog` (in the `/var/log` directory): `messages`, `secure`, and `maillog`. The following lines in the `/etc/syslog.conf` file instruct `syslog` to create those log files:

```
*.info;mail.none;news.none;authpriv.none;cron.none    /var/log/messages
authpriv.*                                             /var/log/secure
mail.*                                                 /var/log/maillog
```

Services on your Red Hat Linux system produce messages of different levels. Message levels, from most critical to least critical, are as listed in Table 14-9.

Table 14-9
Message Levels

Level	What It Means	Level	What It Means
alert	immediate action needed	err	error condition
crit	critical	info	purely informational
debug	detailed processing information	notice	important, but not an error
emerg	system unusable	warning	potential error

The line shown in the example indicates that all messages from the info level (*.info) and above are logged to the /var/log/messages file. However, messages of types mail, news, authpriv, and cron are excluded because they are sent to other log files. All authpriv (authpriv.*) messages are logged to the /var/log/secure file. mail messages (mail.*) are all logged to the /var/log/maillog file.

With this default configuration of syslog, Logcheck should catch all major security related activities. There are a few situations, however, where you may want to modify the /etc/syslog.conf file. For example, if you are receiving a lot of log messages for a particular type of service (such as ppp if you are having trouble with a dial-up connection), you may consider directing messages for that service to its own log file. Then, if Logcheck uncovers a problem, it's easier to go through only that log file for those messages relating to the problem service.

Another temporary change you may want to consider is if you need to debug a problem with your system. Changing *.info to *.debug temporarily can give you more details about a problem. (Just make sure you change it back later, or syslog will chew up too much of your system resources.)

Guarding Your Computer with PortSentry

While Logcheck gathers and sorts log messages that may represent attempts to break into your computer system, the PortSentry takes a more active approach to protecting your system from network intrusions. PortSentry can be installed and configured on a Red Hat Linux system to monitor selected TCP and UDP ports, and can then react to attempts to access these ports (presumably by people trying to break in) in ways that you choose.

Like Logcheck, PortSentry is another software package from Psionic Software, Inc., (www.psionic.com/abacus/portsentry). PortSentry acts as a nice compliment to Logcheck by actively looking for intrusion behavior on network ports. When PortSentry perceives an attack, it reacts to the attack (in ways that you choose) and produces log messages about the activity that can be forwarded to the system administrator by Logcheck.

PortSentry operates in several different modes. Each of these modes can be applied to monitoring of TCP and UDP ports. The PortSentry modes include:

✦ **Basic:** This is the mode PortSentry uses by default. Selected UDP and TCP ports in this mode are bound by PortSentry, giving the monitored ports the appearance of offering a service to the network.

✦ **Stealth:** In this mode, PortSentry listens to the ports at the socket level instead of binding the ports. This mode can detect a variety of scan techniques (strobe-style, SYN, FIN, NULL, XMAS and UDP scans), but because it is more sensitive than basic mode, it is likely to produce more false alarms.

✦ **Advanced Stealth:** This mode offers the same detection method as the regular stealth mode, but instead of monitoring only the selected ports, it monitors all ports below a selected number (port number 1023, by default). You can then exclude monitoring of particular ports. This mode is even more sensitive than Stealth mode and is, therefore, more likely to cause false alarms than regular stealth mode.

Note
When a port is "bound" by PortSentry or any other network service daemon process, all requests that come to that port from the network are handled by the binding process. For example, when the httpd daemon binds to port 80, requests for Web services from the network are processed by httpd.

Besides selecting the PortSentry mode and the ports that are monitored, you can also choose the response to your computer being scanned. By default, PortSentry can log intrusion attempts and block access to the intruder. However, PortSentry also offers ways of using other tools to respond to intrusions, including firewall rules, route changes, and host denial configuration. These methods of response are described later in this chapter.

Downloading and installing PortSentry

The `portsentry` package is not included in the Red Hat Linux distribution. You can download the package from any Red Hat Linux FTP mirror site. For example, you could use the following command to find a PortSentry package from an available FTP site:

```
# rpmfind portsentry
```

After PortSentry is downloaded, run the following command from the directory you downloaded it to:

```
# rpm -i portsentry*
```

The installed `portsentry` package consists of several configuration files (in the `/etc/portsentry` directory), the `portsentry` start-up script (`/etc/init.d/portsentry`), and the `portsentry` command (in `/usr/sbin`). There are also several README files of interest in the `/usr/share/doc/portsentry*` directory.

Note
The PortSentry package used in this example is portsentry-1.0.11.i386.rpm. Procedures described in this section may not work completely if you are using a different version of PortSentry. This version was included with the Red Hat Linux 7.1 PowerTools. The PowerTools CD is no longer being produced.

Using PortSentry as-is

As with Logcheck, you don't need to do anything to get PortSentry to work after it is installed. By default, here is what PortSentry does when you install the portsentry package:

✦ The /etc/init.d/portsentry start-up script runs automatically when you boot to run levels 3, 4, or 5 (levels 3 and 5 are most commonly used).

✦ The following port numbers are configured to be monitored by PortSentry in basic mode:

• **TCP:** 1, 11, 15, 143, 540, 635, 1080, 1524, 2000, 5742, 6667, 12345, 12346, 20034, 31337, 32771, 32772, 32773, 32774, 40421, 49724, 54320

• **UDP:** 1, 513, 635, 640, 641, 700, 32770, 32771, 32772, 32773, 32774, 31337, 54321

✦ In response to attacks (represented by scans of the ports being monitored), all further attempts to connect to any services for the protocol (TCP or UDP) will be blocked.

The computers that are blocked from accessing your system are listed in either the portsentry.blocked.tcp or portsentry.blocked.udp files (in the /var/portsentry directory), depending on which protocol was scanned (TCP or UPD). If you decide to run with just the default configuration, any computers that have access blocked by mistake can have access restored to them by removing entries created for those computers in these files.

Configuring PortSentry

Chances are that you will want to make some changes to the way that PortSentry runs. To change how PortSentry behaves, you can modify the /etc/portsentry/portsentry.conf file. In that file, you can choose which ports to monitor, the mode in which to monitor, and the responses to take when a scan is detected. The responses can include:

✦ Blocking access by the remote computer

✦ Rerouting messages from the remote computer to a dead host

✦ Adding a firewall rule to drop packets from the remote computer

The only other file you may want to change is the /etc/portsentry/portsentry. modes. The portsentry.modes file simply contains the modes that PortSentry can be run in.

Changing the portsentry.conf file

To edit the portsentry.conf file, as root user, open the /etc/portsentry/portsentry.conf file using any text editor. The following sections describe the information that can be changed in that file.

Selecting ports

The `portsentry.conf` file defines which ports are monitored in basic and stealth modes. By default, only basic TCP and UDP modes are active, so only those ports are monitored (unless you change to one of the stealth modes). The `TCP_PORTS` and `UDP_PORTS` options define which ports are monitored. Here is how they appear in the `portsentry.conf` file:

```
TCP_PORTS="1,11,15,143,540,635,1080,1524,2000,5742,6667,12345,12346,20034,31337,
    32771,32772,32773,32774,40421,49724,54320"
UDP_PORTS="1,513,635,640,641,700,32770,32771,32772,32773,32774,31337,54321"
```

Unless you are a TCP/IP expert, you're probably wondering what services these ports represent. The Internet Assigned Numbers Authority (IANA) assigns services to UDP and TCP ports. You can see these assignments at the following Web address:

```
www.iana.org/assignments/port-numbers
```

Network services in Red Hat Linux (as well as other Linux/UNIX systems) obtain port number assignments from the `/etc/services` file. So, in general, you can simply check the `/etc/services` file to find out most of the services that are assigned to ports being scanned.

The ports being assigned for monitoring are chosen based on a couple of different criteria. Lower port numbers (1, 11, 15, etc.) are chosen to catch port scanners that begin at port 1 and scan through a few hundred ports. If the scanner is blocked after accessing port 1, it won't be able to get information about any other ports that may be open on your computer. Another criterion is to include ports that are often checked specifically by intruders because those services may be vulnerable to attack. These include the `systat` (port 11) and `netstat` (port 15) services.

You will want to remove ports from the list in the `portsentry.conf` file if you are actually running the service assigned to that port. On the other hand, you may want to add ports to the list if you are paranoid about attacks and you want a bit more coverage. The `portsentry.conf` file contains some examples that you can uncomment (remove the # sign) so that more ports are monitored.

If you change from basic to stealth scans (as described in the "Changing the portsentry.modes file" section, later in this chapter), the ports that are monitored are those defined by the `ADVANCED_PORTS_TCP` and `ADVANCED_PORTS_UDP` options. Here is how those two options are set by default:

```
ADVANCED_PORTS_TCP="1023"
ADVANCED_PORTS_UDP="1023"
```

The two preceding entries indicate that all ports from 1 to 1023 are monitored. Monitoring higher port numbers can result in many more false alarms, so this practice is not recommended. If you find that PortSentry is being tripped accidentally, you may want to exclude the ports being tripped by using the `ADVANCED_EXCLUDE_TCP` and `ADVANCED_EXCLUDE_UDP` options. The following example shows how these two values are set by default:

```
ADVANCED_EXCLUDE_TCP="111,113,139"
ADVANCED_EXCLUDE_UDP="520,138,137,67"
```

By default, `ident` and NetBIOS services for TCP (ports 111, 113, and 139) and `route`, NetBIOS, and `Bootp` broadcasts for UDP (ports 520, 138, 127, and 67) are excluded from the advanced scan. (The exclusion is because a remote computer may hit these ports without representing any misuse.) If you are running in stealth mode, you should likewise exclude any services that you are running on your system by adding their port numbers to this list.

Identifying configuration files

Besides the portsentry.conf file, there are several other configuration files used by PortSentry. You can identify the locations of these other files within the portsentry.conf file. Here are how those files are defined:# Hosts to ignore
IGNORE_FILE="/etc/portsentry/portsentry.ignore"
# Hosts that have been denied (running history)
HISTORY_FILE="/var/portsentry/portsentry.history"
# Hosts that have been denied this session only (temporary until next restart)
BLOCKED_FILE="/var/portsentry/portsentry.blocked"

Chances are that you will not want to move the location of these configuration files. Here are some descriptions of what these files are used for:

✦ The `portsentry.ignore` file contains a list of all IP addresses that you do not want blocked (even if they improperly try to access ports on your computer). By default, all IP addresses assigned to the local computer are added to this file. You can add IP addresses of trusted computers, if you like.

✦ The `portsentry.history` file contains a list of IP addresses for computers that have been blocked from accessing your computer.

✦ The `portsentry.blocked.*` files contain a list of computers that have been blocked from accessing your computer during the current session. The `portsentry.blocked.tcp` file contains IP addresses of computers that have improperly scanned TCP ports on your computer. Addresses of computers that have been blocked after scanning UDP ports are contained in the `portsentry.blocked.udp` file.

Access to ports on your computer is only blocked during the current session (that is, until the next reboot or restart of PortSentry). So, to more permanently exclude remote computers, you should impose other restrictions (such as by using the `/etc/hosts.deny` file, a firewall command, or a reroute to a dead host). These methods are described later in this chapter.

Choosing responses

Someone scanning a port is like them checking a door in your house to see if it is locked. In most cases, it indicates that someone is checking your system for weaknesses. That is why, when another computer scans your ports, the default response from PortSentry is to block further access from the other computer to your computer for the duration of the current session. No action is taken to permanently block access from that computer. The BLOCK_UDP and BLOCK_TCP options in the portsentry.conf file set which type of automatic response is taken when ports are scanned. Here is how these options are set by default:

```
BLOCK_UDP="2"
BLOCK_TCP="2"
```

The value in quotation marks determines how PortSentry reacts to a scan of your ports by another computer. The following list describes each of these values.

✦ A value of "2" (the default value) causes access to be temporarily blocked to services for the scanned protocol (TCP or UDP) and for the action to be logged. Also, if any commands were defined to be run by a KILL_RUN_CMD option, that command is then run. (This option is not configured by default.)

✦ A value of "0" causes port scans to be logged, but not blocked.

✦ A value of "1" causes the KILL_ROUTE and KILL_HOSTS_DENY options to be run. (See the following list for descriptions of these options.) By default, further requests from the remote computer will be rerouted to a dead host, and the remote host's IP address will be added to the /etc/hosts.deny file, thereby denying access to network services.

Following are some suggestions on options you can use to can change the responses to your ports being scanned:

✦ **KILL_ROUTE:** This option runs the /sbin/route command to reroute requests from the remote computer to a dead host. By default, this option is set to the following value, which effectively drops the request from the remote computer:

```
KILL_ROUTE="/sbin/route add -host $TARGET$ gw 127.0.0.1"
```

Note

Instead of rerouting IP packets from the remote computer, you could use firewall rules to deny access. For example, if your computer uses ipchains firewalls (which Red Hat Linux uses by default), you can uncomment the following line to deny access from the remote computer to your computer:

```
KILL_ROUTE="/sbin/ipchains -I input -s $TARGET$ -j DENY -l"
```

This ipchains rule would deny (in other words, drop) all packets from the remote computer. To make this action permanent, you could add the ipchains options (from the -I to the end of the line) to the /etc/sysconfig/ipchains file, replacing the $TARGET$ with the actual IP address of the computer you want to deny access to.

✦ `KILL_HOSTS_DENY`: This option is used to deny requests for any network services that are protected by TCP wrappers. This option is set by default as follows:

```
KILL_HOSTS_DENY="ALL: $TARGET$"
```

With the preceding option set, `$TARGET$` is replaced by the IP address of the intruding remote computer and the line in quotes is added to the `/etc/hosts.deny` file. For example, if the remote computer's IP address were 10.0.0.59, the line that appears in `/etc/hosts.deny` would be:

```
ALL: 10.0.0.59
```

✦ `KILL_RUN_CMD`: Instead of using firewalls, rerouting, or TCP wrappers to deny an intruding computer from accessing your computer, you can choose any command you like in response. With the `BLOCK_TCP` and `BLOCK_UDP` options set to "2", the value of `KILL_RUN_CMD` is run in response to a scan of your monitored ports.

The value of `KILL_RUN_CMD` should be the full path to the script you want to run, plus any options. To include the IP address of the remote computer or the port number that was scanned, you could include the `$TARGET$` or `$PORT$` variables, respectively. Here is how the example appears that you would want to modify:

```
KILL_RUN_CMD="/some/path/here/script $TARGET$ $PORT$"
```

Caution

It is recommended that you not use any `KILL_RUN_CMD` to retaliate against the intruding remote computer. Firstly, it is quite possible that the computer that is scanning your ports has itself been cracked and is thus not a valid target for retaliations, and secondly, retaliation may simply incite the cracker into further attacks on you.

✦ `PORT_BANNER`: You can send a message to the person who sets off the PortSentry monitor by setting the `PORT_BANNER` option. By default, no message is defined. However, you can uncomment the following line to use that message. (An abusive message is not recommended.)

```
PORT_BANNER="** UNAUTHORIZED ACCESS PROHIBITED ***
    YOUR CONNECTION ATTEMPT HAS BEEN LOGGED. GO AWAY."
```

The number of scans from an intruding computer that PortSentry will accept before setting off the responses described above can be set by using the `SCAN_TRIGGER` option. By default, that option is set as follows:

```
SCAN_TRIGGER="0"
```

The "0" value means that you won't accept any scans from an intruding system. In other words, the first scan will trip the PortSentry monitor. You can increase this value to be tolerant of one or more errant scans (though you probably won't want to).

Changing the portsentry.modes file

The `/etc/portsentry/portsentry.modes` file defines the modes in which the PortSentry command is run at boot time. Here is how that file appears by default:

```
tcp
udp
#stcp
#sudp
#atcp
#audp
```

The `tcp` and `udp` options are the basic PortSentry modes for the TCP and UDP services, respectively. Your other choices of options include *stealth TCP* (`stcp`) and *advanced stealth TCP* (`atcp`) and *stealth UDP* (`sudp`) and *advanced stealth UDP* (`audp`). Only run one TCP service and one UDP service. So, if you uncomment a stealth or advanced stealth service, be sure to add a comment in front of the appropriate basic service.

To activate the new services, you would then execute the following command:

```
# /etc/init.d/portsentry restart
```

The new PortSentry modes will take effect immediately. Those new modes will also be in effect when your computer reboots.

Testing PortSentry

You can test that your ports are properly protected in different ways. What you want to do is run a program that a potential intruder would run and see if it trips the appropriate response from Portsentry. For example, you could use a port scanner to see how your ports appear to the outside world. You could also use a command, such as `telnet`, to try and set off a particular port to see if PortSentry catches it.

`nmap` is a popular software package for scanning TCP and UDP ports. You can give the `nmap` command a host name or IP address, and it will scan about 1500 ports on computer to see which ports are open (and presumably offering services that could potentially be cracked). You can download the `nmap` package from the following Web site: `www.insecure.org/nmap`.

An RPM of `nmap` is also available. You can download the `nmap-frontend` package, which contains a simple graphical interface to `nmap` called `xnmap`. I suggest that you install the packages on the system running PortSentry as well as on another system on your LAN (if one is available). Then run the following procedure on the PortSentry system to test it:

1. If PortSentry is running, shut it down by typing the following:

   ```
   # /etc/init.d/portsentry stop
   ```

2. Type the following `nmap` commands to see which ports are open on the local system:

   ```
   # nmap -sS -O 127.0.0.1
   # nmap -sU -O 127.0.0.1
   ```

   The output shows you which ports are currently offering services on your computer for TCP and UDP protocols, respectively.

3. If there are any services that you don't want open, you should turn off those services by using `chkconfig service off` (replacing *service* with the service name) or by editing the configuration file in the `/etc/xinetd.d` directory that represents the service and changing `disable = no` to `disable = yes`.

4. If there are services that you want to be available from your computer, make sure that the port numbers representing those services are not being monitored by PortSentry. Remove the port number from the `TCP_PORTS` and/or `UDP_PORTS` options in the `/etc/portsentry/portsentry.conf` file, or PortSentry will report that there is a possible stealth scan on the port.

5. Restart PortSentry as follows:

   ```
   # /etc/init.d/portsentry start
   ```

6. Run `nmap` again, as described previously. The ports offering legitimate services, as well as the ports being monitored by PortSentry, should all appear to be open.

7. Check the `/var/log/messages` file to make sure that PortSentry is not trying to monitor any ports on which you are offering services.

When you have determined that PortSentry is set up the way you would like it to be, run the `nmap` command from another computer on your network. This time, replace 127.0.0.1 with the name or IP address of the PortSentry computer. If everything is working properly, the first port that the remote computer scans on your PortSentry computer should cause all subsequent requests to scan ports to be denied.

Tip

Another way to set off PortSentry from another computer is with the `telnet` command. If, for example, PortSentry is monitoring port number 11 on your computer named `jake`, you could run the following command from the remote computer:

```
$ telnet jake 11
```

Telnet would then try to talk to a service on port 11. The attempt will be logged, and further attempts from the remote computer to access `jake` should be denied.

Tracking PortSentry intrusions

Besides blocking access to your system or performing some other action you assign, the activities of PortSentry are logged using your Red Hat Linux system's `syslog` utility. As a result, PortSentry's start-up, shutdown, and scan-detection activities are logged to your /var/log/messages file. The following are some examples of output from PortSentry in your /var/log/messages file.

```
portsentry[13259]: adminalert: Psionic PortSentry 1.0 is starting.
portsentry[13260]: adminalert: Going into listen mode on TCP port: 1
portsentry[13260]: adminalert: Going into listen mode on TCP port: 11
portsentry[13260]: adminalert: Going into listen mode on TCP port: 15
portsentry[13260]: adminalert: Going into listen mode on TCP port: 79
portsentry[13260]: adminalert: Going into listen mode on TCP port: 111
        .
        .
        .
portsentry[13260]: adminalert: PortSentry is now active and listening.

portsentry[]: attackalert:Connect from host:10.0.0.4/10.0.0.4 to TCP port: 31337
portsentry[]: attackalert: Connect from host: 10.0.0.4/10.0.0.4 to TCP port: 11
portsentry[]: attackalert: Host: 10.0.0.40 is already blocked. Ignoring
portsentry[]: attackalert: Connect from host: 10.0.0.4/10.0.0.4 to TCP port: 15
portsentry[]: attackalert: Host: 10.0.0.40 is already blocked. Ignoring
        .
        .
        .
portsentry[13371]: securityalert: Psionic PortSentry is shutting down
portsentry[13371]: adminalert: Psionic PortSentry is shutting down
```

The first part of the previous example of PortSentry log output shows PortSentry starting up. As PortSentry begins listening to each port, that port is noted in a separate log message.

The next set of messages shows the local computer being scanned. Someone from host 10.0.0.4 ran the `nmap` command to scan the ports on the computer being protected by PortSentry. PortSentry caught the scan of port 31337 and blocked all subsequent attempts to scan other ports.

Finally, the last set of messages shows PortSentry being shut down. This is noted as a security alert because someone that wasn't you could be shutting down PortSentry to hide the fact that they had broken into your system.

> **Note**
>
> If you have been running the Logcheck package (described earlier in this chapter), these messages show up in the e-mail messages you receive each hour from Logcheck. In particular, the attack alerts would appear under the "Active System Attack Alerts" heading. Also, the words "ACTIVE SYSTEM ATTACK!" would appear in the e-mail's message line.

Restoring access

If access was cut off to a computer that you wanted to have access, there are several things you can check to correct that problem:

✦ /etc/hosts.deny: See if the computer's IP address was mistakenly added to this file. This would cause network services to be denied to the host at that IP address.

✦ /var/portsentry/portsentry.blocked: Check that an entry for the computer's IP address wasn't added to the portsentry.blocked.udp or portsentry.blocked.tcp files.

✦ route: Run the /sbin/route command to see if messages from the computer are being rerouted to a dead host (probably the localhost).

✦ ipchains: Run the ipchains -L command to see if a new firewall was created to block access from the computer.

Tip   To make sure that access isn't cut off again, you can add the IP address of the remote computer to the /etc/portsentry/portsentry.ignore file. Future improper scans or requests for services won't cause the remote computer to be blocked.

Where to Get More Information about Security

This chapter should be a useful ally in your battle against security problems. Unfortunately, no chapter or book can win the war for you; computer security is an endless conflict fought on an ever-changing battlefield. Each new operating system upgrade brings with it the potential for new security holes. Each new application can have its own hidden perils. Even if you change nothing on your network, crackers may discover some new exploit that had previously remained hidden. Fortunately, resources on the Internet can alert you to the most recently discovered security vulnerabilities and tell you how to combat them.

CERT

The CERT Coordination Center is part of the Survivable Systems Initiative at the Software Engineering Institute, a federally funded research and development center at Carnegie-Mellon University. CERT stands for Computer Emergency Response Team. It was founded in 1988 by DARPA (the Defense Applied Research Projects Agency) in response to the now infamous Internet Worm Incident. Initially, CERT was intended to be the central place where one could report all computer security incidents. Since 1988, CERT has broadened its purpose to include:

    ✦ Assisting in the creation of new incident response teams.

    ✦ Coordinating the efforts of teams when responding to large-scale incidents.

    ✦ Providing training to incident response professionals.

    ✦ Researching the causes of security vulnerabilities, prevention of vulnerabilities, system security improvement, and survivability of large-scale networks.

As part of these efforts, CERT issues advisories that warn of newly discovered security problems and explain how to protect against them. These advisories are available at the CERT Web site at `www.cert.org`. You can also have CERT advisories e-mailed to you by subscribing to the CERT Advisory Mailing List.

To subscribe to the CERT advisory mailing list, send email to majordomo@cert.org. In the body of the message, type:

```
subscribe cert-advisory
```

To remove your name from the CERT mailing list, send email to majordomo@cert.org.   In the body of the message, type:

```
unsubscribe cert-advisory
```

After you have subscribed to the mailing list, you will eventually begin to receive CERT Advisory e-mail messages. In an average month, you can expect several messages from the CERT mailing list. CERT issues warnings on a wide variety of computer security topics encompassing many operating systems and applications, so not every message will apply to your situation. Nevertheless, it is a good idea to read each message carefully to become familiar with the broader security risks of the Internet. A typical CERT Advisory is divided into several sections:

    ✦ **Topic** — A one-line description of the vulnerability.

    ✦ **Effected Systems** — Who is vulnerable. For example, it may say, "This vulnerability affects Red Hat Linux systems versions 5.0 and older."

    ✦ **Overview** — A very brief description of the vulnerability.

    ✦ **Description** — A more in-depth discussion of the exploit and the service it attacks.

    ✦ **Impact** — What sort of damage can occur. For example, "By exploiting this bug, anyone with anonymous FTP access to your system can obtain root access."

    ✦ **Solution** — What you can do to fix the problem, such as instructions for downloading and installing software patches, or the appropriate flags to change in configuration files.

CERT also maintains an online library of security-related instructional materials and software tools. I strongly recommend that you visit CERT's Web site at `www.cert.org`.

CIAC

Another good source for computer security information is the CIAC Web site at `www.ciac.org`. CIAC stands for Computer Incident Advisory Capability and is affiliated with the Department of Energy. Like CERT, it posts advisories and other types of helpful security information.

AntiOnline

If you are really serious about defending your system from cracker attacks, you need to know the tools and resources that crackers have at their disposal. The AntiOnline Web site at `www.antionline.com` is very useful in that respect. AntiOnline has reports on actual computer break-ins and other cracker-related news. AntiOnline even keeps an archive of the actual tools that cracker use (though you will need to sign up as a registered AntiOnline member to access the archive). You may be surprised and frightened at the number of tools crackers have access to.

Caution Remember, breaking into a computer you do not own is ILLEGAL! Don't do it. The last I heard, they don't let you take your Red Hat Linux box with you when they send you to prison. Breaking into your own computers, however, can be a great way to test your security, and that is where AntiOnline can be very useful. Make no mistake; the crackers already have these tools. By giving us a peek into the cracker's tool bag, AntiOnline is helping to level the playing field.

Newsgroups

There are newsgroups that contain a wealth of knowledge about computer security. You may want to consider reading these newsgroups:

✦ comp.security.announce — Contains announcements from CERT about security. This group is moderated.

✦ comp.security.misc — Covers general security issues of computers and networks.

✦ comp.security.pgp.announce — Covers the new PGP versions and utilities.

✦ comp.security.ssh — Contains information about the SSH package, secure remote login, and tunneling tools.

✦ comp.security.unix — Covers UNIX security, including items that relate to Red Hat Linux system security.

Other miscellaneous tools and resources

The following are some useful tools that relate to computer security. Using the Web addresses provided for each, you can usually download the software.

- ✦ FWTK
  - **Homepage:** www.fwtk.org/
  - **Description:** The FireWall Tool Kit. A useful collection of programs and libraries for building your own firewall.
- ✦ Kerberos
  - **Homepage:** http://web.mit.edu/kerberos/www/
  - **Description:** An authentication system for network applications. It uses Private Key Cryptography.
- ✦ Merlin
  - **Homepage:** www.ciac.org/ciac/ToolsUnixSysMon.html#Merlin
  - **Description:** A single, graphical, front-end for a variety of security tools, including SPI-Net, Tiger, COPS, Crack, and Tripwire.
- ✦ SATAN
  - **Homepage:** www.fish.com/~zen/satan
  - **Description:** A security-auditing tool that tests your security by mimicking the behavior of an actual cracker. It tries a broad range of exploits to try and get into your system.
- ✦ Swatch
  - **Homepage:** ftp://coast.cs.purdue.edu/pub/tools/unix/logutils/swatch/
  - **Description:** A program that monitors log files and reacts to unusual system activity, usually by alerting the system administrator.
- ✦ SecurityFocus
  - **Homepage:** www.securityfocus.com
  - **Description:** This Web site was set up to encourage discussion of computer security topics. It contains a database of security resources and information. SecurityFocus maintains the Bugtraq mailing list, which is a popular mailing list for discussing security topics. To subscribe to Bugtraq, send an e-mail message to LISTSERV@SECURITYFOCUS.COM, containing the message: SUBSCRIBE BUGTRAQ *Lastname*, *Firstname*.

Security-related terminology

Here are a few terms that are related to computer security. You may want to refer to these terms if you are posting questions to newsgroups about security.

- ✦ **backdoor:** A hole placed in your security by a cracker. It allows the cracker to bypass normal security and gain easy access to your system.

✦ **buffer overflow:** A security exploit that takes advantage of a specific type of software bug. A cracker sends excessive data to a faulty system program, causing the program to overwrite part of its running program code with code the cracker supplies.

✦ **cracker:** An individual with malicious intent who breaks into computer systems or breaks copy protection on software products.

✦ **DES:** Data Encryption Standard. A common form of private-key encryption. Other, stronger forms of encryption are replacing it.

✦ **exploit:** The method by which a cracker gains access to your system.

✦ **hacker:** Someone who works with or programs computers in a creative way for the pure enjoyment of it.

✦ **NSA:** The National Security Agency. The U.S. government agency that handles encryption and communications-related intelligence work.

✦ **PAM:** Pluggable Authentication Module. The software component on a Linux system that provides password authentication for user logins and other services.

✦ **SSL:** Secure Sockets Layer. A network protocol that uses public-key encryption. It is the primary protocol used for electronic commerce on the Web.

✦ **Trojan horse:** A malicious program that mimics the behavior of a legitimate system program, usually for the purpose of stealing passwords.

✦ **virus:** A self-replicating program that can spread itself from computer to computer, usually by attaching itself to other programs.

✦ **worm:** A program that copies itself from computer to computer over the network, consuming system resources as it goes.

Summary

With the rise of the Internet, security has become a critical issue for nearly all computer users. The Red Hat Linux operating system is a powerful tool that can help you get the most out of the Internet, but care must be taken to prevent break-ins by crackers. Proper use of password security in Red Hat Linux is critical, as is proper configuration of the various network services.

Understanding system log files so that you can recognize a cracker attack is another important part of defending your system from crackers. In general, knowledge is your most important tool. Learn everything you can about how your Linux system works and where the vulnerabilities are.

And remember, good security is not a one-time job; it is an ongoing process that requires constant vigilance. Take advantage of the many great security tools that are available on the Internet. Applications such as Crack, Tiger, and Tripwire can help you keep your system secure. Run them periodically to make sure your system stays secure.

Logcheck and PortSentry are software packages produced by Psionic Software, Inc., to help protect your Red Hat Linux system from intrusions from the network. The Logcheck package scans your system logs for messages that may represent break-in attempts. PortSentry takes an active approach to protecting your system by monitoring ports and responding in a variety of ways to those who try to improperly access those ports.

Subscribe to the CERT and CIAC mailing lists and install security-related patches as soon as they become available. It is better to spend a few minutes upgrading a system program than to spend many hours rebuilding an entire server.

✦   ✦   ✦

Red Hat Linux Network and Server Setup

Setting Up a Local Area Network

In the home or in a small business, Red Hat Linux can help you connect to other Linux, Windows, and Macintosh computers so that you can share your computing equipment (files, printers, and devices). Add a connection to the Internet and routing among multiple LANs (described in Chapter 16), and Red Hat Linux can serve as a focal point for network computing in a larger enterprise.

This chapter helps you set up your own local area network (LAN). The procedures described here provide a foundation for sharing the computing resources in your home or organization. In particular, the chapter describes how to use Ethernet cards, wiring, and protocols to connect computers. It then tells you specifically how to configure your Red Hat Linux computer so that it can communicate with other computers.

Understanding Red Hat Linux and Local Area Networks

Connecting the computers in your organization via a LAN can save you a lot of time and money. The amount of money you put into networking hardware, even in a small configuration (less than five or six users), can save you from buying multiple printers, backup media, and other hardware. Add a single, shared Internet connection and you no longer need multiple modems and Internet accounts.

With a LAN, you don't have to run down the hall anymore with your file on a floppy disk to print it on your friend's printer. Information that had to wait for the mailroom to make the rounds can be sent in an instant to anyone (or everyone) on your LAN.

With a LAN, you begin to open the greatest potential of Red Hat Linux — its ability to act as a server on a network. Because Red Hat Linux is more robust and feature-rich than other computing systems (certainly for the price), adding it to your LAN can provide a focal point to workstations that could use Red Hat Linux as a file server, a mail server, a printer server, or a news server. (Those features are described later in this book.)

Creating a LAN and configuring it to be useful consists of three steps:

1. **Setting up the hardware** — This entails choosing a network topology, purchasing the equipment you need, and installing it (adding cards and connecting wires).

2. **Setting up Ethernet** — Red Hat Linux must be able to recognize the Ethernet card in your computer, install a driver for it, and make it available for use by Linux. (For supported cards, this is done easily during Red Hat Linux installation.) Ethernet is the protocol that enables messages to get from one machine to another on your LAN.

3. **Configuring TCP/IP** — To use most of the networking applications and tools that come with Red Hat Linux, you must have TCP/IP configured. TCP/IP lets you communicate not only with computers on your LAN, but to any computers that you can reach on your LAN, modem, or other network connection.

This chapter focuses on Ethernet as the underlying network because it is by far the most popular LAN protocol. Protocols are rules for communications between computers. To expand beyond your LAN — for example, to share an Internet connection from your LAN to the Internet — there are several other protocols that you could use.

Ethernet is a CSMA-CD type of network, which stands for *Carrier Sense Multiple Access with Collision Detection*. On this type of network, data is broadcast on the network for all to see, then picked up by the computer for which the information is intended. The collision detection part is what helps the network detect and recover from data collisions.

 Information on how to set up routers to communicate beyond your LAN is contained in Chapter 16.

In addition to Ethernet, you need to configure TCP/IP. TCP/IP is the standard that defines the protocols and addressing scheme (unique names and numbers) that allow computers to interoperate around the entire world. TCP/IP is a transport protocol. This means that it provides end-to-end connection service between host computers. The actual underlying physical network can be carried out by a variety of network service providers, which can rely on Ethernet, telephone lines, direct connections, or other media to physically carry messages. Different ways of arranging and connecting your computers in a LAN are discussed in the next section.

Choosing a network topology and equipment

Even with a simple LAN, you need to make some decisions about network topology (how computers are connected). You also need to make some decisions about network equipment (network interface cards, wires, hubs, and so on).

LAN topologies

Most small office and home LANs connect computers together in one of the following topologies:

✦ **Star topology** — In this arrangement, each computer contains a Network Interface Card (NIC) that connects with a cable to a central hub. The cabling is referred to as twisted pair cable, resembling the wires used to plug a telephone into the wall. Other equipment, such as printers and fax machines, can also be connected to the hub in a star topology. Figure 15-1 is an example of a star topology.

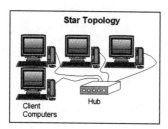

Figure 15-1: In a star topology, machines on the network connect to a central hub.

✦ **Bus topology** — Instead of using hubs, the bus topology connects computers in a chain from one to the next. The cabling usually used is referred to as coaxial, or Thin Ethernet cable. A "T" connector attaches to each computer's NIC, then to two adjacent computers in the chain. At the two ends of the chain, the T connectors are terminated. Figure 15-2 is an example of a bus topology.

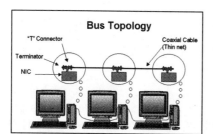

Figure 15-2: A bus topology chains computers together without using a hub.

✦ **Ring topology** — This is a far less popular topology than star and bus topologies. In a ring topology, computers connect to a ring of wires on which tokens are taken and passed by computers that want to send information on the network. This type of topology typically uses IBM's token ring protocols.

For our purposes, we focus on star and bus topologies. Common to both topologies is the protocol used to send data over those wires — the Ethernet protocol.

Star topology is the more common one among small office and home networks. There are several reasons why this is so. It's easy to add and remove computers without disrupting other computers on the network. The star cabling (twisted pair) is more flexible, less expensive, and generally easier to handle than bus cabling (coaxial). Also, many inexpensive NICs do not have the BNC connectors needed for the bus topology.

> I have used bus topology (coaxial cables and BNC connectors) when I had some old 10 Mbps NICs hanging around and only a couple of computers to connect. If you are starting a new installation, I recommend star topology. The equipment is easier to deal with and more readily available. Also, coaxial cables offer no easy way to upgrade to 100 Mbps technology.

Bus topology does have some advantages over star topology, however. Although the cabling is slightly more expensive, cost savings can occur because no hub is needed. The coaxial cables are also considered extremely reliable.

Both topologies have different limitations on the number of machines that can be connected and the distances between machines. Star topology's limit is 1024 nodes on the network; bus topology's limit is 30 nodes. The total length of a bus network cannot be more than 185 meters. For a star topology, each computer must be no more than 100 meters from the farthest computer on the LAN. In other words, a 50-meter cable connecting each of two computers would reach the limit.

LAN equipment

The equipment that you need to connect your LAN can include some or all of the following:

✦ **Network Interface Card (NIC)** — Typically, one of these cards goes into a slot in each computer. For Ethernet networks, the cards can transmit data at 10 Mbps or 100 Mbps. Gigabit (1000 Mbps) NICs are also now available, but are quite a bit more expensive.

> If you are looking to upgrade your network in the near future, but still have a lot of computers around that run at 10 Mbps, you may want to consider buying new NICs that run at both 10 Mbps and 100 Mbps. When you switch over to 100 Mbps, you will have fewer cards to replace.

✦ **Cables** — For star topologies, cables are referred to as *twisted pair*. Connectors at each end of the cable are RJ-45 plugs, similar to those used on telephone cables. Ethernet interfaces are either 10Base-T (10 Mbps speeds) or 100Base-TX (100 Mbps speeds). These cables plug into the computer's NIC on one end and the hub on the other.

For bus topologies, coaxial cables are used. These cables are also referred to as thin Ethernet cables, or *thin net*. (There are also thick net cables, which are more expensive and more cumbersome to deal with. These are rarely used and are primarily for network backbones.)

The connector on coaxial cables is a barrel connector (BNC). A "T" connector attaches to the BNC port on the NIC. In the middle of the daisy chain, each computer connects to two adjacent computers using the T connector. At the two ends of the chain, the computer connects to one adjacent computer, then uses a terminator at the other end of the T to end the chain.

Figure 15-3 shows an example of a twisted pair cable with an RJ-45 connector used for star topologies. Figure 15-4 shows a coaxial (thin net) cable with a BNC connector and a T connector used for bus topologies. A terminator at the end of the T connector shows that this is the end of a chain. If it were in the middle of the chain, the other side of the T would be connected to the next computer in the chain.

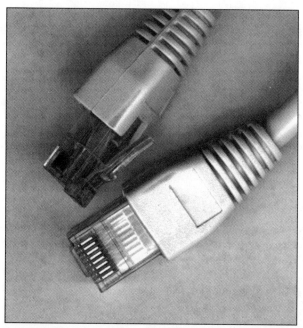

Figure 15-3: A star topology's twisted pair cables have RJ-45 connectors (similar to telephone cable connectors).

Figure 15-4: A bus topology has coaxial cables that must be terminated (as shown) or continued from the T.

✦ **Hubs**—With the star topology, a hub is required to connect the computers. For the bus topology a hub can be used, but is not necessary. Sometimes hubs are also referred to as repeaters or concentrators because they receive signals from the nodes connected to them and send the signals on to other nodes. Intel and 3Com make popular, inexpensive hubs for small offices.

The questions you need to answer when choosing a hub are how many ports you need and how fast you want your network to go. If you need to expand in the future, hubs can be connected together. Choice of speeds is 10 Mbps or 100 Mbps. The higher speed means more expensive cards and a more expensive hub, but significantly better performance. Some 10 Mbps hubs offer one or more coaxial connectors.

✦ **Switches**—A switch lets you divide subnetworks that are getting too large into segments that are more manageable. A switch can reduce network traffic by directing messages intended for a specific computer directly to that computer. This is as opposed to a hub, which broadcasts all data to all nodes.

One piece of equipment that I won't go into yet is a router. A router is used to direct information from the LAN to other LANs or the Internet.

Machines that carry out routing functions are described in Chapter 16.

Choosing peer-to-peer vs. client/server models

Although the Ethernet hub sees all computers on the network as equal, the computers on that hub can actually play different roles. The models used to describe the two general types of computing environments are client/server and peer-to-peer. Red Hat Linux is usually described as a server computer. However, Red Hat Linux can also function quite happily as a client machine or in a peer-to-peer network.

Client/server model

In a client/server model, one or more server computers manage most network services. The server acts as a focal point for administration and security of the network. It may also control printers, databases of information, backup media, and other resources that need to be made available to client computers on the network. The client is the person (or more correctly, the software program) that requests services from the network.

A server computer can act as a server for some or all of these services:

✦ **Print Server** — This maintains and manages one or more printers.

✦ **File Server** — A central repository for documents and databases of information.

✦ **Mail Server** — This gathers e-mail intended for clients on the network and makes it accessible to those clients.

✦ **FTP Server** — This is used to make files available to users who log in to the server over the network. (Anonymous FTP is a way of making files available to strangers.)

✦ **Web Server** — This makes Web pages (HTML) and related content available to users on the network.

✦ **News Server** — This gathers messages from Usenet newsgroups, allowing users to read and respond to topics of interest.

Red Hat Linux can act as any of the server types described above. However, with a growing number of productivity applications becoming available for Linux and friendly X-based desktops (such as KDE and GNOME), Red Hat Linux is beginning to make a better case for becoming a client system as well.

Because Red Hat Linux can run applications as well as offer services, a purer example of a network server is NetWare (from Novell, Inc.). A NetWare server has no way of running applications. It is tuned to store and secure files efficiently, as well as manage groups of printers. With the addition of ZENworks and NDS, NetWare can manage databases of information on all the components on a network.

Chapters 17 through 23 describe how to set up different kinds of servers in Red Hat Linux.

Peer-to-peer model

In a peer-to-peer network, computers generally behave as equals. Each computer has most of what it needs to operate on its own. Any computer on the network may offer services to other computers. One computer may share the contents of a CD-ROM, whereas another may offer its printer for use by others.

A typical peer-to-peer network is one where several employees in a business each have a computer at their desk. A shared printer may be connected to one person's computer, whereas a tape backup system may be connected to another.

The drawback with peer-to-peer networks is that if there is a big demand for your printer or other device, your computer's performance may suffer (and so may your work). That's why larger networks tend to offload shared services to a server.

After you have made a choice about the typology and computing model you are going to use, the following sections tell you how to actually configure your computers so that they can communicate together.

Setting Up an Ethernet LAN

After you physically install your Ethernet card, it is possible that Red Hat Linux will automatically detect your card and assign it to the first Ethernet interface on your system (eth0). If Red Hat Linux does find your card, after you connect your hardware you don't need to do much more than assign addresses.

Follow this procedure to set up your LAN and install your LAN cards:

1. Choose a network topology. Earlier in this chapter, I described several different network topologies. This procedure assumes that you are using either a star or a bus Ethernet topology.

2. Choose your LAN hardware. You need an Ethernet NIC for each computer on your network, as well as cables that reach from each computer to the hub. Also, you need to purchase a hub. (See the description of these components earlier in this chapter.)

   Before you purchase a new NIC, read the following discussion on choosing an Ethernet card. Red Hat Linux does not support all NICs. Choosing one that has already been tested with Red Hat Linux can save you some headaches.

3. Install your NIC cards. Power down your computer and physically install the NIC card (following the manufacturer's instructions).

4. Power up your system.

5. If Red Hat Linux is not installed yet, install the software and reboot (as instructed.) See the discussion on adding Ethernet during Red Hat installation for information on how to answer Ethernet-related questions and the section on configuring host computers for information on adding TCP/IP host names and IP addresses.

   When the system comes up, your Ethernet card and interface (eth0) should be ready to use. See the section "Checking Your Ethernet Connection" later in this chapter to learn how to check if your Ethernet connection is working.

Choosing an Ethernet card

Support for many Ethernet cards is available in Red Hat Linux. If you are adding Red Hat Linux to a computer that already has an Ethernet card installed, you can check the list of supported cards or you can just go ahead and install Red Hat. Red Hat Linux may detect the board automatically. If you have a laptop computer that uses a PCMCIA Ethernet card, the card will probably be detected when you boot your computer.

To find out what Ethernet cards are supported, refer to the descriptions of supported networking hardware in the `/usr/src/linux*/Documentation/networking` directory. To see these descriptions, you need to have the kernel-source package installed.

Recommended Ethernet cards

The Ethernet-HOWTO recommends the following Ethernet cards as being mature and well-tested in Red Hat Linux. If you want to use one of the cards, you just have to make sure that you have the type of card slot in your computer that the card requires. Here are cards for 16-bit ISA and PCI slots:

Recommended 16-Bit ISA Cards:

- ✦ SMC-Ultra/EtherEZ
- ✦ SMC-Elite (WD80x3)
- ✦ 3c509
- ✦ Lance
- ✦ NE2000

Recommended PCI Cards:

- ✦ 3Com Vortex/Boomerang (3c59x/3c9xx)
- ✦ DEC Tulip (21xxx)
- ✦ Intel EtherExpressPro 100

In addition to these cards, there are many, many cards that work well. You need to gauge the demands on your network to decide if you can get by with a 10 Mbps network or if you need 100 Mbps. Of course, if you are used to a 28.8 Kbps modem connection to the Internet, any working LAN will look fast to you. Even an old 8-bit Ethernet card can provide about 20 times the speed of that old modem.

Caution Eight-bit Ethernet cards aren't being made any more. You can, however, find them anywhere that used computer parts are sold. For light performance, you can use wd8003, 3c503, and ne1000 cards. Avoid 3c501 cards because they are said to provide poor performance.

Laptop (PCMCIA) Ethernet cards

There are a large number of Ethernet drivers available for laptop computers (typically using PCMCIA cards). PCMCIA stands for Personal Computer Memory Card International Association. Essentially, it is a standard that enables small, removable cards to be used to connect devices to a laptop computer.

I have a Netgear 10/100 Mbps PCMCIA card (model FA 410Txc) in my laptop. Red Hat Linux detected my card automatically. I simply configured the eth0 interface using the Network Configuration as described in the discussion on adding your host information after installation later in this chapter. (Basically, what you still need to do is assign an IP address to the interface and decide if you want your LAN connection to start automatically at boot time.)

PCMCIA cards that are supported in Red Hat Linux are defined in the file /etc/pcmcia/config. There are more than 100 PCMCIA Ethernet cards listed, a handful of wireless PCMCIA LAN drivers, and a couple of Token Ring PCMCIA cards. The Ethernet-HOWTO is not up to date with all the PCMCIA Ethernet cards that are now supported. Be sure to check this file before buying a card (or giving up on the one that you have).

Note   Linux probes for PCMCIA cards by launching the /etc/init.d/pcmcia script. Options required for your PCMCIA cards are contained in the /etc/sysconfig/ pcmcia file.

Adding Ethernet during Red Hat installation

When you install Red Hat Linux, if your Ethernet card is already installed, the installation procedure will let you set up Ethernet using that card. Figure 15-5 shows the Ethernet setup screen you see during installation.

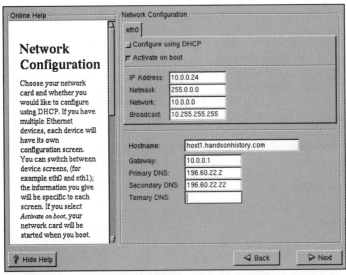

Figure 15-5: Configure your Ethernet card for TCP/IP during installation.

The information you enter into the Network Configuration screen is described in Chapter 2. If you didn't set up your network at that point, you can do it now as described in the next section.

Adding Ethernet after Red Hat is installed

If Red Hat Linux is already installed when you want to add your Ethernet card, simply power down the system, install the card, and reboot the computer. If the card is supported, it is likely that the proper driver will be found and assigned to the board using the eth0 interface. At this point, you simply need to do a bit of configuration (mostly to assign an IP address to the interface) using the Network Configuration window (described in the "Adding host names and IP addresses" section later in this chapter).

Adding two Ethernet cards

If your computer is acting as a router between two LANs (or if it simply is connected to two LANs), you may need to do some special setup to get two LAN cards to work on your computer. If both cards are PCI or EISA LAN cards, they will probably be autodetected so no further configuration will be needed to add the cards. However, if at least one card is an ISA cards, you will need to add some information to your /etc/modules.conf file.

To add two ISA cards to your computer, you need to identify the Ethernet interface associated with each card (eth0, eth1, etc.), then identify the I/O base addresses for each card. Then you must add this information to the /etc/modules.conf file. The following is an example:

```
alias eth0 3c501
alias eth1 3c503
options 3c501 io=0x280
options 3c503 io=0x300
```

In this example, there is a 3Com 3c501 assigned to the eth0 interface and a 3c503 card assigned to eth1. The base addresses are 0x280 for the 3c501 card and 0x300 for the 3c503 card. The modules are loaded after your computer boots. If both cards you are adding are of the same type, you may be able to use a single options line (for example, options wd io=0x280,0x300) or, if the module supports only one card at a time, you may need two options lines (which results in the module being loaded twice).

The best reference for supported Ethernet cards and modules is Appendix A of the Red Hat Linux Reference Guide. This guide contains a listing of Ethernet cards, the modules needed to use them, and the options you need with each module.

For more information on adding multiple Ethernet cards, refer to the Ethernet-HOWTO document. You can also check out the Multiple Ethercards document at `www.scyld.com/expert/multicard.html`.

Cross-Reference

> Chances are that if you are adding two or more LAN cards to one computer, you may want that computer to act as a router between the two networks. Setting up routing functions is described in Chapter 16.

Configuring Host Computers

Each computer you communicate with (including your computer) must have a unique address on the network. In TCP/IP, each computer needs to be assigned an IP address and (usually) a host name. When a user runs a program to communicate with another computer, the user typically enters the computer name (or IP address) that it wants to communicate with. There are two basic ways to assign a host name and IP address to the network interfaces:

✦ **Static Addresses** — With static IP addresses, each computer has its IP address entered in manually. This can be done at Red Hat Linux installation time or later using the Network Configuration window. With this method, the computer has the same IP address each time it boots.

✦ **Dynamic Addresses** — With dynamic addresses, a client computer gets its IP address assigned from a server on the network when the client boots. The most popular protocol for providing dynamic addresses is called Dynamic Host Configuration Protocol. With this method, a client computer wouldn't necessarily have the same IP address each time it boots.

For this first example, let's assume that you are setting up a LAN with no outside connections. So, in this section I describe how to use static IP addresses. This is where each computer has a hard IP address and maintains its own list of host names and IP addresses for the computers it communicates with. This will work fine for communicating with a few computers on a LAN.

Tip

> If you expect to add and remove computers regularly from your LAN or if you have a limited number of IP addresses, you should use DHCP to assign IP addresses. Chapter 23 describes how to set up a DHCP server.

Understanding IP addresses

An IP address is a four-part number, with each part represented by a number from 0 to 255 (256 numbers total). Part of that IP address represents the network the computer exists on, whereas the remainder identifies the specific host on that network. Here is an example of an IP address:

```
192.168.35.121
```

Originally, IP addresses were grouped together and assigned to an organization that needed IP addresses, based on IP address classes. Later, a more efficient method, referred to as Classless Inter-Domain Routing (CIDR), was created to improve routing and waste fewer IP addresses. These two IP address methods are described in the following sections.

IP address classes

Unfortunately, it's not so easy to understand which part of an IP address represents the network and which represents the host without some explanation of how IP addresses are structured. The way IP addresses are assigned is that a network administrator is given a pool of addresses. The administrator can assign specific host addresses within that pool as new computers are added to the organization's local network. There are three basic classes of IP addresses, each representing a different size network:

✦ **Class A** — Each Class A address has a number between 0 and 127 as its first part. Host numbers within a Class A network are represented by any combination of numbers in the next three parts. A class A network therefore contains millions of host numbers (approximately $256 \times 256 \times 256$, with a few special numbers being invalid). Whole Class A networks were once assigned only to the largest organizations but, I have been told, are no longer assigned. A valid Class A network number is:

```
24.
```

✦ **Class B** — A Class B IP address has a number between 128 and 191 in its first part. With a Class B network, however, the second part also represents the network. This enables a Class B network to have more than 64,000 host addresses (256×256). A whole Class B network is also rarely assigned. A valid Class B network number is:

```
135.84
```

✦ **Class C** — A Class C IP address begins with a number between 192 and 223 in its first part. With a Class C network, the first three parts of an IP address represent the network, whereas only the last part represents a specific host. This makes it so each Class C network can have 254 numbers (the numbers 0 and 254 can't be assigned to hosts). Here is an example of a Class C network number:

```
194.122.56
```

When IP addresses were created, nobody expected that, even though this numbering scheme represented millions of potential addresses, there wouldn't be enough to go around. Now, if you get an official pool of addresses assigned to you for the Internet, you will get either a Class C address or part of a Class A or Class B address. The question becomes: How can a network number be divided among several networks? The answer is: by using a netmask.

Understanding netmasks

Let's say that you are assigned the Class B address 135.84, but you are only given the pool of numbers available to the address 135.84.118. How do you tell your network that every address beginning with 135.84.118 represents a host on your network, but that other addresses beginning with 135.84 should be routed to another network? The answer is with the netmask.

The netmask essentially identifies the network number for a network. When you assign the IP address that is associated with your computer's interface to the LAN (eth0), you are asked for a netmask. By default, your computer will fill in a number that masks the part of your IP address that represents the Class of your network. For example, the default netmasks for Class A, B, and C networks are the following:

- ✦ Class A netmask: 255.0.0.0
- ✦ Class B netmask: 255.255.0.0
- ✦ Class C netmask: 255.255.255.0

Now, if your network was assigned the network number 135.84.118, to tell your computer that 135.84.118 is the network number and not 135.84 (as it normally would be for a Class B address), add a netmask of 255.255.255.0. Thus, your network has available host numbers of 1 to 254 (which would go into the fourth part of the number).

To further confuse the issue, you could mask only one or more bits that are part of the IP address. Instead of using the number 255, you could use any other number from 1 to 254 to mask only part of the numbers in that part of the address. (The numbers that you can use for each network get rather strange when you do this.)

Classless Inter-Domain Routing

The class method of allocating IP addresses had several major drawbacks. First, few organizations fell neatly into one class or another. For most organizations, a Class C address (up to 256 IP addresses) was too small, and a Class B address (up to 65,534 IP addresses) was too big. The result was a lot of wasted numbers in a world where IP addresses were running short. Second, IP classes resulted in too many routing table entries. As a result, routers were becoming overloaded with information.

The Classless Inter-Domain Routing addressing scheme set out to deal with these problems. The scheme is similar to IP address classes, but offers much more flexibility in assigning how much of the 32-bit IP address is the network identifer. Instead of the first 8, 16, or 32 bits identifying the network, 13 to 27 bits could identify the network. As a result, groups of assigned IP addresses could contain from 32 to about 524,000 host addresses.

To indicate the network identifier, a CIDR IP address is followed by a slash (/) and then a number from 13 to 27. A smaller number indicates a network containing more hosts. Here is an example of an IP address that uses the CIDR notation:

```
128.8.27.18/16
```

In this example, the first 16 bits (128.8) represent the network number and the remainder (27.18) represent the specific host number. This network number can contain up to 65,536 hosts (the same as a class B address). The following list shows how many hosts can be represented in networks using different numbers to identify the network:

```
/13    524,288 hosts
/14    262,144 hosts
/15    131,072 hosts
/16     65,536 hosts
/17     32,768 hosts
/18     16,382 hosts
/19      8,192 hosts
/20      4,096 hosts
/21      2,048 hosts
/22      1,024 hosts
/23        512 hosts
/24        256 hosts
/25        128 hosts
/26         64 hosts
/27         32 hosts
```

The CIDR addressing scheme also helps reduce the routing overload problem by having a single, high-level route represent many lower level routes. For example, an Internet service provider could be assigned a single /13 IP network and assign the 500,000-plus addresses to its customers. Routers outside the ISP would only need to know how to reach the ISP for those half-million addresses. The ISP would then be responsible for maintaining routing information for all of the host routes with that network address.

Getting IP addresses

So, what is the impact of assigning IP addresses for the computers on your LAN? How you choose which IP addresses to use depends on your situation. If you are part of a large organization, you should get addresses from the network administrator of your organization. Even if you don't connect to other LANs in your organization, having unique addresses can make it easier to connect to other LANs in the future.

If you are setting up a network for yourself (with no other networks to consider in your organization), use private addresses or (if you need the network to be part of the Internet) apply for your own domain name and IP addresses. (You can get unique IP addresses and domain names from Network Solutions at `www.networksolutions.com` or, more likely, from your Internet Service Provider.)

If you don't need to have your LAN accessible from the Internet, choose IP addresses from the set of available general-purpose IP addresses. (Using these private IP addresses, you can still access the Internet from your LAN for such things as Web browsing and accessing e-mail by using a feature described in Chapter 16 called IP masquerading.) Table 15-1 lists the private IP addresses not used on any public part of the Internet.

	Table 15-1 Private IP Addresses	
Network Class	**Network Numbers**	**Addresses per Network Number**
Class A	10.0.0.0	167,777,216
Class B	172.16.0.0 to 172.31.0.0	65,536
Class C	192.168.0.0 to 192.168.255.255	256

So, for a small private LAN, the following numbers are examples of IP addresses that could be assigned to the host computers on your network. (You could use any of the network numbers plus host numbers from the table. These are just examples.)

✦ 192.168.1.1

✦ 192.168.1.2

✦ 192.168.1.3

✦ 192.168.1.4

✦ 192.168.1.5

You could continue that numbering up to 192.168.1.254 on this network, and you could use a network mask of 255.255.255.0.

Adding host names and IP addresses

When you install Red Hat Linux, you are given the opportunity to add your TCP/IP host name and IP address, as well as some other information, to your computer. You also need to set up a way to reach the computers on your LAN. That's done either by adding all computer names and IP addresses to your /etc/hosts file (described here) or by using a DNS server.

Cross-Reference   DNS servers are discussed in Chapter 16.

If you did not identify your IP address during installation of Red Hat Linux, you can do so at a later time using the Network Configuration window (neat command). This procedure lets you attach a particular IP address to your Ethernet interface, so your computer knows what address to listen for.

Note

A computer can have more than one IP address because it can have more than one network interface. Each network interface must have an IP address (even if that address is assigned only temporarily). So, if you have two Ethernet cards on your computer (eth0 and eth1), each needs its own IP address. Also, the address 127.0.0.1 represents the local host, so users on the local computer can access services in loopback.

To define your IP address for your eth0 interface, follow this procedure:

1. Start the Network Configuration. As root user from a Terminal window, type **neat**. The Network Configuration window appears.

2. Click the Devices tab. A listing of your existing network interfaces appears.

3. Double-click the eth0 interface. A pop-up window appears, enabling you to configure your eth0 interface. Figure 15-6 shows the Network Configuration window and the pop-up Ethernet Device window configuring eth0.

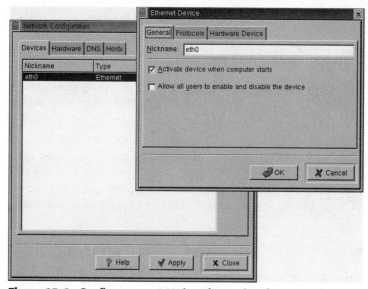

Figure 15-6: Configure your LAN interface using the Network Configuration window.

4. Select "Activate device when computer starts" to have the network interface start at boot time.

5. Click the Protocols tab. You should at least see TCP/IP.

6. Click TCP/IP and select Edit. On the TCP/IP Settings window that appears, you can enter the following information:

- **Automatically obtain IP address settings with:** Make sure that the check box is off next to this box. (If you were getting your IP address from a DHCP server, this box would be on and the rest of the information would be obtained automatically.)

- **Address:** Type the IP address of this computer into the Address box. This number must be unique on your network.

- **Subnet Mask:** Enter the netmask to indicate what part of the IP address represents the network. (Netmask is described earlier in this chapter.)

- **Default Gateway Address:** If there is a computer or router connected to your LAN that is providing routing functions to the Internet or other network, type the IP address of the computer into this box.

7. Click OK in the TCP/IP Settings window to save the current configuration.

8. Click OK in the Ethernet Device window to close that window.

9. Click Apply in the Network Configuration window to apply the changes.

Adding other host addresses

You can use the Network Configuration window to add host names and IP addresses to the Ethernet LAN for the computers on your network as well. This adds host name and IP address pairs to your /etc/hosts file (which you could also edit manually, if you prefer).

Note   If you are using a DHCP server to centralize assignments of your IP addresses, you probably want to centralize host name look-ups as well. In this way, you don't have to change every computer's /etc/hosts file every time a computer is added or removed from your network. Refer to Chapter 23 for information on how to do this.

To add host names and addresses, do the following:

1. Start the Network Configuration. As root user from a Terminal window, type **neat**. The Network Configuration window appears.

2. Click the Hosts tab. A list of IP addresses, host names, and aliases appears.

3. Click Add. A pop-up window appears asking you to add the IP address, host name, and aliases for a host that you can reach on your network. Figure 15-7 shows the Network Configuration window and the pop-up window for adding a host.

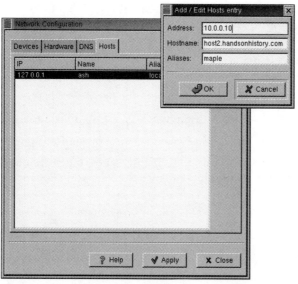

Figure 15-7: Add hosts to /etc/hosts using the Network Configuration.

4. Type in the IP address number, host name, and, optionally, the host alias.

5. Click OK.

6. Repeat this process until you have added every computer on your LAN.

7. Click Apply to apply the changes.

8. Click Close to exit.

Now, when you use programs such as `ftp`, `rlogin`, or other TCP/IP utilities, you can use a host name to identify the computers that you want to communicate with. (Strictly speaking, you don't have to set up your `/etc/hosts` file. You could use IP addresses as arguments to TCP/IP commands. But names are easier to work with.)

Adding Windows computers to your LAN

It is likely that you have other types of computers on your LAN in addition to those running Red Hat Linux systems (at least for a few more years). The following are general steps for adding your Windows computers to the Ethernet LAN we just created:

1. Power down your computer and install an Ethernet card. (Most PC Ethernet cards will run on Windows. Some may need new drivers for Windows 2000.)

2. Connect an Ethernet cable from the card to your hub.

3. Reboot your computer. If your card is detected, Windows will either automatically install a driver or ask you to insert a disk that comes with the card to install the driver.

4. Open the Network configuration window (Start ➪ Settings ➪ Control Panel; then double-click the Network icon). The Network window appears.

5. Find the Ethernet card you just installed in the list and select it.

6. Click Add. The Select Network Component Type pop-up window appears.

7. Double-click Protocol. The Select Network Protocol window appears.

8. Click Microsoft, and then double-click TCP/IP. A new entry should appear in your Network window that looks similar to the following, depending on your card:

```
TCP/IP -> 3Com Etherlink III ISA
```

9. Double-click on that new entry. The TCP/IP Properties window should appear, as shown in Figure 15-8.

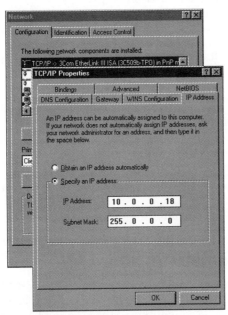

Figure 15-8: Configure TCP/IP on Windows for your Ethernet LAN.

Note   Notice in the figure that the IP address is one of the reserved IP addresses described earlier. Because it is a Class A address, the Netmask is 255.0.0.0, which implies that there could be millions of computers on this network.

10. Click Specify an IP address.

Note

If you were using a DHCP server to assign IP addresses, you would click "Obtain an IP address automatically" instead. See Chapter 23 for information on setting up Red Hat Linux as a DHCP server.

11. Add the host name and IP address for this computer. (These should match the name and IP address that you added for this computer for Linux in your Network Configuration window.)

12. Click OK to exit.

At this point, your Windows computer knows to listen on the network (via its Ethernet card) for messages addressed to the IP address you have just entered. From the Windows system, you can access any of the following services configured on your Red Hat Linux system:

✦ **Printer server** — You can print to a printer connected to Linux that is configured as a Samba print server.

✦ **Web server** — You can display Web pages served from your Linux server via your Netscape Navigator, Internet Explorer, or other Web browser window.

✦ **File server** — You can find file folders shared from Linux (by using the Samba facility) and use them from your Network Neighborhood.

These are just a few examples of the types of services that can be accessed easily from your Windows system once the services have been properly configured on the Red Hat Linux server. (Most of the remaining chapters of this book describe how to configure these services.)

Checking Your Ethernet Connection

After your LAN has been set up, your Ethernet cards installed, and host names and addresses added, there are several methods you can use to check that everything is up and working. For example, you can check your boot messages to make sure that your board was detected and that you can use the `ping` command to make sure you can connect to other computers.

Did Linux find your Ethernet driver at boot-time?

Type the following to check that Linux found your card and installed the Ethernet interface properly:

```
dmesg | grep eth
```

The `dmesg` command lists all the messages that were output by Linux at boot-time. The `grep eth` command causes only those lines that contain the word *eth* to be printed. The first message shown below appeared on my laptop computer with the Netgear card. The second example is from my computer with the EtherExpress Pro/100 card:

```
eth0: NE2000 Compatible: port 0x300, irq3, hw_addr 00:80:C8:8C:8E:49

eth0: OEM i82557/i82558 10/100 Ethernet at 0xccc0, 00:90:27:4E:67:35, IRQ 17.
```

The message in the first example shows that a card was found at IRQ3 with a port address of 0x300 and an Ethernet hardware address of 00:80:C8:8C:8E:49. In the second example, the card is at IRQ 17, the port address is 0xccc0, and the Ethernet address is 00:90:27:4E:67:35.

Tip   If the eth0 interface is not found, but you know that you have a supported Ethernet card, check that your Ethernet card is properly seated in its slot.

Can you reach another computer on the LAN?

Try communicating with another computer on the LAN. The `ping` command can be used to send a packet to another computer and to ask for a packet in return. You could give `ping` either a host name (pine) or an IP address (10.0.0.10). For example, to ping a computer on the network called pine, type the following command:

```
# ping pine
```

If the computer can be reached, the output will look similar to the following:

```
PING pine.trees (10.0.0.10): 56 data bytes
64 bytes from 10.0.0.10: icmp_seq=0 ttl=255 time=0.6 ms
64 bytes from 10.0.0.10: icmp_seq=1 ttl=255 time=0.5 ms
64 bytes from 10.0.0.10: icmp_seq=2 ttl=255 time=0.5 ms
64 bytes from 10.0.0.10: icmp_seq=3 ttl=255 time=0.5 ms
64 bytes from 10.0.0.10: icmp_seq=4 ttl=255 time=0.5 ms
64 bytes from 10.0.0.10: icmp_seq=5 ttl=255 time=0.5 ms
64 bytes from 10.0.0.10: icmp_seq=6 ttl=255 time=0.5 ms
64 bytes from 10.0.0.10: icmp_seq=7 ttl=255 time=0.6 ms
64 bytes from 10.0.0.10: icmp_seq=8 ttl=255 time=0.5 ms
64 bytes from 10.0.0.10: icmp_seq=9 ttl=255 time=0.5 ms

--- pine.trees ping statistics ---
10 packets transmitted, 10 packets received, 0% packet loss
round-trip min/avg/max = 0.5/0.5/0.6 ms
```

A line of output is printed each time a packet is sent and received in return. It shows how much data was sent and how long it took for each package to be received. After you have watched this for a while, type Ctrl+C to stop ping. At that point, it will show you statistics of how many packets were transmitted, received, and lost.

If you don't see output that shows packets have been received, it means that you are not contacting the other computer. Try to verify that the names and addresses of the computers that you want to reach are in your /etc/hosts file or that your DNS server is accessible. Next, confirm that the names and IP addresses you have for the other computers that you are trying to reach are correct (the IP addresses are the most critical).

Is your Ethernet connection up?

Using the ifconfig command, you can determine whether your Ethernet (and other network interfaces) are up and running. Type the following command:

```
# ifconfig
```

The output that appears will be similar to the following:

```
eth   Link encap:Ethernet HWaddr 00:90:27:4E:67:35
      inet addr:10.0.0.11 Bcast:10.255.255.255 Mask:255.0.0.0
      UP BROADCAST RUNNING MULTICAST MTU:1500 Metric:1
      RX packets:156 errors:0 dropped:0 overruns:0 frame:0
      TX packets:104 errors:0 dropped:0 overruns:0 carrier:0
      collisions:0
      RX bytes:20179 (19.7 Kb)   TX bytes:19960 (19.4 Kb)

lo    Link encap:Local Loopback
      inet addr:127.0.0.1 Mask:255.0.0.0
      UP LOOPBACK RUNNING MTU:3924 Metric:1
      RX packets:56 errors:0 dropped:0 overruns:0 frame:0
      TX packets:56 errors:0 dropped:0 overruns:0 carrier:0
      collisions:0
      RX bytes:3148 (3.0 Kb)  TX bytes:3148 (3.0Kb)
```

In this example, there are currently two network interfaces up on the current computer. The first section shows your Ethernet interface (eth0) and its hardware address, Ethernet hardware address, IP address (inet addr), broadcast address, and network mask. The next lines provide information on packets that have been sent, along with the number of errors and collisions that have occurred.

Note   The lo entry is for loopback. This enables you to run TCP/IP commands on your local system without having a physical network up and running. I describe this and other network interfaces in more detail in Chapter 16.

If your eth0 interface does not appear, it may still be configured properly, but not running at the moment. Try to start the eth0 interface by typing the following:

```
# ifconfig eth0 up
```

After this, type `ifconfig` again to see if eth0 is now running. If it is, it may be that eth0 is simply not configured to start automatically at boot time. You can change it so Ethernet starts at boot-time (which I recommend), using the Network Configuration window (described earlier in this chapter).

Tip   If your network interfaces are not running at all, you can try to start them from the network initialization script. This interface reads parameters and basically runs `ifconfig` for all network interfaces on your computer. Type the following to restart your network:

```
# /etc/init.d/network restart
```

Another way to see statistics for your Ethernet driver is to list the contents of the process pseudo file system for network devices. To do that, type the following:

```
# cat /proc/net/dev
```

The output should look similar to the following:

```
Inter-|  Receive                                |  Transmit
face |bytes   packets errs drop fifo frame compressed multicast|bytes    packets
errs drop fifo colls carrier compressed
    lo:  5362    64   0  0  0   0     0        0   5362   64  0 0 0   0      0       0
  eth0:  3083    35   0  0  0   0     0        0   3876   31  0 0 0   0      0       0
```

The output is a bit hard to read (our book isn't wide enough to show it without wrapping around). With this output, you can see Receive and Transmit statistics for each interface. This output also shows you how many Receive and Transmit errors occurred during communication.

For a more detailed look at your network, you can use the Ethereal window. Ethereal is described in the following section.

Watching LAN traffic with Ethereal

If you really want to understand the coming and going of information on your LAN, you need a tool that analyzes network traffic. Ethereal is a graphical tool for capturing and displaying the packets being sent across your network interfaces. Using filters to select particular hosts, protocols, or direction of data, you can specifically monitor activities and track down problems on your network.

In addition to reading Ethernet packet data gathered by Ethereal, the Ethereal window can be used to display captured files from LanAlyzer, Sniffer, Microsoft Network Monitor, Snoop, and a variety of other tools. These files can be read from their native formats or after being compressed with gzip (.gz).

Ethereal can track more than 100 packet types (representing different protocols). It can also display specific fields related to each protocol, such as various data sizes, source and destination addresses, port numbers and other values.

Starting Ethereal

To start Ethereal, choose Programs ➪ Internet ➪ ethereal, or type the following (as root user) from a Terminal window:

```
# ethereal &
```

The Ethereal window appears, as shown in Figure 15-9. (If the `ethereal` command is not found, the package is probably not installed. You can install the ethereal package from the Red Hat Linux installation CD-2.)

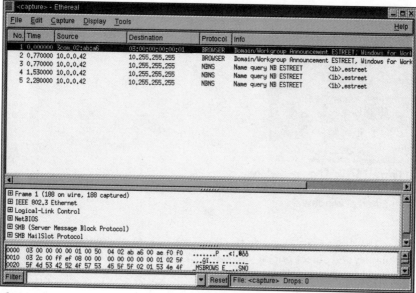

Figure 15-9: Configure your Ethernet card for TCP/IP during installation.

The primary function of Ethereal is to take a snapshot of the packets coming across your network interfaces and display that data in the Ethereal window. You can filter the data based on a variety of filter primitives. When the capture is done, you can step through and sort the data based on the values in different columns. Optionally, you can save the captured data to a file to study the data at a later time.

Tip

If you can't use Ethereal because you don't have a GUI available, you can use the `tcpdump` command from the shell. It is not as friendly as Ethereal, but it supports the same filtering syntax. Because `tcpdump` can produce a lot of output, you will probably want to use some form of filtering and/or direct the output of the command to a file. (Type **man tcpdump** for information on filter options.)

Capturing Ethernet data

With the Ethereal window displayed, you can capture data relating to packet activities on any of your Ethernet network interfaces by doing the following:

1. Click Capture.

2. Click Start. An Ethereal Capture Preferences window appears, as shown in Figure 15-10.

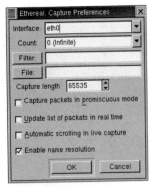

Figure 15-10: Choose preferences for capturing Ethernet data from the Ethereal window.

3. Click the down arrow next to the Interface box, to see what interfaces are available, and select one. If you have an Ethernet card installed, select eth0 to choose to capture data for packets being sent across that card. You can also choose to monitor the lo interface, to watch the loopback driver. (By choosing lo, you can see requests from local users for local TCP/IP services).

4. Choose other options relating to what data is captured:

   • **Count:** By default, Ethereal will capture data from the moment you click OK on the Capture Preferences until you click Stop (with this value set to 0). Optionally, you can type any number into the Count field to capture only that number of packets.

   • **Filter:** This optional field lets you enter a filter that can be used to filter capture data. You can type in filters individually or click the Filter button to use a filter you have stored earlier.

Filtering is one of the most powerful features of Ethereal. See the sidebar "Using Ethereal Filters" for further information on how to enter filters into the Filter field.

- **File:** Enter the name of a file in which you want to capture the data gathered. If you don't enter a file name, the information is displayed on the Ethereal window without being saved to a file.

- **Capture length:** Enter the maximum number of bytes of data that can be displayed for each packet.

- **Capture packets in promiscuous mode:** Any computer on a LAN can see all packets that traverse the LAN, except for those packets intended for switched portions of the LAN. With this option on, all packets that are seen by your network interface are captured. With this mode off, only packets intended specifically for your network interface (including multicast and broadcast packets) are captured. In other words, turn on promiscuous mode to monitor the whole LAN and turn it off to monitor only your interface.

- **Update list of packets in real time:** Select this option to have packet information appear in the Ethereal window as each packet crosses the interface. With this option off, the information is displayed after you stop capturing it.

- **Automatic scrolling in live capture:** If you are updating packets in real time, select this option to have packet information scroll up after the screen fills. With this option off, you will just see the first screen of packets and have to scroll down manually to see the rest.

- **Enable name resolution:** With this option on, Source and Destination IP addresses are displayed as host names (if they can be resolved from /etc/hosts or DNS). With this off, IP addresses appear for the Source and Destination columns.

5. Click OK. Ethereal will begin gathering data on the packets encountered by the selected interface. Figure 15-11 shows an example of the Ethereal capture window that appears.

The Ethereal Capture window displays information on how many incoming and outgoing packets have crossed the interface since the capture began. The number of packets that are associated with each protocol Ethereal monitors is displayed, along with the percentage of total packets associated with each protocol. For this example, I opened a Web page (resulting in TCP packets) and ran the ping command (resulting in ICMP packets).

Using Ethereal Filters

If you are monitoring a busy server or a busy network, Ethereal can gather so much data that it can become almost unusable. If you know what you are looking for, however, you can use Ethereal to filter what packets are captured based on values you enter.

Filters in Ethereal are implemented using the pcap library (type `man pcap` to read about it). The filter expressions you can use with Ethereal are described on the `tcpdump` man page. Here are some examples of filters that you could enter into the Filter box when you capture Ethernet data with Ethereal:

```
host 10.0.0.15
```

The `host` primitive lets you only capture packets that are either to or from a particular host computer (by IP address or host name). By preceding host with `src` or `des`, you can indicate that you only want packages sent from a particular source or to a particular destination host.

```
tcp port 80
```

You can enter a protocol name (such as `tcp`, `ether`, `udp`, or `ip`) to limit captured packets to those that are assigned to that protocol. As shown in the previous example, with tcp you could also indicate a port number (such as 80, to monitor traffic to and from your Web server).

You can filter for certain special activities on the network, using such things as the `gateway`, `broadcast`, or `multicast` primitives. Entering `gateway host` lets you find packets sent to a gateway host that is neither a Source nor Destination for the packet (which is determined because the Ethernet address doesn't match either of those IP addresses). Enter `ether broadcast` to monitor broadcast packets on your Ethernet network, such as announcements from name servers announcing availability. Likewise, you could filter for `multicast` packets on `ether` or `ip` protocols (`ether multicast`).

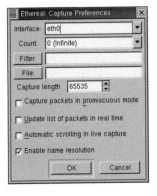

Figure 15-11: Ethernet activity is displayed by protocol as packets are captured.

6. Click Stop. The snapshot of data you just took will appear on the Ethereal window. Packets are displayed in the order in which they traversed the interface.

7. If you did not already ask to save the capture data to a file, you may do so now by choosing File ➪ Save As.

At this point, you can start interpreting the data.

Interpreting captured Ethernet data

With the captured data displayed in your Ethereal window, you can get a detailed view of the network traffic that your computer is exposed to. The Ethereal window is divided into three parts. The top part contains a scrollable list of packets. The protocol tree for the current packet appears in the middle part of the display. A hexadecimal dump of the entire contents of the packet appears in the bottom part.

You can sort data in different ways from the top part of the window by clicking on the column headings. To see more details relating to different items in the protocol tree for the current packet, you can click the plus sign next to the protocol information that interests you.

The following are some tips that will help you interpret what the data means:

✦ The Source and Destination columns show where each packet came from and where it went. If the Enable name resolution option is on (which is recommended), the host name associated with IP packets is displayed. This makes it much easier to see which computer is communicating with you.

✦ To see all activity associated with a particular location, click the Source or Destination column. Packets will be sorted alphabetically, making it easier for you to scroll through activity for the location that interests you.

✦ If you are trying to debug a particular feature, you may want to click the Protocol column to gather activities based on protocol. For example, if you were trying to get Samba to work (for Windows file or printer sharing), sorting by protocol would enable you to see all NetBIOS and NBNS (NetBIOS name server) requests that came to your computer.

✦ To mark a packet of interest to you, click the middle mouse button on it. This will highlight the packet, making it easier to find later. (If you only have a two-button mouse, and you indicated during installation that it should emulate a three-button mouse, you can click both mouse buttons together to emulate the middle mouse button.)

The Info column gives you details about the intention of the packet. For example, you can see the type of service that was requested (such as http for Web service or FTP for file transfer). You can see what information is being broadcast and determine when attempts to find particular host computers are failing. If you believe someone is using your network improperly, you can see which sites they are visiting and the services they are requesting.

Another handy option is one that lets you follow the stream of TCP information. Click Tools ⇨ Follow TCP Stream. The "Contents of TCP stream" window that appears lets you see the total output of the HTTP, SMTP, or other protocol being used.

Summary

Red Hat Linux is at its best when it is connected to a network. Configuring a LAN enables you to share resources with other computers in your home or organization. These resources can include files, printers, CD-ROM drives, and backup media.

This chapter describes how to create a LAN with a Red Hat Linux system being used on one of the computers on that LAN. It helps you determine the kind of equipment you need to obtain, and the layout (topology) of the network.

On the Red Hat Linux side, you learned about choosing and installing Ethernet cards (also called NICs). You also learned to configure TCP/IP so that you can later employ a variety of TCP/IP tools to use the network.

If something isn't working with your Red Hat Linux interface to the LAN, you can use utilities such as ifconfig to check that your Ethernet interface is configured and running properly. You can also check that Linux found and installed the proper driver for your Ethernet card. After an Ethernet interface is working, you can use the Ethereal window to monitor the packets coming and going across the interface between your computer and the network.

✦   ✦   ✦

Connecting to the Internet

This chapter demonstrates how to connect Red Hat Linux to any TCP/IP-based network, such as the Internet, a private intranet, or a company extranet. The differences in how you connect have more to do with the network medium you use (that is, telephone lines, LAN router, and so on) than they do with whether you are connecting to the public Internet or a company's private network.

Connections to the Internet described in this chapter include a simple dial-up connection from your own Red Hat Linux system. The most popular protocols for making dial-up connections to the Internet are Point-to-Point Protocol (PPP) and Serial Line Internet Protocol (SLIP). This chapter focuses on PPP (it is more widely used than SLIP). It also builds on the procedures in Chapter 15 for creating your own Local Area Network (LAN) by teaching you how to connect your LAN to the Internet.

This chapter first provides an overview of the structure of the Internet, including descriptions of domains, routing, and proxy service. It then discusses how to connect your Red Hat Linux system to the Internet using PPP dial-up connections. For those who want to connect a LAN to the Internet, it describes how to use Red Hat Linux as a router and set it up to do IP masquerading (to protect your private LAN addresses). Finally, it describes how to configure Red Hat Linux as a proxy server, including how to configure client proxy applications such as Netscape and Microsoft Internet Explorer.

Understanding How the Internet Is Structured

In order to operate, the Internet relies on maintaining a unique set of names and numbers. The names are domain names and hostnames, which enable the computers connected to the Internet to be identified in a hierarchy. The numbers are Internet Protocol (IP) addresses and port numbers, which enable computers to be grouped together into interconnected sets of subnetworks, yet remain uniquely addressable by the Internet.

An Internet Service Provider (ISP) will give you the information you need to set up a connection to the Internet. You plug that information into the programs used to create that connection, such as scripts to create a Point-to-Point Protocol (PPP) connection over telephone lines. See the section later in this chapter on outgoing dial-up connections for descriptions of the information needed from your ISP and the procedures for configuring PPP to connect to the Internet.

The following list describes basic Internet structure in more detail:

✦ **IP addresses** — These are the numbers that uniquely define each computer known to the Internet. Internet authorities assign pools of IP addresses (along with network masks, or netmasks) so that network administrators can assign addresses to each individual computer that they control. An alternative to assigned addresses is to use a reserved set of private IP addresses.

Cross-Reference

See Chapter 15 for a description of IP addresses.

✦ **Port numbers** — Port numbers provide access points to particular services. A server computer will listen on the network for packets that are addressed to its IP address, along with one or more port numbers. For example, a Web server listens to port 80 to respond to requests for HTTP content.

✦ **Domain names** — On the Internet, computer names are organized in a hierarchy of domain names and hostnames. If you want to have and maintain your own Internet domain, you need to be assigned one that fits into one of the top-level domains (domains such as .com, .org, .net, .edu, .us, and so on).

✦ **Hostnames** — If a domain name is assigned to your organization, you are free to create your own hostnames within that domain. This is a way of associating a name (hostname) with an address (IP address). When you use the Internet, you use a *fully qualified domain name* to identify a host computer. For example, in the domain handsonhistory.com, a host computer named baskets would have a fully qualified domain name of baskets.handsonhistory.com.

Within an organization, you should choose a host-naming scheme that makes sense to you. For example, for handsonhistory.com, you could have hostnames dedicated to different crafts (baskets, decoys, weaving, and so on).

✦ **Routers**—If you have a LAN or other type of network in your home or organization that you want to connect to the Internet, you can share an Internet connection. You do this by setting up a router. The router connects to both your network and the Internet, providing a route for data to pass between your network and the Internet.

✦ **Firewalls and IP masquerading**—To keep your private network somewhat secure, yet still allow some data to pass between it and the Internet, you can set up a firewall. The firewall restricts the kind of data packets or services that can pass through the boundary between the private and public networks. If your network uses private addresses, or if you just want to protect the addresses of computers behind your firewall, you can use a technique called IP masquerading.

Though you can set up a firewall to filter packets on any computer on your private network, firewalls are typically configured on the machine that routes packets between the public and private networks. In this way, intruders can be stopped before they get on your private network and security can be relaxed somewhat between your computers behind the firewall.

✦ **Proxies**—You can bypass some of the configuration required to allow the computers on your LAN to communicate directly with the Internet by configuring a proxy server. With a proxy server, a computer on your LAN can run Internet applications (such as a Web browser) and have them appear to the Internet as if they are actually running on the proxy server.

You can read about firewalls in Chapter 14. IP masquerading is described later in this chapter.

Internet domains

You can't read a magazine, watch a TV commercial, or open a cereal box these days without hitting a "something.com." When a company, organization, or person wants you to connect to them on the Internet, it relies on the uniqueness of its particular domain name. However, within that domain name, the company or organization to which it has been assigned can arrange its content however it chooses.

Internet domains are organized in a structure called the *domain name system* (DNS). At the top of that structure is a set of *top-level domains* (or TLDs). Some of the top-level domains are used commonly in the United States, although they are available for worldwide use. TLDs such as edu (for colleges and universities), gov (for United States government), and mil (for United States military sites) were among the most used TLDs in the early Internet. In more recent years, com (for commercial sites) has experienced the most growth. The us domain was added to include U.S. institutions, such as local governments and elementary schools, as well as to individuals within a geographical region of the United States.

To facilitate the entry of other countries to the Internet, the International Organization for Standardization (ISO) has defined a set of two-letter codes that are assigned to each country. Within each country, there are naming authorities that are responsible for organizing the subdomains. Some subdomains are organized by categories, while others are structured by geographic location.

Tip
Several RFCs (Request for Comments) define the domain name system. RFC 1034 covers domain name concepts and facilities. RFC 1035 is a technical description of how DNS works. RFC 1480 describes the "us" domain. For a more general description of DNS, there is RFC 1591.

Common top-level domain names

Of the generic TLDs in use today, several are used throughout the world, while two are available only in the United States. Here are descriptions of common TLDs:

✦ **com** — Businesses, corporations, and other commercial organizations fall into this TLD. As the Internet has grown into an important tool for commerce, domains in this TLD have grown at a dramatic rate.

✦ **edu** — Colleges and universities fall under this TLD. Although it was originally intended for all educational institutions, two-year colleges, high schools, and elementary schools are now organized by location under country codes (such as US in the United States).

✦ **gov** — This TLD is restricted to U.S. federal government locations. Local government sites are expected to fall under the us domain.

✦ **int** — This domain includes international databases and organizations created by international treaties.

✦ **mil** — U.S. military organizations fall under this domain.

✦ **net** — Computer network providers fall under this domain.

✦ **org** — A variety of organizations that are neither governmental nor commercial in nature fall under this catchall TLD.

Domain name formation

As noted earlier, domain names are hierarchical, which means there can be subdomains beneath second-level domains, as well as host computers. (Second-level domains are the names directly below the TLDs that are assigned to individual people and organizations.) Each subdomain is separated by a dot (.), starting with the top-level domain on the right and with the second-level domain and each subsequent subdomain appearing to the left. Here is an example of a fully qualified domain name for a host:

```
baskets.crafts.handsonhistory.com
```

In this example, the top-level domain is `.com`. The second-level domain name assigned to the organization that controls the domain is `handsonhistory`. Within that domain is a subdomain called `crafts`. The last name (`baskets`) refers to a particular computer within that second-level domain. From other hosts in the second-level domain, the host can be referred to simply as `baskets`. From the Internet, you would refer to it as `baskets.crafts.handsonhistory.com`.

Hostnames and IP addresses

In the early days of the Internet, every known host computer name and address was collected into a file called HOSTS.TXT and distributed throughout the Internet. This quickly became cumbersome because of the size of the list and the constant changes being made to it. The solution was to distribute the responsibility for resolving hostnames and addresses to many DNS servers throughout the Internet.

To make the domain names friendly, the names contain no network addresses, routes, or other information needed to deliver messages. Instead, each computer must rely on some method to translate domain names and hostnames into IP addresses. The DNS server is the primary method of resolving the names to addresses. If you request a service from a computer using a fully qualified domain name (including all domains and subdomains), it will go to the DNS server to resolve that name into an IP address.

If you have a private LAN or other network, you can keep your own list of hostnames and IP addresses. For the computers you work with all the time, it's easier to type `baskets` than `baskets.crafts.handsonhistory.com`. There are a couple of ways (besides DNS) that your computer can resolve the IP address for computers for which you give only the hostname:

✦ **Check the `/etc/hosts` file.** In your computer's `/etc/hosts` file, you can place the names and IP addresses for the computers on your local network. In this way, your computer doesn't need to query the DNS server to get the address (which may not be there anyway if you are on a private network).

✦ **Check specified domains.** You can specify that if the hostname requested doesn't include a fully qualified domain name and the hostname is not in your `/etc/hosts` file, then your computer should check certain specified domain names.

On your Red Hat Linux system, the decisions on how to try to resolve hostnames to IP addresses are taken from the `/etc/resolv.conf` file. That file specifies your local domain, an alternative list of domains, and the location of one or more DNS servers. Here is an example of an `/etc/resolv.conf` file:

```
domain crafts.handsonhistory.com
search crafts.handsonhistory.com handsonhistory.com
nameserver 10.0.0.10
nameserver 10.0.0.12
```

In this example, the local domain is `crafts.handsonhistory.com`. If you try to contact a host by giving only its hostname (with no domain name), your computer can check in both `crafts.handsonhistory.com` and `handsonhistory.com` domains to find the host. If you give the fully qualified domain name, it can contact the name servers (first `10.0.0.10` and then `10.0.0.12`) to resolve the address. (You can specify up to three name servers that your computer will query in order until the address is resolved.)

Tip   Your resolver knows to check your `/etc/hosts` file first because of the contents of the `/etc/host.conf` and `/etc/nsswitch` files. You can change that behavior by modifying those files. See the resolv.conf man page for further information.

Routing

Knowing the IP address of the computer you want to reach is one thing; being able to reach that IP address is another. Even if you connect your computers on a LAN, to have full connectivity to the Internet there must be at least one node (that is, a computer or dedicated device) through which you can route messages that are destined for locations outside your LAN. That is the job of a *router*.

A router is a device that has interfaces to at least two networks and is able to route network traffic between the two networks. In our example of a small business that has a LAN that it wants to connect to the Internet, the router would have a connection and IP address on the LAN, as well as a connection and IP address to a network that provides access to the Internet.

Red Hat Linux can act as a router by connecting to two LANs or by connecting to a LAN and a modem (to dial-up the Internet). Alternatively, you can purchase a dedicated router, such as Cisco ADSL routers, that can exclusively perform routing between your LAN and the Internet or network service provider.

Tip   Unlike regular dial-up modems, xDSL modems have several different standards that are not all compatible. Before purchasing a xDSL modem, check with your ISP. If your ISP supports xDSL, it can tell you the exact models of xDSL modems you can use to get xDSL service.

Proxies

Instead of having direct access to the Internet (as you do with routing), you can have indirect access via the computers on your LAN by setting up a *proxy server*. With a proxy server, you don't have to configure and secure every computer on the LAN for Internet access. When, for example, a client computer tries to access the Internet from a Web browser, the request goes to the proxy server. The proxy server then makes that request to the Internet. Using a proxy server, Internet access is fairly easy to set up and quite secure to use. Red Hat Linux can be configured as a proxy server (as described later in this chapter).

Using Dial-up Connections to the Internet

Most individuals and even many small businesses that need to connect to the Internet do so using modems and telephone lines. Your modem connects to a serial port (COM1, COM2, and so on) on your computer and then into a telephone wall jack. Then your computer dials a modem at your Internet Service Provider or business that has a connection to the Internet.

The two most common protocols for making dial-up connections to the Internet (or other TCP/IP network) are Point-to-Point Protocol (PPP) and Serial Line Internet Protocol (SLIP). Of the two, PPP is more popular and more reliable. SLIP, however, has been around longer. This section describes how to use PPP protocol to connect to the Internet.

Getting information

To establish a PPP connection, you need to get some information from the administrator of the network that you are connecting to. This is either your Internet Service Provider (ISP) when you sign up for Internet service or the person who walks around carrying cables, a cellular phone, and a beeper where you work (when a network goes down, these people are in demand!). Here is the kind of information you need to set up your PPP connection:

✦ **PPP or SLIP** — Does the ISP require SLIP or PPP protocols to connect to it? In this book, I describe how to configure PPP.

✦ **Telephone number** — This telephone number gives you access to the modem (or pool of modems) at the ISP. If it is a national ISP, make sure that you get a local telephone number (otherwise, you will rack up long distance fees on top of your ISP fees).

✦ **Account name and password** — This information is used to verify that you have an Internet account with the ISP. This is typically used when you connect to Red Hat Linux or other UNIX system. (When connecting to an NT server, the account name may be referred to as a system name.)

✦ **An IP number** — Most ISPs use Dynamic IP numbers, which means that you are assigned an IP number temporarily when you are connected. Your ISP assigns a permanent IP number if it uses Static IP addresses. If your computer or all the computers on your LAN need to have a more permanent presence on the network, you may be given one Static IP number or a set of Static IP numbers to use.

✦ **DNS IP numbers** — When you use a Web browser, FTP utility, or other Internet program to request a service from a computer on the network, you need a way to translate that name (for example, whatever.com) into an Internet address. Your computer will do this by querying a Domain Name System (DNS) server. Your ISP should give you at least one, and possibly two or three, IP addresses for a primary (and possibly secondary and tertiary) DNS server.

✦ **PAP or CHAP secrets**—You may need a PAP id or CHAP id and a secret, instead of a login and password when connecting to a Windows NT system. These features are used with authentication on Microsoft operating systems, as well as other systems. Red Hat Linux and other UNIX servers don't typically use this type of authentication, although they support PAP and CHAP on the client side. If Red Hat Linux didn't support PAP or CHAP, you wouldn't be able to connect to a great many ISPs.

Besides providing an Internet connection, your ISP typically also provides services for use with your Internet connection. Although you don't need this information to create your connection, you will need it soon afterward to configure these useful services. Here is some information you should acquire:

✦ **Mail server**—If your ISP is providing you with an e-mail account, you need to know the address of the mail server, the type of mail service (such as Post Office Protocol or POP), and the authentication password for the mail server in order to get your e-mail.

✦ **News server**—To be able to participate in newsgroups, the ISP may provide you with the hostname of a news server. If the server requires you to log on, you will also need a password.

After you have gathered this information, you are ready to set up your connection to the Internet. To configure Red Hat Linux to connect to your ISP, follow the PPP procedure described below.

Setting up dial-up PPP

Point-to-Point Protocol (PPP) is used to create Internet Protocol (IP) connections over serial lines. Most often, the serial connection is established over a modem; however, it will also work over serial cables (null modem cables) or digital lines (including ISDN and DSL digital media). PPP is a common way to connect an individual computer or LAN to a TCP/IP Wide Area Network (such as the Internet).

Although one side must dial out while the other side must receive the call to create a PPP connection over a modem, after the connection is established, information can flow in both directions. For the sake of clarity, however, I refer to the computer placing the call as the client and the computer receiving the call as the server.

To simplify the process of configuring PPP (and other network interfaces), Red Hat Linux provides a dial-up configuration tool for both the GNOME and KDE interfaces. Those interfaces are, respectively, as follows:

✦ **Dialup Configuration Tool**—From the GNOME desktop menu, choose Programs ⇨ Internet ⇨ Dialup Configuration. The Internet Connection window that appears lets you configure and test your dial-up PPP connection.

✦ **Kppp Window**—From the KDE desktop menu, choose Internet ➪ Internet Dialer. This runs the kppp command. From the kppp window you can set up a PPP dial-up connection and launch it.

Before you begin either of the two dial-up procedures, physically connect your modem to your computer, plug it in, and connect it to your telephone line. If you have an internal modem, you will probably see a telephone port on the back of your computer that you need to connect. After the modem is connected, reboot Red Hat Linux so it can automatically detect and configure your modem.

Creating a dial-up connection from GNOME

To configure dial-up networking from the GNOME desktop, you should use the Dialup Configuration window. To start it, choose Programs ➪ Internet ➪ Dialup Configuration from the GNOME menu. A connection wizard appears to help you configure your PPP dial-up connection, as shown in Figure 16-1.

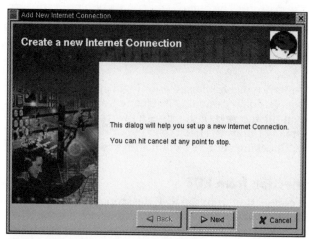

Figure 16-1: The Dialup Configuration Tool steps you through a PPP Internet connection.

Follow the procedure below from the first Dialup Configuration Tool window to configure your dial-up connection.

1. From the Add New Internet Connection window that appears, click Next to continue. If you do not have a modem configured, you are asked if you want to configure one.

2. Click Next to configure a modem. A pop-up window searches your computer for a modem. If it finds your modem, its location will be filled in on the Enter a modem window. Otherwise, you will have to enter the location of the modem yourself.

3. Select the modem you want from the list of modems found (there will probably only be one). Click "Keep this modem," and then click Next to continue. A window appears, asking for your account name and telephone number.

4. Enter the account name (any name to identify the account) and the telephone number of the ISP you want to dial into. Then click Next to continue. (The optional Prefix is in case you need to dial a 9 or some other number to get an outside dial tone before dialing.) The window asks for your user account name and password.

5. Type in the account name and password. You should have received this information from your ISP. The ISP may have called the account name a Login ID or similar name. Click Next to continue. The Other Options window appears.

6. Select Normal ISP (unless your ISP happens to appear in the listing, in which case select it instead). Then click Next to continue. The Create the account window appears.

7. If all the information looks correct, click Finish (otherwise, click the Back button to change any information). The completed connection type appears in the Internet Connections window.

8. To test your connection, select your new PPP account and click the Debug button. The Internet dialer starts up and dials your ISP.

If everything is working properly, you should see your login and password accepted and the PPP connection completed. Try opening Netscape Communicator and see if you can access a Web site on the Internet. If this doesn't work the first time, don't be discouraged. There are many things to check to get your dial-up PPP connection working. Skip ahead to the "Checking your PPP connection" section.

Creating a dial-up connection from KDE

To configure a dial-up PPP connection from the KDE desktop, you can use the kppp window. To open that window, choose Internet ⇨ Internet Dialer from the KDE menu. Then click the Setup button. A kppp Configuration window appears, as shown in Figure 16-2.

Note   Instead of using the Internet Dialer (kppp) window, you can use the Dialup Configuration window described in the section "Creating a dial-up connection from GNOME." Open the Dialup Configuration window from the KDE desktop by selecting Internet ⇨ Dialup Configuration from the KDE menu.

1. From the kppp Configuration window (Accounts tab), click New. A pop-up window asks if you want to use the wizard to create a new account.

2. Click Dialog Setup. A New Account window appears.

Figure 16-2: Configure PPP connections
from KDE using the kppp Configuration window.

3. From the Dial tab on the New Account window, add the following information:

- **Connection Name** — Enter any name you choose to identify the connection. Typically, the name would identify your ISP.

- **Phone Number** — Click on the Add button, enter the telephone number of the ISP's modem pool, and click on OK.

- **Authentication** — Determine from your ISP the type of authentication that is used to establish the connection. Many ISPs use a PAP or CHAP type of authentication (which are used with Windows NT and other types of servers), while universities and other sites where UNIX and Linux servers are used tend to use Terminal and Script-based authentication.

- **Customize pppd arguments** — Click on this button, type an argument you want to add, click on Add, repeat for additional arguments (optional), and click on OK. These arguments are passed to the pppd daemon (which establishes and maintains your PPP connections). Some of these arguments are described later in the section "Checking your PPP connection." See the pppd manual page (type **man pppd**) for information on available arguments.

4. Click the IP tab. Chances are that the ISP will use Dynamic IP addresses. If the ISP gave you a Static IP address, click the Static IP Address box and type in the address and netmask the ISP gave you. You can also click on the "Autoconfigure hostname..." box to have your host name automatically assigned from your ISP.

5. Click the DNS tab. This is where you enter your domain name and the IP address for the DNS server (which is used to resolve Internet host/domain names into IP addresses). If DNS servers are not assigned dynamically (which they probably are), you will typically be given two DNS servers to enter (a primary and a backup).

6. Click the Login Script tab. This is a somewhat advanced feature. It can be used if your dial-up ISP connection doesn't do the standard PAP, CHAP, or terminal login ways of setting up a connection. If that is the case, you can set up a custom "chat" script here that defines what you expect to receive from the remote side and what you will send in response. (When you try your connection a few steps later, you will be able to watch this chat take place.)

7. Click the Execute tab. If you want to run a special command or script before or at the point of connection or disconnection, you can add the full path to the command or script in the appropriate box. (You will typically leave these blank.)

8. Click the Accounting tab. If you need to account for the amount of traffic being received or sent over this connection, you can click the Enable Accounting button on this tab. You must then select the Available rules, based on your country and type of service. This feature is more useful outside of the United States, where billing for Internet service is done differently.

9. Click OK. The new account should appear in the Account Setup box.

10. Click the Device tab. Select the modem device that will be used for the connection. Your modem may already be linked to the /dev/modem device (whether it is on COM1 or COM2). To specifically set the modem to one of those ports, you could select /dev/ttyS0 for COM1, or select /dev/ttyS1 for COM2 (and so on).

11. Click OK to exit from the kppp Configuration window.

12. From the main kppp window (which should still be on your screen), make sure that your new connection type appears in the Connect to window. The first time you try the connection, click the Show Log Window box. Type the login ID and password for your ISP account.

13. Click Connect. The Login Script Debug window will step through the process of initializing the modem, dialing, and making the PPP connection. If all goes well, you should be able to start browsing the Internet. If the connection fails, skip to the "Checking your PPP connection" section for information on hunting down the problem.

Launching your PPP connection

After you have a working PPP connection configured, you can set up that connection to launch easily from the desktop. Here's how:

From the GNOME desktop:

1. Right-click Panel and then choose Panel ⇨ Add to Panel ⇨ Applet ⇨ Network ⇨ RH PPP Dialer from the GNOME menu.

   When the Choose pop-up window appears, click the interface you want to use and then click OK.

2. You can either start the connection now or not. In either case, after you finish Step 1, an icon appears on the panel that you can click to immediately connect to the ISP (click the green button).

From the KDE desktop:

1. Right-click the desktop and choose Create New ⇨ Link to Application.
2. Type **Dialup.kdelnk**.
3. Click the icon and select an icon to represent the application; then click OK. (There is one called kppp that you can use.)
4. Click the Execute tab and then type **kppp** into the Execute box. Click OK.
5. An icon called Dialup appears on your KDE desktop. Click it to open the kppp window. Then select your ISP from the Connect box and click Connect to start your PPP connection.

From this point forward, icons will appear on your desktop that you can select to immediately connect to your ISP over the dial-up connection you configured. Both GNOME and KDE support drag-and-drop, so you can drag the dial-up icon to the desktop to make it even more easily available.

Checking your PPP connection

To debug your PPP connection or simply to better understand how it works, you can run through the steps below. They will help you understand where information is being stored and how tools can be used to track this information.

Check that your PPP interface is working

One way to do this is with the ping command. From the Terminal window, type **ping** along with any Internet address you know. For example:

```
$ ping www.handsonhistory.com
PING handsonhistory.com (198.60.22.8) from 192.168.0.43 : 56(84) bytes of data.
64 bytes from handsonhistory.com (198.60.22.8): icmp_seq=0 ttl=240 time=120 msec
64 bytes from handsonhistory.com (198.60.22.8): icmp_seq=1 ttl=240 time=116 msec
64 bytes from handsonhistory.com (198.60.22.8): icmp_seq=2 ttl=240 time=120 msec

--- www.handsonhistory.com ping statistics ---
4 packets transmitted, 3 packets received, 25% packet loss
round-trip min/avg/max/mdev = 116.816/119.277/120.807/1.779 ms
```

Press Ctrl+C to end the `ping` command. The lines above show the responses from `www.handsonhistory.com`. It sent back packets from the IP address `198.60.22.8` in response to each one it received. You can see the sequence of packets (`icmp_seq`) and the time it took for each response (in milliseconds). If you receive packets in return, you will know two things: first, that your connection is working, and second, that your name to address translation (from the DNS addresses in `/etc/resolv.conf`) is working.

Check the default route

Check that the default route is set using the `route -n` command.

```
# /sbin/route -n
Kernel IP routing table
Destination    Gateway      Genmask          Flags Metric Ref Use Iface
198.62.1.1     0.0.0.0      255.255.255.255  UH    0      0   0 ppp0
10.0.0.0       0.0.0.0      255.0.0.0        U     0      0   0 eth0
127.0.0.0      0.0.0.0      255.0.0.0        U     0      0   0 lo
0.0.0.0        198.62.1.1   0.0.0.0          UG    0      0   0 ppp0
```

This shows that the gateway was set to the remote PPP server (`198.62.1.1`), as well as showing the other interfaces running on my computer. There are two ppp0 entries. The first shows the destination as a host (`UH`). The second shows the destination as a gateway (`UG`). All addresses that can't be resolved on the local LAN are directed to the gateway address.

Check that the name servers are set

If you are able to ping a remote computer by IP address, but are not able to resolve any addresses, your DNS servers may not be set correctly. As root user from a Terminal window, open the `/etc/resolv.conf` file and check that there are lines identifying one or more DNS servers in this file. These should be supplied to you by your ISP. Here are some examples (the numbers are fictitious):

```
nameserver 111.11.11.111
nameserver 222.22.22.222
```

Check the chap-secrets or pap-secrets files

PPP supports two authentication protocols in Red Hat Linux: Challenge Handshake Authentication Protocol (CHAP) and Password Authentication Protocol (PAP). Here is what each protocol does to authenticate:

✦ **CHAP** — The server sends the client a challenge packet (which includes the server name). The client sends back a response that includes its name and a value that combines the secret and the challenge. The client name and secret are stored in your `/etc/ppp/chap-secrets` file.

✦ **PAP** — The client sends its name and a password (clear text) for authentication. The client name and secret are stored in your `/etc/ppp/pap-secrets` file.

By default, PPP in Red Hat Linux will authenticate if the server requests it, unless it has no secrets to share. If it has no secrets, PPP (or, more specifically, the PPP daemon pppd) will refuse authentication. It is likely that if you look in these files you will find the user names and passwords you provided when you set up your PPP connection (Red Hat assumes that you may be using CHAP or PAP authentication).

The chap-secrets and pap-secrets file formats are the same. Each authentication line can contain the client name, the server name, and the secret. The server name can be represented by an * (to allow this secret to be used to authenticate any server). This is useful if you don't know what the server name will be. Also, remember that case is significant (that is, Myserver is not the same as myserver).

Tip

For more details about PAP and CHAP in PPP for Linux, see the pppd man page (type `man pppd`).

In any case, here's an example of what a chap-secrets file may look like:

```
# Secrets for authentication using CHAP
# client              server        secret                    IP addresses
0300584919390921      *             JckMLt4CwZiYo03/bkNTpLmU   *
```

Caution

The pap-secrets and chap-secrets files should not be accessible by anyone but the root user. Anyone gaining this information could use it to access your Internet account. (To close permission, type `chmod 600 /etc/ppp/*-secrets`.)

You need to obtain your own client name and secret from your ISP. The ones shown here are just examples.

Look at the ifcfg-ppp0 file

The ifcg-ppp0 file (`/etc/sysconfig/network-scripts/ifcfg-ppp0`) contains options that are passed to the pppd daemon for features that are negotiated with the remote PPP server. Most of the problems that can occur with your PPP connection result from getting some of these options wrong (particularly asking for features that the server can't or won't provide).

Here is an example of the ifcfg-ppp0 file that you can use to connect to a Windows NT PPP server:

```
DEVICE=ppp0
NAME=Acme_Internet_Service
MODEMPORT=/dev/ttyS0
LINESPEED=115200
PAPNAME=guest
ONBOOT=no
DEFROUTE=yes
DEMAND=yes
IDLETIMEOUT=600
```

The device name is ppp0 (which is associated with the configuration file ifcfg-ppp0). NAME is the name you assigned to the connection. MODEMPORT is the device name associated with the port the modem is connected to (in this case, COM1). LINESPEED sets the speed, in bps, between the computer and the modem (not the dial-up speed, which is typically slower). PAPNAME is the user name that you log in with, assuming you are using PAP authentication.

ONBOOT is set to no, meaning that the connection doesn't start automatically at boot time. DEFROUTE=yes sets the default route to be this PPP connection. DEMAND=yes causes the link to be initiated only when traffic is present. IDLETIMEOUT=600 causes your connection to time out after 600 seconds (that is, ten minutes).

> **Tip**　If you want to see the exact options that each of these parameters set, look at the contents of the /etc/sysconfig/network-scripts/ifup-ppp script. For example, if DEFROUTE=yes, then the option defaultroute is sent to the pppd daemon. See the pppd man page for a description of each option (type man pppd).

You can add PPPOPTIONS lines to set any additional options you want passed to the pppd daemon process. There are some cases where the ISP will require other values that are not included here. Likewise, there are some options that you should not put in this file when connecting to certain types of servers. Here are some suggestions of values that either should not be in this file or should be (in some cases) for some Windows NT servers. For descriptions of these options, see the pppd man page:

✦ remotename=*remotename* — You may need this value for PAP authentication, but it should not be entered for CHAP authentication. (For CHAP, the remote PPP server sends you its name.)

✦ require-chap, require-pap, auth, noauth — It's a nice idea to ask a Windows NT server to authenticate itself (which is what require-chap and require-pap do for their respective protocols). The auth value requires the server to authenticate itself before packets can be sent or received. However, I'm told on good authority that Windows NT will not let you do any of this. Authentication will fail and you will not get a connection. You may need to indicate explicitly that the server is not required to authenticate itself by entering the noauth option.

✦ default-asyncmap — PAP can fail to authenticate because of "link transparency problems." If authentication fails and you are sure you have the authentication information correct, try adding this value.

✦ ipcp-accept-local, ipcp-accept remote — Sometimes a server will request your local IP address, even if it wants to assign one itself. The same is true of the remote address. Try adding these lines to the options file:

```
192.168.0.1:192.168.0.2
ipcp-accept-local
ipcp-accept-remote
demand
```

This gives temporary local and remote addresses and tells the remote server that it can replace those values. Instead of using private IP addresses (as shown here), you could use 0.0.0.0 instead.

✦ bsdcomp, deflate—Certain kinds of compression are not supported with Windows NT PPP servers. So, you should not request BSD compression (bsdcomp) or Deflate compression (deflate). In some cases, you may want to specifically prohibit those types of compression: nobsdcomp, nodeflate, and noccp (for no compression control protocol).

As noted earlier, the best place for descriptions of pppd options is the pppd man page. For a sample options file, look in /usr/share/doc/ppp*/sample.

Run debugging

If you are not getting connected at all, the first thing to do is to turn on logging for PPP. This will help you track down the problem. If you are still stumped after looking at the logging output, take the log file and have an expert review it. Make sure that debugging is turned on by setting DEBUG=yes in the ifcfg-ppp0 file.

Tip

I recommend posting your failed PPP output to the comp.protocol.ppp newsgroup, where some very smart PPP experts can help answer your questions. Before you post, however, read a few days' worth of messages from the group. Chances are that someone has already run into the same problem and has a solution. Also, post only the parts of the log file that are relevant.

To have debugging directed to a separate log file for PPP, add these lines to the /etc/syslog.conf file:

```
daemon.*        /var/log/pppmsg
local2.*        /var/log/pppmsg
```

After this, restart the syslogd daemon process as follows:

```
# service syslog restart
```

It's best to try to do this debugging process from the desktop because it helps to have several Terminal windows open (I would suggest at least three). From the first window, start a command that lists the contents of the log file we just defined above (pppmsg) as debug messages come in:

```
# tail -f /var/log/pppmsg
```

In the next window, start the PPP interface. Assuming ppp0, use the following command as root user:

```
# ifup ppp0
```

Here is a partial listing of the output:

```
Jun  6 20:43:51 maple pppd[2077]: pppd 2.3.7 started by root, uid 0
Jun  6 20:43:51 maple ifup-ppp: pppd started for ppp0 on /dev/modem at 115200
Jun  6 20:43:52 maple chat[2079]: abort on (BUSY)
Jun  6 20:43:52 maple chat[2079]: abort on (ERROR)
Jun  6 20:43:52 maple chat[2079]: abort on (NO CARRIER)
Jun  6 20:43:52 maple chat[2079]: abort on (NO DIALTONE)
Jun  6 20:43:52 maple chat[2079]: abort on (Invalid Login)
Jun  6 20:43:52 maple chat[2079]: abort on (Login incorrect)
Jun  6 20:43:52 maple chat[2079]: send (ATZ^M)
Jun  6 20:43:52 maple chat[2079]: expect (OK)
Jun  6 20:43:53 maple chat[2079]: ATZ^M^M
Jun  6 20:43:53 maple chat[2079]: OK
Jun  6 20:43:53 maple chat[2079]:  -- got it
Jun  6 20:43:53 maple chat[2079]: send (ATDT5551212^M)
Jun  6 20:43:53 maple chat[2079]: expect (CONNECT)
Jun  6 20:43:53 maple chat[2079]: ^M
Jun  6 20:44:10 maple chat[2079]: ATDT5551212^M^M
Jun  6 20:44:10 maple chat[2079]: CONNECT
Jun  6 20:44:10 maple chat[2079]:  -- got it
Jun  6 20:44:10 maple chat[2079]: send (\d)
Jun  6 20:44:14 maple pppd[2077]: Serial connection established.
Jun  6 20:44:14 maple pppd[2077]: Using interface ppp0
Jun  6 20:44:14 maple pppd[2077]: Connect: ppp0 <--> /dev/modem
                .
                .
                .
Jun  6 20:44:17 maple pppd[2077]: local  IP address 222.62.137.121
Jun  6 20:44:17 maple pppd[2077]: remote IP address 222.62.1.105
```

This output shows starting the PPP connection on /dev/modem. After verifying that the modem is working, the chat script sends the telephone number. The connection is made, and the PPP interface is started. After some parameter negotiations, the server assigns IP addresses to both sides of the communication, and the connection is ready to use.

If you do get connected, but none of your applications (Web browser, FTP, and so on) seem to work, check that your PPP interface is noted as the default route (/sbin/route -n). If it is, check that you have the DNS servers specified correctly in your /etc/resolv.conf file. Use the ping command on those DNS server IP addresses to make sure you can get through.

Connecting Your LAN to the Internet

The users on your LAN are happy that you made it so that they can share files and printers with each other. However, if they want to get out to the Internet they may need to use their own modem, telephone line, and Internet account to get there. With your users already connected on a LAN, you can set up a connection to the Internet that everyone can share. The advantages of doing this are as follows:

✦ **Save on modems**—Instead of each computer having its own modem, you can have one high-speed modem (such as a DSL modem) that routes all messages to the Internet.

✦ **Save on telephone lines**—Instead of using a telephone line for each person who wants to get to the Internet, you can use one line to your ISP. (In the case of DSL, the telephone company will even let you use the same telephone line for both analog voice and high-speed digital data.)

✦ **Central maintenance**—If information related to your Internet connection changes (such as your dial-out number or name server addresses), you can administrate those changes in one location instead of having to change it on every computer.

✦ **Central security**—You can better control the Internet traffic that comes in to and goes out of your network.

The procedures in this section assume that you have already set up a LAN, as described in Chapter 15. It is also assumed that you have an outgoing connection from your Red Hat Linux system to the Internet that all traffic between the computers on your LAN and the Internet can pass through. That outgoing connection may be dial-up or through another LAN card connected to a DSL modem or other LAN. This section describes two ways to set up the Red Hat Linux computer so clients on the LAN can access the Internet:

✦ **As a router**—By configuring Red Hat Linux as a router, it can route IP packets from clients on the LAN to the Internet through the dial-up connection.

✦ **As a proxy server**—You can configure Red Hat Linux as a proxy server. In this way, client computers on your LAN can access the Internet as though the connection were coming from the Linux computer.

Setting Up Red Hat Linux as a Router

There are several different ways to set up routing from your LAN to the Internet. You can have a dedicated router (such as the Cisco 675 ADSL router), or you can have a computer already connected to your LAN that will act as a router. This section describes how to use your Red Hat Linux computer as a router.

A computer may have several network interfaces, such as a loopback, an Ethernet LAN, a direct line to another computer, or a dial-up interface. For a client computer to use a router to reach the Internet, it may have private IP addresses assigned to computers on the LAN, while the connection to a routing computer would act as the gateway to all other addresses.

Here is a fairly simple example of a Red Hat Linux computer being used as a router between a LAN and the Internet:

✦ The Red Hat Linux system has at least two network interfaces: one to the office LAN and one to the Internet. The interface to the Internet may be a dial-up PPP connection or a higher-speed DSL or cable modem connection.

✦ Packets on the LAN that are not addressed to a known computer on the LAN are forwarded to the router (that is, the Red Hat Linux system acting as a router). So, each client identifies that Red Hat Linux system as the gateway system.

✦ The Red Hat Linux "router" firewall is set up to receive packets from the local LAN, then forwards those packets to its other interface (possibly a PPP connection to the Internet). If the LAN uses private IP addresses, the firewall is also configured to use IP masquerading.

Tip
You can set up a Linux computer as a dedicated router. The Linux Router Project (www.psychosis.com/linux-router) is a mini-distribution of Linux that fits on one 3.5-inch floppy disk. With it, you can maintain a router and terminal server more simply than with a full Linux system. This is a good way to make use of that old 486 in the closet.

The following sections describe how to set up the Red Hat Linux router, as well as the client computers from your LAN (Red Hat Linux and MS Windows clients) that will use this router. Using Red Hat Linux as a router also provides an excellent opportunity to improve the security of your Internet connection by setting up a firewall to filter traffic and hide the identity of the computers on your LAN (IP masquerading).

Configuring the Red Hat Linux router

To configure your Red Hat Linux computer as a router, you need to have a few things in place. Here's what you need to do before you set up routing:

✦ **Connect to your LAN.** Add a network card and optionally set up the addresses (in /etc/hosts) to the computers on your LAN. (This is described in Chapter 15.)

✦ **Connect to the Internet.** Set up a dial-up or other type of connection from your Red Hat Linux computer to your ISP. This is described earlier in this chapter in the section on setting up outgoing PPP connections.

✦ **Configure your Red Hat Linux computer as a router.** This procedure is described in the rest of this section.

The type of IP addresses you are using on your LAN will have an impact on a couple of steps in this procedure. Here are the differences:

✦ **Private IP addresses** — If the computers on your LAN use private IP addresses (described in Chapter 15), you need to set up IP masquerading. Because those numbers are private, they must be hidden from the Internet when the Red Hat Linux router forwards their requests. Packets forwarded with masquerading look to the outside world as though they came from the Red Hat Linux computer forwarding the packets.

Note IP addresses can be assigned statically (as described in Chapter 15) or using DHCP (as described in Chapter 23).

✦ **Valid IP addresses** — If your LAN uses addresses that were officially assigned by your ISP or other registration authority, you don't need to do any special IP masquerading.

With your Red Hat Linux computer's LAN and Internet interfaces in place, follow the procedure below to set up Red Hat Linux as a router:

1. Open the `/etc/sysconfig/network` file in a text editor as the root user. Then add either a default gateway or default gateway device as described below.

   Your default gateway is where IP addresses are sought that are not on any of your local interfaces. This is where you would identify your Internet connection. Here is how you choose which one to enter:

   • **Default Gateway** — If there is a static IP address you use to reach the Internet, enter that IP address here. For example, if your Internet connection went through a DSL modem on your LAN at address 192.168.0.1, you would enter that address as follows:

   ```
   GATEWAY=192.168.0.1
   ```

   • **Default Gateway Device** — If you reach the Internet using a dynamic address that is assigned when you connect to a particular interface, you would enter that interface here. For example, if you had a dial-up interface to the Internet on the first PPP device, you would enter ppp0 as the default gateway device as follows:

   ```
   GATEWAYDEV=ppp0
   ```

   When you are done, the contents of this file should look similar to the following:

   ```
   NETWORKING=yes
   HOSTNAME=maple
   DOMAINNAME=handsonhistory.com
   #GATEWAY=
   GATEWAYDEV=ppp0
   ```

In this case, the computer is configured to route packets over a dial-up connection to the Internet (ppp0).

2. Turn on IP packet forwarding. One way to do this is to change the value of `net.ipv4.ip_forward` to 1 in the `/etc/sysctl.conf` file. Open that file as root user with any text editor and change the line to appear as follows:

```
net.ipv4.ip_forward = 1
```

3. If the computers on your LAN have valid IP addresses, skip ahead to the section on configuring Red Hat Linux routing clients. If your computers have private IP addresses, continue with this procedure.

Caution

The ipchains example in the next step is not terribly secure, although in most cases it will get routing up and going. I recommend that you read the IP masquerading section later in this chapter, as well as Chapter 14, for information on firewalls and other security issues.

4. To get IP masquerading going on your Red Hat Linux router, you need to define which addresses will be masqueraded and forwarded. Here is an example where all computers on the LAN with a network number of 10.0.0.0 are accepted for forwarding and masquerading:

```
# ipchains -P forward DENY
# ipchains -A forward -i ppp0 -s 10.0.0.0/255.0.0.0 -j MASQ
```

This example shows that, by default, forwarding is denied (DENY). Forwarding is done, however, for a computer on the network 10.0.0.0 (with a netmask of 255.0.0.0); packets will be forwarded to the ppp0 interface and masqueraded (MASQ) as if they came from the local Red Hat Linux system.

You could use a shorter notation for entering the netmask. For a class A, B, or C network, the value is 8, 16, or 24, respectively. Instead of allowing the whole network, you could also just allow individual hosts. For example, you could have separate forward lines for 10.0.0.10, 10.0.0.11, 10.0.0.12, and so forth.

To set up your forwarding rules permanently, you can add them to the ipchains configuration file. This will run the rules each time the system reboots (or the network restarts). If you added the rules described above to the `/etc/sysconfig/ipchains` file, the file would appear as follows:

```
:input ACCEPT
:forward ACCEPT
-P forward DENY
-A forward -i ppp0 -s 10.0.0.0/255.0.0.0 -j MASQ
:output ACCEPT
```

5. At this point, you may want to restart your Linux system.

6. To check that your `ipchains` commands worked, print out the `ip_fwchains` proc file contents as follows:

```
# cat /proc/net/ip_fwchains | grep MASQ
forward 0A000000/FF000000->00000000/00000000 ppp0 0 0 0
     0  0  0  0-65535 0-65535 AFF X00 00000000 0 0  MASQ
```

The output shows that the forwarding policy (`forward`) is set to do masquerading (`MASQ`) for computers on the network 10.0.0.0.

At this point, you should set up the client computers to use your Red Hat Linux router for their Internet connections.

Configuring network clients

In this example, there are a variety of Red Hat Linux and Windows operating system clients on a LAN. One Red Hat Linux computer has a connection to the Internet and is willing to act as a router between the Internet and the other computers on the LAN (as described in the previous section). To be able to reach computers on the Internet, each client must be capable of doing the following things:

✦ Resolve the names it requests (for example, `www.redhat.com`) into IP addresses.

✦ Find a route to get from the local system to the remote system, using the local system's existing network interfaces.

The way each Red Hat Linux client computer knows how to find another computer's address is based on the contents of the `/etc/host.conf`, `/etc/hosts`, and `/etc/resolv.conf` files. The contents of the `host.conf` file by default is the following:

```
order hosts,bind
```

This tells your system to check for any hostnames that you request by first checking the contents of the `/etc/hosts` file and then checking with name servers that are identified in the `/etc/resolv.conf` file. In our case, we will put the addresses of every host we know about on our private network (whether on the LAN, direct connection, or other network interface) in the `/etc/hosts` file. Then, we will add addresses of name servers that we get from our Internet Service Provider to the `/etc/resolv.conf` file.

Next, each client machine must know how to get to the Internet. You do this by adding a default route that identifies the location of the router to the client computer. (Often, this router is indicated on the client as the gateway or gateway device.) This default route is used to try to access any address that the client doesn't specifically know how to reach (that is, hosts that aren't on the local LAN or other direct interface). You can add the default route using the `route` command. Here is an example:

```
# route add default gw 10.0.0.1 eth0
```

To make the default route permanent on the client Red Hat Linux system, do the following:

1. Set the default route to point to the router. This entails setting the GATEWAY or GATEWAYDEV value in the /etc/sysconfig/network file as described in the previous procedure. (This time, the address will point to the LAN interface of the router.)

2. Restart your network interfaces by typing the following as root user:

```
# /etc/init.d/network restart
```

3. When the computer comes back up, type the following:

```
# netstat -r
Kernel IP routing table
Destination  Gateway   Genmask    Flags  MSS Window  irtt
Iface
10.0.0.0     *         255.0.0.0  U      0   0       0
eth0
127.0.0.0    *         255.0.0.0  U      0   0       0    lo
default      10.0.0.1  0.0.0.0    UG     0   0       0
eth0
```

You can see that the default gateway was set to the host at the IP address 10.0.0.1 on the eth0 Ethernet interface. Assuming that router is ready to route your packets to the Internet, your Red Hat Linux client is now ready to use that router to find all IP addresses that you request that you do not already know where to find. (The netstat -r command provides the same output as the /sbin/route command.)

Configuring Windows network clients

If you have some Microsoft systems on your LAN, you need to configure them so that they can connect to the Internet through your router. To set up the Windows operating system computers on your private network to access the Internet through your routing computer, you have to add only a few pieces of information to each Windows system. Here's how to do this from Windows ME and most other Windows systems:

1. Choose Start ⇨ Settings ⇨ Control Panel.

2. Open the Network icon in the Control Panel.

3. Double-click the interface shown that supports connecting to the Linux router. (For a LAN, it may look like this: TCP/IP ⇨ 3Com EtherLink III.)

4. Click the Gateway tab, type the IP address of your Linux router, and then click Add.

5. Click the DNS Configuration tab, type in the number of the DNS server that you use to resolve addresses on the Internet, and then click Add. Repeat this step if you have multiple DNS servers.

6. Click OK.

7. You may need to reboot your computer at this point, if Windows requires you to do so.

At this point, try accessing a Web site from your Internet browser on the Windows computer. If the Internet connection is up on your Red Hat Linux computer, you should be able to connect to the Internet through your LAN connection to the Red Hat Linux computer.

Setting Up Red Hat Linux as a Proxy Server

You have a LAN set up, and your Red Hat Linux computer has both a connection to the LAN and a connection to the Internet. One way to provide Web-browsing services to the computers on the LAN without setting up routing is to configure your Red Hat Linux computer as a proxy server.

The Squid proxy caching server software package comes with Red Hat Linux. In a basic configuration, you can get the software going very quickly. However, the package is full of configuration features that let you adapt it to your needs. You can control which hosts have access to proxy services, how memory is used to cache data, how logging is done, and a variety of other features. Here are the basic proxy services available with Squid:

✦ **HTTP** — Allowing HTTP proxy services is the primary reason to use Squid. This is what lets client computers access Web pages on the Internet from their browsers (through your Red Hat Linux computer). In other words, HTTP proxy services will find and return the content to you for addresses that look similar to this: `www.whatever.com`.

✦ **FTP** — This represents File Transfer Protocol (FTP) proxy services. When you enable HTTP for a client, you enable FTP automatically (for example, `ftp://ftp.whatever.com`).

✦ **Gopher** — The gopher protocol proxy service was one of the first mechanisms for organizing and searching for documents on the Internet (it predates the Web by more than a decade). It isn't used much anymore. However, if you need to use it, gopher is supported when you enable HTTP for a client.

Besides allowing proxy services, Squid can also be part of an Internet cache hierarchy. Internet caching occurs when Internet content is taken from the original server and copied to a caching server that is closer to you. When you, or someone else in the caching hierarchy, requests that content again, it can be taken from the caching server instead of having to be retrieved from the original server.

You don't have to cache Internet content for other computers to participate in caching with Squid. If you know of a parent caching-computer that will allow you access, you can identify that computer in Squid and potentially speed your Web browsing significantly.

Caching services in Squid are provided through your Linux system's ICP port. Besides ICP services, you can also enable Simple Network Management Protocol (SNMP) services. SNMP enables your computer to make statistics and status information about itself available to SNMP agents on the network. SNMP is a feature for monitoring and maintaining computer resources over a network.

 Caution SNMP poses a potential security risk if it is not configured properly. Use caution when configuring SNMP with Squid.

The squid daemon process (/usr/sbin/squid) can be started automatically at system boot time. After that is set up, most of the configuration for Squid is done in the /etc/squid/squid.conf file. The sample squid.conf file (/etc/squid/squid.conf.default) contains lots of information about how to configure Squid (the file contains more than 1800 lines of comments, examples, and default settings).

For further information about the Squid proxy server, refer to the Squid Web Proxy Cache home page (www.squid-cache.org).

Starting the squid daemon

When you install Red Hat Linux, you have an opportunity to install Squid. If you are not sure whether or not Squid was set up, there are a couple of ways to check. First, type the following as root user:

```
# ps x | grep squid
```

If the squid daemon is running, you should see an entry that looks similar to the following:

```
774 ?      S       0:00 squid -D
```

If you don't see a Squid process running, the daemon process may not be set up to start automatically. To set up the daemon to start at boot time, type the following:

```
# chkconfig squid on
```

At this point, the squid daemon should start automatically when your system boots. By default, the squid daemon will run with the -D option. The -D option enables Squid to start without having an active Internet connection. If you want to add other options to the squid daemon, you can edit that startup script. First, make a copy (cp /etc/init.d/squid /etc/init.d/squid.default) and then edit the /etc/rc.d/init.d/squid script. Look for the line that looks similar to the following:

```
SQUID_OPTS="-D"
```

You can add any options, along with the `-D` option, between the quotes. Most of these options are useful for debugging Squid:

✦ `-a` *port#*—Substitute for *port#* a port number that will be used instead of the default port number (3128) for servicing HTTP proxy requests. This is useful for temporarily trying out an alternative port.

✦ `-f` *squidfile*—Use this option to specify an alternative `squid.conf` file (other than `/etc/squid/squid.conf`). Replace *squidfile* with the name of the alternative `squid.conf` file. This is a good way to try out a new `squid.conf` file before you replace the old one.

✦ `-d` *level*—Change the debugging level to a number indicated by *level*. This also causes debugging messages to be sent to `stderr`.

✦ `-X`—Use this option to check that the values are set properly in your `squid.conf` file. It turns on full debugging while the `squid.conf` file is being interpreted.

You can restart the Squid service by typing `/etc/init.d/squid restart`. While the squid daemon is running, there are several ways you can run the `squid` command to change how the daemon works, using these options:

✦ `squid -k reconfigure`—Causes Squid to again read its configuration file.

✦ `squid -k shutdown`—Causes Squid to exit after waiting briefly for current connections to exit.

✦ `squid -k interrupt`—Shuts down Squid immediately, without waiting for connections to close.

✦ `squid -k kill`—Kills Squid immediately, without closing connections or log files. (Use this option only if other methods don't work.)

With the squid daemon ready to run, you now need to set up the `squid.conf` configuration file.

Using a simple squid.conf file

You can use the `/etc/squid/squid.conf` file that comes with squid to get started. Though the file contains lots of comments, the actual settings in that file are quite manageable. The following paragraphs described the lines that are contained in the default `squid.conf` file:

```
hierarchy_stoplist cgi-bin ?
```

The `hierarchy_stoplist` tag indicates that when a certain string of characters appear in a URL, the content should be obtained from the original server and not from a cache peer. In this example, requests for the string `cgi-bin` and the question mark character (?) are all forwarded to the originating server.

```
acl QUERY urlpath_regex cgi-bin \?
no_cache deny QUERY
```

The preceding two lines can be used to cause URLs containing certain characters to never be cached. These go along with the previous line by not caching URLs containing the same strings (cgi-bin and ?) that are always sought from the original server.

```
acl all src 0.0.0.0/0.0.0.0
acl manager proto cache_object
acl localhost src 127.0.0.1/255.255.255.255
```

The acl tags are used to create access control lists. The first line above creates an access control list called "all" that includes all IP addresses. The next acl line assigns the manager acl to handle the cache_object protocol. The localhost source is assigned to the IP address of 127.0.0.1.

The next several entries define how particular ports are handled and how access is assigned to HTTP and ICP services.

```
acl SSL_ports port 443 563
acl Safe_ports port 80                  # http
acl Safe_ports port 21                  # ftp
acl Safe_ports port 443 563             # https, snews
acl Safe_ports port 70                  # gopher
acl Safe_ports port 210                 # wais
acl Safe_ports port 1025-65535          # unregistered ports
acl Safe_ports port 280                 # http-mgmt
acl Safe_ports port 488                 # gss-http
acl Safe_ports port 591                 # filemaker
acl Safe_ports port 777                 # multiling http
acl CONNECT method CONNECT
http_access allow manager localhost
http_access deny manager
http_access deny !Safe_ports
http_access deny CONNECT !SSL_ports
http_access allow localhost
http_access deny all
icp_access allow all
```

The following sections describe these settings in more detail, as well as other tags you may want to set in your squid.conf file.

To make sure that this simple Squid configuration is working, follow the procedure below:

1. On the Squid server, restart the squid daemon. To do this, either reboot your computer or type /etc/init.d/squid restart. (If Squid isn't running, use start instead of restart.)

2. On the Squid server, start your connection to the Internet (if it is not already up).

3. On a client computer on your network, set up Netscape (or another Web browser) to use the Squid server as a proxy server (described later in this chapter). (In Netscape, choose Edit ➪ Preferences ➪ Advanced ➪ Proxies, then choose Manual proxy configuration ➪ View, and add the Squid server's computer name and, by default, port 3128 to each protocol.)

4. On the client computer, try to open any Web page on the Internet with the browser you just configured.

If the Web page doesn't appear, see the section on debugging Squid for ideas on fixing the problem.

Modifying the Squid configuration file

If you want to set up a more complex set of access permissions for Squid, you should start with the default `squid.conf` configuration file (described earlier).

To begin, open the `/etc/squid/squid.conf` file (as the root user). You will see a lot of information describing the values that you can set in this file. In general, most of the tags that you need to configure Squid are used to set up cache and provide host access to your proxy server.

Tip

Don't change the `squid.conf.default` file! If you really mess up your `squid.conf` file, you can start again by making another copy of this file to `squid.conf`. If you want to recall exactly what change you have made so far, type the following from the `/etc/squid` directory:

```
# diff squid.conf squid.conf.default | less
```

This will show you the differences between your actual `squid.conf` and the version you started with.

Configuring access control in squid.conf

To protect your computing resources from being used by anyone, Squid requires that you define which host computers have access to your HTTP (Web) services. By default, all hosts are denied access to Squid HTTP services except for the local host. With the `acl` tag, you can create access lists. Then, with the `http_access` tag, you can authorize access to HTTP (Web) services for the access lists you create.

The form of the access control list tag (`acl`) is:

```
acl  name  type  string
acl  name  type  file
```

The *name* is any name you want to assign to the list. A *string* is a string of text, and *file* is a file of information that applies to the particular *type* of acl. Valid acl types include `dst`, `src`, `dstdomain`, `srcdomain`, `url_path_pattern`, `url_pattern`, `time`, `port`, `proto`, `method`, `browser`, and `user`.

Several access control lists are set up by default. You can use these assigned acl names to assign permissions to HTTP or ICP services. You can also create your own acl names to assign to those services. Here are the default acl names from the /etc/squid/squid.conf file that you can use or change:

```
acl all src 0.0.0.0/0.0.0.0
acl manager proto cache_object
acl localhost src 127.0.0.1/255.255.255.255
acl SSL_ports port 443 563
acl Safe_ports port 80              # http
acl Safe_ports port 21              # ftp
acl Safe_ports port 443 563        # https, snews
acl Safe_ports port 70              # gopher
acl Safe_ports port 210             # wais
acl Safe_ports port 1025-65535     # unregistered ports
acl Safe_ports port 280             # http-mgmt
acl Safe_ports port 488             # gss-http
acl Safe_ports port 591             # filemaker
acl Safe_ports port 777             # multiling http
acl CONNECT method CONNECT
```

When Squid tries to determine which class a particular computer falls in, it goes from top to bottom. In the first line, all host computers (address/netmask are all zeros) are added to the acl group all. In the second line, you create a manager group called manager that has access to your cache_object (the capability to get content from your cache). The group localhost is assigned to your loopback address. Secure socket layer (SSL) ports are assigned to the numbers 443 and 563, whereas Safe_ports are assigned to the numbers shown above. The last line defines a group called CONNECT (which you can use later to allow access to your SSL ports).

To deny or enable access to HTTP services on the Squid computer, the following definitions are set up:

```
http_access allow manager localhost
http_access deny manager
http_access deny !Safe_ports
http_access deny CONNECT !SSL_ports
http_access allow localhost
http_access deny all
```

These definitions are quite restrictive. The first line allows someone requesting cache objects (manager) from the local host to do so, but the second line denies anyone else making such a request. Access is not denied to ports defined as safe ports. Also, secure socket connections via the proxy are denied on all ports, except for SSL ports (!SSL_ports). HTTP access is permitted only from the local host and is denied to all other hosts.

To allow the client computers on your network access to your HTTP service, you need to create your own `http_access` entries. You probably want to do something more restrictive than simply saying `http_access allow all`. Here is an example of a more restrictive `acl` group and how to assign that group to HTTP access:

```
acl ourlan src 10.0.0.1-10.0.0.100/255.0.0.0
http_access allow ourlan
```

In the previous example, all computers at IP addresses 10.0.0.1 through 10.0.0.100 are assigned to the `ourlan` group (the netmask is 255.0.0.0, indicating a Class A network). Access is then allowed for `ourlan` with the `http_access` line.

Configuring caching in squid.conf

Caching, as it relates to a proxy server, is the process of storing data on an intermediate system between the Web server that sent the data and the client that received it. The assumption is that later requests for the same data can be serviced more quickly by not having to go all the way back to the original server. Instead, your proxy server (or other proxy server) can simply send you the content from its copy in cache. Another benefit of caching is that it reduces demands on network resources and on the information servers.

You can arrange caching with other caching proxy servers to form a cache hierarchy. The idea is to have a *parent cache* exist close to an entry to the Internet backbone. When a *child cache* requests an object, if the parent doesn't have it, the parent goes out and gets the object, sends a copy to the child, and keeps a copy itself. That way, if another request for the data comes to the parent, it can probably service that request without making another request to the original server. This hierarchy also supports *sibling caches*, which can, in effect, create a pool of caching servers on the same level.

Here are some cache-related tags that you should consider setting:

✦ `cache_peer` — If there is a cache parent whose resources you can use, you can add the parent cache using this tag. You would need to obtain the parent cache's hostname, the type of cache (parent), proxy port (probably 3128), and ICP port (probably 3130) from the administrator of the parent cache. (If you have no parent cache, you don't have to set this value.) Here's an example of a `cache_peer` entry:

```
cache_peer parent.handsonhistory.com parent 3128 3130
```

You can also add options to the end of the line, such as `proxy-only` (so that what you get from the parent isn't stored locally) and `weight=n` (where *n* is replaced by a number above 1 to indicate that the parent should be used above other parents). Add `default` if the parent is used as a last resort (when all other parents don't have the requested data).

✦ `cache_mem`—Specifies the amount of cache memory (RAM) used to store in-transit objects (ones that are currently being used), hot objects (ones that are used often), and negative-cached objects (recent failed requests). The default is 8MB, though you can raise that value. To set `cache_mem` to 16MB, enter the following:

`cache_mem   16 MB`

Note   Because Squid will probably use a total of three times the amount of space you give it for all its processing, Squid documentation recommends that you use a `cache_mem` size one-third the size of the space that you actually have available for Squid.

✦ `cache_dir`—Specifies the directory (or directories if you want to distribute cache across multiple disks or partitions) in which cache swap files are stored. The default is the `/var/spool/squid` directory. You can also specify how much disk space to use for cache in megabytes (100 is the default), the number of first-level directories to create (16 is the default), and the number of second-level directories (256 is the default). Here is an example:

`cache_dir   /var/spool/squid 100 16 256`

Note   The cache directory must exist. Squid won't create it for you. It will, however, create the first- and second-level directories.

✦ `cache_mgr`—Add the e-mail address of the user who should receive e-mail if the cache daemon dies. By default, e-mail is sent to the local Webmaster. To change that value to the root user, use the following:

`cache_mgr   root`

✦ `cache_effective_user`—After the squid daemon process is started as root, subsequent processes are run as Squid user and group (by default). To change that subsequent user to a different name (for example, to `nobody`) set the `cache_effective_user` as follows:

`cache_effective_user   nobody`

Configuring port numbers in squid.conf

When you configure client computers to use your Squid proxy services, the clients need to know your computer's name (or IP address) and the port numbers associated with the services. For a client wanting to use your proxy to access the Web, the HTTP port is the needed number. Here are the tags that you use to set port values in Squid for different services, along with their default values:

✦ `http_port 3128`—The `http_port` is set to 3128 by default. Client workstations need to know this number (or the number you change this value to) to access your proxy server for HTTP services (that is, Web browsing).

✦ `icp_port 3130`—ICP requests are sent to and from neighboring caches through port 3130 by default.

✦ `htcp_port 4827`—ICP sends HTCP requests to and from neighboring caches on port 4827 by default.

Debugging Squid

If Squid isn't working properly when you set it up, or if you just want to monitor Squid activities, there are several tools and log files to help you. These are discussed below.

Checking the squid.conf file

By running the squid daemon with the `-X` option (described earlier), you can check what is being set from the `squid.conf` file. You can add an `-X` option to the `SQUID_OPTS` line in the `/etc/init.d/squid` file. Then run `/etc/init.d/squid restart`. A whole lot of information is output, which details what is being set from `squid.conf`. If there are syntax errors in the file, they appear here.

Checking Squid log files

Squid log files (in Red Hat Linux) are stored in the `/var/log/squid` directory by default. The following are the log files created there, descriptions of what they contain, and descriptions of how they may help you debug potential problems:

✦ `access.log`—Contains entries that describe each time the cache has been hit or missed when a client requests HTTP content. Along with that information is the identity of the host making the request (IP address) and the content they are requesting. Use this information to find out when content is being used from cache and when the remote server must be accessed to obtain the content. Here is what some of the access result codes mean:

- `TCP_DENIED`—Squid denied access for the request.
- `TCP_HIT`—Cache contained a valid copy of the object.
- `TCP_IMS_HIT`—A fresh version of the requested object was still in cache when the client asked if the content had changed.
- `TCP_IMS_MISS`—An If-Modified-Since request was issued by the client for a stale object.
- `TCP_MEM_HIT`—Memory contained a valid copy of the object.
- `TCP_MISS`—Cache did not contain the object.
- `TCP_NEGATIVE_HIT`—The object was negatively cached, meaning that an error was returned (such as the file not being found) when the object was requested.
- `TCP_REF_FAIL_HIT`—A stale object was returned from cache because of a failed request to validate the object.

- TCP_REFRESH_HIT—A stale copy of the object was in cache, but a request to the server returned information that the object had not been modified.

- TCP_REFRESH_MISS—A stale cache object was replaced by new, updated content.

- TCP_SWAPFAIL—An object could not be accessed from cache, despite the belief that the object should have been there.

✦ cache.log—Contains valuable information about your Squid configuration when the squid daemon starts up. You can see how much memory is available (Max Mem), how much swap space (Max Swap), the location of the cache directory (/var/spool/squid), the types of connections being accepted (HTTP, ICP, and SNMP), and the port on which connections are being accepted. You can also see a lot of information about cached objects (such as how many are loaded, expired, or canceled).

✦ store.log—Contains entries that show when content is being swapped out from memory to the cache (SWAPOUT), swapped back into memory from cache (SWAPIN), or released from cache (RELEASE). You can see where the content comes from originally and where it is being placed in the cache. Time is logged in this file in raw UNIX time (in milliseconds).

Another log file may interest you: /var/log/messages. This file contains entries describing the startup and exit status of the squid daemon.

Note   When I changed the cache_effective_user name so a user other than Squid ran that Squid, the messages file logged several failed attempts to initialize the Squid cache before the process exited. When I changed the user name back to Squid, the process started properly.

Using the top command

Run the top command to see information about running processes, including the Squid process. If you are concerned about performance hits from too much Squid activity, type M from within the top window. The M option displays information about running processes, sorted by the percent of memory each process is using. If you find that Squid is consuming too large a percentage of your system memory, you can reduce the memory usage by resetting the cache_mem value in your squid.conf file. (There is a graphical version of top called gtop that you can run from the desktop to provide a more friendly interface.)

Setting Up Proxy Clients

For your Red Hat Linux proxy server to provide Web-browsing access (HTTP) to the Windows and Red Hat Linux client computers on your network, each client needs to do a bit of set up within the Web browser. The beauty of using proxy servers is in what your client computers don't need to know, such as the following:

✦ Addresses of DNS servers

✦ Telephone numbers of ISPs

✦ Chat scripts to connect to the ISP

There are probably other things that clients don't need to know, but you get the idea. After the proxy server has a connection to the Internet and has allowed a client computer on the LAN access to that service, all the client needs to know is the following:

✦ **Hostname** — The name or IP address of the proxy server. (This assumes that the client can reach the proxy over the company's LAN or other IP-based network.)

✦ **Port numbers** — The port number of the HTTP service (3128 by default). That same port number can be used for FTP and gopher services as well.

How you go about setting up proxy service on the client has more to do with the browser you are using than with the operating system you are using. Follow the procedures below for setting up Netscape Communicator, Microsoft Internet Explorer, Mosaic, or Lynx browsers.

Configuring Netscape to use a proxy

Normally, you would set up Netscape to browse the Web over a TCP/IP connection to the Internet (over telephone lines or via a router on your LAN). Follow this procedure to change Netscape Communicator to access the Web through your proxy server:

1. Open Netscape Communicator.

2. Choose Edit ⇨ Preferences. The Netscape Preferences window appears.

3. Next to the Advanced category, click the down arrow and select Proxies.

4. Click Manual proxy configuration.

5. Click View. The Manual Proxy Configuration window appears.

6. Type the address of the proxy server in the address boxes for HTTP, FTP, and Gopher services.

7. Type the port number for HTTP services on your proxy server (probably 3128) in the Port boxes for HTTP, FTP, and Gopher services.

8. Click OK (in the Manual Proxy Configuration window) and OK again (in the Preferences window).

The next time you request a Web address from Netscape, it will contact the proxy server to try to obtain the content.

Configuring Internet Explorer to use a proxy

To configure Internet Explorer to use a proxy server to get to the Web, you need to change a few Internet options. Follow the procedure below:

1. Open the Internet Explorer window.

2. Choose View ➪ Internet Options. The Internet Options window appears.

3. Click the Connections tab.

4. Assuming you have a LAN already configured, click Local Area Network and then click Settings. The Local Area Network Settings window should appear.

5. Type the address of the proxy server and the port number for HTTP services (probably 3128).

> **Tip** MS Internet Explorer assumes that the same ports are used for HTTP, Gopher, and FTP services. If this is not true, click Advanced and change the port numbers for each service accordingly.

6. Click OK (in the Local Area Network Settings window) and OK again (in the Internet Options window).

The next time you try to access the Web from Internet Explorer, it will try to do so through the proxy server you defined.

Configuring Mosaic and Lynx browsers to use a proxy

To have a Mosaic or Lynx browser use a proxy server to access the Internet, add an environment variable to the shell where the browser will run. Here is how you would set the environment variables for HTTP, Gopher, and FTP proxy services to a proxy computer named maple using a csh or tcsh shell:

```
setenv http_proxy http://maple:3128/
setenv gopher_proxy http://maple:3128/
setenv ftp_proxy http://maple:3128/
```

If you are using a ksh or bash shell, type the following:

```
export http_proxy=http://maple:3128
export gopher_proxy=http://maple:3128
export ftp_proxy=http://maple:3128
```

You can add any of these values to your startup scripts. Or to make them available on a system-wide basis, you could add them to a system configuration file, such as /etc/profile or /etc/skel/.bash_profile.

Summary

Connecting to the Internet opens a whole world of possibilities for your Red Hat Linux computer. Using Red Hat Linux as a Web server, mail server, or FTP server depends on Red Hat Linux's capability to connect to the Internet. Likewise, if your computers are already connected together in a LAN, adding an Internet connection can provide Internet access to everyone on the LAN in one stroke.

Descriptions of how Internet domains are organized built on discussions of IP addresses in the previous chapter. Creating dial-up connections to the Internet focused on descriptions of the PPP protocol. Debugging methods were also described.

For connecting your LAN to the Internet, several different techniques were discussed. You can set up your Red Hat Linux computer as a router. The Red Hat Linux router either can route packets from computers on your network that have valid IP addresses or can use a special packet-forwarding technique so that computers with private IP addresses can use the Internet. This technique is referred to as IP masquerading.

Finally, the last section described how to set up Red Hat Linux as a proxy server. Using Red Hat Linux as a proxy server with the Squid proxy server software, you can save client computers from having to set up DNS and other information themselves. Each client simply has to identify the proxy server to the Web browser to be capable of using that server to gain access to the Internet.

✦   ✦   ✦

Setting Up a Print Server

Sharing printers is a good way to save money and make your printing more efficient. Very few people need to print all the time, but when they do need something printed, they usually need it quickly. Setting up a print server can save money by eliminating the need for a printer at every workstation. Some of those savings can be used to buy special printer features, such as high-speed printing or color.

You can attach printers to your Red Hat Linux system to make them available to users of that system or to other computers on the network. You can configure your Red Hat Linux printer as a remote Linux printer, a Samba printer, or a NetWare printer. With Samba and NetWare, you are emulating those types of servers.

Red Hat Linux can also act as a client, taking advantage of printers on the network. As a client, Red Hat Linux can access local printers, other Linux or UNIX printers, NetWare printers, and printers on Windows or OS/2 systems (using the SMB protocol).

This chapter describes configuring printers and using printers in Red Hat Linux. The discussion includes configuring printers to emulate printing services for NetWare and Server Message Block (SMB), as well as configuring local printers. For printing documents, Red Hat Linux offers both command-line and GUI tools for configuring printers, as well as several commands for processing text in different formats (such as the `troff` and `TeX` commands, which are described in Chapter 6).

Because Red Hat Linux can act as both a print server and a print client, this chapter contains procedures for both types of configurations. The print client is the computer that is sending documents to the printer. The print server is the computer that is configured to access the printer (with the printer often physically attached).

Printing in Red Hat Linux

Beginning with Red Hat Linux 7, printing is provided by the LPRng (LPR Next Generation) print spooling system. The LPRng software offers many security benefits over the old LPR print spooling facility that was originally used with UNIX systems.

LPRng is based on the old Berkeley UNIX line printer package (`lpr`). This new software offers extensive features for managing multiple printers and queues, as well as providing many security features. Companies and college campuses with hundreds of printers often use LPRng print spooling.

If you are adding one printer for your home computer, you probably don't need to know much about LPRng. If you are managing numerous computers whose resources are being demanded by many people (such as at a large business), LPRng gives you a lot of control and security.

Key pieces of LPRng include the `/etc/printcap` and `/etc/printcap.local` files (where printers are defined) and the `lpd` daemon (which manages the print service). The `lpd` daemon relies mainly on two configuration files: `/etc/lpd.conf`, which contains global printing values, and `/etc/lpd.perms`, which sets access permissions to the printing service. These features are described in the following sections.

Before you can use a printer, you have to identify it to your Red Hat Linux system. This is true whether the printer is connected directly to your computer or must be reached over a network. The `printconf-gui` command opens a graphical window for adding a printer. After a printer is configured, print commands (such as `lpr`) are available for carrying out the actual printing. Commands also exist for querying print queues (`lpq`), manipulating print queues (`lpc`), and removing print queues (`lprm`).

Understanding the lpd print daemon

When someone sends a print request in Red Hat Linux, the lpd (line-printer daemon) process handles that request. In Red Hat Linux, the lpd process is started at boot time from the `/etc/init.d/lpd` script (which is actually linked to a file that is sent to run at boot time). The lpd process handles print requests both from local users and from remote users over the network. Its actions are based on configuration information set up in the `/etc/lpd.conf` and `/etc/lpd.perms` files.

Here is a description of what `lpd` does after it starts up, typically at system boot time:

1. Reads the `/etc/printcap` file to see what printers (and related spool files) it needs to manage.

2. Scans spool files for those printers and prints any files that are queued for those printers.

3. Listens for the following types of requests:

- Requests to print files in the queue
- Requests to transfer files to the spool directories
- Requests to display a listing of the current print jobs in the queue
- Requests to remove print jobs from the queue

4. Starts up a child process to handle each request, so it (lpd) can go back to listening for other printing requests.

For a print request from a remote computer to be accepted, that computer must be allowed in the /etc/lpd.perms file on your Linux system. The /etc/lpd.perms file allows a range of options for permitting or denying printer access. If disk space is a problem on your computer, you can limit the amount of space that lpd can consume in your spool directories. You can limit the amount of disk space (in blocks) that each printer's spool files can consume by creating a minfree file in each spool directory. The file should simply contain the number of blocks on the disk that the spool files can consume.

For files that are destined for remote printers (in other words, those files whose printing is handled by other computers), lpd relies on special filters to handle the printing. Special filters exist for printing to NetWare and SMB printers (described later).

Setting permissions in lpd.perms

When a request comes to the lpd daemon to print a document (or otherwise access the spool directories), it consults the /etc/lpd.perms file to determine whether the request should be accepted or rejected. If no specific action is set up for the request, then the lpd daemon takes the default action, which is DEFAULT ACCEPT, to accept the action.

The permissions that you set in this file can be quite specific. When you begin, here are the values that are set in the lpd.perms file (the comment lines in the file are omitted here):

```
ACCEPT SERVICE=C SERVER REMOTEUSER=root
ACCEPT SERVICE=C LPC=lpd,status,printcap
REJECT SERVICE=C
ACCEPT SERVICE=M SAMEHOST SAMEUSER
ACCEPT SERVICE=M SERVER REMOTEUSER=root
REJECT SERVICE=M
DEFAULT ACCEPT
```

In this file, the C service refers to requests from the lpc command to control the print spools (in other words, to change the files that are waiting to print). The M service refers to requests from the lprm command to remove print jobs.

The first line in the preceding block allows a remote root user to control print services on the computer. The second line allows anyone to get information from the print daemon (lpd), the status of print jobs from the print queues (status), and information from the printcap file (printcap). The third line causes all other lpc-related requests to be rejected. The fourth line allows users on any computer to remove their own print jobs. The fifth line allows a remote root user to remove any print job on the local server. The sixth line causes all other remove requests on the local server to be rejected. The last line indicates that all other operations that are not specifically excluded are allowed.

Within the /etc/lpd.perms file are descriptions of the options you can add or modify to suit your situation. In particular, you may be interested in the REMOTEUSER, REMOTEHOST, and REMOTEIP values to address access to printing services from other computers on the network.

After you have made changes to the lpd.perms file, run the lpc reread command (as root user) to activate those changes, as shown here:

```
# lpc reread
lpd server pid 11353 on oak.handsonhistory.com, sending SIGHUP
```

Setting global printing values in lpd.conf

Entries in the lpd.conf file are in the same format as they are in the /etc/printcap file (with the exception that lpd.conf doesn't use colons to separate options and values). All entries begin *commented out*. (This means that though entries are in the file, comment characters prevent the entries from being active.) To change a global printing value, simply remove the comment character (#) and edit the line as you please.

Note Remember, anything you set in lpd.conf can be overridden by settings for a printer in the /etc/printcap file. For example, an entry in the /etc/printcap file may suppress the printing of a header page (containing the user name, time, and so forth) that would otherwise be produced when you print a document on that printer. In this case, even if you enable header pages in lpd.conf, you have to remove the suppress header page option from the printcap entry to enable it for a particular printer.

The default_printer option is an example of an option you may want to set in lpd.conf. To change that value, look for the default_printer line and remove the comment character (#). Then, after the equal sign, add the name of the printer you want as the default. Here is an example of how it would look if you wanted to change the default printer to lp3:

```
default default_printer=lp3
```

To override this setting, users could set their own default printer using the $PRINTER environment variable. If no default printer is set, the first printer in /etc/printcap is used as the default. Other values you may want to change in this file depend on your situation. More than 100 options are available. You can set such things as printing timeout values, banner printing, print filters, locations of log files and lock files, and maximum sizes of log files and status files.

After you have made changes to the lpd.conf file, run the following lpc reread command (as root user) to activate those changes:

```
# lpc reread
lpd server pid 11353 on oak.handsonhistory.com, sending SIGHUP
```

Installing a local printer from the desktop

To install a printer from your desktop, use the printconf-gui tool. This tool enables you to add, delete, and edit printers. It also has features that enable you to send test pages to those printers to make sure they are working properly. With this tool, you can add a printer that is connected directly to your computer (such as on a parallel port) or to another computer on the network (such as from another UNIX system, MS Windows system, or NetWare server).

To add a local printer with the printconf-gui tool (in other words, a printer connected directly to your computer), follow this procedure. (See the "Choosing a Printer" section later in this chapter if you don't have a printer yet.)

Tip You should connect your printer before starting this procedure. Connecting it before starting this procedure enables the printer software to autodetect the printer's location and to immediately test the printer when you are done adding it.

1. To open the printconf-gui tool, either select Programs ➪ System ➪ Printer Configuration from the GNOME menu or type the following as root user from a Terminal window:

   ```
   # printconf-gui &
   ```

   The printconf-gui window appears.

2. Click New. An Add a New Print Queue window appears.

3. Click Next. The window that appears asks you to add a printer type and name for the printer, as shown in Figure 17-1.

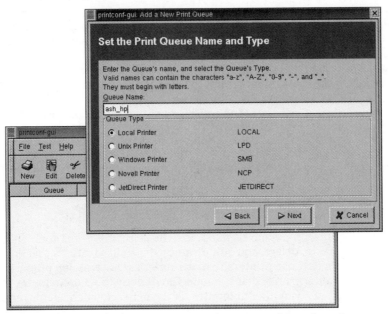

Figure 17-1: The printconf-gui tool enables you to add a printer from those connected locally or remotely.

4. Add the following information; then click Next:

- **Queue Name:** Add the name you want to give to identify the printer. The name must begin with a letter, but after the initial letter, it can contain a combination of letters, numbers, dashes (-), and underscores (_). For example, an HP printer on a computer named ash could be named ash_hp.

- **Queue Type:** Select Local Printer if the printer is connected directly to the parallel (LPT) or serial (COM) ports on your computer. (If the printer is connected to a Windows system, another UNIX/Linux system, or a Netware server, skip ahead to descriptions on configuring those servers.)

The Configure a Local Printer screen appears, displaying a list of devices on which printers were found.

5. Select your printer from the list of devices found and click Next. (/dev/lp0 represents the first parallel port on your computer.) Alternatively, you could do one of the following:

- If your printer is not on the list because you had not connected it yet, you can connect it now and select Rescan Devices to have your computer try again to detect your printer.

- If you intend to connect your printer later, or for some reason it's not being scanned, click on Custom Device and specify the device name where the printer will be found.

The Select a Print Driver window appears.

6. Click the arrow next to the manufacturer of your printer, select the model of printer you are using, and then click Next. The Finish and Create the New Print Queue window appears.

Tip If your printer doesn't appear on the list but supports PCL (which is HP's Printer Control Language), you can try selecting one of the HP printers (such as HP LaserJet). If your printer supports PostScript, you can select PostScript printer from the list.

7. If the information looks correct, click Finish to create the entry for your printer. The printer will appear in the main `printconf-gui` window. If it is your only printer configured, a check mark will appear next to it, indicating that it is the default printer. As you add other printers, you can change the default printer by selecting the one you want and clicking on the Default button.

8. Choose File ⇨ Save Changes to save the changes.

After your printer is installed, check that it is working properly. First, restart the `lpd` daemon by choosing File ⇨ Restart lpd. Next, click the printer's name in the `printconf-gui` window; click Test, and select one of the following:

✦ **Print US Letter Postscript Test Page** — Sends a letter-sized (8.5" x 11") page to the printer in Postscript format. If you have a color printer, the page appears in color.

✦ **Print ASCII test page** — Sends plain text to the named printer.

✦ **Print A4 Postscript test page** — Sends an A4 Postscript-formatted page to the named printer.

Printing should be working fine at this point. If it isn't, and you get an error message such as `device busy` when you try to output text to your printing device, you may need to reboot your Linux computer.

Configuring a remote printer from the desktop

To be able to use a printer that is available on your network, you need to identify that printer to your Red Hat Linux system. Supported remote printer connections include Remote UNIX printers, SMB (MS Windows) printers, and NetWare printers. (Of course, UNIX implies Linux systems, as well as other UNIX systems.)

In each case, you need a network connection from your Red Hat Linux system that enables you to reach the servers to which those printers are connected. To use a remote printer, of course, requires that someone set up that printer on the remote server computer. See the section "Configuring Print Servers," later in this chapter, for information on how to do that in Red Hat Linux.

You can use the `printconf-gui` window to configure each of the remote printer types:

1. From a Terminal window as root user, type **printconf-gui&**.

2. Click New. The Add a New Printer Queue window appears.

3. Click Next. The Set the Print Queue Name and Type window appears.

4. Type the name of the Printer Queue, select one of the following, and click Next:

   - Unix Printer (LPD)

   - Windows Printer (SMB)

   - Novell Printer (NCP)

   - JetDirect Printer (JETDIRECT)

5. Next, continue following the steps in whichever of the following sections is appropriate.

Adding a remote UNIX printer

After you have selected to add a UNIX printer from the `printconf-gui` window, you need to add the following information to the window that appears:

- ✦ **Server**—The host name of the computer to which the printer is attached (or otherwise accessible). This is the TCP/IP name for the computer (the TCP/IP name is accessible from your `/etc/hosts` file or through a DNS name server).

- ✦ **Queue**—The local spool directory on which print jobs destined for the UNIX computer are to be placed.

Note   Click on the Strict RFC1179 Compliance button if you are printing to an older lpd server.

Complete the configuration as you would for a local printer (Click Next to select a print driver, select the appropriate driver and click Next, and then click Finish to create the new print queue). Choose File ⇨ Save Changes from the `printconf-gui` window. Choose File ⇨ Restart `lpd` to have the printer daemon receive the new printer entry.

After you create the remote printer entry, restart the `lpd` daemon by choosing File ⇨ Restart `lpd`.

Tip   If the print job is rejected when you send it to test the printer, the print server computer may not have allowed you access to the printer. Ask the remote computer's administrator to add your host name to the `/etc/lpd.perms` file.

Adding a Windows (SMB) printer

Enabling your computer to access an SMB printer (generally, one that is connected to a Windows OS) involves adding an entry for the printer in the `printconf-gui` window. Ultimately, information about the printer and SMB server is passed to the `smbclient` command (which is part of the Samba-client package) to transmit the print job.

After you have selected to add a Windows printer to the `printconf-gui` window (described previously), fill in the following information in the appropriate fields:

✦ **Share** — The host name and printer name of the computer to which the printer is attached (or otherwise accessible). The share information is in the form: `\\`*hostname*`\`*printername*. The host name is the NetBIOS name for the computer, which may or may not be the same as its TCP/IP name. To translate this name into the IP address needed to reach the SMB host, Samba checks several places where the name may be assigned to an IP address. Samba checks the following (in the order shown) until it finds a match: the local `/etc/hosts` file, the local `/etc/lmhosts` file, a WINS server on the network, or responses to broadcasts on each local network interface to resolve the name.

The *printername* is the name under which the printer is shared with the remote computer. This may be a different name from the one by which local users of the SMB printer know the printer.

Tip

To find a remote printer name on most Windows systems, first go to the Printers folder (Start ⇨ Settings ⇨ Printers), and double-click the printer being shared. From the printer queue window that appears, choose Printer ⇨ Properties, and then select the Sharing tab. The Sharing tab indicates whether the printer is shared and, if so, the name it is shared under.

✦ **Host IP (optional)** — The IP address of the print server. This is not necessary if your computer can get the IP address by resolving the host name.

✦ **User** — The user name that is required by the SMB server system to give you access to the SMB printer. This is not necessary if you are authenticating the printer based on share-level, rather than user-level, access control. With share-level access, you can add a password for each shared printer or file system.

✦ **Password** — The password associated with the SMB user name or the shared resource, depending on the kind of access control being used.

Caution

When you enter a User and Password for SMB, that information is stored on your system unencrypted. You should use a different password for printing access from the one you use for your Red Hat Linux user account. That way, if the password is found, only the printing capability is compromised and not the whole user account. It also recommends that you use different passwords for file sharing and print sharing.

✦ **Workgroup** — The workgroup name assigned to the SMB server. Filling in the workgroup name doesn't seem to be necessary in all cases.

Tip If you are printing to a Windows 95/98 printer, you can find the Workgroup and Hostname of Print Server entries in the Network window. From Windows 95/98, choose Start ⇨ Settings ⇨ Control Panel. Open the Network window, and then click its Identification tab, which will display the computer name and workgroup. If there is no Identification tab, you may need to install the Client for Microsoft Networks client in the Network window.

Click Next after you have set up the configuration you want. When the next screen appears, select the print driver and click Next. If the printer definition looks okay, click Finish. Then choose File ⇨ Save Changes from the printconf-gui window. Choose File ⇨ Restart lpd to have the printer daemon receive the new printer entry.

The result of this input is a new entry in your /etc/printcap file and a new mf.cfg file in the spool directory for the printer (in /var/spool/lpd/*pn*, where *pn* is replaced by the printer name). Here is an example of the /etc/printcap entry that is created:

```
canyonsps:\
:sh:\
:ml=0:\
:mx=0:\
:sd=/var/spool/lpd/canyonsps:\
:af=/var/spool/lpd/canyonsps/canyonsps.acct:\
:lp=|/usr/share/printconf/util/smbprint:\
:lpd_bounce=true:\
:if=/usr/share/printconf/util/mf_wrapper:
```

The /etc/printcap entry identifies the name of the printer and the location of the spool files. The lines most significant to an SMB printer are: the if line, which identifies the filter used to send the file to the SMB printer, and the lp line for the device, which directs printing output to the smbprint command. The printconf-gui window should automatically create the necessary spool directory (/var/spool/lpd/canyonsps) and configuration files (in particular, the script.cfg and mf.cfg files).

The script.cfg file, created in the local spool directory for the printer (/var/spool/lpd/*pn*), contains the share name, IP address, user name, password, workgroup, and other data that is particular to the SMB printer. Here's an example of that file after adding the SMB printer:

```
share="\\canyons\canyonsps"
hostip=""
user=""
password="asecretpwd"
workgroup=""
```

The shared printer, in this case, is named canyonsps on the computer named canyons. The IP address was not needed in my case, so I left it out. Likewise, I was dealing with a printer that used resource-level access, so the user name wasn't needed either. Notice that the password is simply stored as a plain-text file, which is a security risk if you don't keep the file closed to non-root users. Finally, the Windows workgroup is also left empty, although adding it here seems to do no harm.

If everything was set up properly, you should be able to use the standard lpr command to print the file to the printer. With this example, you could use the following form for printing:

```
$ cat file1.ps | lpr -P canyonsps
```

If you are really brave, you can use the smbclient command directly. It uses an interface that is similar to the ftp command. You can either add all the options that you need to the command line, or go to an interactive mode in which you move up and down the directories, get and put files, and run other commands (such as print). Here's an example of using smbclient, relying on the printer definition just entered:

```
$ smbclient "\\\\canyons\\canyonsps" asecretpwd -N -c "print file1.ps"
```

Because the command is being run from the shell, all the backslashes have to be doubled in the host name (canyons) and service name (canyonsps). After that is the unencrypted password. The -N option suppresses the password prompt (it may be superfluous, because the password is given on the command line, but including it doesn't hurt). The -c option is used to enter the command that you would normally type interactively to an smbclient prompt. In this case, it runs the command "print file1.ps" to print the file.

> **Tip** If you are receiving failure messages, make sure that the computer you are printing to is accessible. In this case, you could type smbclient -L canyons. If you get a positive name query response, after you enter a password (or press Enter if no password is used), you should see a list of shared printers and files from that server. Check the names, and try printing again.

Adding a NetWare printer

With this procedure, you set up your Red Hat Linux system to use a printer that is connected to (or otherwise managed by) a NetWare file and print server. As with SMB printing, the key is to use an input filter that knows how to gather the information you input and how to direct print files to the print server. In this case, the filter passes information to the nprint command, which ultimately handles sending files to the NetWare printer.

After you have selected to add a NetWare printer from the `printconf-gui` window (described previously), fill in the following information in the appropriate window:

- ✦ **Server** — The host name of the computer to which the printer is attached (or otherwise accessible). This is the NetWare Server name for the computer.

- ✦ **Queue** — The name of the print queue on the NetWare server.

- ✦ **User** — The user name required by the NetWare server system to enable access to the NetWare printer.

- ✦ **Password** — The password associated with the user name.

Click Next after you have set up the configuration you want. Select the print driver you want and click Next. If the configuration looks correct, click Finish. Then choose File ➪ Save Changes from the `printconf-gui` window. Choose File ➪ Restart `lpd` to have the printer daemon receive the new printer entry.

To send print jobs to the NetWare printer, the new printer entry relies on the `ncpprint` script, which in turn passes the values to the `nprint` command. For NetWare printers, the printconf-gui window fills in this value for you automatically. The other filters needed to handle the printing are set up on the print server.

Here is what the entry you created for the NetWare printer looks like in `/etc/printcap`:

```
nwlps:\
:sh:\
:ml=0:\
:mx=0:\
:sd=/var/spool/lpd/nwlps:\
:lp=|/usr/share/printconf/util/ncpprint:\
:if=/usr/share/printconf/util/mf_wrapper:
```

The location of the spool directory here is `/var/spool/lpd/nwlps`. As noted previously, the print filter passes information for printing to the `ncpprint` script (which, in turn, uses the `nprint` command to transport the file to the NetWare printer).

Other specific information about the NetWare printer is contained in the printer's `script.cfg` file (located in `/var/spool/lpd/`*pn*, where your printer name replaces *pn*). Here is an example of the contents of `script.cfg` for a remote NetWare printer:

```
server="nwlps"
queue="postpr1"
user="joe"
password="123"
```

As you can see, the server, queue, user, and password information are kept in this file. Remember to control access to this file because it is unencrypted and contains the password. (By default, these files should have 600 permissions so that only the lp user account can read and write these files.)

To check that the printer is configured properly, click the printer entry in the `printconf-gui` window and select Test ⇨ Print ASCII Test Page. If all is correct in the configuration, you should be able to print to this printer with the standard `lpr` command. For example:

```
$ cat file1.ps | lpr -P nw1ps
```

Choosing a Printer

If you are choosing a new printer to use with your Red Hat Linux system, look for one that is PostScript-compatible. The PostScript language is the preferred format for Linux and UNIX printing and has been for many years. Every major word-processing product that runs on Red Hat Linux and UNIX systems supports PostScript printing.

If you get a PostScript printer, you simply select the PostScript filter when you install the printer locally. No special drivers are needed. Your next best choice is to choose a printer that supports PCL. In either case, make sure that the PostScript or PCL are implemented in the printer hardware and not in the Windows driver.

When selecting a printer, avoid those that are referred to as *Winprinters*. These are printers that use nonstandard printing interfaces (that is, those other than PostScript or PCL). Support for these low-end printers is hit-or-miss. For example, some low-end HP DeskJet printers use the pnm2ppa driver to print documents in Printing Performance Architecture (PPA) format. Some Lexmark printers use the pbm217k driver to print. Though there are drivers available for many of these Winprinters, many of them are not fully supported.

Instead of a PostScript printer, Ghostscript may support your printer; if it does, you can use that tool to do your printing. Ghostscript (found at `www.aladdin.com`) is a free PostScript-interpreter program. It can convert PostScript content to output that can be interpreted by a variety of printers.

Table 17-1 is a partial list of printers that are supported in Red Hat Linux. How well each printer performs under Linux varies. The list shows printers that work perfectly, mostly, partially, or not at all. A more complete listing is maintained at `www.linuxprinting.org`. I strongly recommend you visit that site before you purchase a printer to work with Linux. Besides showing supported printers, the site also has a page describing how to choose a printer for use with Linux (`www.linuxprinting.org/suggested.html`).

	Table 17-1			
	Red Hat Linux–Supported Printer Models			
Vendor	*Models That Work Perfectly*	*Models That Work Mostly*	*Models That Work Partially*	*Models That Don't Work at All*
Brother	HL-10V, HL-660, HL-720, HL-760			
Canon	BJ-10e, BJ-20, BJ-200, BJC-210, BJC-240, BJC-250, BJC-610, BJC-620, BJC-70, BJC-800, LBP-8II, LIPS-III	BJ-300, BJC-4000, BJC-4100, BJC-4200, BJC-4300, BJC-4400, BJC-7000, BJC-7004	BJC-4550, MultiPASS C2500, MultiPASS C3500	BJC-5000, LBP-460, LBP-660
Epson	ActionLaser 1100, LP 8000, LQ 850, Stylus Color, Stylus Color 400, Stylus Color 500, Stylus Color 600, Stylus Color 640, Stylus Color 850, Stylus Color II, Stylus Color IIs, Stylus Pro XL	Stylus Color 800, Stylus Photo 750	Stylus Color 740	
HP	2000Cse, 2500C, DesignJet 650C, DeskJet 1200C, DeskJet 1600C, DeskJet 1600Cm, DeskJet 400, DeskJet 420C, DeskJet 500, DeskJet 550C, DeskJet 600, DeskJet 660Cse, DeskJet 690C, DeskJet 850C, DeskJet 855C, DeskJet 870, DeskJet 870Cxi, DeskJet 890,	HP 660C	DeskJet 1000C, DeskJet 670C, DeskJet 710, DeskJet 720C, DeskJet 722C, DeskJet 820C	LaserJet 3100

Vendor	Models That Work Perfectly	Models That Work Mostly	Models That Work Partially	Models That Don't Work at All
HP (cont.)	LaserJet 1100, LaserJet 2100, LaserJet 2100M, LaserJet 4000N, LaserJet 4L, LaserJet 5, LaserJet 5L, LaserJet 5MP, LaserJet 6L, LaserJet 6MP, LaserJet 8000, LaserJet 8100, Laserjet 5000, Mopier 320, PaintJet XL300			
IBM	Jetprinter 3852, Lexmark, Optra Color 1200, Optra Color 1275, Optra Color 40, Optra Color 45, Optra E, Optra E+, Optra Ep, Optra S 1250	1020 Business, 3000, 5700, 7000		1000, 1020, 1100, 2030, 2050, 2070, 5000, 7200, Winwriter 100, Winwriter 150c, Winwriter 200
Minolta	PagePro 6, PagePro 8			
NEC	P2X	SuperScript 100C, SuperScript 1260, SuperScript 150C, SuperScript 650C, SuperScript 750C, SuperScript 860, SuperScript 870	SuperScript 660i, SuperScript 660plus	
Okidata	OL 410e, OL 610e/PS, OL 810e/PS, Okipage 6e, Okipage 6ex, Okipage 8c	Okipage 4w		Okipage 8w, Okijet 2010

Continued

Table 17-1 (continued)				
Vendor	Models That Work Perfectly	Models That Work Mostly	Models That Work Partially	Models That Don't Work at All
Olivetti	JP350S			
Panasonic	KX-P1123, KX-P4440, KX-P5400, KX-P8420, KX-P8475	KX-P6500		KX-P6100, KX-P8410
QMS	2425 Turbo EX			
Ricoh	4801, 6000			
Xerox	DocuPrint C55, DocuPrint N17, DocuPrint N32			

Managing Document Printing in Red Hat Linux

Most printing in Red Hat Linux can be done with the lpr command. Word processing applications, such as StarOffice and AbiWord, are set up to use this facility to do their printing.

With the Red Hat printconf-gui command, you can define the filters needed for each printer so that the text can be formatted properly. Options to the lpr command can add filters to properly process the text. Other commands for managing printed documents include lpq (for viewing the contents of print queues), lprm (for removing print jobs from the queue), and lpc (for controlling printers).

Commands also exist for directing print jobs to remote printers (such as those on NetWare or SMB print servers). As previously noted, the smbclient command is used for printing to remote SMB printers. Likewise, for NetWare printing, the nprint command can be used. The lpr command relies on those commands for printing to SMB and NetWare, respectively. However, you can use smbclient or nprint directly if you want to choose different options with your printing.

Cross-Reference   Chapter 6 has examples of how to format and print documents in several different formats, including troff and TeX.

Using lpr to print

With the lpr command, you can print documents to both local and remote printers. Document files can be either added to the end of the lpr command line or directed to the lpr command using a pipe (|). Here is an example of a simple lpr command:

```
$ lpr doc1.ps
```

When you just specify a document file with lpr, output is directed to the default printer. As an individual user, you can change your default printer by setting the value of the PRINTER variable. Typically, you would add the PRINTER variable to one of your startup files, such as $HOME/.bashrc. Here is a line you could add to your .bashrc file to set your default printer to lp3:

```
export PRINTER=lp3
```

To override the default printer, specify a particular printer on the lpr command line. The following example uses the -P option to select a different printer:

```
$ lpr -P canyonps doc1.ps
```

The lpr command has a variety of options that enable lpr to interpret and format several different types of documents. The following are options that you can use on the command line and the types of text those options can process:

- ✦ -c—Processes cifplot data.
- ✦ -d—Processes TeX data in DVI format.
- ✦ -f—Interprets the first character of each line as a standard FORTRAN carriage control character.
- ✦ -g—Processes plot data.
- ✦ -l—Processes content so that control characters can print and page breaks are suppressed.
- ✦ -n—Processes data in ditroff (device independent troff) format.
- ✦ -t—Processes data produced by troff commands.
- ✦ -v—Processes raster images for devices such as the Benson Varian.

The following lpr options are available for handling the print job itself:

- ✦ -m—Sends mail after the job has been printed.
- ✦ -r—Removes the file after it has been spooled.

✦ -s — Uses a symbolic link to obtain the file to print, instead of copying the file to a spool directory. This prevents very large print jobs from taking up space in the print queue. If you do this, however, you must be sure not to delete the original file until after it has been printed.

✦ -#n — Replace the *n* with a number representing the number of copies you want to print.

A burst page can be printed with each document to identify its contents and owner. Here are several options that you can use that relate to the burst page:

✦ -h — Suppresses output of a burst page.

✦ -C *class* — Identifies a job classification to use on the burst page. Replace *class* with a word or words to appear on the page. This value replaces the host name that is usually printed here.

✦ -J *job* — Identifies a job name to appear on the burst page. The value of *job* replaces the name of the first printed file on the burst page.

✦ -P *printer* — Identifies the printer to which the print job will be sent. Without the -P option, the default printer is used.

✦ -U *user* — Identifies the user name that is to appear on the burst page.

Removing print jobs with lprm

Users can remove their own print jobs from the queue with the lprm command. Used alone on the command line, lprm will remove all the user's print jobs from the default printer. To remove jobs from a specific printer, use the -P option, as follows:

```
$ lprm -P lp0
```

To remove all print jobs for the current user, type the following:

```
$ lprm -
```

The root user can remove all the print jobs for a specific user by indicating that user on the lprm command line. For example, to remove all print jobs for the user named mike, the root user would type the following:

```
$ lprm mike
```

To remove an individual print job from the queue, indicate the job number of that print job on the lprm command line. To first find out what the job number is, type the lpq command. Here's what the output of that command may look like:

```
$ lpq
Printer: lp@localhost
 Queue: 2 printable jobs
 Server: pid 4134 active
```

```
Unspooler: pid 4135 active
Status: waiting for subserver to exit at 18:54:05.230
Rank    Owner/ID          Class Job Files              Size Time
active root@localhost+133  A   133 /home/jake/pr1       467 18:53:49
2      root@localhost+197  A   197 /home/jake/mydoc    23948 18:54:05
```

The output shows two printable jobs waiting in the queue. (In this case, they're not printing because the printer is off.) Under the Job column, you can see the job number associated with each document. To remove the first print job, type the following:

```
# lprm 133
```

Controlling printers with lpc

The lpc command enables you to check the status of printers, enable and disable printers, and change the arrangement of jobs in the queue. Any action you do with the lpc command can be done either to an individual printer (by indicating a printer name) or to all printers (by using the word *all*). To disable a specific printer (for example, one named canyonsps), use the disable option and type the following:

```
$ lpc disable canyonsps
Printer: canyonps@localhost
kill server PID 4134 with User defined signal 1
canyonps@localhost.localdomain: disabled
```

To enable a disabled printer (such as the one in the previous example), use the enable option and type the following:

```
$ lpc enable canyonsps
Printer: canyonps@localhost
canyonps@localhost.localdomain: enabled
```

When a printer is disabled, it can still continue to receive print jobs and hold them in the queue until the printer is enabled again. If you want to prevent jobs from being spooled at all, use the stop option as follows:

```
$ lpc stop canyonsps
Printer: canyonps@localhost
canyonps@localhost.localdomain: stopped
```

To start the printing daemon again and resume printing, use the start option, as follows:

```
$ lpc start canyonsps
Printer: canyonps@localhost
canyonps@localhost.localdomain: started
```

To disable a printer and kill the lpd printing daemon (so that no further jobs can be printed), use the `abort` option, as follows:

```
$ lpc abort canyonsps
Printer: canyonps@localhost
kill server PID 4239 with Interrupt
canyonps@localhost.localdomain: aborted job
```

Configuring Print Servers

The printers that are connected to your Red Hat Linux system can be shared in different ways with other computers on your network. Not only can your computer act as a Linux print server, but it can also appear to other client computers as a NetWare or SMB print server. After a local printer is attached to your Red Hat Linux system, and your computer is connected to your local network, you can use the procedures in this section to share it with client computers using a Linux (UNIX), NetWare, or SMB interface.

Configuring a shared Linux printer in lpd.perms

After a local printer is added to your Red Hat Linux computer, making it available to other computers on your network is fairly easy. If a TCP/IP network connection exists between the computers sharing the printer, then you simply have to grant permission to individual hosts or users from remote hosts to access your computer's printing service. The procedures for setting up local printers are discussed earlier in this chapter.

The permissions that users from other computers have to your Red Hat Linux printer are determined based on the values in your /etc/lpd.perms file. By default, you should be able to print from other Linux computers on your network to your shared printer. You can modify your lpd.perms file if you want to restrict access to your printer.

Configuring a shared NetWare printer

NetWare server functions delivered with Red Hat Linux are offered using the mars_nwe package. This package enables you to do file and printer sharing from Red Hat Linux as though the resources being shared were coming from a NetWare server. Although not all NetWare features are offered, the mars_nwe package does well with basic NetWare file and printer sharing.

Cross-Reference

See Chapter 18 for information on setting up the mars_nwe package to share NetWare resources. The mars_nwe service must be running to share your printer as a NetWare print server.

You can make your Red Hat Linux printers available as NetWare printers by adding entries to the /etc/nwserv.conf file. This file is used for configuring most mars_nwe information. Of particular interest for adding printers is the Print Queues section (section 21). Red Hat Linux printers are identified as NetWare print queues by indicating each line as a section 21 entry. Here is an example:

```
21 PSPRINT  SYS:/PRINT/PSPRINT lpr -Ppsprint
```

The number 21 identifies the entry as a NetWare print queue. PSPRINT is the name of the queue. The queue directory is identified as SYS:/PRINT/PSPRINT. Note that the queue directory is different from the lpd spool directory. Finally, the last part of the entry is the lpr command line used to print documents submitted to this print queue.

Assuming you have done your basic NetWare server configuration, as described in Chapter 18, use this procedure to check that you are able to print to the NetWare print server you just set up in Linux:

1. Restart the mars_nwe service to incorporate the changes you just made to nwserv.conf by typing the following:

   ```
   # /etc/init.d/mars-nwe stop
   # /etc/init.d/mars-nwe start
   ```

2. Type the slist command to make sure that the NetWare server you configured is available:

   ```
   # slist
   Known NetWare File Servers          Network   Node Address
   ------------------------------------------------------------
   PINE                                7F000001  000000000001
   ```

   In this example, the NetWare server name (of the NetWare server running on Linux) is called PINE. Your server name will be different.

3. Use the nprint command to print to your NetWare print server in Linux. Type the following commands:

   ```
   $ cd /usr/share/printconf/tests
   $ nprint -S PINE -U GUEST -q PSPRINT testpage.asc
   Logging into PINE as GUEST
   Password:
   ```

   In the previous example, the NetWare server name is PINE, the user name is GUEST, and the print queue name is PSPRINT. By default, the guest account has no password, so you can just press Enter at the Password prompt.

Note You don't need to change to the tests directory in the previous example. I did that because I know that directory contains several test print pages in different formats. The textpage.asc is a plain text file. You can also try printing testpage.ps (a PostScript file) or testpage-a4.ps (an A4 PostScript page).

Configuring a shared Samba printer

Your Red Hat Linux printers can be configured as shared SMB printers by using the Samba SWAT (Samba Web Administration Tool) program. To use SWAT, you need to have the Samba package installed and the swat service configured so that SWAT can be opened in your browser window. You also need a TCP/IP connection between you and the client computers that will use your printer.

 Cross-Reference   Chapter 18 describes how to set up Samba and SWAT to be used in your browser.

With SWAT configured, you can open that program by opening Netscape on your local computer and typing the following address in the location box:

```
http://localhost:901/
```

From the main Samba SWAT screen, click the Printers icon. The Printer Parameters page appears. It is possible that your printers are already made available as shared SMB printers. Click the down arrow next to the Choose Printer box. You should see a list of available printers. Those printers from the pop-up list that have an asterisk preceding their name were automatically loaded as shared printers.

To create a new SMB printer, type a name into the Create Printer box and click Create Printer. Then, fill in the information about the printer (the path, security options, printing options, browse options, and miscellaneous options). When you are done, click Commit Changes. To find out how you would set up an SMB printer from Linux, see the section "Adding a Windows (SMB) printer" earlier in this chapter.

Chances are good that if you are configuring an SMB printer on your Red Hat Linux computer, you will want to share it with Windows clients. If SMB is set up properly on your computer, and the client computers can reach you over the network, finding and using your printer should be fairly straightforward.

The first place a client computer should look for your shared SMB printer is in Network Neighborhood (or My Network Places, for Windows 2000). From the Windows 9*x* desktop, double-click the Network Neighborhood icon. (From Windows 2000, double-click the My Network Places icon.) The name of your host computer (the NetBIOS name, which is probably also your TCP/IP name) should appear on the screen or within a workgroup folder on the screen. Open the icon that represents your computer. The window that opens should show your shared printers and folders.

If your computer's icon doesn't appear in Network Neighborhood, try using the Find: Computer window. From Windows 95, choose Start ➪ Find ➪ Computer. Type your computer's name into the Named box and click Find Now. If the Find window finds your computer, double-click it. A window displaying the shared printers and folders from your computer appears, as shown in Figure 17-2.

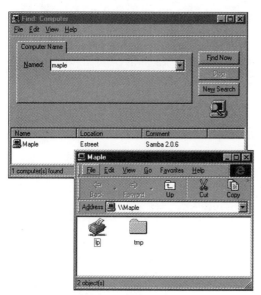

Figure 17-2: Find and display your SMB printer from Find: Computer.

After your shared printer appears in the window, the client can configure a pointer to that printer by opening (double-clicking) the printer icon. You should see a message telling you that you have to set up the printer before you can use it. Click Yes to proceed to configure the printer for local use. The Add Printer Wizard appears. Answer the questions on how you intend to use the printer, and add appropriate drivers. When you are done, the printer will appear in your printer window. It can now be selected as the printer for any application program in Windows 9x.

Another way to configure an SMB printer from a Windows operating system is to go to Start ⇨ Settings ⇨ Printers. Open the Add Printer icon, and then select Network Printer from the first window. Open the Add Printer icon. Then, follow the instructions to add a printer from the network.

Summary

Sharing printers is an economical and efficient way to use your organization's printing resources. A centrally located printer can make it easier to maintain a printer, while still allowing everyone to get his or her printing jobs done.

Printer configuration is done with the `printconf-gui` tool. Printers configured with that tool can be printed using the `lpr` command. A variety of filters make it possible to print to different kinds of printers, as well as to printers that are connected to computers on the network.

Besides being able to set up your computer as a Red Hat Linux print server, you can also have your computer emulate a NetWare or an SMB (Windows 9*x*) print server. After your network is configured properly and a local printer is installed, sharing that printer over the network as a UNIX, NetWare, or SMB print server is not very complicated.

✦   ✦   ✦

Setting Up a File Server

When groups of people need to work together on projects, they usually need to share documents. Likewise, it can be efficient for groups of people on a computer network to share common applications and directories of information needed to do their jobs. A common way to centrally store and share files on a network is by setting up a file server.

Red Hat Linux includes support for each of the most common file server protocols in use today. The Network File System (NFS) has always been the file-sharing protocol of choice for Linux and other UNIX systems. Networks with many Windows and OS/2 computers tend to use Samba (SMB protocol). Prior to Samba, NetWare was the most prominent file-server software used on local area networks (LANs).

This chapter describes how to set up file servers and clients associated with NFS, Samba, and NetWare file servers.

Goals of Setting Up a File Server

By centralizing data and applications on a *file server*, you can accomplish several different goals:

+ **Centralized distribution** — You can add documents or applications to one location and make them accessible to any computer or user that is granted permission. In this way, you don't have to be responsible for placing necessary files on every computer.

+ **Security** — You can control who has access to the file server on one computer instead of distributing the information to every computer and trying to control it.

✦ **Transparency**—Using protocols such as NFS, clients of your file server (Windows, Linux or UNIX systems) can connect your file systems to their local file systems as if your file systems existed locally. (In other words, no drive letters. Just change to the remote system's mount point and you are there.)

Setting Up an NFS File Server in Red Hat Linux

Instead of representing storage devices as drive letters (A, B, C, and so on), as they are in Microsoft operating systems, Red Hat Linux connects file systems from multiple hard disks, floppy disks, CD-ROMs, and other local devices invisibly to form a single Linux file system. The Network File System (NFS) facility lets you extend your Red Hat Linux file system in the same way, to connect file systems on other computers to your local directory structure as well.

Cross-Reference   See Chapter 10 for a description of how to mount local devices on your Linux file system. The same command (`mount`) is used to mount both local devices and NFS file systems.

Creating an NFS file server is an easy way to share large amounts of data among the users and computers in an organization. An administrator of a Red Hat Linux system that is configured to share its file systems using NFS has several things to do to get NFS working:

1. **Set up the network**—If a LAN or other network connection is already connecting the computer on which you want to use NFS (using TCP/IP as the network transport), you already have the network you need.

2. **On the server, choose what to share**—Decide which file systems on your Linux NFS server you want to be available to other computers. You can choose any point in the file system to make all files and directories below that point accessible to other computers.

3. **On the server, set up security**—There are several different security features that you can use to suit the level of security with which you are comfortable. Mount-level security lets you restrict the computers that can mount a resource and, for those allowed to mount it, lets you specify whether it can be mounted read/write or read-only. With user-level security, you map users from the client systems to users on the NFS server. In this way, users can rely on standard Linux read/write/execute permissions, file ownership, and group permissions to access and protect files.

4. **On the client, mount the file system**—Each client computer that is allowed access to the server's NFS shared file system can mount it anywhere the client chooses. For example, you may mount a file system from a computer called

maple on the /mnt/maple directory in your local file system. After it is mounted, you can view the contents of that directory by typing ls /mnt/maple. Then you can use the cd command below the /mnt/maple mount point to see the files and directories it contains.

Figure 18-1 illustrates a Linux file server using NFS to share (export) a file system and a client computer mounting the file system to make it available to its local users.

In this example, a computer named oak makes its /apps/bin directory available to clients on the network (pine, maple, and spruce) by adding an entry to the /etc/exports file. The client computer (pine) sees that the resource is available, then mounts the resource on its local file system at the mount point /oak/apps. At this point, any files, directories, or subdirectories from /apps/bin on oak are available to users on pine (given proper permissions).

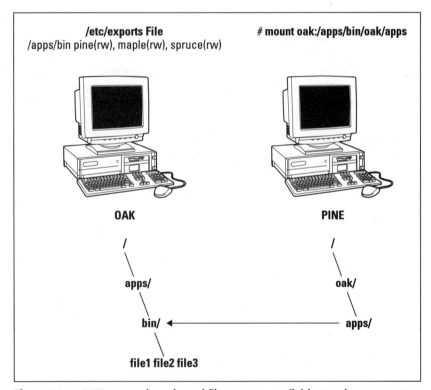

Figure 18-1: NFS can make selected file systems available to other computers.

Although it is often used as a file server (or other type of server), Red Hat Linux is a general-purpose operating system. So, any Red Hat Linux system can share file systems (export) as a server or use other computer's file systems (mount) as a client. Contrast this with dedicated file servers, such as NetWare, which can only share files with client computers (such as Windows workstations) and will never act as a client.

Note   Many people use the term *file system* rather loosely. A file system is usually a structure of files and directories that exists on a single device (such as a hard disk partition or CD-ROM). When I talk about the Linux file system, however, I am referring to the entire directory structure (which may include file systems from several disks or NFS resources), beginning from root (/) on a single computer. A shared directory in NFS may represent all or part of a computer's file system, which can be attached (from the shared directory down the directory tree) to another computer's file system.

Sharing NFS file systems

To share an NFS file system from your Red Hat Linux system, you need to export it. Exporting is done in Red Hat Linux by adding entries into the /etc/exports file. Each entry identifies the directory in your local file system that you want to share. The entry identifies the other computers that can share the resource (or opens it to all computers) and includes other options that reflect permissions associated with the directory.

Remember that when you share a directory, you are sharing all files and subdirectories below that directory as well (by default). So, you need to be sure that you want to share everything in that directory structure. There are still ways to restrict access within that directory structure (those methods are described later).

Configuring the /etc/exports file

As root user, you can use any text editor to configure the /etc/exports file to indicate what directories to share. Here is an example of an /etc/exports file, including some entries that it could include:

```
/cal    *.ourdomain.com(rw)                # Company events
/pub    (ro,insecure,all_squash)           # Public dir
/home   maple(rw,squash uids=0-99) spruce(rw,squash uids=0-99)
```

Here is what the entries in the /etc/exports file mean:

✦ **/cal**—Represents a directory that contains information about events related to the company. It is made accessible to everyone with accounts to any computers in the company's domain (*.ourdomain.com). Users can write files to the directory as well as read them (indicated by the rw option). The comment (# Company events) simply serves as a reminder of what the directory contains.

✦ **/pub** — Represents a public directory. It allows any computer and user to read files from the directory (indicated by the `ro` option), but not to write files. The `insecure` option lets any computer, even those that don't use a secure NFS port, to have access to the directory. The `all_squash` option causes all users (UIDs) and groups (GIDs) to be mapped to the `anonymous` user, giving them minimal permission to files and directories.

✦ **/home** — This is where you enable a set of users to have the same `/home` directory on different computers. Say, for example, that you are sharing `/home` from a computer named oak. The computers named maple and spruce could each mount that directory on their own `/home` directory. If you gave all users the same user name/UIDs on all machines, you could have the same `/home/user` directory available for each user, regardless of which computer they logged in to. The `uids=0-99` is used to exclude any administrative login from another computer from changing any files in the shared directory.

Tip   If you were sharing `/home`, but you didn't want to share a particular user's directory, you could exclude that user's home directory using the `noaccess` option, described later.

Of course, you can share any directories that you choose (these were just examples), including the entire file system (`/`). There are security implications of sharing the whole file system or sensitive parts of it (such as `/etc`). Security options that you can add to your `/etc/exports` file are described below.

Tip   The `linuxconf` command can be used to add exported directories to `/etc/exports`. Select *Exported file systems (NFS)* from the left column (under Config ➪ Networking ➪ Server tasks). Buttons on the page let you choose a few options that affect write privileges, root privileges, symbolic links, and security. (If you add an entry this way, check `/etc/exports` later to see what you have done.)

The format of the `/etc/exports` file is:

```
Directory    Host(Options)    # Comments
```

`Directory` is the name of the directory that you want to share. `Host` indicates the host computer that the sharing of this directory is restricted to. `Options` can include a variety of options to define the security measures attached to the shared directory for the host. (You can repeat Host/Option pairs.) `Comments` are any optional comments you want to add (following the `#` sign).

Hostnames in /etc/exports

You can indicate in the `/etc/exports` file which host computers can have access to your shared directory in the following ways:

✦ **Individual host**—You can enter one or more TCP/IP hostnames or IP Addresses. If the host is in your local domain, you can simply indicate the hostname. Otherwise, you can use the full host.domain format. These are valid ways of indicating individual host computers:

```
maple
maple.handsonhistory.com
10.0.0.11
```

✦ **IP network**—To allow access to all hosts from a particular network address, indicate a network number and its netmask, separated by a slash (/). These are valid ways of indicating network numbers:

```
10.0.0.0/255.0.0.0
172.16.0.0/255.255.0.0
192.168.18.0/255.255.255.0
```

✦ **TCP/IP domain**—Using wild cards, you can include all or some host computers from a particular domain level. Here are some valid uses of the asterisk and question mark wild cards:

```
*.handsonhistory.com
*craft.handsonhistory.com
???.handsonhistory.com
```

The first example matches all hosts in the handsonhistory.com domain. The second example matches woodcraft, basketcraft, or any other hostnames ending in craft in the handsonhistory.com domain. The final example matches any three-letter hostnames in the domain.

Note Using an asterisk doesn't match subdomains. For example, *.handson history.com would *not* cause the hostname mallard.duck.handson history.com to be included in the access list.

✦ **NIS groups**—You can allow access to hosts contained in an NIS group. To indicate a NIS group, precede the group name with an at (@) sign (for example, @*group*).

Link and access options in /etc/exports

You don't have to just give away your files and directories when you export a directory with NFS. In the options part of each entry in /etc/exports, you can add options that allow or limit access based on user ID, subdirectory, and read/write permission. These options, which are passed to NFS, are as follows:

✦ ro—Only allow the client to mount this exported file system read-only. The default is to mount the file system read/write.

✦ rw—Explicitly ask that a shared directory be shared with read/write permissions. (If the client chooses, it can still mount the directory read-only.)

✦ `noaccess`—All files and directories below the given directory are not accessible. This is how you would exclude selected subdirectories of a shared directory from being shared. The directory will still appear to the client that mounts the file system that includes this directory, but the client will not be able to view its contents.

✦ `link_relative`—If absolute symbolic links are included in the shared file system (that is, ones that identify a full path), the full path is converted to a relative path. To do this, each part of the path is converted to two dots and a slash (`../`) to reach the root of the file system.

✦ `Link_absolute`—Don't change any of the symbolic links (default).

User mapping options in /etc/exports

Besides options that define how permissions are handled generally, you can also use options to set the permissions that specific users have to NFS shared file systems.

One method that simplifies this process is to have each user with multiple user accounts have the same user name and UID on each machine. This makes it easier to map users so that they have the same permission on a mounted file system as they do on files stored on their local hard disk. If that method is not convenient, user IDs can be mapped in many other ways. Here are some methods of setting user permissions and the `/etc/exports` option that you use for each method:

✦ **root user**—Normally, the client's root user is mapped into the `anonymous` user ID. This prevents the root user from a client computer from being able to change all files and directories in the shared file system. If you want the client's root user to have root permission on the server, use the `no_root_squash` option.

Tip

There may be other administrative users, in addition to root, that you want to squash. I recommend squashing UIDs 0–99 as follows: `squash_uids=0-99`.

✦ **Anonymous user/group**—By using `anonymous` user ID and group ID, you essentially create a user/group whose permissions will not allow access to files that belong to any users on the server (unless those users open permission to everyone). However, files created by the `anonymous` user/group will be available to anyone assigned as the `anonymous` user/group. To set all remote users to the `anonymous` user/group, use the `all_squash` option.

The `anonymous` user assigned by NFS is typically the "nobody" user name with a UID and GID -2 (because -2 cannot be assigned to a file, UIDs and GIDs of 65534 are assigned when the "nobody" user owns a file). This prevents the ID from running into a valid user or group ID. Using anonuid or anongid, you can change the `anonymous` user or group, respectively. For example, anonuid=175 sets all `anonymous` users to UID 175 and anongid=300 sets the GID to 300.

✦ **User mapping**—If the same users have login accounts for a set of computers (and they have the same IDs), NFS, by default, will map those IDs. This means that if the user named mike (UID 110) on maple has an account on pine (mike, UID 110), from either computer he could use his own remotely mounted files from the other computer.

If a client user that is not set up on the server creates a file on the mounted NFS directory, the file is assigned to the remote client's UID and GID. (An ls -l on the server would show the UID of the owner.) You can identify a file that contains user mappings using the map_static option.

Tip   The exports man page describes the map_static option, which should let you create a file that contains new ID mappings. These mappings should let you remap client IDs into different IDs on the server.

Exporting the shared file systems

After you have added entries to your /etc/exports file, you can actually export the directories listed using the exportfs command. If you reboot your computer, the exportfs command is run automatically to export your directories. However, if you want to export them immediately, you can do so by running exportfs from the command line (as root).

Tip   It's a good idea to run the exportfs command after you change the exports file. If any errors are in the file, exportfs will identify those errors for you.

Here's an example of the exportfs command:

```
# /usr/sbin/exportfs -a -v
exporting :/pub
exporting :/home
```

The -a option indicates that all directories listed in /etc/exports should be exported. The -v option says to print verbose output. In this example, the /pub and /home directories from the local server are now immediately available for mounting by client computers.

Tip   The /var/lib/nfs/xtab file lists all the options, including the default options, assigned to each of the exported directories.

Running the exportfs command temporarily makes your exported NFS directories available. To have your NFS directories available on an ongoing basis (that is, every time your system reboots), you need to configure your nfs start-up scripts to run at boot time. This is described in the next section.

Starting the nfs daemons

For security purposes, the NFS service is probably turned off by default on your Red Hat Linux system. You can use the chkconfig command to turn on the NFS service so that your files are exported and the nfsd daemons are running when your system boots.

There are two start-up scripts you want to turn on for the NFS service to work properly. The nfs service exports file systems (from /etc/exports) and starts the nfsd daemon that listens for service requests. The nfslock service starts the lockd daemon, which helps allow file locking to prevent multiple simultaneous use of critical files over the network.

You can use the chkconfig command to turn on the nfs service by typing the following commands (as root user):

```
# chkconfig nfs on
# chkconfig nfslock on
```

The next time you start your computer, the NFS service will start automatically and your exported directories will be available. If you want to start the service immediately, without waiting for a reboot, you can type the following:

```
# /etc/init.d/nfs start
# /etc/init.d/nfslock start
```

The NFS service should now be running and ready to share directories with other computers on your network.

Using NFS file systems

After a server exports a directory over the network using NFS, a client computer connects that directory to its own file system using the mount command. The mount command is the same one used to mount file systems from local hard disks, CDs, and floppies. Only the options to give to mount are slightly different.

Mount can automatically mount NFS directories that are added to the /etc/fstab file, just as it does with local disks. NFS directories can also be added to the /etc/fstab file in such a way that they are not automatically mounted. With a noauto option, an NFS directory listed in /etc/fstab is inactive until the mount command is used, after the system is up and running, to mount the file system.

Manually mounting an NFS file system

If you know that the directory from a computer on your network has been exported (that is, made available for mounting), you can mount that directory manually using the mount command. This is a good way to make sure that it is available and working before you set it up to mount permanently. Here is an example of mounting the /tmp directory from a computer named maple on your local computer:

```
# mkdir /mnt/maple
# mount maple:/tmp /mnt/maple
```

The first command (mkdir) creates the mount point directory (/mnt is a common place to put temporarily mounted disks and NFS file systems). The mount command then identifies the remote computer and shared file system separated by a colon (maple:/tmp). Then, the local mount point directory follows (/mnt/maple).

Note   If the mount failed, make sure that the NFS service is running on the server and that your firewall rules don't deny access to the service. From the server, type ps ax | nfsd. You should see a list of nfsd server processes. If you don't, try to start your NFS daemons as described in the previous section. To view your firewall rules, type ipchains -L or iptables -L depending on which firewall service you are using (see Chapter 14 for a description of firewalls). By default, the nfsd daemon listens for NFS requests on port number 2049.

To make sure that the mount occurred, type mount. This command lists all mounted disks and NFS file systems. Here is an example of the mount command and its output:

```
# mount
/dev/hda3 on / type ext3 (rw)
none on /proc type proc (rw)
none on /dev/pts type devpts (rw,gid=5,mode=620)
usbdevfs on /proc/bus/usb type usbdevfs (rw)
maple:/tmp on /mnt/maple type nfs (rw,addr=10.0.0.11)
```

The output from the mount command shows your mounted disks and NFS file systems. The first output line shows your hard disk (/dev/hda3), mounted on the root file system (/), with read/write permission (rw), with a file system type of ext3 (the standard Linux file system type). The /proc, /dev/pts, and usbdevfs mount points represent special file system types. The just mounted NFS file system is the /tmp directory from maple (maple:/tmp). It is mounted on /mnt/maple and its mount type is nfs. The file system was mounted read/write (rw) and the IP address of maple is 10.0.0.11 (addr=10.0.0.11).

What I just showed is a simple case of using mount with NFS. The mount is temporary and is not remounted when you reboot your computer. You can also add options to the mount command line for NFS mounts:

✦ -a — Mount all file systems in /etc/fstab (except those indicated as noauto).

✦ -f — This goes through the motions of (fakes) mounting the file systems on the command line (or in /etc/fstab). Used with the -v option, -f is useful for seeing what mount would do before it actually does it.

✦ -r — Mounts the file system as read-only.

✦ -w — Mounts the file system as read/write. (For this to work, the shared file system must have been exported with read/write permission.)

The next section describes how to make the mount more permanent (using the /etc/fstab file) and how to select various options for NFS mounts.

Automatically mounting an NFS file system (/etc/fstab file)

To set up an NFS file system to mount automatically each time you start your Red Hat Linux system, you need to add an entry for that NFS file system to the /etc/fstab file. The /etc/fstab file contains information about all different kinds of mounted (and available to be mounted) file systems for your Red Hat Linux system.

The format for adding an NFS file system to your local system is the following:

```
host:directory     mountpoint     nfs     options     0     0
```

The first item (host:directory)identifies the NFS server computer and shared directory. Mountpoint is the local mount point on which the NFS directory is mounted, followed by the file system type (nfs). Any options related to the mount appear next in a comma-separated list. (The last two zeros just tell Red Hat Linux not to dump the contents of the file system and not to run fsck on the file system.)

The following are two examples of NFS entries in /etc/fstab:

```
maple:/tmp    /mnt/maple nfs    rsize=8192,wsize=8192   0 0
oak:/apps     /oak/apps  nfs    noauto,ro              0 0
```

In the first example, the remote directory /tmp from the computer named maple (maple:/tmp) is mounted on the local directory /mnt/maple (the local directory must already exist). The file system type is nfs, and read (rsize) and write (wsize) buffer sizes are set at 8192 to speed data transfer associated with this connection. In the second example, the remote directory is /apps on the computer named oak. It is set up as an NFS file system (nfs) that can be mounted on the /oak/apps directory locally. This file system is not mounted automatically (noauto), however, and can be mounted only as read only (ro) using the mount command after the system is already running.

 Tip   The default is to mount an NFS file system as read/write. However, the default for exporting a file system is read-only. If you are unable to write to an NFS file system, check that it was exported as read/write from the server.

Mounting noauto file systems

In your /etc/fstab file are devices for other file systems that are not mounted automatically (probably /dev/cdrom and /dev/fd0, for your CD-ROM and floppy disk devices, respectively). A noauto file system can be mounted manually. The advantage is that when you type the mount command, you can type less information and have the rest filled in by the contents of the /etc/fstab file. So, for example, you could type:

```
mount /oak/apps
```

With this command, `mount` knows to check the `/etc/fstab` file to get the file system to mount (`oak:/apps`), the file system type (`nfs`), and the options to use with the mount (in this case `ro` for read-only). Instead of typing the local mount point (`/oak/apps`), you could have typed the remote file system name (`oak:/apps`) instead, and had other information filled in.

Tip   When naming mount points, including the name of the remote NFS server in that name can help you remember where the files are actually being stored. This may not be possible if you are sharing home directories (`/home`) or mail directories (`/var/spool/mail`).

Using mount options

You can add several `mount` options to the `/etc/fstab` file (or to a `mount` command line itself) to impact how the file system is mounted. When you add options to `/etc/fstab`, they must be separated by commas. The following are some options that are valuable for mounting NFS file systems:

✦ `hard`—With this option on, if the NFS server disconnects or goes down while a process is waiting to access it, the process will hang until the server comes back up. This option is helpful if it is critical that the data you are working with not get out of sync with the programs that are accessing it. (This is the default behavior.)

✦ `soft`—If the NFS server disconnects or goes down, a process trying to access data from the server will timeout after a set period of time when this is on.

✦ `rsize`—The number of bytes of data read at a time from an NFS server. The default is 1024. Using a larger number (such as 8192) will get you better performance on a network that is fast (such as a LAN) and is relatively error-free (that is, one that doesn't have a lot of noise or collisions).

✦ `wsize`—The number of bytes of data written at a time to an NFS server. The default is 1024. Performance issues are the same as with the `rsize` option.

✦ `timeo=#`—Sets the time after an RPC timeout occurs that a second transmission is made, where # represents a number in tenths of a second. The default value is seven-tenths of a second. Each successive timeout causes the timeout value to be doubled (up to 60 seconds maximum). You should increase this value if you believe that timeouts are occurring because of slow response from the server or a slow network.

✦ `retrans=#`—Sets the number of minor retransmission timeouts that occur before a major timeout. When a major timeout occurs, the process is either aborted (soft mount) or a Server Not Responding message appears on your console.

✦ `retry=#`—Sets how many minutes to continue to retry failed mount requests, where # is replaced by the number of minutes to retry. The default is 10,000 minutes (which is about one week).

✦ bg—If the first mount attempt times out, try all subsequent mounts in the background. This option is very valuable if you are mounting a slow or sporadically available NFS file system. By placing mount requests in the background, Red Hat Linux can continue to mount other file systems instead of waiting for the current one to complete.

Note If a nested mount point is missing, a timeout to allow for the needed mount point to be added occurs. For example, if you mount /usr/trip and /usr/trip/extra as NFS file systems, if /usr/trip is not yet mounted when /usr/trip/extra tries to mount, /usr/trip/extra will time out. Hopefully, /usr/trip will come up and /usr/trip/extra will mount on the next retry.

✦ fg—If the first mount attempt times out, try subsequent mounts in the foreground. This is the default behavior. Use this option if it is imperative that the mount be successful before continuing (for example, if you were mounting /usr).

Any of the values that don't require a value can have no appended to it to have the opposite effect. For example, nobg indicates that the mount should not be done in the background.

Unmounting NFS file systems

After an NFS file system is mounted, unmounting it is simple. You use the umount command with either the local mount point or the remote file system name. For example, here are two ways you could unmount maple:/tmp from the local directory /mnt/maple.

```
# umount maple:/tmp
# umount /mnt/maple
```

Either form will work. If maple:/tmp is mounted automatically (from a listing in /etc/fstab), the directory will be remounted the next time you boot Red Hat Linux. If it was a temporary mount (or listed as noauto in /etc/fstab), it will not be remounted at boot time.

Tip If you get the message, "device is busy" when you try to unmount a file system, it means that the unmount failed because the file system is being accessed. Most likely, one of the directories in the NFS file system is the current directory for your shell (or the shell of someone else on your system). The other possibility is that a command is holding a file open in the NFS file system (such as a text editor). Check your Terminal windows and other shells, and cd out of the directory if you are in it, or just close the Terminal windows.

Other cool things to do with NFS

You can share some directories to make it consistent for a user to work from any of several different Linux computers on your network. Some examples of useful directories to share are:

✦ `/var/spool /mail`—By sharing this directory from your mail server, and mounting it on the same directory on other computers on your network, users can access their mail from any of those other computers. This saves the user from having to download messages to their current computer or from having to log in to the server just to get mail. There is only one mailbox for each user, no matter from where it is accessed.

✦ `/home`—This is a similar concept to sharing mail, except that all users have access to their home directories from any of the NFS clients. Again, you would mount `/home` on the same mount point on each client computer. When the user logs in, that user has access to all the user's startup files and data files contained in the `/home/user` directory.

> **Tip**
> If your users rely on a shared `/home` directory, you should make sure that the NFS server that exports the directory is fairly reliable. If `/home` isn't available, the user may not have the startup files to login correctly, or any of the data files needed to get work done. One workaround is to have a minimal set of startup files (`.bashrc`, `.Xdefaults`, and so on) available in the user's home directory when the NFS directory is not mounted. Doing so allows the user to log in properly at those times.

✦ `/project`—Although you don't have to use this name, a common practice among users on a project is to share a directory structure containing files that people on the project need to share. This way everyone can work on original files and keep copies of the latest versions in one place.

✦ `/var/log`—An administrator can keep track of log files from several different computers by mounting the `/var/log` file on the administrator's computer. (Each server may need to export the directory to allow root to be mapped between the computers for this to work.) If there are problems with a computer, the administrator can then easily view the shared log files live.

If you are working mostly with Red Hat Linux and other UNIX systems, NFS is probably your best choice for sharing file systems. If your network consists primarily of MS Windows computers, you may want to look into using Samba for file sharing.

Setting Up a Samba File Server in Red Hat Linux

Samba is a software package that comes with Red Hat Linux that lets you share file systems and printers on a network with computers that use the Session Message Block (SMB) protocol. SMB is the protocol that is delivered with Windows operating systems for sharing files and printers. Although you can't always count on NFS being installed on Windows clients (unless you install it yourself), SMB is always available (with a bit of setup).

On the Red Hat Linux side, the Samba software package contains a variety of daemon processes, administrative tools, user tools, and configuration files. The work you need to do with Samba centers on the /etc/samba/smb.conf file. You can either edit /etc/samba/smb.conf by hand or use the SWAT program (which runs in a browser window) to set up the file.

Daemon processes consist of smbd (the SMB daemon) and nmbd (the NetBIOS name server). smbd is what makes the file sharing and printing services you add to your Red Hat Linux computer available to Windows client computers. The client computers this package supports include:

✦ Windows 9*x*

✦ Windows 2000

✦ Windows NT

✦ Windows ME

✦ Windows XP

✦ Windows for Workgroups

✦ MS Client 3.0 for DOS

✦ OS/2

✦ Dave for Macintosh Computers

✦ Samba for Linux

As for administrative tools for Samba, there are several shell commands that you can use. You can check your configuration file using the testparm and testprns commands. The smbstatus command will tell you which computers are currently connected to your shared resources. Using the nmblookup command, you can query for NetBIOS names (the names used to identify host computers in Samba).

Although Samba uses the NetBIOS service to share resources with SMB clients, the underlying network must be configured for TCP/IP. Although other SMB hosts can use TCP/IP, NetBEUI, and IPX/SPX to transport data, Samba for Linux supports only TCP/IP. Messages are carried between host computers with TCP/IP and are then handled by NetBIOS.

Getting and installing Samba

Although not installed with all installation groups in Red Hat Linux, Samba is available on the second Red Hat CD-ROM (CD-2). To install Samba from the CD, mount the CD and run rpm as follows:

```
# mount /mnt/cdrom
# cd /mnt/cdrom/RedHat/RPMS
# rpm -ivh samba*
```

If you prefer, you can obtain the latest version of Samba from www.samba.org. An rpm that is more recent than the one on the Red Hat CD may be available. (Follow the download links from the Samba Web site to obtain the Samba rpm.) A lot of documentation comes with Samba. Before you start trying to configure Samba, read the README file (probably located in /usr/share/doc/samba*). It provides a good overview of the SMB protocol and Samba.

Quick-starting Samba

This procedure is primarily for people who are trying out Samba for the first time in a secure environment. If you are using Samba in an environment that contains critical data and is accessible from the Internet, I urge you to consider more stringent security measures. Read the more complete descriptions of Samba in the rest of this section and refer to documents in the /usr/share/doc/samba*/docs/ directory for information on security.

The procedure in this section steps you through an example of a Red Hat Linux system configured as a Samba server. In this example, the Linux Samba server uses "user" security to share home directories and printers with users from Windows workstations on the local LAN. The procedure consists of three basic steps:

1. Editing the smb.conf file.

2. Adding Samba users.

3. Starting the Samba service.

Editing the smb.conf file

Using either SWAT (described in the "Configuring Samba with SWAT" section) or a regular text editor (as root user), create an /etc/samba/smb.conf file. Here is an example of an smb.conf file (with comment lines removed) that can be used to share printers and directories with several Windows systems on a single LAN:

```
  [global]
workgroup = ESTREET
netbios name = MAPLE
server string = Samba Server on Maple
hosts allow = 192.168.0.
printcap name = /etc/printcap
load printers = yes
printing = lprng
log file = /var/log/samba/%m.log
max log size = 0
```

```
security = user
encrypt passwords = yes
smb passwd file = /etc/samba/smbpasswd
socket options = TCP_NODELAY SO_RCVBUF=8192 SO_SNDBUF=8192
dns proxy = no

[homes]
comment = Home Directories
browseable = no
writable = yes

[printers]
comment = All Printers
path = /var/spool/samba
browseable = no
guest ok = no
printable = yes
```

In the [global] section, the workgroup is set to ESTREET, the server is identified as the Samba Server on Maple, and only computers that are on the local network (192.168.0.) are allowed access to the Samba service. Definitions for the local printers that will be shared are taken from the /etc/printcap file, the printers are loaded (yes), and the lprng printing service (which is the default print service used by Red Hat Linux) is used.

Separate log files for each host that tries to use the service are created in /var/log/samba/%m.log (with %m automatically replaced with each host name). There is no limit to the size of each log file (0).

In this case, we are using user-level security (security = user). This allows a user to log in once and then easily access the printers and the user's home directory on the Red Hat Linux system. Password encryption is on (encrypt passwords = yes) because Windows 95, Windows 98, and other Windows systems have password encryption on by default. Passwords are stored in the /etc/samba/ smbpasswd file on your Linux system.

The dns proxy = no option prevents Linux from looking up system names on the DNS server (used for TCP/IP lookups). You may need to add host names and IP addresses of the computers on your LAN to your /etc/hosts file to resolve these addresses.

The [homes] section allows each user to be able to access his or her Linux home directory from a Windows system on the LAN. The user will be able to write to the home directory. However, other users will not be able see or share this directory. The [printers] section allows all users to print to any printer that is configured on the local Linux system.

Adding Samba users

Doing user-style Samba security means assigning a Linux user account to each person using the Linux file systems and printers from his or her Windows workstation. (You could assign users to a guest account instead, but in this example, all users have their own accounts.) Then you need to add SMB passwords for each user. For example, here is how you would add a user whose Windows 98 workstation login is chuckp:

1. Type the following as root user from a Terminal window to add a Linux user account:

   ```
   # useradd -m chuckp
   ```

2. Add a Linux password for the new user as follows:

   ```
   # passwd chuckp
   Changing password for user chuckp
   New UNIX password: ********
   Retype new UNIX password: ********
   ```

3. Repeat the previous steps to add user accounts for all users from Windows workstations on your LAN that you want to give access to your Linux system to.

4. Type the following command to create the Samba password file (smbpasswd):

   ```
   # cat /etc/passwd | /usr/bin/mksmbpasswd.sh >
   /etc/samba/smbpasswd
   ```

5. Add an SMB password for the user as follows:

   ```
   # smbpasswd chuckp
   New SMB password: **********
   Retype new SMB password: **********
   ```

   Repeat this step for each user. Later, each user can log in to Linux and rerun the passwd and smbpasswd commands to set private passwords.

Starting the Samba service

To start the Samba SMB and NMB daemons, you can run the /etc/init.d/smb start-up script by typing the following as the root user:

```
# /etc/init.d/smb start
```

This runs the Samba service during the current session. To set up Samba to start automatically when your Linux system starts, type the following:

```
# chkconfig smb on
```

This turns on the Samba service to start automatically in run levels 3, 4, or 5.

At this point, you can open the Network Neighborhood icon from the Windows desktop on the local LAN for a user you have just set up. An icon representing the Linux Samba server you just configured should appear in the Network Neighborhood window. When you open the server icon, you should see an icon representing the user's home directory (/home/user) and one icon for each shared printer available from the Linux Samba server.

Configuring Samba with SWAT

The SWAT program lets you set Samba configuration information, the result of which is stored in the /etc/samba/smb.conf file. The advantage of using SWAT, as opposed to editing the /etc/samba/smb.conf file by hand, is that you can get help and some error checking as you configure Samba.

SWAT is an application that runs in your Web browser window. Before you can use swat, you need to do some configuration. To set up the SWAT program to run from your browser, follow these steps:

1. In /etc/services, make sure that the following line exists. This assigns the swat service to port 901, using the TCP protocol.

   ```
   swat   901/tcp    # Samba Web Administration Tool
   ```

2. In the /etc/xinetd.d/swat file, you need to change the disable line from yes to no. This is how the line should appear after that:

   ```
   disable = no
   ```

3. For the changes to xinetd and /etc/services to take effect, you restart the xinetd start-up script as follows:

   ```
   # /etc/init.d/xinetd restart
   ```

When you have finished this procedure, use the SWAT program, described in the next section, to configure Samba.

Creating the Samba server configuration with SWAT

You can run the SWAT program, by typing the following URL from your local browser:

```
http://localhost:901/
```

Instead of running SWAT from your local browser, you can also run the SWAT program from another computer on the network, by substituting the server computer's name for localhost. (To allow computers besides localhost to access the swat service, you must change or remove the only_from = 127.0.0.1 line from the

/etc/xinetd.d/swat file and restart the xinetd service.) At this point, the browser will prompt you for a user name and password. Enter the root user name and password. The SWAT window should appear, as shown in Figure 18-2.

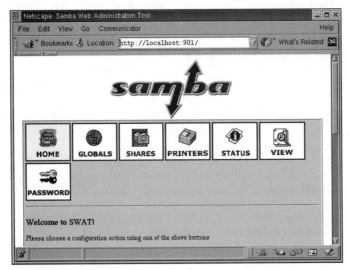

Figure 18-2: Use SWAT from your browser to manage your Samba configuration.

The rest of this section describes how to use SWAT to create your configuration entries (in /etc/samba/smb.conf) and to work with that configuration.

Caution   Any time you use a GUI to change a plain-text configuration file (as you do with SWAT), it is possible that you will lose some of the information that you put in by hand. In this case, SWAT deletes comment lines and rearranges other entries. Make a backup copy of your /etc/samba/smb.conf file if you edit it with SWAT after you have edited it by hand.

Creating global Samba settings

A group of global settings affects how file and print sharing are generally accomplished on a Samba server. They appear under the [global] heading in the /etc/samba/smb.conf file. There are six option types available: Base options, security options, logging options, printing options, browse options, and WINs options. To view and modify your global Samba server settings, click the Globals button. Then add the following options.

Base options
The following options relate to basic information associated with your Samba server.

✦ **Workgroup** — The name of the workgroup associated with the group of SMB hosts. By default, the value for this field is "workgroup."

✦ **Netbios Name** — The name assigned to this Samba server. You can use the same name as your DNS hostname.

✦ **Server String** — A string of text identifying the server. This name appears in places such as the printer comment box. By default, it says Samba Server.

✦ **Interfaces** — Lets you set up more than one network interface. This enables Samba to browse several different subnetworks. The form of this field can be *IP Address/Subnetwork Mask*. Or, you could identify a network interface (such as eth0 for the first Ethernet card on your computer). For example, a Class C network address may appear as:

```
192.168.24.11/255.255.255.0
```

Security options

Of the security options settings, the first option (security) is the most important one to get right. It defines the type of security used to give access to the shared file systems and printers to the client computers.

✦ **Security** — Sets how password and user information is transferred to the Samba server from the client computer. As noted earlier, it's important to get this value right. The default value for security (security=user) is different than the default value for security (security=share) in pre-2.0 versions of Samba. If you are coming from an earlier version of Samba and clients are failing to access your server, this setting is a good place to start. Here are your options:

• **user** — The most common type of security used to share files and printers to Windows 95/98/2000 and Windows NT clients. It is the default set with Samba in the current release. This setting is appropriate if users are doing a lot of file sharing (as opposed to a Samba server used mostly as a print server). It requires that a user provide a user name/password before using the server.

The easiest way to get this method working is to give a Red Hat Linux user account to every client user who will use the Red Hat Linux Samba server. This provides basically the same file permissions to a user account through Samba as the same user would get if he or she were logged in directly to Red Hat Linux.

Caution   Apparently, there is a bug in Windows for Workgroups that causes the password that the user types in to be ignored from a "connect drive" dialog box. Instead, Windows uses the user name and password in effect for the user's current Windows login session. One way around this problem, although it is clumsy from a security standpoint, is to assign the same user name/password combination for each user on the Red Hat computer that they use in Windows.

- **share**—The share value for security works best for just print sharing or for providing file access that is more public (guest sharing). A client doesn't need to provide a valid user name and password to access the server. However, the user will typically have a "guest" level of permission to access and change files. See the sidebar describing guest accounts for further information.

- **server**—The security option that, from the client's point of view, is the same as user security, in that the client still has to provide a valid user name/password combination to use the Samba server at all. The difference is on the server side. With server security, the user name/password is sent to another SMB server for validation. If this fails, Samba will try to validate the client using user security.

- **domain**—The security option that, from the client's point of view, looks the same as *user* security. This setting is used only if the Samba server has been added to a Windows NT domain (using the smbpasswd command). When a client tries to connect to the Samba server in this mode, its user name and password are sent to a Windows NT Primary or Backup Domain controller. This is accomplished the same way that a Windows NT server would perform validation. Valid Red Hat Linux user accounts must still be set up.

✦ **Encrypt Passwords**—Controls whether encrypted passwords can be negotiated with the client. This is off (No) by default. For *domain* security, this value must be true. Later versions of Windows NT (4.0 SP3 or later) and Windows 98 and Windows 2000 expect encrypted passwords to be on.

✦ **Update Encrypted**—Allows users who log in with a plain-text password to automatically have their passwords updated to an encrypted password when they log in. Normally, this option is off. It can be turned on when you want an installation using plain-text passwords to have everyone updated to encrypted password authentication. It saves users the trouble of running the smbpasswd command directly from the server. After everyone is updated, this feature can be turned off. When this option is on, the encrypt passwords option should be set to no.

✦ **Guest Account**—Specifies the user name for the guest account. When a service is specified as Guest OK, the user name entered here will be used to access that service. The account is usually the *nobody* user name.

Tip   Make sure that the guest account is a valid user. (The default of nobody should already be set up to work.) Without a valid user as the guest account, the IPC$ connection that lists the shared resources will fail.

✦ **Hosts Allow**—Contains a list of one or more hosts that are allowed to use your computer's Samba services. By default, users from any computer can connect to the Samba server (of course, they still have to provide valid user names and passwords). Usually, you use this option to allow connections from specific computers or computer networks that are excluded by the Hosts Deny option.

Assigning Guest Accounts

Samba always assigns the permissions level of a valid user on the Red Hat Linux system to clients who use the server. In the case of share security, the user is assigned a guest account (the "nobody" user account by default).

If the guest account value isn't set, Samba goes through a fairly complex set of rules to determine which user account to use. The result is that it can be hard to assure which user permissions will be assigned in each case. This is why it is recommended to use "user security" if you want to provide more specific user access to your Samba server.

✦ **Hosts Deny** — Contains a list of one or more hosts from which users are not allowed to use your computer's Samba services. You can make this option fairly restrictive, and then add the specific hosts and networks you want to use the Samba server. By default, no hosts are denied.

Secure Socket Layer options

The ssl CA certFile option lets you define the location of a file that contains all certificate authorities Samba uses. By default, Red Hat Linux uses the following file: /usr/share/ssl/certs/ca-bundle.crt.

Logging options

The following options help define how logging is done on your Samba server.

✦ **Log File** — Defines the location of the Samba smb log file. By default, Samba log files are contained in /var/log/samba (with file names log.nmbd, log.smbd, and smb.log). In this option, the %m is replaced by smb to set the smb log file as /var/log/samba/smb.log.

✦ **Max Log Size** — Sets the maximum amount of space, in kilobytes, that the log files can consume. By default, the value is set to 0 (no limit).

Tuning option

The Socket Options option lets you pass options to the protocols Samba uses to communicate. The following options are set by default: TCP_NODELAY, SO_RCVBUF=8192, and SO_SNDBUF=8192. The first option disables Nagle's algorithm, which is used to manage the transmission of TCP/IP packets. The other two options set the maximum size of the sockets receive buffer and send buffer to 8192, respectively. These options are set to improve performance (reportedly up to 10 times faster than without setting these options). In general, you shouldn't change these options.

Printing option

The Printing option is used to define how printer status information is presented. For Linux systems (including Red Hat Linux), the value is typically LPRNG. You can use printing styles from other types of operating systems, such as UNIX System V (sysv), AIX (aix), HP UNIX (hpux), and Berkeley UNIX (bsd), to name a few.

Browse options

A browse list is a list of computers that are available on the network to SMB services. Clients use this list to find computers that are not only on their own LAN, but also computers in their workgroups that may be on other reachable networks.

With the latest release of Samba, browsing is supported. In Samba, browsing is configured by options described below and implemented by the nmbd daemon. If you are using Samba for a workgroup within a single LAN, you probably don't need to concern yourself with the browsing options. If, however, you are using Samba to provide services across several physical subnetworks, you may consider configuring Samba as a domain master browser. Here are some points to think about:

✦ Samba can be configured as a master browser. This allows it to gather lists of computers from local browse masters to form a wide-area server list.

✦ If Samba is acting as a domain master browser, Samba should use a WINS server to help browse clients resolve the names from this list.

✦ Samba can be used as a WINS server, although it can also rely on other types of operating systems to provide that service.

✦ There should be only one domain master browser for each workgroup. Don't use Samba as a domain master for a workgroup with the same name as an NT domain.

If you are working in an environment that has a mix of Samba and Windows NT servers, you should use an NT server as your WINS server. If Samba is your only file server, you should choose a single Samba server (nmbd daemon) to supply the WINS services.

Note   A WINS server is basically a name server for NetBIOS names. It provides the same service that a DNS server does with TCP/IP domain names: it can translate names into addresses. A WINS server is particularly useful for allowing computers to communicate with SMB across multiple subnetworks where information is not being broadcast across the subnetworks' boundaries.

To configure the browsing feature in Samba, you must have the workgroup named properly (described earlier in this section). Here are the global options related to SMB browsing.

Note If you have trouble getting browsing to work, check the nmbd log file (/var/log/samba/log.nmb). If you need more detail, increase the debug information level to 2 or 3 (described earlier in this section) and restart Samba. The log can tell you if your Samba server is the master browser and, if so, which computers are on its list.

✦ **OS Level** — Set a value to control whether your Samba server (nmbd daemon) may become the local master browser for your workgroup. Raising this setting increases the Samba server's chance to control the browser list for the workgroup in the local broadcast area.

If the value is 0, a Windows machine will probably be selected. A value of 60 will probably ensure that the Samba server is chosen over an NT server. The default value is 20.

✦ **Preferred Master** — Set this to Yes if you want to force selection of a master browser. By setting this to Yes, the Samba server also has a better chance of being elected. (Setting Domain Master to Yes along with this option should ensure that the Samba server will be selected.) This is set to Auto by default, which causes Samba to try to detect the current master browser before taking that responsibility.

✦ **Local Master** — Set this to Yes if you want the Samba server to become the local browser master. (This is not a guarantee, but gives it a chance.) Set the value to No if you do not want your Samba server selected as the local master. Local Master is Auto by default.

✦ **Domain Master** — Set this to Yes if you want the Samba server (nmbd daemon) to identify itself as the domain master browser for its workgroup. This list will then allow client computers assigned to the workgroup to use SMB-shared files and printers from subnetworks that are outside of their own subnetwork. This is set to No by default.

WINS options

Use the WINS options if you want to have a particular WINS server provide the name-to-address translation of NetBIOS names used by SMB clients. As noted earlier, you probably don't need to use a WINS server if all of the clients and servers in your SMB workgroup are on the same subnetwork. That's because NetBIOS names can be obtained through addresses that are broadcast. It is possible to have your Samba server provide WINS services.

✦ **DNS Proxy** — By setting this to Yes, Samba will use Domain Name Service (DNS) to determine the IP address of each NetBIOS name that is requested. This assumes that your NetBIOS names are the same as your TCP/IP names for each computer. One restriction is that NetBIOS names cannot be more than 15 characters, which could be a problem with long domain/host names. This is set to No by default.

✦ **WINS Server**—If there is a WINS server on your network that you want to use to resolve the NetBIOS names for your workgroup, you can enter the IP address of that server here. Again, you will probably want to use a WINS server if your workgroup extends outside of the local subnetwork.

✦ **WINS Support**—Set this value to Yes if you want your Samba server to act as a WINS server. (It's No by default.) Again, this is not needed if all the computers in your workgroup are on the same subnetwork. Only one computer on your network should be assigned as the WINS server.

Besides the values described here, you can access dozens more options by clicking the Advanced View button. When you have filled in all the fields you need, click Commit Changes at the bottom of the screen to have the changes written to the /etc/samba/smb.conf file.

Configuring shared file systems with SWAT

To make your shared directory available to others, you can add an entry to the SWAT window. To use SWAT to set up Samba to share directories, do the following:

Note   You may see one or more security warnings during the course of this procedure. These are to warn you that someone can potentially view the data you are sending to SWAT. If you are working on your local host or on a private LAN, the risk is minimal.

1. From the main SAMBA window, click Shares.

2. Type the name of the directory that you want to share in the Create Share box, then click Create Share.

3. Add any of these options:

   • **Comment**—A few words to describe the shared directory (optional).

   • **Path**—The path name of the directory you are sharing.

   • **Guest Account**—If Guest OK is selected, then the user name that is defined here is assigned to users accessing the file system. The nobody user account (which is used only by users who access your computer remotely) is the default name used. (The FTP user is also a recommended value.)

   • **Read Only**—If Yes, then files can only be read from this file system, but no remote user can save or modify files on the file system. Select No if you want users to be allowed to save files to this directory over the network.

   • **Guest OK**—Select Yes to enable anyone access to this directory without requiring a password.

- **Hosts Allow** — Add the names of the computers that you want to allow access to this file system. You can separate hostnames by commas, spaces, or tabs. Here are some valid ways of entering hostnames:

  localhost — Allow access to the local host.

  192.168.74.18 — IP address. Enter an individual IP address.

  192.168.74. — Enter a network address to include all hosts on a network. (Be sure to put a dot at the end of the network number or it won't work!)

  maple, pine — Enable access to individual hosts by name.

  EXCEPT *host* — If you are allowing access to a group of hosts (such as by entering a network address), use EXCEPT to specifically deny access from one host from that group.

- **Hosts Deny** — Deny access to specific computers by placing their names here. By default, no particular computers are excluded. Enter hostnames in the same forms you used for Hosts Allow.

- **Browseable** — Indicates whether you can view this directory on the list of shared directories. This is on (Yes) by default. (See Viewing Available Samba File Systems for a description of how to view shared file systems.)

- **Available** — Enables you to leave this entry intact, but turns off the service. This is useful if you want to close access to a directory temporarily. This is on (Yes) by default. Select No to turn it off.

   4. Select Commit Changes.

At this point, the shared file systems should be available to the Samba client computers (Windows 9*x*, Windows NT, Windows 2000, OS/2, Linux, and so on) that have access to your Linux Samba server. Before you try that, however, you can check a few things about your Samba configuration.

Checking your Samba setup with SWAT

From the SWAT window, select Status. From this window you can restart your `smbd` and `nmbd` processes. Likewise, you can see lists of active connections, active shares, and open files. (The preferred way to start the `smbd` and `nmbd` daemons is to set up the smb service to start automatically. Type `chkconfig smb on` to set the service to start automatically at boot time.)

Testing Your Samba permissions

You can run several commands from a shell to work with Samba. One is the `testparm` command. Use the `testparm` command to check the access permissions you have set up. It lists global parameters that are set, along with any shared directories or printers.

Checking the status of shared file systems

The smbstatus command can be used to view who is currently using Samba shared resources offered from your Red Hat Linux system. The following is an example of the output from smbstatus:

```
Samba version 2.2.1a
Service uid     gid      pid    machine
---------------------------------------------
Temp    nobody  nobody   2943   snowbird (10.0.0.12) Mon Nov 22 10:52:22 2001

Locked files:
Pid    DenyMode  R/W    Oplock          Name
---------------------------------------------
2943   DENY_NONE RDONLY EXCLUSIVE+BATCH /tmp/install.log Mon Nov 22 11:17:04 2002

Share mode memory usage (bytes):
    1048360(99%) free + 136(0%) used + 80(0%) overhead = 1048576(100%) total
```

This output shows that from your Red Hat Linux Samba server, the Temp service (which is a share of the /tmp directory) is currently open by the computer named snowbird. The user and group nobody is being used to access the resource. The PID (2943) is the process number of the smbd daemon on the Red Hat Linux server that is handling the service. The only file that has been opened is the /tmp/install.log file. The file is available as read-only (RDONLY).

Setting up Samba clients for Windows systems

To be able to share Samba file systems from your Red Hat Linux system over your network with users on Windows client computers, there is some configuration required of those clients. On Windows 95/98 and similar systems, most of the configuration is done from the Network window. To open the Network window, do the following from Windows 95:

1. Choose Start ➪ Settings ➪ Control Panel.

2. From the Control Panel, double-click on the Network icon.

On the Network window, you can see the network components (protocols, clients, adapters, and services). Samba relies on a working TCP/IP network, so you should have already set up TCP/IP on your LAN (as described in Chapter 15). To be able to use Samba file systems, you also need to have at least the following network components configured:

✦ **Client for Microsoft Networks** — The client that allows print and file sharing. If it is not listed, you can add it by choosing Add ➪ Client ➪ Add ➪ Microsoft ➪ Client for Microsoft Networks ➪ OK.

✦ **NetBEUI protocol** — The protocol used to carry out file and print sharing among MS Windows (and other) systems. If it is not listed, add it by choosing Add ⇨ Protocol ⇨ Add ⇨ Microsoft ⇨ NetBEUI ⇨ OK. (NetBEUI is a raw NetBIOS protocol. If your computer lets you run NetBIOS over TCP and bypass NetBEUI, you should do so.)

✦ **A Network Adapter** — Represents the networking medium that actually connects the computer together. Chances are this represents a LAN card, such as an Ethernet card.

✦ **TCP/IP protocol** — If TCP/IP is not yet added for your network adapter, choose Add ⇨ Protocol ⇨ Add ⇨ Microsoft ⇨ TCP/IP. Then click OK. Click the TCP/IP entry for your network adapter; then click Properties. From the Bindings tab, make sure that Client for Microsoft Networks is checked. From the WINS Configuration tab, click Enable WINS Resolution, type the IP address for your Linux server, and click Add. Then click OK.

Tip

If you want to allow the client to share its own files and printers, you can click File and Print Sharing. Then you can select to turn on file access and/or printer access from the pop-up window that appears.

Other information that you need to add relates to the client computer's identity and access. On the Network window, click the Identification tab. On that tab, enter a name for the client computer, the name of the workgroup and a description of the computer. Next, click the Access Control tab. From there, select either User-level or Share-level access control (to match the type of control set up on the server). Click OK when you are done. (At this point, you may need to reboot Windows.)

To see the file and print services available from your Red Hat Linux Samba server (as well as from other computers on the network), open the Network Neighborhood window. To open the window, double-click the Network Neighborhood icon on the Windows 95 desktop. Figure 18-3 shows an example of the Network Neighborhood window for a small LAN.

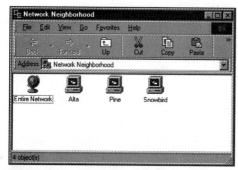

Figure 18-3: View your Red Hat Linux Samba server from the Network Neighborhood window.

The Network Neighborhood window shows the computers that Windows found on your network. If your server appears on the screen (in my case, the server's name is maple), double-click on it. Otherwise, you may need to double-click on Entire Network, then open the workgroup that your server is a part of to find your server. The server should show two kinds of resources:

✦ **Printers** — A name and a printer icon should represent each printer shared from the server. To access a printer, double-click on it. Windows will have you set up the printer for your computer. After that, you can print with it as you would any local printer.

✦ **Directories** — A name and folder icon should represent shared directories from the server. Open the directory to see the files and folders in that directory.

Double-click on a folder to view the contents of that folder. At this point, you may receive a request to enter a password. Type the password and click OK. You should be able to view the contents of the folder, and its subfolders, at this time.

Tip　If you plan to use the directory often, you may want to assign a drive letter to it. Right-click on the folder icon, then select Map Network Drive. Select a drive from the list and, if you like, choose Reconnect at logon to have it available when you log on. Then click OK.

If the file server that you are looking for does not appear in your Network Neighborhood, you can try to search for it. Choose Start ⇨ Find ⇨ Computer. Type the name of the computer to search for, then select Find Now. If the computer name appears, double-click on it. A window should open, displaying the shared directories and printers from the server.

Another thing you can do to help your Windows 95 computer find your Linux Samba server is to create an lmhosts file. Copy the sample C:\windows\lmhosts.sam file to C:\windows\lmhosts. Then edit the file to add the hostnames and IP addresses of the SMB servers on your network.

Setting Up a NetWare File Server in Red Hat Linux

NetWare was once the most popular software for sharing files and printers among PCs connected in LANs. NetWare is referred to as a network operating system. That means that NetWare takes control of the whole computer and manages its resources. Although NetWare is not like client operating systems (such as Windows 95 or 98) that you could keep on your desk at work to do word processing, it is a highly efficient file and print server.

In Linux, there is software available for emulating a NetWare server from your Linux system. One that comes with Red Hat Linux is the Martin Stovers NetWare Emulator (mars_nwe package). Though mars_nwe doesn't do everything a NetWare server can do, it does a good job as a basic file-and-print server. Here are features that mars_nwe includes:

✦ **File Services** — You can share directory structures (referred to as volumes) from Linux using the NetWare Emulator.

✦ **Print Services** — You can share printers associated with NetWare services using the NetWare Emulator.

✦ **RIP/SAP daemon** — This allows your Red Hat Linux computer to function as an IPX router. (IPX is the native protocol used to communicate among NetWare systems.)

Note If the mars_nwe package is not installed on your computer, you can install it from the second Red Hat Linux installation CD (CD-2) that comes with this book.

Another package that offers NetWare file server emulation is the lwared package (short for LinWare Daemon). This package also provides NetWare file and print services. However, it doesn't work very well with Windows clients. (The lwared package is not included with Red Hat Linux and isn't discussed in this section.)

On the client side, the ncpfs package is an additional package that you would need to install if you want your Red Hat Linux computer to take advantage of services from NetWare servers. This package offers a full range of client commands for accessing NetWare services. These commands let you mount NetWare volumes, display information about available services, and work with NetWare bindery objects.

Creating the NetWare file server

To share NetWare services from your Red Hat Linux server, you need to use IPX protocol to communicate with NetWare clients over your physical network. A common situation is to use IPX over an Ethernet LAN (which is what is described in this section).

Cross-Reference See Chapter 15 for information on setting up an Ethernet LAN.

Most of the configuration of your NetWare server in Linux is done in the /etc/nwserv.conf file. The nwserv.conf file that is delivered with mars_nwe contains a lot of commented information that describes what you need to do to configure NetWare services in Red Hat Linux. Refer to the commented text for more details on different ways of configuring NetWare servers in Red Hat Linux.

Configuring /etc/nwserv.conf

Information that you need to add to your `/etc/nwserv.conf` file is organized in sections. Each entry in a section begins with the number of that section. Here are some of the sections that you may need to modify for your NetWare server in Red Hat Linux. (The number assigned to each section is shown in parentheses.)

✦ **Volumes** (1) — The names of the volumes (Red Hat Linux directories) you want to share.

✦ **Server Name** (2) — The identity of your server.

✦ **Internal Network Number** (3) — A number that uniquely identifies your server. The address either must be a hexadecimal number or must include the word *auto* to use your current IP address as your internal network number.

✦ **IPX Devices** (4) — Contains information used by the IPX network. It includes the IP network number, the network interface's device name (such as eth0), the frame type (ethernet_ii, 802.2, 802.3, or SNAP), and the number of ticks (that is, the time it takes packets to travel over a particular interface in $\frac{1}{18}$ of a second). You don't need to do this if your IPX network is already configured.

✦ **Password Handling** (7) — Defines whether (and how) passwords are encrypted from clients. (The default is 0, which enforces encryption of all client passwords.)

✦ **Minimal UID/GID Rights** (10) — Assigns the minimal user rights to the shared volumes from your Linux server. By default, the *nobody* user rights (UID=99) are assigned. Also by default, the *nobody* group rights (GID=99) are assigned.

✦ **Supervisor Login** (12) — Assigns the NetWare supervisor login to a particular login on your Linux system. It is recommended that you assign a special login instead of using root (to limit the security implications). By default, the supervisor login is assigned to the Linux root login (UID=0). This entry is read only once, the first time the server is started. In should also include an initial password for the login.

✦ **User Logins** (13) — Maps regular Linux logins on your computer into Linux NetWare server logins. You can also add a default password, although none is required.

✦ **Automatic Login Mapping** (15) — Defines whether to map your Red Hat Linux user logins (those in `/etc/passwd`) automatically into your Linux NetWare server. For commonly mapped logins, the same password is assigned. By default, logins are reread from `/etc/passwd` and assigned the password `top-secret`.

✦ **Startup Tests** (16) — Runs sanity checks at startup with this value set to 1 (the default).

You can find information about a few other values that are used to set printing, debugging, and timing by reading the descriptions in the `/etc/nwserv.conf` file. Here is an example of the values I set to share a NetWare volume from a Linux system. Some of these values are defaults that are set in the `nwserv.conf` file. (These entries are spread throughout the `/etc/nwserv.conf` file.)

```
1       SYS            /var/mars_nwe/sys      kt   711 600
1       CDROM          /mnt/cdrom             kr   auto     1
2       maple1
4       0x0            eth0      802.3        1
7       1
10      99
11      99
12      SUPERVISOR     root       secret
15      99             top-secret
```

In this sample, the SYS (`/var/mars_nwe/sys` directory) and CDROM (`/mnt/cdrom`) volumes are being shared. The server's name is assigned to `maple1`. The address is being automatically selected (`auto`) from the IP address of the local computer. By using `0x0` the Linux kernel can choose a network number for you. The network interface is `eth0` (the first Ethernet network on the computer) and the frame type used is `802.3`. Minimal user and group permission are assigned to UID 99 (the user named nobody). `SUPERVISOR` permissions are assigned to the root user (with an initial password of `secret`). The password for UID 99 is `top-secret`.

Starting the NetWare server daemon

At this point, all you have to do is start your NetWare server process. You can do that by typing `nwserv`. Your other option, which is better in the long term, is to start the server from a system init script. The mars_nwe package delivers such a script, but it is probably not configured to start automatically on your system. To set the script to start the NetWare server process automatically, type the following:

```
# chkconfig mars-new on
```

This command sets up mars-nwe to start at run levels 3, 4, and 5. The next time you reboot your Linux system, the `nwserv` daemon will start providing your NetWare services. Or, you could start the service immediately by typing the following:

```
# /etc/init.d/mars-nwe start
```

Using NetWare client commands

The ncpfs software package comes with a set of utilities that work with NetWare file and print services. Here are a few of those commands.

✦ `nsend` — Sends a message to a user's workstation. The `nsend` command looks for information about the file server, user name and, optionally, a password, in the .nwclient file in your home directory. For example, to send a message to the system administrator, you could type `nsend supervisor 'Hello, how is your day?'`

✦ nwauth—Authenticates to a NetWare server. You can specify the server (-S *servername*) and user (-U *username*) you want to authenticate. Otherwise, nwauth will look in your $HOME/.nwclient file for that information. If you run this command from the shell, the server will prompt you for a password.

✦ nwbols—Lists the NetWare bindery objects that you specify.

✦ nwboprops—Lists properties associated with a specified NetWare bindery object.

✦ nwbpset—Sets NetWare bindery properties value or creates a bindery property.

✦ nwfsinfo—Displays information about a file server without requiring you to log in to the server.

✦ nwpasswd—Changes your password on a NetWare server.

✦ nwpurge—Purges a directory of files that were previously erased.

✦ nwrights—Displays the NetWare rights associated with a particular file or directory.

✦ nwsfind—Searches for a NetWare server and displays a route (network address) to the server.

✦ nwtrustee—Displays a lot of trustee directory assignments associated with an object.

✦ nwuserlist—Displays a list of users that are currently logged in to a NetWare server.

✦ nwvolinfo—Shows information about a NetWare server volume.

✦ slist—Shows a list of all available NetWare servers.

✦ ncpmount—Mounts volumes from a NetWare file server.

✦ ncpumount—Unmounts volumes from a NetWare file server.

✦ nwbocreate—Creates a bindery object for a NetWare file server.

✦ nwborm—Deletes a bindery object for a NetWare file server.

✦ nwfsctrl—Runs a command on the NetWare file server.

✦ nwgrant—Adds a bindery object and its associated trustee rights to a directory.

✦ nwmsg—Sends a NetWare user broadcast message.

✦ nwrevoke—Revokes a directory's trustee rights.

Many NetWare commands can draw on configuration information in your $HOME/.nwclient file. When you run a NetWare command without specifying a server name, user name, and/or a password, that information can be obtained from the `.nwclient` file. This file must have secure permissions (0600) because it can contain passwords and other private information. Entries in a `.nwclient` file may look similar to the following:

```
nwfs1/mike mypasswd
remserv/guest -
```

The first line is a listing for a file server named `nwfs1` and a user named `mike`, followed by the password for that account, `mypasswd`. On the next line, the server's name is `remserv` and the user account is `guest`. No password is required for this account (indicated by the `-`).

Summary

By providing centralized file servers, an organization can efficiently share information and applications with people within the organization, with customers, or with anyone around the world. Several different technologies are available in Red Hat Linux to enable you to make your Red Hat Linux computer a file server.

The Network File System (NFS) protocol was one of the first file server technologies available. It is particularly well suited for sharing file systems among Red Hat Linux and other UNIX systems, although you can also access NFS file systems from Windows 9*x* operating systems if those systems are configured to do so. NFS uses standard `mount` and `umount` commands to connect file systems into the directory structures of client computers.

The Samba software package that comes with Red Hat Linux contains protocols and utilities for sharing files and printers among Windows and OS/2 operating systems. It uses SMB protocols that are included with all Microsoft Windows systems, and therefore provide a convenient method of sharing resources on LANs containing many Windows systems.

NetWare was once the dominant network operating system used on LANs. It provided file- and printer-sharing services for networked PCs, although in recent years it has branched out to offer a variety of network services. With the mars_nwe package, you can provide basic NetWare file and print services from your Red Hat Linux computer. With the ncpfs package, you can also use many NetWare client services to query NetWare servers and use NetWare file systems and printers.

✦　　✦　　✦

Setting Up a Mail Server

Two decades ago, e-mail was just a way to send a message to a person on the same minicomputer. Ten years ago, it was simply a stream of text exchanged primarily by researchers and scientists. Today, electronic messaging is part of the communication backbone, the core of information dissemination within companies of all sizes. Everyone uses e-mail, from the mailroom to the laboratories to the CEO's office. And if you're in charge of an organization's mail server, you'll be notified (incessantly) when it stops functioning normally.

This chapter explains how to set up a mail server in Red Hat Linux to send and receive messages. This level of communication is possible not just within the local machine, but with any host connected to the Internet. The primary aspects of mail server configuration are discussed in this chapter, but many configuration aspects are well beyond its scope and thus are not addressed. Because security is an important concern when you're connected to the Internet, it is given considerable focus in this chapter.

After you master sending mail, the next challenge is to send mail to large groups of people in a reasonable and orderly fashion. Mailing list configuration and administration are also discussed in this chapter, detailing how mailing list management software integrates and interfaces with the mail server.

Introduction to SMTP and sendmail

Even with multimedia attachments and HTML encoding prevalent in e-mail messages today, the technology behind message transfer hasn't changed significantly since the early 1980s. The framework for the Simple Mail Transfer Protocol (SMTP) was initially described in RFC 821 in 1982. The protocol itself was extended in 1993 (by RFC 1425), yielding the Extended Simple Mail Transfer Protocol (ESMTP), which provides several additional commands and new delivery modes.

The three parts to message transfer are the Mail Transfer Agent (MTA), the Mail Delivery Agent (MDA), and the Mail User Agent (MUA). The MTA (commonly referred to as the mail server, of which sendmail is an example) actually handles distributing outgoing mail and listening for incoming mail from the Internet. The MDA accepts messages from the MTA and copies the message into a user's mailbox. Red Hat Linux uses /usr/bin/procmail as the default MDA, as specified in sendmail's configuration file. For sites that have a centralized mail server, Post Office Protocol (POP) clients are also considered MDAs. An MUA is the program run by a user to read incoming mail or to send messages to others.

See Chapter 9 for details on Mail User Agents available for Red Hat Linux.

Other Mail Servers Available for Red Hat Linux

The open source version of sendmail is not the only mail server available for Red Hat Linux, but it is definitely the most common. Other servers are described in the following list, with URLs that provide further information.

✦ **Exim** — The Exim MTA is a free mail server (under GNU) that runs on Linux and other UNIX systems. This MTA includes enhanced protection against unsolicited junk mail and mail bombs. Find out more about Exim from the Exim Home Page (www.exim.org).

✦ **Postfix** — Written by Wietse Venema (of tcp_wrappers fame), this free mail server was designed with security in mind and executes most functions as an unprivileged user in a restricted chroot environment. The server encompasses more than a dozen small programs (each performing a simple, distinct task) and several single-purpose queues. Information and source code can be found at www.postfix.org/.

✦ **Qmail** — Also conceived with security as a high priority, this mail server (written by Daniel J. Bernstein, a security activist and prolific software developer) offers secure and reliable message transfer, mailbox quotas, virtual domains, and antispam features. More information is available from www.qmail.org/top.html.

✦ **Sendmail (Commercial version)** — Based on the same source code as open source sendmail, this product is distributed as binary executables built specifically for Red Hat Linux (among other Linux and UNIX variants). Pricing for the Sendmail Advanced Message Server is based on the number of mailboxes you are serving. The product offers simple installation, graphical Web-based management, and commercial support. Details can be found at www.sendmail.com/.

✦ **Smail** — Smail offers many of the same features as sendmail but is somewhat easier to configure and requires less memory. The source code can be downloaded from ftp://ftp.planix.com/pub/Smail/.

This chapter focuses on the sendmail MTA, the most common mail server on the Internet. It is estimated that nearly 70 percent of all e-mail messages on the Internet are delivered by sendmail. With the rapidly growing Internet population, several billion e-mail messages are sent and received each day.

Three major releases of sendmail have occurred. The original code (called sendmail V5, or version 5) was written in 1983 by Eric Allman, then a student at the University of California at Berkeley. He maintained the code until 1987, when Lennart Lövstrand enhanced the program, simplified the configuration, and developed IDA sendmail (named for the Institutionen för Datavetenskap, the Computer Science Department at Sweden's University of Linköping). Eric Allman returned to Berkeley in 1991 and embarked on a major code revision, releasing sendmail V8 in 1993, which incorporated the extensions from IDA sendmail. The current version (8.11.4) is based on this "version 8" code.

Installing and Running sendmail

The full sendmail distribution consists of three RPM packages: sendmail, sendmail-cf, and sendmail-doc. Only the first package is truly necessary to send and receive mail on your machine. The second package includes configuration macros and other files that can help you reconfigure your site's sendmail installation if the defaults are insufficient. The third package contains documentation files that help to explain some of the details of the current version.

These binary packages can be downloaded from any Red Hat mirror site and are included in the Red Hat distribution. The sendmail and sendmail-cf packages are on CD-1, while the sendmail-doc package is on CD-2. From the Red Hat RPMS directory on each CD-ROM, the following command installs the packages:

```
# rpm -ivv sendmail*
```

Note If a new version of sendmail is released before an equivalent Red Hat package is available, the full source code distribution can be downloaded from www.sendmail.org. Remember that this involves configuring and compiling the entire distribution, not exactly a task for the uninitiated or fainthearted.

Starting sendmail

To start sendmail, you can either reboot the machine or just execute the command /etc/init.d/sendmail start to run the server. The procedure for starting and stopping sendmail is no different from that of other server processes. The preceding installation process installs the /etc/init.d/sendmail file and uses the chkconfig command to create the appropriate links in the /etc/rcX.d directories.

Cross-Reference   See Chapter 12 for detailed information on the inner workings of the shell scripts that control starting and stopping daemons and server processes.

The `/etc/init.d/sendmail` shell script accepts any of four command-line arguments. If it is called with the `start` argument, the sendmail script starts the daemon process, which, unless otherwise instructed by the `/etc/sysconfig/sendmail` file, processes incoming mail immediately (DAEMON=yes) and attempts to deliver queued mail every 60 minutes (QUEUE=1h). Also, each time the daemon starts, several database maps are created from plain-text configuration files in the `/etc/mail` directory. If called with `stop` as the command-line argument, the mail server shuts down, and further incoming messages are ignored (remaining in the outgoing queue on the machine sending the message).

If given a command-line argument of `restart`, the script simply executes the aforementioned `stop` and `start` procedures in sequence. Using `status` as the argument reports whether the daemon is running and, if it is, print its PID. All other command-line arguments result in an error and cause a usage message to be printed.

Tip   If your machine seems to hang for a few minutes while loading sendmail (after the `Starting sendmail:` message is printed), the machine's hostname cannot be resolved. To remedy this, add the machine's IP address and hostname to the `/etc/hosts` file. This same behavior can occur as the X server attempts to start.

If sendmail is running in daemon mode, incoming messages are processed and stored in the `/var/spool/mail` directory. Each file in this directory represents a valid user name on the local machine. Each individual user's MUA is (either from a value compiled into the program or from an environment variable) set up to use this directory and the user's account name as the incoming mailbox for that user.

Outgoing messages are stored in the `/var/spool/mqueue` directory while they are being processed or if they must be queued for later delivery. The filenames in this directory may look strange, but there is a consistent naming scheme. The first two characters indicate what type of data is stored in the file (as described in Table 19-1). All subsequent characters form a unique random identifier based on the PID of the sendmail process that is handling that message.

Table 19-1	
File Prefixes in /var/spool/mqueue	

Filename Prefix	Type of Data Stored
df	The data that constitutes the body of an e-mail message.
qf	The queue control file that contains the message headers and other administrative details.

Filename Prefix	Type of Data Stored
tf	A temporary copy of the qf file, created if delivery errors are encountered.
xf	Any error messages generated while attempting to send the message.

Other programs

As indicated in the output from the sendmail installation, several other executable programs are included in the distribution. These are described in Table 19-2.

<table>
<tr><td colspan="2" align="center">Table 19-2
Other Related Sendmail Programs</td></tr>
<tr><td>Program</td><td>Description</td></tr>
<tr><td>hoststat</td><td>Displays the status of hosts that have recently communicated with the sendmail daemon on the local machine. The command is equivalent to <code>sendmail -bh</code>, which is not enabled by default.</td></tr>
<tr><td>mailq</td><td>Displays a summary of the messages awaiting processing in the mail queue (the command is equivalent to <code>sendmail -bp</code>).</td></tr>
<tr><td>mailstats</td><td>Displays message quantity and byte count statistics.</td></tr>
<tr><td>makemap</td><td>Translates a plain-text file (i.e., <code>/etc/mail/virtusertable</code>) into a hashed Berkeley database file (i.e., <code>/etc/mail/virtusertable.db</code>). This command runs each time the sendmail script starts at boot time.</td></tr>
<tr><td>newaliases</td><td>Translates the plain-text <code>/etc/aliases</code> file into the hashed Berkeley database file <code>/etc/aliases.db</code> (the command is equivalent to <code>sendmail -bi</code>).</td></tr>
<tr><td>praliases</td><td>Prints out all aliases defined in <code>/etc/aliases</code>.</td></tr>
<tr><td>procmail</td><td>Not included with the sendmail package, but is used as an MDA for sendmail.</td></tr>
<tr><td>purgestat</td><td>Clears the directory where host status information is stored. The command is equivalent to <code>sendmail -bH</code>, which is not enabled by default.</td></tr>
<tr><td>rmail</td><td>Handles incoming mail via UUCP.</td></tr>
<tr><td>smrsh</td><td>Implements a restricted shell for running programs from sendmail.</td></tr>
</table>

Logging performed by sendmail

The amount of logging performed by sendmail is configurable in the `sendmail.cf` file, but the default level provides good coverage of informational notices and error messages. By default, the syslog facility stores logging information from sendmail in the `/var/log/maillog` file. A few examples from this file are shown in this section.

An informational message similar to the following is written in the `/var/log/maillog` file each time the daemon starts (which also causes the hashed alias database to be regenerated):

```
Jul 19 12:52:40 al sendmail[444]: alias database /etc/aliases rebuilt by root
Jul 19 12:52:40 al sendmail[444]: /etc/aliases: 14 aliases, longest 10 bytes,
    15 2 bytes total
Jul 19 12:52:40 al sendmail[460]: starting daemon (8.9.3): SMTP+queueing@
    01:00:0 0
```

Each time a message is sent or received, a log file entry is created:

```
Jul 19 12:54:34 al sendmail[1120]: 0AA01120: from=root, size=161, class=0, pri=3
    0161, nrcpts=1, msgid=<199907191254.0AA01120@al.mybox.com>,
    relay=root@localhost
Jul 19 12:54:35 al sendmail[1127]: 0AA01120: to=jkpat, ctladdr=root (0/0),
    delay=00:00:01, xdelay=00:00:00, mailer=local, stat=Sent
```

The logs even show when people attempt things that perhaps they shouldn't try. The `wiz` and `debug` commands were implemented in earlier versions of sendmail and were found to be a huge security problem. You may log file entries, such as those shown in the code examples below, as people with malicious intent check to make sure that you're not running a vulnerable sendmail daemon. Also, the `expn` and `vrfy` commands (which can be disabled via a configuration option) could give out more information than you'd care to distribute.

```
Jul 19 13:03:27 al sendmail[699]: NOQUEUE: "wiz" command from localhost [127.0.0
    .1] (127.0.0.1)
Jul 19 13:03:29 al sendmail[699]: NOQUEUE: "debug" command from localhost [127.0
    .0.1] (127.0.0.1)
Jul 19 13:03:37 al sendmail[701]: NOQUEUE: localhost [127.0.0.1]: expn oracle
Jul 19 13:03:43 al sendmail[702]: NOQUEUE: localhost [127.0.0.1]: vrfy oracle
```

Configuring sendmail

If you ever find the need to strike up a conversation with a system administrator, simply mention "sendmail.cf file," "address rewriting rules," or "mail loops back to itself," and you will be instantly understood, considered a compatriot, and find yourself the recipient of much sympathy.

The `sendmail.cf` file (or sendmail configuration file) is legendary (and infamous) for arcane syntax, nearly indecipherable rule sets, and its capability to make an administrator tear out his or her hair. In reality, some of this reputation is earned and well deserved, but configuring sendmail has gotten much easier in the past few years with the advent of m4 preprocessor macros, which are discussed at the end of this section. Even better, the default /etc/sendmail.cf file that is included in the sendmail RPM will likely work without modification, although a small amount of tweaking should be performed anyway.

The file /etc/sendmail.cf contains the configuration information and optional values used to direct the behavior of the sendmail daemon. The entire file is well over 1,000 lines in length, at least half of which are not discussed here (and you are to be pitied if you ever find the need to manipulate those lines). Some potentially useful lines are presented in the sections that follow, with comments interjected after related blocks of options.

The generic format of the sendmail.cf file is a single-letter command followed by a parameter (usually represented by a single letter, although not necessarily). For example, options are preceded by a capital *O* (for option). If a value is required, this is specified last. The command must start in the first column of the line, because leading white space indicates a continuation of the previous line. Also, only one command may exist on a single line. The valid commands are described in Table 19-3. Lines that begin with a # are considered comments and are not processed.

Table 19-3
Commands Available in /etc/sendmail.cf

Command	Description
C	Defines a "class macro," a variable that can contain several values.
D	Defines a macro, which may contain only one value.
E	Sets an environment variable.
F	Defines a "file class macro" where the values are obtained from a file or pipe.
H	Selects the format of a header line.
K	Declares a keyed database file.
L	Allows processing restrictions based on the system load average.
M	Defines an MDA and its parameters.
O	Assigns a value to an option.
P	Defines a message priority level.
R	Assembles a rewriting rule.
S	Begins a set of rewriting rules.
T	Classifies a user as "trusted".
V	Defines the major version of the configuration file.

Because setting up a working sendmail.cf file is the key to getting your e-mail service working, the following sections are devoted to breaking this file down, line by line. If you are setting up your first e-mail server, you should go through these sections thoroughly so that you understand how sendmail works and what you need to change to suit your e-mail configuration. The option lines are discussed first, followed by the discussions of the m4 preprocessor, forward files, and alias files.

Note Any line in the sendmail.cf file that begins with a number sign (#) is a comment and is not interpreted. Often, you can uncomment and change these lines to activate a particular feature, as described in the next sections.

sendmail component files

The first part of the sendmail.cf file contains a listing of component files used to create the sendmail.cf file. It also contains information about the configuration file's format and version. The following is an example of the beginning of the sendmail.cf file:

```
#
# Copyright (c) 1998-2001 Sendmail, Inc. and its suppliers.
#       All rights reserved.
# Copyright (c) 1983, 1995 Eric P. Allman. All rights reserved.
# Copyright (c) 1988, 1993
#   The Regents of the University of California. All rights reserved.
#
# By using this file, you agree to the terms and conditions set
# forth in the LICENSE file which can be found at the top level of
# the sendmail distribution.
#
#

#####################################################################
#####################################################################
#####
#####      SENDMAIL CONFIGURATION FILE
#####
#####################################################################
#####################################################################

#####  $Id: cfhead.m4,v 8.76.4.16 2001/03/06 22:56:36 ca Exp $   #####
#####  $Id: cf.m4,v 8.32 1999/02/07 07:26:14 gshapiro Exp $   #####
#####  linux setup for Red Hat Linux   #####
#####  $Id: linux.m4,v 8.11.16.2 2000/09/17 17:04:22 gshapiro Exp $   #####
#####  $Id: local_procmail.m4,v 8.21 1999/11/18 05:06:23 ca Exp $   #####
#####  $Id: no_default_msa.m4,v 8.1.10.1 2000/09/17 17:04:22 gs Exp $   #####
#####  $Id: smrsh.m4,v 8.14 1999/11/18 05:06:23 ca Exp $   #####
```

```
#####   $Id: mailertable.m4,v 8.18 1999/07/22 17:55:35 gshapiro Exp $  #####
#####   $Id: virtusertable.m4,v 8.16 1999/07/22 17:55:36 gshapiro Exp $  #####
#####   $Id: redirect.m4,v 8.15 1999/08/06 01:47:36 gshapiro Exp $  #####
#####   $Id: always_add_domain.m4,v 8.9 1999/02/07 07:26:08 gshapiro Exp $  #####
#####   $Id: use_cw_file.m4,v 8.9 1999/02/07 07:26:13 gshapiro Exp $  #####
#####   $Id: use_ct_file.m4,v 8.9 1999/02/07 07:26:13 gshapiro Exp $  #####
#####   $Id: local_procmail.m4,v 8.21 1999/11/18 05:06:23 ca Exp $  #####
#####   $Id: access_db.m4,v 8.15 1999/07/22 17:55:34 gshapiro Exp $  #####
#####   $Id: blacklist_recipients.m4,v 8.13 1999/04/02 02:25:13 gs Exp $  #####
#####   $Id: accept_unresolvable_domains.m4,v 8.10 1999/02/0707:26:07 gs Exp$ ##
####   $Id: proto.m4,v 8.446.2.5.2.41 2001/05/23 21:32:16 ca Exp $  #####
```

The preceding block of comments is useful, because it indicates which component m4 macro files (from within subdirectories of the /usr/lib/sendmail-cf directory) were used to create this sendmail.cf file. The /etc/sendmail.mc file is the actual configuration file used to build sendmail.cf (using the command m4 /etc/sendmail.mc > /etc/sendmail.cf). The following code from the sendmail.cf file indicates the version and vendor associated with the configuration file.

```
# level 9 config file format
V9/Berkeley
```

The line above identifies this configuration file as corresponding with the open-source Berkeley distribution of sendmail V9. The next lines refer to certain security features:

```
# override file safeties - setting this option compromises system security
# addressing the actual file configuration problem is preferred
# need to set this before any file actions are encountered in the cf file
#O DontBlameSendmail=safe
```

This version of sendmail is, by default, somewhat paranoid, judging from the previous three commented lines. By not setting DontBlameSendmail=safe, sendmail won't accept .forward files, include files, incoming mailboxes, configuration files, class files, or hashed map files that are group- or world-writable, or that are located in a directory that is group- or world-writable. If you need to override these defaults, you can remove the comment character (#) in front of the DontBlameSendmail line. The next lines relate to LDAP maps.

```
# default LDAP map specification
# need to set this now before any LDAP maps are defined
#O LDAPDefaultSpec=-h localhost
```

With the LDAPDefaultSpec option, you can add default LDAP maps that include LDAP-specific settings. These settings apply to all LDAP maps, unless individual maps override those values. Set this option before you define any LDAP maps.

sendmail local info entries

The next entries in the `sendmail.cf` file appear under the local info heading. They enable you to enter configuration information that is specific to your local host computer. Here are the first lines you see in that section:

```
#################
#   local info  #
#################

Cwlocalhost
# file containing names of hosts for which we receive email
Fw/etc/mail/local-host-names
```

The previous lines have similar functions. The Cwlocalhost line defines the class macro w, which contains a list of all possible hostnames given to the machine. This includes any DNS aliases, all references in /etc/hosts, and perhaps even incorrect names used by individuals with accounts on that machine (to avoid having those messages bounced). Because this could become quite an extensive list on some hosts, the Fw/etc/mail/local-host-names line defines the file class macro w, which enables these hostnames to be stored in a separate file, /etc/mail/local-host-name in this case. The next lines are used to set your TCP/IP domain name:

```
# my official domain name
# ... define this only if sendmail cannot automatically determine your domain
#Dj$w.Foo.COM
```

If the last of the previous lines is uncommented, the line sets the predefined macro j (the host's canonical fully qualified domain name) to be the value of the class w (the hostname only), followed by the domain name (alternatively, the class m if it is defined). Of course, you would want to replace Foo.COM with your domain name. It is recommended that you let sendmail determine the canonical name. The next lines let you configure smart relay and other options:

```
CP.
# "Smart" relay host (may be null)
DS
# operators that cannot be in local usernames (i.e., network indicators)
CO @ % !
# a class with just dot (for identifying canonical names)
C..
# a class with just a left bracket (for identifying domain literals)
C[[
```

The preceding DS line could be used to define a smart relay host. Though it is more commonly used with UUCP as a transport mechanism, this can also be useful if the machine doesn't have a reliable connection to the entire network (perhaps it's only on a local network). The relay accepts mail from this machine and handle delivering the mail to the appropriate recipients.

The other lines define class macros that become important within the rewriting rules. The CP. and C.. lines define the classes P and ., each of which consists of only a period (.). The CO @ % ! line defines the class O, which lists three characters that are invalid within user names (@, %, and !). The C[[line defines the class [, which consists of a left bracket. The next lines identify the virtual user table and the access list database:

```
# Virtual user table (maps incoming users)
Kvirtuser hash -o /etc/mail/virtusertable

# Access list database (for spam stomping)
Kaccess hash -o /etc/mail/access
```

The previous Kvirtuser and Kaccess lines define two key database files. The Virtual user table database (/etc/mail/virtusertable.db) is created from the hashed output of the /etc/mail/virtusertable text file. The Access list (/etc/mail/access.db) database, created from the /etc/mail/access file, lets you discard and reject e-mail from certain users to prevent spamming. See the sidebar "Forwarding E-mail and Stopping Spamming," which describes how to set up the virtual user and access list databases.

The FR-o line identifies a file that can be configured to allow mail relaying. The DR and DH lines refer to where e-mail with unqualified names and local e-mail are sent:

```
# Hosts for which relaying is permitted ($=R)
FR-o /etc/mail/relay-domains

# who I send unqualified names to (null means deliver locally)
DR

# who gets all local email traffic ($R has precedence for unqualified names)
DH
```

The first line in the preceding block declares the file class R, which is a list of hosts to which mail can be sent for relaying, stored in the file /etc/mail/relay-domains. The second and third lines can be used to define two macros, R and H, which contain the names of machines to which mail can be relayed. Add hostnames to the relay-domains file for that feature to work. Add a hostname after DR to identify the host to which mail with unqualified names is sent, and add a hostname after DH to identify the host to which all local e-mail is sent. The next lines have to do with dequoting:

```
# dequoting map
Kdequote dequote
```

The Kdequote line declares the dequote database of class dequote. This is used to remove quotation marks from addresses within the rewriting rules. The next lines relate to how user names and domain names are exposed to the outside world:

Forwarding E-mail and Stopping Spamming

The `/etc/mail/virtusertable` and `/etc/mail/access` files can be set up to forward e-mail and to discard e-mail from unwanted users. The `virtusertable` file is most commonly used on machines that receive mail for multiple domains. It enables you to redirect incoming messages. Here are some examples of mappings that could be in the `virtusertable` file:

```
@township.org                    wilhelm@orgnet.com
videotech@myotherbox.org         hadji
sales@verysmallcompany.com       george@wehavenomoney.com
```

The first line delivers all mail sent to a township.org to `wilhelm@orgnet.com`. The second line redirects mail intended for `videotech@myotherbox.org` to the local user account hadji. The third line redirects mail for `sales@verysmallcompany.com` to the remote user `george@wehavenomoney.com`.

Similarly, the Access list database is created from `/etc/mail/access`. It can be used to selectively accept, reject, relay, or discard any message based on the address, hostname, domain name, or IP address contained within the header:

```
ads@freestuff.net      DISCARD
junkmail.com           REJECT
coupons.junkmail.com   OK
spam.junkmail.com      550 Unsolicited bulk email will
                       be stored and handled for a fee of $500/KB
```

The first line in the preceding block discards (without returning any error messages) all mail from `ads@freestuff.net`. The second line rejects all mail from within the junkmail.com domain, returning a general delivery status notification message to the sender. However, the third line overrides the previous setting by allowing mail from coupons.junkmail.com, and the fourth line returns the specified error code to the particularly annoying spam.junkmail.com domain.

```
# class E: names that should be exposed as from this host, even if we masquerade
# class L: names that should be delivered locally, even if we have a relay
# class M: domains that should be converted to $M
# class N: domains that should not be converted to $M
```

The preceding class E line (CE root) indicates that mail from the user root should always have the appropriate full hostname and domain name, even if other directives indicate that the hostname should be masquerading as some other name. The related class L could be used to list those user names that should receive mail on the local host, even if other directives indicate that all mail should be relayed elsewhere. The class M could be used to indicate which domains should have their hostnames masqueraded (as set in the following M macro). The class N could be used to indicate hostnames that should not be masqueraded. The next lines also address masquerading:

```
# who I masquerade as (null for no masquerading) (see also $=M)
DM

# my name for error messages
DnMAILER-DAEMON

CPREDIRECT

# Configuration version number
DZ8.11.4
```

The preceding DM line (the macro M) defines the name used in place of the machine's real hostname. The macro n defines the user name (or alias) that is used as the sender of error messages. The CPREDIRECT line adds the text REDIRECT to the class P, which was defined several blocks earlier. This is used in conjunction with the redirect feature (enabled in the m4 configuration files), which allows aliases to be created for accounts that are no longer active. For example, if the /etc/aliases file contained the following line:

```
jefft: jefft@newplace.com.REDIRECT
```

any mail sent to jefft on the local machine would result in an informational message being returned to the original sender, indicating the changed address. The original mail message will not be forwarded to the address listed in the jefft example above. The DZ8.11.4 line sets the macro Z, which contains the full version information for the sendmail daemon.

sendmail options

The sendmail.cf file contains a long list of options that you can set for sendmail on your Red Hat Linux system. Option definitions start after the Options block. Here is an example of the beginning of the Options section:

```
##############
#   Options   #
##############

# strip message body to 7 bits on input?
O SevenBitInput=False

# 8-bit data handling
# O EightBitMode=pass8
```

The SevenBitInput option indicates that sendmail should not clear the most significant bit from each byte of all mail messages. The EightBitMode option dictates how sendmail should handle message data that is not explicitly labeled as 8-bit. The pass8 option allows any 8-bit data to be delivered unaltered; mimefy converts any unspecified data to a MIME-encoded type; strict rejects any unlabeled 8-bit data.

Note that this option has no effect on data that *is* specified as 8-bit. The next lines relate to alias files:

```
# wait for alias file rebuild (default units: minutes)
O AliasWait=10

# location of alias file
O AliasFile=/etc/aliases
```

Before rebuilding the aliases database, sendmail performs several checks to make sure that no other processes are attempting to do the same. The AliasWait option specifies the number of minutes that sendmail alternates between waiting and performing its checks. The AliasFile option specifies the location of the plain-text file containing mail aliases. The next lines relate to how disk space is allocated for sendmail:

```
# minimum number of free blocks on filesystem
O MinFreeBlocks=100

# maximum message size
#O MaxMessageSize=1000000
```

The MinFreeBlocks option specifies that a message will be rejected if the acceptance of that message would cause there to be less than 100 free blocks (100K) available on the file system where messages are stored. The MaxMessageSize, if uncommented, can impose a limit on the maximum size of an incoming e-mail message (1MB in the preceding line). By default, there is no restriction on the size of a message. The next lines are for substituting characters for blank space:

```
# substitution for space (blank) characters
O BlankSub=.
```

The BlankSub option substitutes the specified character (a . here) in place of a blank space (which is an illegal character) in an e-mail address. The next lines are for avoiding expensive mailers:

```
# avoid connecting to "expensive" mailers on initial submission?
O HoldExpensive=False
```

If an MDA definition (explained later in this section) includes the option F=e, the mailer is classified as expensive, which simply indicates that delivering that mail may involve a slow connection or other processing delay. The HoldExpensive option allows messages handled by an expensive MDA to be queued rather than processed immediately. The preceding line disables this option. The next lines relate to checkpoint queues:

```
# checkpoint queue runs after every N successful deliveries
#O CheckpointInterval=10
```

When delivering messages to many addresses (as in a mailing list scenario), send-mail occasionally needs to record which recipients have already received the message and which have not. The CheckpointInterval option specifies the number of recipient addresses processed between updates of the qf file. The preceding line is commented out, but the default value is 10 anyway. The next lines relate to delivery mode:

```
# default delivery mode
O DeliveryMode=background
```

The four possible DeliveryMode values are as follows:

✦ background — Sendmail forks (splits off) a copy of itself and asynchronously processes the message. The default mode is background.

✦ deferred — The message is queued and all processing, including DNS lookups and database accesses, is deferred until the queue is run.

✦ interactive — The queue is processed synchronously, in the foreground.

✦ queueonly — Much like deferred, but hostnames are resolved and databases are queried immediately.

The next lines relate to rebuilding the alias database:

```
# automatically rebuild the alias database?
# NOTE: There is a potential for a denial of service attack if this is set.
#       This option is deprecated and will be removed from a future version.
O AutoRebuildAliases=
```

If no argument is specified, AutoRebuildAliases is set to true. In this case, if send-mail discovers that the modification time of the /etc/aliases file is newer than that of the /etc/aliases.db file, the Berkeley database file is rebuilt. The next lines relate to error message headers and error modes:

```
# error message header/file
#O ErrorHeader=/etc/mail/error-header
```

```
# error mode
#O ErrorMode=print
```

The ErrorHeader option allows the text of a specified file to be included in all delivery status messages returned to the sender, along with any error messages from the xf file. The ErrorMode option provides five possible methods of displaying error messages to users on the local machine who encounter problems while attempting to send mail:

✦ e — Mail an error message to the sender, but terminate successfully.

✦ m — Mail an error message, and exit with an error code.

✦ p — Print the error message to the user's terminal and save the message in ~/dead.letter. This is the default.

✦ q — Quietly ignore all delivery errors.

✦ w — Write the error message to the user's terminal.

The next lines relate to the From lines in e-mail messages:

```
# save Unix-style "From_" lines at top of header?
#O SaveFromLine=False
```

By default, the SaveFromLine option is disabled (False). The result is that lines within mail messages that begin with the text "From" (a special token that differentiates the end of one message from the headers of the next) will be prefaced by a > in the delivered message. The next lines relate to permissions of temporary files:

```
# temporary file mode
O TempFileMode=0600
```

The TempFileMode option sets the file permissions of temporary files to be readable only by the owner of the file. All other modes are highly discouraged. The next lines relate to the GECOS field:

```
# match recipients against GECOS field?
#O MatchGECOS=False
```

The MatchGECOS option lets sendmail deliver mail to a converted form of a user's full name, as specified in the GECOS field of the /etc/passwd file. For example, if the full name of user wharris (according to the GECOS field) is Wayne Harris, that user could receive mail as wharris@mybox.com, Wayne_Harris@mybox.com, or Wayne.Harris@mybox.com. This option is not recommended, because it could lead to ambiguities, and users could change their GECOS fields in a way that could subvert sendmail's usual delivery mechanisms. The next lines relate to hop counts:

```
# maximum hop count
#O MaxHopCount=17
```

The MaxHopCount option specifies the largest number of hops (a transmission of the message from one machine to another) before a message is returned to the sender as undeliverable. The default value is 17. The next lines relate to the sendmail help file:

```
# location of help file
O HelpFile=/etc/mail/helpfile
```

The HelpFile option lists the name of the file containing the online help text. To view this data, execute the command `telnet localhost 25` and type `help`. Help is also available for most SMTP commands using the `help` command via `help` *command name*. The next lines relate to dots as terminators:

```
# ignore dots as terminators in incoming messages?
#O IgnoreDots=False
```

The IgnoreDots option determines the behavior of sendmail when presented with a message that contains a single . on a line. With the option nonexistent, commented, or set to False, the single dot is treated as the end of the message (the behavior specified in RFC 821). If the option is set to True, the dot assumes no special significance. The next lines relate to resolver options:

```
# name resolver options
#O ResolverOptions=+AAONLY
```

The ResolverOptions option can be used to tune the behavior of DNS lookups. Descriptions of the available flags can be found in the man page for resolver (type `man resolver`). The next lines relate to MIME errors:

```
# deliver MIME-encapsulated error messages?
O SendMimeErrors=True
```

The SendMimeErrors option defines whether delivery status notification messages should be MIME-encoded or left as plain text. The next lines relate to search paths used for forwarding e-mail messages:

```
# Forward file search path
O ForwardPath=$z/.forward.$w:$z/.forward
```

The ForwardPath option specifies the search path for an individual user's .forward file. In the preceding line, $z represents the user's home directory, and $w indicates the local machine's hostname. For example, if `/home/kzabon` were the home directory for the user kzabon on the local machine al, sendmail would first look for the file `/home/kzabon/.forward.al`, followed by `/home/kzabon/.forward`. If neither file existed, the mail would be delivered to the incoming mailbox file `/var/spool/mail/kzabon`. The next lines relate to how caching is used on open connections:

```
# open connection cache size
O ConnectionCacheSize=2
```

```
# open connection cache timeout
O ConnectionCacheTimeout=5m
```

Rather than open a connection to a host, send a message, close the connection, and then open another connection to the same host, connection caching allows send-mail to send multiple mail messages to the same machine over one connection. This ConnectionCacheSize option can reduce the overhead of creating and destroying connections. The default value of 2 indicates that a maximum of two simultaneous connections can be maintained. The ConnectionCacheTimeout value specifies the maximum amount of time that a connection can be maintained. The default value is 300s, which is equivalent to 5m (five minutes). The next lines relate to the host status directory and thread deliveries:

```
# persistent host status directory
#O HostStatusDirectory=.hoststat

# single thread deliveries (requires HostStatusDirectory)?
#O SingleThreadDelivery=False
```

The HostStatusDirectory option can establish a directory (relative to the queue directory /var/spool/mqueue if a full pathname isn't specified) that stores status information for all machines with which sendmail has established a connection. This option is not set by default, because its implementation consumes resources but may not provide a substantial gain.

The SingleThreadDelivery option ensures that there is always a maximum of one connection to any given machine. This, too, may not be desirable. Not only does it require the HostStatusDirectory option, it may also prevent any outgoing messages to a host if the local machine is currently processing a high volume of mail from that same machine. The next lines relate to the Errors-To header:

```
# use Errors-To: header?
O UseErrorsTo=False
```

The UseErrorsTo option allows sendmail to utilize or ignore the "Errors-To:" header line. If set to True, any delivery errors are reported to the address specified in the header line. Otherwise, this line is ignored. The option is set to False by default because this behavior violates RFC 1123. The next lines relate to the log level:

```
# log level
O LogLevel=9
```

The LogLevel option sets the priority and severity of logging messages sent to the syslog facility. Values range from 0 (only severe errors are reported) to 98 (maximum debugging information is logged, along with all the more important messages). Unless you need to view copious amounts of debugging information while tracking down a mail delivery problem, the default value of 9 provides a suitable level of detail. The next lines relate to how messages are sent to the message sender:

```
# send to me too, even in an alias expansion?
#O MeToo=True
```

The MeToo option selects sendmail's behavior when the sender of a message is also on the mailing list's distribution list. Unless a value of True is specified, the sender does not receive the message (based on the assumption that if the sender wrote the message, the sender doesn't need to see it again). The next lines have to do with evaluating addresses:

```
# verify RHS in newaliases?
O CheckAliases=False
```

If the value is set to True, the CheckAliases option evaluates addresses on the left side of the colon and guarantees a valid delivery agent for addresses on the right side. The default value is False. The next lines relate to old-style headers:

```
# default messages to old style headers if no special punctuation?
O OldStyleHeaders=True
```

Lists of recipients were originally delimited by spaces. More recently, commas have been used because recipient names frequently contain spaces. When set to True, the OldStyleHeaders option allows comma-delimited lists, but unquoted spaces are converted to commas. If the option is set to False (the default), uncommented spaces are converted to the character specified by the BlankSub option. The next lines relate to SMTP daemon options:

```
# SMTP daemon options
# DaemonPortOptions=Name=MTA
O DaemonPortOptions=Port=smtp, Addr=127.0.0.1, Name=MTA

# SMTP client options
#O ClientPortOptions=Address=0.0.0.0
```

The DaemonPortOptions option can be used to restrict the port number and network on which sendmail will listen for incoming connections, the number of simultaneous incoming connections, and the size of the TCP/IP send and receive buffers.

Note By default, the DaemonPortOption=Port=smtp line shown above restricts access to the smtp port (Port 25) and only to the local host (Addr=127.0.0.1) for mail transfer (Name=MTA). You must change or comment out the line to allow your mail server to accept mail from host computers other than the local host.

The ClientPortOptions option is the same as DaemonPortOptions, except that it works for outgoing connections rather than incoming connections. The next lines relate to privacy:

```
# privacy flags
O PrivacyOptions=authwarnings,novrfy,noexpn,restrictqrun
```

The PrivacyOptions option can be used to require that incoming connections strictly adhere to correct SMTP behavior, disable the EXPN (noxepn) or VRFY (novrfy) functions, disable return receipts, and restrict the users who may run the `mailq` and `sendmail -q` commands (restrictqrun). The `mailq` command shows all entries in the queue, while the `sendmail -q` command synchronously processes the queue. The PrivacyOptions option also enables utilization of the "X-Authentication-Warning:" header line. The next lines relate to copies of error messages:

```
# who (if anyone) should get extra copies of error messages
#O PostMasterCopy=Postmaster
```

The PostMasterCopy option can specify an address (or several) that should receive copies of any delivery status notifications that are sent to message senders. The default is to send no copies. The next lines relate to the mail queue:

```
# slope of queue-only function
#O QueueFactor=600000

# queue directory
O QueueDirectory=/var/spool/mqueue
```

The QueueFactor option takes the current system load average into consideration and can implement a cutoff value where outbound messages are queued rather than immediately sent. The QueueDirectory option specifies the location of queued outbound messages. The filename prefixes present in this directory are described in Table 19-1 earlier in this chapter. The next lines relate to timeout values used by sendmail:

```
# timeouts (many of these)
#O Timeout.initial=5m
O Timeout.connect=1m
#O Timeout.iconnect=5m
#O Timeout.helo=5m
#O Timeout.mail=10m
#O Timeout.rcpt=1h
#O Timeout.datainit=5m
#O Timeout.datablock=1h
#O Timeout.datafinal=1h
#O Timeout.rset=5m
#O Timeout.quit=2m
#O Timeout.misc=2m
#O Timeout.command=1h
#O Timeout.ident=5s
#O Timeout.fileopen=60s
O Timeout.queuereturn=5d
#O Timeout.queuereturn.normal=5d
#O Timeout.queuereturn.urgent=2d
```

```
#O  Timeout.queuereturn.non-urgent=7d
O   Timeout.queuewarn=4h
#O  Timeout.queuewarn.normal=4h
#O  Timeout.queuewarn.urgent=1h
#O  Timeout.queuewarn.non-urgent=12h
#O  Timeout.hoststatus=30m
#O  Timeout.resolver.retrans=5s
#O  Timeout.resolver.retrans.first=5s
#O  Timeout.resolver.retrans.normal=5s
#O  Timeout.resolver.retry=4
#O  Timeout.resolver.retry.first=4
#O  Timeout.resolver.retry.normal=4
```

Several options relating to timeouts while waiting for events can be specified, as shown in the preceding lines. These values limit the amount of time sendmail spends waiting for an event to occur or complete. The actual time values can be specified in seconds, minutes, hours, or days (with each specified as an integer followed by an s, an m, an h, or a d, respectively). An explanation for each is given in Table 19-4. Each timeout option is in the form `Timeout.event`, where *event* is replaced by the timeout events listed in the table.

Table 19-4 Timeout Events	
Timeout Events	**Waiting for . . .**
Command	the next command
Connect	the acceptance of a connection
Datablock	the read of the DATA block to complete
datafinal	acknowledgment of the final dot or End-Of-File marker
datainit	acknowledgment of the DATA command
fileopen	an NFS file open command to complete
helo	a HELO or EHLO
hoststatus	the results of a host status check
iconnect	the initial connect(2) system call to complete
ident	the results of an identification protocol response
initial	the initial greeting message
mail	acknowledgment of the MAIL command
misc	acknowledgment of other SMTP commands

Continued

Table 19-4 *(continued)*	
Timeout Events	*Waiting for . . .*
queuereturn (any priority)	the message delivery to complete (a bounce message will be delivered)
queuewarn (any priority)	the message delivery to complete (a warning message will be delivered)
quit	acknowledgment of the QUIT command
rcpt	acknowledgment of the RCPT command
rset	acknowledgment of the RSET command

The next lines relate to pruning routes:

```
# should we not prune routes in route-addr syntax addresses?
#O DontPruneRoutes
```

With the DontPruneRoutes option, an address can be specified as a "route address" where an explicit path through a sequence of hosts is indicated. If the option is set to True, this route is followed. Otherwise, the route is pruned. The next lines relate to where messages are stored as they are being delivered:

```
# queue up everything before forking?
O SuperSafe=True
```

If the SuperSafe option is set to False, sendmail reads a message into memory before delivering it. If the machine were to crash at this point, the message would be lost. When the SuperSafe option is set to True, the message always exists on the file system until delivery is completed. No good reason exists for this option to be set to False. The next lines relate to the status file:

```
# status file
O StatusFile=/var/log/sendmail.st
```

The StatusFile option specifies a file where mail delivery statistics can be stored. This file is then parsed by the mailstats program to display the number of messages sent and the size of those messages (in kilobytes), the number of messages received and the size of those messages (also in kilobytes), the number of messages rejected, and the number of messages discarded. The first column and the last column indicate the MDA. The last row displays totals for each column. The following is a sample:

```
Statistics from Mon Jul 19 13:05:24 1999
  M   msgsfr  bytes_from  msgsto  bytes_to  msgsrej  msgsdis  Mailer
  4    414       3845K      23      894K       0        0     smtp
  8     10        19K        8       13K       0        0     local
 ===========================================================
  T    424       3864K      31      907K       0        0
```

The next lines relate to how time zones are handled:

```
# time zone handling:
#  if undefined, use system default
#  if defined but null, use TZ envariable passed in
#  if defined and non-null, use that info
#O TimeZoneSpec=
```

The TimeZoneSpec option allows the explicit selection of the local time zone, over-riding the value in the TZ environment if it exists. The next lines relate to the UID and GID used by sendmail:

```
# default UID (can be username or userid:groupid)
O DefaultUser=8:12
```

The DefaultUser option specifies the UID and GID of the default user to which send-mail switches when delivering mail. In this case, it is set to mail:mail (UID 8 and GID 12). The next lines relate to the location of the user database file:

```
# list of locations of user database file (null means no lookup)
O UserDatabaseSpec=/etc/mail/userdb.db
```

The UserDatabaseSpec option enables the specification of another database that can redirect incoming messages and rewrite the header fields of outgoing messages. The next lines can be used to create fallback connections:

```
# fallback MX host
#O FallbackMXhost=fall.back.host.net

# if we are the best MX host for a site, try it directly instead of config err
O TryNullMXList=true
```

The FallbackMXhost option can be used by sites that don't have a reliable connection to the Internet, where it would be preferable to relay the messages to another host with a better connection rather than queue the mail on the local machine.

If the host sending a message is also an MX (mail exchanger) host for the receiving host, all hosts with a higher MX preference are deemed invalid. If this results in no available mail exchangers, the message will be returned to the sender if the TryNullMXList option is set to False. If the option is set to True, sendmail tries to send mail directly to the receiving host before returning the message as undelivered. The next lines relate to responses to high load averages:

```
# load average at which we just queue messages
#O QueueLA=8
```

```
# load average at which we refuse connections
#O RefuseLA=12
```

The QueueLA option specifies the system load average at which point mail is not delivered immediately but queued for later processing. The RefuseLA option sets the point at which incoming mail is no longer accepted. The next lines relate to the number of child processes and new connections:

```
# maximum number of children we allow at one time
#O MaxDaemonChildren=12
```

```
# maximum number of new connections per second
#O ConnectionRateThrottle=0
```

Sendmail forks a copy of itself to handle each incoming message and to process the queue. The MaxDaemonChildren option restricts the number of children of the original sendmail process that can exist simultaneously. Though this sounds like a good idea, it also makes it easier for someone to implement a Denial-of-Service attack on your machine by keeping all available child processes occupied.

A better solution (if you must limit incoming connections) is to use the ConnectionRateThrottle option. Rather than deny all connections beyond a certain threshold, the ConnectionRateThrottle option slows down the acceptance of messages. Using a value of three as an example, if eight connections arrive simultaneously, three are handled immediately; three more are processed after a one-second delay; and the remaining two are handled after a two-second delay. The next lines relate to processes for queued jobs:

```
# deliver each queued job in a separate process?
#O ForkEachJob=False
```

The ForkEachJob option instructs sendmail to fork a copy of itself to handle each individual message in the queue. This may be useful for machines with limited amounts of memory but should generally not be used (or set to False). The next lines are related to message priority:

```
# work recipient factor
#O RecipientFactor=30000
```

```
# work class factor
#O ClassFactor=1800
```

```
# work time factor
#O RetryFactor=90000
```

```
# shall we sort the queue by hostname first?
#O QueueSortOrder=priority

# minimum time in queue before retry
#O MinQueueAge=30m
```

The ClassFactor and RecipientFactor options can be used to alter the priority of a message in the queue based on its precedence class or number of recipients. The RetryFactor option can be used to alter the priority of a message in the queue that has already been processed but couldn't be delivered. The QueueSortOrder option, which can select the method used to determine the queue priority, can be set to host (the messages in the queue are sorted based on the receiving host and the priority), priority (the traditional precedence scale), and time (based on the order of submission). MinQueueAge sets the minimum amount of time a failed message transfer waits in the buffer before transmission is retried. The next lines relate to the character set:

```
# default character set
#O DefaultCharSet=iso-8859-1
```

The DefaultCharSet option defines the MIME type used when converting 8-bit messages into 7-bit messages. The next lines define the location of the service.switch file:

```
# service switch file (ignored on Solaris, Ultrix, OSF/1, others)
#O ServiceSwitchFile=/etc/mail/service.switch
```

Because the /etc/nsswitch.conf file already dictates the order for resolving various database requests, the ServiceSwitchFile option is ignored, even if defined. It is best to leave it commented out. The next lines let you redefine the location of the /etc/hosts file:

```
# hosts file (normally /etc/hosts)
#O HostsFile=/etc/hosts
```

The HostsFile option specifies the path to the file containing locally customized IP address-to-hostname translations. The default value is /etc/hosts. The next lines relate to dial-up delays when the connection fails:

```
# dialup line delay on connection failure
#O DialDelay=10s
```

When a dial-up connection to the Internet needs to be established, the time required to secure the connection can vary greatly. The DialDelay option allows a number of seconds or minutes to be specified, which represents the amount of time sendmail will sleep if its initial connection attempt fails. The next lines let you define what happens when there is no recipient in the message:

```
# action to take if there are no recipients in the message
#O NoRecipientAction=add-to-undisclosed
```

The NoRecipientAction option instructs sendmail what to do if a message has no recipients specified in the header lines. The valid parameters include add-apparently-to (adds an "Apparently-To:" header line), add-bcc (adds an empty "Bcc:" header line to comply with RFC 821), add-to (adds a "To:" header with recipients from the message "envelope"), add-to-undisclosed (adds an empty "To: undisclosed-recipients:" header line), and none (delivers the message without modification). The next lines can be used to change the root directory used by sendmail:

```
# chrooted environment for writing to files
#O SafeFileEnvironment=/arch
```

The SafeFileEnvironment option provides a more secure location for delivering mail to files by using a chroot system call. The next lines define whether colons are okay in an address:

```
# are colons OK in addresses?
#O ColonOkInAddr=True
```

The ColonOkInAddr option determines whether colons are valid within addresses. The default value is False, indicating that a colon within an e-mail address represents an error. The next lines define how many jobs you can process in the queue:

```
# how many jobs can you process in the queue?
#O MaxQueueRunSize=10000
```

The MaxQueueRunSize option indicates the maximum number of queued messages that can be processed during one run of the queue. The preceding line sets the limit at 10,000 messages. The next lines relate to expanding CNAMES:

```
# shall I avoid expanding CNAMEs (violates protocols)?
#O DontExpandCnames=False
```

The DontExpandCnames option controls whether sendmail accepts a CNAME record as the canonical hostname. If the DontExpandCnames option is set to True, the CNAME record is considered valid within the rewriting rules. If it is set to False (the default value), the CNAME record must be translated into a valid address record for use within the rewriting rules. The next lines relate to the SMTP login message:

```
# SMTP initial login message (old $e macro)
O SmtpGreetingMessage=$j Sendmail $v/$Z; $b
```

The SmtpGreetingMessage option defines the banner text presented when a client connects to the sendmail daemon on the local machine. In the preceding line, $j evaluates to the FQDN of the local machine; $v and $Z represent the configuration file and executable program versions, respectively; and $b is the current local date and time. This prints a line similar to the following:

```
220 al.mybox.com ESMTP Sendmail 8.9.3/8.9.3; Mon, 19 Jul 1999 18:47:23 -0400

# UNIX initial From header format (old $l macro)
O UnixFromLine=From $g  $d
```

The UnixFromLine option defines the format of the "From" header line that is used as a message separator within mailbox files. The default value of $g $d prints the sender's e-mail address, followed by two blank spaces and the local date and time at which the message was received. The next lines define how to handle embedded newlines:

```
# From: lines that have embedded newlines are unwrapped onto one line
#O SingleLineFromHeader=False
```

If the SingleLineFromHeader option is set to True, any new lines within the "From:" header are converted into spaces. Otherwise, the split header lines are retained. The next lines relate to how SMTP responds to a HELO request not associated with a hostname:

```
# Allow HELO SMTP command that does not include a host name
#O AllowBogusHELO=False
```

If the AllowBogusHELO option is set to True, the restriction that a hostname must follow a HELO command is not enforced. If it is set to False (the default), the behavior specified by RFC 1123 is required. The next lines relate to quoting special characters:

```
# Characters to be quoted in a full name phrase (@,;:\()[] are automatic)
#O MustQuoteChars=.
```

By default (and according to RFC 821), the nine characters enumerated in the comment in the first line must be quoted if they appear in a nonaddress portion of an address (for example, the user's name or nickname). The . and ' characters can be specified in the MustQuoteChars option to require quoting as well. The next lines relate to delimiter characters:

```
# delimiter (operator) characters (old $o macro)
O OperatorChars=.:%@!^/[]+
```

The OperatorChars option lists the characters (in addition to the set of ()<>,;"\r\n already defined by sendmail) that can be used as separators within an address. This option should not be altered. The next lines relate to initgroups:

```
# shall I avoid calling initgroups(3) because of high NIS costs?
#O DontInitGroups=False
```

The DontInitGroups option (if set to True) forces sendmail to not process the initgroups system call. This is useful if groups have many members or a slow name service is used. The default value is False. The next lines relate to an obsolete function:

```
# are group-writable :include: and .forward files (un)trustworthy?
#O UnsafeGroupWrites=True
```

The UnsafeGroupWrites option has been effectively replaced by various arguments to the DontBlameSendmail option, which was discussed early in this section. The next lines relate to sending errors:

```
# where do errors that occur when sending errors get sent?
#O DoubleBounceAddress=postmaster
# where to save bounces if all else fails
#O DeadLetterDrop=/var/tmp/dead.letter
```

The DoubleBounceAddress option specifies the recipient of error messages that result from a failure to deliver an earlier error message. The default value is the postmaster alias. The DeadLetterDrop option sets the backup location for saving bounced e-mail if the bounced e-mail can't be written to other locations (by default, it is /var/tmp/dead.letter). The next lines relate to the user ID used for sendmail processing:

```
# what user id do we assume for the majority of the processing?
#O RunAsUser=sendmail
```

By using the RunAsUser option, sendmail can be configured to perform most of its processing (other than reading the configuration file and listening for incoming connections on a privileged port) as an unprivileged user. The RunAsUser option specifies the user name or UID of the user. This may sound like a good idea, but it has the side effect of requiring the unprivileged user to have access to all .forward files, :include: files, and the queue directory. This will likely require liberal use of the DontBlameSendmail options and could cause more problems than it solves. The next lines relate to the recipients in an SMTP envelope:

```
# maximum number of recipients per SMTP envelope
#O MaxRecipientsPerMessage=100
```

The MaxRecipientsPerMessage option specifies the upper boundary on the number of individual recipients per message in an effort to block mail spam (unsolicited commercial e-mail or unsolicited bulk e-mail), which is commonly sent to large distribution lists. By default, there is no restriction. The next lines relate to getting local names:

```
# shall we get local names from our installed interfaces?
O DontProbeInterfaces=true
```

The DontProbeInterfaces option (if set to True) keeps sendmail from automatically modifying the class macro Cw with the hostnames and addresses of all physical network interfaces. By default, the equivalent hosts and addresses are added to Cw. The next lines relate to delivery status notification (DSN):

```
# Return-Receipt-To: header implies DSN request
#O RrtImpliesDsn=False
```

The RtrImpliesDsn option causes a delivery status notification to be sent to the envelope sender instead of to the address contained in the header. The next option lets you override the connection address.

```
# override connection address (for testing)
#O ConnectOnlyTo=0.0.0.0
```

To force delivery of mail to all go to a particular address, you can add an IP address using the ConnectOnlyTo option. This is useful for testing purposes. The next option relates to defining a trusted user:

```
# Trusted user for file ownership and starting the daemon
#O TrustedUser=root
```

The TrustedUser option can be used to set which user on your system is trusted to own sendmail-related files and to run sendmail daemons. The user name can be either the name or user ID contained in the /etc/passwd file. The next set of options can be used to indicate the locations of certificate authority (CA) certificates and private keys on your system:

```
# CA directory
#O CACERTPath
# CA file
#O CACERTFile
# Server Cert
#O ServerCertFile
# Server private key
#O ServerKeyFile
# Client Cert
#O ClientCertFile
# Client private key
#O ClientKeyFile
```

The CACERTPath option lets you indicate a directory that contains CA certificates. CACERTFile lets you indicate an individual CA certificate. ServerCertFile and ServerKeyFile let you identify the CA certificate and associated private key, respectively, that sendmail should use when it is acting as a server. ClientCertFile and ClientKeyFile let you identify the CA certificate and associated private key, respectively, that sendmail should use when it is acting as a client.

Message precedences

Precedences can be associated with e-mail messages in an attempt to give some messages higher authority for transferring than others. The message precedences section of the sendmail.cf file enables you to set how different message precedences are handled. The following lines appear at the beginning of the section:

```
##########################
#   Message precedences    #
##########################

Pfirst-class=0
Pspecial-delivery=100
Plist=-30
Pbulk=-60
Pjunk=-100
```

The previous lines equate precedence values with the possible precedence names in message headers. The meaning of each precedence name is indicated in Table 19-5. The numbers by themselves aren't significant, except in relation to other precedence names. Also note that incoming mail is processed immediately (unless otherwise restricted), so these priority values apply only to messages in the queue.

	Table 19-5 Precedence Names
Name	**Meaning**
special-delivery	A high-priority message that should be delivered from the queue before any others.
first-class	Unless overridden in the message header, this is the default priority.
list	This precedence name should be used for most messages emanating from mailing lists.
bulk	A relatively noncrucial broadcast message. This also indicates that if there are delivery troubles, the body of the message will not be included in bounce notices.
junk	Worthless e-mail that is possibly the output of a program or a test message. The body is also discarded from bounce notices.

Trusted users

You can allow users whom you trust to send messages that have sender names other than their real user names. The following lines appear in the Trusted users section for setting trusted user values:

```
####################
#   Trusted users   #
####################

# this is equivalent to setting class "t"
Ft/etc/sendmail.ct
Troot
Tdaemon
Tuucp
```

These names specify users who are allowed to use sendmail's -f flag to set a sender other than the user running the command. You probably won't want to specify any normal user accounts here. However, if you use a mailing list manager (see the next section) that lets you specify the sender of outgoing messages, you may want to include the line Tmajordomo. Otherwise, all outgoing mail to list recipients will contain the error *X-Authentication-Warning: localhost: majordomo set sender to owner-bigmailinglist using* -f in the message header. If you have a large number of trusted users, the file class t can be used to specify a file that contains the list of names. 0

Format of headers

You can change the format that mail headers use with sendmail in your /etc/sendmail.cf file. The following lines appear at the beginning of that section:

```
#########################
#   Format of headers   #
#########################

H?P?Return-Path: <$g>
HReceived: $?sfrom $s $.$?_($?s$|from $.$_)
        $.$?{auth_type}(authenticated$?{auth_ssf} (${auth_ssf} bits)$.)
        $.by $j ($v/$Z)$?r with $r$. id $i$?{tls_version}
        (using ${tls_version} with cipher ${cipher} (${cipher_bits} bits) \
            verified ${verify})$.$?u
        for $u; $|;
        $.$b
H?D?Resent-Date: $a
H?D?Date: $a
H?F?Resent-From: $?x$x <$g>$|$g$.
H?F?From: $?x$x <$g>$|$g$.
H?x?Full-Name: $x
```

```
# HPosted-Date: $a
# H?l?Received-Date: $b
H?M?Resent-Message-Id: <$t.$i@$j>
H?M?Message-Id: <$t.$i@$j>
```

These lines dictate the format of message headers. After the appropriate values are substituted into the preceding variables, this block of text becomes a qf file in /var/spool/mqueue.

Rewriting rules

The Rewriting Rules section of the sendmail.cf file contains a complex set of rules needed to handle your sendmail service. The rules cover such things as converting addresses and dealing with local hostnames. You should not change entries in this section arbitrarily. The start of the Rewriting Rules section contains a header that appears as follows:

```
###############################################################
###############################################################
#####
#####              REWRITING RULES
#####
###############################################################
###############################################################
```

Again, if you ever need to edit these lines, you deserve at least some degree of pity and sympathy from system administrators everywhere.

Mailer definitions

Mail Delivery Agents (MDAs) are described in the Mailer Definitions section. Specifically, the section enables you to define Mlocal and Mprog MDAs as other than the procmail and smrsh programs, respectively:

```
Mlocal,   P=/usr/bin/procmail, F=lsDFMAw5:/|@qSPfhn9, S=EnvFromL/HdrFromL,
             R=EnvToL/HdrToL,
          T=DNS/RFC822/X-Unix,
          A=procmail -Y -a $h -d $u
Mprog,    P=/usr/sbin/smrsh, F=lsDFMoqeu9, S=EnvFromL/HdrFromL,
             R=EnvToL/HdrToL, D=$z:/,
          T=X-Unix/X-Unix/X-Unix,
          A=smrsh -c $u
```

In general, you shouldn't need to modify the options specified in the mailer definitions. However, the Mlocal and Mprog mailer definitions, shown previously, are worthy of note. The Mlocal definition is for delivering messages to a local account. The procmail MDA is used (rather than the UNIX standard of /bin/mail) to place the file in the appropriate user's mailbox.

The Mprog mailer definition is used when the recipient of a message is actually a program (as in the case of majordomo, described in the next section). To direct a message to a program, sendmail uses a program called smrsh (SendMail Restricted Shell). Allowing mail to be piped directly into a program is not a great idea from a security standpoint, but smrsh makes the process a bit safer. For the program to successfully execute, a link to the program must exist within the /etc/smrsh directory. This restriction ensures that only programs installed by the administrator can directly receive mail, and other random executable programs are denied.

Using the m4 macro preprocessor

Although using an m4 preprocessor macro file doesn't make configuring sendmail a simple task, it is at least considerably more intuitive. For example, the cryptic send-mail.cf file described in this chapter was generated by the following text file (the /etc/mail/sendmail.mc file):

```
divert(-1)
dnl This is the sendmail macro config file. If you make changes to this file,
dnl you need the sendmail-cf rpm installed and then have to generate a
dnl new /etc/sendmail.cf by running the following command:
dnl
dnl          m4 /etc/mail/sendmail.mc > /etc/sendmail.cf
dnl
include(`/usr/lib/sendmail-cf/m4/cf.m4')
VERSIONID(`linux setup for Red Hat Linux')dnl
OSTYPE(`linux')
define(`confDEF_USER_ID',``8:12'')dnl
undefine(`UUCP_RELAY')dnl
undefine(`BITNET_RELAY')dnl
define(`confAUTO_REBUILD')dnl
define(`confTO_CONNECT', `1m')dnl
define(`confTRY_NULL_MX_LIST',true)dnl
define(`confDONT_PROBE_INTERFACES',true)dnl
define(`PROCMAIL_MAILER_PATH',`/usr/bin/procmail')dnl
define(`ALIAS_FILE','/etc/aliases')dnl
define(`STATUS_FILE', `/var/log/sendmail.st')dnl
define(`UUCP_MAILER_MAX', `2000000')dnl
define(`confUSERDB_SPEC', `/etc/mail/userdb.db')dnl
define(`confPRIVACY_FLAGS', `authwarnings,novrfy,noexpn,restrictqrun')dnl
define(`confAUTH_OPTIONS', `A')dnl
dnl TRUST_AUTH_MECH(`DIGEST-MD5 CRAM-MD5 LOGIN PLAIN')dnl
dnl define(`confAUTH_MECHANISMS', `DIGEST-MD5 CRAM-MD5 LOGIN PLAIN')dnl
dnl define(`confTO_QUEUEWARN', `4h')dnl
dnl define(`confTO_QUEUERETURN', `5d')dnl
dnl define(`confQUEUE_LA', `12')dnl
dnl define(`confREFUSE_LA', `18')dnl
dnl FEATURE(delay_checks)dnl
FEATURE(`no_default_msa',`dnl')dnl
```

```
FEATURE(`smrsh',`/usr/sbin/smrsh')dnl
FEATURE(`mailertable',`hash -o /etc/mail/mailertable')dnl
FEATURE(`virtusertable',`hash -o /etc/mail/virtusertable')dnl
FEATURE(redirect)dnl
FEATURE(always_add_domain)dnl
FEATURE(use_cw_file)dnl
FEATURE(use_ct_file)dnl
FEATURE(local_procmail)dnl
FEATURE(`access_db',`hash -o /etc/mail/access.db')dnl
FEATURE(`blacklist_recipients')dnl
EXPOSED_USER(`root')dnl
dnl This changes sendmail to only listen on the loopback device 127.0.0.1
dnl and not on any other network devices. Comment this out if you want
dnl to accept email over the network.
DAEMON_OPTIONS(`Port=smtp,Addr=127.0.0.1, Name=MTA')
dnl NOTE: binding both IPv4 and IPv6 daemon to the same port requires
dnl      a kernel patch
dnl DAEMON_OPTIONS(`port=smtp,Addr=::1, Name=MTA-v6, Family=inet6')
dnl We strongly recommend to comment this one out if you want to protect
dnl yourself from spam. However, the laptop and users on computers that do
dnl not have 24x7 DNS do need this.
FEATURE(`accept_unresolvable_domains')dnl
dnl FEATURE(`relay_based_on_MX')dnl
MAILER(smtp)dnl
MAILER(procmail)dnl
```

Compared with the `sendmail.cf` file, it almost looks readable. Through a series of includes, defines, undefines, and features, this file brings the template-like m4 macro files together to form the `sendmail.cf` file.

The `dnl` command is used to comment out entries, but the technical definition is "Delete through New Line." Notice that the `dnl` command is also used to terminate commands. The `include` command uses the cf.m4 file as a prototype, and the `OSTYPE` command sets any Red Hat Linux–specific configuration options. The `define` commands perform the same task as setting similar options within the sendmail.cf file. For example, beginning with `confAUTO_REBUILD`, the options and macros that are equivalent to those in the preceding `define` commands are, in order, AutoRebuildAliases, Timeout.connect, TryNullMXList, DontProbeInterfaces, and the Mprocmail mailer specification.

This `sendmail.mc` file is finally turned into the `sendmail.cf` file with the following command:

```
m4 /etc/mail/sendmail.mc > /etc/sendmail.cf
```

Details on the configuration options available through the m4 macro preprocessor can be found at `www.sendmail.org/m4/tweakingoptions.html`.

The .forward file

One way for users to redirect their own mail is through the use of the .forward file, as described within the previously listed sendmail.cf file. The format of a plain-text .forward file is a comma-separated list of mail recipients. Common uses of the .forward file include:

✦ Piping mail to a program to filter the mailbox contents:

"| /usr/bin/procmail"

✦ Sending mail destined for one user (for example, jkpat) to another (for example, cht09, on a different machine in this case):

cht09@other.mybox.com

✦ Delivering mail to the local user (jkpat again) *and* sending it to two others (cht09 and brannigan):

\jkpat, cht09@other.mybox.com, brannigan

The aliases file

A more flexible method of handling mail delivery (systemwide rather than being specific to one particular user) involves the /etc/aliases file, which is also a plain-text file. The aliases file (described earlier in the sendmail.cf section) contains a name followed by a colon, and then a user name, another alias, a list of addresses, a file, or a program to which mail will be delivered. The name on the left side of the colon (which can be a valid user name or just an alias) can then be used as an e-mail recipient on the local machine. Using the aliases file for mail-aliasing allows for several extensions to normal mail-handling behavior:

✦ One account can receive mail under several different names:

patterson: jkpat

This indicates that any mail addressed to patterson@mybox.com (just an alias) will arrive in the mailbox of jkpat (an actual user account).

✦ Mail can be received under a name that isn't a valid (or reasonable) user name:

Charlie.Jackson.II@mybox.com: jackson

He wouldn't really want to type Charlie.Jackson.II as a user name, but that doesn't mean he can't receive mail as such.

✦ Messages intended for one user can be redirected to another account (or to several accounts):

```
oldemployee: bradford
consultant: bradford, jackson, patterson
users: :include:/root/mail/lists/users
```

Here, any message for oldemployee@mybox.com would be delivered to the mailbox of user bradford. Also, the users bradford, jackson, and patterson would receive any mail addressed to consultant. The third line indicates that the recipients of the "users" alias are specified in the file /root/mail/lists/users.

✦ Mail can be sent directly to a file on the local machine:

```
acsp-bugs: /dev/null
trouble-ticket: /var/spool/trouble/incoming
```

In the first line, because the fictional ACSP program is no longer used on the machine, there's no need to track its errors, so the mail is effectively ignored. The second line stores incoming trouble tickets in the /var/spool/trouble/incoming file. Remember that if you enable this, anyone anywhere can send you a sufficiently large message to fill up the partition on which that directory resides. This is a security risk and should be carefully evaluated before being implemented.

✦ Incoming messages can be piped directly into an executable program:

```
majordomo: "| /usr/lib/majordomo/wrapper majordomo"
```

Tip When resolving addresses, sendmail doesn't actually use the /etc/aliases text file. For faster accesses, the text file is turned into a Berkeley database-format file, /etc/aliases.db, which is used to resolve aliased addresses. For this reason, the newaliases command (equivalent to sendmail -bi) must be run to rebuild the database file each time the /etc/aliases text file is modified.

Administering a Mailing List

Even though sendmail provides several flexible methods for aliasing addresses, many situations require additional functionality. Mailing list managers (or, more commonly, listservers) offer the ability to handle large distribution lists coupled with advanced features such as moderators, archives with file transfer, digests, automatic subscription, and automatic filtering of bad addresses.

Other Mailing List Managers

Although the basic concept of a listserver is common to all mailing list managers, some packages offer radically different features and approach the task in a different manner. The following are some of the other listservers that are available for Linux:

✦ **CREN ListProc 9.0** — Available for a $2,000 donation to CREN (Corporation for Research and Educational Networking), this mailing list manager features Web-based administration, extensive logging capabilities, and automatic deletion of bad addresses. Further information and a free trial version can be found at www.cren.net/listproc/.

✦ **listar** — This free mailing list manager (created originally for Linux) features nonprivileged execution, secure remote administration via e-mail, and expandability through dynamically loaded modules. More details and source code are available from www.listar.org/.

✦ **L-Soft LISTSERV** — In use for more than a dozen years (originally on IBM mainframe computers), this package features file transfer via e-mail, indexing, digests, and subscription flags. Details, pricing information, and a restricted free trial version can be downloaded from www.lsoft.com/listserv.stm.

Listservers typically provide several options for how each list is configured (replies go to author, replies go to the list, anyone can post to the list, posts are restricted to subscribers, subscriptions are open to anyone, subscriptions must be confirmed, and so forth). They also provide options for how the messages are presented to the recipients (with custom headers and footers, subject prefixes, filtered text in the header or body, and so forth).

This section briefly describes the majordomo mailing list manager. Majordomo is a free listserver written in Perl, with the exception of one wrapper program (which is not written in Perl) that allows switching to the majordomo user. The configuration files (for the listserver as well as each individual list) are in plain text and are simple to edit. Other available mailing list managers are listed in the accompanying sidebar.

Installing majordomo

Majordomo is available in RPM format from any Red Hat mirror site, and the source distribution can be obtained from www.greatcircle.com/majordomo/. The package can be installed with the following command (with the package in the current directory):

```
# rpm -ivv majordomo*
```

Configuring majordomo

Several aliases should be added to the /etc/aliases file. These aliases allow mail-related accounts to be listed under different names:

```
#
#  Majordomo Aliases
#
listserve: listserv
listserver: listserv
majordomo: listserv
listserv: "| /usr/lib/majordomo/wrapper majordomo"
majordomo-owner: owner-majordomo
owner-majordomo: owner-listserv
listserv-owner: owner-listserv
owner-listserv: mailserverguy@mybox.com
#
#  List Aliases
#
#  The BioChemistry List
#
biochem-request: "| /usr/lib/majordomo/wrapper request-answer biochem"
biochem-approval: biochem-owner
biochem-owner: owner-biochem
owner-biochem: emailguy@mybox.com
biochem: "| /usr/lib/majordomo/wrapper resend -l biochem -h mail.mybox.com -R bi
ochem-out"
biochem-out: :include:/var/lib/majordomo/lists/biochem,biochem-archival
biochem-archival: "| /usr/lib/majordomo/wrapper archive2.pl -a -M -f /var/lib/ma
jordomo/archives/biochem/biochem"
```

The first set of aliases establishes the individual who "owns" the listserver (or at least who receives its error messages) and the names by which majordomo will be known. It is most common to send requests to a "listserv" address, and this occasionally gets confused and translated into "listserve" or "listserver," so those are acceptable as well.

The next block establishes a list related to BioChemistry. Similar to the listserver itself, each list has an owner who can control its configuration and is notified of error messages. Each message sent to the address biochem@mail.mybox.com is distributed to the recipients listed in the /var/lib/majordomo/lists/biochem file. The message is also sent to the archive2.pl Perl script. Archived messages are stored in files such as /var/lib/majordomo/archives/biochem/biochem.200107 (the archive for July 2001).

Running majordomo

Unfortunately, none of these wonderful features works quite yet. First, the alias database needs to be rebuilt, using the newaliases command or sendmail -bi. Next, because all mail delivered directly to a program is handled by the smrsh program, the smrsh program needs to be configured to allow majordomo's wrapper program to receive mail. To accomplish this, just create the appropriate symbolic link using the following command:

```
# ln -s /var/lib/majordomo/wrapper /etc/smrsh/wrapper
```

I also recommend that you add the line Tmajordomo to the `/etc/sendmail.cf` file to avoid any extraneous X-Authentication-Warning header lines.

Now the listserver can be tested. Run the following command:

```
# echo "help" | mail majordomo@mail.mybox.com
```

You should quickly receive majordomo's Help Document in your mailbox.

The programs included with the majordomo distribution are summarized in Table 19-6.

Table 19-6 Programs Included with Majordomo	
Program	**Description**
Approve	Approves majordomo requests and handles bounce messages.
Archive2.pl	Archives messages for later retrieval.
Bounce	Automatically removes an address (usually because of repeated delivery failures) from a list and subscribes that address to the "bounce" list (if it exists).
Bounce-remind	Sends a notice to subscribers of the "bounce" list, informing them that they have been removed from the list to which they were once subscribed.
Config-test	Verifies the majordomo installation and points out current and potential problems.
Digest	Packages messages into digests, to be sent when a particular time limit or message size is reached.
Majordomo	Performs most of the tasks involved in managing the distribution lists.
Medit	Locks a majordomo file for editing and unlocks the file when the editing session is completed.
resend	Retransmits outgoing messages to the distribution list.
request-answer	Responds to a subscription request and forwards the request to the list owner.
wrapper	Allows other programs to always run as the majordomo user, and simplifies running under smrsh (only one link to place in /etc/smrsh).

Summary

Installing a mail server in Red Hat Linux is the easy part; it's the configuration that takes patience, resolve, and a fair bit of experimentation. Even though it may be considerably faster and easier to utilize the m4 macros, eventually you'll need to edit the `sendmail.cf` file. Just hope that it's not the rewriting rules that need editing.

Sooner or later, an alias definition in `/etc/aliases` will become unmanageable. At this point, mailing list software can provide the flexibility necessary to manage a large distribution list, with the added benefits of archiving, moderation, digesting, and automated administration.

✦   ✦   ✦

Setting Up an FTP Server

File Transfer Protocol (FTP) has been the standard method for sharing files over the Internet for many years. Even with the popularity of the Web, which made document database services such as Gopher and WAIS almost obsolete, FTP servers are still the most common way to make directories of documents and software available to the public over the Internet.

File-sharing applications, such as NFS and Samba, are excellent tools for sharing files and directories over a private network. For organizations that need to share large numbers of files over public networks, however, FTP server software provides more robust tools for sharing files and protecting your computer systems. Also, FTP client software (for accessing FTP servers) is available for any type of computer that can access a network.

This chapter describes how to set up and maintain an FTP server and focuses on the Washington University FTP Server software (wu-ftpd) provided with Red Hat Linux. This package has been battle tested and includes particularly good tools for monitoring and protecting your FTP server. It is also the FTP server software that is installed by default with Red Hat Linux.

Caution

If you are using an FTP server only to share public files, there are minimal security risks. However, sharing private files or allowing users to upload files to your server involves additional risks. Risks include attackers intercepting and replacing files that are being uploaded or downloaded or denial of service attacks. Refer to the end of this chapter for references to documents from CERT that provide FTP security tips.

Understanding FTP Servers

The first implementations of FTP date back to 1971, predating the Web by more than a decade. FTP was created at a time when most computing was done on large mainframe computers and minicomputers. The predominant platforms using FTP were UNIX systems.

FTP set out to solve the need to publish documents and software so that people could get them easily from other computer systems. On the FTP server, files were organized in a directory structure; users could connect to the server over the network (usually the Internet), move up and down the directory structure to find the files that interested them, and download files from (or possibly upload files to) the server.

Originally, a drawback of FTP servers was that people looking for a file or a document on the Internet had to have an idea of which FTP server held the files they were looking for. Tools such as Gopher and WAIS helped in such searches. With the advent of the Web, however, users can now rely on a variety of search engines and Web pages to help point them to the FTP servers that have the files they want. In fact, when you download files by clicking on a link from a Web page, you may not even be aware that the file is being downloaded from an FTP server.

Attributes of FTP servers

That FTP was implemented on large, multiuser UNIX systems accounts for many of the design decisions that remain a part of FTP today. As the most popular free version of UNIX, Linux in general (and Red Hat Linux in particular) has drawn on FTP features that have resulted from years of testing and experience gained from other UNIX versions of FTP. Some attributes of FTP servers follow:

✦ Because FTP was originally used on multiuser systems, only restricted parts of the file system in Red Hat Linux are devoted to FTP. Those who access FTP from a public user account (usually the anonymous user name) are automatically given an FTP directory (often /var/ftp) as their root directory. From there, the anonymous user can access only files and directories below that point in the file system.

✦ Access to the FTP server relies on a login process that uses standard UNIX login names (that is, those user names found in /etc/passwd). Although anonymous was the user name that strangers would use, users with their own accounts on the system could log in with their own user names through FTP and most likely have access to a greater part of the file system (in particular, their own private files and directories).

✦ The `ftp` command and other FTP client programs let you log in and then operate from a command interpreter (similar to a very simple shell). Many of the commands that you use from that command interpreter are familiar UNIX commands. You change directories with `cd`, list files with `ls`, change permissions with `chmod`, and check your location with `pwd` (to name a few). When you find where you want to be, you use the `get` command to download a file or the `put` command to upload one.

As an administrator of an FTP server, it is your responsibility to make sure that you share your files in a way that gives people access to the information that you want them to have without compromising the security of your system. This means implementing a strong security policy and relentlessly monitoring the system to prevent abuse.

See Chapter 14 for information on computer security issues.

FTP user types

Several different types of users can log in to and use an FTP server. The user name `anonymous` is the most common for providing public access. Real users represent the category of users who have real login accounts to your Red Hat Linux system (that is, you know them and have given them permission for other uses besides FTP). A guest user is similar to a real user account, except that he or she has more restrictive access to the computer's file system. Procedures for setting up these different kinds of users are outlined later in this chapter.

Running the FTP Server

Before you can use Red Hat Linux as an FTP server, you must have installed the `wu-ftpd`, `anonftp`, and `xinetd` packages. You must then turn on the FTP service by editing the `/etc/xinetd.d/wu-ftpd` file and changing the `disable=yes` line to `disable=no`. After you have installed the required packages, your system is set up as an FTP server. However, although users can log in and see the default FTP directories, no files that they can access are there yet. The default setup for your Red Hat Linux FTP server after you install the FTP software follows (the Washington University FTP Server software is the wu-ftpd package):

✦ **FTP Daemon** — The FTP daemon is set up in the `/etc/xinetd.d/wu-ftpd` file as `/usr/sbin/in.ftpd`. When someone requests FTP service from your computer (probably on port 21), the xinetd daemon (which listens to lots of ports) starts the FTP daemon to handle that login request. The daemon runs with the `-l` option (so that FTP requests are logged by `syslog` to `/var/log/messages`) and the `-a` option (so that the `/etc/ftpaccess` file is used to define access permissions).

✦ **Access Permissions** (`/etc/ftpaccess`) — The `ftpaccess` file delivered with Linux is quite restrictive. Although you can change it to be as open or as restrictive as you like, here is how the file is originally set:

- **deny** and **allow** — The following lines are included to set which user accounts are allowed and which are denied access to the FTP service:

```
deny-uid %-99 %65534-
deny-gid %-99 %65534-
allow-uid ftp
allow-gid ftp
```

The `deny-uid` and `deny-gid` entries prevent access to the FTP service from any users with IDs that are 99 or less or 65534 or greater for either user or group accounts. The `allow-uid` and `allow-gid` lines make an exception to the deny rules by allowing the ftp user and group to use the FTP service.

- **email root@localhost** — E-mail related to the administration of the FTP server is directed to the root user on the local computer, by default.

- **loginfails 5** — The FTP connection terminates after five consecutive failed login attempts. (This slows down people who are trying to guess your server's passwords.)

- **readme README*** — When the user logs in (`login`) or changes to any other accessible directory (`cwd=*`), the user is notified of the existence of README files, if they exist. By default, none of these files exist. For any file that begins with the word README, a message is displayed by the server that says "Please read the file README.whatever."

- **message** — This indicates that the message contained in the `/welcome.msg` file should be displayed when a user logs in to FTP. A similar line indicates that the .message file is displayed when the user enters a directory that contains such a file. By default, none of these files exist. If you want them on your FTP server, you have to create them yourself.

> **Note**   The `/welcome.msg` file is relative to the root directory that the FTP user logs in to. A guest user, such as `anonymous`, would have `/var/ftp` as its root directory by default. The `welcome.msg` file would therefore have to be in `/var/ftp`.

- **compress yes all** — This enables compression of files for the FTP site for all users. The `compress` command is the standard compression command used in UNIX systems (though `gzip` is used more often with free operating systems, such as Linux). The `compress` command lines used to carry out the compressions are defined in `/etc/ftpconversions`. (Files stored by compress have a .Z suffix.)

- **tar yes all** — This enables tar compression for all users at the FTP site. The `tar` command is the standard UNIX command used to create archives of multiple files. The `tar` commands used to carry out the compressions are defined in `/etc/ftpconversions`. (Files stored by tar have a .tar, .tar.gz, or .tar.Z suffix.)

- **chmod no guest, anonymous**—This prevents guest and anonymous user names from changing the permissions on any files or directories.

- **delete no anonymous**—This prevents anonymous user name from deleting files or directories.

- **overwrite no anonymous**—This prevents anonymous user name from overwriting existing files or directories.

- **rename no anonymous**—This prevents anonymous user name from renaming any files or directories.

- **log transfers anonymous, guest, real inbound, outbound**—This logs file transfers for the anonymous user, guest user, and any real users (that is, those who have their own user accounts on the Linux system). Both uploads (inbound) and downloads (outbound) transfers are logged.

- **shutdown /etc/shutmsg**—This checks the /etc/shutmsg file to see if the server is about to be shut down. If it is, your FTP server sends a message to current FTP users, warning them that the server is about to go down. It also denies new FTP connections and disconnects current users at a specified time prior to shutdown. (By default, the /etc/shutmsg file does not exist.) See the section on setting up FTP shutdowns later in this chapter for information on how to set up a shutdown file for scheduled FTP shutdowns.

- **passwd-check rfc822 warn**—This checks that passwords for anonymous logins are rfc822-compliant addresses. In other words, the FTP server asks for any valid e-mail address as the password for the anonymous login. If the address is not compliant (that is, is not in the form user@host.domain), the server will "warn" the user but still allow the user to log in.

✦ **FTP Root Directory**—For a user who logs in as an anonymous user, the /var/ftp directory is assigned as the user's root directory. In other words, the anonymous user could not cd above the /var/ftp directory (or even know what files exist outside the /var/ftp directory structure).

Within the /var/ftp directory are those directories and files necessary to make FTP work properly, without your having to access other files in the file system. The /bin directory contains executable commands that FTP may need (such as compress, ls, and gzip). The /etc directory contains passwd and group entries. The /lib directory holds shared object libraries needed by FTP. Finally, the /pub directory is available for placing the files that you want to be generally available to anonymous users.

Note   Previous to Red Hat Linux 7, the location of the FTP home directory was /home/ftp. Because administrators often shared /home directories across a group of computers so users could have access to their files from different computers, it was not useful to share the FTP home directory in this way. The FTP home directory is now /var/ftp. The home directory for your Web server (www directory) has also been moved to /var.

Creating FTP Users

The different types of users who can use the FTP services from your server include the `anonymous` user name, any of the real users who have been added to your computer (in `/etc/passwd`), and any special guest accounts that you set up. The following sections describe each of these types of users and how to set them up.

The anonymous FTP user

Because most visitors to your FTP site from the Internet will not have an individual login account to your computer, the `anonymous` user name is used on public FTP sites. With the `anonymous` user name, anyone who can reach the FTP site from the network can log in to the server and have minimal permission for its use. Typically, minimal means that an anonymous user can only copy files from (and not write files to) the FTP server and that only selected directories are even visible to the `anonymous` user.

Here is an example of a login session from an `anonymous` user:

```
$ ftp maple
Connected to maple.
220 maple FTP server (Version wu-2.6.1-18) Mon Nov 26 09:21:53
EDT 2000) ready.
Name (pine:mike): anonymous
331 Guest login ok, send your complete e-mail address as password.
Password: *********
230 Guest login ok, access restrictions apply.
Remote system type is UNIX.
Using binary mode to transfer files.
ftp>
ftp> bye
221-You have transferred 0 bytes in 0 files.
221-Total traffic for this session was 313 bytes in 0 transfers.
221-Thank you for using the FTP service on maple.trees.
221 Goodbye.
```

After connecting to the server, I typed **anonymous** at the login prompt. The server says that `anonymous` is okay and to enter my e-mail address as the password. (The password doesn't appear; I've used asterisks here to represent the password.) The server accepted my password as valid. If it had been invalid, I could have continued, but the server would have warned me to type a valid e-mail address next time. Because this is an illustration, I just ended the session by typing **bye** and I was logged off.

While I was logged on to the FTP server, I had access to all files and directories that the server allowed to the `anonymous` user. That would probably include only a restricted area of the server's system (the `/var/ftp` directory, by default, on Red Hat Linux systems). There were probably restrictions on what I could change, delete, or create on the server as an `anonymous` user as well.

One of the great advantages of anonymous FTP is that it can easily be automated. Instead of using the `ftp` command, users can simply type the FTP address of the server into a Web browser. Users don't even need to know that they are being logged in as an `anonymous` user when they visit the FTP site. The list of files and directories requested simply appears.

Tip
Assuming you have installed the anonftp software package and started the FTP service, anonymous users are given access to your FTP server by default. This assumes that your firewall is not blocking access to the service and that "disable = yes" was changed to disable = *no* in the file `/etc/xinetd.d/wu-ftpd`. To prevent anonymous users from accessing your FTP server, add the following line to your `/etc/ftpaccess` file:

```
defaultserver private
```

Real users

The users who have valid login accounts to your computer can also access the computer via FTP. These users can have any user name that the administrator defines. To use FTP, they can simply type their user names and passwords to the FTP prompts. At that point, they will be logged in to the FTP server.

Cross-Reference
See Chapter 11 for information on setting up regular real user accounts.

Instead of having `/var/ftp` as their root directory, however, real users have `/` as their root directory and their regular home directories (such as `/home/user`, where *user* is the user name) as their current directory when they log in. Unlike the `anonymous` user, the real user has no special restrictions with regard to the file system. Whatever they can access when they log in through a regular login prompt can be accessed when they log in through FTP.

No special configuration needs to be done in the `/etc/ftpaccess` file to allow a user with a real account to connect to the server through FTP. However, if by some chance a user or a group fell into a guestuser or guestgroup definition you set up, you could redefine that user or group as real again by setting a `realuser` or `realgroup` value for the user or group, respectively.

Tip
To prevent any real user from using the FTP service, you can simply add the person's user name to the `/etc/ftpusers` list. By default, these users are excluded because they are on this list: root, bin, daemon, adm, lp, sync, shutdown, halt, mail, news, uucp, operator, games, and nobody. Most of those users are administrative accounts that could be exploited. In the `/etc/ftpaccess` file, all administrative accounts except the ftp user and group are denied access to the FTP service by default.

Guest users

A guest user is sort of halfway between a real user and an anonymous user. You can assign any name as a guest user. However, the guest user is limited to a restricted area of the file system, typically the user's home directory.

Using guest user accounts is a great way to give specific users permission to add files to and remove them from a specific part of your file system but not allow them to do much else. This is useful, for example, if you want to give users a place to set up their own Web pages.

In general terms, an FTP guest user will have an account set up in the Linux /etc/passwd file, then that user will be defined as either a guestuser or guestgroup in the /etc/ftpaccess file. The following is an example of how to set up an FTP guest user account:

1. Add the user account as you would normally. For example, to add a user named mike with a home directory of /home/mike, type the following (as root user):

```
# useradd mike
```

2. Add a password for mike using the passwd command (entering it twice, as prompted):

```
# passwd mike
Changing password for user mike
New UNIX password:********
Retype new UNIX password: ********
```

3. Edit the user's account information in /etc/passwd so that the user's root directory is changed to the restricted directory (for example, the user's /home directory). Here is an example of how that new entry would look for the user named mike:

```
mike:x:501:501:guest acct:/home/mike/./pub:/etc/ftponly
```

The dot (.) after /home/mike makes the /home/mike directory on the FTP server the root directory for mike. When mike logs in, his current directory is /home/mike/pub. The /etc/ftponly value prevents a shell from starting up (such as /bin/bash) if mike were to log in from a regular Linux prompt.

4. Copy the sample ftponly file to /etc and make it executable as follows:

```
# cp /usr/share/doc/wu-ftpd*/examples/ftponly /etc/
# chmod 755 /etc/ftponly
```

5. Add the line /etc/ftponly to the /etc/shells file.

6. Create directories needed for the guest user's home directory to have everything FTP needs to work properly. To do this, I just copied everything from the /var/ftp directory structure (as root user) to my guest user's home directory (/home/mike). After that, I changed group assignment of /home/mike/pub to mike:

```
# cp -r /var/ftp/* /home/mike
# chgrp mike /home/mike/pub
```

7. Add the necessary definitions to /etc/ftpaccess. At the very least, you need to define the user as a guest login. For example, to define mike as a guest login, add the following to /etc/ftpaccess:

```
guestuser mike
```

With just guestuser mike defined, the user mike has /home/mike as his root directory and he can get files (but not put them on the server). Also, he can browse the directory structure below /home/mike only. To add to or change permissions, see the section on controlling FTP access later in this chapter.

At this point, the guest user can use the ftp command to connect to the server and have access to only those files and directories that are under the user's restricted directory.

Setting Up FTP Directories, Message Files, and Greetings

As an FTP site administrator, you are responsible for setting up the directory structure used on your site. You also have an opportunity to make the navigation of your site easier for users by providing a variety of message files and README files on your site and to change the greetings on your FTP server. The following sections describe these features.

Creating the FTP directory structure

Because you are providing a limited view of the file system to those who use your FTP service, you must provide everything they need within the root file system that they can access (typically, /var/ftp). How to set up the minimal directory structure for FTP is described in the section on setting up guest users.

A viable directory structure is provided in the /var/ftp directory when you install the FTP service in Red Hat Linux (specifically, the anonftp package). After that, most of what you want to share with the public can be arranged in the /pub directory structure that you create. For directories containing information that is restricted to certain classes of user, you may want to create a different root directory (such as /local).

Specific directories can be included or excluded within the directory structure using a variety of parameters in the /etc/ftpaccess file. You can choose which directories allow upload and download. You can also set whether users can rename, delete, overwrite, or change permissions of files. See the sections on controlling FTP access for further information on setting up user directories and files.

Adding helpful information

The FTP service on your Red Hat Linux computer is set up to automatically display messages and to alert the user of the existence of README files at different times in a user's navigation of your site. When FTP is installed, however, none of these files exist. So to help the navigation of your site, you need to create these files.

Creating README files

A README file is a standard method of providing information about the contents of a software package or, in this case, the contents of an FTP directory. Your FTP server is set up, by default, to alert users to the existence of README files when they either log in or change into a directory that contains a README file. Here are the entries in the /etc/ftpaccess file that make this happen:

```
readme   README*   login
readme   README*   cwd=*
```

The asterisk at the end of README indicates that any files that begin with the word README are matched (such as README.info, README-help, or README.txt). The README file is usually in plain text, so anyone can read it. You can create one using any text editor. Add a README file to the /var/ftp directory (to describe the contents of the FTP server) or to any directory where you want to describe the contents to the user who enters.

Users who enter a directory containing a README file will see a message that tells them that the README file is there. They have to open the file themselves to see the contents.

Creating message files

If you want to make sure that the users see a message when they log in or enter a particular directory, you can create welcome.msg and .message files. You can create those files using any text editor. Two entries in the /etc/ftpaccess file define how these message files are set up to be read:

```
message  /welcome.msg   login
message  .message       .cwd=*
```

You can create a welcome.msg in the FTP user's root directory (probably /var/ftp for anonymous users). It should be a plain-text message. It will appear when the user first logs in to your FTP server. In each directory, you can create a .message file. When users enter that directory, the contents of the .message file are displayed. As with the welcome.msg file, the .message file should be in plain text.

Changing FTP login greetings

When users log in to your FTP server, they see several standard greetings. You can change what greetings they see and what those greetings include by adding information to your /etc/ftpaccess file.

Changing the initial greeting

If you don't change anything, a user who logs in to your FTP server won't see that much information. The default greeting when a user logs into your FTP server looks something like this:

```
$ ftp maple
Connected to maple.
220 maple FTP server (Version wu-2.6.1(1) Mon Dec 25 09:21:53 EDT 2000) ready.
Name (maple:mike):
```

That was the full greeting. To shorten the greetings that a user sees, you can set the greeting option to brief or terse in the /etc/ftpaccess file as follows:

```
greeting terse
```

The terse option causes much shorter output to be displayed before the login prompt. Here is an example:

```
$ ftp maple
Connected to pine.
220 FTP server ready.
Name (maple:mike):
```

Changing the FTP server hostname

Normally, your system's hostname is displayed when someone connects to your FTP service. If you want to assign a special hostname that applies only to connections to your FTP server, you can change that name in the /etc/ftpaccess file. Here is an example of the line you would enter:

```
hostname ftppine
```

The next time an FTP user connects, that user will see the hostname as ftppine.

Adding a message before login

If you want to have a message appear after a user connects to your FTP service, but before the login prompt, you can do that with the banner option in the /etc/ftpaccess file. First, you need to create a text file that contains the message you want to print. Next, add a banner line pointing to that file (relative to your system root, not the FTP relative root). For example:

```
banner /etc/ftpbanner.msg
```

With this example, the next time a user connects to the FTP service, the contents of the `/etc/ftpbanner.msg` file are displayed after the connection message and before the login prompt appears.

Controlling FTP Access

Just because you open your computer to public access doesn't mean that you have to let everyone abuse your computing resources. In the `/etc/ftpaccess` file, you can define exactly which directories are readable and writable. You can limit the number of users who can access your FTP server at a time. You can also set permissions or limits to your resources for individuals or groups. The following sections describe some of your options.

Creating user classes

By setting up user classes, you create a method of assigning access to different resources to different groups of users. Any user who does not fall into a class will not have access to your FTP server. That's why the default class includes all users with the following line:

```
class       all       real,guest,anonymous       *
```

The first thing you need to do is decide which groups of users you want to treat separately. An effective technique is to define your local users as one class and all other users as another class. The class keyword lets you assign classes based on network address and types of user within that address (that is, real, guest, or anonymous). For example, you may want to assign one set of permissions for all users within your Internet domain and another set for everyone else. Here's how to do that:

```
class   home    real,guest,anonymous   10.0.0.0/8
class   world   real,guest,anonymous   *
```

In this example, all users who come from a host computer with an address on network number 10.0.0.0 (presumably your local network) are assigned to the "home" class. Users from any other network are assigned to the "world" class. Instead of a network number, you can use a domain name.

Note   The `/8` following the network address is a shorthand for the netmask. It indicates that the eight leftmost bits represent the network. In this example, therefore, the number `10` represents the network number and the next three octets represent individual host addresses.

As discussed earlier, user types defined within each class are represented by one of the following keywords:

✦ **real** — For users who have a login account on the local computer.

✦ **guest** — For users with real login accounts who are designated as guestusers or guestgroups in the `/etc/ftpaccess` file.

✦ **anonymous** — For anyone who logs in under the `anonymous` user name.

With class names assigned, you can assign limitations or permissions to any of those classes.

Allowing uploading of incoming files

By default, `anonymous` users are not permitted to upload files to your FTP server. For uploading to occur, you must specifically allow uploading in the `/etc/ftpaccess` file, using the `upload` parameter. Also, specific parameters deal with whether guest and `anonymous` users can delete, overwrite, rename, or change permissions of files and directories. (Remember that allowing public uploading of files to your FTP server can pose a significant security risk.)

Opening directories for uploading

You need to add information to your `/etc/ftpaccess` to enable FTP users to upload files to your Red Hat Linux system. Here are two examples of using the `upload` parameter to permit ftp users to upload files:

```
upload    /var/ftp   /incoming   yes   mike   sales   0600
upload    /var/ftp   /testdir    yes   ftp    ftp     0666
```

These examples enable you to upload files to the `/incoming` and `/testdir` directories in the `anonymous` user's root directory (`/var/ftp`). The permission the user has to write to the `/incoming` directory (and its subdirectories) is as the user `mike` and the group `sales`. Files are written with 0600 permission (so only `mike` could read and write the files). In the second example, ftp user and group permission are used to create the file and its read/write permissions are open (0666).

Cross-Reference If you don't remember what permission settings such as 0666 and 0600 mean, refer to the description of access permissions in Chapter 3. These are common options used with the `chmod` command to change access permissions.

Allowing upload permission also allows those same users the right to create directories (within the upload areas). To disallow the creation of directories, add the `nodirs` keyword at the end of an upload line (after the permission numbers). To have the ability to create directories turned on for an instance where it may be off, add the `dirs` keyword to the end of the line.

Another useful option with the `upload` parameter is the `class` option. The `class` option lets you set upload permission for a particular class of users. Here is an example of using the `class` option:

```
upload class=home /var/ftp /incoming/local yes ftp guest 0666
```

In this example, along with the previous example, any `anonymous` user could write to the `/incoming` directory, but only those who belonged to the class called `home` can write to the `/incoming/local` directory (within the `/var/ftp` directory). The permissions in this case are open (0666), and files and directories are created with FTP and guest for the user and group who own the file, respectively.

> **Tip**
> Using upload is not enough to ensure that an `anonymous` user can upload files to your FTP directories. Red Hat Linux file and directory ownership also applies. For example, if the incoming directory were owned by root, 700 permission would not allow the `anonymous` user to upload, but 777 permission would.

Preventing files or directories from being retrieved

Using the `noretrieve` parameter, you can prevent files with specific names or from specific directories from being retrieved. Here are some examples:

```
noretrieve relative class=world /pub/homestuff
noretrieve absolute /etc/hosts /etc/inittab
noretrieve core personal money
```

In these examples, `relative` and `absolute` are keywords that indicate whether the files and directories indicated are relative to the FTP user's directory (for example, `/var/ftp`) or an absolute path from the system's root directory. The first line indicates that any users in the class `world` cannot retrieve files from the `/pub/homestuff` directory relative to the `/var/ftp` directory (that is, `/var/ftp/pub/homestuff`). The second line says that the system's `/etc/hosts` and `/etc/inittab` files cannot be retrieved. When no path name is indicated, as in the third line, no files that match the names shown can be downloaded, regardless of where they reside in the file system.

Allowing files or directories to be retrieved

If you have prevented a group of files from being retrieved using the `noretrieve` parameter, you can selectively allow certain files and directories to be retrieved using the `all-retrieve` parameter. Here's an example:

```
all-retrieve relative class=world /pub/homestuff/publicfile.txt
```

In this example, although you restricted download from the `/pub/homestuff` directory in a previous example, you now allow the download of the `/pub/homestuff/publicfile.txt` file to the `world` class of users.

Allowing permission capabilities

Even after you have allowed a user or class of users permission to upload files to your FTP server, you still have a lot of control over different aspects of writing and changing files. Each of these permissions capabilities can be turned on or off for anonymous, guest, or real users. Or you can turn them on or off for a specific class of users. Below are a few examples. By default, all these services are turned on when a user has upload capabilities (that is, the capability to write to an FTP server).

Note Remember that Red Hat Linux ownership permission still applies to files and directories, regardless of how these permission capabilities are set. For example, even if you are allowed to use `chmod`, you still couldn't use it to change permission on someone else's file that was set to `0600`.

Enabling chmod

You can set whether or not a user can change the permissions associated with a file or directory using the `chmod` parameter. You set `chmod` to either `yes` (to allow it) or `no` (to disallow it). Then you can add a comma-separated list of keywords to choose who is assigned that permission. Here is an example:

```
chmod      yes    guest,class=home
chmod      no     anonymous
```

In this example, all guest users are allowed to use the `chmod` command in directories to which they are allowed to upload files. An `anonymous` user, however, is not allowed to use the `chmod` command to change file and directory permissions.

Enabling delete

To allow users with Linux ownership permission to delete files, use the `delete` parameter. Here is an example:

```
delete     yes    class=home
delete     no     anonymous,guest
```

This example enables deletions for any user in the `home` class. However, deletions are not allowed for `anonymous` or guest users who do not belong to that class.

Enabling overwrite

To allow users to overwrite files that currently exist on the FTP server, use the `overwrite` parameter. Here is an example:

```
overwrite   no     anonymous,guest,class=home
```

In this example, no anonymous users, guest users, or users from the class "home" are allowed to overwrite files using the FTP service (regardless of the ownership of the files).

Enabling rename

To allow a user to rename a file with the FTP service, use the `rename` parameter. Here is an example:

```
rename       no      anonymous,guest
```

This prevents anonymous or guest users from renaming files using the FTP service, regardless of file ownership.

Enabling umask

To enable a user to change the default permission bits assigned to the files and directories the user uploads, use the `umask` parameter. Here is an example:

```
umask        yes     anonymous,guest
```

This example enables anonymous and guest users to use `umask`.

Limiting the number of concurrent users

You can limit how many users at a time can be logged in to your FTP server based on the class of the user. This is an excellent way of making sure that your local users can access your server, even when there is extraordinary demand from the outside world. (By not defining any limit values, you ensure that connections will not be refused based on there being too many connections.) Here are some examples of limit entries:

```
limit   home    40      Any        /etc/ftp.overlimit
limit   world   120     Any        /etc/ftp.overlimit
```

The first example limits the number of users in the `home` class (which you assigned your local users to) who can be connected at any one time to 40. The `world` class of users is limited to 120 simultaneous connections to your server. If the maximum number of connections for a group is reached, a connection from the user is refused and a message that you created in `/etc/ftp.overlimit` is presented to the user.

The keyword `Any` indicates that this limitation is in effect on any day. You could, instead, assign the particular limit definition to apply to a particular day or time of day. For example, to set a limit that applies only on weekends, you could do the following:

```
limit    world   140     SaSu    /etc/ftp.overlimit
```

You can also create a limit entry based on time rather than days. To indicate a time period from 10 p.m. to 5 a.m. where access could be extended, you would enter the numbers 2200-0500, instead of SaSu, in the example. If conflicts between limit entries occur, the first matching limit takes precedence.

Limiting uploading and downloading

Downloading is what most people go to FTP sites to do. Typically, the disk area assigned to anonymous users contains documents or software that can be freely downloaded to your computer over the network. Some options, however, enable you to limit how much of the computer's resources someone can consume while downloading files. The following sections describe some of them.

File limits

Using the file-limit parameter, you can limit the number of data files that a user can transfer in a given session based on user class. Here are some examples:

```
file-limit      total   100     home
file-limit      in      5       world
file-limit      out     30      world
```

The first example allows all users in the home class (which we defined as belonging to your domain) to download and/or upload up to 100 files during an FTP session. To place limits on what the outside world can upload to your computer, the world class is limited to 5 incoming file transfers (uploads) and 30 outgoing transfers (downloads) per session. If no class is indicated, the entry applies to all users who don't fall into a class that already has file-limit defined.

Data limits

Instead of limiting the number of files a user can transfer, you can limit the amount of data that can be transferred by a user. Here are some examples:

```
byte-limit      total   102400000       home
byte-limit      out     51200000        world
byte-limit      in      25600000        world
```

The byte-limit parameter limits the amount of data transferred during a session to a certain number of bytes. The first line shows that the total amount of data that a user in the home class can transfer during a session (both in and out) is 102400000 bytes (about 100MB). Someone assigned to the world class can take (out) only 51200000 bytes of data during an FTP session (about 50MB). A user in the world class can also upload only 25600000 bytes of data during a session (about 25MB).

Note   If a user reaches the end of the byte-limit value during a transfer, the transfer is allowed to complete before the connection is dropped.

Connection time limits

You can limit the amount of time that an anonymous or guest user can be connected during an FTP session with the limit-time parameter. There is no way to limit connection time for any real users. By default, anonymous and guest users aren't limited either. For example:

```
limit-time anonymous 120
limit-time guest     240
```

In this example, the anonymous user is limited to sessions that are 120 minutes long. A guest user, however, is limited to 240-minute sessions.

Denying access from hosts and users

You can deny certain host computers from having access to your FTP server. Likewise, you can deny access for anonymous, guest, and real accounts in different ways.

Denying access to host computers

You can deny FTP access to requests coming from specific hosts using the deny parameter. Here's an example:

```
deny  maple,snowbird,oak  /etc/ftpdeny.msg
```

In this example, any user who tries to log in to your FTP service from computers named maple, snowbird, or oak will be denied access to your system. After the user tries to log in, a message from a specified text file (in this example, /etc/ftpdeny.msg) is displayed to the user, and no connection is made.

Limiting host access to anonymous and guest logins

You can use the guestserver parameter to limit which hosts are enabled to access your server using anonymous or guest logins. Here is an example:

```
guestserver maple,pine,snowbird
```

In this example, guest and anonymous logins are limited to connections from the hosts named maple, pine, or snowbird. Logins of those types from other computers are rejected. If you were to use the guestserver parameter alone with no hostnames, all requests for guest and anonymous logins would be denied.

Denying access to real users

You can deny access to your FTP service to a login from a real user (one who has a user account to your system in /etc/passwd) by adding the name to the /etc/ftpusers file. The main reason for doing this is to prevent people from trying to break into your system through administrative accounts. It may seem counterintuitive to deny access to administrative users, but it prevents potential security breaches. User names that are in this file by default are:

```
root
bin
daemon
adm
lp
sync
shutdown
halt
mail
news
uucp
operator
games
nobody
```

If these administrative real user accounts were accessible from your FTP server, crackers may be able to break into your system through FTP. This could gain them access to your entire Red Hat Linux system—not just to the /var/ftp directory structure.

Denying/allowing user access by UID and GID

You can deny access to your FTP service for users who try to log in as users with particular user or group names or numbers. The deny-uid and deny-gid features can be used instead of the /etc/ftpusers file previously described. The allow-uid and allow-gid features can be used to allow permission to use a service that has been denied in the /etc/ftpusers file.

You can identify users and groups by either numbers or names. If you use numbers, those numbers must be preceded by a percent sign (%). Here are some examples:

```
deny-gid    %-110
deny-uid    %-110
allow-uid   uucp news
```

In these examples, all administrative logins and other users up to user id 110 and group id 110 are denied access to your FTP service. The allow-uid line, however, overrides the denial of service for the uucp and news logins.

Shutting Down and Restarting the FTP Server

With ftpshut command, you can either shut down the server immediately or set it to shut down some time in the future. When you run ftpshut, it creates a shut-down file. To restart the FTP service after it has been shut down, you need to remove that file.

Shutting down FTP

The `ftpshut` command shuts down the FTP service. Any users who are currently connected to the FTP service are disconnected. When they type FTP commands, they will see a message such as `FTP server shut down—please try again later` or simply `Not connected`. To shut down the service immediately, type the following:

```
ftpshut now
```

You can set the server to shut down at a specific time by either adding the number of minutes from now that you want the server to shut down or by entering a particular time in the future. Here are some examples:

```
ftpshut 20:18
ftpshut -l 20 -d 3
```

In the first example, the server is set to shut down at 20:18 (or 8:18 p.m. on a 12-hour clock). In the second example, the `-l` option specifies the number of minutes left before the server will be shut down (in this example, 20 minutes). The `-d` option specifies the number of minutes before the FTP service shuts down that users are disconnected from the server. (If no `-d` option is specified, users are disconnected five minutes before the server shuts down.)

To be less antisocial about shutting down your FTP service, it's nice to send a warning message to let users know that FTP is going down. Here's an example of how to send a shutdown-warning message when you shut down your FTP server:

```
ftpshut 20:15 "FTP will go down soon. Finish and disconnect."
```

Restarting FTP

After `ftpshut` is run, it creates a file called `shutmsg` in both the `/etc` and `/var/ftp/etc` directories. When your FTP server shuts down, it stays down until these files are removed. So, to restart your FTP server, all you have to do is the following (as root user):

```
rm /etc/shutmsg /var/ftp/etc/shutmsg
```

The above command removes the files. At this point, users will immediately be able to reconnect to your FTP server. Another command you could use to restart your FTP server is the `ftprestart` command.

Monitoring the FTP Server

Whenever you set up a service from your computer for general consumption, it's a good idea to keep an eye on it. You can use many of the same techniques that you use to monitor your computer's file system in general to monitor your FTP server (for example, various tools for watching disk space consumption). To track the activities of users on your FTP system, however, FTP provides logging features.

Logging connections

When the ftpd daemon is run (from an entry in the `/etc/xinetd.d/wu-ftpd` file), the `-l` option is added to the command line. This option causes each FTP session to be logged to the syslog facility. As a result, messages that provide some of the following information about FTP activities will be sent to your `/var/log/messages` file:

- ✦ The user name, hostname, and IP address of the user who is trying to connect to your FTP service.
- ✦ The user names they log in under (`anonymous`, etc.)
- ✦ How and when the FTP service was disconnected for the user.

You can use this information to monitor the activities on your server. For example, if someone is trying to break into your system, you can see multiple failed login attempts. You can also see if you are getting more anonymous FTP requests than you can handle (which may encourage you to get a more powerful server or look into whether you are under a denial-of-service attack).

Logging file transfers

If there are file transfers during the session, they are logged to the `/var/log/xferlog`. In that file you can see both incoming and outgoing file transfers. Here are two examples of log entries in the `/var/log/xferlog` file:

```
Sat Oct 27 21:26:20 2001 1 oak 1625 /incoming/loginfo b _ i r mike ftp 1 root c
Sat Oct 27 21:27:23 2001 1 pine 124 /pub/README.txt a _ o r mike ftp 1 root c
```

In the first example, the transfer occurred at 21:26:20 on Saturday, October 27, 2001. The transfer time was only one (1) second. The remote hostname is `oak`, and the size of the file is `1625` bytes. The transferred file was named `loginfo` and was put in the `/incoming` directory on the FTP server. The type of transfer was binary (`b`). The underscore (`_`) indicates that no special action (such as file compression or decompression) was taken. The `i` shows that it was an incoming transfer. The user was a real user (`r`) named `mike`. The service invoked was `ftp`. Authentication was done using RFC931 authentication (`1`). The user id returned by the authentication method was `root`. The `c` indicates that the transfer was completed.

In the second example, several items are of interest. The remote computer name was `pine`. The file was transferred using an ASCII transfer method (`a`). The file `/pub/README.txt` was transferred from the file server (`o`).

Getting More Information about FTP Servers

There are plenty of resources for gaining more information about FTP servers. Here are some of your options:

✦ **FAQ** — The latest version of the WU-FTPD frequently asked questions list is available from `www.cetis.hvu.nl/~koos/wu-ftpd-faq.html`. Besides providing some useful answers, this FAQ also includes pointers to other helpful documentation.

✦ **RFCs** — Requests for comments are the documents that define standard protocols used with the Internet. The main RFC for FTP is RFC959. You can obtain RFCs from a variety of locations on the Internet, including the Internet RFC/FYI/STD/BCP Archives: `www.faqs.org/rfcs`.

✦ **CERT** — This organization provides useful documents for setting up FTP servers. Anonymous FTP Abuses describes how to respond to and recover from FTP server abuse. It also tells how to deal with software piracy issues. Anonymous FTP Configuration Guidelines provide general guidance in setting up your FTP area, as well as specific challenges of setting up a writable FTP area. Both of those documents are available from the CERT Tech Tips page (`www.cert.org/tech_tips`).

Tip   I strongly recommend reading the two FTP documents from CERT. The tips contained in these documents will help keep your FTP server secure, while still enabling you to offer the services that you want to share.

✦ **Mailing List** — To subscribe to the WU-FTP mailing list, you simply have to send an e-mail message to `listproc@mail.wustl.edu`, with the following line in the body of the message:

`SUBSCRIBE WU-FTPD <yourfullname>`

If you want to send e-mail to everyone on the list (after you've been subscribed), address the e-mail to:

`wu-ftpd@mail.wustl.edu`

✦ **Mailing List Archive** — An archive of the WU-FTP mailing list is maintained at `www.landfield.com/wu-ftpd/mail-archive`. There is also a search page for that archive at `www.landfield.com/wu-ftpd/mail-archive/search.html`.

Trying Out Your FTP Server

You can use both graphical and command-line tools to access FTP servers. The most common command-line tool in Linux is the `ftp` command. There are, however, graphical FTP programs available, including the gFTP window. Also, your Web browser can provide you with access to FTP servers.

Normally, to visit an FTP site from a Web browser such as Netscape, you either click on a link to the server or type an address similar to `ftp://ftp.whatever.com`. Your browser would, without your knowing or caring, log you into the FTP server as an `anonymous` user. If you want to try out your FTP service from Netscape but log in as a different user, there is a way to do that by adding the user name and password. You type those items with the FTP site's URL into Netscape's location box. Here is an example of what to type:

```
ftp://mike:99pQ15@ftp.whatever.com
```

In this example, you attempt to log in from Netscape to the FTP server named `ftp.whatever.com`. You log in as the user `mike` with a password of `99pQ15`. If the user name and password are correct, you will see that user's initial directory in your Netscape window. (Of course, this can expose your password to onlookers, which is not a good thing.)

Another graphical tool for accessing FTP sites from Red Hat Linux is the gFTP window. To start it, type **gftp&** from a Terminal window. To connect to an FTP site, choose Remote ⇨ Connect, and then enter information about the site that you want to connect to (hostname, port, directory, user name, and password). Then click Connect. Assuming you typed everything correctly, a window will appear.

Remote and local windows appear side by side in the gFTP window. Double-click on folder icons to move down the directory structure. Double-click on the double dots (..) to move up a directory level. To download a file from the remote FTP server, click on the file you want from the right pane, then select the arrow pointing to the left. To upload a file from the local host (if uploading is permitted), click on the file in the left window, then select the arrow pointing to the right.

The `ftp` command that comes with Red Hat Linux provides an even less complex interface to an FTP server. To open a connection to an FTP server, simply type **ftp** *servername*, where *servername* is replaced by the hostname or IP address of the FTP server you want to connect to. Type the user name and password as prompted. Then you can use many standard Linux commands to move up and down the FTP server directory structure. When you find a file that you want to download, type **get** *file* (where *file* is the name of the file to download). When you find a file that you want to upload, type **put** *file* (where *file* is the name of the file to upload).

Summary

The FTP service is the primary method of offering archives of document and software files to users over the Internet and other TCP/IP networks. The FTP package that is delivered with Red Hat Linux (wu-ftpd) contains a full set of features that enable you to set up and maintain your own FTP server.

The FTP server package centers on the ftp daemon process (ftpd, which is run in Red Hat Linux as in.ftpd by the xinetd daemon), which services connection requests to your FTP server. Configuration of features is done in the /etc/ ftpaccess file. A wide range of features are available with the ftpaccess file that enable you to control who can access your server, which areas of your file system they can access, and how they can access them (incoming transfers, outgoing transfers, deleting files, renaming files, and so on).

To check out your FTP server once it is set up, you can use several different tools. The ftp command is available with Linux and with any other UNIX system. For a more graphical interface, there is the gFTP window. To access your FTP site as most others will access it, you can type the URL of your FTP site in the location box of your browser window. (You can even add FTP user and password information to the location of the FTP site.)

✦   ✦   ✦

Setting Up a
Web Server

T he World Wide Web is the fastest growing segment of the Internet, and HTTP traffic makes up over 70 percent of the total network bandwidth. Electronic commerce has provided a new virtual storefront for businesses trying to stay on the cutting edge of technology.

The Web has also been a boon to organizations seeking an inexpensive means to publish and distribute information. And with increasing computing power, decreasing prices, free operating systems such as Linux, and free Web servers such as Apache, it's getting even easier for anyone to establish a presence on "the Web."

This chapter shows you how to install and configure the Apache Web server on your Red Hat Linux machine. Each of the server's configuration files is described and explained in detail. You learn about various options for starting and stopping the server, as well as how to monitor the activity of a running server. Security is an important focal point throughout the descriptions and examples.

Introduction to Web Servers

The World Wide Web, as it is known today, began as a project of Tim Berners-Lee at the European Center for Particle Physics (CERN). The original goal was to provide one consistent interface for geographically dispersed researchers and scientists who needed access to information in a variety of formats. From this idea came the concept of using one client (the Web browser) to access data (text, images, sounds, video, and binary files) from several types of servers (HTTP, FTP, SMTP, Gopher, NNTP, WAIS, Finger, and streaming-media servers).

The Web server usually has a simpler job: to accept HTTP (HyperText Transfer Protocol) requests and send a response to the client. However, this job can get much more complex (as the server can also), executing functions such as:

✦ Performing access-control based on file permissions, user name/password pairs, and hostname/IP address restrictions.

✦ Parsing a document (substituting appropriate values for any conditional fields within the document) before sending it to the client.

✦ Spawning a CGI (Common Gateway Interface) script or custom API (Application Program Interface) program to evaluate the contents of a submitted form, presenting a dynamically created document, or accessing a database.

✦ Sending a Java applet to the client.

✦ Logging any successful accesses, failures, and errors.

The Apache Web server was originally based on HTTPd, a free server from NCSA (the National Center for Supercomputing Applications). At the time, HTTPd was the most common server on the Internet. Unfortunately, the development of the server wasn't keeping up with the needs of Webmasters, and several security problems had been discovered. Many Webmasters had been independently applying their own features and fixes to the NCSA source code. In early 1995, a group of these developers pooled their efforts and created "a patchy server," initially just a collection of patches to the HTTPd code. Since then, the Apache Group has largely rewritten the code and created a stable, multiplatform Web server daemon.

Other Web Servers Available for Red Hat Linux

Apache is not the only Web server that runs on Red Hat Linux, but it is the most popular and the most common server on the Internet, according to recent Netcraft surveys (www.netcraft.com/survey/). Some other servers are described below, with URLs that provide more detailed information.

✦ **Stronghold 3** — Based on Apache 1.3.6, this server features 128-bit SSL encryption and a digital certificate. According to Netcraft, Stronghold is the number one commercial SSL Web server running on UNIX systems. Although it is not a free server, it does include full source code. Details are available from www.c2net.com. Red Hat has acquired C2Net, resulting in a combination of their popular Web technologies.

✦ **iPlanet Web Server** — The iPlanet Web Server is offered by an alliance of Sun Microsystems and Netscape. The FastTrack Edition is a free version that includes support for Java, SSL, and LDAP. It also contains a full GUI. You can download a free copy of the FastTrack Edition or trial of the Enterprise Edition from www.iplanet.com.

✦ **AOLserver 3** — Originally called NaviPress, it features Web-based administration, access-control, SSL encryption, and SQL database drivers. More information and downloadable source code can be found at `www.aolserver.com/`.

✦ **Boa 0.94** — Designed to be fast and simple and not laden with features, Boa requires less system resources than other servers and is ideal for older hardware. It can be downloaded from `www.boa.org/`.

✦ **CERN (W3C) httpd** — The original (HTTP/1.0) "reference server" of the W3C (World Wide Web Consortium), this program is no longer being developed. The code is still available at `www.w3c.org/Daemon/`.

✦ **CERN (W3C) Jigsaw 2.2** — The latest HTTP/1.1 reference server, written completely in Java and freely available, can be found at `www.w3c.org/Jigsaw/`. It features extensive caching, an improved mechanism for executing external programs (although CGI is also supported), and a graphical administration tool.

✦ **NCSA HTTPd** — One of the earliest Web-server daemons and the original code base for the Apache project. Although it is no longer being developed, the source code is still available at `http://hoohoo.ncsa.uiuc.edu/`.

✦ **Servertec iServer 1.1** — Written in Java, this relatively small server provides load balancing and fault tolerance in a clustered environment and can be easily coupled with application and database servers. Further details are available at `www.servertec.com/products/iws/iws.html`.

✦ **WN 2.3** — More features than Boa but still somewhat small, this server features an advanced searching facility, parsed and conditionally served documents, and improved file-security features. Details and source code can be found at `http://hopf.math.nwu.edu/docs/overview.html`.

✦ **Zeus Web Server** — Designed for use by Internet Service Providers (ISPs), it features clustering support, 128-bit SSL encryption, and a GUI for management. More information and pricing details can be found at `www.zeustech.net/products`.

Apache is also the base for several other Web servers, most of which use Apache's freely available source code and add improved security features such as SSL (Secure Sockets Layer) for encrypted data transfer or advanced authentication modules.

Several of the main features of the Apache Web server include:

✦ The stability and rapid development cycle associated with a large group of cooperative volunteer programmers.

✦ Full source code, downloadable at no charge.

✦ Ease of configuration using plain-text files.

✦ Access-control based on client hostname/IP address or user name/password combinations.

✦ Support for server-side scripting as well as CGI scripts.

✦ A custom API that enables external modules (for example, for extended logging capabilities, improved authentication, caching, connection tracking, and so on) to be utilized by the server daemon.

Although Apache is widely used, it is not the only one available for Red Hat Linux. See the accompanying sidebar for descriptions of other Web servers that are available for Red Hat and other Linux flavors.

Quick Starting the Apache Web Server

There are several ways to install Apache on your machine. If it wasn't installed during Red Hat installation, you can install it later from the CD-ROMs that come with this book. The binary package can also be downloaded from any Red Hat mirror site and is included on the official Red Hat distribution CD-ROM set.

Note   It is possible for a new version of Apache to be released before an equivalent Red Hat package is available. Or perhaps you'd prefer to customize the server's compile-time options and build Apache directly from the source code. The full source code distribution can be downloaded from `www.apache.org/dist/` or from any Apache mirror site. You can select your closest mirror from `www.apache.org/dyn/closer.cgi`.

Here is a quick way to get your Apache Web server started. From here, you'll certainly want to customize it to match your needs and your environment (as described in the next section).

1. Make sure that Apache is installed by typing the following from a Terminal window:

```
$ rpm -qa | grep apache
apacheconf-0.8-4
apache-devel-1.3.20-8
apache-1.3.20-8
apache-manual-1.3.20-8
```

The version number you see may be different. You need only the Apache package to get started. I recommend apache-manual because it has excellent information on the whole Apache setup. The apache-devel package includes the apxs tool for building and installing Apache extension modules. The apacheconf package contains a GUI-based Apache Configuration tool.

2. You need to have a valid host name for your computer (for example, `host1.handsonhistory.com`). If you don't, you can edit the `/etc/httpd/conf/httpd.conf` file and define the `ServerName` as your computer's IP address. Open the `httpd.conf` file (as the root user) in any text editor, search for the line containing `ServerName localhost`, and uncomment it. It should appear as follows:

```
ServerName localhost
```

This allows you to work with your Web server from your local computer. To make it available to your LAN, you may want to use your IP address instead of localhost (for example, `ServerName 10.0.0.15`). To be a real Web server, you should get a real DNS host name.

3. Start the http server. As root user, type the following:

```
# /etc/init.d/httpd start
```

If all goes well, this message should appear: `Starting httpd: [OK]`. Now you are ready to go. To have httpd start every time you boot your system, run the `chkconfig httpd on` command as root user.

4. To make sure that it is working, open Netscape (or other browser) and type the following into the location box and press Enter:

```
http://localhost/
```

You should see the Test Page for the Apache Web server, as shown in Figure 21-1. To access this page from another computer, you will need to enter the computer's hostname or IP address.

Figure 21-1: Appearance of the Test Page indicates that the Apache installation succeeded.

Tip   It is not necessary to be connected to a network (or even to have a network connection) just to test the server or to view the files on your machine. Rather than specify the server's real name in the URL, just use the name "localhost" (that is, `http://localhost/` or `http://localhost/index.html`). **In fact, it's best to fully test the configuration before making the server accessible on an unprotected network.**

5. Replace the `index.html` file with your own home page in the `/var/www/html` directory. Then, you can continue to add your own content to that directory structure.

Now that you have gotten your Web server to work (or at least, I hope you have), you should step through the next section. It helps you understand how to set up more complex Web server arrangements and protect your server from misuse.

Configuring the Server

The primary file for configuring your Apache Web server is `httpd.conf` (located in the `/etc/httpd/conf` directory). For older installations, you may also have `srm.conf` and `access.conf` files configured. In recent releases, however, Apache developers are recommending you put all directives into `httpd.conf` and leave the other two files empty.

All Apache configuration files are plain-text files and can be edited with your favorite text editor. The `/etc/httpd/conf/httpd.conf` file is reproduced in its entirety below, with explanations inserted after related blocks of options (intended to supplement the comments provided with each file).

Cross-Reference   More information on Apache can be obtained from your own Web server, as the Apache manual is installed at `http://localhost/manual/`. **(If it is not there, install the apache-manual package.)**

Configuring httpd.conf

The `httpd.conf` file is the primary configuration file for the Apache Web server. It contains options that pertain to the general operation of the server. The default filename (`/etc/httpd/conf/httpd.conf`) can be overridden by the `-f filename` command-line argument to the httpd daemon or the `ServerConfigFile` directive. The following sections list the contents of the `httpd.conf` file and describe how to use the file.

The first section contains comments about the `httpd.conf` file:

```
##
## httpd.conf -- Apache HTTP server configuration file
##
```

```
#
# Based upon the NCSA server configuration files originally by Rob McCool.

#
# This is the main Apache server configuration file. It contains the
# configuration directives that give the server its instructions.
# See <URL:http://www.apache.org/docs/> for detailed information about
# the directives.
#
# Do NOT simply read the instructions in here without understanding
# what they do.  They're here only as hints or reminders.  If you are unsure
# consult the online docs. You have been warned.
#
# After this file is processed, the server will look for and process
# /usr/conf/srm.conf and then /usr/conf/access.conf
# unless you have overridden these with ResourceConfig and/or
# AccessConfig directives here.
#
# The configuration directives are grouped into three basic sections:
#  1. Directives that control the operation of the Apache server process as a
#     whole (the 'global environment').
#  2. Directives that define the parameters of the 'main' or 'default' server,
#     which responds to requests that aren't handled by a virtual host.
#     These directives also provide default values for the settings
#     of all virtual hosts.
#  3. Settings for virtual hosts, which allow Web requests to be sent to
#     different IP addresses or hostnames and have them handled by the
#     same Apache server process.
#
# Configuration and logfile names: If the filenames you specify for many
# of the server's control files begin with "/" (or "drive:/" for Win32), the
# server will use that explicit path.  If the filenames do *not* begin
# with "/", the value of ServerRoot is prepended -- so "logs/foo.log"
# with ServerRoot set to "/usr/local/apache" will be interpreted by the
# server as "/usr/local/apache/logs/foo.log".
#
```

This section consists entirely of comments. It basically tells you how information is grouped together in this file and how the httpd daemon accesses this file, as well as the `srm.conf` and `access.conf` files. By default, log files are in the `/var/log/httpd` directory.

Setting the global environment

In "Section 1: Global Environment" of the `httpd.conf` file, you set directives that affect the general workings of the Apache server. Here is what the different directives are for:

```
### Section 1: Global Environment
#
# The directives in this section affect the overall operation of Apache,
```

```
# such as the number of concurrent requests it can handle or where it
# can find its configuration files.
#
```

Choosing the server type

You can choose how server daemons are spawned to handle http requests. To do that, you can set the `ServerType` value as follows:

```
#
# ServerType is either inetd, or standalone.  Inetd mode is only supported on
# Unix platforms.
#
ServerType standalone
```

Using the "inetd" ServerType, one server is spawned from the xinetd daemon each time a new http request is received. It also requires additional setup of xinetd configuration files. This is not recommended because a new daemon must be loaded and configured for each new request. A ServerType of "standalone" (which starts one master daemon to spawn several servers that wait for incoming requests) results in better response times and allows more requests to be handled at once.

Setting the server root directory

The `ServerRoot` directive specifies the directory that contains the configuration files, a link to the log file directory, and a link to the module directory. An alternative `ServerRoot` pathname can be specified using the `-d` command-line argument to httpd.

```
# ServerRoot: The top of the directory tree under which the server's
# configuration, error, and log files are kept.
#
# NOTE!  If you intend to place this on an NFS (or otherwise network)
# mounted filesystem then please read the LockFile documentation
# (available at <URL:http://www.apache.org/docs/mod/core.html#lockfile>);
# you will save yourself a lot of trouble.
#
# Do NOT add a slash at the end of the directory path.
#
ServerRoot "/etc/httpd"
```

Storing the server's PID, Lock, and ScoreBoard files

The Apache Web server keeps track of the PID for the running server process. It also stores information about lock files. On some systems, a ScoreBoard file is also created, to store internal server process information. You can change the locations of these files using the entries described below:

```
# The LockFile directive sets the path to the lockfile used when Apache
# is compiled with either USE_FCNTL_SERIALIZED_ACCEPT or
# USE_FLOCK_SERIALIZED_ACCEPT. This directive should normally be left at
# its default value. The main reason for changing it is if the logs
# directory is NFS mounted, since the lockfile MUST BE STORED ON A LOCAL
```

```
# DISK. The PID of the main server process is automatically appended to
# the filename.
#
LockFile logs/accept.lock

# PidFile: The file in which the server should record its process
# identification number when it starts.
#
PidFile /var/run/httpd.pid

# ScoreBoardFile: File used to store internal server process information.
# Not all architectures require this.  But if yours does (you'll know because
# this file is created when you run Apache) then you *must* ensure that
# no two invocations of Apache share the same scoreboard file.
ScoreBoardFile logs/apache_runtime_status
```

The default value of the `LockFile` directive (as specified at compile time) is the `accept.lock` file in the Apache configuration directory for logs (`/etc/httpd/logs`). Because `USE_FCNTL_SERIALIZED_ACCEPT` (a method of attempting to secure a lock on a file) is defined at compile time, the lock file is necessary, but it's likely that there's no reason to change the default value.

Apache uses the `PidFile` to store the process ID of the first (root-owned) master daemon process. This information is used by the `/etc/init.d/httpd` script when shutting down the server, and also by the server-status handler (as described later).

Red Hat Linux does not need to use the `ScoreBoardFile`, as the status information usually saved in that file is stored in memory instead.

Bypassing srm.conf and access.conf files

As noted in the comment below, Apache used to process `srm.conf` and `access.conf` files after the `httpd.conf`. Now all information should be put into the `httpd.conf` file. You can uncomment the `ResourceConfig` and `AccessConfig` directives below and change them to `/dev/null` if you want to skip processing of these files.

```
#
# In the standard configuration, the server will process this file,
# srm.conf, and access.conf in that order.  The latter two files are
# now distributed empty, as it is recommended that all directives
# be kept in a single file for simplicity.  The commented-out values
# below are the built-in defaults.  You can have the server ignore
# these files altogether by using "/dev/null" (for Unix) or
# "nul" (for Win32) for the arguments to the directives.
#
#ResourceConfig conf/srm.conf
#AccessConfig conf/access.conf
```

Configuring timeout values

You can set several values that relate to timeout values. Some of these values are described below:

```
#
# Timeout: The number of seconds before receives and sends time out.
#
Timeout 300

#
# KeepAlive: Whether or not to allow persistent connections (more than
# one request per connection). Set to "Off" to deactivate.
#
KeepAlive Off

#
# MaxKeepAliveRequests: The maximum number of requests to allow
# during a persistent connection. Set to 0 to allow an unlimited amount.
# We recommend you leave this number high, for maximum performance.
#
MaxKeepAliveRequests 100

#
# KeepAliveTimeout: Number of seconds to wait for the next request from the
# same client on the same connection.
#
KeepAliveTimeout 15
```

The Timeout directive determines the number of seconds that Apache will hold a connection open between the receipt of packets for a PUT or POST HTTP request method, between the receipt of acknowledgments on sent responses, or while receiving an incoming request. The default of five minutes (300 seconds) can certainly be lowered if you find an excessive number of open, idle connections on your machine.

The KeepAlive directive instructs Apache to hold a connection open for a period of time after a request has been handled. This enables subsequent requests from the same client to be processed faster, as a new connection (to a different server process, most likely) doesn't need to be created for each request.

The MaxKeepAliveRequests directive sets a limit on the number of requests that can be handled with one open connection. The default value is certainly reasonable because most connections will hit the KeepAliveTimeout before MaxKeepAliveRequests.

The KeepAliveTimeout directive specifies the number of seconds to hold the connection while awaiting another request. You may wish to increase the default of 15 seconds, depending on how long it may take a client to peruse your average page and select a link from it.

Setting the number of server processes

You can have Apache dynamically change the number of server processes. To do this, set the `MinSpareServers` and `MaxSpareServers` values, as described below:

```
#
# Server-pool size regulation.  Rather than making you guess how many
# server processes you need, Apache dynamically adapts to the load it
# sees --- that is, it tries to maintain enough server processes to
# handle the current load, plus a few spare servers to handle transient
# load spikes (e.g., multiple simultaneous requests from a single
# Netscape browser).
#
# It does this by periodically checking how many servers are waiting
# for a request.  If there are fewer than MinSpareServers, it creates
# a new spare.  If there are more than MaxSpareServers, some of the
# spares die off.  The default values are probably OK for most sites.
#
MinSpareServers 5
MaxSpareServers 20


#
# Number of servers to start initially --- should be a reasonable ballpark
# figure.
#
StartServers 8


#
# Limit on total number of servers running, i.e., limit on the number
# of clients who can simultaneously connect --- if this limit is ever
# reached, clients will be LOCKED OUT, so it should NOT BE SET TOO LOW.
# It is intended mainly as a brake to keep a runaway server from taking
# the system with it as it spirals down...
#
MaxClients 150


#
# MaxRequestsPerChild: the number of requests each child process is
# allowed to process before the child dies.  The child will exit so
# as to avoid problems after prolonged use when Apache (and maybe the
# libraries it uses) leak memory or other resources.  On most systems, this
# isn't really needed, but a few (such as Solaris) do have notable leaks
# in the libraries. For these platforms, set to something like 10000
# or so; a setting of 0 means unlimited.
#
# NOTE: This value does not include keepalive requests after the initial
#       request per connection. For example, if a child process handles
#       an initial request and 10 subsequent "keptalive" requests, it
#       would only count as 1 request towards this limit.
#
MaxRequestsPerChild 1000
```

In standalone mode (from the `ServerType` directive), Apache will start one master daemon process owned by root that binds to the appropriate Port and then switches to a nonprivileged User. More servers (equivalent to the value of the `StartServers` directive) will then be started as the same nonprivileged User (the Apache user in this case).

Apache attempts to intelligently start and kill servers based on the current load. If the amount of traffic decreases and there are too many idle servers, some will be killed (down to the number of servers noted in `MinSpareServers`). Similarly, if many requests arrive in close proximity and there are too few servers waiting for new connections, more servers will be started (up to the number of servers noted in `MaxSpareServers`).

Using the values specified above, when the daemon is started, eight server processes will run, waiting for connections (as defined by `StartServers`). As more requests arrive, Apache will ensure that at least eight servers are ready to answer requests. When requests have been fulfilled and no new connections arrive, Apache will begin killing processes until the number of idle Web server processes is below 20. The value of `StartServers` should always be somewhere between `MinSpareServers` and `MaxSpareServers`.

Apache limits the total number of simultaneous server processes with the `MaxClients` directive. The default value is 150, which should be sufficiently high. However, if you find that you frequently have nearly that many servers running, remember that any connection beyond the 150th will be rejected. In such cases, if your hardware is sufficiently powerful (and if your network connection can handle the load), you should increase the value of `MaxClients`.

To minimize the effect of possible memory leaks (and to keep the server pool "fresh"), each server process is limited in the number of requests that it can handle (equal to the value of `MaxRequestsPerChild`). After servicing 1000 requests (the value specified above), the process will be killed. It is even more accurate to say that each process can service 1000 *connections* because all `KeepAlive` requests (occurring prior to encountering a `KeepAliveTimeout`) are calculated as just one request.

Binding to specific addresses

You can bind to specific IP addresses using the `Listen` directive. `Listen` directives can be used to add to the default bindings you already have:

```
# Listen: Allows you to bind Apache to specific IP addresses and/or
# ports, in addition to the default. See also the VirtualHost
# directive.
#
#Listen 3000
#Listen 12.34.56.78:80
Listen 80
```

The `Listen` directive is more flexible than the `BindAddress` and `Port` directives. Multiple `Listen` commands can be specified, enabling you to specify several IP address/port number combinations. It can also be used to specify just IP addresses (in which case the `Port` directive is still necessary) or just port numbers. By default, Apache listens to port 80 on the local computer (which is the standard www port listed in `/etc/services`).

Binding on virtual addresses

Apache supports the concept of virtual hosts. Using a `BindAddress` entry, you can tell your server which IP address to listen for:

```
# BindAddress: You can support virtual hosts with this option. This option
# is used to tell the server which IP address to listen to. It can either
# contain "*", an IP address, or a fully qualified Internet domain name.
# See also the VirtualHost and Listen directive.

#BindAddress *
```

By default, the Web server will listen on the specified port for all IP addresses configured for that machine (the same behavior as if the line above were not commented out). Alternatively, the `Listen` directive (described later in this section) can provide greater control over which IP addresses and ports the server uses. The `BindAddress` directive can be used only once.

Selecting modules in httpd.conf

During the compilation process, individual Apache modules can be selected for dynamic linking. Dynamically linked modules are not loaded into memory with the httpd server process unless those modules are explicitly identified to be loaded by the `LoadModule` directive. The blocks of code shown below select several modules to be loaded into memory by using the `LoadModule` directive with the module name and the path to the module (relative to `ServerRoot`). The following text shows a partial listing of these modules:

```
#
# Dynamic Shared Object (DSO) Support
#
# To be able to use the functionality of a module which was built as a DSO you
# have to place corresponding 'LoadModule' lines at this location so the
# directives contained in it are actually available _before_ they are used.
# Please read the file README.DSO in the Apache 1.3 distribution for more
# details about the DSO mechanism and run 'httpd -l' for the list of already
# built-in (statically linked and thus always available) modules in your httpd
# binary.
#
# Note: The order is which modules are loaded is important.  Don't change
# the order below without expert advice.
```

```
#
# Example:
# LoadModule foo_module modules/mod_foo.so

#LoadModule mmap_static_module modules/mod_mmap_static.so
LoadModule vhost_alias_module modules/mod_vhost_alias.so
<IfDefine HAVE_BANDWIDTH>
LoadModule bandwidth_module    modules/mod_bandwidth.so
</IfDefine>
<IfDefine HAVE_THROTTLE>
LoadModule throttle_module    modules/mod_throttle.so
</IfDefine>
LoadModule env_module          modules/mod_env.so
LoadModule config_log_module   modules/mod_log_config.so
LoadModule agent_log_module    modules/mod_log_agent.so
LoadModule referer_log_module modules/mod_log_referer.so
#LoadModule mime_magic_module  modules/mod_mime_magic.so
LoadModule mime_module         modules/mod_mime.so
LoadModule negotiation_module modules/mod_negotiation.so
LoadModule status_module       modules/mod_status.so
LoadModule info_module         modules/mod_info.so
LoadModule includes_module     modules/mod_include.so
        .
        .
        .
        .
        .

#  Reconstruction of the complete module list from all available modules
#  (static and shared ones) to achieve correct module execution order.
#  [WHENEVER YOU CHANGE THE LOADMODULE SECTION ABOVE UPDATE THIS, TOO]
ClearModuleList
#AddModule mod_mmap_static.c
AddModule mod_vhost_alias.c
<IfDefine HAVE_BANDWIDTH>
AddModule mod_bandwidth.c
</IfDefine>
<IfDefine HAVE_THROTTLE>
AddModule mod_throttle.c
</IfDefine>
AddModule mod_env.c
AddModule mod_log_config.c
AddModule mod_log_agent.c
AddModule mod_log_referer.c
#AddModule mod_mime_magic.c
        .
        .
        .
```

Apache modules are included in the list of active modules via the AddModule directive. The ClearModuleList directive removes all entries from the current list of active modules. It is important to synchronize the LoadModule and AddModule blocks above; otherwise, the modules may not be available to the server at runtime. Each of the standard dynamically linked Apache modules is described in Table 21-1.

If a particular module contains features that are not necessary, it can easily be commented out of the above lists. Similarly, you may want to add the features or functionality of a third-party module (for example, mod_perl, which integrates the Perl run-time library for faster Perl script execution, or mod_php, which provides a scripting language embedded within HTML documents) by including those modules in the lists above.

Table 21-1
Dynamic Shared Object (DSO) Modules

Module	Description
mod_access	Provides access-control based on originating hostname/IP address.
mod_actions	Conditionally executes CGI scripts based on the file's MIME type or the request method.
mod_alias	Allows for redirection and mapping parts of the physical file system into logical entities accessible through the Web server.
mod_asis	Enables files to be transferred without adding any HTTP headers (for example, the Status, Location, and Content-type header fields).
mod_auth	Provides access-control based on user name/password pairs. The authentication information is stored in a plain-text file, although the password is encrypted using the crypt() system call.
mod_auth_anon	Similar to anonymous FTP, this module enables predefined user names access to authenticated areas by using a valid e-mail address as a password.
mod_auth_db	Provides access-control based on user name/password pairs. The authentication information is stored in a Berkeley DB binary database file, with encrypted passwords.
mod_auth_dbm	Provides access-control based on user name/password pairs. The authentication information is stored in a DBM binary database file, with encrypted passwords.
mod_autoindex	Implements automatically generated directory indexes.
mod_bandwidth	Allows bandwidth limits to be set based on a per-connection or total server basis.
mod_cgi	Controls the execution of files that are parsed by the "cgi-script" handler or that have a MIME type of x-httpd-cgi.
mod_digest	Provides access-control based on user name/password pairs. The authentication information is MD5-encrypted and stored in a plain-text file.

Continued

Table 21-1 *(continued)*	
Module	**Description**
mod_dir	Sets the list of filenames that may be used if no explicit filename is selected in a URL that references a directory.
mod_env	Controls environment variables passed to CGI scripts.
mod_example	Illustrates how the server handles module references.
mod_expires	Implements time limits on cached documents by using the Expires HTTP header.
mod_headers	Enables the creation and generation of custom HTTP headers.
mod_imap	Controls inline image map files, which have a MIME type of x-httpd-imap or that are parsed by the imap handler.
mod_include	Implements Server-Side Includes (SSI), which are HTML documents that include conditional statements parsed by the server prior to being sent to a client.
mod_info	Provides a detailed summary of the server's configuration, including a list of actively loaded modules and the current settings of every directive defined within each module.
mod_log_agent	Enables logging of the UserAgent field from the HTTP header of incoming client requests.
mod_log_config	Enables a customized format for information contained within the log files.
mod_log_referer	Enables logging of the Referer field from the HTTP header of incoming client requests.
mod_mime	Alters the handling of documents based on predefined values or the MIME type of the file.
mod_mime_magic	Similar to the UNIX `file` command, this module attempts to determine the MIME type of a file based on a few bytes of the file's contents.
mod_mmap_static	If a file is not likely to change, this module enables the file to be loaded into memory when the server starts, eliminating the need to access the disk when the file is requested.
mod_negotiation	Provides for the conditional display of documents based upon the Content-Encoding, Content-Language, Content-Length, and Content-Type HTTP header fields.
mod_rewrite	Provides a flexible and extensible method for redirecting client requests and mapping incoming URLs to other locations in the file system.
mod_setenvif	Conditionally sets environment variables based on the contents of various HTTP header fields.

Module	Description
mod_so	The only module other than http_core that must be statically compiled in the server, this module contains the directives necessary to implement loading dynamic shared objects.
mod_speling	Attempts to automatically correct misspellings in requested URLs.
mod_status	Provides a summary of the activities of each individual httpd server process, including CPU and bandwidth usage levels.
mod_throttle	Allows limiting of bandwidth use based on policies you set for virtual hosts, locations, users, and directories.
mod_unique_id	Attempts to assign a token to each client request that is unique across all server processes on all machines within a cluster.
mod_userdir	Specifies locations that can contain individual users' HTML documents.
mod_usertrack	Uses cookies to track the progress of users through a Web site.
mod_vhost_alias	Contains support for dynamically configured mass virtual hosting.

More information about each module (and the directives that can be defined within it) can be found on your server at `http://localhost/manual/mod/`.

Configuring status information

By default, only basic status information is generated. If you would like to generate full status information, you need to turn on the `ExtendedStatus` directive by uncommenting the last line shown below:

```
#
# ExtendedStatus: controls whether Apache will generate "full" status
# information (ExtendedStatus On) or just basic information (ExtendedStatus
# Off) when the "server-status" handler is called. The default is Off.
#
#ExtendedStatus On
```

Setting the Main server configuration

The second section of the `http.conf` file relates to directives handled by your main server. In other words, these values are used in all cases except virtual host definitions. You can also assign these same directives to particular virtual hosts (by adding them within virtual host containers). The following is the introduction to this section in the `httpd.conf` file:

```
### Section 2: 'Main' server configuration
#
# The directives in this section set up the values used by the 'main'
```

```
# server, which responds to any requests that aren't handled by a
# <VirtualHost> definition.  These values also provide defaults for
# any <VirtualHost> containers you may define later in the file.
#
# All of these directives may appear inside <VirtualHost> containers,
# in which case these default settings will be overridden for the
# virtual host being defined.
#


#
# If your ServerType directive (set earlier in the 'Global Environment'
# section) is set to "inetd", the next few directives don't have any
# effect since their settings are defined by the inetd configuration.
# Skip ahead to the ServerAdmin directive.
#
```

Choosing the HTTP port number

Apache listens on particular ports for HTTP requests. The port that is used is set by the Port entry as follows:

```
#
# Port: The port to which the standalone server listens. For
# ports < 1023, you will need httpd to be run as root initially.
#
Port 80
```

Port 80 is the default for HTTP traffic, which is why the URL http://www.apache.org:80/ is equivalent to http://www.apache.org/. If the server is bound to a different port, the port number must be specified in the URL (for example, http://video.dlib.vt.edu:90/history/). Most Web servers run on port 80, although they can accept connections on any port (below 65536) that is not already bound to a particular service (see the /etc/services file for a list of common services/protocols and the ports they use). Only root can run programs that listen for connections on privileged ports (those below 1024).

Choosing the server's user/group

The httpd daemon doesn't have to run as the root user. By setting User and Group entries, you can have the daemon run by a different user and group:

```
# If you wish httpd to run as a different user or group, you must run
# httpd as root initially and it will switch.
#
# User/Group: The name (or #number) of the user/group to run httpd as.
#  . On SCO (ODT 3) use "User nouser" and "Group nogroup".
#  . On HPUX you may not be able to use shared memory as nobody, and the
#    suggested workaround is to create a user www and use that user.
#  NOTE that some kernels refuse to setgid(Group) or semctl(IPC_SET)
#  when the value of (unsigned)Group is above 60000;
#  don't use Group nobody on these systems!
```

```
#
User apache
Group apache
```

It is recommended that the User and Group directives specify a nonprivileged entity. This minimizes the risk of damage if your site is compromised. The first dae-mon process that is started will run as root. This is necessary to bind the server to a low-numbered port and to switch to the user/group specified by the User and Group directives. All other servers will run under that user ID (UID) and group ID (GID). In this case, the apache user and group name are used.

Setting an e-mail address

You can identify where e-mail should be sent if there is a problem with your server. This is done with the ServerAdmin directive:

```
#
# ServerAdmin: Your address, where problems with the server should be
# e-mailed.  This address appears on some server-generated pages, such
# as error documents.
#
ServerAdmin root@localhost
```

The ServerAdmin directive can be set to any valid e-mail address. It can simply point to the root account (as above), send mail to a user account (on the same or another machine), or redirect mail to an alias (such as Webmaster) that could dis-tribute mail to several individuals.

Setting the server name

If your server name is anything but your exact registered host/domain name, you should identify your server name here. As the comments point out, the ServerName directive can be set to a value other than the actual hostname of your machine. However, this other name should still refer to your machine in DNS if the server is to be a public Internet server. Frequently, www is just an alias for the real name of the machine (for example, a machine may respond to www.mybox.com, but its real name may be a1.mybox.com).

```
#
# ServerName: allows you to set a host name which is sent back to clients for
# your server if it's different than the one the program would get (i.e., use
# "www" instead of the host's real name).
#
# Note: You cannot just invent host names and hope they work. The name you
# define here must be a valid DNS name for your host. If you don't understand
# this, ask your network administrator.
# If your host doesn't have a registered DNS name, enter its IP address here.
# You will have to access it by its address (e.g., http://123.45.67.89/)
# anyway, and this will make redirections work in a sensible way.
#
ServerName localhost
```

Bonus content at www.unltded.com

Identifying HTTP content directories

There are several directives for determining the location of your server's Web content. The main location for your Web content is set to /var/www/html by the DocumentRoot directive. (Note that this location has changed from versions of Red Hat Linux prior to Red Hat 7. The location was formerly in /home/http.)

```
# DocumentRoot: The directory out of which you will serve your
# documents. By default, all requests are taken from this directory, but
# symbolic links and aliases may be used to point to other locations.
DocumentRoot "/var/www/html"
```

Setting access options and overrides

You can set individual access permissions for each directory in the Web server's directory structure. The default is fairly restrictive. Here is the default:

```
<Directory />
    Options FollowSymLinks
    AllowOverride None
</Directory>
```

This segment sets up a default block of permissions for the Options and AllowOverride directives. The <Directory />...</Directory> tags enclose the directives that are to be applied to the / directory (which is /var/www/html by default).

The Options FollowSymLinks directive instructs the server that symbolic links within the directory can be followed to allow content that resides in other locations on the computer. None of the other special server features will be active in the / directory, or in any directory below that, without being explicitly specified later. Next, the following access options are specifically set for the root of your Web server (/var/www/html). (I removed the comments here for clarity.)

```
<Directory "/var/www/html">
Options Indexes FollowSymLinks
AllowOverride None
Order allow,deny
    Allow from all
</Directory>
```

If you have changed the value of DocumentRoot earlier in this file, you need to change the /var/www/html to match that value. The Options set for the directory are Indexes and FollowSysLinks. Those and other special server features are described in Table 21-2. The AllowOverride None directive instructs the server that the .htaccess file (or the value of AccessFileName) cannot override any of the special access features. The special access features are described in Table 21-3.

Note   Remember that unless you specifically enable a feature described in Tables 21-2 and 21-3, that feature is not enabled for your server (with the exceptions of Indexes and FollowSymLinks).

Table 21-2
Special Server Features for the Options Directive

Feature	Description
ExecCGI	The execution of CGI scripts is permitted.
FollowSymLinks	The server will traverse symbolic links.
Includes	Server-Side Includes are permitted.
IncludesNOEXEC	Server-Side Includes are permitted, except the #exec and #include elements.
Indexes	If none of the files specified in the DirectoryIndex directive exists, a directory index will be generated.
MultiViews	The server allows a content-based filename pattern-matching search.
SymLinksIfOwnerMatch	The server will traverse symbolic links only if the owner of the target is the same as the owner of the link.
None	None of the features above are enabled.
All	All the features above are enabled, with the exception of MultiViews. This must be explicitly enabled.

Table 21-3
Special Access Features for the AllowOverride Directive

Feature	Description
AuthConfig	Enables authentication-related directives (AuthName, AuthType, AuthUserFile, AuthGroupFile, Require, and so on).
FileInfo	Enables MIME-related directives (AddType, AddEncoding, AddLanguage, LanguagePriority, and so on).
Indexes	Enables directives related to directory indexing (FancyIndexing, DirectoryIndex, IndexOptions, IndexIgnore, HeaderName, ReadmeName, AddIcon, AddDescription, and so on).
Limit	Enables directives controlling host access (Allow, Deny, and Order).
Options	Enables the Options directive (as described in Table 21-5).
None	None of the access features above can be overridden.
All	All the access features above can be overridden.

Identifying user directories

You can identify the name that is appended to a user's home directory when a request for a user's directory (~user) is received. The default is set to public_html:

```
# UserDir: The name of the directory which is appended onto a user's home
# directory if a ~user request is received.

<IfModule mod_userdir.c>
    UserDir public_html
</IfModule>
```

For the UserDir directive to allow access to a particular user's public_html directory, both the user's home directory and public_html directory must be executable by everyone. For example, a user named cjb could type chmod 711 /home/cjb /home/cjb/public_html to make those directories accessible. For UserDir to work, the mod_userdir module must also be added (which it is by default).

There are two ways in which the UserDir directive can handle an incoming request that includes a user name (for example, ~cjb). One possible format identifies the physical pathname of the individual users' publicly accessible directories. The other can specify a URL to which the request is redirected. A few examples are presented in Table 21-4, using the URL http://www.mybox.com/~cjb/proj/ c004.html as a sample request.

Table 21-4
UserDir Path Name and URL Examples

UserDir Directive	Referenced Path or URL
UserDir public_html	~cjb/public_html/proj/c004.html
UserDir /public/*/WWW	/public/cjb/WWW/proj/c004.html
UserDir /usr/local/web	/usr/local/web/cjb/proj/c004.html
UserDir http://www.mybox.com/users	http://www.mybox.com/users/cjb/ proj/c004.html
UserDir http://www.mybox.com/~*	http://www.mybox.com/~cjb/proj/ c004.html
UserDir http://www.mybox.com/ */html	http://www.mybox.com/cjb/html/ proj/c004.html

The UserDir directive can also be used to explicitly allow or deny URL-to-path name translation for particular users. For example, it is a good idea to include the following line to avoid publishing data that shouldn't be made public:

```
UserDir disable root
```

Alternatively, use the following lines to disable the translations for all but a few users:

```
UserDir disable
UserDir enable wilhelm cjb jsmith
```

The `DirectoryIndex` directive establishes a list of files that is used when an incoming request specifies a directory rather than a file. For example, a client requests the URL `http://www.mybox.com/~jsmith`. Because it's a directory, it is automatically translated to `http://www.mybox.com/~jsmith/`. Now that directory is searched for any of the files listed in the `DirectoryIndex` directive. The first match (from the default list of `index.html`, `index.htm`, `index.shtml`, `index.php`, `index.php4`, `index.php3`, `index.phtml`, and `index.cgi`) is used as the default document in that directory. If none of the files exist and the Indexes option (as in the `httpd.conf` file) is selected, the server will automatically generate an index of the files in the directory.

```
# DirectoryIndex: Name of the file or files to use as a pre-written HTML
# directory index.  Separate multiple entries with spaces.

<IfModule mod_dir.c>
DirectoryIndex index.html index.htm index.shtml index.php index.php4
        index.php3 index.phtml index.cgi
</IfModule>
```

For the `DirectoryIndex` directory to take effect, the `mod_dir.c` modules must have been added.

Setting directory access control

You can add an access file to each directory to control access to that directory. By default, the `AccessFileName` directive sets `.htaccess` as the file containing this information. The following lines set this filename and prevent the contents of that file from being viewed by visitors to the Web site. If you change the file to a name other than `.htaccess`, be sure to change the line below (`"\.ht"`) that denies access to that file.

```
#
# AccessFileName: The name of the file to look for in each directory
# for access control information.
#
AccessFileName .htaccess

<Files ~ "^\.ht">
    Order allow,deny
    Deny from all
</Files>
```

Allowing proxy caching

A proxy server has the ability to store the documents it serves to its clients, so that if a client requests the same document the proxy server doesn't have to retrieve another copy from the Web server. The `CacheNegotiatedDocs` directive indicates that the Web server allows documents to be cached. It is off by default (no caching). Turning this directive on can improve performance, but it risks outdated material being served.

```
#
# CacheNegotiatedDocs: By default, Apache sends "Pragma: no-cache" with each
# document that was negotiated on the basis of content. This asks proxy
# servers not to cache the document. Uncommenting the following line disables
# this behavior, and proxies will be allowed to cache the documents.
#
#CacheNegotiatedDocs
```

Setting canonical names

Use the `UseCanonicalName` directive to create a self-referencing URL, as shown below:

```
# UseCanonicalName:  (new for 1.3)  With this setting turned on, whenever
# Apache needs to construct a self-referencing URL (a URL that refers back
# to the server the response is coming from) it will use ServerName and
# Port to form a "canonical" name.  With this setting off, Apache will
# use the hostname:port that the client supplied, when possible.  This
# also affects SERVER_NAME and SERVER_PORT in CGI scripts.
#
UseCanonicalName On
```

The `UseCanonicalName` directive provides a form of naming consistency. When it is set to on, Apache will always use the `ServerName` and `Port` directives to create a URL that references a file on the same machine (for example, `http://www.mybox.com/docs/`). Otherwise, the URL will consist of whatever the client specified (for example, the URL could be `http://al.mybox.com/docs/` or `http://al/docs/` if the client is within the same domain).

This can be problematic particularly when access-control rules require username/password authentication: if the client is authenticated for the host al.mybox.com but a link sends him or her to `www.mybox.com` (physically the same machine), the client will be prompted to enter a username and password again. It is recommended that `UseCanonicalName` be set to on. In the situation above, the authentication would not need to be repeated, as any reference to the same server would always be interpreted as `www.mybox.com`.

Setting MIME type defaults

The location of the MIME type definitions file is defined by the `TypesConfig` directive. The `DefaultType` directive sets the MIME type:

```
# TypesConfig describes where the mime.types file (or equivalent) is
# to be found.
```

```
#
<IfModule mod_mime.c>
TypesConfig /etc/mime.types
</IfModule>

#
# DefaultType is the default MIME type the server will use for a document
# if it cannot otherwise determine one, such as from filename extensions.
# If your server contains mostly text or HTML documents, "text/plain" is
# a good value.  If most of your content is binary, such as applications
# or images, you may want to use "application/octet-stream" instead to
# keep browsers from trying to display binary files as though they are
# text.
#
DefaultType text/plain
```

Using the mod_mime_magic module, a server can look for hints to help figure out what type of file is being requested. You must make sure this module is added to your system for it to be used. The module can use hints from the /usr/share/magic.mime and /etc/httpd/conf/magic files to determine the contents of a requested file. Here are the directives that cause that module to be used if it is available:

```
<IfModule mod_mime_magic.c>
    MIMEMagicFile /usr/share/magic.mime
    MIMEMagicFile conf/magic
</IfModule>
```

Setting Hostname Lookups
With the Apache Web server, you can have the server look up addresses for incoming client requests. Turning on the HostnameLookups entry can do this:

```
# HostnameLookups: Log the names of clients or just their IP addresses
# e.g.   www.apache.org (on) or 204.62.129.132 (off).
# The default is off because it'd be overall better for the net if people
# had to knowingly turn this feature on, since enabling it means that
# each client request will result in AT LEAST one lookup request to the
# nameserver.
#
HostnameLookups Off
```

If the HostnameLookups directive is turned on, every incoming connection will generate a DNS lookup to translate the client's IP address into a hostname. If your site receives many requests, the server's response time could be adversely affected. The HostnameLookups should be turned off unless you use a log file analysis program or statistics package that requires fully qualified domain names and cannot perform the lookups on its own. The logresolve program that is installed with the Apache distribution can be scheduled to edit log files by performing hostname lookups during off-peak hours.

Configuring HTTP logging

You can set several values related to logging of Apache information. When a relative pathname is shown, the /etc/httpd directory is appended (for example, /etc/httpd/logs/error_log). As shown in the following example, you can set the location of error logs, the level of log warnings, and some log nicknames:

```
#
# ErrorLog: The location of the error log file.
# If you do not specify an ErrorLog directive within a <VirtualHost>
# container, error messages relating to that virtual host will be
# logged here.  If you *do* define an error logfile for a <VirtualHost>
# container, that host's errors will be logged there and not here.
#
ErrorLog logs/error_log


#
# LogLevel: Control the number of messages logged to the error_log.
# Possible values include: debug, info, notice, warn, error, crit,
# alert, emerg.
#
LogLevel warn


#
# The following directives define some format nicknames for use with
# a CustomLog directive (see below).
#
LogFormat "%h %l %u %t \"%r\" %>s %b \"%{Referer}i\"\"%{User-Agent}i\"" combined
LogFormat "%h %l %u %t \"%r\" %>s %b" common
LogFormat "%{Referer}i -> %U" referer
LogFormat "%{User-agent}i" agent


#
# The location and format of the access logfile (Common Logfile Format).
# If you do not define any access logfiles within a <VirtualHost>
# container, they will be logged here.  Contrariwise, if you *do*
# define per-<VirtualHost> access logfiles, transactions will be
# logged therein and *not* in this file.
#
# CustomLog /var/log/httpd/access_log common
CustomLog logs/access_log combined


#
# If you would like to have agent and referer logfiles, uncomment the
# following directives.
#
#CustomLog /var/log/httpd/referer_log referer
#CustomLog /var/log/httpd/agent_log agent
CustomLog logs/agent_log agent


#
```

```
# If you prefer a single logfile with access, agent, and referer information
# (Combined Logfile Format) you can use the following directive.
#
#CustomLog /var/log/httpd/access_log combined
```

The previous several lines deal with how server errors, client tracking information, and incoming requests are logged. The `ErrorLog` directive, which can specify an absolute path name or a path name relative to the `ServerRoot` (which is `/etc/httpd` by default), indicates where the server should store error messages. In this case, the specified file is `logs/error_log`, which expands to `/etc/httpd/logs/error_log`.

The `LogLevel` directive controls the severity and quantity of messages that appear in the error log. The messages can range from the particularly verbose `debug` log level to the particularly silent `emerg` log level. With `debug`, a message is logged anytime the configuration files are read, when an access-control mechanism is used, or if the number of active servers has changed. With `emerg`, only critical system-level failure creates a panic condition for the server.

The level specified by the `LogLevel` directive indicates the least-severe message that will be logged—all messages at that severity and above are recorded. For example, if `LogLevel` is set to `warn`, the error log will contain messages at the `warn`, `error`, `crit`, `alert`, and `emerg` levels. The default value of `warn` is a good choice for normal use (it will log only significant events that may eventually require operator intervention), but `info` and `debug` are perfect for testing a server's configuration or tracking down the exact location of errors.

The four `LogFormat` lines define (for later use) four types of log file formats: combined, common, referer, and agent. The tokens available within the `LogFormat` directive are described in Table 21-5. The `LogFormat` definitions can be modified to your own personal preference, and other custom formats can be created as needed.

	Table 21-5
	Available Tokens within LogFormat

Token	Description
%a	The IP address of the client machine.
%b	The number of bytes sent to the client (excluding header information).
%{VAR}e	The contents of the environment variable VAR.
%f	The filename referenced by the requested URL.
%h	The hostname of the client machine.

Continued

Table 21-5 *(continued)*

Token	Description
%{Header}i	The contents of the specified header line in the HTTP request.
%l	As reported by the identd daemon (if available), the user on the client machine who initiated the request.
%{Note}n	The contents of the message Note from a different module.
%{Header}o	The contents of the specified header line in the HTTP response.
%p	The port number on which the request was received.
%P	The PID of the server process that handled the request.
%r	The actual HTTP request from the client.
%s	The server response code generated by the request.
%t	The current local time and date. The time format can be altered using %{Format}t, where Format is described in the strftime(3) man page.
%T	The number of seconds required to fulfill the client request.
%u	If access-control rules require user name/password authentication, this represents the username supplied by the client.
%U	The URL requested by the client.
%v	The hostname and domain name of the server according to the Domain Name System (DNS).
%V	The hostname and domain name of the server handling the request according to the ServerName directive.

The common format includes the client host's name or IP address, the username as reported by the ident daemon and the server's authentication method (if applicable), the local time at which the request was made, the actual HTTP request, the server response code, and the number of bytes transferred. This format is a de facto standard among Web servers (and lately even among FTP servers).

For the purpose of connection tracking, the referer format will store the URL (from the same site or an external server) that linked to the document just delivered (relative to the ServerRoot). For example, if the page http://www.redhat.com/corp/about_us.html contained a link to your home page at http://www.mybox.com/linuxguy/bio.html, when a client accessed that link, the referer log on www.mybox.com would look like:

```
http://www.redhat.com/corp/about_us.html -> /linuxguy/bio.html
```

This information can be used to determine which path each client took to reach your site.

The agent format stores the contents of the User-agent: HTTP header for each incoming connection. This field typically indicates the browser name and version, the language, and the operating system or architecture upon which the browser was run. On a Pentium II running Red Hat 7, Netscape will produce the following entry:

```
Mozilla/5.0 (X11; U; Linux i686; en-US; rv:0.9.2)
```

The combined format includes all the information from the other three log file formats into one line. This format is useful for storing all connection-related log entries in one centralized file.

The `CustomLog` directives then assign one of the defined LogFormat formats to a filename (again, specified as an absolute path name or a path name relative to the `ServerRoot`). The only uncommented definition above assigns the combined format to the file `/etc/httpd/logs/access_log`. If you need to retain the agent or referer information separately, simply uncomment those definitions. Also, you could choose to comment out the `CustomLog /etc/httpd/logs/access_log` combined line and use the definition for the combined format instead.

Adding a Signature

Any page that is generated by the Apache server can have a signature line added to the bottom of the page. Examples of server-generated pages include a directory listing, error page, a status page, or an info page. The `ServerSignature` directive can be set to On, Off, or EMail. Here is how `ServerSignature` appears by default:

```
# Optionally add a line containing the server version and virtual host
# name to server-generated pages (error documents, FTP directory listings,
# mod_status and mod_info output etc., but not CGI generated documents).
# Set to "EMail" to also include a mailto: link to the ServerAdmin.
# Set to one of:  On | Off | EMail
#
ServerSignature On
```

With the ServerSignature directive On, this line appears at the bottom of server-generated pages:

```
Apache/1.3.20 Server at mycoolserver.com Port 80
```

With `ServerSignature` set to `EMail`, a link to the Web page's administrative e-mail account is added to the signature line (the server name becomes the link). If the directive is Off, the line doesn't appear at all.

Aliasing relocated content

There are various ways to define alias content. These include the `Alias` directive and the `ScriptAlias` directive:

```
#
# Aliases: Add here as many aliases as you need (with no limit). The format is
# Alias fakename realname
#
# Note that if you include a trailing / on fakename then the server will
# require it to be present in the URL.  So "/icons" isn't aliased in this
# example, only "/icons/". If the fakename is slash-terminated, then the
# trailing slash, the realname must also omit it.
#
Alias /icons/ "/var/www/icons/"

<Directory "/var/www/icons">
    Options Indexes MultiViews
    AllowOverride None
    Order allow,deny
    Allow from all
</Directory>


#
# ScriptAlias: This controls which directories contain server scripts.
# ScriptAliases are essentially the same as Aliases, except that
# documents in the realname directory are treated as applications and
# run by the server when requested rather than as documents sent to the client.
# The same rules about trailing "/" apply to ScriptAlias directives as to
# Alias.
#
ScriptAlias /cgi-bin/ "/var/www/cgi-bin/"


#
# "/var/www/cgi-bin" should be changed to whatever your ScriptAliased
# CGI directory exists, if you have that configured.
#
<Directory "/var/www/cgi-bin">
    AllowOverride None
    Options ExecCGI
    Order allow,deny
    Allow from all
</Directory>
```

The `Alias` directive implements a similar feature but points to a file system location (not necessarily within the DocumentRoot, either). For example, with the following line in place:

```
Alias /bigjob /home/newguy/proj
```

any client request for a document in `/bigjob` (`http://www.mybox.com/bigjob/index.html`, for example) would result in the retrieval of `/home/newguy/proj/index.html`.

The ScriptAlias directive also performs a related function, but the directories that it aliases contain executable code (most likely CGI scripts). The syntax is the same as for the Alias directive.

Redirecting requests for old content

As content changes on your Web server, some content will become obsolete while other content may move to a different place in the file system or to a different server. Using the Redirect directive, you can redirect requests for old content to new locations.

By default, there are no Redirect directives set for your Apache server. However, here is the text describing the directive:

```
#
# Redirect allows you to tell clients about documents which used to exist in
# your server's namespace, but do not anymore. This allows you to tell the
# clients where to look for the relocated document.
# Format: Redirect old-URI new-URL
```

Redirect can be used to instruct clients that the document they seek has moved elsewhere (to the same server or to an external location) by simply indicating the old and new locations. If the following Redirect option were in place:

```
Redirect /test http://www.mybox.com/prod
```

a client's attempt to access http://www.mybox.com/test/dmgr.html would result in a redirect to http://www.mybox.com/prod/dmgr.html.

Defining indexing

It's possible to have your Apache server show different icons for different types of files. To use this feature, IndexOptions should be set to FancyIndexing, and AddIconByEncoding, AddIconByType, and AddIcon directives should be used:

```
#
# FancyIndexing: whether you want fancy directory indexing or standard
#
IndexOptions FancyIndexing NameWidth=*


#
# AddIcon* directives tell the server which icon to show for different
# files or filename extensions.  These are only displayed for
# FancyIndexed directories.
#
AddIconByEncoding (CMP,/icons/compressed.gif) x-compress x-gzip

AddIconByType (TXT,/icons/text.gif) text/*
AddIconByType (IMG,/icons/image2.gif) image/*
AddIconByType (SND,/icons/sound2.gif) audio/*
AddIconByType (VID,/icons/movie.gif) video/*
```

```
AddIcon /icons/binary.gif .bin .exe
AddIcon /icons/binhex.gif .hqx
AddIcon /icons/tar.gif .tar
AddIcon /icons/world2.gif .wrl .wrl.gz .vrml .vrm .iv
AddIcon /icons/compressed.gif .Z .z .tgz .gz .zip
AddIcon /icons/a.gif .ps .ai .eps
AddIcon /icons/layout.gif .html .shtml .htm .pdf
AddIcon /icons/text.gif .txt
AddIcon /icons/c.gif .c
AddIcon /icons/p.gif .pl .py
AddIcon /icons/f.gif .for
AddIcon /icons/dvi.gif .dvi
AddIcon /icons/uuencoded.gif .uu
AddIcon /icons/script.gif .conf .sh .shar .csh .ksh .tcl
AddIcon /icons/tex.gif .tex
AddIcon /icons/bomb.gif core

AddIcon /icons/back.gif ..
AddIcon /icons/hand.right.gif README
AddIcon /icons/folder.gif ^^DIRECTORY^^
AddIcon /icons/blank.gif ^^BLANKICON^^

#
# DefaultIcon: which icon to show for files which do not have an icon
# explicitly set.
#
DefaultIcon /icons/unknown.gif

#
# AddDescription: allows you to place a short description after a file in
# server-generated indexes.  These are only displayed for FancyIndexed
# directories.
# Format: AddDescription "description" filename
#
#AddDescription "GZIP compressed document" .gz
#AddDescription "tar archive" .tar
#AddDescription "GZIP compressed tar archive" .tgz

#
# ReadmeName: the name of the README file the server will look for by
# default, and append to directory listings.
#
# HeaderName: the name of a file which should be prepended to
# directory indexes.
#
# The server will first look for name.html and include it if found.
# If name.html doesn't exist, the server will then look for name.txt
# and include it as plaintext if found.
#
```

```
ReadmeName README
HeaderName HEADER

#
# IndexIgnore: a set of filenames which directory indexing should ignore
# and not include in the listing.  Shell-style wildcarding is permitted.
#
IndexIgnore .??* *~ *# HEADER* README* RCS CVS *,v *,t
```

The previous block of options deals with how server-generated directory indexes are handled. The IndexOptions FancyIndexing NameWidth=* directive enables an autogenerated directory index to include several bits of information about each file or directory, including an icon representing the file type, the filename, the last modification time for the file, the file's size, and a description of the file. The NameWidth=* option allows file names of any length to be displayed. You change the * to a number representing the maximum number of characters that can be displayed in the Name column. If the IndexOptions directive is not set to FancyIndexing, only the file's name is listed in the index.

The AddIconByEncoding directive is used to configure the output of the FancyIndexing directive. It forces a particular icon to be displayed for files that match that particular MIME encoding. In the AddIconByEncoding line in the previous example, compressed.gif (with an alternative image tag of "CMP" for browsers that don't load images) will be displayed for files with a MIME encoding of x-compress and x-gzip. The AddIconByType directive has the same syntax but matches files based on their MIME type.

The AddIcon directive performs a similar function, but the icons are displayed based on a pattern in the filename. In the lines above, for example, bomb.gif will be displayed for files ending with core, and binary.gif will be displayed for files ending in .bin and .exe. The folder.gif icon represents a subdirectory, the back.gif file will be displayed to allow navigating back to the parent directory, and files named README will be associated with the hand.right.gif file. The blank.gif file is inserted into the autogenerated list to preserve proper formatting.

If there is a conflict between the AddIcon, AddIconByEncoding, or AddIconByType directives, the AddIcon directive has precedence. The DefaultIcon directive specifies the image to be displayed (unknown.gif, according to the line above) if no previous directive has associated an icon with a particular file.

The HeaderName and ReadmeName directives both specify files that will be inserted at the top and bottom of the autogenerated directory index, if they exist. Using the default values above, the server will first look for HEADER.html, then HEADER, to include at the top of the "fancy index." At the end of the index, README.html or README (whichever is located first) is inserted.

The `IndexIgnore` directive specifies files that should not appear in an autogenerated directory index. The line above excludes:

✦ any filename starting with a dot and containing at least two additional characters.

✦ any filename ending with a tilde (~) or what is commonly called a hash mark (#) (typically used by text editors as temporary files or backup files).

✦ filenames beginning with HEADER or README (the files displayed at the top and bottom of the directory listing, according to the `HeaderName` and `ReadmeName` directives).

✦ the RCS (Revision Control System) directory.

Defining encoding and language

The `AddEncoding` directive lets you set compression definitions that can be used by browsers to encode data as it arrives. The `AddLanguage` directive lets you indicate the language of a document, based on its file suffix.

```
#
# AddEncoding: allows you to have certain browsers (Mosaic/X 2.1+) uncompress
# information on the fly. Note: Not all browsers support this.
# Despite the name similarity, the following Add* directives have nothing
# to do with the FancyIndexing customization directives above.
#
AddEncoding x-compress Z
AddEncoding x-gzip gz tgz


#
# AddLanguage: allows you to specify the language of a document. You can
# then use content negotiation to give a browser a file in a language
# it can understand.
       .
       .
       .
# Danish (da) - Dutch (nl) - English (en) - Estonian (ee)
# French (fr) - German (de) - Greek-Modern (el)
# Italian (it) - Korean (kr) - Norwegian (no)
# Portugese* (pt) - Luxembourgeois* (ltz)
# Spanish (es) - Swedish (sv) - Catalan (ca) - Czech(cz)
# Polish (pl) - Brazilian Portuguese (pt-br) - Japanese (ja)
# Russian (ru)
#
AddLanguage da .dk
AddLanguage nl .nl
AddLanguage en .en
AddLanguage et .ee
AddLanguage fr .fr
       .
       .
       .
# LanguagePriority: allows you to give precedence to some languages
```

```
# in case of a tie during content negotiation.
#
# Just list the languages in decreasing order of preference. We have
# more or less alphabetized them here. You probably want to change this.
#
<IfModule mod_negotiation.c>
LanguagePriority en da nl et fr de el it ja kr no pl pt pt-br ru ltz ca es sv tw
</IfModule>
```

The AddEncoding directive supplements or overrides mappings provided by the TypesConfig file. Knowledge of the MIME type/encoding may allow certain browsers to automatically manipulate files as they are being downloaded or retrieved.

The AddLanguage directive performs similar mappings, associating a MIME language definition with a filename extension. The LanguagePriority directive determines the precedence if a particular file exists in several languages (and if the client does not specify a preference). Using the definition above, if the file index.html were requested from a directory that contained the files index.html.de, index.html.en, index.html.fr, and index.html.it, the index.html.en file would be sent to the client.

Adding MIME types and handlers

With the AddType directive, you can enhance the MIME types assigned for your Apache Web server without editing the mime.types file. With the AddHandler directive, you can map selected file extensions to handlers (that result in certain actions being taken):

```
# AddType: allows you to tweak mime.types without actually editing it, or to
# make certain files to be certain types.
#
# For example, the PHP 3.x module (not part of the Apache distribution - see
# http://www.php.net) will typically use:
#
<IfModule mod_php3.c>
  AddType application/x-httpd-php3 .php3
  AddType application/x-httpd-php3-source .phps
</IfModule>
#
# And for PHP 4.x, use:
#
<IfModule mod_php4.c>
  AddType application/x-httpd-php .php .php4 .php3 .phtml
  AddType application/x-httpd-php-source .phps
</IfModule>

# For PHP/FI (PHP2), use:
<IfModule mod_php.c>
  AddType application/x-httpd-php .phtml
</IfModule>
```

```
AddType application/x-tar .tgz

#
# AddHandler: allows you to map certain file extensions to "handlers",
# actions unrelated to filetype. These can be either built into the server
# or added with the Action command (see below)
#
# If you want to use server side includes, or CGI outside
# ScriptAliased directories, uncomment the following lines.
#
# To use CGI scripts:
#
#AddHandler cgi-script .cgi

#
# To use server-parsed HTML files
#
AddType text/html .shtml
AddHandler server-parsed .shtml

#
# Uncomment the following line to enable Apache's send-asis HTTP file
# feature
#
#AddHandler send-as-is asis

#
# If you wish to use server-parsed imagemap files, use
#
AddHandler imap-file map

#
# To enable type maps, you may want to use
#
#AddHandler type-map var
```

Defining actions and headers

Some types of media can be set to execute a script when they are opened. Likewise, certain handler names, when opened, can be set to perform specified scripts. The Action directive can be used to configure these scripts:

```
# Action lets you define media types that will execute a script whenever
# a matching file is called. This eliminates the need for repeated URL
# pathnames for oft-used CGI file processors.
# Format: Action media/type /cgi-script/location
# Format: Action handler-name /cgi-script/location

# MetaDir: specifies the name of the directory in which Apache can find
# meta information files. These files contain additional HTTP headers
# to include when sending the document

#MetaDir .web
```

```
# MetaSuffix: specifies the file name suffix for the file containing the
# meta information.

#MetaSuffix .meta
```

The `Action` directive maps a CGI script to a handler or a MIME type, whereas the `Script` directive maps a CGI script to a particular HTTP request method (`GET`, `POST`, `PUT`, or `DELETE`). These options allow scripts to be executed whenever a file of the appropriate MIME type is requested, a handler is called, or a request method is invoked.

The `MetaDir` and `MetaSuffix` directives implement a feature of the original CERN httpd daemon, allowing additional HTTP header information to be sent with the requested file. If the two lines above were uncommented, any request for a file would include searching the same directory for a subdirectory called `.web`, and then searching in that directory for a file with the same name as the requested file except with a `.meta` suffix. For example, if a client requested `http://www.mybox.com/services/grant.html` (which is stored as `/home/httpd/html/services/grant.html`), the file `/home/httpd/html/services/.web/grant.html.meta` would provide additional HTTP header information to the client.

Customizing error responses

For different error conditions that occur, you can define specific responses. The responses can be in plain text, redirects to pages on the local server, or redirects to external pages:

```
# Customizable error response (Apache style)
#   these come in three flavors
#
#     1) plain text
#ErrorDocument 500 "The server made a boo boo.
#  n.b.  the (") marks it as text, it does not get output
#
#     2) local redirects
#ErrorDocument 404 /missing.html
#  to redirect to local url /missing.html
#ErrorDocument 404 /cgi-bin/missing_handler.pl
#  N.B. can redirect to a script or a document using server-side-includes.
#
#     3) external redirects
#ErrorDocument 402 http://some.other_server.com/subscription_info.html
#  N.B.: Many of the environment variables associated with the original
#  request will *not* be available to such a script.
```

As the comments suggest, the `ErrorDocument` directive can customize any server response code, redirecting it to an external page, a local file or CGI script, or to a simple text sentence. Table 21-6 lists the most common server response codes and their meanings.

Table 21-6
Server Response Codes

Response Code	Meaning
200 OK	The request was successfully processed.
201 Created	Using the POST request method, a new file was successfully stored on the server.
202 Accepted	The request has been received and is currently being processed.
204 No Content	The request was successful, but there is no change in the current page displayed to the client.
301 Moved Permanently	The requested page has been permanently moved, and future references to that page should use the new URL that is displayed.
302 Moved Temporarily	The requested page has been temporarily relocated. Future references should continue to use the same URL, but the current connection is being redirected.
304 Not Modified	A cached version of the page is identical to the requested page.
400 Bad Request	The client's request contains invalid syntax.
401 Unauthorized	The client specified an invalid user name/password combination.
402 Payment Required	The client must provide a means to complete a monetary transaction.
403 Forbidden	Access-control mechanisms deny the client's request.
404 Not Found	The requested page does not exist on the server.
500 Internal Server Error	Usually encountered when running a CGI program, this response code indicates that the program or script contains invalid code or was given input that it cannot handle.
501 Not Implemented	The request method (for example, GET, POST, PUT, DELETE, HEAD) is not understood by the server.
502 Bad Gateway	Using the Web server as a proxy, an error was encountered in fulfilling the request to an external host.
503 Service Unavailable	The server is currently processing too many requests.
505 HTTP Version Not Supported	The request version (for example, HTTP/1.0, HTTP/1.1) is not understood by the server.

Setting responses to browsers

If file extensions are not enough to determine a file's MIME type, you can define hints with the MimeMagicFile directive. With the BrowserMatch directive, you can set responses to conditions based on particular browser types:

```
# The following directives modify normal HTTP response behavior.
# The first directive disables keepalive for Netscape 2.x and browsers that
# spoof it. There are known problems with these browser implementations.
# The second directive is for Microsoft Internet Explorer 4.0b2
# which has a broken HTTP/1.1 implementation and does not properly
# support keepalive when it is used on 301 or 302 (redirect) responses.
#
BrowserMatch "Mozilla/2" nokeepalive
BrowserMatch "MSIE 4\.0b2;" nokeepalive downgrade-1.0 force-response-1.0


#
# The following directive disables HTTP/1.1 responses to browsers which
# are in violation of the HTTP/1.0 spec by not being able to grok a
# basic 1.1 response.
#
BrowserMatch "RealPlayer 4\.0" force-response-1.0
BrowserMatch "Java/1\.0" force-response-1.0
BrowserMatch "JDK/1\.0" force-response-1.0
```

The BrowserMatch directive allows environment variables to be set based on the contents of the User-agent: header field.

Enabling the perl module

If the perl module is installed (mod_perl.c), the following lines enable the use of Perl scripts. These lines allow perl-script to be used from the /var/www/perl directory. The Options +ExecCGI line allows the execution of CGI scripts.

```
# If the perl module is installed, this will be enabled.
<IfModule mod_perl.c>
    Alias /perl/ /var/www/perl/
    <Directory /var/www/perl>
        SetHandler perl-script
        PerlHandler Apache::Registry
        Options +ExecCGI
    </Directory>
</IfModule>
```

Allowing password updates

By enabling the following lines (which are off by default), you can allow the http put feature to be used to generate new passwords. As noted in the comment, this feature allows an application such as the Netscape Gold publish feature to change user authentication information for HTTP users.

```
#
# Allow http put (such as Netscape Gold's publish feature)
# Use htpasswd to generate /etc/httpd/conf/passwd.
#
#<IfModule mod_put.c>
```

```
#    Alias /upload /tmp
#    <Directory /tmp>
#        EnablePut On
#        AuthType Basic
#        AuthName Temporary
#        AuthUserFile /etc/httpd/conf/passwd
#        EnableDelete Off
#        umask 007
#        <Limit PUT>
#            require valid-user
#        </Limit>
#    </Directory>
#</IfModule>
```

Note   If you are following along in the `httpd.conf` file, you notice that we are skipping descriptions of the server-status lines and server-info lines. Those features are described later in the "Monitoring Server Activities" section.

Allowing access to local documentation

Documentation that comes with each software package installed with Red Hat Linux is stored in the `/usr/share/doc` directory. The following lines make that directory available to users on your local computer through the httpd service (i.e., from their Web browsers):

```
# Allow access to local system documentation from localhost
Alias /doc/ /usr/share/doc/
<Directory /usr/share/doc>
  order deny,allow
  deny from all
  allow from localhost .localdomain
  Options Indexes FollowSymLinks
</Directory>
```

Enabling proxy/caching service

Proxy and caching services are turned off by default. You can turn them on by uncommenting several values that are presented below:

```
#
# Proxy Server directives. Uncomment the following lines to
# enable the proxy server:
#
#<IfModule mod_proxy.c>
#    ProxyRequests On
#
#    <Directory proxy:*>
#        Order deny,allow
#        Deny from all
#        Allow from .your_domain.com
```

```
#     </Directory>

#
# Enable/disable the handling of HTTP/1.1 "Via:" headers.
# ("Full" adds the server version; "Block" removes all outgoing Via: headers)
# Set to one of: Off | On | Full | Block
#
#ProxyVia On

#
# To enable the cache as well, edit and uncomment the following lines:
# (no cacheing without CacheRoot)
#
#CacheRoot "/var/cache/httpd"
#CacheSize 5
#CacheGcInterval 4
#CacheMaxExpire 24
#CacheLastModifiedFactor 0.1
#CacheDefaultExpire 1
#NoCache a_domain.com another_domain.edu joes.garage_sale.com

#</IfModule>
# End of proxy directives.
```

Apache can function as a proxy server, a caching server, or a combination of the two. If `ProxyRequests` is set to off, the server will simply cache files without acting as a proxy. If `CacheRoot` (which specifies the directory used to contain the cache files) is undefined, or if `NoCache` is set to *, no caching will be performed. The `CacheRoot` should exist on a file system with enough free space to accommodate the cache, which is limited by the `CacheSize` directive. However, you should have 20 to 40 percent more space available in the file system because cache cleanup (to maintain the `CacheSize`, in kilobytes) occurs only periodically, as specified by the `CacheGcInterval` directive.

The `CacheMaxExpire` directive indicates the maximum number of hours that a document will exist in the cache without checking the original document for modifications. The `CacheLastModifiedFactor` applies to documents that do not have an expiration time, even though the protocol would support one. To formulate an expiration date, the factor (a floating-point number) is multiplied by the number of hours since the document's last modification. For example, if the document were modified three days ago and the `CacheLastModifiedFactor` were 0.25, the document would expire from the cache in 18 hours (as long as this value is still below the value of `CacheMaxExpire`).

The `CacheDefaultExpire` directive (specifying the number of hours before a document expires) applies to documents received via protocols that do not support expiration times. The `NoCache` directive contains a space-separated list of IP addresses, hostnames, or keywords in hostnames that should not have documents cached.

If the settings above were uncommented, a caching proxy server would be implemented. The cached files would exist in /var/cache/httpd for a maximum of 24 hours, although the server would perform garbage collection (cache cleanup) every four hours to ensure that the cache contained less than 5K of data. Documents received via protocols without expiration times (anonymous FTP, for example) will expire after one hour, whereas documents that don't have an expiration time (even though the protocol supports expiration times, such as HTTP) will use the CacheLastModifiedFactor to determine when the document will expire from the cache. Documents from the domains a_domain.com, another_domain.edu, and joes.garage_sale.com will not be cached.

You'll probably want to allow a much larger CacheSize, and possibly a shorter CacheGcInterval, but otherwise the supplied values are reasonable. Remember that the CacheGcInterval value can be a floating-point number (for example, 1.25 would indicate 75 minutes).

Configuring virtual hosting

The third section of the httpd.conf file is for configuring virtual hosting. You can handle multiple server addresses using the VirtualHost tags.

```
### Section 3: Virtual Hosts
#
# VirtualHost: If you want to maintain multiple domains/hostnames on your
# machine you can setup VirtualHost containers for them. Most configurations
# use only name-based virtual hosts so the server doesn't need to worry about
# IP addresses. This is indicated by the asterisks in the directives below.
#
# Please see the documentation at <URL:http://www.apache.org/docs/vhosts/>
# for further details before you try to setup virtual hosts.
#
# You may use the command line option '-S' to verify your virtual host
# configuration.

#
# Use name-based virtual hosting.
#
#NameVirtualHost *

#
# VirtualHost example:
# Almost any Apache directive may go into a VirtualHost container.
# The first VirtualHost section is used for requests without a known
# server name.
#
#<VirtualHost *>
#    ServerAdmin webmaster@dummy-host.example.com
#    DocumentRoot /www/docs/dummy-host.example.com
```

```
#       ServerName dummy-host.example.com
#       ErrorLog logs/dummy-host.example.com-error_log
#       CustomLog logs/dummy-host.example.com-access_log common
#</VirtualHost>
```

Apache supports the concept of virtual hosts, which means that your Web server can simultaneously exist as a1.mybox.com (which has a DNS alias of www.mybox.com), www.verysmallcompany.com, and www.wehavenomoney.org. Virtual hosting is implemented by simply configuring your machine to accept packets destined for additional IP addresses and supplying Apache with even more configuration directives. The same directives as discussed above can be used between the <VirtualHost>...</VirtualHost> tags.

Starting and Stopping the Server

The procedure for starting and stopping the Apache Web server is no different from that of many other server processes. The apache package installation creates the /etc/init.d/httpd file and uses the chkconfig command to create the appropriate links in the /etc/rcX.d directories.

See Chapter 12 for detailed information on the inner workings of the shell scripts that control starting and stopping daemons and server processes.

The /etc/init.d/httpd shell script accepts any of five command-line arguments. If it is called with the argument start, the httpd script will run one master daemon process (owned by "root"), which will spawn other daemon processes (equal to the number specified by the StartServers directive) owned by the user apache (from the User and Group directives). These processes are responsible for responding to incoming HTTP requests. If called with stop as the command-line argument, the server will be shut down as all httpd processes are terminated.

If given a command-line argument of restart, the script will simply execute the aforementioned stop and start procedures in sequence. Using reload as the argument will send the hangup signal (-HUP) to the master httpd daemon, which causes it to reread its configuration files and restart all the other httpd daemon processes. The shell script also supports an argument of status, which will report if the daemon is running and, if it is, the PIDs of the running processes. All other command-line arguments result in an error and cause a usage message to be printed.

The actual binary program that is being run, /usr/sbin/httpd, supports several command-line arguments, although the default values are typically used. The possible command-line arguments are listed in Table 21-7.

Table 21-7
Command-Line Arguments to httpd

Argument	Description
-c *directive*	Read the configuration files and then process the *directive*. This may supersede a definition for the directive within the configuration files.
-C *directive*	Process the *directive* and then read the configuration files. The directive may alter the evaluation of the configuration file, but it may also be superseded by another definition within the configuration file.
-d *directory*	Use *directory* as the ServerRoot directive, specifying where the module, configuration, and log file directories are located.
-D *parameter*	Define *parameter* to be used for conditional evaluation within the IfDefine directive.
-f *file*	Use *file* as the ServerConfigFile directive, rather than the default of /etc/httpd/conf/httpd.conf.
-h	Display a list of possible command-line arguments.
-l	List the modules linked into the executable at compile-time: Compiled-in modules: http_core.c mod_so.c
-L	Print a verbose list of directives that can be used in the configuration files, along with a short description and the module that contains each directive.
-S	List the configured settings for virtual hosts.
-t	Perform a syntax check on the configuration files. The results will either be: Syntax OK or (for example): Syntax error on line 118 of /etc/httpd/conf/httpd.conf: ServerType must be either 'inetd' or 'standalone'
-T	Same as -t, except that there is no check of the DocumentRoot value.
-v	Print the version information: Server version: Apache/1.3.12 (Unix)(Red Hat/Linux) Server built: Aug 7 2000 06:20:48

Argument	Description
-V	List the version information and any values defined during compilation: Server version: Apache/1.3.12 (Unix)(Red Hat/Linux) Server built: Apr 7 2000 06:20:48 Server's Module Magic Number: 19990320:7 Server compiled with.... -D EAPI -D HAVE_MMAP -D HAVE_SHMGET -D USE_SHMGET_SCOREBOARD -D USE_MMAP_FILES -D USE_FCNTL_SERIALIZED_ACCEPT -D HTTPD_ROOT="/usr" -D SUEXEC_BIN="/usr/sbin/suexec" -D DEFAULT_PIDLOG="/var/httpd/httpd.pid" -D DEFAULT_SCOREBOARD="/var/httpd/httpd.scoreboard" -D DEFAULT_LOCKFILE="/var/httpd/httpd.lock" -D DEFAULT_XFERLOG="/var/log/httpd/access_log" -D DEFAULT_ERRORLOG="/var/log/httpd/error_log" -D TYPES_CONFIG_FILE="/etc/httpd/conf/mime.types" -D SERVER_CONFIG_FILE="/etc/httpd/conf/httpd.conf" -D ACCESS_CONFIG_FILE="/etc/httpd/conf/access.conf" -D RESOURCE_CONFIG_FILE="/etc/httpd/conf/srm.conf"
-X	Only the single master daemon process is started, and no other httpd processes will be spawned. This should be used only for testing purposes.

Monitoring Server Activities

Apache provides two unique built-in methods to check the performance of your Web server. The server-info handler can be configured to display a detailed summary of the Web server's configuration. The server-status handler can be configured to show information about server processes. You can activate these services by adding the following lines to the /etc/httpd/conf/httpd.conf file, respectively:

```
<Location /server-info>
    SetHandler server-info
    order deny,allow
    deny from all
    allow from handsonhistory.com
</Location>
```

```
<Location /server-status>
    SetHandler server-status
    order deny,allow
    deny from all
    allow from handsonhistory.com
</Location>
```

In this example, all computers in the `handsonhistory.com` domain can display the server-info and server-status pages. You can change `handsonhistory.com` to any domain or host that you choose.

Displaying server information

The Server Information (server-info) page contains the server version information and various general configuration parameters and breaks up the rest of the data by module. Each loaded module is listed, with information about all directives supported by that module, and the current value of any defined directives from that module.

The Server Information is usually quite verbose and contains much more information than can be displayed in Figure 21-2, which shows only the links to each module's section and the general Server Settings section.

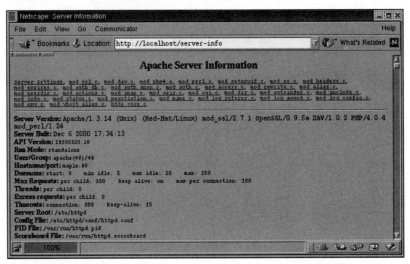

Figure 21-2: The server-info page displays server and module information.

Displaying server status

The contents of the server-status page include version information for the server, the current time, a timestamp of when the server was last started, and the server's uptime. The page also details the status of each server process, choosing from several possible states (waiting for a connection, just starting up, reading a request, sending a reply, waiting to read a request before reaching the number of seconds defined in the KeepAliveTimeout, performing a DNS lookup, logging a transaction, or gracefully exiting).

The bottom of the server-status page lists each server by process ID (PID) and indicates its state, using the same possible values. Figure 21-3 is an example of this page.

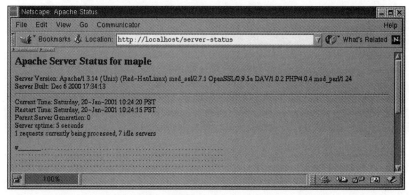

Figure 21-3: The Apache server-status page displays general Apache information and reports on individual server process activities.

The server-status page can also perform automatic updates to provide even closer monitoring of the server. If the URL http://localhost/server-status? refresh=40 is specified, the server-status page displayed in your browser will be updated every 40 seconds. This enables a browser window to be devoted entirely to continually monitoring the activities of the Web server.

Further security of server-info and server-status

Because both the server-info and server-status pages contain private information that should not be accessible to just anyone on the network, there are a few extra ways you can secure that information. You can restrict that information only to the local host; however, in some environments that may not be practical.

If you must allow other machines or networks access to such detailed configuration information, allow only as many machines as is necessary, and preferably only those machines on your local network. Also, be aware that, in the wrong hands, the information displayed by the server-info and server-status pages can make it much easier for the security of your entire machine to be compromised. Figure 21-4 shows the error message that should be presented to hosts that do not have access to the server-status page.

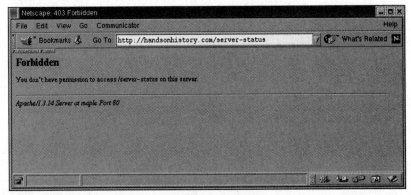

Figure 21-4: Deny server-status and server-info access to hosts on external networks, and perhaps to any machine other than the server.

It may also be beneficial to change the URL used to reference both of the aforementioned pages. This is an example of "security through obscurity," which should not be relied on but which can make it just a little more difficult for unauthorized individuals to obtain information about your Web server's configuration (particularly if you cannot restrict such connections to the local network). To accomplish this, simply change the filename in the Location directive, as in the lines below:

```
<Location /server.information.page>
```

and:

```
<Location /server.status.page>
```

Logging errors

The error log contains messages generated by the server that describe various error conditions. Though the format of the error log cannot be customized, the ErrorLog and LogLevel directives in the httpd.conf file (as described in the section on configuring the server) can modify the filename and the amount of information that is logged. The default file is /etc/httpd/logs/error_log (which is a link to /var/log/httpd/error_log). A few sample lines from the error log are shown below:

```
[Wed Nov 14 10:29:13 2001] [notice] Apache/1.3.12 (Unix)  (Red Hat/Linux)
    configured -- resuming normal operations
[Wed Nov 14 10:43:07 2001] [error] [client 127.0.0.1] client denied by server
    configuration: /home/httpd/html/server-status
[Sat Nov 14 10:06:42 2001] [error] [client 127.0.0.1] File
    does not exist: /home/httpd/html/newfile.html
[Sat Nov 14 01:12:28 2001] [notice] caught SIGTERM, shutting down
```

The first line indicates that the server has just been started and will be logged regardless of the LogLevel directive. The second line indicates an error that was logged to demonstrate a denied request (from Figure 21-4). The third line shows an error, which represents a request for a file that does not exist. The fourth line, also logged regardless of the LogLevel directive, indicates that the server is shutting down. The error log should be monitored periodically because it will also contain the error messages from CGI scripts that may need repair.

Logging transfers

Every incoming HTTP request generates an entry in the transfer log (by default, /etc/httpd/logs/access_log, which is a link to /var/log/httpd/access_log). Statistics packages and log file analysis programs typically use this file because manually reading through it can be a rather tedious exercise. The format of the transfer log can be altered by the LogFormat and CustomLog directives in the httpd.conf file (as described in the "Configuring the Server" section). If you attempted to access http://localhost/ following the installation procedure (from Figure 21-1), the following lines (in the "common" format) were written to the access_log:

```
127.0.0.1 - - [14/Nov/2001:23:32:28 -0400] "GET / HTTP/1.0" 200 1945
127.0.0.1 - - [14/Nov/2001:23:32:36 -0400] "GET /poweredby.gif HTTP/1.0" 200
1817
127.0.0.1 - - [14/Nov/2001:23:32:36 -0400] "GET /icons/apache_pb.gif HTTP/1.0"
200 2326
```

Viewing the server-info and server-status pages (as shown in Figures 21-2 and 21-3, respectively) generated the following entries:

```
127.0.0.1 - - [14/Nov/2001:23:40:41 -0400] "GET /server-info HTTP/1.0" 200 42632
127.0.0.1 - - [14/Nov/2001:23:41:49 -0400] "GET /server-status HTTP/1.0" 200
1504
```

The denied attempt to access the server-status page (from Figure 21-4) logged the following line (note the 403 server response code):

```
127.0.0.1 - - [11/Apr/2001:23:43:07 -0400] "GET /server-status HTTP/1.0" 403 211
```

Analyzing Web server traffic

The `webalizer` command can take Apache log files and produce usage reports for your server. Those reports are created in HTML format so you can display the information graphically. Information is produced in both table and graph form.

To use the `webalizer` command, the webalizer package must be installed. You can run `webalizer` with no options and have it take the values in the `/etc/webalizer.conf` files to get the information it needs. As an alternative, you can use command-line options to override settings in the `webalizer.conf` file. To use the defaults, simply run the following:

```
# webalizer
```

If all goes well, the command should run for a few moments and exit silently. Based on the information in the `/etc/webalizer.conf` file, the `/var/log/httpd/access_log` log file is read and an `index.html` file is copied to the `/var/www/html/usage/` directory. You can view the output by opening the file in any browser window. For example, you could type the following:

```
# netscape /var/www/html/usage/index.html
```

The output report shows a 12-month summary of Web server activity. On the bar chart, for each month a green bar represents the number of hits on the Web site, the dark blue bar shows the number of different files hit, and the light blue bar shows the number of pages opened. It also shows data for the number of visits and the number of sites that visited in the right column. The amount of data transferred, in kilobytes, is displayed as well.

Figure 21-5 shows an example of a `webalizer` output file for a Web server that was launched in the past few days.

Statistics Packages Available for Red Hat Linux

Analyzing the transfer log by hand isn't much fun. Several packages have been written to automate this task, two of which are described below.

✦ **Analog** — This free log file analyzer is very fast and easily configurable, and it produces very detailed output (including bar graphs and hypertext links). More information can be found at www.statslab.cam.ac.uk/~sret1/analog/.

✦ **Wuage** — The output from this statistics program is detailed, graphical, and extremely configurable. A 30-day trial version is downloadable, but the full version can cost between $75 (for a single license) and $295 (for an ISP Multiple-Server license). Details are available at www.boutell.com/wusage/.

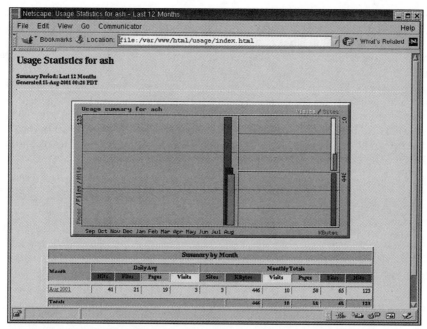

Figure 21-5: Webalizer displays Web data in chart and column formats.

Below the chart, a table shows daily and monthly summaries for activity during each month. Click the name of a month to see detailed activity.

Tip Because webalizer supports both common log format (CLF) and combined log format, it can be used to display information for log files other than those produced for Apache. For example, you could display statistics for your FTP server or Squid server.

Several other software tools are available for analyzing transfer statistics. The accompanying sidebar on statistics packages available for Red Hat Linux describes some of these packages.

Summary

Web servers are responsible for storing and delivering the vast amount of content that is available on the World Wide Web to clients all over the world. Although several software packages are available for Red Hat Linux, the most popular (and the one that comes with Red Hat Linux) is the Apache Web server.

This chapter describes how to install, configure, and run an Apache server in Red Hat Linux. The `httpd` daemon process handles requests for Web content (HTTP). Configuration files define what content is made available and how it can be accessed. In particular, the `/etc/httpd/conf/httpd.conf` file is used to configure the server.

The apache package also includes facilities for logging error and transfer messages. You can look for the `access_log` and `error_log` files in the `/etc/httpd/logs` directory. The `access_log` file contains information on content requests that have been serviced by the server. The `error_log` file contains listings of error conditions that have occurred and times when service has been denied.

✦   ✦   ✦

Setting Up a News Server

Newsgroups, the first popular offshoots of the early success of Internet e-mail, were started by people with common interests collectively maintaining e-mail lists to exchange messages on their subjects. As the lists became larger and harder to maintain, a new solution was needed. The result was Usenet newsgroups.

Today, with literally thousands of newsgroups available (more than 36,000 newsgroups are listed officially with the Internet Software Consortium: isc.org), managing the servers that gather newsgroups and offering the newsgroups to people in an organization can be a daunting task. The difficulty of the task relates more to making decisions about what newsgroups to offer and how you want to manage news feeds with other servers than it does to implementing those decisions (although that is tricky, too).

This chapter describes how to set up a news server on your Red Hat Linux system. It focuses on the most popular news server software—InterNetworkNews (or INN configuration files). INN happens to be free and comes delivered with Red Hat Linux.

Many other configuration files and methods of setting up a news server exist than those that are contained in this chapter. Use this chapter as a jumping-off point for configuring your news server. Then, refer to the man pages in /usr/share/man/*, the documents in /usr/share/doc/inn*, and the configuration files themselves for more information on setting up your news server.

Caution   Because a full INN news feed consumes massive amounts of disk space and network bandwidth, you need to configure it carefully. I strongly recommend getting help from experts as you tune your news server over time. You can get questions answered from the `new.software.nntp` newsgroup. There is also a database of INN information you can subscribe to from Mib Software called the Usenet RKT. To learn how to subscribe to the Usenet RKT, visit the following site: `www.mibsoftware.com/0023.htm`.

Understanding News Transports

In Red Hat Linux, the `innd` and the `nnrpd` daemons handle news transports. The `innd` daemon handles the incoming news feeds. When users request newsgroup articles, the innd daemon starts a nnrpd process to handle the request.

The `innd` daemon is started from the innd script from one of the various system start-up directories. The `innd` daemon decides which incoming news articles to accept and which to reject, based on configuration information that is set up in a variety of configuration files. These include the `active`, `newsfeeds`, and `incoming. conf` files. (The INN configuration files for the INN news server are described later in this chapter.) The `innd` daemon also listens for user connections and manages the article spool directories.

After a user requests an article, `innd` starts a `nnrpd` daemon to handle the request. It does that by checking the active and history fields to get information about the article. It then gets the article (taking it from the local spool directory) and forwards it to the user.

Note
The INN service is turned off by default. To turn it on, I recommend running the `chkconfig` **command (as root user). Type** `chkconfig innd on` **to turn on the** service. The next time your computer enters system state 3 or 5 (normal boot time), the INN service starts.

Planning Your News Server

Setting up a news server can result in huge volumes of information traveling to and from your Red Hat Linux system. The task of setting up a news server to run smoothly can benefit greatly from a little bit of planning. Activities that go into planning a news server include:

✦ Determining whether you need a news server

✦ Choosing which newsgroups to offer from your server

✦ Choosing how articles are stored

✦ Locating one or more servers to provide your news feed

✦ Setting policies on acceptable usage of newsgroups

Do you need a news server?

This may sound strange, but the first thing you need to decide when planning a news server is whether or not you really need one. Unless you have a fairly large group of users who need to access newsgroups on a regular basis, you may simply want to have your people access newsgroups from a news server provided by your ISP.

Maintaining a news server is resource-intensive. It involves a lot of network traffic, demands on the CPU, and disk space consumed. A full news feed can consume about 250GB of disk space per day. You can save a lot of space by not allowing groups that include binary files. Even then, however, you will still be consuming about 2GB of disk space per day.

A news server can be contentious as well. Without firm policies, you can find yourself dealing with demands for newsgroups from your users that may not be appropriate for your organization's goals.

Which newsgroups should you offer?

After you decide to set up a news server, choosing the newsgroups to offer will have an impact on all other aspects of setting up the server. Your decision will affect the amount of traffic coming into the server, the disk space used, and probably, above all, how your users can spend or waste their time with newsgroups. Basically, you will do this by restricting which newsgroups are accepted from the news feeds you define. For example, you may want to exclude many of the newsgroups in the alt.* hierarchy.

How should articles be stored?

The traditional method of storing news articles places each article in a separate file within the news server's directory structure under the name of the newsgroup. This method is inefficient for large volumes of news. Therefore, INN offers several different methods of storing news articles. (See the section "Choosing How Articles Are Stored," later in this chapter, for descriptions of each of these methods.)

How long are articles stored?

Articles that are stored using the traditional news storage method are held for 10 days by default. You can change that value (by resetting entries in the `inn.conf` and `expire.ctl` files). For the `cnfs` method, articles are rotated out automatically after the buffers are full. How to change the amount of time that news articles are stored is described in detail later in this chapter.

How are servers to provide your news feeds located?

You need to find one or more news servers to provide you with news feeds. Likewise, you need to configure your news server to feed other news servers with the articles that you want to pass on. You can ask your ISP whether it can provide you with a news feed or query a newsgroup that discusses how to set up news servers. How to set up news feeds is described later in the chapter.

Tip   Some news feed providers don't want to be bothered with configuring partial news feeds. They will want you to take a full news feed or none at all. One way to use INN to configure a partial feed is by using the `suck` package. You can find the `suck` package using the `rpmfind` command or by visiting a Red Hat FTP mirror site.

What are your newsgroup policies?

Both the best and the worst of humanity seem to be unleashed in newsgroups. You need to set standards for your organization on what is acceptable usage of your newsgroups. For example, you may want to prevent the use of certain "offensive" newsgroups. Because the use of your news server reflects on your organization, you also want to teach your users good netiquette (Internet etiquette) when it comes to participating in newsgroups.

Encourage your users to read articles from the news.announce.newusers newsgroup first. The articles in this newsgroup offer behavior guidelines when participating in newsgroups. Newsgroup primers are available that offer good advice, such as "Never forget that the person on the other side is human" and "Be careful what you say about others." Guidelines for posting to newsgroups also exist. If users of your news server are abusive or antisocial, you as the administrator may find yourself the recipient of many complaints.

Configuring an INN News Server

The INN software lets you turn your Red Hat Linux system into a news server. INN is the most popular news server software for Red Hat Linux and other UNIX systems. All the daemon processes, commands, and configuration files that are needed to run a news server in INN come with your distribution of Red Hat Linux.

The option to install news services is given to you during the Red Hat Linux installation process. If you did not install the news server software during the Linux installation, you can always install it later from the INN RPM file. You will first have to install the cleanfeed RPM, because the INN RPM depends on cleanfeed. Both RPM files are available on your Red Hat Linux media or from any Red Hat distribution mirror site. Obtain the files from the second Red Hat Linux installation CD (CD-2) and then, while logged in as root and within the directory containing the RPM files, type the following commands:

```
# rpm -i cleanfeed-0.95.7b-12.noarch.rpm
# rpm -i inn-2.3.2-5.i386.rpm
```

It is possible that the version numbers of the RPM files you find will be different than those shown here. That is okay. Always use the latest version you can find.

Red Hat Linux does a lot of the initial INN setup for you. You don't need to build INN from source code, and you don't need to set up the news user or create the spool directories. As INN is installed, you need only edit a few configuration files to get it going and turn on the service. (Though there isn't much configuration needed at first, you will find yourself tuning it over time.)

Note One thing you might need to do is run the `makehistory` command to create a `history.hash` file. This initializes the INN history database.

Rich Salz created the INN software package. In recent years, its development was taken over by the Internet Software Consortium (at `www.isc.org/products/INN`). From ISC's home page, you can get other documentation and the latest software updates for INN.

Starting with INN

Because so much of the INN software package that comes with Red Hat Linux is already set up for you, it helps to find out first what you are starting with. Here is a quick rundown of how INN is set up for you after you install it from the Red Hat Linux distribution:

✦ **News user:** A *news* user is created in your `/etc/passwd` file. Ownership of news components (configuration files, spool files, and commands) is assigned to this user. The group name is also *news*. Its home directory is the news user's spool directory (`/var/spool/news`).

✦ **Configuration directory:** Configuration files for INN are contained in the `/etc/news` directory. Sample files that you can use with INN are contained in `/usr/share/doc/inn*/samples`.

✦ **Spool directories:** The INN spool directory structure, created in `/var/spool/news`, contains these directories: archive, articles, incoming, innfeed, outgoing, and overview.

✦ **cron:** Three entries exist for cron (two daily and one hourly). The two daily entries, in `/etc/cron.daily`, clean up the news service (remove old entries) and check that the news service is working once a day. The one hourly cron entry checks that the news service is running and then sends news articles to other NNTP sites.

✦ **Mail command:** The Mail Transfer Agent (MTA) used by news is set to the `sendmail` command in the `inn.conf` file.

✦ **Reading access:** As delivered, INN enables only users from the local host to read and post articles through your news server. Other hosts would have to be added to definitions in the INN server's `/etc/news/readers.conf` file.

Although a lot of the INN configuration is preset for you, some configuration is required before you can use the server. In particular, you must make some changes to the `inn.conf` (for general news server information), newsfeeds (to decide where your news articles are sent), and incoming.conf (where the articles you receive come from).

If you use nontraditional storage methods (discussed later), some other files must also be configured. The `inn.conf` file is discussed in the next section, "Configuring the INN server." Where your news articles are sent (`newsfeeds`) and where the articles you receive come from (`incoming.conf`) are discussed in "Setting Up News Feeds" later in the chapter. The information in these files is used by the `innd` daemon to manage incoming news feeds and by the `nnrpd` daemon to control which users can access the news server.

This chapter frequently refers to headers that appear in the news articles. A news server often reacts to the information in these headers or puts information in these headers. The following is an example of some of the headers that can be contained in a news article:

```
Path: news.cwix.com!newsfeed.cwix.com!192.252.116.205!
From: Caleb Hollatz <news.handsonhistory.com>
Newsgroups: comp.os.linux.misc,comp.os.linux.networking
Subject: Re: Getting a newsgroup server working
Date: 15 Jun 2000 18:37:16 +0100
Organization: Hands on History
Message-ID: <x6k8t5s6ur.fsf@handsonhistory.com>
References: <7k2lad$llu$1@whatever.com>
NNTP-Posting-Host: crafts.handsonhistory.com
X-Complaints-To: abuse@handsonhistory.net
Content-Type: text/plain; charset=us-ascii
NNTP-Posting-Date: 15 Jun 2000 17:37:19 GMT
```

Note   In most newsreaders, you see only the contents of some of the headers, such as the From and Subject headers. To see all the headers, you would have to open the news article in a text editor or choose some sort of view header function. See Chapter 9 for discussions of newsreaders.

Of the headers shown in the preceding example, several should be of interest to a news server administrator. The Path: header indicates where the article has already been sent. This lets your news server know that it doesn't need to forward an article to a host that appears there. The Newsgroups: header shows the newsgroup or newsgroups that the article is posted to. The Organization: is something that you need to set in your `inn.conf` file to identify your organization. Likewise, you need to set an X-Complaints-To value so that problems encountered by users of your server can be forwarded to you (or to whomever's e-mail the complaints related to your server are to be forwarded).

Configuring the INN server

The `inn.conf` file is where most of the general news server information is configured. For your INN news server to work, you must make several changes to this file. Most of the required changes are associated with identifying your server. However, you need to consider other changes that will have a major impact on how your server performs, what and how information is logged and stored, and the location of the directories that have newsgroup information. You add or change parameters in this file to configure INN.

After making a backup copy of the `/etc/news/inn.conf` file, open it in any text editor and make changes based on the following descriptions.

Tip

In general, you shouldn't remove parameters from the `inn.conf` file. If you aren't sure how to set a parameter, leave the default value, if one is given. More than 100 parameters are in the `inn.conf` file. For more information about inn.conf parameters, see the `inn.conf` man page (type `man inn.conf`).

General parameters

The `inn.conf` parameters described in this section identify your news server. They define the names of your organization and news server that appear in the header of local posts, the host path name that identifies how to get to your computer on the network, and the domain your computer is in. The following is a list of the `inn.conf` parameters along with a description of the values that you can set for each of these parameters:

✦ The `mta` parameter sets the particular mail transfer agent that is used by your news server to transfer messages. The following default setting causes the `sendmail` command to be used:

```
mta:            /usr/sbin/sendmail -oi -oem %s
```

✦ The `organization` parameter identifies the name of your organization. When someone in your organization sends a news article, this name appears in the Organization: header of the article. The organization may be something similar to Customer of Hands on History, or Member of the Salt Lake Bird Club, or simply an organization name, such as Acme Realtors. Here is an example:

```
organization:   Hands on History
```

✦ The `ovmethod` parameter sets the type of overview storage method to use, if `enableoverview` is `true` (which it is by default). The default is `tradindexed`, a method that is fast for reading news and slow for writing it. Each newsgroup is stored in two files (a data file and an index file). A value of `buffindexed` causes data and index information to be stored in buffers (based on values set in the `/etc/news/buffindexed.conf` file). A value of `ovdb` causes newsgroups to be stored in a Berkeley DB database format. Here is the default setting of `ovmethod`:

```
ovmethod:       tradindexed
```

✦ The `pathhost` parameter must be set to a name that represents the local site. Each article that passes through your INN server has this name added to its Path header. The fully-qualified host name of the computer is a good choice to use at the `pathhost`. A value for `pathhost` is required; there is no default value. Here is an example:

```
pathhost:        news.handsonhistory.com
```

✦ The `pathnews` parameter sets the root of the news storage hierarchy as well as the news user's home directory. By default, the `pathnews` parameter is set to `/usr` as follows:

```
pathnews:        /usr
```

✦ The `domain` parameter determines the domain name used for your news server. Usually, this parameter is blank, and your computer's domain name is picked up automatically. You can set this option manually if your computer doesn't use an FQDN for other services. Here is an example:

```
domain:          handsonhistory.com
```

✦ The `innflags` parameter lets you add flags to pass to the `innd` daemon process when the server starts up. The flags are the options to the `innd` daemon. (Type **man innd 8** to see available flags.)

✦ The `mailcmd` parameter indicates the command that is used by the INN server to send messages. The default value is as follows:

```
mailcmd:         /usr/bin/innmail
```

✦ The `server` parameter identifies the name of your news server. It can be a fully qualified domain name (FQDN) or an IP address. The server name is added to the Path: header, so that other news servers know not to forward the message to your server again. You can override the server parameter by setting the NNTPSERVER environment variable. Here is an example of a server parameter:

```
server:          news.handsonhistory.com
```

News feed parameters

This set of parameters relates to how INN allocates resources to handle news feeds.

✦ To limit how long an article can be stored on your server, set the `artcutoff` parameter. By default, it is set to 10 days. Articles older than that are dropped. Here is an example of the `artcutoff` parameter with a cutoff date of 14 days:

```
artcutoff:       14
```

✦ The `bindaddress` parameter sets which interface (IP address) the INN server listens on. The default is to listen on all network interfaces on the computer. Setting `bindaddress` to `All` also results in INN listening on all interfaces.

✦ The `hiscachesize` parameter can be used to set the amount of memory to make available (in kilobytes) to store message IDs. Storing these incoming messages can speed up history lookup. The default is 0 (no memory allocated) as follows:

```
hiscachesize:    0
```

✦ The `ignorenewsgroups` parameter can be used to control routing of newsgroup creation control messages. By default, this feature is off (`false`) as follows:

```
ignorenewsgroups:       false
```

✦ If the `immediatecancel` parameter is set to true, it can be used to immediately cancel articles (and not just set them in cache to be cancelled). This option is only available for timecaf storage methods. By default, the feature is off as follows:

```
immediatecancel:        false
```

✦ With the `maxartsize` parameter, you can limit the size of the articles that are accepted by your news server. By default, this value is 1,000,000 bytes. To make the value half that size, you could set the parameter as follows:

```
maxartsize:        500000
```

✦ Use the `maxconnection` parameter to limit the number of incoming NNTP connections that are allowed from your server at the same time. NNTP connections, which enable users to read articles from and post articles to your news server, are handled by the `nnrpd` daemon. Limiting NNTP connections is one way to reduce demand on your server, but it can also prevent people from using it effectively. By default, `maxconnections` is set to 50. To set it to 40, use the following line:

```
maxconnections:        40
```

✦ You can use the `pathalias` parameter to prepend a name to the front of the `pathhost` value that appears on a news article's Path: line. No value is required.

✦ The port parameter lets you indicate which TCP/IP port to listen on. The default is 119, which is the standard news port.

```
port:                   119
```

✦ By setting `refusecybercancels` to true, you can automatically refuse any article that has a message ID that begins with `<cancel`. This is one method, though an inefficient one, of refusing cancelled spam messages. This is off by default:

```
refusecybercancels:     false
```

✦ The `rememertrash` parameter lets your INN server keep a record of rejected articles so that further copies of messages it has received can be refused before they are sent. This is on by default, as follows:

```
remembertrash:          true
```

✦ The `sourceaddress` parameter sets which interface (IP address) the INN server binds to for outgoing traffic. The default is for the INN server to choose which interface to use from the available interfaces. Setting `sourceaddress` to `all` also results in INN listening on all interfaces.

Other parameters related to news feeds can also help limit unwanted news items. The `linecountfuzz` parameter lets you reject mail messages where the line count doesn't match the value of the Lines header. The `pgpverify` parameter lets you choose if you want to verify control messages (other than cancel messages). The `usecontrolchan` parameter lets you choose to handle non-cancel control messages with an external program.

The `verifycancels` parameter lets you verify that a cancel message came from the same person that originated the post. The `wanttrash` parameter, if true, causes messages posted to unknown newsgroups to be sorted into the junk newsgroup. The `wipcheck` parameter sets a time limit (5 seconds by default) in which the server will wait to receive a promised article from a news server peer before accepting the article from another news server. The `wipexpire` parameter sets how long (10 seconds by default) to keep a message ID for an article that was offered but not yet sent.

Article storage parameters

Use these storage-related parameters to set how newsgroup messages are stored on your hard disk.

✦ The `cnfscheckfudgesize` parameter causes the size of CNFS cycbuffs articles to be checked against the value plus the value of `maxartsize` parameter. If the value is larger, the CNF cycbuff is assumed to be corrupt. This parameter is off by default, based on the following value:

```
cnfscheckfudgesize:    0
```

✦ If the `enableoverview` parameter is true (default), overview data is written out for articles. When this parameter is true, the `ovmethod` parameter must be set as well (as described earlier). Here is an example of the default `enableoverview` parameter:

```
enableoverview:        true
```

✦ As the `groupbaseexpiry` parameter is set to true, expiration of newsgroup messages is done based on newsgroup name. If you change it to false, expiration is done based on the storage method class being used. Here is how the parameter is set by default:

```
groupbaseexpiry:       true
```

✦ The `mergetogroups` parameter can be set to true if you want to file articles posted to `.to*` groups to pseudonewsgroups "to". If true, this parameter requires that the `to` newsgroup exist in the active file to allow INN to start. This feature is off (false) by default:

```
mergetogroups:         false
```

✦ The `overcachesize` parameter sets the number of cache slots that are set aside to hold open overview files. INN will store and open overview files just in case articles are received for those newsgroups. This parameter is used only if `enableoverview` is true and `ovmethod` is defined as `tradindexed`. By default, `overcachesize` is set to 15, as shown below:

```
overcachesize:         15
```

✦ The `ovgrouppat` parameter can be used to limit overview information stored by the INN server. With the value set to true, overview information is only stored for newsgroups that match a comma-separated list of expressions (in wildmat format).This option is not set by default.

✦ To have the INN server store articles based on newsgroup name in the Xref header, the `storeonxref` parameter should be true (it is false by default). If this value is false, newsgroup articles are stored by newsgroup name in the Newsgroups header.

```
storeonxref:       false
```

✦ The `useoverchan` parameter can be used to turn on a feature where overview data are stored internally using the `libstorage` function. If false, which it is by default, the INN server will handle creation of overview data on its own. Here is how `useoverchan` is set by default:

```
useoverchan:           false
```

✦ You can turn on the `wireformat` parameter, if you are using the `tradspool` storage method, to write articles in wire format. With wire format, messages are stored with a \r\n ending each line and periods at the beginning of lines doubled. Articles formatted in this way require no conversion. The INN server can operate more efficiently with `wireformat` set to true. By default, the value is false as indicated below:

```
wireformat:            false
```

✦ The `xrefslave` parameter indicates that the INN server should be a slave to another server. In this arrangement, each INN server should have the same article numbering so that the two servers could be used interchangeably. If this value is set to true, you must set the host name of the other server using the `nnrpdposthost` parameter (described later). By default, this value is false as shown below:

```
xrefslave:             false
```

Reading parameters

This set of parameters is used to validate news readers and features related to the news readers.

✦ If the `allownewnews` parameter is set to true, your users can request the NEWNEWS feature from their newsreaders. The NEWNEWS feature enables a user of a newsreader to request all articles that were posted or received for a particular newsgroup since a particular date. By default, this value is on (true), as recommended by the Network News Transfer Protocol RFC (RFC977). However, overuse of this feature can result in serious performance problems for the server. If you want to turn off NEWNEWS, set the value of the `allownewnews` parameter to false, as follows:

```
allownewnews: false
```

✦ With the `articlemmap` parameter on, articles can be mapped into memory using the `mmap` function. By default, this parameter is off (false) and articles are read into memory before going to the newsreader.

```
articlemmap:        false
```

✦ The `clienttimeout` parameter sets the number of seconds a connection to a client can be idle before it is dropped. By default, the value is set to 1800 (30 minutes) as follows:

```
clienttimeout:      1800
```

✦ The `nnrpdcheckart` parameter sets whether or not the INN server daemon should check if an article is on the server before listing it as so. By default, this value is on as follows:

```
nnrpdcheckart:          true
```

✦ The `nnrpperlauth` parameter can be used to cause the INN server to use "Perl hook" to check that readers are valid. If `nnrpperlauth` is true, then the connection is not authenticated using the `readers.conf` file, as it would be otherwise. This value is false by default, as shown here:

```
nnrpperlauth:        false
```

✦ The `nnrppythonauth` parameter can be used to cause the INN server to use "Python hook" to check that readers are valid. If `nnrppythonauth` is true, then the connection is not authenticated using the `readers.conf` file, as it would be otherwise. This value is false by default, as shown here:

```
nnrppythonauth:      false
```

✦ With the `noreader` parameter set to true, incoming connections from unknown hosts (that is, those not listed in `incoming.conf`), will be rejected. With this value set to false, an additional INN server daemon is launched to handle incoming connections from hosts not listed in `incoming.conf`. The default is false, as follows:

```
noreader:           false
```

✦ The `readerswhenstopped` parameter can be used to allow newsreaders to connect to the INN server, even if the server is in a paused or throttled state. This feature is only available if the server is spawned from the `innd` daemon process (which it is not by default in Red Hat Linux). The default is false, as follows:

```
readerswhenstopped:     false
```

✦ The `readertrack` parameter can be used to enable a system that tracks client reading and posting of articles. Client tracking is off by default (false), as follows:

```
readertrack:            false
```

The INN server supports the feature of creating keyword databases from the body of news articles. For large feeds, this could cause a substantial performance hit on the INN server. Before you set any of these parameters, you should stop the INN server (`innd`) and remove the current overview database.

✦ The `keywords` parameter sets whether or not keyword generation should be done at all. By default, a keyword database is not generated based on the following line:

```
keywords:               false
```

✦ The `keyartlimit` parameter limits the maximum size of news articles for which keywords are added to the keyword database. The default is 100000, which represents about 100KB maximum size, as follows:

```
keyartlimit:            100000
```

✦ The `keylimit` parameter sets the maximum amount of space that can be used to store keyword data. The default value is 512 bytes. It that limit is exceeded, further keyword data is discarded. Here is the default value:

```
keylimit:               512
```

✦ The `keymaxwords` parameter indicates the maximum amount of keywords that can be used from any one article. The default value is 250 words. (Some words that are not significant, such as *the* or *and*, are not generated and will not be counted in reaching this maximum.)

keymaxwords: 250Posting parameters

Parameters in this section help define how programs that generate and accept postings behave. Many of these parameters relate particularly to how local postings are handled.

✦ The `addnntppostingdate` parameter indicates whether or not to add the following header to local posts: NNTP-Posting-Date. This is on (true) by default, as follows:

```
addnntppostingdate:     true
```

✦ The `addnntppostinghost` parameter indicates whether or not to add the following header to local posts: NNTP-Posting-Host. The information in this header is either the IP address or the fully-qualified domain name of the INNserver. This is on (true) by default, as follows:

```
addnntppostinghost:     true
```

✦ The `checkincludedtext` parameter restricts how much included text can appear in a news article that is posted from your server. Included text is text from an article the user is responding to (indicated by a > character) that is copied into the current article. By default, this parameter is set to false, so there is no restriction on included text. If you set it to true, however, less than half of the text in a message can contain include lines. Turning this parameter on can result in better performance by not allowing articles that simply repeat previously sent text. Here is an example of having this parameter turned on to restrict articles containing too much included text:

```
checkincludedtext: true
```

✦ The value of the `complaints` parameter can be set to define an e-mail address that is placed in the `X-Complaints-To:` line in articles that originate from your server. Newsgroup participants can use this e-mail address to complain about something your users did. If no value is set, your newsmaster e-mail address is used. Common e-mail addresses are `postmaster@domainname.com` or `abuse@domainname.com`. Here is an example:

```
complaints: abuse@handsonhistory.com
```

✦ The `fromhost` parameter can be used to indicate a domain name to use when the INN server constructs e-mail addresses. If there is no value set for `fromhost` (which is true by default), than the local host computer's fully-qualified domain name is used.

✦ To limit the size of locally posted articles that your news server accepts, use the `localmaxartsize` parameter. The default is the same as for `maxartsize` (1,000,000 bytes). To set that value to half the default, use the following:

```
localmaxartsize:       500000
```

✦ The `moderatormailer` parameter sets the default machine containing aliases for moderated newsgroups. By default, the values in the `/etc/news/moderators` file are used to identify the list of all public moderated news-groups as being available from `moderators.isc.org`, with the newsgroup name prepended (`*.%s@moderators.isc.org`). No value is entered for this parameter by default.

✦ The `nnrpdauthsender` parameter indicates whether or not a Sender header is generated after the reader is authenticated. The Sender header would contain the reader's host name and authenticated user name. By default, this parameter is off (false) as shown here:

```
nnrpdauthsender:       false
```

✦ If the `nnrpdposthost` parameter is set to a host name, all locally posted articles are sent to that host instead of being saved locally. This parameter must be set if `xrefslave` is true. By default, there is no value set for this parameter.

✦ If your INN server is being used as a slave server, the `nnrpdpostport` parameter can be set to indicate which port on the master server to connect to. This parameter is only valid if the xrefslave and nnrpdposthost parameters are set. The default port value is 119, as shown in the following line:

```
nnrpdpostport:          119
```

✦ The spoolfirst parameter can be used to cause articles to be spooled instead of having them sent to the INN server daemon. The default (false) is to only spool articles when an error is received from sending an article to the INN server daemon. This is how the default value is set:

```
spoolfirst:          false
```

✦ The strippostcc parameter can be used to cause To, Cc, and Bcc lines to be removed from locally posted articles. The default is to not strip them out (false), as indicated by the following line:

```
strippostcc:          false
```

Posting exponential backoff parameters

A set of backoff parameters is used to control high-volume news posters. This feature works by indexing news clients by either user name or IP number. After the number of posts from the user or IP number reaches the limit set for the time period you set, *posting backoff* occurs, which is when your server sleeps for a period of time before posting anything. In this way, posts get through at an increasingly slower rate.

The backoff feature is off by default. To turn it on, you need to set the backoffauth parameter to true. The time between postings is used to determine the sleep time. By default, no location is defined for storing backoff information. A common place to put the database of backoff information is in /var/lib/news/backoff (set by backoffdb parameter).

The backoffk parameter lets you set how sleep time is multiplied. If it were set to 3, the sleep time will triple the sleep time for each subsequent post. The backoffpostfast can be used to increase the backoff sleep time when posts from the same identity arrive in less than the backoff time. The backoffpostslow parameter, by default, allows up to 86,400 postings from the same identity (because it is set to 1). Divide 86,400 by the value of backoffpostslow to allow fewer posts per day.

The number of postings that are allowed before the backoff feature kicks in is set to 10,000 by the backofftrigger parameter. The following lines are examples of the default settings for the set of backoff commands.

```
backoffauth:          false
backoffdb:
backoffk:             1
backoffpostfast:      0
backoffpostslow:      1
backofftrigger:       10000
```

Monitoring parameters

The `innwatch` program can be set up to log INN server activities. The `doinnwatch` parameter indicates whether or not to have the innwatch program started from the `/etc/rc.news` script (which starts automatically when the `innd` script starts the INN server at boot time). The logging service is off (false) by default.

Other monitoring-related parameters set thresholds for a variety of INN server attributes that the monitoring service looks out for. These include watching for free space running out in the batch (`innwatchbatchspace`) and database (`innwatchlibspace`) directories. The `innwatchloload` and `innwatchhiload` sets the range of load average, which causes the INN server daemon to be throttled. The following lines contain the default parameters that relate to monitoring:

```
doinnwatch:            false
innwatchbatchspace:    800
innwatchlibspace:      25000
innwatchloload:        1000
innwatchhiload:        2000
```

For other parameters that relate to monitoring INN server resources, refer to the `inn.conf` man page.

Logging parameters

Several parameters in the `inn.conf` file can be used to change what information is logged and how it is logged. News log information is written to log files in a directory set by the `pathlog` parameter. By default, the `pathlog` parameter is set to `/var/log/news`.

✦ The `docnfsstat` parameter lets you turn on or off the cnfsstat program. Cnfsstat monitors the usage of cycbuffs if you are using the Cyclic News File System to store your news articles. The parameter is off (false) by default.

```
docnfsstat:      false
```

✦ To have the size of an article written to the log file, set the `logartsize` parameter to true. By default, `logartsize` is on, as follows:

```
logartsize:      true
```

✦ Use the `logcancelcomm` parameter to log `ctlinnd cancel` commands to syslog. This parameter is off by default, as follows:

```
logcancelcomm:   false
```

✦ To set the number of logs that news.daily keeps before it overwrites them, set the `logcycles` parameter. By default, this number is set to 3, as follows:

```
logcycles        3
```

✦ Use the `logippadr` parameter to have the IP address of the host logged for a received article. By default, this is on, as follows:

```
logipaddr:       true
```

✦ If you want the site names for received articles to be put in the article log file, the `logsitename` parameter should be on. By default, it is on, as follows:

```
logsitename:      true
```

✦ To have overview statistics related to the `nnrpd` daemon process logged to syslog, turn on the `nnrpdoverstats` parameters. By default, this parameter is off, as follows:

```
nnrpdoverstats:   false
```

✦ The `nntpactsync` parameter sets the number of articles that can come on an incoming channel before the activity is logged. The default value is 200 articles, as follows:

```
nntpactsync:         200
```

✦ The `nntplinklog` parameter indicates whether or not to place accepted articles' storage API token. By default, this parameter is not on (false).

```
nntplinklog:         false
```

✦ To enable status monitoring, you need to turn on the `status` parameter by setting the value to a number. By default, this parameter is off (0). To have it turned on, set the value to the number of seconds between which status monitoring statistics are logged. You could set the value to 600 seconds as follows:

```
status:           600
```

✦ To enable performance monitoring, you need to turn on the `timer` parameter. By default, `timer` is off (0). To have it turned on, set the value to the number of seconds between which performance statistics are logged. You could set the value to 600 seconds as follows:

```
timer:         600
```

System tuning parameters

A set of low-level tuning parameters is available for tuning your INN server. In most cases, you shouldn't need to change these parameters. These parameters include: `badiocount`, `blockbackoff`, `chaninacttime`, `chanretrytime`, `icdsynccount`, `maxforks`, `nicekids`, `nicenewnews`, `nicennrpd`, `pauseretrytime`, `peertimeout`, and `rlimitnofile`. If you are interested in learning more about the INN system tuning parameters, refer to the `inn.conf` man page.

News directory parameters

The `inn.conf` file sets the location of directories that contain newsgroup information. Although you shouldn't have a need to change these locations, knowing where they are can be useful. The following text is taken from the `inn.conf` file, to show where the different news directories are located:

```
# Paths
patharchive:          /var/spool/news/archive
patharticles:         /var/spool/news/articles
```

```
pathbin:                /usr/bin
pathcontrol:            /usr/bin/control
pathdb:                 /var/lib/news
pathetc:                /etc/news
pathfilter:             /usr/bin/filter
pathhttp:               /var/log/news
pathincoming:           /var/spool/news/incoming
pathlog:                /var/log/news
pathoutgoing:           /var/spool/news/outgoing
pathoverview:           /var/spool/news/overview
pathrun:                /var/run/news
pathspool:              /var/spool/news
pathtmp:                /var/lib/news/tmp
```

Setting Up News Feeds

For the flow of news articles to take place, news servers need to know about each other and need to be willing to exchange articles. The /etc/news/incoming.conf file lists the host computers that you allow to connect to feed your news. You use the /etc/news/newsfeeds file to set up where your news articles should be sent. You have to set up both of these files.

Configuring hosts to feed you

To configure the host computers that feed articles to your news server, you need to configure the /etc/news/incoming.conf file. In this file, you can set various key/value parameters that affect how these news feeds behave. Other entries are either peer entries or group entries.

The key/value entries set values that are assigned to every peer and group entry. Those values can be overridden for particular peers or groups by adding new key/value entries within peer and group entries. Peer entries identify the FQDN of a computer that can feed news to your server, along with any key/value entries. Group entries are a way of assigning groups of peers to have particular key/value entries.

The whole thing seems a bit complicated when all you are doing is defining which hosts can send news to you and how they are allowed to do that. Here is an example of the contents of an incoming.conf file from its man page:

```
streaming:          true   # streaming allowed by default
max-connections:    8      # per feed

# A peer definition.
peer uunet {
    hostname: usenet1.uu.net
}
```

```
peer vixie {
     hostname: gw.home.vix.com
     max-connections: 10 # override global value.
}

# A group of two peers who can open more
# connections than normal
group fast-sites {
     max-connections: 15

     # Another peer. The ``max-connections'' value from the
     # ``fast-sites'' group scope is used.
     peer data.ramona.vix.com {
          hostname: data.ramona.vix.com
     }

     peer bb.home.vix.com {
          hostname: bb.home.vix.com
          max-connections: 20 # he can really cook.
     }
}
```

The only key/value pair in this example is `max-connections: 8`, which defines the maximum number of connections from any one host to be five (unless overridden in a peer or group value). Two individual hosts are defined as news feeders: uunet (usenet1.uu.net) and vixie (gw.home.vix.com). The vixie definition is an example of using a key/value pair to override a default value.

The group example is just a way to set key/value entries for several hosts at the same time. This example sets the maximum number of connections to 15 and assigns that value to all the peers in the group (`data.ramona.vix.com` and `bb.home.vix.com`). Then, as an illustration, that value is overridden for the second of those two hosts by setting the value to 20.

The hostname can be a full host.domain name or an IP address. As you have already seen, `max-connections` can set the maximum number of connections that are enabled at a time from a host (0 enables unlimited connections). Here are some key/values that you can set globally, for a particular peer, or within a group:

✦ **hostname:** Identifies the host.domain name or IP address of the news server.

✦ **streaming:** Defines whether streaming commands are enabled (true or false).

✦ **password:** Assigns a string to this key that must be used by the host as a password before it can connect. By default, no password is required.

✦ **noresendid:** Causes the innd daemon to send a 431 RESENDID response to an article that has already been received from another peer.

Configuring hosts that you feed

The entries that you place in the /etc/news/newsfeeds file define how the articles that your news server receives are fed to other news servers. This file offers a lot of opportunity for configuration. The main reason this file is so complex is that it enables you to select which newsgroup articles to forward to each news server (based primarily on what they will accept). You can also set up definitions that apply to groups of servers.

Note   Despite its name, a news feed doesn't actually feed news articles to another site. It simply reports that an article is available to be transferred to the other news server.

Within the entries in the newsfeeds file, certain wildcard characters can be used to match or exclude whole sets of newsgroups. You can probably figure out how they work in the context of the examples. If not, however, you can refer to the "Understanding Wildmat Characters" sidebar for information on using the wildcard characters.

The default /etc/news/newsfeeds file has only an ME parameter entry in it (and a lot of comments). The ME entry is required; you can have only one of them in your newsfeeds file, and it must appear before any other newsfeed lines. This entry contains a subscription list that is automatically added first to the subscription list of every other entry. Here is the default ME line:

```
ME:!*/!local,!collabra-internal::
```

This default ME line specifically indicates some articles that are note forwarded. This line causes all incoming articles with local or collabra-internal in the Path header to be rejected. Articles that come in with either of those headers indicate that they are coming from a mis-configured server.

Note   The ME subscription entry defines only the subscription lists that you feed. It has nothing to do with the newsgroups that you receive. Newsgroups that you receive are defined in the active list. See the active(5) man page.

The following is an example of an ME entry that includes additional restrictions:

```
ME\
:*,@alt.binaries.warez.*,!junk,!control*,!local*,!foo.*\
/world,usa,na,gnu,bionet,pubnet,u3b,eunet,vmsnet,inet,ddn,k12\
::
```

With this entry, all newsgroups are propagated to every server, with the exception of junk, control, local, and foo groups. The exclamation mark indicates that the name that follows is to be excluded.

Understanding Wildmat Characters

When you need to identify newsgroups in your newsfeeds configuration file, you can use several different wildcard characters to simplify the process. These characters are defined on the wildmat man page (type `man wildmat`). Here is what they do:

✦ **!**: The exclamation point is used to indicate that the newsgroup name that follows should not be matched.

✦ *****: An asterisk at the end of a newsgroup name indicates that all newsgroups following the one shown (those lower in the hierarchy) should be matched.

✦ **[abc]**: Any single character surrounded by the brackets is matched. For example, [abc]* matches any group name that begins with a, b, or c. You can also specify number or letter ranges, such as 3–9 or a–r, with the braces to include all those numbers or letters.

✦ **?**: A question mark matches any single character. So, c?mp matches comp, camp, and a lot of stuff that makes no sense at all.

✦ **[^abc]**: When a ^ is placed at the beginning of a set of brackets, the letters in the pattern match any character that is not in the brackets. For example, [^abc]* matches any group that does not begin with a, b, or c.

With the ME line set, you can go about defining how your specific newsfeeds are done. Here is an example of an innfeed line you can add to your `newsfeeds` file. This example funnels all newsfeeds to the `startinfeed` command.

```
innfeed!:\
    !*\
    :Tc,Wnm*,S16384:/usr/bin/startinnfeed -y
```

This line runs the `startinnfeed` command to start the innfeed program. The innfeed program, in turn, carries out the actual transfer of news articles between the news servers.

Note   If you have used an earlier version of INN, you should note that the `overchan` and `crosspost` programs are no longer used. The functions they used to perform are now incorporated into the INN server. With `useoverchan` set in the `inn.conf`, you can still use `overchan`. However, `crosspost` is no longer supported.

After the ME and `innfeed!` entries, you need to add entries that define the actual news servers to which you will feed articles. You should have one entry for each news server that you feed. The general format of those entries is as follows:

```
remote-peer.domain.com/name-in-header.domain.com\
    :newsgroup-list\
    :Tm:innfeed!
```

You need to replace *remote-peer.domain.com* with the FQDN of the server that you are feeding the news to. Next, replace the *name-in-header* with any alias names that the remote news server uses. The aliases are names that the remote news server puts in the Path header of the articles it forwards. (If no aliases exist, leave off the entire */name-in-header* part.) You need to enter a newsgroup-list only if you want to feed newsgroups that are different from the newsgroups that are set by default (in your ME entry). The last part of the entry (:Tm:innfeed!) should be left as it is.

If your server has the controlchan feature turned on (usecontrolchan: true in the inn.conf file), you should create an entry for the controlchan program in the newsfeeds file. This entry is meant to reduce the load if, in a short period of time, many control messages arrive at your news server. This entry runs the /usr/bin/controlchan command.

```
controlchan!\
        :!*,control,control.*,!control.cancel\
        :Tc,Wnsm:/usr/bin/controlchan
```

You can use a mind-numbing number of options within the newsfeeds file. If you are interested in delving deeper, read the comments in the newsfeeds file and refer to the newsfeeds manual page (type **man newsfeeds**). That manual page will also point you to related man pages.

Getting a list of active newsgroups

The Internet Software Consortium (www.isc.org) maintains a listing of all officially active newsgroups. ISC stores these newsgroups in two different files: newsgroups and active. The newsgroups file contains each newsgroup name and a short description of the newsgroup. The active file stores the newsgroups to indicate which newsgroups your computer will offer.

You can download the latest copies of the active and newsgroups files from the ISC FTP server: ftp://ftp.isc.org/pub/usenet/CONFIG/. From that directory, you can download either uncompressed versions of those files (each is more than 1MB in size) or compressed versions. Choose the active.gz and newsgroups.gz files, which you can uncompress in Red Hat Linux by using the gunzip command (gunzip active.gz newsgroup.gz).

Place both the active and newsgroups files in your /etc/news directory. The newsgroups file provides the names and descriptions of the newsgroups offered to the users of your news server. The active file is the official list of newsgroups that is read by the innd daemon so that it knows what newsgroups it should accept articles for. You can edit the active file manually.

Choosing How Articles Are Stored

Traditionally, news servers have stored newsgroup articles in a very simple format. In the news spool directory (such as `/var/spool/news`), each article was stored under a subdirectory named after the newsgroup. For example, articles for the comp.os.linux.x newsgroup would be stored in the directory `comp/os/linux/x` in the news spool directory. Each article would be named by its unique message number and placed in that directory.

Unfortunately, the traditional way of storing news articles has become quite inefficient, given the huge volume of newsgroup articles these days. In addition to the traditional method, the INN news server offers the following other methods for storing newsgroup articles:

✦ **timehash:** Articles are stored in directories based on when they arrive. This method makes it easier to control how long articles are kept and prevents any directory from containing too many files.

In the default news directory (`/var/spool/news`), the `timehash` method of storage creates directories based on the time articles are received. A time-hash directory is in the form time-*xx/bb/cc/yyy-aadd*. Here, *xx* is a hexadecimal value of the storage class, and *yyyy* is a hexadecimal value of a sequence number. The other values represent the arrival time.

✦ **cnfs:** Articles are stored in buffer files that are configured before articles arrive. In this arrangement, when a new article arrives and the buffer is full, the new article replaces the oldest article. This is referred to as *cyclical storage*.

When buffers are used instead of the file system, articles can be stored and served much faster. The downside to this method is that, because articles are overwritten automatically after the buffer limit is reached, it is harder to enforce a policy that retains articles for a set period of time. This method also requires more upfront configuration.

✦ **timecaf:** Lots of articles are stored in a single file with this storage method. This method can be about four times faster than the `timehash` method, though it gives you less control over the article spool. Because this method is relatively new, it has not been as well tested as other methods. Like `timehash`, the arrival time is used to name the files where articles are stored.

✦ **tradspool:** This is the original storage method for INN, where each article is stored as a separate file in a directory structure that is named after its newsgroup. While this method makes it easy to access articles on the news server, it has become ineffective for handling the volume of news that today's news servers need to handle.

✦ **trash:** This method is only used for testing and for discarding articles based on your particular storage method. You cannot retrieve articles that have been assigned to the `trash` storage method.

Activating different storage methods

Storage methods used for your INN server are set in the `/etc/news/storage.conf` file. You can activate the `timehash`, `cnfs`, `timecaf`, `tradspool`, or `trash` storage methods by creating method entries in the `storage.conf` file. You can also assign different newsgroups and other attributes to different methods. (After this file is configured, no additional configuration file setup is needed for the `timehash` method; however, the `cnfs` method requires that you set up a `cycbuff.conf` file.)

 Note   The `storage.conf` file replaces the now-obsolete `storage.ctl` file used for the same function in earlier releases.

The format of a `storage.conf` file entry is as follows:

```
method <methodname> {
     class: <storage class number>
     newsgroup: <wildmat>
     size: <minsize> [,<maxsize>]
     expires: <mintime>[,<maxtime>]
     options: <options>
}
```

For each method name (`timehash`, `cnfs`, `timecaf`, `tradspool`, or `trash`), define the newsgroup(s) that applies to the method. Wildcard characters (*, ?, and so on) that can be used are described in the "Understanding Wildmat Characters" sidebar, earlier in this chapter. The `optional` class value can be assigned a number (0, 1, and so on) that matches an entry in the `expire.ctl` file where article expiration times are stored. The optional size value determines the minimum and maximum size an article can be. (A 0 as `maxsize` places no limits on article size.) The optional `expires` value determines the storage class based on the Expires: headers in the article. The `options` value (which is itself optional) can be used to set options that are specific to a method.

Using the timehash storage method

The `timehash` storage method stores newsgroup articles based on when your news server receives them. The following `timehash` method entry examples are contained in the `storage.conf` file itself. You can uncomment and modify these entries to create your own entries:

```
method timehash {
     newsgroups: *
     class: 0
}
method timehash {
     newsgroups: alt.binaries.*
     class: 1
     size: 2,32000
}
```

```
method timehash {
        newsgroups: alt.*
        class: 2
        size: 1
}
```

The first `timehash` entry matches all newsgroups that come in (*). The class number basically identifies a class that matches expiration time settings for newsgroups that are stored with the entry. (See the description of `expire.ctl` in "Setting Up Expiration Times," later in the chapter, for information on how each class is defined.) The second `timehash` entry assigns a class (1) and size (2-byte to 32,000-byte limit) on newsgroups below the alt.binaries hierarchy. The third `timehash` entry is an example of assigning a class (2) and a size (1 to an unlimited number of characters) to all groups under the alt newsgroup hierarchy.

Using the cnfs storage method

The `cnfs` newsgroup storage method is an efficient way to rotate out newsgroup articles based on how many articles have been received (rather than just when they were received). Although this method is more complicated to configure, it is a good way to manage the size of your incoming news article database.

> **Tip** The INN installation instructions recommend the `cnfs` method of storing articles if you have a full news feed. This method is much more efficient than the `timehash` storage method for managing the volume of news that must be handled nowadays.

Here are some examples of `cnfs` method entries from the `storage.conf` file. You can uncomment and modify these entries to suit your configuration:

```
method cnfs {
        newsgroups: *
        class: 1
        size: 0,3999
        expires 4d1s
        options: FAQS
}
method cnfs {
        newsgroups: *
        class: 2
        size: 0,3999
        expires: 0s,4d
        options: SMALLAREA
}
method cnfs {
        newsgroups: *
        class: 3
        size: 4000,1000000
        options: BIGAREA
}
```

Notice that each of the `cnfs` storage methods in these examples applies to all newsgroups. Articles are stored in different buffers based on their class and size. The values in each of the `options` fields need to match entries in the `cycbuff.conf` file, as shown in the following section.

Assigning buffers for cnfs storage

Newsgroup articles are cycled out of your news server, for appropriate storage methods, based on the contents of the `/etc/news/cycbuff.conf` file. Here are some entries from the `cycbuff.conf` file that define the buffers used for the methods previously described:

```
# The order of lines in this file is not important among the same item.
# But all cycbuff items should be presented before any metacycbuff item.


    # 1. Cyclic buffers

    cycbuff:ONE:/export/cycbuffs/one:512000
    cycbuff:TWO:/export/cycbuffs/two:512000
    cycbuff:THREE:/export/cycbuffs/three:512000

    # 2. Meta-cyclic buffers

    metacycbuff:BIGAREA:ONE,TWO
    metacycbuff:SMALLAREA:THREE
```

In the `cycbuff.conf` file, all cyclic buffers (`cycbuff`) entries should appear before metacyclic buffers (`metacycbuff`). The second field of a cycbuff entry identifies the buffer's name. In this example, the three buffer entries are named ONE, TWO, and THREE, respectively. (Each buffer name is later assigned to a `metacyclic` buffer.) The third field in each cycbuff field is the filename that identifies the path to the buffer file. The last field is the size of the buffer in kilobytes (1K equals 1024 bytes).

In the metacycbuff entries, the second field contains the symbolic names of the `metacyclic` buffers (which are used in the options entries of the `storage.conf` file). The third field in each entry then assigns cycbuff entries to each metacyclic class.

You can also add optional entries to this file, such as the following, to affect how buffering is done:

✦ `cycbuffupdate`: Reflects how many articles are stored between header updates. The default value is 25.

✦ `refreshinterval`: Reflects the number of seconds between the time a cycbuff header is read and the time it is reread. The default value is 30.

Creating buffers for cnfs storage

You can use the dd command to create a big file that exists on top of your regular file system. Here is an example of the dd command for creating a buffer file:

```
dd if=/dev/zero of=/var/spool/news/articles/cycbuff bs=32k count=N
```

In this example, *N* would be replaced with the size of the buffer that you want, divided by 32.

The news user and newsgroup must be assigned ownership of the buffer file you create. The permission mode should be 0664 or 0660. For example:

```
chown news /var/spool/news/articles/cycbuff
chgrp news /var/spool/news/articles/cycbuff
chmod 0664 /var/spool/news/articles/cycbuff
```

Setting Up Expiration Times

Expiration times for news articles are set in the /etc/news/expire.ctl file. Existing entries in that file can be used as your default expiration times. With the remember entry, an article (even if it is expired) is remembered for 10 days. In this way, if the article is offered from another news feed, you can accept it. Here is the remember entry included in expire.ctl:

```
/remember/:10
```

If you want the Expires: headers to work, leave the following entry in your expire.ctl file:

```
*:A:1:10:never
```

Some groups are good to keep around forever. Here are two lines in the expire.ctl file that keep articles around longer for all newsgroups that end in .answers and all that begin with news.announce:

```
*.answers:M:1:35:90
news.announce.*:M:1:35:90
```

Three different formats exist for entries in the expire.ctl file. The first format is represented by the /remember/ entry shown previously. The next is an entry for defining the expiration times associated with classes that are set in the storage.conf file. The other format contains five colon-separated fields that assign expiration to particular groups. Here are examples of the latter two formats:

```
classnumber:keep:default:purge
newsgroups:modflag:keep:default:purge
```

The following are descriptions of each of the fields:

✦ *classnumber*: A number (0, 1, and so on) that corresponds with a class that is identified in the `storage.conf` file.

✦ *newsgroups*: The first field specifies which newsgroups are assigned to this expiration rule. As usual, you can use wildmat characters to match news-groups. (Refer to the "Understanding Wildmat Characters" sidebar for details.)

✦ *modflag*: You can use the value in this field to further limit which groups are matched. The field should contain one of the following letters: M (moderated groups only), U (unmoderated groups only), A (all groups), X (removes the article). X results in every article that matches being deleted from every group that it is assigned to.

✦ *keep*: This field identifies how many days the article should be kept. The field should either contain a number or the word *never*. Articles are expired no sooner than the value set by keep.

✦ *default*: This field specifies the default value (in days). If an Expires: value is less than the default value, the default value is used. If the Expires: value is greater than the default, then the Expires: value is also honored.

✦ *purge*: This field identifies the outside boundary, in days, for how long articles should be kept. This boundary allows articles with Expires: headers to be accepted. If an article has an Expires: value that is longer than this purge value, the article is discarded at the time specified by purge.

Tip   Add your default newsgroups first. The *expire* rule that will be used is the last one that is matched.

The contents of this file are less valuable for the `cnfs` storage method, because articles are cycled out when the buffer is full. The `cnfs` storage method therefore makes it difficult to control precisely when articles are purged.

Allowing Users to Access Your Server

As the INN software is delivered, your server will enable anyone with a login to your local host to access (or read) the news server. Requests from all other host computers are denied. To carry this out, the contents of the `/etc/news/readers.conf` file are set as follows:

```
auth "localhost" {
    hosts: "localhost, 127.0.0.1, stdin"
    default: "<localhost>"
}
```

```
access "localhost" {
    users: "<localhost>"
    newsgroups: "*"
    access: RPA
}
```

In the above lines, the auth definition defines the localhost identity as including reader connections that come from different interfaces on the local computer. Access given to users from the localhost identity for all newsgroups consists of the ability to read articles (R), post articles (P), and post articles for moderated newsgroups (A).

You can add access definitions to allow access to your INN server from other host computers. For example, if you wanted to add access to your INN server from all users from computers in the handsonhistory.com domain, you could use the following code:

```
auth handson {
    hosts: "*.handsonhistory.com, handsonhistory.com"
    default: "<LOCAL>"
}
access handson {
    newsgroups: "*"
    access: RPA
}
```

In this example, the handson identity consists of all hosts in the handsonhistory. com domain. As with the localhost example, access is granted to all newsgroups for reading articles, posting articles, and posting articles to moderated newsgroups.

The access letters, shown below, each represent a different permission that is granted to the client hosts you are defining. Here are the available letters:

✦ R: Users from this host can retrieve articles.

✦ P: Users from this host can post articles.

✦ A: Users from this host can post articles to moderated newsgroups. (This includes any articles that have Approved headers.)

✦ N: Users from this host can use the NEWNEWS command, even if that means overriding the global settings (set by the allownewnews parameter in the inn.conf file, described earlier).

✦ L: Users from this host can post to groups that have prohibited local posting.

Summary

Setting up a news server can be a complex task. In general, it is a task that should be avoided for most organizations in which only a few users need to access news. (In this case, get access to your ISP's server if you can.) If, however, you decide that you want to go ahead and build your own news server, the InterNetNews (INN) package comes with Red Hat Linux and is ready to use.

Being the administrator of a news server requires that you perform several tasks. The most important file to configure is the `inn.conf` file (probably located in `/etc/news`). Many of the basic INN options are set up in that file. In addition to setting up `inn.conf`, you need to configure which hosts you get your news feed from and which hosts you feed your users' article to.

An initial task with INN is to choose and configure a storage method for the articles on your server. The traditional method is to store files in spool directories that are associated with each newsgroup. The `timehash` storage method enables you to gather news articles based on when they were received (making it easier to enforce policies on how long articles should be kept). The `cnfs` storage method lets you create buffer files and have them store the articles (rotating out articles when the buffers are full).

✦　　✦　　✦

Setting Up Boot Servers: DHCP and NIS

If your business, organization, or home network has more than a few computers, administering each computer individually can be difficult. Moving your network's domain name server can result in your having to change configuration files on every computer on the network. A new member in your organization could mean having to add a new user account to multiple computers.

Red Hat Linux offers several mechanisms for centrally configuring and distributing critical information associated with your network, its servers, and the people that use your computing resources. DHCP provides a means of dynamically configuring the IP addresses, network numbers, and server locations for the computers on your local network. NIS offers a means of distributing a variety of configuration files (containing such information as user accounts, passwords, and network addresses) to other Linux and UNIX systems on your network.

This chapter describes how to set up Red Hat Linux as a DHCP or NIS server. It then describes how to check that those services are working and tells how to set up client computers to use those services.

Using Dynamic Host Configuration Protocol

Setting up a Dynamic Host Configuration Protocol (DHCP) server allows you to centrally manage the addresses and other network information for client computers on your private network. With DHCP configured on your network, a client computer can simply indicate that it wants to use DHCP and the DHCP server can provide its IP address, network mask, DNS server, NetBIOS server, router (gateway), and other information needed to get up and running on the network.

With DHCP, you can greatly simplify initial network configuration that each client computer on your network needs to do. Later, as your network evolves, you can easily update that information, having changes automatically picked up by clients when they restart their network interfaces.

Assuming you have already set up the physical connections between your DHCP server and the client computers on your network (presumably an Ethernet LAN), the minimum you need to get the DHCP server working are:

✦ A configured `/etc/dhcpd.conf` file

✦ A running `dhcpd` server daemon (which can be started at boot time)

After the DHCP server is running, it broadcasts its availability as a DHCP server to the LAN. A client simply boots up (with a Ethernet network interface turned on and DHCP identified as its method of getting network addresses), and the information it needs to get up and running on the network is fed to it from the server.

The following sections describe how to set up your `/etc/dhcpd.conf` file, start the DHCP server, and configure DHCP clients.

Setting Up a DHCP Server

Configuring a DHCP server in Red Hat Linux consists primarily of setting up the `/etc/dhcpd.conf` file. The following sections describe how to configure your `dhcpd.conf` file.

Note   The `dhcpd.conf` file allows an extraordinary amount of flexibility. To see the full set of options and parameters you can set in that file, refer to the dhcp-options and dhcpd.conf man pages (type `man dhcp-options`).

Configuring the dhcpd.conf file

Let's say that you have a single pool of IP addresses that you want to distribute to a set of computers that are all on the same subnetwork. In other words, all the computers are connected to one hub (or a set of daisy-chained hubs). Here is an example of a simple `dhcpd.conf` file you could start with:

```
# A simple /etc/dhcpd.conf file.
default-lease-time 720;
max-lease-time 86400;
```

```
option subnet-mask 255.0.0.0;
option broadcast-address 10.255.255.255;
option routers 10.0.0.254;
option domain-name-servers 10.0.0.1, 10.0.0.2;
range 10.0.0.10 10.0.0.100;
```

In the previous example, the default lease time is two hours (720 seconds) and the maximum lease time is 24 hours (86400 seconds). These values set the boundaries in which a client can keep its IP address before the DHCP server tries to reclaim it.

The domain-name-servers option set above assumes that you have set up your own DNS servers on your LAN. These numbers may be replaced by IP addresses of DNS servers that you get from your ISP.

The remaining settings determine the information that is actually used by each client to configure its computer. Because the network number is 10, the subnetwork mask is 255.0.0.0, and the broadcast address is 10.255.255.255. The IP address of the computer on the subnetwork that is used to route data to other networks from the local LAN is 10.0.0.24. That address may represent a DSL modem or a Red Hat Linux system configured as a router between your LAN and the Internet.

The IP addresses that are dynamically assigned to clients are defined in the range declaration. In this case, numbers between 10.0.0.10 and 10.0.0.100 are assigned. The domain name servers, used to resolve names to IP addresses, are 10.0.0.1 and 10.0.0.2.

Expanding the dhcpd.conf file

As I note earlier, this is a very simple example that works well for a single network of client computers. Below are some examples of ways that you can expand your dhcpd.conf file.

✦ If you have multiple ranges of addresses on the same subnetwork, you can add multiple range options to a subnet declaration. Here is an example:

```
subnet 10.0.0.0 netmask 255.0.0.0 {
  range 10.0.0.10 10.0.0.100;
  range 10.0.0.200 10.0.0.250;
}
```

This example causes the DHCP server to assign IP addresses between the ranges of 0.0.10 and 0.0.100 and between 0.0.200 and 0.0.250 on network number 10.

✦ You can set fixed addresses for particular host computers. In particular, you would want to do this for your server computers so that their addresses don't change. One way to do this is based on the Ethernet hardware address of the server's Ethernet card. All information for that computer can be contained in a host definition, such as the following:

```
host pine {
    hardware ethernet 00:04:5A:4F:8E:47;
    fixed-address 10.0.0.254;
}
```

Here, when the DHCP server encounters the Ethernet address, the fixed-address (10.0.0.254) is assigned to it. Type **ifconfig -a** on the server computer to see the address of its Ethernet hardware (while the interface is up). Within this host definition, you can add other options as well. For example, you could set the location of different routes (`routers` option).

✦ Many of the options let you define the locations of various server types. These options can be set globally or within particular host or subnet definitions. For example:

```
option netbios-name-servers 10.0.0.252;
option time-servers 10.0.0.253;
```

In these examples, the `netbios-name-servers` option defines the location of the WINS server (if you are doing Windows file and print server sharing using Samba). The `time-servers` option sets the location of a time server on your network.

✦ The DHCP server can be used to provide the information an X Terminal or diskless workstation could use to boot up on the network. The following is an example of a definition you could use to start such a computer on your network:

```
host maple {
    filename "/dwboot/maple.nb";
    hardware ethernet 00:04:5A:4F:8E:47;
    fixed-address 10.0.0.150;
        }
```

In the previous example, the boot file used by the diskless workstation from the DHCP server is located at `/dwboot/maple.nb`. The hardware Ethernet value sets the address of the Ethernet card on the client. The client's IP address is set to 10.0.0.150. All of those lines are contained within a host definition, where the host name is defined as *maple*. (See the Thin Client heading in Table 23-2 for other options that may be useful for configuring Thin Clients.)

Adding options

There are dozens of options you can use in the `/etc/dhcpd.conf` file to pass information from the DHCP server to DHCP clients. Table 23-1 describes data types you can use for different options. Table 23-2 describes options that are available.

Table 23-1 Data Types	
Data Types	**Description**
ip-address	Enter *ip-address* as either an IP address number (11.111.111.11) or a fully-qualified domain name (comp1.handsonhistory.com). To use a domain name, the name must be resolvable to an IP address number.
int32, int16, int8, uint32, uint16, uint8	Used to represent signed and unsigned 32-, 16-, and 8-bit integers, respectively.
"string"	Enter a string of characters, surrounded by double quotes.
boolean	Enter true or false when a boolean value is required.
data-string	Enter a string of characters in quotes ("client1") or a hexadecimal series of octets (00:04:5A:4F:8E:47).

Options contain values that are passed from the DHCP server to clients. Although Table 23-2 lists valid options, the client computer will not be able to use every value you could potentially pass to it. In other words, not all options are appropriate in all cases.

Table 23-2 is divided into the following categories:

✦ **Names, Addresses, and Time:** These options set values that are used by clients to have their host name, domain name, network numbers, and time (offset from GMT) defined.

✦ **Servers and Routers:** These options are used to tell DHCP clients where on the network to find routers and servers. Though more than a dozen server types are listed, most often you will just indicate the address of the router and the DNS servers the client will use.

✦ **Routing:** These options indicate whether or not the client routes packets.

✦ **Thin Clients:** These options are useful if DHCP is being used as a boot server for thin clients. A thin client may be an X Terminal or diskless workstation that has processing power, but no disk (or a very small disk) so it can't store a boot image and a file system itself.

Table 23-2
DHCP Options

Options	Descriptions
Names, Addresses, and Time	
option host-name *string*;	Indicates the name that the client computer can use to identify itself. It can either be a simple host name (for example, *pine*) or a fully-qualified domain name (for example, *pine.handsonhistory.com*). You may use this in a host declaration, where a host computer is identified by an Ethernet address.
option domain-name *string*;	Identifies the default domain name the client should use to resolve DNS host names.
option *subnet-mask ip-address*;	Associates a subnetwork mask with an IP address. For example, option 255.0.0.0 10.0.0.1;.
option time-offset *int32*;	Indicates the offset (in seconds) from the Universal Time Coordinate (UTC). For example, a six-hour UTC offset is set as follows: option time-offset 21600;.
Servers and Routers	
option routers *ip-address* [, *ip-address*...];	Lists, in order of preference, one or more routers connected to the local subnetwork. The client may refer to this value as the gateway.
option domain-name-servers *ip-address* [, *ip-address*...];	Lists one or more Domain Name System (DNS) servers that the client can use to resolve names into IP addresses. List servers in the order in which they should be tried.
option time-servers *ip-address* [, *ip-address*...];	Lists, in order of preference, one or more time servers that can be used by the DHCP client.
option ien116-name-servers *ip-address* [, *ip-address*...];	Lists, in order of preference, one or more IEN 116 name servers that can be used by the client.
option log-servers *ip-address* [, *ip-address*...];	Lists one or more MIT-LCS UDP log servers. List servers in the order in which they should be tried.
option cookie-servers *ip-address* [, *ip-address*...];	Lists one or more Quote of the Day (cookie) servers (see RFC 865). List servers in the order in which they should be tried.
option lpr-servers *ip-address* [, *ip-address*...];	Lists one or more line printer servers that are available. List servers in the order in which they should be tried.
option impress-servers *ip-address* [, *ip-address*...];	Lists one or more Imagen Impress image servers. List servers in the order in which they should be tried.

Options	Descriptions
Servers and Routers	
option resource-location-servers *ip-address* **[,** *ip-address...* **];**	Lists one or more Resource Location servers (RFC 887). List servers in the order in which they should be tried.
option nis-domain *string*;	Indicates the name of the NIS domain, if an NIS server is available to the client.
option nis-servers *ip-address* **[,** *ip-address...* **];**	Lists addresses of NIS servers available to the client, in order of preference.
option ntp-servers *ip-address* **[,** *ip-address...* **];**	Lists addresses of network time protocol servers, in order of preference.
option netbios-name-servers *ip-address* **[,** *ip-address...* **];**	Lists the addresses of WINS servers, used for NetBIOS name resolution (for Windows file and print sharing).
option netbios-dd-server *ip-address* **[,** *ip-address...* **];**	Lists the addresses of NetBIOS datagram distribution (NBDD) servers, in preference order.
option netbios-node-type *uint8*;	Contains a number (a single octet) that indicates how NetBIOS names are determined (used with NetBIOS over TCP/IP). Acceptable values include: 1 (broadcast: no WINS), 2 (peer: WINS only), 4 (mixed: broadcast, then WINS), 8 (hybrid: WINS, then broadcast).
option font-servers *ip-address* **[,** *ip-address...* **];**	Indicates the location of one or more X Window font servers that can be used by the client, listed in preference order.
option nisplus-domain *string*;	Indicates the NIS domain name for the NIS+ domain.
option nisplus-servers *ip-address* **[,** *ip-address...* **];**	Lists addresses of NIS+ servers available to the client, in order of preference.
option smtp-server *ip-address* **[,** *ip-address...* **];**	Lists addresses of SMTP servers available to the client, in order of preference.
option pop-server *ip-address* **[,** *ip-address...* **];**	Lists addresses of POP3 servers available to the client, in order of preference.
option nntp-server *ip-address* **[,** *ip-address...* **];**	Lists addresses of NNTP servers available to the client, in order of preference.
option www-server *ip-address* **[,** *ip-address...* **];**	Lists addresses of WWW servers available to the client, in order of preference.
option finger-server *ip-address* **[,** *ip-address...* **];**	Lists addresses of Finger servers available to the client, in order of preference.
option irc-server *ip-address* **[,** *ip-address...* **];**	Lists addresses of IRC servers available to the client, in order of preference.

Continued

Table 23-2 *(continued)*

Options	Descriptions
Routing	
option ip-forwarding *flag;*	Indicates whether the client should allow (1) or not allow (0) IP forwarding. This would be allowed if the client were acting as a router.
option non-local-source-routing *flag;*	Indicates whether or not the client should allow (1) or disallow (0) datagrams with nonlocal source routes to be forwarded.
option static-routes *ip-address ip-address [, ip-address ip-address...];*	Specifies static routes that the client should use to reach specific hosts. (List multiple routes to the same location in descending priority order.)
option router-discovery *flag;*	Indicates whether the client should try to discover routers (1) or not (0) using the router discovery mechanism.
option router-solicitation-address *ip-address;*	Indicates an address the client should use to transmit router solicitation requests.
Thin Clients	
option boot-size *uint16;*	Indicates the size of the default boot image (in 512-octet blocks) that the client computer uses to boot.
option merit-dump *string;*	Indicates where the core image should be dumped if the client crashes.
option swap-server *ip-address;*	Indicates where the client computer's swap server is located.
option root-path *string;*	Indicates the location (path name) of the root disk used by the client.
option tftp-server-name *string;*	Indicates the name of the TFTP server that the client should use to transfer the boot image. Used more often with DHCP clients than with BOOTP clients.
option bootfile-name *string;*	Indicates the location of the bootstrap file that is used to boot the client. Used more often with DHCP clients than with BOOTP clients.
option x-display-manager *ip-address [, ip-address...];*	Indicates the locations of X Window System Display Manager servers that the client can use, in order of preference.

Starting the DHCP server

After the /etc/dhcpd.conf file is configured, you can start the DHCP server immediately. As root user from a Terminal window, type the following:

```
# /etc/init.d/dhcpd start
```

Your DHCP server should now be available to distribute information to the computers on your LAN. If there are client computers on your LAN waiting on your DHCP server, their network interfaces should now be active.

If everything is working properly, you can have your DHCP server start automatically each time your computer boots by turning on the dhcpd service as follows:

```
# chkconfig dhcpd on
```

There are a few ways you can check that your DHCP server is working:

✦ Check the /var/lib/dhcp/dhcpd.leases file. If a client has successfully been assigned addresses from the DHCP server, a lease line should appear in that file. There should be one set of information for each client that has leased an IP address that looks like the following:

```
lease 10.0.0.100 {
        starts 2 2001/12/04 03:48:12;
        ends 2 2001/12/04 15:48:12;
        hardware ethernet 00:50:ba:d8:03:9e;
        client-hostname "pine:;
}
```

✦ Turn on the Ethereal window (from the GNOME menu, choose Programs ⇨ Internet ⇨ ethereal) and start capturing data (in promiscuous mode). Restart the DHCP server and restart the network interface on the client. You should see a series of DHCP packets that show a sequence that looks like the following: DHCP Offer, DHCP Discover, DHCP Offer, DHCP Request, and DHCP ACK.

✦ From the client computer, you should be able to start communicating on the network. If the client is a Linux system, type the ifconfig -a command. Your Ethernet interface (probably eth0) should appear, with the IP address set to the address assigned by the DHCP server.

When the server is running properly, you can continue to add DHCP clients to your network to draw on the pool of addresses you assign.

Setting Up a DHCP Client

Configuring a network client to get addresses from your DHCP server is fairly easy. Different types of operating systems, however, have different ways of using DHCP. Here are examples for setting up Windows and Red Hat Linux DHCP clients.

Windows:

1. From most Windows operating systems (Windows 95, 98, ME, and so on), you open the Network window from the Control Panel (Start ⇨ Settings ⇨ Control Panel).

2. From the Configuration tab, click the TCP/IP interface associated with your Ethernet card (something like TCP/IP-> 3Com EtherLink III).

3. Click Properties. The Properties window appears.

4. Click the IP Address tab and then select "Obtain an IP Address Automatically".

5. Click OK and reboot the computer so the client can pick up the new IP address.

Red Hat Linux:

1. While you are initially installing Red Hat Linux, click Configure using DHCP on the Network Configuration screen. Your network client should automatically pick up its IP address from your DHCP server when it starts up.

2. To set up DHCP after installation, open the Network Configuration window (neat command).

3. From the Network Configuration window:

   a. Click the Devices tab.

   b. Click on your Ethernet device (probably eth0).

   c. Click Edit.

   d. Click the Protocols tab.

   e. Click on TCP/IP.

   f. Select Edit.

4. From the TCP/IP settings window, click "Automatically Obtain IP Address Settings With:" and select dhcp. Then, from a Terminal window, type:

```
# /etc/init.d/network restart
```

By default, a Red Hat Linux client will not accept all information passed to it from the DHCP server. The way that the Red Hat Linux client handles DHCP server input is based on settings in the /etc/sysconfig/network-scripts/ifup script. If the client has DHCP turned on, when the system starts up networking, the ifup script runs the dhcpcd command in the following ways:

✦ If the dhcpcd client process is currently running, the dhcpcd command sends a signal to it so that it asks the DHCP server to renew the lease on the IP address.

✦ If no host name is currently set on the client, the -H option is passed to dhcpcd to indicate that it should accept the host name supplied by the DHCP server. (If the host name is already set, the client will not reset the host name from the server.)

✦ If your DNS servers are already configured in the `/etc/resolv.conf` file, then the `-R` option is passed to `dhcpcd` to prevent it from updating that file with new DNS server information. (This is prevented with `PEERDNS=no` in the `/etc/sysconfig/network` file.)

To change how the `dhcpcd` command works to accept information from the DHCP server, you can pass options to the `dhcpcd` command. Do this by adding arguments to the `DHCPCDARGS` variable in the `/etc/sysconfig/network` configuration file. (For example, `DHCPCDARGS="-d"` causes the `ifup` script to run `dhcpcd` in debug mode so that messages are sent to the `/var/log/messages` file.)

Understanding Network Information Service

Network Information Service (NIS) was created by Sun Microsystems as a way of managing information that is shared among a group of host computers on a network. Using NIS, computers can share a common set of user accounts, user groups, and TCP/IP hostnames, as well as other information.

Note   NIS was originally called Yellow Pages, but Sun had to change this name because it was trademarked. Some people still refer to NIS as YP, and many of the NIS commands (and even NIS package names) begin with the letters "yp."

The information you share with NIS comes from files that are used with UNIX systems and, therefore, compatible with other UNIX-like systems, such as Red Hat Linux. The group of computers that the master NIS server supports is referred to as an NIS domain. This domain is a defined set of host computers that may or may not be the same group of computers contained in a TCP/IP domain.

With NIS, an administrator creates information databases called *maps* from common UNIX (or Linux) system files. The NIS maps are created on the *master NIS server* and are accessible to other host computers from that server. Just in case the master server is down or inaccessible, one or more slave servers can be defined. The NIS slave servers contain copies of the NIS maps and can provide that information to client computers when the master is unavailable. However, NIS slave servers are not used to create the maps.

When the maps have been shared among the computers in the NIS domain, the main result is that all the computers share a common set of users and network configuration. The following is a list of files that are available for sharing by NIS (not all of them are set up for sharing by default).

✦ `/etc/group`—Defines the groups to which users on the computer belong.

✦ `/etc/passwd`—Defines the users who have accounts set up on the computer.

✦ `/etc/shadow`—Contains encrypted passwords for the users set up in the `/etc/passwd` file.

✦ /etc/gshadow—Contains encrypted passwords associated with groups contained in the /etc/groups file. (This file is optional and is usually not used.)

✦ /etc/passwd.adjunct—Secures password entries if your system doesn't use shadow passwords. (This file is used with SunOS systems.)

✦ /etc/aliases—Contains user aliases used with mail. It allows mail that is sent to a particular user name to be directed to a different user (or set of users). On some systems, this file may be /etc/mailaliases instead.

✦ /etc/ethers—Used by the RARP to map Ethernet addresses into IP numbers. This file is optional. (By default, RARP support is not configured into Red Hat Linux.)

✦ /etc/bootparams—Contains entries needed to start diskless workstations (typically used to boot Sun Microsystems diskless workstations).

✦ /etc/hosts—Contains the names and IP addresses of computers that can be reached on TCP/IP networks. (Often used to contain all the addresses for a private LAN, while Internet addresses would be determined from a DNS server.)

✦ /etc/networks—Used to attach a name to a network. In this way, you can refer to networks by name rather than by number.

✦ /etc/printcap—Contains printer definitions.

✦ /etc/protocols—Identifies numbers that are assigned to different Internet network protocols (such as IP, TCP, UDP, and others).

✦ /etc/publickey—Used on some UNIX systems to contain user names and associated public and private keys for secure networking in NFS and related features.

✦ /etc/rpc—Contains listings of supported Remote Procedure Call (rpc) protocols. These protocols are used with Sun Microsystems UNIX systems to allow requests for network services, such as NIS and others.

✦ /etc/services—Contains listings that identify port number and protocols for supported network services that are used with Internet protocols.

✦ /etc/netgroup—Used to define users (from particular hosts and domains) for permission-checking associated with remote mounts, remote shells, and remote logins.

✦ /etc/netid—Contains information that maps RPC network names to UNIX credentials.

Note   Some of the files just shown may not be applicable to your Red Hat Linux system. Don't worry if some of these files don't exist. In the course of setting up your system (adding users, configuring networks, and so on), you will set up the files you need.

Although these files are created in the /etc directory, the NIS administrator can copy these files to a different location and change them, so as not to share the master NIS server's original configuration files. Files can also be added to this list or removed from the list as the NIS administrator chooses. When an NIS client computer is configured, this configuration information can be obtained from the NIS master server.

Setting Up Red Hat Linux as an NIS Client

If your network uses NIS centrally to administer users, groups, network addresses, and other information, you can set up your Red Hat Linux system to use that information as an NIS client. To configure Red Hat Linux as an NIS client, you need to get the following information from your NIS administrator:

✦ **NIS Domain Name** — This is a keyword used to describe the group of hosts that use the common set of NIS files. Domain name is an unfortunate way of referring to this keyword, because it doesn't have anything to do with the TCP/IP domain name. Its only similarity is that it refers to a group of computers.

✦ **NIS Master Server Name** — This is the name of the computer on your network that maintains the NIS databases and responds to requests from the network for that information.

✦ **NIS Slave Server Names** — An NIS domain may have more than one NIS server that can handle requests for information from the domain's NIS database. An NIS slave server keeps copies of the NIS maps so that it can respond to requests if the master NIS server goes down. (NIS slave servers are optional.)

When you installed Red Hat Linux, if you knew that your network used NIS, you could have selected NIS as the way to handle user names and passwords on your computer. If you have not already configured NIS for your computer, the procedures that follow will describe how to do that. The procedures consist of defining your NIS domain name, setting up the /etc/yp.conf file, and configuring NIS client daemons (ypbind and ypwhich) to start when you boot your system.

Defining an NIS domain name

You can set your Red Hat Linux computer's NIS domain name using the domainname command. For example, if your NIS domain name were trident, you could set it by typing the following as the root user from the shell:

```
domainname trident
```

To verify that your NIS domain name is set, simply type `domainname` and you will see the name. Unfortunately, you're not done yet. Running `domainname` doesn't set the NIS domain name permanently. As soon as you reboot the computer, it is gone. (You can verify this by typing `domainname` again.)

To make the NIS domain name permanent, you need to have the `domainname` command run automatically each time your system boots. There are many ways to do this. What I did was add the command line (`domainname trident`) to a run-level script that runs before the ypbind daemon is started. I edited the `/etc/init.d/network` file and added the following lines just after the first set of comment lines (about line number 9).

```
# Set the NIS domain name.
domainname trident
```

This caused my NIS domain name to be set each time my Red Hat Linux system booted. When you add this entry, make sure you spell the NIS domain name properly (including upper- and lowercase letters). If you get it slightly wrong, you will see `ypbind` failure messages when you boot.

Caution   Be very careful editing a run-level script. Make a copy before you edit it. If you make a mistake editing one of these files, you could find yourself with a network or other essential service that doesn't work.

Setting up the /etc/yp.conf file

The ypbind daemon needs information about your NIS domain and NIS servers for it to work. That information is set up in your `/etc/yp.conf` file. The first entries define your NIS domain name and NIS servers. For example, if you had an NIS domain called trident and a master server called maple, you would have the following entry in your `/etc/yp.conf` file:

```
domain trident server maple
```

If you had other slave NIS servers named *oak* and *pine*, for example, you could also have the following entries:

```
domain trident server oak
domain trident server pine
```

You can also set your computer to broadcast to the local network for your NIS server. If your domain were named trident, for example, you would use the domain/broadcast option as follows:

```
domain trident broadcast
```

If the address of your NIS server is contained in your /etc/hosts file, you can specify that ypbind look in that file to find the server's IP address. For example, if your NIS master server is named maple, you would add the following entry:

```
ypserver maple
```

When ypbind starts, all the information in this file is read. It is then used to contact the appropriate NIS server.

Configuring NIS client daemons

After your NIS client information is all set up, all you need to do to run NIS as a client is start the ypbind and ypwhich daemons. The ypbind daemon runs continuously as two processes: The master ypbind process handles requests for information from your NIS server, and the slave ypbind process checks the bindings from time to time. The ypwhich daemon finds your NIS master server.

Getting these daemons running is pretty easy. You can set up an existing run-level script called ypbind to start automatically at boot time. To do this, you can run the following command (as root user from a Terminal window):

```
# chkconfig ypbind on
```

Alternatively, you can type the following commands (as root user) to link the ypbind run-level script so it starts at boot:

```
# ln -s /etc/init.d/ypbind /etc/rc3.d/S13ypbind
# ln -s /etc/init.d/ypbind /etc/rc5.d/S13ypbind
```

The results of the command lines are that the script to start the ypbind daemon at boot time is added to start at run levels 3 and 5, respectively.

 For more information on run-level scripts, refer to Chapter 12.

Checking that NIS is working

To check that your NIS client is communicating with your NIS master server, follow the instructions below.

 If your NIS server isn't configured yet, refer to the "Setting Up Red Hat Linux as an NIS Master Server" to configure your NIS server. Then return to this procedure to make sure that everything is working properly.

From the NIS client computer, type the following command to make sure that you are communicating with the NIS server:

```
# ypwhich
pine
```

The output shown above indicates that the NIS client is bound to the NIS server named *pine*. Next, check that the maps are being shared using the ypcat command. (To see what files are being shared from the NIS server, look in the server's /var/yp/*nisdomain* directory, where *nisdomain* is replaced by your NIS domain name.) Type one of the files shown in that directory along with the ypcat command. Here is an example:

```
# ypcat hosts
10.0.0.45      ash
10.0.0.46      pine
10.0.0.47      maple
```

If you are communicating with the NIS server and able to access map files, you can now define which maps the NIS client uses of those shared map files.

Using NIS maps

For the information being distributed by the NIS server to be used by the NIS client, you must configure the /etc/nsswitch.conf file to include nis in the search path for each file you want to use.

The following is a listing from the /etc/nsswitch.conf file showing valid values that can be in the search paths for accessing different configuration files.

```
# Legal entries are:
#
#    nisplus or nis+    Use NIS+ (NIS version 3)
#    nis or yp          Use NIS (NIS version 2), also called YP
#    dns                Use DNS (Domain Name Service)
#    files              Use the local files
#    db                 Use the local database (.db) files
#    compat             Use NIS on compat mode
#    hesiod             Use Hesiod for user lookups
#    [NOTFOUND=return]  Stop searching if not found so far
#
```

For our purposes, we want to add nis into the paths for the files we want to distribute from our NIS server to the NIS client. In most cases, the local files are checked first (files), followed by nisplus. The following are examples of how some entries appear:

```
passwd:     files nisplus
shadow:     files nisplus
```

```
group:         files nisplus
hosts:         files nisplus dns
```

For each of these entries, the original files are checked first (/etc/passwd, /etc/shadow, and so on). Then any nisplus server is checked. For host names, the DNS server is checked last. For our purposes, we can change nisplus to nis to access the maps being shared from the NIS server. The lines would then appear as follows:

```
passwd:        files nis
shadow:        files nis
group:         files nis
hosts:         files nis dns
```

As soon as the /etc/nsswitch file is changed, the data from the NIS maps are accessible. No need to restart the NIS service. You can now go through and change any of the files listed in the /etc/nsswitch file so that it is configured to let our system access the NIS maps being shared.

Setting Up Red Hat Linux as an NIS Master Server

To configure your Red Hat Linux system as an NIS master server, you should first configure it as an NIS client (That is, set the NIS domain name, set up /etc/yp.conf, and configure client daemons as described earlier.) Then you create the NIS maps and configure the NIS master server daemon processes (ypserv and rpc.yppasswdd). The next sections describe these procedures.

Creating NIS maps

To create NIS maps so that your Red Hat Linux system can be an NIS master server, start from the /var/yp directory from a Terminal window as root user. In that directory, a Makefile enables you to configure which files are being shared with NIS. The files that are shared by default are listed near the beginning of this chapter and within the Makefile itself.

Choosing files to map

If you don't want to share any file that is set up in the Makefile, you can prevent it from being built. Do this by finding the following line in the Makefile and simply adding a comment character in front of the file you want excluded:

```
all: passwd group hosts rpc services netid protocols mail \
        # netgrp shadow publickey networks ethers bootparams printcap \
        # amd.home auto.master auto.home auto.local passwd.adjunct \
        # timezone locale netmasks
```

You may notice that not all the names in the all: line represent the exact filename. For example, netgrp is for the /etc/netgroup file. The files that each name represents are listed a few lines below the all: line in the Makefile. You may also notice that many of the files are already commented out, including the shadow file.

> **Tip**   The NIS-HOWTO document suggests that using shadow passwords with NIS is "always a bad idea." Options in the Makefile (described in the next section) enable you to automatically merge the shadow and gshadow files into the passwd and group files, respectively.

Choosing mapping options

Within the Makefile, several options are set. You can choose to change these options or leave them as they are. Here are the options:

✦ B=—You can use the B= option to allow NIS to use the domain name resolver to find hosts that are not in the current domain. By default, B= is not set. To turn on this feature, set it to -b (B=-b).

✦ NOPUSH=true—When set to true (the default), the NOPUSH option prevents the maps from being pushed to a slave server. This implies that the NIS master server is the only server for the NIS domain. Set this to false, and place the hostnames of slave servers into the /var/yp/ypservers file if you do not want the NIS master to be the only server for the domain.

✦ MINUID=500—To prevent password entries from being distributed for administrative users, the MINUID is set to 500. This assumes that all regular user accounts on the system that you want to share have UIDs that are 500 or above.

✦ MINGID=500—To prevent password entries from being distributed for administrative groups, the MINGID is set to 500. This assumes that all regular groups that you want to share have GIDs that are 500 or above.

✦ MERGE_PASSWD=true—Keep this option set to true if you want each user's password to be merged from the shadow file back into the passwd file that is shared by NIS.

✦ MERGE_GROUP=true—Keep this option set to true if you want each group's password to be merged from the gshadow file back into the group file that is shared by NIS.

To build the NIS maps, your system must have the awk, make, and umask commands. In the Makefile, the locations of these commands are /usr/bin/gawk, /usr/bin/gmake, and umask, respectively. (The umask command is a shell built-in command, so you don't have to look for its location.) You can use comparable commands in different locations by changing the values of the AWK, MAKE, and UMASK variables in the Makefile.

Besides the options just mentioned, there are several variables you can set to change the location of NIS files. For example, the locations of password files (YPP-WDDIR) and other source files (YPSRCDIR) are both set to /etc by default. The location of YP commands (YPBINDIR) is set to /usr/lib/yp. If you want to change the values of these or other variables, you can do so in the Makefile.

Defining NIS client access

Add the IP addresses of the client computers that are allowed access to your NIS maps to the /var/yp/securenets file. By default, any computer on any network that can reach your NIS master can have access to your maps (which is not a secure situation). So, it is important that you configure this file. IP numbers can be given in the form of netmask/network pairs. For example:

```
255.0.0.0               10.0.0.0
```

This example enables access to your NIS master server maps from all computers on network number 10.

 See Chapter 15 for descriptions of IP addresses and netmasks.

Configuring access to maps

In the /etc/ypserv.conf file, you can define rules regarding which client host computers have access to which maps. You can also set several related options. Access rules in the ypserv.conf file have the following format:

```
host:map:security:mangle[:field]
```

Asterisks can replace *host* and *map* fields to create rules that match any host or map, respectively. The *host* is the IP address for the network or particular host for which the rule applies. The *map* is the name of the map for which you are defining access. The *security* is replaced by none (to always allow access), port (to allow access from a port less than port number 1024), deny (to deny access to this map), or des (to require DES authentication).

The *mangle* is replaced by yes or no (to indicate if a field in the map should be replaced by an x if a request comes from an unprivileged host). If the mangle is set to yes, *field* is replaced by the name of the field that should be mangled (the second field is used by default).

The following options can be set in the ypserv.conf file:

✦ dns — If yes (dns:yes), NIS will query the TCP/IP name server for hostnames when hostnames are not found in maps. By default, dns:no is set.

✦ xfr_check_port — If yes (xfr_check_port:yes), the NIS master server must run on a port that is less than port number 1024. If no, any port number may be used. By default, this is set to yes.

If you make changes to the /etc/ypserv.conf file, the ypserv daemon will pick up those changes the next time your system reboots. Alternatively, you can have ypserv read the contents of the file immediately by sending the ypserv process a SIGHUP signal. By default, the following line in /etc/ypserv.conf allows all hosts access to all maps:

```
* : * : none
```

Generate the NIS map database

To install and build the NIS database, run the ypinit command. To start the ypinit program, type the following:

```
# /usr/lib/yp/ypinit -m
```

The ypinit command should automatically choose your host name to use as an NIS server. After that, it asks you to add slave servers. Add one at a time; then press Ctrl+D after you have entered your last slave server. Verify that the list of NIS servers is correct (type **y**).

The database is built at this point. A new directory that has the name of your NIS domain is created in /var/yp. For example, if your NIS domain name is trident, the directory is /var/yp/trident. All maps built are then placed in that directory.

Adding NIS slave servers

In Red Hat Linux, NIS is configured to have a master NIS server and no slave NIS servers. You can allow your NIS maps to be pushed to one or more slave servers by setting NOPUSH=false in the /var/yp/Makefile file. After that, you need to add the names of the slave servers to your /var/yp/ypservers file. You can either add the hostnames manually or have them added automatically when you run the ypinit command later.

Configuring NIS server daemons

The NIS server must be running several daemon processes to be an NIS server. Red Hat Linux supplies several run-level scripts that you can configure to start NIS server daemon processes. These scripts, located in the /etc/init.d directory, include the following:

✦ ypserv — This script starts the ypserv (/usr/sbin/ypserv) daemon. It reads information from the /etc/ypserv.conf file to determine what to do. Then it listens for requests from NIS client computers on the network.

✦ yppasswdd—This script starts the rpc.yppasswdd
(/usr/sbin/rpc.yppasswdd) daemon. This daemon handles requests from
users on NIS client computers who want to change their user passwords.

Unless you requested that these scripts be configured to start at boot-time when
you installed Red Hat Linux, they will not start automatically. You can use the following chkconfig command to set ypserv and yppasswdd scripts to start automatically at boot time.

```
# chkconfig ypserv on
# chkconfig yppasswdd on
```

If you want to start the services immediately, you can type the following:

```
# /etc/init.d/ypserv start
# /etc/init.d/yppasswdd start
```

The NIS master server should be up and running. If there are any NIS slave servers,
you should configure them now.

Setting Up Red Hat Linux as an NIS Slave Server

To set up an NIS slave server, you must configure it as you do an NIS master server,
but with one exception: Instead of creating the NIS maps, you run the ypinit command so that the NIS maps can be copied from the server. The option that you give
to ypinit is the -s master option, where master is replaced by the name of your
NIS master server. Here is an example of running ypinit where the NIS master
server is named maple:

```
# /usr/lib/yp/ypinit -s maple
```

As long as the NIS slave server is allowed access, the maps should be copied to
your computer from the NIS master server. If the NIS master server goes down, this
slave computer should be able to handle NIS requests from the network.

At this point, you can return to the section on setting up NIS as a client to make
sure that your NIS server is running properly and distributing the maps to its
clients.

Summary

DHCP and NIS both provide mechanisms for centrally administering computers on your network. DHCP can provide information that helps client computers get up and running quickly on the network. NIS lets you distribute a wide range of configuration information among Linux and UNIX systems.

DHCP is used to provide information about your network to Windows, Linux, Mac, or other client computers on your network. IP addresses can be assigned *dynamically*, meaning they are distributed from a pool of IP addresses. Or specific addresses can be assigned to clients, based on specific Ethernet hardware addresses.

You can configure Red Hat Linux as an NIS client, an NIS master server, or an NIS slave server. An NIS client can take advantage of shared information from an NIS server. The NIS master server builds the databases of information (called maps) and enables access to those maps from the network. Optional NIS slave servers can be used to maintain copies of the NIS maps, enabling NIS service to continue on the network in the event that the NIS master server goes down.

✦　　✦　　✦

Setting Up a MySQL Database Server

MySQL is a popular structured query language (SQL) database server. Like other SQL servers, MySQL provides the means of accessing and managing SQL databases. However, MySQL also provides tools for creating database structures, as well as for adding, modifying and removing data from those structures. Because MySQL is a relational database, data can be stored and managed in small, manageable tables. Those tables can be used in combination to create flexible yet complex data structures.

A Swedish company called MySQL AB is responsible for developing MySQL (www.mysql.com). MySQL AB has released MySQL as an Open Source product, gaining revenue by offering a variety of MySQL support packages. The company also supports several application programming interfaces (APIs) to help application developers and Web content creators to access MySQL content.

Because MySQL is an Open Source product, it has been ported to several different operating systems (primarily UNIX and Linux systems, though there are Windows versions as well). As you may have guessed, these include binary versions of MySQL that run on Red Hat Linux. This chapter contains descriptions of and procedures for the version of MySQL that is contained in the Red Hat Linux distribution.

Finding MySQL Packages

To use MySQL in Red Hat Linux, there are several software packages you can install. You need at least the mysql and mysql-server packages installed to set up MySQL using the procedures described in this chapter. The following MySQL packages come with the Red Hat Linux distribution:

✦ **mysql** — This software package contains a lot of MySQL client programs (in /usr/bin), several client shared libraries, the default MySQL configuration file (/etc/my.cnf), a few sample configuration files, general SQL files to support different languages and documentation.

✦ **mysql-server** — This software package contains the MySQL server daemon (mysqld) and the mysqld start-up script (/etc/init.d/mysqld). The package also creates various administrative files and directories needed to set up the MySQL databases.

✦ **mysqlclient** — This software package contains the MySQL C programming language library, which is required by applications that are written to that interface.

✦ **mysql-devel** — This software package contains libraries and header files required for developing MySQL applications.

✦ **mysqlclient9** — This software package is needed to run some MySQL applications written to earlier versions of Red Hat Linux.

✦ **php-mysql** — This software package contains a shared library that allow PHP applications to access MySQL databases.

In the current version of Red Hat Linux, these software packages are contained on CD #2. If those packages are not yet installed, you can install them as follows:

1. Insert the Red Hat Linux CD 2 into the CD-ROM drive.

2. If the CD does not mount automatically, type the following from a Terminal window as root user:

```
# mount /mnt/cdrom
```

3. Type the following to install the necessary mysql packages:

```
# rpm -i /mnt/cdrom/RedHat/RPMS/mysql*
```

At this point, you can begin configuring your MySQL database server.

Configuring the MySQL Server

Like most server software in Red Hat Linux, the MySQL server relies on a start-up script and a configuration file to provide the service. Server activities are logged to a file in the /var/log directory. There are also mysql user and group accounts for managing MySQL activities. The following sections describe how these components all work together.

Tip
For many of the steps described in this section, the MySQL server daemon must be running. Starting the server is described in detail later in this chapter. For the moment, you can start the server temporarily by typing the following:

```
# /etc/init.d/mysqld start
```

Using mysql user/group accounts

When the MySQL software is installed, it automatically creates a `mysql` user and a `mysql` group. These user and group accounts are assigned to MySQL files and activities. In this way, someone can manage the MySQL server without needing to have root permission for the computer.

The mysql user entry appears in the `/etc/password` file as follows:

```
mysql:x:27:27:MySQL Server:/var/lib/mysql:/bin/bash
```

The mysql entry just shown indicates that the UID and GID for the `mysql` user is 27. The text string identifying this user account is "MySQL Server." The home directory is `/var/lib/mysql` and the default shell used by the user is `/bin/bash`. The home directory identified will contain directories that hold each table of data you define for the MySQL server.

The group entry for `mysql` is even simpler. The following entry in the `/etc/group` file indicates that the `mysql` group has a group ID (GID) of 27.

```
mysql:x:27:
```

If you care to check the ownership of files associated with MySQL, you will see that most of these files have mysql assigned as the user account and group account that own each file. This allows daemon processes that are run by the mysql user to access the database files.

Adding administrative users

To administer MySQL, you need to create at least one administrative account. You can do this using the `mysqladmin` command. To add the root user as a MySQL administrator, login as the root user and type the following from a Terminal window:

```
# mysqladmin -u root password my47gmc
```

You want to enter your own password instead of the my47gmc shown above. After this command is run, the root user can run any of the MySQL administrative commands by typing the password when prompted.

If you happen to be logged in as another user when you want to use administrative privilege for a MySQL command, you can do that without re-logging in. Simply add the argument -u root to the command line of the MySQL command you are running. In other words, the Linux root user account has no connection to the MySQL root user account once the MySQL account is created. You would typically use different passwords for the two accounts.

Tip

To save yourself the trouble of typing in the password each time you run a MySQL client command, you can add a password option under the [client] group in one of the option files. The most secure way to do that is to create a .my.cnf file in the root user's home directory that contains the following lines (substituting your password for the last argument shown).[client]

    password=my47gmc

Setting MySQL options

You can set options that effect how the MySQL applications behave by using options files or command line arguments. The MySQL server (as well as other administrative tools) reads the following options files when it starts up (if those files exist):

✦ /etc/my.cnf — Contains global options read by mysqld (server daemon) and mysql.server (script to start the server daemon).

✦ /var/lib/mysql/my.cnf — Contains options that are intended primarily for the mysqld server daemon.

✦ -defaults-extra-file — You can identify a file on the command line that contains options to be used by the server. For example, the following command would cause the file /home/jim/my.cnf to be read for options after the global options and before the user-specific options:

    # mysqld --defaults-extra-file=/home/jim/my.cnf

✦ $HOME/.my.cnf — Contains user-specific options. (The $HOME refers to the user's home directory, such as /home/susyq.)

Table 24-1 shows the MySQL commands that read the options files (in the order shown in the previous bullet list) and use those options in their processing. Options are contained within groups that are identified by single words within brackets. Group names that are read by each command are also shown in the table.

Table 24-1
Option Groups Associated with MySQL Commands

Command	Description	Group names
mysqld (in /usr/libexec)	The MySQL server daemon.	[mysqld] [server]
mysql.server (in /usr/share/mysql)	Used as the start-up script to start and stop the MySQL daemon. (Red Hat Linux uses /etc/init.d/mysql instead.)	[mysql] [server] [mysql.server]
safe_mysqld	Run by the mysql start-up script to start the MySQL server.	[mysql] [server] [mysql.server]
mysql	Offers a text-based interface for displaying and working with MySQL databases.	[mysql] [client]
mysqladmin	Used to create and maintain MySQL databases.	[mysqladmin] [client]
isamchk	Used to check, fix, and optimize ISAM databases (.ism suffix).	[isamchk]
myisamchk	Used to check, fix, and optimize MyISAM databases (.myi suffix).	[myisamchk]
pack_isam	Used to pack ISAM databases (.ism suffix).	[pack_isam]
myisampack	Used to compress MyISAM database tables	[myisampack]
mysqldump	Offers a text-based interface for backing up MySQL databases.	[mysqldump] [client]
mysqlimport	Loads plain-text data files into MySQL databases.	[mysqlimport] [client]
mysqlshow	Shows MySQL databases and tables you select.	[mysqlshow] [client]

Though you can use any of the options files to set your MySQL options, begin by configuring the /etc/my.cnf file. Later, if you want to override any of the values set in that file you can do so using the other options files or command-line arguments.

Creating the my.cnf configuration file

Global options that affect how the MySQL server and related client programs run are defined in the /etc/my.cnf file. The default my.cnf file contains only a few settings needed to get a small MySQL configuration going. The following is an example of the /etc/my.cnf file that comes with MySQL:

```
[mysqld]
datadir=/var/lib/mysql
socket=/var/lib/mysql/mysql.sock

[mysql.server]
user=mysql
basedir=/var/lib

[safe_mysqld]
err-log=/var/log/mysqld.log
pid-file=/var/run/mysqld/mysqld.pid
```

Most of the settings in the default my.cnf file define the locations of files and directories needed by the mysqld server. Each option is associated with a particular group, with each group identified by a name in square brackets. The above options are associated with the mysqld daemon ([mysqld]), the MySQL server ([mysql.server]), and the safe_mysqld script that starts the mysqld daemon ([safe_mysqld]). (See Table 24-1 for a list of these clients.)

The default datadir value indicates that /var/lib/mysql is the directory that stores the mysql databases you create. The socket option identifies /var/lib/mysql/mysql.sock as the socket that is used to create the MySQL communications end-point associated with the mysqld server. The basedir option identifies /var/lib as the base directory in which the mysql software is installed. The user option identifies mysql as the user account that has permission to do administration of the MySQL service.

The err-log and pid-file options tell the safe_mysqld script the locations of the error log (/var/log/mysqld.log) and the file that stores the process ID of the mysqld daemon when it is running (/var/run/mysqld/mysqld.pid). The safe_mysqld script actually starts the mysqld daemon from the mysqld start-up script.

Note   Each option that follows a group name is assigned to that group. Group assignments end when a new group begins or when the end of file is reached.

Choosing options

There are many values that are used by the MySQL server that are not explicitly defined in the my.cnf file. The easiest way to see which options are available for MySQL server and clients is to run each command with the –help option.

For example, to see available mysqld options (as well as other information) type the following from a Terminal window:

```
# /usr/libexec/mysqld --help | less
```

Another way to find what options are available is with the man command. For example, to see which options are available to set for the mysqld daemon, type the following:

```
man mysqld
```

It's quite likely that you can try out your MySQL database server without changing any options at all. However, after you set up you MySQL database server in a production environment, you will almost surely want to tune the server to match the way the server is used. For example, if it is a dedicated MySQL server, you will want to allow MySQL to consume more of the system resources than it would by default.

Below are a few examples of options additional options that you may want to set for your MySQL configuration:

✦ **password = *yourpwd*** — Adding this option to a [client] group in a user's $HOME/.my.cnf file allows the user to run MySQL client commands without having to enter a password each time. (Replace *yourpwd* with the user's password.)

✦ **port = #** — Defines the port number to which the MySQL service listens for MySQL requests. Replace # with the port number you want to use. By default, MySQL listens to port number 3306 on TCP and UDP protocols.

✦ **safe-mode** — Tells the server to skip some optimization steps when the server starts.

✦ **tmpdir = *path*** — Identifies a directory, other than the default /tmp, for MySQL to use for writing temporary files. Substitute a full path name for *path*.

In addition to the options you can set, MySQL clients also have a lot of variables that you can set. Variables set such things a buffer sizes, timeout values, and acceptable packet lengths. These variables are also listed on the –help output. To change a variable value, you use the –set-variable option, followed by the variable name and value. For example, to set the sort_buffer variable to 10MB, you could add the following option under your [mysqld] group:

```
[mysqld]
set-variable = sort_buffer=10M
```

The following is a list of other variables you could set for your server. In general, raising the values of these variables improves performance, but does consume more system resources. So you need to be careful raising this value on machines that are not dedicated to MySQL or that have limited memory resources.

Note For variables that require you to enter a size, indicate Megabytes using an M (e.g. 10M) or Kilobytes using a K (e.g. 256K).

✦ **key_buffer_size** = *size* — Sets the buffer size that is used for holding index blocks that are used by all threads. This is a key value to raise to improve MySQL performance.

✦ **max_allowed_packet** = *size* — Limits the maximum size of a single packet. Raise this limit if you require processing of very large columns.

✦ **myisam_sort_buffer_size** = *size* — Sets the buffer size used for sorting while repairing an index, creating an index, or altering a table.

✦ **record_buffer** = *size* — Sets the buffer size used for threads doing sequential scans. Each process doing a sequential scan allocates a buffer of the size set here.

✦ **sort_buffer** = **size** — Defines how much buffer size is allocated for each thread that needs to do a sort. Raising this value makes sorting threads go faster.

✦ **table_cache** = **#** — Limits the total number of tables that can be open at the same time for all threads. The number of this variable represents the total number of file descriptors that MySQL can have open at the same time.

✦ **thread_cache** = *size* — Sets the number of threads that are kept in cache, awaiting use by MySQL. When a thread is done being used, it is placed back in the cache. If all the threads are used, new threads must be created to service requests.

Checking options

In addition to seeing how options and variables are set in the options files, you can also view how all variables are set on your current system. You can view both the defaults and the current values being used by the MySQL server.

The –help command-line argument lets you see the options and variables as they are set for the server and for each MySQL client. Here is an example of the output showing this information for the `mysqld` server daemon:

```
# /var/libexec/mysqld --help
   .
   .
   .

The default values (after parsing the command line arguments) are:

basedir:      /usr/
datadir:      /var/lib/mysql/
tmpdir:       /tmp/
language:     /usr/share/mysql/english/
pid file:     /var/lib/mysql/maple.pid
TCP port:     3306
```

```
Unix socket: /var/lib/mysql/mysql.sock

system locking is not in use

Possible variables for option --set-variable (-O) are:
back_log                current value: 50
bdb_cache_size          current value: 8388600
bdb_log_buffer_size     current value: 0
bdb_max_lock            current value: 10000
bdb_lock_max            current value: 10000
binlog_cache_size       current value: 32768
connect_timeout         current value: 5
delayed_insert_timeout  current value: 300
delayed_insert_limit    current value: 100
delayed_queue_size      current value: 1000
flush_time              current value: 0
interactive_timeout     current value: 28800
join_buffer_size        current value: 131072
key_buffer_size         current value: 8388600
long_query_time         current value: 10
lower_case_table_names  current value: 0
max_allowed_packet      current value: 1048576
max_binlog_cache_size   current value: 4294967295
max_binlog_size         current value: 1073741824
max_connections         current value: 100
max_connect_errors      current value: 10
max_delayed_threads     current value: 20
max_heap_table_size     current value: 16777216
max_join_size           current value: 4294967295
max_sort_length         current value: 1024
max_tmp_tables          current value: 32
max_user_connections    current value: 0
max_write_lock_count    current value: 4294967295
myisam_sort_buffer_size current value: 8388608
net_buffer_length       current value: 16384
net_retry_count         current value: 10
net_read_timeout        current value: 30
net_write_timeout       current value: 60
open_files_limit        current value: 0
query_buffer_size       current value: 0
record_buffer           current value: 131072
slow_launch_time        current value: 2
sort_buffer             current value: 2097144
table_cache             current value: 64
thread_concurrency      current value: 10
thread_cache_size       current value: 0
tmp_table_size          current value: 1048576
thread_stack            current value: 65536
wait_timeout            current value: 28800
```

After the server is started, you can see the values that are actually in use by running the `mysqladmin` command with the `variables` option. (Pipe the output to the less command so you can page through the information.) Here is an example:

```
# mysqladmin variables | less
+------------------------+--------------------------------------------+
| Variable_name          | Value                                      |
+------------------------+--------------------------------------------+
| ansi_mode              | OFF                                        |
| back_log               | 50                                         |
| basedir                | /usr/                                      |
| bdb_cache_size         | 8388600                                    |
| bdb_log_buffer_size    | 32768                                      |
| bdb_home               | /var/lib/mysql/                            |
| bdb_max_lock           | 10000                                      |
| bdb_logdir             |                                            |
| bdb_shared_data        | OFF                                        |
| bdb_tmpdir             | /tmp/                                      |
                              .
                              .
                              .
| tmp_table_size         | 1048576                                    |
| tmpdir                 | /tmp/                                      |
| version                | 3.23.36                                    |
| wait_timeout           | 28800                                      |
+------------------------+--------------------------------------------+
```

If you decide that the option and variable settings that come with the default MySQL system don't exactly suit you, you don't have to start from scratch. Sample `my.cnf` files that come with the mysql package can let you begin with a set of options and variables that are closer to the ones you need.

Using sample my.cnf files

Sample `my.cnf` files are available in the `/usr/share/mysql` directory. To use one of these files, do the following:

1. Keep a copy of the old `my.cnf` file:

   `# mv /etc/my.cnf /etc/my.cnf.old`

2. Copy the sample `my.cnf` file you want to the `/etc/my.cnf` file. For example, to use the my-medium.cnf file, type the following:

   `# mv /usr/share/mysql/my-medium.cnf /etc/my.cnf`

3. Edit the new `/etc/my.cnf` file (as root user) using any text editor to further tune your MySQL variables and options.

The following paragraphs describe each of the sample `my.cnf` files:

my-small.cnf

This options file is recommended for computer systems that have less than 64MB of memory and are only used occasionally for MySQL. With this options file, MySQL won't be able to handle a lot of usage but it won't be a drag on the performance of your computer.

For the mysqld server buffer sizes are set low — only 64K for the sort_buffer and 16K for the key_buffer. The thread_stack is only set to 64K and net_buffer_length is only 2K. The table_cache is set to 4.

my-medium.cnf

As with the small options file, the my-medium.cnf file is intended for systems where MySQL is not the only important application running. This system also has a small amount of total memory available-between 32MB and 64MB-however more consistent MySQL use is expected.

The key_buffer_size is set to 16M in this file, while the sort_buffer value is raised to 512K for the mysqld server. The table_cache is set to 64 (allowing more simultaneous threads to be active). The net_buffer_length is raised to 8K.

my-large.cnf

The my-large.cnf sample file is intended for computers that are dedicated primarily to MySQL service. It assumes about 512M of available memory. More MySQL services are available and they do perform better.

Server buffers allow more active threads and better sorting performance. Half of the system's assumed 512M of memory is assigned to the key_buffer variable (256M). The sort_buffer size is raised to 1M. The table_cache allows many more simultaneous users (up to 256 active threads).

my-huge.cnf

As with the my-large.cnf file, the my-huge.cnf file expects the computer to be used primarily for MySQL. However, the system for which it is intended offers much more total memory (between 1G and 2G of memory).

Sort buffer size (sort_buffer) is raised to 2M while the key_buffer is set to consume 384M of memory. The table_cache size is doubled to allow up to 512 active threads.

Starting the MySQL Server

For Red Hat Linux, the MySQL server is off by default. To turn it on, however, is fairly simple. The /etc/init.d/mysqld start-up script is delivered with the mysql-server package. To start the server, you can either run the mysqld start-up script manually or set it to start each time your system boots.

To start the MySQL server manually, type the following from a Terminal window as root user:

```
# /etc/init.d/mysqld start
```

To set the MySQL server to start automatically each time your computer reboots, type the following as root user:

```
# chkconfig mysqld on
```

This sets mysqld to start during most multi-user run states (levels 3, 4, and 5). To check that the service is turned on for those levels, type chkconfig –list mysqld from a Terminal window.

Checking that MySQL Server Is Working

You can use the `mysqladmin` or `mysqlshow` commands to check that the MySQL server is up and running. Here is an example of how to check information about the MySQL server using the `mysqladmin` command.

```
# mysqladmin -u root -p version proc
Enter password: ********
mysqladmin  Ver 8.21 Distrib 3.23.40, for redhat-linux-gnu on i386

Copyright (C) 2000 MySQL AB & MySQL Finland AB & TCX DataKonsult AB

This software comes with ABSOLUTELY NO WARRANTY. This is free software,
and you are welcome to modify and redistribute it under the GPL license

Server version       3.23.40
Protocol version     10
Connection           Localhost via UNIX socket
UNIX socket          /var/lib/mysql/mysql.sock
Uptime:              2 days 10 hours 47 min 35 sec

Threads: 1  Questions: 184  Slow queries: 0  Opens: 1  Flush tables: 3
Open tables: 1 Queries per second avg: 0.001

+----+------+-----------+---------+---------+------+-------+------------------+
| Id | User | Host      | db      | Command | Time | State | Info             |
+----+------+-----------+---------+---------+------+-------+------------------+
| 52 | root | localhost | mysql   | Query   | 0    |       | show processlist |
+----+------+-----------+---------+---------+------+-------+------------------+
```

Each of the two options to `mysqladmin` shown here provides useful information. The version information shows the MySQL version is 8.21 and the number assigned to this distribution of the mysql server is 3.23.40. The binary package was created for Red Hat Linux/GNU on the i386 processor. The connection to the server is through a UNIX socket (`mysql.sock`) on the local host. The server has been up for 2 days, 10 hours, 47 minutes and 35 seconds. Statistics show that there is one thread (connection to the server) currently active. There have been 184 requests to the server.

The proc option shows that one client is currently connected to the server. That client is logged into MySQL as the root user on the `localhost`. The client has an Id of 52 (which you could use as the server's administrator if you wanted to disconnect the user) is currently querying the MySQL database.

If the server were not running at the moment, the `mysqladmin` command shown above would result in a failure message:

```
mysqladmin: connect to server at 'localhost' failed.
```

Recommended remedies are to try to restart the server (by typing `/etc/init.d/ mysqld restart`) or to make sure that the socket exists (`/var/lib/mysql/ mysql.sock`).

Working with MySQL Databases

The first time you start the MySQL server (using the start-up script described previously), the system creates the initial grant tables for the MySQL database. It does this by running the `mysql_install_db` command.

Note   If for some reason the grant tables are not initialized, you can run the `mysql_install_db` command yourself (as root user). Running the command more than once won't hurt anything.

The `mysql_install_db` command starts you off with two databases: `mysql` and `test`. As you create data for these databases, that information is stored in the `/var/lib/mysql/mysql` and `/var/lib/mysql/test` directories, respectively.

Starting the mysql command

To get started creating databases and tables, you can use the `mysql` command. From any Terminal window, open the mysql database on your computer by typing the following:

```
# mysql -u root -p mysql
Enter password: *********
Reading table information for completion of table and column names
You can turn off this feature to get a quicker startup with -A
```

```
Welcome to the MySQL monitor. Commands end with ; or \g.
Your MySQL connection id is 39 to server version: 3.23.36
Type 'help;' or '\h' for help. Type '\c' to clear the buffer

mysql>
```

Type in the root user's MySQL password as prompted. The `mysql>` prompt appears, ready to accept commands for working with the mysql default database on the localhost. If you are connecting to the MySQL server from another host computer, add a `-h` *hostname* to the command line (where `hostname` is the name or IP address of the computer on which the MySQL server is running). Remember, you can also login as any valid mysql login you created, regardless of which Linux login account you are currently logged in under.

As the mysql text notes above, be sure to end each command that you type with a semi-colon (;) or a \g. If you type a command and it appears to be waiting for more input, it's probably because you forgot to put a semi-colon at the end.

Before you begin using the mysql interface to create databases, try checking the status of the MySQL server using the status command. The following is an example of output from the status command:

```
mysql> status
--------------
mysql  Ver 11.15 Distrib 3.23.40, for redhat-linux-gnu (i386)

Connection id:  43
Current database:      mysql
Current user:          root@localhost
Current pager:         stdout
Using outfile:         ''
Server version:        3.23.40
Protocol version:      10
Connection:            Localhost via UNIX socket
Client characterset:   latin1
Server characterset:   latin1
UNIX socket:           /var/lib/mysql/mysql.sock
Uptime:                1 day 2 hours 57 min 19 sec

Threads: 1  Questions: 136  Slow queries: 0  Opens: 12
Flush tables: 1  Open tables: 6 Queries per second avg: 0.001
--------------
```

The status information tells you about the version of the MySQL server (11.15) and the distribution (3.23.40). The output also reminds you of the current database (mysql) and your user name (root@localhost). You can see how long the server has been up (Uptime). You can also see how many threads are currently active and how many commands have been run to query this server (Questions).

Creating a database with mysql

Within an interactive `mysql` session, you can create and modify databases and tables. If you are not already connected to a `mysql` session, type the following command (assuming the `mysql` user name of root):

```
# mysql -u root -p
Enter password: *******
mysql>
```

The general steps for creating a MySQL database include creating the database name, identifying the new database as the current database, creating tables, and adding data to the tables. While you are connected to a mysql sessions, you can run the procedure below to create a sample database.

1. To create a new database name, use the CREATE DATABASE command at the mysql> prompt. For example, to create a database named allusers, type the following:

   ```
   mysql> CREATE DATABASE allusers;
   ```

   This action creates a directory called allusers in the `/var/lib/mysql` directory.

Note　You can also create a database from the command line using the `mysqladmin` command. For example, to create the database named allusers with `mysqladmin`, you could type the following:

```
# mysqladmin -u root -p create allusers
```

2. To see what databases are available for your mysql server, type the following from the mysql> command prompt:

   ```
   mysql> SHOW DATABASES;
   +----------+
   | Database |
   +----------+
   | allusers |
   | mysql    |
   | test     |
   +----------+
   3 rows in set (0.00 sec)
   ```

   The databases shown here are named `allusers`, `mysql`, and `test`. The `allusers` database is the one created in the previous step. The `mysql` database contains user access data. The `test` database is created automatically for creating test mysql databases.

3. To work with the database we just created (allusers), you need to make allusers your current database. To do that, type the following from the mysql> command prompt:

```
mysql> USE allusers;
Database changed
```

4. Creating a table for your database requires some planning and understanding of table syntax. You can type in the following commands and column information to try out creating a table. For more detailed information on creating tables and using different data types, refer to the section "Understanding MySQL Tables" later in this chapter.

To create a table called "names," use the following CREATE TABLE command from a mysql> prompt:

```
mysql> CREATE TABLE names (
-> firstname        varchar(20)      not null,
-> lastname         varchar(20)      not null,
-> streetaddr       varchar(30)      not null,
-> city             varchar(20)      not null,
-> state            varchar(20)      not null,
-> zipcode          varchar(10)      not null
-> );
Query OK, 0 rows affected (0.00 sec)
```

You have now created a table called names for a database named allusers. It contains columns called firstname, lastname, streedaddr, city, state, and zip-code. Each column allows record lengths of between 10 and 30 characters. Though MySQL supports several different database formats, because none is specified here, the default MyISAM database type is used.

With a database and one table created, you can now add data to the table.

Adding data to a MySQL database table

After the database is created and the structure of a database table is in place, you can begin working with the database. You can add data to your MySQL database by manually entering each record during a mysql session or by adding the data into a plain text file and loading that file into the database.

Manually entering data

To do the procedure in this section, I assume you have an open interactive mysql session and that you have created a database and table as described in the previous section. If you are not already connected to a mysql session, type the following command (assuming the mysql user name of root):

```
# mysql -u root -p
Enter password: *******
mysql>
```

To add data to an existing MySQL database, the following procedure describes how to view the available tables and load data into those tables manually. Following the procedure is a description of how to create a plain text file containing database data and how to load that file into your database.

1. To make the database you want to use your current database (in this case, allusers), type the following command from the mysql> prompt:

```
mysql> USE allusers;
Database changed
```

2. To see the tables that are associated with the current database, type the following command from the mysql> prompt:

```
mysql> SHOW tables;

+---------------------+
| Tables_in_allusers  |
+---------------------+
| names               |
+---------------------+
1 row in set (0.00 sec)
```

You can see that the only table defined so far for the allusers database is the one called names.

3. To display the format of the "names" table, type the following command from the mysql> prompt:

```
mysql> DESCRIBE names;

+------------+-------------+------+-----+---------+-------+
| Field      | Type        | Null | Key | Default | Extra |
+------------+-------------+------+-----+---------+-------+
| firstname  | varchar(20) |      |     |         |       |
| lastname   | varchar(20) |      |     |         |       |
| streetaddr | varchar(30) |      |     |         |       |
| city       | varchar(20) |      |     |         |       |
| state      | varchar(20) |      |     |         |       |
| zipcode    | varchar(10) |      |     |         |       |
+------------+-------------+------+-----+---------+-------+
```

4. To add data to the new table, you can use the INSERT INTO command from the mysql> prompt. Here is an example of how to add a person's name and address to the new table:

```
mysql> INSERT INTO names
-> VALUES ('Jerry','Wingnut','167 E Street',
-> 'Roy','UT','84103');
```

In this example, the INSERT INTO command identifies the names table. Then it indicates that values for a record in that table include the name Jerry Wingnut at the address 167 E. Street, Roy UT 84103.

5. To check that the data has been properly entered into the new table, type the following command from the mysql> prompt:

```
mysql> SELECT * FROM names;
+------------+----------+--------------+--------+-------+---------+
| firstname  | lastname | streetaddr   | city   | state | zipcode |
+------------+----------+--------------+--------+-------+---------+
| Jerry      | Wingnut  | 167 E Street | Roy    | UT    | 84103   |
+------------+----------+--------------+--------+-------+---------+
```

The resulting output shows the data you just entered, displayed in the columns you defined for the names table. If you like, you can continue adding data in this way.

Typing each data item individually can be tedious. As an alternative, you can add your data to a plain text file and load it into your MySQL database.

Loading data from a file

Using the LOAD DATA command during a mysql session, you can load a file containing database records into your MySQL database. Here are a few things you need to know about creating a data file to be loaded into MySQL.

✦ You can create the file using any Linux text editor.

✦ Each record, consisting of all the columns in the table, must be on its own line. (A line feed indicates the start of the next record.)

✦ Separate each column by a Tab character.

✦ You can leave a column blank for a particular record by placing a \N in that column for the record.

✦ Any blank lines you leave in the file result in blank lines in the database table.

In this example, the text shown below is added into a plain text file. The text is in a format that can be loaded into the "names" table created earlier in this chapter. To try it out, type the following text into a file. Make sure that you insert a tab character between each value (indicated here as multiple spaces).

```
Chris    Smith    175 Harrison Street    Gig Harbor    WA    98999
John     Jones    18 Talbot Road NW      Coventry      NJ    54889
Howard   Manty    1515 Broadway          New York      NY    10028
```

When you are done entering the data, save the text to any accessible file name (for example, /tmp/mysql_names.txt). Remember the file name so that you can enter it later. If you are not already connected to a mysql session, type the following command (assuming the mysql user name of root):

```
# mysql -u root -p
Enter password: *******
mysql>
```

Next, identify the database (allusers in this example) as the current database by typing the following:

```
mysql> USE allusers;
Database changed
```

To actually load the file into the names table in the allusers database, type the following command to load the file (in this case, /tmp/mysql_names.txt) from the mysql> prompt.

Note Either enter the full path to the file or have it in the directory where the mysql command starts. In the latter case, you can type the file name without indicating its full path.

```
mysql> LOAD DATA LOCAL INFILE "/tmp/mysql_names.txt" INTO TABLE names;
Query OK, 3 rows affected (0.02 sec)
Records: 3  Deleted: 0 Skipped: 0 Warnings: 0
```

Type the following at the mysql> prompt to make sure that the records have been added correctly:

```
mysql> SELECT * FROM names;
+-----------+----------+--------------------+------------+-------+---------+
| firstname | lastname | streetaddr         | city       | state | zipcode |
+-----------+----------+--------------------+------------+-------+---------+
| Chris     | Smith    | 175 Harrison Street| Gig Harbor | WA    | 98999   |
| John      | Jones    | 18 Talbot Road NW  | Coventry   | NJ    | 54889   |
| Howard    | Manty    | 1515 Broadway      | New York   | NY    | 10028   |
+-----------+----------+--------------------+------------+-------+---------+
```

Understanding MySQL Tables

You have a lot of flexibility when it comes to setting up MySQL tables. To have your MySQL database operate as efficiently as possible, you want to have the columns be assigned to the most appropriate size and data type to hold the data you need to store.

You can use the following tables as a reference to the different data types that can be assigned to your columns. Data types available for use in MySQL fall into these categories: numbers, time/date, and character strings. Here are a few things you need to know as you read these tables:

✦ The maximum display size for a column is 255 characters. An "M" option to a data type indicates the number of characters that are displayed and, in most cases, stored for the column.

✦ There can be up to 30 of digits following the decimal point for floating-point data types. A "D" option to a data type indicates the number of digits allowed for a floating-point number following the decimal point. (The value should be no more than two digits less than the value of the display size being used.)

✦ The UNSIGNED option (shown in braces) indicates that only positive number to be allowed in the column. This allows the column to hold larger positive numbers.

✦ The ZEROFILL option (shown in braces) indicates that the data in the column will be padded with zeros. For example, the number 25 in a column with a data type of INTEGER(7) ZEROFILL would appear as 0000025. (Any ZEROFILL column automatically becomes UNSIGNED.)

✦ All values shown in braces are optional.

✦ The parentheses shown around the (M) and (D) values are necessary if you enter either of those values. In other words, don't type the braces, but do type the parentheses.

Table 24-2
Numeric Data Types for Columns

Data Type	Description	Space Needed
BIGINT[(M)] [UNSIGNED] [ZEROFILL]	Can contain large integers with the following allowable values: -9223372036854775808 to 9223372036854775807 (unsigned) 0 to 18446744073709551615 (signed)	Uses 8 bytes
DECIMAL[(M[,D])] [ZEROFILL]	Contains an unpacked floating-point number (signed only). Each digit is stored as a single character. When you choose the display value (M), decimal points and minus signs are not counted in that value. The value of (M) is 10 by default. Setting D to zero (which is the default) causes only whole numbers to be used.	Uses M+2 bytes if D is greater than 0 Uses M+1 bytes if D is equal to 0

Data Type	Description	Space Needed
DOUBLE[(M,D)] [ZEROFILL]	Contains a double-precision, floating-point number of an average size. Values that are allowed include: -1.7976931348623157E+308 to -2.2250738585072014E-308 0 2.2250738585072014E-308 to 1.7976931348623157E+308.	Uses 8 bytes
DOUBLE PRECISION	Same as DOUBLE.	Same as DOUBLE.
FLOAT(X) [ZEROFILL]	Contains a floating-point number. For a single-precision floating-point number X can be less than or equal to 24. For a double-precision floating-point number, X can be between 25 and 53. The display size and number of decimals are undefined.	Uses 4 bytes
FLOAT[(M,D)] [ZEROFILL]	Contains a single-precision floating-point number. Values that are allowed include: -3.402823466E+38 to -1.175494351E-38 0 1.175494351E-38 to 3.402823466E+38. If the display value (M) is less than or equal to 24, the number is a single-precision floating-point number.	Uses 4 bytes if X is less than or equal to 24 Uses 8 bytes if X is greater than or equal to 25 and less than or equal to 53
INT[(M)] [UNSIGNED] [ZEROFILL]	Contains an integer of normal size. The range is -2147483648 to 2147483647 if it's signed and 0 to 4294967295 if unsigned.	Uses 4 bytes
INTEGER[(M)] [UNSIGNED] [ZEROFILL]	Same as INT.	Same as INT.
MEDIUMINT[(M)] [UNSIGNED] [ZEROFILL]	Contains an integer of medium size. The range is -8388608 to 8388607 if it's signed and 0 to 16777215 if unsigned.	Uses 3 bytes
NUMERIC(M,D) [ZEROFILL]	Same as DECIMAL.	Same as DECIMAL.
REAL	Same as DOUBLE.	Same as DOUBLE.

Continued

Table 24-2 *(continued)*

Data Type	Description	Space Needed
SMALLINT[(M)] [UNSIGNED] [ZEROFILL]	Contains an integer of small size. The range is -32768 to 32767 if it's signed and 0 to 65535 if it's unsigned.	Uses 2 bytes
TINYINT[(M)] [UNSIGNED] [ZEROFILL]	A very small integer, with a signed range of -128 to 127 and a 0 to 255 unsigned range.	Uses 1 byte

The format of dates in MySQL is YYYY-MM-DD, which stands for the year, month and day. Any improperly formatted date or time values will be converted to zeroes.

Table 24-3
Time/Date Data Types for Columns

Data Type	Description	Space Needed
DATE	Contains a date between the range of January 1, 1000 (1000-01-01) and December 31, 9999 (9999-12-31).	Uses 3 bytes
DATETIME	Contains a combination of date and time between zero hour of January 1, 1000 (1000-01-01 00:00:00) and the last second of December 31, 9999 (9999-12-31 23:59:59).	Uses 8 bytes
TIMESTAMP[(M)]	Contains a timestamp from between zero hour of January 1, 1970 (1970-01-01 00:00:00) and a time in the year 2037. It is stored in the form: YMMDDHHMMSS. Using (M), you can reduce the size of the TIMESTAMP displayed to less than the full 14 characters (though the full 4-byte TIMESTAMP is still stored).	Uses 4 bytes
TIME	Contains a time between -838:59:59 and 838:59:59. The format of the field is in hours, minutes, and seconds (HH:MM:SS).	Uses 3 bytes
YEAR[(2|4)]	Contains a year, represented by either two or four digits. For a four-digit year, YEAR can be between 1901 to 2155 (0000 is also allowed). For a two-digit year, the digits 70-69 can represent the years from 1970-2069.	Uses 1 byte

Table 24-4
String Data Types for Columns

Data Type	Description	Space Needed
BLOB	Contains a binary large object (BLOB) that varies in size, based on the actual value of the data, rather than on the maximum allowable size. Searches on a BLOB column are case-sensitive.	Uses up to L+2 bytes, where L is less than or equal to 65535
[NATIONAL] CHAR(M) [BINARY]	Contains a character string of fixed length, with spaces padded to the right to meet the length. To display the value, the spaces are deleted. The value of (M) determines the number of characters (from 1 to 255). If the BINARY keyword is used, sorting of values is case-sensitive (it is case-insensitive by default). The NATIONAL keyword indicates that the default CHARACTER set should be used.	Uses between 1 and 255 bytes, based on the value of (M)
ENUM('val1','val2',...)	Contains enumerated strings that are typically chosen from a list of values indicated when you create the column. For example, you set a column definition to ENUM("dog","cat","mouse"). Then, if you set the value of that column to "1" the value displayed would be "dog", "2" would be "cat" and "3" would be mouse. It lets you take a number as input and have a string as output. Up to 65535 values are allowed.	Uses either 1 byte (for up to about 255 values) or 2 bytes, (for up to 65535 values)
LONGBLOB	Contains a binary large object (BLOB) that varies in size, based on the actual value of the data, rather than on the maximum allowable size. LONGBLOB allows larger values than MEDIUMBLOB. Searches on a LONGBLOB column are case-sensitive.	Uses up to L+4 bytes, where L is less than or equal to 4294967295
LONGTEXT	Same as LONGBLOB, except that searching is done on these columns in case-insensitive style.	Uses up to L+4 bytes, where L is less than or equal to 4294967295

Continued

Table 24-4 *(continued)*

Data Type	Description	Space Needed
MEDIUMBLOB	Contains a binary large object (BLOB) that varies in size, based on the actual value of the data, rather than on the maximum allowable size. MEDIUMBLOB allows larger values than BLOB. Searches on a MEDIUMBLOB column are case-sensitive.	Uses up to L+3 bytes, where L is less than or equal to 16777215
MEDIUMTEXT	Same as MEDIUMBLOB, except that searching is done on these columns in case-insensitive style.	Uses up to L+3 bytes, where L is less than or equal to 16777215
SET('val1','val2',...)	Contains a set of values. A SET column can display zero or more values from the list of values contained in the SET column definition. Up to 64 members are allowed.	Uses 1, 2, 3, 4 or 8 bytes, varying based on how many of the up to 64 set members are used
TEXT	Same as BLOB, except that searching is done on these columns in case-insensitive style.	Uses up to L+2 bytes, where L is less than or equal to 65535
TINYBLOB	Contains a binary large object (BLOB) that varies in size, based on the actual value of the data, rather than on the maximum allowable size. TINYBLOB allows smaller values than BLOB. Searches on a TINYBLOB column are case-sensitive.	Uses up to L+1 bytes, where L is less than or equal to 255
TINYTEXT	Same as TINYBLOB, except that searching is done on these columns in case-insensitive style.	Uses up to L+1 bytes, where L is less than or equal to 255
[NATIONAL] VARCHAR(M) [BINARY]	Contains a character string of variable length, with no padded spaces added. The value of (M) determines the number of characters (from 1 to 255). If the BINARY keyword is used, sorting of values is case-sensitive (it is case-insensitive by default). The NATIONAL keyword indicates that the default CHARACTER set should be used.	Uses L+1 bytes, where L is less than or equal to M and M is from 1 to 255 characters

Displaying MySQL Databases

There are many different ways of sorting and displaying database records during a mysql session. If you are not already connected to a mysql session, type the following command (assuming the mysql user name of root):

```
# mysql -u root -p
Enter password: *******
mysql>
```

When you are in your mysql session (and have chosen your database), you can display all or selected records from a table, choose which columns are displayed, or choose how displayed records are sorted.

Displaying all or selected records

Assuming that the current database is allusers (as shown in the previous examples), type the following command to choose (SELECT) all records (*) from the "names" table and display them in the order in which they were entered into the database.

```
mysql> SELECT * FROM names;
```

firstname	lastname	streetaddr	city	state	zipcode
Chris	Smith	175 Harrison Street	Gig Harbor	WA	98999
John	Jones	18 Talbot Road NW	Coventry	NJ	54889
Howard	Manty	1515 Broadway	New York	NY	10028

The following command displays all records from the "names" table that have the lastname column set to Jones. Instead of using lastname, you could search for a value from any column name used in the table.

```
mysql> SELECT * FROM names WHERE lastname = "Jones";
```

firstname	lastname	streetaddr	city	state	zipcode
John	Jones	18 Talbot Road NW	Coventry	NJ	54889

Using the OR operator, you can select records that match several different values. In the following command, records that have either Chris or Howard as the firstname are matched and displayed.

```
mysql> SELECT * FROM names WHERE firstname = "Chris" OR firstname = "Howard";
+-----------+----------+--------------------+-------------+-------+---------+
| firstname | lastname | streetaddr         | city        | state | zipcode |
+-----------+----------+--------------------+-------------+-------+---------+
| Chris     | Smith    | 175 Harrison Street| Gig Harbor  | WA    | 98999   |
| Howard    | Manty    | 1515 Broadway      | New York    | NY    | 10028   |
+-----------+----------+--------------------+-------------+-------+---------+
```

To match and display a record based on the value of two columns in a record, you can use the AND operator. In the following, command any record that has Chris as the firstname and Smith as the lastname is matched.

```
mysql> SELECT * FROM names WHERE firstname = "Chris" AND lastname = "Smith";
+-----------+----------+--------------------+-------------+-------+---------+
| firstname | lastname | streetaddr         | city        | state | zipcode |
+-----------+----------+--------------------+-------------+-------+---------+
| Chris     | Smith    | 175 Harrison Street| Gig Harbor  | WA    | 98999   |
+-----------+----------+--------------------+-------------+-------+---------+
```

Displaying selected columns

You don't need to display every column of data. Instead of using the asterisk (*) shown in previous examples to match all columns, you can enter a comma-separated list of column names. The following command displays the firstname, lastname, and zipcode records for all of the records in the "names" table:

```
mysql> SELECT firstname,lastname,zipcode FROM names;
+-----------+----------+---------+
| firstname | lastname | zipcode |
+-----------+----------+---------+
| Chris     | Smith    | 98999   |
| John      | Jones    | 54889   |
| Howard    | Manty    | 10028   |
+-----------+----------+---------+
```

Likewise, you can sort columns in any order you choose. Type the following command to show the same three columns with the zipcode column displayed first:

```
mysql> SELECT zipcode,firstname,lastname FROM names;
+---------+-----------+----------+
| zipcode | firstname | lastname |
+---------+-----------+----------+
| 98999   | Chris     | Smith    |
| 54889   | John      | Jones    |
| 10028   | Howard    | Manty    |
+---------+-----------+----------+
```

Note that you can have the columns displayed in any order you choose. You can also mix column selection with record selection as shown in the following example:

```
mysql> SELECT firstname,lastname,city FROM names WHERE firstname = "Chris";
+-----------+----------+------------+
| firstname | lastname | city       |
+-----------+----------+------------+
| Chris     | Smith    | Gig Harbor |
+-----------+----------+------------+
```

Sorting data

You can sort records based on the values in any column you choose. For example, using the ORDER BY operator, you can display the records based on the lastname column:

```
mysql> SELECT * FROM names ORDER BY lastname;
+-----------+----------+------------------+------------+-------+---------+
| firstname | lastname | streetaddr       | city       | state | zipcode |
+-----------+----------+------------------+------------+-------+---------+
| John      | Jones    | 18 Talbot Road NW| Coventry   | NJ    | 54889   |
| Howard    | Manty    | 1515 Broadway    | New York   | NY    | 10028   |
| Chris     | Smith    | 167 Small Road   | Gig Harbor | WA    | 98999   |
+-----------+----------+------------------+------------+-------+---------+
```

To sort records based on city name, you could use the following command:

```
mysql> SELECT * FROM names ORDER BY city;
+-----------+----------+------------------+------------+-------+---------+
| firstname | lastname | streetaddr       | city       | state | zipcode |
+-----------+----------+------------------+------------+-------+---------+
| John      | Jones    | 18 Talbot Road NW| Coventry   | NJ    | 54889   |
| Chris     | Smith    | 167 Small Road   | Gig Harbor | WA    | 98999   |
| Howard    | Manty    | 1515 Broadway    | New York   | NY    | 10028   |
+-----------+----------+------------------+------------+-------+---------+
```

Now that you have entered and displayed the database records, you may find that you need to change some of them. The following section describes how to update database records during a mysql session.

Making Changes to Tables and Records

As you begin to use your MySQL database, you will find that you need to make changes to both the structure and content of the database tables. The following section describes how you can alter the structure of your MySQL tables and change the content of MySQL records.

If you are not already connected to a mysql session, type the following command (assuming the mysql user name of root):

```
# mysql -u root -p
Enter password: *******
mysql>
```

To use the examples shown in the following sections, identify the database (allusers in this example) as the current database by typing the following:

```
mysql> USE allusers;
Database changed
```

Altering MySQL tables

After you have created your database tables, there will inevitably be changes you want to make to them. This section describes how to use the ALTER command during a mysql session to do the following: add a column, delete a column, rename a column, and change the data type for a column.

To add a column to the end of your table that displays the current date, type the following:

```
mysql> ALTER TABLE names ADD curdate TIMESTAMP;
```

The previous example tells mysql to change the table in the current database called names (ALTER TABLE names), add a column named curdate (ADD curdate), and assign the value of that column to display the current date (TIMESTAMP data type). If you decide later that you want to remove that column, you can remove it by typing the following:

```
mysql> ALTER TABLE names DROP COLUMN curdate;
```

If you want to change the name of an existing column, you can do so using the CHANGE option to ALTER. Here is an example:

```
mysql> ALTER TABLE names CHANGE city town varchar(20);
```

In the previous example, the names table is chosen (ALTER TABLE names) to change the name of the city column to town (CHANGE city town). The data type of the column must be entered as well (varchar(20)), even if you are not changing it. In fact, if you just want to change the data type of a column, you would use the same syntax as the previous example but you would simply repeat the column name twice. Here is an example:

```
mysql> ALTER TABLE names CHANGE zipcode zipcode INTEGER;
```

The previous example changes the data type of the zipcode column from its previous type (varchar) to the INTEGER type.

Updating and deleting MySQL records

You can select records based on any value you choose and update any values in those records. When you are in your mysql session, you can use UPDATE to change the values in a selected table. Here is an example:

```
mysql> UPDATE names SET streetaddr = "933 3rd Avenue" WHERE firstname = "Chris";
Query OK, 1 row affected (0.00 sec)
Rows matched: 1 Changed: 1 Warnings: 0
```

The previous example attempts to update the names table (UPDATE names). In this example, each record that has the firstname column set to "Chris" will have the value of the streetaddr column for that record changed to "933 3rd Avenue" instead. Note that the Query found 1 row that matched. That one row matched was also changed, with no error warnings necessary.

You can use any combination of values to match records (using WHERE) and change column values (using SET) that you would like. After you have made a change, it is a good idea to display the results to make sure that the change was made as you expected.

To remove an entire row (that is, one record), you can use the DELETE command. For example, if you wanted to delete any row where the value of the firstname column is "Chris", you could type the following:

```
mysql> DELETE FROM names WHERE firstname = "Chris";
Query OK, 1 row affected (0.00 sec)
```

The next time you display the table, there will no longer be any records where the first name is Chris.

Adding and Removing User Access

There are several different methods you can use to control user access to your MySQL databases. To begin with, assign a user name and password to every user that accesses your MySQL databases. Then you can use the GRANT and REVOKE commands of mysql to specifically indicate the databases and tables users and host computers can access, as well as the rights they have to those databases and tables.

Cross-Reference

Database servers are common targets of attacks from hackers. While this chapter gives some direction for granting access to your MySQL server, you need to provide much more stringent protection for the server if you are allowing Internet access. Refer to Section 6, The MySQL Access System in the MySQL manual (/usr/share/doc/mysql*/manual.html) for further information on securing your MySQL server.

Adding users and granting access

Though you have a user account defined to create databases (the root user, in this example), to make a database useful, you may want to allow access to other users as well. The following procedure describes how to grant privileges to your MySQL database for other users.

Note   If you are upgrading your MySQL from a version previous to 3.22, run the `mysql_fix_privilege_tables` script. This script adds new GRANT features to your databases. If you don't run the script, you will be denied access to the databases.

In this example, I am adding a user named bobby that can login to the MySQL server from the local host. The password for bobby is i8yer2shuz. (Remember that there does not have to be a Red Hat Linux user account named bobby. So any user on the localhost with the password for bobby can login to that MySQL account.)

1. If you are not already connected to a mysql session, type the following command (assuming the mysql user name of root):

```
# mysql -u root -p
Enter password: *******
mysql>
```

2. To create the user named bobby and a password i8yer2shuz, use the GRANT command as follows:

```
mysql> GRANT USAGE ON *.*
    -> TO bobby@localhost IDENTIFIED BY "i8yer2shuz";
```

At this point, someone could login from the localhost using the name bobby and i8yer2shuz password (`mysql -u bobby -p`). But the user would have no privilege to work with any of the databases. Next you need to grant privileges.

3. To grant bobby privileges to work with the database called allusers, you could type the following:

```
mysql> GRANT DELETE,INSERT,SELECT,UPDATE ON allusers.*
    -> TO bobby@localhost;
```

In this example, the user named bobby is allowed to login to the MySQL server on the local host and access all tables from the allusers database (USE allusers). For that database, bobby will be able to use the DELETE, INSERT, SELECT, and UPDATE commands.

4. To see the privileges that you just granted, you can select mysql as your current database, they select the db table as follows:

```
mysql> USE mysql;
Database changed
mysql> SELECT * FROM db WHERE db="allusers";
+---------+--------+------+------------+------------+------------+-----------
|Host     |Db      |User  |Select_priv |Insert_priv |Update_priv |Delete_priv
+---------+--------+------+------------+------------+------------+-----------
|localhost|allusers|bobby | Y          | Y          | Y          | Y
+---------+--------+------+------------+------------+------------+-----------
```

The output here shows all users who are specifically granted privileges to the allusers database. Only part of the output is shown here because it is very long. You should either make a very wide terminal window to view the output or learn how to read wrapped text. Other privileges on the line will be set to N (no access).

Revoking access

You can revoke privileges you grant using the REVOKE command. To revoke all privileges for a user to a particular database, use the following procedure:

1. If you are not already connected to a mysql session, type the following command (assuming the mysql user name of root):

```
# mysql -u root -p
Enter password: *******
mysql>
```

2. To revoke all privileges of a user named bobby to use a database named allusers on your MySQL server, you could type the following:

```
mysql> REVOKE ALL PRIVILEGES ON allusers.*
    -> FROM bobby@localhost;
```

At this point, bobby has no privileges to use any of the tables in the allusers databases.

3. To see the privileges that you just granted, you can select mysql as your current database, they select the db table as follows:

```
mysql> USE mysql;
Database changed
mysql> SELECT * FROM db WHERE db="allusers";
```

The output should show that the user named bobby is no longer listed as having access to the allusers database. (The results might just say "Empty set.")

Checking and Fixing Databases

Over time, databases can become corrupted or store information inefficiently. MySQL comes with commands that you can use to check and repair your databases. The myisamchk and isamchk commands are available to check MyISAM and ISAM database tables, respectively.

MyISAM tables are used by default with MySQL. The tables are stored in the /var/lib/mysql/*dbname* directory by default, where *dbname* is replaced by the name of the database you are using. For each table, there are three files in this directory. Each file begins with the table name and ends with one of the following three suffixes:

.frm   Contains the definition (or form) or the table

.MYI   Contains the table's index.

.MYD   Contains the table's data.

The following procedure describes how to use the myisamchk command to check your MyISAM tables. (The procedure is the same for checking ISAM tables, except that you use the isamchk command instead.)

Note   Do a backup of your database tables before running a repair with myisamchk. Though myisamchk is unlikely to damage your data, backups are still a good precaution.

1. Stop your MySQL server temporarily by typing the following from a Terminal window as the root user:

   ```
   # /etc/init.d/mysqld stop
   ```

2. You can check all or some of your database tables at once. The first example shows how to check a table called "names" in the "allusers" database.

   ```
   # myisamchk /var/lib/mysql/allusers/names.MYI
   Checking MyISAM file: /var/lib/mysql/allusers/names.MYI
   Data records:       5   Deleted blocks:        0
   - check file-size
   - check key delete-chain
   - check record delete-chain
   - check index reference
   - check record links
   ```

   You could also check tables for all your databases at once as follows:

   ```
   # myisamchk /var/lib/mysql/*/*.MYI
   ```

The example above shows a simple, 5-record database where no errors were encountered. If instead of the output shown above, you see output like the following you may need to repair the database:

```
Checking MyISAM file: names.MYI
Data records:         5    Deleted blocks:        0
- check file-size
myisamchk: warning: Size of datafile is: 689 Should be: 204
- check key delete-chain
- check record delete-chain
- check index reference
- check record links
myisamchk: error: Found wrong record at 0
MyISAM-table 'names.MYI' is corrupted
Fix it using switch "-r" or "-o"
```

3. To fix a corrupted database, you could run the following command

```
# myisamchk -r /var/lib/allusers/names.MYI
- recovering (with keycache) MyISAM-table 'names.MYI'
Data records: 5
Found wrong stored record at 0
Data records: 4
```

4. If for some reason the -r options doesn't work, you can try running the myisamchk command with the -o option. This is a slower, older method of repair, but it can handle a few problems that the -r option cannot. Here is an example:

```
# myisamchk -o /var/lib/allusers/names.MYI
```

Tip

If your computer has a lot of memory, raise the key buffer size value on the myisamchk command line, which will lessen the time it takes to check the databases. For example, you could use the following command line:

```
# myisamchk -r -O --key_buffer_size=64M *.MYI
```

This would set the key buffer size to 64 Megabytes.

Summary

MySQL is a Structured Query Language (SQL) server that runs on Red Hat Linux, as well as other operating systems. Using a start-up script (/etc/init.d/mysqld) and a configuration file (/etc/my.cnf), you can quickly get a MySQL server up and running.

With tools such as the `mysqladmin` and `mysql` commands, you can administer the MySQL server and create databases and tables that are as simple or complex as you need. During mysql sessions, you can modify the structure of your database tables or add, update, or delete database records.

You have a variety of options for querying data and sorting the output. You also have a lot of control over who can access your database tables and what privileges users have to modify, add to, or delete from the databases you control.

✦　　✦　　✦

What's on the CD-ROMs?

The CD-ROMs that accompany this book consist of two Red Hat Linux 7.2 Installation CDs and one Documentation CD. To install Red Hat Linux 7.2:

✦ Follow the instructions contained in Chapter 2 and on the CD-ROM Installation page in the back of this book.

✦ Refer to Appendix B for a complete list of the Red Hat software packages.

If for some reason you don't have your CDs handy, you can download any of these packages from a Red Hat Linux mirror site (see www.redhat.com/download/mirror.html). The RPMfind.net is an excellent resource for finding additional software packages for Red Hat Linux. I also recommend that you consider installing software packages that are available from the Red Hat Linux ContribNet site (http://rhcontrib.bero.org). RPMfind.net and ContribNet locations can help you find extra, useful software packages that were once included with the Red Hat Linux PowerTools CD. Red Hat, Inc., no longer maintains PowerTools.

Note All CD-ROM files are read-only. The CD-ROM is intended primarily for users to install the binary Red Hat Linux software. However, a CD-ROM containing source code for the Red Hat Linux distribution is also available by using a mail-in coupon that's on the CDs. Advanced users can modify this source code to change the behavior of Red Hat Linux. Changing this source code requires some knowledge of programming and software compilation tools.

Linux source code: From time to time, you may want to recompile the Linux kernel. Doing so requires the kernel source code, which usually ships with Red Hat Linux. The source code is available for the cost of shipping and handling from Hungry Minds, Inc. See the coupon in the back of the book for details.

◆   ◆   ◆

Red Hat Linux RPMs

More than 1,200 Red Hat Package Manager (RPM) software packages are delivered with Red Hat Linux 7.2. Many of these packages are added to your computer automatically when you first install Red Hat Linux. Others can be added later, using one of several software installation tools.

This appendix contains an alphabetical listing and descriptions of the Red Hat Linux 7.2 software packages. The descriptions in this appendix will help you determine the contents of those packages.

 Red Hat Linux software packages are contained on the first two CDs packaged with this book (CD-1 and CD-2). The third CD contains FAQs, HOW-TOs, and Red Hat–specific manuals (Installation, Configuration, Getting Started, and Reference guides).

Package Categories

If you prefer a listing of packages that is organized by category, Red Hat supplies the GNOME RPM window (started by the `gnorpm` command). This window organizes packages into the following major categories:

- ✦ **Amusements** — Contains games and graphics packages.

- ✦ **Applications** — Contains application program packages for a dozen subcategories. These categories include Archiving, Communications, Editors, Emulators, Engineering, File, Internet, Multimedia, Productivity, Publishing, System, and Text.

✦ **Development**—Contains software development packages for the following categories: Debuggers, Languages, Libraries, System, and Tools.

✦ **Documentation**—Contains documentation packages, which include such things as the GNOME User's Guide, help tools, man pages, FAQs, HOW-TOs, System Administrator's Guide, and XFree86 documentation.

✦ **System Environment**—Contains basic Red Hat Linux system software packages. Categories of packages include Base, Daemons, Kernel, Libraries, and Shells.

✦ **User Interface**—Contains software packages related to the Desktops (such as window managers), X (the X Window System), and X Hardware Support (such as Xconfigurator for configuring video cards).

A command-line tool for adding, deleting, and displaying the contents of RPMs is the `rpm` command. With the `rpm` command, you can even view the contents of a package that you haven't installed yet.

See Chapter 5 for descriptions of the RPM package format and tools for installing RPM packages.

The Packages

The packages contained on the two installation CD-ROMs are as follows:

✦ **4Suite:** Contains Python programming tools for manipulating XML content and object databases.

✦ **a2ps:** Contains tools for converting text and other types of files into PostScript output for printing.

✦ **abiword:** Contains the AbiWord word processing application.

✦ **adjtimex:** Contains the `adjtimex` command for regulating the system clock.

✦ **alchemist:** Contains back-end configuration tools used by such features as printing, DNS, and Apache Web server.

✦ **alchemist-devel:** Files needed for developing programs that use alchemist.

✦ **alien:** Converts Debian, Stampede, and Slackware packages into Red Hat packages that can be installed with rpm.

✦ **am-utils:** Contains the `amd automount` utility and related configuration files.

✦ **amanda:** Contains the amanda network-capable tape backup application.

✦ **amanda-client:** Contains the client components of the amanda network tape backup application.

✦ **amanda-server:** Contains the server components of the amanda network tape backup application.

✦ **ami:** Contains a Korean input method system.

✦ **ami-gnome:** Contains GNOME applet mode binary of ami.

✦ **anaconda:** Contains the `anaconda` command, which is used to install or reconfigure Linux.

✦ **anaconda-runtime:** Contains the part of the Red Hat Linux installer that is required for new installation.

✦ **anacron:** Contains the `anacron` command, which is used to execute set commands on a periodic basis.

✦ **anonftp:** Contains utilities that are made available to anonymous FTP users.

✦ **apache:** Contains the Apache Web server configuration files, documentation and daemons.

✦ **apache-devel:** Contains Apache Web server header files and `apxs` tool for building extension modules.

✦ **apache-manual:** Contains the Apache manual (in HTML format).

✦ **apacheconf:** Contains the Red Hat apacheconf tool for configuring an Apache Web server.

✦ **apel:** Contains a portable emacs library for interfacing with emacs.

✦ **apmd:** Contains the advanced power management software for monitoring battery power.

✦ **arpwatch:** Contains the `arpwatch` utility for tracking Ethernet/IP address pairings.

✦ **arts:** Contains the analog real-time synthesizer software used with the KDE sound system.

✦ **ash:** Contains the `ash` utility, which is a shell that is similar to the UNIX System V sh shell.

✦ **asp2php:** Contains tools for converting active server pages to PHP format.

✦ **asp2php-gtk:** Contains a gtk front end interface for the asp2php application.

✦ **aspell*:** This set of packages contains the aspell spell checking program for a variety of languages.

✦ **at:** Contains the `at` and `batch` commands, used to queue commands to run in the background.

✦ **atk:** Contains a set of interfaces for adding accessibility support to applications.

✦ **atk-devel:** Contains the libraries, header files, and documentation for atk.

✦ **audiofile:** Contains utilities that implement the SGI Audio File library for processing audio files.

✦ **audiofile-devel:** Contains development tools associated with audio software development.

✦ **aumix:** Contains the `aumix` program (which runs in a Terminal window) for adjusting audio mixing device (`/dev/mixer`) settings.

✦ **aumix-X11:** Contains an X-based version of the aumix program.

✦ **auth_ldap:** Contains the auth_ldap module for authenticating Apache users using the LDAP database.

✦ **authconfig:** Contains tools for configuring system authorization resources.

✦ **autoconf:** Contains tools to create scripts to make source code packages using templates and m4 macros.

✦ **autoconvert:** Contains autoconverter tools for converting Chinese HZ/GB/BIG5 encodings.

✦ **autoconvert-xchat:** Contains autoconvert-xchat plugins.

✦ **autofs:** Contains software for automounting file systems.

✦ **automake:** Contains the automake makefile generator.

✦ **autorun:** Contains software that automatically detects and mounts CD-ROMs.

✦ **awesfx:** Contains AWE32 sound driver utilities.

✦ **balsa:** Contains the balsa e-mail reader (which is part of the GNOME desktop).

✦ **basesystem:** Contains part of the base system.

✦ **bash:** Contains version 2.04 of the GNU Bash shell (Bourne Again SHell).

✦ **bash-doc:** Contains documentation for the GNU Bash shell.

✦ **bc:** Contains the `bc` precision calculator utility.

✦ **bdflush:** Contains the `bdflush` kernel daemon for flushing dirty buffers back to the disk.

✦ **bg5ps:** Contains a tool that converts BIG5 encoded Chinese into printable postscript.

✦ **bind:** Contains Internet domain name server software (named utility and related components).

✦ **bind-devel:** Contains header files needed for domain name server software development.

✦ **bind-utils:** Contains `dig`, `dnsquery`, `nslookup`, `nsupdate` and other DNS-related utilities.

✦ **bindconf:** Contains the `bindconf-gui` tool for configuring DNS settings.

✦ **binutils:** Contains GNU development tools, such as `ar`, `as`, `ld`, `nm`, `size`, and others.

✦ **bison:** Contains the GNU bison parser generator (replacement for `yacc`).

✦ **blas:** Contains the Basic Linear Algebra Subprograms (BLAS) libraries for performing many basic linear algebra algorithms.

✦ **blas-man:** Contains man pages that document the blas package.

✦ **blt:** Contains the BLT library of extensions to the TK library.

✦ **bonobo:** Contains a framework that allows GNOME applications to handle compound documents.

✦ **bonobo-devel:** Contains libraries and header files that enable applications to use the bonobo document model.

✦ **bootparamd:** Contains the `bootparamd` boot parameter server for booting diskless workstations.

✦ **bug-buddy:** Contains the bug-buddy graphical bug reporting tool.

✦ **busybox:** Contains a statically linked binary that provides simplified versions of system commands; useful for recovering from certain types of system failures.

✦ **busybox-anaconda:** Contains a version of busybox for use with anaconda.

✦ **byacc:** Contains the `byacc` (`yacc`) parser generator.

✦ **bzip2:** Contains the `bzip2` and `bzcat` utilities for compressing and uncompressing files.

✦ **bzip2-devel:** Contains programming tools associated with the bzip and bzcat utilities.

✦ **bzip2-libs:** Contains libraries for applications using bzip2.

✦ **caching-nameserver:** Contains configuration files used for caching-only name servers.

✦ **cadaver:** Contains a command-line WebDAV client.

✦ **Canna:** Contains a unified user interface called Canna for inputting Japanese.

✦ **Canna-devel:** Contains developments tools associated with Canna.

✦ **Canna-libs:** Contains programming libraries used to support Canna.

✦ **cdda2wav:** Contains the `cdda2wav` utility for coverting CD audio files into WAV sound files.

✦ **cdecl:** Contains the `cdecl` utility for composing C and C++ type declarations.

✦ **cdlabelgen:** Contains a utility that generates frontcards and traycards for compact disc cases.

✦ **cdp:** Contains the `cdp` and `cdplay` utilities for playing music CDs.

✦ **cdparanoia:** Contains the cdparanoia program for retrieving audio tracks from CD-ROM.

✦ **cdparanoia-devel:** Contains development tools associated with the cdparanoia program.

✦ **cdrdao:** Contains a tool for writing audio CD-R in disc-at-once mode.

✦ **cdrecord:** Contains software for writing data to writable CD-ROMs.

✦ **cdrecord-devel:** Contains software development tools for writing data to writable CD-ROMs.

✦ **cervisia:** Contains a KDE graphical front-end for the CVS client.

✦ **chkconfig:** Contains the `chkconfig` command for changing run-level information for system services.

✦ **chkfontpath:** Contains the `chkfontpath` utility for working with X font server directories.

✦ **chromium:** Contains an arcade-style shooting game.

✦ **cipe:** Contains the Crypto IP Encapsulation tool (cipe), which is used for creating virtual private networks across public networks (such as the Internet) using tunneling.

✦ **cleanfeed:** Contains the cleanfed.conf file and filters for filtering spam from news servers.

✦ **compat-egcs:** Contains a compiler to create backward-compatible applications for Red Hat 5.2.

✦ **compat-egcs-c++:** Contains a C++ compiler that can be used to create applications that run on Red Hat 5.2.

✦ **compat-egcs-g77:** Contains a compiler to create applications that are backward compatible with Red Hat 5.2.

✦ **compat-egcs-objc:** Contains an Objective C compiler that can create backward compatible Red Hat 5.2 programs.

✦ **compat-glibc:** Contains a version of the GNU C library that can compile binaries to run in Red Hat 5.2.

✦ **compat-libs:** Contains run-time libraries that allow you to do development for earlier Red Hat Linux systems (such as Red Hat Linux 6.2).

✦ **compat-libstdc++:** Contains several Run-Time Libraries that provide applications that are backward compatible with C++ in Red Hat 5.2.

✦ **comsat:** Contains the `biff` (mail notification client) and comsat (mail server) components.

✦ **console-tools:** Contains utilities for loading console fonts and keyboard mappings.

✦ **control-center:** Contains the Control-Center configuration tool for configuring your GNOME environment.

✦ **control-center-devel:** Contains components needed to develop capplets used as panels in the GNOME control center.

✦ **cpio:** Contains the `cpio` command for copying files to or from a tar or cpio archive.

✦ **cpp:** Contains the `cpp` (C preprocessor) macro processing utility, for preprocessing C code.

✦ **cproto:** Contains the cproto tool for creating function prototypes and variable declaration for X language source code.

✦ **cracklib:** Contains CrackLib software for testing passwords for their security.

✦ **cracklib-dicts:** Contains the dictionaries that are used by CrackLib when testing password security.

✦ **crontabs:** Contains the root crontabs files, used by the cron daemon to schedule tasks.

✦ **ctags:** Contains the `ctags` tool for generating tag files of objects from C source code and headers.

✦ **curl:** Contains a utility for getting files from remote servers using various Internet protocols.

✦ **curl-devel:** Contains the files needed for building applications that use curl.

✦ **cvs:** Contains the Concurrent Version System for maintaining a history of file changes.

✦ **cWnn:** Contains a Chinese character input system.

✦ **cWnn-common:** Contains files needed by both the cWnn and tWnn Chinese input systems.

✦ **cWnn-devel:** Contains the library and header files required to develop applications that use the cWnn or tWnn Chinese character input system.

✦ **cyrus-sasl:** Contains the Cyrus version of the Simple Authentication and Security Layer, which is used to provide authentication support for connection-based applications.

✦ **cyrus-sasl-devel:** Contains the files needed for developing applications that use cyrus-sasl.

- ✦ **cyrus-sasl-gssapi:** Contains plugins for cyrus-sasl that support GSSAPI authentication.

- ✦ **cyrus-sasl-md5:** Contains plugins for cyrus-sasl that support CRAM-MD5 and DIGEST-MD5 authentication schemes.

- ✦ **cyrus-sasl-plain:** Contains plugins for cyrus-sasl that support PLAIN and LOGIN authentication schemes.

- ✦ **dateconfig:** Contains a graphical interface for modifying system date and time.

- ✦ **db1:** Contains the first part of the Berkeley Database programming toolkit.

- ✦ **db1-devel:** Contains development tools associated with the db1 package.

- ✦ **db2:** Contains the second part of the Berkeley Database programming toolkit.

- ✦ **db2-devel:** Contains development tools associated with the db2 package.

- ✦ **db3:** Contains the third part of the Berkeley Database programming toolkit.

- ✦ **db3-devel:** Contains development tools associated with the db3 package.

- ✦ **db3-utils:** Contains command-line tools for managing Berkeley databases.

- ✦ **dbskkd-cdb:** Contains a dictionary server for the SKK Japanese input method.

- ✦ **ddd:** Contains the Data Display Debugger, a GUI that interacts with several command-line debuggers.

- ✦ **ddskk:** Contains a simple Kanna to Kanji conversion tool for emacs.

- ✦ **dejagnu:** Contains a utility for testing other applications and delivers the outputs in a standard format.

- ✦ **desktop-backgrounds:** Contains a selection of images to use as your screen background.

- ✦ **dev:** Contains many of the most commonly used Linux devices installed in the /dev directory.

- ✦ **dev86:** Contains software development tools, including the as86 assembler and bcc compiler.

- ✦ **dhcp:** Contains components needed to support the dynamic host configuration protocol, which is needed to configure a DHCP server on your network.

- ✦ **dhcpcd:** Contains the DHCP daemon processes needed by a DHCP client to get network configuration information about itself from a DHCP server system.

- ✦ **dia:** Contains the dia diagram drawing program.

- ✦ **dialog:** Contains the dialog utility for showing dialog boxes in text mode interfaces.

✦ **diffstat:** Contains the `diffstat` command for converting `diff` output to display file changes in a form that is easier to read.

✦ **diffutils:** Contains the `diff`, `cmp`, `diff3`, and `sdiff` utilities for comparing files to find differences.

✦ **dip:** Contains the `dip` modem dialer utility, used for PPP, SLIP, and other dialup connections.

✦ **diskcheck:** Contains a utility that monitors the remaining free space on a hard drive.

✦ **Distutils:** Contains modules used to distribute and install Python modules.

✦ **dmalloc:** Contains the `dmalloc` memory management library, which can be used to replace other memory management tools.

✦ **docbook*:** This set of packages contains the DocBook SGML DTD for working with SGML documents, as well as other related tools and style sheets.

✦ **dos2unix:** Contains the dos2unix utility for converting text files from DOS to UNIX format.

✦ **dosfstools:** Contains tools for creating and working with DOS filesystems.

✦ **doxygen:** Contains the `doxygen` command for creating documentation from C or C++ programming language source code that is documented.

✦ **doxygen-doxywizard:** Contains a GUI front-end for creating and editing configuration files that are used by doxygen.

✦ **dump:** Contains the `dump` and `restore` utilities for backing up and restoring files.

✦ **dump-static:** Contains static versions of commands for backing up (`dump-static`) and restoring (`restore-static`) filesystems.

✦ **e2fsprogs:** Contains programs for finding and fixing inconsistencies in ext2 file systems.

✦ **e2fsprogs-devel:** Contains libraries and header files used to develop programs for the ext2 file system.

✦ **ed:** Contains the `ed` line-oriented text editor (which was the original UNIX text editor).

✦ **ee:** Contains the Electric Eyes (`ee`) utility for viewing and manipulating images.

✦ **eel:** Contains the Eazel Extensions Library, a collection of widgets and functions for use with GNOME.

✦ **eel-devel:** Contains libraries and includes files for developing with eel.

✦ **efax:** Contains the `efax` program for sending and receiving faxes.

✦ **eject:** Contains the `eject` program, used to eject CDs, floppy disks, Jazz disks, or other media from their drives.

✦ **ElectricFence:** Contains ElectricFence software for debugging memory problems in applications.

✦ **elm:** Contains the popular `elm` e-mail mail user agent (for reading and sending mail).

✦ **emacs:** Contains the popular emacs text editor along with the libraries needed to run the editor.

✦ **emacs-el:** Contains the emacs-elisp sources of many elisp programs used with the emacs text editor.

✦ **emacs-leim:** Contains the Emacs Lisp code used with international character scripts.

✦ **emacs-nox:** Contains a version of the emacs text editor that does not contain support for the X Window System.

✦ **emacs-X11:** Contains a version of the emacs text editor that is used with the X Window System.

✦ **enlightenment:** Contains Enlightenment, an X-based window manager. Enlightenment is the default window manager used with the GNOME desktop environment.

✦ **enscript:** Contains the `enscript` print filter for formatting ASCII text into PostScript output.

✦ **eruby:** Contains an interpreter of Ruby, the embedded language.

✦ **esound:** Contains the EsounD daemon process to allow many programs to share a sound card.

✦ **esound-devel:** Contains libraries and includes files for developing EsounD applications.

✦ **ethereal:** Contains a tool for analyzing network traffic on UNIX operating systems.

✦ **ethereal-gnome:** Contains integration tools for running ethereal on Red Hat Gnome.

✦ **ethtool:** Contains a tool that allows for the displaying and changing of Ethernet card settings.

✦ **exmh:** Contains the `exmh` mail handling system, which runs under X.

✦ **expat:** Contains the expat stream-oriented XML parsing library.

✦ **expat-devel:** Contains documentation and libraries for developing XML applications with expat.

✦ **expect:** Contains the `expect` tcl extension to automate FTP, fsck, and other interactive applications.

✦ **ext2ed:** Contains the `ext2ed` program for examining ext2 file systems.

✦ **extace:** Contains the extace multimedia window.

✦ **fam:** Contains the File Alteration Monitor tool, which provides notification of changes in specific files or directories to an application.

✦ **fam-devel:** Contains libraries and header files for fam.

✦ **fbset:** Contains the `fbset` utility, which is used to change video modes on fbcon consoles.

✦ **fetchmail:** Contains the `fetchmail` mail retrieval utilities, which are used to get mail over TCP/IP serial connections (such as SLIP and PPP).

✦ **fetchmailconf:** Contains the `fetchmailconf` tcl/tk utility for graphically configuring mail.

✦ **file:** Contains the `file` command for identifying the contents of different types of files.

✦ **filesystem:** Contains the files that create the basic directory layout of the Red Hat Linux system.

✦ **fileutils:** Contains popular file management utilities, such as `chgrp`, `chown`, `cp`, `dd`, and others.

✦ **findutils:** Contains the `find` utility for searching your file systems for selected files.

✦ **finger:** Contains the `finger` utility for displaying information about system users.

✦ **finger-server:** Contains the in.fingerd server for providing the finger service to network clients.

✦ **firewall-config:** Contains tools to configure firewalls and IP masquerading.

✦ **flex:** Contains the `flex` program for scanning files and recognizing patterns in text.

✦ **fnlib:** Contains the fnlib font library, with fonts in png and tif formats.

✦ **fnlib-devel:** Contains header files, libraries, and documentation for developing `fnlib` programs.

✦ **foomatic:** Contains a spooler-independent database of printers, printer drivers, and driver descriptions.

✦ **fortune-mod:** Contains the `fortune` program for printing a random fortune.

✦ **freecdb:** Contains the cdb tools for building and accessing constant databases.

✦ **freeciv:** Contains the freeciv clone of the Civilization II strategy game.

✦ **freetype:** Contains the FreeType font rendering engine for TrueType fonts.

✦ **freetype-devel:** Contains components needed to develop applications that use the FreeType library.

✦ **freetype-utils:** Contains several utilities for managing fonts.

✦ **FreeWnn:** Contains a tool that converts Japanese Kanna characters to Kanji characters and vice versa.

✦ **FreeWynn-common:** Contains common files needed for Wnn Kanna to Kanji conversion.

✦ **FreeWnn-devel:** Contains tools for developing applications for FreeWnn.

✦ **FreeWnn-libs:** Contains run-time libraries for running FreeWnn applications.

✦ **ftp:** Contains the FTP package of utilities for doing FTP file transfers.

✦ **ftpcopy:** Contains tools to mirror FTP sites, by copying files and directories from one FTP server to another.

✦ **fvwm2:** Contains an enhanced version of the F virtual window manager (`fvwm2`).

✦ **fvwm2-icons:** Contains icons used by the `fvwm` and `fvwm2` window managers.

✦ **gaim:** Contains the Gaim graphical window for accessing AOL instant messaging.

✦ **gal:** Contains the GNOME Applications Library (GAL), which includes useful GNOME utilities and widgets.

✦ **gal-devel:** Contains development tools associated with the GNOME Applications Library.

✦ **galeon:** Contains a GNOME browser based on Gecko (Mozilla rendering engine).

✦ **gated:** Contains the `gated` daemon for managing different network routing protocols.

✦ **gawk:** Contains the `gawk` (GNU awk) text processing utility.

✦ **gcc*:** This set of packages contains GNU C language compilers and related tools.

✦ **GConf:** Contains the GNOME configuration database system.

✦ **GConf-devel:** Contains library files required for developing with GConf.

✦ **gd:** Contains the Gd graphics library for creating GIF image files.

✦ **gd-devel:** Contains components needed to develop applications that use the gd gif graphics library.

✦ **gd-progs:** Contains utility programs associated with the JPEG graphics library.

✦ **gdb:** Contains the `gdb` command-driven debugger.

✦ **gdbm:** Contains the Gdbm database indexing library.

✦ **gdbm-devel:** Contains components needed to develop applications that use the GNU database system.

✦ **gdk-pixbuf:** Contains the GDK Pixbuf image loading libraries.

✦ **gdk-pixbuf-devel:** Contains development tools associated with GDK Pixbuf.

✦ **gdk-pixbuf-gnome:** Contains GNOME Canvas support for displaying images.

✦ **gdm:** Contains the GNOME display manager, which provides an X-based graphical login.

✦ **gedit:** Contains the compact gEdit text editor that is compatible with the GNOME GUI.

✦ **genromfs:** Contains utilities for building romfs file systems so they can be used by the Linux kernel.

✦ **gettext:** Contains the `gettext` utilities for creating programs with messages in multiple languages.

✦ **gftp:** Contains the multithreaded `gftp` program for doing simultaneous FTP uploads and downloads.

✦ **ggv:** Contains a front-end for Ghostscript that adds panning and persistent user settings to Ghostscript.

✦ **ghostscript:** Contains the Ghostscript (`gs`) program for displaying PostScript files and for producing output from PostScript files so they can be printed on non-PostScript printers.

✦ **ghostscript-fonts:** Contains a set of type fonts used with the `Ghostscript` program.

✦ **giftrans:** Contains the `giftrans` utility for converting GIF87 files to GIF89 format.

✦ **gimp:** Contains the GIMP image manipulation program, which can be used to retouch photos, create images, and work with images.

✦ **gimp-data-extras:** Contains patterns, gradients, and other graphical elements to use with the GIMP program.

✦ **gimp-devel:** Contains libraries and header files needed to develop GIMP plug-ins and extensions.

✦ **gimp-perl:** Contains libraries used for communications between GIMP and GIMP Perl extensions and plug-in programs.

✦ **gkermit:** Contains the `gkermit` utility for transferring files using the Kermit protocol.

✦ **gkrellm:** Contains a collection of monitoring software that charts the usage of resources including CPU, disk activity, and network traffic.

✦ **glade:** Contains software for developing quick user interfaces for the GTK+ toolkit.

✦ **glib:** Contains the Glib library of common utility functions used to avoid portability problems.

✦ **glib-devel:** Contains static libraries and header files to support the GIMP Xlibrary.

✦ **glib2:** Contains the beta version of the next release of the glib package.

✦ **glib2-devel:** Contains the beta version of the static libraries and header files of the next release of the glib-devel package.

✦ **glib10:** Contains common utility functions used by many Red Hat Linux applications.

✦ **glibc:** Contains standard libraries that are used by many programs in Red Hat Linux.

✦ **glibc-common:** Contains common binary programs used with C language development in Red Hat Linux.

✦ **glibc-devel:** Contains the standard header and object files needed to develop most C language programs.

✦ **glibc-profile:** Contains the libraries that are needed to create programs being profiled with `gprof`.

✦ **glms:** Contains tools for using LM processors (which are hardware sensors that monitor such things as fan speed, processor temperature, and performance of your power supply.

✦ **gmc:** Contains the GNOME version of the Midnight Commander visual shell file manager.

✦ **gmp:** Contains the MP library for handling arithmetic and floating point number functions.

✦ **gmp-devel:** Contains components needed to create applications that use the GNU MP arbitrary precision library.

✦ **gnome-applets:** Contains applets (small graphical applications) that can be used on the GNOME desktop environment.

✦ **gnome-audio:** Contains a set of sounds that you can use with your GNOME environment.

✦ **gnome-audio-extra:** Contains sound files that can be used with the GNOME desktop environment.

✦ **gnome-core:** Contains the core components needed to run the GNOME desktop environment.

✦ **gnome-core-devel:** Contains libraries and header files needed to create GNOME panels.

✦ **gnome-games:** Contains games such as `solitaire`, `gnothello`, and `tetris` that are compatible with the GNOME GUI.

✦ **gnome-games-devel:** Contains components used in developing some GNOME games.

✦ **gnome-kerberos:** Contains the krb5 tools for managing Kerberos 5 tickets.

✦ **gnomeicu:** Contains an ICQ client (an Internet-based chat program) that runs in the GNOME GUI desktop environment.

✦ **gnome-libs:** Contains libraries that are needed by the GNOME desktop environment and applications.

✦ **gnome-libs-devel:** Contains libraries needed to create applications to run on a GNOME desktop environment.

✦ **gnome-linuxconf:** Contains the GNOME front end for the `linuxconf` system configuration utility.

✦ **gnome-lokkit:** Contains the GNOME-lokkit tools for configuring simple network firewalls.

✦ **gnome-media:** Contains the GNOME CD player and other multimedia tools.

✦ **gnome-pim:** Contains the GNOME Personal Information Manager, which includes applications such as `gnomecal` (personal calendar) and `gnomecard` (contact lists).

✦ **gnome-pim-devel:** Contains components needed to develop applications that communicate with GNOME-PIM applications using Corba.

✦ **gnome-print:** Contains fonts and tools needed by GNOME applications to print from the GNOME Desktop Environment.

✦ **gnome-print-devel:** Contains software development tools associated with printing in GNOME.

✦ **gnome-user-docs:** Contains the GNOME glossary, introduction to GNOME, and a UNIX primer for the GNOME Desktop Environment.

✦ **gnome-utils:** Contains several useful GNOME utilities, such as a calculator and a calendar.

✦ **gnome-vfs:** Contains the GNOME virtual file system that forms the foundation of the Nautilus file manager.

✦ **gnome-vfs-devel:** Contains the libraries and header files required to develop in the GNOME-VFS environment.

✦ **gnome-vfs-extras:** Contains extra modules that are not distributed with the core GNOME-VFS package, including a Samba-based smb network browser.

✦ **gnorpm:** Contains the GNOME front end for managing software packages (RPMs).

✦ **gnucash:** Contains an application that tracks personal finance data.

✦ **gnuchess:** Contains the GNU chess program and related utilities.

✦ **gnumeric:** Contains the gnumeric spreadsheet program that runs in the GNOME desktop environment.

✦ **gnumeric-devel:** Contains development tools associated with the gnumeric spreadsheet program.

✦ **gnupg:** Contains the GNU Privacy Guard (gnupg) for providing digital signatures and data encryption.

✦ **gnuplot:** Contains the gnuplot utilities, used to plot scientific and other types of data.

✦ **gperf:** Contains the gperf C++ hash function generator.

✦ **gphoto:** Contains the gphoto application for managing images from digital cameras.

✦ **gpm:** Contains the gpm components needed to support a mouse in text-based applications.

✦ **gpm-devel:** Contains libraries and header files used to develop text-mode programs that use a mouse.

✦ **gq:** Contains the gq graphical LDAP browser.

✦ **gqview:** Contains the gqview utility for browsing and displaying graphics files.

✦ **grep:** Contains the grep utilities for finding matching patterns in text files.

✦ **grip:** Contains a front-end for various compact disc rippers and MP3 encoders.

✦ **groff:** Contains the groff document utilities for formatting documents from plain text and markup commands.

✦ **groff-gxditview:** Contains the gxditview utility for displaying groff output in the X Window System.

✦ **groff-perl:** Contains the afmtodit and grog utilities for working with groff documents.

- ✦ **grub:** Contains the Grand Unified Boot Loader, an experimental utility capable of booting into most of the major free and commercial operating systems.

- ✦ **gsl:** Contains the GNU Scientific Library for numerical analysis and other high-level mathematics.

- ✦ **gsm:** Contains the toast and untoast sound compression utilities.

- ✦ **gsm-devel:** Contains sound compression development tools.

- ✦ **gtk+:** Contains the GIMP graphical toolkit for building graphical X applications.

- ✦ **gtk+-devel:** Contains the `gtk+` development tools for create applications that need the GIMP toolkit.

- ✦ **gtk2:** Contains the beta version of the next release of the gtk+ package.

- ✦ **gtk2devel:** Contains the beta version of the next release of the gtk+-devel package.

- ✦ **gtk+10:** Contains compatibility libraries required for applications that use gtk+ and glib 1.0.

- ✦ **gtk-doc:** Contains tools that generate documentation for GTK+, GNOME, and Glib components.

- ✦ **gtk-engines:** Contains several GTK+ toolkit themes (including Notif, Redmond95, Pixmap, and Metal).

- ✦ **gtkglarea:** Contains an OpenGL widget for the GTK+ GUI library.

- ✦ **gtkhtml:** Contains a lightweight html rendering/printing/editing engine.

- ✦ **gtkhtml-devel:** Contains header files and libraries needed to develop gtkhtml applications.

- ✦ **Gtk-Perl:** Contains Perl extensions for gtk+ that allows graphical interfaces to be written for the X Windows System.

- ✦ **gtoaster:** Contains a compact disc recording package that supports both audio and data files.

- ✦ **gtop:** Contains the GNOME version of the `gtop` system manager for displaying memory graphs.

- ✦ **guile:** Contains the GUILE library for implementing the Scheme programming language.

- ✦ **guile-devel:** Contains libraries and header files required to develop programs that are linked with the GUILE extensibility library.

- ✦ **guppi:** Contains a GNOME-based data analysis and visualization system.

- ✦ **guppi-devel:** Contains header files and libraries needed for developing applications that use Guppi.

◆ **gv:** Contains the `gv` utility to display PostScript or PDF documents in the X Window System.

◆ **g-wrap:** Contains a tool for creating Scheme interfaces to C libraries.

◆ **g-wrap-devel:** Contains files and libraries needed for grap development.

◆ **gzip:** Contains the `gzip` utility for compressing data.

◆ **h2ps:** Contains a tool that converts Korean Hangul to postscript.

◆ **hanterm-xf:** Contains a Hangul terminal for the X Windows system based on the xterm in XFree86.

◆ **hdparm:** Contains the `hdparm` utility for setting hard drive parameters.

◆ **hexedit:** Contains a hexadecimal file viewer and editor.

◆ **hotplug:** Contains hotplug utilities, which loads the necessary modules when a USB device is connected.

◆ **hotplug-gtk:** Contains the gtk control interface for hotplug.

◆ **htdig:** Contains the htdig Web indexing and search system. This system was created specifically for use on private intranets and campuses.

◆ **htdig-web:** Contains CGI scripts and HTML code used by the htdig Web indexing and search tool.

◆ **htmlview:** Contains the `htmlview` command, which is used by some applications to display their help pages.

◆ **hwbrowser:** Contains a browser for the current hardware configuration of the system.

◆ **ical:** Contains the `ical` X-based calendar program for tracking your schedule.

◆ **im:** Contains a set of Internet Message (im*) commands for integrating mail and news programs.

◆ **ImageMagick:** Contains the ImageMagick graphics manipulation program for displaying and editing images.

◆ **ImageMagick-c++:** Contains the ImageMagick C++ tools for displaying and editing images.

◆ **ImageMagick-c++-devel:** Contains libraries used for ImageMagick C++ applications.

◆ **ImageMagick-devel:** Contains libraries needed to implement ImageMagick application programming interfaces.

◆ **ImageMagick-perl:** Contains Perl bindings to ImageMagick that allow Perl scripts to use ImageMagick.

◆ **imap:** Contains the IMAP and POP protocols for handling mail transport from servers to clients.

✦ **imap-devel:** Contains the IMAP Powertools for interfacing with IMAP mail servers.

✦ **imlib:** Contains the imlib image loading and rendering library used with the X Window System.

✦ **imlib-cfgeditor:** Contains the `imlib_conf` program, which is used to control how imlib renders images.

✦ **imlib-devel:** Contains components used to develop programs that need the Imlib image and rendering library.

✦ **indent:** Contains the indent program for beautifying C programming code.

✦ **indexhtml:** Contains the indexhtml package, which includes Red Hat Linux welcome page that appears when you start your Web browser.

✦ **inews:** Contains the `inews` program for posting news articles to the local news server.

✦ **info:** Contains the `info` text-based browser for displaying texinfo files.

✦ **initscripts:** Contains many of the basic Linux system initialization scripts, which are started at different run levels.

✦ **inn:** Contains the InterNetNews server for creating and maintaining a news server in Linux.

✦ **inn-devel:** Contains components needed to develop applications that use the InterNetNews system.

✦ **internet-config:** Contains the `internet-config` graphical tool for configuring the following types of network connections: ADSL or T-DSL, ISDN, or modem.

✦ **ipchains:** Contains components for implementing firewalls and IP masquerading on IP networks.

✦ **iproute:** Contains the `ip` command and related utilities used for routing IP traffic. Features in this package include routing, multicasting, and tunneling, including IPv6 support.

✦ **iptables:** Contains tools for creating firewalls for IP networks.

✦ **iptables-ipv6:** Contains tools for creating firewalls for IP version 6 networks.

✦ **iptraf:** Contains a console-based network monitoring tool.

✦ **iputils:** Contains various TCP/IP utilities, including `ping`, `rdisc`, and `tracepath`.

✦ **ipvsadm:** Contains a utility to administer the Linux Virtual Server.

✦ **ipxutils:** Contains a set of utilities for configuring and working with Novell IPX networks.

✦ **irb:** Contains the Interactive Ruby that evaluates Ruby expressions from the terminal.

✦ **ircii:** Contains the `ircii` Internet Relay Chat (IRC) client program for chatting on the Internet.

✦ **irda-utils:** Contains the IrDA utilities, which are used to communicate with remote devices using wireless protocols.

✦ **isapnptools:** Contains the ISA plug-and-play utilities for automatically configuring PnP hardware.

✦ **iscsi:** Contains the iSCSI daemon and utility programs, which provide distributed disk access over IP networks.

✦ **isdn4k-utils:** Contains tools for configuring ISDN dialup connections.

✦ **isdn4k-utils-vboxgetty:** Contains vboxgetty and vboxputty tools, which are needed for an ISDN voice box.

✦ **isicom:** Contains utilities for loading Multitech Intelligent Serial Internal data files.

✦ **itcl:** Contains an object-oriented extension to the Tcl language.

✦ **jadetex:** Contains the `jadetex` and `pdfjadetex` commands for working with DSSSL documents.

✦ **jed:** Contains the jed text editor, which is based on the slang screen library.

✦ **jed-common:** Contains files needed for the jed text editor to run.

✦ **jed-xjed:** Contains a version of the jed text editor that works on the X Window System.

✦ **jikes:** Contains the jikes java source to bytecode compiler.

✦ **joe:** Contains the joe modeless text editor which uses WordStar keybinding.

✦ **joystick:** Contains commands for attaching and testing a joystick.

✦ **jpilot:** Contains a desktop organizer application for the Palm Pilot.

✦ **junkbuster:** Contains an application that stops the Web browser from displaying advertisements in Web pages.

✦ **kaffe:** Contains the kaffe virtual Java (TM) machine, designed to execute Java bytecode.

✦ **kakasi:** Contains a Japanese character set conversion filter that converts Kanji to Hiragana, Katakana, or Romaji.

✦ **kakasi-devel:** Contains the header files and library for developing applications that use Kakasi.

✦ **kakasi-dict:** Contains the base Kakasi dictionary.

✦ **kappa20:** Contains Japanese fonts in 20pt.

✦ **kbdconfig:** Contains the `kbdconfig` command for configuring keyboard mappings.

✦ **kcc:** Contains a Kanji code converter.

✦ **kdbg:** Contains the KDE graphical front end for the GNU debugger (`gdb`).

✦ **kde1-compat:** Contains libraries that provide compatibility with KDE 1.1.x desktop environments.

✦ **kde1-compat-devel:** Contains tools for compiling applications for the KDE 1.1.x desktop environment.

✦ **kdeaddons-kate:** Contains plugins for the Kate text editor.

✦ **kdeaddons-kicker:** Contains plugins and additional applets for the KDE panel.

✦ **kdeaddons-knewsticker:** Contains scripts that extend the functionality of KNewsTicker.

✦ **kdeaddons-konqueror:** Contains plugins that extend the functionality of Konqeror.

✦ **kdeaddons-noatun:** Contains plugins that extend the functionality of the noatun media player.

✦ **kdeadmin:** Contains tape backup, user administration, and other system tools for use with the KDE desktop.

✦ **kdeartwork:** Contains additional artwork (themes, sound themes, and so on) for KDE.

✦ **kdeartwork-locolor:** Contains low-color icons (256 or less colors) for KDE.

✦ **kdebase:** Contains the basic applications that are used with the KDE desktop environment, including the kwm window manager, kfm file manager, and konsole terminal window.

✦ **kdebase-devel:** Contains header files for developing applications using kdebase.

✦ **kdebindings*:** This set of packages contains KDE/DCOP bindings to various non-C++ languages.

✦ **kdegames:** Contains games such as `kasteroids`, `kblackbox`, and `ksmiletris` that are compatible with the KDE desktop interface.

✦ **kdegraphics:** Contains graphics applications created for the KDE desktop environment, including the `kdvi` TeX display utility, the `kfax` Fax display utility, and the kicon icon editor.

✦ **kdegraphics-devel:** Contains development files needed to develop applications that use kdegraphics.

✦ **kde-i18n*:** This set of packages provides support for various human languages.

✦ **kdelibs:** Contains libraries needed by the K Desktop Environment.

✦ **kdelibs-devel:** Contains tools and documentation for developing KDE desktop applications.

✦ **kdelibs-sound:** Contains support for sound in the KDE desktop environment.

✦ **kdelibs-sound-devel:** Contains support for developing sound applications in the KDE desktop environment.

✦ **kdemultimedia:** Contains multimedia utilities that are suited for the KDE desktop environment.

✦ **kdemultimedia-devel:** Contains development files needed to develop applications that use kdemultimedia, such as plugins for the noatun media player.

✦ **kdenetwork:** Contains network applications used with the KDE environment.

✦ **kdenetwork-ppp:** Contains the kppp utility to configure PPP on the KDE desktop.

✦ **kdepim:** Contains a set of personal information management (PIM) tools for the KDE desktop environment.

✦ **kdepim-cellphone:** Contains KDE support for synchronizing data with cell phones.

✦ **kdepim-devel:** Contains header files and libraries needed for developing applications which use kdepim.

✦ **kdepim-pilot:** Contains KDE support for synchronizing data with a Palm Pilot or compatible PDA device.

✦ **kdesdk:** Contains the KDE software development kit.

✦ **kdesdk-devel:** Contains development files for kdesdk.

✦ **kdetoys:** Contains some fun utilities, such as kmoon (moon phase indicator) and kworldwatch (which indicates areas in sunlight and times around the world).

✦ **kdeutils:** Contains utilities, such as calculators and simple editors, for use with the KDE desktop.

✦ **kdevelop:** Contains development tools for creating applications with consistent interfaces in the KDE desktop environment.

✦ **kdoc:** Contains the kdoc2 program for cross-referencing specially formatted comments in C++ header files.

✦ **kernel:** Contains the Red Hat Linux kernel software, which is the heart of the operating system.

✦ **kernel-BOOT:** Contains a trimmed-down version of the Linux kernel suitable for placing on an installation boot disk.

✦ **kernel-doc:** Contains documentation files that come with parts of the Linux kernel source code.

✦ **kernel-enterprise:** Contains kernel configuration components that are appropriate for large computer installations.

✦ **kernel-headers:** Contains the C header files needed to build the Red Hat Linux kernel.

✦ **kernel-pcmcia-cs:** Contains software that supports PCMCIA devices (typically used on laptop computers).

✦ **kernel-smp:** Contains the SMP (symmetric multiprocessing) Linux kernel version.

✦ **kernel-source:** Contains the source code files that are used to build the Red Hat Linux kernel.

✦ **kinput2-canna-wnn6:** Contains an input server for X11 applications that require Japanese text input in either Canna or Wnn6.

✦ **knm_new:** Contains Kaname-cho font.

✦ **koffice:** Contains the a set of office productivity applications.

✦ **kon2:** Contains a Kanji emulator for the console.

✦ **kon2-fonts:** Contains fonts for kon.

✦ **kpppload:** Contains the `kpppload` utility for visually monitoring the load on your PPP connections.

✦ **krb5*:** This set of packages is used to provide support for Kerberos authentication methods.

✦ **krbafs*:** Contains the krbafs library, for providing support for AFS tokens with Kerberos 5 credentials.

✦ **ksconfig:** Contains the ksconfig graphical tool for creating Kickstart files (for doing unattended Red Hat Linux installations).

✦ **ksymoops:** Contains a utility that reads kernel error messages and converts them to meaningful symbols and offsets.

✦ **kterm:** Contains the kterm multi-lingual terminal window.

✦ **kudzu:** Contains the `kudzu` utility, which detects and configures computer hardware.

✦ **kudzu-devel:** Contains header files used to create kudzu applications.

✦ **kWnn:** Contains a Korean character set input system.

- **kWnn-devel:** Contains header files and library needed to develop applications that use kWnn.
- **lam:** Contains Local Area Management (LAM) software development tools for managing clusters of computers on a network.
- **lapack:** Contains the Linear Algebra Package (LAPACK) for solving simultaneous linear equations.
- **lapack-man:** Contains documentation for the lapack package.
- **lclint:** Contains the lclint utility for scanning C programs for style and errors.
- **less:** Contains the `less` utility, which is used to page through and search text documents.
- **lesstif:** Contains a free replacement for OSF/Motif, providing a full set of widgets for application development.
- **lesstif-devel:** Contains a static library and header files needed to develop Motif-1.2-based applications using LessTif.
- **lftp:** Contains a sophisticated ftp/http file transfer program.
- **lha:** Contains an archiving and compression utility for LHarc format archives.
- **libao:** Contains a cross-platform audio output library.
- **libao-devel:** Contains the header files and documentation needed to develop applications with libao.
- **libcap:** Contains a library for getting and setting POSIX.1e capabilities.
- **libcap-devel:** Contains headers and libraries needed for developing applications that use libcap.
- **libelf:** Contains libraries that let applications access the internals of ELF object files.
- **libesmtp:** Contains a library that manages the posting of e-mail using SMTP.
- **libesmtp-devel:** Contains the header files and libraries needed to develop applications using libesmtp.
- **libgal7:** Contains a variety of GNOME functions and utilities.
- **libgcc:** Contains GCC version 3 shared support library.
- **libgcj:** Contains the Java runtime library for gcc.
- **libgcj-devel:** Contains development tools associated with the Java runtime library for gcc.
- **libgcj3:** Contains the Java runtime library for gcc version 3.
- **libgcj3-devel:** Contains the development tools associated with the Java runtime library for gcc version 3 that are required for compilation.

✦ **libghttp:** Contains the ghttp library, used for making HTTP 1.1 requests.

✦ **libghttp-devel:** Contains the components needed to develop libghttp applications.

✦ **libglade:** Contains libraries that can be used to create GLADE user interface applications.

✦ **libglade-devel:** Contains tools and documentation for developing GLADE applications.

✦ **libgnomeprint15:** Contains components needed to support GNOME printing.

✦ **libgtop:** Contains a library that gets information about system usage.

✦ **libgtop-devel:** Contains basic components needed to develop applications that monitor system usage.

✦ **libgtop-examples:** Contains examples of retrieved systems information used by libgtop.

✦ **libjpeg6a-6a:** Contains backward-compatible versions of the libjpeg libraries for using JPEG images.

✦ **libjpeg-6b:** Contains the libjpeg library for manipulating JPEG images.

✦ **libjpeg-devel-6b:** Contains header files and static libraries for creating programs that use JPEG images.

✦ **libmng:** Contains the libmng library for working with images in MNG and JNG formats.

✦ **libmng-devel:** Contains header files related to the libmng library.

✦ **libmng-static:** Contains static versions of the libmng library.

✦ **libodbc++:** Contains interface components for the JDBC Java protocol within KDE.

✦ **libodbc++-devel:** Contains software development tools for the JDBC Java protocol within KDE.

✦ **libodbc++-qt:** Contains software development tools for the JDBC Java protocol for integration with the QT GUI toolkit.

✦ **libogg:** Contains the libogg library for working with ogg bitstreams.

✦ **libogg-devel:** Contains documentation and header files for developing ogg applications.

✦ **libole2:** Contains the libogg library for working with OLE structured storage files.

✦ **libole2-devel:** Contains documentation and header files for developing applications that manipulate OLE structured storage files.

✦ **libpcap:** Contains components for creating applications that can monitor low-level network traffic.

✦ **libpng:** Contains the libpng library for working with PNG image files.

✦ **libpng-devel:** Contains libraries and header files needed to develop programs that use PNG images.

✦ **libPropList:** The PropList libraries allow programs using configuration files to make them compatible with GNUstep/OpenStep.

✦ **librep:** Contains tools and documentation associated with the librep Lisp dialect.

✦ **librep-devel:** Contains header files and tools associated with the libred Lisp dialect.

✦ **librsvg:** Contains an SVG library based on libart.

✦ **librsvg-devel:** Contains libraries and include files required for developing applications using librsvg.

✦ **libsigc++:** Contains a library which implements a callback system for use in widget libraries.

✦ **libsigc++-devel:** Contains the static libraries and header files required to develop applications using libsigc++.

✦ **libstdc++:** Contains the EGCS libraries needed to run C++ applications.

✦ **libstdc++-devel:** Contains standard C++ development libraries.

✦ **libtabe:** Contains Chinese lexicon libraries for xcin input method.

✦ **libtabe-devel:** Contains the header files and libraries required for developing applications which will use libtabe.

✦ **libtermcap:** Contains libraries needed to access the termcap database for managing character displays.

✦ **libtermcap-devel:** Contains components needed to develop programs that access the termcap database.

✦ **libtiff:** Contains libraries for using and saving GIF image files.

✦ **libtiff-devel:** Contains development tools used to work with TIFF image files in applications.

✦ **libtool:** Contains the libtool shell scripts, which are used to configure Linux to build generic shared libraries.

✦ **libtool-libs13:** Contains runtime libraries associated with libtool utilities (for building generic shared libraries).

✦ **libtool-libs13:** Contains runtime libraries, created to be compatible with libtool 1.3 utilities (for building generic shared libraries).

✦ **libungif:** Contains library functions needed to use and save GIF image files.

✦ **libungif-devel:** Contains development tools used to create applications to load and save GIF image files.

✦ **libungif-progs:** Contains several utilities for working with GIF images.

✦ **libunicode:** Contains the unicode manipulation library, for working with unicode strings.

✦ **libunicode-devel:** Contains static libraries and header files for unicode support.

✦ **libuser:** Contains a standardized interface for administration of user accounts.

✦ **libuser-devel:** Contains header files and static libraries required for developing applications that use libuser.

✦ **libvorbis:** Contains the Ogg Vorbis open audio compression codec and run-time libraries.

✦ **libvorbis-devel:** Contains header files and documentation required to develop applications using libvorbis.

✦ **libxml:** Contains a library of functions for working with XML files.

✦ **libxml-devel:** Contains tools for developing applications that use the libxml library.

✦ **libxml10:** Contains the backward-compatible libxml10 XML parser for GNOME.

✦ **libxml2:** Contains a library that allows manipulation of XML and HTML files, including DTD support.

✦ **libxml2-devel:** Contains libraries and include files required to develop applications using libxml2.

✦ **libxslt:** Contains a tool which translates XML into other structures using the XSLT transformation mechanism.

✦ **libxslt-devel:** Contains libraries and include files required to develop applications using libxslt.

✦ **licq:** Contains the licq ICQ utility for chatting on TCP/IP networks.

✦ **licq-gnome:** Contains a GNOME front-end for licq.

✦ **licq-kde:** Contains a KDE front-end for licq.

✦ **licq-qt:** Contains a Qt front-end for licq.

✦ **licq-text:** Contains a text mode front-end for licq.

✦ **lilo:** Contains the LILO (LInux LOader) program for booting Linux or other systems.

◆ **links:** Contains the `links` text-based Web browser.

◆ **linuxconf:** Contains the comprehensive linuxconf system administration facility.

◆ **linuxconf-devel:** Contains tools for creating modules to use in the linuxconf administration interface.

◆ **lm_sensors:** Contains modules for interfacing with sensors that monitor computer hardware.

◆ **lm_sensors-devel:** Contains software for developing software that interfaces with hardware monitors.

◆ **locale_config:** Contains the `locale_config` command for graphically selecting the default system locale.

◆ **lockdev:** Contains the liblockdev library for locking devices.

◆ **lockdev-devel:** Contains static library versions and headers for the liblockdev library.

◆ **logrotate:** Contains the `logrotate` program for administering multiple log files.

◆ **logwatch:** Contains a customizable log file analysis program.

◆ **lokkit:** Contains the `lokkit` command for creating a simple set of firewall rules for your network.

◆ **losetup:** Contains the Linux loop device, for mapping a regular file into a virtual block device.

◆ **lout:** Contains the lout language tools for formatting documents. It supports several languages.

◆ **lout-doc:** Contains documentation that explains how to use the lout document formatting tools.

◆ **LPRng:** Contains the LPRng printing software, which contains the basic user and administrative printing tools for Red Hat Linux.

◆ **lrzsz:** Contains the `lrz` and `lsz` utilities, which are used to provide Zmodem functions in Linux.

◆ **lslk:** Contains the `lslk` utility for listing lock files.

◆ **lsof:** Contains the `lsof` utility for listing information about open files.

◆ **ltrace:** Contains the `ltrace` tool for running and tracing the activities of a specific command.

◆ **lv:** Contains the lv multilingual file viewer and related utilities.

◆ **lynx:** Contains the `lynx` text-based Internet Web browser.

✦ **m2crypto:** Contains support for OpenSSL in Python scripts.

✦ **m4:** Contains the `m4` macro processor, an implementation of the UNIX m4 processor.

✦ **macutils:** Contains utilities for working with files that are often used with Macintosh computers.

✦ **Maelstrom:** Contains the Maelstrom (shoot-the-asteroids) game.

✦ **magicdev:** Contains the `magicdev` daemon for detecting and playing audio CDs.

✦ **MagicPoint:** Contains an X11-based presentation tool.

✦ **mailcap:** Contains the mailcap configuration file for defining how special data types are handled.

✦ **mailman:** Contains a mailing list manager accessed through a Web page.

✦ **mailx:** Contains the `/bin/mail` program for easily sending plain text e-mail messages.

✦ **make:** Contains the `make` command for building and installing software from source code.

✦ **MAKEDEV:** Contains a program that makes it easier to create and maintain files in the `/dev` directory.

✦ **man:** Contains the `man` command for displaying information and documentation about a UNIX system.

✦ **man-pages*:** This set of man pages contains many man pages from the Linux Documentation Project. Each man-pages package contains man pages that relate to a particular language.

✦ **mars-nwe:** Contains components needed to allow Linux to emulate a NetWare file and print server.

✦ **mawk:** Contains the `mawk` version of the awk programming language processor.

✦ **mc:** Contains the Midnight Commander visual shell for managing a variety of file interfaces, such as FTP, Zip files, Tar files, and RPMs.

✦ **mcserv:** Contains Midnight Commander file management server tools to allow remote access to files.

✦ **memprof:** Contains the `memprof` command for profiling memory usage by applications from the desktop.

✦ **Mesa:** Contains the Mesa 3D graphics library.

✦ **Mesa-demos:** Contains demo programs that run on Mesa 3D graphics cards.

+ **Mesa-devel:** Contains the development environment associated with the Mesa 3D graphics library.

+ **metamail:** Contains utilities for managing multimedia mail with the mailcap file.

+ **mgetty:** Contains the `mgetty` version of getty for allowing logins to Linux over serial lines.

+ **mgetty-sendfax:** Contains the `sendfax` program for sending faxes in conjunction with the `mgetty` program.

+ **mgetty-viewfax:** Contains the `viewfax` utilities for displaying faxes in X that were received by `mgetty`.

+ **mgetty-voice:** Contains `vgetty` utilities for supporting voice communications with `mgetty`.

+ **micq:** Contains a program that is a clone of the ICQ instant messenger.

+ **mikmod:** Contains the MikMod music file player for playing a variety of audio formats.

+ **mingetty:** Contains a minimalist version of getty called `mgetty` to allow logins on virtual consoles.

+ **miniChinput:** Contains a smaller version of Chinput, a Chinese XIM server.

+ **minicom:** Contains the `minicom` text-based modem control for communicating over modems.

+ **mkbootdisk:** Contains the `mkbootdisk` utility for creating a bootable floppy disk.

+ **mkinitrd:** Contains the `mkinitrd` program for creating initial RAM disk images.

+ **mkisofs:** Contains the `mkisofs` program for creating ISO9660 file systems (to make CD-ROMs).

+ **mkkickstart:** Contains the `mkkickstart` utility for building a computer's configuration automatically, so it can be used during a network or CD-ROM installation.

+ **mktemp:** Contains the `mktemp` utility for safely creating /tmp files that can be used by shell scripts.

+ **mkxauth:** Contains the `mkxauth` utility for setting up and controlling X authentication databases.

+ **mm:** Contains a library that provides a shared memory layer for processes.

+ **mm-devel:** Contains the files required for developing applications that use mm.

✦ **modutils:** Contains the `kerneld` program for loading kernel modules.

✦ **mod_auth_any:** Contains basic authentication for the Apache Web server using arbitrary shell commands.

✦ **mod_auth_mysql:** Contains basic authentication for the Apache Web server using MySQL database.

✦ **mod_auth_pgsql:** Contains basic authentication for the Apache Web server using PostgresQL database.

✦ **mod_bandwidth:** Contains an Apache module that can limit bandwidth usage.

✦ **mod_dav:** Contains a module that enables the Apache Web server to handle the DAV (Distributed Authoring and Versioning) protocol, which replaces proprietary Web publishing protocols.

✦ **mod_perl:** Contains a Perl interpreter that is used with an Apache Web server to allow it to interpret Perl code.

✦ **mod_put:** Contains an Apache module that implements the PUT and DELETE client methods.

✦ **mod_python:** Contains an embedded Python interpreter for the Apache Web server.

✦ **mod_roaming:** Contains an Apache module, which allows the Web server to support Netscape Communicator roaming profiles.

✦ **mod_ssl:** Contains the mod_ssl module, which is used by the Apache Web server to provide secure cryptography using the Secure Socket Layer (SSL) cryptography and Transport Layer Security (TLS) protocols.

✦ **mod_throttle:** Contains an Apache Web server module that can throttle the amount of bandwidth the server uses.

✦ **mount:** Contains utilities for mounting and unmounting file systems (`mount`, `umount`, etc.).

✦ **mouseconfig:** Contains the `mouseconfig` utility for configuring attributes of your mouse.

✦ **mozilla*:** Contains the Mozilla Web browser, as well as related utilities and programming libraries.

✦ **mpage:** Contains the `mpage` utility, which allows you to print several pages of PostScript output on a single page.

✦ **mpg123:** Contains the `mpg123` audio player for playing MPEG audio files.

✦ **mrtg:** Contains the Multi Router Traffic Grapher tool, which creates charts of network traffic.

✦ **mt-st:** Contains the `mt` (magnetic tape) and `st` (SCSI tape) programs for managing tape drives.

✦ **mtools:** Contains utilities for managing MS-DOS files and disks.

✦ **mtr:** Contains the mtr network diagnostic tool, which combines ping and traceroute features.

✦ **mtr-gtk:** Contains a GTK interface to the mtr network diagnostic tool.

✦ **mtx:** Contains the mtx program for working with tape libraries and autoloaders.

✦ **mutt:** Contains the `mutt` text-based e-mail mail user agent.

✦ **mx:** Contains a collection of Python software tools.

✦ **MyODBC:** Contains an ODBC driver for MySQL.

✦ **mysql*:** This set of packages contains tools for interfacing with SQL databases.

✦ **nasm:** Contains the nasm Netwide Assembler.

✦ **nasm-doc:** Contains documentation for the nasm Netwide Assembler.

✦ **nasm-rdoff:** Contains tools for the RDOFF binary format, which can be used with nasm.

✦ **nautilus:** Contains a network user environment, which integrates access to files, applications, and Internet resources.

✦ **nautilus-devel:** Contains libraries and include files required for developing Nautilus components.

✦ **nautilus-mozilla:** Contains a component that enables Mozilla to be used as a Nautilus component.

✦ **nc:** Contains the Netcat (`nc`) utility for reading and writing data across TCP/IP connections.

✦ **ncftp:** Contains the `ncftp` FTP client program, which includes improved command line editing and histories.

✦ **ncompress:** Contains the `compress` and `uncompress` utilities to create and expand compressed files.

✦ **ncpfs:** Contains components needed to use Novell NetWare ncpfs file systems.

✦ **ncurses:** Contains the ncurses library needed by applications that control character-based screens.

✦ **ncurses-devel:** Contains components to create applications that use the ncurses screen handling interface.

✦ **ncurses4:** Contains a backward-compatible version of the ncurses library.

✦ **net-tools:** Contains a basic set of tools for configuring networking.

✦ **netconfig:** Contains the `netconfig` utility, which is a graphical tool for configuring network interfaces.

✦ **netpbm:** Contains netpbm tools for working with graphical images.

✦ **netpbm-devel:** Contains static libraries and headers for the netpbm interface.

✦ **netpbm-progs:** Contains scripts for working with graphical images.

✦ **netscape-common:** Contains files that are shared by applications in the Netscape Communicator suite.

✦ **netscape-communicator:** Contains the applications that make up Netscape Communicator.

✦ **netscape-navigator:** Contains the Netscape Navigator Web browser for those who want the browser, but not the other components that make up the Netscape Communicator suite.

✦ **newt:** Contains the Newt library for creating color, text-based, and widget based user interfaces.

✦ **newt-devel:** Contains header files and libraries for developing text-mode applications that use Newt.

✦ **nfs-utils:** Contains utilities that you can use with the Network File System (NFS) facility to share files and directories over the network.

✦ **nhpf:** Contains a utility to create postscript files in the Korean Hangul font.

✦ **njamd:** Contains an advanced debugger for detecting memory allocation errors.

✦ **nkf:** Contains `nkf` network Kanji code conversion filter.

✦ **nmap:** Contains a network exploration tool and security scanner.

✦ **nmap-frontend:** Contains a Gtk+ front-end for nmap.

✦ **nmh:** Contains the nmh e-mail system, which can be used as a replacement for MH mail.

✦ **nscd:** Contains the nscd daemon for caching name services requests from NIS and DNS.

✦ **nss_db:** Contains libraries that allow programs to access basic system information (users, groups, hosts, services, etc.) from Berkeley UNIX databases.

✦ **nss_db-compat:** Contains libraries that provide backward compatibility to access older versions of Berkeley UNIX databases.

✦ **nss_ldap:** Contains the NSS library and PAM (for supporting password and other security features) for handling LDAP clients.

✦ **ntp:** Contains the Network Time Protocol daemon for synchronizing system time from the network.

- ✦ **ntsysv:** Contains the `ntsysv` command for configuring services at different run levels.

- ✦ **nut:** Contains software tools for monitoring uninterruptible power supply (UPS) systems.

- ✦ **nut-cgi:** Contains CGI scripts for monitoring UPS systems.

- ✦ **nut-client:** Contains client utilities for monitoring UPS systems over a network.

- ✦ **nvi-m17n:** Contains common files for the nvi multilingual text editor, which supports Japanese, Korean, Chinese, and other encoding schemes.

- ✦ **nvi-ml17n-canna:** Contains the nvi multilingual text editor with support for the canna input system.

- ✦ **nviml17n-nocanna:** Contains the nvi multilingual text editor without support for the canna input system.

- ✦ **oaf:** Contains an object activation framework for GNOME.

- ✦ **oaf-devel:** Contains libraries and include files for developing applications that use oaf.

- ✦ **octave:** Contains the GNU octave tools for performing numerical computations.

- ✦ **open:** Contains the `open` command for using virtual consoles to run programs.

- ✦ **openjade:** Contains utilities for parsing DSSSL SGML content.

- ✦ **openldap:** Contains configuration files, documentation, and libraries needed to run OpenLDAP programs. LDAP is an standard protocol for accessing information services.

- ✦ **openldap-clients:** Contains client programs used to work with OpenLDAP directories.

- ✦ **openldap-devel:** Contains tools and documentation needed to create LDAP client programs.

- ✦ **openldap-servers:** Contains server programs used to make OpenLDAP directories available.

- ✦ **openldap12:** Contains OpenLDAP development tools required for running OpenLDAP 1.2 applications.

- ✦ **openssh*:** Contains components needed by OpenSSH client and server processes. OpenSSH lets clients login and execute commands securely on remote systems.

- ✦ **openssl*:** Contains components need to provide Secure Socket Layer (SSL) services. These include tools for managing certificates and keys.

✦ **ORBit:** Contains daemon processes used with the ORBit implementation of CORBA ORB.

✦ **ORBit-devel:** Contains header files, libraries, and utilities needed to write programs using Corba ORB.

✦ **p2c:** Contains the P2c system, which is used to translate Pascal code into C language code.

✦ **pam:** Contains the Pluggable Authentication Modules (PAM) libraries for selecting and changing authentication mechanisms used with Red Hat Linux.

✦ **pam-devel:** Contains static libraries and header files needed for PAM applications.

✦ **pam_krb5:** Contains PAM libraries that can be used with Kerberos 5 authentication.

✦ **pam_smb:** Contains a module that can authenticate users using an external SMB server.

✦ **pan:** Contains the pan graphical newsgroup news reader.

✦ **pango:** Contains Pango software for rendering international text.

✦ **pango-devel:** Contains development tools associated with Pango software for rendering international text.

✦ **parted:** Contains the `parted` utility for creating and resizing partitions.

✦ **parted-devel:** Contains the GNU parted library for manipulating disk partitions.

✦ **passwd:** Contains the `passwd` command for adding or changing user passwords.

✦ **patch:** Contains the `patch` program for using the output from running the `diff` command to update code to include changes found from the original to the updated file.

✦ **pax:** Contains the `pax` utility for creating and reading archive files.

✦ **pccts:** Contains software tools that help in the implementation of compilers and other translation systems.

✦ **pciutils:** Contains utilities for viewing and configuring information about devices connected to a PCI bus.

✦ **pciutils-devel:** Contains header files associated with PCI utilities.

✦ **pcre:** Contains a Perl-compatible, regular expression library.

✦ **pcre-devel:** Contains headers and libraries needed for developing applications with pcre.

✦ **pdksh:** Contains the pdksh utility, which is an implementation of the Korn shell.

✦ **perl*:** Contains perl high-level programming language components.

✦ **php:** Contains the PHP scripting language, which can be embedded in HTML for use on Apache servers.

✦ **php-devel:** Contains commands and header files for building PHP extensions.

✦ **php-imap:** Contains the IMAP module that can be used with PHP.

✦ **php-ldap:** Contains the LDAP module that can be used with Apache server applications.

✦ **php-manual:** Contains the PHP manual, in HTML format.

✦ **php-mysql:** Contains a module that allows PHP4 modules to access MySQL databases.

✦ **php-odbc:** Contains a module that allows PHP4 modules to access ODBC.

✦ **php-pgsql:** Contains the PostgreSQL database modules that can be used with PHP.

✦ **pidentd:** Contains the pidentd daemon that returns information about TCP/IP connections.

✦ **pidentd:** Contains an implementation of the RFC1413 identification server.

✦ **pilot-link:** Contains tools for synchronizing a USR Pilot with a Red Hat Linux system.

✦ **pilot-link-devel:** Contains components needed to build the pilot-link application.

✦ **pine:** Contains the pine mail user agent, including the simple pico text editor.

✦ **pinfo:** Contains the pinfo viewer for displaying info pages and man pages.

✦ **pkgconfig:** Contains the pkg-config command for entering package compilation options.

✦ **playmidi:** Contains the playmidi utility for playing MIDI music files.

✦ **playmidi-X11:** Contains the xplaymidi utility for playing MIDI music files in the X Window System.

✦ **plugger:** Contains the plugger Netscape plug-in that can be used as a generic interface for using Linux utilities as plug-ins.

✦ **pmake:** Contains a GNU tool that allows users to build and install programs without knowledge of the build process.

✦ **pnm2ppa:** Contains drivers for printing to HP PNA printers.

✦ **popt:** Contains the Popt C language library for `parsing` command line parameters.

✦ **portmap:** Contains the `portmapper` utility, which manages RPC connections for NFS and NIS.

✦ **postgresql*:** This set of software packages contains utilities and programming interfaces needed to create and maintain a PostgreSQL database server.

✦ **ppp:** Contains the Point-to-Point Protocol daemon (pppd) for managing TCP/IP connections over serial lines.

✦ **prelink:** Contains an ELF pre-linking utility that makes programs start up more quickly.

✦ **printconf:** Contains the `printconf` printer configuration system. This include ncpprint and smbprint tools for printing to NetWare and Samba printers, respectively.

✦ **printconf-gui:** Contains the `printconf-gui` command for configuring printers.

✦ **procinfo:** Contains the `procinfo` command for displaying information about the kernel from the proc file system.

✦ **procmail:** Contains the `procmail` utility for managing local e-mail delivery.

✦ **procps:** Contains utilities, such as `ps`, `free`, and `top`, for displaying system information.

✦ **procps-X11:** Contains the XConsole shell script, which provides a wrapper for the xconsole program.

✦ **psacct:** Contains process accounting utilities, such as `ac`, `lastcomm`, `accton`, and `sa`, for displaying accounting information about users and processes they run.

✦ **psgml:** Contains PSGML software that allows GNU Emacs to edit SGML and XML documents.

✦ **psmisc:** Contains utilities, such as `pstree`, `killall`, and `fuser`, for managing processes on the system.

✦ **pspell:** Contains the pspell spell checking library.

✦ **pspell-devel:** Contains static libraries and headers for the pspell spell checking interface.

✦ **psutils:** Contains utilities for manipulating postscript documents.

✦ **pump:** Contains the pump client daemon, which can retrieve BOOTP or DHCP configuration information from a server.

✦ **pump-devel:** Contains software development libraries to interface with the pump facility.

◆ **pvm:** Contains the `pvmd` daemon and related utilities for coordinating a virtual machine across several UNIX and/or Linux host computers.

◆ **pvm-gui:** Contains the X-based xpvm tools for graphically managing a virtual machine.

◆ **pwdb:** Contains the password database library for managing user and group information.

◆ **pxe:** Contains the `pxe` utility and related libraries for remote booting and installing Linux.

◆ **pychecker:** Contains a Python source code checking tool.

◆ **pygnome:** Contains the PyGNOME extension to Python for providing access to GNOME libraries.

◆ **pygnome-applet:** Contains Python bindings for GNOME panel applets.

◆ **pygnome-capplet:** Contains panel applets for GNOME.

◆ **pygnome-devel:** Contains files required to build wrappers for GTK+ libraries, enabling them to be compatible with PyGNOME.

◆ **pygnome-gtkhtml:** Contains a wrapper for the GTKHTML widget that allows the rendering of html inside a pygtk program.

◆ **pygnome-libglade:** Contains libglade Python wrapper support in GNOME.

◆ **pygtk:** Contains the modules that let gtk features be used in Python.

◆ **pygtk-devel:** Contains the files required to build wrappers for GTK+ libraries, enabling them to be compatible with pygtk.

◆ **pygtk-glarea:** Contains a wrapper for the GTKGLAREA widget that enables the display of OpenGL output in a pygtk program.

◆ **pygtk-libglade:** Contains the libglade module, which provides a wrapper for the libglade library.

◆ **pyqt:** Contains the Python bindings for Qt.

◆ **pyqt-devel:** Contains files needed to build other bindings for C++ classes based on any of the Qt classes.

◆ **pyqt-examples:** Contains sample code demonstrating how to use the Python bindings for Qt.

◆ **python:** Contains the Python interpreter, an interactive object-oriented programming language.

◆ **python-devel:** Contains header files and libraries for adding dynamically loaded Python extensions.

◆ **python-docs:** Contains documentation for the Python programming language (in text and LaTeX).

✦ **python-tools:** Contains tools to provide a Tkinter-based IDE for Python.

✦ **python-xmlrpc:** Contains a library of Python functions that implement the Userland XML RPC protocol.

✦ **pyxml:** Contains xml libraries for Python.

✦ **qt:** Contains the Qt software toolkit for creating X Window System applications.

✦ **qt-designer:** Contains user interface development tools for the Qt toolkit.

✦ **qt-devel:** Contains components needed to develop Qt applications.

✦ **qt-static:** Contains static libraries for the Qt toolkit.

✦ **qt-Xt:** Contains the Xt compatibility add-on for Qt.

✦ **qt1x:** Contains a version of the Qt toolkit that is compatible with version 1.x.

✦ **qt1x-devel:** Contains a version of the Qt development library that is compatible with version 1.x .

✦ **qt1x-GL:** Contains a version of the OpenGL add-on for the Qt toolkit that is compatible with version 1.x.

✦ **qt3*:** This set of packages contains beta versions of the next implementation of Qt.

✦ **quanta:** Contains an html editor for the KDE environment.

✦ **quota:** Contains the `quota`, `quotacheck`, `quotaoff`, and `quotaon` utilities for managing disk space.

✦ **radvd:** Contains the router advertisement daemon for IPv6.

✦ **raidtools:** Contains several raid utilities for configuring raid file system devices.

✦ **rarpd:** Contains the rarpd daemon for providing Reverse Address Resolution Protocol (RARP) features for TCP/IP networks.

✦ **rcs:** Contains the Revision Control System for managing multiple versions of files.

✦ **rdate:** Contains the `rdate` utility for retrieving the date and time from a computer on the network.

✦ **rdist:** Contains the `rdist` program for maintaining exact copies of files on multiple computers.

✦ **readline:** Contains the readline library for allowing programs to edit text lines with emacs keys.

✦ **readline-devel:** Contains components needed to develop applications that need the readline library.

+ **readline2.2.1:** Contains a version of the readline library that is compatible with Red Hat Linux 6.2.

+ **redhat-config-network:** Contains the network administration tool for Red Hat Linux.

+ **redhat-config-users:** Contains a graphical interface for administering users and groups.

+ **redhat-logos:** Contains the Red Hat Shadow Man and RPM trademarked logos.

+ **redhat-release:** Contains the Red Hat Linux release file.

+ **reiserfs-utils:** Contains utilities for checking and repairing ReiserFS file systems.

+ **rep-gtk:** Contains the rep-gtk binding of GTK+ for the rep Lisp interpreter.

+ **rep-gtk-gnome:** Contains bindings to different GNOME libraries for the Lisp interpreter.

+ **rep-gtk-libglade:** Contains the librep binding for the libglade library. This is used for loading libglade user interfaces.

+ **rhmask:** Contains the `rhmask` utility, which creates mask files from original and updated files.

+ **rhn_register:** Contains components that let you register your system with Red Hat Network services.

+ **rhn_register-gnome:** Contains Red Hat Network registration software if an X desktop interface is available.

+ **rmt:** Contains the `rmt` command for accessing remote tape devices.

+ **rootfiles:** Contains the default user configuration files provided to the root user, including .Xdefaults, .bash_logout, .bash_profile, .bashrc, .cshrc, and .tcshrc.

+ **routed:** Contains the routed daemon, which handles routing traffic and maintains routing tables.

+ **rp-pppoe:** Contains PPP over Ethernet software for connecting to an ISP over some ADSL modems.

+ **rp3:** Contains the graphical Red Hat PPP management tool for configuring dial-up connections to the Internet.

+ **rpm:** Contains the `rpm` command for installing and managing RPM (.rpm) software packages.

+ **rpm-build:** Contains development tools for creating RPM packages.

+ **rpm-devel:** Contains components that simplify the process of creating applications that manipulate RPM packages.

✦ **rpm-python:** Contains Python bindings for applications that work with RPM packages.

✦ **rpm2html:** Contains tools for converting RPM data to HTML output.

✦ **rpmdb-redhat:** Contains the database for the entire Red Hat Linux distribution.

✦ **rpmfind:** Contains the rpmfind tool for locating RPM packages on the Web.

✦ **rpmlint:** Contains tools for checking that RPM packages work properly.

✦ **rpm-perl:** Contains native bindings to the RPM API for Perl.

✦ **rpm-python:** Contains native bindings to the RPM API for Python.

✦ **rsh:** Contains `rsh`, `rcp`, `rlogin`, and other "r" commands that are used for remote execution, file copying, login, and other features over a network.

✦ **rsh-server:** Contains the `in.rshd` daemon for providing the rsh (remote shell) service to clients from the network.

✦ **rsync:** Contains the `rsync` utility for synchronizing files between a remote and local host.

✦ **ruby*:** This set of packages contains an object-oriented scripting language called Ruby.

✦ **rusers:** Contains the `rusers` utility, which lets users find out who is logged in other machines on the network.

✦ **rusers-server:** Contains the `in.rusersd` daemon for providing the ruser (remote user) service to clients from the network.

✦ **rwall:** Contains the `rwall` command, which is used to send messages to all users who are currently logged in a computer.

✦ **rwall-server:** Contains the `in.rwalld` daemon for providing the rwall (remote write to all user terminals) service to clients from the network.

✦ **rwho:** The `rwho` command displays information about users on other machines on the network.

✦ **rxvt:** Contains the `rxvt` color VT102 terminal emulator window that runs in the X Window System.

✦ **samba:** Contains the Samba SMB server software for sharing files, folders, and printers on a network with other computers (usually Microsoft Windows, OS/2, or Linux systems).

✦ **samba-client:** Contains Samba utilities needed to provide file and print sharing with Microsoft Windows operating systems.

✦ **samba-common:** Contains Samba configuration files and related utilities for configuring a Samba server.

- **samba-swat:** Contains SWAT Web-based interface for configuring Samba from a Web browser.
- **sane-backends:** Contains SANE utilities for using and managing scanners.
- **sane-backends-devel:** Contains programming libraries for interfacing to scanners.
- **sane-frontends:** Contains graphical front-end to SANE.
- **sash:** Contains the `sash` shell, which includes several simplified shell built-in commands.
- **sawfish:** Contains the sawfish window manager for X11.
- **sawfish-themer:** Contains a graphical tool for creating sawfish window manager themes.
- **screen:** Contains the `screen` utility, which allows you to have multiple logins on a single terminal.
- **scrollkeeper:** Contains a cataloging system for documentation on open systems.
- **SDL:** Contains the Simple DirectMedia Layer utilities for creating audio, keyboard, mouse, and display framebuffer applications.
- **SDL-devel:** Contains the Simple DirectMedia Layer application programming interface for creating audio, keyboard, mouse, and display framebuffer applications.
- **SDL_image:** Contains the `showimage` utility for displaying image files.
- **SDL_image-devel:** Contains a library for loading images for SDL applications.
- **SDL_mixer:** Contains Simple DirectMedia Layer (SDL) sound mixing tools.
- **SDL_mixer-devel:** Contains SDL sound mixing application development tools.
- **SDL_net:** Contains a portable network library for use with SDL.
- **SDL_net-devel:** Contains libraries and include files needed to develop SDL networked applications.
- **SDL11:** Contains a backward-compatible (version 1.1) SDL.
- **sed:** Contains the `sed` utility for doing repeated search and edit functions on groups of files.
- **semi:** Contains libraries that provide MIME and other functions to emacs.
- **semi-xemacs:** Contains libraries that provide MIME and other functions to xemacs.
- **sendmail:** Contains the `sendmail` mail transport agent, which transports mail between e-mail servers.

✦ **sendmail-cf:** Contains the files for generating a sendmail.cf file (the configuration file for sendmail).

✦ **sendmail-doc:** Contains documents relating to the sendmail mail transport agent (Postscript and troff).

✦ **serviceconf:** Contains a utility that configures enabled services on the system.

✦ **setserial:** Contains the `setserial` utility for configuring and showing serial port information.

✦ **setup:** Contains default versions of many basic system configuration files (in /etc/directory), including /etc/exports, /etc/host.conf, /etc/passwd, /etc/profile, /etc/services, and others.

✦ **setuptool:** Contains the text-mode `setuptool` utility for accessing text mode configuration tools in Red Hat Linux.

✦ **sgml-common:** Contains catalog and DTD files used with SGML.

✦ **sgml-tools:** Contains utilities for formatting documents based on SGML (such as LaTeX, HTML, RTF, LyX, and others).

✦ **sh-utils:** Contains a set of GNU shell utilities, such as `date`, `echo`, `logname`, and many others.

✦ **shadow-utils:** Contains utilities for working with shadow passwords and related user and group information.

✦ **shapecfg:** Contains the `shapecfg` command for shaping network traffic transmissions.

✦ **sharutils:** Contains utilities for encoding and decoding packages of files.

✦ **sip:** Contains a tool that generates bindings for C++ classes, enabling them to be accessed as Python classes.

✦ **sip-devel:** Contains files needed to generate Python bindings for any C++ class library.

✦ **skkdic:** Contains a dictionary for a simple Kana-Kanji conversion program.

✦ **skkinput:** Contains a Kana to Kanji converter with multiple input protocols.

✦ **slang:** Contains the S-Lang language extension libraries and related components.

✦ **slang-devel:** Contains components needed to develop S-Lang based applications.

✦ **sliplogin:** Contains `sliplogin` for creating SLIP links on terminal lines.

✦ **slocate:** Contains the `slocate` utility for search databases for selected patterns.

✦ **slrn:** Contains the `slrn` threaded Internet news reader.

✦ **slrn-pull:** Contains the `slrnpull` utility for spooling news for offline news reading.

✦ **smpeg:** Contains the `gtv` and `plaympeg` utilities for playing MPEG video content.

✦ **smpeg-devel:** Contains the static libraries and header files for MPEG software development.

✦ **smpeg-xmms:** Contains an MPEG video plug-in that works with the XMMS player.

✦ **snavigator:** Contains an integrated development environment for a variety of programming languages.

✦ **sndconfig:** Contains the `sndconfig` command, a text-based utility for setting up your sound card.

✦ **sox:** Contains the `sox` utility for converting sound files.

✦ **sox-devel:** Contains libraries needed to develop SoX applications that convert sound file formats.

✦ **specspo:** Contains the specspo portable object catalogues for internationalizing Red Hat packages.

✦ **squid:** Contains the squid proxy caching server for HTTP, FTP, gopher, and other Web clients.

✦ **stat:** Contains the `stat` utility for printing requested information about the file system.

✦ **statserial:** Contains the `statserial` program for displaying signals on 9-pin and 25-pin serial ports.

✦ **strace:** Contains the `strace` utility for tracing the system calls performed by a selected program.

✦ **stunnel:** Contains the stunnel tool, which can be used to add secure SSL services to non-SSL servers.

✦ **sudo:** Contains the `sudo` utility for allowing administrative user access to specific users.

✦ **swig:** Contains a tool that connects C/C++/Objective C to other high-level languages.

✦ **switchdesk:** Contains the desktop switcher utility (`switchdesk`) for changing a user's window manager.

✦ **switchdesk-gnome:** Contains the GNOME look-and-feel version of the desktop switcher utility.

✦ **switchdesk-kde:** Contains the KDE look-and-feel version of the desktop switcher utility.

✦ **sylpheed:** Contains a GTK+–based e-mail and news client.

✦ **symlinks:** Contains the `symlinks` program for checking and correcting symbolic links.

✦ **sysctlconfig:** Contains configuration tools for managing system tunable parameters.

✦ **sysklogd:** Contains the `syslogd` and `klogd` daemon processes, used for logging system messages.

✦ **syslinux:** Contains a simple boot loader that can boot from a DOS (FAT) filesystem.

✦ **sysreport:** Contains the `sysreport` utility, which is used to check your system for hardware problems.

✦ **sysstat:** Contains the sar and iostat system monitoring tools.

✦ **SysVinit:** Contains several basic Linux boot and startup programs.

✦ **taipeifonts:** Contains Chinese Big5 fonts.

✦ **talk:** Contains the `ntalk` client and daemon processes for using the Internet talk protocol.

✦ **talk-server:** Contains the `in.talkd` daemon for providing the talk service to clients from the network.

✦ **tamago:** Contains components that allow multilingual input to emacs-lisp.

✦ **taper:** Contains the `taper` backup and restore utilities.

✦ **tar:** Contains the `tar` utility for creating backup archives and restoring files from those archives.

✦ **tcl:** Contains the `tcl` scripting language that allows scripting to be included within other applications.

✦ **tcllib:** Contains a variety of modules for TCL.

✦ **tclx:** Contains tclX extensions designed to make common Linux programming tasks easier to implement.

✦ **tcpdump:** Contains the `tcpdump` command-line utility for monitoring network traffic.

✦ **tcp_wrappers:** Contains daemons that monitor incoming requests for system services from the network.

✦ **tcsh:** Contains the `tcsh` shell, which is a shell command interpreter that is compatible with csh.

✦ **telnet:** Contains the popular `telnet` utility for logging in to remote systems over the Internet.

✦ **telnet-server:** Contains the `in.telnetd` daemon for providing the telnet service (for remote login) to clients from the network.

✦ **termcap:** Contains the /etc/termcap file, which contains interface information for applications that run on character-cell terminals, such as screen-oriented editors like vi or emacs.

✦ **tetex:** Contains tools for creating TeTeX documents. TeTeX is an implementation of TeX.

✦ **tetex-afm:** Contains the `afm2tfm` utility for converting PostScript font metric files.

✦ **tetex-doc:** Contains documentation that describes how to produce TeX formatted documents.

✦ **tetex-dvilj:** Contains tools for converting TeX output (dvi format) into HP PCL output.

✦ **tetex-dvips:** Contains the `dvips` utility for converting TeX files to PostScript format.

✦ **tetex-fonts:** Contains fonts for use with TeX documents.

✦ **tetex-latex:** Contains LaTeX front-end utilities for producing TeX documents.

✦ **tetex-xdvi:** Contains the `xdvi` program for previewing TeX output files in the X Window System.

✦ **texinfo:** Contains the Texinfo document system for producing online and printed documents from the same source file.

✦ **textutils:** Contains utilities for changing the contents of files, such as comparing or joining files.

✦ **tftp:** Contains the Trivial File Transfer Protocol, which is used to boot diskless workstations.

✦ **tftp-server:** Contains the `in.tftpd` daemon for providing tftp (trivial FTP) service to clients from the network.

✦ **time:** Contains the `time` utility, which is used to monitor processing time of a selected program.

✦ **timeconfig:** Contains the `timeconfig` and `setclock` for configuring time parameters and the hardware clock, respectively.

✦ **timidity++:** Contains the Timidity++ MIDI player and converter.

✦ **tix:** Contains the Tix (Tk Interface Extension) add-on to the Tk widget set.

✦ **tk:** Contains the Tk X Window System widget set, which is designed to work with the `tcl` scripting language.

✦ **tkinter:** Contains the Tkinter graphical interface for the Python scripting language.

✦ **tmake:** Contains a tool that creates and maintains makefiles for software projects.

✦ **tmpwatch:** Contains the `tmpwatch` command for removing files that haven't been used for a time.

✦ **traceroute:** Contains the `traceroute` utility for tracing the route of IP packets across the network.

✦ **transfig:** Contains the `transfig` utility for translating FIG or PIC figures to other formats.

✦ **tree:** Contains the `tree` utility for displaying the contents of directories in a tree format.

✦ **tripwire:** Contains tripwire security tools for monitoring your system for potential security violations.

✦ **ttcp:** Contains a tool for testing the throughput of TCP connections.

✦ **ttfm:** Contains a True Type font manager that handles installation, un-installation, list, and default font settings.

✦ **ttfonts:** Contains TrueType fonts that can be used with Xfree86 and Ghostview.

✦ **ttfonts-ja:** Contains Japanese True Type fonts.

✦ **ttfonts-ko:** Contains Baekmuk Korean True Type fonts.

✦ **ttfonts-zh_CN:** Contains Chinese True Type fonts.

✦ **ttfonts-zh_TW:** Contains Chinese True Type fonts.

✦ **ttfprint:** Contains a utility that converts a Chinese text file to postscript.

✦ **tux:** Contains a kernel-based threaded HTTP server.

✦ **tuxracer:** Contains a simple racing game featuring Tux, the Linux penguin mascot.

✦ **tWnn:** Contains a Chinese character set input system.

✦ **ucd-snmp:** Contains UCD-SNMP tools, such as tools for working with SNMP agents.

✦ **ucd-snmp-devel:** Contains components needed to develop UCD-SNMP network management applications.

✦ **ucd-snmp-utils:** Contains utilities for managing TCP/IP networks using SNMP protocols.

✦ **umb-scheme:** Contains the public version of the Scheme programming language.

✦ **unarj:** Contains the UNARJ program, which is used to uncompress .arj compressed archives.

✦ **units:** Contains the `units` utility for converting units from one type of measurement to another.

✦ **unix2dos:** Contains the `unix2dos` command for converting Linux/UNIX files to DOS files.

✦ **unixODBC*:** This set of packages contains tools associated with the ODBC driver manager.

✦ **unzip:** Contains the `unzip` utility, which is used to test, list and extract files from a zip archive.

✦ **up2date:** Contains the Red Hat Linux update agent (`up2date` command).

✦ **up2date-gnome:** Contains the GNOME interface to the `up2date` command.

✦ **urw-fonts:** Contains a free version of the 35 standard PostScript fonts.

✦ **usbview:** Contains the `usbview` utility for viewing USB devices.

✦ **usermode:** Contains graphical tools, such as `userinfo`, `usermount` and `userpasswd`, for managing user information.

✦ **utempter:** Contains the libutempter shared library and `utempter` command.

✦ **util-linux:** Contains many basic Linux utilities for users and system administrators, such as `kill`, `login`, `more`, `fdisk`, `cal`, `whereis`, and `banner`.

✦ **uucp:** Contains the classic `uucp` utilities for transferring files among remote host computers.

✦ **VFlib2*:** This set of packages contains tools to convert vector fonts to bitmaps.

✦ **vim-common:** Contains files needed for the `vim` editor to run.

✦ **vim-enhanced:** Contains enhancements for the `vim` editor, such as Python and Perl interpreters.

✦ **vim-minimal:** Contains several commands used by the `vim` editor, including `ex`, `rvi`, `rview`, `vi`, and `view` utilities.

✦ **vim-X11:** Contains the vim (VIsual editor iMproved) text editor, which is an enhanced vi editor.

✦ **vixie-cron:** Contains the Vixie implementation of the `cron` utility, adding some security features.

✦ **vlock:** Contains the `vlock` program for locking console sessions.

✦ **vnc:** Contains the vncviewer application for viewing desktops from remote computers over the network.

✦ **vnc-doc:** Contains documentation related to the vnc server and vncviewer applications.

✦ **vnc-server:** Contains the Virtual Network Computing (vnc) server for allowing remote users to run desktops that are displayed from the server.

✦ **vorbis:** Contains the Vorbis run-time library and utilities related to the Vorbis compressed audio format.

✦ **w3c-libwww:** Contains the libwww Web application programming interface, a C language programming interface for Linux, UNIX, and Microsoft Windows systems.

✦ **w3c-libwww-apps:** Contains the w3c and webbot commands.

✦ **w3c-libwww-devel:** Contains libraries and header files needed to create w3c-libwww applications.

✦ **w3m:** Contains a text file viewer that can also be used as a text-mode Web browser.

✦ **w3m-el:** Contains w3m interface for emacsen.

✦ **watanabe:** Contains the Japanese watanabe font.

✦ **webalizer:** Contains a flexible Web server log file analysis program.

✦ **wget:** Contains the wget file retrieval utility, which uses HTTP or FTP protocols.

✦ **which:** Contains the which command for showing the full path of a selected program.

✦ **whois:** Contains the whois command for displaying information about users.

✦ **WindowMaker:** Contains Window Maker, an X-based window manager that emulates NeXTSTEP (TM).

✦ **WindowMaker-libs:** Contains libraries for creating applications that are compatible with the Window Maker window manager.

✦ **wine:** Contains a Windows 16/32 bit emulator that allows Windows binaries to run on Intel UNIX systems.

✦ **wine-devel:** Contains header and include files needed for developing applications with wine.

✦ **wireless-tools:** Contains tools for configuring communication to wireless Ethernet equipment.

✦ **wl:** Contains Wanderlust, an IMAP4, POP, and NNTP client for GNU emacs.

✦ **wl-xemacs:** Contains Wanderlust, an IMAP4, POP, and NNTP client for XEmacs.

✦ **wmakerconf:** Contains the GTK+ based configuration utility used to configure Window Maker.

✦ **Wnn6-SDK:** Contains a runtime Wnn6 client library needed to run Wnn6 clients.

✦ **Wnn6-SDK-devel:** Contains library and header files for Wnn6 client development.

✦ **words:** Contains a dictionary of English words that is placed in the /usr/dict directory.

✦ **wu-ftpd:** Contains the Washington University FTP server software for configuring an FTP server.

✦ **wvdial:** Contains the `wvdial` command, which is an intelligent dialer for PPP.

✦ **x3270:** Contains software for emulating an IBM 3270 terminal on an X Window System display.

✦ **x3270-tcl:** Contains tcl bindings for an IBM 3270 terminal emulator.

✦ **x3270-text:** Contains an IBM 3270 terminal emulator for text mode.

✦ **x3270-x11:** Contains an IBM 3270 terminal emulator for the X Windows system.

✦ **xalf:** Contains a utility that provides feedback when starting X11 applications.

✦ **Xaw3d:** Contains the Xaw3d libraries needed to run programs that contain MIT Athena widgets.

✦ **Xaw3d-devel:** Contains Xaw3d development components, which is an enhanced version of MIT Athena widgets for the X Window System.

✦ **xawtv:** Contains a simple TV application for video4linux-compliant devices.

✦ **xbill:** Contains an X-based game where you seek out and destroy Bill and help new operating systems take over.

✦ **xbl:** Contains the `xbl` 3D game.

✦ **xboard:** Contains a graphical, X-based interface to GNU chess.

✦ **xcdroast:** Contains utilities for burning your own music and data CD-ROMs.

✦ **xchat:** Contains the X-Chat utility, an IRC chat utility that runs on the X Window System.

✦ **xcin:** Contains an X-input method server for Chinese characters.

✦ **Xconfigurator:** Contains the `Xconfigurator` utility for configuring your X server and video card.

✦ **xcpustate:** Contains the X-based `xcpustate` program for displaying information on CPU usage.

✦ **xdaliclock:** Contains the `xdaliclock` program, which displays a digital clock.

✦ **xdelta:** Contains Xdelta tools, which can be used to compare the contents of binary files.

✦ **xdelta-devel:** Contains Xdelta development tools.

✦ **xdialog:** Contains a program that converts any terminal-based program into one with an X Windows interface.

✦ **xemacs:** Contains the libraries needed to run the emacs text editor.

✦ **xemacs-el:** Contains a variety of elisp programs that you can use with the emacs text editor.

✦ **xemacs-info:** Contains info documentation (/usr/share/info/xemacs/*) for the emacs text editor.

✦ **xfig:** Contains the xfig utility for creating vector graphics that can be saved and converted to a variety of formats.

✦ **XFree86-100dpi-fonts:** Contains 100 dpi, high-resolution fonts that can be use on X Window System displays.

✦ **XFree86-3DLabs:** Contains an X Window System server that can be used with video cards that include the Permidia and Glint chip sets.

✦ **XFree86:** Contains the basic software needed to run the X Window System in Red Hat Linux.

✦ **XFree86-75dpi-fonts:** Contains 75 dpi fonts that can be used on X Window System displays.

✦ **XFree86-cyrillic-fonts:** Contains Cyrillic character set fonts used with the X Window System.

✦ **XFree86-devel:** Contains components needed to develop X-based client programs.

✦ **XFree86-doc:** Contains a variety of XFree86-related documentation, mostly in zipped PostScript format.

✦ **XFree86-FBDev:** Contains the X server used for generic frame buffer devices, such as those on Macintosh, Amiga, and Atari computers.

✦ **XFree86-ISO8859:** Contains X Window System fonts that are used with Central European versions of Linux.

✦ **XFree86-ISO8859-2-75dpi-fonts:** Contains 75 dpi X Window System fonts that are used with Central European versions of Linux.

✦ **XFree86-ISO8859-2-100dpi-fonts:** Contains 100 dpi X Window System fonts that are used with Central European versions of Linux.

✦ **XFree86-ISO8859-2-Type1-fonts:** Contains Type 1 X Window System fonts that are used with Central European versions of Linux.

✦ **XFree86-ISO8859-9-100dpi-fonts:** Contains 100 dpi X Window System fonts that are used with Turkish versions of Linux.

✦ **XFree86-ISO8859-9-75dpi-fonts:** Contains 75 dpi X Window System fonts that are used with Turkish versions of Linux.

✦ **XFree86-KOI8-R:** Contains Russian and Ukrainian fonts used with XFree86.

✦ **XFree86-KOI8-R-100dpi-fonts:** Contains 100 dpi X Window System fonts that are used with Russian and Ukrainian versions of Linux.

✦ **XFree86-KOI8-R-75dpi-fonts:** Contains 75 dpi X Window System fonts that are used with Russian and Ukrainian versions of Linux.

✦ **XFree86-libs:** Contains shared libraries required for most X-based programs to run in Linux.

✦ **XFree86-Mach32:** Contains the XFree86 X server used for video cards built using the ATI Mach32 chip.

✦ **XFree86-Mach64:** Contains the XFree86 X server used for video cards built using the ATI Mach64 chip.

✦ **XFree86-Mach8:** Contains the XFree86 X server used for video cards built using the ATI Mach8 chip, such as the ATI 8514 Ultra and Graphics Ultra cards.

✦ **XFree86-Mono:** Contains the XFree86 X server used for generic monochrome video cards.

✦ **XFree86-P9000:** Contains the XFree86 X server used for video cards built using the Weitek P9000 chip.

✦ **XFree86-S3:** Contains the XFree86 X server used for video cards based on S3 chips.

✦ **XFree86-S3V:** Contains the XFree86 X server used for video cards based on the S3 ViRGE chipset.

✦ **XFree86-SVGA:** Contains the XFree86 X server that will work for most simple SVGA video cards.

✦ **XFree86-tools:** Contains a variety of X utilities.

✦ **XFree86-twm:** Contains the simple twm window manager.

✦ **XFree86-V4L:** Contains components that add Video for Linux support to XFree86.

✦ **XFree86-VGA16:** Contains the XFree86 X server used for generic 16-bit video cards.

✦ **XFree86-W32:** Contains the XFree86 X server used for video cards built on the ET4000/W32 chipset.

✦ **XFree86-xdm:** Contains the xdm X display manager.

✦ **XFree86-xf86cfg:** Contains the xf86cfg utility for changing your X configuration.

✦ **XFree86-xfs:** Contains the XFree86 font server.

✦ **XFree86-Xnest:** Contains the Xnest nested window server that runs within the X Window System server.

✦ **XFree86-Xvfb:** Contains the xvfb X server, which is capable of running on computers that have no display hardware.

✦ **xinetd:** Contains the xinetd daemon, which listens to ports to handle a variety of network services (replaces the inetd package).

✦ **xinitrc:** Contains the xinitrc script, which is used to configure how your X Window System starts.

✦ **xisdnload:** Contains a graphical tool for displaying load activity on your ISDN network connections.

✦ **xloadimage:** Contains the xloadimage utility for displaying and manipulating images.

✦ **xlockmore:** Contains the xlockmore utility for allowing users to lock an X session display.

✦ **xmailbox:** Contains the xmailbox program, an X-based utility for notifying you when mail arrives.

✦ **xml-i18n-tools:** Contains utility scripts for internationalizing XML files.

✦ **xmms:** Contains the Xmms multimedia player. This player supports supports MPEG, WAV, and AU formats.

✦ **xmms-devel:** Contains header files needed by the Xmms multimedia player.

✦ **xmms-gnome:** Contains components used to integrate the Xmms player into the GNOME desktop.

✦ **xmms-skins:** Contains skins for the xmms media player.

✦ **xmorph:** Contains the xmorph program for morphing one image into another.

✦ **xosview:** Contains the xosview utility for displaying system state, memory usage, system load, CPU usages, and other information about your system.

✦ **xpdf:** Contains the xpdf utility for displaying Adobe Acrobat PDF files.

✦ **xpilot:** Contains the X-based Xpilot game for playing multiplayer aerial combat.

✦ **xrn:** Contains the X-based xrn program for reading, posting, and replying to news articles.

✦ **xsane:** Contains an X interface to the Sane scanner and digital camera features.

✦ **xsane-gimp:** Contains a Gimp library interface to the xsane scanner and digital camera interface.

✦ **xscreensaver:** Contains a large set of screensaver programs.

✦ **xsnow:** Contains an X Windows system–based dose of Christmas cheer.

✦ **xsri:** Contains the `xsri` command for displaying images on the background of your X display.

✦ **xsysinfo:** Contains the `xsysinfo` utility, which is a graphical tool for monitoring system usage.

✦ **xtoolwait:** Contains the `xtoolwait` utility for efficiently starting X client programs automatically.

✦ **xtraceroute:** Contains an X and GTK+–based graphical display of trace routes output.

✦ **yp-tools:** Contains tools for a version of the Network Information System (NIS) based on the FreeBSD version of YP.

✦ **ypbind:** Contains the ypbind daemon process for binding NIS clients to an NIS domain.

✦ **ypserv:** Contains the ypserv components for setting up an NIS server in Linux.

✦ **ytalk:** Contains the `YTalk` program for chatting with multiple users on multiple connections.

✦ **zebra:** Contains a TCP/IP-based routing protocol that is intended to be used as a route server and a route reflector.

✦ **zip:** Contains the zip utility for compressing and packaging files.

✦ **zlib:** Contains a version of the zlib compression library that only supports the deflation compression method.

✦ **zlib-devel:** Contains header files and libraries used to develop applications that use zlib compression.

✦ **zsh:** Contains the `zsh` shell command line interpreter, which is similar to an enhanced ksh.

✦   ✦   ✦

Running Network Services

✦ ✦ ✦ ✦

In This Appendix

Understanding system services

Working with system services

Individual system services

✦ ✦ ✦ ✦

Because Red Hat Linux is capable of providing so many different kinds of services (serving Web pages, printers, files, and other resources), it's easy to lose track of them. Let's say you install all server software packages with Red Hat Linux. How do you know which servers will start up automatically and which will need special configuration in order to work? Where do you begin to look for configuration files, startup scripts, and daemon processes? How do you know if your firewall configuration is blocking access to the services?

This appendix provides a quick reference to the network services that come with Red Hat Linux. Its purpose is to provide an overview of these services that are described in detail in other chapters. You can use this appendix as a reminder of how to get services working or as a guide to help you step through debugging a service that needs some fixing.

Caution Any services your computer offers to users who can reach it over a network pose a potential security threat. Refer to Chapter 14 for information on security, as well as the sections in the book that describe configuration of each feature in detail.

Checklist to Running Networking Services

As computer security issues rise with the onslaught of computer crackers and viruses, operating systems (such as Red Hat Linux) are moving toward more security rather than more ease-of-use. Simply installing server software isn't enough to get the service up and running.

The following is a set of steps to make sure that everything is in place for a particular service to run:

1. **Is the software package(s) installed?** Each network service is represented by one or more software packages. If you did a workstation or a custom install, most network server software may not be installed on your computer at all. Check Table C-1 to see which package(s) is needed for a service to work. (There may be other package dependencies as well, which you will be alerted to when you try to install the package.) Then use the `rpm` command to install the software from one of the installation CDs.

2. **Does the firewall permit access to the service?** In Red Hat Linux 7.2, the installation procedure lets you configure a firewall. If you choose the default (High security) firewall, most services will not be available to your network. Refer to Chapter 14 for information on how to change your firewall configuration.

3. **Is the start-up script set up to automatically launch the service?** Most network services are launched from start-up scripts that cause daemon processes to continuously listen to the network for requests for the service. See the Networking Service Daemons section for information on how to find start-up scripts and set them up to launch automatically.

4. **Is the configuration file created for the service?** Even if the daemon process is listening for requests for a network service, there are probably one or more configuration files associated with the service that need to be set up before requests will be accepted. Table C-1 lists important configuration files for each type of server.

5. **Does the configuration file permit proper access to the service?** Within the configuration file for a service, there may be several levels of permissions that a user must go through to get permission to the service. For example, a configuration file may allow access to the service from a particular host computer, but deny access to a particular user.

6. **Are there other restrictions to the service being shared?** Some standard Linux security measures may block access to a service that is otherwise open to being shared. For example, you may share a Linux directory using NFS or FTP servers, but local file ownership and permissions may block access to the directory or files within the shared directory.

The rest of this appendix provides an overview of the daemon processes, start-up scripts, configuration files, and software packages that are associated with the networking services that come with Red Hat Linux.

Networking Service Daemons

As a quick review of how networking services (as well as other services) are started in Red Hat Linux, here are the two main directories containing files that define how services are started:

✦ /etc/xinetd.d: contains configuration files used by the xinetd daemon

✦ /etc/init.d: contains start-up scripts that are linked to /etc/rc?.d directories so they can be started at different run levels

Each of these two methods for handling network services is described below.

Note

Some Red Hat Linux configuration tools also store configuration information in the /etc/sysconfig directory. For example, there are configuration files for ipchains and sendmail in /etc/sysconfig. If you search the scripts in the /etc/init.d directory for the word sysconfig, you will see just how many services look in that directory for configuration information.

The xinetd super-server

The xinetd daemon is referred to as the super-server. It listens for incoming requests for services based on information in separate files in the /etc/xinetd.d directory. When a request for a service is received by the xinetd daemon (for a particular network port number), xinetd typically launches a different daemon to handle the request. So instead of there being separate daemons running for every network service, only the xinetd daemon needs to run — plus an additional daemon process for each service currently in use.

To see if a particular service that is handled by xinetd is on or off, go to the /etc/xinetd.d directory and open the file representing that service with a text editor. A default line at the top of the file indicates whether or not the service is on or off by default. The disable line actually sets whether or not the service is currently disabled. The following is an example from the /etc/xinetd.d/ipop3 file:

```
# default: off

# description: The POP3 service allows remote users to access their mail \
#              using an POP3 client such as Netscape Communicator, mutt, \
#              or fetchmail.

service pop3
{
        socket_type        = stream
        wait               = no
        user               = root
        server             = /usr/sbin/ipop3d
        log_on_success     += USERID
        log_on_failure     += USERID
        disable            = yes
}
```

In this example, the ipop3 configuration file represents a Post Office Protocol (POP) version 3 service. By default (as noted at the top of the file), the service is turned off. When the service is on, a request to the xinetd server daemon for a POP3 service from the network is handed off to the /usr/sbin/ipop3d daemon. The ipop3d daemon, in turn, handles the remote user's request to download his or her e-mail from this Linux system that is acting as a POP3 server.

To enable a service in an /etc/xinetd.d file, edit the file using any text editor as the root user. Turning on the service is as easy as changing the disable option from yes to no and restarting the xinetd daemon. For example, you could change the line in the /etc/xinetd.d/ipop3 so that it appears as follows:

```
disable    = no
```

Then you could restart the xinetd daemon as follows:

```
# /etc/init.d/xinetd restart
```

In this case, you could look in the /etc/services file and see that POP3 services are (by default) received on port number 110 for TCP/IP networks. So, any request that comes into your computer for port 110 is first directed to the xinetd daemon, then handled by the ipop3d daemon. If authentication is correct, e-mail is downloaded to the user's mailbox (typically /var/spool/mail/*user*, where *user* represents the user's name).

The xinetd super-server is described in Chapter 12.

The init.d start-up scripts

Network services that are not available via the xinetd daemon are typically handled by scripts in the /etc/init.d directory. For a script in the /etc/init.d directory to activate a service, it must be linked to a file in one of the run level directories (/etc/rc?.d) that begins with the letter "S" followed by a two-digit number.

For example, the script for starting the print service daemon (/etc/init.d/lpd) is linked to the file S60lpd in the /etc/rc2.d, /etc/rc3.d, /etc/rc4.d, and /etc/rc5.d directories. In that way, the print service is started when Red Hat Linux is running in initialization states 2, 3, 4, or 5.

See Chapter 12 for more details on run levels and start-up scripts.

For the most part, system administrators are not expected to modify these start-up scripts. However, to have a service turned on or off for a particular run level, change the script to a filename that begins with an *S* (start) to one that begins with a *K* (kill). You can easily do this with the Service Configuration window. To start that window, type **serviceconf** from a Terminal window while you are logged in as the root user.

Referencing Network Services

This section contains the quick reference information related to Red Hat Linux system services. The table listing these services (Table C-1) contains the following information:

- ✦ **Feature:** What type of service is it?
- ✦ **Package names:** What software packages must be installed for the service to be available?
- ✦ **Start-up scripts:** Which start-up scripts launch the service?
- ✦ **Daemon:** What daemon process is running to provide the service?
- ✦ **Configuration files:** What configuration files can you modify to tailor the service to your specific needs?

The descriptions following the table provide additional information about the service. That information includes whether or not the service is started by default and where you can find more information about the service.

Note When the `xinetd` daemon is noted as the start-up script, the daemon process to which the service is handed off is also noted.

Table C-1
Quick Reference to Network Services

Feature	Package names	Startup script(s)	Daemon	Configuration file(s)
Web Server				
Web Page Server (Apache)	apache apache-docs apache-devel	/etc/init.d/httpd	/usr/sbin/httpd	/etc/httpd/conf/httpd.conf
File Servers				
FTP Server (Wu-FTP)	wu-ftpd	/etc/init.d/xinetd (/etc/xinetd.d/wu-ftpd)	/usr/sbin/xinetd /usr/sbin/in.ftpd	/etc/ftpaccess /etc/ftphosts /etc/ftpusers /etc/ftpgroups
FTP Server with Kerberos support (Gss-FTP)	krb5-workstation	/etc/init.d/xinetd (/etc/xinetd.d/gssftp)	/usr/sbin/xinetd (/usr/kerberos/sbin/ftpd)	/etc/krb5.conf
Samba Windows File & Printers (SMB)	samba samba-common samba-client samba-swat	/etc/init.d/smb	/usr/sbin/smbd /usr/sbin/nmbd	/etc/samba/smb.conf
UNIX Network File System (NFS)	nfs-utils	/etc/init.d/nfs	/usr/sbin/rpc.nfsd /usr/sbin/rpc.mountd	/etc/exports
NetWare Server (Mars-Nwe)	mars-nwe	/etc/init.d/mars-nwe	/usr/sbin/nwserv /usr/sbin/ncpserv /usr/sbin/nwbind	/etc/nwserv.conf
Login Servers				
Telnet	telnet-server	/etc/init.d/xinetd (/etc/xinetd.d/telnet)	/usr/sbin/xinetd (/usr/sbin/in.telnetd)	/etc/issue.net
Telnet w/ Kerberos Support (krb5-telnet)	krb5-workstation	/etc/init.d/xinetd (/etc/xinetd.d/krb5-telnet)	/usr/sbin/xinetd (/usr/kerberos/sbin/telnetd)	/etc/krb5.conf
Open Secure Shell (Openssh)	openssh-server	/etc/init.d/sshd	/usr/sbin/sshd	/etc/ssh/*

Feature	Package names	Startup script(s)	Daemon	Configuration file(s)
Remote Login (Rlogin)	rsh-server	/etc/init.d/xinetd (/etc/xinetd.d/rlogin)	/usr/sbin/xinetd (/usr/sbin/in.rlogind)	/etc/hosts.equiv $HOME/.rhosts
Remote Login w/ Kerberos Support (Eklogin) (Klogin)	krb5-workstation krb5-workstation	/etc/init.d/xinetd (/etc/xinetd.d/eklogin) /etc/init.d/xinetd (/etc/xinetd.d/klogin)	**/usr/sbin/xinetd** (/usr/kerberos/sbin/klogind) /usr/sbin/xinetd (/usr/kerberos/sbin/klogind)	/etc/krb5.conf $HOME/.k5login $HOME/.klogin /etc/krb5.conf $HOME/.k5login $HOME/.klogin
E-mail Servers				
E-mail Reader Servers (IMAP)	imap	/etc/init.d/xinetd (/etc/xinetd.d/imap)	/usr/sbin/xinetd (/usr/sbin/imapd)	/var/spool/mail/user
(IMAP with SSL)	imap	/etc/init.d/xinetd (/etc/xinetd.d/imaps)	/usr/sbin/xinetd (/usr/sbin/stunnel **and** /usr/sbin/imapd)	/var/spool/mail/user
(POP2)	imap	/etc/init.d/xinetd (/etc/xinetd.d/ipop2)	/usr/sbin/xinetd (/usr/sbin/ipop2d)	/var/spool/mail/user
(POP3)	imap	/etc/init.d/xinetd (/etc/xinetd.d/ipop3 **or** /etc/xinet.d/pop3s)	/usr/sbin/xinetd (/usr/sbin/ipop3d)	/var/spool/mail/user
(POP3 with SSL)	imap	/etc/init.d/xinetd (/etc/xinet.d/pop3s)	/usr/sbin/xinetd (/usr/sbin/stunnel **and** /usr/sbin/ipop3d)	/var/spool/mail/user
E-mail Transfer Server (Sendmail)	sendmail sendmail-cf sendmail-doc	/etc/init.d/sendmail	/usr/sbin/sendmail	/etc/sendmail.cf /etc/mail/*
E-mail Notice Server (comsat)	comsat	/etc/init.d/xinetd (/etc/xinetd.d/comsat)	/usr/sbin/xinetd (/usr/sbin/in.comsat)	

Continued

Table C-1 (continued)

Feature	Package names	Startup script(s)	Daemon	Configuration file(s)
News Server				
Internet Network News (INN)	inn	/etc/init.d/innd	/usr/bin/innd	/etc/news/*
Print Server				
LPR New Generation (LPRng)	LPRng	/etc/init.d/lpd	/usr/sbin/lpd	/etc/printcap /etc/printcap.local /etc/lpd.conf /etc/lpd.perms
Network Administration Servers				
Network Time Protocol Server (NTP)	ntp	/etc/init.d/ntpd	/usr/sbin/ntpd	/etc/ntp.conf
Network Portmap (RPC to DARPA)	portmap	/etc/init.d/portmap	/sbin/portmap	/etc/rpc
Samba Administration (SWAT)	samba samba-common samba-client samba-swat	/etc/init.d/xinetd (/etc/xinetd.d/swat)	/usr/sbin/xinetd /usr/sbin/swat	/etc/smb.conf
Network Management (arpwatch)	arpwatch	/etc/init.d/arpwatch	/usr/sbin/arpwatch	
Simple Network Management Protocol (SNMP)	ucd-snmp	/etc/init.d/snmpd	/usr/sbin/snmpd	/etc/snmp/snmpd.conf

Feature	Package names	Startup script(s)	Daemon	Configuration file(s)
Information Servers				
Network Information Server (Ypbind)	ypbind	/etc/init.d/ypbind	/sbin/ypbind	/etc/yp.conf
(Yppasswdd)	ypserv	/etc/init.d/yppasswdd	/usr/sbin/rpc.yppasswd	/etc/passwd/etc/shadow
(Ypserv)	ypserv	/etc/init.d/ypserv	/usr/sbin/ypserv	/etc/ypserv.conf
Dynamic Host Configuration Protocol Server (DHCP)	dhcp	/etc/init.d/dhcp	/usr/sbin/dhcpd	/etc/dhcpd.conf
Lightweight Directory Access Protocol (LDAP)	openldap-servers	/etc/init.d/ldap	/usr/sbin/slapd /usr/sbin/slurpd	/etc/openldap/slapd.at.conf /etc/openldap/slapd.oc.conf /etc/openldap/slapd.conf
Domain Name System Server (DNS)	bind	/etc/init.d/named	/usr/sbin/named	/etc/named.conf
Reverse Address Resolution Protocol Server (RARP)	rarpd	/etc/init.d/rarpd	/usr/sbin/rarpd	/etc/ethers
Database Services				
MySQL Database	mysql mysql-server	/etc/init.d/mysql	/usr/libexec/mysqld	/etc/my.cnf
Postgresql	postgresql-libs postgresql postgresql-server	/etc/init.d/postgresql	/usr/bin/postmaster	/var/lib/pgsql/data

Continued

Table C-1 (continued)

Feature	Package names	Startup script(s)	Daemon	Configuration file(s)
User Services				
Remote Execution Servers (Rsh)	rsh-server	/etc/init.d/xinetd (/etc/xinetd.d/rsh)	/usr/sbin/xinetd (/usr/sbin/in.rshd)	/etc/hosts.equiv $HOME/.rhosts
(Rexec)	rsh-server	/etc/init.d/xinetd (/etc/xinetd.d/rexec) (/usr/sbin/in.rexecd)	/usr/sbin/xinetd	/etc/passwd
(Kshell)	krb5-workstation	/etc/init.d/xinetd (/etc/xinetd.d/kshell)	/usr/sbin/xinetd (/usr/kerberos/sbin/kshd)	/etc/krb5.conf
Talk Server (ntalk)	talk-server	/etc/init.d/xinetd (/etc/xinetd.d/ntalk)	/usr/sbin/xinetd (/usr/sbin/in.ntalkd)	
(talk)	talk-server	/etc/init.d/xinetd (/etc/xinetd.d/talk)	/usr/sbin/xinetd (/usr/sbin/in.talkd)	
Finger Server (Finger)	finger-server	/etc/init.d/xinetd (/etc/xinetd.d/finger)	/usr/sbin/xinetd (/usr/sbin/in.fingerd)	
Identify Users (Rusers)	rusers-server	/etc/init.d/rusersd	/usr/sbin/rpc.rusersd	
Write All Users (Rwall)	rwall-server	/etc/init.d/rwalld	/usr/sbin/rpc.rwalld	
Security Services				
Virtual Private Network Servers (CIPE)	cipe	/etc/init.d/ciped	/usr/sbin/ciped-cb	/etc/sysconfig/cipe
Caching Server (Squid)	squid	/etc/init.d/squid	/usr/sbin/squid	/etc/squid/squid.conf

The following sections provide some additional information about the services described in the table.

Web server

You use the apache software package to create a Web server in Red Hat Linux. If apache is installed, startup will fail unless you have a valid name (and IP address) for your Web server. To define a server name, add a `ServerName` entry to the `httpd.conf` file and restart the service.

By default, users who can access your system from the network will be able to view the contents of the `/var/www/html` directory. The contents include the apache manual (if the `apache-docs` package is installed).

See Chapter 21 for information on configuring an Apache Web server.

File servers

File services in Red Hat Linux can be provided using FTP servers, Samba (Windows) servers, Network File System (NFS) servers, and NetWare servers. The following sections describe each of these.

FTP servers

The Washington University FTP package (wu-ftpd) contains the tools to configure an FTP server. If the wu-ftpd package is installed, the `xinetd` daemon passes all requests for FTP service (by default, port 21) to the `in.ftpd` daemon to present the FTP login prompt.

By default, users with real logins and passwords to the computer have the same permissions as if they had logged in locally. Anonymous users have access only to the `/var/ftp` directory structure (which by default contains no shared files). (Anyone can be an anonymous user by logging in using the name `anonymous` and typing his or her e-mail address as the password.)

See Chapter 20 for information on configuring a wu-ftpd FTP server.

An FTP server with Kerberos 5 support is also included with Red Hat Linux. The `krb5-workstation` package contains the `ftpd` daemon that includes Kerberos 5 support.

Samba server

The Samba server software supports the Server Message Block (SMB) file- and printer-sharing protocol. SMB is most often used to share resources on local networks consisting of computers running Microsoft Windows. You would typically not share SMB files and printers over a public network, such as the Internet.

Samba services are off by default in Red Hat Linux. To have Samba start automatically when you boot your computer, change the `kill` script (K30smb) to a `start` script (S30smb) in the run level directory you boot to (probably `/etc/rc3.d` or `/etc/rc5.d`).

In order for Samba to be useful, edit the Samba configuration file, `/etc/samba/smb.conf`. The best way to configure this file is to use the SWAT service (described later in this appendix).

For more information about configuring Samba, see Chapters 17 and 18.

NetWare server

NetWare is an operating system from Novell, Inc., that provides dedicated file and print services to network users. The `mars-nwe` package that comes with Red Hat Linux lets you set up your computer to emulate a NetWare file server.

Information on setting up NetWare services in Red Hat Linux can be found in Chapter 18.

By default, NetWare file and print services are off in Red Hat Linux. To turn them on, change the `kill` script (K60mars-nwe) to a start-up script (S60mars-nwe). Do this by changing the files in the directories for run levels in which you want the service to run (probably `/etc/rc3.d` or `/etc/rc5.d`). For the service to be usable, you need to edit the `/etc/nwserv.conf` file.

Login servers

A variety of login servers are available for use with Red Hat Linux. Both telnet and rlogin services can be used to allow users from other computers to log in to Red Hat Linux from the network. These days, however, `ssh` is the preferred login service.

If the `telnet-server` package is installed, the telnet service is available by default for run levels 3, 4, and 5 and is made unavailable at run levels 0, 1, 2, and 6. The `xinetd` daemon passes all requests for telnet service (by default, port 23) to the `in.telnetd` daemon to present the telnet login prompt. By default, only users with real logins to the computer can log in to the computer — anonymous users are not supported. Users who log in using telnet are presented with a shell interface for accessing the computer.

Red Hat Linux also includes login daemons that provide Kerberos 5 support. Kerberos 5 provides a higher level of security than is available with other login servers. Kerberos 5–enabled login servers include Klogin (Kerberos 5) and EKlogin (Kerberos 5 with encryption).

The rlogin service has been available for UNIX systems for a long time, though it is generally less secure than the other login services described here. The rlogin service is available by default on your Red Hat Linux system.

A newer addition to the login servers available with Red Hat Linux is the OpenSSH server. This service is on by default. To access this service, use applications that come with the openssh-client software package, such as the ssh and slogin remote login commands. Many Linux administrators use OpenSSH tools, as opposed to older remote login tools such as rlogin and telnet because OpenSSH is believed to be more secure.

E-mail servers

The most common protocols used to download e-mail from a mail server to a client workstation are Post Office Protocol (POP) and Internet Message Protocol (IMAP). If you configure Red Hat Linux as your mail server, you can configure several different POP and IMAP daemons that can allow users to download e-mail to their workstations.

By default, all POP or IMAP services are off. Choose the POP or IMAP server you would like to use from those provided in the e-mail reader servers listing in Table 24-1. To turn on that service, simply change the file in /etc/xinet.d associated with that service so that the disable = yes entry is changed to disable = no. Then restart the xinetd daemon.

The e-mail transfer server that comes with Red Hat Linux is called sendmail. If send-mail software is installed, the sendmail service is started automatically. However, you need to configure the /etc/sendmail.cf file, as well as several files in /etc/mail, for the service to work as you would like it to.

Chapter 19 contains a detailed description of how to configure sendmail.

The comsat service can be turned on to check when e-mail arrives in users' mail-boxes on your Red Hat Linux system. Though comsat is off by default, if you turn it on, you can use the biff or xbiff commands to alert users when e-mail arrives in their mailboxes. To turn on comsat, simply change the comsat file in /etc/xinet.d so that the disable = yes entry is changed to disable = no.

News server

Red Hat Linux comes with the Internet Network News Server (INN) software to let you set up a Red Hat Linux system as a news server. INN can provide your users access to thousands of Internet newsgroups.

By default, INN service is off in Red Hat Linux. To turn it on, change the `kill` script (`K05innd`) to a start-up script (`S05innd`). Do this by changing the files in the directories for run levels in which you want the service to run (probably `/etc/rc3.d` or `/etc/rc5.d`). For the service to be usable, you need to edit files in the `/etc/news` directory.

Caution   Because a news server can potentially consume huge amounts of system resources, you need to think carefully about how you configure it. See Chapter 22 for details about configuring your INN server.

Print server

The LPR New Generation (LPRng) software is included as the printer software for the current release of Red Hat Linux. The LPRng software is particularly well-suited for organizations in which a lot of people share many printers, such as on college campuses.

The LPRng server (lpd) is started automatically when you boot your Red Hat Linux system (in run levels 2, 3, 4, or 5). However, unless you add one or more printers to the `/etc/printcap` file, no printers will actually be available for you to share. To add a printer manually, you must edit the `/etc/printcap.local` file. Also, any remote computer that you want to allow to access your computer must be added to the `/etc/lpd.perms` file. Global printing values (that is, ones that apply to all printers) can be added to the `/etc/lpd.conf` file.

Cross-Reference   Information on setting up printers can be found in Chapter 17.

Network administration servers

Some network servers offer services that monitor or configure network configurations. Several of these services, listed in Table C-1, are described below.

Network Time Protocol Server

The Network Time Protocol (NTP) Server synchronizes time among a set of computers on a network.

By default, the NTP service is off in Red Hat Linux. To turn it on, change the `kill` script (`K10ntpd`) to a start-up script (`S10ntpd`). Do this by changing the files in the directories for run levels in which you want the service to run (probably `/etc/rc3.d` or `/etc/rc5.d`). For the service to be usable, you need to edit the `/etc/ntp.conf` file. The `/etc/ntp.conf` file contains information that identifies the addresses of synchronization sources and modes of operation.

Portmap server

The portmap server translates Remote Procedure Call (RPC) numbers to TCP/IP and UDP port numbers. This server must be running in order for certain network services, such as NFS (nfs), Rusers (rusersd), and Wall (rwalld), to work properly. RPC numbers are stored in the /etc/rpc file.

SWAT

The Samba Web Administration Tool (SWAT) provides a Web-based interface for configuring Samba file and print services. Once properly configured, any Web browser can access the SWAT service (with a root user password).

By default, the SWAT service is off in Red Hat Linux. To turn the service on, edit the /etc/xinetd.d/swat file and change the disable = yes entry to disable = no. This makes the service available to a Web browser on the local host that asks for port number 901 (for example, http://localhost:901). You can remove the line only_from = localhost to allow a Web browser from any computer that has access to your computer on the network to use SWAT. (Of course, someone trying to use the service would also need to know your root password.)

Arpwatch server

The Arpwatch service can be turned on to monitor Ethernet/IP activities on your network. Any potential problems (such as two different computers using the same IP address) are logged to the syslog facility (usually to the /var/log/messages file).

By default, the Arpwatch service is turned off. To turn it on, change the kill script (K45arpwatch) to a start-up script (S45arpwatch). Do this by changing the files in the directories for run levels in which you want the service to run (probably /etc/rc3.d or /etc/rc5.d). You can check the /var/log/messages file to see if the Arpwatch services started successfully and watch for changes on your network.

Simple Network Management Protocol (SNMP) server

The Simple Network Management Protocol (SNMP) server lets your Red Hat Linux system listen for SNMP requests from the network. With this server running, other computers using SNMP tools can monitor (based on configuration files you set up on your system) the activities of your computer.

By default, SNMP is turned off. To turn it on, change the kill script (K50snmpd) to a start-up script (S50snmpd). Do this by changing the files in the directories for run levels in which you want the service to run (probably /etc/rc3.d or /etc/rc5.d). SNMP configuration can be quite complex. Start by referring to the snmpd.conf man page (type **man snmpd.conf**) and going through the tutorial from the UCD-SNMP home page (http://ucd-snmp.ucdavis.edu).

Information servers

By distributing such information as hostnames, user account information, and network addresses, an administrator can more easily manage groups of networked computers. Popular types of servers for managing network information include Network Information System (NIS), Dynamic Host Configuration Protocol (DHCP), and Lightweight Directory Access Protocol (LDAP).

Network Information System servers

Network Information System (NIS) is a software feature that was developed by Sun Microsystems to manage information needed to configure a group of UNIX (and now Linux) computers on a network. Using NIS, a group of computers can share common passwd, groups, hosts, and other configuration files.

By default, NIS services are off. You can turn on NIS services for your Linux computer as either an NIS client (using shared information) or an NIS server (distributing shared information). NIS client computers need to start the /etc/init.d/ypbind script and identify the NIS servers in the /etc/yp.conf file.

If you want to use your Red Hat Linux system as an NIS server, you need to gather up the configuration files you need to share, then start the /etc/init.d/ypserv script. The script runs the /usr/sbin/ypserv daemon, which takes care of the distribution of information to the NIS client computers.

Cross-Reference   Chapter 23 describes the NIS client and server software.

Dynamic Host Configuration Protocol (DHCP) server

Instead of going to each computer on your local network and adding all the TCP/IP information they need in order to work (IP address, netmasks, gateways, and so on), you can configure Red Hat Linux as a Dynamic Host Configuration Protocol (DHCP) server to distribute that information. The client computer simply identifies the IP address of the DHCP server so that when the client starts up its network connection, the DHCP server automatically assigns its network address.

By default, DHCP is turned off. To turn it on, change the kill script (K35dhcpd) to a start-up script (S35dhcpd). Do this by changing the files in the directories for run levels in which you want the service to run (probably /etc/rc3.d or /etc/rc5.d). Along with running the start-up script, you need to configure the /etc/dhcpd.conf file.

Lightweight Directory Access Protocol (LDAP) server

If your organization uses Lightweight Directory Access Protocol (LDAP) databases of information, running the LDAP server that comes with Red Hat Linux enables you to access those databases. Likewise, the LDAP server can let you use LDAP-enabled applications, such as Netscape Roaming Access and sendmail 8.

By default, the LDAP service is turned off. To turn it on, change the `kill` script (`K61ldap`) to a start-up script (`S61ldap`). Do this by changing the files in the directories for run levels in which you want the service to run (probably `/etc/rc3.d` or `/etc/rc5.d`). Along with running the start-up script, you need to configure files in the `/etc/ldap/` directory.

Domain Name System (DNS) server

A Domain Name System (DNS) server is set up to translate hostnames to IP addresses on a TCP/IP network. Red Hat Linux can be configured to be a DNS server using the named daemon.

By default, the DNS server is not configured to start automatically in Red Hat Linux. To start a DNS server, change the `kill` script (`K45named`) to a start-up script (`S45named`). Do this by changing the files in the directories for run levels in which you want the service to run (probably `/etc/rc3.d` or `/etc/rc5.d`). Along with running the start-up script, you need to configure the `/etc/named.conf` file. You also need to configure zone files.

Reverse Address Resolution Protocol (RARP) server

The Reverse Address Resolution Protocol (RARP) daemon responds to requests from RARP clients that need to obtain their own IP addresses. Today, RARP is not used very often.

By default, the RARP service is off. To start an RARP server, change the `kill` script (`K16rarpd`) to a start-up script (`S16rarpd`). Do this by changing the files in the directories for run levels in which you want the service to run (probably `/etc/ rc3.d` or `/etc/rc5.d`). When requests come in for addresses, the `/usr/sbin/rarpd` daemon checks the `/etc/ethers` or NIS+ databases for addresses.

Database services

Database servers provide tools for accessing and managing databases of information. The Postgresql service uses the `postmaster` daemon to handle requests for its services. The MySQL server runs the mysqld daemon to handle access to its databases. Each of these daemons is started from start-up scripts in `/etc/init.d`: postgresql and mysqld scripts, respectively.

User services

Red Hat Linux can provide end users with a variety of network services. These services let users run remote programs, send messages in real time, and get information on active users.

Remote execution servers

Remote execution servers respond to requests from other computers to run commands on the local computer. Three remote execution service daemons are available with Red Hat Linux: Rsh, Rexec, and Kshell.

✦ The Rsh service (/usr/sbin/in.rshd) accepts requests for remote execution requests that were initiated by the rsh command (from other Linux or UNIX systems). By default, the service is on. However, the host and/or user must be allowed access before remote execution is permitted. Access is configured in the /etc/hosts.equiv file or in the .rhosts file in each user's home directory.

✦ The Rexec service (/usr/sbin/in.rexecd) accepts remote execution requests from the rexec command (from other Linux or UNIX systems). By default, the service is on. To allow the remote execution, however, the user making the request must provide a valid username and password.

✦ The Kshell service (/usr/kerberos/sbin/kshd) receives remote execution requests from the rsh command. It uses Kerberos authentication and encryption, making it more secure than the alternative in.rshd daemon. By default, the service is off. However, if you turn it on (by editing the /etc/xinetd.d/kshell file and changing the disable = yes entry to disable = no) it will take precedence over the in.rshd daemon.

Cross-Reference   Login commands that work with the various login daemons are described in Chapter 16.

Talk server

You can use the in.talk or in.ntalk servers to allow users to communicate using the talk command. The talk command lets users type messages back and forth in real time. The talk daemon handles requests on port 517, and the ntalk daemon handles requests on port 518.

Both of these services are turned off by default. To turn on either service, edit the /etc/xinetd.d/talk and/or /etc/xinetd.d/ntalk files and change the disable = yes entry to disable = no.

Finger server

The finger (/usr/sbin/in.fingerd) server lets people use the finger command to request information about active users on Linux and other UNIX systems locally or over a network. This service is on by default. If the in.fingerd server accepts a request from a finger command, the output to the user who made the request looks something like the following:

```
[maple]
Login: jake                Name: Jake W. Jones
Directory: /home/jake      Shell: /bin/bash
Last login Mon Oct 16 13:34 (PDT) on pts/2 from maple
Mail last read Mon Oct 16 12:10 2000 (PDT)
```

The output shows the user's login name, real name, home directory, and shell. It also shows when the user last logged in and accessed his or her e-mail.

Remote user identification

The Rusers server (`/usr/sbin/rpc.rusersd`) allows users to query the system from a remote computer to list who is currently logged in to the Red Hat Linux system. The `rusers` command can be used to query the `rpc.rusersd` server.

By default, the Rusers service is off. To start an Rusers server, change the `kill` script (`K20rusersd`) to a start-up script (`S20rusersd`). Do this by changing the files in the directories for run levels in which you want the service to run (probably `/etc/rc3.d` or `/etc/rc5.d`).

Write-to-All (RWall) server

The Write-to-All (RWall) server (`/user/sbin/rpc.rwalld`) accepts requests to broadcast a text message to the screens of all users currently logged in to the Red Hat Linux or other UNIX system. The request is made with the `rwall` command.

By default, the RWall service is off. To start an RWall server, you need to change the `kill` script (`K20rwalld`) to a start-up script (`S20rwalld`). Do this by changing the files in the directories for run levels in which you want the service to run (probably `/etc/rc3.d` or `/etc/rc5.d`).

Security services

Red Hat Linux provides some services to protect your local network from outside attacks. These services include virtual private network servers and caching servers. The following sections describe those services.

Virtual Private Network servers

By encrypting data that travels across public networks, a virtual private network (VPN) can provide a secure way for users to access your local network from remote locations. Red Hat Linux comes with the Crypto IP Encapsulation (CIPE) virtual private network software. By default, the CIPE daemon (`/usr/sbin/ciped-cb`) is not running. To configure CIPE, set up a VPN between two host systems that communicate over the Internet.

Proxy/Caching server

The Squid server (`/usr/sbin/squid`) can be used as both a proxy server and a caching server. A proxy server can allow computers on your local network to communicate with the Internet by passing all requests through the proxy server. A caching server stores Web content that has been accessed by a local user on a computer that is physically closer to the user than the originating computer.

By default, the Squid server is off. To start the Squid server, change the `kill` script (`K25squid`) to a start-up script (`S25squid`). Do this by changing the files in the directories for run levels in which you want the service to run (probably `/etc/rc3.d` or `/etc/rc5.d`). You also must set up an `/etc/squid/squid.conf` file to identify who has access to the server and what services they can access.

Cross-Reference   Chapter 16 provides details for configuring Squid.

Summary

Daemon processes are used to implement most network services in Red Hat Linux. These processes listen for requests to or from the network and see that (with proper authentication) the request is carried out. In Red Hat Linux, these daemons are launched based on information in the system start-up files (`/etc/init.d/*`) or by the `xinetd` daemon (which listens for requests and hands them off to other daemons for the actual execution of the service).

Among the most popular types of network servers available with Red Hat Linux are the apache Web server, the wu-ftp file server software, and a variety of login servers. Services that are available for individual users to get information or communicate include talk (real-time messages), finger (query users who are logged in), and Rwall (write to terminals of all users on the system).

✦   ✦   ✦

Index

Continued

Continued

Continued

GNU General Public License

Version 2, June 1991

Copyright © 1989, 1991 Free Software Foundation, Inc.

59 Temple Place, Suite 330, Boston, MA 02111-1307, USA

Preamble

The licenses for most software are designed to take away your freedom to share and change it. By contrast, the GNU General Public License is intended to guarantee your freedom to share and change free software—to make sure the software is free for all its users. This General Public License applies to most of the Free Software Foundation's software and to any other program whose authors commit to using it. (Some other Free Software Foundation software is covered by the GNU Library General Public License instead.) You can apply it to your programs, too.

When we speak of free software, we are referring to freedom, not price. Our General Public Licenses are designed to make sure that you have the freedom to distribute copies of free software (and charge for this service if you wish), that you receive source code or can get it if you want it, that you can change the software or use pieces of it in new free programs; and that you know you can do these things.

To protect your rights, we need to make restrictions that forbid anyone to deny you these rights or to ask you to surrender the rights. These restrictions translate to certain responsibilities for you if you distribute copies of the software, or if you modify it.

For example, if you distribute copies of such a program, whether gratis or for a fee, you must give the recipients all the rights that you have. You must make sure that they, too, receive or can get the source code. And you must show them these terms so they know their rights.

We protect your rights with two steps: (1) copyright the software, and (2) offer you this license which gives you legal permission to copy, distribute and/or modify the software.

Also, for each author's protection and ours, we want to make certain that everyone understands that there is no warranty for this free software. If the software is modified by someone else and passed on, we want its recipients to know that what they have is not the original, so that any problems introduced by others will not reflect on the original authors' reputations.

Finally, any free program is threatened constantly by software patents. We wish to avoid the danger that redistributors of a free program will individually obtain patent licenses, in effect making the program proprietary. To prevent this, we have made it clear that any patent must be licensed for everyone's free use or not licensed at all.

The precise terms and conditions for copying, distribution and modification follow.

Terms and Conditions for Copying, Distribution, and Modification

0. This License applies to any program or other work which contains a notice placed by the copyright holder saying it may be distributed under the terms of this General Public License. The "Program", below, refers to any such program or work, and a "work based on the Program" means either the Program or any derivative work under copyright law: that is to say, a work containing the Program or a portion of it, either verbatim or with modifications and/or translated into another language. (Hereinafter, translation is included without limitation in the term "modification".) Each licensee is addressed as "you".

Activities other than copying, distribution and modification are not covered by this License; they are outside its scope. The act of running the Program is not restricted, and the output from the Program is covered only if its contents constitute a work based on the Program (independent of having been made by running the Program). Whether that is true depends on what the Program does.

1. You may copy and distribute verbatim copies of the Program's source code as you receive it, in any medium, provided that you conspicuously and appropriately publish on each copy an appropriate copyright notice and disclaimer of warranty; keep intact all the notices that refer to this License and to the absence of any warranty; and give any other recipients of the Program a copy of this License along with the Program.

You may charge a fee for the physical act of transferring a copy, and you may at your option offer warranty protection in exchange for a fee.

2. You may modify your copy or copies of the Program or any portion of it, thus forming a work based on the Program, and copy and distribute such modifications or work under the terms of Section 1 above, provided that you also meet all of these conditions:

   a) You must cause the modified files to carry prominent notices stating that you changed the files and the date of any change.

   b) You must cause any work that you distribute or publish, that in whole or in part contains or is derived from the Program or any part thereof, to be licensed as a whole at no charge to all third parties under the terms of this License.

   c) If the modified program normally reads commands interactively when run, you must cause it, when started running for such interactive use in the most ordinary way, to print or display an announcement including an appropriate copyright notice and a notice that there is no warranty (or else, saying that you provide a warranty) and that users may redistribute the program under these conditions, and telling the user how to view a copy of this License. (Exception: if the Program itself is interactive but does not normally print such an announcement, your work based on the Program is not required to print an announcement.)

These requirements apply to the modified work as a whole. If identifiable sections of that work are not derived from the Program, and can be reasonably considered independent and separate works in themselves, then this License, and its terms, do not apply to those sections when you distribute them as separate works. But when you distribute the same sections as part of a whole which is a work based on the Program, the distribution of the whole must be on the terms of this License, whose permissions for other licensees extend to the entire whole, and thus to each and every part regardless of who wrote it.

Thus, it is not the intent of this section to claim rights or contest your rights to work written entirely by you; rather, the intent is to exercise the right to control the distribution of derivative or collective works based on the Program.

In addition, mere aggregation of another work not based on the Program with the Program (or with a work based on the Program) on a volume of a storage or distribution medium does not bring the other work under the scope of this License.

3. You may copy and distribute the Program (or a work based on it, under Section 2) in object code or executable form under the terms of Sections 1 and 2 above provided that you also do one of the following:

   a) Accompany it with the complete corresponding machine-readable source code, which must be distributed under the terms of Sections 1 and 2 above on a medium customarily used for software interchange; or,

b) Accompany it with a written offer, valid for at least three years, to give any third party, for a charge no more than your cost of physically performing source distribution, a complete machine-readable copy of the corresponding source code, to be distributed under the terms of Sections 1 and 2 above on a medium customarily used for software interchange; or,

c) Accompany it with the information you received as to the offer to distribute corresponding source code. (This alternative is allowed only for noncommercial distribution and only if you received the program in object code or executable form with such an offer, in accord with Subsection b above.)

The source code for a work means the preferred form of the work for making modifications to it. For an executable work, complete source code means all the source code for all modules it contains, plus any associated interface definition files, plus the scripts used to control compilation and installation of the executable. However, as a special exception, the source code distributed need not include anything that is normally distributed (in either source or binary form) with the major components (compiler, kernel, and so on) of the operating system on which the executable runs, unless that component itself accompanies the executable.

If distribution of executable or object code is made by offering access to copy from a designated place, then offering equivalent access to copy the source code from the same place counts as distribution of the source code, even though third parties are not compelled to copy the source along with the object code.

4. You may not copy, modify, sublicense, or distribute the Program except as expressly provided under this License. Any attempt otherwise to copy, modify, sublicense or distribute the Program is void, and will automatically terminate your rights under this License. However, parties who have received copies, or rights, from you under this License will not have their licenses terminated so long as such parties remain in full compliance.

5. You are not required to accept this License, since you have not signed it. However, nothing else grants you permission to modify or distribute the Program or its derivative works. These actions are prohibited by law if you do not accept this License. Therefore, by modifying or distributing the Program (or any work based on the Program), you indicate your acceptance of this License to do so, and all its terms and conditions for copying, distributing or modifying the Program or works based on it.

6. Each time you redistribute the Program (or any work based on the Program), the recipient automatically receives a license from the original licensor to copy, distribute or modify the Program subject to these terms and conditions. You may not impose any further restrictions on the recipients' exercise of the rights granted herein. You are not responsible for enforcing compliance by third parties to this License.

7. If, as a consequence of a court judgment or allegation of patent infringement or for any other reason (not limited to patent issues), conditions are imposed on you (whether by court order, agreement or otherwise) that contradict the conditions of this License, they do not excuse you from the conditions of this License. If you cannot distribute so as to satisfy simultaneously your obligations under this License and any other pertinent obligations, then as a consequence you may not distribute the Program at all. For example, if a patent license would not permit royalty-free redistribution of the Program by all those who receive copies directly or indirectly through you, then the only way you could satisfy both it and this License would be to refrain entirely from distribution of the Program.

If any portion of this section is held invalid or unenforceable under any particular circumstance, the balance of the section is intended to apply and the section as a whole is intended to apply in other circumstances.

It is not the purpose of this section to induce you to infringe any patents or other property right claims or to contest validity of any such claims; this section has the sole purpose of protecting the integrity of the free software distribution system, which is implemented by public license practices. Many people have made generous contributions to the wide range of software distributed through that system in reliance on consistent application of that system; it is up to the author/donor to decide if he or she is willing to distribute software through any other system and a licensee cannot impose that choice.

This section is intended to make thoroughly clear what is believed to be a consequence of the rest of this License.

8. If the distribution and/or use of the Program is restricted in certain countries either by patents or by copyrighted interfaces, the original copyright holder who places the Program under this License may add an explicit geographical distribution limitation excluding those countries, so that distribution is permitted only in or among countries not thus excluded. In such case, this License incorporates the limitation as if written in the body of this License.

9. The Free Software Foundation may publish revised and/or new versions of the General Public License from time to time. Such new versions will be similar in spirit to the present version, but may differ in detail to address new problems or concerns.

Each version is given a distinguishing version number. If the Program specifies a version number of this License which applies to it and "any later version", you have the option of following the terms and conditions either of that version or of any later version published by the Free Software Foundation. If the Program does not specify a version number of this License, you may choose any version ever published by the Free Software Foundation.

10. If you wish to incorporate parts of the Program into other free programs whose distribution conditions are different, write to the author to ask for permission. For software which is copyrighted by the Free Software Foundation, write to the Free Software Foundation; we sometimes make exceptions for this. Our decision will be guided by the two goals of preserving the free status of all derivatives of our free software and of promoting the sharing and reuse of software generally.

No Warranty

11. BECAUSE THE PROGRAM IS LICENSED FREE OF CHARGE, THERE IS NO WARRANTY FOR THE PROGRAM, TO THE EXTENT PERMITTED BY APPLICABLE LAW. EXCEPT WHEN OTHERWISE STATED IN WRITING THE COPYRIGHT HOLDERS AND/OR OTHER PARTIES PROVIDE THE PROGRAM "AS IS" WITHOUT WARRANTY OF ANY KIND, EITHER EXPRESSED OR IMPLIED, INCLUDING, BUT NOT LIMITED TO, THE IMPLIED WARRANTIES OF MERCHANTABILITY AND FITNESS FOR A PARTICULAR PURPOSE. THE ENTIRE RISK AS TO THE QUALITY AND PERFORMANCE OF THE PROGRAM IS WITH YOU. SHOULD THE PROGRAM PROVE DEFECTIVE, YOU ASSUME THE COST OF ALL NECESSARY SERVICING, REPAIR OR CORRECTION.

12. IN NO EVENT UNLESS REQUIRED BY APPLICABLE LAW OR AGREED TO IN WRITING WILL ANY COPYRIGHT HOLDER, OR ANY OTHER PARTY WHO MAY MODIFY AND/OR REDISTRIBUTE THE PROGRAM AS PERMITTED ABOVE, BE LIABLE TO YOU FOR DAMAGES, INCLUDING ANY GENERAL, SPECIAL, INCIDENTAL OR CONSEQUENTIAL DAMAGES ARISING OUT OF THE USE OR INABILITY TO USE THE PROGRAM (INCLUDING BUT NOT LIMITED TO LOSS OF DATA OR DATA BEING RENDERED INACCURATE OR LOSSES SUSTAINED BY YOU OR THIRD PARTIES OR A FAILURE OF THE PROGRAM TO OPERATE WITH ANY OTHER PROGRAMS), EVEN IF SUCH HOLDER OR OTHER PARTY HAS BEEN ADVISED OF THE POSSIBILITY OF SUCH DAMAGES.

End Of Terms And Conditions